STO

ACPL ITEM
DISCARDED

3 1833 04072 6967

OVERSIZE

REFERENCE

Not to leave the library

S0-BVP-373

Stocks, Bonds, Bills,
and Inflation

# SBBI

**2001 Yearbook**
Market Results for 1926-2000

**Ibbotson**Associates

© Ibbotson Associates, Inc. 2001

**Stocks, Bonds, Bills, and Inflation® 2001 Yearbook.**

Stocks, Bonds, Bills, and Inflation® and SBBI® are registered trademarks of Ibbotson Associates.

The information presented in this publication has been obtained with the greatest of care from sources believed to be reliable, but is not guaranteed. Ibbotson Associates expressly disclaims any liability, including incidental or consequential damages, arising from errors or omissions in this publication.

Copyright © 1983-2001 Ibbotson Associates, Inc. All rights reserved. No part of this publication may be reproduced or used in any form or by any means—graphic, electronic, or mechanical, including photocopying, recording, taping, or information storage and retrieval systems—without written permission from the publisher. To obtain permission, please write to the address below. Specify the data or other information you wish to use and the manner in which it will be used, and attach a copy of any charts, tables, or figures derived from the information. There is a $150 processing fee per request. There may be additional fees depending on usage.

Published by:

**Ibbotson Associates**
**225 North Michigan Avenue, Suite 700**
**Chicago, Illinois 60601-7676**
**Telephone (312) 616-1620**
**Fax (312) 616-0404**
**www.ibbotson.com**

**ISBN 1-882864-12-3**
**ISSN 1047-2436**

Additional copies of this Yearbook may be obtained for $110, plus shipping and handling, by calling or writing to the address above. Order forms are provided inside the back cover. Information about volume discounts, companion publications and consulting services may also be obtained. The data in this Yearbook are also available with our Analyst software, a Microsoft Windows™ application. Statistics and graphs can be quickly accessed over any subperiod. Updates can be obtained annually, semi-annually, quarterly or monthly. For more information about Analyst, call (800) 758-3557 or write to the address listed above.

# Table of Contents

# Most Commonly Used References

## Graph/Table/Equation

# List of Tables

(Text)

## Chapter 5

## Chapter 6

## Chapter 7

# List of Graphs

(Text)

# List of Graphs

(Image)

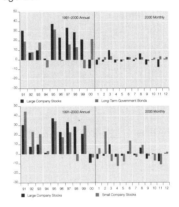
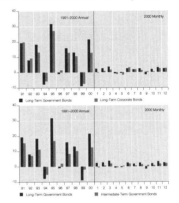
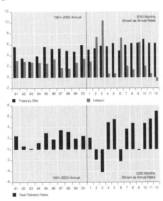
| Series | Geometric Mean | Arithmetic Mean | Standard Deviation | Distribution |
|---|---|---|---|---|
| Large Company Stocks | 11.0% | 13.0% | 20.2% | |
| Small Company Stocks | 12.4 | 17.3 | 33.4 | * |
| Long-Term Corporate Bonds | 5.7 | 6.0 | 8.7 | |
| Long-Term Government | 5.3 | 5.7 | 9.4 | |
| Intermediate-Term Government | 5.3 | 5.5 | 5.8 | |
| U.S. Treasury Bills | 3.8 | 3.9 | 3.2 | |
| Inflation | 3.1 | 3.2 | 4.4 | |

−90%　　　　0%　　　　90%

*The 1933 Small Company Stocks Total Return was 142.9 percent.

**Graph 2-1**
Wealth Indices of Investments in the U.S. Capital Markets (1925–2000). *Page 26.*

**Graph 3-1(a)**
Large Company Stocks: Return Indices (1925–2000). *Page 52.*

**Graph 3-1(b)**
Large Company Stocks: Returns (1926–2000). *Page 52.*

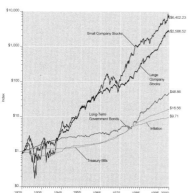

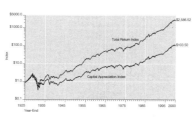

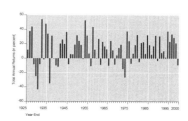

**Graph 3-1(c)**
Large Company Stocks: Yields (1926–2000). *Page 52.*

**Graph 3-2(a)**
Small Company Stocks: Return Index (1925–2000). *Page 54.*

**Graph 3-2(b)**
Small Company Stocks: Returns (1926–2000). *Page 54.*

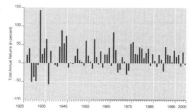

**Graph 3-3(a)**
Long-Term Corporate Bonds: Return Index (1925–2000). *Page 57.*

**Graph 3-3(b)**
Long-Term Corporate Bonds: Returns (1926–2000). *Page 57.*

**Graph 3-4(a)**
Long-Term Government Bonds: Return Indices (1925–2000). *Page 58.*

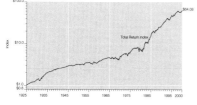

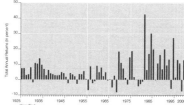

**Graph 3-4(b)**
Long-Term Government Bonds: Returns (1926–2000). *Page 58.*

**Graph 3-4(c)**
Long-Term Government Bonds: Yields (1926–2000). *Page 58.*

**Graph 3-5(a)**
Intermediate-Term Government Bonds: Return Indices (1925–2000). *Page 60.*

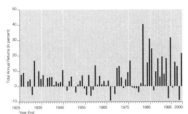

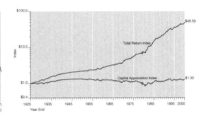

**Graph 3-5(b)**
Intermediate-Term Government Bonds: Returns (1926–2000). *Page 60.*

**Graph 3-5(c)**
Intermediate-Term Government Bonds: Yields (1926–2000). *Page 60.*

**Graph 3-6(a)**
U.S. Treasury Bills: Return Index (1925–2000). *Page 64.*

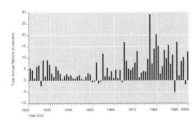

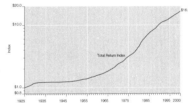

**Graph 3-6(b)**
U.S. Treasury Bills: Returns (1926–2000). *Page 64.*

**Graph 3-7(a)**
Inflation: Cumulative Index (1925–2000). *Page 66.*

**Graph 3-7(b)**
Inflation: Rates of Change (1926–2000). *Page 66.*

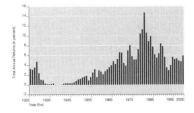

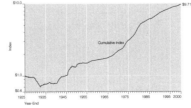

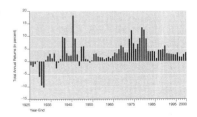

**Graph 4-1**
Equity Risk Premium Annual Returns
(1926–2000). *Page 73.*

**Graph 4-2**
Small Stock Premium Annual Returns
(1926–2000). *Page 74.*

**Graph 4-3**
Bond Default Premium Annual Returns
(1926–2000). *Page 75.*

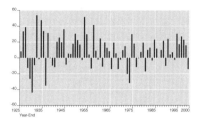

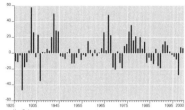

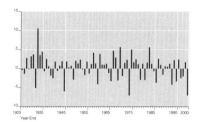

**Graph 4-4**
Bond Horizon Premium Annual Returns
(1926–2000). *Page 77.*

**Graph 4-5**
Large Company Stocks: Real and
Nominal Return Indices (1925–2000).
*Page 78.*

**Graph 4-6**
Small Company Stocks: Real and
Nominal Return Indices (1925–2000).
*Page 80.*

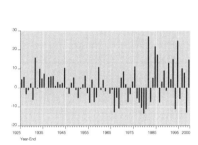

**Graph 4-7**
Long-Term Corporate Bonds: Real and
Nominal Return Indices (1925–2000).
*Page 81.*

**Graph 4-8**
Long-Term Government Bonds: Real
and Nominal Return Indices
(1925–2000). *Page 83.*

**Graph 4-9**
Intermediate-Term Government Bonds:
Real and Nominal Return Indices
(1925–2000). *Page 84.*

**Graph 4-10**
Annual Real Riskless Rates of Return (1926–2000). *Page 85.*

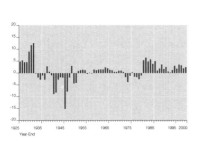

**Graph 4-11**
U.S. Treasury Bills: Real and Nominal Return Indices (1925–2000). *Page 86.*

**Graph 6-1(a)**
Month-by-Month Returns on Large Company Stocks (1926–2000). *Page 104.*

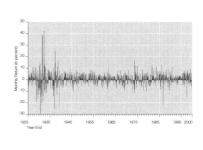

**Graph 6-1(b)**
Month-by-Month Returns on Long-Term Government Bonds (1926–2000). *Page 104.*

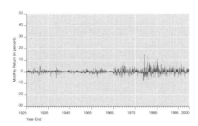

**Graph 6-2(a)**
Rolling 60-Month Standard Deviation: Small Company Stocks, Large Company Stocks, and Long-Term Government Bonds (1930–2000). *Page 114.*

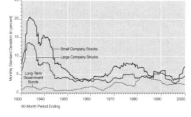

**Graph 6-2(b)**
Rolling 60-Month Standard Deviation: Long-Term Government Bonds, Intermediate-Term Government Bonds, and Treasury Bills (1930–2000). *Page 114.*

**Graph 6-3(a)**
Rolling 60-Month Correlations: Large Company Stocks and Long-Term Government Bonds (1930–2000). *Page 115.*

**Graph 6-3(b)**
Rolling 60-Month Correlations: Treasury Bills and Inflation (1930–2000). *Page 115.*

**Graph 6-4**
10-Year Compound Annual Return Across Mutual Funds. *Page 119.*

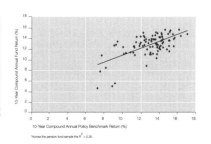

**Graph 6-5a**
Variation of Returns Across Funds
Explained by Asset Allocation.
*Page 120.*

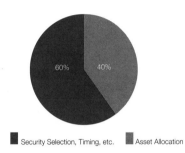

**Graph 6-5b**
Percentage of a Fund's Total Returns
Explained by Asset Allocation.
*Page 120.*

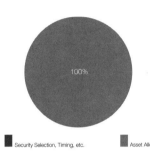

**Graph 7-1**
Size-Decile Portfolios of the NYSE/
AMEX/NASDAQ: Wealth Indices of
Investments in Mid-, Low-, Micro-, and
Total Capitalization Stocks (1925–2000).
*Page 132.*

**Graph 7-2**
Size-Decile Portfolios of the NYSE/
AMEX/NASDAQ: Security Market Line.
*Page 136.*

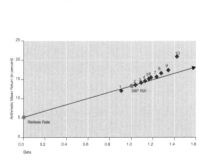

**Graph 8-1**
All Growth Stocks vs. All Value Stocks
(1927–2000). *Page 140.*

**Graph 8-2**
Small Value Stocks, Small Growth
Stocks, Large Value Stocks, Large
Growth Stocks (1927–2000). *Page 144.*

**Graph 8-3**
All Value Premium (in percent)
(1928–2000). *Page 152.*

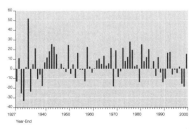

**Graph 8-4**
Small Value Premium (in percent)
(1928–2000). *Page 153.*

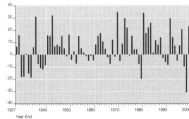

**Graph 8-5**
Large Value Premium (in percent)
(1928–2000). *Page 154.*

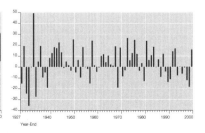

**Graph 8-6**
Excess Return of All Value Stocks Over All Growth Stocks (in percent): 36-Month Rolling Periods (1930–2000). *Page 160.*

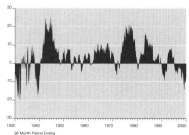

**Graph 8-7**
Excess Return of Small Value Stocks Over Small Growth Stocks (in percent): 36-Month Rolling Periods (1930–2000). *Page 161.*

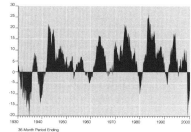

**Graph 8-8**
Excess Return of Large Value Stocks Over Large Growth Stocks (in percent): 36-Month Rolling Periods (1930–2000). *Page 162.*

**Graph 9-1**
Forecasted Distribution and the Realization of Nominal Large Company Stocks Cumulative Wealth Relative for the Period 1976-1999 *Page 167.*

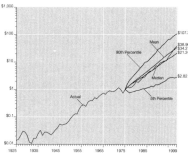

**Graph 9-2**
Efficient Frontier: Large Company Stocks, Long-Term Government Bonds, and U.S. Treasury Bills. *Page 171.*

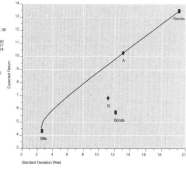

**Graph 9-3**
Twenty Year Rolling Period Correlations of Annual Returns: Large Company Stocks and Intermediate-Term Government Bonds (1945–2000). *Page 176.*

**Graph 9-4**
Forecast Total Distribution: 100 Percent Large Stocks (2001–2020). *Page 177.*

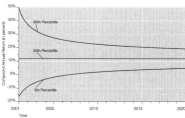

**Graph 9-5**
Forecast Distribution of Wealth Index Value: 100 Percent Large Stocks (2001–2020). *Page 179.*

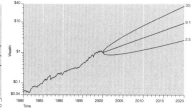

**Graph 10-1**
Distribution of Raw Stock Prices (1815–1925). *Page 184.*

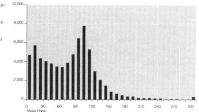

**Graph 10-2**
Large Company Stocks Annual Capital Appreciation Returns (1825–2000). *Page 187.*

**Graph 10-3**
20-Year Rolling Capital Appreciation Returns for Large Company Stocks (1844–2000). *Page 188.*

**Graph 10-4**
Large Company Stocks Annual Income Returns (1825–2000). *Page 189.*

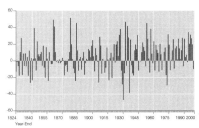

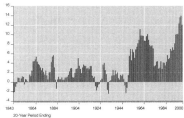

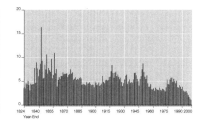

**Graph 10-5**
Large Company Stocks Annual Total Returns (1825–2000). *Page 190.*

**Graph 10-6**
5-Year Rolling Standard Deviation for Large Company Stocks (1829–2000). *Page 191.*

**Graph 10-7**
Large Company Stocks (1824–2000). *Page 192.*

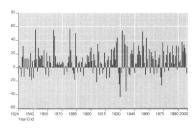

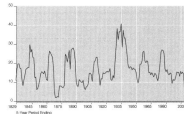

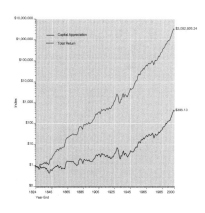

# Acknowledgements

We thank, foremost, Roger G. Ibbotson, professor in the practice of finance at the Yale School of Management and chairman of Ibbotson Associates, for his contribution to this book. Professor Ibbotson and Rex A. Sinquefield, chairman of Dimensional Fund Advisors, Inc. (Santa Monica, CA), wrote the two journal articles and four books upon which this Yearbook is based and formulated much of the philosophy and methodology. Mr. Sinquefield also provides the small stock returns, as he has since 1982.

We thank others who contributed to this book. Rolf W. Banz provided the small stock returns for 1926–1981. Thomas S. Coleman (Greenwich, CT), Professor Lawrence Fisher of Rutgers University, and Roger Ibbotson constructed the model used to generate the intermediate-term government bond series for 1926–1933. The pioneering work of Professors Fisher and James H. Lorie of the University of Chicago inspired the original monograph. Stan V. Smith, President of the Corporate Financial Group, Ltd. and former Managing Director at Ibbotson Associates, originated the idea of the Yearbook and its companion update services. The Center for Research in Security Prices at the University of Chicago contributed the data and methodology for the returns on the NYSE by capitalization decile used in Chapter 7, Firm Size and Return. Ken French, of the Massachusetts Institute of Technology, and Eugene Fama, of the University of Chicago, contributed the data and methodology for the returns on the growth and value portfolios. William N. Goetzmann and Liang Peng, both at the Yale School of Management, helped with the assembly of the New York Stock Exchange database for the period prior to 1926.

### Production Staff

Sandy Penn
Jim Casey
Danna McKenzie
Terrence Evans

### Contributing Editors

Michael Barad
Ian McKenney
Edward Lopez
Sharon Olson
Anne Jablo

### Senior Editors

Michael Annin, CFA
James Licato

# Introduction

## Who Should Read This Book

This book is a history of the returns on the capital markets in the United States from 1926 to the present. It is useful to a wide variety of readers. Foremost, anyone serious about investments or investing needs an appreciation of capital market history. Such an appreciation, which can be gained from this book, is equally valuable to the individual and institutional investor. For students at both the graduate and undergraduate levels, this book is both a source of ideas and a reference. Other intended readers include teachers of these students; practitioners and scholars in finance, economics, and business; portfolio strategists; and security analysts.

Chief financial officers and, in some cases, chief executive officers of corporations will find this book useful. More generally, persons concerned with history may find it valuable to study the detail of economic history as revealed in more than six decades of capital market returns.

To these diverse readers, we provide two resources. One is the data. The other is a thinking person's guide to using historical data to understand the financial markets and make decisions. This historical record raises many questions. This book represents our way of appreciating the past—only one of the many possible ways—but one grounded in real theory. We provide a means for the reader to think about the past and the future of financial markets.

## How to Read This Book

| Intended Reader | Most Important Chapters | Other Related Chapters, Graphs, Tables, and Appendices |
|---|---|---|
| Persons Concerned with Data | Chapters 1, 2, 3, and 10 | Chapters 4, 7, and 8; Graphs 2-1 and 10-7; Tables 2-1, 10-1, and 10-2; and Appendices A, B, and C |
| Financial Planners, Asset Allocators, and Investment Consultants | Chapters 1, 2, 8, 9, and 10 | Chapter 6; Graphs 2-1, 9-1, and 10-7; and Tables 2-7, 6-6, 10-1, and 10-2 |
| Individual Investors | Chapters 1 and 2 | Graph 2-1; and Table 2-1 |
| Institutional Investors, Portfolio Managers, and Security Analysts | Chapters 1 through 10 | Graph 10-7; Tables 2-7, 6-6, 7-1, 10-1, and 10-2 |
| Students, Faculty, and Economists | Chapters 2, 5, 7, 8, 9, and 10 | Graph 10-7; Tables 6-6, 10-1, and 10-2 |
| Brokers and Security Sales Representatives | Chapters 1 and 2 | Graph 2-1; and Tables 2-1 and 2-5 |
| Investment Bankers and Security Sales Representatives | Chapters 2, 7, and 8 | Table 2-1 |
| Executives, Corporate Planners, Chief Financial Officers, Chief Executive Officers, and Treasurers | Chapters 1, 2, and 9 | Chapters 1 and 2; and Graph 9-1 |
| Pension Plan Sponsors | Chapters 1, 2, 6, and 9 | Graph 2-1; and Tables 2-1 and 2-4 |

*The Journal of Business* published Roger G. Ibbotson and Rex A. Sinquefield's two companion papers on security returns in January 1976 and July 1976. In the first paper, the authors collected historical data on the returns from stocks, government and corporate bonds, U.S. Treasury bills, and consumer goods (inflation). To uncover the risk/return and the real/nominal relationship in the historical data, they presented a framework in which the return on an asset class is the sum of two or more elemental parts. These elements, such as real returns (returns in excess of inflation) and risk premia (for example, the net return from investing in large company stocks rather than bills), are referred to throughout the book as derived series.

In the second paper, the authors analyzed the time series behavior of the derived series and the information contained in the U.S. government bond yield curve to obtain inputs for a simulation model of future security price behavior. Using the methods developed in the two papers, they forecast security returns through the year 2000.

The response to these works showed that historical data are fascinating in their own right. Both total and component historical returns have a wide range of applications in investment management, corporate finance, academic research, and industry regulation. Subsequent work—the 1977, 1979, and 1982 Institute of Chartered Financial Analysts (ICFA) monographs; the 1989 Dow Jones-Irwin book; and Ibbotson Associates' 1983 through 2000 *Stocks, Bonds, Bills, and Inflation*™ *Yearbooks*—updated and further developed the historical data and forecasts. (All references to previous works used in the development of Stocks, Bonds, Bills, and Inflation [SBBI] data appear at the end of this introduction in the References section.)

In 1981, Ibbotson and Sinquefield began tracking a new asset class: small company stocks. This class consists of issues listed on the New York Stock Exchange (NYSE) that rank in the ninth and tenth (lowest) deciles when sorted by capitalization (price times number of shares outstanding), plus non-NYSE issues of comparable capitalization. This asset class has been of interest to researchers and investors because of its high long-term returns. Intermediate-term (five years to maturity) government bonds were added in 1988. Monthly and annual total returns, income returns, capital appreciation returns, and yields are presented.

## The Stocks, Bonds, Bills, and Inflation 2001 Yearbook

In the present volume the historical data are updated. The motivations are: 1) to document this history of security market returns; 2) to uncover the relationships between the various asset class returns as revealed by the derived series: inflation, real interest rates, risk premia, and other premia; 3) to encourage deeper understanding of the underlying economic history through the graphic presentation of data; and 4) to answer questions most frequently asked by subscribers.

In keeping with the spirit of the previous work, the asset classes contained in this edition highlight the differences between targeted segments of the financial markets in the United States. Our intent is to show historical trade-offs between risk and return.

In this book, the equity markets are segmented between large and small company stocks. Fixed income markets are segmented on two dimensions. Riskless U.S. government securities are differentiated by maturity or investment horizon. U.S. Treasury bills with approximately 30 days to maturity are used to describe the short end of the horizon; U.S. Treasury securities with approximately five years to maturity are used to describe the middle horizon segment; and U.S. Treasury securities with approximately 20 years to maturity are used to describe the long maturity end of the market. A corporate bond series with a long maturity is used to describe fixed income securities that contain risk of default.

Some indices of the stock and bond markets are broad, capturing most or all of the capitalization of the market. Our indices are intentionally narrow. The large company stock series captures the largest issues (those in the Standard & Poor's 500 Composite Index), while the small company stock series is composed of the smallest issues. By studying these polar cases, we identify the small stock premium (small minus large stock returns) and the premium of large stocks over bonds and bills. Neither series is intended to be representative of the entire stock market. Likewise, our long-term government bond and U.S. Treasury bill indices show the returns for the longest and shortest ends of the yield curve, rather than the return for the entire Treasury float. Readers and investors should understand that our bond indices do not, and are not intended to, describe the experience of the typical bond investor who is diversified across maturities; rather, we present returns on carefully focused segments of the market for U.S. Treasury securities.

## Recent Changes and Additions

Traditionally, *Stocks, Bonds, Bills, and Inflation* attempted to cater to two different audiences—those interested in investment returns and those interested in company valuation. While these two groups of readers sound quite similar, they actually require significantly different types of data. Instead of trying to serve two different audiences with one book, we decided to create different editions of SBBI to better serve these distinctly different markets.

The *Stocks, Bonds, Bills, and Inflation: Valuation Edition* was launched in 1999 and has been revised this year to further help business appraisers and other valuation professionals with a better understanding of issues relating to the determination of an appropriate cost of capital.

Starting with the *Stocks, Bonds, Bills, and Inflation: Classic Edition 2000 Yearbook*, we give added focus primarily on investment related topics. The Classic Edition no longer contains information that directly applies to cost of capital issues. To that end, we have replaced Chapter 8, "Estimating the Cost of Capital or Discount Rate" and revised Chapter 7, "Firm Size and Return."

The most exciting change that the SBBI Classic Edition has undergone this year is the addition of color throughout the book. The Classic Edition now carries the traditional brick red along with black and varying shades of each throughout. Also, the book has been completely reformatted to incorporate a new look and sharper style.

We are pleased to add a new chapter, Chapter 10, that extends New York Stock Exchange data back to the year 1815. The chapter will examine the research of Roger Ibbotson, William N. Goetzmann, and Liang Peng on NYSE data for the period 1815–1925, covering the data sources and collection methods used as well as the results and conclusions of the new database.

Another significant addition to this Classic Edition is a summary of the study conducted by Roger Ibbotson and Paul Kaplan, "Does Asset Allocation Policy Explain 40%, 90%, or 100% of Performance?" This summary can be found in Chapter 6, "Statistical Analysis of Returns."

## The SBBI Data Series

The series presented here are total returns, and where applicable or available, capital appreciation returns and income returns for:

| SBBI Data Series | Series Construction | Index Components | Maturity Approximate |
|---|---|---|---|
| 1. **Large Company Stocks** | S&P 500 Composite with dividends reinvested. (S&P 500, 1957–Present; S&P 90, 1926–1956) | Total Return<br>Income Return<br>Capital Appreciation Return | N/A |
| 2. **Small Company Stocks** | Fifth capitalization quintile of stocks on the NYSE for 1926–1981.<br>Performance of the Dimensional Fund Advisors (DFA) Small Company Fund 1982–Present. | Total Return | N/A |
| 3. **Long-Term Corporate Bonds** | Salomon Brothers Long-Term High Grade Corporate Bond Index | Total Return | 20 Years |
| 4. **Long-Term Government Bonds** | A One-Bond Portfolio | Total Return<br>Income Return<br>Capital Appreciation Return<br>Yield | 20 Years |
| 5. **Intermediate-Term Government Bonds** | A One-Bond Portfolio | Total Return<br>Income Return<br>Capital Appreciation Return<br>Yield | 5 Years |
| 6. **U.S. Treasury Bills** | A One-Bill Portfolio | Total Return | 30 Days |
| 7. **Consumer Price Index** | CPI—All Urban Consumers, not seasonally adjusted | Inflation Rate | N/A |

# References

1. **Stocks, Bonds, Bills, and Inflation Yearbook, annual.**

   1983, 1984, 1985, 1986, 1987, 1988, 1989, 1990, 1991, 1992, 1993, 1994, 1995, 1996, 1997, 1998, 1999, 2000.

   Ibbotson Associates, Chicago.

2. **Banz, Rolf W.**

   "The Relationship Between Return and Market Value of Common Stocks,"

   *Journal of Financial Economics* 9:3–18, 1981.

3. **Brinson, Gary P., L. Randolph Hood, and Gilbert P. Beebower**

   "Determinants of Portfolio Performance,"

   *Financial Analysts Journal*, July/August 1986.

4. **Brinson, Gary P., Brian D. Singer, and Gilbert P. Beebower**

   "Determinants of Portfolio Performance II,"

   *Financial Analysts Journal*, May/June 1991.

5. **Coleman, Thomas S., Lawrence Fisher, and Roger G. Ibbotson**

   *Historical U.S. Treasury Yield Curves 1926–1992* with 1994 update,

   Ibbotson Associates, Chicago, 1994.

6. **Coleman, Thomas S., Lawrence Fisher, and Roger G. Ibbotson**

   *U.S. Treasury Yield Curves 1926–1988,*

   Moody's Investment Service, New York, 1990.

7. **Cottle, Sidney, Roger F. Murray, and Frank E. Block**

   "Graham and Dodd's Security Analysis,"

   Fifth Edition, McGraw-Hill, 1988.

8. **Cowles, Alfred**

   *Common Stock Indices,*

   Principia Press, Bloomington, 1939.

9. **Goetzmann, William N., Roger G. Ibbotson, and Liang Peng**

   "A New Historical Database for the NYSE 1815 to 1925: Performance and Predictability,"

   *Journal of Financial Markets* 4, No. 1 (scheduled publication date February 2001), pp. 1–32.

10. **Ibbotson, Roger G., and Rex A. Sinquefield**

    Speech to the Center for Research in Security Prices, May 1974.

11. **Ibbotson, Roger G., and Paul D. Kaplan**

    "Does Asset Allocation Policy Explain 40, 90, or 100 Percent of Performance?,"

    *Financial Analysts Journal,* January/February 2000.

12. **Ibbotson, Roger G., and Rex A. Sinquefield (foreword by Jack L. Treynor)**

    *Stocks, Bonds, Bills, and Inflation: The Past (1926–1976) and the Future (1977–2000),* 1977 ed.,

    Institute of Chartered Financial Analysts, Charlottesville, VA, 1977.

13. **Ibbotson, Roger G., and Rex A. Sinquefield, (foreword by Laurence B. Siegel)**

    *Stocks, Bonds, Bills, and Inflation: The Past and the Future,* 1982 ed.,

    Institute of Chartered Financial Analysts, Charlottesville, VA, 1982.

14. **Ibbotson, Roger G., and Rex A. Sinquefield**

    *Stocks, Bonds, Bills, and Inflation: Historical Returns (1926–1987)*, 1989 ed.,

    Dow-Jones Irwin, Homewood, IL, 1989.

15. **Ibbotson, Roger G., and Rex A. Sinquefield**

    *Stocks, Bonds, Bills, and Inflation: Historical Returns (1926–1978),*

    Institute of Chartered Financial Analysts, Charlottesville, VA, 1979.

16. **Ibbotson, Roger G., and Rex A. Sinquefield**

    "Stocks, Bonds, Bills, and Inflation: Year-By-Year Historical Returns (1926–1974),"

    *The Journal of Business* 49, No. 1 (January 1976), pp. 11–47.

17. **Ibbotson, Roger G., and Rex A. Sinquefield**

    "Stocks, Bonds, Bills, and Inflation: Simulations of the Future (1976–2000),"

    *The Journal of Business* 49, No. 3 (July 1976), pp. 313–338.

18. **Levy, Haim, and Deborah Gunthorpe**

    "Optimal Investment Proportions in Senior Securities and Equities Under Alternative Holding Periods,"

    *Journal of Portfolio Management*, Summer 1993, page 33.

19. **Lewis, Alan L., Sheen T. Kassouf, R. Dennis Brehm, and Jack Johnston**

    "The Ibbotson-Sinquefield Simulation Made Easy,"

    *The Journal of Business 53*, No. 2 (1980), pp. 205–214.

20. **Markowitz, Harry M.**

    *Portfolio Selection: Efficient Diversification of Investments,*

    John Wiley & Sons, New York, 1959.

21. **Nuttall, Jennifer A., and John Nuttall**

    "Asset Allocation Claims–Truth or Fiction?," (unpublished), 1998.

22. **Sharpe, William F.**

    "The Arithmetic of Active Management,"

    *Financial Analysts Journal*, January/February 1991.

23. **Stevens, Dale H., Ronald J. Surz, and Mark E. Wimer**

    "The Importance of Investment Policy,"

    *The Journal of Investing*, Winter 1999.

Stocks, Bonds, Bills, and Inflation

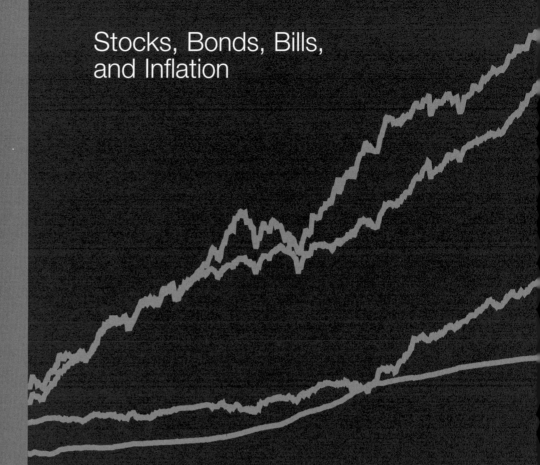

# Chapters

**Ibbotson**Associates

# Chapter 1

## Highlights of the 2000 Markets and the Past Decade

## Events of 2000

The stock market in the year 2000 was marked with extreme volatility and produced returns well below historical averages. Both large and small company stocks posted negative total returns for the year 2000, with small company stocks finishing the year ahead of large company stocks. This effectively ended a nine year run of positive annual total returns for large company stocks.

Bonds demonstrated one of their best years despite the Federal Reserve raising its fed funds rate on three separate occasions early in the year. The raise was in response to signs of excessive economic growth and was increased by a quarter-point in both February and March and by a half-point in May to bring the rate to 6.50 percent. Throughout the remainder of the year, the Fed decided to maintain the existing stance of monetary policy and the rate remained unchanged. Substantial shortfalls in sales and earnings, erosion of consumer confidence, and a drop in demand and profits can serve as signs that economic growth is slowing.

## Strong Economic Growth Continues

The Gross Domestic Product (GDP), a measure of the market value of all goods and services produced within the U.S., grew at a real (inflation-adjusted) rate of 5.0 percent for the year 2000. This rate of growth was higher than the revised growth rate for 1999 of 4.2 percent. The 5.0 percent growth rate was the best performance since the 7.3 percent growth rate recorded in 1984.

The U.S. civilian unemployment rate continued to fall in 2000 to its lowest level in almost 30 years. From a high of 4.1 percent at year-end 1999, unemployment fell slightly to 4.0 percent by year-end 2000. The tightening of the job market did not appear to have a strong impact on wage inflation, with average hourly earnings up from the previous year.

## Indecision 2000

The 2000 Presidential election was filled with a vast amount of uncertainty as well as turmoil. An election that was supposed to have ended around five weeks earlier was finally put to rest when Vice President Al Gore conceded on December 13, 2000. Weeks of ballot recounting, legislative sessions and lawsuits and a number of other delays stemmed from questionable and inconclusive results. The recounting process was triggered by so-called undervotes—ballots that showed no vote for any presidential candidate during the machine count. The United States Supreme Court ruled to stop the process of recounting because it failed to provide a fair and uniform standard for tallying the disputed votes. It is important to note that none of the recounts gave the vice president the votes he needed to overtake President-elect George W. Bush.

## AT&T to Split into Four Companies

AT&T, following a significant drop in its stock price over this past year, informed investors that it will split the troubled company into four parts in the year 2002. The increase of shareholder value is the telephone and cable television giant's main objective. The company's cable-television operations, AT&T Wireless Group and AT&T Broadband, will be represented by independent stocks. AT&T Consumer, which sells long-distance services to homes, will get its own tracking stock and AT&T, the parent company, will own the Business Services division as its principal operation. The goal is that the creation of four units will help each segment prosper independently without having to fight for cash or attention from parent Ma Bell.

## Bridgestone/Firestone Tire Recall

Bridgestone/Firestone tires have been under investigation for their role in over 100 deaths and 400 injuries in the United States. Firestone, the largest unit of Japan's Bridgestone Corporation, has struggled since August, when it recalled 6.5 million tires after reports of tread separation linked to their product. Recall costs most likely will exceed $400 million. The massive recall is a major factor in plunging sales and major layoffs. Sales of replacement tires carrying the Firestone brand name dropped by 40 percent during the two months following the recall. The company is also facing several personal-injury lawsuits. The road ahead to rebuild the company's image in the eyes of U.S. consumers should prove to be a daunting challenge.

The Firestone recall, however, should propel interest in a new revolution of tires. Congress has mandated that within three years all new cars will be equipped with warning systems to indicate to the driver when a tire is considerably underinflated—which is a major cause of tread separation. This development should be just the tip of the tire-technology iceberg.

## Microsoft Antitrust Investigation

The Supreme Court rendered a decision to send Microsoft's appeal to a lower court, which will most likely prolong the final resolution of the landmark case by at least six months and possibly even several years, antitrust experts agree. However, experts remain divided on whether the high court's decision will ultimately help the software powerhouse triumph in its attempt to reverse Judge Thomas Penfield Jackson's order to divide the company into two parts. Microsoft submitted a 150-page document/brief on November 27, 2000, which should be the first formal step toward the next round of courtroom arguments, scheduled for February 26 and 27 before seven members of the U.S. Circuit Court of Appeals for the District of Columbia. The brief asks the court to dismiss the case completely, revisits most of the trial's contested issues and requests that a different judge be assigned to re-hear the case. On January 12, the government is due to file its brief, with Microsoft given a chance to reply by the end of January. Oral arguments are set for late February.

## Oil Prices Soar

Despite four increases by the Organization of Petroleum Exporting Countries, or OPEC, of a total of 3.7 million barrels a day this year, oil prices have refused to cool down. The main reasons for such an increase in oil prices this year include the world's growing thirst for oil, the trillions of dollars of investments needed to finance additional oil production and refining facilities, and the increasing reliance on a select few countries of the Middle East for the immense amounts of oil required to fuel the growing world economy. Also, the importance of Saudi Arabia in the world of oil appears destined to grow. The International Energy Agency believes that only a handful of countries in the Middle East have the reserves needed to adhere to the world's soaring demand for oil.

The President of OPEC, however, believes that world oil prices will moderate next year. Current oversupply and modest demand next year should lead to a rise in inventory, which in turn should cool down oil prices.

## Middle East Violence

Due to continued aggression and fighting in the Middle East, Palestinian leader Yasser Arafat and Israeli Prime Minister Ehud Barak agreed to the formation of an international fact-finding commission to investigate the causes of and possible solutions to the growing violence. The five-member International Commission is headed by former United States senator George Mitchell and is made up of diplomats from the European Union, Norway, Turkey, and the United States. Currently there is no official timetable for the commission to complete its investigation. Analysts state that the commission can help build confidence among leaders in the turbulent region.

## Barak Resigns

Israeli Prime Minister Ehud Barak tendered his resignation on December 10, 2000 to Israeli President Moshe Katzav. Barak's resignation went into effect on December 12, 2000. Barak's decision to resign is viewed by many as a strategic move to obstruct Prime Minister Benjamin Netanyahu's run for the prime minister's position. Under Israeli law, Netanyahu cannot run for the prime minister's post as long as Israel's parliament remains intact. However, this did not stop Netanyahu from declaring his candidacy while also appealing for help among Israeli lawmakers to draft legislation that would allow him to run for office. The law clearly states that until the parliament is dissolved, only sitting members can run for the prime minister's post. Netanyahu is barred from being a candidate due to the fact that he is not a member of the legislature. Palestinian Authority President Yasser Arafat said he hoped Barak's move would not affect the Mideast peace process.

## Montgomery Ward Files for Bankruptcy

Retailer Montgomery Ward announced that it will close its doors for good after 128 years and filed for Chapter 11 bankruptcy-court protection. The move will prompt the closing of 250 stores and 10 distribution centers and will threaten at least 28,000 jobs throughout the United States. Montgomery Ward was a fully owned unit of General Electric Company's GE Capital.

## Mergers and Acquisitions

Merger and acquisition activity in the United States for the year 2000 surpassed last year's total in terms of value despite the high level of stock market volatility. Worldwide, merger activity was slightly up from the previous year. Companies looked to mergers for potential growth opportunities and to gain market share. The opportunity to enter new markets was also a favorable reason to merge. All in all, the main goal is to become more competitive. The state of the economy will undoubtedly be the most significant factor driving mergers and acquisitions next year, and all eyes will be on the Federal Reserve's anticipated rate cut.

This past year experienced a number of large-scale merger agreements within the food group industry. Unilever PLC, one of the world's largest consumer products companies, acquired Bestfoods, a producer of consumer foods, for over $20 billion. Philip Morris Companies, Inc. completed its acquisition of Nabisco Holdings Corp. for a little under $20 billion. The Phillip Morris family of companies is the world's largest producer and marketer of consumer packaged goods. General Mills shareholders approved two key proposals concerning its planned purchase of Pillsbury Co., a unit of Diageo PLC. Diageo shareholders approved the transaction in October. The deal, however, awaits Federal Trade Commission review. Kellogg Co. agreed to acquire Keebler Foods in a deal valued at a little under $4 billion. The deal is subject to the approval of Keebler shareholders and should create a powerful diversified food company boasting more than $10 billion in annual sales. PepsiCo Inc. proposed an acquisition of The Quaker Oats Company for a little over $13 billion. However, the proposed acquisition can be terminated by either party if not complete by June 2, 2001. The transaction is subject to the approval of both companies' shareholders, the European Union's antitrust commission and the expiration of the waiting period.

The financial services industry saw Chase Manhattan Corp., the third largest U.S. bank holding company, receive Federal Reserve approval to proceed with its purchase of commercial and investment bank J.P. Morgan & Co. Inc. for around $30 billion. Their respective shareholders approved the merger of the two banking companies, and the merger was completed on December 31, 2000. The company, with assets of more than $705 billion, will begin trading Tuesday, January 2, 2001, under the symbol JPM. The merged bank, to be called J.P. Morgan Chase & Co. Inc., will be the third-ranked U.S. bank behind Bank of America Corp. and Citigroup Inc. Citigroup Inc. acquired Associates First Capital Corp., a provider of leasing and related services to individual consumers and businesses worldwide, in a deal valued around $30 billion. Firstar Corp. agreed to acquire U.S. Bancorp for around $21 billion. The merger, which is expected to close in the first quarter of 2001, combines a financial holding company (Firstar) with about $74.5 billion in total assets with a financial services holding company with $86 billion in assets. UBS AG agreed to acquire PaineWebber Group Inc., for around $16 billion. The acquisition is designed to increase the global reach of both companies and expand UBS' private client operations.

Another vastly important deal may produce the biggest media merger ever. The Federal Trade Commission unanimously approved, with conditions, the proposed merger between America Online, Inc. and Time Warner, Inc., a merger estimated at over $110 billion. AOL is the world's largest Internet-service provider, and Time Warner is a media conglomerate that holds a major position in the publishing, film, broadcast and cable television markets. The agreed upon conditions include Time Warner having to offer its subscribers the option to sign up to at least one nonaffiliated cable, high-speed Internet service provider via Time Warner's cable system before AOL itself begins offering such service. It must then offer two other service provider options shortly after AOL launches its offering. Also, AOL Time Warner must not interfere with content passed along the networks it has contracted to other Internet service providers. The FCC is currently reviewing the proposed merger and will most likely continue to do so into the early part of 2001.

With oil prices having escalated at an unprecedented level for the year 2000, the creation of an oil mega-merger would most likely be met with serious antitrust scrutiny. When the first wave of deals struck in 1998, oil prices were seriously on the decline. The opposite currently holds true. This, however, has not stopped the agreement between Chevron Corp. and Texaco Inc. which will form the world's fourth-largest publicly traded oil company. The deal is valued at around $35 billion. Exxon Mobil Corp., Royal Dutch/Shell Group and BP Amoco PLC, which have grown in size as a result of recent mergers, would still be ahead of the new company. Chevron is currently gathering information in response to a request from the Federal Trade Commission for more information concerning the proposed merger. The two companies expected such requests with the most recent being the second from the FTC. In other news, natural gas pipeline giants El Paso Energy Corp. and Coastal Corp. announced their plans for a merger valued at around $30 billion. The two companies expected approval from the Federal Trade Commission towards the end of December. Such a deal would place the new merged company up towards the top near the proposed Chevron/Texaco merger.

One of the other bigger-name mergers announced, valued at around $45 billion, was General Electric Company's announcement to acquire Honeywell International Inc., a manufacturer of aircraft engines and parts, turbines, radar systems, motor vehicles, brakes, chemicals, and plastic materials. Antitrust enforcers of the Justice Department currently are investigating the acquisition with a focus on military electronics and engine parts. Federal antitrust approval is unlikely before mid-February, but could come later, those close to the review state. The deal may also face antitrust issues in Europe. After the merger, Honeywell is expected to be divided up among four GE units: GE Aircraft Engines, which would roughly double in size; GE Power Systems, which makes generators and related power equipment; GE Industrial Systems, which makes thousands of industrial-electrical and other products; and GE Plastics, which includes the company's chemicals operations.

In other news, Glaxo Wellcome PLC, a major global pharmaceutical group engaged in the creation and discovery, development, manufacture, and marketing of prescription and non-prescription medicines merged with fellow pharmaceutical company, SmithKline Beecham PLC in a deal valued at around $75 million. Deutsche Telekom, a provider of wireless and personal communications services, agreed to acquire VoiceStream Wireless Corp. in a merger valued at around $50 billion. JDS Uniphase Corp., a provider of advanced fiber optic components and modules, agreed to acquire SDL Inc., a company which designs, manufactures, and markets semiconductor lasers and fiber optic related products. The pending deal is estimated at around $40 billion.

## IPO Roller Coaster

Investors who were once so excited and enthusiastic about Initial Public Offerings (IPOs) have, for the most part, been down in the dumps this past year. The IPO market has been a bit frustrating and somewhat of a disappointment as the U.S. stock market has turned treacherous. Few of the meager number of recent offerings have risen considerably in the days after the IPO and IPOs as a whole have performed rather poorly this past year. Much of the IPO fanfare of 1999 spilled over into the first quarter of 2000—with IPO issuance as well as dollar value up when compared to the previous year. However, offerings fell during the second quarter, bounced back during the third, and fell once again during the fourth. Many companies preparing for an initial public offering have simply decided to wait it out in hopes for a better market environment. At the IPO and technology-stock mania peak of last year and earlier this year, it was quite lucrative for many small investors to purchase an IPO on or around the offer price and watch it take off. Times have changed in the year 2000.

## Results of 2000 Capital Markets

### Large Company Stocks

The market for U.S. large company stocks is represented here by the total return on the S&P 500. (The total return includes reinvestment of dividends.) Large company stocks for the year produced a total return of –9.11 percent, which is substantially below the long-term average return (1926 to 2000) of 11.05 percent. Only four of the twelve months between January and December 2000 produced positive returns. The month of March produced the highest return at 9.78 percent, while the month of November produced the lowest return at –7.88 percent. The year 2000 effectively ended a five-year stretch in which large company stocks produced returns that were substantially above their long-term average.

Considering the relatively poor performance of the market this past year, an index of large company stock total returns, initialized at $1.00 on December 31, 1925, closed down versus the previous year. The index grew to $2,586.52 by the end of 2000, compared with $2,845.63 a year earlier.

### Small Company Stocks

Small company stocks outperformed the equities of larger companies for the second year in a row, even with a total return of –3.59 percent. Five of the twelve months between January and December 2000 produced positive returns. The month of February produced the highest return at 23.58 percent, while the month of April produced the lowest return at –12.51 percent. The small stock premium, or geometric difference of small over large stocks, was positive 6.07 percent (versus 7.22 percent the previous year).

The cumulative wealth index, initialized at $1.00 at the end of 1925, closed down versus the previous year. The index grew to $6,402.23 by the end of 2000, compared with a staggering $6,640.79 a year earlier. The 2000 value ranks as the second highest close since 1926.

## A Fall in Bond Yields

Bond prices rose as yields fell on all categories of bonds in 2000 with the exception of U.S. Treasury bills. Intermediate-term rates fell more than long-term rates. Short-term rates experienced a modest increase. Since long-term bonds are more interest-rate sensitive, they increased in value more than their intermediate-term counterparts.

## Long-Term Government Bonds

Long-term government bonds (with maturity near 20 years) returned 21.48 percent. This return ranks as the fifth highest year-end return over the past 75 years, with 40.36 percent serving as the highest year-end return in 1982. The yield on long-term government bonds was 5.58 percent compared to 6.82 percent by year-end 1999. With the exception of the 5.42 percent yield at year-end 1998, the year-end 2000 yield was the lowest since 1967, which produced a year-end yield of 5.56 percent.

An index of total returns, initialized at $1.00 at year-end 1925, grew to $48.86 by the end of December 2000. The capital appreciation index of long-term government bond returns closed at $0.95, which is still substantially less than its all-time high of $1.43 reached in early 1946.

## Intermediate-Term Government Bonds

The total return on intermediate-term government bonds (with maturity 5 years) in 2000 was 12.59 percent. This return ranks as the tenth highest year-end return over the past 75 years, with 29.10 percent serving as the highest year-end return in 1982. The yield on intermediate-term government bonds was 5.07 percent compared to 6.46 percent by year-end 1999. With the exception of the 4.68 percent yield at year-end 1998, the year-end 2000 yield was the lowest since 1966, which produced a year-end yield of 4.79 percent.

The wealth index of intermediate-term government bonds, initialized at $1.00 at year-end 1925, rose to an all-time high of $48.59 at the end of December 2000.

## Long-Term Corporate Bonds

Long-term corporate bonds (with maturity near 20 years), along with their government counterparts, also experienced a great year, producing a year-end total return of 12.87 percent. Total returns were positive in nine of the twelve months during the year, with negative results occurring only in January, April, and May.

The year-end bond default premium, or net return from investing in long-term corporate bonds rather than long-term government bonds of equal maturity, was −7.09 percent. This marks the second lowest bond default premium during the past 75 years, with the −7.11 percent year-end premium in 1974 being the lowest. This is significantly lower than that of its long-term (1926-2000) average of 0.36 percent. A dollar invested in long-term corporate bonds at year-end 1925, rose to $64.08 by the end of December 2000.

Graph 1-1

**The Decade: Wealth Indices of Investments in U.S. Stocks, Bonds, Bills, and Inflation**
Year-End 1990 = $1.00

from December 1990 to December 2000

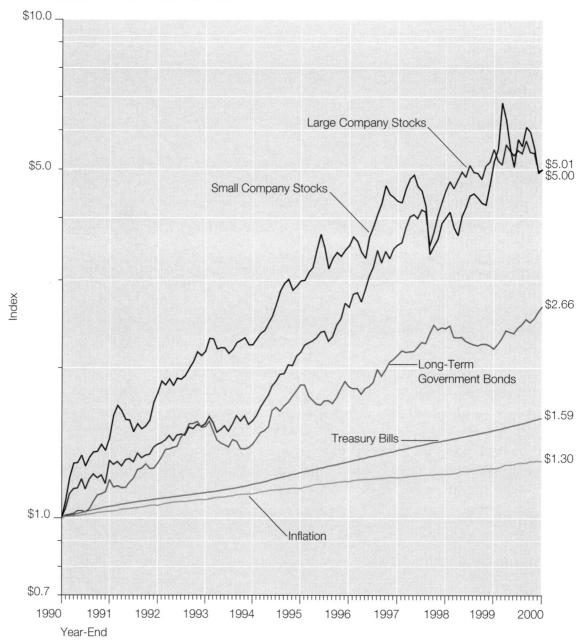

## Treasury Bills

The yield on U.S. Treasury bills experienced a modest increase in 2000, rising from 4.89 percent at the end of 1999 to 5.75 percent at year-end 2000. An investment in bills with approximately 30 days to maturity had a total return of 5.89 percent, the 17th highest return over the past 75 years. The cumulative index of Treasury bill total returns ended the year at $16.56, compared with $15.64 a year earlier. Because monthly Treasury bill returns are nearly always positive, each monthly index value typically sets a new all-time high.

## Inflation

Consumer prices rose at an estimated annualized rate of 3.39 percent in 2000, which is considerably higher than the prior year as well as the long-term historical average (1926-2000) of 3.08 percent. Thus, inflation has remained below 5 percent for eighteen of the last nineteen years. (Inflation was above 5 percent in 1990.)

A cumulative inflation index, initialized at $1.00 at year-end 1925, finished 2000 at $9.71, up from $9.39 at year-end 1999. That is, a "basket" of consumer goods and services that cost $1.00 in 1925 would cost $9.71 today. The two baskets are not identical, but are intended to be comparable.

## A Graphic View of the Decade

The past decade, 1991-2000, has been characterized by a robust rate of increase in stock prices, with the exception of this past year, which produced negative returns for both large and small company stocks. Stock market volatility for the period 1991-1996 fell to levels not seen since the 1960s, as prices slowly climbed. Volatility increased again in 1997 through 2000.

Graph 1-1 shows the market results for the past decade—illustrating the growth of $1.00 invested on December 31, 1990 in stocks, bonds, and bills, along with an index of inflation. A review of the major themes of the past decade, as revealed in the capital markets, appears later in this chapter.

## The Decade in Perspective

The great stock and bond market rise of the 1980s and 1990s was one of the most unusual in the history of the capital markets. In terms of the magnitude of the rise, these decades most closely resembled the 1920s and 1950s. These four decades accounted for a majority of the market's cumulative total return over the past 75 years. While the importance of a long-term view of investing is noted consistently in this book and elsewhere, the counterpart of this observation is: To achieve high returns on your investments, you only need to participate in the few periods of truly outstanding return. The bull markets of 1922 to mid-1929, 1949–1961 (roughly speaking, the Fifties), mid-1982 to mid-1987, and 1991–1999 were such periods. The 2000s have gotten off to a poor start for both large and small company stocks but the bond market demonstrated one of its best years.

Table 1-1

**Compound Annual Rates of Return by Decade (in percent)**

|  | 1920s* | 1930s | 1940s | 1950s | 1960s | 1970s | 1980s | 1990s | 2000s** | 1991-00 |
|---|---|---|---|---|---|---|---|---|---|---|
| Large Company | 19.2 | −0.1 | 9.2 | 19.4 | 7.8 | 5.9 | 17.5 | 18.2 | −9.1 | 17.5 |
| Small Company | −4.5 | 1.4 | 20.7 | 16.9 | 15.5 | 11.5 | 15.8 | 15.1 | −3.6 | 17.5 |
| Long-Term Corporate | 5.2 | 6.9 | 2.7 | 1.0 | 1.7 | 6.2 | 13.0 | 8.4 | 12.9 | 9.0 |
| Long-Term Government | 5.0 | 4.9 | 3.2 | −0.1 | 1.4 | 5.5 | 12.6 | 8.8 | 21.5 | 10.3 |
| Intermediate-Term Government | 4.2 | 4.6 | 1.8 | 1.3 | 3.5 | 7.0 | 11.9 | 7.2 | 12.6 | 7.5 |
| Treasury Bills | 3.7 | 0.6 | 0.4 | 1.9 | 3.9 | 6.3 | 8.9 | 4.9 | 5.9 | 4.7 |
| Inflation | −1.1 | −2.0 | 5.4 | 2.2 | 2.5 | 7.4 | 5.1 | 2.9 | 3.4 | 2.7 |

*Based on the period 1926–1929.

**Based on the period 2000 only.

Table 1-1 compares the returns by decade on all of the basic asset classes covered in this book. It is notable that either large company stocks or small company stocks were the best performing asset class in every full decade save one. In this table, the Twenties cover the period 1926–1929.

It is interesting to place the decades of superior performance in historical context. The Twenties were preceded by mediocre returns and high inflation and were followed by the most devastating stock market crash and economic depression in American history. This sequence of events mitigated the impact of the Twenties bull market on investor wealth. Nevertheless, the stock market became a liquid secondary market in the Twenties, rendering that period important for reasons other than return. In contrast, the Fifties were preceded and followed by decades with roughly average equity returns. The Eighties were preceded by a decade of "stagflation" where modest stock price gains were seriously eroded by inflation and were followed by a period of stability in the Nineties.

The bond market performance of the Eighties and Nineties has no precedent. Bond yields, which had risen consistently since the 1940s, reached unprecedented levels in 1980–1981. (Other countries experiencing massive inflation have had correspondingly high interest rates.) Never before having had so far to fall, bond yields dropped further and faster than at any other time, producing what is indisputably the greatest bond bull market in history. Unfortunately, the boom came to an end in 1994. After falling to 21-year lows one year earlier, bond yields rose in 1994 to their highest level in over three years. After a gradual decline, bond yields rose again in 1999, but fell in 2000.

The historical themes of the past decade, as they relate to the capital markets, can be summarized in three observations. First, the 17½ year period starting in mid-1982 and ending in 1999, comprised a rare span of time in which investors quickly accumulated wealth.

Second, the postwar aberration of ever-higher inflation rates ended with a dramatic disinflation in the early Eighties. In the Nineties, inflation remained low. However, the more deeply embedded aberration of consistently positive inflation rates—that is, ever-higher prices—has not ended. As this decade begins, inflation is above its long-term historical average.

Finally, participation in the returns of the capital markets reached levels not even approached in the Twenties, the Fifties, or the atypical boom period of 1967–1972. The vast size and importance of pension funds, as well as the rapidly increasing popularity of stock and bond mutual funds as a basic savings vehicle, have caused more individuals to experience the returns of the capital markets than ever before.

## Graphic Depiction of Returns in the Decade

Graphs 1-2, 1-3, and 1-4 contain bar graphs of 1991–2000 annual and 2000 monthly total returns on the assets discussed above. The top part of Graph 1-2 compares large company stocks and long-term government bonds. The graph shows that stock and bond returns were quite closely correlated over the decade. [See Chapter 6.] The bottom half of Graph 1-2 compares large company stocks and small company stocks, showing that neither consistently outperformed the other over the past decade.

The top part of Graph 1-3 compares corporate and government bonds of like maturity (approximately 20 years). Clearly, returns of corporate bonds did not always outperform government bonds over the past decade, contradicting their historical trend. The bottom part of Graph 1-3 compares long-term and intermediate-term government bonds. Intermediate-term bonds are less volatile; and, as usual, tended to return less than long-term bonds in rising markets.

Graph 1-4 displays bar graphs of the 1991–2000 annual and 2000 monthly Treasury bill returns, inflation rates, and real riskless rates of return. The top part of Graph 1-4 compares Treasury bills and inflation. The bottom part of Graph 1-4 shows month-by-month real riskless rates of return, defined as Treasury bill returns in excess of inflation.

## Tables of Market Results for 1991–2000

The 1991–2000 annual and 2000 quarterly and monthly total returns on the seven basic asset classes studied in this book are presented in Table 1-2. Table 1-3 displays cumulative indices of the returns shown in Table 1-2, based on a starting value of $1.00 on December 31, 1925.

For the past decade, stocks have had unusually high returns, with the exception of this past year. Bonds and Treasury bills produced returns that were well-above their long-term historical averages and inflation rates fell to levels below their 75-year average.

## Graph 1-2

**1991–2000 Annual and 2000 Monthly Total Returns**
A Comparison of Large Company Stocks with Long-Term Government Bonds, and
Large Company Stocks with Small Company Stocks (in percent)

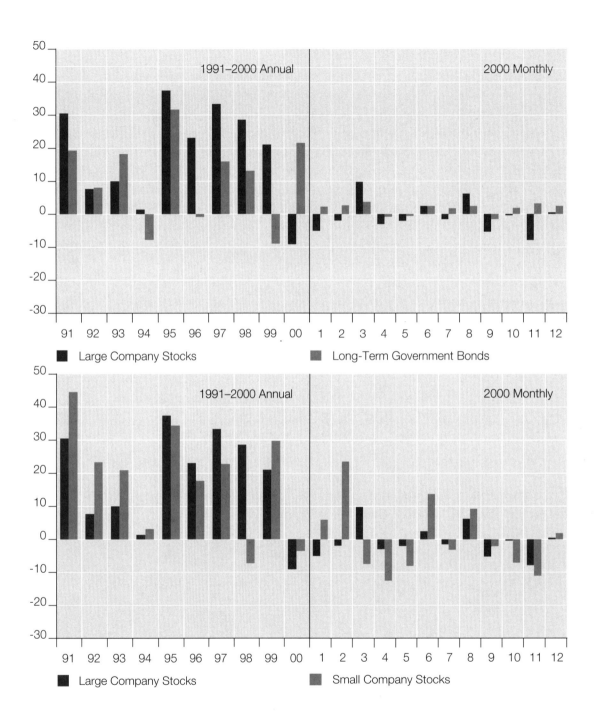

Graph 1-3

## 1991–2000 Annual and 2000 Monthly Total Returns

A Comparison of Long-Term Governement Bonds with Long-Term Corporate Bonds, and Long-Term Government Bonds with Intermediate-Term Government Bonds (in percent)

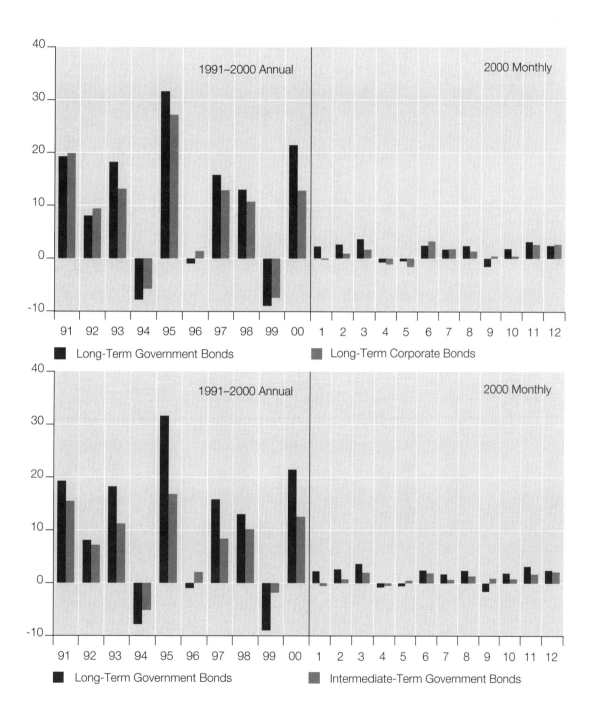

## Graph 1-4

### 1991–2000 Annual and 2000 Monthly Total Returns

Treasury Bills, Inflation and Real Riskless Rates of Return (in percent)

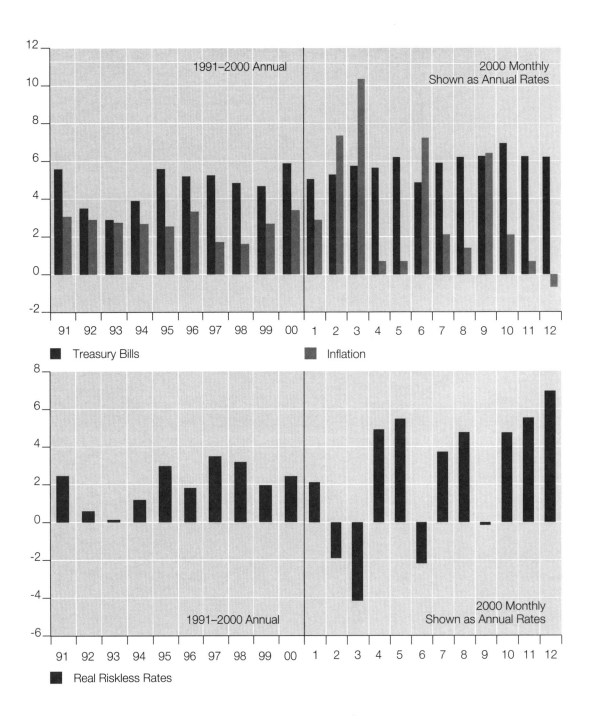

## Table 1-2

### 1991-2000 Annual and 2000 Quarterly and Monthly Market Results

Returns on Stocks, Bonds, Bills, and Inflation (in percent)

| Year | Large Company Stocks | Small Company Stocks | Long-Term Corporate Bonds | Long-Term Government Bonds | Intermediate Government Bonds | U.S. Treasury Bills | Inflation |
|---|---|---|---|---|---|---|---|
| **1991-2000 Annual Returns** | | | | | | | |
| 1991 | 30.55 | 44.63 | 19.89 | 19.30 | 15.46 | 5.60 | 3.06 |
| 1992 | 7.67 | 23.35 | 9.39 | 8.05 | 7.19 | 3.51 | 2.90 |
| 1993 | 9.99 | 20.98 | 13.19 | 18.24 | 11.24 | 2.90 | 2.75 |
| 1994 | 1.31 | 3.11 | −5.76 | −7.77 | −5.14 | 3.90 | 2.67 |
| 1995 | 37.43 | 34.46 | 27.20 | 31.67 | 16.80 | 5.60 | 2.54 |
| 1996 | 23.07 | 17.62 | 1.40 | −0.93 | 2.10 | 5.21 | 3.32 |
| 1997 | 33.36 | 22.78 | 12.95 | 15.85 | 8.38 | 5.26 | 1.70 |
| 1998 | 28.58 | −7.31 | 10.76 | 13.06 | 10.21 | 4.86 | 1.61 |
| 1999 | 21.04 | 29.79 | −7.45 | −8.96 | −1.77 | 4.68 | 2.68 |
| 2000 | −9.11 | −3.59 | 12.87 | 21.48 | 12.59 | 5.89 | 3.39 |
| **2000 Quarterly Returns** | | | | | | | |
| I-00 | 2.29 | 21.1 | 2.41 | 8.83 | 2.28 | 1.32 | 1.66 |
| II-00 | −2.66 | −8.58 | 0.44 | 1.11 | 2.00 | 1.37 | 0.70 |
| III-00 | −0.97 | 3.44 | 3.65 | 2.54 | 3.04 | 1.50 | 0.81 |
| IV-00 | −7.83 | −15.81 | 5.87 | 7.67 | 4.73 | 1.58 | 0.17 |
| **2000 Monthly Returns** | | | | | | | |
| 12-99 | 5.89 | 11.37 | −1.02 | −1.55 | −0.48 | 0.44 | 0.00 |
| 01-00 | −5.02 | 5.95 | −0.21 | 2.28 | −0.53 | 0.41 | 0.24 |
| 02-00 | −1.89 | 23.58 | 0.92 | 2.64 | 0.78 | 0.43 | 0.59 |
| 03-00 | 9.78 | −7.51 | 1.69 | 3.67 | 2.03 | 0.47 | 0.82 |
| 04-00 | −3.01 | −12.51 | −1.15 | −0.76 | −0.43 | 0.46 | 0.06 |
| 05-00 | −2.05 | −8.08 | −1.61 | −0.54 | 0.52 | 0.50 | 0.06 |
| 06-00 | 2.46 | 13.68 | 3.26 | 2.44 | 1.91 | 0.40 | 0.58 |
| 07-00 | −1.56 | −3.22 | 1.79 | 1.73 | 0.72 | 0.48 | 0.17 |
| 08-00 | 6.21 | 9.25 | 1.35 | 2.40 | 1.34 | 0.50 | 0.12 |
| 09-00 | −5.28 | −2.17 | 0.46 | −1.57 | 0.96 | 0.51 | 0.52 |
| 10-00 | −0.42 | −7.06 | 0.45 | 1.87 | 0.79 | 0.56 | 0.17 |
| 11-00 | −7.88 | −11.10 | 2.63 | 3.19 | 1.74 | 0.51 | 0.06 |
| 12-00 | 0.49 | 1.89 | 2.70 | 2.43 | 2.14 | 0.50 | −0.06 |

## Table 1-3

### 1991-2000 Annual and 2000 Monthly Market Results
Indices of Returns on Stocks, Bonds, Bills, and Inflation

Year-End 1925 = $1.00

| Year | Large Company Stocks | Small Company Stocks | Long-Term Corporate Bonds | Long-Term Government Bonds | Intermediate Government Bonds | U.S. Treasury Bills | Inflation |
|---|---|---|---|---|---|---|---|
| **1991-2000 Annual Indices** | | | | | | | |
| 1991 | 675.592 | 1847.629 | 32.577 | 21.942 | 27.270 | 11.012 | 7.693 |
| 1992 | 727.412 | 2279.039 | 35.637 | 23.709 | 29.230 | 11.398 | 7.916 |
| 1993 | 800.078 | 2757.147 | 40.336 | 28.034 | 32.516 | 11.728 | 8.133 |
| 1994 | 810.538 | 2842.773 | 38.012 | 25.856 | 30.843 | 12.186 | 8.351 |
| 1995 | 1113.918 | 3822.398 | 48.353 | 34.044 | 36.025 | 12.868 | 8.563 |
| 1996 | 1370.946 | 4495.993 | 49.031 | 33.727 | 36.782 | 13.538 | 8.847 |
| 1997 | 1828.326 | 5519.969 | 55.380 | 39.074 | 39.864 | 14.250 | 8.998 |
| 1998 | 2350.892 | 5116.648 | 61.339 | 44.178 | 43.933 | 14.942 | 9.143 |
| 1999 | 2845.629 | 6640.788 | 56.772 | 40.218 | 43.155 | 15.641 | 9.389 |
| 2000 | 2586.524 | 6402.228 | 64.077 | 48.856 | 48.589 | 16.563 | 9.707 |
| **2000 Monthly Indices** | | | | | | | |
| 12-99 | 2845.629 | 6640.788 | 56.772 | 40.218 | 43.155 | 15.641 | 9.389 |
| 01-00 | 2702.664 | 7035.915 | 56.652 | 41.135 | 42.925 | 15.706 | 9.411 |
| 02-00 | 2651.503 | 8694.984 | 57.174 | 42.220 | 43.260 | 15.774 | 9.467 |
| 03-00 | 2910.899 | 8041.990 | 58.142 | 43.768 | 44.140 | 15.848 | 9.545 |
| 04-00 | 2823.310 | 7035.937 | 57.476 | 43.437 | 43.950 | 15.920 | 9.550 |
| 05-00 | 2765.376 | 6467.434 | 56.552 | 43.200 | 44.179 | 16.001 | 9.556 |
| 06-00 | 2833.543 | 7352.179 | 58.396 | 44.254 | 45.024 | 16.064 | 9.612 |
| 07-00 | 2789.254 | 7115.438 | 59.442 | 45.018 | 45.347 | 16.141 | 9.628 |
| 08-00 | 2962.495 | 7773.616 | 60.245 | 46.100 | 45.953 | 16.223 | 9.640 |
| 09-00 | 2806.105 | 7604.929 | 60.525 | 45.376 | 46.394 | 16.305 | 9.690 |
| 10-00 | 2794.235 | 7068.021 | 60.797 | 46.227 | 46.760 | 16.397 | 9.707 |
| 11-00 | 2573.937 | 6283.471 | 62.394 | 47.699 | 47.573 | 16.480 | 9.712 |
| 12-00 | 2586.524 | 6402.228 | 64.077 | 48.856 | 48.589 | 16.563 | 9.707 |

# Chapter 2

**The Long Run Perspective**

---

## Motivation

A long view of capital market history, exemplified by the 75-year period (1926–2000) examined here, uncovers the basic relationships between risk and return among the different asset classes and between nominal and real (inflation-adjusted) returns. The goal of this study of asset returns is to provide a period long enough to include most or all of the major types of events that investors have experienced and may experience in the future. Such events include war and peace, growth and decline, bull and bear markets, inflation and deflation, and other less dramatic events that affect asset returns.

By studying the past, one can make inferences about the future. While the actual events that occurred during 1926–2000 will not be repeated, the event-types (not specific events) of that period can be expected to recur. It is sometimes said that only a few periods are unusual, such as the crash of 1929–1932 and World War II. This logic is suspicious because all periods are unusual. Two of the most unusual events of the century—the stock market crash of 1987 and the equally remarkable inflation of the 1970s and early 1980s—took place over the last two decades. From the perspective that historical event-types tend to repeat themselves, a 75-year examination of past capital market returns reveals a great deal about what may be expected in the future. [See Chapter 9.]

---

## Historical Returns on Stocks, Bonds, Bills, and Inflation

Graph 2-1 graphically depicts the growth of $1.00 invested in large company stocks, small company stocks, long-term government bonds, Treasury bills, and a hypothetical asset returning the inflation rate over the period from the end of 1925 to the end of 2000. All results assume reinvestment of dividends on stocks or coupons on bonds and no taxes. Transaction costs are not included, except in the small stock index starting in 1982.

Each of the cumulative index values is initialized at $1.00 at year-end 1925. The graph vividly illustrates that large company stocks and small company stocks were the big winners over the entire 75-year period: investments of $1.00 in these assets would have grown to $2,586.52 and $6,402.23, respectively, by year-end 2000. This phenomenal growth was earned by taking substantial risk. In contrast, long-term government bonds (with an approximate 20-year maturity), which exposed the holder to much less risk, grew to only $48.86.

The lowest-risk strategy over the past 75 years (for those with short-term time horizons) was to buy U.S. Treasury bills. Since Treasury bills tended to track inflation, the resulting real (inflation-adjusted) returns were just above zero for the entire 1926–2000 period.

Graph 2-1

**Wealth Indices of Investments in the U.S. Capital Markets**
Year-End 1925 = $1.00

from 1925 to 2000

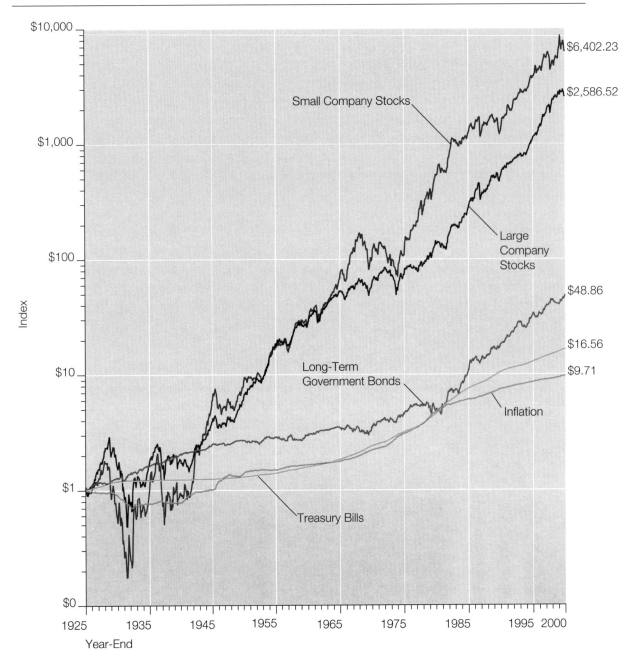

## Logarithmic Scale on the Index Graphs

A logarithmic scale is used on the vertical axis of our index graphs. The date appears on the horizontal axis.

A logarithmic scale allows for the direct comparison of the series' behavior at different points in time. Specifically, the use of a logarithmic scale allows the following interpretation of the data: the same vertical distance, no matter where it is measured on the graph, represents the same percentage change in the series. On the log scale shown below, a 50 percent gain from $10 to $15 occupies the same vertical distance as a 50 percent gain from $100 to $150. On the linear scale, the same percentage gains look different.

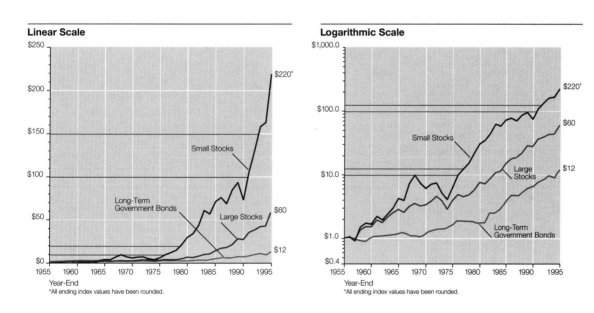

A logarithmic scale allows the viewer to compare investment performance across different time periods; thus the viewer can concentrate on rates of return, without worrying about the number of dollars invested at any given time. An additional benefit of the logarithmic scale is the way the scale spreads the action out over time. This allows the viewer to more carefully examine the fluctuations of the individual time series in different periods.

## Large Company Stocks

As noted above, an index of S&P 500 total returns, initialized on December 31, 1925, at $1.00, closed 2000 at $2,586.52, a compound annual growth rate of 11.0 percent. The inflation-adjusted S&P 500 total return index closed 2000 at a level of $266.47.

## Small Company Stocks

Over the long run, small stock returns surpassed the S&P 500, with the small stock total return index ending 2000 at a level of $6,402.23. This represents a compound annual growth rate of 12.4 percent, the highest rate among the asset classes studied here.

## Long-Term Government Bonds

The long-term government bond total return index, constructed with an approximate 20-year maturity, closed 2000 at a level of $48.86 (based on year-end 1925 equaling $1.00). Based on the capital appreciation component alone, the $1.00 index fell to a level of $0.95, a 5 percent capital loss over the period 1926–2000. This indicates that more than all of the positive historical returns on long-term government bonds were due to income returns. The compound annual total return for long-term government bonds was 5.3 percent.

## Intermediate-Term Government Bonds

Over the 1926–2000 period, intermediate-term government bonds outperformed long-term government bonds. One dollar invested in intermediate-term bonds at the end of 1925, with coupons reinvested, grew to $48.59 by year-end 2000. This compares with $48.86 for long-term government bonds. The compound annual total return for intermediate-term government bonds was 5.3 percent.

Capital appreciation caused $1.00 to increase to $1.30 over the 75-year period, representing a compound annual growth rate of 0.3 percent. This increase was unexpected: Since yields rose on average over the period, capital appreciation on a hypothetical intermediate-term government bond portfolio with a constant five-year maturity should have been negative.

## Long-Term Corporate Bonds

Long-term corporate bonds outperformed both categories of government bonds with a compound annual total return of 5.7 percent. One dollar invested in the long-term corporate bond index at year-end 1925 was worth $64.08 by the end of 2000. This higher return reflected the risk premium that investors require for investing in corporate bonds, which are subject to the risk of default.

## Treasury Bills

One dollar invested in Treasury bills at the end of 1925 was worth $16.56 by year-end 2000, with a compound annual growth rate of 3.8 percent. Treasury bill returns followed distinct patterns, described on the next page. Moreover, Treasury bills tended to track inflation; therefore, the average inflation-adjusted return on Treasury bills (or real riskless rate of return) was only 0.7 percent over the 75-year period. This real return also followed distinct patterns.

### Patterns in Treasury Bill Returns

During the late 1920s and early 1930s, Treasury bill returns were just above zero. (These returns were observed during a largely deflationary period.) Beginning in late 1941, the yields on Treasury bills were pegged by the government at low rates while high inflation was experienced.

Treasury bills closely tracked inflation after March 1951, when Treasury bill yields were deregulated in the U.S. Treasury-Federal Reserve Accord. (Treasury bill returns after that date reflect free market rates.) This tracking relationship has weakened since 1973. From about 1974 to 1980, Treasury bill returns were consistently lower than inflation rates. Then, from about 1981 to 1986, Treasury bills outpaced inflation, yielding substantial positive real returns. Since 1987, real returns on Treasury bills have still been positive, but lower than before.

### Federal Reserve Operating Procedure Changes

The disparity between performance and volatility for the periods prior to and after October 1979 can be attributed to the Federal Reserve's new operating procedures. Prior to this date, the Fed used the federal funds rate as an operating target. Subsequently, the Fed de-emphasized this rate as an operating target and, instead, began to focus on the manipulation of the money supply (through non-borrowed reserves). As a result, the federal funds rate underwent much greater volatility, thereby bringing about greater volatility in Treasury returns.

In the fall of 1982, however, the Federal Reserve again changed the policy procedures regarding its monetary policy. The Fed abandoned its new monetary controls and returned to a strategy of preventing excessive volatility in interest rates. Volatility in Treasury bill returns from the fall of 1979 through the fall of 1982 was nearly 50 percent greater than that which has occurred since.

## Inflation

The compound annual inflation rate over 1926–2000 was 3.1 percent. The inflation index, initiated at $1.00 at year-end 1925, grew to $9.71 by year-end 2000. The entire increase occurred during the postwar period. The years 1926–1933 were marked by deflation; inflation then raised consumer prices to their 1926 levels by the middle of 1945. After a brief postwar spurt of inflation, prices rose slowly over most of the 1950s and 1960s. Then, in the 1970s, inflation reached a pace unprecedented in peacetime, peaking at 13.3 percent in 1979. (On a month-by-month basis, the peak inflation rate was a breathtaking 24.0 percent, stated in annualized terms, in August 1973.) The 1980s saw a reversion to more moderate, though still substantial, inflation rates averaging about 5 percent. Inflation rates continued to decline in the 1990s with a compound annual rate of 2.9 percent.

## Summary Statistics of Total Returns

Table 2-1 presents summary statistics of the annual total returns on each asset class over the entire 75-year period of 1926–2000. The data presented in these exhibits are described in detail in Chapters 3 and 6.

Note that in Table 2-1, the arithmetic mean returns are always higher than the geometric mean returns. (Where they appear the same, it is due to rounding.) The difference between these two means is related to the standard deviation, or variability, of the series. [See Chapter 6.]

The "skylines" or histograms to the right in Table 2-1 show the frequency distribution of returns on each asset class. The height of the common stock skyline in the range between +10 and +20 percent, for example, shows the number of years in 1926–2000 that large company stocks had a return in that range. The histograms are shown in 5 percent increments to fully display the spectrum of returns as seen over the last 75 years, especially in stocks.

Riskier assets, such as large company stocks and small company stocks, have low, spread-out skylines, reflecting the broad distribution of returns from very poor to very good. Less risky assets, such as bonds, have narrow skylines that resemble a single tall building, indicating the tightness of the distribution around the mean of the series. The histogram for Treasury bills is one-sided, lying almost entirely to the right of the vertical line representing a zero return; that is, Treasury bills rarely experienced negative returns on a yearly basis over the 1926–2000 period. The inflation skyline shows both positive and negative annual rates. Although a few deflationary months and quarters have occurred recently, the last negative annual inflation rate occurred in 1954.

The histograms in Tables 2-2 through 2-4 show the total return distributions on the basic series over the past 75 years. These histograms are useful in determining the years with similar returns.

Table 2-1

**Basic Series: Summary Statistics of Annual Total Returns**

from 1926 to 2000

| Series | Geometric Mean | Arithmetic Mean | Standard Deviation | Distribution |
|---|---|---|---|---|
| Large Company Stocks | 11.0% | 13.0% | 20.2% | |
| Small Company Stocks | 12.4 | 17.3 | 33.4 | * |
| Long-Term Corporate Bonds | 5.7 | 6.0 | 8.7 | |
| Long-Term Government | 5.3 | 5.7 | 9.4 | |
| Intermediate-Term Government | 5.3 | 5.5 | 5.8 | |
| U.S. Treasury Bills | 3.8 | 3.9 | 3.2 | |
| Inflation | 3.1 | 3.2 | 4.4 | |

–90%    0%    90%

*The 1933 Small Company Stocks Total Return was 142.9 percent.

## Table 2-2

### Histogram

Large Company Stock and Small Company Stock Total Returns (in percent)

from 1926 to 2000

**Large Company Stocks**

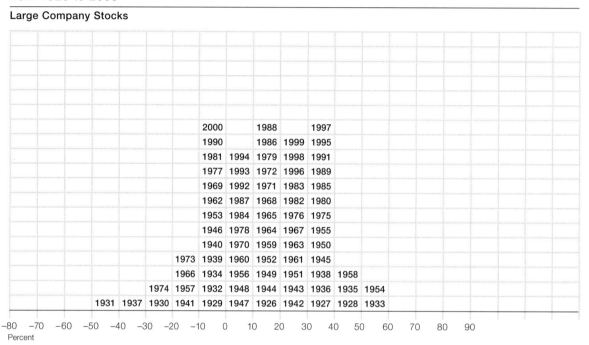

**Small Company Stocks**

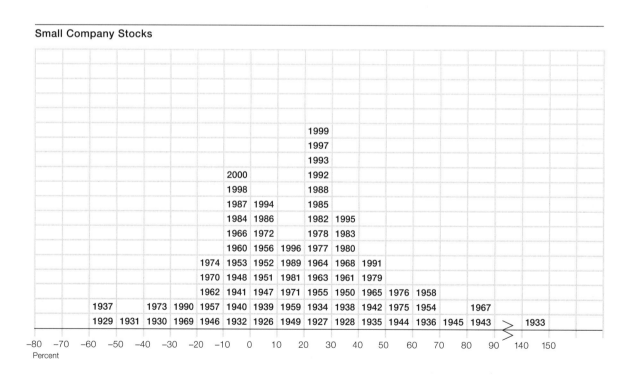

## Table 2-3

### Histogram
Long-Term Government Bond and Intermediate-Term Government Bond Total Returns (in percent)

from 1926 to 2000

**Long-Term Government Bonds**

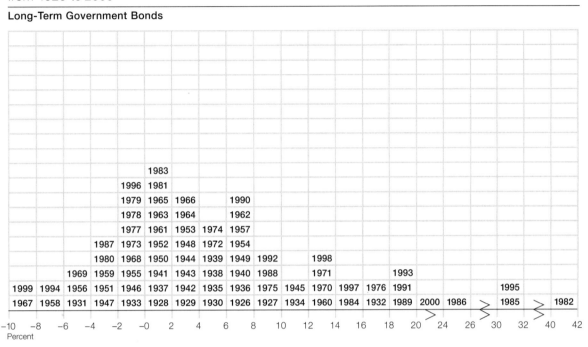

**Intermediate-Term Government Bonds**

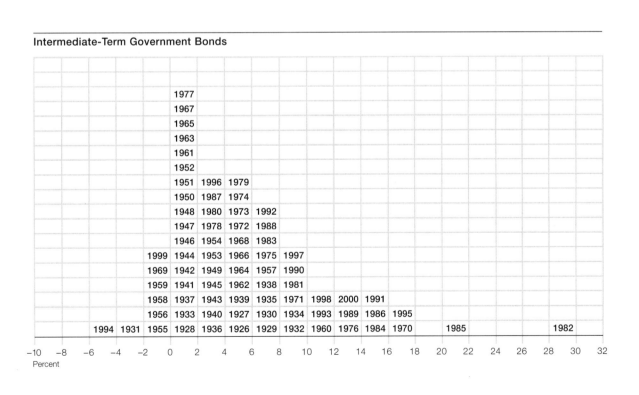

## Table 2-4

### Histogram
U.S. Treasury Bill Total Returns and Inflation (in percent)

from 1926 to 2000

**U.S. Treasury Bills**

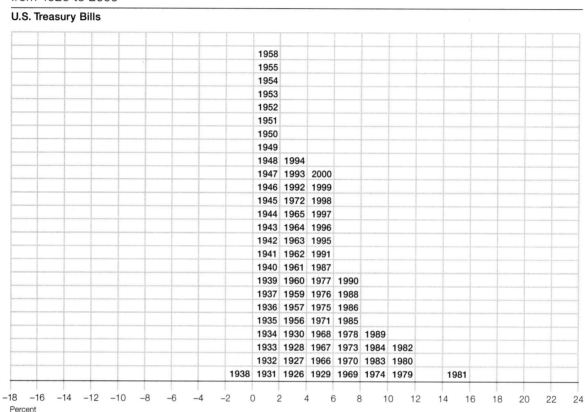

**Inflation**

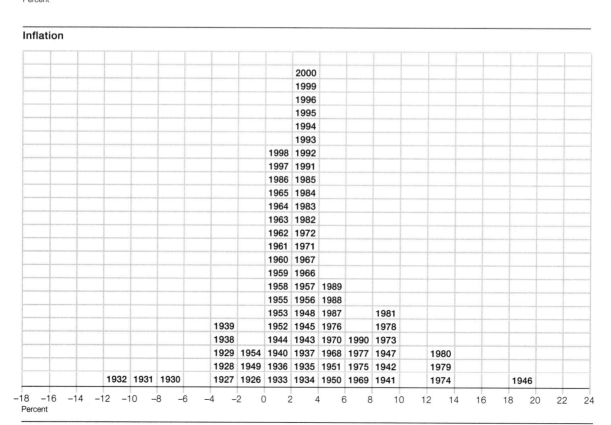

The stock histograms are shown in 10 percent increments while the bond, bill, and inflation histograms are in 2 percent increments. The increments are smaller for the assets with less widely distributed returns. Treasury bills are the most tightly clustered of any of the asset classes, confirming that this asset bears little risk; the annual return usually fell near zero.

## Annual Total Returns

Table 2-5 shows annual total returns for the seven basic asset classes for the full 75-year time period. This table can be used to compare the performance of each asset class for the same annual period. Monthly total returns for large company stocks, small company stocks, long-term corporate bonds, long-term government bonds, intermediate-term government bonds, Treasury bills, and inflation rates are presented in Appendix A: Tables A-1, A-4, A-5, A-6, A-10, A-14, and A-15, respectively.

## Capital Appreciation, Income, and Reinvestment Returns

Table 2-6 provides further detail on the returns of large company stocks, and long- and intermediate-term government bonds. Total annual returns are shown as the sum of three components: capital appreciation returns, income returns, and reinvestment returns. The capital appreciation and income components are explained in Chapter 3. The third component, reinvestment return, reflects monthly income reinvested in the total return index in subsequent months in the year. Thus, for a single month the reinvestment return is zero, but over a longer period of time it is nonzero. Since the returns in Table 2-6 are annual, reinvestment return is relevant.

The annual total return formed by compounding the monthly total returns does not equal the sum of the annual capital appreciation and income components; the difference is reinvestment return. A simple example illustrates this point. In 1995, an "up" year on a total return basis, the total annual return on large company stocks was 37.4 percent. The annual capital appreciation was 34.1 percent and the annual income return was 2.9 percent. These two components sum to 37.0 percent; the remaining 0.4 percent of the total 1995 return came from the reinvestment of dividends in the market. For more information on calculating annual total and income returns, see Chapter 5.

Monthly income and capital appreciation returns for large company stocks are presented in Appendix A: Tables A-2 and A-3, respectively. Monthly income and capital appreciation returns are presented for long-term government bonds in Appendix A: Tables A-7 and A-8; and for intermediate-term government bonds in Tables A-11 and A-12.

## Table 2-5

**Basic Series**
Annual Total Returns (in percent)

### from 1926 to 1970

| Year | Large Company Stocks | Small Company Stocks | Long-Term Corporate Bonds | Long-Term Government Bonds | Intermediate-Term Government Bonds | U.S. Treasury Bills | Inflation |
|------|------|------|------|------|------|------|------|
| 1926 | 11.62 | 0.28 | 7.37 | 7.77 | 5.38 | 3.27 | −1.49 |
| 1927 | 37.49 | 22.10 | 7.44 | 8.93 | 4.52 | 3.12 | −2.08 |
| 1928 | 43.61 | 39.69 | 2.84 | 0.10 | 0.92 | 3.56 | −0.97 |
| 1929 | −8.42 | −51.36 | 3.27 | 3.42 | 6.01 | 4.75 | 0.20 |
| 1930 | −24.90 | −38.15 | 7.98 | 4.66 | 6.72 | 2.41 | −6.03 |
| 1931 | −43.34 | −49.75 | −1.85 | −5.31 | −2.32 | 1.07 | −9.52 |
| 1932 | −8.19 | −5.39 | 10.82 | 16.84 | 8.81 | 0.96 | −10.30 |
| 1933 | 53.99 | 142.87 | 10.38 | −0.07 | 1.83 | 0.30 | 0.51 |
| 1934 | −1.44 | 24.22 | 13.84 | 10.03 | 9.00 | 0.16 | 2.03 |
| 1935 | 47.67 | 40.19 | 9.61 | 4.98 | 7.01 | 0.17 | 2.99 |
| 1936 | 33.92 | 64.80 | 6.74 | 7.52 | 3.06 | 0.18 | 1.21 |
| 1937 | −35.03 | −58.01 | 2.75 | 0.23 | 1.56 | 0.31 | 3.10 |
| 1938 | 31.12 | 32.80 | 6.13 | 5.53 | 6.23 | −0.02 | −2.78 |
| 1939 | −0.41 | 0.35 | 3.97 | 5.94 | 4.52 | 0.02 | −0.48 |
| 1940 | −9.78 | −5.16 | 3.39 | 6.09 | 2.96 | 0.00 | 0.96 |
| 1941 | −11.59 | −9.00 | 2.73 | 0.93 | 0.50 | 0.06 | 9.72 |
| 1942 | 20.34 | 44.51 | 2.60 | 3.22 | 1.94 | 0.27 | 9.29 |
| 1943 | 25.90 | 88.37 | 2.83 | 2.08 | 2.81 | 0.35 | 3.16 |
| 1944 | 19.75 | 53.72 | 4.73 | 2.81 | 1.80 | 0.33 | 2.11 |
| 1945 | 36.44 | 73.61 | 4.08 | 10.73 | 2.22 | 0.33 | 2.25 |
| 1946 | −8.07 | −11.63 | 1.72 | −0.10 | 1.00 | 0.35 | 18.16 |
| 1947 | 5.71 | 0.92 | −2.34 | −2.62 | 0.91 | 0.50 | 9.01 |
| 1948 | 5.50 | −2.11 | 4.14 | 3.40 | 1.85 | 0.81 | 2.71 |
| 1949 | 18.79 | 19.75 | 3.31 | 6.45 | 2.32 | 1.10 | −1.80 |
| 1950 | 31.71 | 38.75 | 2.12 | 0.06 | 0.70 | 1.20 | 5.79 |
| 1951 | 24.02 | 7.80 | −2.69 | −3.93 | 0.36 | 1.49 | 5.87 |
| 1952 | 18.37 | 3.03 | 3.52 | 1.16 | 1.63 | 1.66 | 0.88 |
| 1953 | −0.99 | −6.49 | 3.41 | 3.64 | 3.23 | 1.82 | 0.62 |
| 1954 | 52.62 | 60.58 | 5.39 | 7.19 | 2.68 | 0.86 | −0.50 |
| 1955 | 31.56 | 20.44 | 0.48 | −1.29 | −0.65 | 1.57 | 0.37 |
| 1956 | 6.56 | 4.28 | −6.81 | −5.59 | −0.42 | 2.46 | 2.86 |
| 1957 | −10.78 | −14.57 | 8.71 | 7.46 | 7.84 | 3.14 | 3.02 |
| 1958 | 43.36 | 64.89 | −2.22 | −6.09 | −1.29 | 1.54 | 1.76 |
| 1959 | 11.96 | 16.40 | −0.97 | −2.26 | −0.39 | 2.95 | 1.50 |
| 1960 | 0.47 | −3.29 | 9.07 | 13.78 | 11.76 | 2.66 | 1.48 |
| 1961 | 26.89 | 32.09 | 4.82 | 0.97 | 1.85 | 2.13 | 0.67 |
| 1962 | −8.73 | −11.90 | 7.95 | 6.89 | 5.56 | 2.73 | 1.22 |
| 1963 | 22.80 | 23.57 | 2.19 | 1.21 | 1.64 | 3.12 | 1.65 |
| 1964 | 16.48 | 23.52 | 4.77 | 3.51 | 4.04 | 3.54 | 1.19 |
| 1965 | 12.45 | 41.75 | −0.46 | 0.71 | 1.02 | 3.93 | 1.92 |
| 1966 | −10.06 | −7.01 | 0.20 | 3.65 | 4.69 | 4.76 | 3.35 |
| 1967 | 23.98 | 83.57 | −4.95 | −9.18 | 1.01 | 4.21 | 3.04 |
| 1968 | 11.06 | 35.97 | 2.57 | −0.26 | 4.54 | 5.21 | 4.72 |
| 1969 | −8.50 | −25.05 | −8.09 | −5.07 | −0.74 | 6.58 | 6.11 |
| 1970 | 4.01 | −17.43 | 18.37 | 12.11 | 16.86 | 6.52 | 5.49 |

Table 2-5 (continued)

**Basic Series**
Annual Total Returns (in percent)

from 1971 to 2000

| Year | Large Company Stocks | Small Company Stocks | Long-Term Corporate Bonds | Long-Term Government Bonds | Intermediate- Term Government Bonds | U.S. Treasury Bills | Inflation |
|------|------|------|------|------|------|------|------|
| 1971 | 14.31 | 16.50 | 11.01 | 13.23 | 8.72 | 4.39 | 3.36 |
| 1972 | 18.98 | 4.43 | 7.26 | 5.69 | 5.16 | 3.84 | 3.41 |
| 1973 | −14.66 | −30.90 | 1.14 | −1.11 | 4.61 | 6.93 | 8.80 |
| 1974 | −26.47 | −19.95 | −3.06 | 4.35 | 5.69 | 8.00 | 12.20 |
| 1975 | 37.20 | 52.82 | 14.64 | 9.20 | 7.83 | 5.80 | 7.01 |
| 1976 | 23.84 | 57.38 | 18.65 | 16.75 | 12.87 | 5.08 | 4.81 |
| 1977 | −7.18 | 25.38 | 1.71 | −0.69 | 1.41 | 5.12 | 6.77 |
| 1978 | 6.56 | 23.46 | −0.07 | −1.18 | 3.49 | 7.18 | 9.03 |
| 1979 | 18.44 | 43.46 | −4.18 | −1.23 | 4.09 | 10.38 | 13.31 |
| 1980 | 32.42 | 39.88 | −2.76 | −3.95 | 3.91 | 11.24 | 12.40 |
| 1981 | −4.91 | 13.88 | −1.24 | 1.86 | 9.45 | 14.71 | 8.94 |
| 1982 | 21.41 | 28.01 | 42.56 | 40.36 | 29.10 | 10.54 | 3.87 |
| 1983 | 22.51 | 39.67 | 6.26 | 0.65 | 7.41 | 8.80 | 3.80 |
| 1984 | 6.27 | −6.67 | 16.86 | 15.48 | 14.02 | 9.85 | 3.95 |
| 1985 | 32.16 | 24.66 | 30.09 | 30.97 | 20.33 | 7.72 | 3.77 |
| 1986 | 18.47 | 6.85 | 19.85 | 24.53 | 15.14 | 6.16 | 1.13 |
| 1987 | 5.23 | −9.30 | −0.27 | −2.71 | 2.90 | 5.47 | 4.41 |
| 1988 | 16.81 | 22.87 | 10.70 | 9.67 | 6.10 | 6.35 | 4.42 |
| 1989 | 31.49 | 10.18 | 16.23 | 18.11 | 13.29 | 8.37 | 4.65 |
| 1990 | −3.17 | −21.56 | 6.78 | 6.18 | 9.73 | 7.81 | 6.11 |
| 1991 | 30.55 | 44.63 | 19.89 | 19.30 | 15.46 | 5.60 | 3.06 |
| 1992 | 7.67 | 23.35 | 9.39 | 8.05 | 7.19 | 3.51 | 2.90 |
| 1993 | 9.99 | 20.98 | 13.19 | 18.24 | 11.24 | 2.90 | 2.75 |
| 1994 | 1.31 | 3.11 | −5.76 | −7.77 | −5.14 | 3.90 | 2.67 |
| 1995 | 37.43 | 34.46 | 27.20 | 31.67 | 16.80 | 5.60 | 2.54 |
| 1996 | 23.07 | 17.62 | 1.40 | −0.93 | 2.10 | 5.21 | 3.32 |
| 1997 | 33.36 | 22.78 | 12.95 | 15.85 | 8.38 | 5.26 | 1.70 |
| 1998 | 28.58 | −7.31 | 10.76 | 13.06 | 10.21 | 4.86 | 1.61 |
| 1999 | 21.04 | 29.79 | −7.45 | −8.96 | −1.77 | 4.68 | 2.68 |
| 2000 | −9.11 | −3.59 | 12.87 | 21.48 | 12.59 | 5.89 | 3.39 |

## Table 2-6

### Large Company Stocks, Long-Term Government Bonds, and Intermediate-Term Government Bonds

Annual Total, Income, Capital Appreciation, and Reinvestment Returns (in percent)

from 1926 to 1970

| Year | Large Company Stocks | | | | Long-Term Government Bonds | | | | | Intermediate-Term Government Bonds | | | | |
|---|---|---|---|---|---|---|---|---|---|---|---|---|---|---|
| | Capital Apprec. Return | Income Return | Reinvest- ment Return | Total Return | Capital Apprec. Return | Income Return | Reinvest- ment Return | Total Return | Year- end Yield | Capital Apprec. Return | Income Return | Reinvest- ment Return | Total Return | Year- end Yield |
| 1926 | 5.72 | 5.41 | 0.50 | 11.62 | 3.91 | 3.73 | 0.13 | 7.77 | 3.54 | 1.51 | 3.78 | 0.10 | 5.38 | 3.61 |
| 1927 | 30.91 | 5.71 | 0.87 | 37.49 | 5.40 | 3.41 | 0.12 | 8.93 | 3.16 | 0.96 | 3.49 | 0.07 | 4.52 | 3.40 |
| 1928 | 37.88 | 4.81 | 0.91 | 43.61 | -3.12 | 3.22 | 0.01 | 0.10 | 3.40 | -2.73 | 3.64 | 0.01 | 0.92 | 4.01 |
| 1929 | -11.91 | 3.98 | -0.49 | -8.42 | -0.20 | 3.47 | 0.15 | 3.42 | 3.40 | 1.77 | 4.07 | 0.18 | 6.01 | 3.62 |
| 1930 | -28.48 | 4.57 | -0.98 | -24.90 | 1.28 | 3.32 | 0.05 | 4.66 | 3.30 | 3.30 | 3.30 | 0.11 | 6.72 | 2.91 |
| 1931 | -47.07 | 5.35 | -1.62 | -43.34 | -8.46 | 3.33 | -0.17 | -5.31 | 4.07 | -5.40 | 3.16 | -0.08 | -2.32 | 4.12 |
| 1932 | -15.15 | 6.16 | 0.80 | -8.19 | 12.94 | 3.69 | 0.22 | 16.84 | 3.15 | 5.02 | 3.63 | 0.16 | 8.81 | 3.04 |
| 1933 | 46.59 | 6.39 | 1.01 | 53.99 | -3.14 | 3.12 | -0.05 | -0.07 | 3.36 | -0.99 | 2.83 | -0.02 | 1.83 | 3.25 |
| 1934 | -5.94 | 4.46 | 0.04 | -1.44 | 6.76 | 3.18 | 0.09 | 10.03 | 2.93 | 5.97 | 2.93 | 0.09 | 9.00 | 2.49 |
| 1935 | 41.37 | 4.95 | 1.35 | 47.67 | 2.14 | 2.81 | 0.03 | 4.98 | 2.76 | 4.94 | 2.02 | 0.05 | 7.01 | 1.63 |
| 1936 | 27.92 | 5.36 | 0.64 | 33.92 | 4.64 | 2.77 | 0.10 | 7.52 | 2.55 | 1.60 | 1.44 | 0.02 | 3.06 | 1.29 |
| 1937 | -38.59 | 4.66 | -1.09 | -35.03 | -2.48 | 2.66 | 0.05 | 0.23 | 2.73 | 0.05 | 1.48 | 0.03 | 1.56 | 1.14 |
| 1938 | 25.21 | 4.83 | 1.07 | 31.12 | 2.83 | 2.64 | 0.06 | 5.53 | 2.52 | 4.37 | 1.82 | 0.04 | 6.23 | 1.52 |
| 1939 | -5.45 | 4.69 | 0.35 | -0.41 | 3.48 | 2.40 | 0.06 | 5.94 | 2.26 | 3.18 | 1.31 | 0.03 | 4.52 | 0.98 |
| 1940 | -15.29 | 5.36 | 0.14 | -9.78 | 3.77 | 2.23 | 0.09 | 6.09 | 1.94 | 2.04 | 0.90 | 0.02 | 2.96 | 0.57 |
| 1941 | -17.86 | 6.71 | -0.44 | -11.59 | -1.01 | 1.94 | 0.00 | 0.93 | 2.04 | -0.17 | 0.67 | 0.00 | 0.50 | 0.82 |
| 1942 | 12.43 | 6.79 | 1.12 | 20.34 | 0.74 | 2.46 | 0.02 | 3.22 | 2.46 | 1.17 | 0.76 | 0.00 | 1.94 | 0.72 |
| 1943 | 19.45 | 6.24 | 0.21 | 25.90 | -0.37 | 2.44 | 0.02 | 2.08 | 2.48 | 1.23 | 1.56 | 0.02 | 2.81 | 1.45 |
| 1944 | 13.80 | 5.48 | 0.47 | 19.75 | 0.32 | 2.46 | 0.03 | 2.81 | 2.46 | 0.35 | 1.44 | 0.01 | 1.80 | 1.40 |
| 1945 | 30.72 | 4.97 | 0.74 | 36.44 | 8.27 | 2.34 | 0.12 | 10.73 | 1.99 | 1.02 | 1.19 | 0.01 | 2.22 | 1.03 |
| 1946 | -11.87 | 4.09 | -0.29 | -8.07 | -2.15 | 2.04 | 0.01 | -0.10 | 2.12 | -0.08 | 1.08 | 0.00 | 1.00 | 1.12 |
| 1947 | 0.00 | 5.49 | 0.22 | 5.71 | -4.70 | 2.13 | -0.06 | -2.62 | 2.43 | -0.30 | 1.21 | 0.00 | 0.91 | 1.34 |
| 1948 | -0.65 | 6.08 | 0.08 | 5.50 | 0.96 | 2.40 | 0.04 | 3.40 | 2.37 | 0.27 | 1.56 | 0.01 | 1.85 | 1.51 |
| 1949 | 10.26 | 7.50 | 1.03 | 18.79 | 4.15 | 2.25 | 0.06 | 6.45 | 2.09 | 0.95 | 1.36 | 0.01 | 2.32 | 1.23 |
| 1950 | 21.78 | 8.77 | 1.16 | 31.71 | -2.06 | 2.12 | 0.00 | 0.06 | 2.24 | -0.69 | 1.39 | 0.00 | 0.70 | 1.62 |
| 1951 | 16.46 | 6.91 | 0.65 | 24.02 | -6.27 | 2.38 | -0.04 | -3.93 | 2.69 | -1.63 | 1.98 | 0.01 | 0.36 | 2.17 |
| 1952 | 11.78 | 5.93 | 0.66 | 18.37 | -1.48 | 2.66 | -0.02 | 1.16 | 2.79 | -0.57 | 2.19 | 0.01 | 1.63 | 2.35 |
| 1953 | -6.62 | 5.46 | 0.18 | -0.99 | 0.67 | 2.84 | 0.12 | 3.64 | 2.74 | 0.61 | 2.55 | 0.07 | 3.23 | 2.18 |
| 1954 | 45.02 | 6.21 | 1.39 | 52.62 | 4.35 | 2.79 | 0.05 | 7.19 | 2.72 | 1.08 | 1.60 | 0.01 | 2.68 | 1.72 |
| 1955 | 26.40 | 4.56 | 0.60 | 31.56 | -4.07 | 2.75 | 0.03 | -1.29 | 2.95 | -3.10 | 2.45 | 0.00 | -0.65 | 2.80 |
| 1956 | 2.62 | 3.83 | 0.11 | 6.56 | -8.46 | 2.99 | -0.12 | -5.59 | 3.45 | -3.45 | 3.05 | -0.02 | -0.42 | 3.63 |
| 1957 | -14.31 | 3.84 | -0.30 | -10.78 | 3.82 | 3.44 | 0.20 | 7.46 | 3.23 | 4.05 | 3.59 | 0.20 | 7.84 | 2.84 |
| 1958 | 38.06 | 4.38 | 0.93 | 43.36 | -9.23 | 3.27 | -0.14 | -6.09 | 3.82 | -4.17 | 2.93 | -0.05 | -1.29 | 3.81 |
| 1959 | 8.48 | 3.31 | 0.16 | 11.96 | -6.20 | 4.01 | -0.07 | -2.26 | 4.47 | -4.56 | 4.18 | -0.01 | -0.39 | 4.98 |
| 1960 | -2.97 | 3.26 | 0.19 | 0.47 | 9.29 | 4.26 | 0.23 | 13.78 | 3.80 | 7.42 | 4.15 | 0.19 | 11.76 | 3.31 |
| 1961 | 23.13 | 3.48 | 0.28 | 26.89 | -2.86 | 3.83 | 0.00 | 0.97 | 4.15 | -1.72 | 3.54 | 0.03 | 1.85 | 3.84 |
| 1962 | -11.81 | 2.98 | 0.10 | -8.73 | 2.78 | 4.00 | 0.11 | 6.89 | 3.95 | 1.73 | 3.73 | 0.10 | 5.56 | 3.50 |
| 1963 | 18.89 | 3.61 | 0.30 | 22.80 | -2.70 | 3.89 | 0.02 | 1.21 | 4.17 | -2.10 | 3.71 | 0.03 | 1.64 | 4.04 |
| 1964 | 12.97 | 3.33 | 0.18 | 16.48 | -0.72 | 4.15 | 0.07 | 3.51 | 4.23 | -0.03 | 4.00 | 0.07 | 4.04 | 4.03 |
| 1965 | 9.06 | 3.21 | 0.18 | 12.45 | -3.45 | 4.19 | -0.04 | 0.71 | 4.50 | -3.10 | 4.15 | -0.03 | 1.02 | 4.90 |
| 1966 | -13.09 | 3.11 | -0.08 | -10.06 | -1.06 | 4.49 | 0.22 | 3.65 | 4.55 | -0.41 | 4.93 | 0.17 | 4.69 | 4.79 |
| 1967 | 20.09 | 3.64 | 0.25 | 23.98 | -13.55 | 4.59 | -0.23 | -9.18 | 5.56 | -3.85 | 4.88 | -0.02 | 1.01 | 5.77 |
| 1968 | 7.66 | 3.18 | 0.22 | 11.06 | -5.51 | 5.50 | -0.25 | -0.26 | 5.98 | -0.99 | 5.49 | 0.03 | 4.54 | 5.96 |
| 1969 | -11.42 | 3.04 | -0.13 | -8.50 | -10.83 | 5.95 | -0.19 | -5.07 | 6.87 | -7.27 | 6.65 | -0.11 | -0.74 | 8.29 |
| 1970 | 0.16 | 3.41 | 0.43 | 4.01 | 4.84 | 6.74 | 0.52 | 12.11 | 6.48 | 8.71 | 7.49 | 0.66 | 16.86 | 5.90 |

## Table 2-6 (continued)

## Large Company Stocks, Long-Term Government Bonds, and Intermediate-Term Government Bonds

Annual Total, Income, Capital Appreciation, and Reinvestment Returns (in percent)

from 1971 to 2000

| Year | Large Company Stocks | | | | Long-Term Government Bonds | | | | | Intermediate-Term Government Bonds | | | | |
|---|---|---|---|---|---|---|---|---|---|---|---|---|---|---|
| | Capital Apprec. Return | Income Return | Reinvest-ment Return | Total Return | Capital Apprec. Return | Income Return | Reinvest-ment Return | Total Return | Year-end Yield | Capital Apprec. Return | Income Return | Reinvest-ment Return | Total Return | Year-end Yield |
| 1971 | 10.79 | 3.33 | 0.19 | 14.31 | 6.61 | 6.32 | 0.31 | 13.23 | 5.97 | 2.72 | 5.75 | 0.25 | 8.72 | 5.25 |
| 1972 | 15.63 | 3.09 | 0.26 | 18.98 | −0.35 | 5.87 | 0.17 | 5.69 | 5.99 | −0.75 | 5.75 | 0.16 | 5.16 | 5.85 |
| 1973 | −17.37 | 2.86 | −0.16 | −14.66 | −7.70 | 6.51 | 0.08 | −1.11 | 7.26 | −2.19 | 6.58 | 0.22 | 4.61 | 6.79 |
| 1974 | −29.72 | 3.69 | −0.44 | −26.47 | −3.45 | 7.27 | 0.54 | 4.35 | 7.60 | −1.99 | 7.24 | 0.44 | 5.69 | 7.12 |
| 1975 | 31.55 | 5.37 | 0.29 | 37.20 | 0.73 | 7.99 | 0.47 | 9.20 | 8.05 | 0.12 | 7.35 | 0.36 | 7.83 | 7.19 |
| 1976 | 19.15 | 4.38 | 0.31 | 23.84 | 8.07 | 7.89 | 0.80 | 16.75 | 7.21 | 5.25 | 7.10 | 0.51 | 12.87 | 6.00 |
| 1977 | −11.50 | 4.31 | 0.01 | −7.18 | −7.86 | 7.14 | 0.04 | −0.69 | 8.03 | −5.15 | 6.49 | 0.06 | 1.41 | 7.51 |
| 1978 | 1.06 | 5.33 | 0.17 | 6.56 | −9.05 | 7.90 | −0.03 | −1.18 | 8.98 | −4.49 | 7.83 | 0.14 | 3.49 | 8.83 |
| 1979 | 12.31 | 5.71 | 0.42 | 18.44 | −9.84 | 8.86 | −0.25 | −1.23 | 10.12 | −5.07 | 9.04 | 0.12 | 4.09 | 10.33 |
| 1980 | 25.77 | 5.73 | 0.92 | 32.42 | −14.00 | 9.97 | 0.08 | −3.95 | 11.99 | −6.81 | 10.55 | 0.17 | 3.91 | 12.45 |
| 1981 | −9.72 | 4.89 | −0.08 | −4.91 | −10.33 | 11.55 | 0.64 | 1.86 | 13.34 | −4.55 | 12.97 | 1.03 | 9.45 | 13.96 |
| 1982 | 14.76 | 5.50 | 1.15 | 21.41 | 23.95 | 13.50 | 2.91 | 40.36 | 10.95 | 14.23 | 12.81 | 2.06 | 29.10 | 9.90 |
| 1983 | 17.27 | 5.00 | 0.24 | 22.51 | −9.82 | 10.38 | 0.09 | 0.65 | 11.97 | −3.30 | 10.35 | 0.35 | 7.41 | 11.41 |
| 1984 | 1.39 | 4.56 | 0.31 | 6.27 | 2.32 | 11.74 | 1.42 | 15.48 | 11.70 | 1.22 | 11.68 | 1.12 | 14.02 | 11.04 |
| 1985 | 26.34 | 5.10 | 0.72 | 32.16 | 17.84 | 11.25 | 1.88 | 30.97 | 9.56 | 9.01 | 10.29 | 1.04 | 20.33 | 8.55 |
| 1986 | 14.63 | 3.74 | 0.10 | 18.47 | 14.99 | 8.98 | 0.56 | 24.53 | 7.89 | 6.99 | 7.72 | 0.43 | 15.14 | 6.85 |
| 1987 | 2.03 | 3.64 | −0.44 | 5.23 | −10.69 | 7.92 | 0.06 | −2.71 | 9.20 | −4.75 | 7.47 | 0.19 | 2.90 | 8.32 |
| 1988 | 12.41 | 4.17 | 0.24 | 16.81 | 0.36 | 8.97 | 0.34 | 9.67 | 9.18 | −2.26 | 8.24 | 0.13 | 6.10 | 9.17 |
| 1989 | 27.26 | 3.85 | 0.38 | 31.49 | 8.62 | 8.81 | 0.68 | 18.11 | 8.16 | 4.34 | 8.46 | 0.49 | 13.29 | 7.94 |
| 1990 | −6.56 | 3.36 | 0.03 | −3.17 | −2.61 | 8.19 | 0.61 | 6.18 | 8.44 | 1.02 | 8.15 | 0.56 | 9.73 | 7.70 |
| 1991 | 26.31 | 3.82 | 0.42 | 30.55 | 10.10 | 8.22 | 0.98 | 19.30 | 7.30 | 7.36 | 7.43 | 0.67 | 15.46 | 5.97 |
| 1992 | 4.46 | 3.03 | 0.18 | 7.67 | 0.34 | 7.26 | 0.45 | 8.05 | 7.26 | 0.64 | 6.27 | 0.28 | 7.19 | 6.11 |
| 1993 | 7.06 | 2.83 | 0.11 | 9.99 | 10.71 | 7.17 | 0.35 | 18.24 | 6.54 | 5.56 | 5.53 | 0.15 | 11.24 | 5.22 |
| 1994 | −1.54 | 2.82 | 0.03 | 1.31 | −14.29 | 6.59 | −0.07 | −7.77 | 7.99 | −11.14 | 6.07 | −0.07 | −5.14 | 7.80 |
| 1995 | 34.11 | 2.91 | 0.41 | 37.43 | 23.04 | 7.60 | 1.03 | 31.67 | 6.03 | 9.66 | 6.69 | 0.45 | 16.80 | 5.38 |
| 1996 | 20.26 | 2.54 | 0.27 | 23.07 | −7.37 | 6.18 | 0.26 | −0.93 | 6.73 | −3.90 | 5.82 | 0.18 | 2.10 | 6.16 |
| 1997 | 31.01 | 2.11 | 0.25 | 33.36 | 8.51 | 6.64 | 0.71 | 15.85 | 6.02 | 1.94 | 6.14 | 0.30 | 8.38 | 5.73 |
| 1998 | 26.67 | 1.68 | 0.24 | 28.58 | 6.89 | 5.83 | 0.34 | 13.06 | 5.42 | 4.66 | 5.29 | 0.25 | 10.21 | 4.68 |
| 1999 | 19.53 | 1.36 | 0.15 | 21.04 | −14.35 | 5.57 | −0.19 | −8.96 | 6.82 | −7.06 | 5.30 | −0.01 | −1.77 | 6.45 |
| 2000 | −10.14 | 1.10 | −0.07 | −9.11 | 14.36 | 6.50 | 0.62 | 21.48 | 5.58 | 5.94 | 6.19 | 0.46 | 12.59 | 5.07 |

## Rolling Period Returns

The highest and lowest returns on the basic series, expressed as annual rates, are shown for 1-, 5-, 10-, 15-, and 20-year holding periods in Table 2-7. This exhibit also shows the number of times that an asset had a positive return, and the number of times that an asset's return was the highest among all those studied. The number of times positive (or times highest) is compared to the total number of observations—that is, 75 annual, 71 overlapping five-year, 66 overlapping 10-year, 61 overlapping 15-year, and 56 overlapping 20-year holding periods.

Tables 2-8, 2-9, 2-10, and 2-11 show the compound annual total returns for 5-, 10-, 15-, and 20-year holding periods. Often, these calculations are referred to as rolling period returns as they are obtained by rolling a data window of fixed length along each time series. They are useful for examining the behavior of returns for holding periods similar to those actually experienced by investors and show the effects of time diversification. Holding assets for long periods of time has the effect of lowering the risk of experiencing a loss in asset value.

## Table 2-7

### Basic Series
Maximum and Minimum Values of Returns for 1-, 5-, 10-, 15-, and 20-Year Holding Periods
(compound annual rates of return in percent)

Series

| Annual Returns | Maximum Value Return and Year(s) | | Minimum Value Return and Year(s) | | Times Positive (out of 75 years) | Times Highest Returning Asset |
|---|---|---|---|---|---|---|
| Large Company Stocks | 53.99 | 1933 | −43.34 | 1931 | 54 | 16 |
| Small Company Stocks | 142.87 | 1933 | −58.01 | 1937 | 52 | 32 |
| Long-Term Corporate Bonds | 42.56 | 1982 | −8.09 | 1969 | 58 | 6 |
| Long-Term Government Bonds | 40.36 | 1982 | −9.18 | 1967 | 54 | 7 |
| Intermediate-Term Govt. Bonds | 29.10 | 1982 | −5.14 | 1994 | 67 | 2 |
| U.S. Treasury Bills | 14.71 | 1981 | −0.02 | 1938 | 74 | 6 |
| Inflation | 18.16 | 1946 | −10.30 | 1932 | 65 | 6 |

| 5-Year Rolling Period Returns | Maximum Value Return and Year(s) | | Minimum Value Return and Year(s) | | (out of 71 overlapping 5-year periods) | Times Highest Returning Asset |
|---|---|---|---|---|---|---|
| Large Company Stocks | 28.55 | 1995–99 | −12.47 | 1928–32 | 64 | 23 |
| Small Company Stocks | 45.90 | 1941–45 | −27.54 | 1928–32 | 62 | 37 |
| Long-Term Corporate Bonds | 22.51 | 1982–86 | −2.22 | 1965–69 | 68 | 7 |
| Long-Term Government Bonds | 21.62 | 1982–86 | −2.14 | 1965–69 | 65 | 1 |
| Intermediate-Term Govt. Bonds | 16.98 | 1982–86 | 0.96 | 1955–59 | 71 | 2 |
| U.S. Treasury Bills | 11.12 | 1979–83 | 0.07 | 1938–42 | 71 | 0 |
| Inflation | 10.06 | 1977–81 | −5.42 | 1928–32 | 64 | 1 |

| 10-Year Rolling Period Returns | Maximum Value Return and Year(s) | | Minimum Value Return and Year(s) | | (out of 66 overlapping 10-year periods) | Times Highest Returning Asset |
|---|---|---|---|---|---|---|
| Large Company Stocks | 20.06 | 1949–58 | −0.89 | 1929–38 | 64 | 20 |
| Small Company Stocks | 30.38 | 1975–84 | −5.70 | 1929–38 | 64 | 36 |
| Long-Term Corporate Bonds | 16.32 | 1982–91 | 0.98 | 1947–56 | 66 | 6 |
| Long-Term Government Bonds | 15.56 | 1982–91 | −0.07 | 1950–59 | 65 | 0 |
| Intermediate-Term Govt. Bonds | 13.13 | 1982–91 | 1.25 | 1947–56 | 66 | 2 |
| U.S. Treasury Bills | 9.17 | 1978–87 | 0.15 | 1933–42/1934–43 | 66 | 1 |
| Inflation | 8.67 | 1973–82 | −2.57 | 1926–35 | 60 | 1 |

| 15-Year Rolling Period Returns | Maximum Value Return and Year(s) | | Minimum Value Return and Year(s) | | (out of 61 overlapping 15-year periods) | Times Highest Returning Asset |
|---|---|---|---|---|---|---|
| Large Company Stocks | 18.93 | 1985–99 | 0.64 | 1929–43 | 61 | 13 |
| Small Company Stocks | 23.33 | 1975–89 | −1.30 | 1927–41 | 58 | 44 |
| Long-Term Corporate Bonds | 13.66 | 1982–96 | 1.02 | 1955–69 | 61 | 4 |
| Long-Term Government Bonds | 13.53 | 1981–95 | 0.40 | 1955–69 | 61 | 0 |
| Intermediate-Term Govt. Bonds | 11.27 | 1981–95 | 1.45 | 1945–59 | 61 | 0 |
| U.S. Treasury Bills | 8.32 | 1977–91 | 0.22 | 1933–47 | 61 | 0 |
| Inflation | 7.30 | 1968–82 | −1.59 | 1926–40 | 58 | 0 |

| 20-Year Rolling Period Returns | Maximum Value Return and Year(s) | | Minimum Value Return and Year(s) | | (out of 56 overlapping 20-year periods) | Times Highest Returning Asset |
|---|---|---|---|---|---|---|
| Large Company Stocks | 17.87 | 1980–99 | 3.11 | 1929–48 | 56 | 6 |
| Small Company Stocks | 21.13 | 1942–61 | 5.74 | 1929–48 | 56 | 50 |
| Long-Term Corporate Bonds | 11.49 | 1981–00 | 1.34 | 1950–69 | 56 | 0 |
| Long-Term Government Bonds | 11.99 | 1981–00 | 0.69 | 1950–69 | 56 | 0 |
| Intermediate-Term Govt. Bonds | 9.97 | 1981–00 | 1.58 | 1940–59 | 56 | 0 |
| U.S. Treasury Bills | 7.72 | 1972–91 | 0.42 | 1931–50 | 56 | 0 |
| Inflation | 6.36 | 1966–85 | 0.07 | 1926–45 | 56 | 0 |

## Table 2-8

**Basic Series**

Compound Annual Returns for 5-Year Holding Periods (percent per annum)

from 1926 to 1970

| Period | Large Company Stocks | Small Company Stocks | Long-Term Corporate Bonds | Long-Term Government Bonds | Intermediate Government Bonds | U.S. Treasury Bills | Inflation |
|---|---|---|---|---|---|---|---|
| 1926–1930 | 8.68 | −12.44 | 5.76 | 4.93 | 4.69 | 3.42 | −2.10 |
| 1927–1931 | −5.10 | −23.74 | 3.87 | 2.25 | 3.11 | 2.98 | −3.75 |
| 1928–1932 | −12.47 | −27.54 | 4.52 | 3.69 | 3.95 | 2.54 | −5.42 |
| 1929–1933 | −11.24 | −19.06 | 6.01 | 3.66 | 4.13 | 1.89 | −5.14 |
| 1930–1934 | −9.93 | −2.37 | 8.09 | 4.95 | 4.71 | 0.98 | −4.80 |
| 1931–1935 | 3.12 | 14.99 | 8.42 | 5.01 | 4.77 | 0.53 | −3.04 |
| 1932–1936 | 22.47 | 45.83 | 10.26 | 7.71 | 5.90 | 0.35 | −0.84 |
| 1933–1937 | 14.29 | 23.96 | 8.60 | 4.46 | 4.45 | 0.22 | 1.96 |
| 1934–1938 | 10.67 | 9.86 | 7.75 | 5.61 | 5.33 | 0.16 | 1.29 |
| 1935–1939 | 10.91 | 5.27 | 5.81 | 4.81 | 4.46 | 0.13 | 0.78 |
| 1936–1940 | 0.50 | −2.64 | 4.59 | 5.03 | 3.65 | 0.10 | 0.38 |
| 1937–1941 | −7.51 | −13.55 | 3.79 | 3.71 | 3.13 | 0.08 | 2.02 |
| 1938–1942 | 4.62 | 10.70 | 3.76 | 4.32 | 3.21 | 0.07 | 3.21 |
| 1939–1943 | 3.77 | 18.71 | 3.10 | 3.63 | 2.54 | 0.14 | 4.44 |
| 1940–1944 | 7.67 | 29.28 | 3.25 | 3.01 | 2.00 | 0.20 | 4.98 |
| 1941–1945 | 16.96 | 45.90 | 3.39 | 3.90 | 1.85 | 0.27 | 5.25 |
| 1942–1946 | 17.87 | 45.05 | 3.19 | 3.69 | 1.95 | 0.33 | 6.82 |
| 1943–1947 | 14.86 | 35.00 | 2.17 | 2.49 | 1.75 | 0.37 | 6.77 |
| 1944–1948 | 10.87 | 18.43 | 2.43 | 2.75 | 1.55 | 0.47 | 6.67 |
| 1945–1949 | 10.69 | 12.66 | 2.15 | 3.46 | 1.66 | 0.62 | 5.84 |
| 1946–1950 | 9.91 | 7.72 | 1.76 | 1.39 | 1.36 | 0.79 | 6.57 |
| 1947–1951 | 16.70 | 12.09 | 0.87 | 0.60 | 1.23 | 1.02 | 4.25 |
| 1948–1952 | 19.37 | 12.55 | 2.05 | 1.37 | 1.37 | 1.25 | 2.65 |
| 1949–1953 | 17.86 | 11.53 | 1.91 | 1.41 | 1.64 | 1.45 | 2.23 |
| 1950–1954 | 23.92 | 18.27 | 2.31 | 1.55 | 1.72 | 1.41 | 2.50 |
| 1951–1955 | 23.89 | 14.97 | 1.98 | 1.28 | 1.44 | 1.48 | 1.43 |
| 1952–1956 | 20.18 | 14.21 | 1.10 | 0.93 | 1.28 | 1.67 | 0.84 |
| 1953–1957 | 13.58 | 10.01 | 2.10 | 2.15 | 2.49 | 1.97 | 1.27 |
| 1954–1958 | 22.31 | 23.22 | 0.96 | 0.16 | 1.58 | 1.91 | 1.49 |
| 1955–1959 | 14.96 | 15.54 | −0.29 | −1.67 | 0.96 | 2.33 | 1.90 |
| 1956–1960 | 8.92 | 10.58 | 1.36 | 1.16 | 3.37 | 2.55 | 2.12 |
| 1957–1961 | 12.79 | 15.93 | 3.77 | 2.53 | 3.83 | 2.48 | 1.68 |
| 1958–1962 | 13.31 | 16.65 | 3.63 | 2.42 | 3.39 | 2.40 | 1.33 |
| 1959–1963 | 9.85 | 10.11 | 4.55 | 3.97 | 4.00 | 2.72 | 1.30 |
| 1960–1964 | 10.73 | 11.43 | 5.73 | 5.17 | 4.91 | 2.83 | 1.24 |
| 1961–1965 | 13.25 | 20.28 | 3.82 | 2.63 | 2.81 | 3.09 | 1.33 |
| 1962–1966 | 5.72 | 12.13 | 2.88 | 3.17 | 3.38 | 3.61 | 1.86 |
| 1963–1967 | 12.39 | 29.86 | 0.30 | −0.14 | 2.47 | 3.91 | 2.23 |
| 1964–1968 | 10.16 | 32.37 | 0.37 | −0.43 | 3.04 | 4.33 | 2.84 |
| 1965–1969 | 4.96 | 19.78 | −2.22 | −2.14 | 2.08 | 4.93 | 3.82 |
| 1966–1970 | 3.34 | 7.51 | 1.23 | −0.02 | 5.10 | 5.45 | 4.54 |
| 1967–1971 | 8.42 | 12.47 | 3.32 | 1.77 | 5.90 | 5.38 | 4.54 |
| 1968–1972 | 7.53 | 0.47 | 5.85 | 4.90 | 6.75 | 5.30 | 4.61 |
| 1969–1973 | 2.01 | −12.25 | 5.55 | 4.72 | 6.77 | 5.65 | 5.41 |
| 1970–1974 | −2.36 | −11.09 | 6.68 | 6.72 | 8.11 | 5.93 | 6.60 |

Table 2-8 (continued)

## Basic Series

Compound Annual Returns for 5-Year Holding Periods (percent per annum)

from 1971 to 2000

| Period | Large Company Stocks | Small Company Stocks | Long-Term Corporate Bonds | Long-Term Government Bonds | Intermediate Government Bonds | U.S. Treasury Bills | Inflation |
|---|---|---|---|---|---|---|---|
| 1971–1975 | 3.21 | 0.56 | 6.00 | 6.16 | 6.39 | 5.78 | 6.90 |
| 1972–1976 | 4.87 | 6.80 | 7.42 | 6.82 | 7.19 | 5.92 | 7.20 |
| 1973–1977 | –0.21 | 10.77 | 6.29 | 5.50 | 6.41 | 6.18 | 7.89 |
| 1974–1978 | 4.32 | 24.41 | 6.03 | 5.48 | 6.18 | 6.23 | 7.94 |
| 1975–1979 | 14.76 | 39.80 | 5.78 | 4.33 | 5.86 | 6.69 | 8.15 |
| 1976–1980 | 13.95 | 37.35 | 2.36 | 1.68 | 5.08 | 7.77 | 9.21 |
| 1977–1981 | 8.08 | 28.75 | –1.33 | –1.05 | 4.44 | 9.67 | 10.06 |
| 1978–1982 | 14.05 | 29.28 | 5.57 | 6.03 | 9.60 | 10.78 | 9.46 |
| 1979–1983 | 17.27 | 32.51 | 6.87 | 6.42 | 10.42 | 11.12 | 8.39 |
| 1980–1984 | 14.76 | 21.59 | 11.20 | 9.80 | 12.45 | 11.01 | 6.53 |
| 1981–1985 | 14.71 | 18.82 | 17.86 | 16.83 | 15.80 | 10.30 | 4.85 |
| 1982–1986 | 19.87 | 17.32 | 22.51 | 21.62 | 16.98 | 8.60 | 3.30 |
| 1983–1987 | 16.49 | 9.51 | 14.06 | 13.02 | 11.79 | 7.59 | 3.41 |
| 1984–1988 | 15.38 | 6.74 | 15.00 | 14.98 | 11.52 | 7.10 | 3.53 |
| 1985–1989 | 20.40 | 10.34 | 14.88 | 15.50 | 11.38 | 6.81 | 3.67 |
| 1986–1990 | 13.14 | 0.58 | 10.43 | 10.75 | 9.34 | 6.83 | 4.13 |
| 1987–1991 | 15.36 | 6.86 | 10.44 | 9.81 | 9.40 | 6.71 | 4.52 |
| 1988–1992 | 15.89 | 13.63 | 12.50 | 12.14 | 10.30 | 6.31 | 4.22 |
| 1989–1993 | 14.50 | 13.28 | 13.00 | 13.84 | 11.35 | 5.61 | 3.89 |
| 1990–1994 | 8.69 | 11.79 | 8.36 | 8.34 | 7.46 | 4.73 | 3.49 |
| 1991–1995 | 16.57 | 24.51 | 12.22 | 13.10 | 8.81 | 4.29 | 2.79 |
| 1992–1996 | 15.20 | 19.47 | 8.52 | 8.98 | 6.17 | 4.22 | 2.84 |
| 1993–1997 | 20.24 | 19.35 | 9.22 | 10.51 | 6.40 | 4.57 | 2.60 |
| 1994–1998 | 24.06 | 13.16 | 8.74 | 9.52 | 6.20 | 4.96 | 2.37 |
| 1995–1999 | 28.55 | 18.49 | 8.35 | 9.24 | 6.95 | 5.12 | 2.37 |
| 1996–2000 | 18.35 | 10.87 | 5.79 | 7.49 | 6.17 | 5.18 | 2.54 |

## Table 2-9

**Basic Series**

Compound Annual Returns for 10-Year Holding Periods (percent per annum)

from 1926 to 1970

| Period | Large Company Stocks | Small Company Stocks | Long-Term Corporate Bonds | Long-Term Government Bonds | Intermediate Government Bonds | U.S. Treasury Bills | Inflation |
|---|---|---|---|---|---|---|---|
| 1926–1935 | 5.86 | 0.34 | 7.08 | 4.97 | 4.73 | 1.97 | −2.57 |
| 1927–1936 | 7.81 | 5.45 | 7.02 | 4.95 | 4.50 | 1.66 | −2.30 |
| 1928–1937 | 0.02 | −5.22 | 6.54 | 4.08 | 4.20 | 1.37 | −1.80 |
| 1929–1938 | −0.89 | −5.70 | 6.88 | 4.63 | 4.73 | 1.02 | −1.98 |
| 1930–1939 | −0.05 | 1.38 | 6.95 | 4.88 | 4.58 | 0.55 | −2.05 |
| 1931–1940 | 1.80 | 5.81 | 6.49 | 5.02 | 4.21 | 0.32 | −1.34 |
| 1932–1941 | 6.43 | 12.28 | 6.97 | 5.69 | 4.51 | 0.21 | 0.58 |
| 1933–1942 | 9.35 | 17.14 | 6.15 | 4.39 | 3.83 | 0.15 | 2.59 |
| 1934–1943 | 7.17 | 14.20 | 5.40 | 4.62 | 3.93 | 0.15 | 2.85 |
| 1935–1944 | 9.28 | 16.66 | 4.53 | 3.91 | 3.22 | 0.17 | 2.86 |
| 1936–1945 | 8.42 | 19.18 | 3.99 | 4.46 | 2.75 | 0.18 | 2.79 |
| 1937–1946 | 4.41 | 11.98 | 3.49 | 3.70 | 2.54 | 0.20 | 4.39 |
| 1938–1947 | 9.62 | 22.24 | 2.96 | 3.40 | 2.48 | 0.22 | 4.97 |
| 1939–1948 | 7.26 | 18.57 | 2.77 | 3.19 | 2.04 | 0.30 | 5.55 |
| 1940–1949 | 9.17 | 20.69 | 2.70 | 3.24 | 1.83 | 0.41 | 5.41 |
| 1941–1950 | 13.38 | 25.37 | 2.57 | 2.64 | 1.60 | 0.53 | 5.91 |
| 1942–1951 | 17.28 | 27.51 | 2.02 | 2.13 | 1.59 | 0.67 | 5.53 |
| 1943–1952 | 17.09 | 23.27 | 2.11 | 1.93 | 1.56 | 0.81 | 4.69 |
| 1944–1953 | 14.31 | 14.93 | 2.17 | 2.08 | 1.60 | 0.96 | 4.43 |
| 1945–1954 | 17.12 | 15.43 | 2.23 | 2.51 | 1.69 | 1.01 | 4.16 |
| 1946–1955 | 16.69 | 11.29 | 1.87 | 1.33 | 1.40 | 1.14 | 3.96 |
| 1947–1956 | 18.43 | 13.14 | 0.98 | 0.76 | 1.25 | 1.35 | 2.53 |
| 1948–1957 | 16.44 | 11.27 | 2.07 | 1.76 | 1.93 | 1.61 | 1.96 |
| 1949–1958 | 20.06 | 17.23 | 1.43 | 0.79 | 1.61 | 1.68 | 1.86 |
| 1950–1959 | 19.35 | 16.90 | 1.00 | −0.07 | 1.34 | 1.87 | 2.20 |
| 1951–1960 | 16.16 | 12.75 | 1.67 | 1.22 | 2.40 | 2.01 | 1.77 |
| 1952–1961 | 16.43 | 15.07 | 2.43 | 1.73 | 2.55 | 2.08 | 1.26 |
| 1953–1962 | 13.44 | 13.28 | 2.86 | 2.29 | 2.94 | 2.19 | 1.30 |
| 1954–1963 | 15.91 | 16.48 | 2.74 | 2.05 | 2.78 | 2.31 | 1.40 |
| 1955–1964 | 12.82 | 13.47 | 2.68 | 1.69 | 2.92 | 2.58 | 1.57 |
| 1956–1965 | 11.06 | 15.33 | 2.58 | 1.89 | 3.09 | 2.82 | 1.73 |
| 1957–1966 | 9.20 | 14.02 | 3.33 | 2.85 | 3.60 | 3.05 | 1.77 |
| 1958–1967 | 12.85 | 23.08 | 1.95 | 1.13 | 2.93 | 3.15 | 1.78 |
| 1959–1968 | 10.00 | 20.73 | 2.44 | 1.75 | 3.52 | 3.52 | 2.07 |
| 1960–1969 | 7.81 | 15.53 | 1.68 | 1.45 | 3.48 | 3.88 | 2.52 |
| 1961–1970 | 8.18 | 13.72 | 2.51 | 1.30 | 3.95 | 4.26 | 2.92 |
| 1962–1971 | 7.06 | 12.30 | 3.10 | 2.47 | 4.63 | 4.49 | 3.19 |
| 1963–1972 | 9.93 | 14.22 | 3.04 | 2.35 | 4.59 | 4.60 | 3.41 |
| 1964–1973 | 6.00 | 7.77 | 2.93 | 2.11 | 4.89 | 4.98 | 4.12 |
| 1965–1974 | 1.24 | 3.20 | 2.13 | 2.20 | 5.05 | 5.43 | 5.20 |
| 1966–1975 | 3.27 | 3.98 | 3.59 | 3.03 | 5.74 | 5.62 | 5.71 |
| 1967–1976 | 6.63 | 9.60 | 5.35 | 4.26 | 6.54 | 5.65 | 5.86 |
| 1968–1977 | 3.59 | 5.50 | 6.07 | 5.20 | 6.58 | 5.74 | 6.24 |
| 1969–1978 | 3.16 | 4.48 | 5.79 | 5.10 | 6.47 | 5.94 | 6.67 |
| 1970–1979 | 5.86 | 11.49 | 6.23 | 5.52 | 6.98 | 6.31 | 7.37 |

Table 2-9 (continued)

## Basic Series

Compound Annual Returns for 10-Year Holding Periods (percent per annum)

from 1971 to 2000

| Period | Large Company Stocks | Small Company Stocks | Long-Term Corporate Bonds | Long-Term Government Bonds | Intermediate Government Bonds | U.S. Treasury Bills | Inflation |
|---|---|---|---|---|---|---|---|
| 1971–1980 | 8.44 | 17.53 | 4.16 | 3.90 | 5.73 | 6.77 | 8.05 |
| 1972–1981 | 6.47 | 17.26 | 2.95 | 2.81 | 5.80 | 7.78 | 8.62 |
| 1973–1982 | 6.68 | 19.67 | 5.93 | 5.76 | 8.00 | 8.46 | 8.67 |
| 1974–1983 | 10.61 | 28.40 | 6.45 | 5.95 | 8.28 | 8.65 | 8.16 |
| 1975–1984 | 14.76 | 30.38 | 8.46 | 7.03 | 9.11 | 8.83 | 7.34 |
| 1976–1985 | 14.33 | 27.75 | 9.84 | 8.99 | 10.31 | 9.03 | 7.01 |
| 1977–1986 | 13.82 | 22.90 | 9.95 | 9.70 | 10.53 | 9.14 | 6.63 |
| 1978–1987 | 15.26 | 18.99 | 9.73 | 9.47 | 10.69 | 9.17 | 6.39 |
| 1979–1988 | 16.33 | 18.93 | 10.86 | 10.62 | 10.97 | 9.09 | 5.93 |
| 1980–1989 | 17.55 | 15.83 | 13.02 | 12.62 | 11.91 | 8.89 | 5.09 |
| 1981–1990 | 13.93 | 9.32 | 14.09 | 13.75 | 12.52 | 8.55 | 4.49 |
| 1982–1991 | 17.59 | 11.97 | 16.32 | 15.56 | 13.13 | 7.65 | 3.91 |
| 1983–1992 | 16.19 | 11.55 | 13.28 | 12.58 | 11.04 | 6.95 | 3.81 |
| 1984–1993 | 14.94 | 9.96 | 14.00 | 14.41 | 11.43 | 6.35 | 3.71 |
| 1985–1994 | 14.40 | 11.06 | 11.57 | 11.86 | 9.40 | 5.76 | 3.58 |
| 1986–1995 | 14.84 | 11.90 | 11.32 | 11.92 | 9.08 | 5.55 | 3.46 |
| 1987–1996 | 15.28 | 12.98 | 9.48 | 9.39 | 7.77 | 5.46 | 3.68 |
| 1988–1997 | 18.05 | 16.46 | 10.85 | 11.32 | 8.33 | 5.44 | 3.41 |
| 1989–1998 | 19.19 | 13.22 | 10.85 | 11.66 | 8.74 | 5.29 | 3.12 |
| 1990–1999 | 18.20 | 15.09 | 8.36 | 8.79 | 7.20 | 4.92 | 2.93 |
| 1991–2000 | 17.46 | 17.49 | 8.96 | 10.26 | 7.48 | 4.74 | 2.66 |

## Table 2-10

**Basic Series**
Compound Annual Returns for 15-Year Holding Periods (percent per annum)

from 1926 to 1970

| Period | Large Company Stocks | Small Company Stocks | Long-Term Corporate Bonds | Long-Term Government Bonds | Intermediate Government Bonds | U.S. Treasury Bills | Inflation |
|---|---|---|---|---|---|---|---|
| 1926–1940 | 4.04 | −0.66 | 6.24 | 4.99 | 4.37 | 1.34 | −1.59 |
| 1927–1941 | 2.44 | −1.30 | 5.93 | 4.53 | 4.04 | 1.13 | −0.88 |
| 1928–1942 | 1.53 | −0.19 | 5.60 | 4.16 | 3.87 | 0.94 | −0.16 |
| 1929–1943 | 0.64 | 1.82 | 5.60 | 4.29 | 4.00 | 0.73 | 0.12 |
| 1930–1944 | 2.46 | 9.94 | 5.70 | 4.25 | 3.71 | 0.44 | 0.24 |
| 1931–1945 | 6.62 | 17.77 | 5.44 | 4.65 | 3.42 | 0.30 | 0.81 |
| 1932–1946 | 10.11 | 22.29 | 5.70 | 5.02 | 3.65 | 0.25 | 2.62 |
| 1933–1947 | 11.15 | 22.81 | 4.81 | 3.75 | 3.13 | 0.22 | 3.96 |
| 1934–1948 | 8.39 | 15.59 | 4.40 | 3.99 | 3.13 | 0.26 | 4.11 |
| 1935–1949 | 9.75 | 15.31 | 3.73 | 3.76 | 2.70 | 0.32 | 3.85 |
| 1936–1950 | 8.91 | 15.23 | 3.24 | 3.43 | 2.28 | 0.39 | 4.03 |
| 1937–1951 | 8.36 | 12.02 | 2.61 | 2.66 | 2.10 | 0.47 | 4.34 |
| 1938–1952 | 12.78 | 18.92 | 2.66 | 2.72 | 2.11 | 0.56 | 4.19 |
| 1939–1953 | 10.68 | 16.18 | 2.48 | 2.59 | 1.91 | 0.68 | 4.43 |
| 1940–1954 | 13.88 | 19.88 | 2.57 | 2.67 | 1.79 | 0.74 | 4.43 |
| 1941–1955 | 16.78 | 21.80 | 2.38 | 2.18 | 1.55 | 0.85 | 4.39 |
| 1942–1956 | 18.24 | 22.91 | 1.71 | 1.73 | 1.49 | 1.01 | 3.94 |
| 1943–1957 | 15.91 | 18.68 | 2.11 | 2.00 | 1.87 | 1.20 | 3.53 |
| 1944–1958 | 16.92 | 17.63 | 1.76 | 1.44 | 1.59 | 1.28 | 3.44 |
| 1945–1959 | 16.39 | 15.47 | 1.39 | 1.09 | 1.45 | 1.45 | 3.40 |
| 1946–1960 | 14.04 | 11.05 | 1.70 | 1.28 | 2.05 | 1.61 | 3.35 |
| 1947–1961 | 16.52 | 14.07 | 1.91 | 1.35 | 2.11 | 1.72 | 2.25 |
| 1948–1962 | 15.38 | 13.04 | 2.59 | 1.98 | 2.41 | 1.87 | 1.75 |
| 1949–1963 | 16.56 | 14.81 | 2.46 | 1.84 | 2.40 | 2.03 | 1.67 |
| 1950–1964 | 16.40 | 15.05 | 2.56 | 1.65 | 2.51 | 2.19 | 1.88 |
| 1951–1965 | 15.18 | 15.21 | 2.38 | 1.69 | 2.54 | 2.37 | 1.63 |
| 1952–1966 | 12.74 | 14.08 | 2.58 | 2.21 | 2.82 | 2.59 | 1.46 |
| 1953–1967 | 13.09 | 18.56 | 2.00 | 1.47 | 2.78 | 2.76 | 1.61 |
| 1954–1968 | 13.96 | 21.55 | 1.94 | 1.21 | 2.87 | 2.98 | 1.88 |
| 1955–1969 | 10.14 | 15.53 | 1.02 | 0.40 | 2.64 | 3.36 | 2.31 |
| 1956–1970 | 8.43 | 12.66 | 2.13 | 1.25 | 3.75 | 3.69 | 2.65 |
| 1957–1971 | 8.94 | 13.50 | 3.33 | 2.49 | 4.36 | 3.82 | 2.69 |
| 1958–1972 | 11.05 | 15.03 | 3.23 | 2.37 | 4.19 | 3.86 | 2.71 |
| 1959–1973 | 7.27 | 8.55 | 3.47 | 2.73 | 4.59 | 4.22 | 3.17 |
| 1960–1974 | 4.31 | 5.87 | 3.32 | 3.18 | 5.00 | 4.56 | 3.86 |
| 1961–1975 | 6.50 | 9.15 | 3.66 | 2.89 | 4.75 | 4.77 | 4.23 |
| 1962–1976 | 6.32 | 10.43 | 4.52 | 3.90 | 5.47 | 4.97 | 4.51 |
| 1963–1977 | 6.44 | 13.06 | 4.11 | 3.39 | 5.19 | 5.13 | 4.89 |
| 1964–1978 | 5.44 | 13.06 | 3.95 | 3.22 | 5.32 | 5.40 | 5.38 |
| 1965–1979 | 5.56 | 14.19 | 3.34 | 2.90 | 5.32 | 5.85 | 6.17 |
| 1966–1980 | 6.71 | 14.09 | 3.18 | 2.58 | 5.52 | 6.33 | 6.87 |
| 1967–1981 | 7.11 | 15.64 | 3.08 | 2.46 | 5.83 | 6.97 | 7.24 |
| 1968–1982 | 6.96 | 12.89 | 5.90 | 5.47 | 7.58 | 7.40 | 7.30 |
| 1969–1983 | 7.66 | 13.10 | 6.15 | 5.54 | 7.77 | 7.64 | 7.24 |
| 1970–1984 | 8.74 | 14.76 | 7.86 | 6.93 | 8.77 | 7.85 | 7.09 |

Table 2-10 (continued)

## Basic Series
Compound Annual Returns for 15-Year Holding Periods (percent per annum)

### from 1971 to 2000

| Period | Large Company Stocks | Small Company Stocks | Long-Term Corporate Bonds | Long-Term Government Bonds | Intermediate Government Bonds | U.S. Treasury Bills | Inflation |
|---|---|---|---|---|---|---|---|
| 1971–1985 | 10.50 | 17.96 | 8.54 | 8.04 | 8.99 | 7.93 | 6.97 |
| 1972–1986 | 10.76 | 17.28 | 9.10 | 8.73 | 9.40 | 8.06 | 6.82 |
| 1973–1987 | 9.86 | 16.18 | 8.57 | 8.13 | 9.25 | 8.17 | 6.89 |
| 1974–1988 | 12.18 | 20.73 | 9.23 | 8.88 | 9.35 | 8.13 | 6.59 |
| 1975–1989 | 16.61 | 23.33 | 10.56 | 9.78 | 9.86 | 8.15 | 6.10 |
| 1976–1990 | 13.93 | 17.96 | 10.03 | 9.58 | 9.99 | 8.29 | 6.04 |
| 1977–1991 | 14.33 | 17.30 | 10.11 | 9.73 | 10.15 | 8.32 | 5.92 |
| 1978–1992 | 15.47 | 17.17 | 10.65 | 10.35 | 10.56 | 8.21 | 5.66 |
| 1979–1993 | 15.72 | 17.01 | 11.57 | 11.68 | 11.09 | 7.92 | 5.24 |
| 1980–1994 | 14.52 | 14.47 | 11.45 | 11.17 | 10.41 | 7.48 | 4.55 |
| 1981–1995 | 14.80 | 14.17 | 13.46 | 13.53 | 11.27 | 7.11 | 3.92 |
| 1982–1996 | 16.79 | 14.41 | 13.66 | 13.32 | 10.76 | 6.50 | 3.55 |
| 1983–1997 | 17.52 | 14.09 | 11.91 | 11.88 | 9.47 | 6.15 | 3.41 |
| 1984–1998 | 17.90 | 11.02 | 12.22 | 12.75 | 9.66 | 5.89 | 3.26 |
| 1985–1999 | 18.93 | 13.49 | 10.49 | 10.98 | 8.58 | 5.55 | 3.17 |
| 1986–2000 | 16.00 | 11.56 | 9.45 | 10.43 | 8.10 | 5.43 | 3.15 |

## Table 2-11

**Basic Series**

Compound Annual Returns for 20-Year Holding Periods (percent per annum)

from 1926 to 1970

| Period | Large Company Stocks | Small Company Stocks | Long-Term Corporate Bonds | Long-Term Government Bonds | Intermediate Government Bonds | U.S. Treasury Bills | Inflation |
|---|---|---|---|---|---|---|---|
| 1926–1945 | 7.13 | 9.36 | 5.52 | 4.72 | 3.73 | 1.07 | 0.07 |
| 1927–1946 | 6.10 | 8.67 | 5.24 | 4.32 | 3.51 | 0.93 | 0.99 |
| 1928–1947 | 4.71 | 7.64 | 4.74 | 3.74 | 3.33 | 0.80 | 1.53 |
| 1929–1948 | 3.11 | 5.74 | 4.80 | 3.91 | 3.38 | 0.66 | 1.72 |
| 1930–1949 | 4.46 | 10.61 | 4.80 | 4.06 | 3.20 | 0.48 | 1.61 |
| 1931–1950 | 7.43 | 15.17 | 4.51 | 3.82 | 2.90 | 0.42 | 2.22 |
| 1932–1951 | 11.72 | 19.65 | 4.47 | 3.90 | 3.04 | 0.44 | 3.02 |
| 1933–1952 | 13.15 | 20.16 | 4.11 | 3.15 | 2.69 | 0.48 | 3.63 |
| 1934–1953 | 10.68 | 14.56 | 3.77 | 3.34 | 2.76 | 0.55 | 3.64 |
| 1935–1954 | 13.13 | 16.04 | 3.37 | 3.20 | 2.45 | 0.59 | 3.51 |
| 1936–1955 | 12.48 | 15.17 | 2.92 | 2.89 | 2.07 | 0.66 | 3.37 |
| 1937–1956 | 11.20 | 12.56 | 2.23 | 2.22 | 1.90 | 0.77 | 3.46 |
| 1938–1957 | 12.98 | 16.63 | 2.52 | 2.58 | 2.20 | 0.91 | 3.45 |
| 1939–1958 | 13.48 | 17.90 | 2.10 | 1.98 | 1.83 | 0.99 | 3.69 |
| 1940–1959 | 14.15 | 18.78 | 1.85 | 1.57 | 1.58 | 1.14 | 3.79 |
| 1941–1960 | 14.76 | 18.89 | 2.12 | 1.93 | 2.00 | 1.27 | 3.82 |
| 1942–1961 | 16.86 | 21.13 | 2.22 | 1.93 | 2.07 | 1.37 | 3.37 |
| 1943–1962 | 15.25 | 18.17 | 2.48 | 2.11 | 2.25 | 1.50 | 2.98 |
| 1944–1963 | 15.11 | 15.70 | 2.45 | 2.06 | 2.19 | 1.63 | 2.90 |
| 1945–1964 | 14.95 | 14.44 | 2.45 | 2.10 | 2.30 | 1.79 | 2.86 |
| 1946–1965 | 13.84 | 13.29 | 2.23 | 1.61 | 2.24 | 1.97 | 2.84 |
| 1947–1966 | 13.72 | 13.58 | 2.15 | 1.80 | 2.42 | 2.19 | 2.15 |
| 1948–1967 | 14.63 | 17.03 | 2.01 | 1.45 | 2.43 | 2.38 | 1.87 |
| 1949–1968 | 14.92 | 18.97 | 1.93 | 1.26 | 2.56 | 2.60 | 1.96 |
| 1950–1969 | 13.43 | 16.21 | 1.34 | 0.69 | 2.41 | 2.87 | 2.36 |
| 1951–1970 | 12.10 | 13.23 | 2.09 | 1.26 | 3.17 | 3.13 | 2.35 |
| 1952–1971 | 11.65 | 13.67 | 2.77 | 2.10 | 3.58 | 3.28 | 2.22 |
| 1953–1972 | 11.67 | 13.75 | 2.95 | 2.32 | 3.76 | 3.39 | 2.35 |
| 1954–1973 | 10.85 | 12.04 | 2.83 | 2.08 | 3.83 | 3.64 | 2.75 |
| 1955–1974 | 6.87 | 8.21 | 2.41 | 1.94 | 3.98 | 4.00 | 3.37 |
| 1956–1975 | 7.10 | 9.51 | 3.08 | 2.46 | 4.41 | 4.21 | 3.70 |
| 1957–1976 | 7.91 | 11.78 | 4.34 | 3.55 | 5.06 | 4.34 | 3.80 |
| 1958–1977 | 8.12 | 13.95 | 3.99 | 3.15 | 4.74 | 4.44 | 3.98 |
| 1959–1978 | 6.53 | 12.31 | 4.10 | 3.41 | 4.99 | 4.72 | 4.34 |
| 1960–1979 | 6.83 | 13.49 | 3.93 | 3.46 | 5.22 | 5.09 | 4.92 |
| 1961–1980 | 8.31 | 15.61 | 3.34 | 2.59 | 4.84 | 5.51 | 5.46 |
| 1962–1981 | 6.76 | 14.75 | 3.03 | 2.64 | 5.21 | 6.12 | 5.87 |
| 1963–1982 | 8.30 | 16.92 | 4.47 | 4.04 | 6.28 | 6.51 | 6.01 |
| 1964–1983 | 8.28 | 17.63 | 4.68 | 4.01 | 6.57 | 6.80 | 6.12 |
| 1965–1984 | 7.79 | 16.00 | 5.25 | 4.58 | 7.06 | 7.12 | 6.26 |
| 1966–1985 | 8.66 | 15.25 | 6.67 | 5.97 | 8.00 | 7.31 | 6.36 |
| 1967–1986 | 10.17 | 16.06 | 7.63 | 6.94 | 8.52 | 7.38 | 6.24 |
| 1968–1987 | 9.27 | 12.04 | 7.88 | 7.31 | 8.62 | 7.44 | 6.31 |
| 1969–1988 | 9.54 | 11.47 | 8.30 | 7.82 | 8.70 | 7.50 | 6.30 |
| 1970–1989 | 11.55 | 13.64 | 9.58 | 9.01 | 9.42 | 7.59 | 6.22 |

Table 2-11 (continued)

**Basic Series**
Compound Annual Returns for 20-Year Holding Periods (percent per annum)

from 1971 to 2000

| Period | Large Company Stocks | Small Company Stocks | Long-Term Corporate Bonds | Long-Term Government Bonds | Intermediate Government Bonds | U.S. Treasury Bills | Inflation |
|---|---|---|---|---|---|---|---|
| 1971–1990 | 11.15 | 13.35 | 9.01 | 8.71 | 9.08 | 7.66 | 6.26 |
| 1972–1991 | 11.89 | 14.58 | 9.43 | 9.00 | 9.40 | 7.72 | 6.24 |
| 1973–1992 | 11.33 | 15.54 | 9.54 | 9.12 | 9.51 | 7.70 | 6.21 |
| 1974–1993 | 12.76 | 18.82 | 10.16 | 10.10 | 9.85 | 7.49 | 5.91 |
| 1975–1994 | 14.58 | 20.33 | 10.00 | 9.42 | 9.25 | 7.29 | 5.44 |
| 1976–1995 | 14.59 | 19.57 | 10.58 | 10.45 | 9.69 | 7.28 | 5.22 |
| 1977–1996 | 14.55 | 17.84 | 9.71 | 9.54 | 9.14 | 7.28 | 5.14 |
| 1978–1997 | 16.65 | 17.71 | 10.29 | 10.39 | 9.51 | 7.29 | 4.89 |
| 1979–1998 | 17.75 | 16.04 | 10.86 | 11.14 | 9.85 | 7.17 | 4.52 |
| 1980–1999 | 17.87 | 15.46 | 10.66 | 10.69 | 9.53 | 6.89 | 4.00 |
| 1981–2000 | 15.68 | 13.33 | 11.49 | 11.99 | 9.97 | 6.62 | 3.57 |

# Chapter 3
## Description of the Basic Series

This chapter presents the returns for the seven basic asset classes and describes the construction of these returns. More detail on the construction of some series can be found in the January 1976 *Journal of Business* article, referenced at the end of the Introduction. Annual total returns and capital appreciation returns for each asset class are formed by compounding the monthly returns that appear in Appendix A. Annual income returns are formed by summing the monthly income payments and dividing this sum by the beginning-of-year price. Returns are formed assuming no taxes or transaction costs, except for returns on small company stocks that show the performance of an actual, tax-exempt investment fund including transaction and management costs, starting in 1982.

## Large Company Stocks

### Overview

One dollar invested in large company stocks at year-end 1925, with dividends reinvested, grew to $2,586.52 by year-end 2000; this represents a compound annual growth rate of 11.0 percent. [See Graph 3-1.] Capital appreciation alone caused $1.00 to grow to $103.50 over the 75-year period, a compound annual growth rate of 6.4 percent. Annual total returns ranged from a high of 54.0 percent in 1933 to a low of –43.3 percent in 1931. The 75-year average annual dividend yield was 4.4 percent.

### Total Returns

From September 1997 to the present, the large company stock total return is provided by Standard and Poor's, which calculates the total return based on the daily reinvestment of dividends on the ex-dividend date. Standard and Poor's uses closing pricing (usually from the New York Stock Exchange) in their calculation. From 1977 to August 1997, the total return was provided by the American National Bank and Trust Company of Chicago, which modified monthly income numbers provided by Wilshire Associates, Santa Monica, California. Dividends (measured as of the ex-dividend date) are accumulated over the month and invested on the last trading day of the month in the S&P 500 index at the day's closing level. Wilshire uses the last trading price of the day for the stocks, usually from the Pacific Stock Exchange. Prior to 1977, the total return for a given month was calculated by summing the capital appreciation return and the income return as described on the following pages.

The large company stock total return index is based upon the S&P Composite Index. This index is a readily available, carefully constructed, market-value-weighted benchmark of large company stock performance. Market-value-weighted means that the weight of each stock in the index, for a given month, is proportionate to its market capitalization (price times the number of shares outstanding) at the beginning of that month. Currently, the S&P Composite includes 500 of the largest stocks (in terms of stock market value) in the United States; prior to March 1957 it consisted of 90 of the largest stocks.

## Graph 3-1

**Large Company Stocks**
Return Indices, Returns, and Dividend Yields

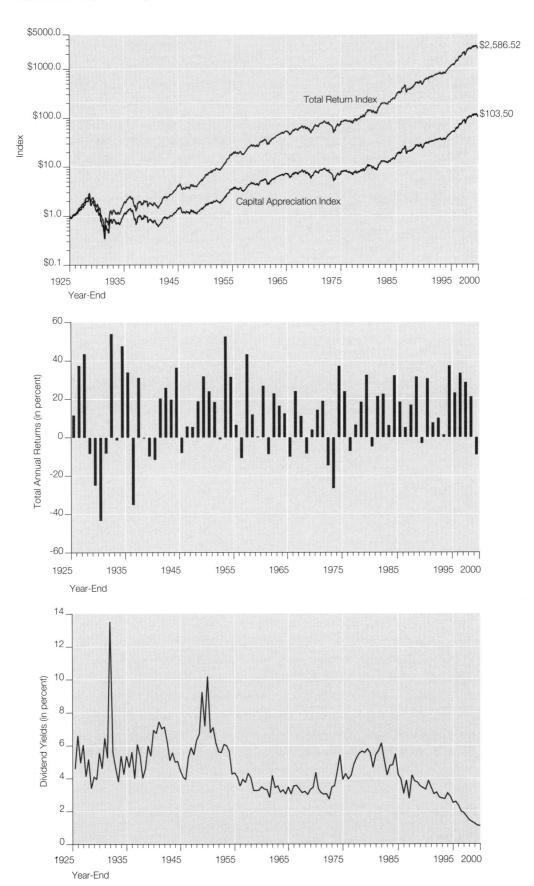

## Capital Appreciation Return

The capital appreciation component of the large company stock total return is the change in the S&P 500-stock index (or 90-stock index) as reported in *The Wall Street Journal* for the period 1977–2000, and in Standard & Poor's *Trade and Securities Statistics* from 1926–1976.

## Income Return

For 1977–2000, the income return was calculated as the difference between the total return and the capital appreciation return. For 1926–1976, quarterly dividends were extracted from rolling yearly dividends reported quarterly in S&P's *Trade and Securities Statistics,* then allocated to months within each quarter using proportions taken from the 1974 actual distribution of monthly dividends within quarters.

The dividend yields depicted in the bottom graph of Graph 3-1 were derived by annualizing the semiannual income return.

## Small Company Stocks

### Overview

One dollar invested in small company stocks at year-end 1925 grew to $6,402.23 by year-end 2000. [See Graph 3-2.] This represents a compound annual growth rate of 12.4 percent over the past 75 years. Total annual returns ranged from a high of 142.9 percent in 1933 to a low of –58.0 percent in 1937.

### DFA Small Company Fund (1982–2000)

For 1982–2000, the small company stock return series is the total return achieved by the Dimensional Fund Advisors (DFA) Small Company 9/10 (for ninth and tenth deciles) Fund. The fund is a market-value-weighted index of the ninth and tenth deciles of the New York Stock Exchange (NYSE), plus stocks listed on the American Stock Exchange (AMEX) and over-the-counter (OTC) with the same or less capitalization as the upper bound of the NYSE ninth decile. The weight of each stock within the fund is proportionate to its market capitalization; therefore, those stocks with a higher market capitalization value will be weighted more than those with a lower market capitalization value. Since the lower bound of the tenth decile is near zero, stocks are not purchased if they are smaller than $10 million in market capitalization (although they are held if they fall below that level). A company's stock is not purchased if it is in bankruptcy; however, a stock already held is retained if the company becomes bankrupt.

Stocks remain in the portfolio if they rise into the eighth NYSE decile, but they are sold when they rise into the seventh NYSE decile or higher. The returns for the DFA Small Company 9/10 Fund represent after-transaction-cost returns, while the returns for the other asset classes and for pre-1982 small company stocks are before-transaction-cost returns.

Graph 3-2

**Small Company Stocks**
Return Index and Returns

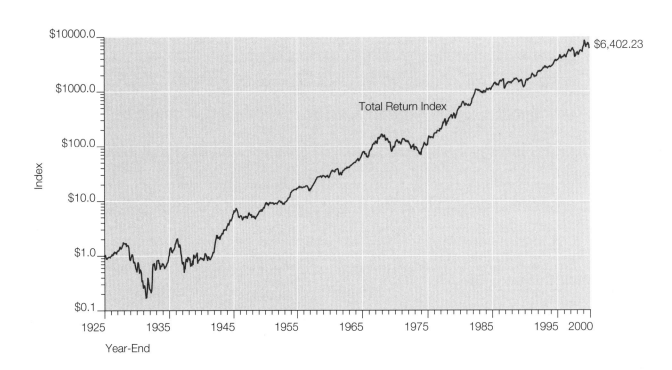

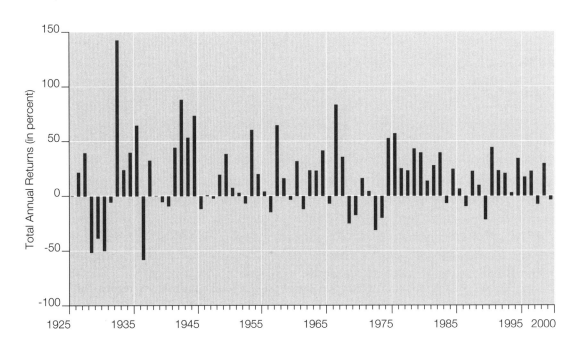

At year-end 2000, the DFA Small Company Fund contained approximately 2,735 stocks, with a weighted average market capitalization of $209 million. The unweighted average market capitalization was $92 million, while the median was $47 million. See Table 7-5 for decile size, bounds, and composition.

### NYSE Fifth Quintile Returns (1926–1981)

The equities of smaller companies from 1926 to 1980 are represented by the historical series developed by Professor Rolf W. Banz (see reference on page 5). This is composed of stocks making up the fifth quintile (i.e., the ninth and tenth deciles) of the New York Stock Exchange (NYSE); the stocks on the NYSE are ranked by capitalization (price times number of shares outstanding), and each decile contains an equal number of stocks at the beginning of each formation period. The ninth and tenth decile portfolio was first ranked and formed as of December 31, 1925. This portfolio was "held" for five years, with value-weighted portfolio returns computed monthly. Every five years the portfolio was rebalanced (i.e., all of the stocks on the NYSE were re-ranked, and a new portfolio of those falling in the ninth and tenth deciles was formed) as of December 31, 1930 and every five years thereafter through December 31, 1980. This method avoided survivorship bias by including the return after the delisting or failure of a stock in constructing the portfolio returns. (Survivorship bias is caused by studying only stocks that have survived events such as bankruptcy and acquisition.)

For 1981, Dimensional Fund Advisors, Inc. updated the returns using Professor Banz' methods. The data for 1981 are significant to only three decimal places (in decimal form) or one decimal place when returns are expressed in percent.

## Long-Term Corporate Bonds

### Overview

One dollar invested in long-term high-grade corporate bonds at the end of 1925 was worth $64.08 by year-end 2000. [See Graph 3-3.] The compound annual growth rate over the 75-year period was 5.7 percent. Total annual returns ranged from a high of 42.6 percent in 1982 to a low of –8.1 percent in 1969.

### Total Returns

For 1969–2000, corporate bond total returns are represented by the Salomon Brothers Long-Term High-Grade Corporate Bond Index. Since most large corporate bond transactions take place over the counter, a major dealer is the natural source of these data. The index includes nearly all Aaa- and Aa-rated bonds. If a bond is downgraded during a particular month, its return for the month is included in the index before removing the bond from future portfolios.

Over 1926–1968 total returns were calculated by summing the capital appreciation returns and the income returns. For the periozd 1946–1968, Ibbotson and Sinquefield backdated the Salomon Brothers' index, using Salomon Brothers' monthly yield data with a methodology similar to that used by Salomon for 1969–2000. Capital appreciation returns were calculated from yields assuming (at the beginning of each monthly holding period) a 20-year maturity, a bond price equal to par, and a coupon equal to the beginning-of-period yield.

For the period 1926–1945, Standard & Poor's monthly High-Grade Corporate Composite yield data were used, assuming a 4 percent coupon and a 20-year maturity. The conventional present-value formula for bond price was used for the beginning and end-of-month prices. (This formula is presented in Ross, Stephen A., and Randolph W. Westerfield, *Corporate Finance*, Times Mirror/Mosby, St. Louis, 1990, p. 97 ["Level-Coupon Bonds"]). The monthly income return was assumed to be one-twelfth the coupon.

## Long-Term Government Bonds

### Overview

One dollar invested in long-term government bonds at year-end 1925, with coupons reinvested, grew to $48.86 by year-end 2000; this represents a compound annual growth rate of 5.3 percent. [See Graph 3-4.] However, returns from the capital appreciation component alone caused $1.00 to decrease to $0.95 over the 75-year period, representing a compound annual growth rate of –0.07 percent. Total annual returns ranged from a high of 40.4 percent in 1982 to a low of –9.2 percent in 1967. The 75-year compounded yield-to-maturity (or yield-to-first-call, where applicable) was 5.2 percent.

### Total Returns

The total returns on long-term government bonds from 1977 to 2000 are constructed with data from *The Wall Street Journal*. The bond used in 2000 is the 8.125 percent issue that matures on August 15, 2021. The data from 1926–1976 are obtained from the Government Bond File at the Center for Research in Security Prices (CRSP) at the University of Chicago Graduate School of Business. The bonds used to construct the index are shown in Table 3-1. To the greatest extent possible, a one-bond portfolio with a term of approximately 20 years and a reasonably current coupon—whose returns did not reflect potential tax benefits, impaired negotiability, or special redemption or call privileges—was used each year. Where "flower" bonds (tenderable to the Treasury at par in payment of estate taxes) had to be used, we chose the bond with the smallest potential tax benefit. Where callable bonds had to be used, the term of the bond was assumed to be a simple average of the maturity and first call dates minus the current date. The bond was "held" for the calendar year and returns were computed.

Graph 3-3

## Long-Term Corporate Bonds
Return Index and Returns

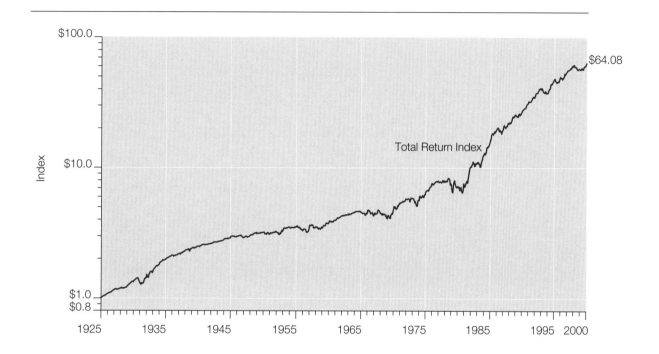

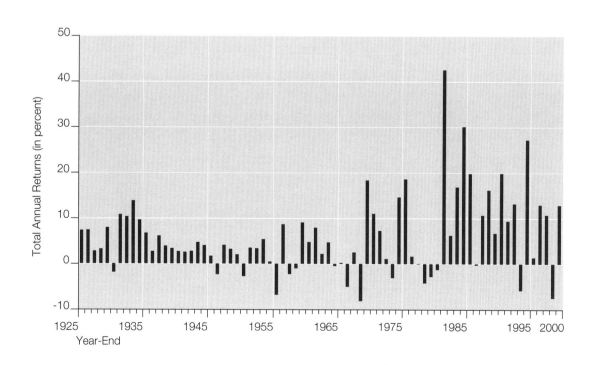

## Graph 3-4

### Long-Term Government Bonds

Return Indices, Returns, and Yields

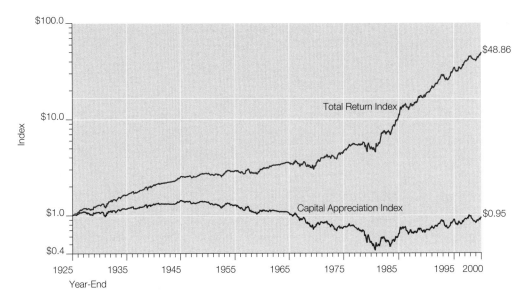

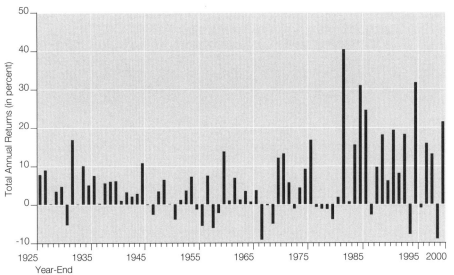

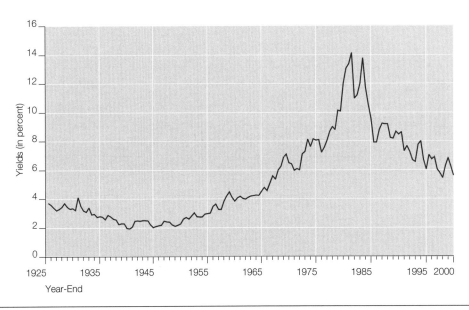

Total returns for 1977–2000 are calculated as the change in the flat or and-interest price.[1] The flat price is the average of the bond's bid and ask prices, plus the accrued coupon.[2] The accrued coupon is equal to zero on the day a coupon is paid, and increases over time until the next coupon payment according to this formula:

$$A = fC \qquad \text{(1)}$$

where,

$A$ = accrued coupon;

$C$ = semiannual coupon rate; and

$f$ = $\dfrac{\text{number of days since last coupon payment}}{\text{number of days from last coupon payment to next coupon payment}}$

## Income Return

For 1977–2000, the income return is calculated as the change in flat price plus any coupon actually paid from one period to the next, holding the yield constant over the period. As in the total return series, the exact number of days comprising the period is used. For 1926–1976, the income return for a given month is calculated as the total return minus the capital appreciation return.

## Capital Appreciation or Return in Excess of Yield

For 1977–2000, capital appreciation is taken as the total return minus the income return for each month. For 1926–1976, the capital appreciation return (also known as the return in excess of yield) is obtained from the CRSP Government Bond File.

A bond's capital appreciation is defined as the total return minus the income return; that is, the return in excess of yield. This definition omits the capital gain or loss that comes from the movement of a bond's price toward par (in the absence of interest rate change) as it matures. Capital appreciation, as defined here, captures changes in bond prices caused by changes in the interest rate.

## Yields

The yield on the long-term government bond series is defined as the internal rate of return that equates the bond's price (the average of bid and ask, plus the accrued coupon) with the stream of cash flows (coupons and principal) promised to the bondholder. The yields reported for 1977–2000 were calculated from *The Wall Street Journal* prices for the bonds listed in Table 3-1. For noncallable bonds, the maturity date is shown. For callable bonds, the first call date and the maturity dates are shown as in the following example: 10/15/47–52 refers to a bond that is first callable on 10/15/1947 and matures on 10/15/1952. Dates from 47–99 refer to 1947–1999; 00–16 refers to 2000–2016. For callable bonds trading below par, the yield to maturity is used; above par, the yield to call is used. The yields for 1926–1976 were obtained from the CRSP Government Bond File.

---

1  "Flat price" is used here to mean the unmodified economic value of the bond, i.e., the and-interest price, or quoted price plus accrued interest. In contrast, some sources use flat price to mean the quoted price.

2  For the purpose of calculating the return in months when a coupon payment is made, the change in the flat price includes the coupon.

## Graph 3-5

### Intermediate-Term Government Bonds

Return Indices, Returns, and Yields

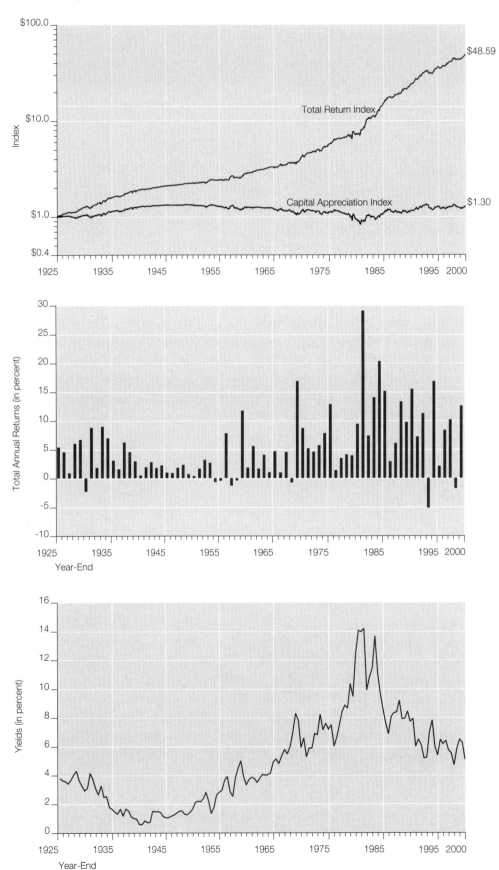

# Intermediate-Term Government Bonds

## Overview

One dollar invested in intermediate-term government bonds at year-end 1925, with coupons reinvested, grew to $48.59 by year-end 2000. [See Graph 3-5.] This represents a 75-year compound annual growth rate of 5.3 percent. Total annual returns ranged from a high of 29.1 percent in 1982 to a low of –5.1 percent in 1994. The compound yield-to-maturity (or yield-to-first-call, where applicable) was 4.8 percent.

Capital appreciation caused $1.00 to increase to $1.30 over the 75-year period, representing a compound annual growth rate of 0.3 percent. This increase was unexpected: Since yields rose on average over the period, capital appreciation on a hypothetical intermediate-term government bond portfolio with a constant five-year maturity should have been negative. An explanation of the positive average return is given at the end of this chapter.

## Total Returns

Total returns of the intermediate-term government bonds for 1987–2000 are calculated from *The Wall Street Journal* prices, using the coupon accrual method described above for long-term government bonds. [See Equation (1).] The bond used in 2000 is the 6.50 percent issue maturing on August 15, 2005. Returns over 1934–1986 are obtained from the CRSP Government Bond File. The bonds used to construct the index over 1934–2000 are shown in Table 3-1.

As with long-term government bonds, one-bond portfolios are used to construct the intermediate-term government bond index. The bond chosen each year is the shortest noncallable bond with a maturity not less than five years, and it is "held" for the calendar year. Monthly returns are computed. (Bonds with impaired negotiability or special redemption privileges are omitted, as are partially or fully tax-exempt bonds starting with 1943.)

Over 1934–1942, almost all bonds with maturities near five years were partially or fully tax-exempt and selected using the rules described above. Personal tax rates were generally low in that period, so that yields on tax-exempt bonds were similar to yields on taxable bonds.

Over 1926–1933, there are few bonds suitable for construction of a series with a five-year maturity. For this period, five-year bond yield estimates are used. These estimates are obtained from Thomas S. Coleman, Lawrence Fisher, and Roger G. Ibbotson, *Historical U.S. Treasury Yield Curves: 1926–1992* with 1995 update (Ibbotson Associates, Chicago, 1995). The estimates reflect what a "pure play" five-year Treasury bond, selling at par and with no special redemption or call provisions, would have yielded had one existed. Estimates are for partially tax-exempt bonds for 1926–1932 and for fully tax-exempt bonds for 1933. Monthly yields are converted to monthly total returns by calculating the beginning and end-of-month flat prices for the hypothetical bonds.

## Table 3-1

## Long-Term and Intermediate-Term Government Bond Issues

### Long-Term Government Bonds

| Period Bond is Held in Index | Coupon (%) | Call/Maturity Date |
|---|---|---|
| 1926–1931 | 4.25 | 10/15/47–52 |
| 1932–1935 | 3.00 | 9/15/51–55 |
| 1936–1941 | 2.875 | 3/15/55–60 |
| 1942–1953 | 2.50 | 9/15/67–72 |
| 1954–1958 | 3.25 | 6/15/78–83 |
| 1959–1960 | 4.00 | 2/15/80 |
| 1961–1965 | 4.25 | 5/15/75–85 |
| 1966–1972 | 4.25 | 8/15/87–92 |
| 1973–1974 | 6.75 | 2/15/93 |
| 1975–1976 | 8.50 | 5/15/94–99 |
| 1977–1980 | 7.875 | 2/15/95–00 |
| 1981 | 8.00 | 8/15/96–01 |
| 1982 | 13.375 | 8/15/01 |
| 1983 | 10.75 | 2/15/03 |
| 1984 | 11.875 | 11/15/03 |
| 1985 | 11.75 | 2/15/05–10 |
| 1986–1989 | 10.00 | 5/15/05–10 |
| 1990–1992 | 10.375 | 11/15/07–12 |
| 1993–1996 | 7.25 | 5/15/16 |
| 1997–1998 | 8.125 | 8/15/19 |
| 1999 | 8.125 | 8/15/21 |
| 2000 | 8.125 | 8/15/21 |

### Intermediate-Term Government Bonds

| Period Bond is Held in Index | Coupon (%) | Call/Maturity Date |
|---|---|---|
| 1934–1936 | 3.25 | 8/01/41 |
| 1937 | 3.375 | 3/15/43 |
| 1938–1940 | 2.50 | 12/15/45 |
| 1941 | 3.00 | 1/01/46 |
| 1942 | 3.00 | 1/01/47 |
| 1943 | 1.75 | 6/15/48 |
| 1944–1945 | 2.00 | 3/15/50 |
| 1946 | 2.00 | 6/15/51 |
| 1947 | 2.00 | 3/15/52 |
| 1948 | 2.00 | 9/15/53 |
| 1949 | 2.50 | 3/15/54 |
| 1950 | 2.25 | 6/15/55 |
| 1951–1952 | 2.50 | 3/15/58 |
| 1953 | 2.375 | 6/15/58 |
| 1954 | 2.375 | 3/15/59 |
| 1955 | 2.125 | 11/15/60 |
| 1956 | 2.75 | 9/15/61 |
| 1957–1958 | 2.50 | 8/15/63 |
| 1959 | 3.00 | 2/15/64 |

### Intermediate-Term Government Bonds (continued)

| Period Bond is Held in Index | Coupon (%) | Call/Maturity Date |
|---|---|---|
| 1960 | 2.625 | 2/15/65 |
| 1961 | 3.75 | 5/15/66 |
| 1962 | 3.625 | 11/15/67 |
| 1963 | 3.875 | 5/15/68 |
| 1964 | 4.00 | 2/15/69 |
| 1965 | 4.00 | 8/15/70 |
| 1966 | 4.00 | 8/15/71 |
| 1967 | 4.00 | 2/15/72 |
| 1968 | 4.00 | 8/15/73 |
| 1969 | 5.625 | 8/15/74 |
| 1970 | 5.75 | 2/15/75 |
| 1971 | 6.25 | 2/15/76 |
| 1972 | 1.50 | 10/01/76 |
| 1973 | 6.25 | 2/15/78 |
| 1974 | 6.25 | 8/15/79 |
| 1975 | 6.875 | 5/15/80 |
| 1976 | 7.00 | 2/15/81 |
| 1977 | 6.375 | 2/15/82 |
| 1978 | 8.00 | 2/15/83 |
| 1979 | 7.25 | 2/15/84 |
| 1980 | 8.00 | 2/15/85 |
| 1981 | 13.50 | 2/15/86 |
| 1982 | 9.00 | 2/15/87 |
| 1983 | 12.375 | 1/01/88 |
| 1984 | 14.625 | 1/15/89 |
| 1985 | 10.50 | 1/15/90 |
| 1986 | 11.75 | 1/15/91 |
| 1987 | 11.625 | 1/15/92 |
| 1988 | 8.75 | 1/15/93 |
| 1989 | 9.00 | 2/15/94 |
| 1990 | 8.625 | 10/15/95 |
| 1991–1992 | 7.875 | 7/15/96 |
| 1993 | 6.375 | 1/15/99 |
| 1994 | 5.50 | 4/15/00 |
| 1995 | 8.50 | 2/15/00 |
| 1996 | 7.75 | 2/15/01 |
| 1997 | 6.375 | 8/15/02 |
| 1998 | 5.75 | 8/15/03 |
| 1999 | 7.25 | 8/15/04 |
| 2000 | 6.50 | 8/15/05 |

The bond is "bought" at the beginning of the month at par (i.e., the coupon equals the previous month-end yield), assuming a maturity of five years. It is "sold" at the end of the month, with the flat price calculated by discounting the coupons and principal at the end-of-month yield, assuming a maturity of 4 years and 11 months. The flat price is the price of the bond including coupon accruals, so that the change in flat price represents total return. Monthly income returns are assumed to be equal to the previous end-of-month yield, stated in monthly terms. Monthly capital appreciation returns are formed as total returns minus income returns.

### Income Return and Capital Appreciation

For the period 1987–2000, the income return is calculated according to the methodology stated under "Long-Term Government Bonds." Monthly capital appreciation (return in excess of yield) over this same period is the difference between total return and income return.

For 1934–1986, capital appreciation (return in excess of yield) is taken directly from the CRSP Government Bond File. The income return is calculated as the total return minus the capital appreciation return. Prior to 1934, the income and capital appreciation components of total return are generated from yield estimates as described earlier under Total Returns.

### Yields

The yield on an intermediate-term government bond is the internal rate of return that equates the bond's price with the stream of cash flows (coupons and principal) promised to the bondholder. The yields reported for 1987–2000 are calculated from *The Wall Street Journal* bond prices listed in Table 3-1. For 1934–1986, yields were obtained from the CRSP Government Bond File. Yields for 1926–1933 are estimates from Coleman, Fisher, and Ibbotson, *Historical U.S. Treasury Yield Curves: 1926–1992* with 1995 update.

## U.S. Treasury Bills

### Overview

One dollar invested in U.S. Treasury bills at year-end 1925 grew to $16.56 by year-end 2000; this represents a compound annual growth rate of 3.8 percent. [See Graph 3-6.] Total annual returns ranged from a high of 14.7 percent in 1981 to a low of 0.0 percent for the period 1938 to 1940.

## Graph 3-6

### U.S. Treasury Bills
Return Index and Returns

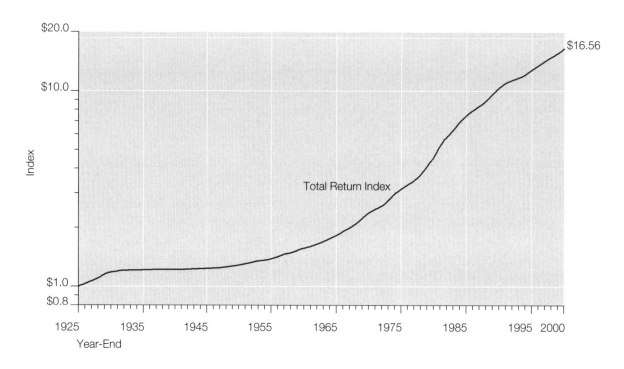

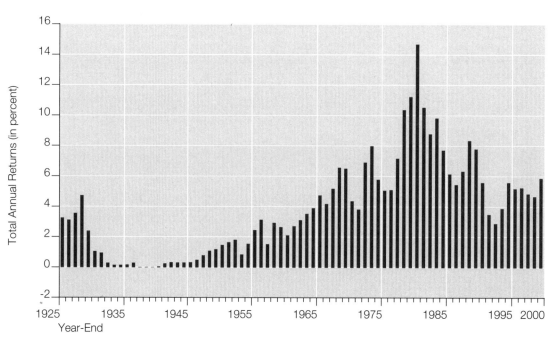

## Total Returns

For the U.S. Treasury bill index, data from *The Wall Street Journal* are used for 1977–2000; the CRSP U.S. Government Bond File is the source until 1976. Each month a one-bill portfolio containing the shortest-term bill having not less than one month to maturity is constructed. (The bill's original term to maturity is not relevant.) To measure holding period returns for the one-bill portfolio, the bill is priced as of the last trading day of the previous month-end and as of the last trading day of the current month.

The price of the bill **(P)** at each time **(t)** is given as:

$$P_t = \left[ 1 - \frac{rd}{360} \right] \qquad (2)$$

where,

**r** = decimal yield (the average of bid and ask quotes) on the bill at time **t**; and,

**d** = number of days to maturity as of time **t**.

The total return on the bill is the month-end price divided by the previous month-end price, minus one.

## Negative Returns on Treasury Bills

Monthly Treasury bill returns (as reported in Appendix A-14) were negative in February 1933, and in 12 months during the 1938–1941 period. Also, the annual Treasury bill return was negative for 1938. Since negative Treasury bill returns contradict logic, an explanation is in order.

Negative yields observed in the data do not imply that investors purchased Treasury bills with a guaranteed negative return. Rather, Treasury bills of that era were exempt from personal property taxes in some states, while cash was not. Further, for a bank to hold U.S. government deposits, Treasury securities were required as collateral. These circumstances created excessive demand for the security, and thus bills were sold at a premium. Given the low interest rates during the period, owners of the bills experienced negative returns.

# Inflation

## Overview

A basket of consumer goods purchased for $1.00 at year-end 1925 would cost $9.71 by year-end 2000. [See Graph 3-7.] Of course, the exact contents of the basket changed over time. This increase represents a compound annual rate of inflation of 3.1 percent over the past 75 years. Inflation rates ranged from a high of 18.2 percent in 1946 to a low of –10.3 percent in 1932.

## Inflation

The Consumer Price Index for All Urban Consumers (CPI-U), not seasonally adjusted, is used to measure inflation, which is the rate of change of consumer goods prices. Unfortunately, the CPI is not measured over the same period as the other asset returns. All of the security returns are measured from one month-end to the next month-end. CPI commodity prices are collected during the

## Graph 3-7

**Inflation**

Cumulative Index and Rates of Change

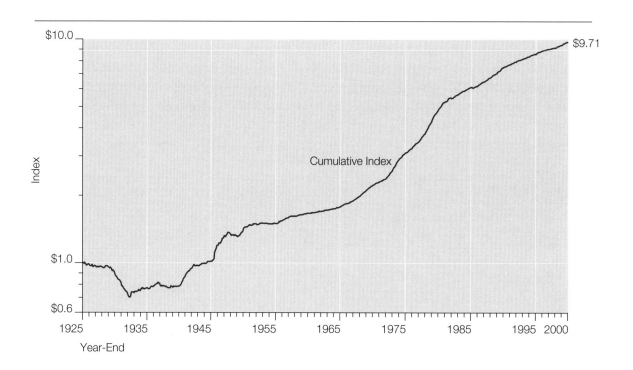

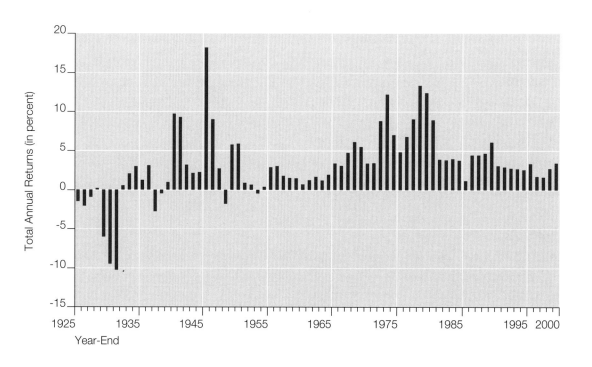

month. Thus, measured inflation rates lag the other series by about one-half month. Prior to January 1978, the CPI (as compared with CPI-U) was used. For the period 1978 through 1987, the index uses the year 1967 in determining the items compromising the basket of goods. Following 1987, a three-year period, 1982 through 1984, was used to determine the items making up the basket of goods. All inflation measures are constructed by the U.S. Department of Labor, Bureau of Labor Statistics, Washington.

## Positive Capital Appreciation on Intermediate-Term Government Bonds

The capital appreciation component of intermediate-term government bond returns caused $1.00 invested at year-end 1925 to grow to $1.30 by the end of 2000, representing a compound annual rate of 0.3 percent. This is surprising because yields, on average, rose over the period.

An investor in a hypothetical five-year constant maturity portfolio, with continuous rebalancing, suffered a capital loss (that is, excluding coupon income) over 1926–2000. An investor who rebalanced yearly, choosing bonds according to the method set forth above, fared better. This investor would have earned the 0.3 percent per year capital gain recorded here.

This performance relates to the construction of the intermediate-term bond series. For 1926–1933, the one-bond portfolio was rebalanced monthly to maintain a constant maturity of five years. For the period 1934–2000, one bond (the shortest bond not less than five years to maturity) was chosen at the beginning of each year and priced monthly. New bonds were not picked each month to maintain a constant five years to maturity intrayear.

There are several possible reasons for the positive capital appreciation return. Chief among these reasons are convexity of the bond portfolio and the substitution of one bond for another at each year-end.

### Convexity

Each year, we "bought" a bond with approximately five years to maturity and held it for one year. During this period, the market yield on the bond fluctuates. Because the duration of the bond shortens (the bond becomes less interest-rate sensitive) as yields rise and the duration lengthens as yields fall, more is gained from a fall in yield than is lost from a rise in yield. This characteristic of a bond is known as convexity.

For example, suppose an 8 percent coupon bond is bought at par at the beginning of a year; the yield fluctuates (but the portfolio is not rebalanced) during the year; and the bond is sold at par at the end of the year. The price of the bond at both the beginning and end of the year is $100; the change in bond price is zero. However, the fluctuations will have caused the gains during periods of falling yields to exceed the losses during periods of rising yields. Thus the total return for the year exceeds 8 percent. Since our measure of capital appreciation is the return in excess of yield, rather than the change in bond price, capital appreciation for this bond (as measured) will be greater than zero.

In 1992, the yield for intermediate-term government bonds started the year at 5.97 percent, rose, fell, and finally rose again to end at 6.11 percent, slightly higher than the starting point. In the absence of convexity, the capital appreciation return for 1992 would be negative. Because of the fluctuation of yields during the year, however, the capital appreciation return on the intermediate-term government bond index was positive 0.64 percent.

It should be noted that the return in excess of yield, or capital gain, from convexity is caused by holding, over the year, a bond whose yield at purchase is different than the current market yield. If the portfolio were rebalanced each time the data were sampled (in this case, monthly), by selling the old bond and buying a new five-year bond selling at par, the portfolio would have no convexity. That is, over a period where yields ended where they started, the measured capital appreciation would be zero. However, this is neither a practical way to construct an index of actual bonds nor to manage a bond portfolio.

## Bond Substitution

Another reason why the intermediate-term government bond series displays positive capital appreciation even though yields rose is the way in which bonds were removed from the portfolio and replaced with other bonds. In general, it was not possible to replace a bond "sold" by buying one with exactly the same yield. This produces a spurious change in the yield of the series—one that should not be associated with a capital gain or loss.

For example: Suppose a five-year bond yielding 8 percent is bought at par at the beginning of the year; at that time, four-year bonds yield 7 percent. Over the year, the yield curve rises in parallel by one percentage point so that when it comes time to sell the bond at year-end, it yields 8 percent and has four years to maturity. Therefore, at both the beginning and end of the year, the price of the bond is $100.

The proceeds from the sale are used to buy a new five-year bond yielding 9 percent. While the bond price change was zero over the year, the yield of the series has risen from 8 percent to 9 percent. Thus it is possible, because of the process of substituting one bond for another, for the yield series to contain a spurious rise that is not, and should not be expected to be, associated with a decline in the price of any particular bond. This phenomenon is likely to be the source of some of the positive capital appreciation in our intermediate-term government bond series.

## Other Issues

While convexity and bond substitution may explain the anomaly of positive capital appreciation in a bond series with rising yields, there are other incomplete-market problems that may also help explain the capital gain. For example, intermediate-term government bonds were scarce in the 1930s and 1940s. As a result, the bonds chosen for this series occasionally had maturities longer than five years, ranging as high as eight years when bought. The 1930s and the first half of the 1940s were bullish for the bond market. Longer bonds included in this series had higher yields and substantially higher capital gain returns than bonds with exactly five years to maturity might have had if any existed. This upward bias is particularly noticeable in 1934, 1937, and 1938.

In addition, callable and fully or partially tax-exempt bonds were used when necessary to obtain a bond for some years. The conversion of the Treasury bond market from tax-exempt to taxable status produced a one-time upward jump in stated yields, but not a capital loss on any given bond. Therefore, part of the increase in stated yields over 1926–2000 was a tax effect that did not cause a capital loss on the intermediate-term bond index. Further, the callable bonds used in the early part of the period may have commanded a return premium for taking this extra risk.

# Chapter 4

**Description of the Derived Series**

Historical data suggests that investors are rewarded for taking risks and that returns are related to inflation rates. The risk/return and the real/nominal relationships in the historical data are revealed by looking at the risk premium and inflation-adjusted series derived from the basic asset series. Monthly total returns for the four risk premia are presented in Appendix A: Tables A-16 through A-19. Monthly inflation-adjusted total returns for the six asset classes are presented in Appendix A: Tables A-20 through A-25.

## Geometric Differences Used to Calculate Derived Series

Derived series are calculated as the geometric differences between two basic asset classes. Returns on basic series **A** and **B** and derived series **C** are related as follows:

$$(1+C) = \left[ \frac{1+A}{1+B} \right] \qquad (3)$$

where the series **A**, **B**, and **C** are in decimal form (i.e., 5 percent is indicated by 0.05). Thus **C** is given by:

$$C = \left[ \frac{1+A}{1+B} \right] - 1 \approx A - B \qquad (4)$$

As an example, suppose return **A** equals 15%, or 0.15; and return **B** is 5%, or 0.05. Then **C** equals (1.15 / 1.05) – 1 = 0.0952, or 9.52 percent. This result, while slightly different from the simple arithmetic difference of 10 percent, is conceptually the same.

## Definitions of the Derived Series

From the seven basic asset classes—large company stocks, small company stocks, long-term corporate bonds, long-term government bonds, intermediate-term government bonds, U.S. Treasury bills, and consumer goods (inflation)—10 additional series are derived representing the component or elemental parts of the asset returns.

## Two Categories of Derived Series

The 10 derived series are categorized as risk premia, or payoffs for taking various types of risk; and as inflation-adjusted asset returns. The risk premia series are the bond horizon premium, the bond default premium, the equity risk premium, and the small stock premium. The inflation-adjusted asset return series are constructed by geometrically subtracting inflation from each of the six asset total return series.

These 10 derived series are:

| Series | Derivation |
|---|---|
| **Risk Premia** | |
| Equity Risk Premium | $\dfrac{(1 + \text{Large Stock TR})}{(1 + \text{Treasury Bill TR})} - 1$ |
| Small Stock Premium | $\dfrac{(1 + \text{Small Stock TR})}{(1 + \text{Large Stock TR})} - 1$ |
| Bond Default Premium | $\dfrac{(1 + \text{LT Corp Bond TR})}{(1 + \text{LT Govt Bond TR})} - 1$ |
| Bond Horizon Premium | $\dfrac{(1 + \text{LT Govt Bond TR})}{(1 + \text{Treasury Bill TR})} - 1$ |
| **Inflation-Adjusted** | |
| Large Company Stock Returns | $\dfrac{(1 + \text{Large Stock TR})}{(1 + \text{Inflation})} - 1$ |
| Small Company Stock Returns | $\dfrac{(1 + \text{Small Stock TR})}{(1 + \text{Inflation})} - 1$ |
| Corporate Bond Returns | $\dfrac{(1 + \text{Corp Bond TR})}{(1 + \text{Inflation})} - 1$ |
| Long-Term Government Bond Returns | $\dfrac{(1 + \text{LT Govt Bond TR})}{(1 + \text{Inflation})} - 1$ |
| Intermediate-Term Government Bond Returns | $\dfrac{(1 + \text{IT Govt Bond TR})}{(1 + \text{Inflation})} - 1$ |
| Treasury Bill Returns (Real Riskless Rate of Returns) | $\dfrac{(1 + \text{Treasury Bill TR})}{(1 + \text{Inflation})} - 1$ |

TR = Total Return

## Equity Risk Premium

Large company stock returns are composed of inflation, the real riskless rate, and the equity risk premium. The equity risk premium is the geometric difference between large company stock total returns and U.S. Treasury bill total returns.

Because large company stocks are not strictly comparable with bonds, horizon and default premia are not used to analyze the components of equity returns. (Large company stocks have characteristics that are analogous to horizon and default risk, but they are not equivalent.)

The monthly equity risk premium is given by:

$$\frac{(1 + \text{Large Stock TR})}{(1 + \text{Treasury Bill TR})} - 1 \qquad (5)$$

Graph 4-1 shows equity risk premium volatility over the last 75 years.

Graph 4-1

**Equity Risk Premium Annual Returns**
(in percent)

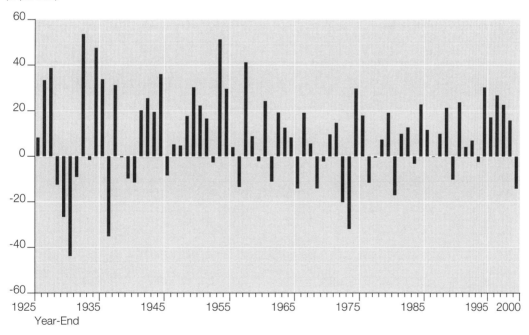

## Small Stock Premium

The small stock premium is the geometric difference between small company stock total returns and large company stock total returns. The monthly small stock premium is given by:

$$\frac{\left(1+\text{Small Stock TR}\right)}{\left(1+\text{Large Stock TR}\right)} - 1 \qquad (6)$$

Graph 4-2 shows small stock premium volatility over the last 75 years.

Graph 4-2

**Small Stock Premium Annual Returns**
(in percent)

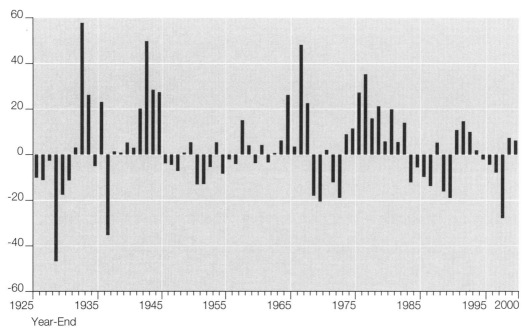

Year-End

## Bond Default Premium

The bond default premium is defined as the net return from investing in long-term corporate bonds rather than long-term government bonds of equal maturity. Since there is a possibility of default on a corporate bond, bondholders receive a premium that reflects this possibility, in addition to inflation, the real riskless rate, and the horizon premium.

The monthly bond default premium is given by:

$$\frac{\left(1+\text{LT Corp Bond TR}\right)}{\left(1+\text{LT Govt Bond TR}\right)} - 1 \qquad (7)$$

## Components of the Default Premium

Bonds susceptible to default have higher returns (when they do not default) than riskless bonds. Default on a bond may be a small loss, such as a late or skipped interest payment; it may be a larger loss, such as the loss of any or all principal as well as interest. In any case, part of the default premium on a portfolio of bonds is consumed by the losses on those bonds that do default.

The remainder of the default premium—over and above the portion consumed by defaults—is a pure risk premium, which the investor demands and, over the long run, receives for taking the risk of default. The expected return on a corporate bond, or portfolio of corporate bonds, is less than the bond's yield. The portion of the yield that is expected to be consumed by defaults must be subtracted. The expected return on a corporate bond is equal to the expected return on a government bond of like maturity, plus the pure risk premium portion of the bond default premium.

## Callability Risk is Captured in the Default Premium

Callability risk is the risk that a bond will be redeemed (at or near par) by its issuer before maturity, at a time when market interest rates are lower than the bond's coupon rate. The possibility of redemption is risky because it would prevent the bondholder of the redeemed issue from reinvesting the proceeds at the original (higher) interest rate. The bond default premium, as measured here, also inadvertently captures any premium investors may demand or receive for this risk.

Graph 4-3 shows bond default premium volatility over the last 75 years.

Graph 4-3

**Bond Default Premium Annual Returns**
(in percent)

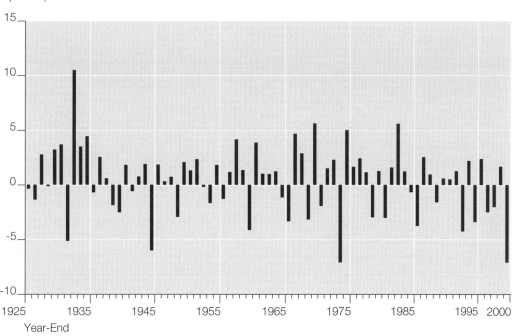

Year-End

## Bond Horizon Premium

Long-term government bonds behave differently than short-term bills in that their prices (and hence returns) are more sensitive to interest rate fluctuations. The bond horizon premium is the premium investors demand for holding long-term bonds instead of U.S. Treasury bills.

The monthly bond horizon premium is given by:

$$\frac{(1 + LT\,Govt\,Bond\,TR)}{(1 + Treasury\,Bill\,TR)} - 1 \qquad \text{(8)}$$

Long-term rather than intermediate-term government bonds are used to derive the bond horizon premium so as to capture a "full unit" of price fluctuation risk. Intermediate-term government bonds may display a partial horizon premium, which is smaller than the difference between long-term bonds and short-term bills.

### Does Maturity or Duration Determine the Bond Premium?

Duration is the present-value-weighted average time to receipt of cash flows (coupons and principal) from holding a bond, and can be calculated from the bond's yield, coupon rate, and term to maturity. The duration of a given bond determines the amount of return premium arising from differences in bond life. The bond horizon premium is also referred to as the "maturity premium," based on the observation that bonds with longer maturities command a return premium over shorter-maturity bonds. Duration, not term to maturity, however, is the bond characteristic that determines this return premium.

### Why a "Horizon" Premium?

Investors often strive to match the duration of their bond holdings (cash inflows) with the estimated duration of their obligations or cash outflows. Consequently, investors with short time horizons regard long-duration bonds as risky (due to price fluctuation risk), and short-term bills as riskless. Conversely, investors with long time horizons regard short-term bills as risky (due to the uncertainty about the yield at which bills can be reinvested), and long-duration bonds as riskless or less risky.

Empirically, long-duration bonds bear higher yields and greater returns than short-term bills; that is, the yield curve slopes upward on average over time. This observation indicates that investors are more averse to the price fluctuation risk of long-duration bonds than to the reinvestment risk of bills.

Bond-duration risk is thus in the eye of the beholder, or bondholder. Therefore, rather than identifying the premium as a payoff for long-bond risk (which implies a judgment that short-horizon investors are "right" in their risk perceptions), it is better to go directly to the source of the return differential (the differing time horizons of investors) and use the label "horizon premium."

Graph 4-4 shows the bond horizon premium over the last 75 years.

Graph 4-4

**Bond Horizon Premium Annual Returns**
(in percent)

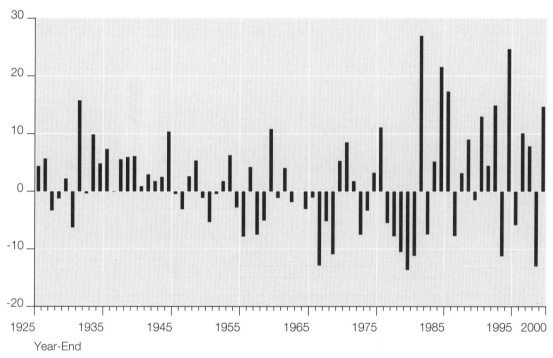

Year-End

## Inflation-Adjusted Large Company Stock Returns

### Overview

Large company stock total returns were 11.0 percent compounded annually over the period 1926–2000 in nominal terms. [See Graph 4-5.] In real (inflation-adjusted) terms, stocks provided a 7.7 percent compound annual return. Thus, a large company stock investor would have experienced a substantial increase in real wealth, or purchasing power, over the 75-year period.

### Construction

The inflation-adjusted return is a geometric difference and is approximately equal to the arithmetic difference between the large company stock total return and the inflation rate. The monthly inflation-adjusted large company stock return is given by:

$$\frac{\left(1+\text{Large Stock TR}\right)}{\left(1+\text{Inflation}\right)} - 1 \qquad (9)$$

Graph 4-5

**Large Company Stocks**
Real and Nominal Return Indices

Year-End 1925 = $1.00

from 1925 to 2000

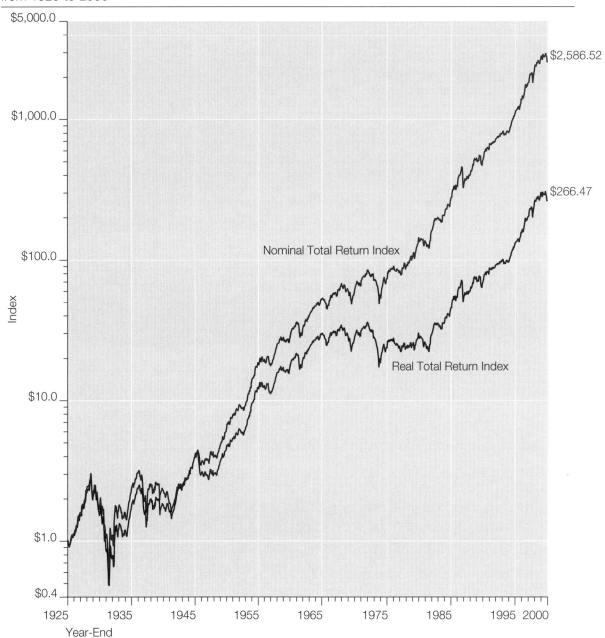

The inflation-adjusted large company stock return may also be expressed as the geometric sum of the real riskless rate and the equity risk premium:

$$[(1 + \text{Real Riskless Rate}) \times (1 + \text{Equity Risk Premium})] - 1 \qquad (10)$$

## Inflation-Adjusted Small Company Stock Returns

### Overview

Small company stock total returns were 12.4 percent compounded annually over the period 1926–2000 in nominal terms. [See Graph 4-6.] In real terms, small company stocks provided an 9.0 percent compound annual return. Thus, long-term a small company stock investor would have experienced a substantial increase in real wealth, or purchasing power, over the 75-year period.

### Construction

The inflation-adjusted return is a geometric difference and is approximately equal to the arithmetic difference between the small company stock total return and the inflation rate. The monthly inflation-adjusted small company stock return is given by:

$$\frac{(1 + \text{Small Stock TR})}{(1 + \text{Inflation})} - 1 \qquad (11)$$

## Inflation-Adjusted Long-Term Corporate Bond Returns

### Overview

Corporate bonds returned 5.7 percent compounded annually over the period 1926–2000 in nominal terms, and a 2.5 percent compound annual return in real (inflation-adjusted) terms. [See Graph 4-7.] Thus, corporate bonds have outpaced inflation over the past 75 years.

### Construction

The inflation-adjusted return is a geometric difference and is approximately equal to the arithmetic difference between the long-term corporate bond total return and the inflation rate. The monthly inflation-adjusted corporate bond total return is given by:

$$\frac{(1 + \text{Corp Bond TR})}{(1 + \text{Inflation})} - 1 \qquad (12)$$

Graph 4-6

## Small Company Stocks
Real and Nominal Return Indices

Year-End 1925 = $1.00

from 1925 to 2000

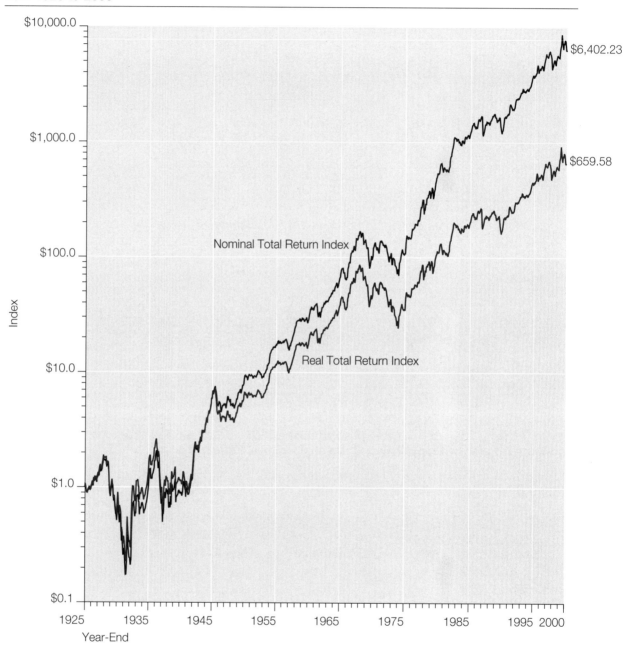

Graph 4-7

**Long-Term Corporate Bonds**
Real and Nominal Return Indices

Year-End 1925 = $1.00

from 1925 to 2000

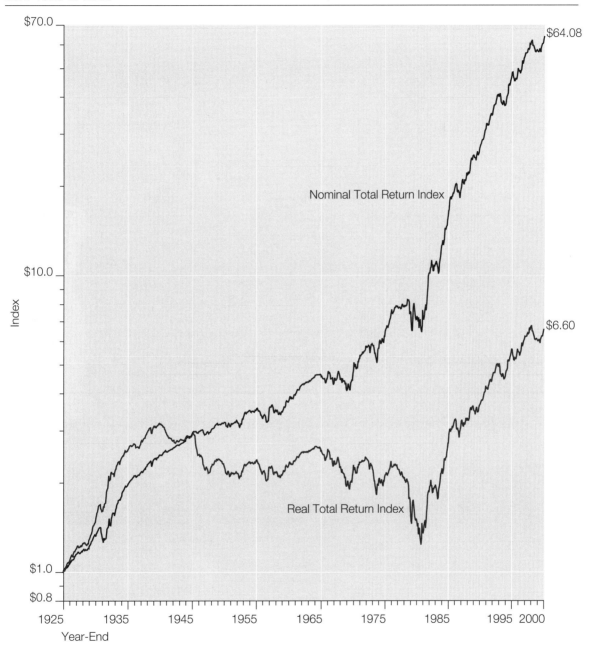

Nominal Total Return Index

$64.08

Real Total Return Index

$6.60

Index

1925    1935    1945    1955    1965    1975    1985    1995  2000

Year-End

## Inflation-Adjusted Long-Term Government Bond Returns

### Overview

Long-term government bonds returned 5.3 percent compounded annually over the period 1926–2000 in nominal terms, and a 2.2 percent compound annual return in real (inflation-adjusted) terms. [See Graph 4-8.] Thus, long-term government bonds have outpaced inflation over the past 75 years despite falling bond prices over most of the period.

### Construction

The inflation-adjusted return is a geometric difference and is approximately equal to the arithmetic difference between the long-term government bond total return and the inflation rate. The monthly inflation-adjusted long-term government bond total return is given by:

$$\frac{(1 + LT\,Govt\,Bond\,TR)}{(1 + Inflation)} - 1 \qquad \text{(13)}$$

Since government bond returns are composed of inflation, the real riskless rate, and the horizon premium, the inflation-adjusted government bond returns may also be expressed as:

$$[(1 + Real\,Riskless\,Rate) \times (1 + Horizon\,Premium)] - 1 \qquad \text{(14)}$$

## Inflation-Adjusted Intermediate-Term Government Bond Returns

### Overview

Intermediate-term government bonds returned 5.3 percent compounded annually in nominal terms, and 2.2 percent in real (inflation-adjusted) terms. [See Graph 4-9.]

### Construction

The inflation-adjusted return is a geometric difference and is approximately equal to the arithmetic difference between the intermediate-term government bond total return and the inflation rate. The monthly inflation-adjusted intermediate-term government bond return is given by:

$$\frac{(1 + IT\,Govt\,Bond\,TR)}{(1 + Inflation)} - 1 \qquad \text{(15)}$$

Graph 4-8

**Long-Term Government Bonds**
Real and Nominal Return Indices

Year-End 1925 = $1.00

from 1925 to 2000

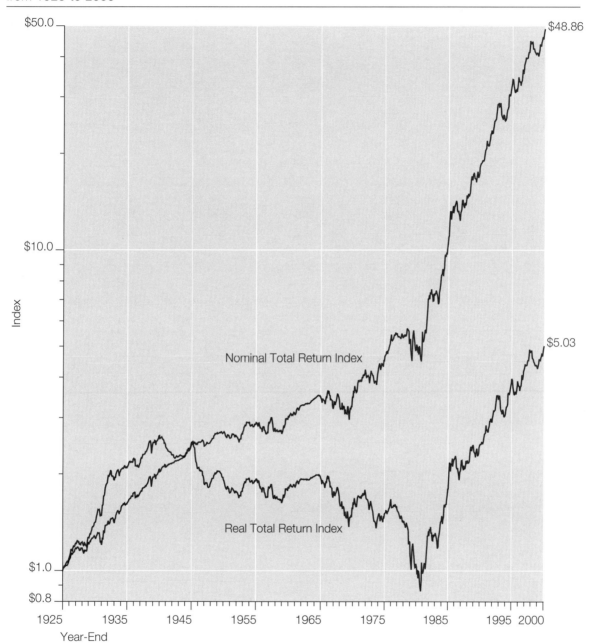

Graph 4-9

**Intermediate-Term Government Bonds**
Real and Nominal Return Indices

Year-End 1925 = $1.00

from 1925 to 2000

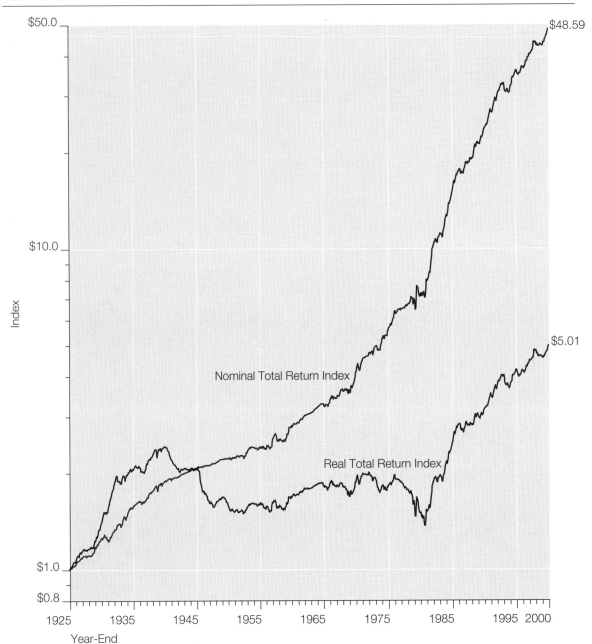

## Inflation-Adjusted U.S. Treasury Bill Returns (Real Riskless Rates of Return)

### Overview

Treasury bills returned 3.8 percent compounded annually over 1926-2000, in nominal terms, but only a 0.7 percent compound annual return in real (inflation-adjusted) terms. [See Graph 4-11.] Thus, an investor in Treasury bills would have barely beaten inflation over the 75-year period.

### Construction

The real riskless rate of return is the difference in returns between riskless U.S. Treasury bills and inflation. This is given by:

$$\frac{(1 + \text{Treasury Bill TR})}{(1 + \text{Inflation})} - 1 \qquad (16)$$

Graph 4-10 shows the levels, volatility, and patterns of real interest rates over the last 75 years.

Graph 4-10

**Annual Real Riskless Rates of Return**
(in percent)

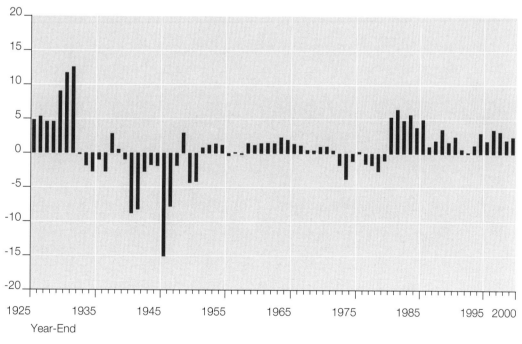

### Returns on the Derived Series

Annual returns for the 10 derived series are calculated from monthly returns in the same manner as the annual basic series. Table 4-1 presents annual returns for each of the 10 derived series. Four of the derived series are risk premia and six are inflation-adjusted total returns on asset classes.

Graph 4-11

**U.S. Treasury Bills**
Real and Nominal Return Indices

Year-End 1925 = $1.00

from 1925 to 2000

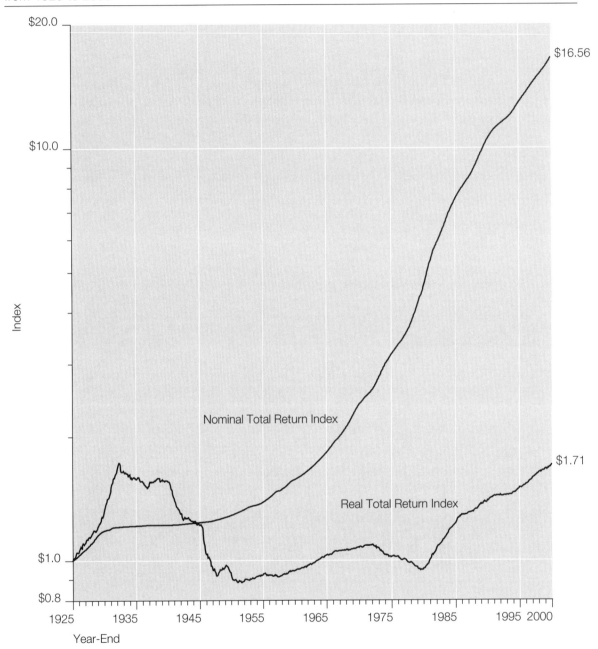

# Table 4-1

**Derived Series**
Annual Returns (in percent)

from 1926 to 1970

| Year | Equity Risk Premia | Small Stock Premia | Default Premia | Horizon Premia | Inflation-Adjusted | | | | | |
|------|-------------------|--------------------|----------------|----------------|---------------------------|------------------------|--------------------------|--------------------------|-------------------------|------------------------|
| | | | | | Large Company Stocks | Small Company Stocks | Long-Term Corp. Bonds | Long-Term Govt. Bonds | Intermed. Govt. Bonds | U.S. Treasury Bills |
| 1926 | 8.09 | −10.17 | −0.37 | 4.36 | 13.31 | 1.79 | 9.00 | 9.40 | 6.97 | 4.83 |
| 1927 | 33.32 | −11.19 | −1.36 | 5.63 | 40.41 | 24.69 | 9.73 | 11.24 | 6.74 | 5.31 |
| 1928 | 38.67 | −2.73 | 2.73 | −3.34 | 45.01 | 41.06 | 3.84 | 1.08 | 1.90 | 4.57 |
| 1929 | −12.57 | −46.89 | −0.14 | −1.27 | −8.59 | −51.45 | 3.07 | 3.22 | 5.81 | 4.54 |
| 1930 | −26.66 | −17.64 | 3.17 | 2.20 | −20.08 | −34.18 | 14.90 | 11.38 | 13.56 | 8.98 |
| 1931 | −43.94 | −11.33 | 3.65 | −6.31 | −37.37 | −44.46 | 8.48 | 4.66 | 7.96 | 11.71 |
| 1932 | −9.07 | 3.05 | −5.15 | 15.73 | 2.35 | 5.47 | 23.54 | 30.26 | 21.30 | 12.55 |
| 1933 | 53.53 | 57.72 | 10.46 | −0.37 | 53.21 | 141.63 | 9.82 | −0.58 | 1.31 | −0.21 |
| 1934 | −1.60 | 26.04 | 3.47 | 9.85 | −3.40 | 21.75 | 11.58 | 7.84 | 6.83 | −1.83 |
| 1935 | 47.42 | −5.06 | 4.41 | 4.81 | 43.39 | 36.13 | 6.44 | 1.94 | 3.91 | −2.73 |
| 1936 | 33.68 | 23.06 | −0.72 | 7.32 | 32.32 | 62.83 | 5.47 | 6.23 | 1.83 | −1.02 |
| 1937 | −35.23 | −35.37 | 2.51 | −0.08 | −36.98 | −59.27 | −0.35 | −2.78 | −1.50 | −2.71 |
| 1938 | 31.14 | 1.28 | 0.57 | 5.55 | 34.87 | 36.59 | 9.16 | 8.55 | 9.27 | 2.84 |
| 1939 | −0.43 | 0.76 | −1.86 | 5.92 | 0.07 | 0.83 | 4.46 | 6.45 | 5.02 | 0.50 |
| 1940 | −9.79 | 5.13 | −2.54 | 6.08 | −10.64 | −6.05 | 2.41 | 5.08 | 1.99 | −0.94 |
| 1941 | −11.64 | 2.93 | 1.78 | 0.87 | −19.42 | −17.06 | −6.37 | −8.01 | −8.40 | −8.80 |
| 1942 | 20.02 | 20.08 | −0.60 | 2.94 | 10.11 | 32.23 | −6.12 | −5.55 | −6.73 | −8.25 |
| 1943 | 25.46 | 49.62 | 0.73 | 1.73 | 22.04 | 82.60 | −0.32 | −1.04 | −0.34 | −2.73 |
| 1944 | 19.36 | 28.37 | 1.87 | 2.48 | 17.28 | 50.55 | 2.57 | 0.69 | −0.31 | −1.74 |
| 1945 | 35.99 | 27.25 | −6.01 | 10.37 | 33.43 | 69.79 | 1.78 | 8.30 | −0.03 | −1.88 |
| 1946 | −8.39 | −3.87 | 1.83 | −0.45 | −22.20 | −25.21 | −13.91 | −15.46 | −14.52 | −15.07 |
| 1947 | 5.18 | −4.53 | 0.29 | −3.11 | −3.03 | −7.42 | −10.41 | −10.67 | −7.43 | −7.80 |
| 1948 | 4.65 | −7.22 | 0.71 | 2.57 | 2.72 | −4.69 | 1.39 | 0.67 | −0.84 | −1.85 |
| 1949 | 17.50 | 0.80 | −2.95 | 5.29 | 20.97 | 21.95 | 5.21 | 8.40 | 4.20 | 2.96 |
| 1950 | 30.16 | 5.34 | 2.05 | −1.12 | 24.50 | 31.15 | −3.47 | −5.42 | −4.81 | −4.34 |
| 1951 | 22.19 | −13.07 | 1.29 | −5.34 | 17.14 | 1.82 | −8.09 | −9.26 | −5.21 | −4.14 |
| 1952 | 16.44 | −12.96 | 2.33 | −0.49 | 17.33 | 2.13 | 2.62 | 0.27 | 0.74 | 0.77 |
| 1953 | −2.76 | −5.55 | −0.22 | 1.78 | −1.60 | −7.07 | 2.77 | 2.99 | 2.59 | 1.19 |
| 1954 | 51.32 | 5.21 | −1.68 | 6.27 | 53.39 | 61.38 | 5.91 | 7.72 | 3.20 | 1.37 |
| 1955 | 29.52 | −8.45 | 1.80 | −2.82 | 31.07 | 19.99 | 0.10 | −1.66 | −1.02 | 1.19 |
| 1956 | 4.00 | −2.13 | −1.30 | −7.85 | 3.59 | 1.38 | −9.41 | −8.21 | −3.19 | −0.39 |
| 1957 | −13.50 | −4.25 | 1.17 | 4.19 | −13.40 | −17.08 | 5.52 | 4.31 | 4.67 | 0.11 |
| 1958 | 41.19 | 15.01 | 4.13 | −7.52 | 40.88 | 62.03 | −3.91 | −7.72 | −3.00 | −0.22 |
| 1959 | 8.75 | 3.97 | 1.32 | −5.06 | 10.30 | 14.68 | −2.43 | −3.70 | −1.86 | 1.43 |
| 1960 | −2.14 | −3.74 | −4.14 | 10.83 | −0.99 | −4.70 | 7.48 | 12.12 | 10.13 | 1.17 |
| 1961 | 24.25 | 4.10 | 3.81 | −1.13 | 26.04 | 31.21 | 4.12 | 0.30 | 1.17 | 1.44 |
| 1962 | −11.16 | −3.48 | 0.99 | 4.04 | −9.83 | −12.97 | 6.64 | 5.59 | 4.29 | 1.49 |
| 1963 | 19.09 | 0.62 | 0.97 | −1.85 | 20.81 | 21.56 | 0.54 | −0.43 | −0.01 | 1.44 |
| 1964 | 12.50 | 6.04 | 1.22 | −0.03 | 15.11 | 22.07 | 3.54 | 2.29 | 2.82 | 2.32 |
| 1965 | 8.20 | 26.06 | −1.16 | −3.10 | 10.33 | 39.08 | −2.33 | −1.19 | −0.89 | 1.97 |
| 1966 | −14.15 | 3.39 | −3.33 | −1.06 | −12.98 | −10.03 | −3.06 | 0.29 | 1.29 | 1.36 |
| 1967 | 18.97 | 48.07 | 4.66 | −12.85 | 20.32 | 78.15 | −7.76 | −11.86 | −1.97 | 1.13 |
| 1968 | 5.57 | 22.43 | 2.84 | −5.20 | 6.05 | 29.84 | −2.05 | −4.76 | −0.18 | 0.46 |
| 1969 | −14.16 | −18.09 | −3.18 | −10.94 | −13.77 | −29.37 | −13.38 | −10.54 | −6.45 | 0.45 |
| 1970 | −2.36 | −20.61 | 5.59 | 5.24 | −1.41 | −21.73 | 12.21 | 6.27 | 10.78 | 0.98 |

Table 4-1 (continued)

**Derived Series**
Annual Returns (in percent)

from 1971 to 2000

| Year | Equity Risk Premia | Small Stock Premia | Default Premia | Horizon Premia | Inflation-Adjusted | | | | | |
|------|------|------|------|------|------|------|------|------|------|------|
| | | | | | Large Company Stocks | Small Company Stocks | Long-Term Corp. Bonds | Long-Term Govt. Bonds | Intermed. Govt. Bonds | U.S. Treasury Bills |
| 1971 | 9.51 | 1.91 | −1.96 | 8.47 | 10.60 | 12.71 | 7.41 | 9.55 | 5.19 | 0.99 |
| 1972 · | 14.58 | −12.22 | 1.49 | 1.78 | 15.05 | 0.99 | 3.72 | 2.20 | 1.69 | 0.41 |
| 1973 | −20.19 | −19.03 | 2.27 | −7.52 | −21.56 | −36.49 | −7.04 | −9.10 | −3.85 | −1.72 |
| 1974 | −31.92 | 8.87 | −7.11 | −3.38 | −34.46 | −28.65 | −13.60 | −6.99 | −5.80 | −3.74 |
| 1975 | 29.68 | 11.38 | 4.99 | 3.21 | 28.21 | 42.80 | 7.13 | 2.04 | 0.76 | −1.13 |
| 1976 | 17.85 | 27.08 | 1.62 | 11.11 | 18.16 | 50.15 | 13.20 | 11.40 | 7.69 | 0.26 |
| 1977 | −11.70 | 35.08 | 2.41 | −5.53 | −13.07 | 17.43 | −4.74 | −6.99 | −5.02 | −1.55 |
| 1978 | −0.58 | 15.86 | 1.12 | −7.80 | −2.26 | 13.24 | −8.34 | −9.36 | −5.08 | −1.69 |
| 1979 | 7.31 | 21.13 | −2.98 | −10.52 | 4.53 | 26.62 | −15.43 | −12.83 | −8.13 | −2.59 |
| 1980 | 19.04 | 5.63 | 1.24 | −13.65 | 17.81 | 24.45 | −13.48 | −14.54 | −7.55 | −1.03 |
| 1981 | −17.10 | 19.76 | −3.04 | −11.20 | −12.71 | 4.53 | −9.34 | −6.50 | 0.47 | 5.30 |
| 1982 | 9.83 | 5.43 | 1.57 | 26.97 | 16.88 | 23.23 | 37.25 | 35.13 | 24.28 | 6.42 |
| 1983 | 12.61 | 14.00 | 5.57 | −7.49 | 18.03 | 34.56 | 2.37 | −3.03 | 3.48 | 4.82 |
| 1984 | −3.26 | −12.17 | 1.20 | 5.12 | 2.22 | −10.22 | 12.42 | 11.08 | 9.68 | 5.67 |
| 1985 | 22.68 | −5.67 | −0.67 | 21.58 | 27.36 | 20.13 | 25.36 | 26.21 | 15.96 | 3.81 |
| 1986 | 11.59 | −9.81 | −3.76 | 17.30 | 17.15 | 5.66 | 18.51 | 23.14 | 13.85 | 4.98 |
| 1987 | −0.22 | −13.81 | 2.51 | −7.76 | 0.79 | −13.13 | −4.48 | −6.82 | −1.44 | 1.01 |
| 1988 | 9.84 | 5.19 | 0.94 | 3.13 | 11.87 | 17.67 | 6.02 | 5.03 | 1.61 | 1.85 |
| 1989 | 21.33 | −16.21 | −1.59 | 8.99 | 25.65 | 5.29 | 11.07 | 12.87 | 8.26 | 3.56 |
| 1990 | −10.19 | −18.99 | 0.57 | −1.51 | −8.74 | −26.08 | 0.64 | 0.07 | 3.42 | 1.61 |
| 1991 | 23.63 | 10.79 | 0.49 | 12.98 | 26.67 | 40.33 | 16.32 | 15.75 | 12.03 | 2.46 |
| 1992 | 4.02 | 14.56 | 1.24 | 4.39 | 4.64 | 19.87 | 6.31 | 5.01 | 4.17 | 0.59 |
| 1993 | 6.89 | 9.99 | −4.28 | 14.91 | 7.05 | 17.74 | 10.16 | 15.08 | 8.26 | 0.14 |
| 1994 | −2.50 | 1.78 | 2.18 | −11.24 | −1.33 | 0.42 | −8.22 | −10.17 | −7.62 | 1.20 |
| 1995 | 30.15 | −2.16 | −3.39 | 24.69 | 34.03 | 31.13 | 24.06 | 28.41 | 13.91 | 2.98 |
| 1996 | 16.98 | −4.43 | 2.35 | −5.83 | 19.12 | 13.84 | −1.86 | −4.12 | −1.18 | 1.82 |
| 1997 | 26.70 | −7.94 | −2.51 | 10.07 | 31.13 | 20.72 | 11.06 | 13.91 | 6.57 | 3.49 |
| 1998 | 22.63 | −27.91 | −2.04 | 7.83 | 26.54 | −8.78 | 9.00 | 11.27 | 8.46 | 3.19 |
| 1999 | 15.63 | 7.22 | 1.67 | −13.04 | 17.88 | 26.39 | −9.87 | −11.34 | −4.34 | 1.95 |
| 2000 | −14.16 | 6.07 | −7.09 | 14.72 | −12.08 | −6.75 | 9.17 | 17.50 | 8.90 | 2.42 |

# Chapter 5
## Annual Returns and Indices

Returns and indices are used to measure the rewards investors earn for holding an asset class. Indices represent levels of wealth or prices, while returns represent changes in levels of wealth. Total returns for specific asset classes consist of component returns that are defined by the nature of the rewards being measured. For example: The total return on a security can be divided into income and capital appreciation components. The income return measures the cash income stream earned by holding the security, such as coupon interest or dividend payments. In contrast, the capital appreciation return results from a change in the price of the security. The method for computing a return varies with the nature of the payment (income or capital appreciation) and the time period of measure (monthly or annual frequency). Indices are computed by establishing a base period and base value and increasing that value by the successive returns. Indices are used to illustrate the cumulative growth of wealth from holding an asset class. This chapter describes the computation of the annual returns and indices.

## Annual and Monthly Returns

### Returns on the Basic Asset Classes

Annual total returns on each of the seven basic asset classes are presented in Table 2-5 in Chapter 2. The monthly total returns on the asset classes appear in Appendix A: Tables A-1, A-4, A-5, A-6, A-10, A-14, and A-15.

### Calculating Annual Returns

Annual returns are formed by compounding the 12 monthly returns. Compounding, or linking, monthly returns is multiplying together the return relatives, or one plus the return, then subtracting one from the result. The equation is denoted as the geometric sum as follows:

$$r_{year} = \left[ (1 + r_{Jan})(1 + r_{Feb}) \ldots (1 + r_{Dec}) \right] - 1 \qquad (17)$$

where,

$r_{year}$ = the compound total return for the year; and,

$r_{Jan}, r_{Feb}, \ldots, r_{Dec}$ = the returns for the 12 months of the year.

The compound return reflects the growth of funds invested in an asset. The following example illustrates the compounding method for a hypothetical year:

| Month | Return (Percent) | Return (Decimal) | Return Relative |
|---|---|---|---|
| January | 1% | 0.01 | 1.01 |
| February | 6 | 0.06 | 1.06 |
| March | 2 | 0.02 | 1.02 |
| April | 1 | 0.01 | 1.01 |
| May | –3 | –0.03 | 0.97 |
| June | 2 | 0.02 | 1.02 |
| July | –4 | –0.04 | 0.96 |
| August | –2 | –0.02 | 0.98 |
| September | 3 | 0.03 | 1.03 |
| October | –3 | –0.03 | 0.97 |
| November | 2 | 0.02 | 1.02 |
| December | 1 | 0.01 | 1.01 |

The return for this hypothetical year is the geometric sum:

$$(1.01 \times 1.06 \times 1.02 \times 1.01 \times 0.97 \times 1.02 \times 0.96 \times 0.98 \times 1.03 \times 0.97 \times 1.02 \times 1.01) - 1 = 1.0567 - 1 = 0.0567$$

or a gain of 5.67 percent. Note that this is different than the simple addition result, $(1 + 6 + 2 + 1 - 3 + 2 - 4 - 2 + 3 - 3 + 2 + 1) = 6$ percent. One dollar invested in this hypothetical asset at the beginning of the year would have grown to slightly less than \$1.06.

## Calculation of Returns from Index Values

Equivalently, annual returns, $r_t$, can be formed by dividing index values according to:

$$r_t = \left[ \frac{V_t}{V_{t-1}} \right] - 1 \tag{18}$$

where,

$r_t$ = the annual return in period $t$;

$V_t$ = the index value as of year-end $t$; and,

$V_{t-1}$ = the index value as of the previous year-end, $t - 1$.

The construction of index values is discussed later in this chapter.

## Calculation of Annual Income Returns

The conversion of monthly income returns to annual income returns is calculated by adding all the cash flows (income payments) for the period, then dividing the sum by the beginning period price:

$$r_I = \frac{\left(I_{Jan} + I_{Feb} + \ldots + I_{Dec}\right)}{P_0}$$

(19)

where,

| | |
|---|---|
| $r_I$ | = the income return for the year; |
| $I_{Jan}, I_{Feb}, \ldots, I_{Dec}$ | = the income payments for the 12 months of the year; and, |
| $P_0$ | = the price of the security at the beginning of the year. |

The following example illustrates the method for a hypothetical year:

| Month | Beginning of Month Price | Income Return (Decimal) | Income Payment |
|---|---|---|---|
| January | $100 | 0.006 | $0.60 |
| February | 102 | 0.004 | 0.41 |
| March | 105 | 0.002 | 0.21 |
| April | 101 | 0.001 | 0.10 |
| May | 99 | 0.005 | 0.50 |
| June | 103 | 0.004 | 0.41 |
| July | 105 | 0.003 | 0.32 |
| August | 103 | 0.002 | 0.21 |
| September | 105 | 0.003 | 0.32 |
| October | 103 | 0.004 | 0.41 |
| November | 106 | 0.001 | 0.11 |
| December | 105 | 0.002 | 0.21 |

Sum the income payments (not the returns), and divide by the price at the beginning of the year:

(0.60 + 0.41 + 0.21 + 0.10 + 0.50 + 0.41 + 0.32 + 0.21 + 0.32 + 0.41
+ 0.11 + 0.21)/100 = 0.0381

or an annual income return of 3.81 percent.

Annual income and capital appreciation returns do not sum to the annual total return. The difference may be viewed as a reinvestment return, which is the return from investing income from a given month into the same asset class in subsequent months within the year.

## Index Values

Index values, or indices, represent the cumulative effect of returns on a dollar invested. For example: One dollar invested in large company stocks (with dividends reinvested) as of December 31, 1925 grew to $1.12 by December 1926, reflecting the 12 percent total return in 1926. [See Table 5-1.] Over the year 1927, the $1.12 grew to $1.53 by December, reflecting the 37.5 percent total return for that year. By the end of 2000, the $1.00 invested at year-end 1925 grew to $2,586.52. Such growth reveals the power of compounding (reinvesting) one's investment returns.

Year-end indices of total returns for all seven basic asset classes are displayed in Table 5-1. This table also shows indices of capital appreciation for large company stocks as well as long- and intermediate-term government bonds. Indices of the inflation-adjusted return series are presented in Table 5-2. Monthly indices of total returns and, where applicable, capital appreciation returns on the basic asset classes are presented in Appendix B: Tables B-1 through B-10. Monthly indices of returns on the inflation-adjusted series are presented in Appendix B: Tables B-11 through B-16.

Graphs of index values, such as Graph 2-1 "Wealth Indices of Investments in the U.S. Capital Markets," depict the growth of wealth. The vertical scale is logarithmic so that equal distances represent equal percentage changes anywhere along the axis.

The inflation-adjusted indices in Table 5-2 are notable in that they show the growth of each asset class in constant dollars, or (synonymously) in real terms. Thus an investor in large company stocks, with dividends reinvested, would have multiplied his or her wealth in real terms, or purchasing power, by a factor of 266.5 between the end of 1925 and the end of 2000.

### Calculation of Index Values

It is possible to mathematically describe the nature of the indices in Tables 5-1 and 5-2 precisely. At the end of each month, a cumulative wealth index ($V_n$) for each of the monthly return series (basic and derived) is formed. This index is initialized as of December 1925 at $1.00 (represented by $V_0 = 1.00$). This index is formed for month $n$ by taking the product of one plus the returns each period, as in the following manner:

$$V_n = V_0 \left[ \prod_{t=1}^{n} (1 + r_t) \right] \quad (20)$$

where,

$V_n$ = the index value at end of period $n$;

$V_0$ = the initial index value at time $0$; and,

$r_t$ = the return in period $t$.

## Using Index Values for Performance Measurement

Index values can be used to determine whether an investment portfolio accumulated more wealth for the investor over a period of time than another portfolio, or whether the investment performed as well as an industry benchmark. In the following example, which produced more wealth—the "investor portfolio" or a hypothetical S&P 500 index fund returning exactly the S&P total return? Each index measures total return and assumes monthly reinvestment of dividends.

|  | Investor Portfolio | S&P 500 |
|---|---|---|
| January 1990 | −5.35% | −6.71% |
| February 1990 | 0.65 | 1.29 |
| March 1990 | 0.23 | 2.63 |
| Accumulated wealth of $1 | $0.955 | $0.970 |

Taking December 1989 as the base period, and using the computation method described above, the S&P 500 outperformed the investor portfolio.

## Computing Returns for Non-Calendar Periods

Index values are also useful for computing returns for non-calendar time periods. To compute the capital appreciation return for long-term government bonds from the end of June 1987 through the end of June 1988, divide the index value in June 1988, 0.661, by the index value in June 1987, 0.683, and subtract 1. [Refer to Table B-6 in Appendix B.]

This yields: $(0.661/ 0.683) − 1 = −0.0322$, or −3.22 percent.

## Table 5-1

**Basic Series**
Indices of Year-End Cumulative Wealth

Year-End 1925 = $1.00

from 1925 to 1970

| Year | Large Stocks Total Returns | Large Stocks Capital Apprec | Small Stocks Total Returns | Long-Term Corp Bonds Total Returns | Long-Term Government Bonds Total Returns | Long-Term Government Bonds Capital Apprec | Intermediate-Term Government Bonds Total Returns | Intermediate-Term Government Bonds Capital Apprec | U.S. T-Bills Total Returns | Inflation |
|------|------|------|------|------|------|------|------|------|------|------|
| 1925 | 1.000 | 1.000 | 1.000 | 1.000 | 1.000 | 1.000 | 1.000 | 1.000 | 1.000 | 1.000 |
| 1926 | 1.116 | 1.057 | 1.003 | 1.074 | 1.078 | 1.039 | 1.054 | 1.015 | 1.033 | 0.985 |
| 1927 | 1.535 | 1.384 | 1.224 | 1.154 | 1.174 | 1.095 | 1.101 | 1.025 | 1.065 | 0.965 |
| 1928 | 2.204 | 1.908 | 1.710 | 1.186 | 1.175 | 1.061 | 1.112 | 0.997 | 1.103 | 0.955 |
| 1929 | 2.018 | 1.681 | 0.832 | 1.225 | 1.215 | 1.059 | 1.178 | 1.014 | 1.155 | 0.957 |
| 1930 | 1.516 | 1.202 | 0.515 | 1.323 | 1.272 | 1.072 | 1.258 | 1.048 | 1.183 | 0.899 |
| 1931 | 0.859 | 0.636 | 0.259 | 1.299 | 1.204 | 0.982 | 1.228 | 0.991 | 1.196 | 0.814 |
| 1932 | 0.789 | 0.540 | 0.245 | 1.439 | 1.407 | 1.109 | 1.337 | 1.041 | 1.207 | 0.730 |
| 1933 | 1.214 | 0.792 | 0.594 | 1.588 | 1.406 | 1.074 | 1.361 | 1.031 | 1.211 | 0.734 |
| 1934 | 1.197 | 0.745 | 0.738 | 1.808 | 1.547 | 1.146 | 1.483 | 1.092 | 1.213 | 0.749 |
| 1935 | 1.767 | 1.053 | 1.035 | 1.982 | 1.624 | 1.171 | 1.587 | 1.146 | 1.215 | 0.771 |
| 1936 | 2.367 | 1.346 | 1.705 | 2.116 | 1.746 | 1.225 | 1.636 | 1.165 | 1.217 | 0.780 |
| 1937 | 1.538 | 0.827 | 0.716 | 2.174 | 1.750 | 1.195 | 1.661 | 1.165 | 1.221 | 0.804 |
| 1938 | 2.016 | 1.035 | 0.951 | 2.307 | 1.847 | 1.229 | 1.765 | 1.216 | 1.221 | 0.782 |
| 1939 | 2.008 | 0.979 | 0.954 | 2.399 | 1.957 | 1.272 | 1.845 | 1.255 | 1.221 | 0.778 |
| 1940 | 1.812 | 0.829 | 0.905 | 2.480 | 2.076 | 1.319 | 1.899 | 1.280 | 1.221 | 0.786 |
| 1941 | 1.602 | 0.681 | 0.823 | 2.548 | 2.096 | 1.306 | 1.909 | 1.278 | 1.222 | 0.862 |
| 1942 | 1.927 | 0.766 | 1.190 | 2.614 | 2.163 | 1.316 | 1.946 | 1.293 | 1.225 | 0.942 |
| 1943 | 2.427 | 0.915 | 2.242 | 2.688 | 2.208 | 1.311 | 2.000 | 1.309 | 1.229 | 0.972 |
| 1944 | 2.906 | 1.041 | 3.446 | 2.815 | 2.270 | 1.315 | 2.036 | 1.314 | 1.233 | 0.993 |
| 1945 | 3.965 | 1.361 | 5.983 | 2.930 | 2.514 | 1.424 | 2.082 | 1.327 | 1.237 | 1.015 |
| 1946 | 3.645 | 1.199 | 5.287 | 2.980 | 2.511 | 1.393 | 2.102 | 1.326 | 1.242 | 1.199 |
| 1947 | 3.853 | 1.199 | 5.335 | 2.911 | 2.445 | 1.328 | 2.122 | 1.322 | 1.248 | 1.307 |
| 1948 | 4.065 | 1.191 | 5.223 | 3.031 | 2.529 | 1.341 | 2.161 | 1.326 | 1.258 | 1.343 |
| 1949 | 4.829 | 1.313 | 6.254 | 3.132 | 2.692 | 1.396 | 2.211 | 1.338 | 1.272 | 1.318 |
| 1950 | 6.360 | 1.600 | 8.677 | 3.198 | 2.693 | 1.367 | 2.227 | 1.329 | 1.287 | 1.395 |
| 1951 | 7.888 | 1.863 | 9.355 | 3.112 | 2.587 | 1.282 | 2.235 | 1.307 | 1.306 | 1.477 |
| 1952 | 9.336 | 2.082 | 9.638 | 3.221 | 2.617 | 1.263 | 2.271 | 1.300 | 1.328 | 1.490 |
| 1953 | 9.244 | 1.944 | 9.013 | 3.331 | 2.713 | 1.271 | 2.345 | 1.308 | 1.352 | 1.499 |
| 1954 | 14.108 | 2.820 | 14.473 | 3.511 | 2.907 | 1.326 | 2.407 | 1.322 | 1.364 | 1.492 |
| 1955 | 18.561 | 3.564 | 17.431 | 3.527 | 2.870 | 1.272 | 2.392 | 1.281 | 1.385 | 1.497 |
| 1956 | 19.778 | 3.658 | 18.177 | 3.287 | 2.710 | 1.165 | 2.382 | 1.237 | 1.419 | 1.540 |
| 1957 | 17.646 | 3.134 | 15.529 | 3.573 | 2.912 | 1.209 | 2.568 | 1.287 | 1.464 | 1.587 |
| 1958 | 25.298 | 4.327 | 25.605 | 3.494 | 2.734 | 1.098 | 2.535 | 1.233 | 1.486 | 1.615 |
| 1959 | 28.322 | 4.694 | 29.804 | 3.460 | 2.673 | 1.030 | 2.525 | 1.177 | 1.530 | 1.639 |
| 1960 | 28.455 | 4.554 | 28.823 | 3.774 | 3.041 | 1.125 | 2.822 | 1.264 | 1.571 | 1.663 |
| 1961 | 36.106 | 5.607 | 38.072 | 3.956 | 3.070 | 1.093 | 2.874 | 1.243 | 1.604 | 1.674 |
| 1962 | 32.954 | 4.945 | 33.540 | 4.270 | 3.282 | 1.124 | 3.034 | 1.264 | 1.648 | 1.695 |
| 1963 | 40.469 | 5.879 | 41.444 | 4.364 | 3.322 | 1.093 | 3.084 | 1.237 | 1.700 | 1.723 |
| 1964 | 47.139 | 6.642 | 51.193 | 4.572 | 3.438 | 1.085 | 3.209 | 1.237 | 1.760 | 1.743 |
| 1965 | 53.008 | 7.244 | 72.567 | 4.552 | 3.462 | 1.048 | 3.242 | 1.199 | 1.829 | 1.777 |
| 1966 | 47.674 | 6.295 | 67.479 | 4.560 | 3.589 | 1.037 | 3.394 | 1.194 | 1.916 | 1.836 |
| 1967 | 59.104 | 7.560 | 123.870 | 4.335 | 3.259 | 0.896 | 3.428 | 1.148 | 1.997 | 1.892 |
| 1968 | 65.642 | 8.139 | 168.429 | 4.446 | 3.251 | 0.847 | 3.583 | 1.136 | 2.101 | 1.981 |
| 1969 | 60.059 | 7.210 | 126.233 | 4.086 | 3.086 | 0.755 | 3.557 | 1.054 | 2.239 | 2.102 |
| 1970 | 62.465 | 7.222 | 104.226 | 4.837 | 3.460 | 0.792 | 4.156 | 1.145 | 2.385 | 2.218 |

## Table 5-1 (continued)

### Basic Series
Indices of Year-End Cumulative Wealth

Year-End 1925 = $1.00

from 1971 to 2000

| Year | Large Stocks Total Returns | Large Stocks Capital Apprec | Small Stocks Total Returns | Long-Term Corp Bonds Total Returns | Long-Term Government Bonds Total Returns | Long-Term Government Bonds Capital Apprec | Intermediate-Term Government Bonds Total Returns | Intermediate-Term Government Bonds Capital Apprec | U.S. T-Bills Total Returns | Inflation |
|------|------|------|------|------|------|------|------|------|------|------|
| 1971 | 71.406 | 8.001 | 121.423 | 5.370 | 3.917 | 0.844 | 4.519 | 1.177 | 2.490 | 2.292 |
| 1972 | 84.956 | 9.252 | 126.807 | 5.760 | 4.140 | 0.841 | 4.752 | 1.168 | 2.585 | 2.371 |
| 1973 | 72.500 | 7.645 | 87.618 | 5.825 | 4.094 | 0.777 | 4.971 | 1.142 | 2.764 | 2.579 |
| 1974 | 53.311 | 5.373 | 70.142 | 5.647 | 4.272 | 0.750 | 5.254 | 1.120 | 2.986 | 2.894 |
| 1975 | 73.144 | 7.068 | 107.189 | 6.474 | 4.665 | 0.755 | 5.665 | 1.121 | 3.159 | 3.097 |
| 1976 | 90.584 | 8.422 | 168.691 | 7.681 | 5.447 | 0.816 | 6.394 | 1.180 | 3.319 | 3.246 |
| 1977 | 84.077 | 7.453 | 211.500 | 7.813 | 5.410 | 0.752 | 6.484 | 1.119 | 3.489 | 3.466 |
| 1978 | 89.592 | 7.532 | 261.120 | 7.807 | 5.346 | 0.684 | 6.710 | 1.069 | 3.740 | 3.778 |
| 1979 | 106.113 | 8.459 | 374.614 | 7.481 | 5.280 | 0.617 | 6.985 | 1.015 | 4.128 | 4.281 |
| 1980 | 140.514 | 10.639 | 523.992 | 7.274 | 5.071 | 0.530 | 7.258 | 0.946 | 4.592 | 4.812 |
| 1981 | 133.616 | 9.605 | 596.717 | 7.185 | 5.166 | 0.476 | 7.944 | 0.903 | 5.267 | 5.242 |
| 1982 | 162.223 | 11.023 | 763.829 | 10.242 | 7.251 | 0.589 | 10.256 | 1.031 | 5.822 | 5.445 |
| 1983 | 198.745 | 12.926 | 1066.828 | 10.883 | 7.298 | 0.532 | 11.015 | 0.997 | 6.335 | 5.652 |
| 1984 | 211.199 | 13.106 | 995.680 | 12.718 | 8.427 | 0.544 | 12.560 | 1.009 | 6.959 | 5.875 |
| 1985 | 279.117 | 16.559 | 1241.234 | 16.546 | 11.037 | 0.641 | 15.113 | 1.100 | 7.496 | 6.097 |
| 1986 | 330.671 | 18.981 | 1326.275 | 19.829 | 13.745 | 0.737 | 17.401 | 1.177 | 7.958 | 6.166 |
| 1987 | 347.967 | 19.366 | 1202.966 | 19.776 | 13.372 | 0.658 | 17.906 | 1.121 | 8.393 | 6.438 |
| 1988 | 406.458 | 21.769 | 1478.135 | 21.893 | 14.665 | 0.661 | 18.999 | 1.096 | 8.926 | 6.722 |
| 1989 | 534.455 | 27.703 | 1628.590 | 25.447 | 17.322 | 0.718 | 21.524 | 1.143 | 9.673 | 7.034 |
| 1990 | 517.499 | 25.886 | 1277.449 | 27.173 | 18.392 | 0.699 | 23.618 | 1.155 | 10.429 | 7.464 |
| 1991 | 675.592 | 32.695 | 1847.629 | 32.577 | 21.942 | 0.769 | 27.270 | 1.240 | 11.012 | 7.693 |
| 1992 | 727.412 | 34.155 | 2279.039 | 35.637 | 23.709 | 0.772 | 29.230 | 1.248 | 11.398 | 7.916 |
| 1993 | 800.078 | 36.565 | 2757.147 | 40.336 | 28.034 | 0.855 | 32.516 | 1.317 | 11.728 | 8.133 |
| 1994 | 810.538 | 36.002 | 2842.773 | 38.012 | 25.856 | 0.733 | 30.843 | 1.170 | 12.186 | 8.351 |
| 1995 | 1113.918 | 48.282 | 3822.398 | 48.353 | 34.044 | 0.901 | 36.025 | 1.283 | 12.868 | 8.563 |
| 1996 | 1370.946 | 58.066 | 4495.993 | 49.031 | 33.727 | 0.835 | 36.782 | 1.233 | 13.538 | 8.847 |
| 1997 | 1828.326 | 76.071 | 5519.969 | 55.380 | 39.074 | 0.906 | 39.864 | 1.257 | 14.250 | 8.998 |
| 1998 | 2350.892 | 96.359 | 5116.648 | 61.339 | 44.178 | 0.968 | 43.933 | 1.316 | 14.942 | 9.143 |
| 1999 | 2845.629 | 115.174 | 6640.788 | 56.772 | 40.218 | 0.829 | 43.155 | 1.223 | 15.641 | 9.389 |
| 2000 | 2586.524 | 103.496 | 6402.228 | 64.077 | 48.856 | 0.949 | 48.589 | 1.296 | 16.563 | 9.707 |

## Table 5-2

**Inflation-Adjusted Series**
Indices of Year-End Cumulative Wealth

Year-End 1925 = $1.00

from 1925 to 1970

| | Inflation-Adjusted | | | | | |
|---|---|---|---|---|---|---|
| | Large Company Stocks | Small Company Stocks | Long-Term Corporate Bonds | Long-Term Government Bonds | Intermediate Government Bonds | U.S. Treasury Bills |
| 1925 | 1.000 | 1.000 | 1.000 | 1.000 | 1.000 | 1.000 |
| 1926 | 1.133 | 1.018 | 1.090 | 1.094 | 1.070 | 1.048 |
| 1927 | 1.591 | 1.269 | 1.196 | 1.217 | 1.142 | 1.104 |
| 1928 | 2.307 | 1.790 | 1.242 | 1.230 | 1.164 | 1.154 |
| 1929 | 2.109 | 0.869 | 1.280 | 1.270 | 1.231 | 1.207 |
| 1930 | 1.685 | 0.572 | 1.471 | 1.414 | 1.398 | 1.315 |
| 1931 | 1.056 | 0.318 | 1.596 | 1.480 | 1.509 | 1.469 |
| 1932 | 1.080 | 0.335 | 1.971 | 1.928 | 1.831 | 1.654 |
| 1933 | 1.655 | 0.810 | 2.165 | 1.917 | 1.855 | 1.650 |
| 1934 | 1.599 | 0.986 | 2.415 | 2.067 | 1.982 | 1.620 |
| 1935 | 2.292 | 1.342 | 2.571 | 2.107 | 2.059 | 1.576 |
| 1936 | 3.033 | 2.185 | 2.712 | 2.238 | 2.097 | 1.560 |
| 1937 | 1.912 | 0.890 | 2.702 | 2.176 | 2.065 | 1.517 |
| 1938 | 2.578 | 1.216 | 2.950 | 2.362 | 2.257 | 1.561 |
| 1939 | 2.580 | 1.226 | 3.082 | 2.514 | 2.370 | 1.568 |
| 1940 | 2.305 | 1.152 | 3.156 | 2.642 | 2.417 | 1.554 |
| 1941 | 1.858 | 0.955 | 2.955 | 2.430 | 2.214 | 1.417 |
| 1942 | 2.046 | 1.263 | 2.774 | 2.295 | 2.065 | 1.300 |
| 1943 | 2.496 | 2.306 | 2.765 | 2.271 | 2.058 | 1.264 |
| 1944 | 2.928 | 3.472 | 2.836 | 2.287 | 2.052 | 1.242 |
| 1945 | 3.907 | 5.895 | 2.887 | 2.477 | 2.051 | 1.219 |
| 1946 | 3.039 | 4.409 | 2.485 | 2.094 | 1.753 | 1.035 |
| 1947 | 2.947 | 4.081 | 2.227 | 1.871 | 1.623 | 0.955 |
| 1948 | 3.027 | 3.890 | 2.258 | 1.883 | 1.609 | 0.937 |
| 1949 | 3.662 | 4.744 | 2.375 | 2.042 | 1.677 | 0.965 |
| 1950 | 4.560 | 6.221 | 2.293 | 1.931 | 1.596 | 0.923 |
| 1951 | 5.341 | 6.335 | 2.107 | 1.752 | 1.513 | 0.885 |
| 1952 | 6.267 | 6.469 | 2.162 | 1.757 | 1.524 | 0.891 |
| 1953 | 6.166 | 6.012 | 2.222 | 1.809 | 1.564 | 0.902 |
| 1954 | 9.458 | 9.703 | 2.354 | 1.949 | 1.614 | 0.914 |
| 1955 | 12.397 | 11.642 | 2.356 | 1.917 | 1.597 | 0.925 |
| 1956 | 12.843 | 11.803 | 2.134 | 1.759 | 1.547 | 0.922 |
| 1957 | 11.122 | 9.788 | 2.252 | 1.835 | 1.619 | 0.923 |
| 1958 | 15.669 | 15.859 | 2.164 | 1.694 | 1.570 | 0.921 |
| 1959 | 17.283 | 18.187 | 2.112 | 1.631 | 1.541 | 0.934 |
| 1960 | 17.111 | 17.333 | 2.270 | 1.829 | 1.697 | 0.945 |
| 1961 | 21.567 | 22.741 | 2.363 | 1.834 | 1.717 | 0.958 |
| 1962 | 19.447 | 19.792 | 2.520 | 1.937 | 1.791 | 0.973 |
| 1963 | 23.494 | 24.060 | 2.534 | 1.928 | 1.790 | 0.987 |
| 1964 | 27.044 | 29.370 | 2.623 | 1.972 | 1.841 | 1.010 |
| 1965 | 29.838 | 40.848 | 2.562 | 1.949 | 1.825 | 1.029 |
| 1966 | 25.964 | 36.751 | 2.484 | 1.955 | 1.848 | 1.043 |
| 1967 | 31.239 | 65.471 | 2.291 | 1.723 | 1.812 | 1.055 |
| 1968 | 33.129 | 85.005 | 2.244 | 1.641 | 1.808 | 1.060 |
| 1969 | 28.567 | 60.042 | 1.944 | 1.468 | 1.692 | 1.065 |
| 1970 | 28.164 | 46.993 | 2.181 | 1.560 | 1.874 | 1.075 |

## Table 5-2 (continued)

### Inflation-Adjusted Series
Indices of Year-End Cumulative Wealth

Year-End 1925 = $1.00

from 1971 to 2000

| | Inflation-Adjusted | | | | | |
|---|---|---|---|---|---|---|
| | Large Company Stocks | Small Company Stocks | Long-Term Corporate Bonds | Long-Term Government Bonds | Intermediate Government Bonds | U.S. Treasury Bills |
| 1971 | 31.149 | 52.968 | 2.343 | 1.709 | 1.971 | 1.086 |
| 1972 | 35.837 | 53.492 | 2.430 | 1.746 | 2.005 | 1.091 |
| 1973 | 28.110 | 33.971 | 2.259 | 1.587 | 1.927 | 1.072 |
| 1974 | 18.422 | 24.238 | 1.951 | 1.476 | 1.815 | 1.032 |
| 1975 | 23.619 | 34.612 | 2.091 | 1.506 | 1.829 | 1.020 |
| 1976 | 27.908 | 51.971 | 2.366 | 1.678 | 1.970 | 1.023 |
| 1977 | 24.260 | 61.029 | 2.254 | 1.561 | 1.871 | 1.007 |
| 1978 | 23.712 | 69.108 | 2.066 | 1.415 | 1.776 | 0.990 |
| 1979 | 24.786 | 87.502 | 1.747 | 1.233 | 1.632 | 0.964 |
| 1980 | 29.201 | 108.894 | 1.512 | 1.054 | 1.508 | 0.954 |
| 1981 | 25.489 | 113.831 | 1.371 | 0.985 | 1.515 | 1.005 |
| 1982 | 29.792 | 140.278 | 1.881 | 1.332 | 1.884 | 1.069 |
| 1983 | 35.165 | 188.759 | 1.926 | 1.291 | 1.949 | 1.121 |
| 1984 | 35.947 | 169.470 | 2.165 | 1.434 | 2.138 | 1.184 |
| 1985 | 45.781 | 203.588 | 2.714 | 1.810 | 2.479 | 1.230 |
| 1986 | 53.631 | 215.106 | 3.216 | 2.229 | 2.822 | 1.291 |
| 1987 | 54.053 | 186.867 | 3.072 | 2.077 | 2.782 | 1.304 |
| 1988 | 60.466 | 219.893 | 3.257 | 2.182 | 2.826 | 1.328 |
| 1989 | 75.977 | 231.516 | 3.617 | 2.462 | 3.060 | 1.375 |
| 1990 | 69.333 | 171.148 | 3.641 | 2.464 | 3.164 | 1.397 |
| 1991 | 87.822 | 240.179 | 4.235 | 2.852 | 3.545 | 1.431 |
| 1992 | 91.893 | 287.908 | 4.502 | 2.995 | 3.693 | 1.440 |
| 1993 | 98.369 | 338.990 | 4.959 | 3.447 | 3.998 | 1.442 |
| 1994 | 97.059 | 340.412 | 4.552 | 3.096 | 3.693 | 1.459 |
| 1995 | 130.085 | 446.387 | 5.647 | 3.976 | 4.207 | 1.503 |
| 1996 | 154.953 | 508.167 | 5.542 | 3.812 | 4.157 | 1.530 |
| 1997 | 203.190 | 613.460 | 6.155 | 4.342 | 4.430 | 1.584 |
| 1998 | 257.121 | 559.616 | 6.709 | 4.832 | 4.805 | 1.634 |
| 1999 | 303.094 | 707.326 | 6.047 | 4.284 | 4.597 | 1.666 |
| 2000 | 266.472 | 659.577 | 6.601 | 5.033 | 5.006 | 1.706 |

# Chapter 6
## Statistical Analysis of Returns

Statistical analysis of historical asset returns can reveal the growth rate of wealth invested in an asset or portfolio, the riskiness or volatility of asset classes, the comovement of assets, and the random or cyclical behavior of asset returns. This chapter focuses on arithmetic and geometric mean returns, standard deviations, and serial and cross-correlation coefficients, and discusses the use of each statistic to characterize the various asset classes by growth rate, variability, and safety.

## Calculating Arithmetic Mean Returns

The arithmetic mean of a series is the simple average of the elements in the series. The arithmetic mean return equation is:

$$r_A = \frac{1}{n} \sum_{t=1}^{n} r_t$$

(21)

where,

$r_A$ = the arithmetic mean return;

$r_t$ = the series return in period **t**, that is, from time **t − 1** to time t; and,

n = the inclusive number of periods.

## Calculating Geometric Mean Returns

The geometric mean of a return series over a period is the compound rate of return over the period. The geometric mean return equation is:

$$r_G = \left[ \prod_{t=1}^{n} (1 + r_t) \right]^{\frac{1}{n}} - 1$$

(22)

where,

$r_G$ = the geometric mean return;

$r_t$ = the series return in period **t**; and,

n = the inclusive number of periods.

The geometric mean return can be restated using beginning and ending period index values. The equation is:

$$r_G = \left[ \frac{V_n}{V_0} \right]^{\frac{1}{n}} - 1$$

(23)

where,

$r_G$ = the geometric mean return;

$V_n$ = the ending period index value at time **n**;

$V_0$ = the initial index value at time **0**; and,

n = the inclusive number of periods.

The annualized geometric mean return over any period of months can also be computed by expressing **n** as a fraction. For example: Starting at the beginning of 1996 to the end of May 1996 is equivalent to five-twelfths of a year, or 0.4167. **V**ₙ would be the index value at the end of May 1996, **V**₀ would be the index value at the beginning of 1996, and **n** would be 0.4167.

## Geometric Mean Versus Arithmetic Mean

A simple example illustrates the difference between geometric and arithmetic means. Suppose $1.00 was invested in a large company stock portfolio that experiences successive annual returns of +50 percent and –50 percent. At the end of the first year, the portfolio is worth $1.50. At the end of the second year, the portfolio is worth $0.75. The annual arithmetic mean is 0.0 percent, whereas the annual geometric mean is –13.4 percent. Both are calculated as follows:

$$r_A = \frac{1}{2}\left(0.50 - 0.50\right) = 0.0, \text{ and}$$

$$r_G = \left[\frac{0.75}{1.00}\right]^{\frac{1}{2}} - 1 = -0.134$$

The geometric mean is backward-looking, measuring the change in wealth over more than one period. On the other hand, the arithmetic mean better represents a typical performance over single periods and serves as the correct rate for forecasting, discounting, and estimating the cost of capital. [See Chapter 9.]

In general, the geometric mean for any time period is less than or equal to the arithmetic mean. The two means are equal only for a return series that is constant (i.e., the same return in every period). For a non-constant series, the difference between the two is positively related to the variability or standard deviation of the returns. For example, in Table 6-7, the difference between the arithmetic and geometric mean is much larger for risky large company stocks than it is for nearly riskless Treasury bills.

The arithmetic mean is the rate of return which, when compounded over multiple periods, gives the mean of the probability distribution of ending wealth values. (A simple example given below shows that this is true.) This makes the arithmetic mean return appropriate for forecasting, discounting, and computing the cost of capital. The discount rate that equates expected (mean) future values with the present value of an investment is that investment's cost of capital. The logic of using the discount rate as the cost of capital is reinforced by noting that investors will discount their expected (mean) ending wealth values from an investment back to the present using the arithmetic mean, for the reason given above. They will, therefore, require such an expected (mean) return prospectively (that is, in the present looking toward the future) to commit their capital to the investment.

For example, assume a stock has an expected return of +10 percent in each year and a standard deviation of 20 percent. Assume further that only two outcomes are possible each year— +30 percent and –10 percent (that is, the mean plus or minus one standard deviation), and that these outcomes are equally likely. (The arithmetic mean of these returns is 10 percent, and the geometric mean is 8.2 percent.) Then the growth of wealth over a two-year period occurs as follows:

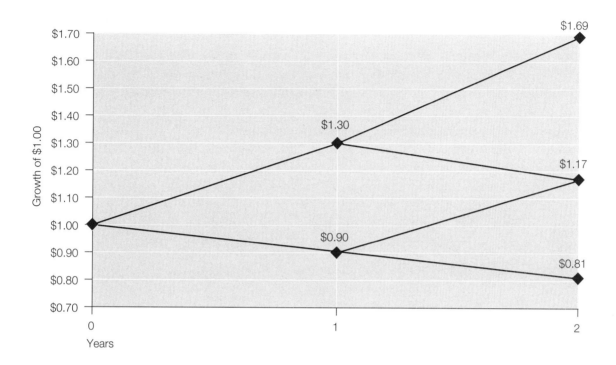

Note that the median (middle outcome) and mode (most common outcome) are given by the geometric mean, 8.2 percent, which compounds up to 17 percent over a two-year period (hence a terminal wealth of $1.17). However, the expected value, or probability-weighted average of all possible outcomes, is equal to:

$$(.25 \times 1.69) = 0.4225$$
$$+ \ (.50 \times 1.17) = 0.5850$$
$$+ \ (.25 \times 0.81) = 0.2025$$

**Total          1.2100**

Now, the rate that must be compounded up to achieve a terminal wealth of $1.21 after 2 years is 10 percent; that is, the expected value of the terminal wealth is given by compounding up the arithmetic, not the geometric mean. Since the arithmetic mean equates the expected future value with the present value, it is the discount rate.

Stated another way, the arithmetic mean is correct because an investment with uncertain returns will have a higher expected ending wealth value than an investment that earns, with certainty, its compound or geometric rate of return every year. In the above example, compounding at the rate of 8.2 percent for two years yields a terminal wealth of $1.17, based on $1.00 invested. But holding the uncertain investment, with a possibility of high returns (two +30 percent years in a row) as well as low returns (two –10 percent years in a row), yields a higher expected terminal wealth, $1.21. In other words, more money is gained by higher-than-expected returns than is lost by lower-than-expected returns. Therefore, in the investment markets, where returns are described by a probability distribution, the arithmetic mean is the measure that accounts for uncertainty, and is the appropriate one for estimating discount rates and the cost of capital.

## Calculating Standard Deviations

The standard deviation of a series is a measure of the extent to which observations in the series differ from the arithmetic mean of the series. For a series of asset returns, the standard deviation is a measure of the volatility, or risk, of the asset. The standard deviation is a measure of the variation around an average or mean.

In a normally distributed series, about two-thirds of the observations lie within one standard deviation of the arithmetic mean; about 95 percent of the observations lie within two standard deviations; and more than 99 percent lie within three standard deviations.

For example, the standard deviation for large company stocks over the period 1926–2000 was 20.2 percent with an annual arithmetic mean of 13.0 percent. Therefore, roughly two-thirds of the observations have annual returns between –7.2 percent and 33.2 percent (13.0 ± 20.2); approximately 95 percent of the observations are between –27.4 percent and 53.4 percent (13.0 ± 40.4).

The equation for the standard deviation of a series of returns ($\sigma_r$) is:

$$\sigma_r = \sqrt{\frac{1}{n-1}\sum_{t=1}^{n}\left(r_t - r_A\right)^2} \tag{24}$$

where,

$r_t$ = the return in period $t$;

$r_A$ = the arithmetic mean of the return series $r$; and,

$n$ = the number of periods.

The scaling of the standard deviation depends on the frequency of the data; therefore, a series of monthly returns produces a monthly standard deviation. For example, using the monthly returns for the hypothetical year on page 90, a monthly standard deviation of 2.94 percent is calculated following equation (24):

$$\left[\frac{1}{12-1}\left((0.01-0.005)^2 + (0.06-0.005)^2 + (0.02-0.005)^2 + (0.01-0.005)^2 \right.\right.$$
$$+ (-0.03-0.005)^2 + (0.02-0.005)^2 + (-0.04-0.005)^2 + (0.02-0.005)^2$$
$$\left.\left.+ (0.03-0.005)^2 + (-0.03-0.005)^2 + (0.02-0.005)^2 + (0.01-0.005)^2\right)\right]^{\frac{1}{2}} = 0.0294$$

It is sometimes useful to express the standard deviation of the series in another time scale. To calculate the annualized monthly standard deviations ($\sigma_n$), one uses equation (25).[1]

$$\sigma_n = \sqrt{\left[\sigma_1^2 + (1+\mu_1)^2\right]^n - (1+\mu_1)^{2n}} \qquad (25)$$

where,

$n$ = the number of periods per year, e.g. 12 for monthly, 4 for quarterly, etc.;

$\sigma_1$ = the monthly standard deviation; and,

$\mu_1$ = the monthly arithmetic mean.

Applying this formula to the prior monthly standard deviation of 2.94 percent results in an annualized monthly standard deviation of 10.78 percent. The annualized monthly standard deviation is calculated with equation (25) as follows:

$$\sqrt{\left[0.0294^2 + (1+0.005)^2\right]^{12} - (1+0.005)^{2(12)}} = 0.1078$$

This equation is the exact form of the common approximation:

$$\sigma_n \approx \sqrt{n}\,\sigma_1$$

The approximation treats an annual return as if it were the sum of 12 independent monthly returns, whereas equation (25) treats an annual return as the compound return of 12 independent monthly returns. [See Equation (17) on page 89.] While the approximation can be used for "back of the envelope" calculations, the exact formula should be used in applications of quantitative analysis. Forming inputs for mean-variance optimization, is one such example. Note that both the exact formula and the approximation assume that there is no monthly autocorrelation.

---

[1] The equation appears in Haim Levy and Deborah Gunthorpe, "Optimal Investment Proportions in Senior Securities and Equities Under Alternative Holding Periods," *Journal of Portfolio Management*, Summer 1993, page 33.

## Graph 6-1

**Month-by-Month Returns on Stocks and Bonds**

Large Company Stocks and Long-Term Government Bonds

from 1926 to 2000

**Large Company Stocks**

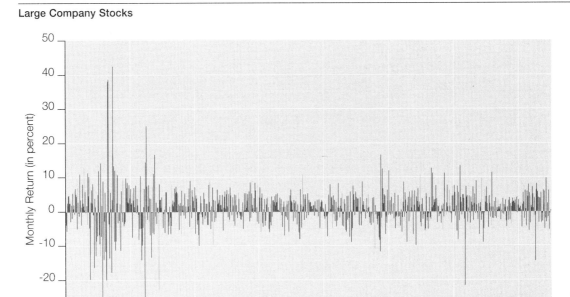

**Long-Term Government Bonds**

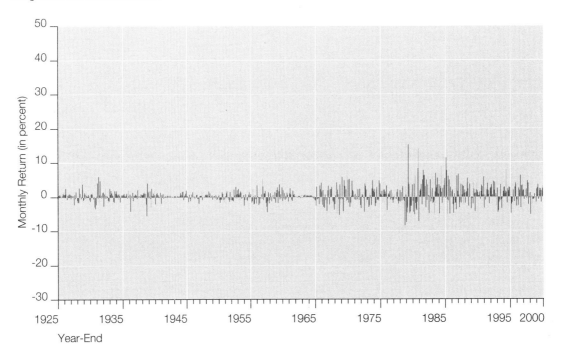

## Volatility of the Markets

The volatility of stocks and long-term government bonds is shown by the bar graphs of monthly returns in Graph 6-1. The stock market was tremendously volatile in the first few years studied; this period was marked by the 1920s boom, the crash of 1929–1932, and the Great Depression years. The market settled after World War II and provided more stable returns in the postwar period. In the 1970s and 1980s, stock market volatility increased, but not to the extreme levels of the 1920s and 1930s, with the exception of October 1987. In the 1990s to date, volatility has been moderate.

Bonds present a mirror image. Long-term government bonds were extremely stable in the 1920s and remained so through the crisis years of the 1930s, providing shelter from the storms of the stock markets. Starting in the late 1960s and early 1970s, however, bond volatility soared; in the 1973–1974 stock market decline, bonds did not provide the shelter they once did. Bond pessimism (i.e., high yields) peaked in 1981 and subsequent returns were sharply positive. While the astronomical interest rates of the 1979–1981 period have passed, the volatility of the bond market remains higher.

## Changes in the Risk of Assets Over Time

Table 6-1

Annualized Monthly Standard Deviations by Decade

|  | 1920s* | 1930s | 1940s | 1950s | 1960s | 1970s | 1980s | 1990s | 2000s** | 1991–2000 |
|---|---|---|---|---|---|---|---|---|---|---|
| Large Company | 23.9% | 41.6% | 17.5% | 14.1% | 13.1% | 17.1% | 19.4% | 15.8% | 16.0 | 15.7 |
| Small Company | 24.7 | 78.6 | 34.5 | 14.4 | 21.5 | 30.8 | 22.5 | 20.2 | 40.4 | 23.4 |
| Long-Term Corp | 1.8 | 5.3 | 1.8 | 4.4 | 4.9 | 8.7 | 14.1 | 6.9 | 5.9 | 6.8 |
| Long-Term Govt | 4.1 | 5.3 | 2.8 | 4.6 | 6.0 | 8.7 | 16.0 | 8.9 | 6.9 | 8.7 |
| Inter-Term Govt | 1.7 | 3.3 | 1.2 | 2.9 | 3.3 | 5.2 | 8.8 | 4.6 | 3.4 | 4.6 |
| Treasury Bills | 0.3 | 0.2 | 0.1 | 0.2 | 0.4 | 0.6 | 0.9 | 0.4 | 0.2 | 0.3 |
| Inflation | 2.0 | 2.5 | 3.1 | 1.2 | 0.7 | 1.2 | 1.3 | 0.7 | 1.0 | 0.6 |

*Based on the period 1926–1929.

**Based on the period 2000 only.

Another time series property of great interest is change in volatility or riskiness over time. Such change is indicated by the standard deviation of the series over different subperiods. Table 6-1 shows the annualized monthly standard deviations of the basic data series by decade beginning in 1926 and illustrates differences and changes in return volatility. In this table, the '20s cover the period 1926–1929. Equity returns have been the most volatile of the basic series, with volatility peaking in the 1930s due to the instability of the market following the 1929 market crash. The significant bond yield fluctuations of the '80s caused the fixed income series' volatility to soar compared to prior decades.

The standard deviation of a series for a particular year is the standard deviation of the 12 monthly returns for that year (around that year's arithmetic mean). This monthly estimate is then annualized according to equation (25). Table 6-2 displays the annualized standard deviation of the monthly returns on each of the basic and derived series from 1926 to 2000. The estimates in this table and in Table 6-1 are not strictly comparable to Table 2-1 and Table 6-7 and 6-8, where the 75-year period standard deviation of annual returns (around the 75-year annual arithmetic mean) was reported. The arithmetic mean drifts for a series that does not follow a random pattern. A series with a drifting mean will have much higher deviations around its long-term mean than it has around the mean during a particular calendar year.

As shown in Table 6-2, large company stocks and equity risk premia have virtually the same annualized monthly standard deviations because there is very little deviation in the U.S. Treasury bill series. These two series also have much higher variability in the pre-World War II period than in the postwar period. On the other hand, the various bond series (long- and intermediate-term government bonds, long-term corporate bonds, horizon premia, and default premia) were quite volatile in the Great Depression and then more so recently.

The series with drifting means (U.S. Treasury bills, inflation rates, and inflation-adjusted U.S. Treasury bills) all tend to have very low annualized monthly standard deviations, since these series are quite predictable from month to month. As seen in Tables 6-7 and 6-8, however, there is much less predictability for these series over the long term. Since it is difficult to forecast the direction and magnitude of the drift in the long-term mean, these series have higher standard deviations over the long term in comparison to their annualized monthly standard deviations.

## Correlation Coefficients: Serial and Cross-Correlations

The behavior of an asset return series over time reveals its predictability. For example, a series may be random or unpredictable; or it may be subject to trends, cycles, or other patterns, making the series predictable to some degree. The serial correlation coefficient of a series determines its predictability given knowledge of the last observation. The cross-correlation coefficient (often shortened to "correlation") between two series determines the predictability of one series, conditional on knowledge of the other.

### Serial Correlations

The serial correlation, also known as the first-order autocorrelation, of a return series describes the extent to which the return in one period is related to the return in the next period. A return series with a high (near one) serial correlation is very predictable from one period to the next, while one with a low (near zero) serial correlation is random and unpredictable.

The serial correlation of a series is closely approximated by the equation for the cross-correlation between two series, which is given in equation (26). The data, however, are the series and its "lagged" self. For example, the lagged series is the series of one-period-old returns:

| Year | Return Series (X) | Lagged Return Series (Y) |
|---|---|---|
| 1 | 0.10 | undefined |
| 2 | −0.10 | 0.10 |
| 3 | 0.15 | −0.10 |
| 4 | 0.00 | 0.15 |

## Table 6-2

**Basic and Derived Series**
Annualized Monthly Standard Deviations (in percent)

### from 1926 to 1970

| Year | Basic Series | | | | | | | Derived Series | | | | |
| | Large Company Stocks | Small Company Stocks | Long-Term Corporate Bonds | Long-Term Govt Bonds | Intermediate-Term Govt Bonds | U.S. Treasury Bills | Inflation | Equity Risk Premia | Small Stock Premia | Bond Default Premia | Bond Horizon Premia | Inflation-Adjusted T-Bills |
|---|---|---|---|---|---|---|---|---|---|---|---|---|
| 1926 | 13.10 | 16.89 | 0.96 | 1.88 | 1.02 | 0.32 | 2.03 | 12.73 | 9.74 | 1.63 | 1.68 | 2.06 |
| 1927 | 17.90 | 21.19 | 1.49 | 2.88 | 1.05 | 0.11 | 2.78 | 17.35 | 11.13 | 2.90 | 2.76 | 3.03 |
| 1928 | 24.62 | 28.68 | 1.87 | 3.21 | 1.27 | 0.32 | 1.72 | 23.65 | 14.48 | 2.74 | 3.06 | 1.84 |
| 1929 | 30.55 | 18.35 | 2.42 | 6.56 | 2.82 | 0.21 | 1.62 | 29.16 | 7.76 | 6.79 | 6.20 | 1.62 |
| 1930 | 21.19 | 25.55 | 2.38 | 2.34 | 2.43 | 0.30 | 2.03 | 20.65 | 11.68 | 2.45 | 2.12 | 2.31 |
| 1931 | 30.04 | 45.35 | 5.91 | 5.24 | 3.72 | 0.16 | 1.35 | 29.72 | 27.44 | 5.25 | 5.18 | 1.75 |
| 1932 | 83.36 | 147.23 | 7.71 | 9.50 | 2.94 | 0.29 | 1.74 | 82.72 | 41.92 | 12.69 | 9.35 | 2.40 |
| 1933 | 99.82 | 286.56 | 11.74 | 5.11 | 3.70 | 0.10 | 4.24 | 99.27 | 72.06 | 7.67 | 5.06 | 4.15 |
| 1934 | 22.64 | 73.85 | 3.10 | 4.50 | 4.07 | 0.04 | 2.03 | 22.59 | 42.03 | 2.52 | 4.46 | 1.94 |
| 1935 | 23.73 | 36.09 | 2.53 | 2.88 | 2.78 | 0.01 | 2.18 | 23.69 | 15.08 | 1.36 | 2.88 | 2.05 |
| 1936 | 19.06 | 66.23 | 1.18 | 2.25 | 1.27 | 0.02 | 1.55 | 19.02 | 37.72 | 1.78 | 2.25 | 1.51 |
| 1937 | 16.33 | 21.81 | 1.99 | 5.04 | 2.44 | 0.05 | 1.74 | 16.28 | 16.46 | 3.93 | 5.01 | 1.63 |
| 1938 | 58.87 | 114.31 | 2.38 | 2.35 | 2.48 | 0.07 | 1.78 | 58.85 | 30.94 | 1.89 | 2.31 | 1.89 |
| 1939 | 31.09 | 95.06 | 5.36 | 8.59 | 5.06 | 0.02 | 2.26 | 31.07 | 43.55 | 8.40 | 8.59 | 2.24 |
| 1940 | 25.56 | 46.88 | 2.02 | 5.20 | 3.25 | 0.02 | 1.09 | 25.55 | 25.68 | 3.92 | 5.19 | 1.07 |
| 1941 | 12.95 | 29.10 | 1.67 | 3.71 | 1.50 | 0.03 | 2.30 | 12.92 | 20.75 | 3.59 | 3.70 | 1.90 |
| 1942 | 17.67 | 37.55 | 0.73 | 1.42 | 0.79 | 0.03 | 1.39 | 17.60 | 25.78 | 1.16 | 1.42 | 1.17 |
| 1943 | 19.59 | 71.56 | 0.90 | 0.65 | 0.51 | 0.01 | 2.35 | 19.53 | 33.94 | 0.58 | 0.65 | 2.21 |
| 1944 | 9.30 | 28.75 | 1.34 | 0.37 | 0.29 | 0.01 | 0.97 | 9.27 | 15.14 | 1.11 | 0.37 | 0.94 |
| 1945 | 17.64 | 37.50 | 1.42 | 2.97 | 0.50 | 0.01 | 1.32 | 17.59 | 16.92 | 1.92 | 2.96 | 1.26 |
| 1946 | 17.72 | 27.25 | 2.15 | 2.73 | 0.94 | 0.00 | 6.65 | 17.65 | 12.20 | 1.74 | 2.72 | 4.66 |
| 1947 | 10.15 | 18.24 | 2.13 | 2.86 | 0.52 | 0.07 | 3.34 | 10.09 | 10.58 | 3.26 | 2.90 | 2.79 |
| 1948 | 21.49 | 24.11 | 2.20 | 1.95 | 0.59 | 0.07 | 2.90 | 21.30 | 6.44 | 1.92 | 1.96 | 2.73 |
| 1949 | 12.02 | 18.75 | 2.17 | 1.83 | 0.47 | 0.02 | 1.63 | 11.89 | 6.72 | 2.44 | 1.80 | 1.71 |
| 1950 | 13.99 | 20.58 | 1.07 | 1.45 | 0.34 | 0.03 | 1.81 | 13.83 | 8.82 | 1.35 | 1.44 | 1.62 |
| 1951 | 15.04 | 16.02 | 3.92 | 3.03 | 1.91 | 0.05 | 1.79 | 14.80 | 6.12 | 2.67 | 2.95 | 1.63 |
| 1952 | 13.32 | 9.66 | 2.85 | 3.24 | 1.32 | 0.08 | 1.15 | 13.11 | 3.78 | 3.82 | 3.23 | 1.14 |
| 1953 | 9.32 | 10.90 | 5.53 | 5.16 | 3.26 | 0.11 | 1.01 | 9.21 | 8.74 | 3.50 | 5.07 | 0.95 |
| 1954 | 19.27 | 20.02 | 2.35 | 3.47 | 1.93 | 0.06 | 0.74 | 19.08 | 10.08 | 2.32 | 3.42 | 0.77 |
| 1955 | 16.11 | 7.70 | 2.17 | 3.60 | 1.65 | 0.14 | 0.67 | 15.91 | 8.83 | 2.36 | 3.47 | 0.71 |
| 1956 | 15.86 | 8.39 | 3.00 | 4.28 | 2.64 | 0.10 | 1.08 | 15.50 | 7.87 | 2.60 | 4.15 | 1.00 |
| 1957 | 11.48 | 10.42 | 9.40 | 8.26 | 5.57 | 0.07 | 0.66 | 11.13 | 9.98 | 5.48 | 8.00 | 0.65 |
| 1958 | 8.74 | 15.44 | 4.56 | 6.29 | 4.50 | 0.27 | 0.90 | 8.47 | 7.99 | 3.73 | 6.16 | 0.88 |
| 1959 | 8.91 | 10.34 | 3.91 | 3.25 | 2.72 | 0.18 | 0.65 | 8.67 | 7.31 | 3.35 | 3.18 | 0.59 |
| 1960 | 13.63 | 13.37 | 3.93 | 6.45 | 4.99 | 0.27 | 0.71 | 13.36 | 7.07 | 3.85 | 6.22 | 0.80 |
| 1961 | 11.16 | 19.02 | 3.63 | 3.55 | 1.57 | 0.07 | 0.51 | 10.94 | 7.72 | 3.93 | 3.51 | 0.50 |
| 1962 | 18.97 | 21.58 | 2.27 | 3.70 | 2.15 | 0.08 | 0.67 | 18.46 | 8.38 | 2.17 | 3.63 | 0.70 |
| 1963 | 11.91 | 13.47 | 1.25 | 0.72 | 0.60 | 0.08 | 0.55 | 11.54 | 7.26 | 1.28 | 0.72 | 0.55 |
| 1964 | 4.63 | 7.05 | 1.46 | 0.91 | 0.78 | 0.06 | 0.41 | 4.47 | 3.78 | 1.84 | 0.87 | 0.38 |
| 1965 | 9.56 | 20.55 | 1.96 | 1.51 | 1.83 | 0.08 | 0.67 | 9.26 | 11.19 | 1.09 | 1.47 | 0.64 |
| 1966 | 9.96 | 17.80 | 4.80 | 8.08 | 4.13 | 0.11 | 0.71 | 9.50 | 13.76 | 5.39 | 7.66 | 0.73 |
| 1967 | 14.89 | 36.96 | 7.33 | 6.58 | 3.81 | 0.16 | 0.44 | 14.24 | 17.30 | 5.14 | 6.27 | 0.54 |
| 1968 | 14.49 | 28.29 | 7.39 | 7.93 | 3.50 | 0.09 | 0.42 | 13.76 | 16.40 | 3.57 | 7.52 | 0.40 |
| 1969 | 12.10 | 18.71 | 6.93 | 9.95 | 5.54 | 0.22 | 0.62 | 11.35 | 9.73 | 7.39 | 9.34 | 0.63 |
| 1970 | 21.60 | 27.68 | 11.28 | 15.07 | 7.05 | 0.22 | 0.44 | 20.33 | 13.19 | 9.22 | 14.11 | 0.47 |

## Table 6-2 (continued)

### Basic and Derived Series
Annualized Monthly Standard Deviations (in percent)

### from 1971 to 2000

| | Basic Series | | | | | | | Derived Series | | | | |
|---|---|---|---|---|---|---|---|---|---|---|---|---|
| Year | Large Company Stocks | Small Company Stocks | Long-Term Corporate Bonds | Long-Term Govt Bonds | Intermediate-Term Govt Bonds | U.S. Treasury Bills | Inflation | Equity Risk Premia | Small Stock Premia | Bond Default Premia | Bond Horizon Premia | Inflation-Adjusted T-Bills |
| 1971 | 15.64 | 29.73 | 11.12 | 10.67 | 6.98 | 0.19 | 0.57 | 14.97 | 14.61 | 6.12 | 10.15 | 0.63 |
| 1972 | 7.80 | 16.60 | 3.21 | 5.85 | 1.97 | 0.17 | 0.41 | 7.51 | 11.39 | 3.97 | 5.61 | 0.42 |
| 1973 | 12.15 | 21.94 | 7.57 | 8.38 | 4.99 | 0.37 | 1.53 | 11.27 | 14.21 | 5.12 | 7.71 | 1.34 |
| 1974 | 18.74 | 20.15 | 11.45 | 8.64 | 5.73 | 0.36 | 0.91 | 17.52 | 22.03 | 5.76 | 8.05 | 0.89 |
| 1975 | 24.38 | 46.28 | 11.49 | 9.13 | 5.68 | 0.21 | 0.78 | 23.00 | 19.98 | 4.43 | 8.55 | 0.77 |
| 1976 | 16.89 | 50.83 | 5.21 | 5.43 | 4.24 | 0.13 | 0.48 | 16.00 | 27.53 | 1.55 | 5.15 | 0.45 |
| 1977 | 8.97 | 17.05 | 4.57 | 5.69 | 2.73 | 0.19 | 0.77 | 8.49 | 13.33 | 1.56 | 5.41 | 0.85 |
| 1978 | 17.92 | 42.56 | 4.45 | 4.45 | 2.07 | 0.36 | 0.67 | 16.75 | 26.56 | 1.66 | 4.21 | 0.78 |
| 1979 | 15.79 | 34.71 | 10.43 | 10.81 | 7.31 | 0.29 | 0.53 | 14.28 | 15.64 | 2.16 | 9.77 | 0.60 |
| 1980 | 24.19 | 39.80 | 20.12 | 21.16 | 16.77 | 0.98 | 1.45 | 22.26 | 14.54 | 4.57 | 18.60 | 1.18 |
| 1981 | 12.44 | 21.37 | 20.21 | 23.25 | 11.84 | 0.51 | 1.15 | 10.85 | 16.03 | 5.23 | 20.23 | 1.00 |
| 1982 | 23.38 | 21.97 | 17.80 | 14.40 | 8.91 | 0.78 | 1.64 | 21.57 | 7.84 | 5.37 | 13.37 | 1.42 |
| 1983 | 12.02 | 21.83 | 10.86 | 11.43 | 5.72 | 0.18 | 0.73 | 11.13 | 14.33 | 3.98 | 10.52 | 0.67 |
| 1984 | 15.00 | 14.57 | 12.97 | 13.34 | 7.17 | 0.34 | 0.61 | 13.63 | 4.37 | 1.92 | 11.97 | 0.61 |
| 1985 | 15.85 | 18.10 | 13.28 | 15.78 | 6.69 | 0.18 | 0.33 | 14.66 | 6.42 | 2.56 | 14.56 | 0.35 |
| 1986 | 21.39 | 15.49 | 9.71 | 21.58 | 6.53 | 0.20 | 1.03 | 20.12 | 6.61 | 9.54 | 20.26 | 1.17 |
| 1987 | 34.04 | 34.45 | 9.67 | 10.09 | 4.93 | 0.23 | 0.68 | 32.38 | 11.21 | 3.03 | 9.49 | 0.64 |
| 1988 | 11.69 | 16.08 | 9.10 | 11.03 | 5.00 | 0.36 | 0.57 | 11.07 | 11.14 | 2.45 | 10.45 | 0.64 |
| 1989 | 16.03 | 11.65 | 7.13 | 9.53 | 6.07 | 0.23 | 0.63 | 14.80 | 6.87 | 2.36 | 8.73 | 0.67 |
| 1990 | 18.25 | 16.85 | 7.55 | 9.89 | 4.75 | 0.18 | 1.16 | 16.92 | 6.83 | 2.67 | 9.18 | 1.16 |
| 1991 | 20.49 | 22.50 | 5.08 | 7.33 | 3.49 | 0.17 | 0.54 | 19.40 | 9.75 | 2.13 | 6.99 | 0.51 |
| 1992 | 7.91 | 21.58 | 5.77 | 7.62 | 5.83 | 0.14 | 0.54 | 7.68 | 19.95 | 2.32 | 7.38 | 0.53 |
| 1993 | 6.69 | 11.43 | 5.53 | 8.38 | 4.44 | 0.05 | 0.57 | 6.52 | 8.37 | 2.38 | 8.15 | 0.57 |
| 1994 | 10.74 | 10.38 | 6.70 | 8.12 | 4.50 | 0.24 | 0.47 | 10.31 | 6.35 | 2.27 | 7.77 | 0.62 |
| 1995 | 6.95 | 12.65 | 7.37 | 9.70 | 3.94 | 0.13 | 0.60 | 6.63 | 8.39 | 1.88 | 9.11 | 0.64 |
| 1996 | 13.29 | 21.06 | 7.62 | 9.33 | 3.89 | 0.09 | 0.61 | 12.67 | 15.16 | 2.14 | 8.87 | 0.62 |
| 1997 | 21.08 | 22.13 | 8.00 | 10.44 | 4.10 | 0.13 | 0.53 | 19.99 | 16.40 | 2.30 | 9.91 | 0.60 |
| 1998 | 27.90 | 25.76 | 5.91 | 7.70 | 4.63 | 0.16 | 0.30 | 26.69 | 6.81 | 4.35 | 7.24 | 0.31 |
| 1999 | 15.78 | 26.31 | 4.57 | 5.25 | 3.44 | 0.10 | 0.77 | 15.02 | 19.21 | 1.91 | 5.00 | 0.77 |
| 2000 | 16.02 | 40.42 | 5.88 | 6.92 | 3.43 | 0.17 | 1.00 | 15.14 | 44.92 | 4.10 | 6.58 | 1.07 |

## Cross-Correlations

The cross-correlation between two series measures the extent to which they are linearly related.[2] The correlation coefficient measures the sensitivity of returns on one asset class or portfolio to the returns of another. The correlation equation between return series **X** and **Y** is:

$$\rho_{X,Y} = \left[ \frac{\mathbf{Cov(X,Y)}}{\sigma_X \sigma_Y} \right]$$

(26)

where,

Cov (X,Y) = the covariance of **X** and **Y**, defined below;

$\sigma_X$ = the standard deviation of **X**; and,

$\sigma_Y$ = the standard deviation of **Y**.

The covariance equation is:

$$\mathbf{Cov(X,Y)} = \frac{1}{n-1} \sum_{t=1}^{n} \left( r_{X,t} - r_{X,A} \right)\left( r_{Y,t} - r_{Y,A} \right)$$

(27)

where,

$r_{X,t}$ = the return for series **X** in period **t**;

$r_{Y,t}$ = the return for series **Y** in period **t**;

$r_{X,A}$ = the arithmetic mean of series **X**;

$r_{Y,A}$ = the arithmetic mean of series **Y**; and,

n = the number of periods.

## Correlations of the Basic Series

Table 6-3 presents the annual cross-correlations and serial correlations for the seven basic series. Long-term government and long-term corporate bond returns are highly correlated with each other but negatively correlated with inflation. Since the inflation was largely unanticipated, it had a negative effect on fixed income securities. In addition, U.S. Treasury bills and inflation are reasonably highly correlated, a result of the post-1951 "tracking" described in Chapter 2. Lastly, both the U.S. Treasury bills and inflation series display high serial correlations.

2  Two series can be related in a non-linear way and have a correlation coefficient of zero. An example is the function y = x$^2$, for which $\rho_{X,Y}$ = 0.

## Table 6-3

**Basic Series**

Serial and Cross Correlations of Historical Annual Returns from 1926 to 2000

| Series | Large Company Stocks | Small Company Stocks | Long-Term Corp Bonds | Long-Term Govt Bonds | Intermediate Govt Bonds | U.S. Treasury Bills | Inflation |
|---|---|---|---|---|---|---|---|
| Large Company Stocks | 1.00 | | | | | | |
| Small Company Stocks | 0.79 | 1.00 | | | | | |
| Long-Term Corporate Bonds | 0.24 | 0.09 | 1.00 | | | | |
| Long-Term Govt Bonds | 0.16 | 0.00 | 0.94 | 1.00 | | | |
| Intermediate-Term Govt Bonds | 0.09 | −0.05 | 0.91 | 0.91 | 1.00 | | |
| U.S. Treasury Bills | −0.03 | −0.10 | 0.22 | 0.24 | 0.49 | 1.00 | |
| Inflation | −0.03 | 0.05 | −0.15 | −0.14 | 0.01 | 0.41 | 1.00 |
| Serial Correlations* | 0.00 | 0.08 | 0.07 | −0.06 | 0.14 | 0.92 | 0.65 |

*The standard error for all estimates is 0.12

## Correlations of the Derived Series

The annual cross-correlations and serial correlations for the four risk premium series and inflation are presented in Table 6-4. These correlations reveal that the small stock premia and bond default premia (each of which is a premium for "economy" risk) are significantly correlated with equity risk premia. With one exception, the remaining series are independent of one another, having cross-correlations that do not differ from zero at the 5 percent statistical significance level. The exception is inflation that is negatively correlated with the horizon premium. Increasing inflation causes long-term bond yields to rise and prices to fall; therefore, a negative horizon premium is observed in times of rising inflation.

## Table 6-4

**Risk Premia and Inflation**

Serial and Cross Correlations of Historical Annual Returns from 1926 to 2000

| Series | Equity Risk Premia | Small Stock Premia | Default Premia | Horizon Premia | Inflation |
|---|---|---|---|---|---|
| Equity Risk Premia | 1.00 | | | | |
| Small Stock Premia | 0.33 | 1.00 | | | |
| Default Premia | 0.20 | 0.14 | 1.00 | | |
| Horizon Premia | 0.18 | −0.08 | −0.36 | 1.00 | |
| Inflation | −0.09 | 0.13 | 0.00 | −0.29 | 1.00 |
| Serial Correlations* | 0.01 | 0.38 | −0.29 | −0.12 | 0.65 |

*The standard error for all estimates is 0.12

Table 6-5 presents annual cross-correlations and serial correlations for the inflation-adjusted asset return series. It is interesting to observe how the relationship between the asset returns are substantially different when these returns are expressed in inflation-adjusted terms (as compared with nominal terms). In general, the cross-correlations between asset classes are higher when one accounts for inflation (i.e., subtracts inflation from the nominal returns).

## Table 6-5

**Inflation-Adjusted Series**
Serial and Cross Correlations of Historical Annual Returns from 1926 to 2000

| Series | Inflation-Adjusted | | | | | | |
|---|---|---|---|---|---|---|---|
| | Large Company Stocks | Small Company Stocks | Long-Term Corp Bonds | Long-Term Govt Bonds | Inter-mediate Govt Bonds | T-Bills (Real Interest Rates) | Inflation |
| Inflation-Adjusted Large Company Stocks | 1.00 | | | | | | |
| Inflation-Adjusted Small Company Stocks | 0.79 | 1.00 | | | | | |
| Inflation-Adjusted Long-Term Corporate Bonds | 0.30 | 0.12 | 1.00 | | | | |
| Inflation-Adjusted Long-Term Govt Bonds | 0.24 | 0.04 | 0.95 | 1.00 | | | |
| Inflation-Adjusted Intermd-Term Govt Bonds | 0.18 | −0.01 | 0.94 | 0.94 | 1.00 | | |
| Inflation-Adjusted T-Bills (Real Interest Rates) | 0.12 | −0.06 | 0.59 | 0.58 | 0.73 | 1.00 | |
| Inflation | −0.23 | −0.08 | −0.56 | −0.53 | −0.61 | −0.74 | 1.00 |
| Serial Correlations* | 0.00 | 0.05 | 0.18 | 0.03 | 0.22 | 0.67 | 0.65 |

*The standard error for all estimates is 0.12

## Serial Correlation in the Derived Series: Trends or Random Behavior?

The risk/return relationships in the historical data are represented in the equity risk premia, the small stock premia, the bond horizon premia, and the bond default premia. The real/nominal historical relationships are represented in the inflation rates and the real interest rates. The objective is to uncover whether each series is random or is subject to any trends, cycles, or other patterns.

The one-year serial correlation coefficients measure the degree of correlation between returns from each year and the previous year for the same series. Highly positive (near 1) serial correlations indicate trends, while highly negative (near −1) serial correlations indicate cycles. There is strong evidence that both inflation rates and real riskless rates follow trends. Serial correlations near zero suggest no patterns (i.e., random behavior); equity risk premia and bond horizon premia are random variables. Small stock premia and bond default premia fall into a middle range where it cannot be determined that they either follow a trend or behave randomly, although the serial correlation of annual small stock premia is high enough to suggest a trend.

Each of the component series' serial correlations can be interpreted as following a random pattern, trend or uncertain path, as given in Table 6-6.

## Table 6-6

**Interpretation of the Annual Serial Correlations**

| Series | Serial Correlation | Interpretation |
|---|---|---|
| Equity Risk Premia | .01 | Random |
| Small Stock Premia | .38 | Likely Trend |
| Bond Default Premia | −.29 | Possible Cycle |
| Bond Horizon Premia | −.12 | Random |
| Inflation Rates | .65 | Trend |
| Real Interest Rates | .67 | Trend |

## Summary Statistics for Basic and Inflation-Adjusted Series

Table 6-7 presents summary statistics of annual total returns, and where applicable, income and capital appreciation, for each asset class. The summary statistics presented here are arithmetic mean, geometric mean, standard deviation, and serial correlation. Table 6-8 presents summary statistics for the six inflation-adjusted total return series.

Table 6-7

**Total Returns, Income Returns, and Capital Appreciation of the Basic Asset Classes**
Summary Statistics of Annual Returns from 1926 to 2000

| Series | Geometric Mean | Arithmetic Mean | Standard Deviation | Serial Correlation |
|---|---|---|---|---|
| **Large Company Stocks** | | | | |
| Total Returns | 11.0% | 13.0% | 20.2% | 0.00 |
| Income | 4.4 | 4.4 | 1.4 | 0.86 |
| Capital Appreciation | 6.4 | 8.3 | 19.5 | 0.01 |
| **Small Company Stocks** (Total Returns) | 12.4 | 17.3 | 33.4 | 0.08 |
| **Long-Term Corporate Bonds** (Total Returns) | 5.7 | 6.0 | 8.7 | 0.07 |
| **Long-Term Government Bonds** | | | | |
| Total Returns | 5.3 | 5.7 | 9.4 | −0.06 |
| Income | 5.2 | 5.2 | 2.8 | 0.96 |
| Capital Appreciation | −0.1 | 0.3 | 8.2 | −0.22 |
| **Intermediate-Term Government Bonds** | | | | |
| Total Returns | 5.3 | 5.5 | 5.8 | 0.14 |
| Income | 4.8 | 4.8 | 3.0 | 0.96 |
| Capital Appreciation | 0.3 | 0.4 | 4.5 | −0.23 |
| **Treasury Bills** (Total Returns) | 3.8 | 3.9 | 3.2 | 0.92 |
| **Inflation** | 3.1 | 3.2 | 4.4 | 0.65 |

Total return is equal to the sum of three component returns; income return, capital appreciation return, and reinvestment return. Annual reinvestment returns for select asset classes are provided in Table 2-6.

### Highlights of the Summary Statistics

Table 6-7 shows that over 1926–2000 small company stocks were the riskiest asset class with a standard deviation of 33.4 percent, but provide the greatest rewards to long-term investors, with an arithmetic mean annual return of 17.3 percent. The geometric mean of the small stock series is 12.4 percent. Large company stocks, long-term government bonds, long-term corporate bonds, and intermediate-term government bonds are progressively less risky, and have correspondingly lower average returns. Treasury bills were nearly riskless and had the lowest return. In general, risk is rewarded by a higher return over the long term.

Inflation-adjusted basic series summary statistics are presented in Table 6-8. Note that the real rate of interest is close to zero (0.7 percent) on average. For the 75-year period, the geometric and arithmetic means are lower by the amount of inflation than those of the nominal series.

The standard deviations of large company stock and small company stock returns remain approximately the same after adjusting for inflation, while inflation-adjusted bonds and bills are more volatile (i.e., have higher standard deviations).

### Table 6-8

**Inflation-Adjusted Series**
Summary Statistics of Annual Returns from 1926 to 2000

| Series | Geometric Mean | Arithmetic Mean | Standard Deviation | Serial Correlation |
|---|---|---|---|---|
| Inflation-Adjusted Large Company Stocks | 7.7% | 9.7% | 20.3% | 0.00 |
| Inflation-Adjusted Small Company Stocks | 9.0 | 13.8 | 32.8 | 0.05 |
| Inflation-Adjusted Long-Term Corporate Bonds | 2.5 | 3.0 | 9.9 | 0.18 |
| Inflation-Adjusted Long-Term Government Bonds | 2.2 | 2.7 | 10.6 | 0.03 |
| Inflation-Adjusted Intermediate-Term Government Bonds | 2.2 | 2.4 | 7.0 | 0.22 |
| Inflation-Adjusted U.S. T-Bills (Real Riskless Rates of Returns) | 0.7 | 0.8 | 4.1 | 0.67 |

## Rolling Period Standard Deviations

Rolling period standard deviations are obtained by rolling a view window of fixed length along each time series and computing the standard deviation for the asset class for each window of time. They are useful for examining the volatility or riskiness of returns for holding periods similar to those actually experienced by investors. Graph 6-2 graphically depicts the volatility. Monthly data are used to maximize the number of data points included in the standard deviation computation.

The upper graph places the 60-month rolling standard deviation for large company stocks, small company stocks, and long-term government bonds on the same scale. It is interesting to see the relatively high standard deviation for small company stocks and large company stocks in the 1930s, with an apparent lessening of volatility for 60-month holding periods during the 1980s. Note also how the standard deviation for long-term government bonds increases and exceeds that for both common stock asset classes during part of the 1980s.

The lower graph places the 60-month rolling standard deviation for long- and intermediate-term government bonds, and Treasury bills on the same scale.

Graph 6-2

## Rolling 60-Month Standard Deviation

Small Company Stocks, Large Company Stocks, Long-Term Government Bonds,
Intermediate Bonds, and Treasury Bills

from January 1926–December 1930 to January 1996–December 2000

**Small Company Stocks, Large Company Stocks, Long-Term Government Bonds**

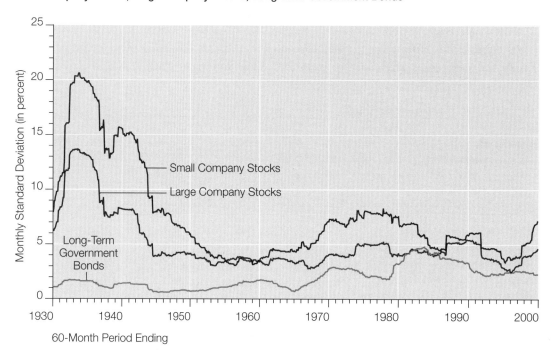

**Long-Term Government Bonds, Intermediate-Term Government Bonds, Treasury Bills**

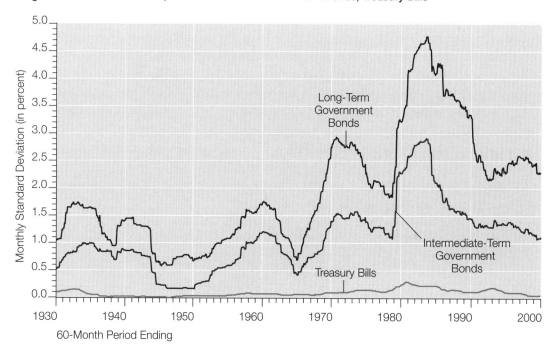

Graph 6-3

**Rolling 60-Month Correlations**
Large Company Stocks, Long-Term Government Bonds, Treasury Bills, and Inflation

from January 1926–December 1930 to January 1996–December 2000

**Large Company Stocks and Long-Term Government Bonds**

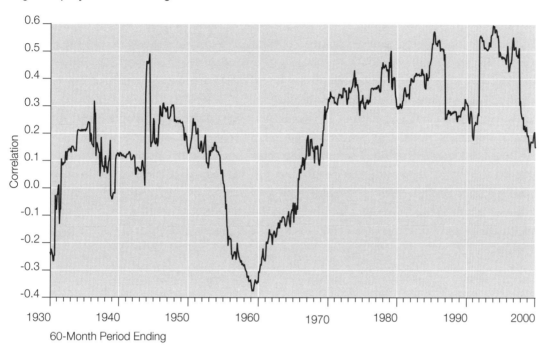

60-Month Period Ending

**Treasury Bills and Inflation**

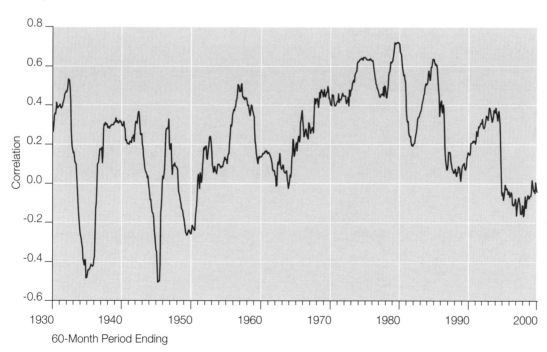

60-Month Period Ending

## Rolling Period Correlations

Rolling period correlations are obtained by moving a view window of fixed length along time series for two asset classes and computing the cross-correlation between the two asset classes for each window of time. They are useful for examining how asset class returns vary together for holding periods similar to those actually experienced by investors. Monthly data are used to maximize the number of data points included in the correlation computation.

Graph 6-3 shows cross correlations between two asset classes for five year (60 months of monthly data) holding periods. The first rolling period covered is January 1926–December 1930 so the graphs begin at December 1930. The top graph shows the volatility of the correlations between large company stocks and long-term government bonds. There are wide fluctuations between strong positive and strong negative correlations over the past 75 years.

The lower graph shows the correlation between Treasury bills and inflation. While there were some wide fluctuations during the 1930s and 1940s, the correlation has generally been positive since the mid-1960s.

## The True Impact of Asset Allocation on Returns

### Universal Misunderstanding

How important is asset allocation policy and what type of impact does it have on fund returns? This is a frequently asked question throughout the financial world, with the answer depending on how you ask the question and what you are trying to explain. Financial professionals generally assert that asset allocation is the most important determinant of returns, accounting for more than 90 percent of fund performance. This assertion stems from the well-known studies by Brinson, Hood, and Beebower[3] which state, "...investment policy dominates investment strategy (market timing and security selection), explaining on average 93.6 percent of the variation in total plan return." Specific claims to the above statement vary, but if you are trying to explain the variability of returns over time, asset allocation is of prime importance.

3  "Determinants of Portfolio Performance," Gary P. Brinson, L. Randolph Hood, and Gilbert P. Beebower, *Financial Analysts Journal*, July/August 1986.

"Determinants of Portfolio Performance II," Gary P. Brinson, Brian D. Singer, and Gilbert P. Beebower, *Financial Analysts Journal*, May/June 1991.

However, a great deal of confusion in both the academic and financial community has arisen, and the results of the Brinson studies are attributed to questions that the studies never intended to answer. A survey by Nuttall & Nuttall[4] reveals that out of fifty writers who quoted Brinson et al., only one quoted them correctly. Thirty-seven writers misinterpreted Brinson's work as an answer to the question, "What percent of total return is explained by asset allocation policy?" while five writers misconstrued the Brinson conclusion as an answer to the question, "What is the impact of choosing one asset allocation over another?"

This section is based upon the work by Roger G. Ibbotson and Paul D. Kaplan.[5] The goal of the study is to clear up this universal misinterpretation and explain the link between asset allocation and investment returns.

## The Brinson Studies

According to the well-known studies by Brinson, Hood, and Beebower, more than 90 percent of the variability of a portfolio's performance over time is due to asset allocation. In other words, Brinson is measuring the relationship between the movement of a portfolio and the movement of the overall stock market. They find that more than 90 percent of a portfolio's movement from quarter to quarter is due to market movement of the asset classes in which the portfolio is invested.

Thus, while the Brinson studies state that more than 90 percent of the variability of a portfolio's performance over time is due to asset allocation, they are frequently misinterpreted and the results are attributed to questions that the studies never intended to answer. Two prime examples being:

- "When choosing between two different asset allocations, how much of a difference does it really make if I choose one over the other?"

- "What portion of my total return is due to asset allocation?"

## Data Analysis Framework

To answer the above questions, as well as to confirm the Brinson result, ten years of monthly returns on 94 balanced mutual funds and five years of quarterly returns on 58 pension funds were analyzed. The 94 funds represent all of the balanced funds in the Morningstar universe that had at least ten years of data ending March 31, 1998. The data collected consist of the total return for each fund for each period of time—either monthly or quarterly.

For the mutual funds, the policy weights were determined by using returns-based style analysis over the entire 120-month period.

---

4 "Asset Allocation Claims—Truth or Fiction?," Jennifer A. Nuttall and John Nuttall (unpublished), 1998.

5 "Does Asset Allocation Policy Explain 40, 90, or 100 Percent of Performance?," Roger G. Ibbotson and Paul D. Kaplan, *Financial Analysts Journal*, January/February 2000.

Dale Stevens[6] provided the same type of analysis on quarterly returns of 58 pension funds over a five-year period 1993–1997. However, rather than using estimated policy weights and the same asset class benchmarks for all funds, the actual policy weights and asset class benchmarks of the pension funds were used. In each quarter, the policy weights are known in advance of the realized returns.

## Questions and Answers

*"How much of the movement in a fund's returns over time is explained by its asset allocation policy?"*

The Brinson studies from 1986 and 1991 answer the above question. To confirm the results of the Brinson study, each fund's total returns is regressed against its policy returns with the R-squared value being reported for each fund.

Our results confirm the Brinson result that approximately 90 percent of the variability of a fund's return across time is explained by asset allocation. However, almost any stock market performance index would explain a high percentage of the time series variation. As Table 6-9 shows, even the S&P 500 index explains about 80 percent of the average fund's performance, almost as high as the fund's specific asset allocation policy benchmark. This is because all benchmarks and funds rise in a bull market and fall in a bear market.

Table 6-9

**Asset Allocation Policy or Market Participation?**
Time-Series R²s Compared to:

|  | Benchmark | |
| --- | --- | --- |
|  | S&P 500 | Fund Policy |
| Mean | 75.2% | 81.4% |
| Median | 81.9% | 87.6% |

*"When choosing between two different asset allocations, how much of a difference does it really make if I choose one over the other?"*

To answer the above question, each fund's return must be compared to the other in order to determine how much of the return variation across funds is explained by the funds' asset allocation variations. A cross-sectional regression of entire-period compound annual total returns on entire-period compound annual policy returns was performed. The R-squared statistic gives us the percentage of the variation explained.

6  "The Importance of Investment Policy," Dale H. Stevens, Ronald J. Surz, and Mark E. Wimer, *The Journal of Investing*, Winter 1999.

For the mutual fund sample, 40 percent of the return difference from one fund to another was explained by asset allocation, while for pension funds the result was 35 percent. Graph 6-4 shows the plot of the 10-year compound annual total returns against the 10-year compound annual policy returns for the mutual fund sample. For example, if one portfolio returns 5 percent more than the other, then on average, about 2 percent of the difference (40 percent of 5 percent) is attributable to the different asset allocations. The remaining 3 percent difference (60 percent of 5 percent) is explained by other factors such as asset class timing, security selection, and fees.

Graph 6-4

**10-Year Compound Annual Return Across Mutual Funds***

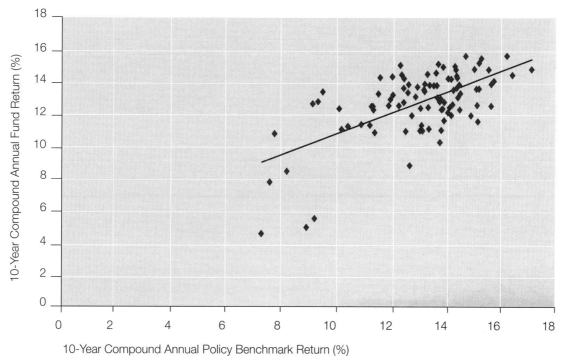

*Across the pension fund sample the $R^2$ = 0.35.

Graph 6-5

Variation of Returns Across Funds Explained by
Asset Allocation

Percentage of a Fund's Total Return Explained by
Asset Allocation

60%   40%

100%

■ Security Selection, Timing, etc.          ■ Asset Allocation

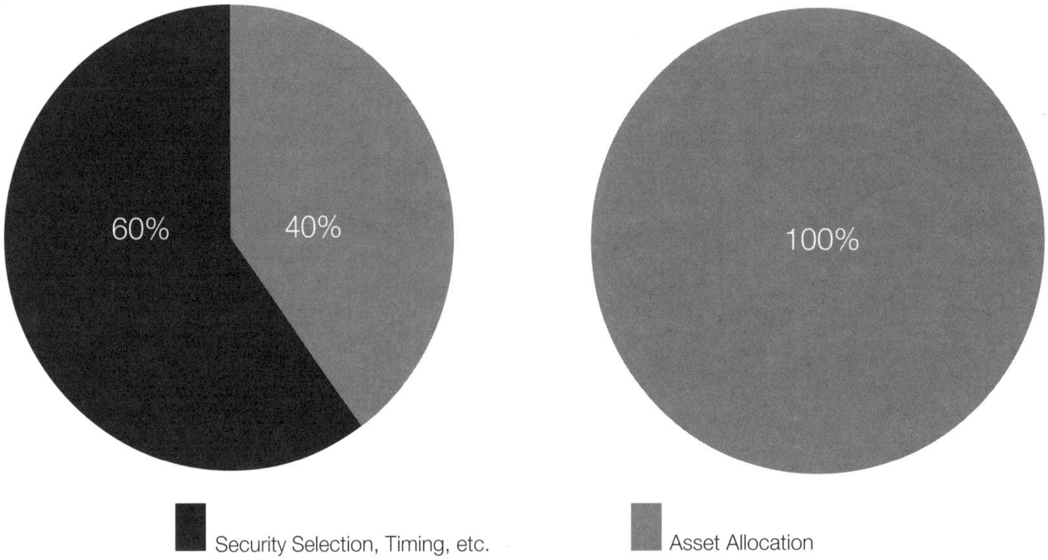

*"What portion of my total return is due to asset allocation?"*

To answer the above question, the percent of fund return explained by asset allocation was calculated for each fund as the ratio of compound annual policy return divided by the compound annual total return. In other words, we create a portfolio of benchmark asset classes that matches a balanced fund's asset allocation policy and then divide the return of the benchmark portfolio by the fund's return. This ratio of compound returns serves as a performance measure. A fund that has stayed exactly at its asset allocation mix and has invested passively will have a ratio of 1.0 or 100 percent. A fund that has outperformed its asset allocation will have a ratio of less than one, while a fund that has underperformed its asset allocation policy will have a ratio of greater than one.

**% of Return due to Policy = $\dfrac{\text{Policy Return}}{\text{Total Return}}$**

We find that, on average, the policy benchmarks perform as well as the actual portfolios producing a ratio of 1.0, or 100 percent. It is safe to say that, on average, the pension funds and balanced mutual funds are not adding value above their asset allocation policy due to their combination of timing, security selection, management fees, and expenses. Thus, about 100 percent of the total return is explained by asset allocation policy.

The above results were anticipated by William Sharpe.[7] Sharpe pointed out that since the aggregation of all investors is the market, the average performance before costs of all investors must equal the performance of the market. This implies that, on average, nearly 100 percent of the level of a fund's total return should be expected from asset allocation. Our results confirm such a prediction.

In summary, much of the recent controversy over the importance of asset allocation is due to the misinterpretation of the Brinson studies. These studies successfully provided an answer to one question, but never intended to address the two questions discussed in the above study. While the Brinson studies show that more than 90 percent of the variability of a portfolio's performance over time is due to asset allocation, through careful analysis, we have also come to the conclusion that asset allocation explains about 40 percent of the variation of returns across funds and about 100 percent of a fund's total return.

7 "The Arithmetic of Active Management," William F. Sharpe, *Financial Analysts Journal*, January/February 1991.

# Chapter 7

## Firm Size and Return

## The Firm Size Phenomenon

One of the most remarkable discoveries of modern finance is the finding of a relationship between firm size and return.[1] On average, small companies have higher returns than large ones. Earlier chapters document this phenomenon for the smallest stocks on the New York Stock Exchange (NYSE). The relationship between firm size and return cuts across the entire size spectrum; it is not restricted to the smallest stocks. In this chapter, the returns across the entire range of firm size are examined.

## Construction of the Decile Portfolios

The portfolios used in this chapter are those created by the Center for Research in Security Prices (CRSP) at the University of Chicago's Graduate School of Business. CRSP has refined the methodology of creating size-based portfolios and has applied this methodology to the entire universe of NYSE/AMEX/NASDAQ-listed securities going back to 1926.

In 1993, CRSP changed the method used to construct these portfolios, thereby causing the return and index values in Table 7-2 and 7-3 to be significantly different from those reported in previous editions of the *Yearbook*. Previously, some eligible companies had been excluded or delayed from inclusion when the portfolios were reformed at the end of each calendar quarter. Also, while in prior editions of the *Yearbook* we used NYSE-listed securities only in the composition of size decile portfolios, starting with the 2001 edition we use the entire population of NYSE, AMEX, and NASDAQ-listed securities for use in the firm size chapter.

The New York Stock Exchange universe is restricted by excluding closed-end mutual funds, preferred stocks, real estate investment trusts, foreign stocks, American Depository Receipts, unit investment trusts, and Americus Trusts. All companies on the NYSE are ranked by the combined market capitalization of all their eligible equity securities. The companies are then split into 10 equally populated groups or deciles. Eligible companies traded on the American Stock Exchange (AMEX) and the Nasdaq National Market (NASDAQ) are then assigned to the appropriate deciles according to their capitalization in relation to the NYSE breakpoints. The portfolios are rebalanced using closing prices for the last trading day of March, June, September, and December. Securities added during the quarter are assigned to the appropriate portfolio when two consecutive month-end prices are available. For securities that become delisted, when the last NYSE price is a month-end price, that month's return is included in the portfolio's quarterly return. When a month-end NYSE price is missing, the month-end value is derived from merger terms, quotations on regional exchanges, and other sources. If a month-end value is not available, the last available daily price is used.

Base security returns are monthly holding period returns. All distributions are added to the month-end prices. Appropriate adjustments are made to prices to account for stock splits and dividends. The return on a portfolio for one month is calculated as the weighted average of the returns for the individual stocks in the portfolio. Annual portfolio returns are calculated by compounding the monthly portfolio returns.

---

1 Rolf W. Banz was the first to document this phenomenon. See Banz, Rolf W., "The Relationship Between Returns and Market Value of Common Stocks," *Journal of Financial Economics*, Volume 9 (1981), pp. 3–18.

## Aspects of the Firm Size Effect

The firm size phenomenon is remarkable in several ways. First, the greater risk of small stocks does not, in the context of the Capital Asset Pricing Model, fully account for their higher returns over the long term. In the CAPM, only systematic or beta risk is rewarded. Small company stocks have had returns in excess of those implied by the betas of small stocks. Secondly, the calendar annual return differences between small and large companies are serially correlated. This suggests that past annual returns may be of some value in predicting future annual returns. Such serial correlation, or auto-correlation, is practically unknown in the market for large stocks and in most other capital markets.

In addition, the firm size effect is seasonal. For example, small company stocks outperformed large company stocks in the month of January in a large majority of the years. Again, such predictability is surprising and suspicious in the light of modern capital market theory. These three aspects of the firm size effect (long-term returns in excess of risk, serial correlation and seasonality) will be analyzed after the data are presented.

Table 7-1
**Size-Decile Portfolios of the NYSE/AMEX/NASDAQ**
Summary Statistics of Annual Returns
from 1926 to 2000

| Decile | Geometric Mean | Arithmetic Mean | Standard Deviation | Serial Correlation |
|---|---|---|---|---|
| 1-Largest | 0.3% | 12.1% | 19.05% | 0.05 |
| 2 | 11.3 | 13.6 | 22.00 | 0.02 |
| 3 | 11.6 | 14.2 | 23.94 | −0.03 |
| 4 | 11.5 | 14.6 | 26.25 | −0.02 |
| 5 | 11.8 | 15.2 | 27.07 | −0.02 |
| 6 | 11.8 | 15.5 | 28.15 | 0.05 |
| 7 | 11.6 | 15.7 | 30.43 | 0.02 |
| 8 | 11.7 | 16.6 | 34.21 | 0.06 |
| 9 | 11.8 | 17.4 | 37.13 | 0.08 |
| 10-Smallest | 13.1 | 20.9 | 45.82 | 0.17 |
| Mid-Cap 3–5 TR | 11.6 | 14.5 | 25.04 | −0.03 |
| Low-Cap 6–8 TR | 11.7 | 15.7 | 29.95 | 0.04 |
| Micro-Cap 9–10 TR | 12.2 | 18.4 | 39.63 | 0.11 |
| NYSE/AMEX/NASDAQ | 10.6 | 12.6 | 20.20 | 0.01 |

Total Value Weighted Index

Results are for quarterly re-ranking for the deciles. The small company stock summary statistics presented in earlier chapters comprise a re-ranking of the portfolios every five years prior to 1982.

## Presentation of the Decile Data

Summary statistics of annual returns of the 10 deciles over 1926–2000 are presented in Table 7-1. Note from this exhibit that the average return tends to increase as one moves from the largest decile to the smallest. (Because securities are ranked quarterly, returns on the ninth and tenth deciles are different than those suggested by the small company stock index presented in earlier chapters. A detailed methodology for the small company stock index is included in Chapter 3.) The total risk, or standard deviation of annual returns, also increases with decreasing firm size. The serial correlations of returns are near zero for all but the smallest two deciles.

Table 7-2 gives the year-by-year history of the returns for the different size categories. Table 7-3 shows the growth of $1.00 invested in each of the categories as of year-end 1925.

The sheer magnitude of the size effect in some years is noteworthy. While the largest stocks actually declined in 1977, the smallest stocks rose more than 20 percent. A more extreme case occurred in the depression-recovery year of 1933, when the difference between the first and tenth decile returns was far more substantial. The divergence in the performance of small and large company stocks is a common occurrence.

In Table 7-4, the decile returns and index values of the NYSE/AMEX/NASDAQ population are broken down into mid-cap, low-cap, and micro-cap stocks. Mid-cap stocks are defined here as the aggregate of deciles 3–5. Based on the most recent data (Table 7-5), companies within this mid-cap range have market capitalizations at or below $4,143,902,000, but greater than $840,000,000. Low-cap stocks include deciles 6–8, and currently include all companies in the NYSE/AMEX/NAS-DAQ with market capitalizations at or below $840,000,000 but greater than $192,598,000. Micro-cap stocks include deciles 9–10, and include companies with market capitalizations at or below $192,598,000. The returns and index values of the entire NYSE/AMEX/NASDAQ population are also included. All returns presented are value-weighted based on the market capitalizations of the deciles contained in each sub-group. Graph 7-1 graphically depicts the growth of $1.00 invested in each of these capitalization groups.

## Table 7-2

**Size-Decile Portfolios of the NYSE/AMEX/NASDAQ**
Year-by-Year Returns

from 1926 to 1970

|  | Decile 1 | Decile 2 | Decile 3 | Decile 4 | Decile 5 | Decile 6 | Decile 7 | Decile 8 | Decile 9 | Decile 10 |
|---|---|---|---|---|---|---|---|---|---|---|
| 1926 | 0.1438 | 0.0545 | 0.0355 | 0.0085 | 0.0033 | 0.0335 | -0.0250 | -0.0932 | -0.0997 | -0.0605 |
| 1927 | 0.3400 | 0.2957 | 0.3116 | 0.4134 | 0.3467 | 0.2312 | 0.3025 | 0.2553 | 0.3190 | 0.3126 |
| 1928 | 0.3889 | 0.3777 | 0.3982 | 0.3736 | 0.4965 | 0.2809 | 0.3530 | 0.3212 | 0.3740 | 0.6974 |
| 1929 | -0.1056 | -0.0793 | -0.2569 | -0.3177 | -0.2448 | -0.4044 | -0.3769 | -0.4082 | -0.4993 | -0.5359 |
| 1930 | -0.2422 | -0.3747 | -0.3465 | -0.3418 | -0.3627 | -0.3781 | -0.3661 | -0.4951 | -0.4570 | -0.4567 |
| 1931 | -0.4215 | -0.5011 | -0.4600 | -0.4569 | -0.4865 | -0.5102 | -0.4787 | -0.4907 | -0.4908 | -0.5010 |
| 1932 | -0.1197 | -0.0078 | -0.0185 | -0.1333 | -0.1144 | 0.0660 | -0.1648 | 0.0129 | -0.0029 | 0.3843 |
| 1933 | 0.4661 | 0.7467 | 1.0331 | 1.1220 | 0.9497 | 1.0972 | 1.1784 | 1.5880 | 1.7361 | 2.2160 |
| 1934 | 0.0223 | 0.0569 | 0.0894 | 0.1782 | 0.0753 | 0.2185 | 0.1480 | 0.2776 | 0.2253 | 0.3185 |
| 1935 | 0.4078 | 0.5846 | 0.3689 | 0.3702 | 0.6401 | 0.5537 | 0.6466 | 0.6423 | 0.6201 | 0.8212 |
| 1936 | 0.2961 | 0.3553 | 0.2857 | 0.4341 | 0.4612 | 0.4999 | 0.5213 | 0.4931 | 0.8344 | 0.8600 |
| 1937 | -0.3185 | -0.3662 | -0.3801 | -0.4352 | -0.4867 | -0.4763 | -0.4918 | -0.5275 | -0.5165 | -0.5562 |
| 1938 | 0.2507 | 0.3455 | 0.3534 | 0.3387 | 0.5054 | 0.4339 | 0.3505 | 0.4541 | 0.3040 | 0.0900 |
| 1939 | 0.0472 | -0.0346 | -0.0253 | 0.0025 | 0.0146 | 0.0386 | 0.0770 | -0.0426 | -0.0627 | 0.1908 |
| 1940 | -0.0709 | -0.0906 | -0.0873 | -0.0388 | -0.0113 | -0.0607 | -0.0617 | -0.0583 | -0.0446 | -0.3104 |
| 1941 | -0.1065 | -0.0650 | -0.0614 | -0.0973 | -0.1207 | -0.1024 | -0.0915 | -0.0933 | -0.1226 | -0.1684 |
| 1942 | 0.1308 | 0.2419 | 0.1969 | 0.2056 | 0.2117 | 0.2466 | 0.2892 | 0.3063 | 0.4322 | 0.7740 |
| 1943 | 0.2353 | 0.3465 | 0.3449 | 0.3967 | 0.4822 | 0.4254 | 0.7373 | 0.7034 | 0.8559 | 1.4216 |
| 1944 | 0.1696 | 0.2627 | 0.2381 | 0.3261 | 0.3951 | 0.4469 | 0.3730 | 0.4935 | 0.5675 | 0.6994 |
| 1945 | 0.2914 | 0.4890 | 0.5354 | 0.6345 | 0.5455 | 0.6075 | 0.6412 | 0.6954 | 0.7647 | 0.9507 |
| 1946 | -0.0448 | -0.0459 | -0.0748 | -0.1312 | -0.0974 | -0.0669 | -0.1563 | -0.1463 | -0.0995 | -0.1837 |
| 1947 | 0.0559 | 0.0064 | -0.0009 | 0.0188 | 0.0343 | -0.0339 | -0.0226 | -0.0291 | -0.0342 | -0.0246 |
| 1948 | 0.0370 | 0.0057 | 0.0208 | -0.0188 | -0.0145 | -0.0370 | -0.0294 | -0.0725 | -0.0670 | -0.0522 |
| 1949 | 0.1870 | 0.2517 | 0.2628 | 0.1999 | 0.1872 | 0.2309 | 0.2202 | 0.1615 | 0.1992 | 0.2485 |
| 1950 | 0.2864 | 0.2851 | 0.2643 | 0.3172 | 0.3700 | 0.3451 | 0.3700 | 0.4076 | 0.4037 | 0.5571 |
| 1951 | 0.2147 | 0.2256 | 0.2187 | 0.1687 | 0.1446 | 0.1414 | 0.1801 | 0.1515 | 0.1128 | 0.0584 |
| 1952 | 0.1429 | 0.1303 | 0.1168 | 0.1240 | 0.1108 | 0.1022 | 0.0984 | 0.0839 | 0.0865 | 0.0180 |
| 1953 | 0.0110 | 0.0157 | 0.0016 | -0.0203 | -0.0258 | -0.0081 | -0.0251 | -0.0780 | -0.0437 | -0.0841 |
| 1954 | 0.4844 | 0.4844 | 0.5839 | 0.5101 | 0.5793 | 0.5945 | 0.5725 | 0.5341 | 0.6359 | 0.6853 |
| 1955 | 0.2838 | 0.1873 | 0.1893 | 0.1897 | 0.1819 | 0.2304 | 0.1794 | 0.2076 | 0.1972 | 0.2648 |
| 1956 | 0.0779 | 0.1160 | 0.0782 | 0.0869 | 0.0845 | 0.0590 | 0.0854 | 0.0478 | 0.0589 | -0.0149 |
| 1957 | -0.0955 | -0.0883 | -0.1342 | -0.1105 | -0.1347 | -0.1831 | -0.1725 | -0.1824 | -0.1448 | -0.1618 |
| 1958 | 0.4078 | 0.4959 | 0.5432 | 0.5889 | 0.5616 | 0.5627 | 0.6697 | 0.6648 | 0.7102 | 0.6963 |
| 1959 | 0.1322 | 0.0967 | 0.1297 | 0.1505 | 0.1885 | 0.1483 | 0.2103 | 0.1719 | 0.1927 | 0.1552 |
| 1960 | -0.0007 | 0.0558 | 0.0455 | 0.0085 | -0.0115 | -0.0147 | -0.0552 | -0.0428 | -0.0377 | -0.0824 |
| 1961 | 0.2699 | 0.2690 | 0.2919 | 0.2955 | 0.2878 | 0.2733 | 0.3034 | 0.3416 | 0.2988 | 0.3183 |
| 1962 | -0.0887 | -0.0961 | -0.1192 | -0.1230 | -0.1669 | -0.1753 | -0.1675 | -0.1467 | -0.1673 | -0.1423 |
| 1963 | 0.2247 | 0.2101 | 0.1695 | 0.1682 | 0.1303 | 0.1845 | 0.1789 | 0.1893 | 0.1335 | 0.1094 |
| 1964 | 0.1596 | 0.1448 | 0.1992 | 0.1667 | 0.1662 | 0.1584 | 0.1580 | 0.1707 | 0.1590 | 0.2091 |
| 1965 | 0.0894 | 0.1909 | 0.2470 | 0.2395 | 0.3106 | 0.3835 | 0.3348 | 0.3180 | 0.3223 | 0.4303 |
| 1966 | -0.1033 | -0.0528 | -0.0516 | -0.0601 | -0.0685 | -0.0532 | -0.0935 | -0.0883 | -0.0577 | -0.1007 |
| 1967 | 0.2191 | 0.2126 | 0.3148 | 0.4513 | 0.5212 | 0.5175 | 0.6489 | 0.8094 | 0.9028 | 1.1453 |
| 1968 | 0.0759 | 0.1670 | 0.1971 | 0.1898 | 0.2663 | 0.3100 | 0.2656 | 0.3998 | 0.3829 | 0.6092 |
| 1969 | -0.0597 | -0.1295 | -0.1158 | -0.1665 | -0.1655 | -0.1978 | -0.2467 | -0.2399 | -0.3195 | -0.3289 |
| 1970 | 0.0229 | 0.0210 | 0.0306 | -0.0651 | -0.0603 | -0.0619 | -0.0988 | -0.1576 | -0.1468 | -0.1793 |

Source: Center for Research in Security Prices, University of Chicago.

Table 7-2 (continued)

## Size-Decile Portfolios of the NYSE/AMEX/NASDAQ
Year-by-Year Returns

from 1971 to 2000

|      | Decile 1 | Decile 2 | Decile 3 | Decile 4 | Decile 5 | Decile 6 | Decile 7 | Decile 8 | Decile 9 | Decile 10 |
|------|----------|----------|----------|----------|----------|----------|----------|----------|----------|-----------|
| 1971 | 0.1491   | 0.1370   | 0.1896   | 0.2401   | 0.1868   | 0.2314   | 0.2030   | 0.1834   | 0.1714   | 0.1879    |
| 1972 | 0.2225   | 0.1297   | 0.0916   | 0.0831   | 0.0805   | 0.0634   | 0.0731   | 0.0259   | -0.0170  | -0.0015   |
| 1973 | -0.1290  | -0.2207  | -0.2464  | -0.2544  | -0.3290  | -0.3187  | -0.3772  | -0.3461  | -0.3884  | -0.4201   |
| 1974 | -0.2802  | -0.2496  | -0.2379  | -0.2757  | -0.2398  | -0.2753  | -0.2694  | -0.2702  | -0.3100  | -0.2895   |
| 1975 | 0.3161   | 0.4702   | 0.5202   | 0.6432   | 0.5737   | 0.5741   | 0.6306   | 0.6813   | 0.6576   | 0.7265    |
| 1976 | 0.2081   | 0.3032   | 0.3785   | 0.4039   | 0.4559   | 0.4620   | 0.5103   | 0.5611   | 0.5350   | 0.5512    |
| 1977 | -0.0868  | -0.0401  | 0.0106   | 0.0479   | 0.1121   | 0.1500   | 0.1843   | 0.2150   | 0.2106   | 0.2282    |
| 1978 | 0.0634   | 0.0255   | 0.1123   | 0.0974   | 0.1201   | 0.1619   | 0.1608   | 0.1721   | 0.1584   | 0.2824    |
| 1979 | 0.1575   | 0.2843   | 0.3214   | 0.3639   | 0.3717   | 0.4443   | 0.4315   | 0.4504   | 0.4487   | 0.4304    |
| 1980 | 0.3253   | 0.3405   | 0.3168   | 0.3141   | 0.3175   | 0.3083   | 0.3656   | 0.3252   | 0.4007   | 0.3038    |
| 1981 | -0.0838  | 0.0145   | 0.0283   | 0.0437   | 0.0501   | 0.0672   | -0.0152  | 0.0174   | 0.0762   | 0.0799    |
| 1982 | 0.1945   | 0.1734   | 0.2066   | 0.2590   | 0.3182   | 0.2919   | 0.2861   | 0.2824   | 0.2694   | 0.2835    |
| 1983 | 0.2069   | 0.1684   | 0.2600   | 0.2683   | 0.2556   | 0.2611   | 0.2807   | 0.3598   | 0.3147   | 0.3699    |
| 1984 | 0.0839   | 0.0740   | 0.0234   | -0.0448  | -0.0270  | 0.0296   | -0.0471  | -0.0713  | -0.0914  | -0.1924   |
| 1985 | 0.3143   | 0.3752   | 0.2957   | 0.3327   | 0.3057   | 0.3153   | 0.3288   | 0.3645   | 0.3046   | 0.2569    |
| 1986 | 0.1789   | 0.1799   | 0.1670   | 0.1788   | 0.1405   | 0.0907   | 0.1191   | 0.0401   | 0.0600   | 0.0050    |
| 1987 | 0.0503   | 0.0072   | 0.0398   | 0.0169   | -0.0412  | -0.0500  | -0.0871  | -0.0768  | -0.1287  | -0.1488   |
| 1988 | 0.1480   | 0.1995   | 0.2137   | 0.2235   | 0.2138   | 0.2340   | 0.2425   | 0.2831   | 0.2273   | 0.1957    |
| 1989 | 0.3314   | 0.2982   | 0.2624   | 0.2336   | 0.2405   | 0.2135   | 0.1782   | 0.1755   | 0.1077   | 0.0651    |
| 1990 | -0.0087  | -0.0864  | -0.1013  | -0.0860  | -0.1412  | -0.1865  | -0.1526  | -0.1959  | -0.2436  | -0.3123   |
| 1991 | 0.3039   | 0.3462   | 0.4148   | 0.3869   | 0.4829   | 0.5387   | 0.4361   | 0.4728   | 0.5127   | 0.4841    |
| 1992 | 0.0475   | 0.1571   | 0.1383   | 0.1279   | 0.2551   | 0.1884   | 0.1890   | 0.1359   | 0.2448   | 0.3360    |
| 1993 | 0.0725   | 0.1342   | 0.1591   | 0.1604   | 0.1685   | 0.1695   | 0.1872   | 0.1847   | 0.1678   | 0.2549    |
| 1994 | 0.0179   | -0.0177  | -0.0406  | -0.0123  | -0.0261  | 0.0120   | -0.0290  | -0.0238  | -0.0343  | -0.0283   |
| 1995 | 0.3938   | 0.3555   | 0.3536   | 0.3248   | 0.3309   | 0.2729   | 0.3186   | 0.2999   | 0.3514   | 0.3034    |
| 1996 | 0.2373   | 0.1981   | 0.1730   | 0.1775   | 0.1562   | 0.1656   | 0.1976   | 0.1771   | 0.2048   | 0.1690    |
| 1997 | 0.3483   | 0.3010   | 0.2460   | 0.2592   | 0.1634   | 0.2820   | 0.3064   | 0.2448   | 0.2621   | 0.2162    |
| 1998 | 0.3531   | 0.1273   | 0.0785   | 0.0699   | 0.0094   | 0.0092   | -0.0091  | 0.0056   | -0.0495  | -0.1132   |
| 1999 | 0.2482   | 0.2075   | 0.3439   | 0.3019   | 0.2656   | 0.3511   | 0.2577   | 0.3956   | 0.3338   | 0.2836    |
| 2000 | -0.1348  | -0.0027  | -0.0651  | -0.0973  | -0.0673  | -0.1010  | -0.1058  | -0.1268  | -0.1285  | -0.1318   |

Source: Center for Research in Security Prices, University of Chicago.

## Table 7-3

**Size-Decile Portfolios of the NYSE/AMEX/NASDAQ**
Year-End Index Values

from 1925 to 1970

| | Decile 1 | Decile 2 | Decile 3 | Decile 4 | Decile 5 | Decile 6 | Decile 7 | Decile 8 | Decile 9 | Decile 10 |
|---|---|---|---|---|---|---|---|---|---|---|
| 1925 | 1.000 | 1.000 | 1.000 | 1.000 | 1.000 | 1.000 | 1.000 | 1.000 | 1.000 | 1.000 |
| 1926 | 1.144 | 1.055 | 1.036 | 1.009 | 1.003 | 1.034 | 0.975 | 0.907 | 0.900 | 0.940 |
| 1927 | 1.533 | 1.366 | 1.358 | 1.425 | 1.351 | 1.272 | 1.270 | 1.138 | 1.188 | 1.233 |
| 1928 | 2.129 | 1.882 | 1.899 | 1.958 | 2.022 | 1.630 | 1.718 | 1.504 | 1.632 | 2.093 |
| 1929 | 1.904 | 1.733 | 1.411 | 1.336 | 1.527 | 0.971 | 1.071 | 0.890 | 0.817 | 0.972 |
| 1930 | 1.443 | 1.084 | 0.922 | 0.879 | 0.973 | 0.604 | 0.679 | 0.449 | 0.444 | 0.528 |
| 1931 | 0.835 | 0.541 | 0.498 | 0.478 | 0.500 | 0.296 | 0.354 | 0.229 | 0.226 | 0.263 |
| 1932 | 0.735 | 0.537 | 0.489 | 0.414 | 0.443 | 0.315 | 0.296 | 0.232 | 0.225 | 0.365 |
| 1933 | 1.077 | 0.937 | 0.994 | 0.878 | 0.863 | 0.661 | 0.644 | 0.600 | 0.616 | 1.173 |
| 1934 | 1.101 | 0.990 | 1.083 | 1.035 | 0.928 | 0.805 | 0.739 | 0.766 | 0.755 | 1.546 |
| 1935 | 1.551 | 1.569 | 1.482 | 1.418 | 1.522 | 1.251 | 1.217 | 1.259 | 1.224 | 2.816 |
| 1936 | 2.010 | 2.127 | 1.905 | 2.034 | 2.223 | 1.877 | 1.851 | 1.879 | 2.244 | 5.238 |
| 1937 | 1.370 | 1.348 | 1.181 | 1.149 | 1.141 | 0.983 | 0.941 | 0.888 | 1.085 | 2.324 |
| 1938 | 1.713 | 1.814 | 1.598 | 1.538 | 1.718 | 1.409 | 1.270 | 1.291 | 1.415 | 2.534 |
| 1939 | 1.794 | 1.751 | 1.558 | 1.542 | 1.743 | 1.464 | 1.368 | 1.236 | 1.326 | 3.017 |
| 1940 | 1.667 | 1.593 | 1.422 | 1.482 | 1.724 | 1.375 | 1.284 | 1.164 | 1.267 | 2.081 |
| 1941 | 1.489 | 1.489 | 1.335 | 1.338 | 1.515 | 1.234 | 1.166 | 1.056 | 1.112 | 1.730 |
| 1942 | 1.684 | 1.849 | 1.597 | 1.613 | 1.836 | 1.538 | 1.503 | 1.379 | 1.592 | 3.069 |
| 1943 | 2.080 | 2.490 | 2.148 | 2.252 | 2.722 | 2.193 | 2.612 | 2.349 | 2.955 | 7.432 |
| 1944 | 2.433 | 3.144 | 2.660 | 2.987 | 3.797 | 3.173 | 3.586 | 3.508 | 4.632 | 12.631 |
| 1945 | 3.142 | 4.681 | 4.084 | 4.882 | 5.868 | 5.100 | 5.885 | 5.947 | 8.174 | 24.638 |
| 1946 | 3.001 | 4.466 | 3.778 | 4.241 | 5.297 | 4.759 | 4.965 | 5.077 | 7.361 | 20.113 |
| 1947 | 3.169 | 4.495 | 3.775 | 4.321 | 5.478 | 4.597 | 4.853 | 4.930 | 7.110 | 19.619 |
| 1948 | 3.286 | 4.521 | 3.853 | 4.240 | 5.399 | 4.427 | 4.711 | 4.572 | 6.633 | 18.594 |
| 1949 | 3.901 | 5.659 | 4.866 | 5.088 | 6.410 | 5.449 | 5.748 | 5.311 | 7.954 | 23.214 |
| 1950 | 5.018 | 7.272 | 6.152 | 6.701 | 8.781 | 7.330 | 7.875 | 7.476 | 11.165 | 36.145 |
| 1951 | 6.095 | 8.913 | 7.497 | 7.832 | 10.051 | 8.366 | 9.292 | 8.608 | 12.425 | 38.255 |
| 1952 | 6.966 | 10.074 | 8.373 | 8.804 | 11.165 | 9.221 | 10.207 | 9.330 | 13.500 | 38.944 |
| 1953 | 7.042 | 10.232 | 8.386 | 8.625 | 10.876 | 9.147 | 9.951 | 8.602 | 12.909 | 35.669 |
| 1954 | 10.454 | 15.189 | 13.283 | 13.025 | 17.177 | 14.584 | 15.647 | 13.197 | 21.118 | 60.112 |
| 1955 | 13.421 | 18.034 | 15.798 | 15.496 | 20.301 | 17.944 | 18.455 | 15.937 | 25.283 | 76.032 |
| 1956 | 14.466 | 20.125 | 17.034 | 16.843 | 22.016 | 19.002 | 20.030 | 16.698 | 26.772 | 74.902 |
| 1957 | 13.085 | 18.349 | 14.748 | 14.982 | 19.051 | 15.524 | 16.575 | 13.653 | 22.895 | 62.781 |
| 1958 | 18.421 | 27.448 | 22.760 | 23.804 | 29.749 | 24.258 | 27.675 | 22.730 | 39.154 | 106.497 |
| 1959 | 20.857 | 30.103 | 25.712 | 27.386 | 35.356 | 27.856 | 33.494 | 26.638 | 46.700 | 123.020 |
| 1960 | 20.842 | 31.783 | 26.881 | 27.618 | 34.951 | 27.446 | 31.645 | 25.497 | 44.941 | 112.881 |
| 1961 | 26.467 | 40.332 | 34.728 | 35.778 | 45.011 | 34.947 | 41.245 | 34.206 | 58.368 | 148.816 |
| 1962 | 24.119 | 36.454 | 30.588 | 31.378 | 37.499 | 28.822 | 34.337 | 29.187 | 48.604 | 127.645 |
| 1963 | 29.538 | 44.112 | 35.772 | 36.655 | 42.384 | 34.139 | 40.480 | 34.712 | 55.095 | 141.604 |
| 1964 | 34.253 | 50.502 | 42.898 | 42.765 | 49.427 | 39.547 | 46.874 | 40.636 | 63.857 | 171.215 |
| 1965 | 37.317 | 60.141 | 53.493 | 53.007 | 64.777 | 54.714 | 62.566 | 53.557 | 84.437 | 244.894 |
| 1966 | 33.463 | 56.965 | 50.732 | 49.819 | 60.337 | 51.802 | 56.718 | 48.829 | 79.567 | 220.233 |
| 1967 | 40.794 | 69.073 | 66.705 | 72.302 | 91.784 | 78.608 | 93.524 | 88.348 | 151.404 | 472.464 |
| 1968 | 43.891 | 80.606 | 79.852 | 86.026 | 116.224 | 102.973 | 118.361 | 123.667 | 209.377 | 760.286 |
| 1969 | 41.270 | 70.168 | 70.604 | 71.703 | 96.993 | 82.603 | 89.164 | 94.002 | 142.476 | 510.191 |
| 1970 | 42.216 | 71.641 | 72.764 | 67.035 | 91.149 | 77.491 | 80.351 | 79.187 | 121.554 | 418.689 |

Source: Center for Research in Security Prices, University of Chicago.

Table 7-3 (continued)

## Size-Decile Portfolios of the NYSE/AMEX/NASDAQ
Year-End Index Values

from 1971 to 2000

|  | Decile 1 | Decile 2 | Decile 3 | Decile 4 | Decile 5 | Decile 6 | Decile 7 | Decile 8 | Decile 9 | Decile 10 |
|---|---|---|---|---|---|---|---|---|---|---|
| 1971 | 48.511 | 81.459 | 86.558 | 83.131 | 108.174 | 95.424 | 96.662 | 93.714 | 142.390 | 497.364 |
| 1972 | 59.305 | 92.026 | 94.490 | 90.037 | 116.882 | 101.469 | 103.730 | 96.137 | 139.971 | 496.640 |
| 1973 | 51.655 | 71.715 | 71.209 | 67.129 | 78.433 | 69.126 | 64.603 | 62.865 | 85.606 | 288.002 |
| 1974 | 37.180 | 53.812 | 54.271 | 48.622 | 59.626 | 50.096 | 47.198 | 45.878 | 59.065 | 204.631 |
| 1975 | 48.934 | 79.113 | 82.501 | 79.895 | 93.831 | 78.856 | 76.962 | 77.136 | 97.907 | 353.295 |
| 1976 | 59.117 | 103.103 | 113.725 | 112.163 | 136.608 | 115.285 | 116.233 | 120.421 | 150.284 | 548.042 |
| 1977 | 53.985 | 98.968 | 114.932 | 117.537 | 151.920 | 132.577 | 137.652 | 146.305 | 181.939 | 673.097 |
| 1978 | 57.408 | 101.490 | 127.833 | 128.981 | 170.164 | 154.044 | 159.789 | 171.478 | 210.757 | 863.193 |
| 1979 | 66.452 | 130.347 | 168.919 | 175.922 | 233.419 | 222.491 | 228.744 | 248.718 | 305.326 | 1234.748 |
| 1980 | 88.068 | 174.724 | 222.437 | 231.179 | 307.530 | 291.082 | 312.369 | 329.594 | 427.670 | 1609.812 |
| 1981 | 80.689 | 177.264 | 228.739 | 241.274 | 322.930 | 310.645 | 307.607 | 335.342 | 460.266 | 1738.404 |
| 1982 | 96.384 | 208.001 | 275.995 | 303.754 | 425.697 | 401.324 | 395.616 | 430.037 | 584.281 | 2231.254 |
| 1983 | 116.326 | 243.025 | 347.746 | 385.257 | 534.511 | 506.122 | 506.671 | 584.779 | 768.127 | 3056.643 |
| 1984 | 126.081 | 261.015 | 355.891 | 368.006 | 520.101 | 521.097 | 482.816 | 543.069 | 697.900 | 2468.535 |
| 1985 | 165.713 | 358.959 | 461.112 | 490.443 | 679.120 | 685.411 | 641.542 | 741.034 | 910.462 | 3102.632 |
| 1986 | 195.360 | 423.523 | 538.115 | 578.141 | 774.520 | 747.552 | 717.941 | 770.782 | 965.113 | 3118.172 |
| 1987 | 205.190 | 426.570 | 559.552 | 587.917 | 742.619 | 710.171 | 655.392 | 711.561 | 840.950 | 2654.171 |
| 1988 | 235.557 | 511.677 | 679.137 | 719.345 | 901.359 | 876.353 | 814.346 | 913.021 | 1032.095 | 3173.665 |
| 1989 | 313.612 | 664.262 | 857.371 | 887.362 | 1118.120 | 1063.422 | 959.477 | 1073.216 | 1143.219 | 3380.150 |
| 1990 | 310.879 | 606.840 | 770.500 | 811.074 | 960.209 | 865.115 | 813.015 | 862.980 | 864.675 | 2324.494 |
| 1991 | 405.358 | 816.936 | 1090.134 | 1124.838 | 1423.882 | 1331.114 | 1167.574 | 1270.995 | 1307.970 | 3449.845 |
| 1992 | 424.605 | 945.253 | 1240.868 | 1268.691 | 1787.159 | 1581.858 | 1388.225 | 1443.690 | 1628.222 | 4608.897 |
| 1993 | 455.390 | 1072.121 | 1438.276 | 1472.201 | 2088.356 | 1849.904 | 1648.078 | 1710.299 | 1901.360 | 5783.583 |
| 1994 | 463.547 | 1053.180 | 1379.846 | 1454.110 | 2033.893 | 1872.110 | 1600.345 | 1669.613 | 1836.202 | 5619.807 |
| 1995 | 646.077 | 1427.589 | 1867.820 | 1926.424 | 2706.957 | 2383.059 | 2110.189 | 2170.317 | 2481.446 | 7324.700 |
| 1996 | 799.398 | 1710.342 | 2191.023 | 2268.310 | 3129.798 | 2777.758 | 2527.097 | 2554.667 | 2989.660 | 8562.717 |
| 1997 | 1077.829 | 2225.088 | 2730.063 | 2856.246 | 3641.131 | 3561.012 | 3301.384 | 3180.068 | 3773.374 | 10414.166 |
| 1998 | 1458.434 | 2508.347 | 2944.442 | 3056.029 | 3675.519 | 3593.802 | 3271.334 | 3197.883 | 3586.414 | 9235.689 |
| 1999 | 1820.479 | 3028.936 | 3956.989 | 3978.680 | 4651.748 | 4855.414 | 4114.203 | 4462.869 | 4783.501 | 11854.826 |
| 2000 | 1575.162 | 3020.830 | 3699.404 | 3591.382 | 4338.508 | 4365.171 | 3678.753 | 3896.802 | 4168.781 | 10291.940 |

Source: Center for Research in Security Prices, University of Chicago.

Table 7-4

**Size-Decile Portfolios of the NYSE/AMEX/NASDAQ**
Mid-, Low-, Micro-, and Total Capitalization Returns and Index Values

from 1926 to 1965

| Year | Total Return | | | | Index Value | | | |
|------|--------------|--|--|--|-------------|--|--|--|
| | Mid-Cap Stocks | Low-Cap Stocks | Micro-Cap Stocks | Total Value Weighted NYSE/ AMEX/ NASDAQ | Mid-Cap Stocks | Low-Cap Stocks | Micro-Cap Stocks | Total Value Weighted NYSE/ AMEX/ NASDAQ |
| 1925 | | | | | 1.000 | 1.000 | 1.000 | 1.000 |
| 1926 | 0.0217 | -0.0129 | -0.0891 | 0.0952 | 1.022 | 0.987 | 0.911 | 1.095 |
| 1927 | 0.3471 | 0.2591 | 0.3151 | 0.3301 | 1.376 | 1.243 | 1.198 | 1.457 |
| 1928 | 0.4100 | 0.3121 | 0.4502 | 0.3872 | 1.941 | 1.631 | 1.737 | 2.021 |
| 1929 | -0.2714 | -0.3967 | -0.5081 | -0.1452 | 1.414 | 0.984 | 0.855 | 1.728 |
| 1930 | -0.3476 | -0.3979 | -0.4569 | -0.2827 | 0.923 | 0.592 | 0.464 | 1.239 |
| 1931 | -0.4637 | -0.4968 | -0.4960 | -0.4392 | 0.495 | 0.298 | 0.234 | 0.695 |
| 1932 | -0.0679 | -0.0223 | 0.0908 | -0.0975 | 0.461 | 0.291 | 0.255 | 0.627 |
| 1933 | 1.0415 | 1.2177 | 1.8718 | 0.5759 | 0.941 | 0.646 | 0.733 | 0.988 |
| 1934 | 0.1137 | 0.2056 | 0.2513 | 0.0435 | 1.048 | 0.779 | 0.917 | 1.031 |
| 1935 | 0.4145 | 0.6020 | 0.6754 | 0.4398 | 1.483 | 1.248 | 1.536 | 1.485 |
| 1936 | 0.3641 | 0.5064 | 0.8447 | 0.3226 | 2.023 | 1.880 | 2.834 | 1.964 |
| 1937 | -0.4194 | -0.4916 | -0.5271 | -0.3463 | 1.174 | 0.956 | 1.340 | 1.284 |
| 1938 | 0.3773 | 0.4110 | 0.2466 | 0.2824 | 1.617 | 1.349 | 1.670 | 1.646 |
| 1939 | -0.0085 | 0.0350 | -0.0015 | 0.0283 | 1.604 | 1.396 | 1.668 | 1.693 |
| 1940 | -0.0574 | -0.0605 | -0.1213 | -0.0717 | 1.512 | 1.312 | 1.466 | 1.572 |
| 1941 | -0.0844 | -0.0968 | -0.1322 | -0.0986 | 1.384 | 1.185 | 1.272 | 1.417 |
| 1942 | 0.2023 | 0.2715 | 0.5101 | 0.1591 | 1.664 | 1.506 | 1.921 | 1.642 |
| 1943 | 0.3869 | 0.5799 | 0.9979 | 0.2836 | 2.308 | 2.380 | 3.837 | 2.107 |
| 1944 | 0.2961 | 0.4325 | 0.6053 | 0.2131 | 2.991 | 3.409 | 6.159 | 2.556 |
| 1945 | 0.5678 | 0.6386 | 0.8224 | 0.3798 | 4.690 | 5.586 | 11.225 | 3.527 |
| 1946 | -0.0975 | -0.1154 | -0.1280 | -0.0592 | 4.233 | 4.941 | 9.789 | 3.319 |
| 1947 | 0.0127 | -0.0293 | -0.0309 | 0.0356 | 4.287 | 4.797 | 9.487 | 3.437 |
| 1948 | 0.0008 | -0.0428 | -0.0615 | 0.0217 | 4.290 | 4.592 | 8.903 | 3.511 |
| 1949 | 0.2272 | 0.2117 | 0.2156 | 0.2034 | 5.264 | 5.564 | 10.822 | 4.226 |
| 1950 | 0.3026 | 0.3675 | 0.4548 | 0.2945 | 6.857 | 7.608 | 15.744 | 5.470 |
| 1951 | 0.1870 | 0.1562 | 0.0941 | 0.2075 | 8.140 | 8.797 | 17.225 | 6.605 |
| 1952 | 0.1179 | 0.0970 | 0.0636 | 0.1342 | 9.100 | 9.650 | 18.321 | 7.492 |
| 1953 | -0.0106 | -0.0288 | -0.0568 | 0.0059 | 9.003 | 9.372 | 17.281 | 7.536 |
| 1954 | 0.5607 | 0.5749 | 0.6513 | 0.5009 | 14.051 | 14.759 | 28.536 | 11.310 |
| 1955 | 0.1876 | 0.2093 | 0.2184 | 0.2521 | 16.687 | 17.848 | 34.767 | 14.161 |
| 1956 | 0.0822 | 0.0649 | 0.0353 | 0.0824 | 18.058 | 19.007 | 35.993 | 15.329 |
| 1957 | -0.1270 | -0.1796 | -0.1503 | -0.1027 | 15.765 | 15.592 | 30.582 | 13.754 |
| 1958 | 0.5607 | 0.6177 | 0.7058 | 0.4500 | 24.604 | 25.224 | 52.168 | 19.943 |
| 1959 | 0.1477 | 0.1729 | 0.1811 | 0.1315 | 28.239 | 29.586 | 61.618 | 22.567 |
| 1960 | 0.0227 | -0.0337 | -0.0511 | 0.0084 | 28.879 | 28.588 | 58.467 | 22.756 |
| 1961 | 0.2922 | 0.2972 | 0.3048 | 0.2743 | 37.318 | 37.085 | 76.285 | 28.999 |
| 1962 | -0.1301 | -0.1674 | -0.1619 | -0.1021 | 32.463 | 30.879 | 63.936 | 26.039 |
| 1963 | 0.1614 | 0.1843 | 0.1209 | 0.2093 | 37.703 | 36.569 | 71.666 | 31.489 |
| 1964 | 0.1832 | 0.1607 | 0.1861 | 0.1616 | 44.608 | 42.446 | 85.003 | 36.577 |
| 1965 | 0.2571 | 0.3514 | 0.3800 | 0.1442 | 56.076 | 57.362 | 117.306 | 41.853 |

Source: Center for Research in Security Prices, University of Chicago.

## Table 7-4 (continued)

### Size-Decile Portfolios of the NYSE/AMEX/NASDAQ
Mid-, Low-, Micro-, and Total Capitalization Returns and Index Values

from 1966 to 2000

| | Total Return | | | | Index Value | | | |
|---|---|---|---|---|---|---|---|---|
| Year | Mid-Cap Stocks | Low-Cap Stocks | Micro-Cap Stocks | Total Value Weighted NYSE/ AMEX/ NASDAQ | Mid-Cap Stocks | Low-Cap Stocks | Micro-Cap Stocks | Total Value Weighted NYSE/ AMEX/ NASDAQ |
| 1966 | -0.0577 | -0.0740 | -0.0819 | -0.0871 | 52.841 | 53.115 | 107.698 | 38.209 |
| 1967 | 0.3985 | 0.6338 | 1.0339 | 0.2872 | 73.896 | 86.778 | 219.044 | 49.181 |
| 1968 | 0.2103 | 0.3187 | 0.5050 | 0.1419 | 89.435 | 114.439 | 329.651 | 56.161 |
| 1969 | -0.1430 | -0.2248 | -0.3251 | -0.1094 | 76.644 | 88.713 | 222.470 | 50.020 |
| 1970 | -0.0198 | -0.0991 | -0.1662 | 0.0003 | 75.130 | 79.918 | 185.502 | 50.033 |
| 1971 | 0.2041 | 0.2090 | 0.1813 | 0.1616 | 90.464 | 96.623 | 219.136 | 58.116 |
| 1972 | 0.0868 | 0.0572 | -0.0088 | 0.1690 | 98.314 | 102.152 | 217.206 | 67.938 |
| 1973 | -0.2655 | -0.3441 | -0.4068 | -0.1816 | 72.207 | 66.999 | 128.854 | 55.603 |
| 1974 | -0.2495 | -0.2723 | -0.2980 | -0.2717 | 54.194 | 48.758 | 90.460 | 40.493 |
| 1975 | 0.5659 | 0.6184 | 0.6957 | 0.3867 | 84.861 | 78.909 | 153.395 | 56.151 |
| 1976 | 0.4011 | 0.5007 | 0.5438 | 0.2673 | 118.895 | 118.419 | 236.809 | 71.158 |
| 1977 | 0.0414 | 0.1753 | 0.2196 | -0.0421 | 123.820 | 139.176 | 288.817 | 68.162 |
| 1978 | 0.1094 | 0.1647 | 0.2226 | 0.0749 | 137.362 | 162.102 | 353.118 | 73.266 |
| 1979 | 0.3442 | 0.4424 | 0.4398 | 0.2301 | 184.644 | 233.811 | 508.424 | 90.121 |
| 1980 | 0.3164 | 0.3297 | 0.3541 | 0.3266 | 243.073 | 310.891 | 688.478 | 119.558 |
| 1981 | 0.0378 | 0.0294 | 0.0769 | -0.0367 | 252.263 | 320.016 | 741.402 | 115.168 |
| 1982 | 0.2464 | 0.2884 | 0.2759 | 0.2088 | 314.431 | 412.299 | 945.978 | 139.211 |
| 1983 | 0.2617 | 0.2887 | 0.3424 | 0.2198 | 396.715 | 531.314 | 1269.875 | 169.814 |
| 1984 | -0.0106 | -0.0209 | -0.1396 | 0.0448 | 392.518 | 520.236 | 1092.660 | 177.423 |
| 1985 | 0.3100 | 0.3319 | 0.2815 | 0.3217 | 514.205 | 692.892 | 1400.198 | 234.492 |
| 1986 | 0.1643 | 0.0875 | 0.0341 | 0.1613 | 598.680 | 753.535 | 1447.986 | 272.326 |
| 1987 | 0.0124 | -0.0678 | -0.1392 | 0.0172 | 606.131 | 702.416 | 1246.375 | 277.023 |
| 1988 | 0.2171 | 0.2481 | 0.2100 | 0.1800 | 737.697 | 876.666 | 1508.152 | 326.879 |
| 1989 | 0.2481 | 0.1925 | 0.0874 | 0.2895 | 920.690 | 1045.420 | 1639.918 | 421.507 |
| 1990 | -0.1048 | -0.1777 | -0.2730 | -0.0595 | 824.197 | 859.635 | 1192.164 | 396.428 |
| 1991 | 0.4195 | 0.4877 | 0.5056 | 0.3469 | 1169.938 | 1278.854 | 1794.958 | 533.941 |
| 1992 | 0.1608 | 0.1750 | 0.2779 | 0.0978 | 1358.009 | 1502.645 | 2293.771 | 586.185 |
| 1993 | 0.1625 | 0.1801 | 0.2018 | 0.1112 | 1578.700 | 1773.310 | 2756.665 | 651.346 |
| 1994 | -0.0283 | -0.0112 | -0.0328 | -0.0005 | 1533.984 | 1753.452 | 2666.191 | 650.991 |
| 1995 | 0.3396 | 0.2948 | 0.3321 | 0.3681 | 2054.999 | 2270.435 | 3551.516 | 890.624 |
| 1996 | 0.1705 | 0.1791 | 0.1901 | 0.2138 | 2405.475 | 2677.159 | 4226.814 | 1081.042 |
| 1997 | 0.2318 | 0.2780 | 0.2417 | 0.3134 | 2963.182 | 3421.402 | 5248.643 | 1419.790 |
| 1998 | 0.0604 | 0.0028 | -0.0801 | 0.2440 | 3142.226 | 3431.055 | 4828.002 | 1766.287 |
| 1999 | 0.3153 | 0.3316 | 0.3126 | 0.2561 | 4132.985 | 4568.762 | 6337.249 | 2218.570 |
| 2000 | -0.0754 | -0.1083 | -0.1287 | -0.1132 | 3821.460 | 4074.145 | 5521.355 | 1967.354 |

Source: Center for Research in Security Prices, University of Chicago.

Graph 7-1

**Size-Decile Portfolios of the NYSE/AMEX/NASDAQ: Wealth Indices of Investments in Mid-,
Low-, Micro-, and Total Capitalization Stocks**
Year-End 1925 = $1.00

from 1925 to 2000

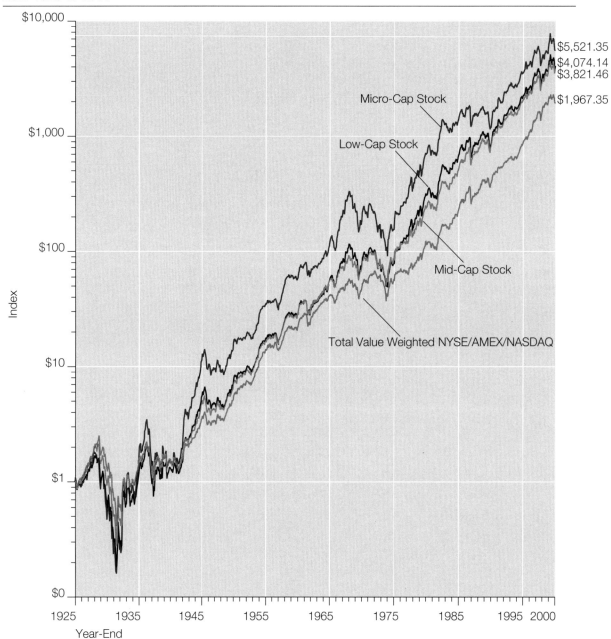

## Size of the Deciles

Table 7-5 reveals that most of the market value of the stocks listed on the NYSE/AMEX/NASDAQ is represented by the top three deciles. Approximately two-thirds of the value is represented by the first decile, which currently consists of 237 stocks. The smallest decile represents less than one percent of the market value of the NYSE/AMEX/NASDAQ. The data in the second column of Table 7-5 are averages across all 75 years. Of course, the proportions represented by the various deciles vary from year to year.

In columns three and four are the number of companies and market capitalization. These present a snapshot of the structure of the deciles near the end of 2000.

The lower portion of Table 7-5 shows the largest firm in each decile and its market capitalization.

Table 7-5
**Size-Decile Portfolios of the NYSE/AMEX/NASDAQ:**
Bounds, Size, and Composition

from 1926 to 2000

| Decile | Historical Average Percentage of Total Capitalization | Recent Number of Companies | Recent Decile Market Capitalization (in thousands) | Recent Percentage of Total Capitalization |
|---|---|---|---|---|
| 1-Largest | 63.13% | 237 | $11,757,098,230 | 72.56% |
| 2 | 14.07% | 262 | 1,797,427,043 | 11.09% |
| 3 | 7.64% | 285 | 864,872,122 | 5.34% |
| 4 | 4.78% | 327 | 546,712,821 | 3.37% |
| 5 | 3.26% | 364 | 400,422,531 | 2.47% |
| 6 | 2.37% | 412 | 286,627,260 | 1.77% |
| 7 | 1.72% | 482 | 221,635,399 | 1.37% |
| 8 | 1.27% | 517 | 137,729,312 | 0.85% |
| 9 | 0.97% | 869 | 116,702,549 | 0.72% |
| 10-Smallest | 0.80% | 1927 | 74,292,170 | 0.46% |
| Mid-Cap 3–5 | 15.68% | 976 | 1,812,007,474 | 11.18% |
| Low-Cap 6–8 | 5.36% | 1411 | 645,991,971 | 3.99% |
| Micro-Cap 9–10 | 1.76% | 2796 | 190,994,719 | 1.18% |

Source: Center for Research in Security Prices, University of Chicago.

Historical average percentage of total capitalization shows the average, over the last 75 years, of the decile market values as a percentage of the total NYSE/AMEX/NASDAQ calculated each year. Number of companies in deciles, recent market capitalization of deciles and recent percentage of total capitalization are as of September 30, 2000.

| Decile | Recent Market Capitalization (in thousands) | Company Name |
|---|---|---|
| 1-Largest | $524,351,578 | General Electric Co. |
| 2 | 10,343,765 | National City Corp. |
| 3 | 4,143,902 | Reader's Digest Association Inc. |
| 4 | 2,177,448 | Engelhard Corp. |
| 5 | 1,327,582 | Price Communications Corp. |
| 6 | 840,000 | Student Loan Corp. |
| 7 | 537,693 | APAC Customer Services Inc. |
| 8 | 333,442 | IHOP Corp. New |
| 9 | 192,598 | SCPIE Holdings Inc. |
| 10-Smallest | 84,521 | Fibermark Inc. |

Source: Center for Research in Security Prices, University of Chicago.

Market capitalization and name of largest company in each decile as of September 30, 2000.

## Long-Term Returns in Excess of Risk

The Capital Asset Pricing Model (CAPM) does not fully account for the higher returns of small company stocks. Table 7-6 shows the returns in excess of risk over the past 75 years for each decile of the NYSE/AMEX/NASDAQ.

The CAPM can be expressed as follows:

$$k_S = r_f + (\beta_s \times ERP) \qquad \text{(28)}$$

where,

| | | |
|---|---|---|
| $k_s$ | = | the expected return for company **s**; |
| $r_f$ | = | the expected return of the riskless asset; |
| $\beta_s$ | = | the beta of the stock of company **s**; and, |
| **ERP** | = | the expected equity risk premium, or the amount by which investors expect the future return on equities to exceed that on the riskless asset. |

The amount of an asset's systematic risk is measured by its beta. A beta greater than 1 indicates that the security is riskier than the market, and according to the CAPM equation, investors are compensated for taking on this additional risk. However, based on historical return data on the NYSE/AMEX/NASDAQ decile portfolios, the smaller deciles have had returns that are not fully explainable by the CAPM. This return in excess of CAPM, grows larger as one moves from the largest companies in decile 1 to the smallest in decile 10. The excess return is especially pronounced for micro-cap stocks (deciles 9–10). This size related phenomenon has prompted a revision to the CAPM, which includes the addition of a size premium.

The CAPM is used here to calculate the CAPM return in excess of the riskless rate and to compare this estimate to historical performance. According to the CAPM, the return on a security should consist of the riskless rate, in this case 5.2 percent, plus an additional return to compensate for the risk of the security. Table 7-6 uses the 75-year arithmetic mean income return component of 20-year government bonds as the historical riskless rate. (However, it is appropriate to match the maturity, or duration, of the riskless asset with the investment horizon.) This CAPM return in excess of the riskless rate is β (beta) multiplied by the realized equity risk premium. The realized equity risk premium is the return that compensates investors for taking on risk equal to the risk of the market as a whole (estimated by the 75-year arithmetic mean return on large company stocks, 13.0 percent, less the historical riskless rate, 5.2 percent). The difference between the excess return predicted by the CAPM and the realized excess return is the size premium, or return in excess of CAPM.

This phenomenon can also be viewed graphically, as depicted in the Graph 7-2. The security market line is based on the pure CAPM without adjusting for the size premium. Based on the risk (or beta) of a security, the expected return should fluctuate along the security market line. However, the expected returns for the smaller deciles of the NYSE/AMEX/NASDAQ lie above the line, indicating that these deciles have had returns in excess of their risk.

## Table 7-6
**Size-Decile Portfolios of the NYSE/AMEX/NASDAQ:**
Long-Term Returns in Excess of CAPM

from 1926 to 2000

| Decile | Beta* | Arithmetic Mean Return | Actual Return in Excess of Riskless Rate** | CAPM Return in Excess of Riskless Rate** | Size Premium (Return in Excess of CAPM) |
|---|---|---|---|---|---|
| 1 | 0.91% | 12.06% | 6.84% | 7.03% | −0.20% |
| 2 | 1.04 | 13.58% | 8.36% | 8.05% | −0.31% |
| 3 | 1.09 | 14.16% | 8.93% | 8.47% | 0.47% |
| 4 | 1.13 | 14.60% | 9.38% | 8.75% | 0.62% |
| 5 | 1.16 | 15.18% | 9.95% | 9.03% | 0.93% |
| 6 | 1.18 | 15.48% | 10.26% | 9.18% | 1.08% |
| 7 | 1.24 | 15.68% | 10.46% | 9.58% | 0.88% |
| 8 | 1.28 | 16.60% | 11.38% | 9.91% | 1.47% |
| 9 | 1.34 | 17.39% | 12.17% | 10.43% | 1.74% |
| 10 | 1.42 | 20.90% | 15.67% | 11.05% | 4.63% |
| Mid-Cap, 3–5 | 1.12 | 14.46% | 9.23% | 8.65% | 0.58% |
| Low-Cap, 6–8 | 1.22 | 15.75% | 10.52% | 9.45% | 1.07% |
| Micro-Cap, 9–10 | 1.36 | 18.41% | 13.18% | 10.56% | 2.62% |

*Betas are estimated from monthly returns in excess of the 30-day U.S. Treasury bill total return,
January 1926–December 2000.

**Historical riskless rate measured by the 75-year arithmetic mean income return component of 20-year
government bonds (5.22).

## Graph 7-2
**Size-Decile Portfolios of the NYSE/AMEX/NASDAQ:**
Security Market Line

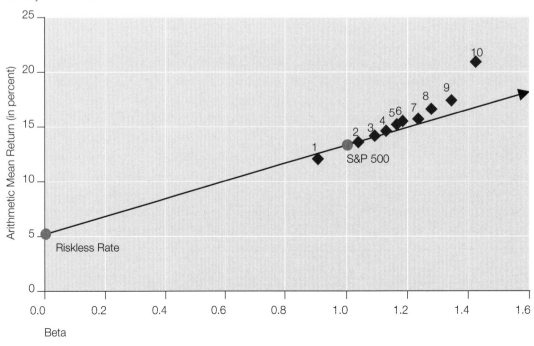

## Serial Correlation in Small Company Stock Returns

The serial correlation, or first-order autocorrelation, of returns on large capitalization stocks is near zero. [See Table 7-1.] If stock returns are serially correlated, then one can gain some information about future performance based on past returns. For the smallest deciles of stocks, the serial correlation is near or above 0.1. This observation bears further examination.

Table 7-7

**Size-Decile Portfolios of the NYSE/ AMEX/NASDAQ:**

Serial Correlations of Annual Returns in Excess of Decile 1 Returns

| Decile | Serial Correlations of Annual Returns in Excess of Decile 1 Return |
|---|---|
| Decile 2 | 0.21 |
| Decile 3 | 0.28 |
| Decile 4 | 0.23 |
| Decile 5 | 0.26 |
| Decile 6 | 0.36 |
| Decile 7 | 0.30 |
| Decile 8 | 0.37 |
| Decile 9 | 0.36 |
| Decile 10 | 0.41 |

To remove the randomizing effect of the market as a whole, the returns for decile 1 are geometrically subtracted from the returns for deciles 2 through 10. The result illustrates that these series differences exhibit greater serial correlation than the decile series themselves. Table 7-7 above presents the serial correlations of the excess returns for deciles 2 through 10. These serial correlations suggest some predictability of smaller company excess returns. However, caution is necessary. The serial correlation of small company excess returns for non-calendar years (February through January, etc.) do not always confirm the results shown here for calendar (January through December) years. The results for the non-calendar years (not shown in this book) suggest that predicting small company excess returns may not be easy.

## Seasonality

Unlike the returns on large company stocks, the returns on small company stocks appear to be seasonal. In January, small company stocks often outperform larger stocks by amounts far greater than in any other month.

Table 7-8 shows the returns of capitalization deciles 2 through 10 in excess of the return on decile 1. This table segregates excess returns into months. For each decile and for each month, the exhibit shows both the average excess return as well as the number of times the excess return is positive. These two statistics measure the seasonality of the excess return in different ways. The average excess return illustrates the size of the effect, while the number of positive excess returns shows the reliability of the effect.

Virtually all of the small stock effect occurs in January. The excess outcomes of the other months are on net, mostly negative for small company stocks. Excess returns in January relate to size in a precisely rank-ordered fashion. This "January effect" seems to pervade all size groups.

Table 7-8
**Size-Decile Portfolios of the NYSE/AMEX/NASDAQ:**
Returns in Excess of Decile 1 (in percent)

from 1926 to 2000

**First row: average excess return in percent**
**Second row: number of times excess return was positive (in 75 years)**

| Decile | Jan | Feb | Mar | Apr | May | Jun | Jul | Aug | Sep | Oct | Nov | Dec | Total (Jan–Dec) |
|---|---|---|---|---|---|---|---|---|---|---|---|---|---|
| 2 | 0.84% | 0.44% | -0.12% | -0.40% | 0.01% | -0.14% | 0.03% | 0.21% | 0.07% | -0.27% | 0.08% | 0.34% | 1.13% |
|   | 54 | 47 | 32 | 27 | 35 | 36 | 36 | 42 | 41 | 33 | 39 | 39 | |
| 3 | 1.20% | 0.31% | -0.02% | -0.21% | -0.30% | -0.20% | 0.04% | 0.33% | 0.05% | -0.44% | 0.44% | 0.26% | 1.53% |
|   | 55 | 49 | 36 | 27 | 31 | 32 | 38 | 45 | 40 | 30 | 41 | 42 | |
| 4 | 1.34% | 0.46% | -0.04% | -0.27% | -0.03% | -0.14% | 0.02% | 0.27% | 0.12% | -0.83% | 0.26% | 0.36% | 1.64% |
|   | 52 | 47 | 36 | 32 | 34 | 32 | 36 | 45 | 37 | 26 | 42 | 42 | |
| 5 | 2.28% | 0.59% | -0.19% | -0.44% | -0.25% | -0.08% | 0.03% | 0.27% | 0.16% | -0.89% | 0.24% | 0.30% | 2.10% |
|   | 56 | 45 | 34 | 28 | 29 | 32 | 37 | 42 | 39 | 28 | 41 | 38 | |
| 6 | 2.65% | 0.58% | -0.38% | -0.25% | 0.13% | -0.29% | 0.03% | 0.50% | 0.23% | -1.39% | 0.14% | 0.19% | 2.34% |
|   | 57 | 48 | 37 | 31 | 34 | 32 | 40 | 42 | 40 | 29 | 39 | 39 | |
| 7 | 3.24% | 0.71% | -0.34% | -0.24% | 0.01% | -0.55% | 0.07% | 0.15% | 0.34% | -1.16% | 0.01% | -0.06% | 2.25% |
|   | 58 | 50 | 37 | 33 | 31 | 30 | 33 | 34 | 41 | 28 | 36 | 35 | |
| 8 | 4.44% | 0.85% | -0.56% | -0.56% | 0.30% | -0.72% | 0.24% | 0.01% | 0.16% | -1.21% | 0.04% | -0.40% | 2.87% |
|   | 58 | 47 | 32 | 30 | 28 | 31 | 34 | 36 | 38 | 29 | 32 | 33 | |
| 9 | 5.89% | 1.11% | -0.31% | -0.35% | 0.03% | -0.65% | 0.17% | 0.09% | -0.05% | -1.41% | -0.11% | -1.19% | 3.39% |
|   | 60 | 44 | 36 | 30 | 30 | 27 | 34 | 38 | 34 | 26 | 31 | 31 | |
| 10 | 9.17% | 1.14% | -0.96% | 0.00% | 0.34% | -0.90% | 0.55% | -0.17% | 0.59% | -1.58% | -0.62% | -1.98% | 6.18% |
|   | 68 | 40 | 31 | 34 | 32 | 27 | 34 | 27 | 38 | 25 | 28 | 24 | |

# Chapter 8
## Growth and Value Investing

## Discussion of Style Investing

The concept of equity investment style has come into being over the past thirty years or so. Investment style can broadly be defined as common types of characteristics that groups of stocks or portfolios share. Probably the first discussion and consideration of style related to large company versus small company investing, and even this distinction was not too prominent until the 1960s. Now, styles of investing are broken down into more detail and used for performance measurement, asset allocation, and other purposes. Mutual funds and other investment portfolios are often measured against broad growth or value benchmarks. In some cases, investment manager-specific style benchmarks are constructed to separate pure stock selection ability from style effects.

Most investors agree on the broad definitions of growth and value, but when it comes to specific definitions, there are many ways of defining a growth stock and a value stock. In fact, a value investor may hold a stock that fits his or her definition of value, while a growth investor may hold the same stock because it fits his or her definition of growth. In general, growth stocks have high relative growth rates of earnings, sales, or return on equity. Growth stocks usually have relatively high price-to-earnings and price-to-book ratios. Value stocks will generally have lower price-to-earnings and price-to-book values, and often have higher dividend yields. Value stocks are often turn-around opportunities, companies that have had disappointing news, or companies with low growth prospects. Value investors generally believe that a value stock has been unfairly beaten down by the market, making the stock sell below its "intrinsic" value. Therefore, they buy the stock with the hope that the market will realize its full value and bid the price up to its fair value.

Using growth and value series that will be described later in this chapter, Graph 8-1 depicts the growth of $1.00 invested in all growth and all value stocks from the end of 1927 to the end of 2000. All results assume reinvestment of dividends and exclude transaction costs. This chart shows that the return of value stocks was much greater than that of growth stocks over the 73-year period. Value stocks grew to $7,755.39 as opposed to $932.13 for growth stocks. The extra return from value stocks was accompanied by higher volatility, as the standard deviation of growth and value stocks were 21.3 percent and 30.5 percent, respectively.

## Different Ways of Measuring Growth and Value

In order to objectively measure the performance of value and growth stocks, several different data providers have constructed value and growth indices, both for large- and small-capitalization stocks. Each index provider uses a different methodology to draw the line between growth and value, but all of the methodologies rely on some combination of accounting data, analyst growth estimates, and market capitalization. Three of the more prominent growth/value index providers are S&P/BARRA, Russell, and Wilshire.

S&P/BARRA starts with the universe of all companies in the S&P 500™ for their large-cap series. Companies are ranked by price-to-book, and the growth/value breakpoint is set where the total market capitalization of the growth and value indices are equal. Low price-to-book stocks are put in the value index, and high price-to-book stocks are put in the growth index. Because many of the growth stocks are also large-cap stocks, the growth index currently has about one-third as many

Graph 8-1

**All Growth Stocks vs. All Value Stocks**
Year-End 1927 = $1.00

from 1927 to 2000

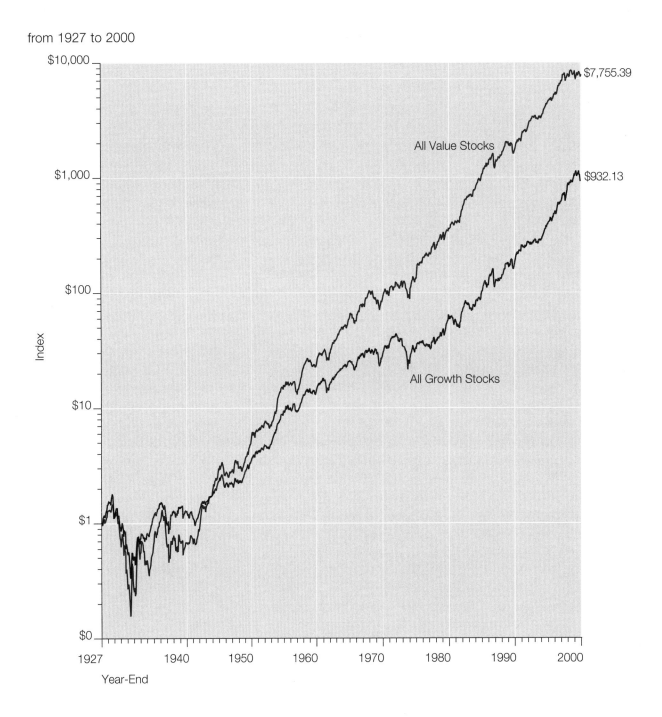

stocks and about three times the weighted average market capitalization as the value index. The large-cap style indices are available from January 1975, and small-cap indices are available from January 1994.

Russell also has large- and small-cap style indices. To determine growth or value, each company is first ranked by a composite score of price-to-book and Institutional Brokers' Estimate System (IBES) mean analyst long-term growth estimate. Using this score and a proprietary algorithm, 70 percent of companies are classified as all value or all growth, and 30 percent are weighted proportionately to both value and growth. Both the large- and small-cap style indices are available from January 1979.

Wilshire uses a proprietary model to determine growth or value using factors that include earnings growth, sales growth, return on equity, dividend yield, and price-to-book. Both the large- and small-cap style indices are available from January 1978.

It is evident that the prominent index providers use different measures to determine value and growth, and use different techniques for constructing portfolios. None of these three providers have growth and value indices going back before 1975. Growth and value stocks were certainly around before then, but much of the accounting data is not readily available today. However, Eugene Fama and Ken French constructed growth and value indices for both large- and small-cap stocks back to 1928 using data from both Compustat and hand-collected data for the early years of the series. The Fama-French series use book-to-market to define value and growth. A detailed description of their index construction methodology follows.

## Growth and Value Index Construction Methodology

As discussed earlier, most growth and value indices go only as far back as the mid-1970s. Due to the long data history of the Fama-French series, we have chosen these indices to use for our analysis of growth and value investing. The indices were constructed by applying the same methodology to define value and growth over the entire time period.

Fama-French use all stocks traded on the New York Stock Exchange (NYSE) to set both growth/value and small/large breakpoints. They then apply these breakpoints to all stocks traded on NYSE, AMEX, and NASDAQ to construct each index.

The market capitalization breakpoint between small and large stocks is set as the median market capitalization of NYSE stocks. This breakpoint is then applied to all stocks traded on NYSE, AMEX, and NASDAQ.

To define value and growth, Fama-French use the book value of equity (BE) divided by market capitalization (ME), which is the inverse of how much investors are willing to pay for a dollar of book value. Value companies will have a high book-to-market ratio, while growth companies will have a low book-to-market ratio. Fama-French used Compustat as their data source to calculate book value from 1963 forward, and hand-collected data for 1928 to 1962.

Book value was calculated as follows:

$$BV = SE + DT + ITC - PS \qquad (29)$$

where,

| | | |
|---|---|---|
| **BV** | = | Fama-French book value; |
| **SE** | = | book value of stockholders' equity; |
| **DT** | = | balance sheet deferred taxes; |
| **ITC** | = | investment tax credit (if available); and, |
| **PS** | = | book value of preferred stock. Depending on availability, either redemption, liquidation, or par value (in that order) is used to estimate book value of preferred stock. |

Stocks are put into three groups based on book-to-market: low, medium, or high. The definition of low, medium, and high is based on the breakpoints for the bottom 30 percent, middle 40 percent, and top 30 percent of the value of book-to-market for NYSE stocks. These breakpoints are then applied to all NYSE, AMEX, and NASDAQ stocks. For the growth/value analysis shown in this chapter, only the low and high portfolios are used. The medium portfolios, which are blends of growth and value, are not shown.

Firms with negative book values are not used when calculating the book-to-market breakpoints or when calculating size-specific book-to-market breakpoints. Also, only firms with ordinary common equity (as classified by CRSP) are included in the portfolios. This excludes ADRs, REITs, and unit trusts.

The four size-specific style indices used in this chapter are small value, small growth, large value, and large growth. These portfolios are defined as the intersections of the two size groups and the low and high book-to-market groups. An all-capitalization value index called "all value" is created by taking the market-cap weighted return of small value and large value, and the same procedure is used to calculate an all-capitalization growth index called "all growth."

## Historical Returns on Growth and Value

Graph 8-2 breaks down the growth of $1.00 chart into small growth, small value, large growth, and large value stocks from the end of 1927 to the end of 2000.

### Small Growth Stocks

One dollar invested in small growth stocks at the end of December 1927 grew to $727.31 by year-end 2000. The compound annual growth rate was 9.4 percent, which was the lowest annualized return among all four series included in this chart.

### Small Value Stocks

Over the period from 1928 to 2000, small value stocks outperformed all other stock series in the graph. One dollar invested in small value stocks at the end of 1927 grew to $16,027.07 by year-end 2000. Its compound annual total return was 14.2 percent for the 73-year period.

### Large Growth Stocks

Large growth stocks outperformed small growth stocks with a compound annual total return of 10.0 percent. One dollar invested in large growth stocks at the end of December 1927 was worth $1,017.38 at the end of 2000.

### Large Value Stocks

Large value stocks, initialized at $1.00 at year-end 1927, closed at $5,169.57 at year-end 2000. The annual compound growth rate was 12.4 percent, well ahead of both small growth and large growth, but lagging behind small value stocks.

## Summary Statistics for Growth and Value Series

Table 8-1 shows summary statistics of annual total returns for small growth, small value, large growth, large value, all growth, and all value stocks. The summary statistics presented are geometric mean, arithmetic mean, and standard deviation.

Value significantly outperformed growth across the market capitalization spectrum. In the large capitalization arena, the extra return of value over growth was at the expense of increased risk, as the standard deviation of large value was 30.1 percent versus 21.2 percent for large growth. Among the small cap series, small value significantly outperformed small growth but did so with higher volatility (35.0 percent versus 30.6 percent).

Graph 8-2

**Small Value Stocks, Small Growth Stocks, Large Value Stocks,
Large Growth Stocks**
Year-End 1927 = $1.00

from 1927 to 2000

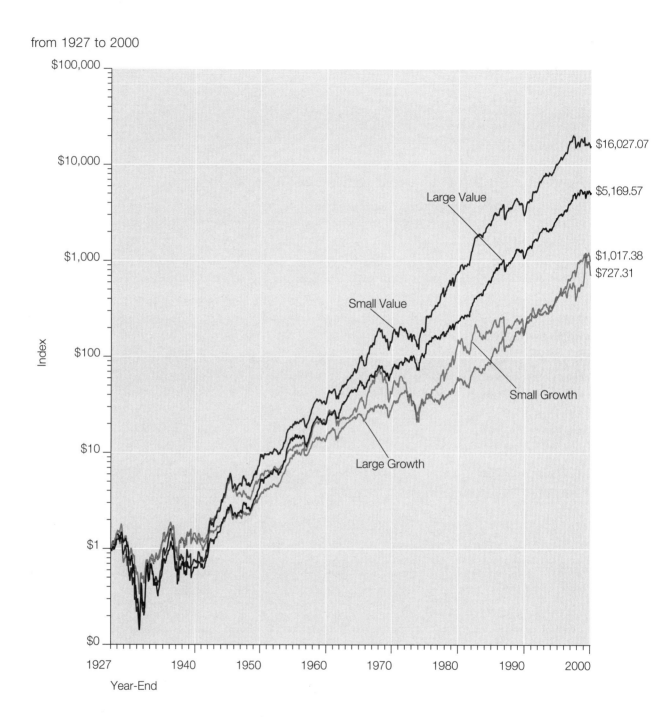

Index

Year-End

## Table 8-1

**Total Returns and Standard Deviation of Value and Growth**
Summary Statistics of Annual Returns

from 1928 to 2000

| Series | Geometric Mean (%) | Arithmetic Mean (%) | Standard Deviation (%) |
|---|---|---|---|
| Large Growth Stocks | 10.0 | 11.8 | 20.0 |
| Large Value Stocks | 12.4 | 15.9 | 27.5 |
| Small Growth Stocks | 9.4 | 14.0 | 33.2 |
| Small Value Stocks | 14.2 | 18.8 | 32.3 |
| All Growth Stocks | 9.8 | 11.7 | 20.1 |
| All Value Stocks | 13.1 | 16.6 | 28.0 |

Table 8-2 shows the compound returns by decade for the growth and value series. It is notable that all value stocks outperformed all growth stocks in every decade except the 1930s and the 1990s. In this table, the 1920s cover the period 1928–1929.

## Table 8-2

**Compound Annual Rates of Return by Decade**

|  | 1920s* | 1930s | 1940s | 1950s | 1960s | 1970s | 1980s | 1990s | 2000s** | 1991-00 |
|---|---|---|---|---|---|---|---|---|---|---|
| Large Growth Stocks | 8.0% | 1.9% | 7.3% | 17.9% | 8.0% | 3.6% | 15.5% | 19.9% | –13.2% | 18.1% |
| Large Value Stocks | 8.5 | –5.8 | 17.1 | 22.0 | 11.1 | 12.0 | 20.7 | 14.4 | 0.5 | 16.1 |
| Small Growth Stocks | –15.8 | 7.4 | 11.3 | 18.0 | 9.8 | 5.3 | 9.9 | 14.3 | –21.2 | 14.0 |
| Small Value Stocks | –6.5 | –0.5 | 21.2 | 20.3 | 15.2 | 15.5 | 20.9 | 14.8 | –3.2 | 17.5 |
| All Growth Stocks | 7.5 | 1.9 | 7.3 | 17.9 | 8.0 | 3.8 | 14.7 | 19.4 | –13.4 | 17.9 |
| All Value Stocks | 5.6 | –4.6 | 17.9 | 21.8 | 12.3 | 13.9 | 20.8 | 14.4 | –0.2 | 16.3 |

*Based on the period 1928–1929

**Based on the period 2000 only

The outperformance of large growth stocks over large value stocks in the 1990s is unusual from a historical perspective, given that the only other decade where this occurred was in the 1930s. The emergence of technology and internet-related companies with high earnings growth rates and high price-to-book and price-to-earnings multiples has led the growth charge. Since the assets of these companies tend to be more intangible, they tend to have lower book values. To a certain extent, a large portion of the performance of the S&P 500 in recent periods can be explained by this phenomenon. Whether or not a fundamental change that favors growth investing has occurred is open to debate. This topic will be discussed in more detail later in this chapter.

Small value stocks beat small growth stocks in all decades except the 1930s. Even in the 1990s where large growth stocks have done well, small value stocks have still outperformed small growth stocks. It is also interesting to note that in any decade small value stocks were never the worst performing among all six stock series.

## Presentation of the Annual Data

Table 8-3 shows the highest and the lowest returns of the growth and value series, expressed as annual rates for 5-, 10-, 15-, and 20-year holding periods. This table also exhibits the number of times that a series had a positive return, and the number of times that the return of the series was the highest among all of the growth and value series listed. The number of times positive and the number of times highest is evaluated with the 73 annual, 69 overlapping 5-year, 64 overlapping 10-year, 59 overlapping 15-year, and 54 overlapping 20-year holding periods.

It is interesting to note that neither large- nor small-cap growth stocks were ever the highest performing series over rolling 20-year periods. Small value stocks were the best-performing series for a large majority of the rolling 10-, 15-, and 20-year periods.

Table 8-4 shows year-by-year total annual returns from 1928 to 2000. This table compares the performance of large growth, large value, small growth, small value, all growth, and all value stocks. Table 8-5 shows the growth of $1.00 invested in each of the categories at year-end 1927.

In addition to the large differences in annual returns between large and small stocks noted in Table 7-2 of this book, there are large differences between growth and value as seen in Table 8-4. In 1998, for instance, all growth stocks returned 33.1 percent while all value stocks returned 12.1 percent. However, we know from the long-term analysis of value versus growth that value outperformed growth a majority of the time. Recent years where this occurred are 1992 and 1993, where value outperformed growth by 17.5 and 17.9 percentage points, respectively.

Table 8-3

## Maximum and Minimum Values of Returns for 1-, 5-, 10-, 15-, and 20-Year Holding Periods
(Compound annual rates of return in percent)

| | Maximum Values Return | Year(s) | Minimum Values Return | Year(s) | Times Positive (out of 73 Years) | Times Highest Return |
|---|---|---|---|---|---|---|
| **Annual Returns** | | | | | | |
| Large Growth Stocks | 50.18 | 1954 | −35.77 | 1931 | 54 | 17 |
| Large Value Stocks | 115.50 | 1933 | −58.70 | 1931 | 52 | 15 |
| Small Growth Stocks | 158.09 | 1933 | −46.29 | 1937 | 48 | 16 |
| Small Value Stocks | 118.08 | 1933 | −52.19 | 1931 | 51 | 25 |
| **5-Year Rolling Period Returns** | | | | | (out of 69 overlapping 5-year periods) | |
| Large Growth Stocks | 30.66 | 1995–99 | −12.50 | 1929–33 | 63 | 11 |
| Large Value Stocks | 31.63 | 1941–45 | −24.00 | 1928–32 | 63 | 19 |
| Small Growth Stocks | 44.98 | 1932–36 | −23.43 | 1928–32 | 59 | 12 |
| Small Value Stocks | 45.53 | 1941–45 | −26.21 | 1928–32 | 62 | 27 |
| **10-Year Rolling Period Returns** | | | | | (out of 64 overlapping 10-year periods) | |
| Large Growth Stocks | 20.56 | 1989–98 | −1.14 | 1929–38 | 62 | 7 |
| Large Value Stocks | 24.33 | 1942–51 | −5.80 | 1930–39 | 60 | 14 |
| Small Growth Stocks | 22.50 | 1975–84 | −1.91 | 1965–74 | 58 | 5 |
| Small Value Stocks | 32.63 | 1975–84 | −4.81 | 1929–38 | 61 | 38 |
| **15-Year Rolling Period Returns** | | | | | (out of 59 overlapping 15-year periods) | |
| Large Growth Stocks | 19.98 | 1985–99 | 0.35 | 1929–43 | 59 | 3 |
| Large Value Stocks | 23.48 | 1942–56 | −1.15 | 1928–42 | 57 | 10 |
| Small Growth Stocks | 19.85 | 1932–46 | −0.42 | 1960–74 | 58 | 3 |
| Small Value Stocks | 26.70 | 1975–89 | −0.13 | 1928–42 | 58 | 43 |
| **20-Year Rolling Period Returns** | | | | | (out of 54 overlapping 20-year periods) | |
| Large Growth Stocks | 17.66 | 1980–99 | 2.36 | 1929–48 | 54 | 0 |
| Large Value Stocks | 20.63 | 1942–61 | 3.89 | 1929–48 | 54 | 6 |
| Small Growth Stocks | 17.68 | 1933–52 | 3.84 | 1955–74 | 54 | 0 |
| Small Value Stocks | 23.39 | 1975–94 | 6.25 | 1929–48 | 54 | 48 |

Table 8-4

**Growth and Value Series**
Year-by-Year Returns

from 1928 to 1970

| | Large Growth Stocks | Large Value Stocks | Small Growth Stocks | Small Value Stocks | All Growth Stocks | All Value Stocks |
|---|---|---|---|---|---|---|
| 1928 | 0.4586 | 0.2358 | 0.3123 | 0.3978 | 0.4552 | 0.2639 |
| 1929 | −0.2005 | −0.0467 | −0.4597 | −0.3743 | −0.2056 | −0.1183 |
| 1930 | −0.2549 | −0.4372 | −0.3520 | −0.4706 | −0.2560 | −0.4447 |
| 1931 | −0.3577 | −0.5870 | −0.4160 | −0.5219 | −0.3580 | −0.5710 |
| 1932 | −0.0719 | −0.0743 | −0.0192 | −0.0118 | −0.0714 | −0.0545 |
| 1933 | 0.4443 | 1.1550 | 1.5809 | 1.1808 | 0.4492 | 1.2009 |
| 1934 | 0.1043 | −0.1979 | 0.3326 | 0.0821 | 0.1057 | −0.1551 |
| 1935 | 0.4181 | 0.4881 | 0.4270 | 0.5118 | 0.4184 | 0.4843 |
| 1936 | 0.2544 | 0.4958 | 0.3307 | 0.7432 | 0.2564 | 0.5217 |
| 1937 | −0.3322 | −0.3960 | −0.4629 | −0.5034 | −0.3353 | −0.4069 |
| 1938 | 0.3255 | 0.2596 | 0.4188 | 0.2634 | 0.3270 | 0.2497 |
| 1939 | 0.0801 | −0.1263 | 0.1086 | −0.0242 | 0.0806 | −0.1120 |
| 1940 | −0.0924 | −0.0179 | −0.0076 | −0.0935 | −0.0915 | −0.0315 |
| 1941 | −0.1231 | −0.0118 | −0.1705 | −0.0406 | −0.1237 | −0.0216 |
| 1942 | 0.1323 | 0.3362 | 0.1762 | 0.3534 | 0.1328 | 0.3369 |
| 1943 | 0.2142 | 0.4217 | 0.4564 | 0.9202 | 0.2168 | 0.5262 |
| 1944 | 0.1597 | 0.4200 | 0.3985 | 0.4907 | 0.1642 | 0.4302 |
| 1945 | 0.3084 | 0.4825 | 0.6242 | 0.7562 | 0.3176 | 0.5165 |
| 1946 | −0.0669 | −0.0746 | −0.1273 | −0.0694 | −0.0702 | −0.0725 |
| 1947 | 0.0326 | 0.0837 | −0.0832 | 0.0546 | 0.0275 | 0.0806 |
| 1948 | 0.0347 | 0.0509 | −0.0758 | −0.0288 | 0.0303 | 0.0411 |
| 1949 | 0.2268 | 0.1852 | 0.2320 | 0.2155 | 0.2260 | 0.1871 |
| 1950 | 0.2421 | 0.5536 | 0.3077 | 0.5191 | 0.2436 | 0.5478 |
| 1951 | 0.1970 | 0.1375 | 0.1662 | 0.1169 | 0.1963 | 0.1335 |
| 1952 | 0.1314 | 0.2024 | 0.0560 | 0.0833 | 0.1299 | 0.1798 |
| 1953 | 0.0220 | −0.0772 | 0.0059 | −0.0665 | 0.0219 | −0.0762 |
| 1954 | 0.5018 | 0.7734 | 0.4268 | 0.6424 | 0.5008 | 0.7462 |
| 1955 | 0.3013 | 0.2991 | 0.1777 | 0.2394 | 0.2995 | 0.2892 |
| 1956 | 0.0665 | 0.0478 | 0.0585 | 0.0748 | 0.0665 | 0.0549 |
| 1957 | −0.0890 | −0.2283 | −0.1436 | −0.1536 | −0.0896 | −0.2079 |
| 1958 | 0.4078 | 0.7458 | 0.7694 | 0.6820 | 0.4112 | 0.7285 |
| 1959 | 0.1317 | 0.1479 | 0.1988 | 0.1860 | 0.1325 | 0.1570 |
| 1960 | −0.0268 | −0.0702 | −0.0103 | −0.0576 | −0.0266 | −0.0657 |
| 1961 | 0.2600 | 0.2526 | 0.2119 | 0.3110 | 0.2593 | 0.2650 |
| 1962 | −0.1051 | −0.0153 | −0.2092 | −0.0883 | −0.1068 | −0.0304 |
| 1963 | 0.2106 | 0.3497 | 0.0822 | 0.2720 | 0.2079 | 0.3328 |
| 1964 | 0.1499 | 0.1984 | 0.1086 | 0.2265 | 0.1491 | 0.2053 |
| 1965 | 0.1358 | 0.2533 | 0.3512 | 0.4148 | 0.1407 | 0.2929 |
| 1966 | −0.1092 | −0.0902 | −0.0556 | −0.0760 | −0.1080 | −0.0804 |
| 1967 | 0.2985 | 0.3136 | 0.7942 | 0.6565 | 0.3144 | 0.3882 |
| 1968 | 0.0408 | 0.2363 | 0.2950 | 0.4515 | 0.0556 | 0.2827 |
| 1969 | 0.0302 | −0.1666 | −0.2452 | −0.2577 | 0.0042 | −0.1793 |
| 1970 | −0.0545 | 0.1122 | −0.2098 | 0.0627 | −0.0677 | 0.1087 |

Source: Eugene Fama and Ken French

Table 8-4 (continued)

**Growth and Value Series**
Year-by-Year Returns

from 1971 to 2000

| | Large Growth Stocks | Large Value Stocks | Small Growth Stocks | Small Value Stocks | All Growth Stocks | All Value Stocks |
|---|---|---|---|---|---|---|
| 1971 | 0.2299 | 0.1240 | 0.2195 | 0.1572 | 0.2308 | 0.1239 |
| 1972 | 0.2186 | 0.1805 | −0.0067 | 0.0806 | 0.2086 | 0.1762 |
| 1973 | −0.2106 | −0.0022 | −0.4284 | −0.2584 | −0.2181 | −0.0493 |
| 1974 | −0.2972 | −0.2546 | −0.3264 | −0.1788 | −0.2979 | −0.2424 |
| 1975 | 0.3383 | 0.5079 | 0.5880 | 0.5776 | 0.3466 | 0.5105 |
| 1976 | 0.1745 | 0.4650 | 0.3690 | 0.5779 | 0.1815 | 0.5120 |
| 1977 | −0.0943 | 0.0131 | 0.1919 | 0.2422 | −0.0809 | 0.0979 |
| 1978 | 0.0730 | 0.0360 | 0.1679 | 0.2177 | 0.0780 | 0.1052 |
| 1979 | 0.1817 | 0.2210 | 0.5006 | 0.3822 | 0.2105 | 0.2563 |
| 1980 | 0.3265 | 0.1515 | 0.5300 | 0.2242 | 0.3473 | 0.1609 |
| 1981 | −0.0757 | 0.1441 | −0.1203 | 0.1780 | −0.0812 | 0.1495 |
| 1982 | 0.1987 | 0.2735 | 0.1993 | 0.4083 | 0.1996 | 0.2914 |
| 1983 | 0.1519 | 0.2745 | 0.2127 | 0.4796 | 0.1609 | 0.2998 |
| 1984 | −0.0059 | 0.1765 | −0.1441 | 0.0768 | −0.0298 | 0.1651 |
| 1985 | 0.3351 | 0.3315 | 0.2836 | 0.3032 | 0.3276 | 0.3290 |
| 1986 | 0.1396 | 0.2171 | 0.0152 | 0.1326 | 0.1224 | 0.2092 |
| 1987 | 0.0763 | −0.0228 | −0.1314 | −0.0626 | 0.0499 | −0.0276 |
| 1988 | 0.1183 | 0.2514 | 0.1379 | 0.2955 | 0.1204 | 0.2539 |
| 1989 | 0.3690 | 0.3122 | 0.1870 | 0.1535 | 0.3479 | 0.2942 |
| 1990 | 0.0060 | −0.1347 | −0.1868 | −0.2361 | −0.0109 | −0.1503 |
| 1991 | 0.4316 | 0.2677 | 0.5379 | 0.4078 | 0.4391 | 0.2884 |
| 1992 | 0.0683 | 0.2205 | 0.0471 | 0.3551 | 0.0677 | 0.2425 |
| 1993 | 0.0252 | 0.1972 | 0.1240 | 0.2823 | 0.0337 | 0.2124 |
| 1994 | 0.0201 | −0.0591 | −0.0392 | 0.0282 | 0.0137 | −0.0466 |
| 1995 | 0.3726 | 0.3760 | 0.3559 | 0.2872 | 0.3709 | 0.3583 |
| 1996 | 0.2080 | 0.1340 | 0.1322 | 0.2145 | 0.2013 | 0.1487 |
| 1997 | 0.3165 | 0.3103 | 0.1526 | 0.3894 | 0.3031 | 0.3291 |
| 1998 | 0.3491 | 0.1820 | 0.0127 | −0.0863 | 0.3311 | 0.1207 |
| 1999 | 0.2931 | 0.0539 | 0.5044 | 0.0386 | 0.2981 | 0.0540 |
| 2000 | −0.1318 | 0.0055 | −0.2120 | −0.0320 | −0.1340 | −0.0016 |

Source: Eugene Fama and Ken French

Table 8-5

## Growth and Value Series
Year-End Index Values

from 1927 to 1970

| | Large Growth Stocks | Large Value Stocks | Small Growth Stocks | Small Value Stocks | All Growth Stocks | All Value Stocks |
|---|---|---|---|---|---|---|
| 1927 | 1.000 | 1.000 | 1.000 | 1.000 | 1.000 | 1.000 |
| 1928 | 1.459 | 1.236 | 1.312 | 1.398 | 1.455 | 1.264 |
| 1929 | 1.166 | 1.178 | 0.709 | 0.875 | 1.156 | 1.114 |
| 1930 | 0.869 | 0.663 | 0.459 | 0.463 | 0.860 | 0.619 |
| 1931 | 0.558 | 0.274 | 0.268 | 0.221 | 0.552 | 0.266 |
| 1932 | 0.518 | 0.254 | 0.263 | 0.219 | 0.513 | 0.251 |
| 1933 | 0.748 | 0.546 | 0.679 | 0.477 | 0.743 | 0.552 |
| 1934 | 0.826 | 0.438 | 0.905 | 0.516 | 0.822 | 0.467 |
| 1935 | 1.172 | 0.652 | 1.292 | 0.781 | 1.165 | 0.693 |
| 1936 | 1.470 | 0.975 | 1.719 | 1.361 | 1.464 | 1.054 |
| 1937 | 0.982 | 0.589 | 0.923 | 0.676 | 0.973 | 0.625 |
| 1938 | 1.301 | 0.742 | 1.310 | 0.854 | 1.292 | 0.781 |
| 1939 | 1.405 | 0.648 | 1.452 | 0.833 | 1.396 | 0.694 |
| 1940 | 1.275 | 0.637 | 1.441 | 0.755 | 1.268 | 0.672 |
| 1941 | 1.118 | 0.629 | 1.195 | 0.725 | 1.111 | 0.657 |
| 1942 | 1.266 | 0.841 | 1.406 | 0.981 | 1.259 | 0.879 |
| 1943 | 1.537 | 1.195 | 2.047 | 1.883 | 1.532 | 1.341 |
| 1944 | 1.783 | 1.697 | 2.863 | 2.807 | 1.783 | 1.919 |
| 1945 | 2.333 | 2.516 | 4.651 | 4.929 | 2.349 | 2.910 |
| 1946 | 2.177 | 2.328 | 4.059 | 4.587 | 2.184 | 2.699 |
| 1947 | 2.248 | 2.523 | 3.721 | 4.837 | 2.244 | 2.916 |
| 1948 | 2.326 | 2.652 | 3.439 | 4.698 | 2.312 | 3.036 |
| 1949 | 2.853 | 3.143 | 4.237 | 5.710 | 2.835 | 3.604 |
| 1950 | 3.544 | 4.883 | 5.541 | 8.674 | 3.525 | 5.578 |
| 1951 | 4.242 | 5.554 | 6.462 | 9.687 | 4.217 | 6.323 |
| 1952 | 4.800 | 6.678 | 6.823 | 10.495 | 4.765 | 7.460 |
| 1953 | 4.905 | 6.163 | 6.863 | 9.797 | 4.869 | 6.892 |
| 1954 | 7.366 | 10.929 | 9.793 | 16.091 | 7.308 | 12.034 |
| 1955 | 9.586 | 14.198 | 11.533 | 19.942 | 9.497 | 15.515 |
| 1956 | 10.224 | 14.876 | 12.207 | 21.433 | 10.129 | 16.367 |
| 1957 | 9.314 | 11.481 | 10.454 | 18.141 | 9.221 | 12.964 |
| 1958 | 13.112 | 20.043 | 18.497 | 30.514 | 13.013 | 22.408 |
| 1959 | 14.840 | 23.007 | 22.175 | 36.190 | 14.737 | 25.926 |
| 1960 | 14.443 | 21.392 | 21.947 | 34.105 | 14.345 | 24.221 |
| 1961 | 18.198 | 26.796 | 26.598 | 44.712 | 18.065 | 30.639 |
| 1962 | 16.285 | 26.386 | 21.033 | 40.765 | 16.135 | 29.707 |
| 1963 | 19.715 | 35.612 | 22.762 | 51.853 | 19.490 | 39.594 |
| 1964 | 22.670 | 42.676 | 25.235 | 63.599 | 22.396 | 47.721 |
| 1965 | 25.749 | 53.487 | 34.098 | 89.982 | 25.547 | 61.698 |
| 1966 | 22.937 | 48.664 | 32.201 | 83.147 | 22.788 | 56.740 |
| 1967 | 29.783 | 63.926 | 57.775 | 137.734 | 29.953 | 78.768 |
| 1968 | 30.998 | 79.032 | 74.821 | 199.918 | 31.617 | 101.034 |
| 1969 | 31.935 | 65.864 | 56.472 | 148.397 | 31.749 | 82.918 |
| 1970 | 30.194 | 73.252 | 44.623 | 157.703 | 29.599 | 91.930 |

Source: Eugene Fama and Ken French

Table 8-5 (continued)

## Growth and Value Series
Year-End Index Values

from 1971 to 2000

| | Large Growth Stocks | Large Value Stocks | Small Growth Stocks | Small Value Stocks | All Growth Stocks | All Value Stocks |
|---|---|---|---|---|---|---|
| 1971 | 37.136 | 82.335 | 54.417 | 182.493 | 36.430 | 103.324 |
| 1972 | 45.254 | 97.198 | 54.054 | 197.203 | 44.028 | 121.533 |
| 1973 | 35.722 | 96.982 | 30.898 | 146.237 | 34.426 | 115.547 |
| 1974 | 25.107 | 72.288 | 20.812 | 120.085 | 24.170 | 87.539 |
| 1975 | 33.600 | 109.000 | 33.051 | 189.443 | 32.547 | 132.224 |
| 1976 | 39.462 | 159.685 | 45.246 | 298.914 | 38.456 | 199.917 |
| 1977 | 35.743 | 161.769 | 53.929 | 371.317 | 35.345 | 219.491 |
| 1978 | 38.351 | 167.585 | 62.982 | 452.167 | 38.104 | 242.576 |
| 1979 | 45.319 | 204.628 | 94.513 | 624.992 | 46.123 | 304.742 |
| 1980 | 60.116 | 235.623 | 144.605 | 765.118 | 62.141 | 353.780 |
| 1981 | 55.565 | 269.584 | 127.203 | 901.287 | 57.098 | 406.684 |
| 1982 | 66.606 | 343.318 | 152.555 | 1269.260 | 68.497 | 525.207 |
| 1983 | 76.726 | 437.548 | 184.999 | 1877.996 | 79.518 | 682.644 |
| 1984 | 76.273 | 514.764 | 158.342 | 2022.319 | 77.147 | 795.360 |
| 1985 | 101.830 | 685.409 | 203.253 | 2635.406 | 102.421 | 1057.033 |
| 1986 | 116.042 | 834.205 | 206.335 | 2984.921 | 114.958 | 1278.135 |
| 1987 | 124.898 | 815.147 | 179.213 | 2798.133 | 120.700 | 1242.901 |
| 1988 | 139.676 | 1020.062 | 203.933 | 3624.846 | 135.233 | 1558.521 |
| 1989 | 191.223 | 1338.508 | 242.071 | 4181.265 | 182.282 | 2016.962 |
| 1990 | 192.373 | 1158.225 | 196.857 | 3193.873 | 180.303 | 1713.901 |
| 1991 | 275.410 | 1468.307 | 302.756 | 4496.213 | 259.468 | 2208.258 |
| 1992 | 294.234 | 1792.001 | 317.030 | 6092.924 | 277.043 | 2743.840 |
| 1993 | 301.635 | 2145.445 | 356.350 | 7813.238 | 286.377 | 3326.538 |
| 1994 | 307.702 | 2018.606 | 342.398 | 8033.436 | 290.297 | 3171.451 |
| 1995 | 422.348 | 2777.624 | 464.268 | 10340.493 | 397.958 | 4307.633 |
| 1996 | 510.208 | 3149.852 | 525.637 | 12558.299 | 478.050 | 4948.048 |
| 1997 | 671.697 | 4127.288 | 605.845 | 17448.659 | 622.947 | 6576.494 |
| 1998 | 906.193 | 4878.387 | 613.514 | 15942.539 | 829.175 | 7370.404 |
| 1999 | 1171.797 | 5141.323 | 922.948 | 16557.203 | 1076.322 | 7768.151 |
| 2000 | 1017.382 | 5169.570 | 727.306 | 16027.071 | 932.127 | 7755.385 |

Source: Eugene Fama and Ken French

## Description of Derived Series

From the four Fama-French series: large growth, large value, small growth and small value, three additional risk premia series are derived. The risk premia series are the large value premium, small value premium, and the all value premium.

### Value Premium

The value premium is the geometric difference between all value total returns and all growth total returns.

The monthly value premium is given by:

$$\frac{\left(1 + \text{All Value TR}\right)}{\left(1 + \text{All Growth TR}\right)} - 1 \tag{30}$$

Graph 8-3

**All Value Premium** (in percent)

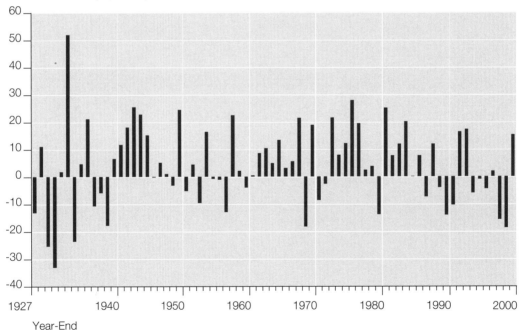

Year-End

The small value premium is the geometric difference between small value total returns and small growth total returns.

The monthly small value premium is given by:

$$\frac{\left(1 + \text{Small Value TR}\right)}{\left(1 + \text{Small Growth TR}\right)} - 1 \tag{31}$$

## Graph 8-4

**Small Value Premium** (in percent)

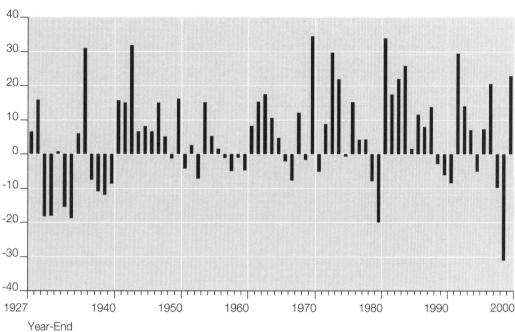

Year-End

The large value premium is the geometric difference between large value total returns and large growth total returns.

The monthly large value premium is given by:

$$\frac{\left(1 + \textbf{Large Value TR}\right)}{\left(1 + \textbf{Large Growth TR}\right)} - 1$$

(32)

Graph 8-5

**Large Value Premium** (in percent)

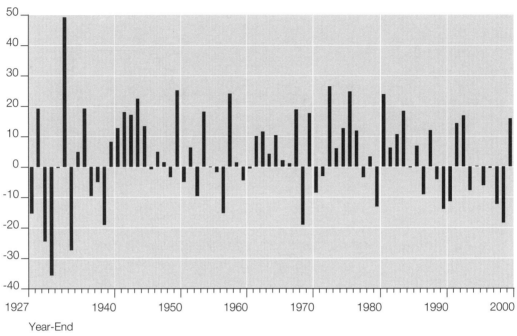

Year-End

Table 8-6 presents annual returns for each of the three value premia series.

**Monthly Standard Deviations**

As shown in Table 8-7, small value and small growth have the highest monthly-annualized standard deviations. These two series along with the other seven all experience extreme volatility during the depression years of 1932 and 1933. These data series also exhibit a higher variability in the pre-World War II period than in the postwar period.

## Table 8-6

**Derived Series**
Annual Returns (in percent)

from 1928 to 2000

| | All Value Premia | Small Value Premia | Large Value Premia | | All Value Premia | Small Value Premia | Large Value Premia |
|---|---|---|---|---|---|---|---|
| 1928 | −13.15 | 6.52 | −15.27 | 1973 | 21.59 | 29.73 | 26.40 |
| 1929 | 10.98 | 15.81 | 19.24 | 1974 | 7.91 | 21.91 | 6.05 |
| 1930 | −25.37 | −18.30 | −24.46 | 1975 | 12.17 | −0.66 | 12.67 |
| 1931 | −33.17 | −18.12 | −35.70 | 1976 | 27.97 | 15.26 | 24.74 |
| 1932 | 1.82 | 0.76 | −0.27 | 1977 | 19.45 | 4.22 | 11.85 |
| 1933 | 51.87 | −15.50 | 49.21 | 1978 | 2.52 | 4.27 | −3.45 |
| 1934 | −23.59 | −18.80 | −27.37 | 1979 | 3.79 | −7.89 | 3.33 |
| 1935 | 4.65 | 5.94 | 4.93 | 1980 | −13.83 | −19.99 | −13.20 |
| 1936 | 21.12 | 31.00 | 19.25 | 1981 | 25.11 | 33.91 | 23.78 |
| 1937 | −10.78 | −7.53 | −9.55 | 1982 | 7.65 | 17.42 | 6.24 |
| 1938 | −5.83 | −10.95 | −4.97 | 1983 | 11.96 | 22.01 | 10.64 |
| 1939 | −17.82 | −11.98 | −19.11 | 1984 | 20.09 | 25.81 | 18.35 |
| 1940 | 6.60 | −8.66 | 8.21 | 1985 | 0.10 | 1.52 | −0.27 |
| 1941 | 11.65 | 15.66 | 12.70 | 1986 | 7.73 | 11.57 | 6.80 |
| 1942 | 18.02 | 15.06 | 18.01 | 1987 | −7.38 | 7.93 | −9.21 |
| 1943 | 25.43 | 31.85 | 17.08 | 1988 | 11.92 | 13.84 | 11.90 |
| 1944 | 22.85 | 6.59 | 22.44 | 1989 | −3.99 | −2.82 | −4.15 |
| 1945 | 15.10 | 8.13 | 13.30 | 1990 | −14.09 | −6.07 | −13.99 |
| 1946 | −0.25 | 6.63 | −0.83 | 1991 | −10.47 | −8.46 | −11.45 |
| 1947 | 5.16 | 15.02 | 4.95 | 1992 | 16.37 | 29.41 | 14.24 |
| 1948 | 1.05 | 5.08 | 1.57 | 1993 | 17.29 | 14.09 | 16.79 |
| 1949 | −3.17 | −1.34 | −3.39 | 1994 | −5.95 | 7.01 | −7.77 |
| 1950 | 24.47 | 16.16 | 25.08 | 1995 | −0.92 | −5.07 | 0.25 |
| 1951 | −5.25 | −4.23 | −4.97 | 1996 | −4.38 | 7.27 | −6.13 |
| 1952 | 4.42 | 2.59 | 6.28 | 1997 | 2.00 | 20.55 | −0.47 |
| 1953 | −9.60 | −7.20 | −9.71 | 1998 | −15.80 | −9.77 | −12.39 |
| 1954 | 16.35 | 15.11 | 18.08 | 1999 | −18.80 | −30.96 | −18.50 |
| 1955 | −0.79 | 5.23 | −0.17 | 2000 | 15.28 | 22.84 | 15.81 |
| 1956 | −1.09 | 1.54 | −1.76 | | | | |
| 1957 | −12.99 | −1.16 | −15.29 | | | | |
| 1958 | 22.48 | −4.94 | 24.01 | | | | |
| 1959 | 2.16 | −1.07 | 1.43 | | | | |
| 1960 | −4.02 | −4.78 | −4.47 | | | | |
| 1961 | 0.45 | 8.18 | −0.59 | | | | |
| 1962 | 8.55 | 15.29 | 10.04 | | | | |
| 1963 | 10.34 | 17.54 | 11.49 | | | | |
| 1964 | 4.89 | 10.63 | 4.22 | | | | |
| 1965 | 13.34 | 4.71 | 10.35 | | | | |
| 1966 | 3.10 | −2.15 | 2.14 | | | | |
| 1967 | 5.61 | −7.67 | 1.16 | | | | |
| 1968 | 21.52 | 12.08 | 18.79 | | | | |
| 1969 | −18.27 | −1.65 | −19.11 | | | | |
| 1970 | 18.93 | 34.49 | 17.63 | | | | |
| 1971 | −8.68 | −5.11 | −8.61 | | | | |
| 1972 | −2.68 | 8.79 | −3.12 | | | | |

Table 8-7

**Basic and Derived Series**

Annualized Monthly Standard Deviations (in percent)

from 1928 to 1970

| | Basic Series | | | | | | Derived Series | | |
|---|---|---|---|---|---|---|---|---|---|
| | Large Growth Stocks | Large Value Stocks | Small Growth Stocks | Small Value Stocks | All Growth Stocks | All Value Stocks | Large Value Premia | Small Value Premia | All Value Premia |
| 1928 | 24.19 | 20.62 | 22.98 | 27.65 | 24.01 | 21.38 | 5.79 | 11.18 | 6.08 |
| 1929 | 30.98 | 18.17 | 16.29 | 18.10 | 30.64 | 17.76 | 27.04 | 9.26 | 22.77 |
| 1930 | 21.59 | 15.62 | 23.78 | 21.81 | 21.61 | 16.42 | 9.29 | 9.04 | 8.49 |
| 1931 | 30.48 | 35.89 | 27.65 | 38.46 | 30.46 | 35.89 | 18.31 | 18.75 | 17.54 |
| 1932 | 61.31 | 193.57 | 98.03 | 224.98 | 61.41 | 191.95 | 61.76 | 41.85 | 60.61 |
| 1933 | 71.14 | 241.57 | 276.25 | 305.89 | 71.60 | 258.27 | 56.61 | 24.24 | 63.04 |
| 1934 | 22.14 | 38.96 | 50.61 | 66.84 | 22.32 | 42.39 | 19.67 | 20.38 | 21.47 |
| 1935 | 17.51 | 50.87 | 30.92 | 50.07 | 17.58 | 48.62 | 25.35 | 20.07 | 23.96 |
| 1936 | 15.03 | 32.10 | 34.37 | 55.48 | 15.15 | 34.07 | 18.56 | 15.90 | 19.68 |
| 1937 | 14.05 | 22.71 | 18.60 | 21.12 | 14.15 | 22.41 | 17.22 | 12.04 | 16.68 |
| 1938 | 53.30 | 76.54 | 84.16 | 81.40 | 53.72 | 76.31 | 17.14 | 5.72 | 16.79 |
| 1939 | 26.35 | 58.10 | 63.99 | 86.22 | 26.73 | 61.98 | 27.52 | 17.06 | 29.54 |
| 1940 | 22.64 | 31.17 | 33.02 | 35.59 | 22.78 | 31.91 | 11.07 | 8.96 | 11.30 |
| 1941 | 12.03 | 15.79 | 15.24 | 27.21 | 12.05 | 17.09 | 13.33 | 13.48 | 13.32 |
| 1942 | 15.75 | 27.36 | 16.54 | 31.88 | 15.65 | 27.72 | 22.07 | 13.65 | 22.16 |
| 1943 | 15.27 | 32.36 | 32.32 | 69.28 | 15.43 | 38.64 | 14.25 | 20.10 | 17.78 |
| 1944 | 8.28 | 17.08 | 14.03 | 24.95 | 8.35 | 18.00 | 9.34 | 9.55 | 9.48 |
| 1945 | 15.23 | 24.68 | 23.90 | 35.21 | 15.36 | 25.82 | 13.47 | 9.23 | 13.79 |
| 1946 | 17.61 | 19.84 | 23.08 | 27.24 | 17.85 | 20.65 | 6.73 | 6.79 | 6.67 |
| 1947 | 10.72 | 13.69 | 13.61 | 16.36 | 10.80 | 13.76 | 6.56 | 4.70 | 6.17 |
| 1948 | 20.26 | 25.64 | 16.95 | 24.05 | 20.10 | 25.39 | 9.70 | 9.73 | 9.52 |
| 1949 | 11.64 | 16.61 | 18.37 | 20.29 | 11.79 | 16.92 | 5.87 | 4.52 | 5.82 |
| 1950 | 14.45 | 24.35 | 16.82 | 30.46 | 14.40 | 25.26 | 22.74 | 16.99 | 22.31 |
| 1951 | 13.84 | 21.36 | 13.78 | 21.26 | 13.80 | 21.25 | 10.06 | 8.14 | 9.90 |
| 1952 | 12.29 | 17.11 | 9.36 | 10.88 | 12.20 | 15.79 | 5.33 | 4.83 | 4.35 |
| 1953 | 9.44 | 10.97 | 8.21 | 9.93 | 9.39 | 10.56 | 5.83 | 5.05 | 5.83 |
| 1954 | 17.79 | 34.73 | 13.48 | 24.38 | 17.64 | 31.89 | 14.13 | 6.76 | 13.21 |
| 1955 | 14.82 | 17.28 | 9.71 | 8.70 | 14.70 | 14.75 | 6.86 | 4.26 | 5.70 |
| 1956 | 15.16 | 16.32 | 9.27 | 8.25 | 15.05 | 14.15 | 5.76 | 4.22 | 4.54 |
| 1957 | 13.39 | 10.49 | 11.35 | 11.16 | 13.34 | 10.54 | 5.57 | 5.06 | 6.46 |
| 1958 | 8.49 | 21.52 | 17.40 | 17.01 | 8.48 | 20.11 | 11.38 | 6.84 | 10.60 |
| 1959 | 10.51 | 10.68 | 11.16 | 10.09 | 10.48 | 10.29 | 7.17 | 5.91 | 7.28 |
| 1960 | 14.48 | 11.12 | 15.35 | 10.78 | 14.47 | 10.75 | 8.32 | 6.63 | 7.82 |
| 1961 | 9.98 | 15.44 | 18.91 | 19.29 | 10.08 | 15.69 | 8.45 | 4.89 | 7.89 |
| 1962 | 20.15 | 19.81 | 23.10 | 21.58 | 20.18 | 20.04 | 11.22 | 9.26 | 10.59 |
| 1963 | 11.59 | 16.13 | 12.47 | 16.07 | 11.58 | 15.78 | 6.13 | 4.97 | 5.91 |
| 1964 | 4.25 | 12.02 | 5.48 | 9.48 | 4.24 | 11.19 | 8.63 | 6.51 | 7.85 |
| 1965 | 9.39 | 12.95 | 20.14 | 20.24 | 9.54 | 14.11 | 6.88 | 4.04 | 6.80 |
| 1966 | 10.01 | 12.92 | 18.85 | 17.86 | 10.11 | 13.92 | 8.73 | 8.58 | 9.26 |
| 1967 | 15.87 | 19.91 | 32.01 | 33.31 | 16.14 | 22.29 | 9.89 | 5.60 | 10.24 |
| 1968 | 17.03 | 18.52 | 30.33 | 23.77 | 17.44 | 19.31 | 8.46 | 10.47 | 9.49 |
| 1969 | 14.00 | 11.64 | 18.99 | 14.78 | 14.50 | 11.92 | 5.96 | 7.58 | 5.80 |
| 1970 | 21.06 | 23.06 | 30.52 | 26.84 | 21.60 | 23.25 | 9.60 | 19.34 | 9.49 |

Table 8-7 (continued)

## Basic and Derived Series
Annualized Monthly Standard Deviations (in percent)

from 1971 to 2000

| | Basic Series | | | | | | Derived Series | | |
|---|---|---|---|---|---|---|---|---|---|
| | Large Growth Stocks | Large Value Stocks | Small Growth Stocks | Small Value Stocks | All Growth Stocks | All Value Stocks | Large Value Premia | Small Value Premia | All Value Premia |
| 1971 | 17.47 | 20.34 | 26.60 | 27.93 | 17.89 | 21.29 | 5.90 | 6.44 | 5.99 |
| 1972 | 6.60 | 17.17 | 13.93 | 15.97 | 6.77 | 16.64 | 12.75 | 6.95 | 12.06 |
| 1973 | 12.47 | 17.96 | 23.50 | 17.71 | 13.14 | 17.81 | 13.74 | 19.26 | 11.61 |
| 1974 | 22.80 | 12.02 | 18.67 | 20.07 | 22.57 | 13.16 | 19.91 | 13.16 | 20.31 |
| 1975 | 25.30 | 36.04 | 44.86 | 51.12 | 25.61 | 38.83 | 16.14 | 7.85 | 17.03 |
| 1976 | 15.71 | 29.41 | 25.76 | 43.39 | 15.89 | 34.76 | 12.12 | 11.68 | 16.41 |
| 1977 | 10.17 | 10.17 | 14.04 | 12.69 | 10.31 | 10.69 | 10.42 | 5.37 | 10.56 |
| 1978 | 21.27 | 16.12 | 39.13 | 30.94 | 22.38 | 19.65 | 8.52 | 10.36 | 9.24 |
| 1979 | 16.66 | 19.11 | 33.08 | 28.26 | 17.96 | 20.78 | 6.74 | 7.13 | 6.82 |
| 1980 | 25.20 | 21.58 | 48.16 | 30.45 | 27.21 | 22.88 | 9.83 | 9.94 | 9.39 |
| 1981 | 14.95 | 10.27 | 20.26 | 16.16 | 15.30 | 11.04 | 13.67 | 16.66 | 13.28 |
| 1982 | 25.44 | 20.82 | 29.96 | 20.66 | 25.89 | 20.40 | 10.43 | 12.95 | 10.50 |
| 1983 | 13.29 | 11.62 | 26.19 | 15.34 | 14.44 | 11.21 | 10.67 | 16.69 | 10.57 |
| 1984 | 15.82 | 16.31 | 17.37 | 14.23 | 16.05 | 15.98 | 13.91 | 13.10 | 13.54 |
| 1985 | 19.97 | 13.80 | 25.25 | 14.19 | 20.62 | 13.59 | 8.53 | 10.01 | 8.81 |
| 1986 | 21.60 | 20.77 | 18.59 | 15.25 | 21.04 | 19.97 | 9.34 | 8.24 | 9.17 |
| 1987 | 37.89 | 26.01 | 38.80 | 33.67 | 37.94 | 26.65 | 9.88 | 12.09 | 10.08 |
| 1988 | 12.01 | 11.34 | 16.66 | 13.66 | 12.01 | 11.17 | 9.17 | 7.72 | 8.86 |
| 1989 | 17.99 | 12.82 | 12.34 | 12.23 | 16.97 | 12.40 | 6.30 | 4.55 | 5.95 |
| 1990 | 21.58 | 15.95 | 22.43 | 14.47 | 21.55 | 15.60 | 5.86 | 7.94 | 5.48 |
| 1991 | 25.72 | 18.91 | 28.74 | 22.62 | 25.74 | 19.08 | 5.40 | 4.31 | 5.26 |
| 1992 | 9.25 | 12.93 | 19.25 | 18.66 | 9.53 | 13.13 | 12.70 | 13.38 | 12.53 |
| 1993 | 9.53 | 8.86 | 14.48 | 9.76 | 9.70 | 8.60 | 11.67 | 11.15 | 11.14 |
| 1994 | 11.01 | 10.00 | 13.28 | 9.99 | 11.12 | 9.55 | 5.51 | 9.94 | 5.36 |
| 1995 | 7.44 | 10.47 | 17.21 | 10.99 | 7.83 | 9.98 | 7.79 | 9.84 | 7.49 |
| 1996 | 14.26 | 10.08 | 26.80 | 12.00 | 14.66 | 9.96 | 6.73 | 16.65 | 6.74 |
| 1997 | 22.93 | 15.32 | 29.63 | 18.32 | 22.52 | 15.15 | 9.30 | 14.95 | 9.52 |
| 1998 | 31.80 | 20.35 | 37.11 | 22.43 | 31.98 | 20.74 | 12.62 | 13.90 | 10.94 |
| 1999 | 19.80 | 17.78 | 39.29 | 20.00 | 20.01 | 17.07 | 15.15 | 13.86 | 14.59 |
| 2000 | 18.70 | 21.74 | 44.34 | 11.80 | 18.91 | 17.48 | 34.00 | 56.45 | 29.13 |

## Standard Deviations by Decade

Table 8-8 shows the annualized monthly standard deviations of the basic data series by decade begin-ning in 1928 and illustrates differences and changes in return volatility. In this table, the 1920s cover the period 1928–1929. Small value and small growth have been predominately the riskiest asset classes in all periods with the exception of the 1920s (which has only two years of annual history) and the 1950s.

Table 8-8

**Annualized Monthly Standard Deviations by Decade**

|  | 1920s* | 1930s | 1940s | 1950s | 1960s | 1970s | 1980s | 1990s | 2000s** | 1991-00 |
|---|---|---|---|---|---|---|---|---|---|---|
| Large Growth Stocks | 31.8% | 35.1% | 15.9% | 13.9% | 13.9% | 18.7% | 21.0% | 18.1% | 18.7% | 18.1% |
| Large Value Stocks | 19.4 | 66.9 | 23.1 | 19.5 | 15.7 | 20.1 | 17.4 | 15.0 | 21.7 | 15.4 |
| Small Growth Stocks | 22.9 | 60.4 | 22.2 | 13.3 | 21.4 | 29.0 | 26.1 | 25.6 | 44.3 | 29.4 |
| Small Value Stocks | 25.2 | 80.2 | 31.6 | 17.0 | 20.1 | 27.4 | 20.3 | 17.6 | 11.8 | 16.9 |
| All Growth Stocks | 31.5 | 35.2 | 16.0 | 13.9 | 14.1 | 19.1 | 21.4 | 18.2 | 18.9 | 18.2 |
| All Value Stocks | 20.0 | 68.2 | 24.3 | 18.6 | 16.3 | 21.6 | 17.5 | 14.9 | 17.5 | 14.8 |

*Based on the period 1928–1929

**Based on the period 2000 only

## Correlation of Basic Series

Table 8-9 presents annual cross-correlations and serial correlations for the seven basic series. Both large value and large growth are perfectly positively correlated to all value and all growth, respec-tively. Likewise, both small value and small growth are highly correlated to all value and all growth, respectively. All series have very low serial correlations, but the two small cap series are slightly more serially correlated, meaning they tend to move more in trends than large cap stocks.

Table 8-9

**Basic Series**
Serial and Cross Correlations of Historical Annual Returns

from 1928 to 2000

| Series | All Value Stocks | All Growth Stocks | Large Value Stocks | Large Growth Stocks | Small Value Stocks | Small Growth Stocks | U.S. Treasury Bills | Inflation |
|---|---|---|---|---|---|---|---|---|
| All Value Stocks | 1.00 | | | | | | | |
| All Growth Stocks | 0.80 | 1.00 | | | | | | |
| Large Value Stocks | 0.99 | 0.80 | 1.00 | | | | | |
| Large Growth Stocks | 0.79 | 1.00 | 0.80 | 1.00 | | | | |
| Small Value Stocks | 0.94 | 0.77 | 0.91 | 0.75 | 1.00 | | | |
| Small Growth Stocks | 0.84 | 0.82 | 0.80 | 0.80 | 0.87 | 1.00 | | |
| U.S. Treasury Bills | −0.06 | −0.04 | −0.06 | −0.03 | −0.07 | −0.12 | 1.00 | |
| Inflation | 0.06 | −0.04 | 0.05 | −0.05 | 0.06 | −0.02 | 0.41 | 1.00 |
| Serial Correlations* | −0.05 | −0.02 | −0.08 | −0.01 | 0.08 | 0.04 | 0.92 | 0.64 |

*The standard error for all estimates is 0.12

## Size and Sector Effects Within Growth and Value

Certain sectors of the equity market are often characterized as growth or value sectors, and where a particular sector lies along the growth/value spectrum is also time-dependent. Sectors such as utilities and finance are usually considered value sectors since these stocks tend to have higher dividend yields and are priced lower relative to their book values when compared to the overall market. Recently the technology and health care sectors would be considered growth sectors as these types of companies have delivered relatively fast earnings growth and sell at a premium in terms of price-to-book and price-to-earnings ratios. Because many of the stocks within a sector may fall into the growth category, for instance, a growth manager will tend to overweight those sectors relative to the broad market. This overweighting may be more due to style considerations than sector considerations, as sector weights are simply a fallout of the style decision.

There is also a distribution of companies within each industry in terms of growth and value. Some companies within an industry may be growing sales and/or earnings rapidly and sell at high price-to-earnings ratios, while others may be having trouble financially and therefore have their prices bid down by the market, making them value companies. Many investors evaluate companies in the context of their industries, trying to evaluate their growth prospects and valuations relative to their competitors in order to make investment decisions.

Historically, small company stocks have been thought of as growth stocks, since small companies have more room to grow sales and earnings, and can be nimble enough to adjust to changing preferences of their customers. Other parts of this book have shown how smaller stocks have outperformed larger stocks over the long term with a higher variability of returns. Some portion of this higher return was undoubtedly due to faster growth in sales and earnings by small companies. However, the past five years have shown us that the very largest stocks can also be growth stocks with great performance, while small stocks have not been able to keep up. Value and growth styles also exist within small cap stocks, and several index providers calculate both large-cap and small-cap growth and value indices, allowing us to evaluate the performance of both size and style at the same time.

## Comparing Growth and Value Return Series

Nearly all of the growth and value analysis done by investment professionals to date has been based on data going back about 25 years. During this period, growth and value have alternated between being in favor, with growth having had the best performance in the most recent five years. Looking at the 36-month rolling excess return of value over growth for the Fama-French series (Graph 8-6), we can see that the alternating performance of growth and value has been more of a recent phenomenon. We have to look back to 36-month periods in the early 1940s to find sustained significant outperformance of growth. Most of the history of growth versus value investing has significantly favored value investing, at least as defined by the book-to-market measure that Fama-French use. The most recent ten or fifteen years have been unusual by historical standards. Whether or not this most recent period shows that investor or market behavior has permanently changed is open to debate, but the long history shows that value has dominated.

Graph 8-6

**Excess Return of All Value Stocks Over All Growth Stocks** (in percent)
36-Month Rolling Periods

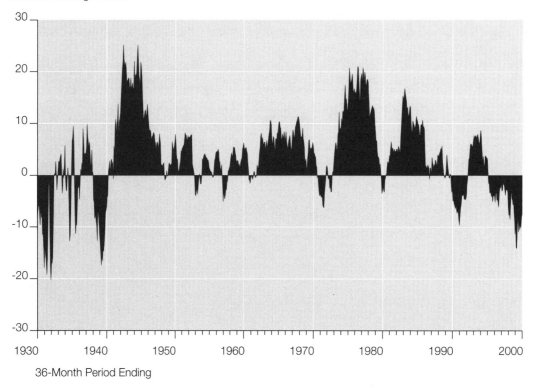

36-Month Period Ending

The dominance of value over growth occurs in both the large-cap and small-cap arena, but is even more pronounced among small-cap stocks. The 36-month rolling period chart for small-cap stocks (Graph 8-7) shows that there have only been a few short periods where small growth has outperformed small value.

Graph 8-7

**Excess Return of Small Value Stocks Over Small Growth Stocks** (in percent)
36-Month Rolling Periods

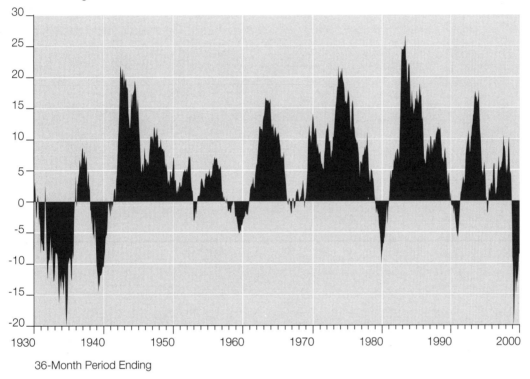

36-Month Period Ending

Graph 8-8 shows the recent cyclicality of large growth and large value, but also shows the long period of dominance of value over growth among large-cap stocks going back to the early 1940s.

Graph 8-8

**Excess Return of Large Value Stocks Over Large Growth Stocks** (in percent)
36-Month Rolling Periods

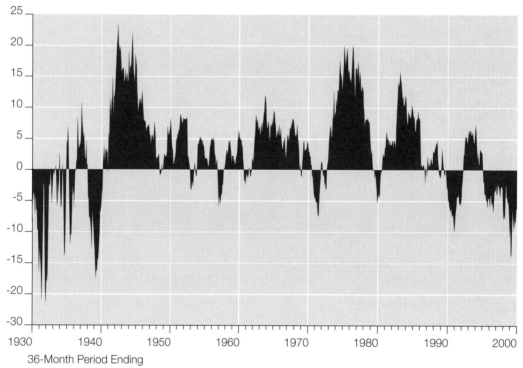

36-Month Period Ending

## Conclusion

What can explain this value effect? Readers of Graham and Dodd's Security Analysis,[1] first published in 1934, would say that the outperformance of value stocks is due to the market coming to realize the full value of a company's securities that were once undervalued. The Graham and Dodd approach to security analysis is to do an independent valuation of a company using accounting data and common market multiples, then look at the stock price to see if the stock is under- or overvalued. Several academic studies have shown that the market overreacts to bad news and underreacts to good news. This would lead us to conclude that there is more room for value stocks (which are more likely to have reported bad news) to improve and outperform growth stocks, which already have high expectations built into them.

Possibly a larger question is whether the recent enormous success of growth stocks can be expected to continue. Advocates of growth investing would argue that technology- and innovation-oriented companies will continue to dominate into the next century as the Internet changes the way the world communicates and does business. Stalwarts of value investing would argue that there are still companies and industries that continue to be ignored and represent long-term investment bargains.

Long-term history favors the value investor. Short-term history favors the growth investor.

---

1 Cottle, Sidney, Murray, Roger F., and Block, Frank E. "Graham and Dodd's Security Analysis," Fifth Edition, McGraw-Hill, 1988.

# Chapter 9

## Using Historical Data in Forecasting and Optimization

### Ibbotson Forecast of the Dow Jones Industrial Average over 100,000

In 1974, Ibbotson and Sinquefield forecasted that the Dow Jones Industrial Average (DJIA) would reach 10,000 in November 1999.[1] This forecast is only eight months shy of the actual record-breaking level hit on March 29, 1999. The forecast for the year-end 1998 DJIA was less than 50 points away from the actual close that year, 9,218 and 9,181 respectively. Table 9-1 outlines the results of the forecast made in that article and the actual realized performances from 1976–1999. The top line shows the 95th percentile or optimistic case. The middle line shows the 50th percentile or median case, and the bottom line shows the 5th percentile or pessimistic case. The bottom panel shows the same projections, redrawn as cumulative values of $1.00 invested at the beginning of 1976. Graph 9-1 shows the forecasted distribution and the realization of nominal large company stocks cumulative wealth relatives for the period 1976–2000 (year-end 1975 = 1.00).

Ibbotson and Sinquefield[2] used a simulation, or random drawing, method of making probabilistic forecasts of asset returns in their 1974 speech and 1976 article in the Journal of Business. Their method, known as a Monte Carlo simulation, relied on drawings from the actual historical data sets. Later, other researchers showed that Ibbotson and Sinquefield's forecasts could be closely replicated by a lognormal distribution with parameters derived from summary statistics of historical returns and current bond yields.[3] This latter, parametric method based on the lognormal distribution was first adopted by Ibbotson and Sinquefield in the 1982 edition of the *Stocks, Bonds, Bills, and Inflation Yearbook* to produce probabilistic forecasts. It has since been incorporated into Ibbotson Associates' software products.

In 1998, Ibbotson updated the forecast for the DJIA using this lognormal method of covering the next 26 years (through 2025).[4] To forecast the growth of the DJIA, first the average compound return for large company stocks was forecasted at 11.6 percent. This forecast is based on the total return of large company stocks, which includes both income return and capital appreciation. Because the DJIA only tracks the capital appreciation of its inclusive stocks, the 11.6 percent total return forecast is an inappropriate measure of the index's growth. A more appropriate measure would be to subtract the dividend yield on the DJIA, which was 1.6 percent at year-end 1998. The total return (11.6 percent) minus the dividend yield (1.6 percent) equals the capital appreciation (10.0 percent). This capital gain rate can be applied to the DJIA to estimate the long-term growth of the index. At year-end 1998, the DJIA closed at 9,181. By applying the 10.0 percent average compound return to the DJIA year-end 1999 close, the DJIA is forecasted to close over 100,000 by year-end 2025. This DJIA forecast is a point estimate that is the average of the probability distribution. The entire company stock return distribution and a detailed description of the lognormal method can be found later in this chapter.

---

1  Ibbotson, Roger G., and Rex A. Sinquefield, (1974) Speech to the Center for Research in Security Prices, May, 1974.
2  More detail on the simulation method can be found in Ibbotson, Roger G., and Rex A. Sinquefield, "Stocks, Bonds, Bills, and Inflation: Simulations of the Future (1976–2000)," *Journal of Business*, vol. 49, No. 3, July 1976.
3  Lewis, Alan L., Sheen T. Kassouf, R. Dennis Brehm, and Jack Johnston, "The Ibbotson-Sinquefield Simulation Made Easy," *Journal of Business*, vol. 53 (1980), pp. 205–214.
4  Published in the April 5, 1999 editions of *Pensions & Investments and Investment News*.

## Table 9-1

### Forecasted Distributions of Compound Annual Returns and End of Period Wealth for the Period 1976–2000

| Percentile | Forecasted Compound Annual Returns 1976–2000 (in percent) | | | |
| | Large Company Stocks | Long-Term Government Bonds | Long-Term Corporate Bonds | Inflation |
| --- | --- | --- | --- | --- |
| 95th | 21.5 | 12.3 | 12.7 | 11.3 |
| 90th | 19.3 | 11.0 | 11.4 | 10.2 |
| 70th | 15.2 | 9.1 | 9.4 | 7.8 |
| 50th | 13.1 | 7.8 | 8.1 | 6.1 |
| 30th | 10.3 | 6.6 | 7.0 | 4.7 |
| 10th | 6.9 | 4.8 | 5.2 | 2.9 |
| 5th | 5.2 | 4.3 | 4.5 | 2.0 |
| Mean | 13.0 | 8.0 | 8.2 | 6.4 |
| Standard Deviations | 4.9 | 2.3 | 2.4 | 2.9 |
| Realizations (1976–1999) | 16.5 | 9.4 | 9.5 | 4.7 |

| Percentile | Forecasted End of Period Wealth 12/31/2000 ($1 invested on 12/31/1975) | | | |
| | Large Company Stocks | Long-Term Government Bonds | Long-Term Corporate Bonds | Inflation |
| --- | --- | --- | --- | --- |
| 95th | 130.14 | 18.18 | 19.87 | 14.53 |
| 90th | 82.42 | 13.59 | 14.86 | 11.34 |
| 70th | 34.38 | 8.82 | 9.45 | 6.54 |
| 50th | 21.71 | 6.54 | 7.01 | 4.39 |
| 30th | 11.60 | 4.94 | 5.43 | 3.15 |
| 10th | 5.30 | 3.23 | 3.55 | 2.04 |
| 5th | 3.55 | 2.86 | 3.01 | 1.64 |
| Mean | 38.31 | 7.81 | 8.43 | 5.81 |
| Standard Deviations | 61.35 | 4.55 | 5.30 | 4.39 |
| Realizations (1976–1999) | 38.90 | 8.62 | 8.77 | 3.03 |

Graph 9-1

**Forecasted Distribution and the Realization of Nominal Large Company Stocks Cumulative Wealth Relatives for the Period 1976–1999**

Year-End 1975 = 1.00

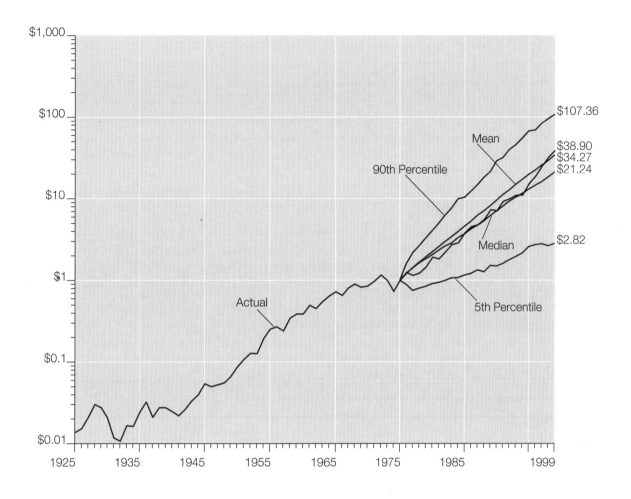

## Probabilistic Forecasts

When forecasting the return on an asset or a portfolio, investors are (or should be) interested in the entire probability distribution of future outcomes, not just the mean or "point estimate." An example of a point estimate forecast is that large company stocks will have a return of 13 percent in 2001. It is more helpful to know the uncertainty surrounding this point estimate than to know the point estimate itself. One measure of uncertainty is standard deviation. The large company stock return forecast can be expressed as 13 percent representing the mean with 20 percent representing the standard deviation.

If the returns on large company stocks are normally distributed, the mean (expected return) and the standard deviation provide enough information to forecast the likelihood of any return. Suppose one wants to ascertain the likelihood that large company stocks will have a return of –25 percent or lower in 2001. Given the above example, a return of –25 percent is [13 – (–25)]/20 = 1.9 standard deviations below the mean. The likelihood of an observation 1.9 or more standard deviations below the mean is 2.9 percent. (This can be looked up in any statistics textbook, in the table showing values of the cumulative probability function for a normal distribution.) Thus, the likelihood that the stock market will fall by 25 percent or more in 2001 is 2.9 percent. This is valuable information, both to the investor who believes that stocks are a sure thing and to the investor who is certain that they will crash tomorrow.

In fact, the historical returns of large company stocks are not exactly normally distributed, and a slightly different method needs to be used to make probabilistic forecasts. The actual model used to forecast the distribution of stock returns is described later in this chapter.

Some people are wary of probabilistic forecasts because they seem too wide to be useful, or because they lack punch. (The most widely quoted forecasters, after all, make very specific predictions.) However, the forecast of a probability distribution actually reveals much more than the point estimate. The point estimate reflects what statisticians call an "expected value"—but one does not actually expect this particular outcome to happen. The actual return will likely be higher or lower than the point estimate. By knowing the extent to which actual returns are likely to deviate from the point estimate, the investor can assess the risk of every asset, and thus compare investment opportunities in terms of their risks as well as their expected returns. As Harry Markowitz showed nearly a half-century ago in his Nobel Prize-winning work on portfolio theory, investors care about avoiding risk as well as seeking return. Probabilistic forecasts enable investors to quantify these concepts.

## Simulation

Simulation is the common method used to generate probabilistic forecasts of the future performance of financial instruments. In its most general sense, simulation is concerned with creating fictitious stories based on factual knowledge of what can happen. The fictitious event may be in the past or the future, or it may have no specific place on the time line. Thus, it is meaningful to talk about using a computer to simulate a thunderstorm, or a random number generator (a tossed coin will do) to simulate returns in the stock market. The kind of simulation with which this chapter is concerned is creating future probability distributions of asset and portfolio returns based on historical and current data.

## The Lognormal Distribution

In the lognormal model, the natural logarithms of asset return relatives are assumed to be normally distributed. (A return relative is one plus the return. That is, if an asset has a return of 15 percent in a given period, its return relative is 1.15.)

The lognormal distribution is skewed to the right. That is, the expected value, or mean, is greater than the median. Furthermore, if return relatives are lognormally distributed, returns cannot fall below negative 100 percent. These properties of the lognormal distribution make it a more accurate characterization of the behavior of market returns than does the normal distribution.

In all normal distributions, moreover, the probability of an observation falling below the mean by as much as one standard deviation equals the probability of falling above the mean by as much as one standard deviation; both probabilities are about 34 percent. In a lognormal distribution, these probabilities differ and depend on the parameters of the distribution.

## Forecasting Wealth Values and Rates of Return

Using the lognormal model, it is fairly simple to form probabilistic forecasts of both compound rates of return and ending period wealth values. Wealth at time $n$ (assuming reinvestment of all income and no taxes) is:

$$W_n = W_0 (1 + r_1)(1 + r_2)...(1 + r_n)$$

(33)

where,

| | |
|---|---|
| $W_n$ | = the wealth value at time $n$; |
| $W_0$ | = the initial investment at time $0$; and, |
| $r_1, r_2,$ etc. | = the total returns on the portfolio for the rebalancing period ending at times 1, 2, and so forth. |

The compound rate of return or geometric mean return over the same period, $r_G$, is:

$$r_G = \left( \frac{W_n}{W_0} \right)^{\frac{1}{n}} - 1$$

(34)

where,

| | |
|---|---|
| $r_G$ | = the geometric mean return; |
| $W_n$ | = the ending period wealth value at time $n$; |
| $W_0$ | = the initial wealth value at time $0$; and, |
| $n$ | = the inclusive number of periods. |

By assuming that all of the $(1 + r_n)$s are lognormally distributed with the same expected value and standard deviation and are all statistically independent of each other, it follows that $W_n$ and $(1 + r_G)$ are lognormally distributed. In fact, even if the $(1 + r_n)$s are not themselves lognormally distributed but are independent and identically distributed, $W_n$ and $(1 + r_G)$ are approximately lognormal for large enough values of $n$. This "central-limit theorem" means that the lognormal model can be useful in long-term forecasting even if short-term returns are not well described by a lognormal distribution.

## Calculating Parameters of the Lognormal Model

To use the lognormal model, we must first calculate the expected value and standard deviation of the natural logarithm of the return relative of the portfolio. These parameters, denoted **m** and **s** respectively, can be calculated from the expected return ($\mu$) and standard deviation ($\sigma$) of the portfolio as follows:

$$m = \ln(1 + \mu) - \left( \frac{s^2}{2} \right) \qquad (35)$$

$$s = \sqrt{\ln\left[ 1 + \left( \frac{\sigma}{1+\mu} \right)^2 \right]} \qquad (36)$$

where,

$\ln$ = the natural logarithm function.

To calculate a particular percentile of wealth or return for a given time horizon, the only remaining parameter needed is the z-score of the percentile. The z-score of a percentile ranking is that percentile ranking expressed as the number of standard deviations that it is above or below the mean of a normal distribution. For example, the z-score of the 95th percentile is 1.645 because in a normal distribution, the 95th percentile is 1.645 standard deviations above the 50th percentile or median, which is also the mean. Z-scores can be obtained from a table of cumulative values of the standard normal distribution or from software that produces such values.

Given the logarithmic parameters of a portfolio (**m** and **s**), a time horizon (**n**), and the z-score of a percentile (**z**), the percentile in question in terms of cumulative wealth at the end of the time horizon ($W_n$) is:

$$e^{(mn + zs\sqrt{n})} \qquad (37)$$

Similarly, the percentile in question in terms of the compound rate of return for the period ($r_G$) is:

$$e^{\left( m + z\frac{s}{\sqrt{n}} \right)} - 1 \qquad (38)$$

Graph 9-2

**Efficient Frontier**

Large Company Stocks, Long-Term Government Bonds, and U.S. Treasury Bills

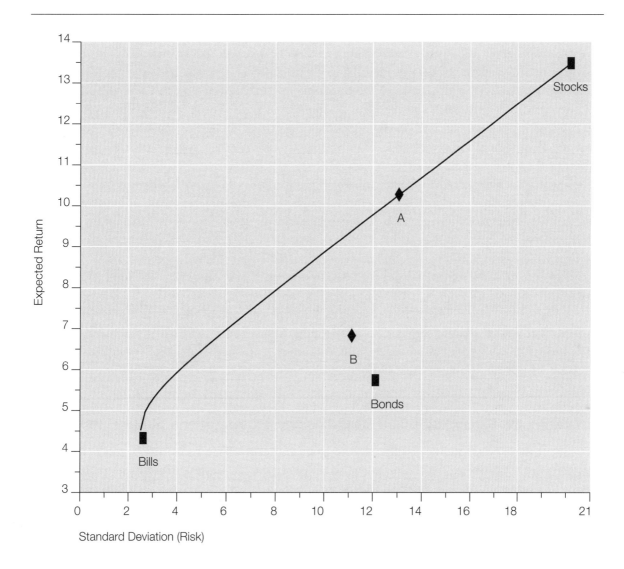

## Mean-Variance Optimization

One important application of the probability forecasts of asset returns is mean-variance optimization. Optimization is the process of identifying portfolios that have the highest possible expected return for a given level of risk, or the lowest possible risk for a given expected return. Such a portfolio is considered "efficient," and the locus of all efficient portfolios is called the efficient frontier. An efficient frontier constructed from large company stocks, long-term government bonds, and Treasury bills is shown in Graph 9-2. All investors should hold portfolios that are efficient with respect to the assets in their opportunity set.

The most widely accepted framework for optimization is Markowitz or mean-variance optimization (MVO), which makes the following assumptions: 1) the forecast mean, or expected return, describes the attribute that investors consider to be desirable about an asset; 2) the risk of the asset is measured by its expected standard deviation of returns; and 3) the interaction between one asset and another is captured by the expected correlation coefficient of the two assets' returns. MVO thus requires forecasts of the return and standard deviation of each asset, and the correlation of each asset with every other asset.[5]

In the 1950s, Harry Markowitz developed both the concept of the efficient frontier and the mathematical means of constructing it (mean-variance optimization)[6]. Currently, there are a number of commercially available mean-variance optimization software packages, including Ibbotson Associates' *Portfolio Strategist*™ and *EnCorr Optimizer*.™[7]

## Estimating the Means, Standard Deviations, and Correlations of Asset Returns

To simulate future probability distributions of asset and portfolio returns, one typically estimates parameters of the historical return data. The parameters that are required to simulate returns on an asset are its mean and standard deviation. To simulate returns on portfolios of assets, one must also estimate the correlation of each asset in the portfolio with every other asset. Thus, the parameters required to conduct a simulation are the same as those required as inputs into a mean-variance optimization.[8]

To illustrate how to estimate the parameters of asset class returns relevant to optimization and forecasting, we construct an example using large company stocks, long-term government bonds, and Treasury bills. The techniques used to estimate these parameters are described below. They are the same techniques as those used in Ibbotson Associates' *Optimizer Inputs*™ data product and *EnCorr InputsGenerator*™ software product.

5 The standard deviation is the square root of the variance; hence the term "mean-variance" in describing this form of the optimization problem.
6 Markowitz, Harry M., Portfolio Selection: Efficient Diversification of Investments, New York: John Wiley & Sons, 1959.
7 For additional information regarding Portfolio Strategist and EnCorr software, refer to the Product Information page at the back of this book.
8 It is also possible to conduct a simulation using entire data sets, that is, without estimating the statistical parameters of the data sets. Typically, in such a nonparametric simulation, the frequency of an event occurring in the simulated history is equal to the frequency of the event occurring in the actual history used to construct the data set.

## Means, or Expected Returns

The mean return (forecast mean, or expected return) on an asset is the probability-weighted average of all possible returns on the asset over a future period. Estimates of expected returns are based on models of asset returns. While many models of asset returns incorporate estimates of GNP, the money supply, and other macroeconomic variables, the model employed in this chapter does not. This is because we assume (for the present purpose) that asset markets are informationally efficient, with all relevant and available information fully incorporated in asset prices. If this assumption holds, investor expectations (forecasts) can be discerned from market-observable data. Such forecasts are not attempts to outguess, or beat, the market. They are attempts to discern the market's expectations, i.e., to read what the market itself is forecasting.

For some assets, expected returns can be estimated using current market data alone. For example, the yield on a riskless bond is an estimate of its expected return. For other assets, current data are not sufficient. Stocks, for example, have no exact analogue to the yield on a bond. In such cases, we use the statistical time series properties of historical data in forming the estimates.

To know which data to use in estimating expected returns, we need to know the rebalancing frequency of the portfolios and the planning horizon. In our example, we will assume an annual rebalancing frequency and a twenty-year planning horizon. The rebalancing frequency gives the time units in which returns are measured.

With a fixed twenty-year planning horizon, the relevant riskless rate is the yield on a zero-coupon, twenty-year bond. At the end of 2000, the yield on a twenty-year "zero" was 5.7 percent. This riskless rate is the baseline, from which the expected return on every other asset class is derived by adding or subtracting risk premia.

## Large Company Stocks

The expected return on large company stocks is the riskless rate, plus the expected risk premium of large company stocks over bonds that are riskless over the planning horizon. With a twenty-year planning horizon, this risk premium is 7.8 percent, shown as the long-horizon expected equity risk premium in Table 9-2. Hence, the expected return on large company stocks is 5.7 (the riskless rate) plus 7.8 (the risk premium) for a total of 13.5 percent (due to rounding).

## Bonds and Bills

For default-free bonds with a maturity equal to the planning horizon, the expected return is the yield on the bond; that is, the expected return is the riskless rate of 5.7 percent. For bonds with other maturities, the expected bond horizon premium should be added to the riskless rate (for longer maturities) or subtracted from the riskless rate (for shorter maturities). Since expected capital gains on a bond are zero, the expected horizon premium is estimated by the historical average difference of the income returns on the bonds.[9]

For Treasury bills, the expected return over a given time horizon is equal to the expected return on a Treasury bond of a similar horizon, less the expected horizon premium of bonds over bills. This

---

9 The expected capital gain on a par bond is self-evidently zero. For a zero-coupon (or other discount) bond, investors expect the price to rise as the bond ages, but the expected portion of this price increase should not be considered a capital gain. It is a form of income return.

premium is estimated by the historical average of the difference of the income return on bonds and the return on bills. From Table 9-2, this is 1.0 percent. Subtracting this from the riskless rate gives us an expected return on bills of 4.1 percent. Of course, this forecast typically differs from the current yield on a Treasury bill, since a portfolio of Treasury bills is rolled over (the proceeds of maturing bills are invested in new bills, at yields not yet known) during the time horizon described.

## Standard Deviations

Standard deviations are estimated from historical data as described in Chapter 6. Since there is no evidence of a major change in the variability of returns on large company stocks, we use the entire period 1926–2000 to estimate the standard deviation of these asset classes. For bonds and bills, we use the period 1970–2000. The use of this more recent period reflects the fact that the volatility of bonds has increased over time.

Table 9-2

**Building Blocks for Expected Return Construction**

|  | **Value** (in percent) |
|---|---|
| **Yields (Riskless Rates)[1]** | |
| Long-Term (20-year) U.S. Treasury Strip Yield | 5.7 |
| Intermediate-Term (5-year) U.S. Treasury Strip Yield | 5.1 |
| Short-Term (30-day) U.S. Treasury Bill Yield | 5.7 |
| **Fixed Income Risk Premia[2]** | |
| Expected default premium: *long-term corporate bond total returns minus long-term government bond total returns* | −0.1 |
| Expected long-term horizon premium: *long-term government bond income returns minus U.S. Treasury bill total returns** | 1.4 |
| Expected intermediate-term horizon premium: *intermediate-term government bond income returns minus U.S. Treasury bill total returns** | 1.0 |
| **Equity Risk Premia[3]** | |
| Long-horizon expected equity risk premium: *large company stock total returns minus long-term government bond income returns* | 7.8 |
| Intermediate-horizon expected equity risk premium: *large company stock total returns minus intermediate-term government bond income returns* | 8.2 |
| Short-horizon expected equity risk premium: *large company stock total returns minus U.S. Treasury bill total returns** | 9.1 |
| Small Stock Premium: *small company stock total return minus large company stock total return* | 4.3 |

[1] As of December 31, 2000. Maturities are approximate.

[2] Expected risk premia for fixed income are based on the differences of historical arithmetic mean returns from 1970–2000.

[3] Expected risk premia for equities are based on the differences of historical arithmetic mean returns from 1926–2000.

*For U.S. Treasury bills, the income return and total return are the same.

## Correlations

Correlations between the asset classes are estimated from historical data as described in Chapter 6. We use the period 1926–2000 to form the estimates for stocks, the same period over which standard deviations are calculated. Correlation coefficients for bonds and bills are derived from 1970–2000. Correlations between major asset classes change over time. Graph 9-3 shows the historical correlation of annual returns on large company stocks and intermediate term bonds over 20 year rolling periods from 1926–1945 through 1981–2000.

## Generating Probabilistic Forecasts

For large company stocks in Table 9-3, the logarithmic parameters are calculated to be $m = 0.1110$ and $s = 0.1766$ based on equations (35) and (36). The z-scores of the 95th, 50th, and 5th percentile are 1.645, 0, and −1.645, respectively. Using these parameters, we can calculate the 95th, 50th, and 5th percentiles of cumulative wealth and compound returns over various time horizons using equations (37) and (38). Graph 9-4 shows percentiles of compound returns over the entire range of one to twenty year horizons in graphical form. This type of graph is sometimes called a "trumpet" graph because the high and low percentile curves taken together make the shape of a trumpet. The "mouthpiece" of the trumpet is on the right side of the graph because for long time horizons, all percentiles converge to the median (50th percentile).

Table 9-3

**Optimizer Inputs: Year-End 2000 Large Company Stocks, Long-Term Government Bonds, and U.S. Treasury Bills** (in percent)

| | Expected Return | Standard Deviation | Correlation with | | |
| | | | Stocks | Bonds | Bills |
|---|---|---|---|---|---|
| Stocks | 13.5 | 20.2 | 1.00 | | |
| Bonds | 5.7 | 12.1 | 0.36 | 1.00 | |
| Bills | 4.3 | 2.6 | −0.09 | 0.00 | 1.00 |

Graph 9-5 is a graph showing percentiles of cumulative wealth over the entire range of zero to twenty year time horizons, along with the back history of the portfolio's performance. The past and forecasted (future) values on the graph are connected by setting the wealth index to $1.00 at the end of 2000. The past index values show how much wealth one would have had to hold in large company stocks to have $1.00 at the end of 2000; the percentiles of future value show the probability distribution of future growth of $1.00 invested in large company stocks. This type of graph is sometimes called a "tulip" graph because of its overall shape.

Table 9-4 shows (in the top panel) the probability distribution of compound annual returns on large company stocks over the next 20 years. The top line shows the 95th percentile or optimistic case, the middle line the 50th percentile or median case, and the bottom line the 5th percentile or pessimistic case. The bottom panel shows the same projections, redrawn as cumulative values of $1.00 invested at the beginning of the period simulated. Simulations such as these are used for asset allocation, funding of liabilities, and other portfolio management-related applications; Ibbotson Associates' *Portfolio Strategist* and *EnCorr Optimizer* can produce these forecasts.

Graph 9-3

**Twenty Year Rolling Period Correlations of Annual Returns**
Large Company Stocks and Intermediate-Term Government Bonds

from 1926–1945 through 1981–2000

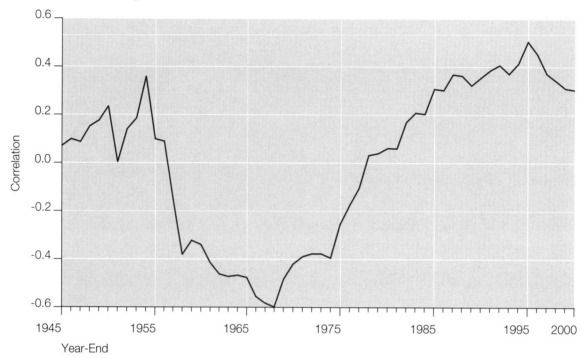

Graph 9-4

**Forecast Total Return Distribution**
100 Percent Large Stocks

from 2001 to 2020

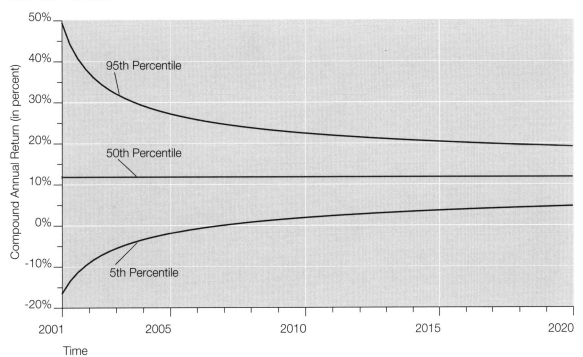

Table 9-4

**Forecast Distributions of Compound Annual Returns
and End of Period Wealth**
Large Company Stocks: Year-End 2000

| Percentile | Compound Annual Return (in percent) | | | | |
| | 2001 | 2002 | 2005 | 2010 | 2020 |
|---|---|---|---|---|---|
| 95th | 49.33 | 37.16 | 27.20 | 22.46 | 19.21 |
| 90th | 40.06 | 31.09 | 23.61 | 20.00 | 17.52 |
| 75th | 25.84 | 21.53 | 17.83 | 16.01 | 14.74 |
| 50th | 11.72 | 11.72 | 11.72 | 11.72 | 11.72 |
| 25th | −0.81 | 2.71 | 5.94 | 7.60 | 8.79 |
| 10th | −10.88 | −4.78 | 0.98 | 4.02 | 6.22 |
| 5th | −16.41 | −9.00 | −1.87 | 1.93 | 4.71 |

| Percentile | End of Period Wealth ($1 Invested on 12/31/00) | | | | |
| | 2001 | 2002 | 2005 | 2010 | 2020 |
|---|---|---|---|---|---|
| 95th | 1.49 | 1.88 | 3.33 | 7.58 | 33.61 |
| 90th | 1.40 | 1.72 | 2.89 | 6.19 | 25.23 |
| 75th | 1.26 | 1.48 | 2.27 | 4.41 | 15.63 |
| 50th | 1.12 | 1.25 | 1.74 | 3.03 | 9.18 |
| 25th | 0.99 | 1.05 | 1.33 | 2.08 | 5.39 |
| 10th | 0.89 | 0.91 | 1.05 | 1.48 | 3.34 |
| 5th | 0.84 | 0.83 | 0.91 | 1.21 | 2.51 |

## Constructing Efficient Portfolios

A mean-variance optimizer uses the complete set of optimizer inputs (the expected return and standard deviation of each asset class and the correlation of returns for each pair of asset classes) to generate an efficient frontier. The efficient frontier shown in Graph 9-2 was generated from the inputs described above and summarized in Table 9-3. Each point on the frontier represents a portfolio mix that is mean-variance efficient. The point labeled A represents a portfolio that contains 65 percent in large company stocks, and 35 percent in Treasury bills. (Recall that other asset classes were not considered in this example.) From the location of point A on the grid, we can find its expected return (10.27 percent) and standard deviation (13.06 percent).

Graph 9-5

**Forecast Distribution of Wealth Index Value**
100 Percent Large Stocks

from 2001 to 2020

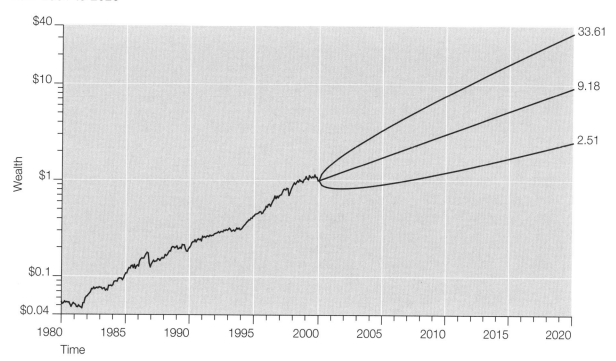

## Using Inputs to Form Other Portfolios

Given a complete set of inputs, the expected return and standard deviation of any portfolio (efficient or other) of the asset classes can be calculated. The expected return of a portfolio is the weighted average of the expected returns of the asset classes:

$$r_p = \sum_{i=1}^{n} x_i r_i$$

(39)

where,

$r_p$ = the expected return of the portfolio $p$;

$n$ = the number of asset classes;

$x_i$ = the portfolio weight of asset class $i$, scaled such that

$$\sum_{i=1}^{n} x_i = 1; \text{ and,}$$

$r_i$ = the expected return of asset class $i$.

The point labeled B in Graph 9-2 represents a portfolio that contains 15 percent in large company stocks (asset class 1), 80 percent in long-term bonds (asset class 2), and 5 percent in Treasury bills (asset class 3). Applying the above formula to this portfolio using the inputs in Table 9-3, we calculate the expected return to be 6.8 percent as follows:

$$(0.15 \times 0.135) + (0.80 \times 0.057) + (0.05 \times 0.043) = 0.068$$

The standard deviation of the portfolio depends not only on the standard deviations of the asset classes, but on all of the correlations as well. It is given by:

$$\sigma_p = \sqrt{\sum_{i=1}^{n} \sum_{j=1}^{n} x_i x_j \sigma_i \sigma_j \rho_{ij}}$$

(40)

where,

$\sigma_p$ = the standard deviation of the portfolio;

$x_i$ and $x_j$ = the portfolio weights of asset classes $i$ and $j$;

$\sigma_i$ and $\sigma_j$ = the standard deviations of returns on asset classes $i$ and $j$; and,

$\rho_{ij}$ = the correlation between returns on asset classes $i$ and $j$.

Note that $\rho_{ii}$ equals one and that $\rho_{ij}$ is equal to $\rho_{ji}$.

The standard deviation for point B in Graph 9-2 (containing three asset classes) would be calculated as follows:

|  | Stocks (asset class 1) | Bonds (asset class 2) | Bills (asset class 3) |
|---|---|---|---|
| Stocks | $x_1^2 \, \sigma_1^2 \, \rho_{1,1} =$<br>$(0.15)^2(0.202)^2(1) =$<br>0.00092 | $x_1 \, x_2 \, \sigma_1 \, \sigma_2 \, \rho_{1,2} =$<br>$(0.15)(0.8)(0.202)(0.121)(0.36)=$<br>0.00106 | $x_1 \, x_3 \, \sigma_1 \, \sigma_3 \, \rho_{1,3} =$<br>$(0.15)(0.05)(0.202)(0.026)(-0.09) =$<br>0.00000 |
| Bonds | $x_1 \, x_2 \, \sigma_1 \, \sigma_2 \, \rho_{1,2} =$<br>$(0.15)(0.8)(0.202)(0.121)(0.36) =$<br>0.00106 | $x_2^2 \, \sigma_2^2 \, \rho_{2,2} =$<br>$(0.8)^2(0.121)^2(1)=$<br>0.00937 | $x_2 \, x_3 \, \sigma_2 \, \sigma_3 \, \rho_{2,3} =$<br>$(0.8)(0.05)(0.121)(0.026)(0.01) =$<br>0.00000 |
| Bills | $x_1 \, x_3 \, \sigma_1 \, \sigma_3 \, \rho_{1,3} =$<br>$(0.15)(0.05)(0.202)(0.026)(-0.09) =$<br>0.00000 | $x_2 \, x_3 \, \sigma_2 \, \sigma_3 \, \rho_{2,3} =$<br>$(0.8)(0.05)(0.121)(0.026)(0.01) =$<br>0.00000 | $x_3^2 \, \sigma_3^2 \, \rho_{3,3} =$<br>$(0.05)^2(0.026)^2(1) =$<br>0.00000 |

By summing these terms and taking the square root of the total, the result is a standard deviation of 11.1 percent.

All tables and graphs presented in this chapter were prepared using Ibbotson Associates' *Portfolio Strategist*™ and *EnCorr*™ suite of asset allocation software and data products. Using these tools, similar analyses can be performed for a wide variety of asset classes, historical time periods, percentiles, and planning horizons. Additionally, Ibbotson Associates offers returns based style analysis products to aid in the evaluation of mutual funds for use in implementing an optimal asset mix. These products include *EnCorr Attribution* and *Fund Strategist* software.

# Chapter 10
## A New Historical Database of the NYSE

## Introduction

Studies on the long-horizon predictability of stock returns, by necessity, require a database of return information that dates as far back as possible. Ibbotson Associates is the leading producer and supplier of a broad set of historical returns on asset classes dating back to 1926. Researchers interested in the dynamics of the U.S. capital markets over earlier decades have had to rely upon indices of uneven quality. Roger Ibbotson and William N. Goetzmann, professors of finance, and Liang Peng, a Ph.D. candidate in finance, all at Yale School of Management, have assembled a New York Stock Exchange database for the period prior to 1926. This chapter covers the sources and construction of this new database extending back to 1815.

We firmly believe that a 1926 starting date was approximately when quality financial data became available. However, the hope is that the new data will allow modern researchers of pre-1926 stock returns, along with future researchers, to test a broad range of hypotheses about the U.S. capital markets as well as open up new areas for more accurate analysis.

## Data Sources and Collection Methods

### Share Price Collection

End-of-month equity prices for companies listed on the New York Stock Exchange (NYSE) were hand-collected from three different sources published over the period January 1815 to December 1870. For the time period 1871 through 1925, end-of-month NYSE stock prices were collected from the major New York newspapers.

*The New York Shipping List*, later called *The New York Shipping and Commercial*, served as the "official" source for NYSE share price collection up until the early 1850s. In the mid-1850s, *The New York Shipping List* reported prices for fewer and fewer stocks. This led to the collection of price quotes from *The New York Herald* and *The New York Times*. While neither claimed to be the official list for the NYSE, the number of securities quoted by each far exceeded the number quoted by *The New York Shipping List*.

It is important to note that in instances where no transaction took place in December, the latest bid and ask prices were averaged to obtain a year-end price. In total, at least two prices from 664 companies were collected. From a low number of eight firms in 1815, the number of firms in the index reached a high point in May of 1883 with 114 listed firms.

One interesting observation was the fact that share prices for much of the period of analysis remained around 100. Graph 10-1 illustrates this point. The graph shows that the typical price of a share of stock was around 100. The distribution of stock prices is significantly skewed to the left with only a few trading above 200. Such a distribution suggests that management maintained a ceiling on stock prices by paying out most of earnings as dividends. No reports of stock splits over the period of data were discovered.

Graph 10-1

**Distribution of Raw Stock Prices**
from 1815 to 1925

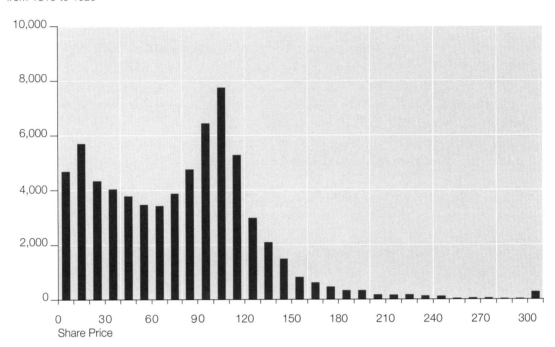

## Dividend Collection

Dividend data was collected for the period 1825–1870 by identifying the semi-annual dividend announcements for equity securities as reported in *The New York Commercial, The Banker's Magazine, The New York Times,* and *The New York Herald.* From 1871 to 1925, aggregate dividend data from the Alfred Cowles[1] series was used. Whether or not the above publications reported dividends for all NYSE stocks is unknown. As a result, there is no way of knowing whether missing dividends meant that they were not paid or possibly not reported. Dividend records were collected for more than 500 stocks in the sample, and most stocks paid dividends semiannually.

In order to estimate the income return for each year, two approaches were implemented. The first approach, the low dividend return estimate, consisted of the summation of all of the dividends paid in a given year by firms whose prices were observed in the preceding year. This number is then divided by the sum of the last available preceding year prices for those firms. The second approach, the high dividend return estimate, focused solely on firms that paid regular dividends and for which price data was collected. The sample is restricted to firms that have two years of dividend payments (four semiannual dividends) and for which there was a price observation. Using the second approach, dividend yields tend to be quite high by modern standards.

---

1 Cowles, Alfred. (1939). *Common Stock Indices.* Principia Press, Bloomington.

It is important to note that when both a high and a low income return series were present, the average was computed. This holds true for the summary statistics table in this chapter as well as the graphs/tables presented throughout. Also, due to missing income return data for the year 1868, an average of the previous forty-three years was computed and used.

## Price Index Estimation

### Index Calculation Concerns

When attempting to construct an index without having market capitalization data readily available, one is left with one of two options: an equal-weighted index or a price-weighted index. One key concern with an equal-weighted index is the effect of a bid-ask bounce. Take for example an illiquid stock that trades at either $1.00 or $2.00 per share. When it rises in price from $1.00 to $2.00, it goes up by 100 percent. When it decreases in price from $2.00 to $1.00, it drops by 50 percent. Equally weighting these returns can produce a substantial upward bias. This led us to the construction of a price-weighted index.

### Calculation of the Price-Weighted Index

The procedure used for calculating the price-weighted index is rather simple. For each month, returns are calculated for all stocks that trade in two consecutive periods. These returns are weighted by the price at the beginning of the two periods.

The return of the price-weighted index closely approximates the return to a "buy and hold" portfolio over the period. Buy and hold portfolios are not sensitive to bid-ask bounce bias. We believe that the price-weighted index does a fairly good job of avoiding such an upward bias.

It was found that companies were rather concentrated into specific industries. In 1815, the index was about evenly split between banks and insurance companies. Banks, transportation firms (primarily canals and railroads), and insurance companies made up the index by the 1850s. By the end of the sample period, the index was dominated by transport companies and other industrials.

## A Look at the Historical Results

It is important to note that there are a few missing months of data that create gaps in the analysis. The NYSE was closed from July 1914 to December 1914 due to World War I. This is obviously an institutional gap. There are additional gaps. The number of available security records was quite lower after 1871. A change in the range of coverage by the financial press is the likely culprit for this. Missing data for the late 1860s quite possibly can be due to the Civil War because the NYSE was definitely open at that time. Further data collection efforts hopefully will allow these missing records to be filled in.

Table 10-1 illustrates summary statistics of annual returns of large company stocks for three different time periods. Note that the three different periods cover the new pre-1926 data, the familiar 1926 to 2000 time period, and a combination of the two.

## Table 10-1

**Large Company Stocks**
Summary Statistics of Annual Returns
from 1825 to 1925

|  | Geometric Mean | Arithmetic Mean | Standard Deviation |
|---|---|---|---|
| Total Return | 7.3% | 8.4% | 16.3% |
| Income Return | 5.9% | 5.9% | 1.9% |
| Capital Appreciation | 1.3% | 2.5% | 16.1% |

from 1926 to 2000

|  | Geometric Mean | Arithmetic Mean | Standard Deviation |
|---|---|---|---|
| Total Return | 11.0% | 13.0% | 20.2% |
| Income Return | 4.4% | 4.4% | 1.4% |
| Capital Appreciation | 6.4% | 8.3% | 19.5% |

from 1825 to 2000

|  | Geometric Mean | Arithmetic Mean | Standard Deviation |
|---|---|---|---|
| Total Return | 8.9% | 10.4% | 18.2% |
| Income Return | 5.2% | 5.3% | 1.8% |
| Capital Appreciation | 3.5% | 5.0% | 17.8% |

## Price Returns

It is interesting to note that the price-weighted index in Table 10-1 has an annual geometric capital appreciation return from 1825 through 1925 of 1.3 percent. This number is significantly lower when compared to the 6.4 percent annual capital appreciation return experienced by large company stocks over the period 1926 through 2000. This once again alludes to the suggestion that dividend policies have evolved over the past two centuries, and that management of old most likely paid out earnings and kept their stock prices lower. In today's financial world, capital appreciation is accepted as a substitute for dividend payments.

Graph 10-2 shows the annual capital appreciation returns for the period 1825 to 2000. The rise in capital appreciation returns over the years is more evident when viewing returns on a twenty-year rolling period basis, as Graph 10-3 demonstrates.

Graph 10-2

**Large Company Stocks Annual Capital Appreciation Returns** (in percent)
from 1825 to 2000

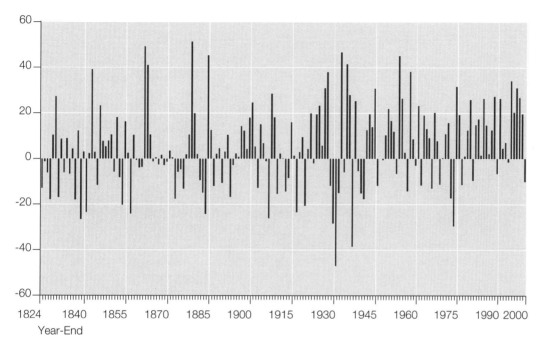

Year-End

Graph 10-3

**20-Year Rolling Capital Appreciation Returns for Large Company Stocks** (in percent)
from 1844 to 2000

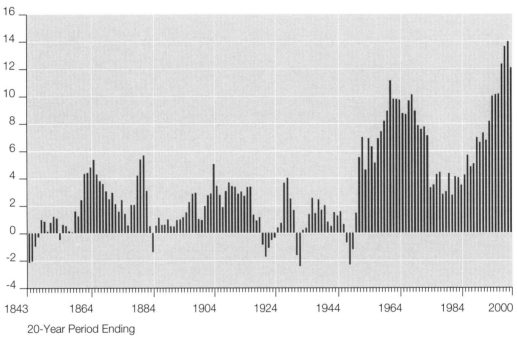

20-Year Period Ending

## Income Returns

Table 10-1 also illustrates the summary statistics for the annual income return series. The higher income return of 5.9 percent in the earlier period, and the fact the many stocks traded near par, once again suggest that most companies paid out a large share of their profits rather than retaining them.

Graph 10-4 shows the annual income returns for the period 1825 to 2000. In fact, when looking at the time distribution of dividend changes over the new time period, dividend decreases were only slightly less common than increases, suggesting that managers may have been less averse to cutting dividends than they are today. Perhaps in the pre-income tax environment of the nineteenth century, investors had a preference for income returns, as opposed to capital appreciation.

Graph 10-4

**Large Company Stocks Annual Income Returns** (in percent)
from 1825 to 2000

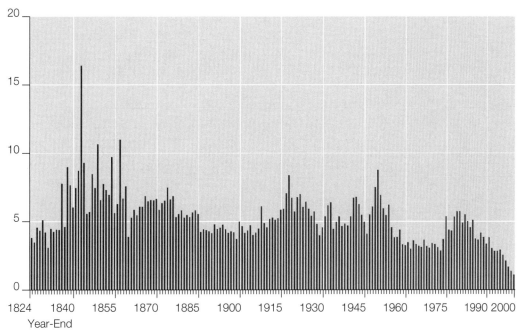

Year-End

## Total Returns

Looking once again at the summary statistics in Table 10-1, it is interesting to notice that the annual geometric total return for large company stocks from 1825 to 1925 was 7.3 percent. This is quite low when compared to the 11.0 percent annual geometric total return of the commonly used 1926 to 2000 time period. For the entire period, the total return seems to fall somewhere in between.

Graph 10-5 illustrates the annual total returns for the period 1825 to 2000.

Graph 10-5

**Large Company Stocks Annual Total Returns** (in percent)
from 1825 to 2000

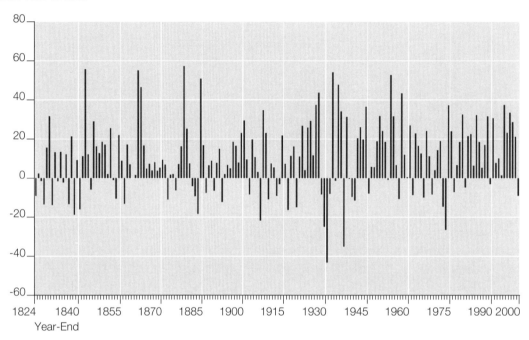

The standard deviation of returns is also slightly lower for the 1825 to 1925 time period (16.3 percent) versus the time period of 1926 to 2000 (20.2 percent). Graph 10-6 illustrates a five-year rolling period standard deviation for the period 1825–2000.

Graph 10-6

**5-Year Rolling Standard Deviation for Large Company Stocks** (in percent)
from 1829 to 2000

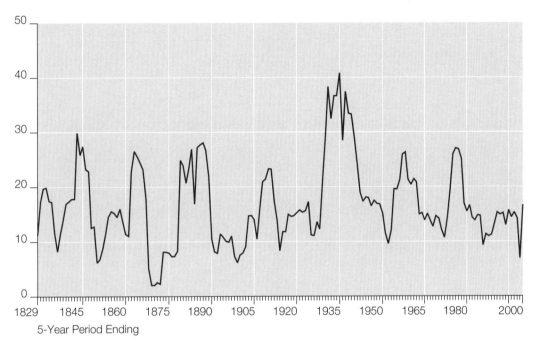

5-Year Period Ending

How much would a dollar be worth today if invested around the beginning of the New York Stock Exchange? Graph 10-7 depicts the growth of $1.00 invested in large company stocks over the period from the end of 1824 to the end of 2000.

Graph 10-7

**Large Company Stocks**
Year-End 1824 = $1.00

from 1824 to 2000

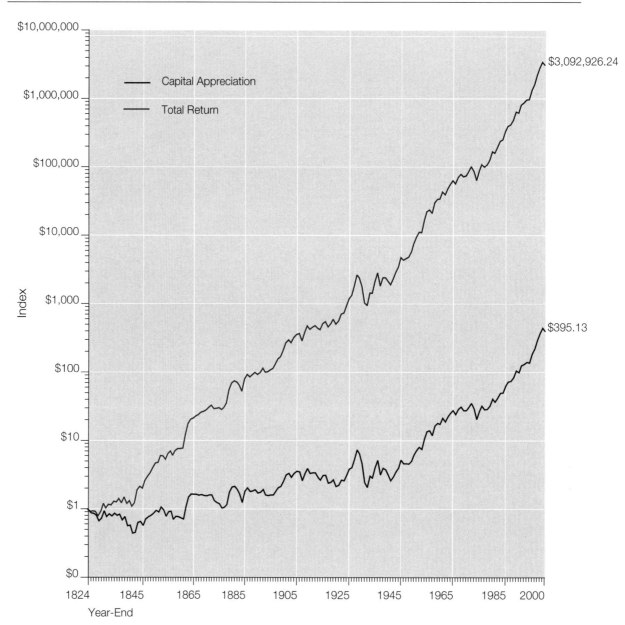

Table 10-2 shows year-by-year capital appreciation, average income, and total returns from 1815 to 1925 of large company stocks. Table 10-3 shows the growth of a dollar invested in large company stocks over the period from the end of 1824 to the end of 2000.

## Conclusion

Data collection efforts over the past eleven years have yielded a comprehensive database of New York Stock Exchange security prices for nearly the entire history of the NYSE. The goal of the study is to assemble an NYSE database for the period prior to 1926. The 1926 starting date was approximately when high-quality financial data became available. However, with such a new database assembled, researchers can expand their analysis back to the early 1800s. It is our hope that the long time series outlined in this chapter will lead to a better understanding of how the New York Stock Exchange evolved from an emerging market at the turn of the eighteenth century to the largest capital market in the world today.

## Table 10-2

**Large Company Stocks**

Annual Capital Appreciation, Income, and Total Returns (in percent)

from 1815 to 1925

| Year | Cap App | Average Income Return | Total Return | Year | Cap App | Average Income Return | Total Return | Year | Cap App | Average Income Return | Total Return |
|---|---|---|---|---|---|---|---|---|---|---|---|
| 1815 | −6.65 | — | — | 1852 | 18.07 | 7.30 | 25.38 | 1889 | 4.49 | 4.28 | 8.77 |
| 1816 | −1.93 | — | — | 1853 | −8.15 | 6.94 | −1.20 | 1890 | −10.72 | 4.14 | −6.59 |
| 1817 | 19.43 | — | — | 1854 | −20.34 | 9.71 | −10.63 | 1891 | 2.95 | 4.78 | 7.74 |
| 1818 | −3.76 | — | — | 1855 | 16.26 | 5.60 | 21.86 | 1892 | 10.35 | 4.44 | 14.79 |
| 1819 | −8.82 | — | — | 1856 | 2.49 | 6.28 | 8.77 | 1893 | −16.86 | 4.54 | −12.33 |
| 1820 | 9.59 | — | — | 1857 | −24.22 | 10.99 | −13.23 | 1894 | −2.82 | 4.76 | 1.94 |
| 1821 | 3.34 | — | — | 1858 | 10.38 | 6.68 | 17.07 | 1895 | 2.14 | 4.42 | 6.56 |
| 1822 | −12.85 | — | — | 1859 | −0.62 | 7.56 | 6.94 | 1896 | 0.69 | 4.17 | 4.86 |
| 1823 | 5.29 | — | — | 1860 | −3.93 | 3.88 | −0.06 | 1897 | 14.15 | 4.27 | 18.41 |
| 1824 | 3.70 | — | — | 1861 | −3.73 | 5.27 | 1.54 | 1898 | 12.17 | 4.21 | 16.38 |
| 1825 | −12.99 | 3.81 | −9.18 | 1862 | 49.15 | 5.85 | 55.00 | 1899 | 4.17 | 3.72 | 7.89 |
| 1826 | −1.22 | 3.48 | 2.27 | 1863 | 40.95 | 5.46 | 46.41 | 1900 | 17.99 | 4.98 | 22.97 |
| 1827 | −6.24 | 4.57 | −1.67 | 1864 | 10.53 | 6.07 | 16.61 | 1901 | 24.60 | 4.66 | 29.26 |
| 1828 | −17.95 | 4.34 | −13.61 | 1865 | −1.33 | 6.08 | 4.75 | 1902 | 5.29 | 4.15 | 9.44 |
| 1829 | 10.33 | 5.10 | 15.43 | 1866 | 0.46 | 6.85 | 7.31 | 1903 | −12.88 | 4.35 | −8.53 |
| 1830 | 27.31 | 4.20 | 31.51 | 1867 | −2.61 | 6.48 | 3.87 | 1904 | 14.94 | 4.72 | 19.66 |
| 1831 | −17.05 | 3.07 | −13.98 | 1868 | 1.52 | 6.56 | 8.08 | 1905 | 6.67 | 4.00 | 10.67 |
| 1832 | 8.60 | 4.48 | 13.08 | 1869 | −2.85 | 6.53 | 3.67 | 1906 | −1.09 | 4.19 | 3.10 |
| 1833 | −6.09 | 4.24 | −1.85 | 1870 | −1.44 | 6.66 | 5.22 | 1907 | −26.26 | 4.47 | −21.79 |
| 1834 | 8.84 | 4.40 | 13.24 | 1871 | 3.34 | 5.86 | 9.20 | 1908 | 28.47 | 6.09 | 34.56 |
| 1835 | −6.74 | 4.38 | −2.36 | 1872 | 0.50 | 6.33 | 6.83 | 1909 | 18.12 | 4.87 | 22.99 |
| 1836 | 4.33 | 7.76 | 12.09 | 1873 | −17.70 | 6.51 | −11.19 | 1910 | −15.50 | 4.56 | −10.94 |
| 1837 | −18.02 | 4.60 | −13.43 | 1874 | −5.77 | 7.47 | 1.70 | 1911 | 2.17 | 5.19 | 7.37 |
| 1838 | 12.20 | 8.99 | 21.19 | 1875 | −4.72 | 6.61 | 1.89 | 1912 | 0.03 | 5.27 | 5.30 |
| 1839 | −26.62 | 7.64 | −18.97 | 1876 | −13.31 | 6.86 | −6.45 | 1913 | −14.44 | 5.12 | −9.32 |
| 1840 | 3.01 | 6.03 | 9.04 | 1877 | 1.74 | 5.31 | 7.05 | 1914 | −8.47 | 5.22 | −3.25 |
| 1841 | −23.52 | 7.46 | −16.06 | 1878 | 10.50 | 5.54 | 16.04 | 1915 | 15.88 | 5.85 | 21.73 |
| 1842 | 2.34 | 8.71 | 11.05 | 1879 | 51.31 | 5.80 | 57.10 | 1916 | 1.29 | 5.91 | 7.19 |
| 1843 | 39.16 | 16.40 | 55.56 | 1880 | 19.83 | 5.28 | 25.12 | 1917 | −23.48 | 7.04 | −16.44 |
| 1844 | 2.81 | 9.29 | 12.11 | 1881 | 1.88 | 5.48 | 7.36 | 1918 | 2.88 | 8.38 | 11.27 |
| 1845 | −11.61 | 5.56 | −6.05 | 1882 | −9.54 | 5.32 | −4.22 | 1919 | 9.38 | 6.71 | 16.09 |
| 1846 | 23.21 | 5.70 | 28.91 | 1883 | −15.04 | 5.65 | −9.39 | 1920 | −20.74 | 5.72 | −15.02 |
| 1847 | 7.65 | 8.48 | 16.13 | 1884 | −24.28 | 5.81 | −18.47 | 1921 | 4.26 | 6.75 | 11.02 |
| 1848 | 5.28 | 7.45 | 12.72 | 1885 | 45.32 | 5.53 | 50.85 | 1922 | 19.74 | 6.98 | 26.72 |
| 1849 | 7.80 | 10.64 | 18.44 | 1886 | 12.46 | 4.23 | 16.69 | 1923 | −2.13 | 6.04 | 3.90 |
| 1850 | 10.48 | 6.57 | 17.05 | 1887 | −12.13 | 4.43 | −7.70 | 1924 | 19.34 | 6.43 | 25.77 |
| 1851 | −5.78 | 7.74 | 1.95 | 1888 | 2.09 | 4.36 | 6.45 | 1925 | 23.22 | 5.91 | 29.12 |

## Table 10-3

### Large-Company Stocks
Annual Capital Appreciation and Total Return Index Values

from 1824 to 1943

| Year | Cap App | Total Return | Year | Cap App | Total Return | Year | Cap App | Total Return |
|------|---------|--------------|------|---------|--------------|------|---------|--------------|
| 1824 | 1.00 | 1.00 | 1864 | 1.65 | 20.48 | 1904 | 3.32 | 322.65 |
| 1825 | 0.87 | 0.91 | 1865 | 1.63 | 21.45 | 1905 | 3.54 | 357.07 |
| 1826 | 0.86 | 0.93 | 1866 | 1.64 | 23.02 | 1906 | 3.51 | 368.14 |
| 1827 | 0.81 | 0.91 | 1867 | 1.59 | 23.91 | 1907 | 2.58 | 287.92 |
| 1828 | 0.66 | 0.79 | 1868 | 1.62 | 25.84 | 1908 | 3.32 | 387.42 |
| 1829 | 0.73 | 0.91 | 1869 | 1.57 | 26.79 | 1909 | 3.92 | 476.49 |
| 1830 | 0.93 | 1.20 | 1870 | 1.55 | 28.19 | 1910 | 3.31 | 424.37 |
| 1831 | 0.77 | 1.03 | 1871 | 1.60 | 30.78 | 1911 | 3.39 | 455.63 |
| 1832 | 0.84 | 1.16 | 1872 | 1.61 | 32.89 | 1912 | 3.39 | 479.76 |
| 1833 | 0.79 | 1.14 | 1873 | 1.32 | 29.21 | 1913 | 2.90 | 435.04 |
| 1834 | 0.86 | 1.29 | 1874 | 1.25 | 29.70 | 1914 | 2.65 | 420.90 |
| 1835 | 0.80 | 1.26 | 1875 | 1.19 | 30.26 | 1915 | 3.07 | 512.38 |
| 1836 | 0.83 | 1.42 | 1876 | 1.03 | 28.31 | 1916 | 3.11 | 549.24 |
| 1837 | 0.68 | 1.23 | 1877 | 1.05 | 30.31 | 1917 | 2.38 | 458.96 |
| 1838 | 0.77 | 1.49 | 1878 | 1.16 | 35.17 | 1918 | 2.45 | 510.66 |
| 1839 | 0.56 | 1.20 | 1879 | 1.75 | 55.25 | 1919 | 2.68 | 592.84 |
| 1840 | 0.58 | 1.31 | 1880 | 2.10 | 69.13 | 1920 | 2.13 | 503.78 |
| 1841 | 0.44 | 1.10 | 1881 | 2.14 | 74.22 | 1921 | 2.22 | 559.27 |
| 1842 | 0.45 | 1.22 | 1882 | 1.93 | 71.09 | 1922 | 2.65 | 708.68 |
| 1843 | 0.63 | 1.90 | 1883 | 1.64 | 64.41 | 1923 | 2.60 | 736.34 |
| 1844 | 0.65 | 2.14 | 1884 | 1.24 | 52.51 | 1924 | 3.10 | 926.09 |
| 1845 | 0.57 | 2.01 | 1885 | 1.81 | 79.21 | 1925 | 3.82 | 1195.79 |
| 1846 | 0.71 | 2.59 | 1886 | 2.03 | 92.44 | 1926 | 4.04 | 1334.79 |
| 1847 | 0.76 | 3.00 | 1887 | 1.79 | 85.32 | 1927 | 5.28 | 1835.18 |
| 1848 | 0.80 | 3.39 | 1888 | 1.82 | 90.83 | 1928 | 7.29 | 2635.47 |
| 1849 | 0.86 | 4.01 | 1889 | 1.91 | 98.79 | 1929 | 6.42 | 2413.68 |
| 1850 | 0.95 | 4.69 | 1890 | 1.70 | 92.28 | 1930 | 4.59 | 1812.75 |
| 1851 | 0.90 | 4.78 | 1891 | 1.75 | 99.42 | 1931 | 2.43 | 1027.17 |
| 1852 | 1.06 | 6.00 | 1892 | 1.93 | 114.12 | 1932 | 2.06 | 943.01 |
| 1853 | 0.97 | 5.93 | 1893 | 1.61 | 100.06 | 1933 | 3.02 | 1452.15 |
| 1854 | 0.78 | 5.30 | 1894 | 1.56 | 102.00 | 1934 | 2.84 | 1431.20 |
| 1855 | 0.90 | 6.45 | 1895 | 1.60 | 108.69 | 1935 | 4.02 | 2113.43 |
| 1856 | 0.92 | 7.02 | 1896 | 1.61 | 113.97 | 1936 | 5.14 | 2830.34 |
| 1857 | 0.70 | 6.09 | 1897 | 1.83 | 134.96 | 1937 | 3.16 | 1838.97 |
| 1858 | 0.77 | 7.13 | 1898 | 2.06 | 157.07 | 1938 | 3.95 | 2411.28 |
| 1859 | 0.77 | 7.63 | 1899 | 2.14 | 169.45 | 1939 | 3.74 | 2401.38 |
| 1860 | 0.74 | 7.62 | 1900 | 2.53 | 208.38 | 1940 | 3.17 | 2166.42 |
| 1861 | 0.71 | 7.74 | 1901 | 3.15 | 269.34 | 1941 | 2.60 | 1915.29 |
| 1862 | 1.06 | 12.00 | 1902 | 3.32 | 294.77 | 1942 | 2.92 | 2304.86 |
| 1863 | 1.49 | 17.56 | 1903 | 2.89 | 269.63 | 1943 | 3.49 | 2901.81 |

## Table 10-3 (continued)

### Large-Company Stocks
Annual Capital Appreciation and Total Return Index Values

from 1944 to 2000

| Year | Cap App | Total Return | Year | Cap App | Total Return | Year | Cap App | Total Return |
|------|---------|--------------|------|---------|--------------|------|---------|--------------|
| 1944 | 3.97 | 3474.99 | 1964 | 25.36 | 56367.95 | 1984 | 50.04 | 252548.89 |
| 1945 | 5.19 | 4741.14 | 1965 | 27.66 | 63386.32 | 1985 | 63.22 | 333763.56 |
| 1946 | 4.58 | 4358.47 | 1966 | 24.03 | 57007.57 | 1986 | 72.47 | 395411.36 |
| 1947 | 4.58 | 4607.25 | 1967 | 28.86 | 70675.53 | 1987 | 73.94 | 416094.53 |
| 1948 | 4.55 | 4860.71 | 1968 | 31.08 | 78493.24 | 1988 | 83.11 | 486037.11 |
| 1949 | 5.01 | 5774.16 | 1969 | 27.53 | 71817.70 | 1989 | 105.76 | 639094.09 |
| 1950 | 6.11 | 7605.31 | 1970 | 27.57 | 74695.15 | 1990 | 98.83 | 618817.55 |
| 1951 | 7.11 | 9431.84 | 1971 | 30.55 | 85386.04 | 1991 | 124.82 | 807863.22 |
| 1952 | 7.95 | 11164.23 | 1972 | 35.32 | 101588.98 | 1992 | 130.40 | 869827.94 |
| 1953 | 7.42 | 11053.79 | 1973 | 29.19 | 86694.82 | 1993 | 139.60 | 956722.01 |
| 1954 | 10.77 | 16870.70 | 1974 | 20.51 | 63748.52 | 1994 | 137.45 | 969229.24 |
| 1955 | 13.61 | 22195.54 | 1975 | 26.98 | 87464.94 | 1995 | 184.33 | 1332006.90 |
| 1956 | 13.96 | 23650.66 | 1976 | 32.15 | 108319.39 | 1996 | 221.69 | 1639356.83 |
| 1957 | 11.97 | 21100.53 | 1977 | 28.45 | 100537.72 | 1997 | 290.43 | 2186285.62 |
| 1958 | 16.52 | 30250.48 | 1978 | 28.76 | 107133.20 | 1998 | 367.88 | 2811163.21 |
| 1959 | 17.92 | 33866.95 | 1979 | 32.30 | 126888.02 | 1999 | 439.71 | 3402761.27 |
| 1960 | 17.39 | 34025.99 | 1980 | 40.62 | 168024.36 | 2000 | 395.13 | 3092926.24 |
| 1961 | 21.41 | 43175.07 | 1981 | 36.67 | 159776.38 | | | |
| 1962 | 18.88 | 39406.53 | 1982 | 42.08 | 193983.54 | | | |
| 1963 | 22.45 | 48391.69 | 1983 | 49.35 | 237656.61 | | | |

| | | | | |
|---|---|---|---|---|
| 0.0478 | 0.0013 | −0.0103 | 0.0096 | 0.0424 |
| −0.0071 | −0.0176 | 0.0020 | 0.0571 | 0.0382 |
| −0.0501 | 0.0034 | 0.0540 | 0.0204 | 0.0052 |
| 0.0589 | −0.0275 | 0.0851 | −0.0167 | 0.0909 |
| 0.0197 | 0.0098 | −0.0030 | 0.0396 | 0.0055 |
| −0.0328 | −0.0440 | 0.0066 | −0.0050 | 0.0370 |
| 0.0449 | 0.0176 | 0.0501 | 0.0270 | 0.0284 |

# Appendix A

| | | | | |
|---|---|---|---|---|
| 0.0209 | −0.0046 | −0.0607 | −0.0811 | −0.0803 |
| −0.0022 | 0.0535 | −0.0097 | 0.0339 | −0.0046 |
| 0.0162 | 0.0178 | 0.0195 | −0.0118 | 0.0301 |
| −0.0133 | 0.0356 | −0.0030 | −0.0473 | 0.0147 |
| 0.0334 | 0.0289 | −0.0031 | 0.0106 | 0.1245 |
| −0.0120 | −0.0725 | −0.0053 | 0.0494 | 0.0095 |
| 0.0190 | 0.0468 | −0.0070 | 0.0342 | −0.0276 |
| 0.0105 | −0.0172 | 0.0164 | 0.0400 | 0.0876 |

**Ibbotson**Associates

# Appendix A

**Monthly Returns on Basic and Derived Series**

## Table A-1

**Large Company Stocks: Total Returns**

from January 1926 to December 1970

| Year | Jan | Feb | Mar | Apr | May | Jun | Jul | Aug | Sep | Oct | Nov | Dec | Year | Jan-Dec* |
|------|-----|-----|-----|-----|-----|-----|-----|-----|-----|-----|-----|-----|------|----------|
| 1926 | 0.0000 | -0.0385 | -0.0575 | 0.0253 | 0.0179 | 0.0457 | 0.0479 | 0.0248 | 0.0252 | -0.0284 | 0.0347 | 0.0196 | 1926 | 0.1162 |
| 1927 | -0.0193 | 0.0537 | 0.0087 | 0.0201 | 0.0607 | -0.0067 | 0.0670 | 0.0515 | 0.0450 | -0.0502 | 0.0721 | 0.0279 | 1927 | 0.3749 |
| 1928 | -0.0040 | -0.0125 | 0.1101 | 0.0345 | 0.0197 | -0.0385 | 0.0141 | 0.0803 | 0.0259 | 0.0168 | 0.1292 | 0.0049 | 1928 | 0.4361 |
| 1929 | 0.0583 | -0.0019 | -0.0012 | 0.0176 | -0.0362 | 0.1140 | 0.0471 | 0.1028 | -0.0476 | -0.1973 | -0.1246 | 0.0282 | 1929 | -0.0842 |
| 1930 | 0.0639 | 0.0259 | 0.0812 | -0.0080 | -0.0096 | -0.1625 | 0.0386 | 0.0141 | -0.1282 | -0.0855 | -0.0089 | -0.0706 | 1930 | -0.2490 |
| 1931 | 0.0502 | 0.1193 | -0.0675 | -0.0935 | -0.1279 | 0.1421 | -0.0722 | 0.0182 | -0.2973 | 0.0896 | -0.0798 | -0.1400 | 1931 | -0.4334 |
| 1932 | -0.0271 | 0.0570 | -0.1158 | -0.1997 | -0.2196 | -0.0022 | 0.3815 | 0.3869 | -0.0346 | -0.1349 | -0.0417 | 0.0565 | 1932 | -0.0819 |
| 1933 | 0.0087 | -0.1772 | 0.0353 | 0.4256 | 0.1683 | 0.1338 | -0.0862 | 0.1206 | -0.1118 | -0.0855 | 0.1127 | 0.0253 | 1933 | 0.5399 |
| 1934 | 0.1069 | -0.0322 | 0.0000 | -0.0251 | -0.0736 | 0.0229 | -0.1132 | 0.0611 | -0.0033 | -0.0286 | 0.0942 | -0.0010 | 1934 | -0.0144 |
| 1935 | -0.0411 | -0.0341 | -0.0286 | 0.0980 | 0.0409 | 0.0699 | 0.0850 | 0.0280 | 0.0256 | 0.0777 | 0.0474 | 0.0394 | 1935 | 0.4767 |
| 1936 | 0.0670 | 0.0224 | 0.0268 | -0.0751 | 0.0545 | 0.0333 | 0.0701 | 0.0151 | 0.0031 | 0.0775 | 0.0134 | -0.0029 | 1936 | 0.3392 |
| 1937 | 0.0390 | 0.0191 | -0.0077 | -0.0809 | -0.0024 | -0.0504 | 0.1045 | -0.0483 | -0.1403 | -0.0981 | -0.0866 | -0.0459 | 1937 | -0.3503 |
| 1938 | 0.0152 | 0.0674 | -0.2487 | 0.1447 | -0.0330 | 0.2503 | 0.0744 | -0.0226 | 0.0166 | 0.0776 | -0.0273 | 0.0401 | 1938 | 0.3112 |
| 1939 | -0.0674 | 0.0390 | -0.1339 | -0.0027 | 0.0733 | -0.0612 | 0.1105 | -0.0648 | 0.1673 | -0.0123 | -0.0398 | 0.0270 | 1939 | -0.0041 |
| 1940 | -0.0336 | 0.0133 | 0.0124 | -0.0024 | -0.2289 | 0.0809 | 0.0341 | 0.0350 | 0.0123 | 0.0422 | -0.0316 | 0.0009 | 1940 | -0.0978 |
| 1941 | -0.0463 | -0.0060 | 0.0071 | -0.0612 | 0.0183 | 0.0578 | 0.0579 | 0.0010 | -0.0068 | -0.0657 | -0.0284 | -0.0407 | 1941 | -0.1159 |
| 1942 | 0.0161 | -0.0159 | -0.0652 | -0.0399 | 0.0796 | 0.0221 | 0.0337 | 0.0164 | 0.0290 | 0.0678 | -0.0021 | 0.0549 | 1942 | 0.2034 |
| 1943 | 0.0737 | 0.0583 | 0.0545 | 0.0035 | 0.0552 | 0.0223 | -0.0526 | 0.0171 | 0.0263 | -0.0108 | -0.0654 | 0.0617 | 1943 | 0.2590 |
| 1944 | 0.0171 | 0.0042 | 0.0195 | -0.0100 | 0.0505 | 0.0543 | -0.0193 | 0.0157 | -0.0008 | 0.0023 | 0.0133 | 0.0374 | 1944 | 0.1975 |
| 1945 | 0.0158 | 0.0683 | -0.0441 | 0.0902 | 0.0195 | -0.0007 | -0.0180 | 0.0641 | 0.0438 | 0.0322 | 0.0396 | 0.0116 | 1945 | 0.3644 |
| 1946 | 0.0714 | -0.0641 | 0.0480 | 0.0393 | 0.0288 | -0.0370 | -0.0239 | -0.0674 | -0.0997 | -0.0060 | -0.0027 | 0.0457 | 1946 | -0.0807 |
| 1947 | 0.0255 | -0.0077 | -0.0149 | -0.0363 | 0.0014 | 0.0554 | 0.0381 | -0.0203 | -0.0111 | 0.0238 | -0.0175 | 0.0233 | 1947 | 0.0571 |
| 1948 | -0.0379 | -0.0388 | 0.0793 | 0.0292 | 0.0879 | 0.0054 | -0.0508 | 0.0158 | -0.0276 | 0.0710 | -0.0961 | 0.0346 | 1948 | 0.0550 |
| 1949 | 0.0039 | -0.0296 | 0.0328 | -0.0179 | -0.0258 | 0.0014 | 0.0650 | 0.0219 | 0.0263 | 0.0340 | 0.0175 | 0.0486 | 1949 | 0.1879 |
| 1950 | 0.0197 | 0.0199 | 0.0070 | 0.0486 | 0.0509 | -0.0548 | 0.0119 | 0.0443 | 0.0592 | 0.0093 | 0.0169 | 0.0513 | 1950 | 0.3171 |
| 1951 | 0.0637 | 0.0157 | -0.0156 | 0.0509 | -0.0299 | -0.0228 | 0.0711 | 0.0478 | 0.0013 | -0.0103 | 0.0096 | 0.0424 | 1951 | 0.2402 |
| 1952 | 0.0181 | -0.0282 | 0.0503 | -0.0402 | 0.0343 | 0.0490 | 0.0196 | -0.0071 | -0.0176 | 0.0020 | 0.0571 | 0.0382 | 1952 | 0.1837 |
| 1953 | -0.0049 | -0.0106 | -0.0212 | -0.0237 | 0.0077 | -0.0134 | 0.0273 | -0.0501 | 0.0034 | 0.0540 | 0.0204 | 0.0052 | 1953 | -0.0099 |
| 1954 | 0.0536 | 0.0111 | 0.0325 | 0.0516 | 0.0418 | 0.0031 | 0.0589 | -0.0275 | 0.0851 | -0.0167 | 0.0909 | 0.0534 | 1954 | 0.5262 |
| 1955 | 0.0197 | 0.0098 | -0.0030 | 0.0396 | 0.0055 | 0.0841 | 0.0622 | -0.0025 | 0.0130 | -0.0284 | 0.0827 | 0.0015 | 1955 | 0.3156 |
| 1956 | -0.0347 | 0.0413 | 0.0710 | -0.0004 | -0.0593 | 0.0409 | 0.0530 | -0.0328 | -0.0440 | 0.0066 | -0.0050 | 0.0370 | 1956 | 0.0656 |
| 1957 | -0.0401 | -0.0264 | 0.0215 | 0.0388 | 0.0437 | 0.0004 | 0.0131 | -0.0505 | -0.0602 | -0.0302 | 0.0231 | -0.0395 | 1957 | -0.1078 |
| 1958 | 0.0445 | -0.0141 | 0.0328 | 0.0337 | 0.0212 | 0.0279 | 0.0449 | 0.0176 | 0.0501 | 0.0270 | 0.0284 | 0.0535 | 1958 | 0.4336 |
| 1959 | 0.0053 | 0.0049 | 0.0020 | 0.0402 | 0.0240 | -0.0022 | 0.0363 | -0.0102 | -0.0443 | 0.0128 | 0.0186 | 0.0292 | 1959 | 0.1196 |
| 1960 | -0.0700 | 0.0147 | -0.0123 | -0.0161 | 0.0326 | 0.0211 | -0.0234 | 0.0317 | -0.0590 | -0.0007 | 0.0465 | 0.0479 | 1960 | 0.0047 |
| 1961 | 0.0645 | 0.0319 | 0.0270 | 0.0051 | 0.0239 | -0.0275 | 0.0342 | 0.0243 | -0.0184 | 0.0298 | 0.0447 | 0.0046 | 1961 | 0.2689 |
| 1962 | -0.0366 | 0.0209 | -0.0046 | -0.0607 | -0.0811 | -0.0803 | 0.0652 | 0.0208 | -0.0465 | 0.0064 | 0.1086 | 0.0153 | 1962 | -0.0873 |
| 1963 | 0.0506 | -0.0239 | 0.0370 | 0.0500 | 0.0193 | -0.0188 | -0.0022 | 0.0535 | -0.0097 | 0.0339 | -0.0046 | 0.0262 | 1963 | 0.2280 |
| 1964 | 0.0283 | 0.0147 | 0.0165 | 0.0075 | 0.0162 | 0.0178 | 0.0195 | -0.0118 | 0.0301 | 0.0096 | 0.0005 | 0.0056 | 1964 | 0.1648 |
| 1965 | 0.0345 | 0.0031 | -0.0133 | 0.0356 | -0.0030 | -0.0473 | 0.0147 | 0.0272 | 0.0334 | 0.0289 | -0.0031 | 0.0106 | 1965 | 0.1245 |
| 1966 | 0.0062 | -0.0131 | -0.0205 | 0.0220 | -0.0492 | -0.0146 | -0.0120 | -0.0725 | -0.0053 | 0.0494 | 0.0095 | 0.0002 | 1966 | -0.1006 |
| 1967 | 0.0798 | 0.0072 | 0.0409 | 0.0437 | -0.0477 | 0.0190 | 0.0468 | -0.0070 | 0.0342 | -0.0276 | 0.0065 | 0.0278 | 1967 | 0.2398 |
| 1968 | -0.0425 | -0.0261 | 0.0110 | 0.0834 | 0.0161 | 0.0105 | -0.0172 | 0.0164 | 0.0400 | 0.0087 | 0.0531 | -0.0402 | 1968 | 0.1106 |
| 1969 | -0.0068 | -0.0426 | 0.0359 | 0.0229 | 0.0026 | -0.0542 | -0.0587 | 0.0454 | -0.0236 | 0.0459 | -0.0297 | -0.0177 | 1969 | -0.0850 |
| 1970 | -0.0743 | 0.0586 | 0.0030 | -0.0889 | -0.0547 | -0.0482 | 0.0752 | 0.0509 | 0.0347 | -0.0097 | 0.0536 | 0.0584 | 1970 | 0.0401 |

* Compound annual return

Table A-1 (continued)

## Large Company Stocks: Total Returns

from January 1971 to December 2000

| Year | Jan | Feb | Mar | Apr | May | Jun | Jul | Aug | Sep | Oct | Nov | Dec | Year | Jan-Dec* |
|------|-----|-----|-----|-----|-----|-----|-----|-----|-----|-----|-----|-----|------|----------|
| 1971 | 0.0419 | 0.0141 | 0.0382 | 0.0377 | −0.0367 | 0.0021 | −0.0399 | 0.0412 | −0.0056 | −0.0404 | 0.0027 | 0.0877 | 1971 | 0.1431 |
| 1972 | 0.0194 | 0.0299 | 0.0072 | 0.0057 | 0.0219 | −0.0205 | 0.0036 | 0.0391 | −0.0036 | 0.0107 | 0.0505 | 0.0131 | 1972 | 0.1898 |
| 1973 | −0.0159 | −0.0333 | −0.0002 | −0.0395 | −0.0139 | −0.0051 | 0.0394 | −0.0318 | 0.0415 | 0.0003 | −0.1082 | 0.0183 | 1973 | −0.1466 |
| 1974 | −0.0085 | 0.0019 | −0.0217 | −0.0373 | −0.0272 | −0.0128 | −0.0759 | −0.0828 | −0.1170 | 0.1657 | −0.0448 | −0.0177 | 1974 | −0.2647 |
| 1975 | 0.1251 | 0.0674 | 0.0237 | 0.0493 | 0.0509 | 0.0462 | −0.0659 | −0.0144 | −0.0328 | 0.0637 | 0.0313 | −0.0096 | 1975 | 0.3720 |
| 1976 | 0.1199 | −0.0058 | 0.0326 | −0.0099 | −0.0073 | 0.0427 | −0.0068 | 0.0014 | 0.0247 | −0.0206 | −0.0009 | 0.0540 | 1976 | 0.2384 |
| 1977 | −0.0489 | −0.0151 | −0.0119 | 0.0014 | −0.0150 | 0.0475 | −0.0151 | −0.0133 | 0.0000 | −0.0415 | 0.0370 | 0.0048 | 1977 | −0.0718 |
| 1978 | −0.0596 | −0.0161 | 0.0276 | 0.0870 | 0.0136 | −0.0152 | 0.0560 | 0.0340 | −0.0048 | −0.0891 | 0.0260 | 0.0172 | 1978 | 0.0656 |
| 1979 | 0.0421 | −0.0284 | 0.0575 | 0.0036 | −0.0168 | 0.0410 | 0.0110 | 0.0611 | 0.0025 | −0.0656 | 0.0514 | 0.0192 | 1979 | 0.1844 |
| 1980 | 0.0610 | 0.0031 | −0.0987 | 0.0429 | 0.0562 | 0.0296 | 0.0676 | 0.0131 | 0.0281 | 0.0187 | 0.1095 | −0.0315 | 1980 | 0.3242 |
| 1981 | −0.0438 | 0.0208 | 0.0380 | −0.0213 | 0.0062 | −0.0080 | 0.0007 | −0.0554 | −0.0502 | 0.0528 | 0.0441 | −0.0265 | 1981 | −0.0491 |
| 1982 | −0.0163 | −0.0512 | −0.0060 | 0.0414 | −0.0288 | −0.0174 | −0.0215 | 0.1267 | 0.0110 | 0.1126 | 0.0438 | 0.0173 | 1982 | 0.2141 |
| 1983 | 0.0348 | 0.0260 | 0.0365 | 0.0758 | −0.0052 | 0.0382 | −0.0313 | 0.0170 | 0.0136 | −0.0134 | 0.0233 | −0.0061 | 1983 | 0.2251 |
| 1984 | −0.0065 | −0.0328 | 0.0171 | 0.0069 | −0.0534 | 0.0221 | −0.0143 | 0.1125 | 0.0002 | 0.0026 | −0.0101 | 0.0253 | 1984 | 0.0627 |
| 1985 | 0.0768 | 0.0137 | 0.0018 | −0.0032 | 0.0615 | 0.0159 | −0.0026 | −0.0061 | −0.0321 | 0.0447 | 0.0716 | 0.0467 | 1985 | 0.3216 |
| 1986 | 0.0044 | 0.0761 | 0.0554 | −0.0124 | 0.0549 | 0.0166 | −0.0569 | 0.0748 | −0.0822 | 0.0556 | 0.0256 | −0.0264 | 1986 | 0.1847 |
| 1987 | 0.1343 | 0.0413 | 0.0272 | −0.0088 | 0.0103 | 0.0499 | 0.0498 | 0.0385 | −0.0220 | −0.2152 | −0.0819 | 0.0738 | 1987 | 0.0523 |
| 1988 | 0.0427 | 0.0470 | −0.0302 | 0.0108 | 0.0078 | 0.0464 | −0.0040 | −0.0331 | 0.0424 | 0.0273 | −0.0142 | 0.0181 | 1988 | 0.1681 |
| 1989 | 0.0723 | −0.0249 | 0.0236 | 0.0516 | 0.0402 | −0.0054 | 0.0898 | 0.0193 | −0.0039 | −0.0233 | 0.0208 | 0.0236 | 1989 | 0.3149 |
| 1990 | −0.0671 | 0.0129 | 0.0263 | −0.0247 | 0.0975 | −0.0070 | −0.0032 | −0.0903 | −0.0492 | −0.0037 | 0.0644 | 0.0274 | 1990 | −0.0317 |
| 1991 | 0.0442 | 0.0716 | 0.0238 | 0.0028 | 0.0428 | −0.0457 | 0.0468 | 0.0235 | −0.0164 | 0.0134 | −0.0404 | 0.1143 | 1991 | 0.3055 |
| 1992 | −0.0186 | 0.0128 | −0.0196 | 0.0291 | 0.0054 | −0.0145 | 0.0403 | −0.0202 | 0.0115 | 0.0036 | 0.0337 | 0.0131 | 1992 | 0.0767 |
| 1993 | 0.0073 | 0.0135 | 0.0215 | −0.0245 | 0.0270 | 0.0033 | −0.0047 | 0.0381 | −0.0074 | 0.0203 | −0.0094 | 0.0123 | 1993 | 0.0999 |
| 1994 | 0.0335 | −0.0270 | −0.0435 | 0.0130 | 0.0163 | −0.0247 | 0.0331 | 0.0407 | −0.0241 | 0.0229 | −0.0367 | 0.0146 | 1994 | 0.0131 |
| 1995 | 0.0260 | 0.0388 | 0.0296 | 0.0291 | 0.0395 | 0.0235 | 0.0333 | 0.0027 | 0.0419 | −0.0035 | 0.0440 | 0.0185 | 1995 | 0.3743 |
| 1996 | 0.0344 | 0.0096 | 0.0096 | 0.0147 | 0.0258 | 0.0041 | −0.0445 | 0.0212 | 0.0562 | 0.0274 | 0.0759 | −0.0196 | 1996 | 0.2307 |
| 1997 | 0.0621 | 0.0081 | −0.0416 | 0.0597 | 0.0614 | 0.0446 | 0.0794 | −0.0556 | 0.0548 | −0.0334 | 0.0463 | 0.0172 | 1997 | 0.3336 |
| 1998 | 0.0111 | 0.0721 | 0.0512 | 0.0101 | −0.0172 | 0.0406 | −0.0107 | −0.1446 | 0.0641 | 0.0813 | 0.0606 | 0.0576 | 1998 | 0.2858 |
| 1999 | 0.0418 | −0.0311 | 0.0400 | 0.0387 | −0.0236 | 0.0555 | −0.0312 | −0.0050 | −0.0274 | 0.0633 | 0.0203 | 0.0589 | 1999 | 0.2104 |
| 2000 | −0.0502 | −0.0189 | 0.0978 | −0.0301 | −0.0205 | 0.0246 | −0.0156 | 0.0621 | −0.0528 | −0.0042 | −0.0788 | 0.0049 | 2000 | −0.0911 |

* Compound annual return

Table A-2

**Large Company Stocks: Income Returns**

from January 1926 to December 1970

| Year | Jan | Feb | Mar | Apr | May | Jun | Jul | Aug | Sep | Oct | Nov | Dec | Year | Jan-Dec* |
|------|-----|-----|-----|-----|-----|-----|-----|-----|-----|-----|-----|-----|------|----------|
| 1926 | 0.0016 | 0.0055 | 0.0016 | 0.0026 | 0.0102 | 0.0025 | 0.0024 | 0.0078 | 0.0023 | 0.0030 | 0.0123 | 0.0030 | 1926 | 0.0541 |
| 1927 | 0.0015 | 0.0061 | 0.0022 | 0.0029 | 0.0085 | 0.0027 | 0.0020 | 0.0070 | 0.0018 | 0.0029 | 0.0105 | 0.0029 | 1927 | 0.0571 |
| 1928 | 0.0011 | 0.0051 | 0.0017 | 0.0021 | 0.0071 | 0.0020 | 0.0016 | 0.0062 | 0.0019 | 0.0023 | 0.0092 | 0.0021 | 1928 | 0.0481 |
| 1929 | 0.0012 | 0.0039 | 0.0012 | 0.0016 | 0.0066 | 0.0016 | 0.0014 | 0.0048 | 0.0013 | 0.0020 | 0.0091 | 0.0029 | 1929 | 0.0398 |
| 1930 | 0.0014 | 0.0044 | 0.0013 | 0.0016 | 0.0068 | 0.0020 | 0.0020 | 0.0066 | 0.0019 | 0.0032 | 0.0130 | 0.0036 | 1930 | 0.0457 |
| 1931 | 0.0013 | 0.0050 | 0.0017 | 0.0024 | 0.0093 | 0.0031 | 0.0020 | 0.0087 | 0.0022 | 0.0051 | 0.0180 | 0.0053 | 1931 | 0.0535 |
| 1932 | 0.0012 | 0.0063 | 0.0024 | 0.0027 | 0.0137 | 0.0067 | 0.0045 | 0.0115 | 0.0024 | 0.0037 | 0.0172 | 0.0046 | 1932 | 0.0616 |
| 1933 | 0.0015 | 0.0072 | 0.0018 | 0.0034 | 0.0096 | 0.0021 | 0.0018 | 0.0060 | 0.0018 | 0.0031 | 0.0100 | 0.0030 | 1933 | 0.0639 |
| 1934 | 0.0010 | 0.0045 | 0.0009 | 0.0019 | 0.0076 | 0.0021 | 0.0020 | 0.0069 | 0.0022 | 0.0033 | 0.0114 | 0.0031 | 1934 | 0.0446 |
| 1935 | 0.0011 | 0.0055 | 0.0023 | 0.0024 | 0.0086 | 0.0021 | 0.0020 | 0.0063 | 0.0018 | 0.0026 | 0.0080 | 0.0023 | 1935 | 0.0495 |
| 1936 | 0.0015 | 0.0056 | 0.0014 | 0.0020 | 0.0087 | 0.0028 | 0.0020 | 0.0063 | 0.0019 | 0.0025 | 0.0093 | 0.0029 | 1936 | 0.0536 |
| 1937 | 0.0012 | 0.0045 | 0.0017 | 0.0022 | 0.0079 | 0.0025 | 0.0019 | 0.0071 | 0.0019 | 0.0036 | 0.0146 | 0.0045 | 1937 | 0.0466 |
| 1938 | 0.0019 | 0.0065 | 0.0018 | 0.0035 | 0.0113 | 0.0032 | 0.0017 | 0.0048 | 0.0017 | 0.0016 | 0.0061 | 0.0024 | 1938 | 0.0483 |
| 1939 | 0.0015 | 0.0065 | 0.0016 | 0.0027 | 0.0110 | 0.0026 | 0.0018 | 0.0066 | 0.0027 | 0.0023 | 0.0094 | 0.0033 | 1939 | 0.0469 |
| 1940 | 0.0016 | 0.0066 | 0.0025 | 0.0024 | 0.0107 | 0.0043 | 0.0030 | 0.0087 | 0.0028 | 0.0028 | 0.0108 | 0.0038 | 1940 | 0.0536 |
| 1941 | 0.0019 | 0.0089 | 0.0030 | 0.0040 | 0.0140 | 0.0043 | 0.0030 | 0.0096 | 0.0029 | 0.0029 | 0.0137 | 0.0044 | 1941 | 0.0671 |
| 1942 | 0.0023 | 0.0091 | 0.0023 | 0.0037 | 0.0157 | 0.0037 | 0.0024 | 0.0093 | 0.0023 | 0.0034 | 0.0117 | 0.0032 | 1942 | 0.0679 |
| 1943 | 0.0020 | 0.0076 | 0.0018 | 0.0026 | 0.0104 | 0.0025 | 0.0016 | 0.0068 | 0.0025 | 0.0025 | 0.0101 | 0.0027 | 1943 | 0.0624 |
| 1944 | 0.0017 | 0.0068 | 0.0025 | 0.0025 | 0.0101 | 0.0032 | 0.0015 | 0.0071 | 0.0023 | 0.0023 | 0.0094 | 0.0023 | 1944 | 0.0548 |
| 1945 | 0.0015 | 0.0067 | 0.0021 | 0.0022 | 0.0081 | 0.0027 | 0.0020 | 0.0061 | 0.0019 | 0.0019 | 0.0072 | 0.0017 | 1945 | 0.0497 |
| 1946 | 0.0017 | 0.0054 | 0.0017 | 0.0017 | 0.0064 | 0.0021 | 0.0016 | 0.0056 | 0.0018 | 0.0020 | 0.0088 | 0.0027 | 1946 | 0.0409 |
| 1947 | 0.0020 | 0.0070 | 0.0019 | 0.0026 | 0.0103 | 0.0028 | 0.0020 | 0.0076 | 0.0026 | 0.0026 | 0.0110 | 0.0027 | 1947 | 0.0549 |
| 1948 | 0.0020 | 0.0082 | 0.0021 | 0.0027 | 0.0097 | 0.0024 | 0.0024 | 0.0082 | 0.0025 | 0.0032 | 0.0121 | 0.0041 | 1948 | 0.0608 |
| 1949 | 0.0026 | 0.0099 | 0.0027 | 0.0033 | 0.0115 | 0.0035 | 0.0028 | 0.0100 | 0.0026 | 0.0045 | 0.0162 | 0.0050 | 1949 | 0.0750 |
| 1950 | 0.0024 | 0.0100 | 0.0029 | 0.0035 | 0.0116 | 0.0032 | 0.0034 | 0.0118 | 0.0033 | 0.0051 | 0.0179 | 0.0051 | 1950 | 0.0877 |
| 1951 | 0.0025 | 0.0092 | 0.0028 | 0.0028 | 0.0107 | 0.0033 | 0.0024 | 0.0085 | 0.0021 | 0.0034 | 0.0122 | 0.0035 | 1951 | 0.0691 |
| 1952 | 0.0025 | 0.0083 | 0.0026 | 0.0029 | 0.0111 | 0.0029 | 0.0020 | 0.0075 | 0.0020 | 0.0029 | 0.0106 | 0.0027 | 1952 | 0.0593 |
| 1953 | 0.0023 | 0.0076 | 0.0023 | 0.0028 | 0.0110 | 0.0029 | 0.0021 | 0.0077 | 0.0021 | 0.0030 | 0.0114 | 0.0032 | 1953 | 0.0546 |
| 1954 | 0.0024 | 0.0084 | 0.0023 | 0.0026 | 0.0088 | 0.0024 | 0.0017 | 0.0065 | 0.0020 | 0.0028 | 0.0101 | 0.0026 | 1954 | 0.0621 |
| 1955 | 0.0017 | 0.0063 | 0.0019 | 0.0019 | 0.0068 | 0.0018 | 0.0015 | 0.0053 | 0.0016 | 0.0021 | 0.0078 | 0.0022 | 1955 | 0.0456 |
| 1956 | 0.0018 | 0.0066 | 0.0018 | 0.0017 | 0.0064 | 0.0018 | 0.0015 | 0.0053 | 0.0015 | 0.0015 | 0.0059 | 0.0018 | 1956 | 0.0383 |
| 1957 | 0.0017 | 0.0063 | 0.0018 | 0.0018 | 0.0068 | 0.0017 | 0.0017 | 0.0056 | 0.0018 | 0.0019 | 0.0071 | 0.0019 | 1957 | 0.0384 |
| 1958 | 0.0017 | 0.0065 | 0.0020 | 0.0019 | 0.0062 | 0.0018 | 0.0018 | 0.0057 | 0.0017 | 0.0016 | 0.0060 | 0.0015 | 1958 | 0.0438 |
| 1959 | 0.0014 | 0.0051 | 0.0014 | 0.0014 | 0.0050 | 0.0014 | 0.0014 | 0.0048 | 0.0013 | 0.0016 | 0.0054 | 0.0015 | 1959 | 0.0331 |
| 1960 | 0.0015 | 0.0056 | 0.0016 | 0.0014 | 0.0057 | 0.0016 | 0.0014 | 0.0056 | 0.0014 | 0.0017 | 0.0062 | 0.0016 | 1960 | 0.0326 |
| 1961 | 0.0014 | 0.0050 | 0.0014 | 0.0012 | 0.0047 | 0.0014 | 0.0014 | 0.0046 | 0.0013 | 0.0015 | 0.0054 | 0.0014 | 1961 | 0.0348 |
| 1962 | 0.0013 | 0.0046 | 0.0013 | 0.0013 | 0.0049 | 0.0015 | 0.0016 | 0.0055 | 0.0017 | 0.0020 | 0.0071 | 0.0018 | 1962 | 0.0298 |
| 1963 | 0.0014 | 0.0050 | 0.0016 | 0.0015 | 0.0050 | 0.0014 | 0.0013 | 0.0048 | 0.0014 | 0.0017 | 0.0059 | 0.0018 | 1963 | 0.0361 |
| 1964 | 0.0013 | 0.0048 | 0.0013 | 0.0014 | 0.0048 | 0.0014 | 0.0012 | 0.0044 | 0.0013 | 0.0015 | 0.0057 | 0.0017 | 1964 | 0.0333 |
| 1965 | 0.0013 | 0.0046 | 0.0013 | 0.0014 | 0.0047 | 0.0014 | 0.0013 | 0.0047 | 0.0014 | 0.0016 | 0.0056 | 0.0016 | 1965 | 0.0321 |
| 1966 | 0.0013 | 0.0047 | 0.0013 | 0.0015 | 0.0049 | 0.0015 | 0.0014 | 0.0053 | 0.0017 | 0.0018 | 0.0064 | 0.0017 | 1966 | 0.0311 |
| 1967 | 0.0016 | 0.0052 | 0.0015 | 0.0014 | 0.0048 | 0.0015 | 0.0014 | 0.0047 | 0.0014 | 0.0014 | 0.0054 | 0.0015 | 1967 | 0.0364 |
| 1968 | 0.0013 | 0.0051 | 0.0016 | 0.0014 | 0.0049 | 0.0014 | 0.0013 | 0.0049 | 0.0014 | 0.0015 | 0.0051 | 0.0014 | 1968 | 0.0318 |
| 1969 | 0.0013 | 0.0048 | 0.0014 | 0.0014 | 0.0048 | 0.0014 | 0.0014 | 0.0053 | 0.0015 | 0.0016 | 0.0056 | 0.0016 | 1969 | 0.0304 |
| 1970 | 0.0015 | 0.0059 | 0.0016 | 0.0016 | 0.0063 | 0.0018 | 0.0019 | 0.0064 | 0.0017 | 0.0017 | 0.0061 | 0.0016 | 1970 | 0.0341 |

* Compound annual return

## Table A-2 (continued)

## Large Company Stocks: Income Returns

from January 1971 to December 2000

| Year | Jan | Feb | Mar | Apr | May | Jun | Jul | Aug | Sep | Oct | Nov | Dec | Year | Jan-Dec* |
|------|-----|-----|-----|-----|-----|-----|-----|-----|-----|-----|-----|-----|------|----------|
| 1971 | 0.0014 | 0.0050 | 0.0014 | 0.0014 | 0.0048 | 0.0014 | 0.0014 | 0.0051 | 0.0014 | 0.0014 | 0.0052 | 0.0015 | 1971 | 0.0333 |
| 1972 | 0.0013 | 0.0046 | 0.0013 | 0.0013 | 0.0046 | 0.0013 | 0.0013 | 0.0047 | 0.0013 | 0.0014 | 0.0048 | 0.0013 | 1972 | 0.0309 |
| 1973 | 0.0012 | 0.0042 | 0.0013 | 0.0013 | 0.0050 | 0.0014 | 0.0014 | 0.0049 | 0.0014 | 0.0016 | 0.0056 | 0.0018 | 1973 | 0.0286 |
| 1974 | 0.0015 | 0.0055 | 0.0016 | 0.0017 | 0.0063 | 0.0018 | 0.0019 | 0.0074 | 0.0024 | 0.0027 | 0.0084 | 0.0024 | 1974 | 0.0369 |
| 1975 | 0.0023 | 0.0075 | 0.0020 | 0.0020 | 0.0068 | 0.0019 | 0.0018 | 0.0066 | 0.0018 | 0.0020 | 0.0066 | 0.0019 | 1975 | 0.0537 |
| 1976 | 0.0016 | 0.0056 | 0.0019 | 0.0011 | 0.0071 | 0.0018 | 0.0012 | 0.0065 | 0.0020 | 0.0017 | 0.0069 | 0.0015 | 1976 | 0.0438 |
| 1977 | 0.0016 | 0.0065 | 0.0021 | 0.0012 | 0.0086 | 0.0021 | 0.0011 | 0.0078 | 0.0025 | 0.0019 | 0.0100 | 0.0020 | 1977 | 0.0431 |
| 1978 | 0.0019 | 0.0086 | 0.0027 | 0.0016 | 0.0094 | 0.0023 | 0.0020 | 0.0081 | 0.0024 | 0.0025 | 0.0093 | 0.0023 | 1978 | 0.0533 |
| 1979 | 0.0024 | 0.0081 | 0.0024 | 0.0020 | 0.0095 | 0.0023 | 0.0022 | 0.0080 | 0.0025 | 0.0030 | 0.0088 | 0.0024 | 1979 | 0.0571 |
| 1980 | 0.0034 | 0.0075 | 0.0031 | 0.0018 | 0.0096 | 0.0026 | 0.0026 | 0.0073 | 0.0029 | 0.0026 | 0.0072 | 0.0024 | 1980 | 0.0573 |
| 1981 | 0.0019 | 0.0075 | 0.0020 | 0.0022 | 0.0079 | 0.0021 | 0.0032 | 0.0066 | 0.0036 | 0.0036 | 0.0075 | 0.0036 | 1981 | 0.0489 |
| 1982 | 0.0012 | 0.0093 | 0.0042 | 0.0014 | 0.0104 | 0.0029 | 0.0015 | 0.0107 | 0.0034 | 0.0022 | 0.0077 | 0.0021 | 1982 | 0.0550 |
| 1983 | 0.0017 | 0.0070 | 0.0034 | 0.0009 | 0.0071 | 0.0030 | 0.0017 | 0.0057 | 0.0034 | 0.0018 | 0.0059 | 0.0027 | 1983 | 0.0500 |
| 1984 | 0.0027 | 0.0061 | 0.0036 | 0.0014 | 0.0060 | 0.0046 | 0.0022 | 0.0062 | 0.0037 | 0.0027 | 0.0050 | 0.0029 | 1984 | 0.0456 |
| 1985 | 0.0027 | 0.0051 | 0.0047 | 0.0014 | 0.0074 | 0.0038 | 0.0022 | 0.0059 | 0.0026 | 0.0022 | 0.0065 | 0.0016 | 1985 | 0.0510 |
| 1986 | 0.0020 | 0.0046 | 0.0026 | 0.0017 | 0.0047 | 0.0025 | 0.0018 | 0.0036 | 0.0032 | 0.0009 | 0.0041 | 0.0019 | 1986 | 0.0374 |
| 1987 | 0.0025 | 0.0044 | 0.0008 | 0.0027 | 0.0043 | 0.0020 | 0.0016 | 0.0035 | 0.0022 | 0.0024 | 0.0034 | 0.0009 | 1987 | 0.0364 |
| 1988 | 0.0023 | 0.0052 | 0.0031 | 0.0014 | 0.0046 | 0.0031 | 0.0014 | 0.0055 | 0.0027 | 0.0013 | 0.0047 | 0.0034 | 1988 | 0.0417 |
| 1989 | 0.0012 | 0.0040 | 0.0028 | 0.0015 | 0.0051 | 0.0025 | 0.0014 | 0.0038 | 0.0026 | 0.0019 | 0.0043 | 0.0022 | 1989 | 0.0385 |
| 1990 | 0.0017 | 0.0044 | 0.0020 | 0.0022 | 0.0055 | 0.0019 | 0.0020 | 0.0040 | 0.0020 | 0.0030 | 0.0045 | 0.0026 | 1990 | 0.0336 |
| 1991 | 0.0027 | 0.0043 | 0.0016 | 0.0025 | 0.0042 | 0.0022 | 0.0019 | 0.0039 | 0.0027 | 0.0015 | 0.0035 | 0.0027 | 1991 | 0.0382 |
| 1992 | 0.0013 | 0.0032 | 0.0022 | 0.0012 | 0.0044 | 0.0028 | 0.0009 | 0.0038 | 0.0024 | 0.0015 | 0.0034 | 0.0030 | 1992 | 0.0303 |
| 1993 | 0.0003 | 0.0030 | 0.0028 | 0.0009 | 0.0043 | 0.0025 | 0.0006 | 0.0037 | 0.0026 | 0.0009 | 0.0035 | 0.0022 | 1993 | 0.0283 |
| 1994 | 0.0010 | 0.0030 | 0.0022 | 0.0015 | 0.0039 | 0.0021 | 0.0016 | 0.0031 | 0.0028 | 0.0020 | 0.0028 | 0.0023 | 1994 | 0.0282 |
| 1995 | 0.0017 | 0.0027 | 0.0023 | 0.0011 | 0.0032 | 0.0022 | 0.0015 | 0.0030 | 0.0018 | 0.0015 | 0.0030 | 0.0011 | 1995 | 0.0291 |
| 1996 | 0.0018 | 0.0027 | 0.0017 | 0.0013 | 0.0029 | 0.0018 | 0.0012 | 0.0024 | 0.0020 | 0.0013 | 0.0025 | 0.0019 | 1996 | 0.0254 |
| 1997 | 0.0008 | 0.0022 | 0.0010 | 0.0013 | 0.0028 | 0.0011 | 0.0013 | 0.0018 | 0.0016 | 0.0011 | 0.0017 | 0.0014 | 1997 | 0.0211 |
| 1998 | 0.0009 | 0.0017 | 0.0013 | 0.0010 | 0.0016 | 0.0012 | 0.0010 | 0.0012 | 0.0017 | 0.0010 | 0.0015 | 0.0012 | 1998 | 0.0168 |
| 1999 | 0.0008 | 0.0012 | 0.0012 | 0.0008 | 0.0014 | 0.0011 | 0.0008 | 0.0013 | 0.0011 | 0.0007 | 0.0013 | 0.0011 | 1999 | 0.0136 |
| 2000 | 0.0007 | 0.0012 | 0.0011 | 0.0007 | 0.0014 | 0.0007 | 0.0007 | 0.0014 | 0.0007 | 0.0007 | 0.0012 | 0.0008 | 2000 | 0.0110 |

* Compound annual return

## Table A-3

**Large Company Stocks: Capital Appreciation Returns**

from January 1926 to December 1970

| Year | Jan | Feb | Mar | Apr | May | Jun | Jul | Aug | Sep | Oct | Nov | Dec | Year | Jan-Dec* |
|------|-----|-----|-----|-----|-----|-----|-----|-----|-----|-----|-----|-----|------|----------|
| 1926 | −0.0016 | −0.0440 | −0.0591 | 0.0227 | 0.0077 | 0.0432 | 0.0455 | 0.0171 | 0.0229 | −0.0313 | 0.0223 | 0.0166 | 1926 | 0.0572 |
| 1927 | −0.0208 | 0.0477 | 0.0065 | 0.0172 | 0.0522 | −0.0094 | 0.0650 | 0.0445 | 0.0432 | −0.0531 | 0.0616 | 0.0250 | 1927 | 0.3091 |
| 1928 | −0.0051 | −0.0176 | 0.1083 | 0.0324 | 0.0127 | −0.0405 | 0.0125 | 0.0741 | 0.0240 | 0.0145 | 0.1199 | 0.0029 | 1928 | 0.3788 |
| 1929 | 0.0571 | −0.0058 | −0.0023 | 0.0161 | −0.0428 | 0.1124 | 0.0456 | 0.0980 | −0.0489 | −0.1993 | −0.1337 | 0.0253 | 1929 | −0.1191 |
| 1930 | 0.0625 | 0.0215 | 0.0799 | −0.0095 | −0.0165 | −0.1646 | 0.0367 | 0.0075 | −0.1301 | −0.0888 | −0.0218 | −0.0742 | 1930 | −0.2848 |
| 1931 | 0.0489 | 0.1144 | −0.0692 | −0.0959 | −0.1372 | 0.1390 | −0.0742 | 0.0095 | −0.2994 | 0.0844 | −0.0978 | −0.1453 | 1931 | −0.4707 |
| 1932 | −0.0283 | 0.0507 | −0.1182 | −0.2025 | −0.2333 | −0.0089 | 0.3770 | 0.3754 | −0.0369 | −0.1386 | −0.0589 | 0.0519 | 1932 | −0.1515 |
| 1933 | 0.0073 | −0.1844 | 0.0336 | 0.4222 | 0.1587 | 0.1317 | −0.0880 | 0.1146 | −0.1136 | −0.0885 | 0.1027 | 0.0223 | 1933 | 0.4659 |
| 1934 | 0.1059 | −0.0367 | −0.0009 | −0.0270 | −0.0813 | 0.0208 | −0.1152 | 0.0541 | −0.0055 | −0.0319 | 0.0829 | −0.0042 | 1934 | −0.0594 |
| 1935 | −0.0421 | −0.0396 | −0.0309 | 0.0956 | 0.0323 | 0.0679 | 0.0831 | 0.0217 | 0.0239 | 0.0751 | 0.0393 | 0.0371 | 1935 | 0.4137 |
| 1936 | 0.0655 | 0.0168 | 0.0254 | −0.0771 | 0.0458 | 0.0306 | 0.0681 | 0.0088 | 0.0013 | 0.0750 | 0.0041 | −0.0058 | 1936 | 0.2792 |
| 1937 | 0.0378 | 0.0146 | −0.0094 | −0.0831 | −0.0103 | −0.0529 | 0.1026 | −0.0554 | −0.1421 | −0.1017 | −0.1011 | −0.0504 | 1937 | −0.3859 |
| 1938 | 0.0133 | 0.0608 | −0.2504 | 0.1412 | −0.0443 | 0.2470 | 0.0727 | −0.0274 | 0.0149 | 0.0760 | −0.0334 | 0.0377 | 1938 | 0.2521 |
| 1939 | −0.0689 | 0.0325 | −0.1354 | −0.0055 | 0.0623 | −0.0638 | 0.1087 | −0.0714 | 0.1646 | −0.0146 | −0.0491 | 0.0238 | 1939 | −0.0545 |
| 1940 | −0.0352 | 0.0066 | 0.0099 | −0.0049 | −0.2395 | 0.0766 | 0.0311 | 0.0262 | 0.0095 | 0.0394 | −0.0424 | −0.0028 | 1940 | −0.1529 |
| 1941 | −0.0482 | −0.0149 | 0.0040 | −0.0653 | 0.0043 | 0.0535 | 0.0548 | −0.0087 | −0.0097 | −0.0686 | −0.0421 | −0.0451 | 1941 | −0.1786 |
| 1942 | 0.0138 | −0.0250 | −0.0675 | −0.0437 | 0.0640 | 0.0184 | 0.0313 | 0.0070 | 0.0267 | 0.0644 | −0.0138 | 0.0517 | 1942 | 0.1243 |
| 1943 | 0.0716 | 0.0506 | 0.0527 | 0.0009 | 0.0449 | 0.0198 | −0.0543 | 0.0103 | 0.0237 | −0.0132 | −0.0755 | 0.0590 | 1943 | 0.1945 |
| 1944 | 0.0154 | −0.0025 | 0.0169 | −0.0125 | 0.0404 | 0.0510 | −0.0208 | 0.0087 | −0.0031 | 0.0000 | 0.0039 | 0.0351 | 1944 | 0.1380 |
| 1945 | 0.0143 | 0.0616 | −0.0462 | 0.0880 | 0.0115 | −0.0033 | −0.0201 | 0.0580 | 0.0419 | 0.0303 | 0.0324 | 0.0099 | 1945 | 0.3072 |
| 1946 | 0.0697 | −0.0695 | 0.0463 | 0.0376 | 0.0224 | −0.0391 | −0.0255 | −0.0729 | −0.1015 | −0.0080 | −0.0115 | 0.0429 | 1946 | −0.1187 |
| 1947 | 0.0235 | −0.0147 | −0.0169 | −0.0389 | −0.0089 | 0.0526 | 0.0362 | −0.0279 | −0.0137 | 0.0212 | −0.0285 | 0.0207 | 1947 | 0.0000 |
| 1948 | −0.0399 | −0.0470 | 0.0771 | 0.0265 | 0.0782 | 0.0030 | −0.0532 | 0.0076 | −0.0301 | 0.0678 | −0.1082 | 0.0305 | 1948 | −0.0065 |
| 1949 | 0.0013 | −0.0394 | 0.0301 | −0.0212 | −0.0373 | −0.0021 | 0.0621 | 0.0120 | 0.0237 | 0.0295 | 0.0012 | 0.0436 | 1949 | 0.1026 |
| 1950 | 0.0173 | 0.0100 | 0.0041 | 0.0451 | 0.0393 | −0.0580 | 0.0085 | 0.0325 | 0.0559 | 0.0041 | −0.0010 | 0.0461 | 1950 | 0.2178 |
| 1951 | 0.0612 | 0.0065 | −0.0183 | 0.0481 | −0.0406 | −0.0260 | 0.0687 | 0.0393 | −0.0009 | −0.0138 | −0.0026 | 0.0389 | 1951 | 0.1646 |
| 1952 | 0.0156 | −0.0365 | 0.0477 | −0.0431 | 0.0232 | 0.0461 | 0.0176 | −0.0146 | −0.0196 | −0.0008 | 0.0465 | 0.0355 | 1952 | 0.1178 |
| 1953 | −0.0072 | −0.0182 | −0.0236 | −0.0265 | −0.0032 | −0.0163 | 0.0253 | −0.0578 | 0.0013 | 0.0510 | 0.0090 | 0.0020 | 1953 | −0.0662 |
| 1954 | 0.0512 | 0.0027 | 0.0302 | 0.0490 | 0.0329 | 0.0007 | 0.0572 | −0.0340 | 0.0831 | −0.0195 | 0.0808 | 0.0508 | 1954 | 0.4502 |
| 1955 | 0.0181 | 0.0035 | −0.0049 | 0.0377 | −0.0013 | 0.0823 | 0.0607 | −0.0078 | 0.0113 | −0.0305 | 0.0749 | −0.0007 | 1955 | 0.2640 |
| 1956 | −0.0365 | 0.0347 | 0.0693 | −0.0021 | −0.0657 | 0.0392 | 0.0515 | −0.0381 | −0.0455 | 0.0051 | −0.0110 | 0.0353 | 1956 | 0.0262 |
| 1957 | −0.0418 | −0.0326 | 0.0196 | 0.0370 | 0.0369 | −0.0013 | 0.0114 | −0.0561 | −0.0619 | −0.0321 | 0.0161 | −0.0415 | 1957 | −0.1431 |
| 1958 | 0.0428 | −0.0206 | 0.0309 | 0.0318 | 0.0150 | 0.0261 | 0.0431 | 0.0119 | 0.0484 | 0.0254 | 0.0224 | 0.0520 | 1958 | 0.3806 |
| 1959 | 0.0038 | −0.0002 | 0.0005 | 0.0388 | 0.0189 | −0.0036 | 0.0349 | −0.0150 | −0.0456 | 0.0113 | 0.0132 | 0.0276 | 1959 | 0.0848 |
| 1960 | −0.0715 | 0.0092 | −0.0139 | −0.0175 | 0.0269 | 0.0195 | −0.0248 | 0.0261 | −0.0604 | −0.0024 | 0.0403 | 0.0463 | 1960 | −0.0297 |
| 1961 | 0.0632 | 0.0269 | 0.0255 | 0.0038 | 0.0191 | −0.0288 | 0.0328 | 0.0196 | −0.0197 | 0.0283 | 0.0393 | 0.0032 | 1961 | 0.2313 |
| 1962 | −0.0379 | 0.0163 | −0.0059 | −0.0620 | −0.0860 | −0.0818 | 0.0636 | 0.0153 | −0.0482 | 0.0044 | 0.1016 | 0.0135 | 1962 | −0.1181 |
| 1963 | 0.0491 | −0.0289 | 0.0355 | 0.0485 | 0.0143 | −0.0202 | −0.0035 | 0.0487 | −0.0110 | 0.0322 | −0.0105 | 0.0244 | 1963 | 0.1889 |
| 1964 | 0.0269 | 0.0099 | 0.0152 | 0.0061 | 0.0115 | 0.0164 | 0.0182 | −0.0162 | 0.0287 | 0.0081 | −0.0052 | 0.0039 | 1964 | 0.1297 |
| 1965 | 0.0332 | −0.0015 | −0.0145 | 0.0342 | −0.0077 | −0.0486 | 0.0134 | 0.0225 | 0.0320 | 0.0273 | −0.0088 | 0.0090 | 1965 | 0.0906 |
| 1966 | 0.0049 | −0.0179 | −0.0218 | 0.0205 | −0.0541 | −0.0161 | −0.0135 | −0.0778 | −0.0070 | 0.0475 | 0.0031 | −0.0015 | 1966 | −0.1309 |
| 1967 | 0.0782 | 0.0020 | 0.0394 | 0.0422 | −0.0524 | 0.0175 | 0.0453 | −0.0117 | 0.0328 | −0.0291 | 0.0011 | 0.0263 | 1967 | 0.2009 |
| 1968 | −0.0438 | −0.0312 | 0.0094 | 0.0819 | 0.0112 | 0.0091 | −0.0185 | 0.0115 | 0.0385 | 0.0072 | 0.0480 | −0.0416 | 1968 | 0.0766 |
| 1969 | −0.0082 | −0.0474 | 0.0344 | 0.0215 | −0.0022 | −0.0556 | −0.0602 | 0.0401 | −0.0250 | 0.0442 | −0.0353 | −0.0193 | 1969 | −0.1142 |
| 1970 | −0.0759 | 0.0527 | 0.0015 | −0.0905 | −0.0610 | −0.0500 | 0.0733 | 0.0445 | 0.0330 | −0.0114 | 0.0474 | 0.0568 | 1970 | 0.0016 |

* Compound annual return

# Table A-3 (continued)

## Large Company Stocks: Capital Appreciation Returns

from January 1971 to December 2000

| Year | Jan | Feb | Mar | Apr | May | Jun | Jul | Aug | Sep | Oct | Nov | Dec | Year | Jan-Dec* |
|------|-----|-----|-----|-----|-----|-----|-----|-----|-----|-----|-----|-----|------|----------|
| 1971 | 0.0405 | 0.0091 | 0.0368 | 0.0363 | −0.0416 | 0.0007 | −0.0413 | 0.0361 | −0.0070 | −0.0418 | −0.0025 | 0.0862 | 1971 | 0.1079 |
| 1972 | 0.0181 | 0.0253 | 0.0059 | 0.0044 | 0.0173 | −0.0218 | 0.0023 | 0.0345 | −0.0049 | 0.0093 | 0.0456 | 0.0118 | 1972 | 0.1563 |
| 1973 | −0.0171 | −0.0375 | −0.0014 | −0.0408 | −0.0189 | −0.0066 | 0.0380 | −0.0367 | 0.0401 | −0.0013 | −0.1139 | 0.0166 | 1973 | −0.1737 |
| 1974 | −0.0100 | −0.0036 | −0.0233 | −0.0391 | −0.0336 | −0.0147 | −0.0778 | −0.0903 | −0.1193 | 0.1630 | −0.0532 | −0.0202 | 1974 | −0.2972 |
| 1975 | 0.1228 | 0.0599 | 0.0217 | 0.0473 | 0.0441 | 0.0443 | −0.0677 | −0.0211 | −0.0346 | 0.0616 | 0.0247 | −0.0115 | 1975 | 0.3155 |
| 1976 | 0.1183 | −0.0114 | 0.0307 | −0.0110 | −0.0144 | 0.0409 | −0.0081 | −0.0051 | 0.0226 | −0.0222 | −0.0078 | 0.0525 | 1976 | 0.1915 |
| 1977 | −0.0505 | −0.0217 | −0.0140 | 0.0002 | −0.0236 | 0.0454 | −0.0162 | −0.0210 | −0.0025 | −0.0434 | 0.0270 | 0.0028 | 1977 | −0.1150 |
| 1978 | −0.0615 | −0.0248 | 0.0249 | 0.0854 | 0.0042 | −0.0176 | 0.0539 | 0.0259 | −0.0073 | −0.0916 | 0.0166 | 0.0149 | 1978 | 0.0106 |
| 1979 | 0.0397 | −0.0365 | 0.0551 | 0.0017 | −0.0263 | 0.0387 | 0.0088 | 0.0531 | 0.0000 | −0.0686 | 0.0426 | 0.0168 | 1979 | 0.1231 |
| 1980 | 0.0576 | −0.0044 | −0.1018 | 0.0411 | 0.0466 | 0.0270 | 0.0650 | 0.0058 | 0.0252 | 0.0160 | 0.1023 | −0.0339 | 1980 | 0.2577 |
| 1981 | −0.0457 | 0.0133 | 0.0360 | −0.0235 | −0.0017 | −0.0101 | −0.0025 | −0.0620 | −0.0538 | 0.0492 | 0.0366 | −0.0301 | 1981 | −0.0972 |
| 1982 | −0.0175 | −0.0605 | −0.0102 | 0.0400 | −0.0392 | −0.0203 | −0.0230 | 0.1160 | 0.0076 | 0.1104 | 0.0361 | 0.0152 | 1982 | 0.1476 |
| 1983 | 0.0331 | 0.0190 | 0.0331 | 0.0749 | −0.0123 | 0.0352 | −0.0330 | 0.0113 | 0.0102 | −0.0152 | 0.0174 | −0.0088 | 1983 | 0.1727 |
| 1984 | −0.0092 | −0.0389 | 0.0135 | 0.0055 | −0.0594 | 0.0175 | −0.0165 | 0.1063 | −0.0035 | −0.0001 | −0.0151 | 0.0224 | 1984 | 0.0139 |
| 1985 | 0.0741 | 0.0086 | −0.0029 | −0.0046 | 0.0541 | 0.0121 | −0.0048 | −0.0120 | −0.0347 | 0.0425 | 0.0651 | 0.0451 | 1985 | 0.2634 |
| 1986 | 0.0024 | 0.0715 | 0.0528 | −0.0141 | 0.0502 | 0.0141 | −0.0587 | 0.0712 | −0.0854 | 0.0547 | 0.0215 | −0.0283 | 1986 | 0.1463 |
| 1987 | 0.1318 | 0.0369 | 0.0264 | −0.0115 | 0.0060 | 0.0479 | 0.0482 | 0.0350 | −0.0242 | −0.2176 | −0.0853 | 0.0729 | 1987 | 0.0203 |
| 1988 | 0.0404 | 0.0418 | −0.0333 | 0.0094 | 0.0032 | 0.0433 | −0.0054 | −0.0386 | 0.0397 | 0.0260 | −0.0189 | 0.0147 | 1988 | 0.1241 |
| 1989 | 0.0711 | −0.0289 | 0.0208 | 0.0501 | 0.0351 | −0.0079 | 0.0884 | 0.0155 | −0.0065 | −0.0252 | 0.0165 | 0.0214 | 1989 | 0.2726 |
| 1990 | −0.0688 | 0.0085 | 0.0243 | −0.0269 | 0.0920 | −0.0089 | −0.0052 | −0.0943 | −0.0512 | −0.0067 | 0.0599 | 0.0248 | 1990 | −0.0656 |
| 1991 | 0.0415 | 0.0673 | 0.0222 | 0.0003 | 0.0386 | −0.0479 | 0.0449 | 0.0196 | −0.0191 | 0.0119 | −0.0439 | 0.1116 | 1991 | 0.2631 |
| 1992 | −0.0199 | 0.0096 | −0.0218 | 0.0279 | 0.0010 | −0.0174 | 0.0394 | −0.0240 | 0.0091 | 0.0021 | 0.0303 | 0.0101 | 1992 | 0.0446 |
| 1993 | 0.0070 | 0.0105 | 0.0187 | −0.0254 | 0.0227 | 0.0008 | −0.0053 | 0.0344 | −0.0100 | 0.0194 | −0.0129 | 0.0101 | 1993 | 0.0706 |
| 1994 | 0.0325 | −0.0300 | −0.0457 | 0.0115 | 0.0124 | −0.0268 | 0.0315 | 0.0376 | −0.0269 | 0.0209 | −0.0395 | 0.0123 | 1994 | −0.0154 |
| 1995 | 0.0243 | 0.0361 | 0.0273 | 0.0280 | 0.0363 | 0.0213 | 0.0318 | −0.0003 | 0.0401 | −0.0050 | 0.0410 | 0.0174 | 1995 | 0.3411 |
| 1996 | 0.0326 | 0.0069 | 0.0079 | 0.0134 | 0.0229 | 0.0023 | −0.0457 | 0.0188 | 0.0542 | 0.0261 | 0.0734 | −0.0215 | 1996 | 0.2026 |
| 1997 | 0.0613 | 0.0059 | −0.0426 | 0.0584 | 0.0586 | 0.0435 | 0.0781 | −0.0574 | 0.0532 | −0.0345 | 0.0446 | 0.0157 | 1997 | 0.3101 |
| 1998 | 0.0102 | 0.0704 | 0.0499 | 0.0091 | −0.0188 | 0.0394 | −0.0116 | −0.1458 | 0.0624 | 0.0803 | 0.0591 | 0.0564 | 1998 | 0.2667 |
| 1999 | 0.0410 | −0.0323 | 0.0388 | 0.0379 | −0.0250 | 0.0544 | −0.0320 | −0.0063 | −0.0286 | 0.0625 | 0.0191 | 0.0578 | 1999 | 0.1953 |
| 2000 | −0.0509 | −0.0201 | 0.0967 | −0.0308 | −0.0219 | 0.0239 | −0.0163 | 0.0607 | −0.0535 | −0.0049 | −0.0801 | 0.0041 | 2000 | −0.1014 |

* Compound annual return

# Table A-4

## Small Company Stocks: Total Returns

from January 1926 to December 1970

| Year | Jan | Feb | Mar | Apr | May | Jun | Jul | Aug | Sep | Oct | Nov | Dec | Year | Jan-Dec* |
|------|-----|-----|-----|-----|-----|-----|-----|-----|-----|-----|-----|-----|------|----------|
| 1926 | 0.0699 | −0.0639 | −0.1073 | 0.0179 | −0.0066 | 0.0378 | 0.0112 | 0.0256 | −0.0001 | −0.0227 | 0.0207 | 0.0332 | 1926 | 0.0028 |
| 1927 | 0.0296 | 0.0547 | −0.0548 | 0.0573 | 0.0734 | −0.0303 | 0.0516 | −0.0178 | 0.0047 | −0.0659 | 0.0808 | 0.0316 | 1927 | 0.2210 |
| 1928 | 0.0482 | −0.0236 | 0.0531 | 0.0910 | 0.0438 | −0.0842 | 0.0059 | 0.0442 | 0.0890 | 0.0276 | 0.1147 | −0.0513 | 1928 | 0.3969 |
| 1929 | 0.0035 | −0.0026 | −0.0200 | 0.0306 | −0.1336 | 0.0533 | 0.0114 | −0.0164 | −0.0922 | −0.2768 | −0.1500 | −0.0501 | 1929 | −0.5136 |
| 1930 | 0.1293 | 0.0643 | 0.1007 | −0.0698 | −0.0542 | −0.2168 | 0.0301 | −0.0166 | −0.1459 | −0.1097 | −0.0028 | −0.1166 | 1930 | −0.3815 |
| 1931 | 0.2103 | 0.2566 | −0.0708 | −0.2164 | −0.1379 | 0.1819 | −0.0557 | −0.0763 | −0.3246 | 0.0770 | −0.1008 | −0.2195 | 1931 | −0.4975 |
| 1932 | 0.1019 | 0.0291 | −0.1311 | −0.2220 | −0.1193 | 0.0033 | 0.3523 | 0.7346 | −0.1320 | −0.1775 | −0.1227 | −0.0492 | 1932 | −0.0539 |
| 1933 | −0.0083 | −0.1278 | 0.1118 | 0.5038 | 0.6339 | 0.2617 | −0.0550 | 0.0924 | −0.1595 | −0.1236 | 0.0654 | 0.0055 | 1933 | 1.4287 |
| 1934 | 0.3891 | 0.0166 | −0.0012 | 0.0240 | −0.1275 | −0.0024 | −0.2259 | 0.1546 | −0.0167 | 0.0097 | 0.0948 | 0.0172 | 1934 | 0.2422 |
| 1935 | −0.0328 | −0.0592 | −0.1189 | 0.0791 | −0.0024 | 0.0305 | 0.0855 | 0.0545 | 0.0357 | 0.0994 | 0.1412 | 0.0598 | 1935 | 0.4019 |
| 1936 | 0.3009 | 0.0602 | 0.0066 | −0.1795 | 0.0272 | −0.0231 | 0.0873 | 0.0210 | 0.0542 | 0.0635 | 0.1400 | 0.0160 | 1936 | 0.6480 |
| 1937 | 0.1267 | 0.0658 | 0.0120 | −0.1679 | −0.0408 | −0.1183 | 0.1235 | −0.0736 | −0.2539 | −0.1093 | −0.1453 | −0.1694 | 1937 | −0.5801 |
| 1938 | 0.0534 | 0.0343 | −0.3600 | 0.2776 | −0.0849 | 0.3498 | 0.1499 | −0.1001 | −0.0157 | 0.2136 | −0.0689 | 0.0487 | 1938 | 0.3280 |
| 1939 | −0.0848 | 0.0107 | −0.2466 | 0.0142 | 0.1088 | −0.1042 | 0.2535 | −0.1590 | 0.5145 | −0.0397 | −0.1053 | 0.0422 | 1939 | 0.0035 |
| 1940 | 0.0009 | 0.0821 | 0.0632 | 0.0654 | −0.3674 | 0.1051 | 0.0231 | 0.0255 | 0.0213 | 0.0545 | 0.0245 | −0.0447 | 1940 | −0.0516 |
| 1941 | 0.0025 | −0.0288 | 0.0319 | −0.0669 | 0.0044 | 0.0753 | 0.2165 | −0.0060 | −0.0469 | −0.0672 | −0.0495 | −0.1204 | 1941 | −0.0900 |
| 1942 | 0.1894 | −0.0073 | −0.0709 | −0.0353 | −0.0032 | 0.0336 | 0.0737 | 0.0325 | 0.0912 | 0.1087 | −0.0511 | 0.0413 | 1942 | 0.4451 |
| 1943 | 0.2132 | 0.1931 | 0.1445 | 0.0933 | 0.1156 | −0.0083 | −0.1083 | −0.0002 | 0.0428 | 0.0123 | −0.1113 | 0.1241 | 1943 | 0.8837 |
| 1944 | 0.0641 | 0.0295 | 0.0749 | −0.0532 | 0.0740 | 0.1384 | −0.0299 | 0.0318 | −0.0020 | −0.0108 | 0.0499 | 0.0869 | 1944 | 0.5372 |
| 1945 | 0.0482 | 0.1009 | −0.0861 | 0.1157 | 0.0500 | 0.0855 | −0.0556 | 0.0557 | 0.0679 | 0.0701 | 0.1172 | 0.0171 | 1945 | 0.7361 |
| 1946 | 0.1562 | −0.0637 | 0.0273 | 0.0696 | 0.0591 | −0.0462 | −0.0530 | −0.0849 | −0.1603 | −0.0118 | −0.0141 | 0.0373 | 1946 | −0.1163 |
| 1947 | 0.0421 | −0.0041 | −0.0336 | −0.1031 | −0.0534 | 0.0552 | 0.0789 | −0.0037 | 0.0115 | 0.0282 | −0.0303 | 0.0359 | 1947 | 0.0092 |
| 1948 | −0.0154 | −0.0783 | 0.0986 | 0.0368 | 0.1059 | 0.0048 | −0.0578 | 0.0006 | −0.0526 | 0.0647 | −0.1116 | 0.0088 | 1948 | −0.0211 |
| 1949 | 0.0182 | −0.0481 | 0.0629 | −0.0336 | −0.0564 | −0.0096 | 0.0671 | 0.0256 | 0.0489 | 0.0472 | 0.0016 | 0.0690 | 1949 | 0.1975 |
| 1950 | 0.0492 | 0.0221 | −0.0037 | 0.0411 | 0.0255 | −0.0777 | 0.0591 | 0.0530 | 0.0521 | −0.0059 | 0.0322 | 0.0953 | 1950 | 0.3875 |
| 1951 | 0.0830 | 0.0061 | −0.0477 | 0.0367 | −0.0331 | −0.0529 | 0.0373 | 0.0605 | 0.0215 | −0.0222 | −0.0083 | 0.0044 | 1951 | 0.0780 |
| 1952 | 0.0191 | −0.0300 | 0.0175 | −0.0519 | 0.0032 | 0.0272 | 0.0112 | −0.0006 | −0.0161 | −0.0103 | 0.0485 | 0.0160 | 1952 | 0.0303 |
| 1953 | 0.0409 | 0.0269 | −0.0067 | −0.0287 | 0.0141 | −0.0486 | 0.0152 | −0.0628 | −0.0262 | 0.0292 | 0.0126 | −0.0266 | 1953 | −0.0649 |
| 1954 | 0.0756 | 0.0094 | 0.0183 | 0.0140 | 0.0451 | 0.0086 | 0.0808 | 0.0014 | 0.0410 | 0.0068 | 0.0779 | 0.1112 | 1954 | 0.6058 |
| 1955 | 0.0201 | 0.0479 | 0.0085 | 0.0150 | 0.0078 | 0.0293 | 0.0064 | −0.0028 | 0.0109 | −0.0170 | 0.0468 | 0.0163 | 1955 | 0.2044 |
| 1956 | −0.0047 | 0.0278 | 0.0431 | 0.0047 | −0.0398 | 0.0056 | 0.0283 | −0.0134 | −0.0260 | 0.0104 | 0.0053 | 0.0038 | 1956 | 0.0428 |
| 1957 | 0.0236 | −0.0200 | 0.0167 | 0.0248 | 0.0075 | 0.0073 | −0.0060 | −0.0386 | −0.0452 | −0.0832 | 0.0113 | −0.0481 | 1957 | −0.1457 |
| 1958 | 0.1105 | −0.0170 | 0.0471 | 0.0376 | 0.0387 | 0.0324 | 0.0492 | 0.0428 | 0.0518 | 0.0407 | 0.0496 | 0.0313 | 1958 | 0.6489 |
| 1959 | 0.0575 | 0.0295 | 0.0027 | 0.0117 | 0.0014 | −0.0042 | 0.0327 | −0.0088 | −0.0431 | 0.0227 | 0.0222 | 0.0322 | 1959 | 0.1640 |
| 1960 | −0.0306 | 0.0050 | −0.0315 | −0.0187 | 0.0204 | 0.0340 | −0.0189 | 0.0525 | −0.0738 | −0.0401 | 0.0437 | 0.0332 | 1960 | −0.0329 |
| 1961 | 0.0915 | 0.0589 | 0.0619 | 0.0127 | 0.0427 | −0.0543 | 0.0031 | 0.0130 | −0.0339 | 0.0262 | 0.0613 | 0.0079 | 1961 | 0.3209 |
| 1962 | 0.0136 | 0.0187 | 0.0057 | −0.0777 | −0.1009 | −0.0785 | 0.0763 | 0.0289 | −0.0659 | −0.0373 | 0.1248 | −0.0089 | 1962 | −0.1190 |
| 1963 | 0.0906 | 0.0034 | 0.0149 | 0.0312 | 0.0436 | −0.0118 | 0.0033 | 0.0517 | −0.0163 | 0.0236 | −0.0106 | −0.0048 | 1963 | 0.2357 |
| 1964 | 0.0274 | 0.0365 | 0.0219 | 0.0093 | 0.0157 | 0.0163 | 0.0398 | −0.0029 | 0.0402 | 0.0205 | 0.0011 | −0.0112 | 1964 | 0.2352 |
| 1965 | 0.0529 | 0.0390 | 0.0238 | 0.0509 | −0.0078 | −0.0901 | 0.0449 | 0.0595 | 0.0347 | 0.0572 | 0.0371 | 0.0622 | 1965 | 0.4175 |
| 1966 | 0.0756 | 0.0311 | −0.0192 | 0.0343 | −0.0961 | −0.0012 | −0.0012 | −0.1080 | −0.0164 | −0.0107 | 0.0491 | 0.0065 | 1966 | −0.0701 |
| 1967 | 0.1838 | 0.0450 | 0.0615 | 0.0271 | −0.0085 | 0.1017 | 0.0951 | 0.0020 | 0.0565 | −0.0311 | 0.0117 | 0.0965 | 1967 | 0.8357 |
| 1968 | 0.0154 | −0.0709 | −0.0109 | 0.1461 | 0.0999 | 0.0030 | −0.0345 | 0.0367 | 0.0599 | 0.0030 | 0.0764 | 0.0062 | 1968 | 0.3597 |
| 1969 | −0.0166 | −0.0990 | 0.0396 | 0.0395 | 0.0173 | −0.1165 | −0.1070 | 0.0732 | −0.0261 | 0.0610 | −0.0557 | −0.0687 | 1969 | −0.2505 |
| 1970 | −0.0608 | 0.0387 | −0.0285 | −0.1728 | −0.1031 | −0.0929 | 0.0554 | 0.0949 | 0.1086 | −0.0706 | 0.0137 | 0.0726 | 1970 | −0.1743 |

* Compound annual return

Table A-4 (continued)

**Small Company Stocks: Total Returns**

from January 1971 to December 2000

| Year | Jan | Feb | Mar | Apr | May | Jun | Jul | Aug | Sep | Oct | Nov | Dec | Year | Jan-Dec* |
|------|-----|-----|-----|-----|-----|-----|-----|-----|-----|-----|-----|-----|------|----------|
| 1971 | 0.1592 | 0.0317 | 0.0564 | 0.0247 | –0.0605 | –0.0319 | –0.0563 | 0.0583 | –0.0226 | –0.0551 | –0.0373 | 0.1144 | 1971 | 0.1650 |
| 1972 | 0.1130 | 0.0296 | –0.0143 | 0.0129 | –0.0191 | –0.0305 | –0.0413 | 0.0186 | –0.0349 | –0.0175 | 0.0592 | –0.0214 | 1972 | 0.0443 |
| 1973 | –0.0432 | –0.0799 | –0.0208 | –0.0621 | –0.0811 | –0.0290 | 0.1194 | –0.0445 | 0.1064 | 0.0084 | –0.1962 | –0.0014 | 1973 | –0.3090 |
| 1974 | 0.1326 | –0.0085 | –0.0074 | –0.0464 | –0.0793 | –0.0147 | –0.0219 | –0.0681 | –0.0653 | 0.1063 | –0.0438 | –0.0788 | 1974 | –0.1995 |
| 1975 | 0.2767 | 0.0285 | 0.0618 | 0.0531 | 0.0663 | 0.0750 | –0.0254 | –0.0574 | –0.0182 | –0.0050 | 0.0320 | –0.0197 | 1975 | 0.5282 |
| 1976 | 0.2684 | 0.1390 | –0.0015 | –0.0359 | –0.0361 | 0.0459 | 0.0045 | –0.0290 | 0.0104 | –0.0209 | 0.0404 | 0.1180 | 1976 | 0.5738 |
| 1977 | 0.0450 | –0.0039 | 0.0131 | 0.0228 | –0.0028 | 0.0772 | 0.0030 | –0.0107 | 0.0092 | –0.0330 | 0.1086 | 0.0081 | 1977 | 0.2538 |
| 1978 | –0.0189 | 0.0347 | 0.1032 | 0.0788 | 0.0820 | –0.0189 | 0.0684 | 0.0939 | –0.0032 | –0.2427 | 0.0732 | 0.0168 | 1978 | 0.2346 |
| 1979 | 0.1321 | –0.0282 | 0.1120 | 0.0387 | 0.0035 | 0.0472 | 0.0171 | 0.0756 | –0.0344 | –0.1154 | 0.0858 | 0.0588 | 1979 | 0.4346 |
| 1980 | 0.0836 | –0.0284 | –0.1778 | 0.0694 | 0.0750 | 0.0452 | 0.1323 | 0.0604 | 0.0418 | 0.0333 | 0.0766 | –0.0338 | 1980 | 0.3988 |
| 1981 | 0.0207 | 0.0094 | 0.0943 | 0.0657 | 0.0422 | 0.0076 | –0.0316 | –0.0684 | –0.0733 | 0.0742 | 0.0276 | –0.0220 | 1981 | 0.1388 |
| 1982 | –0.0196 | –0.0296 | –0.0086 | 0.0383 | –0.0248 | –0.0159 | –0.0015 | 0.0698 | 0.0327 | 0.1305 | 0.0779 | 0.0132 | 1982 | 0.2801 |
| 1983 | 0.0628 | 0.0712 | 0.0525 | 0.0767 | 0.0870 | 0.0348 | –0.0088 | –0.0197 | 0.0133 | –0.0568 | 0.0516 | –0.0145 | 1983 | 0.3967 |
| 1984 | –0.0008 | –0.0645 | 0.0174 | –0.0085 | –0.0521 | 0.0300 | –0.0420 | 0.0998 | 0.0027 | –0.0217 | –0.0336 | 0.0150 | 1984 | –0.0667 |
| 1985 | 0.1059 | 0.0272 | –0.0214 | –0.0174 | 0.0276 | 0.0106 | 0.0260 | –0.0072 | –0.0544 | 0.0261 | 0.0620 | 0.0470 | 1985 | 0.2466 |
| 1986 | 0.0112 | 0.0719 | 0.0477 | 0.0064 | 0.0360 | 0.0026 | –0.0710 | 0.0218 | –0.0559 | 0.0346 | –0.0031 | –0.0262 | 1986 | 0.0685 |
| 1987 | 0.0943 | 0.0809 | 0.0233 | –0.0313 | –0.0039 | 0.0266 | 0.0364 | 0.0287 | –0.0081 | –0.2919 | –0.0397 | 0.0520 | 1987 | –0.0930 |
| 1988 | 0.0556 | 0.0760 | 0.0408 | 0.0209 | –0.0179 | 0.0612 | –0.0025 | –0.0246 | 0.0227 | –0.0123 | –0.0437 | 0.0394 | 1988 | 0.2287 |
| 1989 | 0.0404 | 0.0083 | 0.0358 | 0.0279 | 0.0362 | –0.0201 | 0.0407 | 0.0122 | 0.0000 | –0.0604 | –0.0051 | –0.0134 | 1989 | 0.1018 |
| 1990 | –0.0764 | 0.0187 | 0.0368 | –0.0266 | 0.0561 | 0.0144 | –0.0382 | –0.1296 | –0.0829 | –0.0572 | 0.0450 | 0.0194 | 1990 | –0.2156 |
| 1991 | 0.0841 | 0.1113 | 0.0680 | 0.0034 | 0.0334 | –0.0485 | 0.0407 | 0.0261 | 0.0032 | 0.0317 | –0.0276 | 0.0601 | 1991 | 0.4463 |
| 1992 | 0.1128 | 0.0452 | –0.0249 | –0.0403 | –0.0014 | –0.0519 | 0.0370 | –0.0228 | 0.0131 | 0.0259 | 0.0885 | 0.0441 | 1992 | 0.2335 |
| 1993 | 0.0543 | –0.0180 | 0.0289 | –0.0306 | 0.0342 | –0.0038 | 0.0166 | 0.0339 | 0.0316 | 0.0471 | –0.0175 | 0.0194 | 1993 | 0.2098 |
| 1994 | 0.0618 | –0.0023 | –0.0446 | 0.0060 | –0.0012 | –0.0262 | 0.0184 | 0.0337 | 0.0105 | 0.0115 | –0.0326 | 0.0002 | 1994 | 0.0311 |
| 1995 | 0.0283 | 0.0252 | 0.0145 | 0.0352 | 0.0298 | 0.0568 | 0.0645 | 0.0358 | 0.0195 | –0.0487 | 0.0192 | 0.0239 | 1995 | 0.3446 |
| 1996 | 0.0028 | 0.0369 | 0.0228 | 0.0848 | 0.0749 | –0.0582 | –0.0943 | 0.0476 | 0.0291 | –0.0175 | 0.0288 | 0.0204 | 1996 | 0.1762 |
| 1997 | 0.0420 | –0.0206 | –0.0490 | –0.0276 | 0.1022 | 0.0498 | 0.0605 | 0.0509 | 0.0844 | –0.0386 | –0.0155 | –0.0171 | 1997 | 0.2278 |
| 1998 | –0.0059 | 0.0649 | 0.0481 | 0.0168 | –0.0497 | –0.0206 | –0.0671 | –0.2010 | 0.0369 | 0.0356 | 0.0758 | 0.0252 | 1998 | –0.0731 |
| 1999 | 0.0279 | –0.0687 | –0.0379 | 0.0949 | 0.0387 | 0.0568 | 0.0092 | –0.0191 | –0.0221 | –0.0087 | 0.0971 | 0.1137 | 1999 | 0.2979 |
| 2000 | 0.0595 | 0.2358 | –0.0751 | –0.1251 | –0.0808 | 0.1368 | –0.0322 | 0.0925 | –0.0217 | –0.0706 | –0.1110 | 0.0189 | 2000 | –0.0359 |

* Compound annual return

## Table A-5

**Long-Term Corporate Bonds: Total Returns**

from January 1926 to December 1970

| Year | Jan | Feb | Mar | Apr | May | Jun | Jul | Aug | Sep | Oct | Nov | Dec | Year | Jan-Dec* |
|------|-----|-----|-----|-----|-----|-----|-----|-----|-----|-----|-----|-----|------|----------|
| 1926 | 0.0072 | 0.0045 | 0.0084 | 0.0097 | 0.0044 | 0.0004 | 0.0057 | 0.0044 | 0.0057 | 0.0097 | 0.0057 | 0.0056 | 1926 | 0.0737 |
| 1927 | 0.0056 | 0.0069 | 0.0083 | 0.0055 | −0.0011 | 0.0043 | 0.0003 | 0.0083 | 0.0149 | 0.0055 | 0.0068 | 0.0068 | 1927 | 0.0744 |
| 1928 | 0.0027 | 0.0068 | 0.0041 | 0.0014 | −0.0078 | −0.0024 | −0.0010 | 0.0083 | 0.0030 | 0.0083 | −0.0036 | 0.0084 | 1928 | 0.0284 |
| 1929 | 0.0043 | 0.0030 | −0.0087 | 0.0019 | 0.0045 | −0.0046 | 0.0020 | 0.0020 | 0.0034 | 0.0073 | −0.0018 | 0.0192 | 1929 | 0.0327 |
| 1930 | 0.0059 | 0.0072 | 0.0138 | 0.0084 | 0.0057 | 0.0110 | 0.0056 | 0.0136 | 0.0108 | 0.0054 | −0.0012 | −0.0090 | 1930 | 0.0798 |
| 1931 | 0.0203 | 0.0068 | 0.0094 | 0.0067 | 0.0134 | 0.0052 | 0.0052 | 0.0012 | −0.0014 | −0.0363 | −0.0189 | −0.0286 | 1931 | −0.0185 |
| 1932 | −0.0052 | −0.0238 | 0.0356 | −0.0176 | 0.0107 | −0.0009 | 0.0043 | 0.0436 | 0.0301 | 0.0074 | 0.0073 | 0.0139 | 1932 | 0.1082 |
| 1933 | 0.0547 | −0.0523 | 0.0047 | −0.0095 | 0.0588 | 0.0190 | 0.0161 | 0.0093 | −0.0014 | 0.0040 | −0.0248 | 0.0257 | 1933 | 0.1038 |
| 1934 | 0.0257 | 0.0146 | 0.0187 | 0.0104 | 0.0090 | 0.0158 | 0.0047 | 0.0047 | −0.0061 | 0.0102 | 0.0129 | 0.0101 | 1934 | 0.1384 |
| 1935 | 0.0211 | 0.0141 | 0.0043 | 0.0112 | 0.0042 | 0.0112 | 0.0111 | −0.0042 | 0.0000 | 0.0042 | 0.0069 | 0.0083 | 1935 | 0.0961 |
| 1936 | 0.0082 | 0.0054 | 0.0082 | 0.0026 | 0.0040 | 0.0082 | 0.0011 | 0.0067 | 0.0067 | 0.0025 | 0.0109 | 0.0010 | 1936 | 0.0674 |
| 1937 | 0.0024 | −0.0046 | −0.0114 | 0.0068 | 0.0040 | 0.0053 | 0.0039 | −0.0017 | 0.0025 | 0.0067 | 0.0067 | 0.0067 | 1937 | 0.0275 |
| 1938 | 0.0038 | 0.0010 | −0.0087 | 0.0138 | 0.0010 | 0.0095 | 0.0066 | −0.0019 | 0.0109 | 0.0080 | 0.0037 | 0.0122 | 1938 | 0.0613 |
| 1939 | 0.0022 | 0.0064 | 0.0022 | 0.0064 | 0.0049 | 0.0035 | −0.0007 | −0.0392 | 0.0151 | 0.0237 | 0.0079 | 0.0078 | 1939 | 0.0397 |
| 1940 | 0.0049 | 0.0021 | 0.0049 | −0.0092 | −0.0021 | 0.0121 | 0.0021 | 0.0007 | 0.0092 | 0.0049 | 0.0063 | −0.0023 | 1940 | 0.0339 |
| 1941 | 0.0006 | 0.0006 | −0.0022 | 0.0078 | 0.0049 | 0.0063 | 0.0063 | 0.0034 | 0.0048 | 0.0034 | −0.0094 | 0.0006 | 1941 | 0.0273 |
| 1942 | 0.0006 | −0.0008 | 0.0063 | 0.0006 | 0.0020 | 0.0034 | 0.0020 | 0.0035 | 0.0020 | 0.0006 | 0.0006 | 0.0049 | 1942 | 0.0260 |
| 1943 | 0.0049 | 0.0006 | 0.0020 | 0.0049 | 0.0048 | 0.0048 | 0.0019 | 0.0019 | 0.0005 | −0.0009 | −0.0023 | 0.0049 | 1943 | 0.0283 |
| 1944 | 0.0020 | 0.0034 | 0.0048 | 0.0034 | 0.0005 | 0.0020 | 0.0034 | 0.0034 | 0.0019 | 0.0019 | 0.0048 | 0.0149 | 1944 | 0.0473 |
| 1945 | 0.0076 | 0.0046 | 0.0018 | 0.0018 | −0.0011 | 0.0032 | −0.0011 | 0.0004 | 0.0032 | 0.0032 | 0.0032 | 0.0133 | 1945 | 0.0408 |
| 1946 | 0.0128 | 0.0034 | 0.0034 | −0.0043 | 0.0019 | 0.0019 | −0.0012 | −0.0088 | −0.0026 | 0.0020 | −0.0025 | 0.0113 | 1946 | 0.0172 |
| 1947 | 0.0005 | 0.0005 | 0.0067 | 0.0020 | 0.0020 | 0.0004 | 0.0020 | −0.0071 | −0.0131 | −0.0099 | −0.0098 | 0.0024 | 1947 | −0.0234 |
| 1948 | 0.0024 | 0.0039 | 0.0115 | 0.0038 | 0.0008 | −0.0083 | −0.0052 | 0.0055 | 0.0024 | 0.0024 | 0.0085 | 0.0131 | 1948 | 0.0414 |
| 1949 | 0.0038 | 0.0038 | 0.0007 | 0.0023 | 0.0038 | 0.0084 | 0.0099 | 0.0037 | 0.0021 | 0.0067 | 0.0021 | −0.0145 | 1949 | 0.0331 |
| 1950 | 0.0037 | 0.0007 | 0.0022 | −0.0008 | −0.0008 | 0.0023 | 0.0069 | 0.0038 | −0.0039 | −0.0008 | 0.0054 | 0.0023 | 1950 | 0.0212 |
| 1951 | 0.0019 | −0.0044 | −0.0237 | −0.0009 | −0.0015 | −0.0093 | 0.0205 | 0.0114 | −0.0057 | −0.0145 | −0.0061 | 0.0058 | 1951 | −0.0269 |
| 1952 | 0.0199 | −0.0085 | 0.0076 | −0.0004 | 0.0031 | 0.0016 | 0.0016 | 0.0063 | −0.0018 | 0.0039 | 0.0108 | −0.0091 | 1952 | 0.0352 |
| 1953 | −0.0080 | −0.0040 | −0.0033 | −0.0248 | −0.0030 | 0.0109 | 0.0177 | −0.0085 | 0.0253 | 0.0227 | −0.0073 | 0.0172 | 1953 | 0.0341 |
| 1954 | 0.0124 | 0.0198 | 0.0039 | −0.0034 | −0.0042 | 0.0063 | 0.0040 | 0.0018 | 0.0040 | 0.0040 | 0.0025 | 0.0017 | 1954 | 0.0539 |
| 1955 | −0.0097 | −0.0063 | 0.0092 | −0.0001 | −0.0018 | 0.0029 | −0.0041 | −0.0038 | 0.0076 | 0.0078 | −0.0030 | 0.0063 | 1955 | 0.0048 |
| 1956 | 0.0104 | 0.0026 | −0.0146 | −0.0115 | 0.0052 | −0.0018 | −0.0093 | −0.0208 | 0.0012 | −0.0105 | −0.0126 | −0.0082 | 1956 | −0.0681 |
| 1957 | 0.0197 | 0.0093 | 0.0050 | −0.0066 | −0.0075 | −0.0322 | −0.0110 | −0.0009 | 0.0095 | 0.0023 | 0.0311 | 0.0685 | 1957 | 0.0871 |
| 1958 | 0.0099 | −0.0008 | −0.0046 | 0.0163 | 0.0031 | −0.0038 | −0.0153 | −0.0320 | −0.0096 | 0.0107 | 0.0105 | −0.0058 | 1958 | −0.0222 |
| 1959 | −0.0028 | 0.0126 | −0.0083 | −0.0172 | −0.0114 | 0.0044 | 0.0089 | −0.0068 | −0.0088 | 0.0165 | 0.0135 | −0.0096 | 1959 | −0.0097 |
| 1960 | 0.0107 | 0.0128 | 0.0191 | −0.0022 | −0.0021 | 0.0141 | 0.0257 | 0.0117 | −0.0063 | 0.0008 | −0.0070 | 0.0104 | 1960 | 0.0907 |
| 1961 | 0.0148 | 0.0210 | −0.0029 | −0.0116 | 0.0049 | −0.0080 | 0.0040 | −0.0018 | 0.0144 | 0.0127 | 0.0028 | −0.0026 | 1961 | 0.0482 |
| 1962 | 0.0080 | 0.0052 | 0.0151 | 0.0142 | 0.0000 | −0.0026 | −0.0015 | 0.0143 | 0.0089 | 0.0068 | 0.0062 | 0.0023 | 1962 | 0.0795 |
| 1963 | 0.0059 | 0.0023 | 0.0026 | −0.0051 | 0.0048 | 0.0043 | 0.0028 | 0.0035 | −0.0023 | 0.0049 | 0.0015 | −0.0034 | 1963 | 0.0219 |
| 1964 | 0.0087 | 0.0054 | −0.0062 | 0.0040 | 0.0057 | 0.0048 | 0.0052 | 0.0037 | 0.0021 | 0.0050 | −0.0004 | 0.0088 | 1964 | 0.0477 |
| 1965 | 0.0081 | 0.0009 | 0.0012 | 0.0021 | −0.0008 | 0.0003 | 0.0019 | −0.0006 | −0.0015 | 0.0046 | −0.0057 | −0.0149 | 1965 | −0.0046 |
| 1966 | 0.0022 | −0.0113 | −0.0059 | 0.0013 | −0.0026 | 0.0030 | −0.0098 | −0.0259 | 0.0078 | 0.0261 | −0.0020 | 0.0201 | 1966 | 0.0020 |
| 1967 | 0.0450 | −0.0201 | 0.0117 | −0.0071 | −0.0254 | −0.0223 | 0.0041 | −0.0007 | 0.0094 | −0.0281 | −0.0272 | 0.0127 | 1967 | −0.0495 |
| 1968 | 0.0361 | 0.0037 | −0.0197 | 0.0048 | 0.0032 | 0.0122 | 0.0341 | 0.0206 | −0.0053 | −0.0160 | −0.0226 | −0.0233 | 1968 | 0.0257 |
| 1969 | 0.0139 | −0.0160 | −0.0200 | 0.0335 | −0.0227 | 0.0035 | 0.0005 | −0.0020 | −0.0244 | 0.0127 | −0.0471 | −0.0134 | 1969 | −0.0809 |
| 1970 | 0.0141 | 0.0401 | −0.0045 | −0.0250 | −0.0163 | 0.0001 | 0.0556 | 0.0100 | 0.0139 | −0.0096 | 0.0584 | 0.0372 | 1970 | 0.1837 |

* Compound annual return

Table A-5 (continued)

## Long-Term Corporate Bonds: Total Returns

from January 1971 to December 2000

| Year | Jan | Feb | Mar | Apr | May | Jun | Jul | Aug | Sep | Oct | Nov | Dec | Year | Jan-Dec* |
|------|-----|-----|-----|-----|-----|-----|-----|-----|-----|-----|-----|-----|------|----------|
| 1971 | 0.0532 | −0.0366 | 0.0258 | −0.0236 | −0.0161 | 0.0107 | −0.0025 | 0.0554 | −0.0102 | 0.0282 | 0.0029 | 0.0223 | 1971 | 0.1101 |
| 1972 | −0.0033 | 0.0107 | 0.0024 | 0.0035 | 0.0163 | −0.0068 | 0.0030 | 0.0072 | 0.0031 | 0.0101 | 0.0249 | −0.0004 | 1972 | 0.0726 |
| 1973 | −0.0054 | 0.0023 | 0.0045 | 0.0061 | −0.0039 | −0.0056 | −0.0476 | 0.0356 | 0.0356 | −0.0066 | 0.0078 | −0.0089 | 1973 | 0.0114 |
| 1974 | −0.0053 | 0.0009 | −0.0307 | −0.0341 | 0.0105 | −0.0285 | −0.0211 | −0.0268 | 0.0174 | 0.0885 | 0.0117 | −0.0075 | 1974 | −0.0306 |
| 1975 | 0.0596 | 0.0137 | −0.0247 | −0.0052 | 0.0106 | 0.0304 | −0.0030 | −0.0175 | −0.0126 | 0.0553 | −0.0088 | 0.0442 | 1975 | 0.1464 |
| 1976 | 0.0188 | 0.0061 | 0.0167 | −0.0015 | −0.0103 | 0.0150 | 0.0149 | 0.0231 | 0.0167 | 0.0070 | 0.0319 | 0.0347 | 1976 | 0.1865 |
| 1977 | −0.0303 | −0.0020 | 0.0094 | 0.0100 | 0.0106 | 0.0175 | −0.0005 | 0.0136 | −0.0022 | −0.0038 | 0.0061 | −0.0105 | 1977 | 0.0171 |
| 1978 | −0.0089 | 0.0051 | 0.0042 | −0.0023 | −0.0108 | 0.0023 | 0.0101 | 0.0257 | −0.0048 | −0.0205 | 0.0134 | −0.0133 | 1978 | −0.0007 |
| 1979 | 0.0184 | −0.0128 | 0.0106 | −0.0052 | 0.0228 | 0.0269 | −0.0031 | 0.0006 | −0.0179 | −0.0890 | 0.0222 | −0.0108 | 1979 | −0.0418 |
| 1980 | −0.0645 | −0.0665 | −0.0062 | 0.1376 | 0.0560 | 0.0341 | −0.0429 | −0.0445 | −0.0237 | −0.0159 | 0.0017 | 0.0248 | 1980 | −0.0276 |
| 1981 | −0.0130 | −0.0269 | 0.0311 | −0.0769 | 0.0595 | 0.0023 | −0.0372 | −0.0345 | −0.0199 | 0.0521 | 0.1267 | −0.0580 | 1981 | −0.0124 |
| 1982 | −0.0129 | 0.0312 | 0.0306 | 0.0338 | 0.0245 | −0.0468 | 0.0540 | 0.0837 | 0.0623 | 0.0759 | 0.0201 | 0.0108 | 1982 | 0.4256 |
| 1983 | −0.0094 | 0.0428 | 0.0072 | 0.0548 | −0.0324 | −0.0046 | −0.0455 | 0.0051 | 0.0392 | −0.0025 | 0.0142 | −0.0033 | 1983 | 0.0626 |
| 1984 | 0.0270 | −0.0172 | −0.0235 | −0.0073 | −0.0483 | 0.0199 | 0.0586 | 0.0307 | 0.0314 | 0.0572 | 0.0212 | 0.0128 | 1984 | 0.1686 |
| 1985 | 0.0325 | −0.0373 | 0.0179 | 0.0296 | 0.0820 | 0.0083 | −0.0121 | 0.0260 | 0.0071 | 0.0329 | 0.0370 | 0.0469 | 1985 | 0.3009 |
| 1986 | 0.0045 | 0.0752 | 0.0256 | 0.0016 | −0.0164 | 0.0218 | 0.0031 | 0.0275 | −0.0114 | 0.0189 | 0.0233 | 0.0117 | 1986 | 0.1985 |
| 1987 | 0.0216 | 0.0058 | −0.0087 | −0.0502 | −0.0052 | 0.0155 | −0.0119 | −0.0075 | −0.0422 | 0.0507 | 0.0125 | 0.0212 | 1987 | −0.0027 |
| 1988 | 0.0517 | 0.0138 | −0.0188 | −0.0149 | −0.0057 | 0.0379 | −0.0111 | 0.0054 | 0.0326 | 0.0273 | −0.0169 | 0.0039 | 1988 | 0.1070 |
| 1989 | 0.0202 | −0.0129 | 0.0064 | 0.0213 | 0.0379 | 0.0395 | 0.0178 | −0.0163 | 0.0040 | 0.0276 | 0.0070 | 0.0006 | 1989 | 0.1623 |
| 1990 | −0.0191 | −0.0012 | −0.0011 | −0.0191 | 0.0385 | 0.0216 | 0.0102 | −0.0292 | 0.0091 | 0.0132 | 0.0285 | 0.0167 | 1990 | 0.0678 |
| 1991 | 0.0150 | 0.0121 | 0.0108 | 0.0138 | 0.0039 | −0.0018 | 0.0167 | 0.0275 | 0.0271 | 0.0043 | 0.0106 | 0.0436 | 1991 | 0.1989 |
| 1992 | −0.0173 | 0.0096 | −0.0073 | 0.0016 | 0.0254 | 0.0156 | 0.0308 | 0.0090 | 0.0099 | −0.0156 | 0.0069 | 0.0228 | 1992 | 0.0939 |
| 1993 | 0.0250 | 0.0256 | 0.0025 | 0.0052 | 0.0020 | 0.0293 | 0.0100 | 0.0287 | 0.0043 | 0.0051 | −0.0188 | 0.0067 | 1993 | 0.1319 |
| 1994 | 0.0202 | −0.0286 | −0.0383 | −0.0097 | −0.0062 | −0.0081 | 0.0309 | −0.0031 | −0.0265 | −0.0050 | 0.0018 | 0.0157 | 1994 | −0.0576 |
| 1995 | 0.0256 | 0.0289 | 0.0095 | 0.0175 | 0.0631 | 0.0079 | −0.0101 | 0.0214 | 0.0153 | 0.0185 | 0.0242 | 0.0228 | 1995 | 0.2720 |
| 1996 | 0.0014 | −0.0373 | −0.0130 | −0.0160 | 0.0005 | 0.0172 | 0.0010 | −0.0070 | 0.0259 | 0.0361 | 0.0263 | −0.0186 | 1996 | 0.0140 |
| 1997 | −0.0028 | 0.0028 | −0.0221 | 0.0184 | 0.0128 | 0.0187 | 0.0528 | −0.0240 | 0.0226 | 0.0191 | 0.0101 | 0.0163 | 1997 | 0.1295 |
| 1998 | 0.0137 | −0.0007 | 0.0038 | 0.0053 | 0.0167 | 0.0115 | −0.0056 | 0.0089 | 0.0413 | −0.0190 | 0.0270 | 0.0010 | 1998 | 0.1076 |
| 1999 | 0.0123 | −0.0401 | 0.0002 | −0.0024 | −0.0176 | −0.0160 | −0.0113 | −0.0026 | 0.0093 | 0.0047 | −0.0024 | −0.0102 | 1999 | −0.0745 |
| 2000 | −0.0021 | 0.0092 | 0.0169 | −0.0115 | −0.0161 | 0.0326 | 0.0179 | 0.0135 | 0.0046 | 0.0045 | 0.0263 | 0.0270 | 2000 | 0.1287 |

* Compound annual return

## Table A-6

**Long-Term Government Bonds: Total Returns**

from January 1926 to December 1970

| Year | Jan | Feb | Mar | Apr | May | Jun | Jul | Aug | Sep | Oct | Nov | Dec | Year | Jan-Dec* |
|---|---|---|---|---|---|---|---|---|---|---|---|---|---|---|
| 1926 | 0.0138 | 0.0063 | 0.0041 | 0.0076 | 0.0014 | 0.0038 | 0.0004 | 0.0000 | 0.0038 | 0.0102 | 0.0160 | 0.0078 | 1926 | 0.0777 |
| 1927 | 0.0075 | 0.0088 | 0.0253 | -0.0005 | 0.0109 | -0.0069 | 0.0050 | 0.0076 | 0.0018 | 0.0099 | 0.0097 | 0.0072 | 1927 | 0.0893 |
| 1928 | -0.0036 | 0.0061 | 0.0045 | -0.0004 | -0.0077 | 0.0041 | -0.0217 | 0.0076 | -0.0041 | 0.0158 | 0.0003 | 0.0004 | 1928 | 0.0010 |
| 1929 | -0.0090 | -0.0157 | -0.0144 | 0.0275 | -0.0162 | 0.0110 | 0.0000 | -0.0034 | 0.0027 | 0.0382 | 0.0236 | -0.0089 | 1929 | 0.0342 |
| 1930 | -0.0057 | 0.0129 | 0.0083 | -0.0016 | 0.0139 | 0.0051 | 0.0034 | 0.0013 | 0.0074 | 0.0035 | 0.0042 | -0.0070 | 1930 | 0.0466 |
| 1931 | -0.0121 | 0.0085 | 0.0104 | 0.0086 | 0.0145 | 0.0004 | -0.0042 | 0.0012 | -0.0281 | -0.0330 | 0.0027 | -0.0220 | 1931 | -0.0531 |
| 1932 | 0.0034 | 0.0413 | -0.0018 | 0.0604 | -0.0188 | 0.0065 | 0.0481 | 0.0003 | 0.0057 | -0.0017 | 0.0032 | 0.0131 | 1932 | 0.1684 |
| 1933 | 0.0148 | -0.0258 | 0.0097 | -0.0032 | 0.0303 | 0.0050 | -0.0017 | 0.0044 | 0.0023 | -0.0091 | -0.0149 | -0.0113 | 1933 | -0.0007 |
| 1934 | 0.0257 | 0.0081 | 0.0197 | 0.0126 | 0.0131 | 0.0067 | 0.0040 | -0.0118 | -0.0146 | 0.0182 | 0.0037 | 0.0112 | 1934 | 0.1003 |
| 1935 | 0.0182 | 0.0092 | 0.0041 | 0.0079 | -0.0057 | 0.0092 | 0.0046 | -0.0133 | 0.0009 | 0.0061 | 0.0010 | 0.0070 | 1935 | 0.0498 |
| 1936 | 0.0055 | 0.0081 | 0.0106 | 0.0035 | 0.0040 | 0.0021 | 0.0060 | 0.0111 | -0.0031 | 0.0006 | 0.0205 | 0.0038 | 1936 | 0.0752 |
| 1937 | -0.0013 | 0.0086 | -0.0411 | 0.0039 | 0.0053 | -0.0018 | 0.0138 | -0.0104 | 0.0045 | 0.0042 | 0.0096 | 0.0082 | 1937 | 0.0023 |
| 1938 | 0.0057 | 0.0052 | -0.0037 | 0.0210 | 0.0044 | 0.0004 | 0.0043 | 0.0000 | 0.0022 | 0.0087 | -0.0022 | 0.0080 | 1938 | 0.0553 |
| 1939 | 0.0059 | 0.0080 | 0.0125 | 0.0118 | 0.0171 | -0.0027 | 0.0113 | -0.0201 | -0.0545 | 0.0410 | 0.0162 | 0.0145 | 1939 | 0.0594 |
| 1940 | -0.0017 | 0.0027 | 0.0177 | -0.0035 | -0.0299 | 0.0258 | 0.0052 | 0.0028 | 0.0110 | 0.0031 | 0.0205 | 0.0067 | 1940 | 0.0609 |
| 1941 | -0.0201 | 0.0020 | 0.0096 | 0.0129 | 0.0027 | 0.0066 | 0.0022 | 0.0018 | -0.0012 | 0.0140 | -0.0029 | -0.0177 | 1941 | 0.0093 |
| 1942 | 0.0069 | 0.0011 | 0.0092 | -0.0029 | 0.0075 | 0.0003 | 0.0018 | 0.0038 | 0.0003 | 0.0024 | -0.0035 | 0.0049 | 1942 | 0.0322 |
| 1943 | 0.0033 | -0.0005 | 0.0009 | 0.0048 | 0.0050 | 0.0018 | -0.0001 | 0.0021 | 0.0011 | 0.0005 | 0.0000 | 0.0018 | 1943 | 0.0208 |
| 1944 | 0.0021 | 0.0032 | 0.0021 | 0.0013 | 0.0028 | 0.0008 | 0.0036 | 0.0027 | 0.0014 | 0.0012 | 0.0024 | 0.0042 | 1944 | 0.0281 |
| 1945 | 0.0127 | 0.0077 | 0.0021 | 0.0160 | 0.0056 | 0.0169 | -0.0086 | 0.0026 | 0.0054 | 0.0104 | 0.0125 | 0.0194 | 1945 | 0.1073 |
| 1946 | 0.0025 | 0.0032 | 0.0010 | -0.0135 | -0.0012 | 0.0070 | -0.0040 | -0.0111 | -0.0009 | 0.0074 | -0.0054 | 0.0145 | 1946 | -0.0010 |
| 1947 | -0.0006 | 0.0021 | 0.0020 | -0.0037 | 0.0033 | 0.0010 | 0.0063 | 0.0081 | -0.0044 | -0.0037 | -0.0174 | -0.0192 | 1947 | -0.0262 |
| 1948 | 0.0020 | 0.0046 | 0.0034 | 0.0045 | 0.0141 | -0.0084 | -0.0021 | 0.0001 | 0.0014 | 0.0007 | 0.0076 | 0.0056 | 1948 | 0.0340 |
| 1949 | 0.0082 | 0.0049 | 0.0074 | 0.0011 | 0.0019 | 0.0167 | 0.0033 | 0.0111 | -0.0011 | 0.0019 | 0.0021 | 0.0052 | 1949 | 0.0645 |
| 1950 | -0.0061 | 0.0021 | 0.0008 | 0.0030 | 0.0033 | -0.0025 | 0.0055 | 0.0014 | -0.0072 | -0.0048 | 0.0035 | 0.0016 | 1950 | 0.0006 |
| 1951 | 0.0058 | -0.0074 | -0.0157 | -0.0063 | -0.0069 | -0.0062 | 0.0138 | 0.0099 | -0.0080 | 0.0010 | -0.0136 | -0.0061 | 1951 | -0.0393 |
| 1952 | 0.0028 | 0.0014 | 0.0111 | 0.0171 | -0.0033 | 0.0003 | -0.0020 | -0.0070 | -0.0130 | 0.0148 | -0.0015 | -0.0086 | 1952 | 0.0116 |
| 1953 | 0.0012 | -0.0087 | -0.0088 | -0.0105 | -0.0148 | 0.0223 | 0.0039 | -0.0008 | 0.0299 | 0.0074 | -0.0049 | 0.0206 | 1953 | 0.0364 |
| 1954 | 0.0089 | 0.0240 | 0.0058 | 0.0104 | -0.0087 | 0.0163 | 0.0134 | -0.0036 | -0.0010 | 0.0006 | -0.0025 | 0.0064 | 1954 | 0.0719 |
| 1955 | -0.0241 | -0.0078 | 0.0087 | 0.0001 | 0.0073 | -0.0076 | -0.0102 | 0.0004 | 0.0073 | 0.0144 | -0.0045 | 0.0037 | 1955 | -0.0129 |
| 1956 | 0.0083 | -0.0002 | -0.0149 | -0.0113 | 0.0225 | 0.0027 | -0.0209 | -0.0187 | 0.0050 | -0.0054 | -0.0057 | -0.0179 | 1956 | -0.0559 |
| 1957 | 0.0346 | 0.0025 | -0.0024 | -0.0222 | -0.0023 | -0.0180 | -0.0041 | 0.0002 | 0.0076 | -0.0050 | 0.0533 | 0.0307 | 1957 | 0.0746 |
| 1958 | -0.0084 | 0.0100 | 0.0102 | 0.0186 | 0.0001 | -0.0160 | -0.0278 | -0.0435 | -0.0117 | 0.0138 | 0.0120 | -0.0181 | 1958 | -0.0609 |
| 1959 | -0.0080 | 0.0117 | 0.0017 | -0.0117 | -0.0005 | 0.0010 | 0.0060 | -0.0041 | -0.0057 | 0.0150 | -0.0119 | -0.0159 | 1959 | -0.0226 |
| 1960 | 0.0112 | 0.0204 | 0.0282 | -0.0170 | 0.0152 | 0.0173 | 0.0368 | -0.0067 | 0.0075 | -0.0028 | -0.0066 | 0.0279 | 1960 | 0.1378 |
| 1961 | -0.0107 | 0.0200 | -0.0037 | 0.0115 | -0.0046 | -0.0075 | 0.0035 | -0.0038 | 0.0129 | 0.0071 | -0.0020 | -0.0125 | 1961 | 0.0097 |
| 1962 | -0.0014 | 0.0103 | 0.0253 | 0.0082 | 0.0046 | -0.0076 | -0.0109 | 0.0187 | 0.0061 | 0.0084 | 0.0021 | 0.0035 | 1962 | 0.0689 |
| 1963 | -0.0001 | 0.0008 | 0.0009 | -0.0012 | 0.0023 | 0.0019 | 0.0031 | 0.0021 | 0.0004 | -0.0026 | 0.0051 | -0.0006 | 1963 | 0.0121 |
| 1964 | -0.0014 | -0.0011 | 0.0037 | 0.0047 | 0.0050 | 0.0069 | 0.0008 | 0.0020 | 0.0050 | 0.0043 | 0.0017 | 0.0030 | 1964 | 0.0351 |
| 1965 | 0.0040 | 0.0014 | 0.0054 | 0.0036 | 0.0018 | 0.0047 | 0.0022 | -0.0013 | -0.0034 | 0.0027 | -0.0062 | -0.0078 | 1965 | 0.0071 |
| 1966 | -0.0104 | -0.0250 | 0.0296 | -0.0063 | -0.0059 | -0.0016 | -0.0037 | -0.0206 | 0.0332 | 0.0228 | -0.0148 | 0.0413 | 1966 | 0.0365 |
| 1967 | 0.0154 | -0.0221 | 0.0198 | -0.0291 | -0.0039 | -0.0312 | 0.0068 | -0.0084 | -0.0004 | -0.0400 | -0.0196 | 0.0192 | 1967 | -0.0918 |
| 1968 | 0.0328 | -0.0033 | -0.0212 | 0.0227 | 0.0043 | 0.0230 | 0.0289 | -0.0003 | -0.0102 | -0.0132 | -0.0269 | -0.0363 | 1968 | -0.0026 |
| 1969 | -0.0206 | 0.0042 | 0.0010 | 0.0427 | -0.0490 | 0.0214 | 0.0079 | -0.0069 | -0.0531 | 0.0365 | -0.0243 | -0.0068 | 1969 | -0.0507 |
| 1970 | -0.0021 | 0.0587 | -0.0068 | -0.0413 | -0.0468 | 0.0486 | 0.0319 | -0.0019 | 0.0228 | -0.0109 | 0.0791 | -0.0084 | 1970 | 0.1211 |

* Compound annual return

Table A-6 (continued)

## Long-Term Government Bonds: Total Returns

from January 1971 to December 2000

| Year | Jan | Feb | Mar | Apr | May | Jun | Jul | Aug | Sep | Oct | Nov | Dec | Year | Jan-Dec* |
|------|-----|-----|-----|-----|-----|-----|-----|-----|-----|-----|-----|-----|------|----------|
| 1971 | 0.0506 | −0.0163 | 0.0526 | −0.0283 | −0.0006 | −0.0159 | 0.0030 | 0.0471 | 0.0204 | 0.0167 | −0.0047 | 0.0044 | 1971 | 0.1323 |
| 1972 | −0.0063 | 0.0088 | −0.0082 | 0.0027 | 0.0270 | −0.0065 | 0.0216 | 0.0029 | −0.0083 | 0.0234 | 0.0226 | −0.0229 | 1972 | 0.0569 |
| 1973 | −0.0321 | 0.0014 | 0.0082 | 0.0046 | −0.0105 | −0.0021 | −0.0433 | 0.0391 | 0.0318 | 0.0215 | −0.0183 | −0.0082 | 1973 | −0.0111 |
| 1974 | −0.0083 | −0.0024 | −0.0292 | −0.0253 | 0.0123 | 0.0045 | −0.0029 | −0.0232 | 0.0247 | 0.0489 | 0.0295 | 0.0171 | 1974 | 0.0435 |
| 1975 | 0.0225 | 0.0131 | −0.0267 | −0.0182 | 0.0212 | 0.0292 | −0.0087 | −0.0068 | −0.0098 | 0.0475 | −0.0109 | 0.0390 | 1975 | 0.0920 |
| 1976 | 0.0090 | 0.0062 | 0.0166 | 0.0018 | −0.0158 | 0.0208 | 0.0078 | 0.0211 | 0.0145 | 0.0084 | 0.0339 | 0.0327 | 1976 | 0.1675 |
| 1977 | −0.0388 | −0.0049 | 0.0091 | 0.0071 | 0.0125 | 0.0164 | −0.0070 | 0.0198 | −0.0029 | −0.0093 | 0.0093 | −0.0168 | 1977 | −0.0069 |
| 1978 | −0.0080 | 0.0004 | −0.0021 | −0.0005 | −0.0058 | −0.0062 | 0.0143 | 0.0218 | −0.0106 | −0.0200 | 0.0189 | −0.0130 | 1978 | −0.0118 |
| 1979 | 0.0191 | −0.0135 | 0.0129 | −0.0112 | 0.0261 | 0.0311 | −0.0085 | −0.0035 | −0.0122 | −0.0841 | 0.0311 | 0.0057 | 1979 | −0.0123 |
| 1980 | −0.0741 | −0.0467 | −0.0315 | 0.1523 | 0.0419 | 0.0359 | −0.0476 | −0.0432 | −0.0262 | −0.0263 | 0.0100 | 0.0352 | 1980 | −0.0395 |
| 1981 | −0.0115 | −0.0435 | 0.0384 | −0.0518 | 0.0622 | −0.0179 | −0.0353 | −0.0386 | −0.0145 | 0.0829 | 0.1410 | −0.0713 | 1981 | 0.0186 |
| 1982 | 0.0046 | 0.0182 | 0.0231 | 0.0373 | 0.0034 | −0.0223 | 0.0501 | 0.0781 | 0.0618 | 0.0634 | −0.0002 | 0.0312 | 1982 | 0.4036 |
| 1983 | −0.0309 | 0.0492 | −0.0094 | 0.0350 | −0.0386 | 0.0039 | −0.0486 | 0.0020 | 0.0505 | −0.0132 | 0.0183 | −0.0059 | 1983 | 0.0065 |
| 1984 | 0.0244 | −0.0178 | −0.0156 | −0.0105 | −0.0516 | 0.0150 | 0.0693 | 0.0266 | 0.0342 | 0.0561 | 0.0118 | 0.0091 | 1984 | 0.1548 |
| 1985 | 0.0364 | −0.0493 | 0.0307 | 0.0242 | 0.0896 | 0.0142 | −0.0180 | 0.0259 | −0.0021 | 0.0338 | 0.0401 | 0.0541 | 1985 | 0.3097 |
| 1986 | −0.0025 | 0.1145 | 0.0770 | −0.0080 | −0.0505 | 0.0613 | −0.0108 | 0.0499 | −0.0500 | 0.0289 | 0.0267 | −0.0018 | 1986 | 0.2453 |
| 1987 | 0.0161 | 0.0202 | −0.0223 | −0.0473 | −0.0105 | 0.0098 | −0.0178 | −0.0165 | −0.0369 | 0.0623 | 0.0037 | 0.0165 | 1987 | −0.0271 |
| 1988 | 0.0666 | 0.0052 | −0.0307 | −0.0160 | −0.0102 | 0.0368 | −0.0170 | 0.0058 | 0.0345 | 0.0308 | −0.0196 | 0.0110 | 1988 | 0.0967 |
| 1989 | 0.0203 | −0.0179 | 0.0122 | 0.0159 | 0.0401 | 0.0550 | 0.0238 | −0.0259 | 0.0019 | 0.0379 | 0.0078 | −0.0006 | 1989 | 0.1811 |
| 1990 | −0.0343 | −0.0025 | −0.0044 | −0.0202 | 0.0415 | 0.0230 | 0.0107 | −0.0419 | 0.0117 | 0.0215 | 0.0402 | 0.0187 | 1990 | 0.0618 |
| 1991 | 0.0130 | 0.0030 | 0.0038 | 0.0140 | 0.0000 | −0.0063 | 0.0157 | 0.0340 | 0.0303 | 0.0054 | 0.0082 | 0.0581 | 1991 | 0.1930 |
| 1992 | −0.0324 | 0.0051 | −0.0094 | 0.0016 | 0.0243 | 0.0200 | 0.0398 | 0.0067 | 0.0185 | −0.0198 | 0.0010 | 0.0246 | 1992 | 0.0805 |
| 1993 | 0.0280 | 0.0354 | 0.0021 | 0.0072 | 0.0047 | 0.0449 | 0.0191 | 0.0434 | 0.0005 | 0.0096 | −0.0259 | 0.0020 | 1993 | 0.1824 |
| 1994 | 0.0257 | −0.0450 | −0.0395 | −0.0150 | −0.0082 | −0.0100 | 0.0363 | −0.0086 | −0.0331 | −0.0025 | 0.0066 | 0.0161 | 1994 | −0.0777 |
| 1995 | 0.0273 | 0.0287 | 0.0091 | 0.0169 | 0.0790 | 0.0139 | −0.0168 | 0.0236 | 0.0175 | 0.0294 | 0.0249 | 0.0272 | 1995 | 0.3167 |
| 1996 | −0.0011 | −0.0483 | −0.0210 | −0.0165 | −0.0054 | 0.0203 | 0.0018 | −0.0139 | 0.0290 | 0.0404 | 0.0351 | −0.0256 | 1996 | −0.0093 |
| 1997 | −0.0079 | 0.0005 | −0.0252 | 0.0255 | 0.0097 | 0.0195 | 0.0626 | −0.0317 | 0.0316 | 0.0341 | 0.0148 | 0.0184 | 1997 | 0.1585 |
| 1998 | 0.0200 | −0.0072 | 0.0025 | 0.0026 | 0.0182 | 0.0228 | −0.0040 | 0.0465 | 0.0395 | −0.0218 | 0.0097 | −0.0032 | 1998 | 0.1306 |
| 1999 | 0.0121 | −0.0520 | −0.0008 | 0.0021 | −0.0185 | −0.0078 | −0.0077 | −0.0053 | 0.0084 | −0.0012 | −0.0061 | −0.0155 | 1999 | −0.0896 |
| 2000 | 0.0228 | 0.0264 | 0.0367 | −0.0076 | −0.0054 | 0.0244 | 0.0173 | 0.0240 | −0.0157 | 0.0187 | 0.0319 | 0.0243 | 2000 | 0.2148 |

* Compound annual return

## Table A-7

## Long-Term Government Bonds: Income Returns

from January 1926 to December 1970

| Year | Jan | Feb | Mar | Apr | May | Jun | Jul | Aug | Sep | Oct | Nov | Dec | Year | Jan-Dec* |
|------|-----|-----|-----|-----|-----|-----|-----|-----|-----|-----|-----|-----|------|----------|
| 1926 | 0.0031 | 0.0028 | 0.0032 | 0.0030 | 0.0028 | 0.0033 | 0.0031 | 0.0031 | 0.0030 | 0.0030 | 0.0031 | 0.0030 | 1926 | 0.0373 |
| 1927 | 0.0030 | 0.0027 | 0.0029 | 0.0027 | 0.0028 | 0.0027 | 0.0027 | 0.0029 | 0.0027 | 0.0028 | 0.0027 | 0.0027 | 1927 | 0.0341 |
| 1928 | 0.0027 | 0.0025 | 0.0027 | 0.0026 | 0.0027 | 0.0027 | 0.0027 | 0.0029 | 0.0027 | 0.0030 | 0.0027 | 0.0029 | 1928 | 0.0322 |
| 1929 | 0.0029 | 0.0027 | 0.0028 | 0.0034 | 0.0030 | 0.0029 | 0.0032 | 0.0030 | 0.0032 | 0.0031 | 0.0026 | 0.0031 | 1929 | 0.0347 |
| 1930 | 0.0029 | 0.0026 | 0.0029 | 0.0027 | 0.0027 | 0.0029 | 0.0028 | 0.0026 | 0.0029 | 0.0027 | 0.0026 | 0.0028 | 1930 | 0.0332 |
| 1931 | 0.0028 | 0.0026 | 0.0029 | 0.0027 | 0.0026 | 0.0028 | 0.0027 | 0.0027 | 0.0027 | 0.0029 | 0.0031 | 0.0032 | 1931 | 0.0333 |
| 1932 | 0.0032 | 0.0032 | 0.0031 | 0.0030 | 0.0028 | 0.0028 | 0.0028 | 0.0028 | 0.0026 | 0.0027 | 0.0026 | 0.0027 | 1932 | 0.0369 |
| 1933 | 0.0027 | 0.0023 | 0.0027 | 0.0025 | 0.0028 | 0.0025 | 0.0026 | 0.0026 | 0.0025 | 0.0026 | 0.0025 | 0.0028 | 1933 | 0.0312 |
| 1934 | 0.0029 | 0.0024 | 0.0027 | 0.0025 | 0.0025 | 0.0024 | 0.0024 | 0.0024 | 0.0023 | 0.0027 | 0.0025 | 0.0025 | 1934 | 0.0318 |
| 1935 | 0.0025 | 0.0021 | 0.0022 | 0.0023 | 0.0023 | 0.0022 | 0.0024 | 0.0023 | 0.0023 | 0.0023 | 0.0024 | 0.0024 | 1935 | 0.0281 |
| 1936 | 0.0024 | 0.0023 | 0.0024 | 0.0022 | 0.0022 | 0.0024 | 0.0023 | 0.0023 | 0.0021 | 0.0023 | 0.0022 | 0.0022 | 1936 | 0.0277 |
| 1937 | 0.0021 | 0.0020 | 0.0022 | 0.0023 | 0.0022 | 0.0025 | 0.0024 | 0.0023 | 0.0023 | 0.0023 | 0.0024 | 0.0023 | 1937 | 0.0266 |
| 1938 | 0.0023 | 0.0021 | 0.0023 | 0.0022 | 0.0022 | 0.0021 | 0.0021 | 0.0022 | 0.0021 | 0.0022 | 0.0021 | 0.0022 | 1938 | 0.0264 |
| 1939 | 0.0021 | 0.0019 | 0.0021 | 0.0019 | 0.0020 | 0.0018 | 0.0019 | 0.0018 | 0.0019 | 0.0023 | 0.0020 | 0.0019 | 1939 | 0.0240 |
| 1940 | 0.0020 | 0.0018 | 0.0019 | 0.0018 | 0.0019 | 0.0019 | 0.0020 | 0.0019 | 0.0018 | 0.0018 | 0.0018 | 0.0017 | 1940 | 0.0223 |
| 1941 | 0.0016 | 0.0016 | 0.0018 | 0.0017 | 0.0017 | 0.0016 | 0.0016 | 0.0016 | 0.0016 | 0.0016 | 0.0014 | 0.0016 | 1941 | 0.0194 |
| 1942 | 0.0021 | 0.0019 | 0.0021 | 0.0020 | 0.0019 | 0.0021 | 0.0021 | 0.0021 | 0.0020 | 0.0021 | 0.0020 | 0.0021 | 1942 | 0.0246 |
| 1943 | 0.0020 | 0.0019 | 0.0021 | 0.0020 | 0.0019 | 0.0021 | 0.0021 | 0.0021 | 0.0020 | 0.0020 | 0.0021 | 0.0021 | 1943 | 0.0244 |
| 1944 | 0.0021 | 0.0020 | 0.0021 | 0.0020 | 0.0022 | 0.0020 | 0.0021 | 0.0021 | 0.0020 | 0.0021 | 0.0020 | 0.0020 | 1944 | 0.0246 |
| 1945 | 0.0021 | 0.0018 | 0.0020 | 0.0019 | 0.0019 | 0.0019 | 0.0018 | 0.0019 | 0.0018 | 0.0019 | 0.0018 | 0.0018 | 1945 | 0.0234 |
| 1946 | 0.0017 | 0.0015 | 0.0016 | 0.0017 | 0.0018 | 0.0016 | 0.0019 | 0.0017 | 0.0018 | 0.0019 | 0.0018 | 0.0019 | 1946 | 0.0204 |
| 1947 | 0.0018 | 0.0016 | 0.0018 | 0.0017 | 0.0017 | 0.0019 | 0.0018 | 0.0017 | 0.0018 | 0.0018 | 0.0017 | 0.0021 | 1947 | 0.0213 |
| 1948 | 0.0020 | 0.0019 | 0.0022 | 0.0020 | 0.0018 | 0.0021 | 0.0019 | 0.0021 | 0.0020 | 0.0019 | 0.0021 | 0.0020 | 1948 | 0.0240 |
| 1949 | 0.0020 | 0.0018 | 0.0019 | 0.0018 | 0.0020 | 0.0019 | 0.0017 | 0.0019 | 0.0017 | 0.0018 | 0.0017 | 0.0017 | 1949 | 0.0225 |
| 1950 | 0.0018 | 0.0016 | 0.0018 | 0.0016 | 0.0019 | 0.0017 | 0.0018 | 0.0018 | 0.0017 | 0.0019 | 0.0018 | 0.0018 | 1950 | 0.0212 |
| 1951 | 0.0020 | 0.0017 | 0.0019 | 0.0020 | 0.0021 | 0.0020 | 0.0023 | 0.0021 | 0.0019 | 0.0023 | 0.0021 | 0.0022 | 1951 | 0.0238 |
| 1952 | 0.0023 | 0.0021 | 0.0023 | 0.0022 | 0.0020 | 0.0022 | 0.0022 | 0.0021 | 0.0023 | 0.0023 | 0.0021 | 0.0024 | 1952 | 0.0266 |
| 1953 | 0.0023 | 0.0021 | 0.0025 | 0.0024 | 0.0024 | 0.0027 | 0.0025 | 0.0025 | 0.0025 | 0.0023 | 0.0024 | 0.0024 | 1953 | 0.0284 |
| 1954 | 0.0023 | 0.0022 | 0.0025 | 0.0022 | 0.0020 | 0.0025 | 0.0022 | 0.0023 | 0.0022 | 0.0021 | 0.0023 | 0.0023 | 1954 | 0.0279 |
| 1955 | 0.0022 | 0.0022 | 0.0024 | 0.0022 | 0.0025 | 0.0023 | 0.0023 | 0.0027 | 0.0024 | 0.0025 | 0.0024 | 0.0024 | 1955 | 0.0275 |
| 1956 | 0.0025 | 0.0023 | 0.0023 | 0.0026 | 0.0026 | 0.0023 | 0.0026 | 0.0026 | 0.0025 | 0.0029 | 0.0027 | 0.0028 | 1956 | 0.0299 |
| 1957 | 0.0029 | 0.0025 | 0.0026 | 0.0029 | 0.0029 | 0.0025 | 0.0033 | 0.0030 | 0.0031 | 0.0031 | 0.0029 | 0.0029 | 1957 | 0.0344 |
| 1958 | 0.0027 | 0.0025 | 0.0027 | 0.0026 | 0.0024 | 0.0027 | 0.0027 | 0.0027 | 0.0032 | 0.0032 | 0.0028 | 0.0033 | 1958 | 0.0327 |
| 1959 | 0.0031 | 0.0031 | 0.0035 | 0.0033 | 0.0033 | 0.0036 | 0.0035 | 0.0035 | 0.0034 | 0.0035 | 0.0035 | 0.0036 | 1959 | 0.0401 |
| 1960 | 0.0035 | 0.0037 | 0.0036 | 0.0032 | 0.0037 | 0.0034 | 0.0032 | 0.0034 | 0.0032 | 0.0033 | 0.0032 | 0.0033 | 1960 | 0.0426 |
| 1961 | 0.0033 | 0.0030 | 0.0031 | 0.0031 | 0.0034 | 0.0032 | 0.0033 | 0.0033 | 0.0032 | 0.0034 | 0.0032 | 0.0031 | 1961 | 0.0383 |
| 1962 | 0.0037 | 0.0032 | 0.0033 | 0.0033 | 0.0032 | 0.0030 | 0.0034 | 0.0034 | 0.0030 | 0.0035 | 0.0031 | 0.0032 | 1962 | 0.0400 |
| 1963 | 0.0032 | 0.0029 | 0.0031 | 0.0034 | 0.0033 | 0.0030 | 0.0036 | 0.0033 | 0.0034 | 0.0034 | 0.0032 | 0.0036 | 1963 | 0.0389 |
| 1964 | 0.0035 | 0.0032 | 0.0037 | 0.0035 | 0.0032 | 0.0038 | 0.0035 | 0.0035 | 0.0034 | 0.0034 | 0.0035 | 0.0035 | 1964 | 0.0415 |
| 1965 | 0.0033 | 0.0032 | 0.0038 | 0.0033 | 0.0033 | 0.0038 | 0.0034 | 0.0037 | 0.0035 | 0.0034 | 0.0037 | 0.0037 | 1965 | 0.0419 |
| 1966 | 0.0038 | 0.0034 | 0.0040 | 0.0036 | 0.0041 | 0.0039 | 0.0038 | 0.0043 | 0.0041 | 0.0040 | 0.0038 | 0.0039 | 1966 | 0.0449 |
| 1967 | 0.0040 | 0.0034 | 0.0039 | 0.0035 | 0.0043 | 0.0039 | 0.0043 | 0.0042 | 0.0040 | 0.0045 | 0.0045 | 0.0044 | 1967 | 0.0459 |
| 1968 | 0.0050 | 0.0042 | 0.0043 | 0.0049 | 0.0046 | 0.0042 | 0.0048 | 0.0042 | 0.0044 | 0.0045 | 0.0043 | 0.0049 | 1968 | 0.0550 |
| 1969 | 0.0050 | 0.0046 | 0.0047 | 0.0055 | 0.0047 | 0.0055 | 0.0052 | 0.0048 | 0.0055 | 0.0057 | 0.0049 | 0.0060 | 1969 | 0.0595 |
| 1970 | 0.0056 | 0.0052 | 0.0056 | 0.0054 | 0.0055 | 0.0064 | 0.0059 | 0.0057 | 0.0056 | 0.0055 | 0.0058 | 0.0053 | 1970 | 0.0674 |

* Compound annual return

Table A-7 (continued)

**Long-Term Government Bonds: Income Returns**

from January 1971 to December 2000

| Year | Jan | Feb | Mar | Apr | May | Jun | Jul | Aug | Sep | Oct | Nov | Dec | Year | Jan-Dec* |
|------|-----|-----|-----|-----|-----|-----|-----|-----|-----|-----|-----|-----|------|----------|
| 1971 | 0.0051 | 0.0046 | 0.0056 | 0.0048 | 0.0047 | 0.0056 | 0.0052 | 0.0055 | 0.0049 | 0.0047 | 0.0051 | 0.0050 | 1971 | 0.0632 |
| 1972 | 0.0050 | 0.0047 | 0.0049 | 0.0048 | 0.0055 | 0.0049 | 0.0051 | 0.0049 | 0.0047 | 0.0052 | 0.0048 | 0.0045 | 1972 | 0.0587 |
| 1973 | 0.0054 | 0.0051 | 0.0056 | 0.0057 | 0.0058 | 0.0055 | 0.0061 | 0.0062 | 0.0055 | 0.0063 | 0.0056 | 0.0060 | 1973 | 0.0651 |
| 1974 | 0.0061 | 0.0055 | 0.0058 | 0.0068 | 0.0068 | 0.0061 | 0.0072 | 0.0065 | 0.0071 | 0.0070 | 0.0062 | 0.0067 | 1974 | 0.0727 |
| 1975 | 0.0068 | 0.0060 | 0.0066 | 0.0067 | 0.0067 | 0.0070 | 0.0068 | 0.0065 | 0.0073 | 0.0072 | 0.0061 | 0.0074 | 1975 | 0.0799 |
| 1976 | 0.0065 | 0.0060 | 0.0071 | 0.0064 | 0.0059 | 0.0073 | 0.0065 | 0.0069 | 0.0064 | 0.0061 | 0.0066 | 0.0063 | 1976 | 0.0789 |
| 1977 | 0.0059 | 0.0057 | 0.0065 | 0.0061 | 0.0067 | 0.0062 | 0.0059 | 0.0067 | 0.0061 | 0.0063 | 0.0063 | 0.0062 | 1977 | 0.0714 |
| 1978 | 0.0069 | 0.0060 | 0.0069 | 0.0063 | 0.0075 | 0.0069 | 0.0073 | 0.0070 | 0.0065 | 0.0073 | 0.0071 | 0.0068 | 1978 | 0.0790 |
| 1979 | 0.0079 | 0.0065 | 0.0074 | 0.0076 | 0.0077 | 0.0071 | 0.0076 | 0.0073 | 0.0068 | 0.0082 | 0.0083 | 0.0083 | 1979 | 0.0886 |
| 1980 | 0.0083 | 0.0084 | 0.0099 | 0.0100 | 0.0087 | 0.0086 | 0.0084 | 0.0081 | 0.0097 | 0.0097 | 0.0091 | 0.0108 | 1980 | 0.0997 |
| 1981 | 0.0094 | 0.0088 | 0.0111 | 0.0101 | 0.0104 | 0.0109 | 0.0109 | 0.0110 | 0.0114 | 0.0117 | 0.0113 | 0.0100 | 1981 | 0.1155 |
| 1982 | 0.0108 | 0.0103 | 0.0124 | 0.0112 | 0.0101 | 0.0120 | 0.0114 | 0.0112 | 0.0100 | 0.0091 | 0.0094 | 0.0093 | 1982 | 0.1350 |
| 1983 | 0.0087 | 0.0081 | 0.0089 | 0.0085 | 0.0091 | 0.0090 | 0.0088 | 0.0103 | 0.0096 | 0.0095 | 0.0094 | 0.0094 | 1983 | 0.1038 |
| 1984 | 0.0103 | 0.0092 | 0.0098 | 0.0104 | 0.0103 | 0.0106 | 0.0116 | 0.0106 | 0.0094 | 0.0108 | 0.0091 | 0.0098 | 1984 | 0.1174 |
| 1985 | 0.0096 | 0.0082 | 0.0094 | 0.0102 | 0.0097 | 0.0080 | 0.0094 | 0.0085 | 0.0088 | 0.0089 | 0.0081 | 0.0086 | 1985 | 0.1125 |
| 1986 | 0.0079 | 0.0073 | 0.0071 | 0.0063 | 0.0062 | 0.0070 | 0.0066 | 0.0063 | 0.0065 | 0.0069 | 0.0059 | 0.0070 | 1986 | 0.0898 |
| 1987 | 0.0064 | 0.0059 | 0.0066 | 0.0065 | 0.0066 | 0.0075 | 0.0073 | 0.0075 | 0.0075 | 0.0079 | 0.0075 | 0.0078 | 1987 | 0.0792 |
| 1988 | 0.0072 | 0.0071 | 0.0072 | 0.0070 | 0.0078 | 0.0076 | 0.0071 | 0.0083 | 0.0076 | 0.0076 | 0.0070 | 0.0075 | 1988 | 0.0897 |
| 1989 | 0.0080 | 0.0069 | 0.0079 | 0.0070 | 0.0080 | 0.0070 | 0.0068 | 0.0066 | 0.0065 | 0.0072 | 0.0064 | 0.0064 | 1989 | 0.0881 |
| 1990 | 0.0073 | 0.0066 | 0.0071 | 0.0075 | 0.0075 | 0.0068 | 0.0074 | 0.0071 | 0.0069 | 0.0081 | 0.0071 | 0.0072 | 1990 | 0.0819 |
| 1991 | 0.0071 | 0.0064 | 0.0064 | 0.0076 | 0.0068 | 0.0063 | 0.0076 | 0.0068 | 0.0068 | 0.0065 | 0.0060 | 0.0068 | 1991 | 0.0822 |
| 1992 | 0.0061 | 0.0059 | 0.0067 | 0.0065 | 0.0061 | 0.0067 | 0.0063 | 0.0060 | 0.0058 | 0.0057 | 0.0061 | 0.0063 | 1992 | 0.0726 |
| 1993 | 0.0059 | 0.0055 | 0.0063 | 0.0057 | 0.0052 | 0.0062 | 0.0054 | 0.0056 | 0.0050 | 0.0049 | 0.0053 | 0.0055 | 1993 | 0.0717 |
| 1994 | 0.0055 | 0.0049 | 0.0058 | 0.0057 | 0.0063 | 0.0061 | 0.0060 | 0.0066 | 0.0061 | 0.0066 | 0.0064 | 0.0066 | 1994 | 0.0659 |
| 1995 | 0.0070 | 0.0059 | 0.0064 | 0.0058 | 0.0065 | 0.0054 | 0.0056 | 0.0057 | 0.0052 | 0.0057 | 0.0051 | 0.0049 | 1995 | 0.0760 |
| 1996 | 0.0054 | 0.0048 | 0.0052 | 0.0059 | 0.0058 | 0.0054 | 0.0062 | 0.0057 | 0.0060 | 0.0058 | 0.0052 | 0.0056 | 1996 | 0.0618 |
| 1997 | 0.0056 | 0.0051 | 0.0059 | 0.0059 | 0.0059 | 0.0057 | 0.0058 | 0.0049 | 0.0058 | 0.0054 | 0.0047 | 0.0054 | 1997 | 0.0664 |
| 1998 | 0.0048 | 0.0044 | 0.0052 | 0.0049 | 0.0048 | 0.0052 | 0.0049 | 0.0048 | 0.0044 | 0.0042 | 0.0045 | 0.0045 | 1998 | 0.0583 |
| 1999 | 0.0042 | 0.0040 | 0.0053 | 0.0048 | 0.0045 | 0.0055 | 0.0053 | 0.0053 | 0.0052 | 0.0050 | 0.0056 | 0.0055 | 1999 | 0.0557 |
| 2000 | 0.0057 | 0.0051 | 0.0054 | 0.0047 | 0.0056 | 0.0052 | 0.0052 | 0.0050 | 0.0046 | 0.0053 | 0.0048 | 0.0045 | 2000 | 0.0650 |

* Compound annual return

## Table A-8

**Long-Term Government Bonds: Capital Appreciation Returns**

from January 1926 to December 1970

| Year | Jan | Feb | Mar | Apr | May | Jun | Jul | Aug | Sep | Oct | Nov | Dec | Year | Jan-Dec* |
|------|-----|-----|-----|-----|-----|-----|-----|-----|-----|-----|-----|-----|------|----------|
| 1926 | 0.0106 | 0.0035 | 0.0009 | 0.0046 | -0.0014 | 0.0005 | -0.0027 | -0.0031 | 0.0007 | 0.0072 | 0.0129 | 0.0048 | 1926 | 0.0391 |
| 1927 | 0.0045 | 0.0061 | 0.0224 | -0.0032 | 0.0081 | -0.0096 | 0.0022 | 0.0047 | -0.0009 | 0.0071 | 0.0071 | 0.0045 | 1927 | 0.0540 |
| 1928 | -0.0063 | 0.0036 | 0.0019 | -0.0029 | -0.0104 | 0.0015 | -0.0245 | 0.0047 | -0.0067 | 0.0128 | -0.0024 | -0.0024 | 1928 | -0.0312 |
| 1929 | -0.0119 | -0.0183 | -0.0171 | 0.0242 | -0.0192 | 0.0081 | -0.0032 | -0.0064 | -0.0004 | 0.0351 | 0.0211 | -0.0120 | 1929 | -0.0020 |
| 1930 | -0.0086 | 0.0102 | 0.0055 | -0.0043 | 0.0113 | 0.0022 | 0.0007 | -0.0013 | 0.0045 | 0.0008 | 0.0017 | -0.0098 | 1930 | 0.0128 |
| 1931 | -0.0149 | 0.0059 | 0.0076 | 0.0059 | 0.0119 | -0.0024 | -0.0069 | -0.0015 | -0.0307 | -0.0360 | -0.0004 | -0.0252 | 1931 | -0.0846 |
| 1932 | 0.0002 | 0.0382 | -0.0049 | 0.0574 | -0.0216 | 0.0037 | 0.0453 | -0.0025 | 0.0031 | -0.0044 | 0.0006 | 0.0104 | 1932 | 0.1294 |
| 1933 | 0.0122 | -0.0282 | 0.0070 | -0.0057 | 0.0274 | 0.0025 | -0.0043 | 0.0018 | -0.0002 | -0.0117 | -0.0174 | -0.0140 | 1933 | -0.0314 |
| 1934 | 0.0228 | 0.0057 | 0.0170 | 0.0101 | 0.0106 | 0.0043 | 0.0016 | -0.0143 | -0.0169 | 0.0155 | 0.0013 | 0.0087 | 1934 | 0.0676 |
| 1935 | 0.0157 | 0.0070 | 0.0019 | 0.0056 | -0.0079 | 0.0070 | 0.0022 | -0.0156 | -0.0014 | 0.0038 | -0.0014 | 0.0047 | 1935 | 0.0214 |
| 1936 | 0.0031 | 0.0059 | 0.0083 | 0.0013 | 0.0019 | -0.0003 | 0.0037 | 0.0088 | -0.0053 | -0.0017 | 0.0183 | 0.0017 | 1936 | 0.0464 |
| 1937 | -0.0034 | 0.0067 | -0.0433 | 0.0016 | 0.0031 | -0.0043 | 0.0114 | -0.0128 | 0.0022 | 0.0019 | 0.0072 | 0.0059 | 1937 | -0.0248 |
| 1938 | 0.0034 | 0.0031 | -0.0059 | 0.0187 | 0.0022 | -0.0016 | 0.0022 | -0.0022 | 0.0001 | 0.0065 | -0.0043 | 0.0059 | 1938 | 0.0283 |
| 1939 | 0.0038 | 0.0061 | 0.0105 | 0.0099 | 0.0151 | -0.0045 | 0.0095 | -0.0219 | -0.0564 | 0.0386 | 0.0142 | 0.0125 | 1939 | 0.0348 |
| 1940 | -0.0037 | 0.0009 | 0.0158 | -0.0053 | -0.0318 | 0.0239 | 0.0032 | 0.0009 | 0.0092 | 0.0013 | 0.0187 | 0.0050 | 1940 | 0.0377 |
| 1941 | -0.0217 | 0.0004 | 0.0078 | 0.0112 | 0.0011 | 0.0050 | 0.0005 | 0.0002 | -0.0028 | 0.0124 | -0.0044 | -0.0194 | 1941 | -0.0101 |
| 1942 | 0.0048 | -0.0008 | 0.0071 | -0.0049 | 0.0056 | -0.0018 | -0.0003 | 0.0017 | -0.0016 | 0.0004 | -0.0055 | 0.0028 | 1942 | 0.0074 |
| 1943 | 0.0013 | -0.0024 | -0.0012 | 0.0028 | 0.0031 | -0.0003 | -0.0021 | 0.0000 | -0.0009 | -0.0015 | -0.0021 | -0.0003 | 1943 | -0.0037 |
| 1944 | 0.0000 | 0.0012 | 0.0000 | -0.0006 | 0.0006 | -0.0012 | 0.0015 | 0.0006 | -0.0006 | -0.0009 | 0.0003 | 0.0022 | 1944 | 0.0032 |
| 1945 | 0.0105 | 0.0058 | 0.0001 | 0.0141 | 0.0037 | 0.0150 | -0.0104 | 0.0007 | 0.0037 | 0.0085 | 0.0108 | 0.0177 | 1945 | 0.0827 |
| 1946 | 0.0008 | 0.0017 | -0.0006 | -0.0152 | -0.0030 | 0.0054 | -0.0058 | -0.0129 | -0.0028 | 0.0055 | -0.0072 | 0.0126 | 1946 | -0.0215 |
| 1947 | -0.0024 | 0.0005 | 0.0002 | -0.0054 | 0.0016 | -0.0009 | 0.0044 | 0.0064 | -0.0062 | -0.0055 | -0.0191 | -0.0213 | 1947 | -0.0470 |
| 1948 | 0.0000 | 0.0028 | 0.0013 | 0.0025 | 0.0123 | -0.0105 | -0.0041 | -0.0019 | -0.0006 | -0.0012 | 0.0055 | 0.0036 | 1948 | 0.0096 |
| 1949 | 0.0062 | 0.0031 | 0.0055 | -0.0006 | 0.0000 | 0.0148 | 0.0016 | 0.0092 | -0.0029 | 0.0001 | 0.0004 | 0.0035 | 1949 | 0.0415 |
| 1950 | -0.0080 | 0.0005 | -0.0010 | 0.0014 | 0.0014 | -0.0042 | 0.0037 | -0.0004 | -0.0089 | -0.0067 | 0.0017 | -0.0001 | 1950 | -0.0206 |
| 1951 | 0.0038 | -0.0091 | -0.0176 | -0.0083 | -0.0090 | -0.0082 | 0.0116 | 0.0077 | -0.0098 | -0.0012 | -0.0157 | -0.0083 | 1951 | -0.0627 |
| 1952 | 0.0005 | -0.0007 | 0.0088 | 0.0149 | -0.0054 | -0.0019 | -0.0041 | -0.0091 | -0.0153 | 0.0124 | -0.0036 | -0.0110 | 1952 | -0.0148 |
| 1953 | -0.0011 | -0.0108 | -0.0113 | -0.0129 | -0.0171 | 0.0195 | 0.0014 | -0.0033 | 0.0275 | 0.0051 | -0.0073 | 0.0182 | 1953 | 0.0067 |
| 1954 | 0.0066 | 0.0218 | 0.0034 | 0.0081 | -0.0107 | 0.0138 | 0.0113 | -0.0059 | -0.0031 | -0.0015 | -0.0048 | 0.0042 | 1954 | 0.0435 |
| 1955 | -0.0264 | -0.0100 | 0.0063 | -0.0022 | 0.0048 | -0.0099 | -0.0125 | -0.0022 | 0.0049 | 0.0119 | -0.0069 | 0.0013 | 1955 | -0.0407 |
| 1956 | 0.0058 | -0.0025 | -0.0172 | -0.0139 | 0.0199 | 0.0004 | -0.0234 | -0.0213 | 0.0025 | -0.0083 | -0.0084 | -0.0206 | 1956 | -0.0846 |
| 1957 | 0.0317 | 0.0000 | -0.0050 | -0.0250 | -0.0052 | -0.0206 | -0.0074 | -0.0028 | 0.0045 | -0.0081 | 0.0504 | 0.0277 | 1957 | 0.0382 |
| 1958 | -0.0112 | 0.0075 | 0.0075 | 0.0160 | -0.0023 | -0.0187 | -0.0305 | -0.0463 | -0.0149 | 0.0106 | 0.0092 | -0.0213 | 1958 | -0.0923 |
| 1959 | -0.0111 | 0.0087 | -0.0018 | -0.0150 | -0.0038 | -0.0026 | 0.0025 | -0.0076 | -0.0091 | 0.0115 | -0.0154 | -0.0195 | 1959 | -0.0620 |
| 1960 | 0.0077 | 0.0167 | 0.0246 | -0.0202 | 0.0115 | 0.0139 | 0.0335 | -0.0101 | 0.0043 | -0.0061 | -0.0098 | 0.0247 | 1960 | 0.0929 |
| 1961 | -0.0140 | 0.0170 | -0.0069 | 0.0085 | -0.0080 | -0.0106 | 0.0001 | -0.0071 | 0.0097 | 0.0037 | -0.0052 | -0.0156 | 1961 | -0.0286 |
| 1962 | -0.0051 | 0.0071 | 0.0220 | 0.0049 | 0.0014 | -0.0106 | -0.0143 | 0.0153 | 0.0031 | 0.0049 | -0.0010 | 0.0003 | 1962 | 0.0278 |
| 1963 | -0.0033 | -0.0022 | -0.0022 | -0.0046 | -0.0010 | -0.0011 | -0.0005 | -0.0011 | -0.0029 | -0.0060 | 0.0019 | -0.0042 | 1963 | -0.0270 |
| 1964 | -0.0048 | -0.0043 | 0.0000 | 0.0012 | 0.0018 | 0.0031 | -0.0027 | -0.0015 | 0.0015 | 0.0009 | -0.0018 | -0.0005 | 1964 | -0.0072 |
| 1965 | 0.0007 | -0.0018 | 0.0016 | 0.0003 | -0.0015 | 0.0009 | -0.0012 | -0.0050 | -0.0069 | -0.0007 | -0.0099 | -0.0115 | 1965 | -0.0345 |
| 1966 | -0.0142 | -0.0284 | 0.0256 | -0.0099 | -0.0100 | -0.0054 | -0.0074 | -0.0249 | 0.0292 | 0.0188 | -0.0187 | 0.0374 | 1966 | -0.0106 |
| 1967 | 0.0115 | -0.0255 | 0.0159 | -0.0326 | -0.0082 | -0.0351 | 0.0026 | -0.0126 | -0.0045 | -0.0445 | -0.0241 | 0.0148 | 1967 | -0.1355 |
| 1968 | 0.0278 | -0.0075 | -0.0254 | 0.0178 | -0.0003 | 0.0188 | 0.0241 | -0.0044 | -0.0146 | -0.0177 | -0.0312 | -0.0412 | 1968 | -0.0551 |
| 1969 | -0.0256 | -0.0004 | -0.0036 | 0.0371 | -0.0537 | 0.0159 | 0.0027 | -0.0117 | -0.0586 | 0.0309 | -0.0293 | -0.0129 | 1969 | -0.1083 |
| 1970 | -0.0077 | 0.0535 | -0.0124 | -0.0467 | -0.0523 | 0.0422 | 0.0260 | -0.0076 | 0.0172 | -0.0164 | 0.0733 | -0.0137 | 1970 | 0.0484 |

* Compound annual return

## Table A-8 (continued)

## Long-Term Government Bonds: Capital Appreciation Returns

from January 1971 to December 2000

| Year | Jan | Feb | Mar | Apr | May | Jun | Jul | Aug | Sep | Oct | Nov | Dec | Year | Jan-Dec* |
|------|-----|-----|-----|-----|-----|-----|-----|-----|-----|-----|-----|-----|------|----------|
| 1971 | 0.0455 | −0.0209 | 0.0470 | −0.0331 | −0.0053 | −0.0214 | −0.0022 | 0.0416 | 0.0154 | 0.0120 | −0.0098 | −0.0006 | 1971 | 0.0661 |
| 1972 | −0.0114 | 0.0041 | −0.0131 | −0.0021 | 0.0215 | −0.0113 | 0.0165 | −0.0021 | −0.0129 | 0.0182 | 0.0178 | −0.0275 | 1972 | −0.0035 |
| 1973 | −0.0375 | −0.0037 | 0.0026 | −0.0012 | −0.0162 | −0.0076 | −0.0495 | 0.0329 | 0.0263 | 0.0153 | −0.0238 | −0.0142 | 1973 | −0.0770 |
| 1974 | −0.0144 | −0.0079 | −0.0350 | −0.0320 | 0.0055 | −0.0016 | −0.0101 | −0.0298 | 0.0176 | 0.0419 | 0.0233 | 0.0105 | 1974 | −0.0345 |
| 1975 | 0.0157 | 0.0071 | −0.0333 | −0.0248 | 0.0145 | 0.0222 | −0.0155 | −0.0133 | −0.0171 | 0.0403 | −0.0170 | 0.0316 | 1975 | 0.0073 |
| 1976 | 0.0025 | 0.0001 | 0.0094 | −0.0046 | −0.0217 | 0.0135 | 0.0013 | 0.0142 | 0.0081 | 0.0023 | 0.0273 | 0.0265 | 1976 | 0.0807 |
| 1977 | −0.0447 | −0.0106 | 0.0026 | 0.0010 | 0.0058 | 0.0102 | −0.0130 | 0.0131 | −0.0089 | −0.0156 | 0.0031 | −0.0230 | 1977 | −0.0786 |
| 1978 | −0.0149 | −0.0056 | −0.0090 | −0.0068 | −0.0133 | −0.0132 | 0.0070 | 0.0148 | −0.0171 | −0.0273 | 0.0117 | −0.0198 | 1978 | −0.0905 |
| 1979 | 0.0112 | −0.0200 | 0.0056 | −0.0188 | 0.0184 | 0.0240 | −0.0161 | −0.0108 | −0.0190 | −0.0922 | 0.0229 | −0.0026 | 1979 | −0.0984 |
| 1980 | −0.0824 | −0.0551 | −0.0413 | 0.1424 | 0.0332 | 0.0272 | −0.0560 | −0.0513 | −0.0358 | −0.0360 | 0.0009 | 0.0244 | 1980 | −0.1400 |
| 1981 | −0.0209 | −0.0524 | 0.0274 | −0.0618 | 0.0518 | −0.0288 | −0.0462 | −0.0496 | −0.0259 | 0.0712 | 0.1297 | −0.0813 | 1981 | −0.1033 |
| 1982 | −0.0062 | 0.0079 | 0.0107 | 0.0262 | −0.0067 | −0.0343 | 0.0387 | 0.0669 | 0.0519 | 0.0543 | −0.0097 | 0.0219 | 1982 | 0.2395 |
| 1983 | −0.0396 | 0.0410 | −0.0183 | 0.0265 | −0.0477 | −0.0051 | −0.0574 | −0.0083 | 0.0408 | −0.0227 | 0.0089 | −0.0152 | 1983 | −0.0982 |
| 1984 | 0.0141 | −0.0270 | −0.0254 | −0.0210 | −0.0619 | 0.0044 | 0.0577 | 0.0160 | 0.0248 | 0.0453 | 0.0027 | −0.0007 | 1984 | 0.0232 |
| 1985 | 0.0268 | −0.0575 | 0.0212 | 0.0140 | 0.0798 | 0.0061 | −0.0274 | 0.0173 | −0.0109 | 0.0248 | 0.0320 | 0.0455 | 1985 | 0.1784 |
| 1986 | −0.0105 | 0.1073 | 0.0699 | −0.0142 | −0.0567 | 0.0543 | −0.0173 | 0.0437 | −0.0565 | 0.0220 | 0.0208 | −0.0087 | 1986 | 0.1499 |
| 1987 | 0.0096 | 0.0143 | −0.0289 | −0.0538 | −0.0171 | 0.0023 | −0.0251 | −0.0239 | −0.0443 | 0.0544 | −0.0038 | 0.0088 | 1987 | −0.1069 |
| 1988 | 0.0595 | −0.0019 | −0.0378 | −0.0230 | −0.0180 | 0.0292 | −0.0241 | −0.0025 | 0.0269 | 0.0232 | −0.0266 | 0.0035 | 1988 | 0.0036 |
| 1989 | 0.0124 | −0.0248 | 0.0044 | 0.0088 | 0.0321 | 0.0480 | 0.0170 | −0.0325 | −0.0046 | 0.0307 | 0.0014 | −0.0070 | 1989 | 0.0862 |
| 1990 | −0.0416 | −0.0090 | −0.0115 | −0.0277 | 0.0340 | 0.0162 | 0.0033 | −0.0490 | 0.0048 | 0.0135 | 0.0331 | 0.0114 | 1990 | −0.0261 |
| 1991 | 0.0059 | −0.0033 | −0.0026 | 0.0065 | −0.0068 | −0.0126 | 0.0082 | 0.0272 | 0.0236 | −0.0011 | 0.0022 | 0.0513 | 1991 | 0.1010 |
| 1992 | −0.0385 | −0.0008 | −0.0161 | −0.0049 | 0.0181 | 0.0133 | 0.0334 | 0.0007 | 0.0127 | −0.0255 | −0.0051 | 0.0183 | 1992 | 0.0034 |
| 1993 | 0.0222 | 0.0299 | −0.0042 | 0.0015 | −0.0006 | 0.0387 | 0.0138 | 0.0378 | −0.0045 | 0.0048 | −0.0312 | −0.0035 | 1993 | 0.1071 |
| 1994 | 0.0202 | −0.0498 | −0.0453 | −0.0208 | −0.0146 | −0.0161 | 0.0303 | −0.0152 | −0.0392 | −0.0091 | 0.0002 | 0.0095 | 1994 | −0.1429 |
| 1995 | 0.0203 | 0.0227 | 0.0028 | 0.0112 | 0.0725 | 0.0084 | −0.0223 | 0.0179 | 0.0122 | 0.0237 | 0.0198 | 0.0223 | 1995 | 0.2304 |
| 1996 | −0.0065 | −0.0530 | −0.0262 | −0.0224 | −0.0112 | 0.0149 | −0.0045 | −0.0196 | 0.0230 | 0.0345 | 0.0299 | −0.0312 | 1996 | −0.0737 |
| 1997 | −0.0135 | −0.0046 | −0.0311 | 0.0196 | 0.0037 | 0.0138 | 0.0567 | −0.0367 | 0.0258 | 0.0287 | 0.0101 | 0.0130 | 1997 | 0.0851 |
| 1998 | 0.0152 | −0.0116 | −0.0028 | −0.0023 | 0.0135 | 0.0176 | −0.0088 | 0.0416 | 0.0350 | −0.0260 | 0.0052 | −0.0077 | 1998 | 0.0689 |
| 1999 | 0.0079 | −0.0560 | −0.0061 | −0.0028 | −0.0230 | −0.0133 | −0.0130 | −0.0105 | 0.0032 | −0.0062 | −0.0117 | −0.0210 | 1999 | −0.1435 |
| 2000 | 0.0171 | 0.0213 | 0.0312 | −0.0123 | −0.0111 | 0.0192 | 0.0120 | 0.0190 | −0.0203 | 0.0135 | 0.0270 | 0.0198 | 2000 | 0.1436 |

* Compound annual return

Table A-9

**Long-Term Government Bonds: Yields**

from January 1926 to December 1970

| Year | Jan | Feb | Mar | Apr | May | Jun | Jul | Aug | Sep | Oct | Nov | Dec | Year | Jan-Dec |
|------|------|------|------|------|------|------|------|------|------|------|------|------|------|---------|
| 1926 | 0.0374 | 0.0372 | 0.0371 | 0.0368 | 0.0369 | 0.0368 | 0.0370 | 0.0373 | 0.0372 | 0.0367 | 0.0358 | 0.0354 | 1926 | 0.0354 |
| 1927 | 0.0351 | 0.0347 | 0.0331 | 0.0333 | 0.0327 | 0.0334 | 0.0333 | 0.0329 | 0.0330 | 0.0325 | 0.0320 | 0.0316 | 1927 | 0.0316 |
| 1928 | 0.0321 | 0.0318 | 0.0317 | 0.0319 | 0.0327 | 0.0326 | 0.0344 | 0.0341 | 0.0346 | 0.0336 | 0.0338 | 0.0340 | 1928 | 0.0340 |
| 1929 | 0.0349 | 0.0363 | 0.0377 | 0.0358 | 0.0373 | 0.0367 | 0.0369 | 0.0375 | 0.0375 | 0.0347 | 0.0331 | 0.0340 | 1929 | 0.0340 |
| 1930 | 0.0347 | 0.0339 | 0.0335 | 0.0338 | 0.0329 | 0.0328 | 0.0327 | 0.0328 | 0.0324 | 0.0324 | 0.0322 | 0.0330 | 1930 | 0.0330 |
| 1931 | 0.0343 | 0.0338 | 0.0332 | 0.0327 | 0.0317 | 0.0319 | 0.0325 | 0.0326 | 0.0353 | 0.0385 | 0.0385 | 0.0407 | 1931 | 0.0407 |
| 1932 | 0.0390 | 0.0367 | 0.0370 | 0.0336 | 0.0349 | 0.0347 | 0.0320 | 0.0321 | 0.0319 | 0.0322 | 0.0322 | 0.0315 | 1932 | 0.0315 |
| 1933 | 0.0308 | 0.0325 | 0.0321 | 0.0325 | 0.0308 | 0.0306 | 0.0309 | 0.0308 | 0.0308 | 0.0315 | 0.0327 | 0.0336 | 1933 | 0.0336 |
| 1934 | 0.0321 | 0.0317 | 0.0307 | 0.0300 | 0.0292 | 0.0289 | 0.0288 | 0.0299 | 0.0310 | 0.0300 | 0.0299 | 0.0293 | 1934 | 0.0293 |
| 1935 | 0.0281 | 0.0275 | 0.0274 | 0.0269 | 0.0276 | 0.0270 | 0.0268 | 0.0281 | 0.0282 | 0.0279 | 0.0280 | 0.0276 | 1935 | 0.0276 |
| 1936 | 0.0285 | 0.0281 | 0.0275 | 0.0274 | 0.0273 | 0.0273 | 0.0271 | 0.0264 | 0.0268 | 0.0269 | 0.0257 | 0.0255 | 1936 | 0.0255 |
| 1937 | 0.0258 | 0.0253 | 0.0285 | 0.0284 | 0.0282 | 0.0285 | 0.0277 | 0.0286 | 0.0284 | 0.0283 | 0.0278 | 0.0273 | 1937 | 0.0273 |
| 1938 | 0.0271 | 0.0268 | 0.0273 | 0.0259 | 0.0257 | 0.0259 | 0.0257 | 0.0259 | 0.0259 | 0.0254 | 0.0257 | 0.0252 | 1938 | 0.0252 |
| 1939 | 0.0249 | 0.0245 | 0.0237 | 0.0229 | 0.0217 | 0.0221 | 0.0213 | 0.0231 | 0.0278 | 0.0247 | 0.0236 | 0.0226 | 1939 | 0.0226 |
| 1940 | 0.0229 | 0.0228 | 0.0215 | 0.0220 | 0.0246 | 0.0227 | 0.0224 | 0.0223 | 0.0215 | 0.0214 | 0.0199 | 0.0194 | 1940 | 0.0194 |
| 1941 | 0.0213 | 0.0213 | 0.0206 | 0.0196 | 0.0195 | 0.0191 | 0.0191 | 0.0190 | 0.0193 | 0.0182 | 0.0186 | 0.0204 | 1941 | 0.0204 |
| 1942 | 0.0247 | 0.0247 | 0.0244 | 0.0246 | 0.0243 | 0.0244 | 0.0244 | 0.0244 | 0.0244 | 0.0244 | 0.0247 | 0.0246 | 1942 | 0.0246 |
| 1943 | 0.0245 | 0.0246 | 0.0247 | 0.0246 | 0.0244 | 0.0244 | 0.0245 | 0.0245 | 0.0246 | 0.0247 | 0.0248 | 0.0248 | 1943 | 0.0248 |
| 1944 | 0.0248 | 0.0247 | 0.0247 | 0.0248 | 0.0247 | 0.0248 | 0.0247 | 0.0247 | 0.0247 | 0.0247 | 0.0247 | 0.0246 | 1944 | 0.0246 |
| 1945 | 0.0240 | 0.0236 | 0.0236 | 0.0228 | 0.0226 | 0.0217 | 0.0224 | 0.0223 | 0.0221 | 0.0216 | 0.0210 | 0.0199 | 1945 | 0.0199 |
| 1946 | 0.0199 | 0.0198 | 0.0198 | 0.0207 | 0.0209 | 0.0206 | 0.0209 | 0.0217 | 0.0219 | 0.0216 | 0.0220 | 0.0212 | 1946 | 0.0212 |
| 1947 | 0.0214 | 0.0214 | 0.0213 | 0.0217 | 0.0216 | 0.0216 | 0.0214 | 0.0210 | 0.0213 | 0.0217 | 0.0229 | 0.0243 | 1947 | 0.0243 |
| 1948 | 0.0243 | 0.0241 | 0.0241 | 0.0239 | 0.0231 | 0.0238 | 0.0241 | 0.0242 | 0.0242 | 0.0243 | 0.0239 | 0.0237 | 1948 | 0.0237 |
| 1949 | 0.0233 | 0.0231 | 0.0227 | 0.0227 | 0.0227 | 0.0217 | 0.0216 | 0.0210 | 0.0212 | 0.0212 | 0.0212 | 0.0209 | 1949 | 0.0209 |
| 1950 | 0.0215 | 0.0214 | 0.0215 | 0.0214 | 0.0213 | 0.0216 | 0.0214 | 0.0214 | 0.0220 | 0.0225 | 0.0224 | 0.0224 | 1950 | 0.0224 |
| 1951 | 0.0221 | 0.0228 | 0.0241 | 0.0248 | 0.0254 | 0.0259 | 0.0252 | 0.0246 | 0.0253 | 0.0254 | 0.0264 | 0.0269 | 1951 | 0.0269 |
| 1952 | 0.0268 | 0.0269 | 0.0263 | 0.0254 | 0.0257 | 0.0259 | 0.0261 | 0.0267 | 0.0277 | 0.0269 | 0.0272 | 0.0279 | 1952 | 0.0279 |
| 1953 | 0.0279 | 0.0287 | 0.0294 | 0.0303 | 0.0314 | 0.0301 | 0.0301 | 0.0303 | 0.0284 | 0.0281 | 0.0286 | 0.0274 | 1953 | 0.0274 |
| 1954 | 0.0291 | 0.0279 | 0.0278 | 0.0273 | 0.0279 | 0.0272 | 0.0266 | 0.0269 | 0.0271 | 0.0271 | 0.0274 | 0.0272 | 1954 | 0.0272 |
| 1955 | 0.0286 | 0.0292 | 0.0288 | 0.0290 | 0.0287 | 0.0293 | 0.0300 | 0.0301 | 0.0298 | 0.0292 | 0.0295 | 0.0295 | 1955 | 0.0295 |
| 1956 | 0.0292 | 0.0293 | 0.0303 | 0.0311 | 0.0299 | 0.0299 | 0.0313 | 0.0325 | 0.0324 | 0.0329 | 0.0333 | 0.0345 | 1956 | 0.0345 |
| 1957 | 0.0328 | 0.0328 | 0.0331 | 0.0345 | 0.0348 | 0.0361 | 0.0365 | 0.0367 | 0.0364 | 0.0369 | 0.0340 | 0.0323 | 1957 | 0.0323 |
| 1958 | 0.0330 | 0.0325 | 0.0321 | 0.0311 | 0.0313 | 0.0324 | 0.0343 | 0.0371 | 0.0380 | 0.0374 | 0.0368 | 0.0382 | 1958 | 0.0382 |
| 1959 | 0.0408 | 0.0402 | 0.0403 | 0.0414 | 0.0417 | 0.0419 | 0.0417 | 0.0423 | 0.0429 | 0.0421 | 0.0432 | 0.0447 | 1959 | 0.0447 |
| 1960 | 0.0441 | 0.0429 | 0.0411 | 0.0426 | 0.0417 | 0.0407 | 0.0382 | 0.0390 | 0.0387 | 0.0391 | 0.0399 | 0.0380 | 1960 | 0.0380 |
| 1961 | 0.0404 | 0.0392 | 0.0397 | 0.0391 | 0.0397 | 0.0404 | 0.0404 | 0.0410 | 0.0403 | 0.0400 | 0.0404 | 0.0415 | 1961 | 0.0415 |
| 1962 | 0.0419 | 0.0414 | 0.0398 | 0.0394 | 0.0393 | 0.0401 | 0.0412 | 0.0401 | 0.0398 | 0.0395 | 0.0396 | 0.0395 | 1962 | 0.0395 |
| 1963 | 0.0398 | 0.0400 | 0.0401 | 0.0405 | 0.0406 | 0.0407 | 0.0407 | 0.0408 | 0.0410 | 0.0415 | 0.0414 | 0.0417 | 1963 | 0.0417 |
| 1964 | 0.0421 | 0.0424 | 0.0424 | 0.0423 | 0.0422 | 0.0419 | 0.0421 | 0.0423 | 0.0421 | 0.0421 | 0.0422 | 0.0423 | 1964 | 0.0423 |
| 1965 | 0.0422 | 0.0424 | 0.0422 | 0.0422 | 0.0423 | 0.0423 | 0.0424 | 0.0428 | 0.0433 | 0.0433 | 0.0441 | 0.0450 | 1965 | 0.0450 |
| 1966 | 0.0457 | 0.0477 | 0.0460 | 0.0467 | 0.0473 | 0.0477 | 0.0482 | 0.0499 | 0.0480 | 0.0467 | 0.0480 | 0.0455 | 1966 | 0.0455 |
| 1967 | 0.0448 | 0.0465 | 0.0455 | 0.0477 | 0.0482 | 0.0507 | 0.0505 | 0.0514 | 0.0517 | 0.0549 | 0.0567 | 0.0556 | 1967 | 0.0556 |
| 1968 | 0.0536 | 0.0542 | 0.0560 | 0.0547 | 0.0547 | 0.0534 | 0.0517 | 0.0520 | 0.0531 | 0.0543 | 0.0566 | 0.0598 | 1968 | 0.0598 |
| 1969 | 0.0617 | 0.0618 | 0.0620 | 0.0593 | 0.0635 | 0.0623 | 0.0621 | 0.0630 | 0.0677 | 0.0653 | 0.0676 | 0.0687 | 1969 | 0.0687 |
| 1970 | 0.0693 | 0.0651 | 0.0661 | 0.0699 | 0.0743 | 0.0709 | 0.0687 | 0.0694 | 0.0680 | 0.0693 | 0.0637 | 0.0648 | 1970 | 0.0648 |

Table A-9 (continued)

## Long-Term Government Bonds: Yields

from January 1971 to December 2000

| Year | Jan | Feb | Mar | Apr | May | Jun | Jul | Aug | Sep | Oct | Nov | Dec | Year | Jan-Dec |
|------|-----|-----|-----|-----|-----|-----|-----|-----|-----|-----|-----|-----|------|---------|
| 1971 | 0.0612 | 0.0629 | 0.0593 | 0.0619 | 0.0624 | 0.0641 | 0.0643 | 0.0610 | 0.0598 | 0.0588 | 0.0596 | 0.0597 | 1971 | 0.0597 |
| 1972 | 0.0606 | 0.0602 | 0.0613 | 0.0615 | 0.0597 | 0.0607 | 0.0593 | 0.0595 | 0.0606 | 0.0591 | 0.0577 | 0.0599 | 1972 | 0.0599 |
| 1973 | 0.0685 | 0.0688 | 0.0686 | 0.0687 | 0.0703 | 0.0710 | 0.0760 | 0.0728 | 0.0703 | 0.0689 | 0.0712 | 0.0726 | 1973 | 0.0726 |
| 1974 | 0.0740 | 0.0748 | 0.0783 | 0.0816 | 0.0810 | 0.0812 | 0.0823 | 0.0855 | 0.0837 | 0.0795 | 0.0771 | 0.0760 | 1974 | 0.0760 |
| 1975 | 0.0796 | 0.0788 | 0.0824 | 0.0852 | 0.0836 | 0.0813 | 0.0829 | 0.0844 | 0.0862 | 0.0819 | 0.0838 | 0.0805 | 1975 | 0.0805 |
| 1976 | 0.0802 | 0.0802 | 0.0792 | 0.0797 | 0.0821 | 0.0807 | 0.0805 | 0.0790 | 0.0781 | 0.0779 | 0.0749 | 0.0721 | 1976 | 0.0721 |
| 1977 | 0.0764 | 0.0775 | 0.0772 | 0.0771 | 0.0765 | 0.0754 | 0.0768 | 0.0754 | 0.0764 | 0.0781 | 0.0777 | 0.0803 | 1977 | 0.0803 |
| 1978 | 0.0816 | 0.0822 | 0.0831 | 0.0838 | 0.0852 | 0.0865 | 0.0858 | 0.0843 | 0.0860 | 0.0889 | 0.0877 | 0.0898 | 1978 | 0.0898 |
| 1979 | 0.0886 | 0.0908 | 0.0902 | 0.0922 | 0.0903 | 0.0877 | 0.0895 | 0.0907 | 0.0927 | 0.1034 | 0.1009 | 0.1012 | 1979 | 0.1012 |
| 1980 | 0.1114 | 0.1186 | 0.1239 | 0.1076 | 0.1037 | 0.1006 | 0.1074 | 0.1140 | 0.1185 | 0.1231 | 0.1230 | 0.1199 | 1980 | 0.1199 |
| 1981 | 0.1211 | 0.1283 | 0.1248 | 0.1332 | 0.1265 | 0.1304 | 0.1370 | 0.1445 | 0.1482 | 0.1384 | 0.1220 | 0.1334 | 1981 | 0.1334 |
| 1982 | 0.1415 | 0.1402 | 0.1387 | 0.1348 | 0.1358 | 0.1412 | 0.1352 | 0.1254 | 0.1183 | 0.1112 | 0.1125 | 0.1095 | 1982 | 0.1095 |
| 1983 | 0.1113 | 0.1060 | 0.1083 | 0.1051 | 0.1112 | 0.1119 | 0.1198 | 0.1210 | 0.1157 | 0.1188 | 0.1176 | 0.1197 | 1983 | 0.1197 |
| 1984 | 0.1180 | 0.1217 | 0.1253 | 0.1284 | 0.1381 | 0.1374 | 0.1293 | 0.1270 | 0.1235 | 0.1173 | 0.1169 | 0.1170 | 1984 | 0.1170 |
| 1985 | 0.1127 | 0.1209 | 0.1181 | 0.1162 | 0.1062 | 0.1055 | 0.1091 | 0.1068 | 0.1082 | 0.1051 | 0.1011 | 0.0956 | 1985 | 0.0956 |
| 1986 | 0.0958 | 0.0841 | 0.0766 | 0.0782 | 0.0848 | 0.0790 | 0.0809 | 0.0763 | 0.0827 | 0.0803 | 0.0779 | 0.0789 | 1986 | 0.0789 |
| 1987 | 0.0778 | 0.0763 | 0.0795 | 0.0859 | 0.0880 | 0.0877 | 0.0907 | 0.0936 | 0.0992 | 0.0926 | 0.0931 | 0.0920 | 1987 | 0.0920 |
| 1988 | 0.0852 | 0.0854 | 0.0901 | 0.0929 | 0.0952 | 0.0917 | 0.0947 | 0.0950 | 0.0917 | 0.0889 | 0.0923 | 0.0918 | 1988 | 0.0918 |
| 1989 | 0.0903 | 0.0935 | 0.0929 | 0.0918 | 0.0878 | 0.0821 | 0.0801 | 0.0841 | 0.0847 | 0.0810 | 0.0808 | 0.0816 | 1989 | 0.0816 |
| 1990 | 0.0865 | 0.0876 | 0.0889 | 0.0924 | 0.0883 | 0.0864 | 0.0860 | 0.0920 | 0.0914 | 0.0898 | 0.0858 | 0.0844 | 1990 | 0.0844 |
| 1991 | 0.0837 | 0.0841 | 0.0844 | 0.0837 | 0.0845 | 0.0860 | 0.0850 | 0.0818 | 0.0790 | 0.0791 | 0.0789 | 0.0730 | 1991 | 0.0730 |
| 1992 | 0.0776 | 0.0777 | 0.0797 | 0.0803 | 0.0781 | 0.0765 | 0.0726 | 0.0725 | 0.0710 | 0.0741 | 0.0748 | 0.0726 | 1992 | 0.0726 |
| 1993 | 0.0725 | 0.0698 | 0.0702 | 0.0701 | 0.0701 | 0.0668 | 0.0656 | 0.0623 | 0.0627 | 0.0623 | 0.0651 | 0.0654 | 1993 | 0.0654 |
| 1994 | 0.0637 | 0.0682 | 0.0725 | 0.0745 | 0.0759 | 0.0774 | 0.0746 | 0.0761 | 0.0800 | 0.0809 | 0.0808 | 0.0799 | 1994 | 0.0799 |
| 1995 | 0.0780 | 0.0758 | 0.0755 | 0.0745 | 0.0677 | 0.0670 | 0.0691 | 0.0674 | 0.0663 | 0.0641 | 0.0623 | 0.0603 | 1995 | 0.0603 |
| 1996 | 0.0609 | 0.0659 | 0.0684 | 0.0706 | 0.0717 | 0.0703 | 0.0707 | 0.0726 | 0.0704 | 0.0671 | 0.0643 | 0.0673 | 1996 | 0.0673 |
| 1997 | 0.0689 | 0.0694 | 0.0723 | 0.0705 | 0.0701 | 0.0688 | 0.0637 | 0.0672 | 0.0649 | 0.0623 | 0.0614 | 0.0602 | 1997 | 0.0602 |
| 1998 | 0.0589 | 0.0599 | 0.0602 | 0.0604 | 0.0592 | 0.0576 | 0.0584 | 0.0547 | 0.0517 | 0.0540 | 0.0535 | 0.0542 | 1998 | 0.0542 |
| 1999 | 0.0536 | 0.0587 | 0.0592 | 0.0594 | 0.0615 | 0.0627 | 0.0639 | 0.0649 | 0.0646 | 0.0651 | 0.0662 | 0.0682 | 1999 | 0.0682 |
| 2000 | 0.0666 | 0.0646 | 0.0618 | 0.0630 | 0.0640 | 0.0622 | 0.0611 | 0.0594 | 0.0612 | 0.0600 | 0.0576 | 0.0558 | 2000 | 0.0558 |

## Table A-10

**Intermediate-Term Government Bonds: Total Returns**

from January 1926 to December 1970

| Year | Jan | Feb | Mar | Apr | May | Jun | Jul | Aug | Sep | Oct | Nov | Dec | Year | Jan-Dec* |
|---|---|---|---|---|---|---|---|---|---|---|---|---|---|---|
| 1926 | 0.0068 | 0.0032 | 0.0041 | 0.0090 | 0.0008 | 0.0027 | 0.0013 | 0.0009 | 0.0050 | 0.0054 | 0.0045 | 0.0089 | 1926 | 0.0538 |
| 1927 | 0.0057 | 0.0038 | 0.0038 | 0.0016 | 0.0020 | 0.0029 | 0.0043 | 0.0056 | 0.0060 | −0.0034 | 0.0083 | 0.0037 | 1927 | 0.0452 |
| 1928 | 0.0046 | −0.0004 | 0.0010 | −0.0003 | −0.0006 | 0.0017 | −0.0089 | 0.0050 | 0.0028 | 0.0032 | 0.0019 | −0.0007 | 1928 | 0.0092 |
| 1929 | −0.0029 | −0.0018 | 0.0005 | 0.0089 | −0.0061 | 0.0107 | 0.0066 | 0.0052 | −0.0014 | 0.0168 | 0.0180 | 0.0044 | 1929 | 0.0601 |
| 1930 | −0.0041 | 0.0094 | 0.0161 | −0.0071 | 0.0061 | 0.0142 | 0.0054 | 0.0022 | 0.0063 | 0.0076 | 0.0070 | 0.0024 | 1930 | 0.0672 |
| 1931 | −0.0071 | 0.0099 | 0.0052 | 0.0083 | 0.0119 | −0.0214 | 0.0016 | 0.0017 | −0.0113 | −0.0105 | 0.0049 | −0.0159 | 1931 | −0.0232 |
| 1932 | −0.0032 | 0.0128 | 0.0078 | 0.0194 | −0.0090 | 0.0108 | 0.0120 | 0.0124 | 0.0027 | 0.0045 | 0.0031 | 0.0118 | 1932 | 0.0881 |
| 1933 | −0.0016 | −0.0001 | 0.0099 | 0.0057 | 0.0199 | 0.0008 | −0.0006 | 0.0073 | 0.0026 | −0.0025 | 0.0027 | −0.0253 | 1933 | 0.0183 |
| 1934 | 0.0130 | 0.0052 | 0.0189 | 0.0182 | 0.0120 | 0.0091 | −0.0024 | −0.0092 | −0.0138 | 0.0190 | 0.0046 | 0.0125 | 1934 | 0.0900 |
| 1935 | 0.0114 | 0.0105 | 0.0125 | 0.0107 | −0.0035 | 0.0113 | 0.0037 | −0.0071 | −0.0057 | 0.0109 | 0.0014 | 0.0120 | 1935 | 0.0701 |
| 1936 | −0.0003 | 0.0069 | 0.0031 | 0.0024 | 0.0038 | 0.0012 | 0.0022 | 0.0050 | 0.0010 | 0.0025 | 0.0081 | −0.0057 | 1936 | 0.0306 |
| 1937 | −0.0031 | 0.0007 | −0.0164 | 0.0047 | 0.0080 | −0.0012 | 0.0059 | −0.0043 | 0.0081 | 0.0032 | 0.0042 | 0.0062 | 1937 | 0.0156 |
| 1938 | 0.0085 | 0.0052 | −0.0012 | 0.0230 | 0.0023 | 0.0075 | 0.0010 | 0.0015 | −0.0013 | 0.0093 | −0.0001 | 0.0052 | 1938 | 0.0623 |
| 1939 | 0.0029 | 0.0082 | 0.0081 | 0.0038 | 0.0095 | 0.0002 | 0.0040 | −0.0147 | −0.0262 | 0.0315 | 0.0074 | 0.0108 | 1939 | 0.0452 |
| 1940 | −0.0014 | 0.0035 | 0.0088 | 0.0002 | −0.0214 | 0.0187 | 0.0003 | 0.0043 | 0.0047 | 0.0036 | 0.0056 | 0.0028 | 1940 | 0.0296 |
| 1941 | 0.0001 | −0.0047 | 0.0069 | 0.0033 | 0.0012 | 0.0056 | 0.0000 | 0.0011 | 0.0000 | 0.0023 | −0.0092 | −0.0016 | 1941 | 0.0050 |
| 1942 | 0.0074 | 0.0015 | 0.0023 | 0.0022 | 0.0016 | 0.0013 | 0.0000 | 0.0017 | −0.0023 | 0.0017 | 0.0017 | 0.0000 | 1942 | 0.0194 |
| 1943 | 0.0039 | 0.0013 | 0.0021 | 0.0024 | 0.0057 | 0.0033 | 0.0021 | 0.0002 | 0.0014 | 0.0017 | 0.0015 | 0.0021 | 1943 | 0.0281 |
| 1944 | 0.0011 | 0.0016 | 0.0019 | 0.0028 | 0.0005 | 0.0007 | 0.0029 | 0.0024 | 0.0011 | 0.0011 | 0.0009 | 0.0010 | 1944 | 0.0180 |
| 1945 | 0.0052 | 0.0038 | 0.0004 | 0.0014 | 0.0012 | 0.0019 | 0.0000 | 0.0016 | 0.0017 | 0.0016 | 0.0010 | 0.0021 | 1945 | 0.0222 |
| 1946 | 0.0039 | 0.0048 | −0.0038 | −0.0020 | 0.0006 | 0.0033 | −0.0010 | 0.0004 | −0.0011 | 0.0026 | −0.0008 | 0.0032 | 1946 | 0.0100 |
| 1947 | 0.0023 | 0.0006 | 0.0024 | −0.0013 | 0.0008 | 0.0008 | 0.0006 | 0.0026 | 0.0000 | −0.0023 | 0.0006 | 0.0021 | 1947 | 0.0091 |
| 1948 | 0.0015 | 0.0018 | 0.0018 | 0.0019 | 0.0053 | −0.0008 | −0.0002 | −0.0004 | 0.0010 | 0.0013 | 0.0021 | 0.0032 | 1948 | 0.0185 |
| 1949 | 0.0028 | 0.0011 | 0.0025 | 0.0015 | 0.0023 | 0.0050 | 0.0020 | 0.0031 | 0.0008 | 0.0006 | 0.0002 | 0.0012 | 1949 | 0.0232 |
| 1950 | −0.0005 | 0.0008 | 0.0000 | 0.0008 | 0.0020 | 0.0003 | 0.0020 | −0.0007 | −0.0004 | 0.0001 | 0.0018 | 0.0008 | 1950 | 0.0070 |
| 1951 | 0.0022 | 0.0007 | −0.0127 | 0.0057 | −0.0040 | 0.0050 | 0.0058 | 0.0036 | −0.0057 | 0.0016 | 0.0032 | −0.0016 | 1951 | 0.0036 |
| 1952 | 0.0038 | −0.0020 | 0.0067 | 0.0054 | 0.0019 | −0.0035 | −0.0034 | −0.0024 | 0.0019 | 0.0066 | −0.0006 | 0.0019 | 1952 | 0.0163 |
| 1953 | −0.0002 | 0.0003 | −0.0017 | −0.0096 | −0.0117 | 0.0155 | 0.0056 | −0.0008 | 0.0194 | 0.0038 | 0.0014 | 0.0103 | 1953 | 0.0323 |
| 1954 | 0.0065 | 0.0100 | 0.0027 | 0.0043 | −0.0073 | 0.0125 | −0.0005 | 0.0011 | −0.0020 | −0.0009 | −0.0001 | 0.0005 | 1954 | 0.0268 |
| 1955 | −0.0032 | −0.0052 | 0.0024 | 0.0004 | 0.0001 | −0.0036 | −0.0071 | 0.0007 | 0.0082 | 0.0072 | −0.0053 | −0.0011 | 1955 | −0.0065 |
| 1956 | 0.0105 | 0.0003 | −0.0100 | −0.0001 | 0.0112 | 0.0003 | −0.0095 | −0.0103 | 0.0092 | −0.0019 | −0.0047 | 0.0011 | 1956 | −0.0042 |
| 1957 | 0.0237 | −0.0012 | 0.0018 | −0.0101 | −0.0017 | −0.0106 | −0.0015 | 0.0109 | 0.0002 | 0.0043 | 0.0396 | 0.0215 | 1957 | 0.0784 |
| 1958 | 0.0034 | 0.0139 | 0.0053 | 0.0052 | 0.0060 | −0.0068 | −0.0091 | −0.0356 | −0.0017 | 0.0002 | 0.0132 | −0.0061 | 1958 | −0.0129 |
| 1959 | −0.0013 | 0.0107 | −0.0037 | −0.0052 | −0.0001 | −0.0077 | 0.0034 | −0.0078 | 0.0020 | 0.0174 | −0.0092 | −0.0020 | 1959 | −0.0039 |
| 1960 | 0.0154 | 0.0072 | 0.0292 | −0.0064 | 0.0031 | 0.0217 | 0.0267 | −0.0004 | 0.0029 | 0.0016 | −0.0094 | 0.0210 | 1960 | 0.1176 |
| 1961 | −0.0059 | 0.0090 | 0.0037 | 0.0054 | −0.0028 | −0.0025 | 0.0007 | 0.0019 | 0.0079 | 0.0014 | −0.0019 | 0.0018 | 1961 | 0.0185 |
| 1962 | −0.0045 | 0.0155 | 0.0089 | 0.0025 | 0.0049 | −0.0028 | −0.0012 | 0.0125 | 0.0021 | 0.0051 | 0.0060 | 0.0056 | 1962 | 0.0556 |
| 1963 | −0.0029 | 0.0017 | 0.0027 | 0.0030 | 0.0014 | 0.0014 | 0.0003 | 0.0019 | 0.0014 | 0.0011 | 0.0040 | 0.0003 | 1963 | 0.0164 |
| 1964 | 0.0033 | 0.0012 | 0.0016 | 0.0033 | 0.0081 | 0.0036 | 0.0027 | 0.0027 | 0.0045 | 0.0032 | −0.0004 | 0.0058 | 1964 | 0.0404 |
| 1965 | 0.0042 | 0.0018 | 0.0043 | 0.0026 | 0.0035 | 0.0049 | 0.0017 | 0.0019 | −0.0005 | 0.0000 | 0.0007 | −0.0149 | 1965 | 0.0102 |
| 1966 | 0.0003 | −0.0083 | 0.0187 | −0.0019 | 0.0011 | −0.0024 | −0.0025 | −0.0125 | 0.0216 | 0.0075 | 0.0027 | 0.0223 | 1966 | 0.0469 |
| 1967 | 0.0118 | −0.0013 | 0.0183 | −0.0089 | 0.0044 | −0.0227 | 0.0133 | −0.0036 | 0.0007 | −0.0049 | 0.0028 | 0.0007 | 1967 | 0.0101 |
| 1968 | 0.0145 | 0.0040 | −0.0026 | −0.0016 | 0.0064 | 0.0167 | 0.0176 | 0.0021 | 0.0055 | 0.0009 | −0.0013 | −0.0173 | 1968 | 0.0454 |
| 1969 | 0.0086 | −0.0013 | 0.0097 | 0.0079 | −0.0082 | −0.0084 | 0.0082 | −0.0018 | −0.0300 | 0.0333 | −0.0047 | −0.0193 | 1969 | −0.0074 |
| 1970 | 0.0030 | 0.0439 | 0.0087 | −0.0207 | 0.0110 | 0.0061 | 0.0152 | 0.0116 | 0.0196 | 0.0095 | 0.0451 | 0.0054 | 1970 | 0.1686 |

* Compound annual return

Table A-10 (continued)

## Intermediate-Term Government Bonds: Total Returns

from January 1971 to December 2000

| Year | Jan | Feb | Mar | Apr | May | Jun | Jul | Aug | Sep | Oct | Nov | Dec | Year | Jan-Dec* |
|------|-----|-----|-----|-----|-----|-----|-----|-----|-----|-----|-----|-----|------|----------|
| 1971 | 0.0168 | 0.0224 | 0.0186 | -0.0327 | 0.0011 | -0.0187 | 0.0027 | 0.0350 | 0.0026 | 0.0220 | 0.0052 | 0.0110 | 1971 | 0.0872 |
| 1972 | 0.0106 | 0.0014 | 0.0015 | 0.0014 | 0.0016 | 0.0045 | 0.0015 | 0.0015 | 0.0014 | 0.0016 | 0.0045 | 0.0192 | 1972 | 0.0516 |
| 1973 | -0.0006 | -0.0075 | 0.0046 | 0.0064 | 0.0057 | -0.0006 | -0.0276 | 0.0254 | 0.0250 | 0.0050 | 0.0064 | 0.0040 | 1973 | 0.0461 |
| 1974 | 0.0009 | 0.0035 | -0.0212 | -0.0152 | 0.0130 | -0.0087 | 0.0007 | -0.0012 | 0.0319 | 0.0109 | 0.0236 | 0.0185 | 1974 | 0.0569 |
| 1975 | 0.0053 | 0.0148 | -0.0059 | -0.0186 | 0.0260 | 0.0027 | -0.0030 | -0.0009 | 0.0010 | 0.0366 | -0.0010 | 0.0198 | 1975 | 0.0783 |
| 1976 | 0.0057 | 0.0084 | 0.0075 | 0.0116 | -0.0145 | 0.0159 | 0.0119 | 0.0189 | 0.0076 | 0.0147 | 0.0321 | 0.0026 | 1976 | 0.1287 |
| 1977 | -0.0190 | 0.0048 | 0.0055 | 0.0051 | 0.0056 | 0.0102 | 0.0001 | 0.0008 | 0.0015 | -0.0060 | 0.0079 | -0.0023 | 1977 | 0.0141 |
| 1978 | 0.0013 | 0.0017 | 0.0037 | 0.0024 | -0.0002 | -0.0021 | 0.0098 | 0.0079 | 0.0057 | -0.0112 | 0.0092 | 0.0063 | 1978 | 0.0349 |
| 1979 | 0.0055 | -0.0059 | 0.0112 | 0.0033 | 0.0193 | 0.0205 | -0.0011 | -0.0091 | 0.0006 | -0.0468 | 0.0363 | 0.0087 | 1979 | 0.0409 |
| 1980 | -0.0135 | -0.0641 | 0.0143 | 0.1198 | 0.0490 | -0.0077 | -0.0106 | -0.0387 | -0.0038 | -0.0152 | 0.0029 | 0.0171 | 1980 | 0.0391 |
| 1981 | 0.0032 | -0.0235 | 0.0263 | -0.0216 | 0.0245 | 0.0060 | -0.0270 | -0.0178 | 0.0164 | 0.0611 | 0.0624 | -0.0142 | 1981 | 0.0945 |
| 1982 | 0.0050 | 0.0148 | 0.0042 | 0.0299 | 0.0146 | -0.0135 | 0.0464 | 0.0469 | 0.0325 | 0.0531 | 0.0080 | 0.0185 | 1982 | 0.2910 |
| 1983 | 0.0007 | 0.0252 | -0.0049 | 0.0259 | -0.0122 | 0.0016 | -0.0198 | 0.0081 | 0.0315 | 0.0019 | 0.0103 | 0.0047 | 1983 | 0.0741 |
| 1984 | 0.0177 | -0.0064 | -0.0035 | -0.0003 | -0.0250 | 0.0099 | 0.0393 | 0.0101 | 0.0202 | 0.0383 | 0.0192 | 0.0143 | 1984 | 0.1402 |
| 1985 | 0.0206 | -0.0179 | 0.0166 | 0.0264 | 0.0485 | 0.0108 | -0.0045 | 0.0148 | 0.0113 | 0.0162 | 0.0195 | 0.0257 | 1985 | 0.2033 |
| 1986 | 0.0082 | 0.0275 | 0.0338 | 0.0081 | -0.0215 | 0.0276 | 0.0157 | 0.0266 | -0.0110 | 0.0162 | 0.0113 | 0.0007 | 1986 | 0.1514 |
| 1987 | 0.0107 | 0.0059 | -0.0031 | -0.0244 | -0.0038 | 0.0122 | 0.0025 | -0.0038 | -0.0141 | 0.0299 | 0.0083 | 0.0093 | 1987 | 0.0290 |
| 1988 | 0.0316 | 0.0123 | -0.0086 | -0.0044 | -0.0049 | 0.0181 | -0.0047 | -0.0009 | 0.0196 | 0.0148 | -0.0115 | -0.0010 | 1988 | 0.0610 |
| 1989 | 0.0121 | -0.0051 | 0.0049 | 0.0220 | 0.0212 | 0.0324 | 0.0235 | -0.0246 | 0.0069 | 0.0237 | 0.0084 | 0.0012 | 1989 | 0.1329 |
| 1990 | -0.0104 | 0.0007 | 0.0002 | -0.0077 | 0.0261 | 0.0151 | 0.0174 | -0.0092 | 0.0094 | 0.0171 | 0.0193 | 0.0161 | 1990 | 0.0973 |
| 1991 | 0.0107 | 0.0048 | 0.0023 | 0.0117 | 0.0059 | -0.0023 | 0.0129 | 0.0247 | 0.0216 | 0.0134 | 0.0128 | 0.0265 | 1991 | 0.1546 |
| 1992 | -0.0195 | 0.0022 | -0.0079 | 0.0098 | 0.0222 | 0.0177 | 0.0242 | 0.0150 | 0.0194 | -0.0182 | -0.0084 | 0.0146 | 1992 | 0.0719 |
| 1993 | 0.0270 | 0.0243 | 0.0043 | 0.0088 | -0.0009 | 0.0201 | 0.0005 | 0.0223 | 0.0056 | 0.0018 | -0.0093 | 0.0032 | 1993 | 0.1124 |
| 1994 | 0.0138 | -0.0258 | -0.0257 | -0.0105 | -0.0002 | -0.0028 | 0.0169 | 0.0026 | -0.0158 | -0.0023 | -0.0070 | 0.0053 | 1994 | -0.0514 |
| 1995 | 0.0182 | 0.0234 | 0.0063 | 0.0143 | 0.0369 | 0.0079 | -0.0016 | 0.0086 | 0.0064 | 0.0121 | 0.0149 | 0.0095 | 1995 | 0.1680 |
| 1996 | 0.0006 | -0.0138 | -0.0118 | -0.0050 | -0.0032 | 0.0117 | 0.0025 | -0.0005 | 0.0155 | 0.0183 | 0.0149 | -0.0078 | 1996 | 0.0210 |
| 1997 | 0.0025 | 0.0002 | -0.0114 | 0.0148 | 0.0079 | 0.0102 | 0.0264 | -0.0098 | 0.0151 | 0.0150 | -0.0001 | 0.0106 | 1997 | 0.0838 |
| 1998 | 0.0180 | -0.0039 | 0.0026 | 0.0061 | 0.0070 | 0.0079 | 0.0027 | 0.0271 | 0.0330 | 0.0041 | -0.0098 | 0.0037 | 1998 | 0.1021 |
| 1999 | 0.0055 | -0.0262 | 0.0086 | 0.0021 | -0.0147 | 0.0032 | -0.0003 | 0.0013 | 0.0097 | -0.0008 | -0.0008 | -0.0048 | 1999 | -0.0177 |
| 2000 | -0.0053 | 0.0078 | 0.0203 | -0.0043 | 0.0052 | 0.0191 | 0.0072 | 0.0134 | 0.0096 | 0.0079 | 0.0174 | 0.0214 | 2000 | 0.1259 |

* Compound annual return

## Table A-11

**Intermediate-Term Government Bonds: Income Returns**

from January 1926 to December 1970

| Year | Jan | Feb | Mar | Apr | May | Jun | Jul | Aug | Sep | Oct | Nov | Dec | Year | Jan-Dec* |
|------|------|------|------|------|------|------|------|------|------|------|------|------|------|----------|
| 1926 | 0.0032 | 0.0032 | 0.0032 | 0.0031 | 0.0031 | 0.0031 | 0.0032 | 0.0032 | 0.0032 | 0.0031 | 0.0031 | 0.0030 | 1926 | 0.0378 |
| 1927 | 0.0029 | 0.0029 | 0.0029 | 0.0029 | 0.0029 | 0.0029 | 0.0029 | 0.0029 | 0.0028 | 0.0029 | 0.0028 | 0.0028 | 1927 | 0.0349 |
| 1928 | 0.0028 | 0.0028 | 0.0029 | 0.0029 | 0.0030 | 0.0030 | 0.0032 | 0.0032 | 0.0032 | 0.0032 | 0.0032 | 0.0033 | 1928 | 0.0364 |
| 1929 | 0.0034 | 0.0035 | 0.0036 | 0.0035 | 0.0037 | 0.0035 | 0.0035 | 0.0034 | 0.0035 | 0.0033 | 0.0030 | 0.0030 | 1929 | 0.0407 |
| 1930 | 0.0031 | 0.0030 | 0.0028 | 0.0030 | 0.0029 | 0.0027 | 0.0026 | 0.0026 | 0.0026 | 0.0025 | 0.0024 | 0.0024 | 1930 | 0.0330 |
| 1931 | 0.0026 | 0.0025 | 0.0024 | 0.0023 | 0.0021 | 0.0026 | 0.0026 | 0.0026 | 0.0028 | 0.0031 | 0.0031 | 0.0034 | 1931 | 0.0316 |
| 1932 | 0.0035 | 0.0034 | 0.0033 | 0.0030 | 0.0032 | 0.0031 | 0.0029 | 0.0027 | 0.0027 | 0.0027 | 0.0027 | 0.0025 | 1932 | 0.0363 |
| 1933 | 0.0026 | 0.0026 | 0.0025 | 0.0025 | 0.0021 | 0.0022 | 0.0022 | 0.0021 | 0.0021 | 0.0022 | 0.0022 | 0.0027 | 1933 | 0.0283 |
| 1934 | 0.0030 | 0.0024 | 0.0027 | 0.0024 | 0.0023 | 0.0021 | 0.0021 | 0.0021 | 0.0021 | 0.0026 | 0.0022 | 0.0023 | 1934 | 0.0293 |
| 1935 | 0.0021 | 0.0018 | 0.0018 | 0.0017 | 0.0016 | 0.0015 | 0.0015 | 0.0014 | 0.0015 | 0.0016 | 0.0015 | 0.0016 | 1935 | 0.0202 |
| 1936 | 0.0014 | 0.0013 | 0.0013 | 0.0012 | 0.0012 | 0.0013 | 0.0012 | 0.0012 | 0.0011 | 0.0011 | 0.0011 | 0.0010 | 1936 | 0.0144 |
| 1937 | 0.0010 | 0.0010 | 0.0012 | 0.0015 | 0.0013 | 0.0014 | 0.0014 | 0.0013 | 0.0014 | 0.0012 | 0.0012 | 0.0011 | 1937 | 0.0148 |
| 1938 | 0.0018 | 0.0016 | 0.0017 | 0.0017 | 0.0015 | 0.0014 | 0.0013 | 0.0014 | 0.0013 | 0.0014 | 0.0013 | 0.0013 | 1938 | 0.0182 |
| 1939 | 0.0013 | 0.0011 | 0.0012 | 0.0010 | 0.0011 | 0.0009 | 0.0009 | 0.0009 | 0.0011 | 0.0015 | 0.0010 | 0.0009 | 1939 | 0.0131 |
| 1940 | 0.0009 | 0.0008 | 0.0008 | 0.0007 | 0.0007 | 0.0010 | 0.0008 | 0.0008 | 0.0007 | 0.0007 | 0.0006 | 0.0005 | 1940 | 0.0090 |
| 1941 | 0.0006 | 0.0006 | 0.0008 | 0.0006 | 0.0006 | 0.0006 | 0.0005 | 0.0005 | 0.0005 | 0.0005 | 0.0004 | 0.0007 | 1941 | 0.0067 |
| 1942 | 0.0008 | 0.0006 | 0.0007 | 0.0006 | 0.0006 | 0.0006 | 0.0006 | 0.0006 | 0.0006 | 0.0006 | 0.0006 | 0.0006 | 1942 | 0.0076 |
| 1943 | 0.0014 | 0.0013 | 0.0014 | 0.0013 | 0.0013 | 0.0013 | 0.0013 | 0.0012 | 0.0012 | 0.0012 | 0.0012 | 0.0012 | 1943 | 0.0156 |
| 1944 | 0.0013 | 0.0012 | 0.0013 | 0.0012 | 0.0013 | 0.0012 | 0.0012 | 0.0012 | 0.0011 | 0.0012 | 0.0011 | 0.0011 | 1944 | 0.0144 |
| 1945 | 0.0012 | 0.0010 | 0.0010 | 0.0010 | 0.0010 | 0.0010 | 0.0010 | 0.0010 | 0.0009 | 0.0010 | 0.0009 | 0.0009 | 1945 | 0.0119 |
| 1946 | 0.0009 | 0.0008 | 0.0007 | 0.0009 | 0.0009 | 0.0009 | 0.0009 | 0.0009 | 0.0010 | 0.0010 | 0.0009 | 0.0010 | 1946 | 0.0108 |
| 1947 | 0.0010 | 0.0009 | 0.0010 | 0.0009 | 0.0010 | 0.0011 | 0.0010 | 0.0010 | 0.0010 | 0.0010 | 0.0010 | 0.0012 | 1947 | 0.0121 |
| 1948 | 0.0013 | 0.0012 | 0.0014 | 0.0013 | 0.0012 | 0.0013 | 0.0012 | 0.0013 | 0.0013 | 0.0013 | 0.0014 | 0.0013 | 1948 | 0.0156 |
| 1949 | 0.0013 | 0.0012 | 0.0013 | 0.0012 | 0.0013 | 0.0012 | 0.0010 | 0.0011 | 0.0010 | 0.0010 | 0.0010 | 0.0010 | 1949 | 0.0136 |
| 1950 | 0.0011 | 0.0010 | 0.0011 | 0.0010 | 0.0012 | 0.0011 | 0.0012 | 0.0011 | 0.0011 | 0.0013 | 0.0013 | 0.0013 | 1950 | 0.0139 |
| 1951 | 0.0016 | 0.0014 | 0.0015 | 0.0018 | 0.0017 | 0.0017 | 0.0018 | 0.0017 | 0.0015 | 0.0019 | 0.0017 | 0.0018 | 1951 | 0.0198 |
| 1952 | 0.0018 | 0.0017 | 0.0019 | 0.0017 | 0.0016 | 0.0017 | 0.0018 | 0.0018 | 0.0021 | 0.0020 | 0.0017 | 0.0021 | 1952 | 0.0219 |
| 1953 | 0.0019 | 0.0018 | 0.0021 | 0.0021 | 0.0022 | 0.0027 | 0.0024 | 0.0023 | 0.0023 | 0.0020 | 0.0020 | 0.0020 | 1953 | 0.0255 |
| 1954 | 0.0016 | 0.0014 | 0.0014 | 0.0013 | 0.0011 | 0.0016 | 0.0011 | 0.0012 | 0.0011 | 0.0012 | 0.0014 | 0.0014 | 1954 | 0.0160 |
| 1955 | 0.0018 | 0.0017 | 0.0020 | 0.0019 | 0.0021 | 0.0020 | 0.0020 | 0.0025 | 0.0023 | 0.0023 | 0.0021 | 0.0022 | 1955 | 0.0245 |
| 1956 | 0.0025 | 0.0021 | 0.0022 | 0.0026 | 0.0026 | 0.0023 | 0.0025 | 0.0027 | 0.0026 | 0.0030 | 0.0028 | 0.0030 | 1956 | 0.0305 |
| 1957 | 0.0030 | 0.0025 | 0.0026 | 0.0029 | 0.0030 | 0.0027 | 0.0036 | 0.0032 | 0.0032 | 0.0033 | 0.0031 | 0.0028 | 1957 | 0.0359 |
| 1958 | 0.0024 | 0.0021 | 0.0022 | 0.0021 | 0.0019 | 0.0021 | 0.0021 | 0.0022 | 0.0032 | 0.0032 | 0.0029 | 0.0032 | 1958 | 0.0293 |
| 1959 | 0.0031 | 0.0030 | 0.0033 | 0.0032 | 0.0033 | 0.0037 | 0.0038 | 0.0037 | 0.0039 | 0.0039 | 0.0038 | 0.0041 | 1959 | 0.0418 |
| 1960 | 0.0039 | 0.0039 | 0.0039 | 0.0032 | 0.0037 | 0.0035 | 0.0031 | 0.0030 | 0.0028 | 0.0029 | 0.0028 | 0.0031 | 1960 | 0.0415 |
| 1961 | 0.0030 | 0.0028 | 0.0029 | 0.0027 | 0.0030 | 0.0029 | 0.0031 | 0.0031 | 0.0030 | 0.0032 | 0.0030 | 0.0030 | 1961 | 0.0354 |
| 1962 | 0.0035 | 0.0031 | 0.0031 | 0.0031 | 0.0031 | 0.0029 | 0.0033 | 0.0032 | 0.0028 | 0.0033 | 0.0029 | 0.0030 | 1962 | 0.0373 |
| 1963 | 0.0030 | 0.0028 | 0.0029 | 0.0032 | 0.0031 | 0.0029 | 0.0034 | 0.0031 | 0.0033 | 0.0033 | 0.0031 | 0.0034 | 1963 | 0.0371 |
| 1964 | 0.0034 | 0.0030 | 0.0035 | 0.0033 | 0.0031 | 0.0036 | 0.0034 | 0.0033 | 0.0033 | 0.0033 | 0.0034 | 0.0034 | 1964 | 0.0400 |
| 1965 | 0.0033 | 0.0031 | 0.0037 | 0.0033 | 0.0033 | 0.0037 | 0.0034 | 0.0036 | 0.0034 | 0.0034 | 0.0038 | 0.0037 | 1965 | 0.0415 |
| 1966 | 0.0040 | 0.0036 | 0.0043 | 0.0038 | 0.0042 | 0.0040 | 0.0040 | 0.0047 | 0.0046 | 0.0044 | 0.0042 | 0.0042 | 1966 | 0.0493 |
| 1967 | 0.0041 | 0.0035 | 0.0039 | 0.0033 | 0.0042 | 0.0038 | 0.0045 | 0.0042 | 0.0041 | 0.0047 | 0.0046 | 0.0044 | 1967 | 0.0488 |
| 1968 | 0.0051 | 0.0043 | 0.0043 | 0.0049 | 0.0048 | 0.0043 | 0.0049 | 0.0042 | 0.0044 | 0.0044 | 0.0041 | 0.0047 | 1968 | 0.0549 |
| 1969 | 0.0054 | 0.0048 | 0.0049 | 0.0057 | 0.0050 | 0.0058 | 0.0059 | 0.0054 | 0.0061 | 0.0067 | 0.0056 | 0.0068 | 1969 | 0.0665 |
| 1970 | 0.0066 | 0.0061 | 0.0063 | 0.0059 | 0.0062 | 0.0067 | 0.0065 | 0.0062 | 0.0060 | 0.0057 | 0.0058 | 0.0050 | 1970 | 0.0749 |

* Compound annual return

# Table A-11 (continued)

## Intermediate-Term Government Bonds: Income Returns

from January 1971 to December 2000

| Year | Jan | Feb | Mar | Apr | May | Jun | Jul | Aug | Sep | Oct | Nov | Dec | Year | Jan-Dec* |
|------|-----|-----|-----|-----|-----|-----|-----|-----|-----|-----|-----|-----|------|----------|
| 1971 | 0.0047 | 0.0043 | 0.0047 | 0.0040 | 0.0044 | 0.0053 | 0.0053 | 0.0056 | 0.0048 | 0.0046 | 0.0047 | 0.0046 | 1971 | 0.0575 |
| 1972 | 0.0048 | 0.0044 | 0.0046 | 0.0044 | 0.0052 | 0.0048 | 0.0049 | 0.0050 | 0.0047 | 0.0053 | 0.0051 | 0.0049 | 1972 | 0.0575 |
| 1973 | 0.0056 | 0.0048 | 0.0054 | 0.0056 | 0.0056 | 0.0053 | 0.0059 | 0.0064 | 0.0055 | 0.0060 | 0.0055 | 0.0056 | 1973 | 0.0658 |
| 1974 | 0.0057 | 0.0051 | 0.0054 | 0.0065 | 0.0067 | 0.0059 | 0.0073 | 0.0067 | 0.0072 | 0.0067 | 0.0061 | 0.0064 | 1974 | 0.0724 |
| 1975 | 0.0061 | 0.0055 | 0.0059 | 0.0060 | 0.0063 | 0.0063 | 0.0063 | 0.0061 | 0.0069 | 0.0068 | 0.0055 | 0.0067 | 1975 | 0.0735 |
| 1976 | 0.0060 | 0.0055 | 0.0066 | 0.0059 | 0.0054 | 0.0069 | 0.0060 | 0.0062 | 0.0056 | 0.0054 | 0.0058 | 0.0050 | 1976 | 0.0710 |
| 1977 | 0.0051 | 0.0050 | 0.0056 | 0.0053 | 0.0058 | 0.0055 | 0.0052 | 0.0059 | 0.0056 | 0.0059 | 0.0059 | 0.0059 | 1977 | 0.0649 |
| 1978 | 0.0066 | 0.0057 | 0.0066 | 0.0060 | 0.0071 | 0.0066 | 0.0070 | 0.0068 | 0.0065 | 0.0072 | 0.0072 | 0.0069 | 1978 | 0.0783 |
| 1979 | 0.0079 | 0.0066 | 0.0075 | 0.0077 | 0.0077 | 0.0070 | 0.0074 | 0.0073 | 0.0070 | 0.0084 | 0.0089 | 0.0086 | 1979 | 0.0904 |
| 1980 | 0.0086 | 0.0083 | 0.0107 | 0.0103 | 0.0081 | 0.0075 | 0.0079 | 0.0076 | 0.0097 | 0.0094 | 0.0096 | 0.0111 | 1980 | 0.1055 |
| 1981 | 0.0101 | 0.0095 | 0.0117 | 0.0106 | 0.0110 | 0.0118 | 0.0116 | 0.0120 | 0.0130 | 0.0129 | 0.0121 | 0.0108 | 1981 | 0.1297 |
| 1982 | 0.0107 | 0.0102 | 0.0122 | 0.0112 | 0.0101 | 0.0118 | 0.0113 | 0.0109 | 0.0097 | 0.0089 | 0.0087 | 0.0085 | 1982 | 0.1281 |
| 1983 | 0.0084 | 0.0079 | 0.0084 | 0.0081 | 0.0086 | 0.0085 | 0.0082 | 0.0103 | 0.0094 | 0.0092 | 0.0091 | 0.0091 | 1983 | 0.1035 |
| 1984 | 0.0096 | 0.0088 | 0.0095 | 0.0101 | 0.0104 | 0.0105 | 0.0113 | 0.0105 | 0.0095 | 0.0110 | 0.0093 | 0.0093 | 1984 | 0.1168 |
| 1985 | 0.0090 | 0.0081 | 0.0089 | 0.0097 | 0.0090 | 0.0073 | 0.0083 | 0.0081 | 0.0082 | 0.0081 | 0.0074 | 0.0078 | 1985 | 0.1029 |
| 1986 | 0.0071 | 0.0066 | 0.0068 | 0.0060 | 0.0060 | 0.0068 | 0.0062 | 0.0057 | 0.0058 | 0.0060 | 0.0052 | 0.0060 | 1986 | 0.0772 |
| 1987 | 0.0055 | 0.0052 | 0.0060 | 0.0058 | 0.0062 | 0.0071 | 0.0066 | 0.0068 | 0.0068 | 0.0073 | 0.0070 | 0.0070 | 1987 | 0.0747 |
| 1988 | 0.0065 | 0.0066 | 0.0064 | 0.0063 | 0.0072 | 0.0070 | 0.0064 | 0.0077 | 0.0072 | 0.0071 | 0.0067 | 0.0071 | 1988 | 0.0824 |
| 1989 | 0.0077 | 0.0066 | 0.0078 | 0.0071 | 0.0080 | 0.0070 | 0.0067 | 0.0061 | 0.0065 | 0.0071 | 0.0063 | 0.0060 | 1989 | 0.0846 |
| 1990 | 0.0071 | 0.0064 | 0.0069 | 0.0071 | 0.0075 | 0.0067 | 0.0072 | 0.0068 | 0.0065 | 0.0074 | 0.0067 | 0.0067 | 1990 | 0.0815 |
| 1991 | 0.0064 | 0.0059 | 0.0059 | 0.0070 | 0.0065 | 0.0059 | 0.0069 | 0.0062 | 0.0061 | 0.0058 | 0.0052 | 0.0056 | 1991 | 0.0743 |
| 1992 | 0.0052 | 0.0052 | 0.0060 | 0.0058 | 0.0056 | 0.0058 | 0.0053 | 0.0050 | 0.0047 | 0.0044 | 0.0050 | 0.0053 | 1992 | 0.0627 |
| 1993 | 0.0049 | 0.0045 | 0.0049 | 0.0045 | 0.0041 | 0.0050 | 0.0041 | 0.0044 | 0.0041 | 0.0038 | 0.0042 | 0.0043 | 1993 | 0.0553 |
| 1994 | 0.0045 | 0.0039 | 0.0048 | 0.0049 | 0.0058 | 0.0055 | 0.0055 | 0.0060 | 0.0055 | 0.0060 | 0.0061 | 0.0063 | 1994 | 0.0607 |
| 1995 | 0.0067 | 0.0056 | 0.0060 | 0.0054 | 0.0062 | 0.0050 | 0.0051 | 0.0051 | 0.0047 | 0.0052 | 0.0047 | 0.0043 | 1995 | 0.0669 |
| 1996 | 0.0046 | 0.0041 | 0.0045 | 0.0053 | 0.0054 | 0.0050 | 0.0058 | 0.0052 | 0.0056 | 0.0053 | 0.0047 | 0.0050 | 1996 | 0.0582 |
| 1997 | 0.0052 | 0.0047 | 0.0054 | 0.0055 | 0.0055 | 0.0053 | 0.0054 | 0.0046 | 0.0054 | 0.0050 | 0.0043 | 0.0052 | 1997 | 0.0614 |
| 1998 | 0.0046 | 0.0041 | 0.0049 | 0.0046 | 0.0045 | 0.0049 | 0.0047 | 0.0046 | 0.0041 | 0.0035 | 0.0036 | 0.0039 | 1998 | 0.0529 |
| 1999 | 0.0037 | 0.0035 | 0.0048 | 0.0043 | 0.0041 | 0.0052 | 0.0049 | 0.0049 | 0.0048 | 0.0046 | 0.0052 | 0.0052 | 1999 | 0.0530 |
| 2000 | 0.0054 | 0.0052 | 0.0056 | 0.0048 | 0.0059 | 0.0054 | 0.0053 | 0.0051 | 0.0047 | 0.0051 | 0.0047 | 0.0043 | 2000 | 0.0619 |

* Compound annual return

## Table A-12

**Intermediate-Term Government Bonds: Capital Appreciation Returns**

from January 1926 to December 1970

| Year | Jan | Feb | Mar | Apr | May | Jun | Jul | Aug | Sep | Oct | Nov | Dec | Year | Jan-Dec* |
|------|-----|-----|-----|-----|-----|-----|-----|-----|-----|-----|-----|-----|------|----------|
| 1926 | 0.0036 | 0.0000 | 0.0009 | 0.0059 | −0.0023 | −0.0004 | −0.0018 | −0.0023 | 0.0018 | 0.0023 | 0.0014 | 0.0059 | 1926 | 0.0151 |
| 1927 | 0.0027 | 0.0009 | 0.0009 | −0.0014 | −0.0009 | 0.0000 | 0.0014 | 0.0027 | 0.0032 | −0.0064 | 0.0055 | 0.0009 | 1927 | 0.0096 |
| 1928 | 0.0018 | −0.0032 | −0.0018 | −0.0032 | −0.0036 | −0.0014 | −0.0122 | 0.0018 | −0.0004 | 0.0000 | −0.0014 | −0.0041 | 1928 | −0.0273 |
| 1929 | −0.0063 | −0.0054 | −0.0031 | 0.0054 | −0.0098 | 0.0072 | 0.0031 | 0.0018 | −0.0049 | 0.0135 | 0.0150 | 0.0014 | 1929 | 0.0177 |
| 1930 | −0.0072 | 0.0064 | 0.0133 | −0.0100 | 0.0032 | 0.0115 | 0.0028 | −0.0005 | 0.0037 | 0.0051 | 0.0046 | 0.0000 | 1930 | 0.0330 |
| 1931 | −0.0097 | 0.0074 | 0.0028 | 0.0060 | 0.0098 | −0.0240 | −0.0009 | −0.0009 | −0.0142 | −0.0136 | 0.0018 | −0.0193 | 1931 | −0.0540 |
| 1932 | −0.0067 | 0.0094 | 0.0045 | 0.0164 | −0.0122 | 0.0077 | 0.0091 | 0.0096 | 0.0000 | 0.0018 | 0.0005 | 0.0092 | 1932 | 0.0502 |
| 1933 | −0.0041 | −0.0028 | 0.0074 | 0.0032 | 0.0178 | −0.0014 | −0.0028 | 0.0051 | 0.0005 | −0.0047 | 0.0005 | −0.0280 | 1933 | −0.0099 |
| 1934 | 0.0100 | 0.0028 | 0.0162 | 0.0158 | 0.0097 | 0.0070 | −0.0044 | −0.0113 | −0.0160 | 0.0164 | 0.0024 | 0.0102 | 1934 | 0.0597 |
| 1935 | 0.0093 | 0.0088 | 0.0107 | 0.0090 | −0.0050 | 0.0098 | 0.0022 | −0.0086 | −0.0072 | 0.0093 | −0.0002 | 0.0105 | 1935 | 0.0494 |
| 1936 | −0.0017 | 0.0056 | 0.0018 | 0.0012 | 0.0026 | −0.0001 | 0.0010 | 0.0038 | −0.0001 | 0.0014 | 0.0070 | −0.0067 | 1936 | 0.0160 |
| 1937 | −0.0041 | −0.0003 | −0.0176 | 0.0032 | 0.0067 | −0.0027 | 0.0045 | −0.0056 | 0.0068 | 0.0020 | 0.0030 | 0.0051 | 1937 | 0.0005 |
| 1938 | 0.0067 | 0.0036 | −0.0030 | 0.0214 | 0.0008 | 0.0061 | −0.0003 | 0.0000 | −0.0026 | 0.0079 | −0.0014 | 0.0039 | 1938 | 0.0437 |
| 1939 | 0.0016 | 0.0071 | 0.0069 | 0.0028 | 0.0084 | −0.0007 | 0.0030 | −0.0155 | −0.0273 | 0.0300 | 0.0063 | 0.0098 | 1939 | 0.0318 |
| 1940 | −0.0023 | 0.0027 | 0.0080 | −0.0005 | −0.0221 | 0.0177 | −0.0005 | 0.0035 | 0.0040 | 0.0030 | 0.0050 | 0.0023 | 1940 | 0.0204 |
| 1941 | −0.0006 | −0.0052 | 0.0061 | 0.0027 | 0.0006 | 0.0051 | −0.0004 | 0.0006 | −0.0004 | 0.0018 | −0.0096 | −0.0023 | 1941 | −0.0017 |
| 1942 | 0.0066 | 0.0009 | 0.0016 | 0.0016 | 0.0010 | 0.0006 | −0.0006 | 0.0011 | −0.0029 | 0.0011 | 0.0011 | −0.0006 | 1942 | 0.0117 |
| 1943 | 0.0025 | 0.0001 | 0.0007 | 0.0010 | 0.0044 | 0.0020 | 0.0008 | −0.0010 | 0.0002 | 0.0005 | 0.0002 | 0.0008 | 1943 | 0.0123 |
| 1944 | −0.0002 | 0.0004 | 0.0007 | 0.0016 | −0.0008 | −0.0005 | 0.0016 | 0.0012 | 0.0000 | −0.0001 | −0.0003 | −0.0001 | 1944 | 0.0035 |
| 1945 | 0.0040 | 0.0028 | −0.0005 | 0.0005 | 0.0002 | 0.0009 | −0.0010 | 0.0006 | 0.0008 | 0.0006 | 0.0001 | 0.0012 | 1945 | 0.0102 |
| 1946 | 0.0030 | 0.0040 | −0.0045 | −0.0028 | −0.0003 | 0.0024 | −0.0019 | −0.0005 | −0.0020 | 0.0015 | −0.0018 | 0.0022 | 1946 | −0.0008 |
| 1947 | 0.0012 | −0.0003 | 0.0014 | −0.0022 | −0.0002 | −0.0003 | −0.0004 | 0.0016 | −0.0010 | −0.0033 | −0.0004 | 0.0008 | 1947 | −0.0030 |
| 1948 | 0.0002 | 0.0006 | 0.0003 | 0.0006 | 0.0042 | −0.0021 | −0.0014 | −0.0018 | −0.0003 | 0.0000 | 0.0006 | 0.0019 | 1948 | 0.0027 |
| 1949 | 0.0015 | 0.0000 | 0.0012 | 0.0003 | 0.0010 | 0.0038 | 0.0010 | 0.0019 | −0.0002 | −0.0004 | −0.0008 | 0.0002 | 1949 | 0.0095 |
| 1950 | −0.0016 | −0.0002 | −0.0011 | −0.0003 | 0.0007 | −0.0008 | 0.0009 | −0.0019 | −0.0015 | −0.0012 | 0.0005 | −0.0004 | 1950 | −0.0069 |
| 1951 | 0.0006 | −0.0007 | −0.0142 | 0.0040 | −0.0058 | 0.0033 | 0.0040 | 0.0019 | −0.0072 | −0.0003 | 0.0015 | −0.0033 | 1951 | −0.0163 |
| 1952 | 0.0019 | −0.0037 | 0.0048 | 0.0037 | 0.0004 | −0.0052 | −0.0052 | −0.0042 | −0.0002 | 0.0046 | −0.0023 | −0.0002 | 1952 | −0.0057 |
| 1953 | −0.0022 | −0.0016 | −0.0038 | −0.0117 | −0.0138 | 0.0129 | 0.0032 | −0.0031 | 0.0171 | 0.0018 | −0.0006 | 0.0083 | 1953 | 0.0061 |
| 1954 | 0.0049 | 0.0086 | 0.0013 | 0.0031 | −0.0084 | 0.0109 | −0.0016 | −0.0001 | −0.0032 | −0.0021 | −0.0015 | −0.0010 | 1954 | 0.0108 |
| 1955 | −0.0050 | −0.0070 | 0.0004 | −0.0014 | −0.0019 | −0.0057 | −0.0091 | −0.0018 | 0.0059 | 0.0050 | −0.0074 | −0.0033 | 1955 | −0.0310 |
| 1956 | 0.0080 | −0.0018 | −0.0122 | −0.0027 | 0.0086 | −0.0020 | −0.0120 | −0.0130 | 0.0066 | −0.0049 | −0.0075 | −0.0019 | 1956 | −0.0345 |
| 1957 | 0.0207 | −0.0037 | −0.0009 | −0.0130 | −0.0047 | −0.0133 | −0.0051 | 0.0077 | −0.0030 | 0.0010 | 0.0365 | 0.0188 | 1957 | 0.0405 |
| 1958 | 0.0010 | 0.0117 | 0.0031 | 0.0031 | 0.0041 | −0.0088 | −0.0112 | −0.0378 | −0.0048 | −0.0029 | 0.0103 | −0.0093 | 1958 | −0.0417 |
| 1959 | −0.0045 | 0.0078 | −0.0070 | −0.0084 | −0.0033 | −0.0113 | −0.0004 | −0.0116 | −0.0019 | 0.0134 | −0.0130 | −0.0060 | 1959 | −0.0456 |
| 1960 | 0.0115 | 0.0032 | 0.0253 | −0.0096 | −0.0006 | 0.0182 | 0.0236 | −0.0034 | 0.0001 | −0.0012 | −0.0122 | 0.0180 | 1960 | 0.0742 |
| 1961 | −0.0089 | 0.0063 | 0.0008 | 0.0026 | −0.0058 | −0.0054 | −0.0024 | −0.0012 | 0.0049 | −0.0018 | −0.0049 | −0.0012 | 1961 | −0.0172 |
| 1962 | −0.0080 | 0.0124 | 0.0058 | −0.0006 | 0.0018 | −0.0056 | −0.0045 | 0.0092 | −0.0007 | 0.0018 | 0.0031 | 0.0026 | 1962 | 0.0173 |
| 1963 | −0.0059 | −0.0011 | −0.0002 | −0.0002 | −0.0017 | −0.0015 | −0.0030 | −0.0012 | −0.0019 | −0.0022 | 0.0008 | −0.0032 | 1963 | −0.0210 |
| 1964 | −0.0001 | −0.0019 | −0.0019 | 0.0000 | 0.0049 | 0.0000 | −0.0006 | −0.0006 | 0.0012 | 0.0000 | −0.0037 | 0.0024 | 1964 | −0.0003 |
| 1965 | 0.0009 | −0.0013 | 0.0006 | −0.0007 | 0.0002 | 0.0012 | −0.0016 | −0.0017 | −0.0039 | −0.0033 | −0.0031 | −0.0186 | 1965 | −0.0310 |
| 1966 | −0.0037 | −0.0120 | 0.0145 | −0.0056 | −0.0032 | −0.0064 | −0.0065 | −0.0171 | 0.0170 | 0.0031 | −0.0015 | 0.0180 | 1966 | −0.0041 |
| 1967 | 0.0077 | −0.0048 | 0.0144 | −0.0122 | 0.0002 | −0.0265 | 0.0089 | −0.0078 | −0.0035 | −0.0095 | −0.0018 | −0.0038 | 1967 | −0.0385 |
| 1968 | 0.0095 | −0.0003 | −0.0069 | −0.0065 | 0.0015 | 0.0123 | 0.0128 | −0.0021 | 0.0011 | −0.0034 | −0.0054 | −0.0220 | 1968 | −0.0099 |
| 1969 | 0.0032 | −0.0061 | 0.0048 | 0.0021 | −0.0131 | −0.0142 | 0.0024 | −0.0072 | −0.0361 | 0.0266 | −0.0103 | −0.0260 | 1969 | −0.0727 |
| 1970 | −0.0035 | 0.0378 | 0.0024 | −0.0266 | 0.0049 | −0.0006 | 0.0087 | 0.0054 | 0.0136 | 0.0037 | 0.0393 | 0.0005 | 1970 | 0.0871 |

* Compound annual return

## Table A-12 (continued)

## Intermediate-Term Government Bonds: Capital Appreciation Returns

from January 1971 to December 2000

| Year | Jan | Feb | Mar | Apr | May | Jun | Jul | Aug | Sep | Oct | Nov | Dec | Year | Jan-Dec* |
|------|-----|-----|-----|-----|-----|-----|-----|-----|-----|-----|-----|-----|------|----------|
| 1971 | 0.0121 | 0.0181 | 0.0139 | −0.0367 | −0.0034 | −0.0240 | −0.0027 | 0.0294 | −0.0022 | 0.0173 | 0.0005 | 0.0064 | 1971 | 0.0272 |
| 1972 | 0.0058 | −0.0030 | −0.0031 | −0.0030 | −0.0035 | −0.0003 | −0.0034 | −0.0035 | −0.0033 | −0.0037 | −0.0006 | 0.0143 | 1972 | −0.0075 |
| 1973 | −0.0062 | −0.0123 | −0.0008 | 0.0007 | 0.0001 | −0.0059 | −0.0336 | 0.0190 | 0.0195 | −0.0010 | 0.0009 | −0.0016 | 1973 | −0.0219 |
| 1974 | −0.0048 | −0.0016 | −0.0266 | −0.0217 | 0.0063 | −0.0147 | −0.0066 | −0.0078 | 0.0247 | 0.0043 | 0.0175 | 0.0120 | 1974 | −0.0199 |
| 1975 | −0.0008 | 0.0092 | −0.0119 | −0.0246 | 0.0197 | −0.0035 | −0.0093 | −0.0070 | −0.0059 | 0.0298 | −0.0065 | 0.0131 | 1975 | 0.0012 |
| 1976 | −0.0003 | 0.0028 | 0.0010 | 0.0057 | −0.0200 | 0.0090 | 0.0059 | 0.0127 | 0.0019 | 0.0093 | 0.0264 | −0.0024 | 1976 | 0.0525 |
| 1977 | −0.0241 | −0.0002 | −0.0001 | −0.0001 | −0.0002 | 0.0048 | −0.0051 | −0.0052 | −0.0041 | −0.0118 | 0.0019 | −0.0082 | 1977 | −0.0515 |
| 1978 | −0.0053 | −0.0041 | −0.0029 | −0.0036 | −0.0073 | −0.0087 | 0.0028 | 0.0010 | −0.0008 | −0.0184 | 0.0020 | −0.0005 | 1978 | −0.0449 |
| 1979 | −0.0024 | −0.0125 | 0.0038 | −0.0044 | 0.0116 | 0.0135 | −0.0086 | −0.0163 | −0.0065 | −0.0553 | 0.0274 | 0.0001 | 1979 | −0.0507 |
| 1980 | −0.0221 | −0.0724 | 0.0036 | 0.1095 | 0.0409 | −0.0152 | −0.0185 | −0.0463 | −0.0135 | −0.0246 | −0.0067 | 0.0060 | 1980 | −0.0681 |
| 1981 | −0.0069 | −0.0331 | 0.0146 | −0.0322 | 0.0135 | −0.0058 | −0.0386 | −0.0298 | 0.0034 | 0.0482 | 0.0502 | −0.0250 | 1981 | −0.0455 |
| 1982 | −0.0057 | 0.0046 | −0.0080 | 0.0186 | 0.0045 | −0.0253 | 0.0351 | 0.0359 | 0.0228 | 0.0442 | −0.0007 | 0.0100 | 1982 | 0.1423 |
| 1983 | −0.0076 | 0.0173 | −0.0133 | 0.0177 | −0.0208 | −0.0069 | −0.0280 | −0.0022 | 0.0220 | −0.0073 | 0.0012 | −0.0043 | 1983 | −0.0330 |
| 1984 | 0.0081 | −0.0153 | −0.0129 | −0.0104 | −0.0353 | −0.0007 | 0.0280 | −0.0005 | 0.0106 | 0.0274 | 0.0099 | 0.0050 | 1984 | 0.0122 |
| 1985 | 0.0116 | −0.0260 | 0.0077 | 0.0167 | 0.0395 | 0.0035 | −0.0129 | 0.0067 | 0.0031 | 0.0081 | 0.0121 | 0.0178 | 1985 | 0.0901 |
| 1986 | 0.0011 | 0.0210 | 0.0270 | 0.0021 | −0.0274 | 0.0208 | 0.0095 | 0.0209 | −0.0168 | 0.0102 | 0.0061 | −0.0053 | 1986 | 0.0699 |
| 1987 | 0.0051 | 0.0007 | −0.0091 | −0.0302 | −0.0100 | 0.0051 | −0.0040 | −0.0105 | −0.0209 | 0.0226 | 0.0013 | 0.0023 | 1987 | −0.0475 |
| 1988 | 0.0251 | 0.0057 | −0.0151 | −0.0107 | −0.0121 | 0.0111 | −0.0111 | −0.0086 | 0.0124 | 0.0077 | −0.0182 | −0.0081 | 1988 | −0.0226 |
| 1989 | 0.0044 | −0.0117 | −0.0029 | 0.0149 | 0.0132 | 0.0254 | 0.0168 | −0.0307 | 0.0004 | 0.0166 | 0.0021 | −0.0048 | 1989 | 0.0434 |
| 1990 | −0.0176 | −0.0057 | −0.0067 | −0.0148 | 0.0186 | 0.0084 | 0.0102 | −0.0160 | 0.0030 | 0.0096 | 0.0126 | 0.0095 | 1990 | 0.0102 |
| 1991 | 0.0042 | −0.0011 | −0.0036 | 0.0046 | −0.0006 | −0.0081 | 0.0060 | 0.0184 | 0.0155 | 0.0077 | 0.0076 | 0.0209 | 1991 | 0.0736 |
| 1992 | −0.0247 | −0.0030 | −0.0139 | 0.0039 | 0.0166 | 0.0118 | 0.0189 | 0.0100 | 0.0147 | −0.0226 | −0.0134 | 0.0093 | 1992 | 0.0064 |
| 1993 | 0.0221 | 0.0198 | −0.0006 | 0.0043 | −0.0051 | 0.0152 | −0.0036 | 0.0179 | 0.0015 | −0.0020 | −0.0135 | −0.0011 | 1993 | 0.0556 |
| 1994 | 0.0093 | −0.0297 | −0.0306 | −0.0154 | −0.0060 | −0.0084 | 0.0115 | −0.0034 | −0.0213 | −0.0084 | −0.0131 | −0.0010 | 1994 | −0.1114 |
| 1995 | 0.0115 | 0.0178 | 0.0003 | 0.0090 | 0.0307 | 0.0030 | −0.0066 | 0.0035 | 0.0017 | 0.0069 | 0.0102 | 0.0052 | 1995 | 0.0966 |
| 1996 | −0.0040 | −0.0178 | −0.0164 | −0.0103 | −0.0086 | 0.0067 | −0.0033 | −0.0057 | 0.0100 | 0.0129 | 0.0102 | −0.0128 | 1996 | −0.0390 |
| 1997 | −0.0027 | −0.0045 | −0.0168 | 0.0093 | 0.0024 | 0.0048 | 0.0210 | −0.0143 | 0.0098 | 0.0100 | −0.0045 | 0.0054 | 1997 | 0.0194 |
| 1998 | 0.0134 | −0.0080 | −0.0024 | 0.0015 | 0.0025 | 0.0030 | −0.0020 | 0.0225 | 0.0289 | 0.0006 | −0.0134 | −0.0002 | 1998 | 0.0466 |
| 1999 | 0.0018 | −0.0297 | 0.0038 | −0.0023 | −0.0188 | −0.0020 | −0.0052 | −0.0035 | 0.0049 | −0.0054 | −0.0060 | −0.0100 | 1999 | −0.0706 |
| 2000 | −0.0107 | 0.0026 | 0.0147 | −0.0091 | −0.0007 | 0.0138 | 0.0019 | 0.0083 | 0.0049 | 0.0028 | 0.0127 | 0.0171 | 2000 | 0.0594 |

* Compound annual return

## Table A-13

**Intermediate-Term Government Bonds: Yields**

from January 1926 to December 1970

| Year | Jan | Feb | Mar | Apr | May | Jun | Jul | Aug | Sep | Oct | Nov | Dec | Year | Jan-Dec |
|------|------|------|------|------|------|------|------|------|------|------|------|------|------|---------|
| 1926 | 0.0386 | 0.0386 | 0.0384 | 0.0371 | 0.0376 | 0.0377 | 0.0381 | 0.0386 | 0.0382 | 0.0377 | 0.0374 | 0.0361 | 1926 | 0.0361 |
| 1927 | 0.0355 | 0.0353 | 0.0351 | 0.0354 | 0.0356 | 0.0356 | 0.0353 | 0.0347 | 0.0340 | 0.0354 | 0.0342 | 0.0340 | 1927 | 0.0340 |
| 1928 | 0.0336 | 0.0343 | 0.0347 | 0.0354 | 0.0362 | 0.0365 | 0.0392 | 0.0388 | 0.0389 | 0.0389 | 0.0392 | 0.0401 | 1928 | 0.0401 |
| 1929 | 0.0415 | 0.0427 | 0.0434 | 0.0422 | 0.0444 | 0.0428 | 0.0421 | 0.0417 | 0.0428 | 0.0398 | 0.0365 | 0.0362 | 1929 | 0.0362 |
| 1930 | 0.0378 | 0.0364 | 0.0335 | 0.0357 | 0.0350 | 0.0325 | 0.0319 | 0.0320 | 0.0312 | 0.0301 | 0.0291 | 0.0291 | 1930 | 0.0291 |
| 1931 | 0.0312 | 0.0296 | 0.0290 | 0.0277 | 0.0256 | 0.0308 | 0.0310 | 0.0312 | 0.0343 | 0.0373 | 0.0369 | 0.0412 | 1931 | 0.0412 |
| 1932 | 0.0427 | 0.0406 | 0.0396 | 0.0360 | 0.0387 | 0.0370 | 0.0350 | 0.0329 | 0.0329 | 0.0325 | 0.0324 | 0.0304 | 1932 | 0.0304 |
| 1933 | 0.0313 | 0.0319 | 0.0303 | 0.0296 | 0.0258 | 0.0261 | 0.0267 | 0.0256 | 0.0255 | 0.0265 | 0.0264 | 0.0325 | 1933 | 0.0325 |
| 1934 | 0.0325 | 0.0321 | 0.0296 | 0.0272 | 0.0257 | 0.0246 | 0.0253 | 0.0271 | 0.0298 | 0.0271 | 0.0267 | 0.0249 | 1934 | 0.0249 |
| 1935 | 0.0233 | 0.0218 | 0.0199 | 0.0184 | 0.0193 | 0.0175 | 0.0171 | 0.0187 | 0.0201 | 0.0183 | 0.0183 | 0.0163 | 1935 | 0.0163 |
| 1936 | 0.0166 | 0.0155 | 0.0151 | 0.0149 | 0.0143 | 0.0143 | 0.0141 | 0.0133 | 0.0133 | 0.0130 | 0.0114 | 0.0129 | 1936 | 0.0129 |
| 1937 | 0.0134 | 0.0135 | 0.0184 | 0.0175 | 0.0156 | 0.0164 | 0.0151 | 0.0168 | 0.0147 | 0.0141 | 0.0131 | 0.0114 | 1937 | 0.0114 |
| 1938 | 0.0205 | 0.0200 | 0.0204 | 0.0174 | 0.0173 | 0.0164 | 0.0164 | 0.0164 | 0.0168 | 0.0156 | 0.0158 | 0.0152 | 1938 | 0.0152 |
| 1939 | 0.0149 | 0.0138 | 0.0127 | 0.0122 | 0.0108 | 0.0110 | 0.0105 | 0.0131 | 0.0180 | 0.0127 | 0.0116 | 0.0098 | 1939 | 0.0098 |
| 1940 | 0.0103 | 0.0098 | 0.0083 | 0.0084 | 0.0127 | 0.0092 | 0.0093 | 0.0086 | 0.0078 | 0.0072 | 0.0061 | 0.0057 | 1940 | 0.0057 |
| 1941 | 0.0077 | 0.0089 | 0.0075 | 0.0069 | 0.0067 | 0.0055 | 0.0056 | 0.0055 | 0.0056 | 0.0051 | 0.0076 | 0.0082 | 1941 | 0.0082 |
| 1942 | 0.0083 | 0.0081 | 0.0077 | 0.0074 | 0.0071 | 0.0070 | 0.0071 | 0.0069 | 0.0076 | 0.0073 | 0.0070 | 0.0072 | 1942 | 0.0072 |
| 1943 | 0.0166 | 0.0166 | 0.0164 | 0.0162 | 0.0153 | 0.0149 | 0.0147 | 0.0149 | 0.0149 | 0.0147 | 0.0147 | 0.0145 | 1943 | 0.0145 |
| 1944 | 0.0150 | 0.0150 | 0.0148 | 0.0143 | 0.0146 | 0.0147 | 0.0142 | 0.0139 | 0.0139 | 0.0139 | 0.0140 | 0.0140 | 1944 | 0.0140 |
| 1945 | 0.0127 | 0.0118 | 0.0120 | 0.0118 | 0.0117 | 0.0114 | 0.0118 | 0.0115 | 0.0112 | 0.0109 | 0.0109 | 0.0103 | 1945 | 0.0103 |
| 1946 | 0.0099 | 0.0087 | 0.0101 | 0.0111 | 0.0112 | 0.0103 | 0.0110 | 0.0112 | 0.0120 | 0.0114 | 0.0121 | 0.0112 | 1946 | 0.0112 |
| 1947 | 0.0116 | 0.0117 | 0.0112 | 0.0120 | 0.0121 | 0.0122 | 0.0124 | 0.0117 | 0.0121 | 0.0136 | 0.0138 | 0.0134 | 1947 | 0.0134 |
| 1948 | 0.0160 | 0.0158 | 0.0157 | 0.0155 | 0.0142 | 0.0149 | 0.0154 | 0.0160 | 0.0161 | 0.0161 | 0.0158 | 0.0151 | 1948 | 0.0151 |
| 1949 | 0.0153 | 0.0153 | 0.0148 | 0.0147 | 0.0144 | 0.0129 | 0.0125 | 0.0117 | 0.0118 | 0.0120 | 0.0124 | 0.0123 | 1949 | 0.0123 |
| 1950 | 0.0131 | 0.0132 | 0.0137 | 0.0138 | 0.0134 | 0.0139 | 0.0134 | 0.0145 | 0.0154 | 0.0162 | 0.0159 | 0.0162 | 1950 | 0.0162 |
| 1951 | 0.0179 | 0.0180 | 0.0211 | 0.0202 | 0.0215 | 0.0208 | 0.0199 | 0.0194 | 0.0212 | 0.0212 | 0.0209 | 0.0217 | 1951 | 0.0217 |
| 1952 | 0.0212 | 0.0222 | 0.0209 | 0.0199 | 0.0198 | 0.0213 | 0.0228 | 0.0241 | 0.0242 | 0.0227 | 0.0235 | 0.0235 | 1952 | 0.0235 |
| 1953 | 0.0242 | 0.0245 | 0.0253 | 0.0277 | 0.0307 | 0.0279 | 0.0272 | 0.0279 | 0.0241 | 0.0237 | 0.0238 | 0.0218 | 1953 | 0.0218 |
| 1954 | 0.0187 | 0.0157 | 0.0153 | 0.0142 | 0.0173 | 0.0131 | 0.0138 | 0.0138 | 0.0152 | 0.0161 | 0.0168 | 0.0172 | 1954 | 0.0172 |
| 1955 | 0.0227 | 0.0240 | 0.0240 | 0.0242 | 0.0246 | 0.0257 | 0.0276 | 0.0280 | 0.0267 | 0.0257 | 0.0273 | 0.0280 | 1955 | 0.0280 |
| 1956 | 0.0271 | 0.0275 | 0.0300 | 0.0305 | 0.0287 | 0.0292 | 0.0317 | 0.0346 | 0.0331 | 0.0342 | 0.0359 | 0.0363 | 1956 | 0.0363 |
| 1957 | 0.0326 | 0.0333 | 0.0334 | 0.0357 | 0.0366 | 0.0390 | 0.0399 | 0.0385 | 0.0390 | 0.0388 | 0.0320 | 0.0284 | 1957 | 0.0284 |
| 1958 | 0.0282 | 0.0259 | 0.0253 | 0.0246 | 0.0238 | 0.0250 | 0.0281 | 0.0365 | 0.0376 | 0.0382 | 0.0359 | 0.0381 | 1958 | 0.0381 |
| 1959 | 0.0395 | 0.0378 | 0.0393 | 0.0413 | 0.0420 | 0.0447 | 0.0448 | 0.0477 | 0.0482 | 0.0448 | 0.0482 | 0.0498 | 1959 | 0.0498 |
| 1960 | 0.0471 | 0.0464 | 0.0409 | 0.0431 | 0.0432 | 0.0390 | 0.0334 | 0.0343 | 0.0343 | 0.0346 | 0.0377 | 0.0331 | 1960 | 0.0331 |
| 1961 | 0.0363 | 0.0350 | 0.0348 | 0.0342 | 0.0355 | 0.0368 | 0.0373 | 0.0376 | 0.0365 | 0.0369 | 0.0381 | 0.0384 | 1961 | 0.0384 |
| 1962 | 0.0402 | 0.0377 | 0.0366 | 0.0367 | 0.0363 | 0.0375 | 0.0384 | 0.0365 | 0.0366 | 0.0362 | 0.0355 | 0.0350 | 1962 | 0.0350 |
| 1963 | 0.0368 | 0.0370 | 0.0370 | 0.0371 | 0.0374 | 0.0378 | 0.0385 | 0.0388 | 0.0392 | 0.0398 | 0.0396 | 0.0404 | 1963 | 0.0404 |
| 1964 | 0.0402 | 0.0407 | 0.0411 | 0.0411 | 0.0399 | 0.0399 | 0.0401 | 0.0402 | 0.0399 | 0.0399 | 0.0409 | 0.0403 | 1964 | 0.0403 |
| 1965 | 0.0413 | 0.0416 | 0.0414 | 0.0416 | 0.0415 | 0.0413 | 0.0416 | 0.0420 | 0.0429 | 0.0437 | 0.0444 | 0.0490 | 1965 | 0.0490 |
| 1966 | 0.0482 | 0.0507 | 0.0477 | 0.0489 | 0.0496 | 0.0510 | 0.0525 | 0.0565 | 0.0526 | 0.0519 | 0.0522 | 0.0479 | 1966 | 0.0479 |
| 1967 | 0.0459 | 0.0470 | 0.0437 | 0.0466 | 0.0465 | 0.0530 | 0.0508 | 0.0528 | 0.0537 | 0.0562 | 0.0566 | 0.0577 | 1967 | 0.0577 |
| 1968 | 0.0548 | 0.0549 | 0.0563 | 0.0577 | 0.0574 | 0.0547 | 0.0518 | 0.0523 | 0.0520 | 0.0528 | 0.0541 | 0.0596 | 1968 | 0.0596 |
| 1969 | 0.0637 | 0.0651 | 0.0640 | 0.0636 | 0.0666 | 0.0699 | 0.0693 | 0.0711 | 0.0799 | 0.0735 | 0.0761 | 0.0829 | 1969 | 0.0829 |
| 1970 | 0.0820 | 0.0730 | 0.0724 | 0.0790 | 0.0778 | 0.0780 | 0.0757 | 0.0743 | 0.0707 | 0.0697 | 0.0591 | 0.0590 | 1970 | 0.0590 |

Table A-13 (continued)

## Intermediate-Term Government Bonds: Yields

from January 1971 to December 2000

| Year | Jan | Feb | Mar | Apr | May | Jun | Jul | Aug | Sep | Oct | Nov | Dec | Year | Jan-Dec |
|------|-----|-----|-----|-----|-----|-----|-----|-----|-----|-----|-----|-----|------|---------|
| 1971 | 0.0570 | 0.0526 | 0.0493 | 0.0585 | 0.0593 | 0.0656 | 0.0663 | 0.0585 | 0.0591 | 0.0545 | 0.0543 | 0.0525 | 1971 | 0.0525 |
| 1972 | 0.0556 | 0.0563 | 0.0570 | 0.0577 | 0.0586 | 0.0587 | 0.0595 | 0.0604 | 0.0613 | 0.0623 | 0.0625 | 0.0585 | 1972 | 0.0585 |
| 1973 | 0.0641 | 0.0671 | 0.0673 | 0.0671 | 0.0671 | 0.0686 | 0.0776 | 0.0725 | 0.0674 | 0.0677 | 0.0674 | 0.0679 | 1973 | 0.0679 |
| 1974 | 0.0687 | 0.0691 | 0.0751 | 0.0801 | 0.0786 | 0.0822 | 0.0838 | 0.0857 | 0.0797 | 0.0787 | 0.0743 | 0.0712 | 1974 | 0.0712 |
| 1975 | 0.0730 | 0.0709 | 0.0737 | 0.0798 | 0.0749 | 0.0758 | 0.0782 | 0.0800 | 0.0815 | 0.0736 | 0.0754 | 0.0719 | 1975 | 0.0719 |
| 1976 | 0.0743 | 0.0736 | 0.0733 | 0.0719 | 0.0771 | 0.0747 | 0.0732 | 0.0697 | 0.0692 | 0.0667 | 0.0594 | 0.0600 | 1976 | 0.0600 |
| 1977 | 0.0673 | 0.0673 | 0.0673 | 0.0674 | 0.0674 | 0.0662 | 0.0675 | 0.0689 | 0.0700 | 0.0733 | 0.0727 | 0.0751 | 1977 | 0.0751 |
| 1978 | 0.0773 | 0.0784 | 0.0791 | 0.0800 | 0.0820 | 0.0843 | 0.0836 | 0.0833 | 0.0835 | 0.0887 | 0.0882 | 0.0883 | 1978 | 0.0883 |
| 1979 | 0.0895 | 0.0928 | 0.0918 | 0.0929 | 0.0899 | 0.0864 | 0.0887 | 0.0933 | 0.0951 | 0.1112 | 0.1033 | 0.1033 | 1979 | 0.1033 |
| 1980 | 0.1093 | 0.1294 | 0.1285 | 0.1009 | 0.0903 | 0.0944 | 0.0996 | 0.1133 | 0.1171 | 0.1244 | 0.1264 | 0.1245 | 1980 | 0.1245 |
| 1981 | 0.1275 | 0.1371 | 0.1328 | 0.1427 | 0.1385 | 0.1404 | 0.1533 | 0.1636 | 0.1625 | 0.1472 | 0.1311 | 0.1396 | 1981 | 0.1396 |
| 1982 | 0.1397 | 0.1385 | 0.1406 | 0.1355 | 0.1343 | 0.1417 | 0.1315 | 0.1209 | 0.1144 | 0.1018 | 0.1020 | 0.0990 | 1982 | 0.0990 |
| 1983 | 0.1057 | 0.1010 | 0.1048 | 0.0997 | 0.1059 | 0.1080 | 0.1168 | 0.1175 | 0.1108 | 0.1131 | 0.1127 | 0.1141 | 1983 | 0.1141 |
| 1984 | 0.1137 | 0.1181 | 0.1219 | 0.1251 | 0.1363 | 0.1365 | 0.1274 | 0.1276 | 0.1242 | 0.1154 | 0.1121 | 0.1104 | 1984 | 0.1104 |
| 1985 | 0.1081 | 0.1152 | 0.1131 | 0.1084 | 0.0974 | 0.0963 | 0.1002 | 0.0982 | 0.0973 | 0.0949 | 0.0911 | 0.0855 | 1985 | 0.0855 |
| 1986 | 0.0870 | 0.0815 | 0.0743 | 0.0737 | 0.0816 | 0.0756 | 0.0728 | 0.0668 | 0.0718 | 0.0687 | 0.0669 | 0.0685 | 1986 | 0.0685 |
| 1987 | 0.0685 | 0.0683 | 0.0708 | 0.0793 | 0.0821 | 0.0806 | 0.0818 | 0.0849 | 0.0912 | 0.0844 | 0.0840 | 0.0832 | 1987 | 0.0832 |
| 1988 | 0.0782 | 0.0768 | 0.0807 | 0.0836 | 0.0870 | 0.0839 | 0.0871 | 0.0895 | 0.0859 | 0.0837 | 0.0892 | 0.0917 | 1988 | 0.0917 |
| 1989 | 0.0896 | 0.0927 | 0.0934 | 0.0895 | 0.0860 | 0.0791 | 0.0745 | 0.0834 | 0.0833 | 0.0786 | 0.0779 | 0.0794 | 1989 | 0.0794 |
| 1990 | 0.0842 | 0.0855 | 0.0871 | 0.0907 | 0.0864 | 0.0843 | 0.0819 | 0.0859 | 0.0851 | 0.0826 | 0.0795 | 0.0770 | 1990 | 0.0770 |
| 1991 | 0.0772 | 0.0774 | 0.0783 | 0.0772 | 0.0773 | 0.0793 | 0.0778 | 0.0732 | 0.0693 | 0.0673 | 0.0653 | 0.0597 | 1991 | 0.0597 |
| 1992 | 0.0683 | 0.0690 | 0.0720 | 0.0711 | 0.0674 | 0.0647 | 0.0604 | 0.0581 | 0.0547 | 0.0601 | 0.0634 | 0.0611 | 1992 | 0.0611 |
| 1993 | 0.0588 | 0.0547 | 0.0549 | 0.0540 | 0.0551 | 0.0517 | 0.0526 | 0.0486 | 0.0483 | 0.0488 | 0.0519 | 0.0522 | 1993 | 0.0522 |
| 1994 | 0.0515 | 0.0575 | 0.0638 | 0.0670 | 0.0682 | 0.0699 | 0.0675 | 0.0683 | 0.0730 | 0.0749 | 0.0778 | 0.0780 | 1994 | 0.0780 |
| 1995 | 0.0754 | 0.0708 | 0.0707 | 0.0685 | 0.0606 | 0.0598 | 0.0616 | 0.0606 | 0.0601 | 0.0582 | 0.0553 | 0.0538 | 1995 | 0.0538 |
| 1996 | 0.0528 | 0.0573 | 0.0614 | 0.0640 | 0.0663 | 0.0645 | 0.0654 | 0.0670 | 0.0643 | 0.0607 | 0.0578 | 0.0616 | 1996 | 0.0616 |
| 1997 | 0.0629 | 0.0639 | 0.0677 | 0.0656 | 0.0650 | 0.0639 | 0.0589 | 0.0624 | 0.0601 | 0.0576 | 0.0587 | 0.0573 | 1997 | 0.0573 |
| 1998 | 0.0545 | 0.0562 | 0.0567 | 0.0564 | 0.0558 | 0.0551 | 0.0556 | 0.0503 | 0.0435 | 0.0434 | 0.0467 | 0.0468 | 1998 | 0.0468 |
| 1999 | 0.0467 | 0.0535 | 0.0526 | 0.0532 | 0.0576 | 0.0581 | 0.0593 | 0.0602 | 0.0590 | 0.0604 | 0.0619 | 0.0645 | 1999 | 0.0645 |
| 2000 | 0.0675 | 0.0669 | 0.0636 | 0.0657 | 0.0658 | 0.0626 | 0.0621 | 0.0601 | 0.0589 | 0.0582 | 0.0551 | 0.0507 | 2000 | 0.0507 |

## Table A-14

## U.S. Treasury Bills: Total Returns

from January 1926 to December 1970

| Year | Jan | Feb | Mar | Apr | May | Jun | Jul | Aug | Sep | Oct | Nov | Dec | Year | Jan-Dec* |
|------|-----|-----|-----|-----|-----|-----|-----|-----|-----|-----|-----|-----|------|----------|
| 1926 | 0.0034 | 0.0027 | 0.0030 | 0.0034 | 0.0001 | 0.0035 | 0.0022 | 0.0025 | 0.0023 | 0.0032 | 0.0031 | 0.0028 | 1926 | 0.0327 |
| 1927 | 0.0025 | 0.0026 | 0.0030 | 0.0025 | 0.0030 | 0.0026 | 0.0030 | 0.0028 | 0.0021 | 0.0025 | 0.0021 | 0.0022 | 1927 | 0.0312 |
| 1928 | 0.0025 | 0.0033 | 0.0029 | 0.0022 | 0.0032 | 0.0031 | 0.0032 | 0.0032 | 0.0027 | 0.0041 | 0.0038 | 0.0006 | 1928 | 0.0356 |
| 1929 | 0.0034 | 0.0036 | 0.0034 | 0.0036 | 0.0044 | 0.0052 | 0.0033 | 0.0040 | 0.0035 | 0.0046 | 0.0037 | 0.0037 | 1929 | 0.0475 |
| 1930 | 0.0014 | 0.0030 | 0.0035 | 0.0021 | 0.0026 | 0.0027 | 0.0020 | 0.0009 | 0.0022 | 0.0009 | 0.0013 | 0.0014 | 1930 | 0.0241 |
| 1931 | 0.0015 | 0.0004 | 0.0013 | 0.0008 | 0.0009 | 0.0008 | 0.0006 | 0.0003 | 0.0003 | 0.0010 | 0.0017 | 0.0012 | 1931 | 0.0107 |
| 1932 | 0.0023 | 0.0023 | 0.0016 | 0.0011 | 0.0006 | 0.0002 | 0.0003 | 0.0003 | 0.0003 | 0.0002 | 0.0002 | 0.0001 | 1932 | 0.0096 |
| 1933 | 0.0001 | −0.0003 | 0.0004 | 0.0010 | 0.0004 | 0.0002 | 0.0002 | 0.0003 | 0.0002 | 0.0001 | 0.0002 | 0.0002 | 1933 | 0.0030 |
| 1934 | 0.0005 | 0.0002 | 0.0002 | 0.0001 | 0.0001 | 0.0001 | 0.0001 | 0.0001 | 0.0001 | 0.0001 | 0.0001 | 0.0001 | 1934 | 0.0016 |
| 1935 | 0.0001 | 0.0002 | 0.0001 | 0.0001 | 0.0001 | 0.0001 | 0.0001 | 0.0001 | 0.0001 | 0.0001 | 0.0002 | 0.0001 | 1935 | 0.0017 |
| 1936 | 0.0001 | 0.0001 | 0.0002 | 0.0002 | 0.0002 | 0.0003 | 0.0001 | 0.0002 | 0.0001 | 0.0002 | 0.0001 | 0.0000 | 1936 | 0.0018 |
| 1937 | 0.0001 | 0.0002 | 0.0001 | 0.0003 | 0.0006 | 0.0003 | 0.0003 | 0.0002 | 0.0004 | 0.0002 | 0.0002 | 0.0000 | 1937 | 0.0031 |
| 1938 | 0.0000 | 0.0000 | −0.0001 | 0.0001 | 0.0000 | 0.0000 | −0.0001 | 0.0000 | 0.0002 | 0.0001 | −0.0006 | 0.0000 | 1938 | −0.0002 |
| 1939 | −0.0001 | 0.0001 | −0.0001 | 0.0000 | 0.0001 | 0.0001 | 0.0000 | −0.0001 | 0.0001 | 0.0000 | 0.0000 | 0.0000 | 1939 | 0.0002 |
| 1940 | 0.0000 | 0.0000 | 0.0000 | 0.0000 | −0.0002 | 0.0000 | 0.0001 | −0.0001 | 0.0000 | 0.0000 | 0.0000 | 0.0000 | 1940 | 0.0000 |
| 1941 | −0.0001 | −0.0001 | 0.0001 | −0.0001 | 0.0000 | 0.0000 | 0.0003 | 0.0001 | 0.0001 | 0.0000 | 0.0000 | 0.0001 | 1941 | 0.0006 |
| 1942 | 0.0002 | 0.0001 | 0.0001 | 0.0001 | 0.0003 | 0.0002 | 0.0003 | 0.0003 | 0.0003 | 0.0003 | 0.0003 | 0.0003 | 1942 | 0.0027 |
| 1943 | 0.0003 | 0.0003 | 0.0003 | 0.0003 | 0.0003 | 0.0003 | 0.0003 | 0.0003 | 0.0003 | 0.0003 | 0.0003 | 0.0003 | 1943 | 0.0035 |
| 1944 | 0.0003 | 0.0003 | 0.0002 | 0.0003 | 0.0003 | 0.0003 | 0.0003 | 0.0003 | 0.0002 | 0.0003 | 0.0003 | 0.0002 | 1944 | 0.0033 |
| 1945 | 0.0003 | 0.0002 | 0.0002 | 0.0003 | 0.0003 | 0.0002 | 0.0003 | 0.0003 | 0.0003 | 0.0003 | 0.0002 | 0.0003 | 1945 | 0.0033 |
| 1946 | 0.0003 | 0.0003 | 0.0003 | 0.0003 | 0.0003 | 0.0003 | 0.0003 | 0.0003 | 0.0003 | 0.0003 | 0.0003 | 0.0003 | 1946 | 0.0035 |
| 1947 | 0.0003 | 0.0003 | 0.0003 | 0.0003 | 0.0003 | 0.0003 | 0.0003 | 0.0003 | 0.0006 | 0.0006 | 0.0006 | 0.0008 | 1947 | 0.0050 |
| 1948 | 0.0007 | 0.0007 | 0.0009 | 0.0008 | 0.0008 | 0.0009 | 0.0008 | 0.0009 | 0.0004 | 0.0004 | 0.0004 | 0.0004 | 1948 | 0.0081 |
| 1949 | 0.0010 | 0.0009 | 0.0010 | 0.0009 | 0.0010 | 0.0010 | 0.0009 | 0.0009 | 0.0009 | 0.0009 | 0.0008 | 0.0009 | 1949 | 0.0110 |
| 1950 | 0.0009 | 0.0009 | 0.0010 | 0.0009 | 0.0010 | 0.0010 | 0.0010 | 0.0010 | 0.0010 | 0.0012 | 0.0011 | 0.0011 | 1950 | 0.0120 |
| 1951 | 0.0013 | 0.0010 | 0.0011 | 0.0013 | 0.0012 | 0.0012 | 0.0013 | 0.0013 | 0.0012 | 0.0016 | 0.0011 | 0.0012 | 1951 | 0.0149 |
| 1952 | 0.0015 | 0.0012 | 0.0011 | 0.0012 | 0.0013 | 0.0015 | 0.0015 | 0.0015 | 0.0016 | 0.0014 | 0.0010 | 0.0016 | 1952 | 0.0166 |
| 1953 | 0.0016 | 0.0014 | 0.0018 | 0.0016 | 0.0017 | 0.0018 | 0.0015 | 0.0017 | 0.0016 | 0.0013 | 0.0008 | 0.0013 | 1953 | 0.0182 |
| 1954 | 0.0011 | 0.0007 | 0.0008 | 0.0009 | 0.0005 | 0.0006 | 0.0005 | 0.0005 | 0.0009 | 0.0007 | 0.0006 | 0.0008 | 1954 | 0.0086 |
| 1955 | 0.0008 | 0.0009 | 0.0010 | 0.0010 | 0.0014 | 0.0010 | 0.0010 | 0.0016 | 0.0016 | 0.0018 | 0.0017 | 0.0018 | 1955 | 0.0157 |
| 1956 | 0.0022 | 0.0019 | 0.0015 | 0.0019 | 0.0023 | 0.0020 | 0.0022 | 0.0017 | 0.0018 | 0.0025 | 0.0020 | 0.0024 | 1956 | 0.0246 |
| 1957 | 0.0027 | 0.0024 | 0.0023 | 0.0025 | 0.0026 | 0.0024 | 0.0030 | 0.0025 | 0.0026 | 0.0029 | 0.0028 | 0.0024 | 1957 | 0.0314 |
| 1958 | 0.0028 | 0.0012 | 0.0009 | 0.0008 | 0.0011 | 0.0003 | 0.0007 | 0.0004 | 0.0019 | 0.0018 | 0.0011 | 0.0022 | 1958 | 0.0154 |
| 1959 | 0.0021 | 0.0019 | 0.0022 | 0.0020 | 0.0022 | 0.0025 | 0.0025 | 0.0019 | 0.0031 | 0.0030 | 0.0026 | 0.0034 | 1959 | 0.0295 |
| 1960 | 0.0033 | 0.0029 | 0.0035 | 0.0019 | 0.0027 | 0.0024 | 0.0013 | 0.0017 | 0.0016 | 0.0022 | 0.0013 | 0.0016 | 1960 | 0.0266 |
| 1961 | 0.0019 | 0.0014 | 0.0020 | 0.0017 | 0.0018 | 0.0020 | 0.0018 | 0.0014 | 0.0017 | 0.0019 | 0.0015 | 0.0019 | 1961 | 0.0213 |
| 1962 | 0.0024 | 0.0020 | 0.0020 | 0.0022 | 0.0024 | 0.0020 | 0.0027 | 0.0023 | 0.0021 | 0.0026 | 0.0020 | 0.0023 | 1962 | 0.0273 |
| 1963 | 0.0025 | 0.0023 | 0.0023 | 0.0025 | 0.0024 | 0.0023 | 0.0027 | 0.0025 | 0.0027 | 0.0029 | 0.0027 | 0.0029 | 1963 | 0.0312 |
| 1964 | 0.0030 | 0.0026 | 0.0031 | 0.0029 | 0.0026 | 0.0030 | 0.0030 | 0.0028 | 0.0028 | 0.0029 | 0.0029 | 0.0031 | 1964 | 0.0354 |
| 1965 | 0.0028 | 0.0030 | 0.0036 | 0.0031 | 0.0031 | 0.0035 | 0.0031 | 0.0033 | 0.0031 | 0.0031 | 0.0035 | 0.0033 | 1965 | 0.0393 |
| 1966 | 0.0038 | 0.0035 | 0.0038 | 0.0034 | 0.0041 | 0.0038 | 0.0035 | 0.0041 | 0.0040 | 0.0045 | 0.0040 | 0.0040 | 1966 | 0.0476 |
| 1967 | 0.0043 | 0.0036 | 0.0039 | 0.0032 | 0.0033 | 0.0027 | 0.0032 | 0.0031 | 0.0032 | 0.0039 | 0.0036 | 0.0033 | 1967 | 0.0421 |
| 1968 | 0.0040 | 0.0039 | 0.0038 | 0.0043 | 0.0045 | 0.0043 | 0.0048 | 0.0042 | 0.0043 | 0.0044 | 0.0042 | 0.0043 | 1968 | 0.0521 |
| 1969 | 0.0053 | 0.0046 | 0.0046 | 0.0053 | 0.0048 | 0.0051 | 0.0053 | 0.0050 | 0.0062 | 0.0060 | 0.0052 | 0.0064 | 1969 | 0.0658 |
| 1970 | 0.0060 | 0.0062 | 0.0057 | 0.0050 | 0.0053 | 0.0058 | 0.0052 | 0.0053 | 0.0054 | 0.0046 | 0.0046 | 0.0042 | 1970 | 0.0652 |

* Compound annual return

## Table A-14 (continued)

### U.S. Treasury Bills: Total Returns

from January 1971 to December 2000

| Year | Jan | Feb | Mar | Apr | May | Jun | Jul | Aug | Sep | Oct | Nov | Dec | Year | Jan-Dec* |
|------|-----|-----|-----|-----|-----|-----|-----|-----|-----|-----|-----|-----|------|----------|
| 1971 | 0.0038 | 0.0033 | 0.0030 | 0.0028 | 0.0029 | 0.0037 | 0.0040 | 0.0047 | 0.0037 | 0.0037 | 0.0037 | 0.0037 | 1971 | 0.0439 |
| 1972 | 0.0029 | 0.0025 | 0.0027 | 0.0029 | 0.0030 | 0.0029 | 0.0031 | 0.0029 | 0.0034 | 0.0040 | 0.0037 | 0.0037 | 1972 | 0.0384 |
| 1973 | 0.0044 | 0.0041 | 0.0046 | 0.0052 | 0.0051 | 0.0051 | 0.0064 | 0.0070 | 0.0068 | 0.0065 | 0.0056 | 0.0064 | 1973 | 0.0693 |
| 1974 | 0.0063 | 0.0058 | 0.0056 | 0.0075 | 0.0075 | 0.0060 | 0.0070 | 0.0060 | 0.0081 | 0.0051 | 0.0054 | 0.0070 | 1974 | 0.0800 |
| 1975 | 0.0058 | 0.0043 | 0.0041 | 0.0044 | 0.0044 | 0.0041 | 0.0048 | 0.0048 | 0.0053 | 0.0056 | 0.0041 | 0.0048 | 1975 | 0.0580 |
| 1976 | 0.0047 | 0.0034 | 0.0040 | 0.0042 | 0.0037 | 0.0043 | 0.0047 | 0.0042 | 0.0044 | 0.0041 | 0.0040 | 0.0040 | 1976 | 0.0508 |
| 1977 | 0.0036 | 0.0035 | 0.0038 | 0.0038 | 0.0037 | 0.0040 | 0.0042 | 0.0044 | 0.0043 | 0.0049 | 0.0050 | 0.0049 | 1977 | 0.0512 |
| 1978 | 0.0049 | 0.0046 | 0.0053 | 0.0054 | 0.0051 | 0.0054 | 0.0056 | 0.0055 | 0.0062 | 0.0068 | 0.0070 | 0.0078 | 1978 | 0.0718 |
| 1979 | 0.0077 | 0.0073 | 0.0081 | 0.0080 | 0.0082 | 0.0081 | 0.0077 | 0.0077 | 0.0083 | 0.0087 | 0.0099 | 0.0095 | 1979 | 0.1038 |
| 1980 | 0.0080 | 0.0089 | 0.0121 | 0.0126 | 0.0081 | 0.0061 | 0.0053 | 0.0064 | 0.0075 | 0.0095 | 0.0096 | 0.0131 | 1980 | 0.1124 |
| 1981 | 0.0104 | 0.0107 | 0.0121 | 0.0108 | 0.0115 | 0.0135 | 0.0124 | 0.0128 | 0.0124 | 0.0121 | 0.0107 | 0.0087 | 1981 | 0.1471 |
| 1982 | 0.0080 | 0.0092 | 0.0098 | 0.0113 | 0.0106 | 0.0096 | 0.0105 | 0.0076 | 0.0051 | 0.0059 | 0.0063 | 0.0067 | 1982 | 0.1054 |
| 1983 | 0.0069 | 0.0062 | 0.0063 | 0.0071 | 0.0069 | 0.0067 | 0.0074 | 0.0076 | 0.0076 | 0.0076 | 0.0070 | 0.0073 | 1983 | 0.0880 |
| 1984 | 0.0076 | 0.0071 | 0.0073 | 0.0081 | 0.0078 | 0.0075 | 0.0082 | 0.0083 | 0.0086 | 0.0100 | 0.0073 | 0.0064 | 1984 | 0.0985 |
| 1985 | 0.0065 | 0.0058 | 0.0062 | 0.0072 | 0.0066 | 0.0055 | 0.0062 | 0.0055 | 0.0060 | 0.0065 | 0.0061 | 0.0065 | 1985 | 0.0772 |
| 1986 | 0.0056 | 0.0053 | 0.0060 | 0.0052 | 0.0049 | 0.0052 | 0.0052 | 0.0046 | 0.0045 | 0.0046 | 0.0039 | 0.0049 | 1986 | 0.0616 |
| 1987 | 0.0042 | 0.0043 | 0.0047 | 0.0044 | 0.0038 | 0.0048 | 0.0046 | 0.0047 | 0.0045 | 0.0060 | 0.0035 | 0.0039 | 1987 | 0.0547 |
| 1988 | 0.0029 | 0.0046 | 0.0044 | 0.0046 | 0.0051 | 0.0049 | 0.0051 | 0.0059 | 0.0062 | 0.0061 | 0.0057 | 0.0063 | 1988 | 0.0635 |
| 1989 | 0.0055 | 0.0061 | 0.0067 | 0.0067 | 0.0079 | 0.0071 | 0.0070 | 0.0074 | 0.0065 | 0.0068 | 0.0069 | 0.0061 | 1989 | 0.0837 |
| 1990 | 0.0057 | 0.0057 | 0.0064 | 0.0069 | 0.0068 | 0.0063 | 0.0068 | 0.0066 | 0.0060 | 0.0068 | 0.0057 | 0.0060 | 1990 | 0.0781 |
| 1991 | 0.0052 | 0.0048 | 0.0044 | 0.0053 | 0.0047 | 0.0042 | 0.0049 | 0.0046 | 0.0046 | 0.0042 | 0.0039 | 0.0038 | 1991 | 0.0560 |
| 1992 | 0.0034 | 0.0028 | 0.0034 | 0.0032 | 0.0028 | 0.0032 | 0.0031 | 0.0026 | 0.0026 | 0.0023 | 0.0023 | 0.0028 | 1992 | 0.0351 |
| 1993 | 0.0023 | 0.0022 | 0.0025 | 0.0024 | 0.0022 | 0.0025 | 0.0024 | 0.0025 | 0.0026 | 0.0022 | 0.0025 | 0.0023 | 1993 | 0.0290 |
| 1994 | 0.0025 | 0.0021 | 0.0027 | 0.0027 | 0.0032 | 0.0031 | 0.0028 | 0.0037 | 0.0037 | 0.0038 | 0.0037 | 0.0044 | 1994 | 0.0390 |
| 1995 | 0.0042 | 0.0040 | 0.0046 | 0.0044 | 0.0054 | 0.0047 | 0.0045 | 0.0047 | 0.0043 | 0.0047 | 0.0042 | 0.0049 | 1995 | 0.0560 |
| 1996 | 0.0043 | 0.0039 | 0.0039 | 0.0046 | 0.0042 | 0.0040 | 0.0045 | 0.0041 | 0.0044 | 0.0042 | 0.0041 | 0.0046 | 1996 | 0.0521 |
| 1997 | 0.0045 | 0.0039 | 0.0043 | 0.0043 | 0.0049 | 0.0037 | 0.0043 | 0.0041 | 0.0044 | 0.0042 | 0.0039 | 0.0048 | 1997 | 0.0526 |
| 1998 | 0.0043 | 0.0039 | 0.0039 | 0.0043 | 0.0040 | 0.0041 | 0.0040 | 0.0043 | 0.0046 | 0.0032 | 0.0031 | 0.0038 | 1998 | 0.0486 |
| 1999 | 0.0035 | 0.0035 | 0.0043 | 0.0037 | 0.0034 | 0.0040 | 0.0038 | 0.0039 | 0.0039 | 0.0039 | 0.0036 | 0.0044 | 1999 | 0.0468 |
| 2000 | 0.0041 | 0.0043 | 0.0047 | 0.0046 | 0.0050 | 0.0040 | 0.0048 | 0.0050 | 0.0051 | 0.0056 | 0.0051 | 0.0050 | 2000 | 0.0589 |

* Compound annual return

## Table A-15

**Inflation**

from January 1926 to December 1970

| Year | Jan | Feb | Mar | Apr | May | Jun | Jul | Aug | Sep | Oct | Nov | Dec | Year | Jan-Dec* |
|------|------|------|------|------|------|------|------|------|------|------|------|------|------|----------|
| 1926 | 0.0000 | −0.0037 | −0.0056 | 0.0094 | −0.0056 | −0.0075 | −0.0094 | −0.0057 | 0.0057 | 0.0038 | 0.0038 | 0.0000 | 1926 | −0.0149 |
| 1927 | −0.0076 | −0.0076 | −0.0058 | 0.0000 | 0.0077 | 0.0096 | −0.0190 | −0.0058 | 0.0058 | 0.0058 | −0.0019 | −0.0019 | 1927 | −0.0208 |
| 1928 | −0.0019 | −0.0097 | 0.0000 | 0.0020 | 0.0058 | −0.0078 | 0.0000 | 0.0020 | 0.0078 | −0.0019 | −0.0019 | −0.0039 | 1928 | −0.0097 |
| 1929 | −0.0019 | −0.0020 | −0.0039 | −0.0039 | 0.0059 | 0.0039 | 0.0098 | 0.0039 | −0.0019 | 0.0000 | −0.0019 | −0.0058 | 1929 | 0.0020 |
| 1930 | −0.0039 | −0.0039 | −0.0059 | 0.0059 | −0.0059 | −0.0059 | −0.0139 | −0.0060 | 0.0061 | −0.0060 | −0.0081 | −0.0143 | 1930 | −0.0603 |
| 1931 | −0.0145 | −0.0147 | −0.0064 | −0.0064 | −0.0108 | −0.0109 | −0.0022 | −0.0022 | −0.0044 | −0.0067 | −0.0112 | −0.0091 | 1931 | −0.0952 |
| 1932 | −0.0206 | −0.0140 | −0.0047 | −0.0071 | −0.0144 | −0.0073 | 0.0000 | −0.0123 | −0.0050 | −0.0075 | −0.0050 | −0.0101 | 1932 | −0.1030 |
| 1933 | −0.0153 | −0.0155 | −0.0079 | −0.0027 | 0.0027 | 0.0106 | 0.0289 | 0.0102 | 0.0000 | 0.0000 | 0.0000 | −0.0051 | 1933 | 0.0051 |
| 1934 | 0.0051 | 0.0076 | 0.0000 | −0.0025 | 0.0025 | 0.0025 | 0.0000 | 0.0025 | 0.0150 | −0.0074 | −0.0025 | −0.0025 | 1934 | 0.0203 |
| 1935 | 0.0149 | 0.0074 | −0.0024 | 0.0098 | −0.0048 | −0.0024 | −0.0049 | 0.0000 | 0.0049 | 0.0000 | 0.0049 | 0.0024 | 1935 | 0.0299 |
| 1936 | 0.0000 | −0.0048 | −0.0049 | 0.0000 | 0.0000 | 0.0098 | 0.0048 | 0.0072 | 0.0024 | −0.0024 | 0.0000 | 0.0000 | 1936 | 0.0121 |
| 1937 | 0.0072 | 0.0024 | 0.0071 | 0.0047 | 0.0047 | 0.0023 | 0.0046 | 0.0023 | 0.0092 | −0.0046 | −0.0069 | −0.0023 | 1937 | 0.0310 |
| 1938 | −0.0139 | −0.0094 | 0.0000 | 0.0047 | −0.0047 | 0.0000 | 0.0024 | −0.0024 | 0.0000 | −0.0047 | −0.0024 | 0.0024 | 1938 | −0.0278 |
| 1939 | −0.0048 | −0.0048 | −0.0024 | −0.0024 | 0.0000 | 0.0000 | 0.0000 | 0.0000 | 0.0193 | −0.0047 | 0.0000 | −0.0048 | 1939 | −0.0048 |
| 1940 | −0.0024 | 0.0072 | −0.0024 | 0.0000 | 0.0024 | 0.0024 | −0.0024 | −0.0024 | 0.0024 | 0.0000 | 0.0000 | 0.0048 | 1940 | 0.0096 |
| 1941 | 0.0000 | 0.0000 | 0.0047 | 0.0094 | 0.0070 | 0.0186 | 0.0046 | 0.0091 | 0.0180 | 0.0110 | 0.0087 | 0.0022 | 1941 | 0.0972 |
| 1942 | 0.0130 | 0.0085 | 0.0127 | 0.0063 | 0.0104 | 0.0021 | 0.0041 | 0.0061 | 0.0020 | 0.0101 | 0.0060 | 0.0080 | 1942 | 0.0929 |
| 1943 | 0.0000 | 0.0020 | 0.0158 | 0.0116 | 0.0077 | −0.0019 | −0.0076 | −0.0038 | 0.0039 | 0.0038 | −0.0019 | 0.0019 | 1943 | 0.0316 |
| 1944 | −0.0019 | −0.0019 | 0.0000 | 0.0058 | 0.0038 | 0.0019 | 0.0057 | 0.0038 | 0.0000 | 0.0000 | 0.0000 | 0.0038 | 1944 | 0.0211 |
| 1945 | 0.0000 | −0.0019 | 0.0000 | 0.0019 | 0.0075 | 0.0093 | 0.0018 | 0.0000 | −0.0037 | 0.0000 | 0.0037 | 0.0037 | 1945 | 0.0225 |
| 1946 | 0.0000 | −0.0037 | 0.0074 | 0.0055 | 0.0055 | 0.0109 | 0.0590 | 0.0220 | 0.0116 | 0.0196 | 0.0240 | 0.0078 | 1946 | 0.1816 |
| 1947 | 0.0000 | −0.0016 | 0.0218 | 0.0000 | −0.0030 | 0.0076 | 0.0091 | 0.0105 | 0.0238 | 0.0000 | 0.0058 | 0.0130 | 1947 | 0.0901 |
| 1948 | 0.0114 | −0.0085 | −0.0028 | 0.0142 | 0.0070 | 0.0070 | 0.0125 | 0.0041 | 0.0000 | −0.0041 | −0.0068 | −0.0069 | 1948 | 0.0271 |
| 1949 | −0.0014 | −0.0111 | 0.0028 | 0.0014 | −0.0014 | 0.0014 | −0.0070 | 0.0028 | 0.0042 | −0.0056 | 0.0014 | −0.0056 | 1949 | −0.0180 |
| 1950 | −0.0042 | −0.0028 | 0.0043 | 0.0014 | 0.0042 | 0.0056 | 0.0098 | 0.0083 | 0.0069 | 0.0055 | 0.0041 | 0.0135 | 1950 | 0.0579 |
| 1951 | 0.0160 | 0.0118 | 0.0039 | 0.0013 | 0.0039 | −0.0013 | 0.0013 | 0.0000 | 0.0064 | 0.0051 | 0.0051 | 0.0038 | 1951 | 0.0587 |
| 1952 | 0.0000 | −0.0063 | 0.0000 | 0.0038 | 0.0013 | 0.0025 | 0.0076 | 0.0012 | −0.0012 | 0.0012 | 0.0000 | −0.0012 | 1952 | 0.0088 |
| 1953 | −0.0025 | −0.0050 | 0.0025 | 0.0013 | 0.0025 | 0.0038 | 0.0025 | 0.0025 | 0.0012 | 0.0025 | −0.0037 | −0.0012 | 1953 | 0.0062 |
| 1954 | 0.0025 | −0.0012 | −0.0012 | −0.0025 | 0.0037 | 0.0012 | 0.0000 | −0.0012 | −0.0025 | −0.0025 | 0.0012 | −0.0025 | 1954 | −0.0050 |
| 1955 | 0.0000 | 0.0000 | 0.0000 | 0.0000 | 0.0000 | 0.0000 | 0.0037 | −0.0025 | 0.0037 | 0.0000 | 0.0012 | −0.0025 | 1955 | 0.0037 |
| 1956 | −0.0012 | 0.0000 | 0.0012 | 0.0012 | 0.0050 | 0.0062 | 0.0074 | −0.0012 | 0.0012 | 0.0061 | 0.0000 | 0.0024 | 1956 | 0.0286 |
| 1957 | 0.0012 | 0.0036 | 0.0024 | 0.0036 | 0.0024 | 0.0060 | 0.0047 | 0.0012 | 0.0012 | 0.0000 | 0.0035 | 0.0000 | 1957 | 0.0302 |
| 1958 | 0.0059 | 0.0012 | 0.0070 | 0.0023 | 0.0000 | 0.0012 | 0.0012 | −0.0012 | 0.0000 | 0.0000 | 0.0012 | −0.0012 | 1958 | 0.0176 |
| 1959 | 0.0012 | −0.0012 | 0.0000 | 0.0012 | 0.0012 | 0.0046 | 0.0023 | −0.0011 | 0.0034 | 0.0034 | 0.0000 | 0.0000 | 1959 | 0.0150 |
| 1960 | −0.0011 | 0.0011 | 0.0000 | 0.0057 | 0.0000 | 0.0023 | 0.0000 | 0.0000 | 0.0011 | 0.0045 | 0.0011 | 0.0000 | 1960 | 0.0148 |
| 1961 | 0.0000 | 0.0000 | 0.0000 | 0.0000 | 0.0000 | 0.0011 | 0.0045 | −0.0011 | 0.0022 | 0.0000 | 0.0000 | 0.0000 | 1961 | 0.0067 |
| 1962 | 0.0000 | 0.0022 | 0.0022 | 0.0022 | 0.0000 | 0.0000 | 0.0022 | 0.0000 | 0.0055 | −0.0011 | 0.0000 | −0.0011 | 1962 | 0.0122 |
| 1963 | 0.0011 | 0.0011 | 0.0011 | 0.0000 | 0.0000 | 0.0044 | 0.0044 | 0.0000 | 0.0000 | 0.0011 | 0.0011 | 0.0022 | 1963 | 0.0165 |
| 1964 | 0.0011 | −0.0011 | 0.0011 | 0.0011 | 0.0000 | 0.0022 | 0.0022 | −0.0011 | 0.0022 | 0.0011 | 0.0021 | 0.0011 | 1964 | 0.0119 |
| 1965 | 0.0000 | 0.0000 | 0.0011 | 0.0032 | 0.0021 | 0.0053 | 0.0011 | −0.0021 | 0.0021 | 0.0011 | 0.0021 | 0.0032 | 1965 | 0.0192 |
| 1966 | 0.0000 | 0.0063 | 0.0031 | 0.0042 | 0.0010 | 0.0031 | 0.0031 | 0.0051 | 0.0020 | 0.0041 | 0.0000 | 0.0010 | 1966 | 0.0335 |
| 1967 | 0.0000 | 0.0010 | 0.0020 | 0.0020 | 0.0030 | 0.0030 | 0.0050 | 0.0030 | 0.0020 | 0.0030 | 0.0030 | 0.0030 | 1967 | 0.0304 |
| 1968 | 0.0039 | 0.0029 | 0.0049 | 0.0029 | 0.0029 | 0.0058 | 0.0048 | 0.0029 | 0.0029 | 0.0057 | 0.0038 | 0.0028 | 1968 | 0.0472 |
| 1969 | 0.0028 | 0.0037 | 0.0084 | 0.0065 | 0.0028 | 0.0064 | 0.0046 | 0.0045 | 0.0045 | 0.0036 | 0.0054 | 0.0062 | 1969 | 0.0611 |
| 1970 | 0.0035 | 0.0053 | 0.0053 | 0.0061 | 0.0043 | 0.0052 | 0.0034 | 0.0017 | 0.0051 | 0.0051 | 0.0034 | 0.0051 | 1970 | 0.0549 |

* Compound annual return

# Table A-15 (continued)

## Inflation

from January 1971 to December 2000

| Year | Jan | Feb | Mar | Apr | May | Jun | Jul | Aug | Sep | Oct | Nov | Dec | Year | Jan-Dec* |
|------|-----|-----|-----|-----|-----|-----|-----|-----|-----|-----|-----|-----|------|----------|
| 1971 | 0.0008 | 0.0017 | 0.0033 | 0.0033 | 0.0050 | 0.0058 | 0.0025 | 0.0025 | 0.0008 | 0.0016 | 0.0016 | 0.0041 | 1971 | 0.0336 |
| 1972 | 0.0008 | 0.0049 | 0.0016 | 0.0024 | 0.0032 | 0.0024 | 0.0040 | 0.0016 | 0.0040 | 0.0032 | 0.0024 | 0.0032 | 1972 | 0.0341 |
| 1973 | 0.0031 | 0.0070 | 0.0093 | 0.0069 | 0.0061 | 0.0068 | 0.0023 | 0.0181 | 0.0030 | 0.0081 | 0.0073 | 0.0065 | 1973 | 0.0880 |
| 1974 | 0.0087 | 0.0129 | 0.0113 | 0.0056 | 0.0111 | 0.0096 | 0.0075 | 0.0128 | 0.0120 | 0.0086 | 0.0085 | 0.0071 | 1974 | 0.1220 |
| 1975 | 0.0045 | 0.0070 | 0.0038 | 0.0051 | 0.0044 | 0.0082 | 0.0106 | 0.0031 | 0.0049 | 0.0061 | 0.0061 | 0.0042 | 1975 | 0.0701 |
| 1976 | 0.0024 | 0.0024 | 0.0024 | 0.0042 | 0.0059 | 0.0053 | 0.0059 | 0.0047 | 0.0041 | 0.0041 | 0.0029 | 0.0029 | 1976 | 0.0481 |
| 1977 | 0.0057 | 0.0103 | 0.0062 | 0.0079 | 0.0056 | 0.0066 | 0.0044 | 0.0038 | 0.0038 | 0.0027 | 0.0049 | 0.0038 | 1977 | 0.0677 |
| 1978 | 0.0054 | 0.0069 | 0.0069 | 0.0090 | 0.0099 | 0.0103 | 0.0072 | 0.0051 | 0.0071 | 0.0080 | 0.0055 | 0.0055 | 1978 | 0.0903 |
| 1979 | 0.0089 | 0.0117 | 0.0097 | 0.0115 | 0.0123 | 0.0093 | 0.0130 | 0.0100 | 0.0104 | 0.0090 | 0.0093 | 0.0105 | 1979 | 0.1331 |
| 1980 | 0.0144 | 0.0137 | 0.0144 | 0.0113 | 0.0099 | 0.0110 | 0.0008 | 0.0065 | 0.0092 | 0.0087 | 0.0091 | 0.0086 | 1980 | 0.1240 |
| 1981 | 0.0081 | 0.0104 | 0.0072 | 0.0064 | 0.0082 | 0.0086 | 0.0114 | 0.0077 | 0.0101 | 0.0021 | 0.0029 | 0.0029 | 1981 | 0.0894 |
| 1982 | 0.0036 | 0.0032 | −0.0011 | 0.0042 | 0.0098 | 0.0122 | 0.0055 | 0.0021 | 0.0017 | 0.0027 | −0.0017 | −0.0041 | 1982 | 0.0387 |
| 1983 | 0.0024 | 0.0003 | 0.0007 | 0.0072 | 0.0054 | 0.0034 | 0.0040 | 0.0033 | 0.0050 | 0.0027 | 0.0017 | 0.0013 | 1983 | 0.0380 |
| 1984 | 0.0056 | 0.0046 | 0.0023 | 0.0049 | 0.0029 | 0.0032 | 0.0032 | 0.0042 | 0.0048 | 0.0025 | 0.0000 | 0.0006 | 1984 | 0.0395 |
| 1985 | 0.0019 | 0.0041 | 0.0044 | 0.0041 | 0.0037 | 0.0031 | 0.0016 | 0.0022 | 0.0031 | 0.0031 | 0.0034 | 0.0025 | 1985 | 0.0377 |
| 1986 | 0.0031 | −0.0027 | −0.0046 | −0.0021 | 0.0031 | 0.0049 | 0.0003 | 0.0018 | 0.0049 | 0.0009 | 0.0009 | 0.0009 | 1986 | 0.0113 |
| 1987 | 0.0060 | 0.0039 | 0.0045 | 0.0054 | 0.0030 | 0.0041 | 0.0021 | 0.0056 | 0.0050 | 0.0026 | 0.0014 | −0.0003 | 1987 | 0.0441 |
| 1988 | 0.0026 | 0.0026 | 0.0043 | 0.0052 | 0.0034 | 0.0043 | 0.0042 | 0.0042 | 0.0067 | 0.0033 | 0.0008 | 0.0017 | 1988 | 0.0442 |
| 1989 | 0.0050 | 0.0041 | 0.0058 | 0.0065 | 0.0057 | 0.0024 | 0.0024 | 0.0016 | 0.0032 | 0.0048 | 0.0024 | 0.0016 | 1989 | 0.0465 |
| 1990 | 0.0103 | 0.0047 | 0.0055 | 0.0016 | 0.0023 | 0.0054 | 0.0038 | 0.0092 | 0.0084 | 0.0060 | 0.0022 | 0.0000 | 1990 | 0.0611 |
| 1991 | 0.0060 | 0.0015 | 0.0015 | 0.0015 | 0.0030 | 0.0029 | 0.0015 | 0.0029 | 0.0044 | 0.0015 | 0.0029 | 0.0007 | 1991 | 0.0306 |
| 1992 | 0.0015 | 0.0036 | 0.0051 | 0.0014 | 0.0014 | 0.0036 | 0.0021 | 0.0028 | 0.0028 | 0.0035 | 0.0014 | −0.0007 | 1992 | 0.0290 |
| 1993 | 0.0049 | 0.0035 | 0.0035 | 0.0028 | 0.0014 | 0.0014 | 0.0000 | 0.0028 | 0.0021 | 0.0041 | 0.0007 | 0.0000 | 1993 | 0.0275 |
| 1994 | 0.0027 | 0.0034 | 0.0034 | 0.0014 | 0.0007 | 0.0034 | 0.0027 | 0.0040 | 0.0027 | 0.0007 | 0.0013 | 0.0000 | 1994 | 0.0267 |
| 1995 | 0.0040 | 0.0040 | 0.0033 | 0.0033 | 0.0020 | 0.0020 | 0.0000 | 0.0026 | 0.0020 | 0.0033 | −0.0007 | −0.0007 | 1995 | 0.0254 |
| 1996 | 0.0059 | 0.0032 | 0.0052 | 0.0039 | 0.0019 | 0.0006 | 0.0019 | 0.0019 | 0.0032 | 0.0032 | 0.0019 | 0.0000 | 1996 | 0.0332 |
| 1997 | 0.0032 | 0.0031 | 0.0025 | 0.0013 | −0.0006 | 0.0012 | 0.0012 | 0.0019 | 0.0025 | 0.0025 | −0.0006 | −0.0012 | 1997 | 0.0170 |
| 1998 | 0.0019 | 0.0019 | 0.0019 | 0.0018 | 0.0018 | 0.0012 | 0.0012 | 0.0012 | 0.0012 | 0.0024 | 0.0000 | −0.0006 | 1998 | 0.0161 |
| 1999 | 0.0024 | 0.0012 | 0.0030 | 0.0073 | 0.0000 | 0.0000 | 0.0030 | 0.0024 | 0.0048 | 0.0018 | 0.0006 | 0.0000 | 1999 | 0.0268 |
| 2000 | 0.0024 | 0.0059 | 0.0082 | 0.0006 | 0.0006 | 0.0058 | 0.0017 | 0.0012 | 0.0052 | 0.0017 | 0.0006 | −0.0006 | 2000 | 0.0339 |

* Compound annual return

## Table A-16

**Equity Risk Premia**

from January 1926 to December 1970

| Year | Jan | Feb | Mar | Apr | May | Jun | Jul | Aug | Sep | Oct | Nov | Dec | Year | Jan-Dec* |
|------|-----|-----|-----|-----|-----|-----|-----|-----|-----|-----|-----|-----|------|----------|
| 1926 | −0.0034 | −0.0410 | −0.0603 | 0.0218 | 0.0178 | 0.0421 | 0.0455 | 0.0223 | 0.0229 | −0.0315 | 0.0315 | 0.0168 | 1926 | 0.0809 |
| 1927 | −0.0217 | 0.0510 | 0.0057 | 0.0175 | 0.0575 | −0.0093 | 0.0638 | 0.0486 | 0.0429 | −0.0526 | 0.0699 | 0.0256 | 1927 | 0.3332 |
| 1928 | −0.0065 | −0.0158 | 0.1068 | 0.0322 | 0.0165 | −0.0415 | 0.0108 | 0.0768 | 0.0231 | 0.0127 | 0.1248 | 0.0043 | 1928 | 0.3867 |
| 1929 | 0.0547 | −0.0055 | −0.0046 | 0.0140 | −0.0404 | 0.1082 | 0.0436 | 0.0984 | −0.0510 | −0.2009 | −0.1279 | 0.0245 | 1929 | −0.1257 |
| 1930 | 0.0624 | 0.0229 | 0.0774 | −0.0100 | −0.0122 | −0.1648 | 0.0366 | 0.0132 | −0.1301 | −0.0863 | −0.0101 | −0.0719 | 1930 | −0.2666 |
| 1931 | 0.0487 | 0.1189 | −0.0687 | −0.0942 | −0.1287 | 0.1412 | −0.0727 | 0.0179 | −0.2974 | 0.0885 | −0.0813 | −0.1411 | 1931 | −0.4394 |
| 1932 | −0.0293 | 0.0546 | −0.1172 | −0.2006 | −0.2200 | −0.0025 | 0.3811 | 0.3864 | −0.0349 | −0.1351 | −0.0418 | 0.0564 | 1932 | −0.0907 |
| 1933 | 0.0086 | −0.1770 | 0.0349 | 0.4242 | 0.1678 | 0.1335 | −0.0863 | 0.1203 | −0.1119 | −0.0855 | 0.1125 | 0.0251 | 1933 | 0.5353 |
| 1934 | 0.1064 | −0.0325 | −0.0002 | −0.0252 | −0.0737 | 0.0228 | −0.1132 | 0.0610 | −0.0033 | −0.0287 | 0.0941 | −0.0012 | 1934 | −0.0160 |
| 1935 | −0.0412 | −0.0342 | −0.0287 | 0.0979 | 0.0408 | 0.0698 | 0.0849 | 0.0278 | 0.0255 | 0.0775 | 0.0471 | 0.0392 | 1935 | 0.4742 |
| 1936 | 0.0669 | 0.0222 | 0.0266 | −0.0752 | 0.0543 | 0.0330 | 0.0699 | 0.0150 | 0.0030 | 0.0772 | 0.0133 | −0.0029 | 1936 | 0.3368 |
| 1937 | 0.0389 | 0.0189 | −0.0079 | −0.0812 | −0.0031 | −0.0507 | 0.1042 | −0.0485 | −0.1406 | −0.0983 | −0.0868 | −0.0459 | 1937 | −0.3523 |
| 1938 | 0.0151 | 0.0673 | −0.2486 | 0.1446 | −0.0330 | 0.2503 | 0.0745 | −0.0226 | 0.0164 | 0.0775 | −0.0267 | 0.0400 | 1938 | 0.3114 |
| 1939 | −0.0673 | 0.0389 | −0.1338 | −0.0027 | 0.0732 | −0.0613 | 0.1105 | −0.0647 | 0.1671 | −0.0123 | −0.0398 | 0.0270 | 1939 | −0.0043 |
| 1940 | −0.0336 | 0.0133 | 0.0124 | −0.0025 | −0.2288 | 0.0809 | 0.0339 | 0.0350 | 0.0123 | 0.0422 | −0.0316 | 0.0009 | 1940 | −0.0979 |
| 1941 | −0.0462 | −0.0059 | 0.0069 | −0.0612 | 0.0182 | 0.0577 | 0.0576 | 0.0009 | −0.0069 | −0.0657 | −0.0285 | −0.0407 | 1941 | −0.1164 |
| 1942 | 0.0159 | −0.0160 | −0.0653 | −0.0400 | 0.0794 | 0.0218 | 0.0335 | 0.0161 | 0.0287 | 0.0675 | −0.0024 | 0.0546 | 1942 | 0.2002 |
| 1943 | 0.0734 | 0.0580 | 0.0542 | 0.0032 | 0.0550 | 0.0220 | −0.0529 | 0.0168 | 0.0260 | −0.0110 | −0.0657 | 0.0614 | 1943 | 0.2546 |
| 1944 | 0.0168 | 0.0039 | 0.0192 | −0.0103 | 0.0503 | 0.0539 | −0.0195 | 0.0154 | −0.0010 | 0.0020 | 0.0130 | 0.0372 | 1944 | 0.1936 |
| 1945 | 0.0156 | 0.0681 | −0.0443 | 0.0899 | 0.0192 | −0.0009 | −0.0183 | 0.0638 | 0.0436 | 0.0319 | 0.0394 | 0.0113 | 1945 | 0.3599 |
| 1946 | 0.0711 | −0.0643 | 0.0477 | 0.0390 | 0.0285 | −0.0373 | −0.0242 | −0.0676 | −0.1000 | −0.0063 | −0.0030 | 0.0454 | 1946 | −0.0839 |
| 1947 | 0.0252 | −0.0079 | −0.0152 | −0.0365 | 0.0011 | 0.0550 | 0.0378 | −0.0206 | −0.0117 | 0.0232 | −0.0181 | 0.0225 | 1947 | 0.0518 |
| 1948 | −0.0386 | −0.0395 | 0.0783 | 0.0283 | 0.0870 | 0.0045 | −0.0516 | 0.0149 | −0.0279 | 0.0706 | −0.0965 | 0.0341 | 1948 | 0.0465 |
| 1949 | 0.0030 | −0.0304 | 0.0318 | −0.0188 | −0.0268 | 0.0005 | 0.0641 | 0.0210 | 0.0254 | 0.0331 | 0.0166 | 0.0476 | 1949 | 0.1750 |
| 1950 | 0.0187 | 0.0191 | 0.0060 | 0.0477 | 0.0498 | −0.0558 | 0.0109 | 0.0433 | 0.0581 | 0.0081 | 0.0158 | 0.0501 | 1950 | 0.3016 |
| 1951 | 0.0624 | 0.0146 | −0.0166 | 0.0496 | −0.0311 | −0.0239 | 0.0696 | 0.0464 | 0.0001 | −0.0119 | 0.0085 | 0.0411 | 1951 | 0.2219 |
| 1952 | 0.0165 | −0.0293 | 0.0492 | −0.0413 | 0.0330 | 0.0475 | 0.0181 | −0.0085 | −0.0192 | 0.0006 | 0.0560 | 0.0365 | 1952 | 0.1644 |
| 1953 | −0.0065 | −0.0120 | −0.0230 | −0.0253 | 0.0060 | −0.0153 | 0.0258 | −0.0517 | 0.0018 | 0.0526 | 0.0196 | 0.0040 | 1953 | −0.0276 |
| 1954 | 0.0525 | 0.0104 | 0.0317 | 0.0507 | 0.0412 | 0.0025 | 0.0583 | −0.0280 | 0.0842 | −0.0174 | 0.0902 | 0.0526 | 1954 | 0.5132 |
| 1955 | 0.0189 | 0.0090 | −0.0040 | 0.0386 | 0.0041 | 0.0830 | 0.0611 | −0.0041 | 0.0113 | −0.0302 | 0.0808 | −0.0003 | 1955 | 0.2952 |
| 1956 | −0.0369 | 0.0393 | 0.0694 | −0.0023 | −0.0615 | 0.0389 | 0.0507 | −0.0344 | −0.0457 | 0.0041 | −0.0071 | 0.0346 | 1956 | 0.0400 |
| 1957 | −0.0426 | −0.0287 | 0.0191 | 0.0362 | 0.0411 | −0.0020 | 0.0101 | −0.0529 | −0.0626 | −0.0330 | 0.0203 | −0.0418 | 1957 | −0.1350 |
| 1958 | 0.0416 | −0.0153 | 0.0318 | 0.0329 | 0.0201 | 0.0276 | 0.0442 | 0.0171 | 0.0481 | 0.0251 | 0.0273 | 0.0512 | 1958 | 0.4119 |
| 1959 | 0.0032 | 0.0030 | −0.0002 | 0.0382 | 0.0217 | −0.0047 | 0.0337 | −0.0121 | −0.0472 | 0.0098 | 0.0160 | 0.0257 | 1959 | 0.0875 |
| 1960 | −0.0730 | 0.0118 | −0.0157 | −0.0180 | 0.0297 | 0.0187 | −0.0247 | 0.0300 | −0.0605 | −0.0029 | 0.0451 | 0.0463 | 1960 | −0.0214 |
| 1961 | 0.0625 | 0.0304 | 0.0249 | 0.0033 | 0.0221 | −0.0294 | 0.0323 | 0.0228 | −0.0200 | 0.0279 | 0.0431 | 0.0028 | 1961 | 0.2425 |
| 1962 | −0.0389 | 0.0189 | −0.0066 | −0.0628 | −0.0833 | −0.0821 | 0.0624 | 0.0184 | −0.0485 | 0.0038 | 0.1064 | 0.0129 | 1962 | −0.1116 |
| 1963 | 0.0479 | −0.0261 | 0.0346 | 0.0474 | 0.0169 | −0.0210 | −0.0048 | 0.0509 | −0.0124 | 0.0309 | −0.0073 | 0.0232 | 1963 | 0.1909 |
| 1964 | 0.0252 | 0.0120 | 0.0133 | 0.0045 | 0.0136 | 0.0147 | 0.0164 | −0.0146 | 0.0272 | 0.0067 | −0.0024 | 0.0024 | 1964 | 0.1250 |
| 1965 | 0.0315 | 0.0001 | −0.0168 | 0.0325 | −0.0061 | −0.0506 | 0.0116 | 0.0238 | 0.0302 | 0.0257 | −0.0066 | 0.0073 | 1965 | 0.0820 |
| 1966 | 0.0024 | −0.0166 | −0.0243 | 0.0185 | −0.0531 | −0.0183 | −0.0155 | −0.0763 | −0.0093 | 0.0446 | 0.0055 | −0.0038 | 1966 | −0.1415 |
| 1967 | 0.0752 | 0.0036 | 0.0369 | 0.0403 | −0.0508 | 0.0163 | 0.0435 | −0.0100 | 0.0309 | −0.0314 | 0.0029 | 0.0244 | 1967 | 0.1897 |
| 1968 | −0.0464 | −0.0299 | 0.0071 | 0.0787 | 0.0116 | 0.0063 | −0.0218 | 0.0121 | 0.0355 | 0.0043 | 0.0486 | −0.0443 | 1968 | 0.0557 |
| 1969 | −0.0120 | −0.0470 | 0.0311 | 0.0174 | −0.0022 | −0.0590 | −0.0637 | 0.0402 | −0.0296 | 0.0397 | −0.0347 | −0.0240 | 1969 | −0.1416 |
| 1970 | −0.0799 | 0.0521 | −0.0027 | −0.0935 | −0.0597 | −0.0537 | 0.0696 | 0.0453 | 0.0292 | −0.0143 | 0.0488 | 0.0539 | 1970 | −0.0236 |

* Compound annual return

## Table A-16 (continued)

## Equity Risk Premia

from January 1971 to December 2000

| Year | Jan | Feb | Mar | Apr | May | Jun | Jul | Aug | Sep | Oct | Nov | Dec | Year | Jan-Dec* |
|------|-----|-----|-----|-----|-----|-----|-----|-----|-----|-----|-----|-----|------|----------|
| 1971 | 0.0379 | 0.0107 | 0.0352 | 0.0348 | −0.0396 | −0.0016 | −0.0438 | 0.0364 | −0.0092 | −0.0439 | −0.0011 | 0.0837 | 1971 | 0.0951 |
| 1972 | 0.0165 | 0.0274 | 0.0045 | 0.0028 | 0.0188 | −0.0234 | 0.0005 | 0.0361 | −0.0070 | 0.0067 | 0.0466 | 0.0093 | 1972 | 0.1458 |
| 1973 | −0.0202 | −0.0373 | −0.0047 | −0.0444 | −0.0189 | −0.0102 | 0.0328 | −0.0385 | 0.0345 | −0.0062 | −0.1132 | 0.0119 | 1973 | −0.2019 |
| 1974 | −0.0147 | −0.0039 | −0.0271 | −0.0446 | −0.0345 | −0.0188 | −0.0824 | −0.0883 | −0.1240 | 0.1599 | −0.0499 | −0.0245 | 1974 | −0.3192 |
| 1975 | 0.1186 | 0.0628 | 0.0194 | 0.0447 | 0.0463 | 0.0419 | −0.0704 | −0.0191 | −0.0379 | 0.0578 | 0.0271 | −0.0144 | 1975 | 0.2968 |
| 1976 | 0.1147 | −0.0091 | 0.0285 | −0.0140 | −0.0110 | 0.0382 | −0.0114 | −0.0028 | 0.0202 | −0.0245 | −0.0049 | 0.0497 | 1976 | 0.1785 |
| 1977 | −0.0523 | −0.0186 | −0.0156 | −0.0024 | −0.0186 | 0.0433 | −0.0192 | −0.0176 | −0.0043 | −0.0462 | 0.0318 | −0.0001 | 1977 | −0.1170 |
| 1978 | −0.0642 | −0.0206 | 0.0222 | 0.0812 | 0.0085 | −0.0205 | 0.0501 | 0.0283 | −0.0109 | −0.0952 | 0.0189 | 0.0093 | 1978 | −0.0058 |
| 1979 | 0.0342 | −0.0355 | 0.0490 | −0.0043 | −0.0248 | 0.0326 | 0.0033 | 0.0530 | −0.0057 | −0.0737 | 0.0411 | 0.0096 | 1979 | 0.0731 |
| 1980 | 0.0526 | −0.0057 | −0.1094 | 0.0300 | 0.0477 | 0.0233 | 0.0620 | 0.0067 | 0.0204 | 0.0091 | 0.0990 | −0.0440 | 1980 | 0.1904 |
| 1981 | −0.0536 | 0.0100 | 0.0256 | −0.0317 | −0.0053 | −0.0212 | −0.0116 | −0.0673 | −0.0619 | 0.0403 | 0.0331 | −0.0349 | 1981 | −0.1710 |
| 1982 | −0.0241 | −0.0599 | −0.0156 | 0.0298 | −0.0390 | −0.0267 | −0.0317 | 0.1182 | 0.0059 | 0.1061 | 0.0372 | 0.0105 | 1982 | 0.0983 |
| 1983 | 0.0277 | 0.0197 | 0.0300 | 0.0682 | −0.0120 | 0.0313 | −0.0384 | 0.0093 | 0.0059 | −0.0209 | 0.0162 | −0.0133 | 1983 | 0.1261 |
| 1984 | −0.0140 | −0.0397 | 0.0097 | −0.0012 | −0.0608 | 0.0145 | −0.0223 | 0.1033 | −0.0083 | −0.0073 | −0.0173 | 0.0188 | 1984 | −0.0326 |
| 1985 | 0.0699 | 0.0079 | −0.0043 | −0.0103 | 0.0545 | 0.0103 | −0.0088 | −0.0115 | −0.0379 | 0.0380 | 0.0651 | 0.0399 | 1985 | 0.2268 |
| 1986 | −0.0012 | 0.0704 | 0.0492 | −0.0175 | 0.0497 | 0.0113 | −0.0618 | 0.0699 | −0.0863 | 0.0507 | 0.0216 | −0.0311 | 1986 | 0.1159 |
| 1987 | 0.1296 | 0.0368 | 0.0224 | −0.0132 | 0.0065 | 0.0449 | 0.0450 | 0.0336 | −0.0264 | −0.2199 | −0.0851 | 0.0696 | 1987 | −0.0022 |
| 1988 | 0.0396 | 0.0423 | −0.0345 | 0.0062 | 0.0027 | 0.0413 | −0.0090 | −0.0388 | 0.0360 | 0.0211 | −0.0198 | 0.0117 | 1988 | 0.0984 |
| 1989 | 0.0664 | −0.0308 | 0.0168 | 0.0446 | 0.0321 | −0.0124 | 0.0823 | 0.0118 | −0.0104 | −0.0299 | 0.0138 | 0.0174 | 1989 | 0.2133 |
| 1990 | −0.0724 | 0.0072 | 0.0197 | −0.0314 | 0.0901 | −0.0132 | −0.0099 | −0.0962 | −0.0549 | −0.0104 | 0.0584 | 0.0213 | 1990 | −0.1019 |
| 1991 | 0.0388 | 0.0665 | 0.0193 | −0.0025 | 0.0379 | −0.0497 | 0.0417 | 0.0188 | −0.0209 | 0.0091 | −0.0441 | 0.1101 | 1991 | 0.2363 |
| 1992 | −0.0219 | 0.0099 | −0.0229 | 0.0258 | 0.0026 | −0.0176 | 0.0371 | −0.0227 | 0.0089 | 0.0013 | 0.0313 | 0.0102 | 1992 | 0.0402 |
| 1993 | 0.0050 | 0.0113 | 0.0189 | −0.0268 | 0.0248 | 0.0008 | −0.0071 | 0.0355 | −0.0099 | 0.0181 | −0.0119 | 0.0100 | 1993 | 0.0689 |
| 1994 | 0.0309 | −0.0291 | −0.0461 | 0.0103 | 0.0131 | −0.0277 | 0.0303 | 0.0369 | −0.0277 | 0.0190 | −0.0402 | 0.0101 | 1994 | −0.0250 |
| 1995 | 0.0218 | 0.0347 | 0.0249 | 0.0245 | 0.0340 | 0.0187 | 0.0286 | −0.0020 | 0.0374 | −0.0082 | 0.0396 | 0.0136 | 1995 | 0.3015 |
| 1996 | 0.0300 | 0.0057 | 0.0056 | 0.0101 | 0.0215 | 0.0001 | −0.0488 | 0.0170 | 0.0516 | 0.0231 | 0.0715 | −0.0241 | 1996 | 0.1698 |
| 1997 | 0.0573 | 0.0042 | −0.0457 | 0.0552 | 0.0562 | 0.0408 | 0.0748 | −0.0595 | 0.0501 | −0.0375 | 0.0422 | 0.0124 | 1997 | 0.2670 |
| 1998 | 0.0068 | 0.0679 | 0.0471 | 0.0057 | −0.0211 | 0.0364 | −0.0146 | −0.1482 | 0.0592 | 0.0778 | 0.0574 | 0.0537 | 1998 | 0.2263 |
| 1999 | 0.0381 | −0.0345 | 0.0356 | 0.0349 | −0.0269 | 0.0513 | −0.0349 | −0.0088 | −0.0312 | 0.0592 | 0.0166 | 0.0543 | 1999 | 0.1563 |
| 2000 | −0.0541 | −0.0231 | 0.0927 | −0.0345 | −0.0254 | 0.0206 | −0.0203 | 0.0568 | −0.0576 | −0.0098 | −0.0835 | −0.0002 | 2000 | −0.1416 |

* Compound annual return

## Table A-17

**Small Stock Premia**

from January 1926 to December 1970

| Year | Jan | Feb | Mar | Apr | May | Jun | Jul | Aug | Sep | Oct | Nov | Dec | Year | Jan-Dec* |
|------|-----|-----|-----|-----|-----|-----|-----|-----|-----|-----|-----|-----|------|----------|
| 1926 | 0.0699 | -0.0265 | -0.0529 | -0.0072 | -0.0241 | -0.0076 | -0.0350 | 0.0008 | -0.0246 | 0.0058 | -0.0135 | 0.0133 | 1926 | -0.1017 |
| 1927 | 0.0498 | 0.0009 | -0.0629 | 0.0365 | 0.0120 | -0.0237 | -0.0145 | -0.0659 | -0.0386 | -0.0166 | 0.0081 | 0.0037 | 1927 | -0.1119 |
| 1928 | 0.0523 | -0.0112 | -0.0514 | 0.0546 | 0.0236 | -0.0476 | -0.0081 | -0.0334 | 0.0615 | 0.0106 | -0.0128 | -0.0560 | 1928 | -0.0273 |
| 1929 | -0.0518 | -0.0007 | -0.0189 | 0.0128 | -0.1011 | -0.0545 | -0.0341 | -0.1081 | -0.0468 | -0.0991 | -0.0290 | -0.0761 | 1929 | -0.4689 |
| 1930 | 0.0615 | 0.0374 | 0.0180 | -0.0623 | -0.0450 | -0.0648 | -0.0082 | -0.0304 | -0.0203 | -0.0264 | 0.0061 | -0.0495 | 1930 | -0.1764 |
| 1931 | 0.1525 | 0.1226 | -0.0035 | -0.1356 | -0.0114 | 0.0349 | 0.0177 | -0.0928 | -0.0389 | -0.0116 | -0.0229 | -0.0924 | 1931 | -0.1133 |
| 1932 | 0.1326 | -0.0265 | -0.0173 | -0.0278 | 0.1284 | 0.0055 | -0.0212 | 0.2507 | -0.1009 | -0.0493 | -0.0846 | -0.1000 | 1932 | 0.0305 |
| 1933 | -0.0168 | 0.0601 | 0.0738 | 0.0548 | 0.3986 | 0.1128 | 0.0341 | -0.0251 | -0.0537 | -0.0417 | -0.0425 | -0.0193 | 1933 | 0.5772 |
| 1934 | 0.2549 | 0.0505 | -0.0012 | 0.0503 | -0.0582 | -0.0248 | -0.1271 | 0.0882 | -0.0134 | 0.0394 | 0.0005 | 0.0183 | 1934 | 0.2604 |
| 1935 | 0.0086 | -0.0260 | -0.0929 | -0.0172 | -0.0417 | -0.0369 | 0.0004 | 0.0258 | 0.0098 | 0.0201 | 0.0896 | 0.0197 | 1935 | -0.0506 |
| 1936 | 0.2192 | 0.0370 | -0.0197 | -0.1129 | -0.0258 | -0.0546 | 0.0160 | 0.0058 | 0.0509 | -0.0129 | 0.1250 | 0.0190 | 1936 | 0.2306 |
| 1937 | 0.0844 | 0.0458 | 0.0199 | -0.0947 | -0.0385 | -0.0715 | 0.0172 | -0.0266 | -0.1321 | -0.0124 | -0.0643 | -0.1294 | 1937 | -0.3537 |
| 1938 | 0.0377 | -0.0310 | -0.1482 | 0.1161 | -0.0537 | 0.0796 | 0.0703 | -0.0793 | -0.0318 | 0.1261 | -0.0427 | 0.0083 | 1938 | 0.0128 |
| 1939 | -0.0187 | -0.0273 | -0.1302 | 0.0169 | 0.0331 | -0.0458 | 0.1288 | -0.1007 | 0.2975 | -0.0277 | -0.0683 | 0.0148 | 1939 | 0.0076 |
| 1940 | 0.0358 | 0.0679 | 0.0502 | 0.0681 | -0.1796 | 0.0223 | -0.0106 | -0.0092 | 0.0088 | 0.0117 | 0.0579 | -0.0456 | 1940 | 0.0513 |
| 1941 | 0.0512 | -0.0230 | 0.0247 | -0.0061 | -0.0136 | 0.0166 | 0.1500 | -0.0070 | -0.0404 | -0.0016 | -0.0217 | -0.0831 | 1941 | 0.0293 |
| 1942 | 0.1706 | 0.0087 | -0.0061 | 0.0049 | -0.0767 | 0.0112 | 0.0386 | 0.0159 | 0.0605 | 0.0383 | -0.0491 | -0.0129 | 1942 | 0.2008 |
| 1943 | 0.1299 | 0.1274 | 0.0853 | 0.0895 | 0.0572 | -0.0299 | -0.0588 | -0.0171 | 0.0161 | 0.0233 | -0.0490 | 0.0588 | 1943 | 0.4962 |
| 1944 | 0.0461 | 0.0252 | 0.0544 | -0.0437 | 0.0223 | 0.0799 | -0.0108 | 0.0159 | -0.0012 | -0.0131 | 0.0361 | 0.0477 | 1944 | 0.2837 |
| 1945 | 0.0319 | 0.0305 | -0.0440 | 0.0234 | 0.0299 | 0.0862 | -0.0383 | -0.0080 | 0.0231 | 0.0367 | 0.0746 | 0.0054 | 1945 | 0.2725 |
| 1946 | 0.0791 | 0.0004 | -0.0198 | 0.0292 | 0.0295 | -0.0096 | -0.0298 | -0.0187 | -0.0673 | -0.0058 | -0.0114 | -0.0080 | 1946 | -0.0387 |
| 1947 | 0.0162 | 0.0036 | -0.0190 | -0.0694 | -0.0547 | -0.0002 | 0.0393 | 0.0170 | 0.0229 | 0.0043 | -0.0130 | 0.0123 | 1947 | -0.0453 |
| 1948 | 0.0234 | -0.0411 | 0.0179 | 0.0074 | 0.0166 | -0.0006 | -0.0074 | -0.0149 | -0.0257 | -0.0059 | -0.0172 | -0.0250 | 1948 | -0.0722 |
| 1949 | 0.0142 | -0.0191 | 0.0291 | -0.0160 | -0.0314 | -0.0110 | 0.0020 | 0.0036 | 0.0221 | 0.0128 | -0.0156 | 0.0195 | 1949 | 0.0080 |
| 1950 | 0.0289 | 0.0021 | -0.0106 | -0.0071 | -0.0242 | -0.0242 | 0.0467 | 0.0083 | -0.0067 | -0.0150 | 0.0151 | 0.0419 | 1950 | 0.0534 |
| 1951 | 0.0182 | -0.0095 | -0.0326 | -0.0136 | -0.0033 | -0.0308 | -0.0315 | 0.0121 | 0.0202 | -0.0120 | -0.0177 | -0.0365 | 1951 | -0.1307 |
| 1952 | 0.0010 | -0.0018 | -0.0312 | -0.0122 | -0.0301 | -0.0208 | -0.0082 | 0.0066 | 0.0015 | -0.0123 | -0.0082 | -0.0214 | 1952 | -0.1296 |
| 1953 | 0.0460 | 0.0379 | 0.0149 | -0.0051 | 0.0064 | -0.0357 | -0.0118 | -0.0134 | -0.0296 | -0.0235 | -0.0076 | -0.0316 | 1953 | -0.0555 |
| 1954 | 0.0209 | -0.0017 | -0.0138 | -0.0357 | 0.0033 | 0.0055 | 0.0207 | 0.0298 | -0.0407 | 0.0239 | -0.0119 | 0.0549 | 1954 | 0.0521 |
| 1955 | 0.0004 | 0.0377 | 0.0115 | -0.0237 | 0.0022 | -0.0506 | -0.0525 | -0.0003 | -0.0020 | 0.0118 | -0.0331 | 0.0147 | 1955 | -0.0845 |
| 1956 | 0.0311 | -0.0130 | -0.0261 | 0.0051 | 0.0208 | -0.0340 | -0.0235 | 0.0200 | 0.0188 | 0.0038 | 0.0104 | -0.0320 | 1956 | -0.0213 |
| 1957 | 0.0663 | 0.0066 | -0.0047 | -0.0134 | -0.0347 | 0.0069 | -0.0189 | 0.0126 | 0.0159 | -0.0547 | -0.0115 | -0.0089 | 1957 | -0.0425 |
| 1958 | 0.0632 | -0.0029 | 0.0138 | 0.0037 | 0.0172 | 0.0044 | 0.0041 | 0.0248 | 0.0017 | 0.0134 | 0.0206 | -0.0211 | 1958 | 0.1501 |
| 1959 | 0.0519 | 0.0245 | 0.0007 | -0.0274 | -0.0221 | -0.0020 | -0.0034 | 0.0015 | 0.0013 | 0.0097 | 0.0036 | 0.0030 | 1959 | 0.0397 |
| 1960 | 0.0423 | -0.0096 | -0.0194 | -0.0026 | -0.0117 | 0.0126 | 0.0045 | 0.0201 | -0.0158 | -0.0394 | -0.0026 | -0.0140 | 1960 | -0.0374 |
| 1961 | 0.0253 | 0.0262 | 0.0340 | 0.0076 | 0.0184 | -0.0276 | -0.0300 | -0.0110 | -0.0158 | -0.0035 | 0.0159 | 0.0033 | 1961 | 0.0410 |
| 1962 | 0.0522 | -0.0021 | 0.0103 | -0.0182 | -0.0215 | 0.0020 | 0.0104 | 0.0080 | -0.0203 | -0.0434 | 0.0146 | -0.0238 | 1962 | -0.0348 |
| 1963 | 0.0381 | 0.0280 | -0.0214 | -0.0180 | 0.0238 | 0.0071 | 0.0055 | -0.0017 | -0.0067 | -0.0099 | -0.0061 | -0.0302 | 1963 | 0.0062 |
| 1964 | -0.0008 | 0.0215 | 0.0053 | 0.0019 | -0.0005 | -0.0015 | 0.0200 | 0.0090 | 0.0099 | 0.0108 | 0.0006 | -0.0167 | 1964 | 0.0604 |
| 1965 | 0.0178 | 0.0358 | 0.0376 | 0.0147 | -0.0048 | -0.0449 | 0.0297 | 0.0314 | 0.0013 | 0.0275 | 0.0404 | 0.0511 | 1965 | 0.2606 |
| 1966 | 0.0690 | 0.0448 | 0.0013 | 0.0121 | -0.0493 | 0.0136 | 0.0109 | -0.0382 | -0.0111 | -0.0573 | 0.0393 | 0.0063 | 1966 | 0.0339 |
| 1967 | 0.0963 | 0.0375 | 0.0198 | -0.0159 | 0.0411 | 0.0812 | 0.0461 | 0.0091 | 0.0216 | -0.0036 | 0.0051 | 0.0669 | 1967 | 0.4807 |
| 1968 | 0.0605 | -0.0460 | -0.0216 | 0.0579 | 0.0825 | -0.0074 | -0.0177 | 0.0200 | 0.0192 | -0.0056 | 0.0221 | 0.0484 | 1968 | 0.2243 |
| 1969 | -0.0098 | -0.0589 | 0.0036 | 0.0162 | 0.0147 | -0.0658 | -0.0512 | 0.0266 | -0.0026 | 0.0145 | -0.0268 | -0.0520 | 1969 | -0.1809 |
| 1970 | 0.0146 | -0.0188 | -0.0314 | -0.0920 | -0.0512 | -0.0469 | -0.0185 | 0.0419 | 0.0714 | -0.0615 | -0.0378 | 0.0135 | 1970 | -0.2061 |

* Compound annual return

Table A-17 (continued)

**Small Stock Premia**

from January 1971 to December 2000

| Year | Jan | Feb | Mar | Apr | May | Jun | Jul | Aug | Sep | Oct | Nov | Dec | Year | Jan-Dec* |
|---|---|---|---|---|---|---|---|---|---|---|---|---|---|---|
| 1971 | 0.1126 | 0.0174 | 0.0175 | −0.0125 | −0.0247 | −0.0340 | −0.0171 | 0.0164 | −0.0172 | −0.0154 | −0.0399 | 0.0246 | 1971 | 0.0191 |
| 1972 | 0.0918 | −0.0003 | −0.0214 | 0.0072 | −0.0401 | −0.0102 | −0.0448 | −0.0197 | −0.0314 | −0.0279 | 0.0084 | −0.0340 | 1972 | −0.1222 |
| 1973 | −0.0277 | −0.0482 | −0.0206 | −0.0236 | −0.0681 | −0.0240 | 0.0769 | −0.0132 | 0.0622 | 0.0082 | −0.0987 | −0.0193 | 1973 | −0.1903 |
| 1974 | 0.1423 | −0.0104 | 0.0146 | −0.0094 | −0.0535 | −0.0019 | 0.0585 | 0.0161 | 0.0585 | −0.0510 | 0.0011 | −0.0622 | 1974 | 0.0887 |
| 1975 | 0.1347 | −0.0364 | 0.0373 | 0.0036 | 0.0147 | 0.0275 | 0.0433 | −0.0436 | 0.0151 | −0.0646 | 0.0006 | −0.0101 | 1975 | 0.1138 |
| 1976 | 0.1326 | 0.1456 | −0.0330 | −0.0262 | −0.0290 | 0.0031 | 0.0114 | −0.0304 | −0.0139 | −0.0003 | 0.0413 | 0.0608 | 1976 | 0.2708 |
| 1977 | 0.0987 | 0.0114 | 0.0252 | 0.0214 | 0.0124 | 0.0284 | 0.0184 | 0.0026 | 0.0092 | 0.0089 | 0.0691 | 0.0033 | 1977 | 0.3508 |
| 1978 | 0.0433 | 0.0517 | 0.0736 | −0.0076 | 0.0675 | −0.0037 | 0.0118 | 0.0579 | 0.0017 | −0.1687 | 0.0460 | −0.0004 | 1978 | 0.1586 |
| 1979 | 0.0864 | 0.0002 | 0.0515 | 0.0349 | 0.0206 | 0.0060 | 0.0061 | 0.0137 | −0.0368 | −0.0534 | 0.0327 | 0.0389 | 1979 | 0.2113 |
| 1980 | 0.0213 | −0.0313 | −0.0878 | 0.0253 | 0.0178 | 0.0152 | 0.0606 | 0.0467 | 0.0134 | 0.0144 | −0.0297 | −0.0024 | 1980 | 0.0563 |
| 1981 | 0.0675 | −0.0112 | 0.0542 | 0.0889 | 0.0358 | 0.0157 | −0.0323 | −0.0138 | −0.0243 | 0.0203 | −0.0158 | 0.0046 | 1981 | 0.1976 |
| 1982 | −0.0034 | 0.0228 | −0.0026 | −0.0030 | 0.0041 | 0.0015 | 0.0204 | −0.0505 | 0.0215 | 0.0161 | 0.0327 | −0.0040 | 1982 | 0.0543 |
| 1983 | 0.0271 | 0.0441 | 0.0154 | 0.0008 | 0.0926 | −0.0032 | 0.0232 | −0.0361 | −0.0003 | −0.0440 | 0.0276 | −0.0085 | 1983 | 0.1400 |
| 1984 | 0.0057 | −0.0328 | 0.0003 | −0.0153 | 0.0014 | 0.0077 | −0.0281 | −0.0114 | 0.0025 | −0.0242 | −0.0237 | −0.0100 | 1984 | −0.1217 |
| 1985 | 0.0270 | 0.0133 | −0.0232 | −0.0142 | −0.0319 | −0.0052 | 0.0287 | −0.0011 | −0.0230 | −0.0178 | −0.0090 | 0.0003 | 1985 | −0.0567 |
| 1986 | 0.0068 | −0.0039 | −0.0073 | 0.0190 | −0.0179 | −0.0138 | −0.0150 | −0.0493 | 0.0287 | −0.0199 | −0.0280 | 0.0002 | 1986 | −0.0981 |
| 1987 | −0.0353 | 0.0380 | −0.0038 | −0.0227 | −0.0141 | −0.0222 | −0.0128 | −0.0094 | 0.0142 | −0.0977 | 0.0460 | −0.0203 | 1987 | −0.1381 |
| 1988 | 0.0124 | 0.0277 | 0.0732 | 0.0100 | −0.0255 | 0.0141 | 0.0015 | 0.0088 | −0.0189 | −0.0385 | −0.0299 | 0.0209 | 1988 | 0.0519 |
| 1989 | −0.0297 | 0.0340 | 0.0119 | −0.0225 | −0.0038 | −0.0148 | −0.0451 | −0.0070 | 0.0039 | −0.0380 | −0.0254 | −0.0361 | 1989 | −0.1621 |
| 1990 | −0.0100 | 0.0057 | 0.0102 | −0.0019 | −0.0377 | 0.0216 | −0.0351 | −0.0432 | −0.0354 | −0.0537 | −0.0182 | −0.0078 | 1990 | −0.1899 |
| 1991 | 0.0382 | 0.0370 | 0.0432 | 0.0006 | −0.0090 | −0.0029 | −0.0058 | 0.0025 | 0.0199 | 0.0181 | 0.0133 | −0.0486 | 1991 | 0.1079 |
| 1992 | 0.1339 | 0.0320 | −0.0054 | −0.0674 | −0.0068 | −0.0380 | −0.0032 | −0.0027 | 0.0016 | 0.0222 | 0.0530 | 0.0306 | 1992 | 0.1456 |
| 1993 | 0.0467 | −0.0311 | 0.0072 | −0.0063 | 0.0070 | −0.0071 | 0.0214 | −0.0040 | 0.0393 | 0.0263 | −0.0082 | 0.0070 | 1993 | 0.0999 |
| 1994 | 0.0274 | 0.0254 | −0.0012 | −0.0069 | −0.0172 | −0.0015 | −0.0142 | −0.0067 | 0.0355 | −0.0111 | 0.0043 | −0.0142 | 1994 | 0.0178 |
| 1995 | 0.0022 | −0.0131 | −0.0147 | 0.0059 | −0.0093 | 0.0325 | 0.0302 | 0.0330 | −0.0215 | −0.0454 | −0.0238 | 0.0053 | 1995 | −0.0216 |
| 1996 | −0.0305 | 0.0270 | 0.0131 | 0.0691 | 0.0479 | −0.0620 | −0.0521 | 0.0259 | −0.0257 | −0.0437 | −0.0438 | 0.0408 | 1996 | −0.0443 |
| 1997 | −0.0189 | −0.0285 | −0.0077 | −0.0824 | 0.0384 | 0.0050 | −0.0175 | 0.1128 | 0.0281 | −0.0054 | −0.0591 | −0.0337 | 1997 | −0.0794 |
| 1998 | −0.0168 | −0.0067 | −0.0030 | 0.0067 | −0.0331 | −0.0588 | −0.0571 | −0.0660 | −0.0255 | −0.0423 | 0.0143 | −0.0307 | 1998 | −0.2791 |
| 1999 | −0.0134 | −0.0388 | −0.0749 | 0.0541 | 0.0638 | 0.0012 | 0.0417 | −0.0142 | 0.0055 | −0.0677 | 0.0752 | 0.0518 | 1999 | 0.0722 |
| 2000 | 0.1155 | 0.2596 | −0.1575 | −0.0980 | −0.0615 | 0.1095 | −0.0168 | 0.0286 | 0.0328 | −0.0667 | −0.0349 | 0.0139 | 2000 | 0.0607 |

* Compound annual return

## Table A-18

**Bond Default Premia**

from January 1926 to December 1970

| Year | Jan | Feb | Mar | Apr | May | Jun | Jul | Aug | Sep | Oct | Nov | Dec | Year | Jan-Dec* |
|------|-----|-----|-----|-----|-----|-----|-----|-----|-----|-----|-----|-----|------|----------|
| 1926 | −0.0065 | −0.0018 | 0.0043 | 0.0021 | 0.0030 | −0.0034 | 0.0053 | 0.0044 | 0.0019 | −0.0005 | −0.0101 | −0.0022 | 1926 | −0.0037 |
| 1927 | −0.0019 | −0.0019 | −0.0166 | 0.0060 | −0.0118 | 0.0113 | −0.0046 | 0.0007 | 0.0131 | −0.0043 | −0.0029 | −0.0003 | 1927 | −0.0136 |
| 1928 | 0.0063 | 0.0007 | −0.0004 | 0.0018 | −0.0001 | −0.0065 | 0.0212 | 0.0006 | 0.0071 | −0.0073 | −0.0039 | 0.0080 | 1928 | 0.0273 |
| 1929 | 0.0134 | 0.0190 | 0.0058 | −0.0249 | 0.0210 | −0.0154 | 0.0020 | 0.0054 | 0.0006 | −0.0298 | −0.0249 | 0.0284 | 1929 | −0.0014 |
| 1930 | 0.0117 | −0.0056 | 0.0054 | 0.0100 | −0.0081 | 0.0059 | 0.0021 | 0.0123 | 0.0034 | 0.0018 | −0.0054 | −0.0020 | 1930 | 0.0317 |
| 1931 | 0.0328 | −0.0017 | −0.0010 | −0.0019 | −0.0011 | 0.0048 | 0.0095 | 0.0000 | 0.0274 | −0.0034 | −0.0216 | −0.0068 | 1931 | 0.0365 |
| 1932 | −0.0086 | −0.0625 | 0.0375 | −0.0735 | 0.0301 | −0.0074 | −0.0418 | 0.0433 | 0.0243 | 0.0091 | 0.0041 | 0.0008 | 1932 | −0.0515 |
| 1933 | 0.0393 | −0.0272 | −0.0049 | −0.0063 | 0.0277 | 0.0140 | 0.0178 | 0.0049 | −0.0037 | 0.0132 | −0.0100 | 0.0374 | 1933 | 0.1046 |
| 1934 | 0.0000 | 0.0064 | −0.0010 | −0.0021 | −0.0041 | 0.0090 | 0.0007 | 0.0167 | 0.0086 | −0.0079 | 0.0091 | −0.0011 | 1934 | 0.0347 |
| 1935 | 0.0029 | 0.0049 | 0.0002 | 0.0033 | 0.0099 | 0.0020 | 0.0065 | 0.0093 | −0.0009 | −0.0019 | 0.0059 | 0.0013 | 1935 | 0.0441 |
| 1936 | 0.0027 | −0.0027 | −0.0024 | −0.0009 | 0.0000 | 0.0061 | −0.0049 | −0.0043 | 0.0098 | 0.0019 | −0.0094 | −0.0028 | 1936 | −0.0072 |
| 1937 | 0.0037 | −0.0131 | 0.0310 | 0.0029 | −0.0013 | 0.0071 | −0.0098 | 0.0088 | −0.0020 | 0.0025 | −0.0028 | −0.0015 | 1937 | 0.0251 |
| 1938 | −0.0019 | −0.0042 | −0.0051 | −0.0070 | −0.0034 | 0.0090 | 0.0023 | −0.0019 | 0.0086 | −0.0007 | 0.0059 | 0.0041 | 1938 | 0.0057 |
| 1939 | −0.0037 | −0.0016 | −0.0102 | −0.0053 | −0.0120 | 0.0062 | −0.0119 | −0.0195 | 0.0736 | −0.0166 | −0.0081 | −0.0066 | 1939 | −0.0186 |
| 1940 | 0.0066 | −0.0006 | −0.0126 | −0.0057 | 0.0287 | −0.0134 | −0.0031 | −0.0021 | −0.0018 | 0.0018 | −0.0139 | −0.0089 | 1940 | −0.0254 |
| 1941 | 0.0211 | −0.0014 | −0.0117 | −0.0051 | 0.0022 | −0.0003 | 0.0041 | 0.0016 | 0.0060 | −0.0105 | −0.0065 | 0.0187 | 1941 | 0.0178 |
| 1942 | −0.0063 | −0.0019 | −0.0028 | 0.0035 | −0.0055 | 0.0031 | 0.0002 | −0.0003 | 0.0017 | −0.0018 | 0.0041 | 0.0000 | 1942 | −0.0060 |
| 1943 | 0.0016 | 0.0012 | 0.0011 | 0.0001 | −0.0002 | 0.0030 | 0.0020 | −0.0002 | −0.0006 | −0.0014 | −0.0023 | 0.0031 | 1943 | 0.0073 |
| 1944 | −0.0001 | 0.0002 | 0.0027 | 0.0021 | −0.0023 | 0.0012 | −0.0002 | 0.0007 | 0.0005 | 0.0007 | 0.0024 | 0.0106 | 1944 | 0.0187 |
| 1945 | −0.0050 | −0.0030 | −0.0003 | −0.0140 | −0.0067 | −0.0135 | 0.0076 | −0.0022 | −0.0022 | −0.0072 | −0.0092 | −0.0060 | 1945 | −0.0601 |
| 1946 | 0.0103 | 0.0002 | 0.0024 | 0.0094 | 0.0031 | −0.0051 | 0.0028 | 0.0024 | −0.0017 | −0.0053 | 0.0029 | −0.0031 | 1946 | 0.0183 |
| 1947 | 0.0011 | −0.0016 | 0.0047 | 0.0057 | −0.0013 | −0.0006 | −0.0042 | −0.0151 | −0.0088 | −0.0062 | 0.0077 | 0.0220 | 1947 | 0.0029 |
| 1948 | 0.0004 | −0.0007 | 0.0081 | −0.0007 | −0.0131 | 0.0001 | −0.0031 | 0.0054 | 0.0010 | 0.0017 | 0.0009 | 0.0074 | 1948 | 0.0071 |
| 1949 | −0.0043 | −0.0011 | −0.0067 | 0.0012 | 0.0019 | −0.0082 | 0.0065 | −0.0073 | 0.0032 | 0.0048 | 0.0000 | −0.0196 | 1949 | −0.0295 |
| 1950 | 0.0099 | −0.0014 | 0.0014 | −0.0038 | −0.0041 | 0.0048 | 0.0013 | 0.0024 | 0.0034 | 0.0040 | 0.0019 | 0.0007 | 1950 | 0.0205 |
| 1951 | −0.0039 | 0.0030 | −0.0081 | 0.0054 | 0.0054 | −0.0032 | 0.0066 | 0.0015 | 0.0023 | −0.0155 | 0.0076 | 0.0120 | 1951 | 0.0129 |
| 1952 | 0.0170 | −0.0099 | −0.0034 | −0.0172 | 0.0065 | 0.0013 | 0.0036 | 0.0134 | 0.0113 | −0.0107 | 0.0124 | −0.0005 | 1952 | 0.0233 |
| 1953 | −0.0092 | 0.0047 | 0.0056 | −0.0144 | 0.0119 | −0.0111 | 0.0137 | −0.0078 | −0.0045 | 0.0151 | −0.0024 | −0.0033 | 1953 | −0.0022 |
| 1954 | 0.0034 | −0.0041 | −0.0019 | −0.0136 | 0.0045 | −0.0098 | −0.0093 | 0.0054 | 0.0050 | 0.0034 | 0.0050 | −0.0047 | 1954 | −0.0168 |
| 1955 | 0.0148 | 0.0015 | 0.0005 | −0.0002 | −0.0090 | 0.0106 | 0.0062 | −0.0042 | 0.0003 | −0.0065 | 0.0015 | 0.0026 | 1955 | 0.0180 |
| 1956 | 0.0021 | 0.0028 | 0.0003 | −0.0002 | −0.0170 | −0.0045 | 0.0118 | −0.0022 | −0.0037 | −0.0051 | −0.0069 | 0.0098 | 1956 | −0.0130 |
| 1957 | −0.0144 | 0.0068 | 0.0074 | 0.0159 | −0.0052 | −0.0144 | −0.0069 | −0.0011 | 0.0019 | 0.0074 | −0.0211 | 0.0367 | 1957 | 0.0117 |
| 1958 | 0.0185 | −0.0107 | −0.0147 | −0.0023 | 0.0030 | 0.0124 | 0.0129 | 0.0121 | 0.0021 | −0.0031 | −0.0015 | 0.0125 | 1958 | 0.0413 |
| 1959 | 0.0053 | 0.0009 | −0.0099 | −0.0056 | −0.0109 | 0.0033 | 0.0029 | −0.0027 | −0.0032 | 0.0014 | 0.0257 | 0.0064 | 1959 | 0.0132 |
| 1960 | −0.0005 | −0.0074 | −0.0089 | 0.0150 | −0.0170 | −0.0031 | −0.0107 | 0.0186 | −0.0137 | 0.0036 | −0.0004 | −0.0170 | 1960 | −0.0414 |
| 1961 | 0.0258 | 0.0010 | 0.0009 | −0.0228 | 0.0095 | −0.0005 | 0.0005 | 0.0020 | 0.0015 | 0.0055 | 0.0048 | 0.0100 | 1961 | 0.0381 |
| 1962 | 0.0094 | −0.0050 | −0.0100 | 0.0059 | −0.0046 | 0.0050 | 0.0095 | −0.0043 | 0.0028 | −0.0016 | 0.0041 | −0.0012 | 1962 | 0.0099 |
| 1963 | 0.0060 | 0.0015 | 0.0017 | −0.0039 | 0.0025 | 0.0024 | −0.0003 | 0.0014 | −0.0027 | 0.0075 | −0.0036 | −0.0028 | 1963 | 0.0097 |
| 1964 | 0.0101 | 0.0065 | −0.0099 | −0.0007 | 0.0007 | −0.0021 | 0.0044 | 0.0017 | −0.0028 | 0.0007 | −0.0021 | 0.0058 | 1964 | 0.0122 |
| 1965 | 0.0041 | −0.0005 | −0.0041 | −0.0015 | −0.0026 | −0.0044 | −0.0003 | 0.0007 | 0.0019 | 0.0019 | 0.0005 | −0.0072 | 1965 | −0.0116 |
| 1966 | 0.0127 | 0.0141 | −0.0345 | 0.0076 | 0.0034 | 0.0046 | −0.0061 | −0.0054 | −0.0246 | 0.0032 | 0.0130 | −0.0204 | 1966 | −0.0333 |
| 1967 | 0.0291 | 0.0020 | −0.0079 | 0.0227 | −0.0216 | 0.0092 | −0.0027 | 0.0078 | 0.0099 | 0.0124 | −0.0077 | −0.0064 | 1967 | 0.0466 |
| 1968 | 0.0032 | 0.0070 | 0.0015 | −0.0175 | −0.0011 | −0.0106 | 0.0050 | 0.0209 | 0.0050 | −0.0028 | 0.0044 | 0.0135 | 1968 | 0.0284 |
| 1969 | 0.0352 | −0.0201 | −0.0210 | −0.0088 | 0.0277 | −0.0176 | −0.0074 | 0.0049 | 0.0303 | −0.0230 | −0.0233 | −0.0066 | 1969 | −0.0318 |
| 1970 | 0.0163 | −0.0176 | 0.0023 | 0.0170 | 0.0320 | −0.0463 | 0.0229 | 0.0119 | −0.0087 | 0.0013 | −0.0192 | 0.0460 | 1970 | 0.0559 |

* Compound annual return

## Table A-18 (continued)
## Bond Default Premia

from January 1971 to December 2000

| Year | Jan | Feb | Mar | Apr | May | Jun | Jul | Aug | Sep | Oct | Nov | Dec | Year | Jan-Dec* |
|------|-----|-----|-----|-----|-----|-----|-----|-----|-----|-----|-----|-----|------|----------|
| 1971 | 0.0025 | −0.0206 | −0.0255 | 0.0048 | −0.0155 | 0.0270 | −0.0054 | 0.0079 | −0.0299 | 0.0113 | 0.0076 | 0.0178 | 1971 | −0.0196 |
| 1972 | 0.0031 | 0.0019 | 0.0107 | 0.0008 | −0.0105 | −0.0003 | −0.0182 | 0.0043 | 0.0115 | −0.0130 | 0.0022 | 0.0231 | 1972 | 0.0149 |
| 1973 | 0.0276 | 0.0009 | −0.0037 | 0.0015 | 0.0066 | −0.0035 | −0.0045 | −0.0034 | 0.0037 | −0.0275 | 0.0265 | −0.0007 | 1973 | 0.0227 |
| 1974 | 0.0030 | 0.0033 | −0.0016 | −0.0091 | −0.0017 | −0.0328 | −0.0183 | −0.0037 | −0.0072 | 0.0377 | −0.0173 | −0.0242 | 1974 | −0.0711 |
| 1975 | 0.0363 | 0.0005 | 0.0021 | 0.0132 | −0.0104 | 0.0012 | 0.0057 | −0.0108 | −0.0028 | 0.0075 | 0.0021 | 0.0050 | 1975 | 0.0499 |
| 1976 | 0.0097 | −0.0001 | 0.0001 | −0.0033 | 0.0056 | −0.0056 | 0.0071 | 0.0019 | 0.0022 | −0.0014 | −0.0019 | 0.0019 | 1976 | 0.0162 |
| 1977 | 0.0088 | 0.0029 | 0.0003 | 0.0029 | −0.0019 | 0.0011 | 0.0066 | −0.0061 | 0.0007 | 0.0056 | −0.0032 | 0.0064 | 1977 | 0.0241 |
| 1978 | −0.0009 | 0.0047 | 0.0063 | −0.0018 | −0.0050 | 0.0086 | −0.0041 | 0.0038 | 0.0058 | −0.0005 | −0.0054 | −0.0003 | 1978 | 0.0112 |
| 1979 | −0.0007 | 0.0007 | −0.0023 | 0.0061 | −0.0032 | −0.0041 | 0.0055 | 0.0042 | −0.0057 | −0.0054 | −0.0087 | −0.0164 | 1979 | −0.0298 |
| 1980 | 0.0104 | −0.0208 | 0.0261 | −0.0128 | 0.0136 | −0.0017 | 0.0049 | −0.0014 | 0.0025 | 0.0107 | −0.0082 | −0.0100 | 1980 | 0.0124 |
| 1981 | −0.0015 | 0.0174 | −0.0071 | −0.0265 | −0.0025 | 0.0206 | −0.0020 | 0.0043 | −0.0055 | −0.0284 | −0.0125 | 0.0143 | 1981 | −0.0304 |
| 1982 | −0.0174 | 0.0128 | 0.0073 | −0.0034 | 0.0210 | −0.0251 | 0.0037 | 0.0052 | 0.0004 | 0.0117 | 0.0203 | −0.0198 | 1982 | 0.0157 |
| 1983 | 0.0222 | −0.0061 | 0.0167 | 0.0192 | 0.0064 | −0.0085 | 0.0033 | 0.0031 | −0.0107 | 0.0108 | −0.0041 | 0.0026 | 1983 | 0.0557 |
| 1984 | 0.0026 | 0.0006 | −0.0080 | 0.0033 | 0.0035 | 0.0049 | −0.0100 | 0.0040 | −0.0028 | 0.0011 | 0.0093 | 0.0037 | 1984 | 0.0120 |
| 1985 | −0.0038 | 0.0126 | −0.0124 | 0.0052 | −0.0069 | −0.0058 | 0.0060 | 0.0001 | 0.0092 | −0.0008 | −0.0030 | −0.0068 | 1985 | −0.0067 |
| 1986 | 0.0070 | −0.0353 | −0.0477 | 0.0097 | 0.0359 | −0.0373 | 0.0141 | −0.0214 | 0.0406 | −0.0097 | −0.0033 | 0.0135 | 1986 | −0.0376 |
| 1987 | 0.0054 | −0.0141 | 0.0139 | −0.0030 | 0.0054 | 0.0057 | 0.0060 | 0.0091 | −0.0055 | −0.0109 | 0.0088 | 0.0046 | 1987 | 0.0251 |
| 1988 | −0.0140 | 0.0085 | 0.0122 | 0.0011 | 0.0045 | 0.0010 | 0.0060 | −0.0004 | −0.0018 | −0.0033 | 0.0028 | −0.0070 | 1988 | 0.0094 |
| 1989 | −0.0001 | 0.0051 | −0.0058 | 0.0053 | −0.0021 | −0.0147 | −0.0058 | 0.0098 | 0.0021 | −0.0100 | −0.0008 | 0.0012 | 1989 | −0.0159 |
| 1990 | 0.0157 | 0.0013 | 0.0033 | 0.0011 | −0.0029 | −0.0014 | −0.0005 | 0.0132 | −0.0026 | −0.0081 | −0.0112 | −0.0019 | 1990 | 0.0057 |
| 1991 | 0.0019 | 0.0090 | 0.0070 | −0.0002 | 0.0039 | 0.0045 | 0.0009 | −0.0063 | −0.0031 | −0.0011 | 0.0024 | −0.0137 | 1991 | 0.0049 |
| 1992 | 0.0156 | 0.0045 | 0.0021 | 0.0000 | 0.0011 | −0.0043 | −0.0086 | 0.0023 | −0.0085 | 0.0043 | 0.0059 | −0.0018 | 1992 | 0.0124 |
| 1993 | −0.0030 | −0.0095 | 0.0004 | −0.0020 | −0.0026 | −0.0149 | −0.0090 | −0.0141 | 0.0038 | −0.0045 | 0.0073 | 0.0047 | 1993 | −0.0428 |
| 1994 | −0.0054 | 0.0171 | 0.0012 | 0.0054 | 0.0021 | 0.0020 | −0.0052 | 0.0055 | 0.0068 | −0.0026 | −0.0048 | −0.0004 | 1994 | 0.0218 |
| 1995 | −0.0016 | 0.0002 | 0.0004 | 0.0006 | −0.0148 | −0.0059 | 0.0068 | −0.0022 | −0.0021 | −0.0106 | −0.0007 | −0.0043 | 1995 | −0.0339 |
| 1996 | 0.0025 | 0.0115 | 0.0082 | 0.0005 | 0.0060 | −0.0030 | −0.0008 | 0.0070 | −0.0030 | −0.0041 | −0.0085 | 0.0072 | 1996 | 0.0235 |
| 1997 | 0.0052 | 0.0023 | 0.0032 | −0.0069 | 0.0031 | −0.0008 | −0.0092 | 0.0080 | −0.0087 | −0.0145 | −0.0046 | −0.0021 | 1997 | −0.0251 |
| 1998 | −0.0062 | 0.0065 | 0.0013 | 0.0027 | −0.0015 | −0.0111 | −0.0016 | −0.0359 | 0.0018 | 0.0029 | 0.0172 | 0.0043 | 1998 | −0.0204 |
| 1999 | 0.0001 | 0.0126 | 0.0011 | −0.0045 | 0.0009 | −0.0083 | −0.0036 | 0.0026 | 0.0009 | 0.0059 | 0.0037 | 0.0053 | 1999 | 0.0167 |
| 2000 | −0.0244 | −0.0167 | −0.0190 | −0.0039 | −0.0107 | 0.0080 | 0.0006 | −0.0103 | 0.0207 | −0.0140 | −0.0054 | 0.0027 | 2000 | −0.0709 |

* Compound annual return

## Table A-19

### Bond Horizon Premia

from January 1926 to December 1970

| Year | Jan | Feb | Mar | Apr | May | Jun | Jul | Aug | Sep | Oct | Nov | Dec | Year | Jan-Dec* |
|---|---|---|---|---|---|---|---|---|---|---|---|---|---|---|
| 1926 | 0.0103 | 0.0036 | 0.0011 | 0.0041 | 0.0013 | 0.0004 | −0.0018 | −0.0025 | 0.0015 | 0.0070 | 0.0129 | 0.0050 | 1926 | 0.0436 |
| 1927 | 0.0050 | 0.0062 | 0.0223 | −0.0030 | 0.0078 | −0.0094 | 0.0020 | 0.0048 | −0.0003 | 0.0073 | 0.0076 | 0.0049 | 1927 | 0.0563 |
| 1928 | −0.0061 | 0.0028 | 0.0016 | −0.0026 | −0.0109 | 0.0010 | −0.0249 | 0.0044 | −0.0067 | 0.0116 | −0.0035 | −0.0002 | 1928 | −0.0334 |
| 1929 | −0.0124 | −0.0192 | −0.0177 | 0.0239 | −0.0205 | 0.0058 | −0.0034 | −0.0074 | −0.0008 | 0.0335 | 0.0198 | −0.0125 | 1929 | −0.0127 |
| 1930 | −0.0071 | 0.0099 | 0.0048 | −0.0037 | 0.0113 | 0.0024 | 0.0015 | 0.0004 | 0.0052 | 0.0027 | 0.0029 | −0.0084 | 1930 | 0.0220 |
| 1931 | −0.0136 | 0.0081 | 0.0091 | 0.0078 | 0.0136 | −0.0004 | −0.0048 | 0.0009 | −0.0283 | −0.0340 | 0.0010 | −0.0232 | 1931 | −0.0631 |
| 1932 | 0.0011 | 0.0389 | −0.0035 | 0.0592 | −0.0194 | 0.0063 | 0.0479 | −0.0001 | 0.0054 | −0.0019 | 0.0030 | 0.0130 | 1932 | 0.1573 |
| 1933 | 0.0147 | −0.0256 | 0.0093 | −0.0042 | 0.0298 | 0.0047 | −0.0019 | 0.0042 | 0.0022 | −0.0092 | −0.0151 | −0.0115 | 1933 | −0.0037 |
| 1934 | 0.0252 | 0.0079 | 0.0195 | 0.0125 | 0.0130 | 0.0066 | 0.0039 | −0.0119 | −0.0146 | 0.0181 | 0.0036 | 0.0111 | 1934 | 0.0985 |
| 1935 | 0.0180 | 0.0090 | 0.0040 | 0.0077 | −0.0058 | 0.0091 | 0.0044 | −0.0135 | 0.0007 | 0.0060 | 0.0007 | 0.0069 | 1935 | 0.0481 |
| 1936 | 0.0054 | 0.0080 | 0.0105 | 0.0034 | 0.0039 | 0.0018 | 0.0059 | 0.0109 | −0.0032 | 0.0004 | 0.0204 | 0.0038 | 1936 | 0.0732 |
| 1937 | −0.0014 | 0.0085 | −0.0413 | 0.0035 | 0.0046 | −0.0021 | 0.0135 | −0.0107 | 0.0041 | 0.0041 | 0.0094 | 0.0082 | 1937 | −0.0008 |
| 1938 | 0.0057 | 0.0051 | −0.0036 | 0.0208 | 0.0044 | 0.0004 | 0.0044 | 0.0000 | 0.0021 | 0.0086 | −0.0016 | 0.0080 | 1938 | 0.0555 |
| 1939 | 0.0059 | 0.0079 | 0.0126 | 0.0118 | 0.0170 | −0.0028 | 0.0113 | −0.0200 | −0.0546 | 0.0410 | 0.0162 | 0.0144 | 1939 | 0.0592 |
| 1940 | −0.0017 | 0.0027 | 0.0177 | −0.0035 | −0.0298 | 0.0258 | 0.0051 | 0.0029 | 0.0110 | 0.0031 | 0.0204 | 0.0067 | 1940 | 0.0608 |
| 1941 | −0.0200 | 0.0021 | 0.0095 | 0.0130 | 0.0027 | 0.0065 | 0.0019 | 0.0017 | −0.0012 | 0.0140 | −0.0030 | −0.0178 | 1941 | 0.0087 |
| 1942 | 0.0068 | 0.0010 | 0.0091 | −0.0030 | 0.0073 | 0.0000 | 0.0015 | 0.0035 | 0.0000 | 0.0021 | −0.0038 | 0.0046 | 1942 | 0.0294 |
| 1943 | 0.0030 | −0.0008 | 0.0006 | 0.0045 | 0.0048 | 0.0015 | −0.0004 | 0.0018 | 0.0008 | 0.0002 | −0.0003 | 0.0015 | 1943 | 0.0173 |
| 1944 | 0.0018 | 0.0029 | 0.0018 | 0.0011 | 0.0025 | 0.0005 | 0.0033 | 0.0024 | 0.0012 | 0.0009 | 0.0021 | 0.0040 | 1944 | 0.0248 |
| 1945 | 0.0124 | 0.0074 | 0.0018 | 0.0157 | 0.0053 | 0.0166 | −0.0089 | 0.0023 | 0.0051 | 0.0101 | 0.0123 | 0.0191 | 1945 | 0.1037 |
| 1946 | 0.0022 | 0.0029 | 0.0007 | −0.0138 | −0.0015 | 0.0067 | −0.0043 | −0.0114 | −0.0012 | 0.0071 | −0.0057 | 0.0142 | 1946 | −0.0045 |
| 1947 | −0.0009 | 0.0018 | 0.0017 | −0.0040 | 0.0031 | 0.0007 | 0.0059 | 0.0079 | −0.0050 | −0.0044 | −0.0180 | −0.0200 | 1947 | −0.0311 |
| 1948 | 0.0013 | 0.0039 | 0.0025 | 0.0036 | 0.0133 | −0.0093 | −0.0029 | −0.0007 | 0.0010 | 0.0003 | 0.0072 | 0.0052 | 1948 | 0.0257 |
| 1949 | 0.0072 | 0.0040 | 0.0065 | 0.0002 | 0.0009 | 0.0157 | 0.0025 | 0.0102 | −0.0020 | 0.0010 | 0.0013 | 0.0043 | 1949 | 0.0529 |
| 1950 | −0.0070 | 0.0013 | −0.0001 | 0.0021 | 0.0023 | −0.0035 | 0.0046 | 0.0004 | −0.0083 | −0.0059 | 0.0024 | 0.0005 | 1950 | −0.0112 |
| 1951 | 0.0045 | −0.0084 | −0.0168 | −0.0075 | −0.0081 | −0.0073 | 0.0125 | 0.0085 | −0.0092 | −0.0005 | −0.0147 | −0.0073 | 1951 | −0.0534 |
| 1952 | 0.0013 | 0.0002 | 0.0100 | 0.0159 | −0.0046 | −0.0012 | −0.0035 | −0.0084 | −0.0146 | 0.0134 | −0.0026 | −0.0102 | 1952 | −0.0049 |
| 1953 | −0.0004 | −0.0101 | −0.0106 | −0.0121 | −0.0164 | 0.0204 | 0.0025 | −0.0024 | 0.0283 | 0.0062 | −0.0057 | 0.0193 | 1953 | 0.0178 |
| 1954 | 0.0078 | 0.0232 | 0.0050 | 0.0095 | −0.0092 | 0.0157 | 0.0129 | −0.0041 | −0.0018 | −0.0001 | −0.0031 | 0.0056 | 1954 | 0.0627 |
| 1955 | −0.0249 | −0.0087 | 0.0077 | −0.0010 | 0.0059 | −0.0086 | −0.0112 | −0.0012 | 0.0057 | 0.0126 | −0.0062 | 0.0019 | 1955 | −0.0282 |
| 1956 | 0.0061 | −0.0021 | −0.0164 | −0.0131 | 0.0202 | 0.0007 | −0.0230 | −0.0203 | 0.0031 | −0.0079 | −0.0078 | −0.0202 | 1956 | −0.0785 |
| 1957 | 0.0318 | 0.0001 | −0.0047 | −0.0246 | −0.0048 | −0.0204 | −0.0070 | −0.0023 | 0.0050 | −0.0079 | 0.0504 | 0.0282 | 1957 | 0.0419 |
| 1958 | −0.0112 | 0.0088 | 0.0093 | 0.0178 | −0.0010 | −0.0163 | −0.0285 | −0.0440 | −0.0136 | 0.0120 | 0.0109 | −0.0203 | 1958 | −0.0752 |
| 1959 | −0.0101 | 0.0098 | −0.0005 | −0.0136 | −0.0027 | −0.0014 | 0.0035 | −0.0060 | −0.0087 | 0.0120 | −0.0144 | −0.0192 | 1959 | −0.0506 |
| 1960 | 0.0078 | 0.0175 | 0.0247 | −0.0189 | 0.0124 | 0.0148 | 0.0354 | −0.0084 | 0.0059 | −0.0050 | −0.0079 | 0.0263 | 1960 | 0.1083 |
| 1961 | −0.0126 | 0.0185 | −0.0058 | 0.0097 | −0.0064 | −0.0095 | 0.0016 | −0.0052 | 0.0112 | 0.0052 | −0.0036 | −0.0143 | 1961 | −0.0113 |
| 1962 | −0.0038 | 0.0083 | 0.0232 | 0.0059 | 0.0022 | −0.0095 | −0.0135 | 0.0163 | 0.0040 | 0.0058 | 0.0001 | 0.0012 | 1962 | 0.0404 |
| 1963 | −0.0026 | −0.0015 | −0.0014 | −0.0037 | −0.0002 | −0.0003 | 0.0004 | −0.0003 | −0.0023 | −0.0055 | 0.0024 | −0.0035 | 1963 | −0.0185 |
| 1964 | −0.0043 | −0.0037 | 0.0006 | 0.0017 | 0.0025 | 0.0038 | −0.0022 | −0.0008 | 0.0021 | 0.0014 | −0.0012 | −0.0001 | 1964 | −0.0003 |
| 1965 | 0.0012 | −0.0016 | 0.0018 | 0.0006 | −0.0013 | 0.0012 | −0.0009 | −0.0046 | −0.0065 | −0.0004 | −0.0097 | −0.0110 | 1965 | −0.0310 |
| 1966 | −0.0141 | −0.0284 | 0.0257 | −0.0097 | −0.0100 | −0.0053 | −0.0072 | −0.0246 | 0.0291 | 0.0182 | −0.0188 | 0.0371 | 1966 | −0.0106 |
| 1967 | 0.0111 | −0.0256 | 0.0158 | −0.0323 | −0.0072 | −0.0338 | 0.0037 | −0.0115 | −0.0036 | −0.0438 | −0.0231 | 0.0158 | 1967 | −0.1285 |
| 1968 | 0.0286 | −0.0072 | −0.0249 | 0.0183 | −0.0002 | 0.0187 | 0.0240 | −0.0045 | −0.0144 | −0.0175 | −0.0310 | −0.0404 | 1968 | −0.0520 |
| 1969 | −0.0257 | −0.0004 | −0.0036 | 0.0371 | −0.0536 | 0.0162 | 0.0026 | −0.0119 | −0.0590 | 0.0304 | −0.0293 | −0.0132 | 1969 | −0.1094 |
| 1970 | −0.0081 | 0.0522 | −0.0124 | −0.0461 | −0.0518 | 0.0426 | 0.0266 | −0.0072 | 0.0173 | −0.0154 | 0.0742 | −0.0126 | 1970 | 0.0524 |

* Compound annual return

Table A-19 (continued)

**Bond Horizon Premia**

from January 1971 to December 2000

| Year | Jan | Feb | Mar | Apr | May | Jun | Jul | Aug | Sep | Oct | Nov | Dec | Year | Jan-Dec* |
|------|------|------|------|------|------|------|------|------|------|------|------|------|------|------|
| 1971 | 0.0466 | −0.0196 | 0.0495 | −0.0310 | −0.0035 | −0.0195 | −0.0011 | 0.0422 | 0.0166 | 0.0130 | −0.0084 | 0.0007 | 1971 | 0.0847 |
| 1972 | −0.0092 | 0.0063 | −0.0109 | −0.0002 | 0.0240 | −0.0094 | 0.0184 | 0.0000 | −0.0116 | 0.0194 | 0.0188 | −0.0266 | 1972 | 0.0178 |
| 1973 | −0.0363 | −0.0027 | 0.0036 | −0.0007 | −0.0155 | −0.0072 | −0.0494 | 0.0319 | 0.0248 | 0.0149 | −0.0237 | −0.0145 | 1973 | −0.0752 |
| 1974 | −0.0145 | −0.0082 | −0.0346 | −0.0326 | 0.0047 | −0.0016 | −0.0099 | −0.0290 | 0.0165 | 0.0436 | 0.0240 | 0.0101 | 1974 | −0.0338 |
| 1975 | 0.0166 | 0.0088 | −0.0307 | −0.0225 | 0.0168 | 0.0250 | −0.0135 | −0.0115 | −0.0150 | 0.0417 | −0.0149 | 0.0340 | 1975 | 0.0321 |
| 1976 | 0.0043 | 0.0028 | 0.0125 | −0.0023 | −0.0195 | 0.0163 | 0.0031 | 0.0169 | 0.0101 | 0.0043 | 0.0298 | 0.0286 | 1976 | 0.1111 |
| 1977 | −0.0422 | −0.0084 | 0.0053 | 0.0033 | 0.0088 | 0.0124 | −0.0111 | 0.0153 | −0.0072 | −0.0142 | 0.0043 | −0.0215 | 1977 | −0.0553 |
| 1978 | −0.0129 | −0.0042 | −0.0073 | −0.0058 | −0.0109 | −0.0115 | 0.0086 | 0.0161 | −0.0167 | −0.0266 | 0.0118 | −0.0207 | 1978 | −0.0780 |
| 1979 | 0.0113 | −0.0207 | 0.0048 | −0.0190 | 0.0178 | 0.0228 | −0.0160 | −0.0111 | −0.0203 | −0.0920 | 0.0211 | −0.0038 | 1979 | −0.1052 |
| 1980 | −0.0814 | −0.0551 | −0.0430 | 0.1381 | 0.0335 | 0.0296 | −0.0526 | −0.0492 | −0.0334 | −0.0355 | 0.0004 | 0.0218 | 1980 | −0.1365 |
| 1981 | −0.0217 | −0.0537 | 0.0260 | −0.0618 | 0.0501 | −0.0310 | −0.0471 | −0.0507 | −0.0266 | 0.0700 | 0.1290 | −0.0793 | 1981 | −0.1120 |
| 1982 | −0.0034 | 0.0089 | 0.0132 | 0.0258 | −0.0071 | −0.0316 | 0.0392 | 0.0699 | 0.0564 | 0.0572 | −0.0065 | 0.0243 | 1982 | 0.2697 |
| 1983 | −0.0375 | 0.0427 | −0.0156 | 0.0276 | −0.0452 | −0.0027 | −0.0556 | −0.0056 | 0.0425 | −0.0206 | 0.0112 | −0.0130 | 1983 | −0.0749 |
| 1984 | 0.0166 | −0.0248 | −0.0228 | −0.0185 | −0.0590 | 0.0074 | 0.0606 | 0.0182 | 0.0254 | 0.0457 | 0.0044 | 0.0026 | 1984 | 0.0512 |
| 1985 | 0.0297 | −0.0548 | 0.0244 | 0.0169 | 0.0824 | 0.0086 | −0.0241 | 0.0203 | −0.0081 | 0.0271 | 0.0338 | 0.0473 | 1985 | 0.2158 |
| 1986 | −0.0081 | 0.1087 | 0.0706 | −0.0131 | −0.0552 | 0.0558 | −0.0159 | 0.0451 | −0.0543 | 0.0241 | 0.0227 | −0.0066 | 1986 | 0.1730 |
| 1987 | 0.0119 | 0.0158 | −0.0268 | −0.0515 | −0.0142 | 0.0050 | −0.0223 | −0.0211 | −0.0412 | 0.0560 | 0.0002 | 0.0126 | 1987 | −0.0776 |
| 1988 | 0.0635 | 0.0007 | −0.0349 | −0.0205 | −0.0152 | 0.0318 | −0.0219 | −0.0002 | 0.0281 | 0.0245 | −0.0251 | 0.0046 | 1988 | 0.0313 |
| 1989 | 0.0147 | −0.0239 | 0.0055 | 0.0091 | 0.0320 | 0.0476 | 0.0167 | −0.0330 | −0.0046 | 0.0310 | 0.0009 | −0.0067 | 1989 | 0.0899 |
| 1990 | −0.0397 | −0.0081 | −0.0108 | −0.0269 | 0.0345 | 0.0167 | 0.0039 | −0.0481 | 0.0057 | 0.0146 | 0.0344 | 0.0126 | 1990 | −0.0151 |
| 1991 | 0.0078 | −0.0017 | −0.0006 | 0.0086 | −0.0047 | −0.0104 | 0.0108 | 0.0293 | 0.0257 | 0.0012 | 0.0043 | 0.0541 | 1991 | 0.1298 |
| 1992 | −0.0357 | 0.0023 | −0.0127 | −0.0017 | 0.0214 | 0.0167 | 0.0366 | 0.0041 | 0.0159 | −0.0220 | −0.0013 | 0.0217 | 1992 | 0.0439 |
| 1993 | 0.0256 | 0.0331 | −0.0004 | 0.0048 | 0.0025 | 0.0422 | 0.0167 | 0.0408 | −0.0020 | 0.0074 | −0.0283 | −0.0003 | 1993 | 0.1491 |
| 1994 | 0.0232 | −0.0470 | −0.0421 | −0.0177 | −0.0114 | −0.0131 | 0.0335 | −0.0122 | −0.0366 | −0.0063 | 0.0029 | 0.0116 | 1994 | −0.1124 |
| 1995 | 0.0230 | 0.0246 | 0.0045 | 0.0124 | 0.0733 | 0.0091 | −0.0212 | 0.0189 | 0.0131 | 0.0246 | 0.0206 | 0.0222 | 1995 | 0.2469 |
| 1996 | −0.0053 | −0.0520 | −0.0248 | −0.0210 | −0.0096 | 0.0162 | −0.0027 | −0.0180 | 0.0245 | 0.0360 | 0.0309 | −0.0301 | 1996 | −0.0583 |
| 1997 | −0.0124 | −0.0033 | −0.0294 | 0.0211 | 0.0047 | 0.0157 | 0.0580 | −0.0357 | 0.0270 | 0.0297 | 0.0108 | 0.0136 | 1997 | 0.1007 |
| 1998 | 0.0157 | −0.0110 | −0.0015 | −0.0017 | 0.0141 | 0.0186 | −0.0079 | 0.0420 | 0.0347 | −0.0250 | 0.0066 | −0.0069 | 1998 | 0.0783 |
| 1999 | 0.0086 | −0.0553 | −0.0050 | −0.0016 | −0.0218 | −0.0117 | −0.0114 | −0.0091 | 0.0045 | −0.0050 | −0.0097 | −0.0197 | 1999 | −0.1304 |
| 2000 | 0.0186 | 0.0220 | 0.0318 | −0.0121 | −0.0104 | 0.0203 | 0.0124 | 0.0189 | −0.0207 | 0.0131 | 0.0266 | 0.0191 | 2000 | 0.1472 |

* Compound annual return

## Table A-20

**Large Company Stocks: Inflation-Adjusted Total Returns**

from January 1926 to December 1970

| Year | Jan | Feb | Mar | Apr | May | Jun | Jul | Aug | Sep | Oct | Nov | Dec | Year | Jan-Dec* |
|------|-----|-----|-----|-----|-----|-----|-----|-----|-----|-----|-----|-----|------|----------|
| 1926 | 0.0000 | −0.0349 | −0.0522 | 0.0158 | 0.0236 | 0.0536 | 0.0579 | 0.0307 | 0.0193 | −0.0320 | 0.0308 | 0.0196 | 1926 | 0.1331 |
| 1927 | −0.0118 | 0.0618 | 0.0145 | 0.0201 | 0.0526 | −0.0161 | 0.0877 | 0.0576 | 0.0390 | −0.0557 | 0.0742 | 0.0298 | 1927 | 0.4041 |
| 1928 | −0.0020 | −0.0029 | 0.1101 | 0.0325 | 0.0138 | −0.0310 | 0.0141 | 0.0782 | 0.0179 | 0.0188 | 0.1313 | 0.0089 | 1928 | 0.4501 |
| 1929 | 0.0604 | 0.0000 | 0.0028 | 0.0216 | −0.0419 | 0.1096 | 0.0369 | 0.0986 | −0.0458 | −0.1973 | −0.1229 | 0.0342 | 1929 | −0.0859 |
| 1930 | 0.0680 | 0.0299 | 0.0876 | −0.0138 | −0.0038 | −0.1575 | 0.0532 | 0.0203 | −0.1335 | −0.0800 | −0.0008 | −0.0571 | 1930 | −0.2008 |
| 1931 | 0.0656 | 0.1360 | −0.0615 | −0.0876 | −0.1184 | 0.1547 | −0.0701 | 0.0205 | −0.2941 | 0.0969 | −0.0693 | −0.1321 | 1931 | −0.3737 |
| 1932 | −0.0066 | 0.0721 | −0.1116 | −0.1940 | −0.2082 | 0.0051 | 0.3815 | 0.4041 | −0.0297 | −0.1284 | −0.0368 | 0.0673 | 1932 | 0.0235 |
| 1933 | 0.0244 | −0.1642 | 0.0436 | 0.4294 | 0.1652 | 0.1219 | −0.1118 | 0.1093 | −0.1118 | −0.0855 | 0.1127 | 0.0305 | 1933 | 0.5321 |
| 1934 | 0.1013 | −0.0395 | 0.0000 | −0.0227 | −0.0759 | 0.0203 | −0.1132 | 0.0584 | −0.0180 | −0.0214 | 0.0969 | 0.0014 | 1934 | −0.0340 |
| 1935 | −0.0552 | −0.0411 | −0.0262 | 0.0874 | 0.0460 | 0.0725 | 0.0903 | 0.0280 | 0.0206 | 0.0777 | 0.0423 | 0.0369 | 1935 | 0.4339 |
| 1936 | 0.0670 | 0.0273 | 0.0318 | −0.0751 | 0.0545 | 0.0233 | 0.0649 | 0.0079 | 0.0007 | 0.0800 | 0.0134 | −0.0029 | 1936 | 0.3232 |
| 1937 | 0.0316 | 0.0167 | −0.0147 | −0.0852 | −0.0071 | −0.0526 | 0.0994 | −0.0505 | −0.1481 | −0.0940 | −0.0802 | −0.0437 | 1937 | −0.3698 |
| 1938 | 0.0295 | 0.0775 | −0.2487 | 0.1393 | −0.0284 | 0.2503 | 0.0719 | −0.0203 | 0.0166 | 0.0827 | −0.0250 | 0.0376 | 1938 | 0.3487 |
| 1939 | −0.0629 | 0.0440 | −0.1318 | −0.0003 | 0.0733 | −0.0612 | 0.1105 | −0.0648 | 0.1451 | −0.0076 | −0.0398 | 0.0320 | 1939 | 0.0007 |
| 1940 | −0.0313 | 0.0060 | 0.0148 | −0.0024 | −0.2307 | 0.0783 | 0.0365 | 0.0375 | 0.0099 | 0.0422 | −0.0316 | −0.0038 | 1940 | −0.1064 |
| 1941 | −0.0463 | −0.0060 | 0.0023 | −0.0700 | 0.0112 | 0.0385 | 0.0531 | −0.0080 | −0.0243 | −0.0759 | −0.0368 | −0.0427 | 1941 | −0.1942 |
| 1942 | 0.0031 | −0.0242 | −0.0769 | −0.0459 | 0.0685 | 0.0200 | 0.0295 | 0.0102 | 0.0269 | 0.0571 | −0.0081 | 0.0466 | 1942 | 0.1011 |
| 1943 | 0.0737 | 0.0562 | 0.0382 | −0.0081 | 0.0472 | 0.0242 | −0.0453 | 0.0210 | 0.0223 | −0.0146 | −0.0636 | 0.0597 | 1943 | 0.2204 |
| 1944 | 0.0191 | 0.0061 | 0.0195 | −0.0157 | 0.0465 | 0.0522 | −0.0248 | 0.0119 | −0.0008 | 0.0023 | 0.0133 | 0.0335 | 1944 | 0.1728 |
| 1945 | 0.0158 | 0.0703 | −0.0441 | 0.0881 | 0.0119 | −0.0099 | −0.0199 | 0.0641 | 0.0477 | 0.0322 | 0.0358 | 0.0079 | 1945 | 0.3343 |
| 1946 | 0.0714 | −0.0606 | 0.0404 | 0.0336 | 0.0232 | −0.0474 | −0.0783 | −0.0874 | −0.1100 | −0.0251 | −0.0261 | 0.0376 | 1946 | −0.2220 |
| 1947 | 0.0255 | −0.0061 | −0.0359 | −0.0363 | 0.0044 | 0.0474 | 0.0288 | −0.0305 | −0.0341 | 0.0238 | −0.0232 | 0.0102 | 1947 | −0.0303 |
| 1948 | −0.0487 | −0.0306 | 0.0824 | 0.0147 | 0.0803 | −0.0016 | −0.0625 | 0.0116 | −0.0276 | 0.0754 | −0.0899 | 0.0418 | 1948 | 0.0272 |
| 1949 | 0.0053 | −0.0187 | 0.0299 | −0.0193 | −0.0244 | 0.0000 | 0.0725 | 0.0191 | 0.0220 | 0.0398 | 0.0160 | 0.0545 | 1949 | 0.2097 |
| 1950 | 0.0240 | 0.0228 | 0.0027 | 0.0471 | 0.0465 | −0.0601 | 0.0020 | 0.0357 | 0.0519 | 0.0038 | 0.0128 | 0.0372 | 1950 | 0.2450 |
| 1951 | 0.0469 | 0.0038 | −0.0194 | 0.0496 | −0.0336 | −0.0215 | 0.0697 | 0.0478 | −0.0051 | −0.0154 | 0.0045 | 0.0385 | 1951 | 0.1714 |
| 1952 | 0.0181 | −0.0220 | 0.0503 | −0.0439 | 0.0330 | 0.0464 | 0.0120 | −0.0083 | −0.0164 | 0.0008 | 0.0571 | 0.0395 | 1952 | 0.1733 |
| 1953 | −0.0024 | −0.0056 | −0.0237 | −0.0249 | 0.0052 | −0.0171 | 0.0248 | −0.0525 | 0.0022 | 0.0514 | 0.0242 | 0.0065 | 1953 | −0.0160 |
| 1954 | 0.0510 | 0.0124 | 0.0338 | 0.0542 | 0.0379 | 0.0018 | 0.0589 | −0.0263 | 0.0878 | −0.0143 | 0.0896 | 0.0561 | 1954 | 0.5339 |
| 1955 | 0.0197 | 0.0098 | −0.0030 | 0.0396 | 0.0055 | 0.0841 | 0.0582 | 0.0000 | 0.0092 | −0.0284 | 0.0813 | 0.0040 | 1955 | 0.3107 |
| 1956 | −0.0335 | 0.0413 | 0.0697 | −0.0017 | −0.0640 | 0.0345 | 0.0453 | −0.0316 | −0.0452 | 0.0005 | −0.0050 | 0.0345 | 1956 | 0.0359 |
| 1957 | −0.0412 | −0.0299 | 0.0190 | 0.0350 | 0.0412 | −0.0055 | 0.0083 | −0.0516 | −0.0613 | −0.0302 | 0.0195 | −0.0395 | 1957 | −0.1340 |
| 1958 | 0.0384 | −0.0153 | 0.0256 | 0.0313 | 0.0212 | 0.0267 | 0.0437 | 0.0188 | 0.0501 | 0.0270 | 0.0273 | 0.0548 | 1958 | 0.4088 |
| 1959 | 0.0041 | 0.0060 | 0.0020 | 0.0390 | 0.0228 | −0.0068 | 0.0339 | −0.0091 | −0.0476 | 0.0094 | 0.0186 | 0.0292 | 1959 | 0.1030 |
| 1960 | −0.0689 | 0.0136 | −0.0123 | −0.0216 | 0.0326 | 0.0188 | −0.0234 | 0.0317 | −0.0600 | −0.0052 | 0.0453 | 0.0479 | 1960 | −0.0099 |
| 1961 | 0.0645 | 0.0319 | 0.0270 | 0.0051 | 0.0239 | −0.0286 | 0.0296 | 0.0254 | −0.0205 | 0.0298 | 0.0447 | 0.0046 | 1961 | 0.2604 |
| 1962 | −0.0366 | 0.0187 | −0.0068 | −0.0628 | −0.0811 | −0.0803 | 0.0629 | 0.0208 | −0.0517 | 0.0075 | 0.1086 | 0.0164 | 1962 | −0.0983 |
| 1963 | 0.0494 | −0.0249 | 0.0359 | 0.0500 | 0.0193 | −0.0231 | −0.0065 | 0.0535 | −0.0097 | 0.0328 | −0.0057 | 0.0240 | 1963 | 0.2081 |
| 1964 | 0.0271 | 0.0158 | 0.0154 | 0.0064 | 0.0162 | 0.0156 | 0.0173 | −0.0107 | 0.0279 | 0.0085 | −0.0017 | 0.0045 | 1964 | 0.1511 |
| 1965 | 0.0345 | 0.0031 | −0.0143 | 0.0323 | −0.0051 | −0.0523 | 0.0137 | 0.0294 | 0.0312 | 0.0278 | −0.0052 | 0.0074 | 1965 | 0.1033 |
| 1966 | 0.0062 | −0.0193 | −0.0236 | 0.0177 | −0.0502 | −0.0177 | −0.0151 | −0.0772 | −0.0073 | 0.0451 | 0.0095 | −0.0008 | 1966 | −0.1298 |
| 1967 | 0.0798 | 0.0061 | 0.0388 | 0.0416 | −0.0505 | 0.0159 | 0.0416 | −0.0099 | 0.0321 | −0.0305 | 0.0035 | 0.0247 | 1967 | 0.2032 |
| 1968 | −0.0463 | −0.0290 | 0.0060 | 0.0802 | 0.0131 | 0.0047 | −0.0219 | 0.0135 | 0.0370 | 0.0029 | 0.0491 | −0.0429 | 1968 | 0.0605 |
| 1969 | −0.0096 | −0.0462 | 0.0272 | 0.0163 | −0.0002 | −0.0603 | −0.0630 | 0.0407 | −0.0279 | 0.0421 | −0.0349 | −0.0238 | 1969 | −0.1377 |
| 1970 | −0.0776 | 0.0530 | −0.0022 | −0.0945 | −0.0588 | −0.0531 | 0.0715 | 0.0491 | 0.0294 | −0.0148 | 0.0500 | 0.0530 | 1970 | −0.0141 |

* Compound annual return

Table A-20 (continued)

## Large Company Stocks: Inflation-Adjusted Total Returns

from January 1971 to December 2000

| Year | Jan | Feb | Mar | Apr | May | Jun | Jul | Aug | Sep | Oct | Nov | Dec | Year | Jan-Dec* |
|------|-----|-----|-----|-----|-----|-----|-----|-----|-----|-----|-----|-----|------|----------|
| 1971 | 0.0410 | 0.0124 | 0.0348 | 0.0342 | −0.0415 | −0.0037 | −0.0423 | 0.0387 | −0.0064 | −0.0419 | 0.0010 | 0.0833 | 1971 | 0.1060 |
| 1972 | 0.0186 | 0.0249 | 0.0056 | 0.0033 | 0.0186 | −0.0229 | −0.0004 | 0.0375 | −0.0075 | 0.0075 | 0.0480 | 0.0099 | 1972 | 0.1505 |
| 1973 | −0.0190 | −0.0400 | −0.0094 | −0.0461 | −0.0199 | −0.0119 | 0.0371 | −0.0490 | 0.0385 | −0.0078 | −0.1147 | 0.0117 | 1973 | −0.2156 |
| 1974 | −0.0170 | −0.0109 | −0.0327 | −0.0427 | −0.0379 | −0.0223 | −0.0828 | −0.0945 | −0.1275 | 0.1558 | −0.0528 | −0.0247 | 1974 | −0.3446 |
| 1975 | 0.1201 | 0.0600 | 0.0198 | 0.0440 | 0.0462 | 0.0377 | −0.0757 | −0.0175 | −0.0375 | 0.0572 | 0.0251 | −0.0138 | 1975 | 0.2821 |
| 1976 | 0.1172 | −0.0082 | 0.0301 | −0.0140 | −0.0132 | 0.0372 | −0.0126 | −0.0032 | 0.0205 | −0.0245 | −0.0038 | 0.0509 | 1976 | 0.1816 |
| 1977 | −0.0544 | −0.0251 | −0.0180 | −0.0064 | −0.0204 | 0.0406 | −0.0194 | −0.0170 | −0.0038 | −0.0441 | 0.0320 | 0.0010 | 1977 | −0.1307 |
| 1978 | −0.0647 | −0.0229 | 0.0206 | 0.0774 | 0.0037 | −0.0253 | 0.0484 | 0.0288 | −0.0118 | −0.0963 | 0.0204 | 0.0117 | 1978 | −0.0226 |
| 1979 | 0.0330 | −0.0396 | 0.0474 | −0.0078 | −0.0288 | 0.0314 | −0.0020 | 0.0505 | −0.0078 | −0.0739 | 0.0417 | 0.0086 | 1979 | 0.0453 |
| 1980 | 0.0460 | −0.0105 | −0.1114 | 0.0313 | 0.0459 | 0.0183 | 0.0667 | 0.0066 | 0.0187 | 0.0098 | 0.0996 | −0.0398 | 1980 | 0.1781 |
| 1981 | −0.0515 | 0.0103 | 0.0306 | −0.0275 | −0.0020 | −0.0164 | −0.0106 | −0.0626 | −0.0597 | 0.0505 | 0.0411 | −0.0293 | 1981 | −0.1271 |
| 1982 | −0.0198 | −0.0542 | −0.0049 | 0.0370 | −0.0383 | −0.0292 | −0.0269 | 0.1244 | 0.0093 | 0.1096 | 0.0456 | 0.0215 | 1982 | 0.1688 |
| 1983 | 0.0323 | 0.0257 | 0.0358 | 0.0682 | −0.0106 | 0.0347 | −0.0352 | 0.0136 | 0.0086 | −0.0160 | 0.0216 | −0.0074 | 1983 | 0.1803 |
| 1984 | −0.0120 | −0.0372 | 0.0148 | 0.0020 | −0.0562 | 0.0188 | −0.0175 | 0.1079 | −0.0046 | 0.0001 | −0.0101 | 0.0247 | 1984 | 0.0222 |
| 1985 | 0.0748 | 0.0095 | −0.0026 | −0.0072 | 0.0575 | 0.0128 | −0.0041 | −0.0083 | −0.0351 | 0.0415 | 0.0680 | 0.0441 | 1985 | 0.2736 |
| 1986 | 0.0013 | 0.0791 | 0.0603 | −0.0103 | 0.0517 | 0.0116 | −0.0572 | 0.0729 | −0.0867 | 0.0546 | 0.0247 | −0.0273 | 1986 | 0.1715 |
| 1987 | 0.1275 | 0.0373 | 0.0226 | −0.0141 | 0.0073 | 0.0456 | 0.0476 | 0.0327 | −0.0268 | −0.2172 | −0.0832 | 0.0741 | 1987 | 0.0079 |
| 1988 | 0.0400 | 0.0443 | −0.0344 | 0.0056 | 0.0044 | 0.0420 | −0.0082 | −0.0372 | 0.0354 | 0.0239 | −0.0150 | 0.0164 | 1988 | 0.1187 |
| 1989 | 0.0670 | −0.0289 | 0.0177 | 0.0448 | 0.0343 | −0.0078 | 0.0872 | 0.0177 | −0.0071 | −0.0280 | 0.0184 | 0.0220 | 1989 | 0.2565 |
| 1990 | −0.0766 | 0.0082 | 0.0207 | −0.0262 | 0.0950 | −0.0124 | −0.0070 | −0.0986 | −0.0571 | −0.0097 | 0.0620 | 0.0274 | 1990 | −0.0874 |
| 1991 | 0.0380 | 0.0700 | 0.0223 | 0.0013 | 0.0397 | −0.0485 | 0.0453 | 0.0205 | −0.0207 | 0.0119 | −0.0432 | 0.1135 | 1991 | 0.2667 |
| 1992 | −0.0200 | 0.0091 | −0.0245 | 0.0276 | 0.0040 | −0.0180 | 0.0381 | −0.0230 | 0.0086 | 0.0001 | 0.0322 | 0.0138 | 1992 | 0.0464 |
| 1993 | 0.0024 | 0.0100 | 0.0179 | −0.0272 | 0.0256 | 0.0019 | −0.0047 | 0.0352 | −0.0095 | 0.0161 | −0.0101 | 0.0123 | 1993 | 0.0705 |
| 1994 | 0.0307 | −0.0303 | −0.0467 | 0.0116 | 0.0156 | −0.0280 | 0.0303 | 0.0365 | −0.0267 | 0.0222 | −0.0380 | 0.0146 | 1994 | −0.0133 |
| 1995 | 0.0219 | 0.0347 | 0.0262 | 0.0257 | 0.0375 | 0.0215 | 0.0333 | 0.0001 | 0.0399 | −0.0067 | 0.0447 | 0.0192 | 1995 | 0.3403 |
| 1996 | 0.0284 | 0.0063 | 0.0044 | 0.0108 | 0.0238 | 0.0035 | −0.0463 | 0.0193 | 0.0529 | 0.0242 | 0.0739 | −0.0196 | 1996 | 0.1912 |
| 1997 | 0.0588 | 0.0049 | −0.0440 | 0.0584 | 0.0621 | 0.0433 | 0.0781 | −0.0574 | 0.0522 | −0.0358 | 0.0469 | 0.0185 | 1997 | 0.3113 |
| 1998 | 0.0092 | 0.0701 | 0.0493 | 0.0082 | −0.0190 | 0.0393 | −0.0119 | −0.1456 | 0.0628 | 0.0787 | 0.0606 | 0.0583 | 1998 | 0.2654 |
| 1999 | 0.0393 | −0.0323 | 0.0369 | 0.0312 | −0.0236 | 0.0555 | −0.0341 | −0.0073 | −0.0320 | 0.0614 | 0.0197 | 0.0589 | 1999 | 0.1788 |
| 2000 | −0.0525 | −0.0247 | 0.0888 | −0.0307 | −0.0211 | 0.0187 | −0.0173 | 0.0609 | −0.0577 | −0.0059 | −0.0794 | 0.0055 | 2000 | −0.1208 |

* Compound annual return

## Table A-21

**Small Company Stocks: Inflation-Adjusted Total Returns**

from January 1926 to December 1970

| Year | Jan | Feb | Mar | Apr | May | Jun | Jul | Aug | Sep | Oct | Nov | Dec | Year | Jan-Dec* |
|------|-----|-----|-----|-----|-----|-----|-----|-----|-----|-----|-----|-----|------|----------|
| 1926 | 0.0699 | −0.0604 | −0.1023 | 0.0084 | −0.0010 | 0.0456 | 0.0208 | 0.0315 | −0.0058 | −0.0264 | 0.0169 | 0.0332 | 1926 | 0.0179 |
| 1927 | 0.0374 | 0.0628 | −0.0493 | 0.0573 | 0.0652 | −0.0395 | 0.0719 | −0.0121 | −0.0011 | −0.0713 | 0.0829 | 0.0336 | 1927 | 0.2469 |
| 1928 | 0.0502 | −0.0141 | 0.0531 | 0.0889 | 0.0377 | −0.0771 | 0.0059 | 0.0421 | 0.0806 | 0.0296 | 0.1169 | −0.0476 | 1928 | 0.4106 |
| 1929 | 0.0054 | −0.0007 | −0.0162 | 0.0347 | −0.1387 | 0.0492 | 0.0016 | −0.0201 | −0.0904 | −0.2768 | −0.1484 | −0.0445 | 1929 | −0.5145 |
| 1930 | 0.1337 | 0.0685 | 0.1072 | −0.0753 | −0.0487 | −0.2121 | 0.0446 | −0.0107 | −0.1511 | −0.1043 | 0.0054 | −0.1038 | 1930 | −0.3418 |
| 1931 | 0.2281 | 0.2754 | −0.0648 | −0.2113 | −0.1284 | 0.1950 | −0.0536 | −0.0742 | −0.3216 | 0.0842 | −0.0907 | −0.2124 | 1931 | −0.4446 |
| 1932 | 0.1251 | 0.0437 | −0.1270 | −0.2164 | −0.1065 | 0.0107 | 0.3523 | 0.7561 | −0.1277 | −0.1713 | −0.1183 | −0.0395 | 1932 | 0.0547 |
| 1933 | 0.0071 | −0.1140 | 0.1206 | 0.5078 | 0.6296 | 0.2484 | −0.0816 | 0.0814 | −0.1595 | −0.1236 | 0.0654 | 0.0106 | 1933 | 1.4163 |
| 1934 | 0.3821 | 0.0090 | −0.0012 | 0.0265 | −0.1297 | −0.0049 | −0.2259 | 0.1517 | −0.0312 | 0.0172 | 0.0975 | 0.0198 | 1934 | 0.2175 |
| 1935 | −0.0470 | −0.0661 | −0.1167 | 0.0687 | 0.0024 | 0.0330 | 0.0908 | 0.0545 | 0.0306 | 0.0994 | 0.1357 | 0.0573 | 1935 | 0.3613 |
| 1936 | 0.3009 | 0.0654 | 0.0115 | −0.1795 | 0.0272 | −0.0326 | 0.0820 | 0.0137 | 0.0517 | 0.0661 | 0.1400 | 0.0160 | 1936 | 0.6283 |
| 1937 | 0.1186 | 0.0632 | 0.0048 | −0.1718 | −0.0453 | −0.1203 | 0.1183 | −0.0758 | −0.2607 | −0.1052 | −0.1394 | −0.1674 | 1937 | −0.5927 |
| 1938 | 0.0683 | 0.0441 | −0.3600 | 0.2716 | −0.0806 | 0.3498 | 0.1472 | −0.0980 | −0.0157 | 0.2193 | −0.0666 | 0.0462 | 1938 | 0.3659 |
| 1939 | −0.0805 | 0.0155 | −0.2448 | 0.0166 | 0.1088 | −0.1042 | 0.2535 | −0.1590 | 0.4858 | −0.0351 | −0.1053 | 0.0472 | 1939 | 0.0083 |
| 1940 | 0.0033 | 0.0743 | 0.0657 | 0.0654 | −0.3689 | 0.1024 | 0.0256 | 0.0279 | 0.0188 | 0.0545 | 0.0245 | −0.0492 | 1940 | −0.0605 |
| 1941 | 0.0025 | −0.0288 | 0.0271 | −0.0757 | −0.0025 | 0.0557 | 0.2110 | −0.0150 | −0.0638 | −0.0774 | −0.0577 | −0.1223 | 1941 | −0.1706 |
| 1942 | 0.1742 | −0.0157 | −0.0826 | −0.0413 | −0.0134 | 0.0315 | 0.0693 | 0.0262 | 0.0890 | 0.0976 | −0.0567 | 0.0331 | 1942 | 0.3223 |
| 1943 | 0.2132 | 0.1908 | 0.1267 | 0.0807 | 0.1071 | −0.0064 | −0.1014 | 0.0036 | 0.0388 | 0.0084 | −0.1096 | 0.1219 | 1943 | 0.8260 |
| 1944 | 0.0661 | 0.0315 | 0.0749 | −0.0587 | 0.0699 | 0.1363 | −0.0354 | 0.0280 | −0.0020 | −0.0108 | 0.0499 | 0.0829 | 1944 | 0.5055 |
| 1945 | 0.0482 | 0.1030 | −0.0861 | 0.1136 | 0.0422 | 0.0755 | −0.0574 | 0.0557 | 0.0719 | 0.0701 | 0.1131 | 0.0133 | 1945 | 0.6979 |
| 1946 | 0.1562 | −0.0602 | 0.0198 | 0.0638 | 0.0534 | −0.0565 | −0.1057 | −0.1045 | −0.1699 | −0.0308 | −0.0373 | 0.0292 | 1946 | −0.2521 |
| 1947 | 0.0421 | −0.0025 | −0.0542 | −0.1031 | −0.0505 | 0.0472 | 0.0692 | −0.0141 | −0.0120 | 0.0282 | −0.0359 | 0.0227 | 1947 | −0.0742 |
| 1948 | −0.0264 | −0.0704 | 0.1017 | 0.0222 | 0.0982 | −0.0022 | −0.0694 | −0.0035 | −0.0526 | 0.0691 | −0.1055 | 0.0157 | 1948 | −0.0469 |
| 1949 | 0.0196 | −0.0374 | 0.0599 | −0.0350 | −0.0551 | −0.0110 | 0.0746 | 0.0228 | 0.0445 | 0.0531 | 0.0002 | 0.0750 | 1949 | 0.2195 |
| 1950 | 0.0536 | 0.0250 | −0.0079 | 0.0397 | 0.0212 | −0.0829 | 0.0489 | 0.0443 | 0.0449 | −0.0113 | 0.0281 | 0.0807 | 1950 | 0.3115 |
| 1951 | 0.0660 | −0.0057 | −0.0514 | 0.0353 | −0.0368 | −0.0516 | 0.0360 | 0.0605 | 0.0150 | −0.0272 | −0.0133 | 0.0006 | 1951 | 0.0182 |
| 1952 | 0.0191 | −0.0238 | 0.0175 | −0.0555 | 0.0019 | 0.0246 | 0.0036 | −0.0018 | −0.0149 | −0.0115 | 0.0485 | 0.0173 | 1952 | 0.0213 |
| 1953 | 0.0435 | 0.0321 | −0.0092 | −0.0300 | 0.0116 | −0.0522 | 0.0127 | −0.0651 | −0.0274 | 0.0266 | 0.0164 | −0.0253 | 1953 | −0.0707 |
| 1954 | 0.0730 | 0.0107 | 0.0196 | 0.0165 | 0.0413 | 0.0073 | 0.0808 | 0.0027 | 0.0436 | 0.0093 | 0.0766 | 0.1140 | 1954 | 0.6138 |
| 1955 | 0.0201 | 0.0479 | 0.0085 | 0.0150 | 0.0078 | 0.0293 | 0.0026 | −0.0003 | 0.0072 | −0.0170 | 0.0455 | 0.0188 | 1955 | 0.1999 |
| 1956 | −0.0035 | 0.0278 | 0.0418 | 0.0034 | −0.0445 | −0.0006 | 0.0208 | −0.0122 | −0.0272 | 0.0043 | 0.0053 | 0.0014 | 1956 | 0.0138 |
| 1957 | 0.0224 | −0.0235 | 0.0143 | 0.0212 | 0.0051 | 0.0013 | −0.0107 | −0.0397 | −0.0463 | −0.0832 | 0.0078 | −0.0481 | 1957 | −0.1708 |
| 1958 | 0.1040 | −0.0181 | 0.0398 | 0.0352 | 0.0387 | 0.0312 | 0.0479 | 0.0440 | 0.0518 | 0.0407 | 0.0484 | 0.0325 | 1958 | 0.6203 |
| 1959 | 0.0562 | 0.0307 | 0.0027 | 0.0105 | 0.0002 | −0.0088 | 0.0304 | −0.0076 | −0.0464 | 0.0192 | 0.0222 | 0.0322 | 1959 | 0.1468 |
| 1960 | −0.0295 | 0.0038 | −0.0315 | −0.0242 | 0.0204 | 0.0317 | −0.0189 | 0.0525 | −0.0749 | −0.0444 | 0.0425 | 0.0332 | 1960 | −0.0470 |
| 1961 | 0.0915 | 0.0589 | 0.0619 | 0.0127 | 0.0427 | −0.0554 | −0.0013 | 0.0142 | −0.0360 | 0.0262 | 0.0613 | 0.0079 | 1961 | 0.3121 |
| 1962 | 0.0136 | 0.0165 | 0.0034 | −0.0798 | −0.1009 | −0.0785 | 0.0739 | 0.0289 | −0.0710 | −0.0363 | 0.1248 | −0.0078 | 1962 | −0.1297 |
| 1963 | 0.0894 | 0.0023 | 0.0138 | 0.0312 | 0.0436 | −0.0162 | −0.0011 | 0.0517 | −0.0163 | 0.0225 | −0.0117 | −0.0069 | 1963 | 0.2156 |
| 1964 | 0.0263 | 0.0376 | 0.0208 | 0.0082 | 0.0157 | 0.0141 | 0.0376 | −0.0018 | 0.0380 | 0.0194 | −0.0011 | −0.0122 | 1964 | 0.2207 |
| 1965 | 0.0529 | 0.0390 | 0.0227 | 0.0475 | −0.0099 | −0.0949 | 0.0437 | 0.0617 | 0.0325 | 0.0561 | 0.0349 | 0.0588 | 1965 | 0.3908 |
| 1966 | 0.0756 | 0.0247 | −0.0222 | 0.0301 | −0.0971 | −0.0043 | −0.0043 | −0.1125 | −0.0184 | −0.0147 | 0.0491 | 0.0055 | 1966 | −0.1003 |
| 1967 | 0.1838 | 0.0439 | 0.0593 | 0.0250 | −0.0115 | 0.0984 | 0.0896 | −0.0009 | 0.0544 | −0.0340 | 0.0087 | 0.0933 | 1967 | 0.7815 |
| 1968 | 0.0114 | −0.0736 | −0.0157 | 0.1427 | 0.0967 | −0.0028 | −0.0392 | 0.0337 | 0.0569 | −0.0027 | 0.0724 | 0.0034 | 1968 | 0.2984 |
| 1969 | −0.0194 | −0.1024 | 0.0309 | 0.0328 | 0.0145 | −0.1221 | −0.1110 | 0.0684 | −0.0305 | 0.0572 | −0.0608 | −0.0745 | 1969 | −0.2937 |
| 1970 | −0.0641 | 0.0332 | −0.0335 | −0.1778 | −0.1070 | −0.0976 | 0.0517 | 0.0930 | 0.1029 | −0.0753 | 0.0103 | 0.0672 | 1970 | −0.2173 |

* Compound annual return

# Table A-21 (continued)

## Small Company Stocks: Inflation-Adjusted Total Returns

from January 1971 to December 2000

| Year | Jan | Feb | Mar | Apr | May | Jun | Jul | Aug | Sep | Oct | Nov | Dec | Year | Jan-Dec* |
|------|-----|-----|-----|-----|-----|-----|-----|-----|-----|-----|-----|-----|------|----------|
| 1971 | 0.1582 | 0.0299 | 0.0529 | 0.0213 | −0.0652 | −0.0375 | −0.0586 | 0.0557 | −0.0234 | −0.0567 | −0.0389 | 0.1099 | 1971 | 0.1271 |
| 1972 | 0.1121 | 0.0246 | −0.0159 | 0.0104 | −0.0223 | −0.0328 | −0.0451 | 0.0170 | −0.0387 | −0.0206 | 0.0567 | −0.0244 | 1972 | 0.0099 |
| 1973 | −0.0462 | −0.0863 | −0.0298 | −0.0686 | −0.0867 | −0.0356 | 0.1169 | −0.0615 | 0.1031 | 0.0003 | −0.2021 | −0.0078 | 1973 | −0.3649 |
| 1974 | 0.1229 | −0.0211 | −0.0185 | −0.0517 | −0.0894 | −0.0241 | −0.0291 | −0.0799 | −0.0764 | 0.0969 | −0.0518 | −0.0853 | 1974 | −0.2865 |
| 1975 | 0.2710 | 0.0213 | 0.0578 | 0.0478 | 0.0616 | 0.0662 | −0.0356 | −0.0603 | −0.0230 | −0.0111 | 0.0257 | −0.0238 | 1975 | 0.4280 |
| 1976 | 0.2654 | 0.1362 | −0.0039 | −0.0399 | −0.0418 | 0.0404 | −0.0014 | −0.0336 | 0.0063 | −0.0248 | 0.0374 | 0.1148 | 1976 | 0.5015 |
| 1977 | 0.0390 | −0.0140 | 0.0068 | 0.0149 | −0.0083 | 0.0701 | −0.0014 | −0.0145 | 0.0054 | −0.0357 | 0.1032 | 0.0043 | 1977 | 0.1743 |
| 1978 | −0.0241 | 0.0276 | 0.0957 | 0.0692 | 0.0714 | −0.0290 | 0.0608 | 0.0883 | −0.0102 | −0.2488 | 0.0673 | 0.0113 | 1978 | 0.1324 |
| 1979 | 0.1222 | −0.0395 | 0.1013 | 0.0269 | −0.0087 | 0.0375 | 0.0041 | 0.0649 | −0.0443 | −0.1233 | 0.0758 | 0.0478 | 1979 | 0.2662 |
| 1980 | 0.0683 | −0.0415 | −0.1894 | 0.0574 | 0.0645 | 0.0338 | 0.1314 | 0.0536 | 0.0323 | 0.0244 | 0.0670 | −0.0420 | 1980 | 0.2445 |
| 1981 | 0.0125 | −0.0010 | 0.0865 | 0.0589 | 0.0337 | −0.0009 | −0.0425 | −0.0755 | −0.0826 | 0.0719 | 0.0247 | −0.0248 | 1981 | 0.0453 |
| 1982 | −0.0231 | −0.0327 | −0.0075 | 0.0339 | −0.0343 | −0.0278 | −0.0070 | 0.0676 | 0.0309 | 0.1274 | 0.0797 | 0.0174 | 1982 | 0.2323 |
| 1983 | 0.0603 | 0.0709 | 0.0518 | 0.0690 | 0.0811 | 0.0314 | −0.0128 | −0.0229 | 0.0083 | −0.0593 | 0.0498 | −0.0158 | 1983 | 0.3456 |
| 1984 | −0.0064 | −0.0688 | 0.0151 | −0.0133 | −0.0549 | 0.0267 | −0.0451 | 0.0952 | −0.0021 | −0.0242 | −0.0336 | 0.0144 | 1984 | −0.1022 |
| 1985 | 0.1038 | 0.0230 | −0.0257 | −0.0214 | 0.0238 | 0.0075 | 0.0244 | −0.0093 | −0.0573 | 0.0229 | 0.0584 | 0.0444 | 1985 | 0.2013 |
| 1986 | 0.0081 | 0.0748 | 0.0525 | 0.0086 | 0.0328 | −0.0023 | −0.0713 | 0.0200 | −0.0605 | 0.0337 | −0.0040 | −0.0271 | 1986 | 0.0566 |
| 1987 | 0.0877 | 0.0767 | 0.0187 | −0.0365 | −0.0068 | 0.0224 | 0.0343 | 0.0230 | −0.0130 | −0.2937 | −0.0411 | 0.0523 | 1987 | −0.1313 |
| 1988 | 0.0529 | 0.0732 | 0.0363 | 0.0157 | −0.0212 | 0.0567 | −0.0067 | −0.0287 | 0.0159 | −0.0156 | −0.0445 | 0.0377 | 1988 | 0.1767 |
| 1989 | 0.0352 | 0.0042 | 0.0299 | 0.0212 | 0.0303 | −0.0225 | 0.0382 | 0.0106 | −0.0032 | −0.0649 | −0.0075 | −0.0150 | 1989 | 0.0529 |
| 1990 | −0.0858 | 0.0139 | 0.0312 | −0.0281 | 0.0536 | 0.0089 | −0.0419 | −0.1375 | −0.0905 | −0.0629 | 0.0427 | 0.0194 | 1990 | −0.2608 |
| 1991 | 0.0777 | 0.1097 | 0.0664 | 0.0019 | 0.0304 | −0.0513 | 0.0392 | 0.0231 | −0.0012 | 0.0302 | −0.0304 | 0.0593 | 1991 | 0.4033 |
| 1992 | 0.1112 | 0.0414 | −0.0298 | −0.0417 | −0.0028 | −0.0553 | 0.0348 | −0.0256 | 0.0102 | 0.0223 | 0.0870 | 0.0448 | 1992 | 0.1987 |
| 1993 | 0.0491 | −0.0214 | 0.0253 | −0.0333 | 0.0328 | −0.0052 | 0.0166 | 0.0310 | 0.0295 | 0.0428 | −0.0182 | 0.0194 | 1993 | 0.1774 |
| 1994 | 0.0589 | −0.0057 | −0.0478 | 0.0046 | −0.0019 | −0.0295 | 0.0157 | 0.0295 | 0.0078 | 0.0108 | −0.0339 | 0.0002 | 1994 | 0.0042 |
| 1995 | 0.0242 | 0.0211 | 0.0111 | 0.0318 | 0.0278 | 0.0547 | 0.0645 | 0.0331 | 0.0175 | −0.0518 | 0.0199 | 0.0246 | 1995 | 0.3113 |
| 1996 | −0.0030 | 0.0336 | 0.0175 | 0.0806 | 0.0728 | −0.0588 | −0.0960 | 0.0456 | 0.0258 | −0.0206 | 0.0269 | 0.0204 | 1996 | 0.1384 |
| 1997 | 0.0387 | −0.0237 | −0.0514 | −0.0288 | 0.1029 | 0.0485 | 0.0592 | 0.0489 | 0.0817 | −0.0410 | −0.0149 | −0.0159 | 1997 | 0.2072 |
| 1998 | −0.0077 | 0.0629 | 0.0462 | 0.0149 | −0.0515 | −0.0218 | −0.0682 | −0.2020 | 0.0356 | 0.0331 | 0.0758 | 0.0258 | 1998 | −0.0878 |
| 1999 | 0.0254 | −0.0698 | −0.0408 | 0.0870 | 0.0387 | 0.0568 | 0.0062 | −0.0214 | −0.0268 | −0.0105 | 0.0964 | 0.1137 | 1999 | 0.2639 |
| 2000 | 0.0570 | 0.2285 | −0.0827 | −0.1256 | −0.0813 | 0.1302 | −0.0339 | 0.0912 | −0.0268 | −0.0722 | −0.1115 | 0.0195 | 2000 | −0.0675 |

* Compound annual return

Table A-22

**Long-Term Corporate Bonds: Inflation-Adjusted Total Returns**

from January 1926 to December 1970

| Year | Jan | Feb | Mar | Apr | May | Jun | Jul | Aug | Sep | Oct | Nov | Dec | Year | Jan-Dec* |
|------|-----|-----|-----|-----|-----|-----|-----|-----|-----|-----|-----|-----|------|----------|
| 1926 | 0.0072 | 0.0083 | 0.0141 | 0.0003 | 0.0100 | 0.0080 | 0.0153 | 0.0102 | 0.0000 | 0.0059 | 0.0019 | 0.0056 | 1926 | 0.0900 |
| 1927 | 0.0133 | 0.0146 | 0.0141 | 0.0055 | −0.0088 | −0.0052 | 0.0196 | 0.0142 | 0.0090 | −0.0003 | 0.0087 | 0.0087 | 1927 | 0.0973 |
| 1928 | 0.0046 | 0.0166 | 0.0041 | −0.0006 | −0.0136 | 0.0054 | −0.0010 | 0.0063 | −0.0048 | 0.0103 | −0.0017 | 0.0123 | 1928 | 0.0384 |
| 1929 | 0.0063 | 0.0050 | −0.0048 | 0.0059 | −0.0014 | −0.0085 | −0.0077 | −0.0019 | 0.0053 | 0.0073 | 0.0001 | 0.0251 | 1929 | 0.0307 |
| 1930 | 0.0098 | 0.0111 | 0.0198 | 0.0025 | 0.0117 | 0.0170 | 0.0198 | 0.0198 | 0.0047 | 0.0115 | 0.0070 | 0.0054 | 1930 | 0.1490 |
| 1931 | 0.0353 | 0.0218 | 0.0159 | 0.0132 | 0.0245 | 0.0163 | 0.0074 | 0.0034 | 0.0030 | −0.0298 | −0.0078 | −0.0197 | 1931 | 0.0848 |
| 1932 | 0.0157 | −0.0099 | 0.0405 | −0.0105 | 0.0255 | 0.0064 | 0.0043 | 0.0565 | 0.0352 | 0.0150 | 0.0124 | 0.0242 | 1932 | 0.2354 |
| 1933 | 0.0711 | −0.0373 | 0.0127 | −0.0069 | 0.0560 | 0.0083 | −0.0124 | −0.0009 | −0.0014 | 0.0040 | −0.0248 | 0.0309 | 1933 | 0.0982 |
| 1934 | 0.0205 | 0.0070 | 0.0187 | 0.0129 | 0.0065 | 0.0133 | 0.0047 | 0.0022 | −0.0208 | 0.0177 | 0.0154 | 0.0126 | 1934 | 0.1158 |
| 1935 | 0.0061 | 0.0067 | 0.0067 | 0.0014 | 0.0091 | 0.0137 | 0.0160 | −0.0042 | −0.0049 | 0.0042 | 0.0020 | 0.0059 | 1935 | 0.0644 |
| 1936 | 0.0082 | 0.0103 | 0.0131 | 0.0026 | 0.0040 | −0.0015 | −0.0037 | −0.0005 | 0.0043 | 0.0049 | 0.0109 | 0.0010 | 1936 | 0.0547 |
| 1937 | −0.0047 | −0.0070 | −0.0184 | 0.0021 | −0.0007 | 0.0030 | −0.0007 | −0.0040 | −0.0067 | 0.0113 | 0.0137 | 0.0090 | 1937 | −0.0035 |
| 1938 | 0.0179 | 0.0105 | −0.0087 | 0.0090 | 0.0057 | 0.0095 | 0.0042 | 0.0005 | 0.0109 | 0.0128 | 0.0061 | 0.0098 | 1938 | 0.0916 |
| 1939 | 0.0070 | 0.0112 | 0.0046 | 0.0088 | 0.0049 | 0.0035 | −0.0007 | −0.0392 | −0.0041 | 0.0286 | 0.0079 | 0.0126 | 1939 | 0.0446 |
| 1940 | 0.0073 | −0.0051 | 0.0073 | −0.0092 | −0.0045 | 0.0097 | 0.0045 | 0.0031 | 0.0068 | 0.0049 | 0.0063 | −0.0070 | 1940 | 0.0241 |
| 1941 | 0.0006 | 0.0006 | −0.0069 | −0.0016 | −0.0021 | −0.0120 | 0.0017 | −0.0056 | −0.0129 | −0.0076 | −0.0180 | −0.0016 | 1941 | −0.0637 |
| 1942 | −0.0122 | −0.0093 | −0.0063 | −0.0056 | −0.0083 | 0.0013 | −0.0021 | −0.0026 | 0.0000 | −0.0094 | −0.0054 | −0.0030 | 1942 | −0.0612 |
| 1943 | 0.0049 | −0.0014 | −0.0136 | −0.0067 | −0.0029 | 0.0067 | 0.0096 | 0.0058 | −0.0033 | −0.0047 | −0.0004 | 0.0030 | 1943 | −0.0032 |
| 1944 | 0.0039 | 0.0053 | 0.0048 | −0.0024 | −0.0033 | 0.0001 | −0.0023 | −0.0004 | 0.0019 | 0.0019 | 0.0048 | 0.0111 | 1944 | 0.0257 |
| 1945 | 0.0076 | 0.0065 | 0.0018 | −0.0001 | −0.0085 | −0.0061 | −0.0029 | 0.0004 | 0.0069 | 0.0032 | −0.0005 | 0.0096 | 1945 | 0.0178 |
| 1946 | 0.0128 | 0.0071 | −0.0039 | −0.0097 | −0.0035 | −0.0089 | −0.0569 | −0.0301 | −0.0140 | −0.0173 | −0.0259 | 0.0034 | 1946 | −0.1391 |
| 1947 | 0.0005 | 0.0021 | −0.0148 | 0.0020 | 0.0051 | −0.0072 | −0.0070 | −0.0174 | −0.0360 | −0.0099 | −0.0155 | −0.0105 | 1947 | −0.1041 |
| 1948 | −0.0089 | 0.0125 | 0.0144 | −0.0103 | −0.0062 | −0.0152 | −0.0174 | 0.0014 | 0.0024 | 0.0065 | 0.0154 | 0.0201 | 1948 | 0.0139 |
| 1949 | 0.0052 | 0.0151 | −0.0021 | 0.0009 | 0.0052 | 0.0070 | 0.0170 | 0.0009 | −0.0021 | 0.0124 | 0.0007 | −0.0089 | 1949 | 0.0521 |
| 1950 | 0.0080 | 0.0035 | −0.0021 | −0.0022 | −0.0050 | −0.0033 | −0.0029 | −0.0045 | −0.0107 | −0.0062 | 0.0013 | −0.0111 | 1950 | −0.0347 |
| 1951 | −0.0139 | −0.0160 | −0.0275 | −0.0022 | −0.0054 | −0.0080 | 0.0192 | 0.0114 | −0.0121 | −0.0195 | −0.0111 | 0.0020 | 1951 | −0.0809 |
| 1952 | 0.0199 | −0.0022 | 0.0076 | −0.0042 | 0.0018 | −0.0009 | −0.0059 | 0.0050 | −0.0006 | 0.0026 | 0.0108 | −0.0079 | 1952 | 0.0262 |
| 1953 | −0.0055 | 0.0010 | −0.0058 | −0.0260 | −0.0055 | 0.0071 | 0.0152 | −0.0110 | 0.0240 | 0.0202 | −0.0036 | 0.0185 | 1953 | 0.0277 |
| 1954 | 0.0099 | 0.0211 | 0.0051 | −0.0009 | −0.0079 | 0.0051 | 0.0040 | 0.0030 | 0.0065 | 0.0065 | 0.0013 | 0.0042 | 1954 | 0.0591 |
| 1955 | −0.0097 | −0.0063 | 0.0092 | −0.0001 | −0.0018 | 0.0029 | −0.0078 | −0.0013 | 0.0038 | 0.0078 | −0.0042 | 0.0088 | 1955 | 0.0010 |
| 1956 | 0.0117 | 0.0026 | −0.0158 | −0.0127 | 0.0002 | −0.0079 | −0.0165 | −0.0196 | 0.0000 | −0.0165 | −0.0126 | −0.0106 | 1956 | −0.0941 |
| 1957 | 0.0185 | 0.0057 | 0.0026 | −0.0102 | −0.0099 | −0.0379 | −0.0157 | −0.0021 | 0.0083 | 0.0023 | 0.0275 | 0.0685 | 1957 | 0.0552 |
| 1958 | 0.0040 | −0.0020 | −0.0115 | 0.0140 | 0.0031 | −0.0049 | −0.0164 | −0.0309 | −0.0096 | 0.0107 | 0.0093 | −0.0047 | 1958 | −0.0391 |
| 1959 | −0.0039 | 0.0138 | −0.0083 | −0.0183 | −0.0125 | −0.0002 | 0.0066 | −0.0057 | −0.0122 | 0.0130 | 0.0135 | −0.0096 | 1959 | −0.0243 |
| 1960 | 0.0118 | 0.0116 | 0.0191 | −0.0078 | −0.0021 | 0.0118 | 0.0257 | 0.0117 | −0.0074 | −0.0037 | −0.0081 | 0.0104 | 1960 | 0.0748 |
| 1961 | 0.0148 | 0.0210 | −0.0029 | −0.0116 | 0.0049 | −0.0091 | −0.0005 | −0.0007 | 0.0121 | 0.0127 | 0.0028 | −0.0026 | 1961 | 0.0412 |
| 1962 | 0.0080 | 0.0030 | 0.0129 | 0.0120 | 0.0000 | −0.0026 | −0.0037 | 0.0143 | 0.0034 | 0.0079 | 0.0062 | 0.0034 | 1962 | 0.0664 |
| 1963 | 0.0048 | 0.0012 | 0.0015 | −0.0051 | 0.0048 | −0.0001 | −0.0016 | 0.0035 | −0.0023 | 0.0038 | 0.0004 | −0.0056 | 1963 | 0.0054 |
| 1964 | 0.0076 | 0.0065 | −0.0073 | 0.0029 | 0.0057 | 0.0026 | 0.0030 | 0.0048 | −0.0001 | 0.0039 | −0.0025 | 0.0077 | 1964 | 0.0354 |
| 1965 | 0.0081 | 0.0009 | 0.0001 | −0.0011 | −0.0029 | −0.0050 | 0.0008 | 0.0015 | −0.0036 | 0.0035 | −0.0078 | −0.0180 | 1965 | −0.0233 |
| 1966 | 0.0022 | −0.0175 | −0.0090 | −0.0028 | −0.0036 | −0.0001 | −0.0129 | −0.0309 | 0.0057 | 0.0219 | −0.0020 | 0.0191 | 1966 | −0.0306 |
| 1967 | 0.0450 | −0.0211 | 0.0097 | −0.0091 | −0.0283 | −0.0252 | −0.0009 | −0.0037 | 0.0074 | −0.0310 | −0.0301 | 0.0097 | 1967 | −0.0776 |
| 1968 | 0.0320 | 0.0008 | −0.0245 | 0.0019 | 0.0003 | 0.0064 | 0.0292 | 0.0177 | −0.0081 | −0.0216 | −0.0263 | −0.0261 | 1968 | −0.0205 |
| 1969 | 0.0110 | −0.0197 | −0.0282 | 0.0268 | −0.0254 | −0.0029 | −0.0040 | −0.0065 | −0.0288 | 0.0091 | −0.0522 | −0.0195 | 1969 | −0.1338 |
| 1970 | 0.0105 | 0.0346 | −0.0097 | −0.0309 | −0.0206 | −0.0051 | 0.0520 | 0.0083 | 0.0087 | −0.0146 | 0.0548 | 0.0320 | 1970 | 0.1221 |

* Compound annual return

# Table A-22 (continued)

## Long-Term Corporate Bonds: Inflation-Adjusted Total Returns

from January 1971 to December 2000

| Year | Jan | Feb | Mar | Apr | May | Jun | Jul | Aug | Sep | Oct | Nov | Dec | Year | Jan-Dec* |
|------|-----|-----|-----|-----|-----|-----|-----|-----|-----|-----|-----|-----|------|----------|
| 1971 | 0.0523 | −0.0382 | 0.0224 | −0.0268 | −0.0210 | 0.0049 | −0.0050 | 0.0528 | −0.0110 | 0.0265 | 0.0013 | 0.0181 | 1971 | 0.0741 |
| 1972 | −0.0041 | 0.0058 | 0.0008 | 0.0011 | 0.0130 | −0.0092 | −0.0010 | 0.0056 | −0.0009 | 0.0069 | 0.0225 | −0.0035 | 1972 | 0.0372 |
| 1973 | −0.0085 | −0.0047 | −0.0048 | −0.0008 | −0.0100 | −0.0124 | −0.0498 | 0.0172 | 0.0325 | −0.0146 | 0.0005 | −0.0153 | 1973 | −0.0704 |
| 1974 | −0.0138 | −0.0118 | −0.0415 | −0.0395 | −0.0006 | −0.0378 | −0.0284 | −0.0391 | 0.0053 | 0.0793 | 0.0032 | −0.0145 | 1974 | −0.1360 |
| 1975 | 0.0548 | 0.0066 | −0.0284 | −0.0102 | 0.0062 | 0.0221 | −0.0134 | −0.0205 | −0.0174 | 0.0489 | −0.0148 | 0.0398 | 1975 | 0.0713 |
| 1976 | 0.0164 | 0.0037 | 0.0143 | −0.0057 | −0.0161 | 0.0096 | 0.0090 | 0.0183 | 0.0126 | 0.0029 | 0.0289 | 0.0317 | 1976 | 0.1320 |
| 1977 | −0.0358 | −0.0121 | 0.0032 | 0.0021 | 0.0050 | 0.0108 | −0.0049 | 0.0097 | −0.0060 | −0.0065 | 0.0012 | −0.0142 | 1977 | −0.0474 |
| 1978 | −0.0142 | −0.0018 | −0.0027 | −0.0112 | −0.0205 | −0.0080 | 0.0029 | 0.0205 | −0.0118 | −0.0283 | 0.0079 | −0.0186 | 1978 | −0.0834 |
| 1979 | 0.0094 | −0.0242 | 0.0010 | −0.0164 | 0.0104 | 0.0174 | −0.0158 | −0.0093 | −0.0280 | −0.0971 | 0.0127 | −0.0211 | 1979 | −0.1543 |
| 1980 | −0.0777 | −0.0791 | −0.0203 | 0.1249 | 0.0457 | 0.0228 | −0.0437 | −0.0506 | −0.0326 | −0.0244 | −0.0073 | 0.0161 | 1980 | −0.1348 |
| 1981 | −0.0210 | −0.0369 | 0.0237 | −0.0828 | 0.0508 | −0.0062 | −0.0481 | −0.0418 | −0.0297 | 0.0498 | 0.1235 | −0.0607 | 1981 | −0.0934 |
| 1982 | −0.0164 | 0.0279 | 0.0317 | 0.0294 | 0.0145 | −0.0583 | 0.0482 | 0.0815 | 0.0605 | 0.0730 | 0.0218 | 0.0150 | 1982 | 0.3725 |
| 1983 | −0.0118 | 0.0424 | 0.0065 | 0.0473 | −0.0376 | −0.0079 | −0.0493 | 0.0018 | 0.0340 | −0.0051 | 0.0125 | −0.0046 | 1983 | 0.0237 |
| 1984 | 0.0213 | −0.0217 | −0.0257 | −0.0121 | −0.0511 | 0.0166 | 0.0552 | 0.0264 | 0.0265 | 0.0545 | 0.0212 | 0.0122 | 1984 | 0.1242 |
| 1985 | 0.0305 | −0.0412 | 0.0134 | 0.0254 | 0.0780 | 0.0052 | −0.0136 | 0.0238 | 0.0040 | 0.0297 | 0.0335 | 0.0443 | 1985 | 0.2536 |
| 1986 | 0.0014 | 0.0782 | 0.0303 | 0.0038 | −0.0194 | 0.0168 | 0.0028 | 0.0257 | −0.0162 | 0.0180 | 0.0224 | 0.0108 | 1986 | 0.1851 |
| 1987 | 0.0155 | 0.0019 | −0.0131 | −0.0553 | −0.0081 | 0.0113 | −0.0139 | −0.0130 | −0.0469 | 0.0480 | 0.0110 | 0.0215 | 1987 | −0.0448 |
| 1988 | 0.0490 | 0.0112 | −0.0230 | −0.0199 | −0.0091 | 0.0335 | −0.0153 | 0.0012 | 0.0257 | 0.0239 | −0.0177 | 0.0022 | 1988 | 0.0602 |
| 1989 | 0.0151 | −0.0170 | 0.0006 | 0.0147 | 0.0320 | 0.0370 | 0.0153 | −0.0179 | 0.0008 | 0.0227 | 0.0046 | −0.0010 | 1989 | 0.1107 |
| 1990 | −0.0291 | −0.0059 | −0.0065 | −0.0206 | 0.0361 | 0.0161 | 0.0063 | −0.0381 | 0.0007 | 0.0071 | 0.0262 | 0.0167 | 1990 | 0.0064 |
| 1991 | 0.0090 | 0.0106 | 0.0093 | 0.0123 | 0.0009 | −0.0047 | 0.0152 | 0.0245 | 0.0226 | 0.0028 | 0.0077 | 0.0428 | 1991 | 0.1632 |
| 1992 | −0.0187 | 0.0060 | −0.0123 | 0.0002 | 0.0239 | 0.0120 | 0.0286 | 0.0061 | 0.0070 | −0.0191 | 0.0055 | 0.0235 | 1992 | 0.0631 |
| 1993 | 0.0200 | 0.0220 | −0.0010 | 0.0024 | 0.0006 | 0.0279 | 0.0100 | 0.0259 | 0.0022 | 0.0010 | −0.0195 | 0.0067 | 1993 | 0.1016 |
| 1994 | 0.0174 | −0.0319 | −0.0416 | −0.0110 | −0.0069 | −0.0115 | 0.0281 | −0.0071 | −0.0291 | −0.0057 | 0.0005 | 0.0157 | 1994 | −0.0822 |
| 1995 | 0.0215 | 0.0248 | 0.0062 | 0.0142 | 0.0610 | 0.0059 | −0.0101 | 0.0187 | 0.0133 | 0.0152 | 0.0249 | 0.0235 | 1995 | 0.2406 |
| 1996 | −0.0044 | −0.0404 | −0.0181 | −0.0198 | −0.0014 | 0.0166 | −0.0009 | −0.0089 | 0.0226 | 0.0328 | 0.0244 | −0.0186 | 1996 | −0.0186 |
| 1997 | −0.0059 | −0.0003 | −0.0245 | 0.0171 | 0.0134 | 0.0174 | 0.0515 | −0.0258 | 0.0201 | 0.0166 | 0.0107 | 0.0176 | 1997 | 0.1106 |
| 1998 | 0.0118 | −0.0026 | 0.0019 | 0.0034 | 0.0148 | 0.0103 | −0.0068 | 0.0077 | 0.0400 | −0.0214 | 0.0270 | 0.0017 | 1998 | 0.0900 |
| 1999 | 0.0098 | −0.0412 | −0.0028 | −0.0096 | −0.0176 | −0.0160 | −0.0143 | −0.0050 | 0.0045 | 0.0029 | −0.0030 | −0.0102 | 1999 | −0.0987 |
| 2000 | −0.0045 | 0.0033 | 0.0086 | −0.0120 | −0.0166 | 0.0266 | 0.0161 | 0.0123 | −0.0006 | 0.0028 | 0.0257 | 0.0276 | 2000 | 0.0917 |

* Compound annual return

## Table A-23

**Long-Term Government Bonds: Inflation-Adjusted Total Returns**

from January 1926 to December 1970

| Year | Jan | Feb | Mar | Apr | May | Jun | Jul | Aug | Sep | Oct | Nov | Dec | Year | Jan-Dec* |
|------|------|------|------|------|------|------|------|------|------|------|------|------|------|------|
| 1926 | 0.0138 | 0.0101 | 0.0098 | -0.0018 | 0.0070 | 0.0114 | 0.0100 | 0.0058 | -0.0020 | 0.0063 | 0.0122 | 0.0078 | 1926 | 0.0940 |
| 1927 | 0.0151 | 0.0165 | 0.0313 | -0.0005 | 0.0031 | -0.0163 | 0.0244 | 0.0135 | -0.0040 | 0.0040 | 0.0117 | 0.0091 | 1927 | 0.1124 |
| 1928 | -0.0017 | 0.0159 | 0.0045 | -0.0023 | -0.0135 | 0.0120 | -0.0217 | 0.0057 | -0.0118 | 0.0177 | 0.0023 | 0.0043 | 1928 | 0.0108 |
| 1929 | -0.0071 | -0.0138 | -0.0105 | 0.0316 | -0.0220 | 0.0070 | -0.0097 | -0.0072 | 0.0047 | 0.0382 | 0.0256 | -0.0031 | 1929 | 0.0322 |
| 1930 | -0.0018 | 0.0169 | 0.0143 | -0.0075 | 0.0199 | 0.0111 | 0.0176 | 0.0074 | 0.0013 | 0.0096 | 0.0124 | 0.0074 | 1930 | 0.1138 |
| 1931 | 0.0024 | 0.0236 | 0.0169 | 0.0151 | 0.0256 | 0.0114 | -0.0020 | 0.0035 | -0.0237 | -0.0265 | 0.0141 | -0.0130 | 1931 | 0.0466 |
| 1932 | 0.0245 | 0.0561 | 0.0029 | 0.0680 | -0.0045 | 0.0139 | 0.0481 | 0.0127 | 0.0107 | 0.0058 | 0.0083 | 0.0234 | 1932 | 0.3026 |
| 1933 | 0.0306 | -0.0105 | 0.0177 | -0.0006 | 0.0275 | -0.0056 | -0.0297 | -0.0057 | 0.0023 | -0.0091 | -0.0149 | -0.0062 | 1933 | -0.0058 |
| 1934 | 0.0205 | 0.0005 | 0.0197 | 0.0151 | 0.0106 | 0.0042 | 0.0040 | -0.0143 | -0.0291 | 0.0258 | 0.0062 | 0.0138 | 1934 | 0.0784 |
| 1935 | 0.0032 | 0.0018 | 0.0066 | -0.0019 | -0.0008 | 0.0117 | 0.0095 | -0.0133 | -0.0040 | 0.0061 | -0.0039 | 0.0046 | 1935 | 0.0194 |
| 1936 | 0.0055 | 0.0130 | 0.0156 | 0.0035 | 0.0040 | -0.0076 | 0.0012 | 0.0039 | -0.0055 | 0.0030 | 0.0205 | 0.0038 | 1936 | 0.0623 |
| 1937 | -0.0084 | 0.0063 | -0.0479 | -0.0008 | 0.0006 | -0.0041 | 0.0091 | -0.0127 | -0.0047 | 0.0088 | 0.0166 | 0.0106 | 1937 | -0.0278 |
| 1938 | 0.0199 | 0.0147 | -0.0037 | 0.0162 | 0.0092 | 0.0004 | 0.0020 | 0.0024 | 0.0022 | 0.0135 | 0.0002 | 0.0056 | 1938 | 0.0855 |
| 1939 | 0.0107 | 0.0128 | 0.0149 | 0.0142 | 0.0171 | -0.0027 | 0.0113 | -0.0201 | -0.0724 | 0.0459 | 0.0162 | 0.0193 | 1939 | 0.0645 |
| 1940 | 0.0007 | -0.0045 | 0.0201 | -0.0035 | -0.0322 | 0.0234 | 0.0076 | 0.0052 | 0.0086 | 0.0031 | 0.0205 | 0.0019 | 1940 | 0.0508 |
| 1941 | -0.0201 | 0.0020 | 0.0048 | 0.0035 | -0.0042 | -0.0118 | -0.0024 | -0.0072 | -0.0188 | 0.0029 | -0.0116 | -0.0199 | 1941 | -0.0801 |
| 1942 | -0.0060 | -0.0073 | -0.0035 | -0.0091 | -0.0028 | -0.0018 | -0.0023 | -0.0024 | -0.0017 | -0.0076 | -0.0095 | -0.0030 | 1942 | -0.0555 |
| 1943 | 0.0033 | -0.0025 | -0.0146 | -0.0068 | -0.0026 | 0.0037 | 0.0076 | 0.0059 | -0.0028 | -0.0033 | 0.0019 | -0.0001 | 1943 | -0.0104 |
| 1944 | 0.0040 | 0.0051 | 0.0021 | -0.0044 | -0.0010 | -0.0011 | -0.0021 | -0.0011 | 0.0014 | 0.0012 | 0.0024 | 0.0005 | 1944 | 0.0069 |
| 1945 | 0.0127 | 0.0096 | 0.0021 | 0.0141 | -0.0019 | 0.0075 | -0.0104 | 0.0026 | 0.0091 | 0.0104 | 0.0088 | 0.0157 | 1945 | 0.0830 |
| 1946 | 0.0025 | 0.0069 | -0.0063 | -0.0189 | -0.0066 | -0.0038 | -0.0595 | -0.0324 | -0.0124 | -0.0120 | -0.0288 | 0.0066 | 1946 | -0.1546 |
| 1947 | -0.0006 | 0.0037 | -0.0194 | -0.0037 | 0.0064 | -0.0066 | -0.0028 | -0.0024 | -0.0275 | -0.0037 | -0.0231 | -0.0318 | 1947 | -0.1067 |
| 1948 | -0.0093 | 0.0132 | 0.0063 | -0.0096 | 0.0070 | -0.0153 | -0.0144 | -0.0039 | 0.0014 | 0.0048 | 0.0145 | 0.0126 | 1948 | 0.0067 |
| 1949 | 0.0096 | 0.0162 | 0.0046 | -0.0003 | 0.0033 | 0.0153 | 0.0104 | 0.0083 | -0.0053 | 0.0075 | 0.0007 | 0.0109 | 1949 | 0.0840 |
| 1950 | -0.0019 | 0.0050 | -0.0034 | 0.0016 | -0.0009 | -0.0081 | -0.0042 | -0.0069 | -0.0140 | -0.0102 | -0.0006 | -0.0117 | 1950 | -0.0542 |
| 1951 | -0.0101 | -0.0190 | -0.0195 | -0.0075 | -0.0107 | -0.0049 | 0.0125 | 0.0099 | -0.0143 | -0.0041 | -0.0186 | -0.0098 | 1951 | -0.0926 |
| 1952 | 0.0028 | 0.0077 | 0.0111 | 0.0132 | -0.0046 | -0.0022 | -0.0094 | -0.0082 | -0.0118 | 0.0135 | -0.0015 | -0.0073 | 1952 | 0.0027 |
| 1953 | 0.0037 | -0.0037 | -0.0113 | -0.0118 | -0.0172 | 0.0184 | 0.0014 | -0.0032 | 0.0287 | 0.0049 | -0.0012 | 0.0219 | 1953 | 0.0299 |
| 1954 | 0.0064 | 0.0252 | 0.0071 | 0.0129 | -0.0124 | 0.0150 | 0.0134 | -0.0024 | 0.0015 | 0.0031 | -0.0037 | 0.0089 | 1954 | 0.0772 |
| 1955 | -0.0241 | -0.0078 | 0.0087 | 0.0001 | 0.0073 | -0.0076 | -0.0139 | 0.0029 | 0.0035 | 0.0144 | -0.0057 | 0.0062 | 1955 | -0.0166 |
| 1956 | 0.0096 | -0.0002 | -0.0161 | -0.0125 | 0.0175 | -0.0034 | -0.0280 | -0.0175 | 0.0037 | -0.0115 | -0.0057 | -0.0202 | 1956 | -0.0821 |
| 1957 | 0.0333 | -0.0011 | -0.0048 | -0.0257 | -0.0047 | -0.0239 | -0.0088 | -0.0010 | 0.0064 | -0.0050 | 0.0496 | 0.0307 | 1957 | 0.0431 |
| 1958 | -0.0142 | 0.0089 | 0.0032 | 0.0163 | 0.0001 | -0.0171 | -0.0289 | -0.0424 | -0.0117 | 0.0138 | 0.0109 | -0.0169 | 1958 | -0.0772 |
| 1959 | -0.0092 | 0.0129 | 0.0017 | -0.0128 | -0.0017 | -0.0035 | 0.0037 | -0.0030 | -0.0091 | 0.0116 | -0.0119 | -0.0159 | 1959 | -0.0370 |
| 1960 | 0.0123 | 0.0192 | 0.0282 | -0.0225 | 0.0152 | 0.0150 | 0.0368 | -0.0067 | 0.0064 | -0.0073 | -0.0077 | 0.0279 | 1960 | 0.1212 |
| 1961 | -0.0107 | 0.0200 | -0.0037 | 0.0115 | -0.0046 | -0.0086 | -0.0010 | -0.0027 | 0.0107 | 0.0071 | -0.0020 | -0.0125 | 1961 | 0.0030 |
| 1962 | -0.0014 | 0.0081 | 0.0231 | 0.0060 | 0.0046 | -0.0076 | -0.0131 | 0.0187 | 0.0006 | 0.0095 | 0.0021 | 0.0046 | 1962 | 0.0559 |
| 1963 | -0.0012 | -0.0003 | -0.0002 | -0.0012 | 0.0023 | -0.0024 | -0.0013 | 0.0021 | 0.0004 | -0.0037 | 0.0040 | -0.0028 | 1963 | -0.0043 |
| 1964 | -0.0024 | 0.0000 | 0.0026 | 0.0036 | 0.0050 | 0.0047 | -0.0014 | 0.0031 | 0.0028 | 0.0032 | -0.0005 | 0.0019 | 1964 | 0.0229 |
| 1965 | 0.0040 | 0.0014 | 0.0043 | 0.0004 | -0.0004 | -0.0006 | 0.0011 | 0.0008 | -0.0055 | 0.0017 | -0.0083 | -0.0109 | 1965 | -0.0119 |
| 1966 | -0.0104 | -0.0311 | 0.0264 | -0.0104 | -0.0070 | -0.0047 | -0.0068 | -0.0256 | 0.0311 | 0.0187 | -0.0148 | 0.0403 | 1966 | 0.0029 |
| 1967 | 0.0154 | -0.0231 | 0.0177 | -0.0311 | -0.0069 | -0.0341 | 0.0018 | -0.0114 | -0.0024 | -0.0428 | -0.0226 | 0.0162 | 1967 | -0.1186 |
| 1968 | 0.0287 | -0.0062 | -0.0259 | 0.0197 | 0.0014 | 0.0171 | 0.0240 | -0.0032 | -0.0131 | -0.0188 | -0.0306 | -0.0390 | 1968 | -0.0476 |
| 1969 | -0.0233 | 0.0004 | -0.0073 | 0.0359 | -0.0516 | 0.0149 | 0.0034 | -0.0114 | -0.0574 | 0.0328 | -0.0296 | -0.0130 | 1969 | -0.1054 |
| 1970 | -0.0057 | 0.0531 | -0.0120 | -0.0471 | -0.0510 | 0.0432 | 0.0284 | -0.0036 | 0.0176 | -0.0159 | 0.0755 | -0.0134 | 1970 | 0.0627 |

* Compound annual return

# Table A-23 (continued)

## Long-Term Government Bonds: Inflation-Adjusted Total Returns

from January 1971 to December 2000

| Year | Jan | Feb | Mar | Apr | May | Jun | Jul | Aug | Sep | Oct | Nov | Dec | Year | Jan-Dec* |
|------|------|------|------|------|------|------|------|------|------|------|------|------|------|------|
| 1971 | 0.0497 | −0.0180 | 0.0491 | −0.0315 | −0.0056 | −0.0215 | 0.0005 | 0.0445 | 0.0195 | 0.0150 | −0.0063 | 0.0003 | 1971 | 0.0955 |
| 1972 | −0.0072 | 0.0039 | −0.0098 | 0.0003 | 0.0237 | −0.0088 | 0.0175 | 0.0013 | −0.0122 | 0.0202 | 0.0202 | −0.0260 | 1972 | 0.0220 |
| 1973 | −0.0351 | −0.0056 | −0.0011 | −0.0024 | −0.0165 | −0.0089 | −0.0455 | 0.0207 | 0.0287 | 0.0133 | −0.0254 | −0.0147 | 1973 | −0.0910 |
| 1974 | −0.0168 | −0.0151 | −0.0400 | −0.0307 | 0.0011 | −0.0051 | −0.0103 | −0.0356 | 0.0126 | 0.0400 | 0.0209 | 0.0099 | 1974 | −0.0699 |
| 1975 | 0.0179 | 0.0061 | −0.0304 | −0.0231 | 0.0167 | 0.0209 | −0.0191 | −0.0099 | −0.0147 | 0.0411 | −0.0169 | 0.0347 | 1975 | 0.0204 |
| 1976 | 0.0066 | 0.0037 | 0.0141 | −0.0023 | −0.0216 | 0.0154 | 0.0019 | 0.0164 | 0.0104 | 0.0043 | 0.0309 | 0.0298 | 1976 | 0.1140 |
| 1977 | −0.0443 | −0.0150 | 0.0029 | −0.0008 | 0.0069 | 0.0097 | −0.0114 | 0.0159 | −0.0066 | −0.0120 | 0.0044 | −0.0205 | 1977 | −0.0699 |
| 1978 | −0.0133 | −0.0065 | −0.0089 | −0.0094 | −0.0156 | −0.0164 | 0.0071 | 0.0166 | −0.0175 | −0.0278 | 0.0133 | −0.0184 | 1978 | −0.0936 |
| 1979 | 0.0102 | −0.0249 | 0.0032 | −0.0224 | 0.0137 | 0.0216 | −0.0212 | −0.0134 | −0.0224 | −0.0922 | 0.0216 | −0.0048 | 1979 | −0.1283 |
| 1980 | −0.0872 | −0.0596 | −0.0452 | 0.1395 | 0.0317 | 0.0246 | −0.0484 | −0.0493 | −0.0351 | −0.0347 | 0.0009 | 0.0263 | 1980 | −0.1454 |
| 1981 | −0.0195 | −0.0534 | 0.0310 | −0.0578 | 0.0535 | −0.0263 | −0.0462 | −0.0459 | −0.0244 | 0.0806 | 0.1378 | −0.0739 | 1981 | −0.0650 |
| 1982 | 0.0010 | 0.0150 | 0.0242 | 0.0330 | −0.0064 | −0.0341 | 0.0444 | 0.0759 | 0.0600 | 0.0605 | 0.0015 | 0.0354 | 1982 | 0.3513 |
| 1983 | −0.0332 | 0.0488 | −0.0101 | 0.0276 | −0.0438 | 0.0005 | −0.0525 | −0.0013 | 0.0452 | −0.0158 | 0.0167 | −0.0072 | 1983 | −0.0303 |
| 1984 | 0.0187 | −0.0223 | −0.0179 | −0.0154 | −0.0544 | 0.0117 | 0.0659 | 0.0224 | 0.0293 | 0.0534 | 0.0118 | 0.0084 | 1984 | 0.1108 |
| 1985 | 0.0344 | −0.0532 | 0.0262 | 0.0201 | 0.0855 | 0.0110 | −0.0195 | 0.0237 | −0.0052 | 0.0306 | 0.0366 | 0.0515 | 1985 | 0.2621 |
| 1986 | −0.0056 | 0.1176 | 0.0819 | −0.0059 | −0.0534 | 0.0562 | −0.0111 | 0.0480 | −0.0546 | 0.0280 | 0.0258 | −0.0027 | 1986 | 0.2314 |
| 1987 | 0.0100 | 0.0162 | −0.0266 | −0.0524 | −0.0135 | 0.0056 | −0.0198 | −0.0219 | −0.0416 | 0.0595 | 0.0022 | 0.0168 | 1987 | −0.0682 |
| 1988 | 0.0639 | 0.0026 | −0.0348 | −0.0210 | −0.0135 | 0.0324 | −0.0211 | 0.0016 | 0.0276 | 0.0273 | −0.0204 | 0.0093 | 1988 | 0.0503 |
| 1989 | 0.0153 | −0.0220 | 0.0064 | 0.0093 | 0.0342 | 0.0525 | 0.0213 | −0.0274 | −0.0013 | 0.0330 | 0.0054 | −0.0022 | 1989 | 0.1287 |
| 1990 | −0.0441 | −0.0071 | −0.0098 | −0.0217 | 0.0391 | 0.0175 | 0.0068 | −0.0506 | 0.0033 | 0.0154 | 0.0379 | 0.0187 | 1990 | 0.0007 |
| 1991 | 0.0070 | 0.0016 | 0.0023 | 0.0125 | −0.0029 | −0.0092 | 0.0143 | 0.0310 | 0.0258 | 0.0040 | 0.0053 | 0.0573 | 1991 | 0.1575 |
| 1992 | −0.0338 | 0.0015 | −0.0143 | 0.0002 | 0.0228 | 0.0164 | 0.0376 | 0.0038 | 0.0157 | −0.0233 | −0.0004 | 0.0253 | 1992 | 0.0501 |
| 1993 | 0.0230 | 0.0318 | −0.0014 | 0.0044 | 0.0033 | 0.0434 | 0.0191 | 0.0405 | −0.0015 | 0.0055 | −0.0265 | 0.0020 | 1993 | 0.1508 |
| 1994 | 0.0229 | −0.0482 | −0.0428 | −0.0164 | −0.0089 | −0.0134 | 0.0335 | −0.0126 | −0.0357 | −0.0031 | 0.0053 | 0.0161 | 1994 | −0.1017 |
| 1995 | 0.0232 | 0.0246 | 0.0058 | 0.0136 | 0.0769 | 0.0119 | −0.0168 | 0.0209 | 0.0155 | 0.0261 | 0.0256 | 0.0279 | 1995 | 0.2841 |
| 1996 | −0.0069 | −0.0513 | −0.0260 | −0.0203 | −0.0073 | 0.0196 | −0.0002 | −0.0158 | 0.0257 | 0.0371 | 0.0331 | −0.0256 | 1996 | −0.0412 |
| 1997 | −0.0110 | −0.0026 | −0.0276 | 0.0242 | 0.0103 | 0.0182 | 0.0612 | −0.0336 | 0.0290 | 0.0315 | 0.0154 | 0.0197 | 1997 | 0.1391 |
| 1998 | 0.0181 | −0.0090 | 0.0006 | 0.0008 | 0.0164 | 0.0216 | −0.0052 | 0.0452 | 0.0382 | −0.0242 | 0.0097 | −0.0026 | 1998 | 0.1127 |
| 1999 | 0.0097 | −0.0531 | −0.0038 | −0.0052 | −0.0185 | −0.0078 | −0.0107 | −0.0076 | 0.0036 | −0.0030 | −0.0067 | −0.0155 | 1999 | −0.1134 |
| 2000 | 0.0204 | 0.0203 | 0.0282 | −0.0081 | −0.0060 | 0.0185 | 0.0155 | 0.0229 | −0.0208 | 0.0170 | 0.0313 | 0.0248 | 2000 | 0.1750 |

* Compound annual return

## Table A-24

## Intermediate-Term Government Bonds: Inflation-Adjusted Total Returns

from January 1926 to December 1970

| Year | Jan | Feb | Mar | Apr | May | Jun | Jul | Aug | Sep | Oct | Nov | Dec | Year | Jan-Dec* |
|------|-----|-----|-----|-----|-----|-----|-----|-----|-----|-----|-----|-----|------|----------|
| 1926 | 0.0068 | 0.0069 | 0.0097 | −0.0004 | 0.0065 | 0.0102 | 0.0109 | 0.0067 | −0.0008 | 0.0016 | 0.0007 | 0.0089 | 1926 | 0.0697 |
| 1927 | 0.0133 | 0.0115 | 0.0096 | 0.0016 | −0.0056 | −0.0066 | 0.0237 | 0.0115 | 0.0002 | −0.0092 | 0.0103 | 0.0057 | 1927 | 0.0674 |
| 1928 | 0.0066 | 0.0094 | 0.0010 | −0.0022 | −0.0065 | 0.0095 | −0.0089 | 0.0031 | −0.0050 | 0.0052 | 0.0038 | 0.0032 | 1928 | 0.0190 |
| 1929 | −0.0009 | 0.0001 | 0.0044 | 0.0128 | −0.0120 | 0.0067 | −0.0031 | 0.0014 | 0.0005 | 0.0168 | 0.0200 | 0.0102 | 1929 | 0.0581 |
| 1930 | −0.0002 | 0.0133 | 0.0221 | −0.0129 | 0.0120 | 0.0202 | 0.0196 | 0.0083 | 0.0002 | 0.0137 | 0.0153 | 0.0169 | 1930 | 0.1356 |
| 1931 | 0.0075 | 0.0249 | 0.0117 | 0.0149 | 0.0230 | −0.0106 | 0.0039 | 0.0039 | −0.0069 | −0.0039 | 0.0163 | −0.0069 | 1931 | 0.0796 |
| 1932 | 0.0178 | 0.0272 | 0.0126 | 0.0267 | 0.0055 | 0.0182 | 0.0120 | 0.0249 | 0.0077 | 0.0121 | 0.0082 | 0.0221 | 1932 | 0.2130 |
| 1933 | 0.0140 | 0.0157 | 0.0179 | 0.0084 | 0.0172 | −0.0097 | −0.0286 | −0.0029 | 0.0026 | −0.0025 | 0.0027 | −0.0204 | 1933 | 0.0131 |
| 1934 | 0.0078 | −0.0023 | 0.0189 | 0.0208 | 0.0094 | 0.0065 | −0.0024 | −0.0117 | −0.0283 | 0.0265 | 0.0071 | 0.0150 | 1934 | 0.0683 |
| 1935 | −0.0034 | 0.0031 | 0.0150 | 0.0009 | 0.0014 | 0.0138 | 0.0087 | −0.0071 | −0.0105 | 0.0109 | −0.0035 | 0.0096 | 1935 | 0.0391 |
| 1936 | −0.0003 | 0.0118 | 0.0080 | 0.0024 | 0.0038 | −0.0085 | −0.0026 | −0.0022 | −0.0014 | 0.0049 | 0.0081 | −0.0057 | 1936 | 0.0183 |
| 1937 | −0.0102 | −0.0017 | −0.0233 | 0.0000 | 0.0033 | −0.0036 | 0.0012 | −0.0066 | −0.0011 | 0.0078 | 0.0111 | 0.0085 | 1937 | −0.0150 |
| 1938 | 0.0227 | 0.0147 | −0.0012 | 0.0182 | 0.0070 | 0.0075 | −0.0013 | 0.0038 | −0.0013 | 0.0142 | 0.0023 | 0.0028 | 1938 | 0.0927 |
| 1939 | 0.0077 | 0.0131 | 0.0105 | 0.0063 | 0.0095 | 0.0002 | 0.0040 | −0.0147 | −0.0447 | 0.0364 | 0.0074 | 0.0156 | 1939 | 0.0502 |
| 1940 | 0.0010 | −0.0036 | 0.0112 | 0.0002 | −0.0237 | 0.0162 | 0.0027 | 0.0067 | 0.0024 | 0.0036 | 0.0056 | −0.0020 | 1940 | 0.0199 |
| 1941 | 0.0001 | −0.0047 | 0.0021 | −0.0060 | −0.0058 | −0.0127 | −0.0045 | −0.0079 | −0.0176 | −0.0087 | −0.0177 | −0.0038 | 1941 | −0.0840 |
| 1942 | −0.0055 | −0.0069 | −0.0102 | −0.0040 | −0.0087 | −0.0008 | −0.0041 | −0.0044 | −0.0043 | −0.0083 | −0.0043 | −0.0079 | 1942 | −0.0673 |
| 1943 | 0.0039 | −0.0006 | −0.0134 | −0.0092 | −0.0020 | 0.0053 | 0.0098 | 0.0041 | −0.0024 | −0.0021 | 0.0034 | 0.0001 | 1943 | −0.0034 |
| 1944 | 0.0030 | 0.0035 | 0.0019 | −0.0030 | −0.0033 | −0.0012 | −0.0028 | −0.0014 | 0.0011 | 0.0011 | 0.0009 | −0.0027 | 1944 | −0.0031 |
| 1945 | 0.0052 | 0.0057 | 0.0004 | −0.0004 | −0.0063 | −0.0074 | −0.0019 | 0.0016 | 0.0054 | 0.0016 | −0.0027 | −0.0015 | 1945 | −0.0003 |
| 1946 | 0.0039 | 0.0085 | −0.0111 | −0.0074 | −0.0048 | −0.0075 | −0.0567 | −0.0211 | −0.0125 | −0.0167 | −0.0243 | −0.0046 | 1946 | −0.1452 |
| 1947 | 0.0023 | 0.0021 | −0.0190 | −0.0013 | 0.0038 | −0.0068 | −0.0084 | −0.0078 | −0.0232 | −0.0023 | −0.0052 | −0.0108 | 1947 | −0.0743 |
| 1948 | −0.0098 | 0.0104 | 0.0046 | −0.0122 | −0.0017 | −0.0078 | −0.0125 | −0.0045 | 0.0010 | 0.0054 | 0.0090 | 0.0102 | 1948 | −0.0084 |
| 1949 | 0.0042 | 0.0124 | −0.0003 | 0.0001 | 0.0037 | 0.0036 | 0.0091 | 0.0002 | −0.0034 | 0.0062 | −0.0012 | 0.0069 | 1949 | 0.0420 |
| 1950 | 0.0038 | 0.0036 | −0.0042 | −0.0006 | −0.0022 | −0.0053 | −0.0077 | −0.0090 | −0.0072 | −0.0053 | −0.0023 | −0.0125 | 1950 | −0.0481 |
| 1951 | −0.0136 | −0.0110 | −0.0165 | 0.0044 | −0.0079 | 0.0063 | 0.0045 | 0.0036 | −0.0120 | −0.0035 | −0.0018 | −0.0054 | 1951 | −0.0521 |
| 1952 | 0.0038 | 0.0043 | 0.0067 | 0.0016 | 0.0007 | −0.0060 | −0.0109 | −0.0036 | 0.0031 | 0.0054 | −0.0006 | 0.0032 | 1952 | 0.0074 |
| 1953 | 0.0023 | 0.0053 | −0.0042 | −0.0109 | −0.0141 | 0.0117 | 0.0030 | −0.0033 | 0.0181 | 0.0013 | 0.0051 | 0.0116 | 1953 | 0.0259 |
| 1954 | 0.0040 | 0.0113 | 0.0039 | 0.0068 | −0.0110 | 0.0112 | −0.0005 | 0.0023 | 0.0005 | 0.0016 | −0.0013 | 0.0030 | 1954 | 0.0320 |
| 1955 | −0.0032 | −0.0052 | 0.0024 | 0.0004 | 0.0001 | −0.0036 | −0.0108 | 0.0032 | 0.0044 | 0.0072 | −0.0066 | 0.0014 | 1955 | −0.0102 |
| 1956 | 0.0118 | 0.0003 | −0.0113 | −0.0014 | 0.0062 | −0.0059 | −0.0167 | −0.0091 | 0.0079 | −0.0080 | −0.0047 | −0.0013 | 1956 | −0.0319 |
| 1957 | 0.0225 | −0.0049 | −0.0006 | −0.0137 | −0.0041 | −0.0165 | −0.0062 | 0.0097 | −0.0009 | 0.0043 | 0.0359 | 0.0215 | 1957 | 0.0467 |
| 1958 | −0.0025 | 0.0127 | −0.0017 | 0.0029 | 0.0060 | −0.0079 | −0.0102 | −0.0345 | −0.0017 | 0.0002 | 0.0121 | −0.0050 | 1958 | −0.0300 |
| 1959 | −0.0025 | 0.0119 | −0.0037 | −0.0064 | −0.0013 | −0.0122 | 0.0011 | −0.0067 | −0.0015 | 0.0139 | −0.0092 | −0.0020 | 1959 | −0.0186 |
| 1960 | 0.0166 | 0.0060 | 0.0292 | −0.0120 | 0.0031 | 0.0194 | 0.0267 | −0.0004 | 0.0017 | −0.0029 | −0.0105 | 0.0210 | 1960 | 0.1013 |
| 1961 | −0.0059 | 0.0090 | 0.0037 | 0.0054 | −0.0028 | −0.0037 | −0.0038 | 0.0030 | 0.0056 | 0.0014 | −0.0019 | 0.0018 | 1961 | 0.0117 |
| 1962 | −0.0045 | 0.0132 | 0.0067 | 0.0002 | 0.0049 | −0.0028 | −0.0034 | 0.0125 | −0.0034 | 0.0062 | 0.0060 | 0.0067 | 1962 | 0.0429 |
| 1963 | −0.0040 | 0.0006 | 0.0016 | 0.0030 | 0.0014 | −0.0030 | −0.0040 | 0.0019 | 0.0014 | 0.0000 | 0.0029 | −0.0019 | 1963 | −0.0001 |
| 1964 | 0.0022 | 0.0022 | 0.0006 | 0.0022 | 0.0081 | 0.0014 | 0.0006 | 0.0038 | 0.0024 | 0.0022 | −0.0025 | 0.0047 | 1964 | 0.0282 |
| 1965 | 0.0042 | 0.0018 | 0.0032 | −0.0006 | 0.0014 | −0.0004 | 0.0007 | 0.0040 | −0.0026 | −0.0010 | −0.0014 | −0.0180 | 1965 | −0.0089 |
| 1966 | 0.0003 | −0.0145 | 0.0155 | −0.0060 | 0.0000 | −0.0055 | −0.0056 | −0.0175 | 0.0195 | 0.0034 | 0.0027 | 0.0212 | 1966 | 0.0129 |
| 1967 | 0.0118 | −0.0023 | 0.0163 | −0.0109 | 0.0013 | −0.0256 | 0.0083 | −0.0065 | −0.0013 | −0.0078 | −0.0002 | −0.0023 | 1967 | −0.0197 |
| 1968 | 0.0106 | 0.0011 | −0.0075 | −0.0045 | 0.0034 | 0.0108 | 0.0128 | −0.0008 | 0.0027 | −0.0048 | −0.0050 | −0.0201 | 1968 | −0.0018 |
| 1969 | 0.0058 | −0.0051 | 0.0013 | 0.0014 | −0.0109 | −0.0147 | 0.0037 | −0.0063 | −0.0344 | 0.0296 | −0.0101 | −0.0253 | 1969 | −0.0645 |
| 1970 | −0.0005 | 0.0384 | 0.0035 | −0.0267 | 0.0067 | 0.0009 | 0.0117 | 0.0099 | 0.0144 | 0.0043 | 0.0416 | 0.0003 | 1970 | 0.1078 |

* Compound annual return

## Table A-24 (continued)

## Intermediate-Term Government Bonds: Inflation-Adjusted Total Returns

from January 1971 to December 2000

| Year | Jan | Feb | Mar | Apr | May | Jun | Jul | Aug | Sep | Oct | Nov | Dec | Year | Jan-Dec* |
|------|-----|-----|-----|-----|-----|-----|-----|-----|-----|-----|-----|-----|------|----------|
| 1971 | 0.0160 | 0.0207 | 0.0152 | −0.0359 | −0.0039 | −0.0244 | 0.0002 | 0.0325 | 0.0017 | 0.0203 | 0.0036 | 0.0069 | 1971 | 0.0519 |
| 1972 | 0.0097 | −0.0034 | −0.0002 | −0.0010 | −0.0016 | 0.0020 | −0.0025 | −0.0001 | −0.0026 | −0.0016 | 0.0021 | 0.0160 | 1972 | 0.0169 |
| 1973 | −0.0038 | −0.0145 | −0.0047 | −0.0006 | −0.0004 | −0.0074 | −0.0298 | 0.0072 | 0.0220 | −0.0031 | −0.0009 | −0.0025 | 1973 | −0.0385 |
| 1974 | −0.0077 | −0.0092 | −0.0321 | −0.0207 | 0.0019 | −0.0182 | −0.0067 | −0.0138 | 0.0196 | 0.0023 | 0.0150 | 0.0112 | 1974 | −0.0580 |
| 1975 | 0.0008 | 0.0077 | −0.0097 | −0.0235 | 0.0215 | −0.0054 | −0.0135 | −0.0039 | −0.0039 | 0.0303 | −0.0070 | 0.0155 | 1975 | 0.0076 |
| 1976 | 0.0032 | 0.0059 | 0.0051 | 0.0074 | −0.0203 | 0.0105 | 0.0060 | 0.0141 | 0.0035 | 0.0106 | 0.0292 | −0.0003 | 1976 | 0.0769 |
| 1977 | −0.0246 | −0.0054 | −0.0007 | −0.0027 | 0.0001 | 0.0036 | −0.0043 | −0.0031 | −0.0023 | −0.0087 | 0.0030 | −0.0061 | 1977 | −0.0502 |
| 1978 | −0.0041 | −0.0052 | −0.0032 | −0.0065 | −0.0100 | −0.0123 | 0.0027 | 0.0028 | −0.0013 | −0.0191 | 0.0037 | 0.0009 | 1978 | −0.0508 |
| 1979 | −0.0034 | −0.0174 | 0.0016 | −0.0081 | 0.0069 | 0.0110 | −0.0139 | −0.0189 | −0.0097 | −0.0553 | 0.0268 | −0.0018 | 1979 | −0.0813 |
| 1980 | −0.0274 | −0.0768 | −0.0001 | 0.1074 | 0.0387 | −0.0185 | −0.0114 | −0.0449 | −0.0129 | −0.0238 | −0.0061 | 0.0085 | 1980 | −0.0755 |
| 1981 | −0.0049 | −0.0335 | 0.0190 | −0.0278 | 0.0161 | −0.0026 | −0.0380 | −0.0252 | 0.0062 | 0.0588 | 0.0594 | −0.0170 | 1981 | 0.0047 |
| 1982 | 0.0014 | 0.0116 | 0.0053 | 0.0255 | 0.0047 | −0.0254 | 0.0406 | 0.0447 | 0.0307 | 0.0502 | 0.0097 | 0.0227 | 1982 | 0.2428 |
| 1983 | −0.0017 | 0.0249 | −0.0055 | 0.0186 | −0.0175 | −0.0017 | −0.0238 | 0.0047 | 0.0263 | −0.0008 | 0.0086 | 0.0034 | 1983 | 0.0348 |
| 1984 | 0.0121 | −0.0110 | −0.0057 | −0.0052 | −0.0278 | 0.0066 | 0.0359 | 0.0059 | 0.0153 | 0.0357 | 0.0192 | 0.0137 | 1984 | 0.0968 |
| 1985 | 0.0187 | −0.0220 | 0.0122 | 0.0222 | 0.0445 | 0.0077 | −0.0061 | 0.0126 | 0.0081 | 0.0131 | 0.0161 | 0.0232 | 1985 | 0.1596 |
| 1986 | 0.0052 | 0.0303 | 0.0386 | 0.0103 | −0.0245 | 0.0226 | 0.0154 | 0.0247 | −0.0158 | 0.0153 | 0.0103 | −0.0002 | 1986 | 0.1385 |
| 1987 | 0.0046 | 0.0020 | −0.0076 | −0.0296 | −0.0067 | 0.0081 | 0.0005 | −0.0093 | −0.0189 | 0.0272 | 0.0068 | 0.0096 | 1987 | −0.0144 |
| 1988 | 0.0289 | 0.0096 | −0.0129 | −0.0095 | −0.0083 | 0.0138 | −0.0089 | −0.0051 | 0.0127 | 0.0115 | −0.0123 | −0.0026 | 1988 | 0.0161 |
| 1989 | 0.0071 | −0.0092 | −0.0008 | 0.0154 | 0.0155 | 0.0299 | 0.0210 | −0.0261 | 0.0037 | 0.0188 | 0.0060 | −0.0004 | 1989 | 0.0826 |
| 1990 | −0.0205 | −0.0040 | −0.0052 | −0.0092 | 0.0238 | 0.0096 | 0.0135 | −0.0182 | 0.0010 | 0.0110 | 0.0170 | 0.0161 | 1990 | 0.0342 |
| 1991 | 0.0046 | 0.0033 | 0.0008 | 0.0102 | 0.0030 | −0.0052 | 0.0115 | 0.0217 | 0.0171 | 0.0119 | 0.0099 | 0.0258 | 1991 | 0.1203 |
| 1992 | −0.0209 | −0.0014 | −0.0129 | 0.0083 | 0.0207 | 0.0140 | 0.0220 | 0.0121 | 0.0165 | −0.0216 | −0.0098 | 0.0153 | 1992 | 0.0417 |
| 1993 | 0.0220 | 0.0207 | 0.0008 | 0.0060 | −0.0023 | 0.0187 | 0.0005 | 0.0194 | 0.0035 | −0.0024 | −0.0100 | 0.0032 | 1993 | 0.0826 |
| 1994 | 0.0110 | −0.0291 | −0.0291 | −0.0119 | −0.0009 | −0.0062 | 0.0142 | −0.0015 | −0.0185 | −0.0030 | −0.0083 | 0.0053 | 1994 | −0.0762 |
| 1995 | 0.0141 | 0.0194 | 0.0029 | 0.0110 | 0.0348 | 0.0060 | −0.0016 | 0.0060 | 0.0044 | 0.0088 | 0.0155 | 0.0101 | 1995 | 0.1391 |
| 1996 | −0.0052 | −0.0169 | −0.0169 | −0.0088 | −0.0051 | 0.0111 | 0.0005 | −0.0024 | 0.0123 | 0.0150 | 0.0130 | −0.0078 | 1996 | −0.0118 |
| 1997 | −0.0007 | −0.0029 | −0.0139 | 0.0135 | 0.0085 | 0.0089 | 0.0251 | −0.0116 | 0.0126 | 0.0125 | 0.0005 | 0.0119 | 1997 | 0.0657 |
| 1998 | 0.0161 | −0.0057 | 0.0007 | 0.0043 | 0.0051 | 0.0066 | 0.0014 | 0.0258 | 0.0317 | 0.0016 | −0.0098 | 0.0043 | 1998 | 0.0846 |
| 1999 | 0.0031 | −0.0274 | 0.0056 | −0.0052 | −0.0147 | 0.0032 | −0.0033 | −0.0010 | 0.0049 | −0.0026 | −0.0014 | −0.0048 | 1999 | −0.0434 |
| 2000 | −0.0077 | 0.0019 | 0.0120 | −0.0049 | 0.0046 | 0.0132 | 0.0054 | 0.0122 | 0.0044 | 0.0062 | 0.0168 | 0.0219 | 2000 | 0.0890 |

* Compound annual return

## Table A-25

### U.S. Treasury Bills: Inflation-Adjusted Total Returns

from January 1926 to December 1970

| Year | Jan | Feb | Mar | Apr | May | Jun | Jul | Aug | Sep | Oct | Nov | Dec | Year | Jan-Dec* |
|------|-----|-----|-----|-----|-----|-----|-----|-----|-----|-----|-----|-----|------|----------|
| 1926 | 0.0034 | 0.0064 | 0.0086 | −0.0059 | 0.0057 | 0.0110 | 0.0118 | 0.0083 | −0.0035 | −0.0006 | −0.0007 | 0.0028 | 1926 | 0.0483 |
| 1927 | 0.0101 | 0.0103 | 0.0088 | 0.0025 | −0.0047 | −0.0069 | 0.0224 | 0.0086 | −0.0037 | −0.0033 | 0.0040 | 0.0042 | 1927 | 0.0531 |
| 1928 | 0.0045 | 0.0131 | 0.0029 | 0.0003 | −0.0026 | 0.0110 | 0.0032 | 0.0013 | −0.0051 | 0.0060 | 0.0058 | 0.0045 | 1928 | 0.0457 |
| 1929 | 0.0054 | 0.0055 | 0.0074 | 0.0075 | −0.0015 | 0.0013 | −0.0064 | 0.0002 | 0.0055 | 0.0046 | 0.0057 | 0.0095 | 1929 | 0.0454 |
| 1930 | 0.0053 | 0.0069 | 0.0094 | −0.0038 | 0.0085 | 0.0087 | 0.0161 | 0.0070 | −0.0039 | 0.0069 | 0.0095 | 0.0159 | 1930 | 0.0898 |
| 1931 | 0.0162 | 0.0153 | 0.0077 | 0.0072 | 0.0118 | 0.0118 | 0.0028 | 0.0026 | 0.0047 | 0.0078 | 0.0130 | 0.0104 | 1931 | 0.1171 |
| 1932 | 0.0234 | 0.0166 | 0.0064 | 0.0083 | 0.0152 | 0.0076 | 0.0003 | 0.0127 | 0.0053 | 0.0077 | 0.0052 | 0.0103 | 1932 | 0.1255 |
| 1933 | 0.0157 | 0.0155 | 0.0084 | 0.0036 | −0.0022 | −0.0103 | −0.0279 | −0.0098 | 0.0002 | 0.0001 | 0.0002 | 0.0053 | 1933 | −0.0021 |
| 1934 | −0.0046 | −0.0073 | 0.0002 | 0.0026 | −0.0024 | −0.0024 | 0.0001 | −0.0024 | −0.0147 | 0.0075 | 0.0026 | 0.0026 | 1934 | −0.0183 |
| 1935 | −0.0146 | −0.0071 | 0.0026 | −0.0095 | 0.0050 | 0.0026 | 0.0050 | 0.0001 | −0.0047 | 0.0001 | −0.0046 | −0.0023 | 1935 | −0.0273 |
| 1936 | 0.0001 | 0.0050 | 0.0051 | 0.0002 | 0.0002 | −0.0094 | −0.0047 | −0.0070 | −0.0023 | 0.0026 | 0.0001 | 0.0000 | 1936 | −0.0102 |
| 1937 | −0.0070 | −0.0022 | −0.0069 | −0.0043 | −0.0040 | −0.0020 | −0.0043 | −0.0021 | −0.0088 | 0.0048 | 0.0071 | 0.0024 | 1937 | −0.0271 |
| 1938 | 0.0141 | 0.0095 | −0.0001 | −0.0046 | 0.0048 | 0.0000 | −0.0024 | 0.0024 | 0.0002 | 0.0049 | 0.0018 | −0.0024 | 1938 | 0.0284 |
| 1939 | 0.0047 | 0.0049 | 0.0023 | 0.0024 | 0.0001 | 0.0001 | 0.0000 | −0.0001 | −0.0189 | 0.0048 | 0.0000 | 0.0048 | 1939 | 0.0050 |
| 1940 | 0.0024 | −0.0071 | 0.0024 | 0.0000 | −0.0025 | −0.0023 | 0.0025 | 0.0023 | −0.0024 | 0.0000 | 0.0000 | −0.0047 | 1940 | −0.0094 |
| 1941 | −0.0001 | −0.0001 | −0.0046 | −0.0094 | −0.0069 | −0.0182 | −0.0042 | −0.0089 | −0.0176 | −0.0109 | −0.0086 | −0.0021 | 1941 | −0.0880 |
| 1942 | −0.0126 | −0.0083 | −0.0124 | −0.0062 | −0.0100 | −0.0018 | −0.0038 | −0.0058 | −0.0017 | −0.0097 | −0.0057 | −0.0076 | 1942 | −0.0825 |
| 1943 | 0.0003 | −0.0017 | −0.0152 | −0.0112 | −0.0074 | 0.0022 | 0.0080 | 0.0042 | −0.0036 | −0.0035 | 0.0022 | −0.0016 | 1943 | −0.0273 |
| 1944 | 0.0022 | 0.0022 | 0.0002 | −0.0055 | −0.0036 | −0.0016 | −0.0054 | −0.0035 | 0.0002 | 0.0003 | 0.0003 | −0.0035 | 1944 | −0.0174 |
| 1945 | 0.0003 | 0.0021 | 0.0002 | −0.0016 | −0.0072 | −0.0090 | −0.0015 | 0.0003 | 0.0040 | 0.0003 | −0.0034 | −0.0034 | 1945 | −0.0188 |
| 1946 | 0.0003 | 0.0040 | −0.0070 | −0.0052 | −0.0051 | −0.0105 | −0.0554 | −0.0212 | −0.0111 | −0.0189 | −0.0232 | −0.0075 | 1946 | −0.1507 |
| 1947 | 0.0003 | 0.0018 | −0.0210 | 0.0003 | 0.0033 | −0.0073 | −0.0087 | −0.0101 | −0.0226 | 0.0006 | −0.0052 | −0.0120 | 1947 | −0.0780 |
| 1948 | −0.0105 | 0.0093 | 0.0037 | −0.0132 | −0.0062 | −0.0060 | −0.0115 | −0.0032 | 0.0004 | 0.0045 | 0.0073 | 0.0074 | 1948 | −0.0185 |
| 1949 | 0.0023 | 0.0121 | −0.0018 | −0.0005 | 0.0024 | −0.0004 | 0.0079 | −0.0019 | −0.0033 | 0.0065 | −0.0006 | 0.0065 | 1949 | 0.0296 |
| 1950 | 0.0052 | 0.0037 | −0.0033 | −0.0006 | −0.0032 | −0.0046 | −0.0087 | −0.0073 | −0.0058 | −0.0043 | −0.0030 | −0.0123 | 1950 | −0.0434 |
| 1951 | −0.0145 | −0.0107 | −0.0028 | 0.0000 | −0.0026 | 0.0025 | 0.0001 | 0.0013 | −0.0052 | −0.0035 | −0.0040 | −0.0026 | 1951 | −0.0414 |
| 1952 | 0.0015 | 0.0075 | 0.0011 | −0.0026 | 0.0000 | −0.0010 | −0.0060 | 0.0002 | 0.0029 | 0.0001 | 0.0010 | 0.0029 | 1952 | 0.0077 |
| 1953 | 0.0041 | 0.0064 | −0.0007 | 0.0004 | −0.0008 | −0.0019 | −0.0010 | −0.0008 | 0.0004 | −0.0012 | 0.0045 | 0.0025 | 1953 | 0.0119 |
| 1954 | −0.0014 | 0.0019 | 0.0020 | 0.0034 | −0.0032 | −0.0007 | 0.0005 | 0.0017 | 0.0034 | 0.0032 | −0.0006 | 0.0033 | 1954 | 0.0137 |
| 1955 | 0.0008 | 0.0009 | 0.0010 | 0.0010 | 0.0014 | 0.0010 | −0.0027 | 0.0041 | −0.0021 | 0.0018 | 0.0005 | 0.0043 | 1955 | 0.0119 |
| 1956 | 0.0035 | 0.0019 | 0.0003 | 0.0006 | −0.0027 | −0.0042 | −0.0052 | 0.0029 | 0.0006 | −0.0036 | 0.0020 | 0.0000 | 1956 | −0.0039 |
| 1957 | 0.0015 | −0.0012 | −0.0001 | −0.0011 | 0.0002 | −0.0035 | −0.0018 | 0.0013 | 0.0014 | 0.0029 | −0.0008 | 0.0024 | 1957 | 0.0011 |
| 1958 | −0.0031 | 0.0000 | −0.0060 | −0.0015 | 0.0011 | −0.0009 | −0.0005 | 0.0016 | 0.0019 | 0.0018 | −0.0001 | 0.0034 | 1958 | −0.0022 |
| 1959 | 0.0009 | 0.0030 | 0.0022 | 0.0008 | 0.0010 | −0.0021 | 0.0002 | 0.0030 | −0.0003 | −0.0004 | 0.0026 | 0.0034 | 1959 | 0.0143 |
| 1960 | 0.0045 | 0.0017 | 0.0035 | −0.0037 | 0.0027 | 0.0001 | 0.0013 | 0.0017 | 0.0005 | −0.0023 | 0.0002 | 0.0016 | 1960 | 0.0117 |
| 1961 | 0.0019 | 0.0014 | 0.0020 | 0.0017 | 0.0018 | 0.0009 | −0.0026 | 0.0025 | −0.0006 | 0.0019 | 0.0015 | 0.0019 | 1961 | 0.0144 |
| 1962 | 0.0024 | −0.0002 | −0.0002 | 0.0000 | 0.0024 | 0.0020 | 0.0005 | 0.0023 | −0.0034 | 0.0037 | 0.0020 | 0.0034 | 1962 | 0.0149 |
| 1963 | 0.0014 | 0.0012 | 0.0012 | 0.0025 | 0.0024 | −0.0021 | −0.0017 | 0.0025 | 0.0027 | 0.0018 | 0.0016 | 0.0008 | 1963 | 0.0144 |
| 1964 | 0.0019 | 0.0037 | 0.0020 | 0.0018 | 0.0026 | 0.0009 | 0.0008 | 0.0039 | 0.0006 | 0.0019 | 0.0008 | 0.0020 | 1964 | 0.0232 |
| 1965 | 0.0028 | 0.0030 | 0.0025 | −0.0001 | 0.0010 | −0.0018 | 0.0020 | 0.0054 | 0.0010 | 0.0021 | 0.0014 | 0.0002 | 1965 | 0.0197 |
| 1966 | 0.0038 | −0.0028 | 0.0007 | −0.0007 | 0.0031 | 0.0007 | 0.0005 | −0.0010 | 0.0020 | 0.0005 | 0.0040 | 0.0030 | 1966 | 0.0136 |
| 1967 | 0.0043 | 0.0026 | 0.0019 | 0.0012 | 0.0003 | −0.0004 | −0.0019 | 0.0001 | 0.0012 | 0.0010 | 0.0006 | 0.0004 | 1967 | 0.0113 |
| 1968 | 0.0001 | 0.0009 | −0.0011 | 0.0014 | 0.0015 | −0.0015 | 0.0000 | 0.0013 | 0.0014 | −0.0013 | 0.0005 | 0.0014 | 1968 | 0.0046 |
| 1969 | 0.0024 | 0.0009 | −0.0037 | −0.0011 | 0.0021 | −0.0013 | 0.0008 | 0.0005 | 0.0017 | 0.0024 | −0.0002 | 0.0002 | 1969 | 0.0045 |
| 1970 | 0.0025 | 0.0009 | 0.0004 | −0.0011 | 0.0009 | 0.0006 | 0.0018 | 0.0036 | 0.0002 | −0.0005 | 0.0012 | −0.0008 | 1970 | 0.0098 |

* Compound annual return

Table A-25 (continued)

## U.S. Treasury Bills: Inflation-Adjusted Total Returns

from January 1971 to December 2000

| Year | Jan | Feb | Mar | Apr | May | Jun | Jul | Aug | Sep | Oct | Nov | Dec | Year | Jan–Dec* |
|------|-----|-----|-----|-----|-----|-----|-----|-----|-----|-----|-----|-----|------|----------|
| 1971 | 0.0030 | 0.0016 | −0.0004 | −0.0006 | −0.0020 | −0.0020 | 0.0015 | 0.0022 | 0.0029 | 0.0020 | 0.0021 | −0.0004 | 1971 | 0.0099 |
| 1972 | 0.0021 | −0.0024 | 0.0011 | 0.0005 | −0.0002 | 0.0005 | −0.0009 | 0.0013 | −0.0006 | 0.0008 | 0.0013 | 0.0006 | 1972 | 0.0041 |
| 1973 | 0.0012 | −0.0029 | −0.0047 | −0.0017 | −0.0010 | −0.0017 | 0.0041 | −0.0109 | 0.0038 | −0.0016 | −0.0017 | −0.0002 | 1973 | −0.0172 |
| 1974 | −0.0024 | −0.0070 | −0.0057 | 0.0019 | −0.0035 | −0.0036 | −0.0004 | −0.0068 | −0.0039 | −0.0035 | −0.0031 | −0.0002 | 1974 | −0.0374 |
| 1975 | 0.0013 | −0.0027 | 0.0003 | −0.0007 | −0.0001 | −0.0040 | −0.0057 | 0.0017 | 0.0004 | −0.0006 | −0.0020 | 0.0006 | 1975 | −0.0113 |
| 1976 | 0.0023 | 0.0010 | 0.0016 | 0.0000 | −0.0022 | −0.0010 | −0.0012 | −0.0005 | 0.0003 | 0.0000 | 0.0011 | 0.0012 | 1976 | 0.0026 |
| 1977 | −0.0021 | −0.0067 | −0.0024 | −0.0041 | −0.0018 | −0.0026 | −0.0002 | 0.0006 | 0.0005 | 0.0022 | 0.0001 | 0.0011 | 1977 | −0.0155 |
| 1978 | −0.0005 | −0.0023 | −0.0016 | −0.0036 | −0.0048 | −0.0049 | −0.0016 | 0.0005 | −0.0009 | −0.0012 | 0.0015 | 0.0024 | 1978 | −0.0169 |
| 1979 | −0.0011 | −0.0043 | −0.0015 | −0.0035 | −0.0041 | −0.0012 | −0.0052 | −0.0024 | −0.0021 | −0.0002 | 0.0005 | −0.0010 | 1979 | −0.0259 |
| 1980 | −0.0063 | −0.0048 | −0.0023 | 0.0013 | −0.0018 | −0.0049 | 0.0045 | −0.0001 | −0.0017 | 0.0008 | 0.0005 | 0.0044 | 1980 | −0.0103 |
| 1981 | 0.0022 | 0.0003 | 0.0048 | 0.0043 | 0.0033 | 0.0049 | 0.0010 | 0.0051 | 0.0023 | 0.0099 | 0.0078 | 0.0059 | 1981 | 0.0530 |
| 1982 | 0.0044 | 0.0060 | 0.0109 | 0.0070 | 0.0007 | −0.0026 | 0.0050 | 0.0056 | 0.0034 | 0.0032 | 0.0081 | 0.0109 | 1982 | 0.0642 |
| 1983 | 0.0045 | 0.0058 | 0.0056 | 0.0000 | 0.0015 | 0.0033 | 0.0034 | 0.0043 | 0.0026 | 0.0049 | 0.0054 | 0.0059 | 1983 | 0.0482 |
| 1984 | 0.0020 | 0.0025 | 0.0050 | 0.0032 | 0.0049 | 0.0043 | 0.0050 | 0.0041 | 0.0038 | 0.0074 | 0.0073 | 0.0058 | 1984 | 0.0567 |
| 1985 | 0.0046 | 0.0017 | 0.0017 | 0.0031 | 0.0029 | 0.0024 | 0.0047 | 0.0033 | 0.0029 | 0.0034 | 0.0027 | 0.0040 | 1985 | 0.0381 |
| 1986 | 0.0025 | 0.0081 | 0.0106 | 0.0074 | 0.0019 | 0.0003 | 0.0049 | 0.0028 | −0.0004 | 0.0037 | 0.0030 | 0.0040 | 1986 | 0.0498 |
| 1987 | −0.0019 | 0.0004 | 0.0002 | −0.0009 | 0.0008 | 0.0007 | 0.0025 | −0.0009 | −0.0004 | 0.0034 | 0.0020 | 0.0042 | 1987 | 0.0101 |
| 1988 | 0.0003 | 0.0020 | 0.0001 | −0.0005 | 0.0016 | 0.0006 | 0.0008 | 0.0017 | −0.0006 | 0.0028 | 0.0048 | 0.0047 | 1988 | 0.0185 |
| 1989 | 0.0005 | 0.0020 | 0.0009 | 0.0002 | 0.0022 | 0.0047 | 0.0045 | 0.0058 | 0.0033 | 0.0020 | 0.0045 | 0.0045 | 1989 | 0.0356 |
| 1990 | −0.0046 | 0.0010 | 0.0010 | 0.0053 | 0.0044 | 0.0008 | 0.0029 | −0.0026 | −0.0024 | 0.0008 | 0.0034 | 0.0060 | 1990 | 0.0161 |
| 1991 | −0.0008 | 0.0033 | 0.0029 | 0.0038 | 0.0018 | 0.0012 | 0.0034 | 0.0017 | 0.0002 | 0.0028 | 0.0010 | 0.0031 | 1991 | 0.0246 |
| 1992 | 0.0019 | −0.0008 | −0.0017 | 0.0018 | 0.0013 | −0.0004 | 0.0009 | −0.0002 | −0.0003 | −0.0012 | 0.0009 | 0.0035 | 1992 | 0.0059 |
| 1993 | −0.0026 | −0.0013 | −0.0010 | −0.0004 | 0.0008 | 0.0011 | 0.0024 | −0.0003 | 0.0005 | −0.0019 | 0.0018 | 0.0023 | 1993 | 0.0014 |
| 1994 | −0.0002 | −0.0013 | −0.0007 | 0.0014 | 0.0025 | −0.0003 | 0.0000 | −0.0004 | 0.0010 | 0.0032 | 0.0023 | 0.0044 | 1994 | 0.0120 |
| 1995 | 0.0001 | 0.0000 | 0.0013 | 0.0011 | 0.0034 | 0.0027 | 0.0045 | 0.0020 | 0.0023 | 0.0014 | 0.0049 | 0.0055 | 1995 | 0.0298 |
| 1996 | −0.0016 | 0.0007 | −0.0012 | 0.0007 | 0.0023 | 0.0034 | 0.0026 | 0.0022 | 0.0012 | 0.0011 | 0.0022 | 0.0046 | 1996 | 0.0182 |
| 1997 | 0.0013 | 0.0007 | 0.0018 | 0.0031 | 0.0056 | 0.0024 | 0.0030 | 0.0022 | 0.0019 | 0.0017 | 0.0045 | 0.0060 | 1997 | 0.0349 |
| 1998 | 0.0024 | 0.0020 | 0.0021 | 0.0024 | 0.0022 | 0.0029 | 0.0028 | 0.0031 | 0.0033 | 0.0008 | 0.0031 | 0.0044 | 1998 | 0.0319 |
| 1999 | 0.0011 | 0.0023 | 0.0012 | −0.0035 | 0.0034 | 0.0040 | 0.0008 | 0.0015 | −0.0009 | 0.0021 | 0.0030 | 0.0044 | 1999 | 0.0195 |
| 2000 | 0.0017 | −0.0016 | −0.0035 | 0.0040 | 0.0045 | −0.0018 | 0.0031 | 0.0039 | −0.0001 | 0.0039 | 0.0045 | 0.0056 | 2000 | 0.0242 |

* Compound annual return

# Stocks, Bonds, Bills, and Inflation

| | | | | |
|---|---|---|---|---|
| 1.000 | 0.962 | 0.906 | 0.929 | 0.946 |
| 1.095 | 1.154 | 1.164 | 1.187 | 1.259 |
| 1.529 | 1.509 | 1.676 | 1.733 | 1.768 |
| 2.332 | 2.328 | 2.325 | 2.366 | 2.280 |
| 2.147 | 2.203 | 2.382 | 2.363 | 2.340 |
| 1.592 | 1.782 | 1.662 | 1.506 | 1.314 |
| 0.836 | 0.883 | 0.781 | 0.625 | 0.488 |

# Appendix B

| | | | | |
|---|---|---|---|---|
| 0.795 | 0.654 | 0.678 | 0.966 | 1.129 |
| 1.344 | 1.301 | 1.301 | 1.268 | 1.175 |
| 1.148 | 1.109 | 1.077 | 1.182 | 1.231 |
| 1.886 | 1.928 | 1.980 | 1.831 | 1.931 |
| 2.459 | 2.506 | 2.487 | 2.286 | 2.280 |
| 1.561 | 1.666 | 1.252 | 1.433 | 1.386 |
| 1.881 | 1.954 | 1.692 | 1.688 | 1.811 |
| 1.941 | 1.966 | 1.991 | 1.986 | 1.531 |

**Ibbotson**Associates

# Appendix B

## Cumulative Wealth Indices of Basic and Inflation-Adjusted Series

## Table B-1

**Large Company Stocks: Total Return Index**

from December 1925 to December 1970

| Year | Jan | Feb | Mar | Apr | May | Jun | Jul | Aug | Sep | Oct | Nov | Dec | Yr-end | Index |
|------|-----|-----|-----|-----|-----|-----|-----|-----|-----|-----|-----|-----|--------|-------|
| 1925 | | | | | | | | | | | | 1.000 | 1925 | 1.000 |
| 1926 | 1.000 | 0.962 | 0.906 | 0.929 | 0.946 | 0.989 | 1.036 | 1.062 | 1.089 | 1.058 | 1.095 | 1.116 | 1926 | 1.116 |
| 1927 | 1.095 | 1.154 | 1.164 | 1.187 | 1.259 | 1.251 | 1.334 | 1.403 | 1.466 | 1.393 | 1.493 | 1.535 | 1927 | 1.535 |
| 1928 | 1.529 | 1.509 | 1.676 | 1.733 | 1.768 | 1.700 | 1.724 | 1.862 | 1.910 | 1.942 | 2.193 | 2.204 | 1928 | 2.204 |
| 1929 | 2.332 | 2.328 | 2.325 | 2.366 | 2.280 | 2.540 | 2.660 | 2.933 | 2.794 | 2.243 | 1.963 | 2.018 | 1929 | 2.018 |
| 1930 | 2.147 | 2.203 | 2.382 | 2.363 | 2.340 | 1.960 | 2.035 | 2.064 | 1.800 | 1.646 | 1.631 | 1.516 | 1930 | 1.516 |
| 1931 | 1.592 | 1.782 | 1.662 | 1.506 | 1.314 | 1.500 | 1.392 | 1.418 | 0.996 | 1.085 | 0.999 | 0.859 | 1931 | 0.859 |
| 1932 | 0.836 | 0.883 | 0.781 | 0.625 | 0.488 | 0.487 | 0.672 | 0.933 | 0.900 | 0.779 | 0.746 | 0.789 | 1932 | 0.789 |
| 1933 | 0.795 | 0.654 | 0.678 | 0.966 | 1.129 | 1.280 | 1.169 | 1.310 | 1.164 | 1.064 | 1.184 | 1.214 | 1933 | 1.214 |
| 1934 | 1.344 | 1.301 | 1.301 | 1.268 | 1.175 | 1.202 | 1.066 | 1.131 | 1.127 | 1.095 | 1.198 | 1.197 | 1934 | 1.197 |
| 1935 | 1.148 | 1.109 | 1.077 | 1.182 | 1.231 | 1.317 | 1.429 | 1.469 | 1.507 | 1.624 | 1.700 | 1.767 | 1935 | 1.767 |
| 1936 | 1.886 | 1.928 | 1.980 | 1.831 | 1.931 | 1.995 | 2.135 | 2.167 | 2.174 | 2.342 | 2.374 | 2.367 | 1936 | 2.367 |
| 1937 | 2.459 | 2.506 | 2.487 | 2.286 | 2.280 | 2.165 | 2.391 | 2.276 | 1.957 | 1.765 | 1.612 | 1.538 | 1937 | 1.538 |
| 1938 | 1.561 | 1.666 | 1.252 | 1.433 | 1.386 | 1.733 | 1.862 | 1.820 | 1.850 | 1.993 | 1.939 | 2.016 | 1938 | 2.016 |
| 1939 | 1.881 | 1.954 | 1.692 | 1.688 | 1.811 | 1.701 | 1.889 | 1.766 | 2.062 | 2.036 | 1.955 | 2.008 | 1939 | 2.008 |
| 1940 | 1.941 | 1.966 | 1.991 | 1.986 | 1.531 | 1.655 | 1.712 | 1.772 | 1.793 | 1.869 | 1.810 | 1.812 | 1940 | 1.812 |
| 1941 | 1.728 | 1.718 | 1.730 | 1.624 | 1.653 | 1.749 | 1.850 | 1.852 | 1.839 | 1.718 | 1.670 | 1.602 | 1941 | 1.602 |
| 1942 | 1.627 | 1.602 | 1.497 | 1.437 | 1.552 | 1.586 | 1.640 | 1.666 | 1.715 | 1.831 | 1.827 | 1.927 | 1942 | 1.927 |
| 1943 | 2.070 | 2.190 | 2.310 | 2.318 | 2.446 | 2.500 | 2.368 | 2.409 | 2.472 | 2.446 | 2.286 | 2.427 | 1943 | 2.427 |
| 1944 | 2.468 | 2.479 | 2.527 | 2.502 | 2.628 | 2.771 | 2.717 | 2.760 | 2.758 | 2.764 | 2.801 | 2.906 | 1944 | 2.906 |
| 1945 | 2.952 | 3.154 | 3.015 | 3.287 | 3.351 | 3.349 | 3.288 | 3.499 | 3.652 | 3.770 | 3.919 | 3.965 | 1945 | 3.965 |
| 1946 | 4.248 | 3.976 | 4.167 | 4.330 | 4.455 | 4.290 | 4.188 | 3.906 | 3.516 | 3.495 | 3.486 | 3.645 | 1946 | 3.645 |
| 1947 | 3.738 | 3.709 | 3.654 | 3.521 | 3.526 | 3.721 | 3.863 | 3.785 | 3.743 | 3.832 | 3.765 | 3.853 | 1947 | 3.853 |
| 1948 | 3.707 | 3.563 | 3.846 | 3.958 | 4.305 | 4.329 | 4.109 | 4.174 | 4.059 | 4.347 | 3.929 | 4.065 | 1948 | 4.065 |
| 1949 | 4.081 | 3.960 | 4.090 | 4.017 | 3.913 | 3.919 | 4.174 | 4.265 | 4.377 | 4.526 | 4.605 | 4.829 | 1949 | 4.829 |
| 1950 | 4.924 | 5.022 | 5.057 | 5.303 | 5.573 | 5.267 | 5.330 | 5.566 | 5.895 | 5.949 | 6.050 | 6.360 | 1950 | 6.360 |
| 1951 | 6.765 | 6.871 | 6.764 | 7.109 | 6.896 | 6.739 | 7.218 | 7.563 | 7.573 | 7.495 | 7.567 | 7.888 | 1951 | 7.888 |
| 1952 | 8.030 | 7.804 | 8.197 | 7.867 | 8.137 | 8.536 | 8.703 | 8.642 | 8.490 | 8.507 | 8.993 | 9.336 | 1952 | 9.336 |
| 1953 | 9.291 | 9.192 | 8.997 | 8.783 | 8.851 | 8.732 | 8.971 | 8.521 | 8.551 | 9.012 | 9.196 | 9.244 | 1953 | 9.244 |
| 1954 | 9.739 | 9.848 | 10.168 | 10.693 | 11.139 | 11.173 | 11.831 | 11.506 | 12.485 | 12.277 | 13.393 | 14.108 | 1954 | 14.108 |
| 1955 | 14.387 | 14.528 | 14.485 | 15.059 | 15.142 | 16.416 | 17.437 | 17.393 | 17.618 | 17.118 | 18.533 | 18.561 | 1955 | 18.561 |
| 1956 | 17.917 | 18.657 | 19.982 | 19.973 | 18.788 | 19.557 | 20.594 | 19.919 | 19.043 | 19.169 | 19.072 | 19.778 | 1956 | 19.778 |
| 1957 | 18.986 | 18.485 | 18.882 | 19.614 | 20.472 | 20.481 | 20.749 | 19.701 | 18.516 | 17.957 | 18.372 | 17.646 | 1957 | 17.646 |
| 1958 | 18.431 | 18.170 | 18.767 | 19.400 | 19.810 | 20.363 | 21.277 | 21.651 | 22.735 | 23.348 | 24.012 | 25.298 | 1958 | 25.298 |
| 1959 | 25.430 | 25.554 | 25.605 | 26.635 | 27.273 | 27.213 | 28.199 | 27.911 | 26.674 | 27.017 | 27.519 | 28.322 | 1959 | 28.322 |
| 1960 | 26.340 | 26.729 | 26.400 | 25.976 | 26.821 | 27.388 | 26.748 | 27.596 | 25.968 | 25.949 | 27.154 | 28.455 | 1960 | 28.455 |
| 1961 | 30.291 | 31.257 | 32.100 | 32.262 | 33.033 | 32.125 | 33.223 | 34.029 | 33.404 | 34.401 | 35.940 | 36.106 | 1961 | 36.106 |
| 1962 | 34.784 | 35.511 | 35.349 | 33.204 | 30.512 | 28.061 | 29.891 | 30.512 | 29.092 | 29.279 | 32.459 | 32.954 | 1962 | 32.954 |
| 1963 | 34.620 | 33.794 | 35.045 | 36.798 | 37.510 | 36.805 | 36.726 | 38.692 | 38.318 | 39.617 | 39.435 | 40.469 | 1963 | 40.469 |
| 1964 | 41.612 | 42.222 | 42.917 | 43.238 | 43.940 | 44.721 | 45.592 | 45.055 | 46.409 | 46.856 | 46.878 | 47.139 | 1964 | 47.139 |
| 1965 | 48.763 | 48.913 | 48.264 | 49.984 | 49.833 | 47.477 | 48.177 | 49.488 | 51.140 | 52.618 | 52.453 | 53.008 | 1965 | 53.008 |
| 1966 | 53.335 | 52.634 | 51.555 | 52.688 | 50.096 | 49.363 | 48.769 | 45.234 | 44.993 | 47.214 | 47.662 | 47.674 | 1966 | 47.674 |
| 1967 | 51.478 | 51.846 | 53.967 | 56.325 | 53.641 | 54.658 | 57.215 | 56.817 | 58.758 | 57.136 | 57.507 | 59.104 | 1967 | 59.104 |
| 1968 | 56.592 | 55.113 | 55.718 | 60.363 | 61.334 | 61.980 | 60.916 | 61.913 | 64.387 | 64.945 | 68.393 | 65.642 | 1968 | 65.642 |
| 1969 | 65.193 | 62.414 | 64.653 | 66.131 | 66.303 | 62.708 | 59.024 | 61.705 | 60.251 | 63.014 | 61.141 | 60.059 | 1969 | 60.059 |
| 1970 | 55.594 | 58.850 | 59.028 | 53.779 | 50.837 | 48.386 | 52.026 | 54.672 | 56.570 | 56.019 | 59.020 | 62.465 | 1970 | 62.465 |

Table B-1 (continued)

## Large Company Stocks: Total Return Index

from January 1971 to December 2000

| Year | Jan | Feb | Mar | Apr | May | Jun | Jul | Aug | Sep | Oct | Nov | Dec | Yr-end | Index |
|------|-----|-----|-----|-----|-----|-----|-----|-----|-----|-----|-----|-----|--------|-------|
| 1971 | 65.082 | 65.998 | 68.522 | 71.104 | 68.491 | 68.636 | 65.896 | 68.612 | 68.231 | 65.477 | 65.650 | 71.406 | 1971 | 71.406 |
| 1972 | 72.791 | 74.969 | 75.510 | 75.940 | 77.605 | 76.010 | 76.287 | 79.271 | 78.985 | 79.828 | 83.856 | 84.956 | 1972 | 84.956 |
| 1973 | 83.603 | 80.822 | 80.807 | 77.619 | 76.538 | 76.144 | 79.146 | 76.630 | 79.813 | 79.835 | 71.194 | 72.500 | 1973 | 72.500 |
| 1974 | 71.883 | 72.017 | 70.453 | 67.822 | 65.974 | 65.127 | 60.183 | 55.197 | 48.740 | 56.818 | 54.273 | 53.311 | 1974 | 53.311 |
| 1975 | 59.983 | 64.027 | 65.541 | 68.773 | 72.270 | 75.608 | 70.628 | 69.610 | 67.326 | 71.613 | 73.857 | 73.144 | 1975 | 73.144 |
| 1976 | 81.916 | 81.441 | 84.095 | 83.262 | 82.654 | 86.185 | 85.596 | 85.717 | 87.830 | 86.025 | 85.946 | 90.584 | 1976 | 90.584 |
| 1977 | 86.151 | 84.849 | 83.841 | 83.956 | 82.699 | 86.626 | 85.317 | 84.186 | 84.187 | 80.690 | 83.675 | 84.077 | 1977 | 84.077 |
| 1978 | 79.062 | 77.786 | 79.933 | 86.888 | 88.072 | 86.730 | 91.583 | 94.696 | 94.240 | 85.847 | 88.078 | 89.592 | 1978 | 89.592 |
| 1979 | 93.368 | 90.717 | 95.934 | 96.280 | 94.661 | 98.541 | 99.620 | 105.703 | 105.970 | 99.022 | 104.113 | 106.113 | 1979 | 106.113 |
| 1980 | 112.589 | 112.934 | 101.792 | 106.162 | 112.130 | 115.445 | 123.249 | 124.865 | 128.369 | 130.763 | 145.085 | 140.514 | 1980 | 140.514 |
| 1981 | 134.359 | 137.154 | 142.366 | 139.333 | 140.197 | 139.076 | 139.173 | 131.463 | 124.863 | 131.456 | 137.253 | 133.616 | 1981 | 133.616 |
| 1982 | 131.438 | 124.709 | 123.960 | 129.092 | 125.374 | 123.193 | 120.544 | 135.817 | 137.311 | 152.772 | 159.464 | 162.223 | 1982 | 162.223 |
| 1983 | 167.868 | 172.233 | 178.519 | 192.051 | 191.052 | 198.350 | 192.142 | 195.408 | 198.066 | 195.412 | 199.965 | 198.745 | 1983 | 198.745 |
| 1984 | 197.453 | 190.977 | 194.242 | 195.583 | 185.139 | 189.230 | 186.524 | 207.508 | 207.550 | 208.089 | 205.988 | 211.199 | 1984 | 211.199 |
| 1985 | 227.419 | 230.535 | 230.950 | 230.211 | 244.369 | 248.254 | 247.609 | 246.098 | 238.199 | 248.846 | 266.663 | 279.117 | 1985 | 279.117 |
| 1986 | 280.345 | 301.679 | 318.392 | 314.444 | 331.707 | 337.213 | 318.026 | 341.814 | 313.717 | 331.160 | 339.637 | 330.671 | 1986 | 330.671 |
| 1987 | 375.080 | 390.571 | 401.194 | 397.664 | 401.760 | 421.808 | 442.814 | 459.862 | 449.745 | 352.960 | 324.052 | 347.967 | 1987 | 347.967 |
| 1988 | 362.826 | 379.878 | 368.406 | 372.385 | 375.290 | 392.703 | 391.132 | 378.186 | 394.221 | 404.983 | 399.232 | 406.458 | 1988 | 406.458 |
| 1989 | 435.845 | 424.993 | 435.023 | 457.470 | 475.860 | 473.290 | 515.792 | 525.747 | 523.696 | 511.494 | 522.133 | 534.455 | 1989 | 534.455 |
| 1990 | 498.594 | 505.025 | 518.308 | 505.505 | 554.792 | 550.909 | 549.146 | 499.558 | 474.980 | 473.222 | 503.698 | 517.499 | 1990 | 517.499 |
| 1991 | 540.372 | 579.063 | 592.845 | 594.505 | 619.950 | 591.618 | 619.306 | 633.859 | 623.464 | 631.818 | 606.293 | 675.592 | 1991 | 675.592 |
| 1992 | 663.026 | 671.513 | 658.351 | 677.509 | 681.168 | 671.291 | 698.344 | 684.237 | 692.106 | 694.598 | 718.006 | 727.412 | 1992 | 727.412 |
| 1993 | 732.722 | 742.613 | 758.580 | 739.994 | 759.974 | 762.482 | 758.898 | 787.812 | 781.983 | 797.857 | 790.357 | 800.078 | 1993 | 800.078 |
| 1994 | 826.881 | 804.555 | 769.557 | 779.561 | 792.268 | 772.699 | 798.276 | 830.765 | 810.744 | 829.310 | 798.874 | 810.538 | 1994 | 810.538 |
| 1995 | 831.612 | 863.878 | 889.449 | 915.332 | 951.488 | 973.848 | 1006.227 | 1008.994 | 1051.271 | 1047.591 | 1093.685 | 1113.918 | 1995 | 1113.918 |
| 1996 | 1152.237 | 1163.299 | 1174.466 | 1191.731 | 1222.478 | 1227.490 | 1172.867 | 1197.731 | 1265.044 | 1299.706 | 1398.354 | 1370.946 | 1996 | 1370.946 |
| 1997 | 1456.082 | 1467.876 | 1406.812 | 1490.799 | 1582.334 | 1652.906 | 1784.147 | 1684.948 | 1777.233 | 1717.873 | 1797.411 | 1828.326 | 1997 | 1828.326 |
| 1998 | 1848.621 | 1981.943 | 2083.439 | 2104.398 | 2068.223 | 2152.235 | 2129.313 | 1821.457 | 1938.140 | 2095.788 | 2222.814 | 2350.892 | 1998 | 2350.892 |
| 1999 | 2449.207 | 2373.085 | 2468.032 | 2563.619 | 2503.092 | 2642.014 | 2559.530 | 2546.861 | 2477.051 | 2633.799 | 2687.344 | 2845.629 | 1999 | 2845.629 |
| 2000 | 2702.664 | 2651.503 | 2910.899 | 2823.310 | 2765.376 | 2833.543 | 2789.254 | 2962.495 | 2806.105 | 2794.235 | 2573.937 | 2586.524 | 2000 | 2586.524 |

## Table B-2

**Large Company Stocks: Capital Appreciation Index**

from December 1925 to December 1970

| Year | Jan | Feb | Mar | Apr | May | Jun | Jul | Aug | Sep | Oct | Nov | Dec | Yr-end | Index |
|------|-----|-----|-----|-----|-----|-----|-----|-----|-----|-----|-----|-----|--------|-------|
| 1925 |     |     |     |     |     |     |     |     |     |     |     | 1.000 | 1925 | 1.000 |
| 1926 | 0.998 | 0.955 | 0.898 | 0.918 | 0.926 | 0.966 | 1.009 | 1.027 | 1.050 | 1.017 | 1.040 | 1.057 | 1926 | 1.057 |
| 1927 | 1.035 | 1.085 | 1.092 | 1.111 | 1.168 | 1.158 | 1.233 | 1.288 | 1.343 | 1.272 | 1.350 | 1.384 | 1927 | 1.384 |
| 1928 | 1.377 | 1.353 | 1.499 | 1.548 | 1.567 | 1.504 | 1.523 | 1.636 | 1.675 | 1.699 | 1.903 | 1.908 | 1928 | 1.908 |
| 1929 | 2.017 | 2.005 | 2.001 | 2.033 | 1.946 | 2.165 | 2.263 | 2.485 | 2.364 | 1.893 | 1.640 | 1.681 | 1929 | 1.681 |
| 1930 | 1.786 | 1.824 | 1.970 | 1.951 | 1.919 | 1.603 | 1.662 | 1.675 | 1.457 | 1.328 | 1.299 | 1.202 | 1930 | 1.202 |
| 1931 | 1.261 | 1.405 | 1.308 | 1.183 | 1.020 | 1.162 | 1.076 | 1.086 | 0.761 | 0.825 | 0.745 | 0.636 | 1931 | 0.636 |
| 1932 | 0.618 | 0.650 | 0.573 | 0.457 | 0.350 | 0.347 | 0.478 | 0.658 | 0.633 | 0.545 | 0.513 | 0.540 | 1932 | 0.540 |
| 1933 | 0.544 | 0.444 | 0.458 | 0.652 | 0.755 | 0.855 | 0.780 | 0.869 | 0.770 | 0.702 | 0.774 | 0.792 | 1933 | 0.792 |
| 1934 | 0.875 | 0.843 | 0.842 | 0.820 | 0.753 | 0.769 | 0.680 | 0.717 | 0.713 | 0.690 | 0.748 | 0.745 | 1934 | 0.745 |
| 1935 | 0.713 | 0.685 | 0.664 | 0.727 | 0.751 | 0.802 | 0.868 | 0.887 | 0.908 | 0.976 | 1.015 | 1.053 | 1935 | 1.053 |
| 1936 | 1.121 | 1.140 | 1.169 | 1.079 | 1.129 | 1.163 | 1.242 | 1.253 | 1.255 | 1.349 | 1.354 | 1.346 | 1936 | 1.346 |
| 1937 | 1.397 | 1.418 | 1.404 | 1.288 | 1.274 | 1.207 | 1.331 | 1.257 | 1.078 | 0.969 | 0.871 | 0.827 | 1937 | 0.827 |
| 1938 | 0.838 | 0.889 | 0.666 | 0.760 | 0.726 | 0.906 | 0.972 | 0.945 | 0.959 | 1.032 | 0.998 | 1.035 | 1938 | 1.035 |
| 1939 | 0.964 | 0.995 | 0.861 | 0.856 | 0.909 | 0.851 | 0.944 | 0.876 | 1.020 | 1.005 | 0.956 | 0.979 | 1939 | 0.979 |
| 1940 | 0.944 | 0.951 | 0.960 | 0.955 | 0.726 | 0.782 | 0.806 | 0.828 | 0.835 | 0.868 | 0.832 | 0.829 | 1940 | 0.829 |
| 1941 | 0.789 | 0.777 | 0.781 | 0.730 | 0.733 | 0.772 | 0.814 | 0.807 | 0.799 | 0.745 | 0.713 | 0.681 | 1941 | 0.681 |
| 1942 | 0.690 | 0.673 | 0.628 | 0.600 | 0.639 | 0.650 | 0.671 | 0.676 | 0.694 | 0.738 | 0.728 | 0.766 | 1942 | 0.766 |
| 1943 | 0.821 | 0.862 | 0.908 | 0.908 | 0.949 | 0.968 | 0.915 | 0.925 | 0.947 | 0.934 | 0.864 | 0.915 | 1943 | 0.915 |
| 1944 | 0.929 | 0.926 | 0.942 | 0.930 | 0.968 | 1.017 | 0.996 | 1.005 | 1.002 | 1.002 | 1.005 | 1.041 | 1944 | 1.041 |
| 1945 | 1.056 | 1.121 | 1.069 | 1.163 | 1.176 | 1.172 | 1.149 | 1.216 | 1.266 | 1.305 | 1.347 | 1.361 | 1945 | 1.361 |
| 1946 | 1.455 | 1.354 | 1.417 | 1.470 | 1.503 | 1.444 | 1.408 | 1.305 | 1.172 | 1.163 | 1.150 | 1.199 | 1946 | 1.199 |
| 1947 | 1.227 | 1.209 | 1.189 | 1.143 | 1.132 | 1.192 | 1.235 | 1.201 | 1.184 | 1.209 | 1.175 | 1.199 | 1947 | 1.199 |
| 1948 | 1.151 | 1.097 | 1.182 | 1.213 | 1.308 | 1.312 | 1.242 | 1.252 | 1.214 | 1.296 | 1.156 | 1.191 | 1948 | 1.191 |
| 1949 | 1.193 | 1.146 | 1.180 | 1.155 | 1.112 | 1.110 | 1.179 | 1.193 | 1.221 | 1.257 | 1.259 | 1.313 | 1949 | 1.313 |
| 1950 | 1.336 | 1.350 | 1.355 | 1.416 | 1.472 | 1.386 | 1.398 | 1.444 | 1.524 | 1.531 | 1.529 | 1.600 | 1950 | 1.600 |
| 1951 | 1.697 | 1.708 | 1.677 | 1.758 | 1.687 | 1.643 | 1.755 | 1.824 | 1.823 | 1.798 | 1.793 | 1.863 | 1951 | 1.863 |
| 1952 | 1.892 | 1.823 | 1.910 | 1.828 | 1.870 | 1.956 | 1.991 | 1.962 | 1.923 | 1.922 | 2.011 | 2.082 | 1952 | 2.082 |
| 1953 | 2.067 | 2.030 | 1.982 | 1.929 | 1.923 | 1.892 | 1.940 | 1.828 | 1.830 | 1.923 | 1.940 | 1.944 | 1953 | 1.944 |
| 1954 | 2.044 | 2.049 | 2.111 | 2.215 | 2.288 | 2.289 | 2.420 | 2.338 | 2.532 | 2.483 | 2.683 | 2.820 | 1954 | 2.820 |
| 1955 | 2.871 | 2.881 | 2.867 | 2.975 | 2.971 | 3.216 | 3.411 | 3.384 | 3.422 | 3.318 | 3.567 | 3.564 | 1955 | 3.564 |
| 1956 | 3.434 | 3.553 | 3.799 | 3.792 | 3.542 | 3.681 | 3.871 | 3.723 | 3.554 | 3.572 | 3.533 | 3.658 | 1956 | 3.658 |
| 1957 | 3.505 | 3.390 | 3.457 | 3.585 | 3.717 | 3.712 | 3.755 | 3.544 | 3.324 | 3.218 | 3.270 | 3.134 | 1957 | 3.134 |
| 1958 | 3.268 | 3.201 | 3.299 | 3.404 | 3.455 | 3.545 | 3.698 | 3.742 | 3.923 | 4.023 | 4.113 | 4.327 | 1958 | 4.327 |
| 1959 | 4.343 | 4.342 | 4.345 | 4.513 | 4.599 | 4.582 | 4.742 | 4.671 | 4.458 | 4.508 | 4.567 | 4.694 | 1959 | 4.694 |
| 1960 | 4.358 | 4.398 | 4.337 | 4.261 | 4.375 | 4.461 | 4.350 | 4.464 | 4.194 | 4.184 | 4.353 | 4.554 | 1960 | 4.554 |
| 1961 | 4.842 | 4.972 | 5.099 | 5.118 | 5.216 | 5.066 | 5.232 | 5.335 | 5.230 | 5.378 | 5.589 | 5.607 | 1961 | 5.607 |
| 1962 | 5.395 | 5.483 | 5.451 | 5.113 | 4.673 | 4.291 | 4.563 | 4.633 | 4.410 | 4.429 | 4.879 | 4.945 | 1962 | 4.945 |
| 1963 | 5.188 | 5.038 | 5.217 | 5.470 | 5.549 | 5.437 | 5.418 | 5.682 | 5.619 | 5.800 | 5.739 | 5.879 | 1963 | 5.879 |
| 1964 | 6.038 | 6.097 | 6.190 | 6.227 | 6.299 | 6.402 | 6.519 | 6.413 | 6.597 | 6.650 | 6.616 | 6.642 | 1964 | 6.642 |
| 1965 | 6.862 | 6.852 | 6.752 | 6.984 | 6.929 | 6.592 | 6.681 | 6.832 | 7.050 | 7.243 | 7.179 | 7.244 | 1965 | 7.244 |
| 1966 | 7.279 | 7.149 | 6.993 | 7.136 | 6.750 | 6.641 | 6.552 | 6.042 | 6.000 | 6.285 | 6.305 | 6.295 | 1966 | 6.295 |
| 1967 | 6.788 | 6.801 | 7.069 | 7.368 | 6.981 | 7.103 | 7.426 | 7.339 | 7.579 | 7.359 | 7.367 | 7.560 | 1967 | 7.560 |
| 1968 | 7.229 | 7.003 | 7.069 | 7.648 | 7.734 | 7.804 | 7.660 | 7.748 | 8.046 | 8.104 | 8.493 | 8.139 | 1968 | 8.139 |
| 1969 | 8.073 | 7.690 | 7.955 | 8.126 | 8.108 | 7.658 | 7.197 | 7.485 | 7.298 | 7.621 | 7.352 | 7.210 | 1969 | 7.210 |
| 1970 | 6.663 | 7.014 | 7.024 | 6.389 | 5.999 | 5.699 | 6.117 | 6.389 | 6.600 | 6.524 | 6.834 | 7.222 | 1970 | 7.222 |

Table B-2 (continued)

**Large Company Stocks: Capital Appreciation Index**

from January 1971 to December 2000

| Year | Jan | Feb | Mar | Apr | May | Jun | Jul | Aug | Sep | Oct | Nov | Dec | Yr-end | Index |
|------|-----|-----|-----|-----|-----|-----|-----|-----|-----|-----|-----|-----|--------|-------|
| 1971 | 7.514 | 7.582 | 7.861 | 8.147 | 7.808 | 7.813 | 7.491 | 7.761 | 7.707 | 7.385 | 7.366 | 8.001 | 1971 | 8.001 |
| 1972 | 8.146 | 8.352 | 8.401 | 8.438 | 8.584 | 8.397 | 8.416 | 8.706 | 8.664 | 8.744 | 9.143 | 9.252 | 1972 | 9.252 |
| 1973 | 9.093 | 8.752 | 8.740 | 8.383 | 8.225 | 8.171 | 8.481 | 8.170 | 8.498 | 8.487 | 7.520 | 7.645 | 1973 | 7.645 |
| 1974 | 7.568 | 7.541 | 7.365 | 7.078 | 6.840 | 6.740 | 6.215 | 5.654 | 4.980 | 5.792 | 5.484 | 5.373 | 1974 | 5.373 |
| 1975 | 6.033 | 6.394 | 6.533 | 6.842 | 7.143 | 7.460 | 6.955 | 6.809 | 6.573 | 6.978 | 7.150 | 7.068 | 1975 | 7.068 |
| 1976 | 7.904 | 7.814 | 8.054 | 7.965 | 7.851 | 8.172 | 8.107 | 8.065 | 8.248 | 8.064 | 8.002 | 8.422 | 1976 | 8.422 |
| 1977 | 7.996 | 7.823 | 7.713 | 7.715 | 7.533 | 7.875 | 7.747 | 7.584 | 7.565 | 7.237 | 7.432 | 7.453 | 1977 | 7.453 |
| 1978 | 6.995 | 6.821 | 6.991 | 7.589 | 7.621 | 7.487 | 7.890 | 8.095 | 8.036 | 7.300 | 7.422 | 7.532 | 1978 | 7.532 |
| 1979 | 7.831 | 7.545 | 7.962 | 7.975 | 7.765 | 8.065 | 8.135 | 8.567 | 8.567 | 7.980 | 8.320 | 8.459 | 1979 | 8.459 |
| 1980 | 8.947. | 8.907 | 8.001 | 8.330 | 8.718 | 8.953 | 9.535 | 9.591 | 9.832 | 9.989 | 11.012 | 10.639 | 1980 | 10.639 |
| 1981 | 10.153 | 10.288 | 10.658 | 10.407 | 10.390 | 10.285 | 10.259 | 9.623 | 9.105 | 9.553 | 9.903 | 9.605 | 1981 | 9.605 |
| 1982 | 9.436 | 8.865 | 8.775 | 9.126 | 8.769 | 8.591 | 8.393 | 9.367 | 9.438 | 10.480 | 10.858 | 11.023 | 1982 | 11.023 |
| 1983 | 11.388 | 11.604 | 11.988 | 12.886 | 12.727 | 13.175 | 12.741 | 12.885 | 13.016 | 12.818 | 13.041 | 12.926 | 1983 | 12.926 |
| 1984 | 12.807 | 12.309 | 12.475 | 12.544 | 11.799 | 12.005 | 11.807 | 13.062 | 13.017 | 13.015 | 12.819 | 13.106 | 1984 | 13.106 |
| 1985 | 14.077 | 14.198 | 14.157 | 14.092 | 14.854 | 15.034 | 14.962 | 14.783 | 14.269 | 14.876 | 15.844 | 16.559 | 1985 | 16.559 |
| 1986 | 16.598 | 17.785 | 18.724 | 18.460 | 19.387 | 19.660 | 18.506 | 19.824 | 18.131 | 19.123 | 19.534 | 18.981 | 1986 | 18.981 |
| 1987 | 21.483 | 22.275 | 22.864 | 22.601 | 22.736 | 23.825 | 24.974 | 25.848 | 25.222 | 19.734 | 18.051 | 19.366 | 1987 | 19.366 |
| 1988 | 20.149 | 20.991 | 20.292 | 20.483 | 20.548 | 21.438 | 21.322 | 20.499 | 21.313 | 21.867 | 21.454 | 21.769 | 1988 | 21.769 |
| 1989 | 23.317 | 22.643 | 23.114 | 24.272 | 25.124 | 24.926 | 27.129 | 27.550 | 27.370 | 26.680 | 27.122 | 27.703 | 1989 | 27.703 |
| 1990 | 25.796 | 26.016 | 26.648 | 25.931 | 28.316 | 28.065 | 27.918 | 25.285 | 23.991 | 23.830 | 25.259 | 25.886 | 1990 | 25.886 |
| 1991 | 26.961 | 28.774 | 29.413 | 29.424 | 30.559 | 29.095 | 30.400 | 30.998 | 30.404 | 30.765 | 29.413 | 32.695 | 1991 | 32.695 |
| 1992 | 32.045 | 32.351 | 31.645 | 32.528 | 32.559 | 31.994 | 33.254 | 32.456 | 32.751 | 32.820 | 33.813 | 34.155 | 1992 | 34.155 |
| 1993 | 34.396 | 34.756 | 35.406 | 34.506 | 35.290 | 35.317 | 35.129 | 36.338 | 35.975 | 36.673 | 36.199 | 36.565 | 1993 | 36.565 |
| 1994 | 37.753 | 36.619 | 34.944 | 35.347 | 35.785 | 34.826 | 35.923 | 37.273 | 36.270 | 37.027 | 35.565 | 36.002 | 1994 | 36.002 |
| 1995 | 36.876 | 38.206 | 39.250 | 40.348 | 41.814 | 42.703 | 44.060 | 44.045 | 45.812 | 45.583 | 47.455 | 48.282 | 1995 | 48.282 |
| 1996 | 49.857 | 50.203 | 50.600 | 51.280 | 52.452 | 52.570 | 50.165 | 51.109 | 53.878 | 55.286 | 59.342 | 58.066 | 1996 | 58.066 |
| 1997 | 61.627 | 61.992 | 59.350 | 62.817 | 66.496 | 69.386 | 74.806 | 70.509 | 74.257 | 71.697 | 74.893 | 76.071 | 1997 | 76.071 |
| 1998 | 76.844 | 82.257 | 86.366 | 87.149 | 85.509 | 88.881 | 87.849 | 75.041 | 79.723 | 86.124 | 91.216 | 96.359 | 1998 | 96.359 |
| 1999 | 100.310 | 97.072 | 100.838 | 104.664 | 102.050 | 107.606 | 104.158 | 103.506 | 100.551 | 106.839 | 108.876 | 115.174 | 1999 | 115.174 |
| 2000 | 109.311 | 107.113 | 117.473 | 113.855 | 111.360 | 114.025 | 112.162 | 118.970 | 112.607 | 112.050 | 103.078 | 103.496 | 2000 | 103.496 |

**Large Company Stocks: Capital Appreciation Index**

## Table B-3

**Small Company Stocks: Total Return Index**

from December 1925 to December 1970

| Year | Jan | Feb | Mar | Apr | May | Jun | Jul | Aug | Sep | Oct | Nov | Dec | Yr-end | Index |
|------|-----|-----|-----|-----|-----|-----|-----|-----|-----|-----|-----|-----|--------|-------|
| 1925 | | | | | | | | | | | | 1.000 | 1925 | 1.000 |
| 1926 | 1.070 | 1.001 | 0.894 | 0.910 | 0.904 | 0.938 | 0.949 | 0.973 | 0.973 | 0.951 | 0.971 | 1.003 | 1926 | 1.003 |
| 1927 | 1.032 | 1.089 | 1.029 | 1.088 | 1.168 | 1.133 | 1.191 | 1.170 | 1.176 | 1.098 | 1.187 | 1.224 | 1927 | 1.224 |
| 1928 | 1.283 | 1.253 | 1.319 | 1.440 | 1.503 | 1.376 | 1.384 | 1.445 | 1.574 | 1.617 | 1.803 | 1.710 | 1928 | 1.710 |
| 1929 | 1.716 | 1.712 | 1.677 | 1.729 | 1.498 | 1.578 | 1.596 | 1.569 | 1.425 | 1.030 | 0.876 | 0.832 | 1929 | 0.832 |
| 1930 | 0.939 | 1.000 | 1.101 | 1.024 | 0.968 | 0.758 | 0.781 | 0.768 | 0.656 | 0.584 | 0.583 | 0.515 | 1930 | 0.515 |
| 1931 | 0.623 | 0.783 | 0.727 | 0.570 | 0.491 | 0.581 | 0.548 | 0.507 | 0.342 | 0.368 | 0.331 | 0.259 | 1931 | 0.259 |
| 1932 | 0.285 | 0.293 | 0.255 | 0.198 | 0.175 | 0.175 | 0.237 | 0.411 | 0.357 | 0.293 | 0.257 | 0.245 | 1932 | 0.245 |
| 1933 | 0.243 | 0.212 | 0.235 | 0.354 | 0.578 | 0.729 | 0.689 | 0.753 | 0.633 | 0.555 | 0.591 | 0.594 | 1933 | 0.594 |
| 1934 | 0.825 | 0.839 | 0.838 | 0.858 | 0.749 | 0.747 | 0.578 | 0.667 | 0.656 | 0.663 | 0.726 | 0.738 | 1934 | 0.738 |
| 1935 | 0.714 | 0.672 | 0.592 | 0.639 | 0.637 | 0.656 | 0.713 | 0.751 | 0.778 | 0.855 | 0.976 | 1.035 | 1935 | 1.035 |
| 1936 | 1.346 | 1.427 | 1.436 | 1.179 | 1.211 | 1.183 | 1.286 | 1.313 | 1.384 | 1.472 | 1.678 | 1.705 | 1936 | 1.705 |
| 1937 | 1.921 | 2.047 | 2.072 | 1.724 | 1.654 | 1.458 | 1.638 | 1.517 | 1.132 | 1.008 | 0.862 | 0.716 | 1937 | 0.716 |
| 1938 | 0.754 | 0.780 | 0.499 | 0.638 | 0.584 | 0.788 | 0.906 | 0.815 | 0.802 | 0.974 | 0.907 | 0.951 | 1938 | 0.951 |
| 1939 | 0.870 | 0.879 | 0.663 | 0.672 | 0.745 | 0.667 | 0.837 | 0.704 | 1.066 | 1.023 | 0.915 | 0.954 | 1939 | 0.954 |
| 1940 | 0.955 | 1.033 | 1.099 | 1.171 | 0.741 | 0.818 | 0.837 | 0.859 | 0.877 | 0.925 | 0.947 | 0.905 | 1940 | 0.905 |
| 1941 | 0.907 | 0.881 | 0.909 | 0.848 | 0.852 | 0.916 | 1.115 | 1.108 | 1.056 | 0.985 | 0.936 | 0.823 | 1941 | 0.823 |
| 1942 | 0.979 | 0.972 | 0.903 | 0.872 | 0.869 | 0.898 | 0.964 | 0.995 | 1.086 | 1.204 | 1.143 | 1.190 | 1942 | 1.190 |
| 1943 | 1.444 | 1.723 | 1.971 | 2.155 | 2.404 | 2.384 | 2.126 | 2.126 | 2.217 | 2.244 | 1.994 | 2.242 | 1943 | 2.242 |
| 1944 | 2.385 | 2.456 | 2.640 | 2.499 | 2.684 | 3.055 | 2.964 | 3.059 | 3.053 | 3.020 | 3.170 | 3.446 | 1944 | 3.446 |
| 1945 | 3.612 | 3.977 | 3.634 | 4.055 | 4.257 | 4.621 | 4.364 | 4.607 | 4.920 | 5.265 | 5.882 | 5.983 | 1945 | 5.983 |
| 1946 | 6.917 | 6.476 | 6.653 | 7.117 | 7.537 | 7.189 | 6.808 | 6.230 | 5.232 | 5.170 | 5.097 | 5.287 | 1946 | 5.287 |
| 1947 | 5.509 | 5.487 | 5.303 | 4.756 | 4.502 | 4.750 | 5.125 | 5.106 | 5.165 | 5.311 | 5.150 | 5.335 | 1947 | 5.335 |
| 1948 | 5.254 | 4.842 | 5.320 | 5.515 | 6.099 | 6.128 | 5.774 | 5.778 | 5.474 | 5.828 | 5.177 | 5.223 | 1948 | 5.223 |
| 1949 | 5.318 | 5.062 | 5.380 | 5.199 | 4.906 | 4.859 | 5.185 | 5.318 | 5.578 | 5.841 | 5.851 | 6.254 | 1949 | 6.254 |
| 1950 | 6.562 | 6.706 | 6.682 | 6.956 | 7.134 | 6.580 | 6.969 | 7.338 | 7.720 | 7.675 | 7.922 | 8.677 | 1950 | 8.677 |
| 1951 | 9.398 | 9.455 | 9.004 | 9.334 | 9.026 | 8.548 | 8.867 | 9.403 | 9.606 | 9.392 | 9.314 | 9.355 | 1951 | 9.355 |
| 1952 | 9.533 | 9.248 | 9.410 | 8.922 | 8.950 | 9.193 | 9.296 | 9.291 | 9.142 | 9.047 | 9.486 | 9.638 | 1952 | 9.638 |
| 1953 | 10.032 | 10.302 | 10.233 | 9.939 | 10.079 | 9.589 | 9.735 | 9.123 | 8.884 | 9.143 | 9.258 | 9.013 | 1953 | 9.013 |
| 1954 | 9.694 | 9.786 | 9.965 | 10.104 | 10.561 | 10.651 | 11.512 | 11.528 | 12.000 | 12.082 | 13.024 | 14.473 | 1954 | 14.473 |
| 1955 | 14.764 | 15.471 | 15.602 | 15.837 | 15.960 | 16.428 | 16.533 | 16.487 | 16.667 | 16.384 | 17.152 | 17.431 | 1955 | 17.431 |
| 1956 | 17.348 | 17.830 | 18.598 | 18.685 | 17.942 | 18.042 | 18.552 | 18.303 | 17.827 | 18.013 | 18.108 | 18.177 | 1956 | 18.177 |
| 1957 | 18.607 | 18.234 | 18.540 | 19.000 | 19.143 | 19.283 | 19.167 | 18.427 | 17.595 | 16.131 | 16.314 | 15.529 | 1957 | 15.529 |
| 1958 | 17.245 | 16.952 | 17.750 | 18.418 | 19.131 | 19.752 | 20.722 | 21.610 | 22.730 | 23.655 | 24.828 | 25.605 | 1958 | 25.605 |
| 1959 | 27.076 | 27.875 | 27.951 | 28.277 | 28.315 | 28.196 | 29.118 | 28.863 | 27.619 | 28.245 | 28.873 | 29.804 | 1959 | 29.804 |
| 1960 | 28.891 | 29.034 | 28.120 | 27.594 | 28.158 | 29.116 | 28.565 | 30.064 | 27.844 | 26.728 | 27.896 | 28.823 | 1960 | 28.823 |
| 1961 | 31.460 | 33.314 | 35.376 | 35.825 | 37.355 | 35.326 | 35.436 | 35.898 | 34.682 | 35.590 | 37.772 | 38.072 | 1961 | 38.072 |
| 1962 | 38.591 | 39.314 | 39.537 | 36.464 | 32.786 | 30.213 | 32.518 | 33.458 | 31.254 | 30.087 | 33.842 | 33.540 | 1962 | 33.540 |
| 1963 | 36.580 | 36.705 | 37.251 | 38.412 | 40.088 | 39.613 | 39.744 | 41.799 | 41.118 | 42.090 | 41.642 | 41.444 | 1963 | 41.444 |
| 1964 | 42.581 | 44.134 | 45.099 | 45.520 | 46.234 | 46.985 | 48.857 | 48.715 | 50.676 | 51.716 | 51.772 | 51.193 | 1964 | 51.193 |
| 1965 | 53.902 | 56.003 | 57.335 | 60.252 | 59.782 | 54.398 | 56.837 | 60.220 | 62.310 | 65.876 | 68.319 | 72.567 | 1965 | 72.567 |
| 1966 | 78.051 | 80.479 | 78.935 | 81.645 | 73.797 | 73.709 | 73.617 | 65.669 | 64.595 | 63.902 | 67.041 | 67.479 | 1966 | 67.479 |
| 1967 | 79.884 | 83.475 | 88.606 | 91.003 | 90.232 | 99.411 | 108.862 | 109.085 | 115.244 | 111.662 | 112.965 | 123.870 | 1967 | 123.870 |
| 1968 | 125.779 | 116.861 | 115.586 | 132.468 | 145.698 | 146.137 | 141.088 | 146.266 | 155.034 | 155.505 | 167.388 | 168.429 | 1968 | 168.429 |
| 1969 | 165.634 | 149.238 | 155.142 | 161.265 | 164.063 | 144.954 | 129.449 | 138.925 | 135.301 | 143.552 | 135.552 | 126.233 | 1969 | 126.233 |
| 1970 | 118.554 | 123.145 | 119.641 | 98.970 | 88.762 | 80.519 | 84.975 | 93.037 | 103.140 | 95.856 | 97.170 | 104.226 | 1970 | 104.226 |

## Table B-3 (continued)

## Small Company Stocks: Total Return Index

from January 1971 to December 2000

| Year | Jan | Feb | Mar | Apr | May | Jun | Jul | Aug | Sep | Oct | Nov | Dec | Yr-end | Index |
|------|-----|-----|-----|-----|-----|-----|-----|-----|-----|-----|-----|-----|--------|-------|
| 1971 | 120.820 | 124.647 | 131.676 | 134.923 | 126.760 | 122.710 | 115.802 | 122.555 | 119.780 | 113.180 | 108.954 | 121.423 | 1971 | 121.423 |
| 1972 | 135.142 | 139.141 | 137.144 | 138.912 | 136.257 | 132.100 | 126.645 | 129.005 | 124.506 | 122.329 | 129.576 | 126.807 | 1972 | 126.807 |
| 1973 | 121.329 | 111.635 | 109.318 | 102.527 | 94.211 | 91.476 | 102.398 | 97.837 | 108.242 | 109.155 | 87.737 | 87.618 | 1973 | 87.618 |
| 1974 | 99.238 | 98.393 | 97.661 | 93.129 | 85.745 | 84.485 | 82.637 | 77.009 | 71.978 | 79.629 | 76.143 | 70.142 | 1974 | 70.142 |
| 1975 | 89.551 | 92.105 | 97.799 | 102.990 | 109.821 | 118.053 | 115.056 | 108.456 | 106.488 | 105.954 | 109.341 | 107.189 | 1975 | 107.189 |
| 1976 | 135.960 | 154.854 | 154.626 | 149.081 | 143.698 | 150.298 | 150.976 | 146.592 | 148.123 | 145.028 | 150.881 | 168.691 | 1976 | 168.691 |
| 1977 | 176.275 | 175.587 | 177.880 | 181.941 | 181.434 | 195.445 | 196.028 | 193.924 | 195.715 | 189.249 | 209.804 | 211.500 | 1977 | 211.500 |
| 1978 | 207.502 | 214.707 | 236.868 | 255.528 | 276.484 | 271.254 | 289.807 | 317.010 | 316.002 | 239.303 | 256.811 | 261.120 | 1978 | 261.120 |
| 1979 | 295.623 | 287.279 | 319.448 | 331.805 | 332.955 | 348.676 | 354.642 | 381.457 | 368.351 | 325.827 | 353.796 | 374.614 | 1979 | 374.614 |
| 1980 | 405.926 | 394.411 | 324.303 | 346.795 | 372.814 | 389.666 | 441.224 | 467.894 | 487.473 | 503.725 | 542.326 | 523.992 | 1980 | 523.992 |
| 1981 | 534.839 | 539.866 | 590.776 | 629.590 | 656.158 | 661.145 | 640.253 | 596.460 | 552.739 | 593.752 | 610.140 | 596.717 | 1981 | 596.717 |
| 1982 | 585.021 | 567.705 | 562.822 | 584.378 | 569.886 | 560.825 | 559.983 | 599.070 | 618.660 | 699.395 | 753.878 | 763.829 | 1982 | 763.829 |
| 1983 | 811.793 | 869.617 | 915.267 | 985.448 | 1071.150 | 1108.462 | 1098.662 | 1077.054 | 1091.419 | 1029.455 | 1082.532 | 1066.828 | 1983 | 1066.828 |
| 1984 | 1065.974 | 997.219 | 1014.571 | 1005.947 | 953.537 | 982.143 | 940.893 | 1034.794 | 1037.588 | 1015.072 | 980.966 | 995.680 | 1984 | 995.680 |
| 1985 | 1101.123 | 1131.074 | 1106.869 | 1087.609 | 1117.627 | 1129.474 | 1158.840 | 1150.497 | 1087.910 | 1116.304 | 1185.515 | 1241.234 | 1985 | 1241.234 |
| 1986 | 1255.136 | 1345.380 | 1409.555 | 1418.576 | 1469.645 | 1473.466 | 1368.850 | 1398.691 | 1320.504 | 1366.193 | 1361.958 | 1326.275 | 1986 | 1326.275 |
| 1987 | 1451.342 | 1568.756 | 1605.308 | 1555.062 | 1548.997 | 1590.201 | 1648.084 | 1695.384 | 1681.651 | 1190.777 | 1143.503 | 1202.966 | 1987 | 1202.966 |
| 1988 | 1269.850 | 1366.359 | 1422.107 | 1451.829 | 1425.841 | 1513.102 | 1509.320 | 1472.190 | 1505.609 | 1487.090 | 1422.104 | 1478.135 | 1988 | 1478.135 |
| 1989 | 1537.852 | 1550.616 | 1606.128 | 1650.939 | 1710.703 | 1676.318 | 1744.544 | 1765.827 | 1765.827 | 1659.171 | 1650.710 | 1628.590 | 1989 | 1628.590 |
| 1990 | 1504.166 | 1532.294 | 1588.682 | 1546.423 | 1633.178 | 1656.695 | 1593.410 | 1386.904 | 1271.929 | 1199.175 | 1253.138 | 1277.449 | 1990 | 1277.449 |
| 1991 | 1384.882 | 1539.020 | 1643.673 | 1649.261 | 1704.347 | 1621.686 | 1687.688 | 1731.737 | 1737.279 | 1792.350 | 1742.882 | 1847.629 | 1991 | 1847.629 |
| 1992 | 2056.041 | 2148.974 | 2095.465 | 2011.018 | 2008.202 | 1903.977 | 1974.424 | 1929.407 | 1954.682 | 2005.308 | 2182.778 | 2279.039 | 1992 | 2279.039 |
| 1993 | 2402.790 | 2359.540 | 2427.731 | 2353.442 | 2433.930 | 2424.681 | 2464.931 | 2548.492 | 2629.024 | 2752.851 | 2704.676 | 2757.147 | 1993 | 2757.147 |
| 1994 | 2927.539 | 2920.806 | 2790.538 | 2807.281 | 2803.912 | 2730.450 | 2780.690 | 2874.399 | 2904.580 | 2937.983 | 2842.205 | 2842.773 | 1994 | 2842.773 |
| 1995 | 2923.224 | 2996.889 | 3040.344 | 3147.364 | 3241.155 | 3425.253 | 3646.182 | 3776.715 | 3850.361 | 3662.848 | 3733.175 | 3822.398 | 1995 | 3822.398 |
| 1996 | 3833.101 | 3974.542 | 4065.162 | 4409.887 | 4740.188 | 4464.309 | 4043.325 | 4235.787 | 4359.048 | 4282.765 | 4406.109 | 4495.993 | 1996 | 4495.993 |
| 1997 | 4684.825 | 4588.318 | 4363.490 | 4243.058 | 4676.698 | 4909.598 | 5206.628 | 5471.646 | 5933.453 | 5704.421 | 5616.003 | 5519.969 | 1997 | 5519.969 |
| 1998 | 5487.401 | 5843.534 | 6124.608 | 6227.501 | 5917.994 | 5796.084 | 5407.166 | 4320.326 | 4479.746 | 4639.225 | 4990.878 | 5116.648 | 1998 | 5116.648 |
| 1999 | 5259.403 | 4898.082 | 4712.445 | 5159.656 | 5359.334 | 5663.744 | 5715.851 | 5606.678 | 5482.771 | 5435.070 | 5962.816 | 6640.788 | 1999 | 6640.788 |
| 2000 | 7053.915 | 8694.984 | 8041.990 | 7035.937 | 6467.434 | 7352.179 | 7115.438 | 7773.616 | 7604.929 | 7068.021 | 6283.471 | 6402.228 | 2000 | 6402.228 |

## Table B-4

**Long-Term Corporate Bonds: Total Return Index**

from December 1925 to December 1970

| Year | Jan | Feb | Mar | Apr | May | Jun | Jul | Aug | Sep | Oct | Nov | Dec | Yr-end | Index |
|------|-----|-----|-----|-----|-----|-----|-----|-----|-----|-----|-----|-----|--------|-------|
| 1925 | | | | | | | | | | | | 1.000 | 1925 | 1.000 |
| 1926 | 1.007 | 1.012 | 1.020 | 1.030 | 1.035 | 1.035 | 1.041 | 1.046 | 1.052 | 1.062 | 1.068 | 1.074 | 1926 | 1.074 |
| 1927 | 1.080 | 1.087 | 1.096 | 1.102 | 1.101 | 1.106 | 1.106 | 1.115 | 1.132 | 1.138 | 1.146 | 1.154 | 1927 | 1.154 |
| 1928 | 1.157 | 1.165 | 1.169 | 1.171 | 1.162 | 1.159 | 1.158 | 1.168 | 1.171 | 1.181 | 1.177 | 1.186 | 1928 | 1.186 |
| 1929 | 1.192 | 1.195 | 1.185 | 1.187 | 1.192 | 1.187 | 1.189 | 1.192 | 1.196 | 1.204 | 1.202 | 1.225 | 1929 | 1.225 |
| 1930 | 1.233 | 1.241 | 1.259 | 1.269 | 1.276 | 1.290 | 1.298 | 1.315 | 1.329 | 1.337 | 1.335 | 1.323 | 1930 | 1.323 |
| 1931 | 1.350 | 1.359 | 1.372 | 1.381 | 1.400 | 1.407 | 1.414 | 1.416 | 1.414 | 1.362 | 1.337 | 1.299 | 1931 | 1.299 |
| 1932 | 1.292 | 1.261 | 1.306 | 1.283 | 1.297 | 1.295 | 1.301 | 1.358 | 1.399 | 1.409 | 1.419 | 1.439 | 1932 | 1.439 |
| 1933 | 1.518 | 1.438 | 1.445 | 1.431 | 1.516 | 1.544 | 1.569 | 1.584 | 1.582 | 1.588 | 1.549 | 1.588 | 1933 | 1.588 |
| 1934 | 1.629 | 1.653 | 1.684 | 1.701 | 1.717 | 1.744 | 1.752 | 1.760 | 1.749 | 1.767 | 1.790 | 1.808 | 1934 | 1.808 |
| 1935 | 1.846 | 1.872 | 1.880 | 1.901 | 1.909 | 1.931 | 1.952 | 1.944 | 1.944 | 1.952 | 1.966 | 1.982 | 1935 | 1.982 |
| 1936 | 1.998 | 2.009 | 2.026 | 2.031 | 2.039 | 2.056 | 2.058 | 2.072 | 2.086 | 2.091 | 2.114 | 2.116 | 1936 | 2.116 |
| 1937 | 2.121 | 2.111 | 2.087 | 2.101 | 2.110 | 2.121 | 2.129 | 2.125 | 2.131 | 2.145 | 2.159 | 2.174 | 1937 | 2.174 |
| 1938 | 2.182 | 2.184 | 2.165 | 2.195 | 2.197 | 2.218 | 2.233 | 2.229 | 2.253 | 2.271 | 2.279 | 2.307 | 1938 | 2.307 |
| 1939 | 2.312 | 2.327 | 2.332 | 2.347 | 2.359 | 2.367 | 2.365 | 2.272 | 2.307 | 2.361 | 2.380 | 2.399 | 1939 | 2.399 |
| 1940 | 2.410 | 2.415 | 2.427 | 2.405 | 2.400 | 2.429 | 2.434 | 2.436 | 2.458 | 2.470 | 2.486 | 2.480 | 1940 | 2.480 |
| 1941 | 2.482 | 2.483 | 2.478 | 2.497 | 2.509 | 2.525 | 2.541 | 2.550 | 2.562 | 2.570 | 2.546 | 2.548 | 1941 | 2.548 |
| 1942 | 2.549 | 2.547 | 2.563 | 2.565 | 2.570 | 2.579 | 2.584 | 2.593 | 2.598 | 2.600 | 2.601 | 2.614 | 1942 | 2.614 |
| 1943 | 2.627 | 2.628 | 2.634 | 2.647 | 2.659 | 2.672 | 2.677 | 2.682 | 2.684 | 2.681 | 2.675 | 2.688 | 1943 | 2.688 |
| 1944 | 2.693 | 2.703 | 2.716 | 2.725 | 2.726 | 2.732 | 2.741 | 2.750 | 2.755 | 2.761 | 2.774 | 2.815 | 1944 | 2.815 |
| 1945 | 2.837 | 2.850 | 2.855 | 2.860 | 2.857 | 2.866 | 2.863 | 2.864 | 2.873 | 2.882 | 2.892 | 2.930 | 1945 | 2.930 |
| 1946 | 2.968 | 2.978 | 2.988 | 2.975 | 2.981 | 2.986 | 2.983 | 2.956 | 2.949 | 2.955 | 2.947 | 2.980 | 1946 | 2.980 |
| 1947 | 2.982 | 2.983 | 3.003 | 3.009 | 3.015 | 3.017 | 3.023 | 3.001 | 2.962 | 2.933 | 2.904 | 2.911 | 1947 | 2.911 |
| 1948 | 2.918 | 2.929 | 2.963 | 2.974 | 2.977 | 2.952 | 2.936 | 2.953 | 2.960 | 2.967 | 2.992 | 3.031 | 1948 | 3.031 |
| 1949 | 3.043 | 3.054 | 3.056 | 3.063 | 3.075 | 3.101 | 3.132 | 3.143 | 3.150 | 3.171 | 3.178 | 3.132 | 1949 | 3.132 |
| 1950 | 3.143 | 3.145 | 3.152 | 3.150 | 3.147 | 3.154 | 3.176 | 3.188 | 3.176 | 3.173 | 3.190 | 3.198 | 1950 | 3.198 |
| 1951 | 3.204 | 3.190 | 3.114 | 3.111 | 3.107 | 3.078 | 3.141 | 3.177 | 3.159 | 3.113 | 3.094 | 3.112 | 1951 | 3.112 |
| 1952 | 3.174 | 3.147 | 3.171 | 3.169 | 3.179 | 3.184 | 3.189 | 3.209 | 3.204 | 3.216 | 3.251 | 3.221 | 1952 | 3.221 |
| 1953 | 3.196 | 3.183 | 3.172 | 3.094 | 3.084 | 3.118 | 3.173 | 3.146 | 3.226 | 3.299 | 3.275 | 3.331 | 1953 | 3.331 |
| 1954 | 3.373 | 3.439 | 3.453 | 3.441 | 3.427 | 3.448 | 3.462 | 3.468 | 3.482 | 3.496 | 3.505 | 3.511 | 1954 | 3.511 |
| 1955 | 3.477 | 3.455 | 3.486 | 3.486 | 3.480 | 3.490 | 3.476 | 3.462 | 3.489 | 3.516 | 3.505 | 3.527 | 1955 | 3.527 |
| 1956 | 3.564 | 3.573 | 3.521 | 3.481 | 3.499 | 3.493 | 3.460 | 3.388 | 3.392 | 3.357 | 3.314 | 3.287 | 1956 | 3.287 |
| 1957 | 3.352 | 3.383 | 3.400 | 3.377 | 3.352 | 3.244 | 3.209 | 3.206 | 3.236 | 3.244 | 3.344 | 3.573 | 1957 | 3.573 |
| 1958 | 3.609 | 3.606 | 3.589 | 3.648 | 3.659 | 3.645 | 3.590 | 3.475 | 3.441 | 3.478 | 3.515 | 3.494 | 1958 | 3.494 |
| 1959 | 3.484 | 3.528 | 3.499 | 3.439 | 3.400 | 3.415 | 3.445 | 3.422 | 3.392 | 3.447 | 3.494 | 3.460 | 1959 | 3.460 |
| 1960 | 3.498 | 3.542 | 3.610 | 3.602 | 3.594 | 3.645 | 3.739 | 3.783 | 3.759 | 3.762 | 3.735 | 3.774 | 1960 | 3.774 |
| 1961 | 3.830 | 3.911 | 3.899 | 3.854 | 3.873 | 3.842 | 3.857 | 3.850 | 3.906 | 3.955 | 3.966 | 3.956 | 1961 | 3.956 |
| 1962 | 3.988 | 4.008 | 4.069 | 4.127 | 4.127 | 4.116 | 4.110 | 4.169 | 4.206 | 4.234 | 4.261 | 4.270 | 1962 | 4.270 |
| 1963 | 4.296 | 4.305 | 4.317 | 4.295 | 4.315 | 4.334 | 4.346 | 4.361 | 4.351 | 4.372 | 4.379 | 4.364 | 1963 | 4.364 |
| 1964 | 4.402 | 4.426 | 4.398 | 4.416 | 4.441 | 4.463 | 4.486 | 4.502 | 4.512 | 4.534 | 4.533 | 4.572 | 1964 | 4.572 |
| 1965 | 4.609 | 4.614 | 4.619 | 4.629 | 4.625 | 4.627 | 4.635 | 4.633 | 4.626 | 4.647 | 4.620 | 4.552 | 1965 | 4.552 |
| 1966 | 4.562 | 4.510 | 4.483 | 4.489 | 4.478 | 4.491 | 4.447 | 4.332 | 4.366 | 4.480 | 4.471 | 4.560 | 1966 | 4.560 |
| 1967 | 4.766 | 4.670 | 4.724 | 4.691 | 4.572 | 4.470 | 4.488 | 4.485 | 4.527 | 4.400 | 4.280 | 4.335 | 1967 | 4.335 |
| 1968 | 4.491 | 4.508 | 4.419 | 4.440 | 4.454 | 4.509 | 4.662 | 4.758 | 4.733 | 4.658 | 4.552 | 4.446 | 1968 | 4.446 |
| 1969 | 4.508 | 4.436 | 4.347 | 4.493 | 4.391 | 4.406 | 4.408 | 4.400 | 4.292 | 4.347 | 4.142 | 4.086 | 1969 | 4.086 |
| 1970 | 4.144 | 4.310 | 4.291 | 4.184 | 4.115 | 4.116 | 4.345 | 4.388 | 4.449 | 4.406 | 4.664 | 4.837 | 1970 | 4.837 |

## Table B-4 (continued)

## Long-Term Corporate Bonds: Total Return Index

from January 1971 to December 2000

| Year | Jan | Feb | Mar | Apr | May | Jun | Jul | Aug | Sep | Oct | Nov | Dec | Yr-end | Index |
|------|-----|-----|-----|-----|-----|-----|-----|-----|-----|-----|-----|-----|--------|-------|
| 1971 | 5.095 | 4.908 | 5.035 | 4.916 | 4.837 | 4.889 | 4.876 | 5.146 | 5.094 | 5.238 | 5.253 | 5.370 | 1971 | 5.370 |
| 1972 | 5.352 | 5.409 | 5.422 | 5.441 | 5.530 | 5.493 | 5.509 | 5.549 | 5.566 | 5.622 | 5.762 | 5.760 | 1972 | 5.760 |
| 1973 | 5.729 | 5.742 | 5.768 | 5.803 | 5.780 | 5.748 | 5.474 | 5.669 | 5.871 | 5.832 | 5.878 | 5.825 | 1973 | 5.825 |
| 1974 | 5.795 | 5.800 | 5.622 | 5.430 | 5.487 | 5.331 | 5.218 | 5.078 | 5.167 | 5.624 | 5.690 | 5.647 | 1974 | 5.647 |
| 1975 | 5.984 | 6.066 | 5.916 | 5.885 | 5.947 | 6.128 | 6.110 | 6.003 | 5.927 | 6.255 | 6.200 | 6.474 | 1975 | 6.474 |
| 1976 | 6.596 | 6.636 | 6.747 | 6.737 | 6.667 | 6.767 | 6.868 | 7.027 | 7.144 | 7.194 | 7.424 | 7.681 | 1976 | 7.681 |
| 1977 | 7.448 | 7.434 | 7.503 | 7.579 | 7.659 | 7.793 | 7.789 | 7.895 | 7.878 | 7.848 | 7.895 | 7.813 | 1977 | 7.813 |
| 1978 | 7.743 | 7.783 | 7.815 | 7.797 | 7.713 | 7.731 | 7.809 | 8.010 | 7.971 | 7.808 | 7.912 | 7.807 | 1978 | 7.807 |
| 1979 | 7.951 | 7.849 | 7.932 | 7.892 | 8.072 | 8.289 | 8.263 | 8.269 | 8.121 | 7.398 | 7.563 | 7.481 | 1979 | 7.481 |
| 1980 | 6.998 | 6.533 | 6.492 | 7.386 | 7.799 | 8.065 | 7.719 | 7.376 | 7.201 | 7.086 | 7.098 | 7.274 | 1980 | 7.274 |
| 1981 | 7.180 | 6.987 | 7.204 | 6.650 | 7.046 | 7.062 | 6.799 | 6.565 | 6.434 | 6.769 | 7.627 | 7.185 | 1981 | 7.185 |
| 1982 | 7.092 | 7.313 | 7.537 | 7.792 | 7.983 | 7.609 | 8.020 | 8.691 | 9.233 | 9.933 | 10.133 | 10.242 | 1982 | 10.242 |
| 1983 | 10.146 | 10.580 | 10.657 | 11.241 | 10.876 | 10.826 | 10.334 | 10.386 | 10.794 | 10.767 | 10.920 | 10.883 | 1983 | 10.883 |
| 1984 | 11.177 | 10.985 | 10.727 | 10.649 | 10.134 | 10.336 | 10.942 | 11.278 | 11.632 | 12.297 | 12.558 | 12.718 | 1984 | 12.718 |
| 1985 | 13.132 | 12.642 | 12.868 | 13.249 | 14.336 | 14.455 | 14.280 | 14.651 | 14.755 | 15.240 | 15.804 | 16.546 | 1985 | 16.546 |
| 1986 | 16.620 | 17.870 | 18.327 | 18.357 | 18.056 | 18.449 | 18.506 | 19.015 | 18.799 | 19.154 | 19.600 | 19.829 | 1986 | 19.829 |
| 1987 | 20.258 | 20.375 | 20.198 | 19.184 | 19.084 | 19.380 | 19.149 | 19.006 | 18.204 | 19.127 | 19.366 | 19.776 | 1987 | 19.776 |
| 1988 | 20.799 | 21.086 | 20.689 | 20.381 | 20.265 | 21.033 | 20.800 | 20.912 | 21.594 | 22.183 | 21.808 | 21.893 | 1988 | 21.893 |
| 1989 | 22.335 | 22.047 | 22.188 | 22.661 | 23.520 | 24.449 | 24.884 | 24.479 | 24.576 | 25.255 | 25.432 | 25.447 | 1989 | 25.447 |
| 1990 | 24.961 | 24.931 | 24.903 | 24.428 | 25.368 | 25.916 | 26.181 | 25.416 | 25.647 | 25.986 | 26.726 | 27.173 | 1990 | 27.173 |
| 1991 | 27.580 | 27.914 | 28.216 | 28.605 | 28.717 | 28.665 | 29.144 | 29.945 | 30.757 | 30.889 | 31.216 | 32.577 | 1991 | 32.577 |
| 1992 | 32.014 | 32.321 | 32.085 | 32.136 | 32.953 | 33.467 | 34.497 | 34.808 | 35.153 | 34.604 | 34.843 | 35.637 | 1992 | 35.637 |
| 1993 | 36.528 | 37.463 | 37.557 | 37.752 | 37.828 | 38.936 | 39.326 | 40.454 | 40.628 | 40.835 | 40.068 | 40.336 | 1993 | 40.336 |
| 1994 | 41.151 | 39.974 | 38.443 | 38.070 | 37.834 | 37.528 | 38.687 | 38.567 | 37.545 | 37.358 | 37.425 | 38.012 | 1994 | 38.012 |
| 1995 | 38.985 | 40.112 | 40.493 | 41.202 | 43.802 | 44.148 | 43.702 | 44.637 | 45.320 | 46.158 | 47.275 | 48.353 | 1995 | 48.353 |
| 1996 | 48.421 | 46.615 | 46.009 | 45.273 | 45.295 | 46.074 | 46.121 | 45.798 | 46.984 | 48.680 | 49.960 | 49.031 | 1996 | 49.031 |
| 1997 | 48.894 | 49.031 | 47.947 | 48.829 | 49.454 | 50.379 | 53.039 | 51.766 | 52.936 | 53.947 | 54.492 | 55.380 | 1997 | 55.380 |
| 1998 | 56.139 | 56.100 | 56.313 | 56.611 | 57.557 | 58.219 | 57.893 | 58.408 | 60.820 | 59.664 | 61.275 | 61.339 | 1998 | 61.339 |
| 1999 | 62.091 | 59.603 | 59.617 | 59.473 | 58.427 | 57.493 | 56.843 | 56.693 | 57.221 | 57.492 | 57.356 | 56.772 | 1999 | 56.772 |
| 2000 | 56.652 | 57.174 | 58.142 | 57.476 | 56.552 | 58.396 | 59.442 | 60.245 | 60.525 | 60.797 | 62.394 | 64.077 | 2000 | 64.077 |

## Table B-5

**Long-Term Government Bonds: Total Return Index**

from December 1925 to December 1970

| Year | Jan | Feb | Mar | Apr | May | Jun | Jul | Aug | Sep | Oct | Nov | Dec | Yr-end | Index |
|------|-----|-----|-----|-----|-----|-----|-----|-----|-----|-----|-----|-----|--------|-------|
| 1925 | | | | | | | | | | | | 1.000 | 1925 | 1.000 |
| 1926 | 1.014 | 1.020 | 1.024 | 1.032 | 1.034 | 1.038 | 1.038 | 1.038 | 1.042 | 1.053 | 1.069 | 1.078 | 1926 | 1.078 |
| 1927 | 1.086 | 1.095 | 1.123 | 1.122 | 1.135 | 1.127 | 1.132 | 1.141 | 1.143 | 1.154 | 1.166 | 1.174 | 1927 | 1.174 |
| 1928 | 1.170 | 1.177 | 1.182 | 1.182 | 1.173 | 1.178 | 1.152 | 1.161 | 1.156 | 1.174 | 1.175 | 1.175 | 1928 | 1.175 |
| 1929 | 1.165 | 1.146 | 1.130 | 1.161 | 1.142 | 1.155 | 1.155 | 1.151 | 1.154 | 1.198 | 1.226 | 1.215 | 1929 | 1.215 |
| 1930 | 1.208 | 1.224 | 1.234 | 1.232 | 1.249 | 1.256 | 1.260 | 1.262 | 1.271 | 1.276 | 1.281 | 1.272 | 1930 | 1.272 |
| 1931 | 1.257 | 1.267 | 1.280 | 1.291 | 1.310 | 1.311 | 1.305 | 1.307 | 1.270 | 1.228 | 1.231 | 1.204 | 1931 | 1.204 |
| 1932 | 1.208 | 1.258 | 1.256 | 1.332 | 1.307 | 1.315 | 1.379 | 1.379 | 1.387 | 1.385 | 1.389 | 1.407 | 1932 | 1.407 |
| 1933 | 1.428 | 1.391 | 1.405 | 1.400 | 1.443 | 1.450 | 1.447 | 1.454 | 1.457 | 1.444 | 1.422 | 1.406 | 1933 | 1.406 |
| 1934 | 1.442 | 1.454 | 1.483 | 1.501 | 1.521 | 1.531 | 1.537 | 1.519 | 1.497 | 1.524 | 1.530 | 1.547 | 1934 | 1.547 |
| 1935 | 1.575 | 1.590 | 1.596 | 1.609 | 1.600 | 1.615 | 1.622 | 1.600 | 1.602 | 1.611 | 1.613 | 1.624 | 1935 | 1.624 |
| 1936 | 1.633 | 1.647 | 1.664 | 1.670 | 1.677 | 1.680 | 1.690 | 1.709 | 1.704 | 1.705 | 1.740 | 1.746 | 1936 | 1.746 |
| 1937 | 1.744 | 1.759 | 1.687 | 1.693 | 1.702 | 1.699 | 1.723 | 1.705 | 1.712 | 1.720 | 1.736 | 1.750 | 1937 | 1.750 |
| 1938 | 1.760 | 1.770 | 1.763 | 1.800 | 1.808 | 1.809 | 1.817 | 1.817 | 1.821 | 1.837 | 1.833 | 1.847 | 1938 | 1.847 |
| 1939 | 1.858 | 1.873 | 1.896 | 1.919 | 1.951 | 1.946 | 1.968 | 1.929 | 1.824 | 1.898 | 1.929 | 1.957 | 1939 | 1.957 |
| 1940 | 1.954 | 1.959 | 1.994 | 1.987 | 1.927 | 1.977 | 1.987 | 1.993 | 2.015 | 2.021 | 2.062 | 2.076 | 1940 | 2.076 |
| 1941 | 2.034 | 2.039 | 2.058 | 2.085 | 2.090 | 2.104 | 2.109 | 2.113 | 2.110 | 2.140 | 2.133 | 2.096 | 1941 | 2.096 |
| 1942 | 2.110 | 2.112 | 2.132 | 2.126 | 2.142 | 2.142 | 2.146 | 2.154 | 2.155 | 2.160 | 2.152 | 2.163 | 1942 | 2.163 |
| 1943 | 2.170 | 2.169 | 2.171 | 2.181 | 2.192 | 2.196 | 2.196 | 2.201 | 2.203 | 2.204 | 2.204 | 2.208 | 1943 | 2.208 |
| 1944 | 2.213 | 2.220 | 2.224 | 2.227 | 2.234 | 2.235 | 2.243 | 2.249 | 2.253 | 2.255 | 2.261 | 2.270 | 1944 | 2.270 |
| 1945 | 2.299 | 2.317 | 2.321 | 2.358 | 2.372 | 2.412 | 2.391 | 2.397 | 2.410 | 2.435 | 2.466 | 2.514 | 1945 | 2.514 |
| 1946 | 2.520 | 2.528 | 2.531 | 2.497 | 2.493 | 2.511 | 2.501 | 2.473 | 2.471 | 2.489 | 2.475 | 2.511 | 1946 | 2.511 |
| 1947 | 2.510 | 2.515 | 2.520 | 2.511 | 2.519 | 2.522 | 2.537 | 2.558 | 2.547 | 2.537 | 2.493 | 2.445 | 1947 | 2.445 |
| 1948 | 2.450 | 2.462 | 2.470 | 2.481 | 2.516 | 2.495 | 2.490 | 2.490 | 2.494 | 2.496 | 2.514 | 2.529 | 1948 | 2.529 |
| 1949 | 2.549 | 2.562 | 2.581 | 2.584 | 2.589 | 2.632 | 2.641 | 2.670 | 2.667 | 2.672 | 2.678 | 2.692 | 1949 | 2.692 |
| 1950 | 2.675 | 2.681 | 2.683 | 2.691 | 2.700 | 2.693 | 2.708 | 2.712 | 2.692 | 2.679 | 2.689 | 2.693 | 1950 | 2.693 |
| 1951 | 2.709 | 2.689 | 2.646 | 2.630 | 2.612 | 2.596 | 2.632 | 2.657 | 2.636 | 2.639 | 2.603 | 2.587 | 1951 | 2.587 |
| 1952 | 2.595 | 2.598 | 2.627 | 2.672 | 2.663 | 2.664 | 2.658 | 2.640 | 2.606 | 2.644 | 2.640 | 2.617 | 1952 | 2.617 |
| 1953 | 2.620 | 2.598 | 2.575 | 2.548 | 2.510 | 2.566 | 2.576 | 2.574 | 2.651 | 2.671 | 2.658 | 2.713 | 1953 | 2.713 |
| 1954 | 2.737 | 2.802 | 2.819 | 2.848 | 2.823 | 2.869 | 2.908 | 2.897 | 2.894 | 2.896 | 2.889 | 2.907 | 1954 | 2.907 |
| 1955 | 2.837 | 2.815 | 2.840 | 2.840 | 2.861 | 2.839 | 2.810 | 2.811 | 2.832 | 2.872 | 2.859 | 2.870 | 1955 | 2.870 |
| 1956 | 2.894 | 2.893 | 2.850 | 2.818 | 2.881 | 2.889 | 2.829 | 2.776 | 2.790 | 2.775 | 2.759 | 2.710 | 1956 | 2.710 |
| 1957 | 2.803 | 2.810 | 2.804 | 2.741 | 2.735 | 2.686 | 2.675 | 2.675 | 2.696 | 2.682 | 2.825 | 2.912 | 1957 | 2.912 |
| 1958 | 2.887 | 2.916 | 2.946 | 3.001 | 3.001 | 2.953 | 2.871 | 2.746 | 2.714 | 2.751 | 2.785 | 2.734 | 1958 | 2.734 |
| 1959 | 2.712 | 2.744 | 2.749 | 2.717 | 2.715 | 2.718 | 2.734 | 2.723 | 2.708 | 2.748 | 2.716 | 2.673 | 1959 | 2.673 |
| 1960 | 2.702 | 2.757 | 2.835 | 2.787 | 2.829 | 2.878 | 2.984 | 2.964 | 2.986 | 2.978 | 2.958 | 3.041 | 1960 | 3.041 |
| 1961 | 3.008 | 3.068 | 3.057 | 3.092 | 3.078 | 3.055 | 3.065 | 3.054 | 3.093 | 3.115 | 3.109 | 3.070 | 1961 | 3.070 |
| 1962 | 3.066 | 3.098 | 3.176 | 3.202 | 3.217 | 3.192 | 3.158 | 3.217 | 3.236 | 3.263 | 3.270 | 3.282 | 1962 | 3.282 |
| 1963 | 3.281 | 3.284 | 3.287 | 3.283 | 3.290 | 3.297 | 3.307 | 3.314 | 3.315 | 3.307 | 3.324 | 3.322 | 1963 | 3.322 |
| 1964 | 3.317 | 3.313 | 3.326 | 3.341 | 3.358 | 3.381 | 3.384 | 3.390 | 3.407 | 3.422 | 3.428 | 3.438 | 1964 | 3.438 |
| 1965 | 3.452 | 3.457 | 3.475 | 3.488 | 3.494 | 3.511 | 3.518 | 3.514 | 3.502 | 3.511 | 3.490 | 3.462 | 1965 | 3.462 |
| 1966 | 3.427 | 3.341 | 3.440 | 3.418 | 3.398 | 3.393 | 3.380 | 3.310 | 3.420 | 3.498 | 3.447 | 3.589 | 1966 | 3.589 |
| 1967 | 3.644 | 3.564 | 3.634 | 3.528 | 3.515 | 3.405 | 3.428 | 3.399 | 3.398 | 3.262 | 3.198 | 3.259 | 1967 | 3.259 |
| 1968 | 3.366 | 3.355 | 3.284 | 3.359 | 3.373 | 3.451 | 3.550 | 3.549 | 3.513 | 3.466 | 3.373 | 3.251 | 1968 | 3.251 |
| 1969 | 3.184 | 3.197 | 3.201 | 3.337 | 3.174 | 3.242 | 3.267 | 3.245 | 3.073 | 3.185 | 3.107 | 3.086 | 1969 | 3.086 |
| 1970 | 3.079 | 3.260 | 3.238 | 3.104 | 2.959 | 3.103 | 3.202 | 3.196 | 3.269 | 3.233 | 3.489 | 3.460 | 1970 | 3.460 |

Table B-5 (continued)

**Long-Term Government Bonds: Total Return Index**

from January 1971 to December 2000

| Year | Jan | Feb | Mar | Apr | May | Jun | Jul | Aug | Sep | Oct | Nov | Dec | Yr-end | Index |
|------|-----|-----|-----|-----|-----|-----|-----|-----|-----|-----|-----|-----|--------|-------|
| 1971 | 3.634 | 3.575 | 3.763 | 3.657 | 3.655 | 3.597 | 3.607 | 3.777 | 3.854 | 3.918 | 3.900 | 3.917 | 1971 | 3.917 |
| 1972 | 3.892 | 3.927 | 3.895 | 3.905 | 4.011 | 3.985 | 4.071 | 4.082 | 4.049 | 4.143 | 4.237 | 4.140 | 1972 | 4.140 |
| 1973 | 4.007 | 4.013 | 4.046 | 4.064 | 4.021 | 4.013 | 3.839 | 3.989 | 4.116 | 4.205 | 4.128 | 4.094 | 1973 | 4.094 |
| 1974 | 4.060 | 4.050 | 3.932 | 3.833 | 3.880 | 3.897 | 3.886 | 3.796 | 3.890 | 4.080 | 4.200 | 4.272 | 1974 | 4.272 |
| 1975 | 4.368 | 4.426 | 4.308 | 4.229 | 4.319 | 4.445 | 4.407 | 4.377 | 4.334 | 4.539 | 4.490 | 4.665 | 1975 | 4.665 |
| 1976 | 4.707 | 4.736 | 4.815 | 4.824 | 4.747 | 4.846 | 4.884 | 4.987 | 5.059 | 5.102 | 5.274 | 5.447 | 1976 | 5.447 |
| 1977 | 5.236 | 5.210 | 5.257 | 5.295 | 5.361 | 5.449 | 5.411 | 5.518 | 5.502 | 5.451 | 5.502 | 5.410 | 1977 | 5.410 |
| 1978 | 5.366 | 5.368 | 5.357 | 5.355 | 5.323 | 5.290 | 5.366 | 5.483 | 5.425 | 5.316 | 5.416 | 5.346 | 1978 | 5.346 |
| 1979 | 5.448 | 5.375 | 5.444 | 5.383 | 5.524 | 5.696 | 5.647 | 5.627 | 5.559 | 5.091 | 5.250 | 5.280 | 1979 | 5.280 |
| 1980 | 4.889 | 4.660 | 4.514 | 5.201 | 5.419 | 5.613 | 5.346 | 5.115 | 4.982 | 4.851 | 4.899 | 5.071 | 1980 | 5.071 |
| 1981 | 5.013 | 4.795 | 4.979 | 4.721 | 5.015 | 4.925 | 4.751 | 4.568 | 4.502 | 4.875 | 5.562 | 5.166 | 1981 | 5.166 |
| 1982 | 5.189 | 5.284 | 5.406 | 5.608 | 5.627 | 5.501 | 5.777 | 6.228 | 6.613 | 7.033 | 7.031 | 7.251 | 1982 | 7.251 |
| 1983 | 7.027 | 7.372 | 7.303 | 7.558 | 7.267 | 7.295 | 6.940 | 6.954 | 7.305 | 7.209 | 7.341 | 7.298 | 1983 | 7.298 |
| 1984 | 7.476 | 7.343 | 7.228 | 7.152 | 6.782 | 6.884 | 7.361 | 7.557 | 7.816 | 8.254 | 8.352 | 8.427 | 1984 | 8.427 |
| 1985 | 8.734 | 8.304 | 8.558 | 8.766 | 9.551 | 9.686 | 9.512 | 9.759 | 9.738 | 10.067 | 10.471 | 11.037 | 1985 | 11.037 |
| 1986 | 11.009 | 12.270 | 13.215 | 13.109 | 12.447 | 13.210 | 13.068 | 13.720 | 13.034 | 13.410 | 13.769 | 13.745 | 1986 | 13.745 |
| 1987 | 13.966 | 14.247 | 13.930 | 13.271 | 13.132 | 13.260 | 13.024 | 12.810 | 12.337 | 13.106 | 13.154 | 13.372 | 1987 | 13.372 |
| 1988 | 14.263 | 14.337 | 13.897 | 13.675 | 13.536 | 14.035 | 13.797 | 13.876 | 14.355 | 14.796 | 14.506 | 14.665 | 1988 | 14.665 |
| 1989 | 14.963 | 14.695 | 14.875 | 15.111 | 15.717 | 16.582 | 16.977 | 16.537 | 16.569 | 17.198 | 17.332 | 17.322 | 1989 | 17.322 |
| 1990 | 16.728 | 16.686 | 16.613 | 16.278 | 16.954 | 17.344 | 17.530 | 16.796 | 16.992 | 17.358 | 18.056 | 18.392 | 1990 | 18.392 |
| 1991 | 18.632 | 18.689 | 18.760 | 19.023 | 19.024 | 18.904 | 19.202 | 19.855 | 20.458 | 20.569 | 20.738 | 21.942 | 1991 | 21.942 |
| 1992 | 21.231 | 21.339 | 21.140 | 21.173 | 21.687 | 22.121 | 23.001 | 23.155 | 23.584 | 23.117 | 23.140 | 23.709 | 1992 | 23.709 |
| 1993 | 24.374 | 25.237 | 25.290 | 25.472 | 25.591 | 26.739 | 27.251 | 28.433 | 28.448 | 28.722 | 27.979 | 28.034 | 1993 | 28.034 |
| 1994 | 28.755 | 27.462 | 26.378 | 25.981 | 25.767 | 25.508 | 26.435 | 26.209 | 25.342 | 25.280 | 25.447 | 25.856 | 1994 | 25.856 |
| 1995 | 26.561 | 27.322 | 27.572 | 28.039 | 30.255 | 30.675 | 30.161 | 30.873 | 31.413 | 32.337 | 33.143 | 34.044 | 1995 | 34.044 |
| 1996 | 34.007 | 32.366 | 31.687 | 31.163 | 30.994 | 31.622 | 31.678 | 31.237 | 32.142 | 33.440 | 34.612 | 33.727 | 1996 | 33.727 |
| 1997 | 33.459 | 33.476 | 32.633 | 33.465 | 33.790 | 34.448 | 36.603 | 35.441 | 36.560 | 37.807 | 38.366 | 39.074 | 1997 | 39.074 |
| 1998 | 39.856 | 39.570 | 39.668 | 39.771 | 40.497 | 41.421 | 41.256 | 43.173 | 44.876 | 43.896 | 44.320 | 44.178 | 1998 | 44.178 |
| 1999 | 44.713 | 42.390 | 42.355 | 42.444 | 41.660 | 41.337 | 41.019 | 40.803 | 41.147 | 41.099 | 40.849 | 40.218 | 1999 | 40.218 |
| 2000 | 41.135 | 42.220 | 43.768 | 43.437 | 43.200 | 44.254 | 45.018 | 46.100 | 45.376 | 46.227 | 47.699 | 48.856 | 2000 | 48.856 |

## Table B-6

### Long-Term Government Bonds: Capital Appreciation Index

from December 1925 to December 1970

| Year | Jan | Feb | Mar | Apr | May | Jun | Jul | Aug | Sep | Oct | Nov | Dec | Yr-end | Index |
|------|-----|-----|-----|-----|-----|-----|-----|-----|-----|-----|-----|-----|--------|-------|
| 1925 | | | | | | | | | | | | 1.000 | 1925 | 1.000 |
| 1926 | 1.011 | 1.014 | 1.015 | 1.020 | 1.018 | 1.019 | 1.016 | 1.013 | 1.014 | 1.021 | 1.034 | 1.039 | 1926 | 1.039 |
| 1927 | 1.044 | 1.050 | 1.074 | 1.070 | 1.079 | 1.069 | 1.071 | 1.076 | 1.075 | 1.083 | 1.090 | 1.095 | 1927 | 1.095 |
| 1928 | 1.088 | 1.092 | 1.094 | 1.091 | 1.080 | 1.081 | 1.055 | 1.060 | 1.053 | 1.066 | 1.064 | 1.061 | 1928 | 1.061 |
| 1929 | 1.048 | 1.029 | 1.011 | 1.036 | 1.016 | 1.024 | 1.021 | 1.014 | 1.014 | 1.050 | 1.072 | 1.059 | 1929 | 1.059 |
| 1930 | 1.050 | 1.061 | 1.066 | 1.062 | 1.074 | 1.076 | 1.077 | 1.075 | 1.080 | 1.081 | 1.083 | 1.072 | 1930 | 1.072 |
| 1931 | 1.056 | 1.063 | 1.071 | 1.077 | 1.090 | 1.087 | 1.080 | 1.078 | 1.045 | 1.007 | 1.007 | 0.982 | 1931 | 0.982 |
| 1932 | 0.982 | 1.019 | 1.014 | 1.072 | 1.049 | 1.053 | 1.101 | 1.098 | 1.101 | 1.097 | 1.097 | 1.109 | 1932 | 1.109 |
| 1933 | 1.122 | 1.091 | 1.098 | 1.092 | 1.122 | 1.124 | 1.120 | 1.122 | 1.122 | 1.108 | 1.089 | 1.074 | 1933 | 1.074 |
| 1934 | 1.098 | 1.105 | 1.123 | 1.135 | 1.147 | 1.152 | 1.153 | 1.137 | 1.118 | 1.135 | 1.137 | 1.146 | 1934 | 1.146 |
| 1935 | 1.164 | 1.173 | 1.175 | 1.181 | 1.172 | 1.180 | 1.183 | 1.164 | 1.163 | 1.167 | 1.166 | 1.171 | 1935 | 1.171 |
| 1936 | 1.175 | 1.182 | 1.191 | 1.193 | 1.195 | 1.195 | 1.199 | 1.210 | 1.203 | 1.201 | 1.223 | 1.225 | 1936 | 1.225 |
| 1937 | 1.221 | 1.229 | 1.176 | 1.178 | 1.182 | 1.176 | 1.190 | 1.175 | 1.177 | 1.180 | 1.188 | 1.195 | 1937 | 1.195 |
| 1938 | 1.199 | 1.203 | 1.196 | 1.218 | 1.221 | 1.219 | 1.222 | 1.219 | 1.219 | 1.227 | 1.222 | 1.229 | 1938 | 1.229 |
| 1939 | 1.233 | 1.241 | 1.254 | 1.266 | 1.285 | 1.280 | 1.292 | 1.263 | 1.192 | 1.238 | 1.256 | 1.272 | 1939 | 1.272 |
| 1940 | 1.267 | 1.268 | 1.288 | 1.281 | 1.241 | 1.270 | 1.274 | 1.275 | 1.287 | 1.289 | 1.313 | 1.319 | 1940 | 1.319 |
| 1941 | 1.291 | 1.291 | 1.301 | 1.316 | 1.317 | 1.324 | 1.325 | 1.325 | 1.321 | 1.338 | 1.332 | 1.306 | 1941 | 1.306 |
| 1942 | 1.312 | 1.311 | 1.321 | 1.314 | 1.322 | 1.319 | 1.319 | 1.321 | 1.319 | 1.319 | 1.312 | 1.316 | 1942 | 1.316 |
| 1943 | 1.317 | 1.314 | 1.313 | 1.316 | 1.320 | 1.320 | 1.317 | 1.317 | 1.316 | 1.314 | 1.311 | 1.311 | 1943 | 1.311 |
| 1944 | 1.311 | 1.312 | 1.312 | 1.312 | 1.312 | 1.311 | 1.313 | 1.314 | 1.313 | 1.312 | 1.312 | 1.315 | 1944 | 1.315 |
| 1945 | 1.329 | 1.337 | 1.337 | 1.356 | 1.361 | 1.381 | 1.367 | 1.368 | 1.373 | 1.384 | 1.399 | 1.424 | 1945 | 1.424 |
| 1946 | 1.425 | 1.427 | 1.427 | 1.405 | 1.401 | 1.408 | 1.400 | 1.382 | 1.378 | 1.386 | 1.376 | 1.393 | 1946 | 1.393 |
| 1947 | 1.390 | 1.390 | 1.391 | 1.383 | 1.385 | 1.384 | 1.390 | 1.399 | 1.391 | 1.383 | 1.357 | 1.328 | 1947 | 1.328 |
| 1948 | 1.328 | 1.332 | 1.333 | 1.337 | 1.353 | 1.339 | 1.333 | 1.331 | 1.330 | 1.328 | 1.336 | 1.341 | 1948 | 1.341 |
| 1949 | 1.349 | 1.353 | 1.360 | 1.360 | 1.360 | 1.380 | 1.382 | 1.395 | 1.391 | 1.391 | 1.391 | 1.396 | 1949 | 1.396 |
| 1950 | 1.385 | 1.386 | 1.384 | 1.386 | 1.388 | 1.382 | 1.387 | 1.387 | 1.374 | 1.365 | 1.367 | 1.367 | 1950 | 1.367 |
| 1951 | 1.372 | 1.360 | 1.336 | 1.325 | 1.313 | 1.302 | 1.317 | 1.328 | 1.315 | 1.313 | 1.292 | 1.282 | 1951 | 1.282 |
| 1952 | 1.282 | 1.281 | 1.293 | 1.312 | 1.305 | 1.302 | 1.297 | 1.285 | 1.266 | 1.281 | 1.277 | 1.263 | 1952 | 1.263 |
| 1953 | 1.261 | 1.248 | 1.233 | 1.218 | 1.197 | 1.220 | 1.222 | 1.218 | 1.251 | 1.258 | 1.248 | 1.271 | 1953 | 1.271 |
| 1954 | 1.280 | 1.307 | 1.312 | 1.322 | 1.308 | 1.326 | 1.341 | 1.333 | 1.329 | 1.327 | 1.321 | 1.326 | 1954 | 1.326 |
| 1955 | 1.291 | 1.279 | 1.287 | 1.284 | 1.290 | 1.277 | 1.261 | 1.258 | 1.265 | 1.280 | 1.271 | 1.272 | 1955 | 1.272 |
| 1956 | 1.280 | 1.277 | 1.255 | 1.237 | 1.262 | 1.262 | 1.233 | 1.207 | 1.210 | 1.200 | 1.189 | 1.165 | 1956 | 1.165 |
| 1957 | 1.202 | 1.202 | 1.196 | 1.166 | 1.160 | 1.136 | 1.127 | 1.124 | 1.129 | 1.120 | 1.177 | 1.209 | 1957 | 1.209 |
| 1958 | 1.196 | 1.205 | 1.214 | 1.233 | 1.230 | 1.207 | 1.170 | 1.116 | 1.100 | 1.111 | 1.122 | 1.098 | 1958 | 1.098 |
| 1959 | 1.085 | 1.095 | 1.093 | 1.076 | 1.072 | 1.070 | 1.072 | 1.064 | 1.054 | 1.067 | 1.050 | 1.030 | 1959 | 1.030 |
| 1960 | 1.038 | 1.055 | 1.081 | 1.059 | 1.071 | 1.086 | 1.122 | 1.111 | 1.116 | 1.109 | 1.098 | 1.125 | 1960 | 1.125 |
| 1961 | 1.109 | 1.128 | 1.121 | 1.130 | 1.121 | 1.109 | 1.109 | 1.101 | 1.112 | 1.116 | 1.110 | 1.093 | 1961 | 1.093 |
| 1962 | 1.088 | 1.095 | 1.119 | 1.125 | 1.126 | 1.115 | 1.099 | 1.115 | 1.119 | 1.124 | 1.123 | 1.124 | 1962 | 1.124 |
| 1963 | 1.120 | 1.117 | 1.115 | 1.110 | 1.109 | 1.107 | 1.107 | 1.106 | 1.102 | 1.096 | 1.098 | 1.093 | 1963 | 1.093 |
| 1964 | 1.088 | 1.083 | 1.083 | 1.085 | 1.087 | 1.090 | 1.087 | 1.085 | 1.087 | 1.088 | 1.086 | 1.085 | 1964 | 1.085 |
| 1965 | 1.086 | 1.084 | 1.086 | 1.086 | 1.085 | 1.086 | 1.084 | 1.079 | 1.072 | 1.071 | 1.060 | 1.048 | 1965 | 1.048 |
| 1966 | 1.033 | 1.004 | 1.030 | 1.019 | 1.009 | 1.004 | 0.996 | 0.971 | 1.000 | 1.019 | 1.000 | 1.037 | 1966 | 1.037 |
| 1967 | 1.049 | 1.022 | 1.038 | 1.005 | 0.996 | 0.961 | 0.964 | 0.952 | 0.947 | 0.905 | 0.883 | 0.896 | 1967 | 0.896 |
| 1968 | 0.921 | 0.914 | 0.891 | 0.907 | 0.907 | 0.924 | 0.946 | 0.942 | 0.928 | 0.912 | 0.883 | 0.847 | 1968 | 0.847 |
| 1969 | 0.825 | 0.825 | 0.822 | 0.853 | 0.807 | 0.820 | 0.822 | 0.812 | 0.765 | 0.788 | 0.765 | 0.755 | 1969 | 0.755 |
| 1970 | 0.750 | 0.790 | 0.780 | 0.743 | 0.705 | 0.734 | 0.753 | 0.748 | 0.761 | 0.748 | 0.803 | 0.792 | 1970 | 0.792 |

## Table B-6 (continued)

## Long-Term Government Bonds: Capital Appreciation Index

from January 1971 to December 2000

| Year | Jan | Feb | Mar | Apr | May | Jun | Jul | Aug | Sep | Oct | Nov | Dec | Yr-end | Index |
|------|------|------|------|------|------|------|------|------|------|------|------|------|--------|-------|
| 1971 | 0.828 | 0.811 | 0.849 | 0.821 | 0.816 | 0.799 | 0.797 | 0.830 | 0.843 | 0.853 | 0.845 | 0.844 | 1971 | 0.844 |
| 1972 | 0.835 | 0.838 | 0.827 | 0.825 | 0.843 | 0.834 | 0.847 | 0.846 | 0.835 | 0.850 | 0.865 | 0.841 | 1972 | 0.841 |
| 1973 | 0.810 | 0.807 | 0.809 | 0.808 | 0.795 | 0.789 | 0.750 | 0.774 | 0.795 | 0.807 | 0.788 | 0.777 | 1973 | 0.777 |
| 1974 | 0.765 | 0.759 | 0.733 | 0.709 | 0.713 | 0.712 | 0.705 | 0.684 | 0.696 | 0.725 | 0.742 | 0.750 | 1974 | 0.750 |
| 1975 | 0.761 | 0.767 | 0.741 | 0.723 | 0.733 | 0.750 | 0.738 | 0.728 | 0.716 | 0.745 | 0.732 | 0.755 | 1975 | 0.755 |
| 1976 | 0.757 | 0.757 | 0.764 | 0.761 | 0.744 | 0.754 | 0.755 | 0.766 | 0.772 | 0.774 | 0.795 | 0.816 | 1976 | 0.816 |
| 1977 | 0.780 | 0.771 | 0.773 | 0.774 | 0.779 | 0.787 | 0.776 | 0.787 | 0.780 | 0.767 | 0.770 | 0.752 | 1977 | 0.752 |
| 1978 | 0.741 | 0.737 | 0.730 | 0.725 | 0.715 | 0.706 | 0.711 | 0.721 | 0.709 | 0.690 | 0.698 | 0.684 | 1978 | 0.684 |
| 1979 | 0.692 | 0.678 | 0.682 | 0.669 | 0.681 | 0.697 | 0.686 | 0.679 | 0.666 | 0.604 | 0.618 | 0.617 | 1979 | 0.617 |
| 1980 | 0.566 | 0.535 | 0.512 | 0.585 | 0.605 | 0.621 | 0.587 | 0.556 | 0.537 | 0.517 | 0.518 | 0.530 | 1980 | 0.530 |
| 1981 | 0.519 | 0.492 | 0.505 | 0.474 | 0.499 | 0.484 | 0.462 | 0.439 | 0.428 | 0.458 | 0.518 | 0.476 | 1981 | 0.476 |
| 1982 | 0.473 | 0.476 | 0.481 | 0.494 | 0.491 | 0.474 | 0.492 | 0.525 | 0.552 | 0.582 | 0.577 | 0.589 | 1982 | 0.589 |
| 1983 | 0.566 | 0.589 | 0.578 | 0.594 | 0.565 | 0.563 | 0.530 | 0.526 | 0.547 | 0.535 | 0.540 | 0.532 | 1983 | 0.532 |
| 1984 | 0.539 | 0.524 | 0.511 | 0.500 | 0.469 | 0.472 | 0.499 | 0.507 | 0.519 | 0.543 | 0.544 | 0.544 | 1984 | 0.544 |
| 1985 | 0.558 | 0.526 | 0.538 | 0.545 | 0.589 | 0.592 | 0.576 | 0.586 | 0.580 | 0.594 | 0.613 | 0.641 | 1985 | 0.641 |
| 1986 | 0.634 | 0.702 | 0.751 | 0.741 | 0.699 | 0.737 | 0.724 | 0.755 | 0.713 | 0.728 | 0.743 | 0.737 | 1986 | 0.737 |
| 1987 | 0.744 | 0.755 | 0.733 | 0.693 | 0.682 | 0.683 | 0.666 | 0.650 | 0.621 | 0.655 | 0.652 | 0.658 | 1987 | 0.658 |
| 1988 | 0.697 | 0.696 | 0.670 | 0.654 | 0.642 | 0.661 | 0.645 | 0.644 | 0.661 | 0.676 | 0.658 | 0.661 | 1988 | 0.661 |
| 1989 | 0.669 | 0.652 | 0.655 | 0.661 | 0.682 | 0.715 | 0.727 | 0.703 | 0.700 | 0.722 | 0.723 | 0.718 | 1989 | 0.718 |
| 1990 | 0.688 | 0.681 | 0.674 | 0.655 | 0.677 | 0.688 | 0.691 | 0.657 | 0.660 | 0.669 | 0.691 | 0.699 | 1990 | 0.699 |
| 1991 | 0.703 | 0.701 | 0.699 | 0.703 | 0.699 | 0.690 | 0.695 | 0.714 | 0.731 | 0.730 | 0.732 | 0.769 | 1991 | 0.769 |
| 1992 | 0.740 | 0.739 | 0.727 | 0.724 | 0.737 | 0.747 | 0.772 | 0.772 | 0.782 | 0.762 | 0.758 | 0.772 | 1992 | 0.772 |
| 1993 | 0.789 | 0.813 | 0.809 | 0.811 | 0.810 | 0.841 | 0.853 | 0.885 | 0.881 | 0.885 | 0.858 | 0.855 | 1993 | 0.855 |
| 1994 | 0.872 | 0.829 | 0.791 | 0.775 | 0.763 | 0.751 | 0.774 | 0.762 | 0.732 | 0.726 | 0.726 | 0.733 | 1994 | 0.733 |
| 1995 | 0.748 | 0.765 | 0.767 | 0.775 | 0.831 | 0.838 | 0.820 | 0.834 | 0.845 | 0.865 | 0.882 | 0.901 | 1995 | 0.901 |
| 1996 | 0.896 | 0.848 | 0.826 | 0.807 | 0.798 | 0.810 | 0.807 | 0.791 | 0.809 | 0.837 | 0.862 | 0.835 | 1996 | 0.835 |
| 1997 | 0.824 | 0.820 | 0.794 | 0.810 | 0.813 | 0.824 | 0.871 | 0.839 | 0.861 | 0.885 | 0.894 | 0.906 | 1997 | 0.906 |
| 1998 | 0.920 | 0.909 | 0.907 | 0.904 | 0.917 | 0.933 | 0.925 | 0.963 | 0.997 | 0.971 | 0.976 | 0.968 | 1998 | 0.968 |
| 1999 | 0.976 | 0.921 | 0.916 | 0.913 | 0.892 | 0.880 | 0.869 | 0.860 | 0.863 | 0.857 | 0.847 | 0.829 | 1999 | 0.829 |
| 2000 | 0.844 | 0.862 | 0.889 | 0.878 | 0.868 | 0.885 | 0.895 | 0.912 | 0.894 | 0.906 | 0.930 | 0.949 | 2000 | 0.949 |

## Table B-7

**Intermediate-Term Government Bonds: Total Return Index**

from December 1925 to December 1970

| Year | Jan | Feb | Mar | Apr | May | Jun | Jul | Aug | Sep | Oct | Nov | Dec | Yr-end | Index |
|------|-----|-----|-----|-----|-----|-----|-----|-----|-----|-----|-----|-----|--------|-------|
| 1925 | | | | | | | | | | | | 1.000 | 1925 | 1.000 |
| 1926 | 1.007 | 1.010 | 1.014 | 1.023 | 1.024 | 1.027 | 1.028 | 1.029 | 1.034 | 1.040 | 1.044 | 1.054 | 1926 | 1.054 |
| 1927 | 1.060 | 1.064 | 1.068 | 1.070 | 1.072 | 1.075 | 1.079 | 1.086 | 1.092 | 1.088 | 1.097 | 1.101 | 1927 | 1.101 |
| 1928 | 1.107 | 1.106 | 1.107 | 1.107 | 1.106 | 1.108 | 1.098 | 1.104 | 1.107 | 1.110 | 1.112 | 1.112 | 1928 | 1.112 |
| 1929 | 1.108 | 1.106 | 1.107 | 1.117 | 1.110 | 1.122 | 1.129 | 1.135 | 1.133 | 1.153 | 1.173 | 1.178 | 1929 | 1.178 |
| 1930 | 1.174 | 1.185 | 1.204 | 1.195 | 1.202 | 1.219 | 1.226 | 1.229 | 1.236 | 1.246 | 1.255 | 1.258 | 1930 | 1.258 |
| 1931 | 1.249 | 1.261 | 1.267 | 1.278 | 1.293 | 1.266 | 1.268 | 1.270 | 1.255 | 1.242 | 1.248 | 1.228 | 1931 | 1.228 |
| 1932 | 1.224 | 1.240 | 1.250 | 1.274 | 1.263 | 1.276 | 1.292 | 1.307 | 1.311 | 1.317 | 1.321 | 1.337 | 1932 | 1.337 |
| 1933 | 1.335 | 1.334 | 1.348 | 1.355 | 1.382 | 1.383 | 1.382 | 1.393 | 1.396 | 1.393 | 1.396 | 1.361 | 1933 | 1.361 |
| 1934 | 1.379 | 1.386 | 1.412 | 1.438 | 1.455 | 1.468 | 1.465 | 1.451 | 1.431 | 1.458 | 1.465 | 1.483 | 1934 | 1.483 |
| 1935 | 1.500 | 1.516 | 1.535 | 1.552 | 1.546 | 1.564 | 1.570 | 1.558 | 1.550 | 1.566 | 1.569 | 1.587 | 1935 | 1.587 |
| 1936 | 1.587 | 1.598 | 1.603 | 1.607 | 1.613 | 1.615 | 1.618 | 1.626 | 1.628 | 1.632 | 1.645 | 1.636 | 1936 | 1.636 |
| 1937 | 1.631 | 1.632 | 1.605 | 1.613 | 1.625 | 1.623 | 1.633 | 1.626 | 1.639 | 1.644 | 1.651 | 1.661 | 1937 | 1.661 |
| 1938 | 1.676 | 1.684 | 1.682 | 1.721 | 1.725 | 1.738 | 1.740 | 1.742 | 1.740 | 1.756 | 1.756 | 1.765 | 1938 | 1.765 |
| 1939 | 1.770 | 1.785 | 1.799 | 1.806 | 1.823 | 1.823 | 1.831 | 1.804 | 1.756 | 1.812 | 1.825 | 1.845 | 1939 | 1.845 |
| 1940 | 1.842 | 1.849 | 1.865 | 1.865 | 1.825 | 1.860 | 1.860 | 1.868 | 1.877 | 1.884 | 1.894 | 1.899 | 1940 | 1.899 |
| 1941 | 1.900 | 1.891 | 1.904 | 1.910 | 1.912 | 1.923 | 1.923 | 1.925 | 1.925 | 1.930 | 1.912 | 1.909 | 1941 | 1.909 |
| 1942 | 1.923 | 1.926 | 1.930 | 1.935 | 1.938 | 1.940 | 1.940 | 1.944 | 1.939 | 1.943 | 1.946 | 1.946 | 1942 | 1.946 |
| 1943 | 1.953 | 1.956 | 1.960 | 1.965 | 1.976 | 1.983 | 1.987 | 1.987 | 1.990 | 1.993 | 1.996 | 2.000 | 1943 | 2.000 |
| 1944 | 2.003 | 2.006 | 2.010 | 2.015 | 2.016 | 2.017 | 2.023 | 2.028 | 2.030 | 2.033 | 2.034 | 2.036 | 1944 | 2.036 |
| 1945 | 2.047 | 2.055 | 2.056 | 2.059 | 2.061 | 2.065 | 2.065 | 2.068 | 2.072 | 2.075 | 2.077 | 2.082 | 1945 | 2.082 |
| 1946 | 2.090 | 2.100 | 2.092 | 2.088 | 2.089 | 2.096 | 2.094 | 2.094 | 2.092 | 2.098 | 2.096 | 2.102 | 1946 | 2.102 |
| 1947 | 2.107 | 2.109 | 2.114 | 2.111 | 2.112 | 2.114 | 2.115 | 2.121 | 2.121 | 2.116 | 2.117 | 2.122 | 1947 | 2.122 |
| 1948 | 2.125 | 2.129 | 2.132 | 2.136 | 2.148 | 2.146 | 2.146 | 2.145 | 2.147 | 2.149 | 2.154 | 2.161 | 1948 | 2.161 |
| 1949 | 2.167 | 2.169 | 2.175 | 2.178 | 2.183 | 2.194 | 2.198 | 2.205 | 2.207 | 2.208 | 2.208 | 2.211 | 1949 | 2.211 |
| 1950 | 2.210 | 2.212 | 2.212 | 2.213 | 2.218 | 2.218 | 2.223 | 2.221 | 2.220 | 2.221 | 2.225 | 2.227 | 1950 | 2.227 |
| 1951 | 2.231 | 2.233 | 2.205 | 2.217 | 2.208 | 2.219 | 2.232 | 2.240 | 2.227 | 2.231 | 2.238 | 2.235 | 1951 | 2.235 |
| 1952 | 2.243 | 2.239 | 2.253 | 2.266 | 2.270 | 2.262 | 2.254 | 2.249 | 2.253 | 2.268 | 2.267 | 2.271 | 1952 | 2.271 |
| 1953 | 2.271 | 2.271 | 2.267 | 2.246 | 2.219 | 2.254 | 2.266 | 2.265 | 2.309 | 2.317 | 2.321 | 2.345 | 1953 | 2.345 |
| 1954 | 2.360 | 2.383 | 2.390 | 2.400 | 2.382 | 2.412 | 2.411 | 2.414 | 2.409 | 2.406 | 2.406 | 2.407 | 1954 | 2.407 |
| 1955 | 2.400 | 2.387 | 2.393 | 2.394 | 2.394 | 2.386 | 2.369 | 2.370 | 2.390 | 2.407 | 2.394 | 2.392 | 1955 | 2.392 |
| 1956 | 2.417 | 2.418 | 2.393 | 2.393 | 2.420 | 2.421 | 2.398 | 2.373 | 2.395 | 2.390 | 2.379 | 2.382 | 1956 | 2.382 |
| 1957 | 2.438 | 2.435 | 2.439 | 2.415 | 2.411 | 2.385 | 2.382 | 2.408 | 2.408 | 2.418 | 2.514 | 2.568 | 1957 | 2.568 |
| 1958 | 2.577 | 2.613 | 2.627 | 2.640 | 2.656 | 2.638 | 2.614 | 2.521 | 2.517 | 2.518 | 2.551 | 2.535 | 1958 | 2.535 |
| 1959 | 2.532 | 2.559 | 2.550 | 2.536 | 2.536 | 2.517 | 2.525 | 2.505 | 2.510 | 2.554 | 2.530 | 2.525 | 1959 | 2.525 |
| 1960 | 2.564 | 2.583 | 2.658 | 2.641 | 2.649 | 2.707 | 2.779 | 2.778 | 2.786 | 2.790 | 2.764 | 2.822 | 1960 | 2.822 |
| 1961 | 2.805 | 2.831 | 2.841 | 2.856 | 2.848 | 2.841 | 2.843 | 2.848 | 2.871 | 2.875 | 2.869 | 2.874 | 1961 | 2.874 |
| 1962 | 2.861 | 2.906 | 2.932 | 2.939 | 2.953 | 2.945 | 2.941 | 2.978 | 2.984 | 3.000 | 3.018 | 3.034 | 1962 | 3.034 |
| 1963 | 3.026 | 3.031 | 3.039 | 3.048 | 3.053 | 3.057 | 3.058 | 3.064 | 3.068 | 3.071 | 3.083 | 3.084 | 1963 | 3.084 |
| 1964 | 3.094 | 3.098 | 3.103 | 3.113 | 3.138 | 3.150 | 3.158 | 3.167 | 3.181 | 3.191 | 3.190 | 3.209 | 1964 | 3.209 |
| 1965 | 3.222 | 3.228 | 3.242 | 3.250 | 3.262 | 3.278 | 3.283 | 3.290 | 3.288 | 3.288 | 3.290 | 3.242 | 1965 | 3.242 |
| 1966 | 3.242 | 3.215 | 3.275 | 3.269 | 3.273 | 3.265 | 3.257 | 3.216 | 3.286 | 3.311 | 3.320 | 3.394 | 1966 | 3.394 |
| 1967 | 3.434 | 3.429 | 3.492 | 3.461 | 3.476 | 3.397 | 3.443 | 3.430 | 3.433 | 3.416 | 3.425 | 3.428 | 1967 | 3.428 |
| 1968 | 3.478 | 3.491 | 3.482 | 3.477 | 3.499 | 3.557 | 3.620 | 3.628 | 3.648 | 3.651 | 3.646 | 3.583 | 1968 | 3.583 |
| 1969 | 3.614 | 3.609 | 3.644 | 3.673 | 3.643 | 3.613 | 3.642 | 3.636 | 3.527 | 3.644 | 3.627 | 3.557 | 1969 | 3.557 |
| 1970 | 3.568 | 3.724 | 3.757 | 3.679 | 3.720 | 3.742 | 3.799 | 3.843 | 3.919 | 3.956 | 4.134 | 4.156 | 1970 | 4.156 |

Table B-7 (continued)

## Intermediate-Term Government Bonds: Total Return Index

from January 1971 to December 2000

| Year | Jan | Feb | Mar | Apr | May | Jun | Jul | Aug | Sep | Oct | Nov | Dec | Yr-end | Index |
|------|-----|-----|-----|-----|-----|-----|-----|-----|-----|-----|-----|-----|--------|-------|
| 1971 | 4.226 | 4.321 | 4.401 | 4.257 | 4.262 | 4.182 | 4.193 | 4.340 | 4.351 | 4.447 | 4.470 | 4.519 | 1971 | 4.519 |
| 1972 | 4.567 | 4.573 | 4.580 | 4.586 | 4.594 | 4.614 | 4.621 | 4.628 | 4.635 | 4.642 | 4.662 | 4.752 | 1972 | 4.752 |
| 1973 | 4.749 | 4.713 | 4.735 | 4.765 | 4.792 | 4.790 | 4.657 | 4.776 | 4.895 | 4.920 | 4.951 | 4.971 | 1973 | 4.971 |
| 1974 | 4.975 | 4.993 | 4.887 | 4.813 | 4.876 | 4.833 | 4.837 | 4.831 | 4.985 | 5.040 | 5.159 | 5.254 | 1974 | 5.254 |
| 1975 | 5.282 | 5.360 | 5.328 | 5.229 | 5.365 | 5.380 | 5.363 | 5.359 | 5.364 | 5.561 | 5.555 | 5.665 | 1975 | 5.665 |
| 1976 | 5.697 | 5.745 | 5.788 | 5.855 | 5.770 | 5.862 | 5.932 | 6.044 | 6.089 | 6.179 | 6.378 | 6.394 | 1976 | 6.394 |
| 1977 | 6.273 | 6.303 | 6.338 | 6.371 | 6.407 | 6.472 | 6.473 | 6.478 | 6.487 | 6.449 | 6.499 | 6.484 | 1977 | 6.484 |
| 1978 | 6.492 | 6.503 | 6.527 | 6.543 | 6.542 | 6.528 | 6.592 | 6.644 | 6.682 | 6.608 | 6.668 | 6.710 | 1978 | 6.710 |
| 1979 | 6.747 | 6.707 | 6.783 | 6.805 | 6.936 | 7.079 | 7.071 | 7.006 | 7.010 | 6.682 | 6.925 | 6.985 | 1979 | 6.985 |
| 1980 | 6.891 | 6.449 | 6.542 | 7.325 | 7.684 | 7.625 | 7.544 | 7.252 | 7.225 | 7.115 | 7.136 | 7.258 | 1980 | 7.258 |
| 1981 | 7.281 | 7.110 | 7.297 | 7.140 | 7.315 | 7.358 | 7.160 | 7.033 | 7.148 | 7.585 | 8.058 | 7.944 | 1981 | 7.944 |
| 1982 | 7.984 | 8.102 | 8.137 | 8.379 | 8.502 | 8.387 | 8.776 | 9.188 | 9.486 | 9.990 | 10.070 | 10.256 | 1982 | 10.256 |
| 1983 | 10.263 | 10.522 | 10.471 | 10.742 | 10.611 | 10.628 | 10.417 | 10.501 | 10.832 | 10.852 | 10.964 | 11.015 | 1983 | 11.015 |
| 1984 | 11.211 | 11.139 | 11.100 | 11.097 | 10.819 | 10.926 | 11.355 | 11.469 | 11.701 | 12.149 | 12.382 | 12.560 | 1984 | 12.560 |
| 1985 | 12.818 | 12.588 | 12.798 | 13.136 | 13.772 | 13.922 | 13.859 | 14.064 | 14.222 | 14.453 | 14.735 | 15.113 | 1985 | 15.113 |
| 1986 | 15.238 | 15.657 | 16.186 | 16.318 | 15.968 | 16.409 | 16.667 | 17.109 | 16.921 | 17.195 | 17.389 | 17.401 | 1986 | 17.401 |
| 1987 | 17.587 | 17.691 | 17.636 | 17.205 | 17.140 | 17.350 | 17.394 | 17.328 | 17.085 | 17.596 | 17.741 | 17.906 | 1987 | 17.906 |
| 1988 | 18.472 | 18.698 | 18.537 | 18.455 | 18.364 | 18.698 | 18.610 | 18.593 | 18.957 | 19.238 | 19.017 | 18.999 | 1988 | 18.999 |
| 1989 | 19.230 | 19.133 | 19.227 | 19.650 | 20.067 | 20.717 | 21.203 | 20.682 | 20.824 | 21.318 | 21.497 | 21.524 | 1989 | 21.524 |
| 1990 | 21.299 | 21.313 | 21.318 | 21.154 | 21.707 | 22.035 | 22.418 | 22.213 | 22.422 | 22.804 | 23.243 | 23.618 | 1990 | 23.618 |
| 1991 | 23.870 | 23.984 | 24.039 | 24.320 | 24.464 | 24.409 | 24.725 | 25.335 | 25.881 | 26.228 | 26.565 | 27.270 | 1991 | 27.270 |
| 1992 | 26.737 | 26.796 | 26.583 | 26.843 | 27.438 | 27.923 | 28.600 | 29.029 | 29.592 | 29.054 | 28.810 | 29.230 | 1992 | 29.230 |
| 1993 | 30.021 | 30.749 | 30.883 | 31.156 | 31.126 | 31.753 | 31.769 | 32.477 | 32.657 | 32.714 | 32.411 | 32.516 | 1993 | 32.516 |
| 1994 | 32.964 | 32.113 | 31.286 | 30.957 | 30.951 | 30.863 | 31.385 | 31.466 | 30.968 | 30.896 | 30.680 | 30.843 | 1994 | 30.843 |
| 1995 | 31.404 | 32.140 | 32.341 | 32.805 | 34.014 | 34.285 | 34.231 | 34.525 | 34.745 | 35.164 | 35.687 | 36.025 | 1995 | 36.025 |
| 1996 | 36.048 | 35.551 | 35.131 | 34.955 | 34.844 | 35.253 | 35.340 | 35.323 | 35.872 | 36.527 | 37.072 | 36.782 | 1996 | 36.782 |
| 1997 | 36.873 | 36.880 | 36.460 | 37.000 | 37.293 | 37.671 | 38.666 | 38.289 | 38.867 | 39.451 | 39.446 | 39.864 | 1997 | 39.864 |
| 1998 | 40.583 | 40.426 | 40.530 | 40.777 | 41.062 | 41.385 | 41.495 | 42.619 | 44.023 | 44.203 | 43.772 | 43.933 | 1998 | 43.933 |
| 1999 | 44.175 | 43.015 | 43.387 | 43.476 | 42.834 | 42.972 | 42.958 | 43.016 | 43.435 | 43.401 | 43.365 | 43.155 | 1999 | 43.155 |
| 2000 | 42.925 | 43.260 | 44.140 | 43.950 | 44.179 | 45.024 | 45.347 | 45.953 | 46.394 | 46.760 | 47.573 | 48.589 | 2000 | 48.589 |

## Table B-8

**Intermediate-Term Government Bonds: Capital Appreciation Index**

from December 1925 to December 1970

| Year | Jan | Feb | Mar | Apr | May | Jun | Jul | Aug | Sep | Oct | Nov | Dec | Yr-end | Index |
|------|------|------|------|------|------|------|------|------|------|------|------|------|--------|-------|
| 1925 | | | | | | | | | | | | 1.000 | 1925 | 1.000 |
| 1926 | 1.004 | 1.004 | 1.005 | 1.010 | 1.008 | 1.008 | 1.006 | 1.004 | 1.005 | 1.008 | 1.009 | 1.015 | 1926 | 1.015 |
| 1927 | 1.018 | 1.019 | 1.020 | 1.018 | 1.017 | 1.017 | 1.019 | 1.022 | 1.025 | 1.018 | 1.024 | 1.025 | 1927 | 1.025 |
| 1928 | 1.027 | 1.023 | 1.022 | 1.018 | 1.015 | 1.013 | 1.001 | 1.003 | 1.002 | 1.002 | 1.001 | 0.997 | 1928 | 0.997 |
| 1929 | 0.991 | 0.985 | 0.982 | 0.987 | 0.978 | 0.985 | 0.988 | 0.990 | 0.985 | 0.998 | 1.013 | 1.014 | 1929 | 1.014 |
| 1930 | 1.007 | 1.013 | 1.027 | 1.017 | 1.020 | 1.032 | 1.034 | 1.034 | 1.038 | 1.043 | 1.048 | 1.048 | 1930 | 1.048 |
| 1931 | 1.038 | 1.045 | 1.048 | 1.055 | 1.065 | 1.040 | 1.039 | 1.038 | 1.023 | 1.009 | 1.011 | 0.991 | 1931 | 0.991 |
| 1932 | 0.985 | 0.994 | 0.998 | 1.015 | 1.002 | 1.010 | 1.019 | 1.029 | 1.029 | 1.031 | 1.032 | 1.041 | 1932 | 1.041 |
| 1933 | 1.037 | 1.034 | 1.042 | 1.045 | 1.063 | 1.062 | 1.059 | 1.064 | 1.065 | 1.060 | 1.061 | 1.031 | 1933 | 1.031 |
| 1934 | 1.041 | 1.044 | 1.061 | 1.078 | 1.088 | 1.096 | 1.091 | 1.079 | 1.061 | 1.079 | 1.081 | 1.092 | 1934 | 1.092 |
| 1935 | 1.103 | 1.112 | 1.124 | 1.134 | 1.129 | 1.140 | 1.142 | 1.132 | 1.124 | 1.135 | 1.134 | 1.146 | 1935 | 1.146 |
| 1936 | 1.144 | 1.151 | 1.153 | 1.154 | 1.157 | 1.157 | 1.158 | 1.163 | 1.163 | 1.164 | 1.172 | 1.165 | 1936 | 1.165 |
| 1937 | 1.160 | 1.159 | 1.139 | 1.143 | 1.150 | 1.147 | 1.152 | 1.146 | 1.154 | 1.156 | 1.159 | 1.165 | 1937 | 1.165 |
| 1938 | 1.173 | 1.177 | 1.174 | 1.199 | 1.200 | 1.207 | 1.207 | 1.207 | 1.204 | 1.213 | 1.211 | 1.216 | 1938 | 1.216 |
| 1939 | 1.218 | 1.227 | 1.235 | 1.239 | 1.249 | 1.248 | 1.252 | 1.232 | 1.199 | 1.235 | 1.243 | 1.255 | 1939 | 1.255 |
| 1940 | 1.252 | 1.255 | 1.265 | 1.265 | 1.237 | 1.259 | 1.258 | 1.262 | 1.267 | 1.271 | 1.278 | 1.280 | 1940 | 1.280 |
| 1941 | 1.280 | 1.273 | 1.281 | 1.284 | 1.285 | 1.292 | 1.291 | 1.292 | 1.291 | 1.294 | 1.281 | 1.278 | 1941 | 1.278 |
| 1942 | 1.287 | 1.288 | 1.290 | 1.292 | 1.293 | 1.294 | 1.293 | 1.295 | 1.291 | 1.293 | 1.294 | 1.293 | 1942 | 1.293 |
| 1943 | 1.296 | 1.297 | 1.297 | 1.299 | 1.304 | 1.307 | 1.308 | 1.307 | 1.307 | 1.308 | 1.308 | 1.309 | 1943 | 1.309 |
| 1944 | 1.309 | 1.309 | 1.310 | 1.312 | 1.311 | 1.311 | 1.313 | 1.314 | 1.314 | 1.314 | 1.314 | 1.314 | 1944 | 1.314 |
| 1945 | 1.319 | 1.323 | 1.322 | 1.323 | 1.323 | 1.324 | 1.323 | 1.324 | 1.325 | 1.325 | 1.326 | 1.327 | 1945 | 1.327 |
| 1946 | 1.331 | 1.336 | 1.330 | 1.327 | 1.326 | 1.329 | 1.327 | 1.326 | 1.324 | 1.326 | 1.323 | 1.326 | 1946 | 1.326 |
| 1947 | 1.328 | 1.327 | 1.329 | 1.326 | 1.326 | 1.326 | 1.325 | 1.327 | 1.326 | 1.322 | 1.321 | 1.322 | 1947 | 1.322 |
| 1948 | 1.322 | 1.323 | 1.323 | 1.324 | 1.330 | 1.327 | 1.325 | 1.323 | 1.322 | 1.322 | 1.323 | 1.326 | 1948 | 1.326 |
| 1949 | 1.328 | 1.328 | 1.329 | 1.330 | 1.331 | 1.336 | 1.337 | 1.340 | 1.340 | 1.339 | 1.338 | 1.338 | 1949 | 1.338 |
| 1950 | 1.336 | 1.336 | 1.334 | 1.334 | 1.335 | 1.334 | 1.335 | 1.333 | 1.331 | 1.329 | 1.330 | 1.329 | 1950 | 1.329 |
| 1951 | 1.330 | 1.329 | 1.310 | 1.315 | 1.308 | 1.312 | 1.317 | 1.320 | 1.310 | 1.310 | 1.312 | 1.307 | 1951 | 1.307 |
| 1952 | 1.310 | 1.305 | 1.311 | 1.316 | 1.317 | 1.310 | 1.303 | 1.297 | 1.297 | 1.303 | 1.300 | 1.300 | 1952 | 1.300 |
| 1953 | 1.297 | 1.295 | 1.290 | 1.275 | 1.257 | 1.274 | 1.278 | 1.274 | 1.295 | 1.298 | 1.297 | 1.308 | 1953 | 1.308 |
| 1954 | 1.314 | 1.326 | 1.327 | 1.331 | 1.320 | 1.334 | 1.332 | 1.332 | 1.328 | 1.325 | 1.323 | 1.322 | 1954 | 1.322 |
| 1955 | 1.315 | 1.306 | 1.307 | 1.305 | 1.302 | 1.295 | 1.283 | 1.281 | 1.288 | 1.295 | 1.285 | 1.281 | 1955 | 1.281 |
| 1956 | 1.291 | 1.289 | 1.273 | 1.270 | 1.281 | 1.278 | 1.263 | 1.246 | 1.255 | 1.248 | 1.239 | 1.237 | 1956 | 1.237 |
| 1957 | 1.262 | 1.258 | 1.257 | 1.240 | 1.234 | 1.218 | 1.212 | 1.221 | 1.217 | 1.219 | 1.263 | 1.287 | 1957 | 1.287 |
| 1958 | 1.288 | 1.303 | 1.307 | 1.311 | 1.317 | 1.305 | 1.290 | 1.242 | 1.236 | 1.232 | 1.245 | 1.233 | 1958 | 1.233 |
| 1959 | 1.228 | 1.237 | 1.228 | 1.218 | 1.214 | 1.200 | 1.200 | 1.186 | 1.184 | 1.200 | 1.184 | 1.177 | 1959 | 1.177 |
| 1960 | 1.190 | 1.194 | 1.224 | 1.213 | 1.212 | 1.234 | 1.263 | 1.259 | 1.259 | 1.257 | 1.242 | 1.264 | 1960 | 1.264 |
| 1961 | 1.253 | 1.261 | 1.262 | 1.265 | 1.258 | 1.251 | 1.248 | 1.246 | 1.252 | 1.250 | 1.244 | 1.243 | 1961 | 1.243 |
| 1962 | 1.233 | 1.248 | 1.255 | 1.254 | 1.257 | 1.250 | 1.244 | 1.255 | 1.255 | 1.257 | 1.261 | 1.264 | 1962 | 1.264 |
| 1963 | 1.257 | 1.255 | 1.255 | 1.255 | 1.253 | 1.251 | 1.247 | 1.246 | 1.243 | 1.240 | 1.241 | 1.237 | 1963 | 1.237 |
| 1964 | 1.237 | 1.235 | 1.233 | 1.233 | 1.239 | 1.239 | 1.238 | 1.237 | 1.239 | 1.239 | 1.234 | 1.237 | 1964 | 1.237 |
| 1965 | 1.238 | 1.237 | 1.237 | 1.236 | 1.237 | 1.238 | 1.236 | 1.234 | 1.229 | 1.225 | 1.221 | 1.199 | 1965 | 1.199 |
| 1966 | 1.194 | 1.180 | 1.197 | 1.190 | 1.186 | 1.179 | 1.171 | 1.151 | 1.171 | 1.174 | 1.173 | 1.194 | 1966 | 1.194 |
| 1967 | 1.203 | 1.197 | 1.214 | 1.200 | 1.200 | 1.168 | 1.178 | 1.169 | 1.165 | 1.154 | 1.152 | 1.148 | 1967 | 1.148 |
| 1968 | 1.159 | 1.158 | 1.150 | 1.143 | 1.145 | 1.159 | 1.173 | 1.171 | 1.172 | 1.168 | 1.162 | 1.136 | 1968 | 1.136 |
| 1969 | 1.140 | 1.133 | 1.139 | 1.141 | 1.126 | 1.110 | 1.113 | 1.105 | 1.065 | 1.093 | 1.082 | 1.054 | 1969 | 1.054 |
| 1970 | 1.050 | 1.090 | 1.092 | 1.063 | 1.068 | 1.068 | 1.077 | 1.083 | 1.098 | 1.102 | 1.145 | 1.145 | 1970 | 1.145 |

Table B-8 (continued)

## Intermediate-Term Government Bonds: Capital Appreciation Index

from January 1971 to December 2000

| Year | Jan | Feb | Mar | Apr | May | Jun | Jul | Aug | Sep | Oct | Nov | Dec | Yr-end | Index |
|------|-----|-----|-----|-----|-----|-----|-----|-----|-----|-----|-----|-----|--------|-------|
| 1971 | 1.159 | 1.180 | 1.197 | 1.153 | 1.149 | 1.121 | 1.118 | 1.151 | 1.149 | 1.169 | 1.169 | 1.177 | 1971 | 1.177 |
| 1972 | 1.183 | 1.180 | 1.176 | 1.173 | 1.169 | 1.168 | 1.164 | 1.160 | 1.156 | 1.152 | 1.151 | 1.168 | 1972 | 1.168 |
| 1973 | 1.161 | 1.146 | 1.145 | 1.146 | 1.146 | 1.140 | 1.101 | 1.122 | 1.144 | 1.143 | 1.144 | 1.142 | 1973 | 1.142 |
| 1974 | 1.137 | 1.135 | 1.105 | 1.081 | 1.088 | 1.072 | 1.065 | 1.056 | 1.083 | 1.087 | 1.106 | 1.120 | 1974 | 1.120 |
| 1975 | 1.119 | 1.129 | 1.116 | 1.088 | 1.110 | 1.106 | 1.095 | 1.088 | 1.081 | 1.114 | 1.106 | 1.121 | 1975 | 1.121 |
| 1976 | 1.121 | 1.124 | 1.125 | 1.131 | 1.109 | 1.119 | 1.125 | 1.139 | 1.142 | 1.152 | 1.183 | 1.180 | 1976 | 1.180 |
| 1977 | 1.151 | 1.151 | 1.151 | 1.151 | 1.151 | 1.156 | 1.150 | 1.144 | 1.140 | 1.126 | 1.128 | 1.119 | 1977 | 1.119 |
| 1978 | 1.113 | 1.109 | 1.105 | 1.101 | 1.093 | 1.084 | 1.087 | 1.088 | 1.087 | 1.067 | 1.069 | 1.069 | 1978 | 1.069 |
| 1979 | 1.066 | 1.053 | 1.057 | 1.052 | 1.064 | 1.079 | 1.069 | 1.052 | 1.045 | 0.987 | 1.015 | 1.015 | 1979 | 1.015 |
| 1980 | 0.992 | 0.920 | 0.924 | 1.025 | 1.067 | 1.051 | 1.031 | 0.983 | 0.970 | 0.946 | 0.940 | 0.946 | 1980 | 0.946 |
| 1981 | 0.939 | 0.908 | 0.921 | 0.892 | 0.904 | 0.898 | 0.864 | 0.838 | 0.841 | 0.881 | 0.926 | 0.903 | 1981 | 0.903 |
| 1982 | 0.897 | 0.902 | 0.894 | 0.911 | 0.915 | 0.892 | 0.923 | 0.956 | 0.978 | 1.021 | 1.021 | 1.031 | 1982 | 1.031 |
| 1983 | 1.023 | 1.041 | 1.027 | 1.045 | 1.023 | 1.016 | 0.988 | 0.986 | 1.007 | 1.000 | 1.001 | 0.997 | 1983 | 0.997 |
| 1984 | 1.005 | 0.990 | 0.977 | 0.967 | 0.933 | 0.932 | 0.958 | 0.958 | 0.968 | 0.994 | 1.004 | 1.009 | 1984 | 1.009 |
| 1985 | 1.021 | 0.994 | 1.002 | 1.019 | 1.059 | 1.063 | 1.049 | 1.056 | 1.059 | 1.068 | 1.081 | 1.100 | 1985 | 1.100 |
| 1986 | 1.101 | 1.124 | 1.155 | 1.157 | 1.125 | 1.149 | 1.160 | 1.184 | 1.164 | 1.176 | 1.183 | 1.177 | 1986 | 1.177 |
| 1987 | 1.183 | 1.184 | 1.173 | 1.138 | 1.126 | 1.132 | 1.127 | 1.116 | 1.092 | 1.117 | 1.118 | 1.121 | 1987 | 1.121 |
| 1988 | 1.149 | 1.156 | 1.138 | 1.126 | 1.112 | 1.125 | 1.112 | 1.103 | 1.116 | 1.125 | 1.105 | 1.096 | 1988 | 1.096 |
| 1989 | 1.100 | 1.088 | 1.085 | 1.101 | 1.115 | 1.144 | 1.163 | 1.127 | 1.128 | 1.146 | 1.149 | 1.143 | 1989 | 1.143 |
| 1990 | 1.123 | 1.117 | 1.109 | 1.093 | 1.113 | 1.122 | 1.134 | 1.116 | 1.119 | 1.130 | 1.144 | 1.155 | 1990 | 1.155 |
| 1991 | 1.160 | 1.158 | 1.154 | 1.160 | 1.159 | 1.150 | 1.156 | 1.178 | 1.196 | 1.205 | 1.214 | 1.240 | 1991 | 1.240 |
| 1992 | 1.209 | 1.206 | 1.189 | 1.193 | 1.213 | 1.228 | 1.251 | 1.263 | 1.282 | 1.253 | 1.236 | 1.248 | 1992 | 1.248 |
| 1993 | 1.275 | 1.301 | 1.300 | 1.305 | 1.299 | 1.318 | 1.314 | 1.337 | 1.339 | 1.336 | 1.318 | 1.317 | 1993 | 1.317 |
| 1994 | 1.329 | 1.290 | 1.250 | 1.231 | 1.224 | 1.213 | 1.227 | 1.223 | 1.197 | 1.187 | 1.171 | 1.170 | 1994 | 1.170 |
| 1995 | 1.184 | 1.205 | 1.205 | 1.216 | 1.253 | 1.257 | 1.249 | 1.253 | 1.255 | 1.264 | 1.277 | 1.283 | 1995 | 1.283 |
| 1996 | 1.278 | 1.255 | 1.235 | 1.222 | 1.212 | 1.220 | 1.216 | 1.209 | 1.221 | 1.237 | 1.249 | 1.233 | 1996 | 1.233 |
| 1997 | 1.230 | 1.225 | 1.204 | 1.215 | 1.218 | 1.224 | 1.250 | 1.232 | 1.244 | 1.256 | 1.251 | 1.257 | 1997 | 1.257 |
| 1998 | 1.274 | 1.264 | 1.261 | 1.263 | 1.266 | 1.270 | 1.267 | 1.296 | 1.333 | 1.334 | 1.316 | 1.316 | 1998 | 1.316 |
| 1999 | 1.318 | 1.279 | 1.284 | 1.281 | 1.257 | 1.255 | 1.248 | 1.244 | 1.250 | 1.243 | 1.235 | 1.223 | 1999 | 1.223 |
| 2000 | 1.210 | 1.213 | 1.231 | 1.220 | 1.219 | 1.236 | 1.238 | 1.248 | 1.254 | 1.258 | 1.274 | 1.296 | 2000 | 1.296 |

## Table B-9

**U.S. Treasury Bills: Total Return Index**

from December 1925 to December 1970

| Year | Jan | Feb | Mar | Apr | May | Jun | Jul | Aug | Sep | Oct | Nov | Dec | Yr-end | Index |
|------|-----|-----|-----|-----|-----|-----|-----|-----|-----|-----|-----|-----|--------|-------|
| 1925 | | | | | | | | | | | | 1.000 | 1925 | 1.000 |
| 1926 | 1.003 | 1.006 | 1.009 | 1.013 | 1.013 | 1.016 | 1.018 | 1.021 | 1.023 | 1.027 | 1.030 | 1.033 | 1926 | 1.033 |
| 1927 | 1.035 | 1.038 | 1.041 | 1.044 | 1.047 | 1.049 | 1.053 | 1.055 | 1.058 | 1.060 | 1.063 | 1.065 | 1927 | 1.065 |
| 1928 | 1.068 | 1.071 | 1.074 | 1.077 | 1.080 | 1.084 | 1.087 | 1.091 | 1.093 | 1.098 | 1.102 | 1.103 | 1928 | 1.103 |
| 1929 | 1.107 | 1.111 | 1.114 | 1.118 | 1.123 | 1.129 | 1.133 | 1.137 | 1.141 | 1.147 | 1.151 | 1.155 | 1929 | 1.155 |
| 1930 | 1.157 | 1.160 | 1.164 | 1.167 | 1.170 | 1.173 | 1.175 | 1.176 | 1.179 | 1.180 | 1.181 | 1.183 | 1930 | 1.183 |
| 1931 | 1.185 | 1.185 | 1.187 | 1.188 | 1.189 | 1.190 | 1.190 | 1.191 | 1.191 | 1.192 | 1.194 | 1.196 | 1931 | 1.196 |
| 1932 | 1.198 | 1.201 | 1.203 | 1.205 | 1.205 | 1.206 | 1.206 | 1.206 | 1.207 | 1.207 | 1.207 | 1.207 | 1932 | 1.207 |
| 1933 | 1.207 | 1.207 | 1.208 | 1.209 | 1.209 | 1.210 | 1.210 | 1.210 | 1.210 | 1.210 | 1.211 | 1.211 | 1933 | 1.211 |
| 1934 | 1.211 | 1.212 | 1.212 | 1.212 | 1.212 | 1.212 | 1.212 | 1.212 | 1.212 | 1.213 | 1.213 | 1.213 | 1934 | 1.213 |
| 1935 | 1.213 | 1.213 | 1.213 | 1.213 | 1.214 | 1.214 | 1.214 | 1.214 | 1.214 | 1.214 | 1.215 | 1.215 | 1935 | 1.215 |
| 1936 | 1.215 | 1.215 | 1.215 | 1.216 | 1.216 | 1.216 | 1.216 | 1.216 | 1.217 | 1.217 | 1.217 | 1.217 | 1936 | 1.217 |
| 1937 | 1.217 | 1.217 | 1.218 | 1.218 | 1.219 | 1.219 | 1.219 | 1.220 | 1.220 | 1.220 | 1.221 | 1.221 | 1937 | 1.221 |
| 1938 | 1.221 | 1.221 | 1.221 | 1.221 | 1.221 | 1.221 | 1.221 | 1.221 | 1.221 | 1.221 | 1.221 | 1.221 | 1938 | 1.221 |
| 1939 | 1.220 | 1.221 | 1.220 | 1.220 | 1.220 | 1.221 | 1.221 | 1.221 | 1.221 | 1.221 | 1.221 | 1.221 | 1939 | 1.221 |
| 1940 | 1.221 | 1.221 | 1.221 | 1.221 | 1.221 | 1.221 | 1.221 | 1.221 | 1.221 | 1.221 | 1.221 | 1.221 | 1940 | 1.221 |
| 1941 | 1.221 | 1.221 | 1.221 | 1.221 | 1.221 | 1.221 | 1.221 | 1.221 | 1.221 | 1.221 | 1.221 | 1.222 | 1941 | 1.222 |
| 1942 | 1.222 | 1.222 | 1.222 | 1.222 | 1.222 | 1.223 | 1.223 | 1.223 | 1.224 | 1.224 | 1.225 | 1.225 | 1942 | 1.225 |
| 1943 | 1.225 | 1.226 | 1.226 | 1.226 | 1.227 | 1.227 | 1.227 | 1.228 | 1.228 | 1.228 | 1.229 | 1.229 | 1943 | 1.229 |
| 1944 | 1.229 | 1.230 | 1.230 | 1.230 | 1.231 | 1.231 | 1.231 | 1.232 | 1.232 | 1.233 | 1.233 | 1.233 | 1944 | 1.233 |
| 1945 | 1.233 | 1.234 | 1.234 | 1.234 | 1.235 | 1.235 | 1.235 | 1.236 | 1.236 | 1.237 | 1.237 | 1.237 | 1945 | 1.237 |
| 1946 | 1.238 | 1.238 | 1.238 | 1.239 | 1.239 | 1.239 | 1.240 | 1.240 | 1.240 | 1.241 | 1.241 | 1.242 | 1946 | 1.242 |
| 1947 | 1.242 | 1.242 | 1.243 | 1.243 | 1.243 | 1.244 | 1.244 | 1.244 | 1.245 | 1.246 | 1.247 | 1.248 | 1947 | 1.248 |
| 1948 | 1.249 | 1.250 | 1.251 | 1.252 | 1.253 | 1.254 | 1.255 | 1.256 | 1.256 | 1.257 | 1.257 | 1.258 | 1948 | 1.258 |
| 1949 | 1.259 | 1.260 | 1.262 | 1.263 | 1.264 | 1.265 | 1.266 | 1.267 | 1.269 | 1.270 | 1.271 | 1.272 | 1949 | 1.272 |
| 1950 | 1.273 | 1.274 | 1.275 | 1.276 | 1.278 | 1.279 | 1.280 | 1.281 | 1.283 | 1.284 | 1.286 | 1.287 | 1950 | 1.287 |
| 1951 | 1.289 | 1.290 | 1.291 | 1.293 | 1.295 | 1.296 | 1.298 | 1.300 | 1.301 | 1.303 | 1.305 | 1.306 | 1951 | 1.306 |
| 1952 | 1.308 | 1.310 | 1.311 | 1.313 | 1.314 | 1.316 | 1.318 | 1.320 | 1.322 | 1.324 | 1.326 | 1.328 | 1952 | 1.328 |
| 1953 | 1.330 | 1.332 | 1.334 | 1.337 | 1.339 | 1.341 | 1.343 | 1.345 | 1.348 | 1.349 | 1.350 | 1.352 | 1953 | 1.352 |
| 1954 | 1.354 | 1.355 | 1.356 | 1.357 | 1.357 | 1.358 | 1.359 | 1.360 | 1.361 | 1.362 | 1.363 | 1.364 | 1954 | 1.364 |
| 1955 | 1.365 | 1.366 | 1.367 | 1.369 | 1.371 | 1.372 | 1.373 | 1.376 | 1.378 | 1.380 | 1.383 | 1.385 | 1955 | 1.385 |
| 1956 | 1.388 | 1.391 | 1.393 | 1.396 | 1.399 | 1.402 | 1.405 | 1.407 | 1.410 | 1.413 | 1.416 | 1.419 | 1956 | 1.419 |
| 1957 | 1.423 | 1.426 | 1.430 | 1.433 | 1.437 | 1.441 | 1.445 | 1.448 | 1.452 | 1.456 | 1.460 | 1.464 | 1957 | 1.464 |
| 1958 | 1.468 | 1.470 | 1.471 | 1.472 | 1.474 | 1.474 | 1.475 | 1.476 | 1.479 | 1.481 | 1.483 | 1.486 | 1958 | 1.486 |
| 1959 | 1.489 | 1.492 | 1.496 | 1.499 | 1.502 | 1.505 | 1.509 | 1.512 | 1.517 | 1.521 | 1.525 | 1.530 | 1959 | 1.530 |
| 1960 | 1.535 | 1.540 | 1.545 | 1.548 | 1.552 | 1.556 | 1.558 | 1.561 | 1.563 | 1.567 | 1.569 | 1.571 | 1960 | 1.571 |
| 1961 | 1.574 | 1.576 | 1.579 | 1.582 | 1.585 | 1.588 | 1.591 | 1.593 | 1.596 | 1.599 | 1.601 | 1.604 | 1961 | 1.604 |
| 1962 | 1.608 | 1.612 | 1.615 | 1.618 | 1.622 | 1.626 | 1.630 | 1.634 | 1.637 | 1.641 | 1.645 | 1.648 | 1962 | 1.648 |
| 1963 | 1.652 | 1.656 | 1.660 | 1.664 | 1.668 | 1.672 | 1.677 | 1.681 | 1.685 | 1.690 | 1.695 | 1.700 | 1963 | 1.700 |
| 1964 | 1.705 | 1.709 | 1.715 | 1.720 | 1.724 | 1.729 | 1.734 | 1.739 | 1.744 | 1.749 | 1.754 | 1.760 | 1964 | 1.760 |
| 1965 | 1.765 | 1.770 | 1.776 | 1.782 | 1.787 | 1.794 | 1.799 | 1.805 | 1.811 | 1.817 | 1.823 | 1.829 | 1965 | 1.829 |
| 1966 | 1.836 | 1.842 | 1.849 | 1.856 | 1.863 | 1.870 | 1.877 | 1.885 | 1.892 | 1.901 | 1.908 | 1.916 | 1966 | 1.916 |
| 1967 | 1.924 | 1.931 | 1.939 | 1.945 | 1.951 | 1.957 | 1.963 | 1.969 | 1.975 | 1.983 | 1.990 | 1.997 | 1967 | 1.997 |
| 1968 | 2.005 | 2.012 | 2.020 | 2.029 | 2.038 | 2.046 | 2.056 | 2.065 | 2.074 | 2.083 | 2.092 | 2.101 | 1968 | 2.101 |
| 1969 | 2.112 | 2.121 | 2.131 | 2.143 | 2.153 | 2.164 | 2.175 | 2.186 | 2.200 | 2.213 | 2.225 | 2.239 | 1969 | 2.239 |
| 1970 | 2.252 | 2.266 | 2.279 | 2.291 | 2.303 | 2.316 | 2.328 | 2.341 | 2.353 | 2.364 | 2.375 | 2.385 | 1970 | 2.385 |

## Table B-9 (continued)

### U.S. Treasury Bills: Total Return Index

from January 1971 to December 2000

| Year | Jan | Feb | Mar | Apr | May | Jun | Jul | Aug | Sep | Oct | Nov | Dec | Yr-end | Index |
|---|---|---|---|---|---|---|---|---|---|---|---|---|---|---|
| 1971 | 2.394 | 2.402 | 2.409 | 2.416 | 2.423 | 2.432 | 2.442 | 2.453 | 2.462 | 2.471 | 2.480 | 2.490 | 1971 | 2.490 |
| 1972 | 2.497 | 2.503 | 2.510 | 2.517 | 2.525 | 2.532 | 2.540 | 2.547 | 2.556 | 2.566 | 2.575 | 2.585 | 1972 | 2.585 |
| 1973 | 2.596 | 2.607 | 2.619 | 2.633 | 2.646 | 2.660 | 2.677 | 2.695 | 2.714 | 2.732 | 2.747 | 2.764 | 1973 | 2.764 |
| 1974 | 2.782 | 2.798 | 2.813 | 2.835 | 2.856 | 2.873 | 2.893 | 2.911 | 2.934 | 2.949 | 2.965 | 2.986 | 1974 | 2.986 |
| 1975 | 3.003 | 3.016 | 3.028 | 3.042 | 3.055 | 3.067 | 3.082 | 3.097 | 3.113 | 3.131 | 3.144 | 3.159 | 1975 | 3.159 |
| 1976 | 3.174 | 3.184 | 3.197 | 3.210 | 3.222 | 3.237 | 3.252 | 3.265 | 3.280 | 3.293 | 3.306 | 3.319 | 1976 | 3.319 |
| 1977 | 3.331 | 3.343 | 3.356 | 3.368 | 3.381 | 3.394 | 3.408 | 3.423 | 3.438 | 3.455 | 3.472 | 3.489 | 1977 | 3.489 |
| 1978 | 3.506 | 3.522 | 3.541 | 3.560 | 3.578 | 3.597 | 3.618 | 3.638 | 3.660 | 3.685 | 3.711 | 3.740 | 1978 | 3.740 |
| 1979 | 3.769 | 3.796 | 3.827 | 3.858 | 3.889 | 3.921 | 3.951 | 3.981 | 4.014 | 4.049 | 4.089 | 4.128 | 1979 | 4.128 |
| 1980 | 4.161 | 4.198 | 4.248 | 4.302 | 4.336 | 4.363 | 4.386 | 4.414 | 4.447 | 4.489 | 4.532 | 4.592 | 1980 | 4.592 |
| 1981 | 4.639 | 4.689 | 4.746 | 4.797 | 4.852 | 4.917 | 4.978 | 5.042 | 5.105 | 5.166 | 5.221 | 5.267 | 1981 | 5.267 |
| 1982 | 5.309 | 5.358 | 5.411 | 5.472 | 5.530 | 5.583 | 5.641 | 5.684 | 5.713 | 5.747 | 5.783 | 5.822 | 1982 | 5.822 |
| 1983 | 5.862 | 5.899 | 5.936 | 5.978 | 6.020 | 6.060 | 6.105 | 6.151 | 6.198 | 6.245 | 6.289 | 6.335 | 1983 | 6.335 |
| 1984 | 6.383 | 6.428 | 6.475 | 6.528 | 6.579 | 6.629 | 6.683 | 6.738 | 6.796 | 6.864 | 6.914 | 6.959 | 1984 | 6.959 |
| 1985 | 7.004 | 7.044 | 7.088 | 7.138 | 7.186 | 7.225 | 7.271 | 7.311 | 7.355 | 7.403 | 7.448 | 7.496 | 1985 | 7.496 |
| 1986 | 7.538 | 7.578 | 7.623 | 7.663 | 7.700 | 7.741 | 7.781 | 7.817 | 7.852 | 7.889 | 7.919 | 7.958 | 1986 | 7.958 |
| 1987 | 7.991 | 8.025 | 8.063 | 8.099 | 8.129 | 8.169 | 8.206 | 8.245 | 8.282 | 8.331 | 8.360 | 8.393 | 1987 | 8.393 |
| 1988 | 8.418 | 8.456 | 8.493 | 8.532 | 8.576 | 8.617 | 8.661 | 8.712 | 8.766 | 8.819 | 8.869 | 8.926 | 1988 | 8.926 |
| 1989 | 8.975 | 9.030 | 9.090 | 9.152 | 9.224 | 9.289 | 9.354 | 9.423 | 9.485 | 9.549 | 9.614 | 9.673 | 1989 | 9.673 |
| 1990 | 9.728 | 9.783 | 9.846 | 9.914 | 9.981 | 10.043 | 10.111 | 10.178 | 10.238 | 10.308 | 10.366 | 10.429 | 1990 | 10.429 |
| 1991 | 10.483 | 10.533 | 10.579 | 10.635 | 10.685 | 10.730 | 10.782 | 10.832 | 10.881 | 10.928 | 10.970 | 11.012 | 1991 | 11.012 |
| 1992 | 11.049 | 11.081 | 11.118 | 11.154 | 11.185 | 11.221 | 11.255 | 11.285 | 11.314 | 11.340 | 11.366 | 11.398 | 1992 | 11.398 |
| 1993 | 11.425 | 11.450 | 11.479 | 11.506 | 11.531 | 11.561 | 11.588 | 11.617 | 11.647 | 11.673 | 11.702 | 11.728 | 1993 | 11.728 |
| 1994 | 11.758 | 11.783 | 11.814 | 11.846 | 11.884 | 11.921 | 11.954 | 11.998 | 12.042 | 12.088 | 12.132 | 12.186 | 1994 | 12.186 |
| 1995 | 12.237 | 12.286 | 12.342 | 12.397 | 12.464 | 12.522 | 12.579 | 12.638 | 12.692 | 12.752 | 12.806 | 12.868 | 1995 | 12.868 |
| 1996 | 12.923 | 12.974 | 13.025 | 13.084 | 13.140 | 13.192 | 13.252 | 13.306 | 13.365 | 13.421 | 13.476 | 13.538 | 1996 | 13.538 |
| 1997 | 13.599 | 13.652 | 13.710 | 13.769 | 13.837 | 13.888 | 13.948 | 14.005 | 14.067 | 14.127 | 14.182 | 14.250 | 1997 | 14.250 |
| 1998 | 14.311 | 14.367 | 14.423 | 14.485 | 14.544 | 14.603 | 14.662 | 14.725 | 14.792 | 14.840 | 14.886 | 14.942 | 1998 | 14.942 |
| 1999 | 14.994 | 15.048 | 15.112 | 15.168 | 15.219 | 15.280 | 15.338 | 15.397 | 15.457 | 15.517 | 15.573 | 15.641 | 1999 | 15.641 |
| 2000 | 15.706 | 15.774 | 15.848 | 15.920 | 16.001 | 16.064 | 16.141 | 16.223 | 16.305 | 16.397 | 16.480 | 16.563 | 2000 | 16.563 |

## Table B-10

**Inflation Index**

from December 1925 to December 1970

| Year | Jan | Feb | Mar | Apr | May | Jun | Jul | Aug | Sep | Oct | Nov | Dec | Yr-end | Index |
|------|-----|-----|-----|-----|-----|-----|-----|-----|-----|-----|-----|-----|--------|-------|
| 1925 | | | | | | | | | | | | 1.000 | 1925 | 1.000 |
| 1926 | 1.000 | 0.996 | 0.991 | 1.000 | 0.994 | 0.987 | 0.978 | 0.972 | 0.978 | 0.981 | 0.985 | 0.985 | 1926 | 0.985 |
| 1927 | 0.978 | 0.970 | 0.965 | 0.965 | 0.972 | 0.981 | 0.963 | 0.957 | 0.963 | 0.968 | 0.966 | 0.965 | 1927 | 0.965 |
| 1928 | 0.963 | 0.953 | 0.953 | 0.955 | 0.961 | 0.953 | 0.953 | 0.955 | 0.963 | 0.961 | 0.959 | 0.955 | 1928 | 0.955 |
| 1929 | 0.953 | 0.952 | 0.948 | 0.944 | 0.950 | 0.953 | 0.963 | 0.966 | 0.965 | 0.965 | 0.963 | 0.957 | 1929 | 0.957 |
| 1930 | 0.953 | 0.950 | 0.944 | 0.950 | 0.944 | 0.939 | 0.926 | 0.920 | 0.926 | 0.920 | 0.912 | 0.899 | 1930 | 0.899 |
| 1931 | 0.886 | 0.873 | 0.868 | 0.862 | 0.853 | 0.844 | 0.842 | 0.840 | 0.836 | 0.831 | 0.821 | 0.814 | 1931 | 0.814 |
| 1932 | 0.797 | 0.786 | 0.782 | 0.777 | 0.765 | 0.760 | 0.760 | 0.750 | 0.747 | 0.741 | 0.737 | 0.730 | 1932 | 0.730 |
| 1933 | 0.719 | 0.708 | 0.702 | 0.700 | 0.702 | 0.709 | 0.730 | 0.737 | 0.737 | 0.737 | 0.737 | 0.734 | 1933 | 0.734 |
| 1934 | 0.737 | 0.743 | 0.743 | 0.741 | 0.743 | 0.745 | 0.745 | 0.747 | 0.758 | 0.752 | 0.750 | 0.749 | 1934 | 0.749 |
| 1935 | 0.760 | 0.765 | 0.764 | 0.771 | 0.767 | 0.765 | 0.762 | 0.762 | 0.765 | 0.765 | 0.769 | 0.771 | 1935 | 0.771 |
| 1936 | 0.771 | 0.767 | 0.764 | 0.764 | 0.764 | 0.771 | 0.775 | 0.780 | 0.782 | 0.780 | 0.780 | 0.780 | 1936 | 0.780 |
| 1937 | 0.786 | 0.788 | 0.793 | 0.797 | 0.801 | 0.803 | 0.806 | 0.808 | 0.816 | 0.812 | 0.806 | 0.804 | 1937 | 0.804 |
| 1938 | 0.793 | 0.786 | 0.786 | 0.790 | 0.786 | 0.786 | 0.788 | 0.786 | 0.786 | 0.782 | 0.780 | 0.782 | 1938 | 0.782 |
| 1939 | 0.778 | 0.775 | 0.773 | 0.771 | 0.771 | 0.771 | 0.771 | 0.771 | 0.786 | 0.782 | 0.782 | 0.778 | 1939 | 0.778 |
| 1940 | 0.777 | 0.782 | 0.780 | 0.780 | 0.782 | 0.784 | 0.782 | 0.780 | 0.782 | 0.782 | 0.782 | 0.786 | 1940 | 0.786 |
| 1941 | 0.786 | 0.786 | 0.790 | 0.797 | 0.803 | 0.818 | 0.821 | 0.829 | 0.844 | 0.853 | 0.860 | 0.862 | 1941 | 0.862 |
| 1942 | 0.873 | 0.881 | 0.892 | 0.898 | 0.907 | 0.909 | 0.912 | 0.918 | 0.920 | 0.929 | 0.935 | 0.942 | 1942 | 0.942 |
| 1943 | 0.942 | 0.944 | 0.959 | 0.970 | 0.978 | 0.976 | 0.968 | 0.965 | 0.968 | 0.972 | 0.970 | 0.972 | 1943 | 0.972 |
| 1944 | 0.970 | 0.968 | 0.968 | 0.974 | 0.978 | 0.980 | 0.985 | 0.989 | 0.989 | 0.989 | 0.989 | 0.993 | 1944 | 0.993 |
| 1945 | 0.993 | 0.991 | 0.991 | 0.993 | 1.000 | 1.009 | 1.011 | 1.011 | 1.007 | 1.007 | 1.011 | 1.015 | 1945 | 1.015 |
| 1946 | 1.015 | 1.011 | 1.019 | 1.024 | 1.030 | 1.041 | 1.102 | 1.127 | 1.140 | 1.162 | 1.190 | 1.199 | 1946 | 1.199 |
| 1947 | 1.199 | 1.197 | 1.223 | 1.223 | 1.220 | 1.229 | 1.240 | 1.253 | 1.283 | 1.283 | 1.291 | 1.307 | 1947 | 1.307 |
| 1948 | 1.322 | 1.311 | 1.307 | 1.326 | 1.335 | 1.345 | 1.361 | 1.367 | 1.367 | 1.361 | 1.352 | 1.343 | 1948 | 1.343 |
| 1949 | 1.341 | 1.326 | 1.330 | 1.331 | 1.330 | 1.331 | 1.322 | 1.326 | 1.331 | 1.324 | 1.326 | 1.318 | 1949 | 1.318 |
| 1950 | 1.313 | 1.309 | 1.315 | 1.317 | 1.322 | 1.330 | 1.343 | 1.354 | 1.363 | 1.371 | 1.376 | 1.395 | 1950 | 1.395 |
| 1951 | 1.417 | 1.434 | 1.439 | 1.441 | 1.447 | 1.445 | 1.447 | 1.447 | 1.456 | 1.464 | 1.471 | 1.477 | 1951 | 1.477 |
| 1952 | 1.477 | 1.467 | 1.467 | 1.473 | 1.475 | 1.479 | 1.490 | 1.492 | 1.490 | 1.492 | 1.492 | 1.490 | 1952 | 1.490 |
| 1953 | 1.486 | 1.479 | 1.482 | 1.484 | 1.488 | 1.493 | 1.497 | 1.501 | 1.503 | 1.507 | 1.501 | 1.499 | 1953 | 1.499 |
| 1954 | 1.503 | 1.501 | 1.499 | 1.495 | 1.501 | 1.503 | 1.503 | 1.501 | 1.497 | 1.493 | 1.495 | 1.492 | 1954 | 1.492 |
| 1955 | 1.492 | 1.492 | 1.492 | 1.492 | 1.492 | 1.492 | 1.497 | 1.493 | 1.499 | 1.499 | 1.501 | 1.497 | 1955 | 1.497 |
| 1956 | 1.495 | 1.495 | 1.497 | 1.499 | 1.507 | 1.516 | 1.527 | 1.525 | 1.527 | 1.536 | 1.536 | 1.540 | 1956 | 1.540 |
| 1957 | 1.542 | 1.547 | 1.551 | 1.557 | 1.561 | 1.570 | 1.577 | 1.579 | 1.581 | 1.581 | 1.587 | 1.587 | 1957 | 1.587 |
| 1958 | 1.596 | 1.598 | 1.609 | 1.613 | 1.613 | 1.615 | 1.616 | 1.615 | 1.615 | 1.615 | 1.616 | 1.615 | 1958 | 1.615 |
| 1959 | 1.616 | 1.615 | 1.615 | 1.616 | 1.618 | 1.626 | 1.629 | 1.628 | 1.633 | 1.639 | 1.639 | 1.639 | 1959 | 1.639 |
| 1960 | 1.637 | 1.639 | 1.639 | 1.648 | 1.648 | 1.652 | 1.652 | 1.652 | 1.654 | 1.661 | 1.663 | 1.663 | 1960 | 1.663 |
| 1961 | 1.663 | 1.663 | 1.663 | 1.663 | 1.663 | 1.665 | 1.672 | 1.670 | 1.674 | 1.674 | 1.674 | 1.674 | 1961 | 1.674 |
| 1962 | 1.674 | 1.678 | 1.682 | 1.685 | 1.685 | 1.685 | 1.689 | 1.689 | 1.698 | 1.696 | 1.696 | 1.695 | 1962 | 1.695 |
| 1963 | 1.696 | 1.698 | 1.700 | 1.700 | 1.700 | 1.708 | 1.715 | 1.715 | 1.715 | 1.717 | 1.719 | 1.723 | 1963 | 1.723 |
| 1964 | 1.724 | 1.723 | 1.724 | 1.726 | 1.726 | 1.730 | 1.734 | 1.732 | 1.736 | 1.737 | 1.741 | 1.743 | 1964 | 1.743 |
| 1965 | 1.743 | 1.743 | 1.745 | 1.750 | 1.754 | 1.764 | 1.765 | 1.762 | 1.765 | 1.767 | 1.771 | 1.777 | 1965 | 1.777 |
| 1966 | 1.777 | 1.788 | 1.793 | 1.801 | 1.803 | 1.808 | 1.814 | 1.823 | 1.827 | 1.834 | 1.834 | 1.836 | 1966 | 1.836 |
| 1967 | 1.836 | 1.838 | 1.842 | 1.845 | 1.851 | 1.857 | 1.866 | 1.872 | 1.875 | 1.881 | 1.886 | 1.892 | 1967 | 1.892 |
| 1968 | 1.899 | 1.905 | 1.914 | 1.920 | 1.926 | 1.937 | 1.946 | 1.952 | 1.957 | 1.968 | 1.976 | 1.981 | 1968 | 1.981 |
| 1969 | 1.987 | 1.994 | 2.011 | 2.024 | 2.030 | 2.043 | 2.052 | 2.061 | 2.071 | 2.078 | 2.089 | 2.102 | 1969 | 2.102 |
| 1970 | 2.110 | 2.121 | 2.132 | 2.145 | 2.155 | 2.166 | 2.173 | 2.177 | 2.188 | 2.199 | 2.207 | 2.218 | 1970 | 2.218 |

# Table B-10 (continued)

## Inflation Index

from January 1971 to December 2000

| Year | Jan | Feb | Mar | Apr | May | Jun | Jul | Aug | Sep | Oct | Nov | Dec | Yr-end | Index |
|------|------|------|------|------|------|------|------|------|------|------|------|------|--------|-------|
| 1971 | 2.220 | 2.223 | 2.231 | 2.238 | 2.250 | 2.263 | 2.268 | 2.274 | 2.276 | 2.279 | 2.283 | 2.292 | 1971 | 2.292 |
| 1972 | 2.294 | 2.305 | 2.309 | 2.315 | 2.322 | 2.328 | 2.337 | 2.341 | 2.350 | 2.358 | 2.363 | 2.371 | 1972 | 2.371 |
| 1973 | 2.378 | 2.395 | 2.417 | 2.434 | 2.449 | 2.466 | 2.471 | 2.516 | 2.523 | 2.544 | 2.562 | 2.579 | 1973 | 2.579 |
| 1974 | 2.602 | 2.635 | 2.665 | 2.680 | 2.710 | 2.736 | 2.756 | 2.791 | 2.825 | 2.849 | 2.873 | 2.894 | 1974 | 2.894 |
| 1975 | 2.907 | 2.927 | 2.939 | 2.953 | 2.967 | 2.991 | 3.022 | 3.032 | 3.047 | 3.065 | 3.084 | 3.097 | 1975 | 3.097 |
| 1976 | 3.104 | 3.112 | 3.119 | 3.132 | 3.151 | 3.168 | 3.186 | 3.201 | 3.214 | 3.227 | 3.237 | 3.246 | 1976 | 3.246 |
| 1977 | 3.264 | 3.298 | 3.318 | 3.345 | 3.363 | 3.386 | 3.400 | 3.413 | 3.426 | 3.436 | 3.453 | 3.466 | 1977 | 3.466 |
| 1978 | 3.484 | 3.508 | 3.533 | 3.564 | 3.600 | 3.637 | 3.663 | 3.682 | 3.708 | 3.737 | 3.758 | 3.778 | 1978 | 3.778 |
| 1979 | 3.812 | 3.857 | 3.894 | 3.939 | 3.987 | 4.024 | 4.076 | 4.117 | 4.160 | 4.197 | 4.237 | 4.281 | 1979 | 4.281 |
| 1980 | 4.343 | 4.402 | 4.466 | 4.516 | 4.561 | 4.611 | 4.615 | 4.644 | 4.687 | 4.728 | 4.771 | 4.812 | 1980 | 4.812 |
| 1981 | 4.851 | 4.901 | 4.937 | 4.968 | 5.009 | 5.052 | 5.110 | 5.149 | 5.201 | 5.212 | 5.227 | 5.242 | 1981 | 5.242 |
| 1982 | 5.261 | 5.278 | 5.272 | 5.294 | 5.346 | 5.412 | 5.441 | 5.453 | 5.462 | 5.477 | 5.467 | 5.445 | 1982 | 5.445 |
| 1983 | 5.458 | 5.460 | 5.464 | 5.503 | 5.533 | 5.551 | 5.574 | 5.592 | 5.620 | 5.635 | 5.644 | 5.652 | 1983 | 5.652 |
| 1984 | 5.683 | 5.710 | 5.723 | 5.750 | 5.767 | 5.786 | 5.805 | 5.829 | 5.857 | 5.872 | 5.872 | 5.875 | 1984 | 5.875 |
| 1985 | 5.886 | 5.911 | 5.937 | 5.961 | 5.983 | 6.002 | 6.011 | 6.024 | 6.043 | 6.061 | 6.082 | 6.097 | 1985 | 6.097 |
| 1986 | 6.115 | 6.099 | 6.071 | 6.058 | 6.076 | 6.106 | 6.108 | 6.119 | 6.149 | 6.155 | 6.160 | 6.166 | 1986 | 6.166 |
| 1987 | 6.203 | 6.227 | 6.255 | 6.289 | 6.307 | 6.333 | 6.346 | 6.382 | 6.413 | 6.430 | 6.439 | 6.438 | 1987 | 6.438 |
| 1988 | 6.454 | 6.471 | 6.499 | 6.532 | 6.555 | 6.583 | 6.610 | 6.638 | 6.683 | 6.705 | 6.711 | 6.722 | 1988 | 6.722 |
| 1989 | 6.756 | 6.783 | 6.822 | 6.867 | 6.906 | 6.923 | 6.940 | 6.951 | 6.973 | 7.007 | 7.023 | 7.034 | 1989 | 7.034 |
| 1990 | 7.107 | 7.140 | 7.180 | 7.191 | 7.207 | 7.246 | 7.274 | 7.341 | 7.403 | 7.447 | 7.464 | 7.464 | 1990 | 7.464 |
| 1991 | 7.509 | 7.520 | 7.531 | 7.542 | 7.564 | 7.587 | 7.598 | 7.620 | 7.654 | 7.665 | 7.687 | 7.693 | 1991 | 7.693 |
| 1992 | 7.704 | 7.732 | 7.771 | 7.782 | 7.793 | 7.821 | 7.838 | 7.860 | 7.882 | 7.910 | 7.921 | 7.916 | 1992 | 7.916 |
| 1993 | 7.955 | 7.983 | 8.011 | 8.033 | 8.044 | 8.055 | 8.055 | 8.078 | 8.094 | 8.128 | 8.133 | 8.133 | 1993 | 8.133 |
| 1994 | 8.156 | 8.184 | 8.212 | 8.223 | 8.228 | 8.256 | 8.278 | 8.312 | 8.334 | 8.340 | 8.351 | 8.351 | 1994 | 8.351 |
| 1995 | 8.384 | 8.418 | 8.446 | 8.474 | 8.490 | 8.507 | 8.507 | 8.530 | 8.546 | 8.574 | 8.569 | 8.563 | 1995 | 8.563 |
| 1996 | 8.613 | 8.641 | 8.686 | 8.719 | 8.736 | 8.741 | 8.758 | 8.775 | 8.803 | 8.831 | 8.847 | 8.847 | 1996 | 8.847 |
| 1997 | 8.875 | 8.903 | 8.926 | 8.937 | 8.931 | 8.942 | 8.953 | 8.970 | 8.993 | 9.015 | 9.009 | 8.998 | 1997 | 8.998 |
| 1998 | 9.015 | 9.032 | 9.048 | 9.065 | 9.082 | 9.093 | 9.104 | 9.115 | 9.126 | 9.149 | 9.149 | 9.143 | 1998 | 9.143 |
| 1999 | 9.165 | 9.177 | 9.204 | 9.271 | 9.271 | 9.271 | 9.299 | 9.322 | 9.366 | 9.383 | 9.389 | 9.389 | 1999 | 9.389 |
| 2000 | 9.411 | 9.467 | 9.545 | 9.550 | 9.556 | 9.612 | 9.628 | 9.640 | 9.690 | 9.707 | 9.712 | 9.707 | 2000 | 9.707 |

## Table B-11

## Large Company Stocks: Inflation-Adjusted Total Return Index

from December 1925 to December 1970

| Year | Jan | Feb | Mar | Apr | May | Jun | Jul | Aug | Sep | Oct | Nov | Dec | Yr-end | Index |
|------|-----|-----|-----|-----|-----|-----|-----|-----|-----|-----|-----|-----|--------|-------|
| 1925 | | | | | | | | | | | | 1.000 | 1925 | 1.000 |
| 1926 | 1.000 | 0.965 | 0.915 | 0.929 | 0.951 | 1.002 | 1.060 | 1.093 | 1.114 | 1.078 | 1.111 | 1.133 | 1926 | 1.133 |
| 1927 | 1.120 | 1.189 | 1.206 | 1.230 | 1.295 | 1.274 | 1.386 | 1.466 | 1.523 | 1.438 | 1.545 | 1.591 | 1927 | 1.591 |
| 1928 | 1.588 | 1.583 | 1.757 | 1.815 | 1.840 | 1.783 | 1.808 | 1.949 | 1.984 | 2.021 | 2.287 | 2.307 | 1928 | 2.307 |
| 1929 | 2.446 | 2.446 | 2.453 | 2.506 | 2.401 | 2.664 | 2.763 | 3.035 | 2.896 | 2.325 | 2.039 | 2.109 | 1929 | 2.109 |
| 1930 | 2.252 | 2.320 | 2.523 | 2.488 | 2.479 | 2.088 | 2.199 | 2.244 | 1.944 | 1.789 | 1.788 | 1.685 | 1930 | 1.685 |
| 1931 | 1.796 | 2.040 | 1.915 | 1.747 | 1.540 | 1.779 | 1.654 | 1.688 | 1.191 | 1.307 | 1.216 | 1.056 | 1931 | 1.056 |
| 1932 | 1.049 | 1.124 | 0.999 | 0.805 | 0.637 | 0.641 | 0.885 | 1.243 | 1.206 | 1.051 | 1.012 | 1.080 | 1932 | 1.080 |
| 1933 | 1.107 | 0.925 | 0.965 | 1.380 | 1.608 | 1.804 | 1.602 | 1.777 | 1.578 | 1.443 | 1.606 | 1.655 | 1933 | 1.655 |
| 1934 | 1.823 | 1.751 | 1.751 | 1.711 | 1.581 | 1.613 | 1.431 | 1.514 | 1.487 | 1.455 | 1.596 | 1.599 | 1934 | 1.599 |
| 1935 | 1.511 | 1.449 | 1.410 | 1.534 | 1.604 | 1.721 | 1.876 | 1.929 | 1.968 | 2.121 | 2.211 | 2.292 | 1935 | 2.292 |
| 1936 | 2.446 | 2.513 | 2.593 | 2.398 | 2.529 | 2.588 | 2.756 | 2.778 | 2.780 | 3.002 | 3.042 | 3.033 | 1936 | 3.033 |
| 1937 | 3.129 | 3.182 | 3.135 | 2.868 | 2.847 | 2.697 | 2.966 | 2.816 | 2.399 | 2.173 | 1.999 | 1.912 | 1937 | 1.912 |
| 1938 | 1.968 | 2.120 | 1.593 | 1.815 | 1.764 | 2.205 | 2.363 | 2.315 | 2.354 | 2.549 | 2.485 | 2.578 | 1938 | 2.578 |
| 1939 | 2.416 | 2.522 | 2.190 | 2.189 | 2.350 | 2.206 | 2.450 | 2.291 | 2.623 | 2.603 | 2.500 | 2.580 | 1939 | 2.580 |
| 1940 | 2.499 | 2.514 | 2.551 | 2.545 | 1.958 | 2.111 | 2.188 | 2.270 | 2.293 | 2.390 | 2.314 | 2.305 | 1940 | 2.305 |
| 1941 | 2.199 | 2.186 | 2.191 | 2.037 | 2.060 | 2.139 | 2.253 | 2.235 | 2.180 | 2.015 | 1.941 | 1.858 | 1941 | 1.858 |
| 1942 | 1.863 | 1.818 | 1.679 | 1.601 | 1.711 | 1.745 | 1.797 | 1.815 | 1.864 | 1.970 | 1.955 | 2.046 | 1942 | 2.046 |
| 1943 | 2.196 | 2.320 | 2.408 | 2.389 | 2.501 | 2.562 | 2.446 | 2.497 | 2.553 | 2.516 | 2.356 | 2.496 | 1943 | 2.496 |
| 1944 | 2.544 | 2.560 | 2.610 | 2.569 | 2.688 | 2.829 | 2.758 | 2.791 | 2.789 | 2.796 | 2.833 | 2.928 | 1944 | 2.928 |
| 1945 | 2.974 | 3.183 | 3.043 | 3.311 | 3.351 | 3.318 | 3.252 | 3.460 | 3.625 | 3.742 | 3.876 | 3.907 | 1945 | 3.907 |
| 1946 | 4.186 | 3.932 | 4.091 | 4.228 | 4.326 | 4.121 | 3.799 | 3.467 | 3.085 | 3.008 | 2.929 | 3.039 | 1946 | 3.039 |
| 1947 | 3.117 | 3.098 | 2.986 | 2.878 | 2.891 | 3.028 | 3.115 | 3.020 | 2.917 | 2.987 | 2.917 | 2.947 | 1947 | 2.947 |
| 1948 | 2.804 | 2.718 | 2.942 | 2.985 | 3.225 | 3.219 | 3.018 | 3.053 | 2.969 | 3.193 | 2.906 | 3.027 | 1948 | 3.027 |
| 1949 | 3.044 | 2.987 | 3.076 | 3.017 | 2.943 | 2.943 | 3.157 | 3.217 | 3.287 | 3.418 | 3.473 | 3.662 | 1949 | 3.662 |
| 1950 | 3.750 | 3.836 | 3.846 | 4.028 | 4.215 | 3.961 | 3.969 | 4.111 | 4.325 | 4.341 | 4.396 | 4.560 | 1950 | 4.560 |
| 1951 | 4.774 | 4.792 | 4.699 | 4.932 | 4.766 | 4.664 | 4.989 | 5.227 | 5.200 | 5.121 | 5.143 | 5.341 | 1951 | 5.341 |
| 1952 | 5.438 | 5.318 | 5.586 | 5.341 | 5.517 | 5.773 | 5.842 | 5.794 | 5.699 | 5.703 | 6.029 | 6.267 | 1952 | 6.267 |
| 1953 | 6.252 | 6.217 | 6.069 | 5.918 | 5.949 | 5.847 | 5.992 | 5.677 | 5.690 | 5.982 | 6.127 | 6.166 | 1953 | 6.166 |
| 1954 | 6.481 | 6.561 | 6.783 | 7.151 | 7.421 | 7.435 | 7.873 | 7.666 | 8.339 | 8.220 | 8.956 | 9.458 | 1954 | 9.458 |
| 1955 | 9.645 | 9.740 | 9.711 | 10.096 | 10.152 | 11.006 | 11.646 | 11.646 | 11.753 | 11.419 | 12.348 | 12.397 | 1955 | 12.397 |
| 1956 | 11.982 | 12.476 | 13.346 | 13.324 | 12.471 | 12.902 | 13.487 | 13.060 | 12.471 | 12.477 | 12.414 | 12.843 | 1956 | 12.843 |
| 1957 | 12.313 | 11.945 | 12.173 | 12.599 | 13.119 | 13.046 | 13.155 | 12.475 | 11.711 | 11.358 | 11.580 | 11.122 | 1957 | 11.122 |
| 1958 | 11.549 | 11.372 | 11.664 | 12.029 | 12.284 | 12.612 | 13.163 | 13.410 | 14.081 | 14.461 | 14.855 | 15.669 | 1958 | 15.669 |
| 1959 | 15.733 | 15.828 | 15.859 | 16.478 | 16.854 | 16.739 | 17.306 | 17.149 | 16.333 | 16.486 | 16.793 | 17.283 | 1959 | 17.283 |
| 1960 | 16.092 | 16.311 | 16.110 | 15.761 | 16.275 | 16.581 | 16.194 | 16.707 | 15.704 | 15.622 | 16.329 | 17.111 | 1960 | 17.111 |
| 1961 | 18.215 | 18.796 | 19.303 | 19.401 | 19.864 | 19.296 | 19.867 | 20.372 | 19.953 | 20.549 | 21.468 | 21.567 | 1961 | 21.567 |
| 1962 | 20.777 | 21.165 | 21.022 | 19.702 | 18.105 | 16.650 | 17.697 | 18.065 | 17.130 | 17.259 | 19.133 | 19.447 | 1962 | 19.447 |
| 1963 | 20.407 | 19.899 | 20.613 | 21.644 | 22.062 | 21.553 | 21.413 | 22.560 | 22.342 | 23.074 | 22.943 | 23.494 | 1963 | 23.494 |
| 1964 | 24.131 | 24.512 | 24.888 | 25.047 | 25.454 | 25.851 | 26.297 | 26.015 | 26.740 | 26.968 | 26.923 | 27.044 | 1964 | 27.044 |
| 1965 | 27.976 | 28.062 | 27.660 | 28.555 | 28.408 | 26.922 | 27.290 | 28.092 | 28.968 | 29.774 | 29.618 | 29.838 | 1965 | 29.838 |
| 1966 | 30.022 | 29.442 | 28.749 | 29.259 | 27.791 | 27.299 | 26.888 | 24.811 | 24.629 | 25.740 | 25.984 | 25.964 | 1966 | 25.964 |
| 1967 | 28.036 | 28.208 | 29.303 | 30.521 | 28.979 | 29.440 | 30.663 | 30.359 | 31.334 | 30.378 | 30.485 | 31.239 | 1967 | 31.239 |
| 1968 | 29.794 | 28.930 | 29.105 | 31.440 | 31.853 | 32.003 | 31.303 | 31.725 | 32.898 | 32.995 | 34.615 | 33.129 | 1968 | 33.129 |
| 1969 | 32.810 | 31.295 | 32.147 | 32.670 | 32.665 | 30.697 | 28.762 | 29.932 | 29.096 | 30.321 | 29.263 | 28.567 | 1969 | 28.567 |
| 1970 | 26.349 | 27.746 | 27.684 | 25.069 | 23.595 | 22.342 | 23.940 | 25.114 | 25.854 | 25.472 | 26.746 | 28.164 | 1970 | 28.164 |

Table B-11 (continued)

**Large Company Stocks: Inflation-Adjusted Total Return Index**

from January 1971 to December 2000

| Year | Jan | Feb | Mar | Apr | May | Jun | Jul | Aug | Sep | Oct | Nov | Dec | Yr-end | Index |
|------|-----|-----|-----|-----|-----|-----|-----|-----|-----|-----|-----|-----|--------|-------|
| 1971 | 29.319 | 29.682 | 30.715 | 31.766 | 30.447 | 30.335 | 29.052 | 30.176 | 29.984 | 28.726 | 28.755 | 31.149 | 1971 | 31.149 |
| 1972 | 31.728 | 32.519 | 32.701 | 32.807 | 33.419 | 32.654 | 32.642 | 33.865 | 33.609 | 33.861 | 35.485 | 35.837 | 1972 | 35.837 |
| 1973 | 35.156 | 33.749 | 33.431 | 31.891 | 31.255 | 30.883 | 32.028 | 30.459 | 31.630 | 31.384 | 27.784 | 28.110 | 1973 | 28.110 |
| 1974 | 27.631 | 27.331 | 26.438 | 25.309 | 24.349 | 23.807 | 21.836 | 19.774 | 17.253 | 19.942 | 18.888 | 18.422 | 1974 | 18.422 |
| 1975 | 20.634 | 21.872 | 22.304 | 23.285 | 24.362 | 25.281 | 23.368 | 22.961 | 22.099 | 23.363 | 23.950 | 23.619 | 1975 | 23.619 |
| 1976 | 26.388 | 26.172 | 26.960 | 26.582 | 26.232 | 27.208 | 26.864 | 26.777 | 27.326 | 26.656 | 26.555 | 27.908 | 1976 | 27.908 |
| 1977 | 26.391 | 25.728 | 25.265 | 25.102 | 24.590 | 25.587 | 25.090 | 24.663 | 24.570 | 23.485 | 24.236 | 24.260 | 1977 | 24.260 |
| 1978 | 22.692 | 22.171 | 22.627 | 24.377 | 24.467 | 23.847 | 25.002 | 25.722 | 25.418 | 22.969 | 23.438 | 23.712 | 1978 | 23.712 |
| 1979 | 24.493 | 23.522 | 24.637 | 24.445 | 23.742 | 24.487 | 24.438 | 25.673 | 25.473 | 23.591 | 24.575 | 24.786 | 1979 | 24.786 |
| 1980 | 25.926 | 25.654 | 22.795 | 23.509 | 24.587 | 25.038 | 26.709 | 26.885 | 27.387 | 27.656 | 30.410 | 29.201 | 1980 | 29.201 |
| 1981 | 27.697 | 27.983 | 28.838 | 28.044 | 27.987 | 27.528 | 27.236 | 25.532 | 24.007 | 25.220 | 26.257 | 25.489 | 1981 | 25.489 |
| 1982 | 24.985 | 23.630 | 23.513 | 24.383 | 23.450 | 22.765 | 22.153 | 24.909 | 25.140 | 27.895 | 29.166 | 29.792 | 1982 | 29.792 |
| 1983 | 30.756 | 31.544 | 32.674 | 34.900 | 34.532 | 35.731 | 34.474 | 34.943 | 35.242 | 34.678 | 35.427 | 35.165 | 1983 | 35.165 |
| 1984 | 34.742 | 33.449 | 33.943 | 34.011 | 32.102 | 32.706 | 32.134 | 35.601 | 35.438 | 35.440 | 35.082 | 35.947 | 1984 | 35.947 |
| 1985 | 38.634 | 39.003 | 38.902 | 38.620 | 40.842 | 41.363 | 41.192 | 40.852 | 39.419 | 41.054 | 43.845 | 45.781 | 1985 | 45.781 |
| 1986 | 45.842 | 49.466 | 52.447 | 51.908 | 54.590 | 55.226 | 52.068 | 55.862 | 51.020 | 53.808 | 55.135 | 53.631 | 1986 | 53.631 |
| 1987 | 60.468 | 62.721 | 64.139 | 63.236 | 63.698 | 66.602 | 69.775 | 72.059 | 70.126 | 54.892 | 50.323 | 54.053 | 1987 | 54.053 |
| 1988 | 56.215 | 58.704 | 56.687 | 57.006 | 57.255 | 59.658 | 59.168 | 56.970 | 58.988 | 60.397 | 59.490 | 60.466 | 1988 | 60.466 |
| 1989 | 64.517 | 62.652 | 63.763 | 66.618 | 68.904 | 68.366 | 74.326 | 75.638 | 75.102 | 73.002 | 74.343 | 75.977 | 1989 | 75.977 |
| 1990 | 70.155 | 70.727 | 72.193 | 70.300 | 76.975 | 76.025 | 75.491 | 68.048 | 64.164 | 63.543 | 67.484 | 69.333 | 1990 | 69.333 |
| 1991 | 71.967 | 77.005 | 78.721 | 78.825 | 81.956 | 77.981 | 81.510 | 83.181 | 81.459 | 82.431 | 78.871 | 87.822 | 1991 | 87.822 |
| 1992 | 86.064 | 86.851 | 84.721 | 87.061 | 87.406 | 85.832 | 89.100 | 87.052 | 87.804 | 87.809 | 90.641 | 91.893 | 1992 | 91.893 |
| 1993 | 92.109 | 93.027 | 94.696 | 92.119 | 94.475 | 94.656 | 94.211 | 97.530 | 96.608 | 98.163 | 97.174 | 98.369 | 1993 | 98.369 |
| 1994 | 101.386 | 98.313 | 93.717 | 94.806 | 96.286 | 93.591 | 96.428 | 99.948 | 97.279 | 99.440 | 95.662 | 97.059 | 1994 | 97.059 |
| 1995 | 99.185 | 102.624 | 105.312 | 108.020 | 112.066 | 114.474 | 118.285 | 118.295 | 123.010 | 122.180 | 127.639 | 130.085 | 1995 | 130.085 |
| 1996 | 133.776 | 134.624 | 135.218 | 136.679 | 139.937 | 140.421 | 133.916 | 136.494 | 143.708 | 147.180 | 158.051 | 154.953 | 1996 | 154.953 |
| 1997 | 164.059 | 164.869 | 157.616 | 166.817 | 177.170 | 184.841 | 199.269 | 187.838 | 197.635 | 190.561 | 199.507 | 203.190 | 1997 | 203.190 |
| 1998 | 205.064 | 219.446 | 230.257 | 232.144 | 227.733 | 236.693 | 233.885 | 199.825 | 212.366 | 229.080 | 242.965 | 257.121 | 1998 | 257.121 |
| 1999 | 267.222 | 258.602 | 268.133 | 276.507 | 269.979 | 284.963 | 275.238 | 273.220 | 264.465 | 280.699 | 286.235 | 303.094 | 1999 | 303.094 |
| 2000 | 287.184 | 280.088 | 304.973 | 295.623 | 289.388 | 294.801 | 289.688 | 307.325 | 289.593 | 287.871 | 265.023 | 266.472 | 2000 | 266.472 |

## Table B-12

### Small Company Stocks: Inflation-Adjusted Total Return Index

from December 1925 to December 1970

| Year | Jan | Feb | Mar | Apr | May | Jun | Jul | Aug | Sep | Oct | Nov | Dec | Yr-end | Index |
|------|-----|-----|-----|-----|-----|-----|-----|-----|-----|-----|-----|-----|--------|-------|
| 1925 | | | | | | | | | | | | 1.000 | 1925 | 1.000 |
| 1926 | 1.070 | 1.005 | 0.902 | 0.910 | 0.909 | 0.951 | 0.970 | 1.001 | 0.995 | 0.969 | 0.985 | 1.018 | 1926 | 1.018 |
| 1927 | 1.056 | 1.122 | 1.067 | 1.128 | 1.202 | 1.154 | 1.237 | 1.222 | 1.221 | 1.134 | 1.228 | 1.269 | 1927 | 1.269 |
| 1928 | 1.333 | 1.314 | 1.384 | 1.507 | 1.564 | 1.443 | 1.452 | 1.513 | 1.635 | 1.683 | 1.880 | 1.790 | 1928 | 1.790 |
| 1929 | 1.800 | 1.799 | 1.770 | 1.831 | 1.577 | 1.655 | 1.657 | 1.624 | 1.477 | 1.068 | 0.910 | 0.869 | 1929 | 0.869 |
| 1930 | 0.985 | 1.053 | 1.166 | 1.078 | 1.026 | 0.808 | 0.844 | 0.835 | 0.709 | 0.635 | 0.638 | 0.572 | 1930 | 0.572 |
| 1931 | 0.703 | 0.896 | 0.838 | 0.661 | 0.576 | 0.688 | 0.651 | 0.603 | 0.409 | 0.444 | 0.403 | 0.318 | 1931 | 0.318 |
| 1932 | 0.357 | 0.373 | 0.326 | 0.255 | 0.228 | 0.230 | 0.312 | 0.547 | 0.477 | 0.396 | 0.349 | 0.335 | 1932 | 0.335 |
| 1933 | 0.337 | 0.299 | 0.335 | 0.505 | 0.823 | 1.028 | 0.944 | 1.021 | 0.858 | 0.752 | 0.801 | 0.810 | 1933 | 0.810 |
| 1934 | 1.119 | 1.129 | 1.128 | 1.158 | 1.008 | 1.003 | 0.776 | 0.894 | 0.866 | 0.881 | 0.967 | 0.986 | 1934 | 0.986 |
| 1935 | 0.939 | 0.877 | 0.775 | 0.828 | 0.830 | 0.858 | 0.936 | 0.986 | 1.017 | 1.118 | 1.269 | 1.342 | 1935 | 1.342 |
| 1936 | 1.746 | 1.860 | 1.881 | 1.544 | 1.586 | 1.534 | 1.660 | 1.683 | 1.770 | 1.887 | 2.151 | 2.185 | 1936 | 2.185 |
| 1937 | 2.445 | 2.599 | 2.612 | 2.163 | 2.065 | 1.817 | 2.031 | 1.878 | 1.388 | 1.242 | 1.069 | 0.890 | 1937 | 0.890 |
| 1938 | 0.951 | 0.993 | 0.635 | 0.808 | 0.743 | 1.003 | 1.150 | 1.037 | 1.021 | 1.245 | 1.162 | 1.216 | 1938 | 1.216 |
| 1939 | 1.118 | 1.135 | 0.857 | 0.872 | 0.966 | 0.866 | 1.085 | 0.913 | 1.356 | 1.308 | 1.171 | 1.226 | 1939 | 1.226 |
| 1940 | 1.230 | 1.321 | 1.408 | 1.500 | 0.947 | 1.044 | 1.071 | 1.100 | 1.121 | 1.182 | 1.211 | 1.152 | 1940 | 1.152 |
| 1941 | 1.154 | 1.121 | 1.151 | 1.064 | 1.062 | 1.121 | 1.357 | 1.337 | 1.252 | 1.155 | 1.088 | 0.955 | 1941 | 0.955 |
| 1942 | 1.121 | 1.104 | 1.013 | 0.971 | 0.958 | 0.988 | 1.057 | 1.084 | 1.181 | 1.296 | 1.222 | 1.263 | 1942 | 1.263 |
| 1943 | 1.532 | 1.824 | 2.056 | 2.221 | 2.459 | 2.444 | 2.196 | 2.204 | 2.289 | 2.308 | 2.055 | 2.306 | 1943 | 2.306 |
| 1944 | 2.459 | 2.536 | 2.726 | 2.566 | 2.745 | 3.119 | 3.009 | 3.093 | 3.087 | 3.054 | 3.206 | 3.472 | 1944 | 3.472 |
| 1945 | 3.639 | 4.014 | 3.668 | 4.085 | 4.257 | 4.579 | 4.316 | 4.556 | 4.884 | 5.226 | 5.817 | 5.895 | 1945 | 5.895 |
| 1946 | 6.815 | 6.405 | 6.532 | 6.948 | 7.319 | 6.906 | 6.176 | 5.530 | 4.591 | 4.449 | 4.283 | 4.409 | 1946 | 4.409 |
| 1947 | 4.594 | 4.582 | 4.334 | 3.887 | 3.691 | 3.865 | 4.133 | 4.074 | 4.026 | 4.139 | 3.991 | 4.081 | 1947 | 4.081 |
| 1948 | 3.973 | 3.694 | 4.069 | 4.160 | 4.568 | 4.558 | 4.242 | 4.227 | 4.005 | 4.281 | 3.830 | 3.890 | 1948 | 3.890 |
| 1949 | 3.966 | 3.818 | 4.046 | 3.905 | 3.690 | 3.649 | 3.921 | 4.011 | 4.189 | 4.412 | 4.413 | 4.744 | 1949 | 4.744 |
| 1950 | 4.998 | 5.123 | 5.082 | 5.284 | 5.395 | 4.948 | 5.190 | 5.420 | 5.664 | 5.600 | 5.757 | 6.221 | 1950 | 6.221 |
| 1951 | 6.632 | 6.594 | 6.255 | 6.476 | 6.238 | 5.916 | 6.128 | 6.499 | 6.596 | 6.417 | 6.331 | 6.335 | 1951 | 6.335 |
| 1952 | 6.456 | 6.302 | 6.413 | 6.057 | 6.068 | 6.217 | 6.240 | 6.229 | 6.136 | 6.066 | 6.359 | 6.469 | 1952 | 6.469 |
| 1953 | 6.751 | 6.967 | 6.903 | 6.696 | 6.774 | 6.421 | 6.502 | 6.078 | 5.912 | 6.069 | 6.168 | 6.012 | 1953 | 6.012 |
| 1954 | 6.451 | 6.520 | 6.647 | 6.757 | 7.036 | 7.088 | 7.660 | 7.681 | 8.015 | 8.090 | 8.709 | 9.703 | 1954 | 9.703 |
| 1955 | 9.898 | 10.372 | 10.460 | 10.617 | 10.700 | 11.014 | 11.043 | 11.039 | 11.118 | 10.930 | 11.427 | 11.642 | 1955 | 11.642 |
| 1956 | 11.602 | 11.924 | 12.422 | 12.464 | 11.909 | 11.902 | 12.149 | 12.001 | 11.674 | 11.725 | 11.787 | 11.803 | 1956 | 11.803 |
| 1957 | 12.067 | 11.783 | 11.952 | 12.205 | 12.267 | 12.284 | 12.152 | 11.669 | 11.129 | 10.203 | 10.282 | 9.788 | 1957 | 9.788 |
| 1958 | 10.806 | 10.610 | 11.032 | 11.421 | 11.863 | 12.234 | 12.820 | 13.385 | 14.078 | 14.651 | 15.360 | 15.859 | 1958 | 15.859 |
| 1959 | 16.751 | 17.265 | 17.312 | 17.494 | 17.497 | 17.344 | 17.870 | 17.734 | 16.911 | 17.236 | 17.619 | 18.187 | 1959 | 18.187 |
| 1960 | 17.650 | 17.717 | 17.159 | 16.744 | 17.086 | 17.627 | 17.293 | 18.201 | 16.838 | 16.091 | 16.775 | 17.333 | 1960 | 17.333 |
| 1961 | 18.918 | 20.033 | 21.273 | 21.543 | 22.463 | 21.219 | 21.191 | 21.491 | 20.717 | 21.259 | 22.562 | 22.741 | 1961 | 22.741 |
| 1962 | 23.052 | 23.431 | 23.512 | 21.637 | 19.454 | 17.927 | 19.252 | 19.809 | 18.403 | 17.735 | 19.948 | 19.792 | 1962 | 19.792 |
| 1963 | 21.562 | 21.613 | 21.910 | 22.593 | 23.579 | 23.198 | 23.173 | 24.371 | 23.974 | 24.514 | 24.227 | 24.060 | 1963 | 24.060 |
| 1964 | 24.693 | 25.622 | 26.154 | 26.369 | 26.783 | 27.159 | 28.181 | 28.129 | 29.198 | 29.766 | 29.734 | 29.370 | 1964 | 29.370 |
| 1965 | 30.924 | 32.130 | 32.859 | 34.420 | 34.079 | 30.846 | 32.196 | 34.184 | 35.296 | 37.276 | 38.577 | 40.848 | 1965 | 40.848 |
| 1966 | 43.934 | 45.018 | 44.016 | 45.339 | 40.939 | 40.763 | 40.587 | 36.021 | 35.359 | 34.838 | 36.549 | 36.751 | 1966 | 36.751 |
| 1967 | 43.507 | 45.416 | 48.111 | 49.313 | 48.747 | 53.544 | 58.342 | 58.287 | 61.456 | 59.369 | 59.883 | 65.471 | 1967 | 65.471 |
| 1968 | 66.219 | 61.343 | 60.379 | 68.997 | 75.667 | 75.457 | 72.502 | 74.947 | 79.213 | 79.003 | 84.719 | 85.005 | 1968 | 85.005 |
| 1969 | 83.360 | 74.828 | 77.140 | 79.668 | 80.827 | 70.957 | 63.080 | 67.392 | 65.339 | 69.075 | 64.876 | 60.042 | 1969 | 60.042 |
| 1970 | 56.190 | 58.058 | 56.111 | 46.134 | 41.197 | 37.178 | 39.102 | 42.738 | 47.137 | 43.586 | 44.034 | 46.993 | 1970 | 46.993 |

## Table B-12 (continued)

## Small Company Stocks: Inflation-Adjusted Total Return Index

from January 1971 to December 2000

| Year | Jan | Feb | Mar | Apr | May | Jun | Jul | Aug | Sep | Oct | Nov | Dec | Yr-end | Index |
|---|---|---|---|---|---|---|---|---|---|---|---|---|---|---|
| 1971 | 54.430 | 56.060 | 59.023 | 60.277 | 56.349 | 54.235 | 51.055 | 53.900 | 52.637 | 49.655 | 47.723 | 52.968 | 1971 | 52.968 |
| 1972 | 58.905 | 60.354 | 59.392 | 60.012 | 58.677 | 56.750 | 54.190 | 55.112 | 52.979 | 51.888 | 54.832 | 53.492 | 1972 | 53.492 |
| 1973 | 51.020 | 46.616 | 45.226 | 42.124 | 38.472 | 37.102 | 41.437 | 38.888 | 42.897 | 42.911 | 34.240 | 33.971 | 1973 | 33.971 |
| 1974 | 38.146 | 37.340 | 36.648 | 34.753 | 31.646 | 30.884 | 29.984 | 27.587 | 25.479 | 27.948 | 26.499 | 24.238 | 1974 | 24.238 |
| 1975 | 30.806 | 31.463 | 33.281 | 34.871 | 37.020 | 39.473 | 38.068 | 35.774 | 34.953 | 34.567 | 35.456 | 34.612 | 1975 | 34.612 |
| 1976 | 43.797 | 49.764 | 49.572 | 47.596 | 45.606 | 47.448 | 47.384 | 45.794 | 46.084 | 44.939 | 46.618 | 51.971 | 1976 | 51.971 |
| 1977 | 53.998 | 53.241 | 53.603 | 54.400 | 53.948 | 57.730 | 57.649 | 56.812 | 57.118 | 55.082 | 60.768 | 61.029 | 1977 | 61.029 |
| 1978 | 59.555 | 61.198 | 67.052 | 71.691 | 76.808 | 74.584 | 79.118 | 86.107 | 85.229 | 64.028 | 68.338 | 69.108 | 1978 | 69.108 |
| 1979 | 77.552 | 74.489 | 82.038 | 84.245 | 83.510 | 86.644 | 86.999 | 92.646 | 88.542 | 77.625 | 83.511 | 87.502 | 1979 | 87.502 |
| 1980 | 93.474 | 89.593 | 72.623 | 76.795 | 81.748 | 84.511 | 95.616 | 100.745 | 104.001 | 106.537 | 113.672 | 108.894 | 1980 | 108.894 |
| 1981 | 110.252 | 110.147 | 119.670 | 126.719 | 130.987 | 130.863 | 125.296 | 115.840 | 106.272 | 113.913 | 116.723 | 113.831 | 1981 | 113.831 |
| 1982 | 111.205 | 107.571 | 106.759 | 110.380 | 106.592 | 103.634 | 102.912 | 109.870 | 113.269 | 127.702 | 137.885 | 140.278 | 1982 | 140.278 |
| 1983 | 148.731 | 159.271 | 167.517 | 179.081 | 193.606 | 199.678 | 197.119 | 192.599 | 194.198 | 182.688 | 191.790 | 188.759 | 1983 | 188.759 |
| 1984 | 187.557 | 174.659 | 177.293 | 174.932 | 165.336 | 169.748 | 162.097 | 177.534 | 177.164 | 172.880 | 167.071 | 169.470 | 1984 | 169.470 |
| 1985 | 187.061 | 191.362 | 186.444 | 182.456 | 186.792 | 188.188 | 192.782 | 190.980 | 180.034 | 184.165 | 194.925 | 203.588 | 1985 | 203.588 |
| 1986 | 205.241 | 220.603 | 232.189 | 234.177 | 241.864 | 241.310 | 224.110 | 228.584 | 214.754 | 221.983 | 221.094 | 215.106 | 1986 | 215.106 |
| 1987 | 233.977 | 251.922 | 256.641 | 247.283 | 245.591 | 251.086 | 259.691 | 265.663 | 262.211 | 185.188 | 177.578 | 186.867 | 1987 | 186.867 |
| 1988 | 196.745 | 211.150 | 218.822 | 222.250 | 217.529 | 229.864 | 228.322 | 221.769 | 225.289 | 221.777 | 211.909 | 219.893 | 1988 | 219.893 |
| 1989 | 227.643 | 228.589 | 235.417 | 240.412 | 247.707 | 242.141 | 251.389 | 254.047 | 253.234 | 236.802 | 235.033 | 231.516 | 1989 | 231.516 |
| 1990 | 211.646 | 214.593 | 221.280 | 215.060 | 226.597 | 228.622 | 219.045 | 188.919 | 171.821 | 161.022 | 167.891 | 171.148 | 1990 | 171.148 |
| 1991 | 184.439 | 204.663 | 218.256 | 218.674 | 225.311 | 213.753 | 222.126 | 227.256 | 226.986 | 233.841 | 226.727 | 240.179 | 1991 | 240.179 |
| 1992 | 266.884 | 277.941 | 269.658 | 258.420 | 257.689 | 243.443 | 251.912 | 245.469 | 247.981 | 253.506 | 275.553 | 287.908 | 1992 | 287.908 |
| 1993 | 302.051 | 295.578 | 303.061 | 292.971 | 302.571 | 301.003 | 306.000 | 315.500 | 324.796 | 338.694 | 332.538 | 338.990 | 1993 | 338.990 |
| 1994 | 358.954 | 356.908 | 339.832 | 341.407 | 340.766 | 330.717 | 335.894 | 345.816 | 348.511 | 352.283 | 340.343 | 340.412 | 1994 | 340.412 |
| 1995 | 348.648 | 356.012 | 359.982 | 371.427 | 381.741 | 402.630 | 428.600 | 442.783 | 450.533 | 427.198 | 435.683 | 446.387 | 1995 | 446.387 |
| 1996 | 445.027 | 459.959 | 468.029 | 505.769 | 542.610 | 510.704 | 461.661 | 482.713 | 495.186 | 484.984 | 498.007 | 508.167 | 1996 | 508.167 |
| 1997 | 527.846 | 515.353 | 488.875 | 474.789 | 523.639 | 549.030 | 581.521 | 609.980 | 659.821 | 632.782 | 623.360 | 613.460 | 1997 | 613.460 |
| 1998 | 608.708 | 647.012 | 676.879 | 686.980 | 651.634 | 637.428 | 593.927 | 473.967 | 490.856 | 507.090 | 545.528 | 559.616 | 1998 | 559.616 |
| 1999 | 573.829 | 533.757 | 511.972 | 556.511 | 578.048 | 610.881 | 614.652 | 601.469 | 585.374 | 579.246 | 635.113 | 707.326 | 1999 | 707.326 |
| 2000 | 747.634 | 918.482 | 842.553 | 736.719 | 676.797 | 764.917 | 739.000 | 806.424 | 784.836 | 728.169 | 646.971 | 659.577 | 2000 | 659.577 |

Table B-13

## Long-Term Corporate Bonds: Inflation-Adjusted Total Return Index

from December 1925 to December 1970

| Year | Jan | Feb | Mar | Apr | May | Jun | Jul | Aug | Sep | Oct | Nov | Dec | Yr-end | Index |
|------|-----|-----|-----|-----|-----|-----|-----|-----|-----|-----|-----|-----|--------|-------|
| 1925 | | | | | | | | | | | | 1.000 | 1925 | 1.000 |
| 1926 | 1.007 | 1.016 | 1.030 | 1.030 | 1.040 | 1.049 | 1.065 | 1.076 | 1.076 | 1.082 | 1.084 | 1.090 | 1926 | 1.090 |
| 1927 | 1.104 | 1.121 | 1.136 | 1.143 | 1.133 | 1.127 | 1.149 | 1.165 | 1.176 | 1.175 | 1.186 | 1.196 | 1927 | 1.196 |
| 1928 | 1.202 | 1.222 | 1.227 | 1.226 | 1.209 | 1.216 | 1.215 | 1.222 | 1.216 | 1.229 | 1.227 | 1.242 | 1928 | 1.242 |
| 1929 | 1.250 | 1.256 | 1.250 | 1.257 | 1.255 | 1.245 | 1.235 | 1.233 | 1.239 | 1.249 | 1.249 | 1.280 | 1929 | 1.280 |
| 1930 | 1.293 | 1.307 | 1.333 | 1.336 | 1.352 | 1.375 | 1.402 | 1.430 | 1.436 | 1.453 | 1.463 | 1.471 | 1930 | 1.471 |
| 1931 | 1.523 | 1.556 | 1.581 | 1.602 | 1.641 | 1.668 | 1.680 | 1.686 | 1.691 | 1.640 | 1.628 | 1.596 | 1931 | 1.596 |
| 1932 | 1.621 | 1.605 | 1.670 | 1.652 | 1.694 | 1.705 | 1.712 | 1.809 | 1.873 | 1.901 | 1.925 | 1.971 | 1932 | 1.971 |
| 1933 | 2.111 | 2.033 | 2.058 | 2.044 | 2.159 | 2.177 | 2.150 | 2.148 | 2.145 | 2.153 | 2.100 | 2.165 | 1933 | 2.165 |
| 1934 | 2.209 | 2.225 | 2.266 | 2.296 | 2.310 | 2.341 | 2.352 | 2.357 | 2.308 | 2.349 | 2.385 | 2.415 | 1934 | 2.415 |
| 1935 | 2.430 | 2.446 | 2.463 | 2.466 | 2.489 | 2.523 | 2.563 | 2.553 | 2.540 | 2.551 | 2.556 | 2.571 | 1935 | 2.571 |
| 1936 | 2.592 | 2.619 | 2.653 | 2.660 | 2.671 | 2.666 | 2.657 | 2.655 | 2.667 | 2.680 | 2.709 | 2.712 | 1936 | 2.712 |
| 1937 | 2.699 | 2.680 | 2.631 | 2.636 | 2.635 | 2.642 | 2.640 | 2.630 | 2.612 | 2.642 | 2.678 | 2.702 | 1937 | 2.702 |
| 1938 | 2.751 | 2.780 | 2.755 | 2.780 | 2.796 | 2.823 | 2.835 | 2.836 | 2.867 | 2.904 | 2.921 | 2.950 | 1938 | 2.950 |
| 1939 | 2.970 | 3.004 | 3.018 | 3.044 | 3.059 | 3.070 | 3.068 | 2.948 | 2.935 | 3.019 | 3.043 | 3.082 | 1939 | 3.082 |
| 1940 | 3.104 | 3.088 | 3.111 | 3.082 | 3.068 | 3.098 | 3.112 | 3.122 | 3.143 | 3.158 | 3.178 | 3.156 | 1940 | 3.156 |
| 1941 | 3.158 | 3.160 | 3.138 | 3.133 | 3.126 | 3.089 | 3.094 | 3.077 | 3.037 | 3.014 | 2.960 | 2.955 | 1941 | 2.955 |
| 1942 | 2.919 | 2.892 | 2.874 | 2.858 | 2.834 | 2.838 | 2.832 | 2.824 | 2.824 | 2.798 | 2.783 | 2.774 | 1942 | 2.774 |
| 1943 | 2.788 | 2.784 | 2.746 | 2.728 | 2.720 | 2.738 | 2.765 | 2.781 | 2.771 | 2.758 | 2.757 | 2.765 | 1943 | 2.765 |
| 1944 | 2.776 | 2.791 | 2.804 | 2.798 | 2.788 | 2.789 | 2.782 | 2.781 | 2.787 | 2.792 | 2.805 | 2.836 | 1944 | 2.836 |
| 1945 | 2.858 | 2.876 | 2.882 | 2.881 | 2.857 | 2.840 | 2.831 | 2.832 | 2.852 | 2.861 | 2.860 | 2.887 | 1945 | 2.887 |
| 1946 | 2.924 | 2.945 | 2.933 | 2.905 | 2.894 | 2.869 | 2.706 | 2.624 | 2.587 | 2.543 | 2.477 | 2.485 | 1946 | 2.485 |
| 1947 | 2.487 | 2.492 | 2.455 | 2.460 | 2.472 | 2.454 | 2.437 | 2.395 | 2.309 | 2.286 | 2.250 | 2.227 | 1947 | 2.227 |
| 1948 | 2.207 | 2.234 | 2.266 | 2.243 | 2.229 | 2.195 | 2.157 | 2.160 | 2.165 | 2.179 | 2.213 | 2.258 | 1948 | 2.258 |
| 1949 | 2.269 | 2.304 | 2.299 | 2.301 | 2.313 | 2.329 | 2.369 | 2.371 | 2.366 | 2.395 | 2.397 | 2.375 | 1949 | 2.375 |
| 1950 | 2.394 | 2.403 | 2.398 | 2.392 | 2.380 | 2.372 | 2.366 | 2.355 | 2.330 | 2.315 | 2.318 | 2.293 | 1950 | 2.293 |
| 1951 | 2.261 | 2.225 | 2.163 | 2.159 | 2.147 | 2.130 | 2.171 | 2.195 | 2.169 | 2.127 | 2.103 | 2.107 | 1951 | 2.107 |
| 1952 | 2.149 | 2.144 | 2.161 | 2.152 | 2.156 | 2.154 | 2.141 | 2.152 | 2.150 | 2.156 | 2.179 | 2.162 | 1952 | 2.162 |
| 1953 | 2.150 | 2.153 | 2.140 | 2.084 | 2.073 | 2.088 | 2.119 | 2.096 | 2.146 | 2.190 | 2.182 | 2.222 | 1953 | 2.222 |
| 1954 | 2.244 | 2.291 | 2.303 | 2.301 | 2.283 | 2.294 | 2.304 | 2.311 | 2.326 | 2.341 | 2.344 | 2.354 | 1954 | 2.354 |
| 1955 | 2.331 | 2.316 | 2.337 | 2.337 | 2.333 | 2.340 | 2.321 | 2.318 | 2.327 | 2.345 | 2.335 | 2.356 | 1955 | 2.356 |
| 1956 | 2.383 | 2.390 | 2.352 | 2.322 | 2.322 | 2.304 | 2.266 | 2.221 | 2.221 | 2.185 | 2.157 | 2.134 | 1956 | 2.134 |
| 1957 | 2.174 | 2.186 | 2.192 | 2.170 | 2.148 | 2.067 | 2.034 | 2.030 | 2.047 | 2.052 | 2.108 | 2.252 | 1957 | 2.252 |
| 1958 | 2.261 | 2.257 | 2.231 | 2.262 | 2.269 | 2.258 | 2.221 | 2.152 | 2.131 | 2.154 | 2.174 | 2.164 | 1958 | 2.164 |
| 1959 | 2.156 | 2.185 | 2.167 | 2.128 | 2.101 | 2.100 | 2.114 | 2.102 | 2.077 | 2.104 | 2.132 | 2.112 | 1959 | 2.112 |
| 1960 | 2.137 | 2.162 | 2.203 | 2.186 | 2.181 | 2.207 | 2.264 | 2.290 | 2.273 | 2.265 | 2.246 | 2.270 | 1960 | 2.270 |
| 1961 | 2.303 | 2.352 | 2.345 | 2.318 | 2.329 | 2.308 | 2.307 | 2.305 | 2.333 | 2.363 | 2.369 | 2.363 | 1961 | 2.363 |
| 1962 | 2.382 | 2.389 | 2.420 | 2.449 | 2.449 | 2.442 | 2.433 | 2.468 | 2.476 | 2.496 | 2.511 | 2.520 | 1962 | 2.520 |
| 1963 | 2.532 | 2.535 | 2.539 | 2.526 | 2.538 | 2.538 | 2.534 | 2.543 | 2.537 | 2.547 | 2.548 | 2.534 | 1963 | 2.534 |
| 1964 | 2.553 | 2.569 | 2.551 | 2.558 | 2.573 | 2.580 | 2.587 | 2.600 | 2.600 | 2.610 | 2.603 | 2.623 | 1964 | 2.623 |
| 1965 | 2.645 | 2.647 | 2.647 | 2.644 | 2.637 | 2.623 | 2.626 | 2.630 | 2.620 | 2.629 | 2.609 | 2.562 | 1965 | 2.562 |
| 1966 | 2.568 | 2.523 | 2.500 | 2.493 | 2.484 | 2.484 | 2.452 | 2.376 | 2.390 | 2.442 | 2.437 | 2.484 | 1966 | 2.484 |
| 1967 | 2.595 | 2.541 | 2.565 | 2.542 | 2.470 | 2.408 | 2.405 | 2.396 | 2.414 | 2.339 | 2.269 | 2.291 | 1967 | 2.291 |
| 1968 | 2.364 | 2.366 | 2.308 | 2.313 | 2.313 | 2.328 | 2.396 | 2.438 | 2.418 | 2.366 | 2.304 | 2.244 | 1968 | 2.244 |
| 1969 | 2.269 | 2.224 | 2.161 | 2.220 | 2.163 | 2.157 | 2.148 | 2.134 | 2.073 | 2.092 | 1.982 | 1.944 | 1969 | 1.944 |
| 1970 | 1.964 | 2.032 | 2.012 | 1.950 | 1.910 | 1.900 | 1.999 | 2.016 | 2.033 | 2.004 | 2.113 | 2.181 | 1970 | 2.181 |

## Table B-13 (continued)

## Long-Term Corporate Bonds: Inflation-Adjusted Total Return Index

from January 1971 to December 2000

| Year | Jan | Feb | Mar | Apr | May | Jun | Jul | Aug | Sep | Oct | Nov | Dec | Yr-end | Index |
|------|-----|-----|-----|-----|-----|-----|-----|-----|-----|-----|-----|-----|--------|-------|
| 1971 | 2.295 | 2.207 | 2.257 | 2.196 | 2.150 | 2.161 | 2.150 | 2.263 | 2.238 | 2.298 | 2.301 | 2.343 | 1971 | 2.343 |
| 1972 | 2.333 | 2.346 | 2.348 | 2.351 | 2.381 | 2.360 | 2.357 | 2.370 | 2.368 | 2.385 | 2.438 | 2.430 | 1972 | 2.430 |
| 1973 | 2.409 | 2.398 | 2.386 | 2.384 | 2.360 | 2.331 | 2.215 | 2.253 | 2.327 | 2.293 | 2.294 | 2.259 | 1973 | 2.259 |
| 1974 | 2.227 | 2.201 | 2.110 | 2.026 | 2.025 | 1.949 | 1.893 | 1.819 | 1.829 | 1.974 | 1.980 | 1.951 | 1974 | 1.951 |
| 1975 | 2.058 | 2.072 | 2.013 | 1.993 | 2.005 | 2.049 | 2.022 | 1.980 | 1.946 | 2.041 | 2.010 | 2.091 | 1975 | 2.091 |
| 1976 | 2.125 | 2.133 | 2.163 | 2.151 | 2.116 | 2.136 | 2.156 | 2.195 | 2.223 | 2.229 | 2.294 | 2.366 | 1976 | 2.366 |
| 1977 | 2.282 | 2.254 | 2.261 | 2.266 | 2.277 | 2.302 | 2.291 | 2.313 | 2.299 | 2.284 | 2.287 | 2.254 | 1977 | 2.254 |
| 1978 | 2.222 | 2.218 | 2.212 | 2.188 | 2.143 | 2.126 | 2.132 | 2.176 | 2.150 | 2.089 | 2.105 | 2.066 | 1978 | 2.066 |
| 1979 | 2.086 | 2.035 | 2.037 | 2.004 | 2.024 | 2.060 | 2.027 | 2.008 | 1.952 | 1.763 | 1.785 | 1.747 | 1979 | 1.747 |
| 1980 | 1.611 | 1.484 | 1.454 | 1.635 | 1.710 | 1.749 | 1.673 | 1.588 | 1.536 | 1.499 | 1.488 | 1.512 | 1980 | 1.512 |
| 1981 | 1.480 | 1.425 | 1.459 | 1.338 | 1.407 | 1.398 | 1.331 | 1.275 | 1.237 | 1.299 | 1.459 | 1.371 | 1981 | 1.371 |
| 1982 | 1.348 | 1.386 | 1.430 | 1.472 | 1.493 | 1.406 | 1.474 | 1.594 | 1.690 | 1.814 | 1.853 | 1.881 | 1982 | 1.881 |
| 1983 | 1.859 | 1.938 | 1.950 | 2.043 | 1.966 | 1.950 | 1.854 | 1.857 | 1.921 | 1.911 | 1.935 | 1.926 | 1983 | 1.926 |
| 1984 | 1.967 | 1.924 | 1.874 | 1.852 | 1.757 | 1.786 | 1.885 | 1.935 | 1.986 | 2.094 | 2.139 | 2.165 | 1984 | 2.165 |
| 1985 | 2.231 | 2.139 | 2.168 | 2.223 | 2.396 | 2.408 | 2.376 | 2.432 | 2.442 | 2.514 | 2.599 | 2.714 | 1985 | 2.714 |
| 1986 | 2.718 | 2.930 | 3.019 | 3.030 | 2.971 | 3.021 | 3.030 | 3.108 | 3.057 | 3.112 | 3.182 | 3.216 | 1986 | 3.216 |
| 1987 | 3.266 | 3.272 | 3.229 | 3.051 | 3.026 | 3.060 | 3.017 | 2.978 | 2.838 | 2.975 | 3.007 | 3.072 | 1987 | 3.072 |
| 1988 | 3.222 | 3.258 | 3.184 | 3.120 | 3.092 | 3.195 | 3.146 | 3.150 | 3.231 | 3.308 | 3.250 | 3.257 | 1988 | 3.257 |
| 1989 | 3.306 | 3.250 | 3.252 | 3.300 | 3.406 | 3.532 | 3.586 | 3.522 | 3.524 | 3.604 | 3.621 | 3.617 | 1989 | 3.617 |
| 1990 | 3.512 | 3.491 | 3.469 | 3.397 | 3.520 | 3.576 | 3.599 | 3.462 | 3.465 | 3.489 | 3.581 | 3.641 | 1990 | 3.641 |
| 1991 | 3.673 | 3.712 | 3.747 | 3.793 | 3.796 | 3.778 | 3.836 | 3.930 | 4.019 | 4.030 | 4.061 | 4.235 | 1991 | 4.235 |
| 1992 | 4.156 | 4.180 | 4.129 | 4.130 | 4.228 | 4.279 | 4.401 | 4.428 | 4.460 | 4.375 | 4.399 | 4.502 | 1992 | 4.502 |
| 1993 | 4.592 | 4.693 | 4.688 | 4.700 | 4.703 | 4.834 | 4.882 | 5.008 | 5.019 | 5.024 | 4.926 | 4.959 | 1993 | 4.959 |
| 1994 | 5.046 | 4.885 | 4.682 | 4.630 | 4.598 | 4.545 | 4.673 | 4.640 | 4.505 | 4.479 | 4.481 | 4.552 | 1994 | 4.552 |
| 1995 | 4.650 | 4.765 | 4.794 | 4.862 | 5.159 | 5.189 | 5.137 | 5.233 | 5.303 | 5.383 | 5.517 | 5.647 | 1995 | 5.647 |
| 1996 | 5.622 | 5.395 | 5.297 | 5.192 | 5.185 | 5.271 | 5.266 | 5.219 | 5.337 | 5.513 | 5.647 | 5.542 | 1996 | 5.542 |
| 1997 | 5.509 | 5.507 | 5.372 | 5.464 | 5.537 | 5.634 | 5.924 | 5.771 | 5.887 | 5.984 | 6.048 | 6.155 | 1997 | 6.155 |
| 1998 | 6.227 | 6.212 | 6.224 | 6.245 | 6.338 | 6.403 | 6.359 | 6.408 | 6.664 | 6.522 | 6.698 | 6.709 | 1998 | 6.709 |
| 1999 | 6.774 | 6.495 | 6.477 | 6.415 | 6.302 | 6.201 | 6.113 | 6.082 | 6.109 | 6.127 | 6.109 | 6.047 | 1999 | 6.047 |
| 2000 | 6.020 | 6.039 | 6.092 | 6.018 | 5.918 | 6.075 | 6.174 | 6.250 | 6.246 | 6.263 | 6.424 | 6.601 | 2000 | 6.601 |

# Table B-14

## Long-Term Government Bonds: Inflation-Adjusted Total Return Index

from December 1925 to December 1970

| Year | Jan | Feb | Mar | Apr | May | Jun | Jul | Aug | Sep | Oct | Nov | Dec | Yr-end | Index |
|------|-----|-----|-----|-----|-----|-----|-----|-----|-----|-----|-----|-----|--------|-------|
| 1925 | | | | | | | | | | | | 1.000 | 1925 | 1.000 |
| 1926 | 1.014 | 1.024 | 1.034 | 1.032 | 1.039 | 1.051 | 1.062 | 1.068 | 1.066 | 1.072 | 1.086 | 1.094 | 1926 | 1.094 |
| 1927 | 1.111 | 1.129 | 1.164 | 1.164 | 1.167 | 1.148 | 1.176 | 1.192 | 1.187 | 1.192 | 1.206 | 1.217 | 1927 | 1.217 |
| 1928 | 1.215 | 1.234 | 1.240 | 1.237 | 1.220 | 1.235 | 1.208 | 1.215 | 1.201 | 1.222 | 1.225 | 1.230 | 1928 | 1.230 |
| 1929 | 1.221 | 1.205 | 1.192 | 1.230 | 1.203 | 1.211 | 1.199 | 1.191 | 1.196 | 1.242 | 1.274 | 1.270 | 1929 | 1.270 |
| 1930 | 1.267 | 1.289 | 1.307 | 1.297 | 1.323 | 1.338 | 1.362 | 1.372 | 1.373 | 1.387 | 1.404 | 1.414 | 1930 | 1.414 |
| 1931 | 1.418 | 1.451 | 1.476 | 1.498 | 1.536 | 1.554 | 1.551 | 1.556 | 1.519 | 1.479 | 1.500 | 1.480 | 1931 | 1.480 |
| 1932 | 1.516 | 1.601 | 1.606 | 1.715 | 1.708 | 1.731 | 1.815 | 1.838 | 1.857 | 1.868 | 1.884 | 1.928 | 1932 | 1.928 |
| 1933 | 1.987 | 1.966 | 2.001 | 2.000 | 2.055 | 2.043 | 1.983 | 1.971 | 1.976 | 1.958 | 1.929 | 1.917 | 1933 | 1.917 |
| 1934 | 1.956 | 1.957 | 1.996 | 2.026 | 2.047 | 2.056 | 2.064 | 2.034 | 1.975 | 2.026 | 2.039 | 2.067 | 1934 | 2.067 |
| 1935 | 2.073 | 2.077 | 2.091 | 2.087 | 2.085 | 2.110 | 2.130 | 2.101 | 2.093 | 2.105 | 2.097 | 2.107 | 1935 | 2.107 |
| 1936 | 2.119 | 2.146 | 2.180 | 2.187 | 2.196 | 2.179 | 2.182 | 2.190 | 2.178 | 2.185 | 2.230 | 2.238 | 1936 | 2.238 |
| 1937 | 2.219 | 2.233 | 2.126 | 2.125 | 2.126 | 2.117 | 2.137 | 2.109 | 2.100 | 2.118 | 2.153 | 2.176 | 1937 | 2.176 |
| 1938 | 2.219 | 2.252 | 2.244 | 2.280 | 2.301 | 2.302 | 2.306 | 2.312 | 2.317 | 2.348 | 2.349 | 2.362 | 1938 | 2.362 |
| 1939 | 2.387 | 2.418 | 2.454 | 2.489 | 2.531 | 2.524 | 2.553 | 2.502 | 2.321 | 2.427 | 2.467 | 2.514 | 1939 | 2.514 |
| 1940 | 2.516 | 2.505 | 2.555 | 2.546 | 2.464 | 2.522 | 2.541 | 2.554 | 2.576 | 2.584 | 2.637 | 2.642 | 1940 | 2.642 |
| 1941 | 2.589 | 2.594 | 2.607 | 2.616 | 2.605 | 2.574 | 2.568 | 2.549 | 2.501 | 2.509 | 2.480 | 2.430 | 1941 | 2.430 |
| 1942 | 2.416 | 2.398 | 2.390 | 2.368 | 2.361 | 2.357 | 2.352 | 2.346 | 2.342 | 2.324 | 2.302 | 2.295 | 1942 | 2.295 |
| 1943 | 2.303 | 2.297 | 2.264 | 2.248 | 2.242 | 2.251 | 2.268 | 2.281 | 2.275 | 2.267 | 2.272 | 2.271 | 1943 | 2.271 |
| 1944 | 2.281 | 2.292 | 2.297 | 2.287 | 2.285 | 2.282 | 2.277 | 2.275 | 2.278 | 2.281 | 2.286 | 2.287 | 1944 | 2.287 |
| 1945 | 2.316 | 2.338 | 2.343 | 2.376 | 2.372 | 2.390 | 2.365 | 2.371 | 2.392 | 2.417 | 2.439 | 2.477 | 1945 | 2.477 |
| 1946 | 2.483 | 2.500 | 2.485 | 2.438 | 2.421 | 2.412 | 2.269 | 2.195 | 2.168 | 2.142 | 2.080 | 2.094 | 1946 | 2.094 |
| 1947 | 2.093 | 2.100 | 2.060 | 2.052 | 2.065 | 2.052 | 2.046 | 2.041 | 1.985 | 1.978 | 1.932 | 1.871 | 1947 | 1.871 |
| 1948 | 1.853 | 1.878 | 1.890 | 1.871 | 1.885 | 1.856 | 1.829 | 1.822 | 1.824 | 1.833 | 1.860 | 1.883 | 1948 | 1.883 |
| 1949 | 1.901 | 1.932 | 1.941 | 1.940 | 1.947 | 1.977 | 1.997 | 2.014 | 2.003 | 2.018 | 2.020 | 2.042 | 1949 | 2.042 |
| 1950 | 2.038 | 2.048 | 2.041 | 2.044 | 2.042 | 2.026 | 2.017 | 2.003 | 1.975 | 1.955 | 1.954 | 1.931 | 1950 | 1.931 |
| 1951 | 1.911 | 1.875 | 1.838 | 1.825 | 1.805 | 1.796 | 1.819 | 1.837 | 1.810 | 1.803 | 1.769 | 1.752 | 1951 | 1.752 |
| 1952 | 1.757 | 1.771 | 1.790 | 1.814 | 1.806 | 1.802 | 1.784 | 1.770 | 1.749 | 1.773 | 1.770 | 1.757 | 1952 | 1.757 |
| 1953 | 1.763 | 1.757 | 1.737 | 1.717 | 1.687 | 1.718 | 1.721 | 1.715 | 1.764 | 1.773 | 1.771 | 1.809 | 1953 | 1.809 |
| 1954 | 1.821 | 1.867 | 1.880 | 1.905 | 1.881 | 1.909 | 1.935 | 1.930 | 1.933 | 1.939 | 1.932 | 1.949 | 1954 | 1.949 |
| 1955 | 1.902 | 1.887 | 1.904 | 1.904 | 1.918 | 1.903 | 1.877 | 1.882 | 1.889 | 1.916 | 1.905 | 1.917 | 1955 | 1.917 |
| 1956 | 1.935 | 1.935 | 1.904 | 1.880 | 1.913 | 1.906 | 1.853 | 1.820 | 1.827 | 1.806 | 1.796 | 1.759 | 1956 | 1.759 |
| 1957 | 1.818 | 1.816 | 1.807 | 1.761 | 1.753 | 1.711 | 1.696 | 1.694 | 1.705 | 1.696 | 1.781 | 1.835 | 1957 | 1.835 |
| 1958 | 1.809 | 1.825 | 1.831 | 1.861 | 1.861 | 1.829 | 1.776 | 1.701 | 1.681 | 1.704 | 1.723 | 1.694 | 1958 | 1.694 |
| 1959 | 1.678 | 1.700 | 1.702 | 1.681 | 1.678 | 1.672 | 1.678 | 1.673 | 1.658 | 1.677 | 1.657 | 1.631 | 1959 | 1.631 |
| 1960 | 1.651 | 1.683 | 1.730 | 1.691 | 1.717 | 1.743 | 1.807 | 1.794 | 1.806 | 1.793 | 1.779 | 1.829 | 1960 | 1.829 |
| 1961 | 1.809 | 1.845 | 1.838 | 1.859 | 1.851 | 1.835 | 1.833 | 1.828 | 1.848 | 1.861 | 1.857 | 1.834 | 1961 | 1.834 |
| 1962 | 1.831 | 1.846 | 1.889 | 1.900 | 1.909 | 1.894 | 1.870 | 1.905 | 1.906 | 1.924 | 1.928 | 1.937 | 1962 | 1.937 |
| 1963 | 1.934 | 1.934 | 1.933 | 1.931 | 1.935 | 1.931 | 1.928 | 1.932 | 1.933 | 1.926 | 1.934 | 1.928 | 1963 | 1.928 |
| 1964 | 1.924 | 1.924 | 1.929 | 1.936 | 1.945 | 1.954 | 1.952 | 1.958 | 1.963 | 1.970 | 1.969 | 1.972 | 1964 | 1.972 |
| 1965 | 1.980 | 1.983 | 1.992 | 1.993 | 1.992 | 1.991 | 1.993 | 1.995 | 1.984 | 1.987 | 1.970 | 1.949 | 1965 | 1.949 |
| 1966 | 1.929 | 1.869 | 1.918 | 1.898 | 1.885 | 1.876 | 1.864 | 1.816 | 1.872 | 1.907 | 1.879 | 1.955 | 1966 | 1.955 |
| 1967 | 1.985 | 1.939 | 1.973 | 1.912 | 1.899 | 1.834 | 1.837 | 1.816 | 1.812 | 1.734 | 1.695 | 1.723 | 1967 | 1.723 |
| 1968 | 1.772 | 1.761 | 1.716 | 1.749 | 1.752 | 1.782 | 1.824 | 1.819 | 1.795 | 1.761 | 1.707 | 1.641 | 1968 | 1.641 |
| 1969 | 1.602 | 1.603 | 1.591 | 1.649 | 1.563 | 1.587 | 1.592 | 1.574 | 1.484 | 1.532 | 1.487 | 1.468 | 1969 | 1.468 |
| 1970 | 1.460 | 1.537 | 1.519 | 1.447 | 1.373 | 1.433 | 1.473 | 1.468 | 1.494 | 1.470 | 1.581 | 1.560 | 1970 | 1.560 |

## Table B-14 (continued)

## Long-Term Government Bonds: Inflation-Adjusted Total Return Index

from January 1971 to December 2000

| Year | Jan | Feb | Mar | Apr | May | Jun | Jul | Aug | Sep | Oct | Nov | Dec | Yr-end | Index |
|------|-----|-----|-----|-----|-----|-----|-----|-----|-----|-----|-----|-----|--------|-------|
| 1971 | 1.637 | 1.608 | 1.687 | 1.634 | 1.625 | 1.590 | 1.590 | 1.661 | 1.694 | 1.719 | 1.708 | 1.709 | 1971 | 1.709 |
| 1972 | 1.697 | 1.703 | 1.687 | 1.687 | 1.727 | 1.712 | 1.742 | 1.744 | 1.723 | 1.758 | 1.793 | 1.746 | 1972 | 1.746 |
| 1973 | 1.685 | 1.676 | 1.674 | 1.670 | 1.642 | 1.628 | 1.554 | 1.586 | 1.631 | 1.653 | 1.611 | 1.587 | 1973 | 1.587 |
| 1974 | 1.561 | 1.537 | 1.476 | 1.430 | 1.432 | 1.425 | 1.410 | 1.360 | 1.377 | 1.432 | 1.462 | 1.476 | 1974 | 1.476 |
| 1975 | 1.503 | 1.512 | 1.466 | 1.432 | 1.456 | 1.486 | 1.458 | 1.444 | 1.422 | 1.481 | 1.456 | 1.506 | 1975 | 1.506 |
| 1976 | 1.516 | 1.522 | 1.544 | 1.540 | 1.507 | 1.530 | 1.533 | 1.558 | 1.574 | 1.581 | 1.630 | 1.678 | 1976 | 1.678 |
| 1977 | 1.604 | 1.580 | 1.584 | 1.583 | 1.594 | 1.610 | 1.591 | 1.617 | 1.606 | 1.587 | 1.594 | 1.561 | 1977 | 1.561 |
| 1978 | 1.540 | 1.530 | 1.516 | 1.502 | 1.479 | 1.455 | 1.465 | 1.489 | 1.463 | 1.422 | 1.441 | 1.415 | 1978 | 1.415 |
| 1979 | 1.429 | 1.394 | 1.398 | 1.367 | 1.385 | 1.415 | 1.385 | 1.367 | 1.336 | 1.213 | 1.239 | 1.233 | 1979 | 1.233 |
| 1980 | 1.126 | 1.059 | 1.011 | 1.152 | 1.188 | 1.217 | 1.159 | 1.101 | 1.063 | 1.026 | 1.027 | 1.054 | 1980 | 1.054 |
| 1981 | 1.033 | 0.978 | 1.009 | 0.950 | 1.001 | 0.975 | 0.930 | 0.887 | 0.866 | 0.935 | 1.064 | 0.985 | 1981 | 0.985 |
| 1982 | 0.986 | 1.001 | 1.025 | 1.059 | 1.052 | 1.017 | 1.062 | 1.142 | 1.211 | 1.284 | 1.286 | 1.332 | 1982 | 1.332 |
| 1983 | 1.287 | 1.350 | 1.337 | 1.374 | 1.313 | 1.314 | 1.245 | 1.244 | 1.300 | 1.279 | 1.301 | 1.291 | 1983 | 1.291 |
| 1984 | 1.315 | 1.286 | 1.263 | 1.244 | 1.176 | 1.190 | 1.268 | 1.297 | 1.335 | 1.406 | 1.422 | 1.434 | 1984 | 1.434 |
| 1985 | 1.484 | 1.405 | 1.442 | 1.471 | 1.596 | 1.614 | 1.582 | 1.620 | 1.612 | 1.661 | 1.722 | 1.810 | 1985 | 1.810 |
| 1986 | 1.800 | 2.012 | 2.177 | 2.164 | 2.048 | 2.163 | 2.139 | 2.242 | 2.120 | 2.179 | 2.235 | 2.229 | 1986 | 2.229 |
| 1987 | 2.251 | 2.288 | 2.227 | 2.110 | 2.082 | 2.094 | 2.052 | 2.007 | 1.924 | 2.038 | 2.043 | 2.077 | 1987 | 2.077 |
| 1988 | 2.210 | 2.216 | 2.138 | 2.093 | 2.065 | 2.132 | 2.087 | 2.090 | 2.148 | 2.207 | 2.162 | 2.182 | 1988 | 2.182 |
| 1989 | 2.215 | 2.166 | 2.180 | 2.201 | 2.276 | 2.395 | 2.446 | 2.379 | 2.376 | 2.455 | 2.468 | 2.462 | 1989 | 2.462 |
| 1990 | 2.354 | 2.337 | 2.314 | 2.264 | 2.352 | 2.394 | 2.410 | 2.288 | 2.295 | 2.331 | 2.419 | 2.464 | 1990 | 2.464 |
| 1991 | 2.481 | 2.485 | 2.491 | 2.522 | 2.515 | 2.492 | 2.527 | 2.606 | 2.673 | 2.684 | 2.698 | 2.852 | 1991 | 2.852 |
| 1992 | 2.756 | 2.760 | 2.720 | 2.721 | 2.783 | 2.828 | 2.935 | 2.946 | 2.992 | 2.922 | 2.921 | 2.995 | 1992 | 2.995 |
| 1993 | 3.064 | 3.161 | 3.157 | 3.171 | 3.181 | 3.319 | 3.383 | 3.520 | 3.515 | 3.534 | 3.440 | 3.447 | 1993 | 3.447 |
| 1994 | 3.526 | 3.356 | 3.212 | 3.160 | 3.132 | 3.090 | 3.193 | 3.153 | 3.041 | 3.031 | 3.047 | 3.096 | 1994 | 3.096 |
| 1995 | 3.168 | 3.246 | 3.265 | 3.309 | 3.563 | 3.606 | 3.545 | 3.620 | 3.676 | 3.771 | 3.868 | 3.976 | 1995 | 3.976 |
| 1996 | 3.948 | 3.746 | 3.648 | 3.574 | 3.548 | 3.617 | 3.617 | 3.560 | 3.651 | 3.787 | 3.912 | 3.812 | 1996 | 3.812 |
| 1997 | 3.770 | 3.760 | 3.656 | 3.745 | 3.783 | 3.852 | 4.088 | 3.951 | 4.066 | 4.194 | 4.259 | 4.342 | 1997 | 4.342 |
| 1998 | 4.421 | 4.381 | 4.384 | 4.387 | 4.459 | 4.555 | 4.532 | 4.736 | 4.917 | 4.798 | 4.844 | 4.832 | 1998 | 4.832 |
| 1999 | 4.878 | 4.619 | 4.602 | 4.578 | 4.493 | 4.458 | 4.411 | 4.377 | 4.393 | 4.380 | 4.351 | 4.284 | 1999 | 4.284 |
| 2000 | 4.371 | 4.460 | 4.586 | 4.548 | 4.521 | 4.604 | 4.675 | 4.782 | 4.683 | 4.762 | 4.911 | 5.033 | 2000 | 5.033 |

## Table B-15

**Intermediate-Term Government Bonds: Inflation-Adjusted Total Return Index**

from December 1925 to December 1970

| Year | Jan | Feb | Mar | Apr | May | Jun | Jul | Aug | Sep | Oct | Nov | Dec | Yr-end | Index |
|------|-----|-----|-----|-----|-----|-----|-----|-----|-----|-----|-----|-----|--------|-------|
| 1925 | | | | | | | | | | | | 1.000 | 1925 | 1.000 |
| 1926 | 1.007 | 1.014 | 1.024 | 1.023 | 1.030 | 1.040 | 1.052 | 1.059 | 1.058 | 1.060 | 1.060 | 1.070 | 1926 | 1.070 |
| 1927 | 1.084 | 1.096 | 1.107 | 1.109 | 1.103 | 1.095 | 1.121 | 1.134 | 1.134 | 1.124 | 1.135 | 1.142 | 1927 | 1.142 |
| 1928 | 1.149 | 1.160 | 1.161 | 1.159 | 1.151 | 1.162 | 1.152 | 1.155 | 1.150 | 1.155 | 1.160 | 1.164 | 1928 | 1.164 |
| 1929 | 1.163 | 1.163 | 1.168 | 1.183 | 1.169 | 1.176 | 1.173 | 1.174 | 1.175 | 1.195 | 1.219 | 1.231 | 1929 | 1.231 |
| 1930 | 1.231 | 1.247 | 1.275 | 1.258 | 1.274 | 1.299 | 1.325 | 1.336 | 1.336 | 1.354 | 1.375 | 1.398 | 1930 | 1.398 |
| 1931 | 1.409 | 1.444 | 1.461 | 1.482 | 1.516 | 1.500 | 1.506 | 1.512 | 1.501 | 1.496 | 1.520 | 1.509 | 1931 | 1.509 |
| 1932 | 1.536 | 1.578 | 1.598 | 1.641 | 1.650 | 1.680 | 1.700 | 1.742 | 1.756 | 1.777 | 1.791 | 1.831 | 1932 | 1.831 |
| 1933 | 1.857 | 1.886 | 1.920 | 1.936 | 1.969 | 1.950 | 1.894 | 1.888 | 1.893 | 1.889 | 1.894 | 1.855 | 1933 | 1.855 |
| 1934 | 1.870 | 1.865 | 1.901 | 1.940 | 1.958 | 1.971 | 1.966 | 1.944 | 1.888 | 1.939 | 1.952 | 1.982 | 1934 | 1.982 |
| 1935 | 1.975 | 1.981 | 2.011 | 2.013 | 2.015 | 2.043 | 2.061 | 2.046 | 2.025 | 2.047 | 2.040 | 2.059 | 1935 | 2.059 |
| 1936 | 2.058 | 2.083 | 2.099 | 2.104 | 2.112 | 2.094 | 2.089 | 2.084 | 2.082 | 2.092 | 2.109 | 2.097 | 1936 | 2.097 |
| 1937 | 2.075 | 2.072 | 2.023 | 2.023 | 2.030 | 2.023 | 2.025 | 2.012 | 2.010 | 2.025 | 2.048 | 2.065 | 1937 | 2.065 |
| 1938 | 2.112 | 2.143 | 2.140 | 2.179 | 2.195 | 2.211 | 2.208 | 2.217 | 2.214 | 2.245 | 2.250 | 2.257 | 1938 | 2.257 |
| 1939 | 2.274 | 2.304 | 2.328 | 2.342 | 2.365 | 2.365 | 2.374 | 2.340 | 2.235 | 2.316 | 2.334 | 2.370 | 1939 | 2.370 |
| 1940 | 2.372 | 2.364 | 2.390 | 2.391 | 2.334 | 2.372 | 2.378 | 2.394 | 2.400 | 2.408 | 2.422 | 2.417 | 1940 | 2.417 |
| 1941 | 2.417 | 2.406 | 2.411 | 2.397 | 2.383 | 2.352 | 2.342 | 2.323 | 2.282 | 2.262 | 2.222 | 2.214 | 1941 | 2.214 |
| 1942 | 2.202 | 2.187 | 2.164 | 2.156 | 2.137 | 2.135 | 2.126 | 2.117 | 2.108 | 2.090 | 2.081 | 2.065 | 1942 | 2.065 |
| 1943 | 2.073 | 2.072 | 2.044 | 2.025 | 2.021 | 2.032 | 2.052 | 2.060 | 2.055 | 2.051 | 2.058 | 2.058 | 1943 | 2.058 |
| 1944 | 2.064 | 2.071 | 2.075 | 2.069 | 2.062 | 2.060 | 2.054 | 2.051 | 2.053 | 2.056 | 2.057 | 2.052 | 1944 | 2.052 |
| 1945 | 2.062 | 2.074 | 2.075 | 2.074 | 2.061 | 2.046 | 2.042 | 2.045 | 2.056 | 2.060 | 2.054 | 2.051 | 1945 | 2.051 |
| 1946 | 2.059 | 2.077 | 2.054 | 2.038 | 2.028 | 2.013 | 1.899 | 1.859 | 1.836 | 1.805 | 1.761 | 1.753 | 1946 | 1.753 |
| 1947 | 1.757 | 1.761 | 1.728 | 1.725 | 1.732 | 1.720 | 1.706 | 1.692 | 1.653 | 1.649 | 1.641 | 1.623 | 1947 | 1.623 |
| 1948 | 1.607 | 1.624 | 1.631 | 1.611 | 1.609 | 1.596 | 1.576 | 1.569 | 1.571 | 1.579 | 1.593 | 1.609 | 1948 | 1.609 |
| 1949 | 1.616 | 1.636 | 1.636 | 1.636 | 1.642 | 1.648 | 1.663 | 1.663 | 1.657 | 1.668 | 1.666 | 1.677 | 1949 | 1.677 |
| 1950 | 1.683 | 1.689 | 1.682 | 1.681 | 1.677 | 1.669 | 1.656 | 1.641 | 1.629 | 1.620 | 1.617 | 1.596 | 1950 | 1.596 |
| 1951 | 1.575 | 1.557 | 1.532 | 1.538 | 1.526 | 1.536 | 1.543 | 1.548 | 1.529 | 1.524 | 1.521 | 1.513 | 1951 | 1.513 |
| 1952 | 1.519 | 1.525 | 1.536 | 1.538 | 1.539 | 1.530 | 1.513 | 1.508 | 1.512 | 1.520 | 1.520 | 1.524 | 1952 | 1.524 |
| 1953 | 1.528 | 1.536 | 1.530 | 1.513 | 1.492 | 1.509 | 1.514 | 1.509 | 1.536 | 1.538 | 1.546 | 1.564 | 1953 | 1.564 |
| 1954 | 1.570 | 1.588 | 1.594 | 1.605 | 1.587 | 1.605 | 1.604 | 1.608 | 1.609 | 1.611 | 1.609 | 1.614 | 1954 | 1.614 |
| 1955 | 1.609 | 1.600 | 1.604 | 1.605 | 1.605 | 1.599 | 1.582 | 1.587 | 1.594 | 1.606 | 1.595 | 1.597 | 1955 | 1.597 |
| 1956 | 1.616 | 1.617 | 1.599 | 1.596 | 1.606 | 1.597 | 1.570 | 1.556 | 1.568 | 1.556 | 1.548 | 1.547 | 1956 | 1.547 |
| 1957 | 1.581 | 1.574 | 1.573 | 1.551 | 1.545 | 1.519 | 1.510 | 1.525 | 1.523 | 1.530 | 1.585 | 1.619 | 1957 | 1.619 |
| 1958 | 1.615 | 1.635 | 1.632 | 1.637 | 1.647 | 1.634 | 1.617 | 1.562 | 1.559 | 1.559 | 1.578 | 1.570 | 1958 | 1.570 |
| 1959 | 1.566 | 1.585 | 1.579 | 1.569 | 1.567 | 1.548 | 1.550 | 1.539 | 1.537 | 1.558 | 1.544 | 1.541 | 1959 | 1.541 |
| 1960 | 1.567 | 1.576 | 1.622 | 1.602 | 1.608 | 1.639 | 1.682 | 1.682 | 1.685 | 1.680 | 1.662 | 1.697 | 1960 | 1.697 |
| 1961 | 1.687 | 1.702 | 1.709 | 1.718 | 1.713 | 1.707 | 1.700 | 1.705 | 1.715 | 1.717 | 1.714 | 1.717 | 1961 | 1.717 |
| 1962 | 1.709 | 1.732 | 1.743 | 1.744 | 1.752 | 1.748 | 1.742 | 1.763 | 1.757 | 1.768 | 1.779 | 1.791 | 1962 | 1.791 |
| 1963 | 1.784 | 1.785 | 1.788 | 1.793 | 1.795 | 1.790 | 1.783 | 1.786 | 1.789 | 1.789 | 1.794 | 1.790 | 1963 | 1.790 |
| 1964 | 1.794 | 1.799 | 1.800 | 1.804 | 1.818 | 1.821 | 1.822 | 1.829 | 1.833 | 1.837 | 1.832 | 1.841 | 1964 | 1.841 |
| 1965 | 1.849 | 1.852 | 1.858 | 1.857 | 1.859 | 1.859 | 1.860 | 1.867 | 1.863 | 1.861 | 1.858 | 1.825 | 1965 | 1.825 |
| 1966 | 1.825 | 1.799 | 1.827 | 1.816 | 1.816 | 1.806 | 1.796 | 1.764 | 1.799 | 1.805 | 1.810 | 1.848 | 1966 | 1.848 |
| 1967 | 1.870 | 1.866 | 1.896 | 1.875 | 1.878 | 1.830 | 1.845 | 1.833 | 1.831 | 1.816 | 1.816 | 1.812 | 1967 | 1.812 |
| 1968 | 1.831 | 1.833 | 1.819 | 1.811 | 1.817 | 1.837 | 1.860 | 1.859 | 1.864 | 1.855 | 1.846 | 1.808 | 1968 | 1.808 |
| 1969 | 1.819 | 1.810 | 1.812 | 1.815 | 1.795 | 1.768 | 1.775 | 1.764 | 1.703 | 1.753 | 1.736 | 1.692 | 1969 | 1.692 |
| 1970 | 1.691 | 1.756 | 1.762 | 1.715 | 1.726 | 1.728 | 1.748 | 1.765 | 1.791 | 1.799 | 1.873 | 1.874 | 1970 | 1.874 |

## Table B-15 (continued)

## Intermediate-Term Government Bonds: Inflation-Adjusted Total Return Index

from January 1971 to December 2000

| Year | Jan | Feb | Mar | Apr | May | Jun | Jul | Aug | Sep | Oct | Nov | Dec | Yr-end | Index |
|------|-----|-----|-----|-----|-----|-----|-----|-----|-----|-----|-----|-----|--------|-------|
| 1971 | 1.904 | 1.943 | 1.973 | 1.902 | 1.895 | 1.848 | 1.849 | 1.909 | 1.912 | 1.951 | 1.958 | 1.971 | 1971 | 1.971 |
| 1972 | 1.990 | 1.984 | 1.983 | 1.981 | 1.978 | 1.982 | 1.977 | 1.977 | 1.972 | 1.969 | 1.973 | 2.005 | 1972 | 2.005 |
| 1973 | 1.997 | 1.968 | 1.959 | 1.958 | 1.957 | 1.943 | 1.885 | 1.898 | 1.940 | 1.934 | 1.932 | 1.927 | 1973 | 1.927 |
| 1974 | 1.912 | 1.895 | 1.834 | 1.796 | 1.799 | 1.767 | 1.755 | 1.731 | 1.765 | 1.769 | 1.795 | 1.815 | 1974 | 1.815 |
| 1975 | 1.817 | 1.831 | 1.813 | 1.770 | 1.808 | 1.799 | 1.775 | 1.768 | 1.761 | 1.814 | 1.801 | 1.829 | 1975 | 1.829 |
| 1976 | 1.835 | 1.846 | 1.856 | 1.869 | 1.831 | 1.851 | 1.862 | 1.888 | 1.895 | 1.915 | 1.971 | 1.970 | 1976 | 1.970 |
| 1977 | 1.922 | 1.911 | 1.910 | 1.905 | 1.905 | 1.912 | 1.904 | 1.898 | 1.893 | 1.877 | 1.882 | 1.871 | 1977 | 1.871 |
| 1978 | 1.863 | 1.854 | 1.848 | 1.836 | 1.817 | 1.795 | 1.800 | 1.805 | 1.802 | 1.768 | 1.774 | 1.776 | 1978 | 1.776 |
| 1979 | 1.770 | 1.739 | 1.742 | 1.728 | 1.740 | 1.759 | 1.735 | 1.702 | 1.685 | 1.592 | 1.635 | 1.632 | 1979 | 1.632 |
| 1980 | 1.587 | 1.465 | 1.465 | 1.622 | 1.685 | 1.654 | 1.635 | 1.562 | 1.541 | 1.505 | 1.496 | 1.508 | 1980 | 1.508 |
| 1981 | 1.501 | 1.451 | 1.478 | 1.437 | 1.460 | 1.456 | 1.401 | 1.366 | 1.374 | 1.455 | 1.542 | 1.515 | 1981 | 1.515 |
| 1982 | 1.518 | 1.535 | 1.543 | 1.583 | 1.590 | 1.550 | 1.613 | 1.685 | 1.737 | 1.824 | 1.842 | 1.884 | 1982 | 1.884 |
| 1983 | 1.880 | 1.927 | 1.916 | 1.952 | 1.918 | 1.915 | 1.869 | 1.878 | 1.927 | 1.926 | 1.942 | 1.949 | 1983 | 1.949 |
| 1984 | 1.973 | 1.951 | 1.940 | 1.930 | 1.876 | 1.888 | 1.956 | 1.968 | 1.998 | 2.069 | 2.109 | 2.138 | 1984 | 2.138 |
| 1985 | 2.178 | 2.130 | 2.156 | 2.204 | 2.302 | 2.320 | 2.305 | 2.335 | 2.354 | 2.384 | 2.423 | 2.479 | 1985 | 2.479 |
| 1986 | 2.492 | 2.567 | 2.666 | 2.694 | 2.628 | 2.687 | 2.729 | 2.796 | 2.752 | 2.794 | 2.823 | 2.822 | 1986 | 2.822 |
| 1987 | 2.835 | 2.841 | 2.819 | 2.736 | 2.718 | 2.740 | 2.741 | 2.715 | 2.664 | 2.736 | 2.755 | 2.782 | 1987 | 2.782 |
| 1988 | 2.862 | 2.889 | 2.852 | 2.825 | 2.802 | 2.840 | 2.815 | 2.801 | 2.837 | 2.869 | 2.834 | 2.826 | 1988 | 2.826 |
| 1989 | 2.847 | 2.820 | 2.818 | 2.861 | 2.906 | 2.993 | 3.055 | 2.975 | 2.986 | 3.043 | 3.061 | 3.060 | 1989 | 3.060 |
| 1990 | 2.997 | 2.985 | 2.969 | 2.942 | 3.012 | 3.041 | 3.082 | 3.026 | 3.029 | 3.062 | 3.114 | 3.164 | 1990 | 3.164 |
| 1991 | 3.179 | 3.189 | 3.192 | 3.225 | 3.234 | 3.217 | 3.254 | 3.325 | 3.382 | 3.422 | 3.456 | 3.545 | 1991 | 3.545 |
| 1992 | 3.471 | 3.466 | 3.421 | 3.449 | 3.521 | 3.570 | 3.649 | 3.693 | 3.754 | 3.673 | 3.637 | 3.693 | 1992 | 3.693 |
| 1993 | 3.774 | 3.852 | 3.855 | 3.878 | 3.869 | 3.942 | 3.944 | 4.021 | 4.035 | 4.025 | 3.985 | 3.998 | 1993 | 3.998 |
| 1994 | 4.042 | 3.924 | 3.810 | 3.765 | 3.762 | 3.738 | 3.791 | 3.786 | 3.716 | 3.705 | 3.674 | 3.693 | 1994 | 3.693 |
| 1995 | 3.746 | 3.818 | 3.829 | 3.871 | 4.006 | 4.030 | 4.024 | 4.048 | 4.066 | 4.101 | 4.165 | 4.207 | 1995 | 4.207 |
| 1996 | 4.185 | 4.114 | 4.045 | 4.009 | 3.989 | 4.033 | 4.035 | 4.025 | 4.075 | 4.136 | 4.190 | 4.157 | 1996 | 4.157 |
| 1997 | 4.155 | 4.142 | 4.085 | 4.140 | 4.176 | 4.213 | 4.319 | 4.268 | 4.322 | 4.376 | 4.378 | 4.430 | 1997 | 4.430 |
| 1998 | 4.502 | 4.476 | 4.479 | 4.498 | 4.521 | 4.551 | 4.558 | 4.676 | 4.824 | 4.832 | 4.784 | 4.805 | 1998 | 4.805 |
| 1999 | 4.820 | 4.687 | 4.714 | 4.689 | 4.620 | 4.635 | 4.619 | 4.615 | 4.637 | 4.625 | 4.619 | 4.597 | 1999 | 4.597 |
| 2000 | 4.561 | 4.570 | 4.625 | 4.602 | 4.623 | 4.684 | 4.710 | 4.767 | 4.788 | 4.817 | 4.898 | 5.006 | 2000 | 5.006 |

## Table B-16

**U.S. Treasury Bills: Inflation-Adjusted Total Return Index**

from December 1925 to December 1970

| Year | Jan | Feb | Mar | Apr | May | Jun | Jul | Aug | Sep | Oct | Nov | Dec | Yr-end | Index |
|------|-----|-----|-----|-----|-----|-----|-----|-----|-----|-----|-----|-----|--------|-------|
| 1925 | | | | | | | | | | | | 1.000 | 1925 | 1.000 |
| 1926 | 1.003 | 1.010 | 1.019 | 1.013 | 1.018 | 1.030 | 1.042 | 1.050 | 1.047 | 1.046 | 1.045 | 1.048 | 1926 | 1.048 |
| 1927 | 1.059 | 1.070 | 1.079 | 1.082 | 1.077 | 1.069 | 1.093 | 1.103 | 1.099 | 1.095 | 1.099 | 1.104 | 1927 | 1.104 |
| 1928 | 1.109 | 1.123 | 1.127 | 1.127 | 1.124 | 1.136 | 1.140 | 1.142 | 1.136 | 1.143 | 1.149 | 1.154 | 1928 | 1.154 |
| 1929 | 1.161 | 1.167 | 1.176 | 1.185 | 1.183 | 1.184 | 1.177 | 1.177 | 1.183 | 1.189 | 1.195 | 1.207 | 1929 | 1.207 |
| 1930 | 1.213 | 1.222 | 1.233 | 1.228 | 1.239 | 1.250 | 1.270 | 1.279 | 1.274 | 1.283 | 1.295 | 1.315 | 1930 | 1.315 |
| 1931 | 1.337 | 1.357 | 1.368 | 1.377 | 1.394 | 1.410 | 1.414 | 1.418 | 1.424 | 1.435 | 1.454 | 1.469 | 1931 | 1.469 |
| 1932 | 1.504 | 1.529 | 1.538 | 1.551 | 1.575 | 1.587 | 1.587 | 1.607 | 1.616 | 1.628 | 1.637 | 1.654 | 1932 | 1.654 |
| 1933 | 1.680 | 1.706 | 1.720 | 1.726 | 1.722 | 1.705 | 1.657 | 1.641 | 1.641 | 1.641 | 1.642 | 1.650 | 1933 | 1.650 |
| 1934 | 1.643 | 1.631 | 1.631 | 1.635 | 1.631 | 1.627 | 1.627 | 1.623 | 1.600 | 1.612 | 1.616 | 1.620 | 1934 | 1.620 |
| 1935 | 1.596 | 1.585 | 1.589 | 1.574 | 1.582 | 1.586 | 1.594 | 1.594 | 1.586 | 1.587 | 1.579 | 1.576 | 1935 | 1.576 |
| 1936 | 1.576 | 1.584 | 1.592 | 1.592 | 1.592 | 1.577 | 1.570 | 1.559 | 1.556 | 1.560 | 1.560 | 1.560 | 1936 | 1.560 |
| 1937 | 1.549 | 1.545 | 1.535 | 1.528 | 1.522 | 1.519 | 1.512 | 1.509 | 1.496 | 1.503 | 1.514 | 1.517 | 1937 | 1.517 |
| 1938 | 1.539 | 1.554 | 1.553 | 1.546 | 1.554 | 1.554 | 1.550 | 1.554 | 1.554 | 1.561 | 1.564 | 1.561 | 1938 | 1.561 |
| 1939 | 1.568 | 1.576 | 1.579 | 1.583 | 1.583 | 1.583 | 1.583 | 1.583 | 1.553 | 1.561 | 1.561 | 1.568 | 1939 | 1.568 |
| 1940 | 1.572 | 1.561 | 1.565 | 1.565 | 1.561 | 1.557 | 1.561 | 1.565 | 1.561 | 1.561 | 1.561 | 1.554 | 1940 | 1.554 |
| 1941 | 1.553 | 1.553 | 1.546 | 1.532 | 1.521 | 1.493 | 1.487 | 1.474 | 1.448 | 1.432 | 1.420 | 1.417 | 1941 | 1.417 |
| 1942 | 1.399 | 1.387 | 1.370 | 1.362 | 1.348 | 1.346 | 1.340 | 1.333 | 1.330 | 1.317 | 1.310 | 1.300 | 1942 | 1.300 |
| 1943 | 1.300 | 1.298 | 1.278 | 1.264 | 1.255 | 1.257 | 1.267 | 1.273 | 1.268 | 1.264 | 1.266 | 1.264 | 1943 | 1.264 |
| 1944 | 1.267 | 1.270 | 1.270 | 1.263 | 1.259 | 1.257 | 1.250 | 1.246 | 1.246 | 1.246 | 1.247 | 1.242 | 1944 | 1.242 |
| 1945 | 1.243 | 1.245 | 1.246 | 1.244 | 1.235 | 1.224 | 1.222 | 1.222 | 1.227 | 1.227 | 1.223 | 1.219 | 1945 | 1.219 |
| 1946 | 1.219 | 1.224 | 1.216 | 1.209 | 1.203 | 1.191 | 1.125 | 1.101 | 1.088 | 1.068 | 1.043 | 1.035 | 1946 | 1.035 |
| 1947 | 1.036 | 1.038 | 1.016 | 1.016 | 1.019 | 1.012 | 1.003 | 0.993 | 0.971 | 0.971 | 0.966 | 0.955 | 1947 | 0.955 |
| 1948 | 0.944 | 0.953 | 0.957 | 0.944 | 0.938 | 0.933 | 0.922 | 0.919 | 0.919 | 0.923 | 0.930 | 0.937 | 1948 | 0.937 |
| 1949 | 0.939 | 0.951 | 0.949 | 0.948 | 0.951 | 0.950 | 0.958 | 0.956 | 0.953 | 0.959 | 0.958 | 0.965 | 1949 | 0.965 |
| 1950 | 0.970 | 0.973 | 0.970 | 0.969 | 0.966 | 0.962 | 0.954 | 0.947 | 0.941 | 0.937 | 0.934 | 0.923 | 1950 | 0.923 |
| 1951 | 0.909 | 0.900 | 0.897 | 0.897 | 0.895 | 0.897 | 0.897 | 0.898 | 0.894 | 0.890 | 0.887 | 0.885 | 1951 | 0.885 |
| 1952 | 0.886 | 0.893 | 0.894 | 0.891 | 0.891 | 0.890 | 0.885 | 0.885 | 0.888 | 0.888 | 0.889 | 0.891 | 1952 | 0.891 |
| 1953 | 0.895 | 0.901 | 0.900 | 0.901 | 0.900 | 0.898 | 0.897 | 0.896 | 0.897 | 0.896 | 0.900 | 0.902 | 1953 | 0.902 |
| 1954 | 0.901 | 0.902 | 0.904 | 0.907 | 0.904 | 0.904 | 0.904 | 0.906 | 0.909 | 0.912 | 0.911 | 0.914 | 1954 | 0.914 |
| 1955 | 0.915 | 0.916 | 0.917 | 0.918 | 0.919 | 0.920 | 0.917 | 0.921 | 0.919 | 0.921 | 0.921 | 0.925 | 1955 | 0.925 |
| 1956 | 0.928 | 0.930 | 0.930 | 0.931 | 0.929 | 0.925 | 0.920 | 0.923 | 0.923 | 0.920 | 0.922 | 0.922 | 1956 | 0.922 |
| 1957 | 0.923 | 0.922 | 0.922 | 0.921 | 0.921 | 0.918 | 0.916 | 0.917 | 0.918 | 0.921 | 0.920 | 0.923 | 1957 | 0.923 |
| 1958 | 0.920 | 0.920 | 0.914 | 0.913 | 0.914 | 0.913 | 0.913 | 0.914 | 0.916 | 0.918 | 0.918 | 0.921 | 1958 | 0.921 |
| 1959 | 0.921 | 0.924 | 0.926 | 0.927 | 0.928 | 0.926 | 0.926 | 0.929 | 0.929 | 0.928 | 0.931 | 0.934 | 1959 | 0.934 |
| 1960 | 0.938 | 0.940 | 0.943 | 0.939 | 0.942 | 0.942 | 0.943 | 0.945 | 0.945 | 0.943 | 0.943 | 0.945 | 1960 | 0.945 |
| 1961 | 0.947 | 0.948 | 0.950 | 0.951 | 0.953 | 0.954 | 0.951 | 0.954 | 0.953 | 0.955 | 0.957 | 0.958 | 1961 | 0.958 |
| 1962 | 0.961 | 0.961 | 0.960 | 0.960 | 0.963 | 0.965 | 0.965 | 0.967 | 0.964 | 0.967 | 0.969 | 0.973 | 1962 | 0.973 |
| 1963 | 0.974 | 0.975 | 0.976 | 0.979 | 0.981 | 0.979 | 0.978 | 0.980 | 0.983 | 0.984 | 0.986 | 0.987 | 1963 | 0.987 |
| 1964 | 0.989 | 0.992 | 0.994 | 0.996 | 0.999 | 1.000 | 1.000 | 1.004 | 1.005 | 1.007 | 1.008 | 1.010 | 1964 | 1.010 |
| 1965 | 1.012 | 1.015 | 1.018 | 1.018 | 1.019 | 1.017 | 1.019 | 1.025 | 1.026 | 1.028 | 1.029 | 1.029 | 1965 | 1.029 |
| 1966 | 1.033 | 1.030 | 1.031 | 1.030 | 1.034 | 1.034 | 1.035 | 1.034 | 1.036 | 1.036 | 1.040 | 1.043 | 1966 | 1.043 |
| 1967 | 1.048 | 1.051 | 1.053 | 1.054 | 1.054 | 1.054 | 1.052 | 1.052 | 1.053 | 1.054 | 1.055 | 1.055 | 1967 | 1.055 |
| 1968 | 1.055 | 1.056 | 1.055 | 1.057 | 1.058 | 1.057 | 1.057 | 1.058 | 1.060 | 1.058 | 1.059 | 1.060 | 1968 | 1.060 |
| 1969 | 1.063 | 1.064 | 1.060 | 1.058 | 1.061 | 1.059 | 1.060 | 1.061 | 1.062 | 1.065 | 1.065 | 1.065 | 1969 | 1.065 |
| 1970 | 1.068 | 1.068 | 1.069 | 1.068 | 1.069 | 1.069 | 1.071 | 1.075 | 1.075 | 1.075 | 1.076 | 1.075 | 1970 | 1.075 |

## Table B-16 (continued)

### U.S. Treasury Bills: Inflation-Adjusted Total Return Index

from January 1971 to December 2000

| Year | Jan | Feb | Mar | Apr | May | Jun | Jul | Aug | Sep | Oct | Nov | Dec | Yr-end | Index |
|------|-----|-----|-----|-----|-----|-----|-----|-----|-----|-----|-----|-----|--------|-------|
| 1971 | 1.079 | 1.080 | 1.080 | 1.079 | 1.077 | 1.075 | 1.077 | 1.079 | 1.082 | 1.084 | 1.086 | 1.086 | 1971 | 1.086 |
| 1972 | 1.088 | 1.086 | 1.087 | 1.087 | 1.087 | 1.088 | 1.087 | 1.088 | 1.088 | 1.088 | 1.090 | 1.091 | 1972 | 1.091 |
| 1973 | 1.092 | 1.089 | 1.084 | 1.082 | 1.081 | 1.079 | 1.083 | 1.071 | 1.076 | 1.074 | 1.072 | 1.072 | 1973 | 1.072 |
| 1974 | 1.069 | 1.062 | 1.056 | 1.058 | 1.054 | 1.050 | 1.050 | 1.043 | 1.039 | 1.035 | 1.032 | 1.032 | 1974 | 1.032 |
| 1975 | 1.033 | 1.030 | 1.031 | 1.030 | 1.030 | 1.026 | 1.020 | 1.022 | 1.022 | 1.021 | 1.019 | 1.020 | 1975 | 1.020 |
| 1976 | 1.022 | 1.023 | 1.025 | 1.025 | 1.023 | 1.022 | 1.021 | 1.020 | 1.020 | 1.020 | 1.021 | 1.023 | 1976 | 1.023 |
| 1977 | 1.020 | 1.014 | 1.011 | 1.007 | 1.005 | 1.003 | 1.002 | 1.003 | 1.003 | 1.006 | 1.006 | 1.007 | 1977 | 1.007 |
| 1978 | 1.006 | 1.004 | 1.002 | 0.999 | 0.994 | 0.989 | 0.988 | 0.988 | 0.987 | 0.986 | 0.987 | 0.990 | 1978 | 0.990 |
| 1979 | 0.989 | 0.984 | 0.983 | 0.979 | 0.975 | 0.974 | 0.969 | 0.967 | 0.965 | 0.965 | 0.965 | 0.964 | 1979 | 0.964 |
| 1980 | 0.958 | 0.954 | 0.951 | 0.953 | 0.951 | 0.946 | 0.950 | 0.950 | 0.949 | 0.950 | 0.950 | 0.954 | 1980 | 0.954 |
| 1981 | 0.956 | 0.957 | 0.961 | 0.965 | 0.969 | 0.973 | 0.974 | 0.979 | 0.981 | 0.991 | 0.999 | 1.005 | 1981 | 1.005 |
| 1982 | 1.009 | 1.015 | 1.026 | 1.034 | 1.034 | 1.032 | 1.037 | 1.042 | 1.046 | 1.049 | 1.058 | 1.069 | 1982 | 1.069 |
| 1983 | 1.074 | 1.080 | 1.086 | 1.086 | 1.088 | 1.092 | 1.095 | 1.100 | 1.103 | 1.108 | 1.114 | 1.121 | 1983 | 1.121 |
| 1984 | 1.123 | 1.126 | 1.132 | 1.135 | 1.141 | 1.146 | 1.151 | 1.156 | 1.160 | 1.169 | 1.178 | 1.184 | 1984 | 1.184 |
| 1985 | 1.190 | 1.192 | 1.194 | 1.198 | 1.201 | 1.204 | 1.210 | 1.214 | 1.217 | 1.221 | 1.225 | 1.230 | 1985 | 1.230 |
| 1986 | 1.233 | 1.243 | 1.256 | 1.265 | 1.267 | 1.268 | 1.274 | 1.277 | 1.277 | 1.282 | 1.286 | 1.291 | 1986 | 1.291 |
| 1987 | 1.288 | 1.289 | 1.289 | 1.288 | 1.289 | 1.290 | 1.293 | 1.292 | 1.291 | 1.296 | 1.298 | 1.304 | 1987 | 1.304 |
| 1988 | 1.304 | 1.307 | 1.307 | 1.306 | 1.308 | 1.309 | 1.310 | 1.312 | 1.312 | 1.315 | 1.322 | 1.328 | 1988 | 1.328 |
| 1989 | 1.329 | 1.331 | 1.332 | 1.333 | 1.336 | 1.342 | 1.348 | 1.356 | 1.360 | 1.363 | 1.369 | 1.375 | 1989 | 1.375 |
| 1990 | 1.369 | 1.370 | 1.371 | 1.379 | 1.385 | 1.386 | 1.390 | 1.386 | 1.383 | 1.384 | 1.389 | 1.397 | 1990 | 1.397 |
| 1991 | 1.396 | 1.401 | 1.405 | 1.410 | 1.413 | 1.414 | 1.419 | 1.421 | 1.422 | 1.426 | 1.427 | 1.431 | 1991 | 1.431 |
| 1992 | 1.434 | 1.433 | 1.431 | 1.433 | 1.435 | 1.435 | 1.436 | 1.436 | 1.435 | 1.434 | 1.435 | 1.440 | 1992 | 1.440 |
| 1993 | 1.436 | 1.434 | 1.433 | 1.432 | 1.433 | 1.435 | 1.439 | 1.438 | 1.439 | 1.436 | 1.439 | 1.442 | 1993 | 1.442 |
| 1994 | 1.442 | 1.440 | 1.439 | 1.441 | 1.444 | 1.444 | 1.444 | 1.443 | 1.445 | 1.449 | 1.453 | 1.459 | 1994 | 1.459 |
| 1995 | 1.459 | 1.459 | 1.461 | 1.463 | 1.468 | 1.472 | 1.479 | 1.482 | 1.485 | 1.487 | 1.494 | 1.503 | 1995 | 1.503 |
| 1996 | 1.500 | 1.501 | 1.500 | 1.501 | 1.504 | 1.509 | 1.513 | 1.516 | 1.518 | 1.520 | 1.523 | 1.530 | 1996 | 1.530 |
| 1997 | 1.532 | 1.533 | 1.536 | 1.541 | 1.549 | 1.553 | 1.558 | 1.561 | 1.564 | 1.567 | 1.574 | 1.584 | 1997 | 1.584 |
| 1998 | 1.587 | 1.591 | 1.594 | 1.598 | 1.601 | 1.606 | 1.610 | 1.615 | 1.621 | 1.622 | 1.627 | 1.634 | 1998 | 1.634 |
| 1999 | 1.636 | 1.640 | 1.642 | 1.636 | 1.642 | 1.648 | 1.649 | 1.652 | 1.650 | 1.654 | 1.659 | 1.666 | 1999 | 1.666 |
| 2000 | 1.669 | 1.666 | 1.660 | 1.667 | 1.674 | 1.671 | 1.676 | 1.683 | 1.683 | 1.689 | 1.697 | 1.706 | 2000 | 1.706 |

# Stocks, Bonds, Bills, and Inflation

| | | | | | |
|---:|---:|---:|---:|---:|---:|
| –7.2 | 7.2 | –6.7 | 6.1 | –6.4 | –7.1 |
| 7.2 | 7.2 | 6.7 | 6.1 | 6.4 | 7.1 |
| 7.3 | –7.3 | 6.8 | 6.2 | –6.5 | –7.2 |
| 7.1 | 7.1 | 6.6 | 6.0 | 6.3 | 7.0 |
| 7.3 | 7.3 | –6.9 | –6.3 | 6.6 | 7.2 |
| 7.4 | –7.3 | 6.9 | 6.3 | –6.6 | –7.3 |
| –7.2 | 7.2 | –6.7 | 6.2 | –6.5 | 7.1 |
| 7.2 | –7.2 | 6.8 | –6.2 | –6.5 | 7.1 |

# Appendix C

| | | | | | |
|---:|---:|---:|---:|---:|---:|
| 7.3 | –7.3 | –6.9 | 6.3 | 6.6 | –7.2 |
| –7.2 | 7.2 | 6.8 | –6.3 | –6.6 | 7.1 |
| 7.0 | –7.0 | –6.6 | –6.1 | 6.4 | –6.9 |
| –7.4 | 7.4 | –7.0 | –6.5 | 6.7 | –7.3 |
| 7.5 | –7.5 | –7.1 | 6.6 | –6.9 | 7.4 |
| –7.8 | 7.8 | –7.4 | –6.9 | –7.2 | –7.7 |
| –8.0 | 8.0 | –7.6 | 7.1 | –7.4 | 7.9 |
| 8.1 | –8.1 | 7.7 | –7.3 | 7.5 | –8.0 |
| 9.2 | –9.2 | 8.7 | –8.5 | –8.9 | 9.1 |

**Ibbotson**Associates

# Appendix C
**Rates of Return for All Yearly Holding Periods: 1926–2000**

Each table in this section consists of five pages.

## Table C-1 (page 1 of 5)

### Large Company Stocks Total Returns
Rates of Return for all holding periods
Percent per annum compounded annually

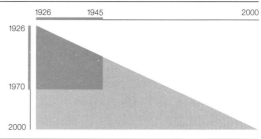

from 1926 to 2000

| To the end of | From the beginning of 1926 | 1927 | 1928 | 1929 | 1930 | 1931 | 1932 | 1933 | 1934 | 1935 | 1936 | 1937 | 1938 | 1939 | 1940 | 1941 | 1942 | 1943 | 1944 | 1945 |
|---|---|---|---|---|---|---|---|---|---|---|---|---|---|---|---|---|---|---|---|---|
| 1926 | 11.6 | | | | | | | | | | | | | | | | | | | |
| 1927 | 23.9 | 37.5 | | | | | | | | | | | | | | | | | | |
| 1928 | 30.1 | 40.5 | 43.6 | | | | | | | | | | | | | | | | | |
| 1929 | 19.2 | 21.8 | 14.7 | -8.4 | | | | | | | | | | | | | | | | |
| 1930 | 8.7 | 8.0 | -0.4 | -17.1 | -24.9 | | | | | | | | | | | | | | | |
| 1931 | -2.5 | -5.1 | -13.5 | -27.0 | -34.8 | -43.3 | | | | | | | | | | | | | | |
| 1932 | -3.3 | -5.6 | -12.5 | -22.7 | -26.9 | -27.9 | -8.2 | | | | | | | | | | | | | |
| 1933 | 2.5 | 1.2 | -3.8 | -11.2 | -11.9 | -7.1 | 18.9 | 54.0 | | | | | | | | | | | | |
| 1934 | 2.0 | 0.9 | -3.5 | -9.7 | -9.9 | -5.7 | 11.7 | 23.2 | -1.4 | | | | | | | | | | | |
| 1935 | 5.9 | 5.2 | 1.8 | -3.1 | -2.2 | 3.1 | 19.8 | 30.9 | 20.6 | 47.7 | | | | | | | | | | |
| 1936 | 8.1 | 7.8 | 4.9 | 0.9 | 2.3 | 7.7 | 22.5 | 31.6 | 24.9 | 40.6 | 33.9 | | | | | | | | | |
| 1937 | 3.7 | 3.0 | 0.0 | -3.9 | -3.3 | 0.2 | 10.2 | 14.3 | 6.1 | 8.7 | -6.7 | -35.0 | | | | | | | | |
| 1938 | 5.5 | 5.1 | 2.5 | -0.9 | 0.0 | 3.6 | 13.0 | 16.9 | 10.7 | 13.9 | 4.5 | -7.7 | 31.1 | | | | | | | |
| 1939 | 5.1 | 4.6 | 2.3 | -0.8 | -0.1 | 3.2 | 11.2 | 14.3 | 8.7 | 10.9 | 3.2 | -5.3 | 14.3 | -0.4 | | | | | | |
| 1940 | 4.0 | 3.5 | 1.3 | -1.6 | -1.0 | 1.8 | 8.6 | 11.0 | 5.9 | 7.2 | 0.5 | -6.5 | 5.6 | -5.2 | -9.8 | | | | | |
| 1941 | 3.0 | 2.4 | 0.3 | -2.4 | -1.9 | 0.5 | 6.4 | 8.2 | 3.5 | 4.3 | -1.6 | -7.5 | 1.0 | -7.4 | -10.7 | -11.6 | | | | |
| 1942 | 3.9 | 3.5 | 1.5 | -1.0 | -0.4 | 2.0 | 7.6 | 9.3 | 5.3 | 6.1 | 1.2 | -3.4 | 4.6 | -1.1 | -1.4 | 3.1 | 20.3 | | | |
| 1943 | 5.0 | 4.7 | 2.9 | 0.6 | 1.3 | 3.7 | 9.0 | 10.8 | 7.2 | 8.2 | 4.0 | 0.4 | 7.9 | 3.8 | 4.8 | 10.2 | 23.1 | 25.9 | | |
| 1944 | 5.8 | 5.5 | 3.8 | 1.7 | 2.5 | 4.8 | 9.8 | 11.5 | 8.3 | 9.3 | 5.7 | 2.6 | 9.5 | 6.3 | 7.7 | 12.5 | 22.0 | 22.8 | 19.8 | |
| 1945 | 7.1 | 6.9 | 5.4 | 3.5 | 4.3 | 6.6 | 11.5 | 13.2 | 10.4 | 11.5 | 8.4 | 5.9 | 12.6 | 10.1 | 12.0 | 17.0 | 25.4 | 27.2 | 27.8 | 36.4 |
| 1946 | 6.4 | 6.1 | 4.7 | 2.8 | 3.5 | 5.6 | 10.1 | 11.6 | 8.8 | 9.7 | 6.8 | 4.4 | 10.1 | 7.7 | 8.9 | 12.4 | 17.9 | 17.3 | 14.5 | 12.0 |
| 1947 | 6.3 | 6.1 | 4.7 | 3.0 | 3.7 | 5.6 | 9.8 | 11.2 | 8.6 | 9.4 | 6.7 | 4.5 | 9.6 | 7.5 | 8.5 | 11.4 | 15.8 | 14.9 | 12.3 | 9.9 |
| 1948 | 6.3 | 6.1 | 4.7 | 3.1 | 3.8 | 5.6 | 9.6 | 10.8 | 8.4 | 9.1 | 6.6 | 4.6 | 9.2 | 7.3 | 8.2 | 10.6 | 14.2 | 13.2 | 10.9 | 8.8 |
| 1949 | 6.8 | 6.6 | 5.3 | 3.8 | 4.5 | 6.3 | 10.1 | 11.2 | 9.0 | 9.7 | 7.4 | 5.6 | 10.0 | 8.3 | 9.2 | 11.5 | 14.8 | 14.0 | 12.2 | 10.7 |
| 1950 | 7.7 | 7.5 | 6.4 | 4.9 | 5.6 | 7.4 | 11.1 | 12.3 | 10.2 | 11.0 | 8.9 | 7.3 | 11.5 | 10.0 | 11.0 | 13.4 | 16.6 | 16.1 | 14.8 | 13.9 |
| 1951 | 8.3 | 8.1 | 7.1 | 5.7 | 6.4 | 8.2 | 11.7 | 12.9 | 11.0 | 11.7 | 9.8 | 8.4 | 12.4 | 11.1 | 12.1 | 14.3 | 17.3 | 16.9 | 15.9 | 15.3 |
| 1952 | 8.6 | 8.5 | 7.5 | 6.2 | 6.9 | 8.6 | 12.0 | 13.2 | 11.3 | 12.1 | 10.3 | 9.0 | 12.8 | 11.6 | 12.5 | 14.6 | 17.4 | 17.1 | 16.1 | 15.7 |
| 1953 | 8.3 | 8.1 | 7.2 | 5.9 | 6.5 | 8.2 | 11.4 | 12.4 | 10.7 | 11.4 | 9.6 | 8.3 | 11.9 | 10.7 | 11.5 | 13.4 | 15.7 | 15.3 | 14.3 | 13.7 |
| 1954 | 9.6 | 9.5 | 8.6 | 7.4 | 8.1 | 9.7 | 12.9 | 14.0 | 12.4 | 13.1 | 11.6 | 10.4 | 13.9 | 12.9 | 13.9 | 15.8 | 18.2 | 18.0 | 17.4 | 17.1 |
| 1955 | 10.2 | 10.2 | 9.3 | 8.2 | 8.9 | 10.5 | 13.7 | 14.7 | 13.2 | 13.9 | 12.5 | 11.4 | 14.8 | 13.9 | 14.9 | 16.8 | 19.1 | 19.0 | 18.5 | 18.4 |
| 1956 | 10.1 | 10.1 | 9.2 | 8.2 | 8.8 | 10.4 | 13.4 | 14.4 | 12.9 | 13.6 | 12.2 | 11.2 | 14.4 | 13.5 | 14.4 | 16.1 | 18.2 | 18.1 | 17.5 | 17.3 |
| 1957 | 9.4 | 9.3 | 8.5 | 7.4 | 8.1 | 9.5 | 12.3 | 13.2 | 11.8 | 12.4 | 11.0 | 10.0 | 13.0 | 12.1 | 12.8 | 14.3 | 16.2 | 15.9 | 15.2 | 14.9 |
| 1958 | 10.3 | 10.2 | 9.5 | 8.5 | 9.1 | 10.6 | 13.3 | 14.3 | 12.9 | 13.6 | 12.3 | 11.4 | 14.3 | 13.5 | 14.3 | 15.8 | 17.6 | 17.5 | 16.9 | 16.7 |
| 1959 | 10.3 | 10.3 | 9.5 | 8.6 | 9.2 | 10.6 | 13.3 | 14.2 | 12.9 | 13.5 | 12.3 | 11.4 | 14.2 | 13.4 | 14.1 | 15.6 | 17.3 | 17.1 | 16.6 | 16.4 |
| 1960 | 10.0 | 10.0 | 9.3 | 8.3 | 8.9 | 10.3 | 12.8 | 13.7 | 12.4 | 13.0 | 11.8 | 10.9 | 13.5 | 12.8 | 13.5 | 14.8 | 16.4 | 16.1 | 15.6 | 15.3 |
| 1961 | 10.5 | 10.4 | 9.7 | 8.8 | 9.4 | 10.8 | 13.3 | 14.1 | 12.9 | 13.4 | 12.3 | 11.5 | 14.1 | 13.4 | 14.0 | 15.3 | 16.9 | 16.7 | 16.2 | 16.0 |
| 1962 | 9.9 | 9.9 | 9.2 | 8.3 | 8.8 | 10.1 | 12.5 | 13.2 | 12.1 | 12.6 | 11.4 | 10.7 | 13.0 | 12.3 | 12.9 | 14.1 | 15.5 | 15.3 | 14.7 | 14.4 |
| 1963 | 10.2 | 10.2 | 9.5 | 8.7 | 9.2 | 10.5 | 12.8 | 13.5 | 12.4 | 12.9 | 11.8 | 11.1 | 13.4 | 12.7 | 13.3 | 14.5 | 15.8 | 15.6 | 15.1 | 14.9 |
| 1964 | 10.4 | 10.4 | 9.7 | 8.9 | 9.4 | 10.6 | 12.9 | 13.6 | 12.5 | 13.0 | 12.0 | 11.3 | 13.5 | 12.9 | 13.5 | 14.5 | 15.8 | 15.6 | 15.2 | 14.9 |
| 1965 | 10.4 | 10.4 | 9.8 | 9.0 | 9.5 | 10.7 | 12.9 | 13.6 | 12.5 | 13.0 | 12.0 | 11.3 | 13.5 | 12.9 | 13.4 | 14.5 | 15.7 | 15.5 | 15.0 | 14.8 |
| 1966 | 9.9 | 9.8 | 9.2 | 8.4 | 8.9 | 10.1 | 12.2 | 12.8 | 11.8 | 12.2 | 11.2 | 10.5 | 12.6 | 12.0 | 12.4 | 13.4 | 14.5 | 14.3 | 13.8 | 13.6 |
| 1967 | 10.2 | 10.2 | 9.6 | 8.8 | 9.3 | 10.4 | 12.5 | 13.1 | 12.1 | 12.5 | 11.6 | 10.9 | 12.9 | 12.4 | 12.8 | 13.8 | 14.9 | 14.7 | 14.2 | 14.0 |
| 1968 | 10.2 | 10.2 | 9.6 | 8.9 | 9.3 | 10.4 | 12.4 | 13.1 | 12.1 | 12.5 | 11.6 | 10.9 | 12.9 | 12.3 | 12.8 | 13.7 | 14.7 | 14.5 | 14.1 | 13.9 |
| 1969 | 9.8 | 9.7 | 9.1 | 8.4 | 8.9 | 9.9 | 11.8 | 12.4 | 11.4 | 11.8 | 10.9 | 10.3 | 12.1 | 11.6 | 12.0 | 12.8 | 13.8 | 13.6 | 13.1 | 12.9 |
| 1970 | 9.6 | 9.6 | 9.0 | 8.3 | 8.7 | 9.7 | 11.6 | 12.2 | 11.2 | 11.6 | 10.7 | 10.1 | 11.9 | 11.3 | 11.7 | 12.5 | 13.5 | 13.2 | 12.8 | 12.5 |

# Table C-1 (page 2 of 5)

## Large Company Stocks Total Returns
Rates of Return for all holding periods
Percent per annum compounded annually

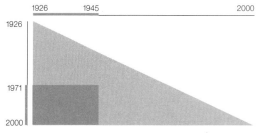

from 1926 to 2000

| To the end of | From the beginning of | | | | | | | | | | | | | | | | | | | |
|---|---|---|---|---|---|---|---|---|---|---|---|---|---|---|---|---|---|---|---|---|
| | 1926 | 1927 | 1928 | 1929 | 1930 | 1931 | 1932 | 1933 | 1934 | 1935 | 1936 | 1937 | 1938 | 1939 | 1940 | 1941 | 1942 | 1943 | 1944 | 1945 |
| 1971 | 9.7 | 9.7 | 9.1 | 8.4 | 8.9 | 9.9 | 11.7 | 12.2 | 11.3 | 11.7 | 10.8 | 10.2 | 11.9 | 11.4 | 11.8 | 12.6 | 13.5 | 13.3 | 12.8 | 12.6 |
| 1972 | 9.9 | 9.9 | 9.3 | 8.7 | 9.1 | 10.1 | 11.9 | 12.4 | 11.5 | 11.9 | 11.0 | 10.5 | 12.1 | 11.6 | 12.0 | 12.8 | 13.7 | 13.5 | 13.0 | 12.8 |
| 1973 | 9.3 | 9.3 | 8.7 | 8.1 | 8.5 | 9.4 | 11.1 | 11.7 | 10.8 | 11.1 | 10.3 | 9.7 | 11.3 | 10.8 | 11.1 | 11.8 | 12.7 | 12.4 | 12.0 | 11.7 |
| 1974 | 8.5 | 8.4 | 7.8 | 7.2 | 7.5 | 8.4 | 10.1 | 10.6 | 9.7 | 10.0 | 9.1 | 8.5 | 10.1 | 9.5 | 9.8 | 10.5 | 11.2 | 10.9 | 10.5 | 10.2 |
| 1975 | 9.0 | 8.9 | 8.4 | 7.7 | 8.1 | 9.0 | 10.6 | 11.1 | 10.2 | 10.6 | 9.8 | 9.2 | 10.7 | 10.2 | 10.5 | 11.1 | 11.9 | 11.6 | 11.2 | 11.0 |
| 1976 | 9.2 | 9.2 | 8.7 | 8.0 | 8.4 | 9.3 | 10.9 | 11.4 | 10.5 | 10.9 | 10.1 | 9.5 | 11.0 | 10.5 | 10.8 | 11.5 | 12.2 | 12.0 | 11.6 | 11.3 |
| 1977 | 8.9 | 8.8 | 8.3 | 7.7 | 8.1 | 8.9 | 10.5 | 10.9 | 10.1 | 10.4 | 9.6 | 9.1 | 10.5 | 10.0 | 10.3 | 10.9 | 11.6 | 11.4 | 11.0 | 10.7 |
| 1978 | 8.9 | 8.8 | 8.3 | 7.7 | 8.0 | 8.9 | 10.4 | 10.8 | 10.0 | 10.3 | 9.6 | 9.0 | 10.4 | 9.9 | 10.2 | 10.8 | 11.5 | 11.3 | 10.9 | 10.6 |
| 1979 | 9.0 | 9.0 | 8.5 | 7.9 | 8.2 | 9.1 | 10.6 | 11.0 | 10.2 | 10.5 | 9.8 | 9.2 | 10.6 | 10.1 | 10.4 | 11.0 | 11.7 | 11.4 | 11.1 | 10.8 |
| 1980 | 9.4 | 9.4 | 8.9 | 8.3 | 8.7 | 9.5 | 11.0 | 11.4 | 10.6 | 10.9 | 10.2 | 9.7 | 11.1 | 10.6 | 10.9 | 11.5 | 12.2 | 11.9 | 11.6 | 11.4 |
| 1981 | 9.1 | 9.1 | 8.6 | 8.1 | 8.4 | 9.2 | 10.6 | 11.0 | 10.3 | 10.6 | 9.9 | 9.4 | 10.7 | 10.2 | 10.5 | 11.1 | 11.7 | 11.5 | 11.1 | 10.9 |
| 1982 | 9.3 | 9.3 | 8.8 | 8.3 | 8.6 | 9.4 | 10.8 | 11.2 | 10.5 | 10.8 | 10.1 | 9.6 | 10.9 | 10.5 | 10.8 | 11.3 | 11.9 | 11.7 | 11.4 | 11.2 |
| 1983 | 9.6 | 9.5 | 9.1 | 8.5 | 8.9 | 9.6 | 11.0 | 11.5 | 10.7 | 11.0 | 10.3 | 9.9 | 11.1 | 10.7 | 11.0 | 11.5 | 12.2 | 12.0 | 11.6 | 11.4 |
| 1984 | 9.5 | 9.5 | 9.0 | 8.5 | 8.8 | 9.6 | 10.9 | 11.3 | 10.6 | 10.9 | 10.3 | 9.8 | 11.0 | 10.6 | 10.9 | 11.4 | 12.0 | 11.8 | 11.5 | 11.3 |
| 1985 | 9.8 | 9.8 | 9.4 | 8.9 | 9.2 | 9.9 | 11.3 | 11.7 | 11.0 | 11.3 | 10.7 | 10.2 | 11.4 | 11.1 | 11.3 | 11.8 | 12.4 | 12.3 | 12.0 | 11.8 |
| 1986 | 10.0 | 9.9 | 9.5 | 9.0 | 9.4 | 10.1 | 11.4 | 11.8 | 11.2 | 11.4 | 10.8 | 10.4 | 11.6 | 11.2 | 11.5 | 12.0 | 12.6 | 12.4 | 12.1 | 11.9 |
| 1987 | 9.9 | 9.9 | 9.5 | 9.0 | 9.3 | 10.0 | 11.3 | 11.7 | 11.0 | 11.3 | 10.7 | 10.3 | 11.5 | 11.1 | 11.3 | 11.8 | 12.4 | 12.2 | 11.9 | 11.8 |
| 1988 | 10.0 | 10.0 | 9.6 | 9.1 | 9.4 | 10.1 | 11.4 | 11.8 | 11.1 | 11.4 | 10.8 | 10.4 | 11.6 | 11.2 | 11.4 | 11.9 | 12.5 | 12.3 | 12.1 | 11.9 |
| 1989 | 10.3 | 10.3 | 9.9 | 9.4 | 9.7 | 10.5 | 11.7 | 12.1 | 11.5 | 11.7 | 11.2 | 10.8 | 11.9 | 11.6 | 11.8 | 12.3 | 12.9 | 12.7 | 12.4 | 12.3 |
| 1990 | 10.1 | 10.1 | 9.7 | 9.2 | 9.5 | 10.2 | 11.5 | 11.8 | 11.2 | 11.4 | 10.9 | 10.5 | 11.6 | 11.3 | 11.5 | 12.0 | 12.5 | 12.4 | 12.1 | 11.9 |
| 1991 | 10.4 | 10.4 | 10.0 | 9.5 | 9.8 | 10.5 | 11.8 | 12.1 | 11.5 | 11.8 | 11.2 | 10.8 | 11.9 | 11.6 | 11.8 | 12.3 | 12.9 | 12.7 | 12.4 | 12.3 |
| 1992 | 10.3 | 10.3 | 9.9 | 9.5 | 9.8 | 10.5 | 11.7 | 12.1 | 11.4 | 11.7 | 11.1 | 10.8 | 11.8 | 11.5 | 11.8 | 12.2 | 12.7 | 12.6 | 12.3 | 12.2 |
| 1993 | 10.3 | 10.3 | 9.9 | 9.5 | 9.8 | 10.5 | 11.7 | 12.0 | 11.4 | 11.7 | 11.1 | 10.8 | 11.8 | 11.5 | 11.7 | 12.2 | 12.7 | 12.5 | 12.3 | 12.1 |
| 1994 | 10.2 | 10.2 | 9.8 | 9.4 | 9.7 | 10.3 | 11.5 | 11.8 | 11.3 | 11.5 | 10.9 | 10.6 | 11.6 | 11.3 | 11.5 | 12.0 | 12.5 | 12.3 | 12.1 | 11.9 |
| 1995 | 10.5 | 10.5 | 10.2 | 9.7 | 10.0 | 10.7 | 11.9 | 12.2 | 11.6 | 11.9 | 11.3 | 11.0 | 12.0 | 11.7 | 11.9 | 12.4 | 12.9 | 12.7 | 12.5 | 12.4 |
| 1996 | 10.7 | 10.7 | 10.3 | 9.9 | 10.2 | 10.9 | 12.0 | 12.4 | 11.8 | 12.0 | 11.5 | 11.2 | 12.2 | 11.9 | 12.1 | 12.6 | 13.1 | 12.9 | 12.7 | 12.6 |
| 1997 | 11.0 | 11.0 | 10.6 | 10.2 | 10.5 | 11.2 | 12.3 | 12.7 | 12.1 | 12.3 | 11.8 | 11.5 | 12.5 | 12.2 | 12.5 | 12.9 | 13.4 | 13.3 | 13.1 | 12.9 |
| 1998 | 11.2 | 11.2 | 10.9 | 10.5 | 10.8 | 11.4 | 12.5 | 12.9 | 12.3 | 12.6 | 12.1 | 11.8 | 12.8 | 12.5 | 12.7 | 13.2 | 13.6 | 13.5 | 13.3 | 13.2 |
| 1999 | 11.3 | 11.3 | 11.0 | 10.6 | 10.9 | 11.5 | 12.7 | 13.0 | 12.5 | 12.7 | 12.2 | 11.9 | 12.9 | 12.6 | 12.9 | 13.3 | 13.8 | 13.7 | 13.5 | 13.3 |
| 2000 | 11.0 | 11.0 | 10.7 | 10.3 | 10.6 | 11.2 | 12.3 | 12.6 | 12.1 | 12.3 | 11.9 | 11.6 | 12.5 | 12.2 | 12.5 | 12.9 | 13.3 | 13.2 | 13.0 | 12.9 |

## Table C-1 (page 3 of 5)

**Large Company Stocks Total Returns**
Rates of Return for all holding periods
Percent per annum compounded annually

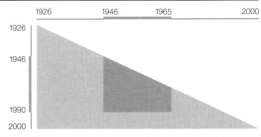

from 1926 to 2000

| To the end of | From the beginning of 1946 | 1947 | 1948 | 1949 | 1950 | 1951 | 1952 | 1953 | 1954 | 1955 | 1956 | 1957 | 1958 | 1959 | 1960 | 1961 | 1962 | 1963 | 1964 | 1965 |
|---|---|---|---|---|---|---|---|---|---|---|---|---|---|---|---|---|---|---|---|---|
| 1946 | -8.1 | | | | | | | | | | | | | | | | | | | |
| 1947 | -1.4 | 5.7 | | | | | | | | | | | | | | | | | | |
| 1948 | 0.8 | 5.6 | 5.5 | | | | | | | | | | | | | | | | | |
| 1949 | 5.1 | 9.8 | 11.9 | 18.8 | | | | | | | | | | | | | | | | |
| 1950 | 9.9 | 14.9 | 18.2 | 25.1 | 31.7 | | | | | | | | | | | | | | | |
| 1951 | 12.1 | 16.7 | 19.6 | 24.7 | 27.8 | 24.0 | | | | | | | | | | | | | | |
| 1952 | 13.0 | 17.0 | 19.4 | 23.1 | 24.6 | 21.2 | 18.4 | | | | | | | | | | | | | |
| 1953 | 11.2 | 14.2 | 15.7 | 17.9 | 17.6 | 13.3 | 8.3 | -1.0 | | | | | | | | | | | | |
| 1954 | 15.1 | 18.4 | 20.4 | 23.0 | 23.9 | 22.0 | 21.4 | 22.9 | 52.6 | | | | | | | | | | | |
| 1955 | 16.7 | 19.8 | 21.7 | 24.2 | 25.2 | 23.9 | 23.9 | 25.7 | 41.7 | 31.6 | | | | | | | | | | |
| 1956 | 15.7 | 18.4 | 19.9 | 21.9 | 22.3 | 20.8 | 20.2 | 20.6 | 28.9 | 18.4 | 6.6 | | | | | | | | | |
| 1957 | 13.2 | 15.4 | 16.4 | 17.7 | 17.6 | 15.7 | 14.4 | 13.6 | 17.5 | 7.7 | -2.5 | -10.8 | | | | | | | | |
| 1958 | 15.3 | 17.5 | 18.7 | 20.1 | 20.2 | 18.8 | 18.1 | 18.1 | 22.3 | 15.7 | 10.9 | 13.1 | 43.4 | | | | | | | |
| 1959 | 15.1 | 17.1 | 18.1 | 19.3 | 19.4 | 18.1 | 17.3 | 17.2 | 20.5 | 15.0 | 11.1 | 12.7 | 26.7 | 12.0 | | | | | | |
| 1960 | 14.0 | 15.8 | 16.6 | 17.6 | 17.5 | 16.2 | 15.3 | 14.9 | 17.4 | 12.4 | 8.9 | 9.5 | 17.3 | 6.1 | 0.5 | | | | | |
| 1961 | 14.8 | 16.5 | 17.3 | 18.3 | 18.3 | 17.1 | 16.4 | 16.2 | 18.6 | 14.4 | 11.7 | 12.8 | 19.6 | 12.6 | 12.9 | 26.9 | | | | |
| 1962 | 13.3 | 14.8 | 15.4 | 16.1 | 15.9 | 14.7 | 13.9 | 13.4 | 15.2 | 11.2 | 8.5 | 8.9 | 13.3 | 6.8 | 5.2 | 7.6 | -8.7 | | | |
| 1963 | 13.8 | 15.2 | 15.8 | 16.6 | 16.4 | 15.3 | 14.6 | 14.3 | 15.9 | 12.4 | 10.2 | 10.8 | 14.8 | 9.9 | 9.3 | 12.5 | 5.9 | 22.8 | | |
| 1964 | 13.9 | 15.3 | 15.9 | 16.6 | 16.4 | 15.4 | 14.7 | 14.4 | 16.0 | 12.8 | 10.9 | 11.5 | 15.1 | 10.9 | 10.7 | 13.5 | 9.3 | 19.6 | 16.5 | |
| 1965 | 13.8 | 15.1 | 15.7 | 16.3 | 16.2 | 15.2 | 14.6 | 14.3 | 15.7 | 12.8 | 11.1 | 11.6 | 14.7 | 11.1 | 11.0 | 13.2 | 10.1 | 17.2 | 14.4 | 12.5 |
| 1966 | 12.6 | 13.7 | 14.2 | 14.7 | 14.4 | 13.4 | 12.7 | 12.4 | 13.4 | 10.7 | 9.0 | 9.2 | 11.7 | 8.2 | 7.7 | 9.0 | 5.7 | 9.7 | 5.6 | 0.6 |
| 1967 | 13.1 | 14.2 | 14.6 | 15.1 | 14.9 | 14.0 | 13.4 | 13.1 | 14.2 | 11.6 | 10.1 | 10.5 | 12.8 | 9.9 | 9.6 | 11.0 | 8.6 | 12.4 | 9.9 | 7.8 |
| 1968 | 13.0 | 14.0 | 14.5 | 14.9 | 14.7 | 13.8 | 13.3 | 13.0 | 14.0 | 11.6 | 10.2 | 10.5 | 12.7 | 10.0 | 9.8 | 11.0 | 8.9 | 12.2 | 10.2 | 8.6 |
| 1969 | 12.0 | 13.0 | 13.3 | 13.7 | 13.4 | 12.5 | 11.9 | 11.6 | 12.4 | 10.1 | 8.7 | 8.9 | 10.7 | 8.2 | 7.8 | 8.7 | 6.6 | 9.0 | 6.8 | 5.0 |
| 1970 | 11.7 | 12.6 | 12.9 | 13.2 | 13.0 | 12.1 | 11.5 | 11.1 | 11.9 | 9.7 | 8.4 | 8.6 | 10.2 | 7.8 | 7.5 | 8.2 | 6.3 | 8.3 | 6.4 | 4.8 |
| 1971 | 11.8 | 12.6 | 12.9 | 13.3 | 13.0 | 12.2 | 11.6 | 11.3 | 12.0 | 10.0 | 8.8 | 8.9 | 10.5 | 8.3 | 8.0 | 8.0 | 7.1 | 9.0 | 7.4 | 6.1 |
| 1972 | 12.0 | 12.9 | 13.2 | 13.5 | 13.3 | 12.5 | 12.0 | 11.7 | 12.4 | 10.5 | 9.4 | 9.5 | 11.0 | 9.0 | 8.8 | 9.5 | 8.1 | 9.9 | 8.6 | 7.6 |
| 1973 | 10.9 | 11.7 | 11.9 | 12.2 | 11.9 | 11.2 | 10.6 | 10.3 | 10.8 | 9.0 | 7.9 | 7.9 | 9.2 | 7.3 | 6.9 | 7.5 | 6.0 | 7.4 | 6.0 | 4.9 |
| 1974 | 9.4 | 10.1 | 10.2 | 10.4 | 10.1 | 9.3 | 8.7 | 8.2 | 8.7 | 6.9 | 5.7 | 5.7 | 6.7 | 4.8 | 4.3 | 4.6 | 3.0 | 4.1 | 2.5 | 1.2 |
| 1975 | 10.2 | 10.9 | 11.1 | 11.3 | 11.0 | 10.3 | 9.7 | 9.4 | 9.9 | 8.2 | 7.1 | 7.1 | 8.2 | 6.4 | 6.1 | 6.5 | 5.2 | 6.3 | 5.1 | 4.1 |
| 1976 | 10.6 | 11.3 | 11.5 | 11.7 | 11.5 | 10.8 | 10.3 | 9.9 | 10.4 | 8.8 | 7.8 | 7.9 | 9.0 | 7.3 | 7.1 | 7.5 | 6.3 | 7.5 | 6.4 | 5.6 |
| 1977 | 10.0 | 10.7 | 10.8 | 11.0 | 10.7 | 10.0 | 9.5 | 9.2 | 9.6 | 8.1 | 7.1 | 7.1 | 8.1 | 6.5 | 6.2 | 6.6 | 5.4 | 6.4 | 5.4 | 4.6 |
| 1978 | 9.9 | 10.5 | 10.7 | 10.9 | 10.6 | 9.9 | 9.4 | 9.1 | 9.5 | 8.0 | 7.1 | 7.1 | 8.0 | 6.5 | 6.2 | 6.6 | 5.5 | 6.5 | 5.4 | 4.7 |
| 1979 | 10.2 | 10.8 | 10.9 | 11.1 | 10.8 | 10.2 | 9.7 | 9.4 | 9.8 | 8.4 | 7.5 | 7.6 | 8.5 | 7.1 | 6.8 | 7.2 | 6.2 | 7.1 | 6.2 | 5.6 |
| 1980 | 10.7 | 11.3 | 11.5 | 11.7 | 11.5 | 10.9 | 10.4 | 10.2 | 10.6 | 9.2 | 8.4 | 8.5 | 9.4 | 8.1 | 7.9 | 8.3 | 7.4 | 8.4 | 7.6 | 7.1 |
| 1981 | 10.3 | 10.8 | 11.0 | 11.2 | 10.9 | 10.3 | 9.9 | 9.6 | 10.0 | 8.7 | 7.9 | 7.9 | 8.8 | 7.5 | 7.3 | 7.6 | 6.8 | 7.6 | 6.9 | 6.3 |
| 1982 | 10.6 | 11.1 | 11.3 | 11.5 | 11.2 | 10.7 | 10.2 | 10.0 | 10.4 | 9.1 | 8.4 | 8.4 | 9.3 | 8.1 | 7.9 | 8.2 | 7.4 | 8.3 | 7.6 | 7.1 |
| 1983 | 10.9 | 11.4 | 11.6 | 11.8 | 11.6 | 11.0 | 10.6 | 10.4 | 10.8 | 9.6 | 8.8 | 8.9 | 9.8 | 8.6 | 8.5 | 8.8 | 8.1 | 8.9 | 8.3 | 7.9 |
| 1984 | 10.7 | 11.3 | 11.4 | 11.6 | 11.4 | 10.9 | 10.5 | 10.2 | 10.6 | 9.4 | 8.7 | 8.8 | 9.6 | 8.5 | 8.4 | 8.7 | 8.0 | 8.8 | 8.2 | 7.8 |
| 1985 | 11.2 | 11.8 | 11.9 | 12.1 | 11.9 | 11.4 | 11.1 | 10.8 | 11.2 | 10.1 | 9.5 | 9.6 | 10.4 | 9.3 | 9.2 | 9.6 | 8.9 | 9.7 | 9.2 | 8.8 |
| 1986 | 11.4 | 11.9 | 12.1 | 12.3 | 12.1 | 11.6 | 11.3 | 11.1 | 11.4 | 10.4 | 9.7 | 9.8 | 10.6 | 9.6 | 9.5 | 9.9 | 9.3 | 10.1 | 9.6 | 9.3 |
| 1987 | 11.2 | 11.8 | 11.9 | 12.1 | 11.9 | 11.4 | 11.1 | 10.9 | 11.3 | 10.2 | 9.6 | 9.7 | 10.4 | 9.5 | 9.4 | 9.7 | 9.1 | 9.9 | 9.4 | 9.1 |
| 1988 | 11.4 | 11.9 | 12.0 | 12.2 | 12.0 | 11.6 | 11.2 | 11.1 | 11.4 | 10.4 | 9.8 | 9.9 | 10.6 | 9.7 | 9.6 | 10.0 | 9.4 | 10.1 | 9.7 | 9.4 |
| 1989 | 11.8 | 12.3 | 12.5 | 12.6 | 12.5 | 12.0 | 11.7 | 11.6 | 11.9 | 10.9 | 10.4 | 10.5 | 11.2 | 10.3 | 10.3 | 10.6 | 10.1 | 10.9 | 10.4 | 10.2 |
| 1990 | 11.4 | 11.9 | 12.1 | 12.2 | 12.1 | 11.6 | 11.3 | 11.1 | 11.5 | 10.5 | 10.0 | 10.1 | 10.8 | 9.9 | 9.8 | 10.2 | 9.6 | 10.3 | 9.9 | 9.7 |

## Table C-1 (page 4 of 5)

### Large Company Stocks Total Returns
Rates of Return for all holding periods
Percent per annum compounded annually

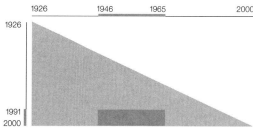

from 1926 to 2000

| To the end of | From the beginning of 1946 | 1947 | 1948 | 1949 | 1950 | 1951 | 1952 | 1953 | 1954 | 1955 | 1956 | 1957 | 1958 | 1959 | 1960 | 1961 | 1962 | 1963 | 1964 | 1965 |
|---|---|---|---|---|---|---|---|---|---|---|---|---|---|---|---|---|---|---|---|---|
| 1991 | 11.8 | 12.3 | 12.5 | 12.6 | 12.5 | 12.1 | 11.8 | 11.6 | 12.0 | 11.0 | 10.5 | 10.6 | 11.3 | 10.5 | 10.4 | 10.8 | 10.3 | 11.0 | 10.6 | 10.4 |
| 1992 | 11.7 | 12.2 | 12.4 | 12.5 | 12.4 | 11.9 | 11.7 | 11.5 | 11.8 | 10.9 | 10.4 | 10.5 | 11.2 | 10.4 | 10.3 | 10.7 | 10.2 | 10.9 | 10.5 | 10.3 |
| 1993 | 11.7 | 12.2 | 12.3 | 12.5 | 12.3 | 11.9 | 11.6 | 11.5 | 11.8 | 10.9 | 10.4 | 10.5 | 11.2 | 10.4 | 10.3 | 10.6 | 10.2 | 10.8 | 10.5 | 10.3 |
| 1994 | 11.5 | 11.9 | 12.1 | 12.2 | 12.1 | 11.6 | 11.4 | 11.2 | 11.5 | 10.7 | 10.2 | 10.3 | 10.9 | 10.1 | 10.1 | 10.4 | 9.9 | 10.5 | 10.2 | 9.9 |
| 1995 | 11.9 | 12.4 | 12.5 | 12.7 | 12.6 | 12.2 | 11.9 | 11.8 | 12.1 | 11.2 | 10.8 | 10.9 | 11.5 | 10.8 | 10.7 | 11.0 | 10.6 | 11.3 | 10.9 | 10.7 |
| 1996 | 12.1 | 12.6 | 12.7 | 12.9 | 12.8 | 12.4 | 12.1 | 12.0 | 12.3 | 11.5 | 11.1 | 11.2 | 11.8 | 11.1 | 11.1 | 11.4 | 10.9 | 11.6 | 11.3 | 11.1 |
| 1997 | 12.5 | 13.0 | 13.1 | 13.3 | 13.2 | 12.8 | 12.6 | 12.4 | 12.8 | 12.0 | 11.5 | 11.7 | 12.3 | 11.6 | 11.6 | 11.9 | 11.5 | 12.2 | 11.9 | 11.7 |
| 1998 | 12.8 | 13.2 | 13.4 | 13.6 | 13.5 | 13.1 | 12.9 | 12.8 | 13.1 | 12.3 | 11.9 | 12.0 | 12.7 | 12.0 | 12.0 | 12.3 | 11.9 | 12.6 | 12.3 | 12.2 |
| 1999 | 13.0 | 13.4 | 13.5 | 13.7 | 13.6 | 13.3 | 13.1 | 12.9 | 13.3 | 12.5 | 12.1 | 12.2 | 12.9 | 12.2 | 12.2 | 12.5 | 12.2 | 12.8 | 12.5 | 12.4 |
| 2000 | 12.5 | 12.9 | 13.1 | 13.2 | 13.1 | 12.8 | 12.5 | 12.4 | 12.7 | 12.0 | 11.6 | 11.7 | 12.3 | 11.6 | 11.6 | 11.9 | 11.6 | 12.2 | 11.9 | 11.8 |

# Table C-1 (page 5 of 5)

## Large Company Stocks Total Returns
Rates of Return for all holding periods
Percent per annum compounded annually

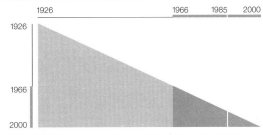

from 1926 to 2000

| To the end of | From the beginning of 1966 | 1967 | 1968 | 1969 | 1970 | 1971 | 1972 | 1973 | 1974 | 1975 | 1976 | 1977 | 1978 | 1979 | 1980 | 1981 | 1982 | 1983 | 1984 | 1985 |
|---|---|---|---|---|---|---|---|---|---|---|---|---|---|---|---|---|---|---|---|---|
| 1966 | -10.1 | | | | | | | | | | | | | | | | | | | |
| 1967 | 5.6 | 24.0 | | | | | | | | | | | | | | | | | | |
| 1968 | 7.4 | 17.3 | 11.1 | | | | | | | | | | | | | | | | | |
| 1969 | 3.2 | 8.0 | 0.8 | -8.5 | | | | | | | | | | | | | | | | |
| 1970 | 3.3 | 7.0 | 1.9 | -2.4 | 4.0 | | | | | | | | | | | | | | | |
| 1971 | 5.1 | 8.4 | 4.8 | 2.8 | 9.0 | 14.3 | | | | | | | | | | | | | | |
| 1972 | 7.0 | 10.1 | 7.5 | 6.7 | 12.3 | 16.6 | 19.0 | | | | | | | | | | | | | |
| 1973 | 4.0 | 6.2 | 3.5 | 2.0 | 4.8 | 5.1 | 0.8 | -14.7 | | | | | | | | | | | | |
| 1974 | 0.1 | 1.4 | -1.5 | -3.4 | -2.4 | -3.9 | -9.3 | -20.8 | -26.5 | | | | | | | | | | | |
| 1975 | 3.3 | 4.9 | 2.7 | 1.6 | 3.3 | 3.2 | 0.6 | -4.9 | 0.4 | 37.2 | | | | | | | | | | |
| 1976 | 5.0 | 6.6 | 4.9 | 4.1 | 6.0 | 6.4 | 4.9 | 1.6 | 7.7 | 30.4 | 23.8 | | | | | | | | | |
| 1977 | 3.9 | 5.3 | 3.6 | 2.8 | 4.3 | 4.3 | 2.8 | -0.2 | 3.8 | 16.4 | 7.2 | -7.2 | | | | | | | | |
| 1978 | 4.1 | 5.4 | 3.9 | 3.2 | 4.5 | 4.6 | 3.3 | 0.9 | 4.3 | 13.9 | 7.0 | -0.5 | 6.6 | | | | | | | |
| 1979 | 5.1 | 6.3 | 5.0 | 4.5 | 5.9 | 6.1 | 5.1 | 3.2 | 6.6 | 14.8 | 9.7 | 5.4 | 12.3 | 18.4 | | | | | | |
| 1980 | 6.7 | 8.0 | 6.9 | 6.5 | 8.0 | 8.4 | 7.8 | 6.5 | 9.9 | 17.5 | 13.9 | 11.6 | 18.7 | 25.2 | 32.4 | | | | | |
| 1981 | 5.9 | 7.1 | 6.0 | 5.6 | 6.9 | 7.2 | 6.5 | 5.2 | 7.9 | 14.0 | 10.6 | 8.1 | 12.3 | 14.3 | 12.2 | -4.9 | | | | |
| 1982 | 6.8 | 8.0 | 7.0 | 6.7 | 7.9 | 8.3 | 7.7 | 6.7 | 9.4 | 14.9 | 12.1 | 10.2 | 14.0 | 16.0 | 15.2 | 7.4 | 21.4 | | | |
| 1983 | 7.6 | 8.8 | 7.9 | 7.7 | 8.9 | 9.3 | 8.9 | 8.0 | 10.6 | 15.7 | 13.3 | 11.9 | 15.4 | 17.3 | 17.0 | 12.3 | 22.0 | 22.5 | | |
| 1984 | 7.5 | 8.6 | 7.8 | 7.6 | 8.7 | 9.1 | 8.7 | 7.9 | 10.2 | 14.8 | 12.5 | 11.2 | 14.1 | 15.4 | 14.8 | 10.7 | 16.5 | 14.1 | 6.3 | |
| 1985 | 8.7 | 9.7 | 9.0 | 8.9 | 10.1 | 10.5 | 10.2 | 9.6 | 11.9 | 16.2 | 14.3 | 13.3 | 16.2 | 17.6 | 17.5 | 14.7 | 20.2 | 19.8 | 18.5 | 32.2 |
| 1986 | 9.1 | 10.2 | 9.5 | 9.4 | 10.6 | 11.0 | 10.8 | 10.2 | 12.4 | 16.4 | 14.7 | 13.8 | 16.4 | 17.7 | 17.6 | 15.3 | 19.9 | 19.5 | 18.5 | 25.1 |
| 1987 | 8.9 | 9.9 | 9.3 | 9.2 | 10.3 | 10.6 | 10.4 | 9.9 | 11.9 | 15.5 | 13.9 | 13.0 | 15.3 | 16.3 | 16.0 | 13.8 | 17.3 | 16.5 | 15.0 | 18.1 |
| 1988 | 9.3 | 10.2 | 9.6 | 9.5 | 10.6 | 11.0 | 10.8 | 10.3 | 12.2 | 15.6 | 14.1 | 13.3 | 15.4 | 16.3 | 16.1 | 14.2 | 17.2 | 16.5 | 15.4 | 17.8 |
| 1989 | 10.1 | 11.1 | 10.5 | 10.5 | 11.5 | 12.0 | 11.8 | 11.4 | 13.3 | 16.6 | 15.3 | 14.6 | 16.7 | 17.6 | 17.5 | 16.0 | 18.9 | 18.6 | 17.9 | 20.4 |
| 1990 | 9.5 | 10.4 | 9.9 | 9.8 | 10.8 | 11.2 | 11.0 | 10.6 | 12.3 | 15.3 | 13.9 | 13.3 | 15.0 | 15.7 | 15.5 | 13.9 | 16.2 | 15.6 | 14.6 | 16.1 |
| 1991 | 10.3 | 11.2 | 10.7 | 10.7 | 11.6 | 12.0 | 11.9 | 11.5 | 13.2 | 16.1 | 14.9 | 14.3 | 16.0 | 16.8 | 16.7 | 15.3 | 17.6 | 17.2 | 16.5 | 18.1 |
| 1992 | 10.2 | 11.1 | 10.6 | 10.5 | 11.5 | 11.8 | 11.7 | 11.3 | 12.9 | 15.6 | 14.5 | 13.9 | 15.5 | 16.1 | 16.0 | 14.7 | 16.7 | 16.2 | 15.5 | 16.7 |
| 1993 | 10.2 | 11.0 | 10.5 | 10.5 | 11.4 | 11.7 | 11.6 | 11.3 | 12.8 | 15.3 | 14.2 | 13.7 | 15.1 | 15.7 | 15.5 | 14.3 | 16.1 | 15.6 | 14.9 | 16.0 |
| 1994 | 9.9 | 10.6 | 10.2 | 10.1 | 11.0 | 11.3 | 11.1 | 10.8 | 12.2 | 14.6 | 13.5 | 12.9 | 14.3 | 14.8 | 14.5 | 13.3 | 14.9 | 14.3 | 13.6 | 14.4 |
| 1995 | 10.7 | 11.5 | 11.1 | 11.1 | 11.9 | 12.2 | 12.1 | 11.8 | 13.2 | 15.6 | 14.6 | 14.1 | 15.4 | 16.0 | 15.8 | 14.8 | 16.4 | 16.0 | 15.4 | 16.3 |
| 1996 | 11.1 | 11.8 | 11.5 | 11.5 | 12.3 | 12.6 | 12.5 | 12.3 | 13.6 | 15.9 | 15.0 | 14.6 | 15.8 | 16.4 | 16.2 | 15.3 | 16.8 | 16.5 | 16.0 | 16.9 |
| 1997 | 11.7 | 12.5 | 12.1 | 12.2 | 13.0 | 13.3 | 13.3 | 13.1 | 14.4 | 16.6 | 15.8 | 15.4 | 16.6 | 17.2 | 17.1 | 16.3 | 17.8 | 17.5 | 17.2 | 18.1 |
| 1998 | 12.2 | 13.0 | 12.6 | 12.7 | 13.5 | 13.8 | 13.8 | 13.6 | 14.9 | 17.1 | 16.3 | 16.0 | 17.2 | 17.7 | 17.7 | 16.9 | 18.4 | 18.2 | 17.9 | 18.8 |
| 1999 | 12.4 | 13.2 | 12.9 | 12.9 | 13.7 | 14.1 | 14.1 | 13.9 | 15.2 | 17.2 | 16.5 | 16.2 | 17.4 | 17.9 | 17.9 | 17.2 | 18.5 | 18.4 | 18.1 | 18.9 |
| 2000 | 11.7 | 12.5 | 12.1 | 12.2 | 12.9 | 13.2 | 13.2 | 13.0 | 14.2 | 16.1 | 15.3 | 15.0 | 16.1 | 16.5 | 16.4 | 15.7 | 16.9 | 16.6 | 16.3 | 17.0 |

| To the end of | From the beginning of 1986 | 1987 | 1988 | 1989 | 1990 | 1991 | 1992 | 1993 | 1994 | 1995 | 1996 | 1997 | 1998 | 1999 | 2000 |
|---|---|---|---|---|---|---|---|---|---|---|---|---|---|---|---|
| 1986 | 18.5 | | | | | | | | | | | | | | |
| 1987 | 11.7 | 5.2 | | | | | | | | | | | | | |
| 1988 | 13.3 | 10.9 | 16.8 | | | | | | | | | | | | |
| 1989 | 17.6 | 17.4 | 23.9 | 31.5 | | | | | | | | | | | |
| 1990 | 13.1 | 11.8 | 14.1 | 12.8 | -3.2 | | | | | | | | | | |
| 1991 | 15.9 | 15.4 | 18.0 | 18.5 | 12.4 | 30.5 | | | | | | | | | |
| 1992 | 14.7 | 14.0 | 15.9 | 15.7 | 10.8 | 18.6 | 7.7 | | | | | | | | |
| 1993 | 14.1 | 13.5 | 14.9 | 14.5 | 10.6 | 15.6 | 8.8 | 10.0 | | | | | | | |
| 1994 | 12.6 | 11.9 | 12.8 | 12.2 | 8.7 | 11.9 | 6.3 | 5.6 | 1.3 | | | | | | |
| 1995 | 14.8 | 14.4 | 15.7 | 15.5 | 13.0 | 16.6 | 13.3 | 15.3 | 18.0 | 37.4 | | | | | |
| 1996 | 15.6 | 15.3 | 16.5 | 16.4 | 14.4 | 17.6 | 15.2 | 17.2 | 19.7 | 30.1 | 23.1 | | | | |
| 1997 | 17.0 | 16.8 | 18.0 | 18.2 | 16.6 | 19.8 | 18.0 | 20.2 | 23.0 | 31.1 | 28.1 | 33.4 | | | |
| 1998 | 17.8 | 17.8 | 19.0 | 19.2 | 17.9 | 20.8 | 19.5 | 21.6 | 24.1 | 30.5 | 28.3 | 31.0 | 28.6 | | |
| 1999 | 18.0 | 18.0 | 19.1 | 19.4 | 18.2 | 20.9 | 19.7 | 21.5 | 23.5 | 28.6 | 26.4 | 27.6 | 24.8 | 21.0 | |
| 2000 | 16.0 | 15.8 | 16.7 | 16.7 | 15.4 | 17.5 | 16.1 | 17.2 | 18.2 | 21.3 | 18.4 | 17.2 | 12.3 | 4.9 | -9.1 |

## Table C-2 (Page 1 of 5)

### Small Company Stocks Total Returns
Rates of Return for all holding periods
Percent per annum compounded annually

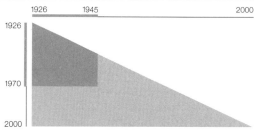

from 1926 to 2000

| To the end of | From the beginning of 1926 | 1927 | 1928 | 1929 | 1930 | 1931 | 1932 | 1933 | 1934 | 1935 | 1936 | 1937 | 1938 | 1939 | 1940 | 1941 | 1942 | 1943 | 1944 | 1945 |
|---|---|---|---|---|---|---|---|---|---|---|---|---|---|---|---|---|---|---|---|---|
| 1926 | 0.3 | | | | | | | | | | | | | | | | | | | |
| 1927 | 10.7 | 22.1 | | | | | | | | | | | | | | | | | | |
| 1928 | 19.6 | 30.6 | 39.7 | | | | | | | | | | | | | | | | | |
| 1929 | −4.5 | −6.0 | −17.6 | −51.4 | | | | | | | | | | | | | | | | |
| 1930 | −12.4 | −15.4 | −25.1 | −45.1 | −38.1 | | | | | | | | | | | | | | | |
| 1931 | −20.2 | −23.7 | −32.2 | −46.7 | −44.3 | −49.8 | | | | | | | | | | | | | | |
| 1932 | −18.2 | −21.0 | −27.5 | −38.5 | −33.5 | −31.1 | −5.4 | | | | | | | | | | | | | |
| 1933 | −6.3 | −7.2 | −11.4 | −19.1 | −8.1 | 4.9 | 51.6 | 142.9 | | | | | | | | | | | | |
| 1934 | −3.3 | −3.8 | −7.0 | −13.1 | −2.4 | 9.4 | 41.9 | 73.7 | 24.2 | | | | | | | | | | | |
| 1935 | 0.3 | 0.3 | −2.1 | −6.9 | 3.7 | 15.0 | 41.4 | 61.7 | 32.0 | 40.2 | | | | | | | | | | |
| 1936 | 5.0 | 5.5 | 3.7 | 0.0 | 10.8 | 22.1 | 45.8 | 62.5 | 42.1 | 52.0 | 64.8 | | | | | | | | | |
| 1937 | −2.7 | −3.0 | −5.2 | −9.2 | −1.9 | 4.8 | 18.5 | 24.0 | 4.8 | −1.0 | −16.8 | −58.0 | | | | | | | | |
| 1938 | −0.4 | −0.4 | −2.3 | −5.7 | 1.5 | 8.0 | 20.4 | 25.4 | 9.9 | 6.5 | −2.8 | −25.3 | 32.8 | | | | | | | |
| 1939 | −0.3 | −0.4 | −2.1 | −5.2 | 1.4 | 7.1 | 17.7 | 21.5 | 8.2 | 5.3 | −2.0 | −17.6 | 15.4 | 0.3 | | | | | | |
| 1940 | −0.7 | −0.7 | −2.3 | −5.2 | 0.8 | 5.8 | 14.9 | 17.8 | 6.2 | 3.5 | −2.6 | −14.6 | 8.1 | −2.4 | −5.2 | | | | | |
| 1941 | −1.2 | −1.3 | −2.8 | −5.5 | −0.1 | 4.4 | 12.3 | 14.4 | 4.2 | 1.6 | −3.7 | −13.5 | 3.6 | −4.7 | −7.1 | −9.0 | | | | |
| 1942 | 1.0 | 1.1 | −0.2 | −2.6 | 2.8 | 7.2 | 14.9 | 17.1 | 8.0 | 6.2 | 2.0 | −5.8 | 10.7 | 5.8 | 7.6 | 14.7 | 44.5 | | | |
| 1943 | 4.6 | 4.8 | 3.9 | 1.8 | 7.3 | 12.0 | 19.7 | 22.3 | 14.2 | 13.1 | 10.1 | 4.0 | 21.0 | 18.7 | 23.8 | 35.3 | 65.0 | 88.4 | | |
| 1944 | 6.7 | 7.1 | 6.3 | 4.5 | 9.9 | 14.5 | 22.0 | 24.7 | 17.3 | 16.7 | 14.3 | 9.2 | 25.2 | 23.9 | 29.3 | 39.7 | 61.1 | 70.2 | 53.7 | |
| 1945 | 9.4 | 9.9 | 9.2 | 7.6 | 13.1 | 17.8 | 25.2 | 27.9 | 21.2 | 21.0 | 19.2 | 15.0 | 30.4 | 30.1 | 35.8 | 45.9 | 64.2 | 71.3 | 63.4 | 73.6 |
| 1946 | 8.3 | 8.7 | 8.0 | 6.5 | 11.5 | 15.7 | 22.3 | 24.5 | 18.3 | 17.8 | 16.0 | 12.0 | 24.9 | 23.9 | 27.7 | 34.2 | 45.0 | 45.2 | 33.1 | 23.9 |
| 1947 | 7.9 | 8.3 | 7.6 | 6.2 | 10.9 | 14.7 | 20.8 | 22.8 | 17.0 | 16.4 | 14.6 | 10.9 | 22.2 | 21.1 | 24.0 | 28.8 | 36.5 | 35.0 | 24.2 | 15.7 |
| 1948 | 7.5 | 7.8 | 7.2 | 5.7 | 10.2 | 13.7 | 19.3 | 21.1 | 15.6 | 15.0 | 13.3 | 9.8 | 19.8 | 18.6 | 20.8 | 24.5 | 30.2 | 28.0 | 18.4 | 11.0 |
| 1949 | 7.9 | 8.3 | 7.7 | 6.4 | 10.6 | 14.0 | 19.4 | 21.0 | 15.8 | 15.3 | 13.7 | 10.5 | 19.8 | 18.7 | 20.7 | 24.0 | 28.8 | 26.7 | 18.6 | 12.7 |
| 1950 | 9.0 | 9.4 | 8.9 | 7.7 | 11.8 | 15.2 | 20.3 | 21.9 | 17.1 | 16.7 | 15.2 | 12.3 | 21.2 | 20.2 | 22.2 | 25.4 | 29.9 | 28.2 | 21.3 | 16.6 |
| 1951 | 9.0 | 9.3 | 8.8 | 7.7 | 11.6 | 14.8 | 19.7 | 21.1 | 16.5 | 16.1 | 14.8 | 12.0 | 20.1 | 19.2 | 21.0 | 23.7 | 27.5 | 25.7 | 19.6 | 15.3 |
| 1952 | 8.8 | 9.1 | 8.6 | 7.5 | 11.2 | 14.2 | 18.8 | 20.2 | 15.8 | 15.3 | 14.0 | 11.4 | 18.9 | 18.0 | 19.5 | 21.8 | 25.1 | 23.3 | 17.6 | 13.7 |
| 1953 | 8.2 | 8.5 | 8.0 | 6.9 | 10.4 | 13.3 | 17.5 | 18.7 | 14.6 | 14.1 | 12.8 | 10.3 | 17.2 | 16.2 | 17.4 | 19.3 | 22.1 | 20.2 | 14.9 | 11.3 |
| 1954 | 9.7 | 10.0 | 9.6 | 8.6 | 12.1 | 14.9 | 19.1 | 20.4 | 16.4 | 16.0 | 14.9 | 12.6 | 19.3 | 18.6 | 19.9 | 21.9 | 24.7 | 23.1 | 18.5 | 15.4 |
| 1955 | 10.0 | 10.3 | 9.9 | 9.0 | 12.4 | 15.1 | 19.2 | 20.4 | 16.6 | 16.3 | 15.2 | 13.0 | 19.4 | 18.7 | 19.9 | 21.8 | 24.4 | 22.9 | 18.6 | 15.9 |
| 1956 | 9.8 | 10.1 | 9.7 | 8.8 | 12.1 | 14.7 | 18.5 | 19.7 | 16.0 | 15.7 | 14.6 | 12.6 | 18.6 | 17.8 | 18.9 | 20.6 | 22.9 | 21.5 | 17.5 | 14.9 |
| 1957 | 8.9 | 9.2 | 8.8 | 7.9 | 11.0 | 13.4 | 17.1 | 18.1 | 14.6 | 14.2 | 13.1 | 11.1 | 16.6 | 15.8 | 16.8 | 18.2 | 20.1 | 18.7 | 14.8 | 12.3 |
| 1958 | 10.3 | 10.7 | 10.3 | 9.4 | 12.5 | 15.0 | 18.6 | 19.6 | 16.2 | 15.9 | 15.0 | 13.1 | 18.6 | 17.9 | 18.9 | 20.4 | 22.4 | 21.1 | 17.6 | 15.4 |
| 1959 | 10.5 | 10.8 | 10.5 | 9.7 | 12.7 | 15.0 | 18.5 | 19.5 | 16.3 | 15.9 | 15.0 | 13.2 | 18.5 | 17.8 | 18.8 | 20.2 | 22.1 | 20.9 | 17.6 | 15.5 |
| 1960 | 10.1 | 10.4 | 10.0 | 9.2 | 12.1 | 14.4 | 17.7 | 18.6 | 15.5 | 15.1 | 14.2 | 12.5 | 17.4 | 16.8 | 17.6 | 18.9 | 20.6 | 19.4 | 16.2 | 14.2 |
| 1961 | 10.6 | 10.9 | 10.6 | 9.9 | 12.7 | 14.9 | 18.1 | 19.0 | 16.0 | 15.7 | 14.9 | 13.2 | 18.0 | 17.4 | 18.2 | 19.5 | 21.1 | 20.0 | 17.0 | 15.2 |
| 1962 | 10.0 | 10.2 | 9.9 | 9.1 | 11.9 | 13.9 | 17.0 | 17.8 | 14.9 | 14.6 | 13.8 | 12.1 | 16.6 | 16.0 | 16.7 | 17.8 | 19.3 | 18.2 | 15.3 | 13.5 |
| 1963 | 10.3 | 10.6 | 10.3 | 9.5 | 12.2 | 14.2 | 17.2 | 18.0 | 15.2 | 14.9 | 14.1 | 12.5 | 16.9 | 16.3 | 17.0 | 18.1 | 19.5 | 18.4 | 15.7 | 14.0 |
| 1964 | 10.6 | 10.9 | 10.6 | 9.9 | 12.5 | 14.5 | 17.4 | 18.2 | 15.5 | 15.2 | 14.4 | 12.9 | 17.1 | 16.6 | 17.3 | 18.3 | 19.7 | 18.6 | 16.1 | 14.4 |
| 1965 | 11.3 | 11.6 | 11.3 | 10.7 | 13.2 | 15.2 | 18.0 | 18.8 | 16.2 | 16.0 | 15.2 | 13.8 | 17.9 | 17.4 | 18.1 | 19.2 | 20.5 | 19.6 | 17.1 | 15.6 |
| 1966 | 10.8 | 11.1 | 10.8 | 10.2 | 12.6 | 14.5 | 17.2 | 18.0 | 15.4 | 15.2 | 14.4 | 13.0 | 17.0 | 16.4 | 17.1 | 18.0 | 19.3 | 18.3 | 16.0 | 14.5 |
| 1967 | 12.2 | 12.5 | 12.2 | 11.6 | 14.1 | 16.0 | 18.7 | 19.5 | 17.0 | 16.8 | 16.1 | 14.8 | 18.7 | 18.3 | 19.0 | 20.0 | 21.3 | 20.4 | 18.2 | 16.9 |
| 1968 | 12.7 | 13.0 | 12.8 | 12.2 | 14.6 | 16.5 | 19.1 | 19.9 | 17.5 | 17.3 | 16.7 | 15.4 | 19.3 | 18.8 | 19.5 | 20.5 | 21.8 | 21.0 | 18.9 | 17.6 |
| 1969 | 11.6 | 11.9 | 11.7 | 11.1 | 13.4 | 15.2 | 17.7 | 18.4 | 16.1 | 15.8 | 15.2 | 13.9 | 17.5 | 17.1 | 17.7 | 18.6 | 19.7 | 18.9 | 16.8 | 15.5 |
| 1970 | 10.9 | 11.1 | 10.9 | 10.3 | 12.5 | 14.2 | 16.6 | 17.3 | 15.0 | 14.7 | 14.1 | 12.9 | 16.3 | 15.8 | 16.3 | 17.1 | 18.2 | 17.3 | 15.3 | 14.0 |

## Table C-2 (Page 2 of 5)

### Small Company Stocks Total Returns
Rates of Return for all holding periods
Percent per annum compounded annually

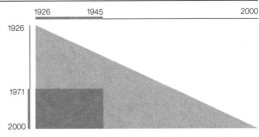

### from 1926 to 2000

| To the end of | From the beginning of 1926 | 1927 | 1928 | 1929 | 1930 | 1931 | 1932 | 1933 | 1934 | 1935 | 1936 | 1937 | 1938 | 1939 | 1940 | 1941 | 1942 | 1943 | 1944 | 1945 |
|---|---|---|---|---|---|---|---|---|---|---|---|---|---|---|---|---|---|---|---|---|
| 1971 | 11.0 | 11.2 | 11.0 | 10.4 | 12.6 | 14.3 | 16.6 | 17.3 | 15.0 | 14.8 | 14.2 | 13.0 | 16.3 | 15.8 | 16.4 | 17.1 | 18.1 | 17.3 | 15.3 | 14.1 |
| 1972 | 10.9 | 11.1 | 10.9 | 10.3 | 12.4 | 14.0 | 16.3 | 16.9 | 14.7 | 14.5 | 13.9 | 12.7 | 15.9 | 15.5 | 16.0 | 16.7 | 17.6 | 16.8 | 14.9 | 13.7 |
| 1973 | 9.8 | 10.0 | 9.7 | 9.1 | 11.2 | 12.7 | 14.9 | 15.4 | 13.3 | 13.0 | 12.4 | 11.2 | 14.3 | 13.8 | 14.2 | 14.9 | 15.7 | 14.9 | 13.0 | 11.8 |
| 1974 | 9.1 | 9.3 | 9.0 | 8.4 | 10.4 | 11.8 | 13.9 | 14.4 | 12.3 | 12.1 | 11.4 | 10.3 | 13.2 | 12.7 | 13.1 | 13.7 | 14.4 | 13.6 | 11.7 | 10.6 |
| 1975 | 9.8 | 10.0 | 9.8 | 9.2 | 11.1 | 12.6 | 14.7 | 15.2 | 13.2 | 12.9 | 12.3 | 11.2 | 14.1 | 13.6 | 14.0 | 14.6 | 15.4 | 14.6 | 12.8 | 11.7 |
| 1976 | 10.6 | 10.8 | 10.6 | 10.0 | 12.0 | 13.4 | 15.5 | 16.0 | 14.0 | 13.8 | 13.2 | 12.2 | 15.0 | 14.6 | 15.0 | 15.6 | 16.4 | 15.7 | 14.0 | 12.9 |
| 1977 | 10.8 | 11.1 | 10.9 | 10.3 | 12.2 | 13.7 | 15.7 | 16.2 | 14.3 | 14.1 | 13.5 | 12.5 | 15.3 | 14.9 | 15.3 | 15.9 | 16.7 | 16.0 | 14.3 | 13.3 |
| 1978 | 11.1 | 11.3 | 11.1 | 10.6 | 12.4 | 13.9 | 15.9 | 16.4 | 14.5 | 14.3 | 13.7 | 12.7 | 15.5 | 15.1 | 15.5 | 16.1 | 16.8 | 16.2 | 14.6 | 13.6 |
| 1979 | 11.6 | 11.8 | 11.6 | 11.1 | 13.0 | 14.4 | 16.4 | 16.9 | 15.0 | 14.8 | 14.3 | 13.4 | 16.1 | 15.7 | 16.1 | 16.7 | 17.5 | 16.8 | 15.3 | 14.3 |
| 1980 | 12.1 | 12.3 | 12.1 | 11.6 | 13.5 | 14.9 | 16.8 | 17.3 | 15.5 | 15.3 | 14.8 | 13.9 | 16.6 | 16.2 | 16.6 | 17.2 | 18.0 | 17.4 | 15.9 | 15.0 |
| 1981 | 12.1 | 12.3 | 12.1 | 11.7 | 13.5 | 14.8 | 16.8 | 17.3 | 15.5 | 15.3 | 14.8 | 13.9 | 16.5 | 16.2 | 16.6 | 17.2 | 17.9 | 17.3 | 15.8 | 14.9 |
| 1982 | 12.4 | 12.6 | 12.4 | 12.0 | 13.7 | 15.1 | 17.0 | 17.5 | 15.7 | 15.6 | 15.1 | 14.2 | 16.8 | 16.4 | 16.8 | 17.4 | 18.1 | 17.5 | 16.1 | 15.3 |
| 1983 | 12.8 | 13.0 | 12.9 | 12.4 | 14.2 | 15.5 | 17.4 | 17.9 | 16.2 | 16.0 | 15.6 | 14.7 | 17.2 | 16.9 | 17.3 | 17.9 | 18.6 | 18.0 | 16.7 | 15.8 |
| 1984 | 12.4 | 12.6 | 12.5 | 12.0 | 13.8 | 15.0 | 16.9 | 17.3 | 15.7 | 15.5 | 15.0 | 14.2 | 16.6 | 16.3 | 16.7 | 17.3 | 17.9 | 17.4 | 16.0 | 15.2 |
| 1985 | 12.6 | 12.8 | 12.7 | 12.3 | 13.9 | 15.2 | 17.0 | 17.5 | 15.8 | 15.7 | 15.2 | 14.4 | 16.8 | 16.5 | 16.9 | 17.4 | 18.1 | 17.5 | 16.2 | 15.4 |
| 1986 | 12.5 | 12.7 | 12.6 | 12.2 | 13.8 | 15.1 | 16.8 | 17.3 | 15.7 | 15.5 | 15.1 | 14.2 | 16.6 | 16.3 | 16.6 | 17.2 | 17.8 | 17.3 | 16.0 | 15.2 |
| 1987 | 12.1 | 12.3 | 12.2 | 11.8 | 13.4 | 14.6 | 16.3 | 16.7 | 15.1 | 15.0 | 14.5 | 13.7 | 16.0 | 15.7 | 16.0 | 16.5 | 17.2 | 16.6 | 15.4 | 14.6 |
| 1988 | 12.3 | 12.5 | 12.3 | 11.9 | 13.5 | 14.7 | 16.4 | 16.8 | 15.3 | 15.1 | 14.7 | 13.9 | 16.1 | 15.8 | 16.2 | 16.7 | 17.3 | 16.8 | 15.5 | 14.8 |
| 1989 | 12.2 | 12.5 | 12.3 | 11.9 | 13.5 | 14.6 | 16.3 | 16.7 | 15.2 | 15.0 | 14.6 | 13.8 | 16.0 | 15.7 | 16.0 | 16.5 | 17.1 | 16.6 | 15.4 | 14.7 |
| 1990 | 11.6 | 11.8 | 11.7 | 11.3 | 12.8 | 13.9 | 15.5 | 15.9 | 14.4 | 14.2 | 13.8 | 13.0 | 15.2 | 14.9 | 15.2 | 15.6 | 16.2 | 15.6 | 14.5 | 13.7 |
| 1991 | 12.1 | 12.3 | 12.1 | 11.7 | 13.2 | 14.4 | 15.9 | 16.3 | 14.9 | 14.7 | 14.3 | 13.5 | 15.7 | 15.4 | 15.7 | 16.1 | 16.7 | 16.2 | 15.0 | 14.3 |
| 1992 | 12.2 | 12.4 | 12.3 | 11.9 | 13.4 | 14.5 | 16.1 | 16.5 | 15.0 | 14.9 | 14.5 | 13.7 | 15.8 | 15.5 | 15.8 | 16.3 | 16.8 | 16.3 | 15.2 | 14.5 |
| 1993 | 12.4 | 12.5 | 12.4 | 12.0 | 13.5 | 14.6 | 16.1 | 16.5 | 15.1 | 15.0 | 14.6 | 13.8 | 15.9 | 15.6 | 15.9 | 16.3 | 16.9 | 16.4 | 15.3 | 14.6 |
| 1994 | 12.2 | 12.4 | 12.3 | 11.9 | 13.3 | 14.4 | 15.9 | 16.3 | 14.9 | 14.8 | 14.4 | 13.6 | 15.6 | 15.4 | 15.7 | 16.1 | 16.6 | 16.1 | 15.0 | 14.4 |
| 1995 | 12.5 | 12.7 | 12.6 | 12.2 | 13.6 | 14.7 | 16.2 | 16.6 | 15.2 | 15.1 | 14.7 | 14.0 | 15.9 | 15.7 | 16.0 | 16.4 | 16.9 | 16.5 | 15.4 | 14.7 |
| 1996 | 12.6 | 12.8 | 12.6 | 12.3 | 13.7 | 14.7 | 16.2 | 16.6 | 15.2 | 15.1 | 14.7 | 14.0 | 16.0 | 15.7 | 16.0 | 16.4 | 16.9 | 16.5 | 15.4 | 14.8 |
| 1997 | 12.7 | 12.9 | 12.8 | 12.4 | 13.8 | 14.9 | 16.3 | 16.7 | 15.3 | 15.2 | 14.8 | 14.2 | 16.1 | 15.8 | 16.1 | 16.5 | 17.0 | 16.6 | 15.6 | 14.9 |
| 1998 | 12.4 | 12.6 | 12.5 | 12.1 | 13.5 | 14.5 | 15.9 | 16.3 | 15.0 | 14.8 | 14.5 | 13.8 | 15.7 | 15.4 | 15.7 | 16.1 | 16.6 | 16.1 | 15.1 | 14.5 |
| 1999 | 12.6 | 12.8 | 12.7 | 12.3 | 13.7 | 14.7 | 16.1 | 16.5 | 15.2 | 15.0 | 14.7 | 14.0 | 15.9 | 15.6 | 15.9 | 16.3 | 16.8 | 16.3 | 15.3 | 14.7 |
| 2000 | 12.4 | 12.6 | 12.4 | 12.1 | 13.4 | 14.4 | 15.8 | 16.1 | 14.9 | 14.7 | 14.4 | 13.7 | 15.5 | 15.3 | 15.5 | 15.9 | 16.4 | 16.0 | 15.0 | 14.4 |

# Table C-2 (Page 3 of 5)

## Small Company Stocks Total Returns
Rates of Return for all holding periods
Percent per annum compounded annually

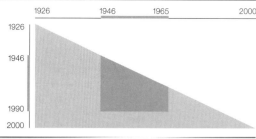

from 1926 to 2000

| To the end of | From the beginning of 1946 | 1947 | 1948 | 1949 | 1950 | 1951 | 1952 | 1953 | 1954 | 1955 | 1956 | 1957 | 1958 | 1959 | 1960 | 1961 | 1962 | 1963 | 1964 | 1965 |
|---|---|---|---|---|---|---|---|---|---|---|---|---|---|---|---|---|---|---|---|---|
| 1946 | -11.6 | | | | | | | | | | | | | | | | | | | |
| 1947 | -5.6 | 0.9 | | | | | | | | | | | | | | | | | | |
| 1948 | -4.4 | -0.6 | -2.1 | | | | | | | | | | | | | | | | | |
| 1949 | 1.1 | 5.8 | 8.3 | 19.7 | | | | | | | | | | | | | | | | |
| 1950 | 7.7 | 13.2 | 17.6 | 28.9 | 38.7 | | | | | | | | | | | | | | | |
| 1951 | 7.7 | 12.1 | 15.1 | 21.4 | 22.3 | 7.8 | | | | | | | | | | | | | | |
| 1952 | 7.0 | 10.5 | 12.6 | 16.6 | 15.5 | 5.4 | 3.0 | | | | | | | | | | | | | |
| 1953 | 5.3 | 7.9 | 9.1 | 11.5 | 9.6 | 1.3 | -1.8 | -6.5 | | | | | | | | | | | | |
| 1954 | 10.3 | 13.4 | 15.3 | 18.5 | 18.3 | 13.6 | 15.7 | 22.5 | 60.6 | | | | | | | | | | | |
| 1955 | 11.3 | 14.2 | 15.9 | 18.8 | 18.6 | 15.0 | 16.8 | 21.8 | 39.1 | 20.4 | | | | | | | | | | |
| 1956 | 10.6 | 13.1 | 14.6 | 16.9 | 16.5 | 13.1 | 14.2 | 17.2 | 26.3 | 12.1 | 4.3 | | | | | | | | | |
| 1957 | 8.3 | 10.3 | 11.3 | 12.9 | 12.0 | 8.7 | 8.8 | 10.0 | 14.6 | 2.4 | -5.6 | -14.6 | | | | | | | | |
| 1958 | 11.8 | 14.0 | 15.3 | 17.2 | 17.0 | 14.5 | 15.5 | 17.7 | 23.2 | 15.3 | 13.7 | 18.7 | 64.9 | | | | | | | |
| 1959 | 12.2 | 14.2 | 15.4 | 17.2 | 16.9 | 14.7 | 15.6 | 17.5 | 22.1 | 15.5 | 14.4 | 17.9 | 38.5 | 16.4 | | | | | | |
| 1960 | 11.1 | 12.9 | 13.9 | 15.3 | 14.9 | 12.8 | 13.3 | 14.7 | 18.1 | 12.2 | 10.6 | 12.2 | 22.9 | 6.1 | -3.3 | | | | | |
| 1961 | 12.3 | 14.1 | 15.1 | 16.5 | 16.2 | 14.4 | 15.1 | 16.5 | 19.7 | 14.8 | 13.9 | 15.9 | 25.1 | 14.1 | 13.0 | 32.1 | | | | |
| 1962 | 10.7 | 12.2 | 13.0 | 14.2 | 13.8 | 11.9 | 12.3 | 13.3 | 15.7 | 11.1 | 9.8 | 10.7 | 16.6 | 7.0 | 4.0 | 7.9 | -11.9 | | | |
| 1963 | 11.4 | 12.9 | 13.7 | 14.8 | 14.5 | 12.8 | 13.2 | 14.2 | 16.5 | 12.4 | 11.4 | 12.5 | 17.8 | 10.1 | 8.6 | 12.9 | 4.3 | 23.6 | | |
| 1964 | 12.0 | 13.4 | 14.2 | 15.3 | 15.0 | 13.5 | 14.0 | 14.9 | 17.1 | 13.5 | 12.7 | 13.8 | 18.6 | 12.2 | 11.4 | 15.4 | 10.4 | 23.5 | 23.5 | |
| 1965 | 13.3 | 14.8 | 15.6 | 16.7 | 16.6 | 15.2 | 15.8 | 16.8 | 19.0 | 15.8 | 15.3 | 16.6 | 21.3 | 16.0 | 16.0 | 20.3 | 17.5 | 29.3 | 32.3 | 41.8 |
| 1966 | 12.2 | 13.6 | 14.3 | 15.3 | 15.0 | 13.7 | 14.1 | 14.9 | 16.7 | 13.7 | 13.1 | 14.0 | 17.7 | 12.9 | 12.4 | 15.2 | 12.1 | 19.1 | 17.6 | 14.8 |
| 1967 | 14.8 | 16.2 | 17.0 | 18.1 | 18.0 | 16.9 | 17.5 | 18.6 | 20.6 | 18.0 | 17.8 | 19.1 | 23.1 | 19.1 | 19.5 | 23.2 | 21.7 | 29.9 | 31.5 | 34.3 |
| 1968 | 15.6 | 17.0 | 17.9 | 19.0 | 18.9 | 17.9 | 18.5 | 19.6 | 21.6 | 19.2 | 19.1 | 20.4 | 24.2 | 20.7 | 21.2 | 24.7 | 23.7 | 30.9 | 32.4 | 34.7 |
| 1969 | 13.5 | 14.8 | 15.5 | 16.4 | 16.2 | 15.1 | 15.6 | 16.3 | 17.9 | 15.5 | 15.2 | 16.1 | 19.1 | 15.6 | 15.5 | 17.8 | 16.2 | 20.8 | 20.4 | 19.8 |
| 1970 | 12.1 | 13.2 | 13.8 | 14.6 | 14.3 | 13.2 | 13.5 | 14.1 | 15.5 | 13.1 | 12.7 | 13.3 | 15.8 | 12.4 | 12.1 | 13.7 | 11.8 | 15.2 | 14.1 | 12.6 |
| 1971 | 12.3 | 13.4 | 13.9 | 14.7 | 14.4 | 13.4 | 13.7 | 14.3 | 15.5 | 13.3 | 12.9 | 13.5 | 15.8 | 12.7 | 12.4 | 14.0 | 12.3 | 15.4 | 14.4 | 13.1 |
| 1972 | 12.0 | 13.0 | 13.5 | 14.2 | 14.0 | 13.0 | 13.2 | 13.8 | 14.9 | 12.8 | 12.4 | 12.9 | 15.0 | 12.1 | 11.8 | 13.1 | 11.6 | 14.2 | 13.2 | 12.0 |
| 1973 | 10.1 | 11.0 | 11.4 | 11.9 | 11.6 | 10.6 | 10.7 | 11.1 | 12.0 | 9.9 | 9.4 | 9.7 | 11.4 | 8.5 | 8.0 | 8.9 | 7.2 | 9.1 | 7.8 | 6.2 |
| 1974 | 8.9 | 9.7 | 10.0 | 10.5 | 10.2 | 9.1 | 9.2 | 9.4 | 10.3 | 8.2 | 7.6 | 7.8 | 9.3 | 6.5 | 5.9 | 6.6 | 4.8 | 6.3 | 4.9 | 3.2 |
| 1975 | 10.1 | 10.9 | 11.3 | 11.8 | 11.5 | 10.6 | 10.7 | 11.0 | 11.9 | 10.0 | 9.5 | 9.8 | 11.3 | 8.8 | 8.3 | 9.2 | 7.7 | 9.3 | 8.2 | 6.9 |
| 1976 | 11.4 | 12.2 | 12.6 | 13.2 | 13.0 | 12.1 | 12.3 | 12.7 | 13.6 | 11.8 | 11.4 | 11.8 | 13.4 | 11.0 | 10.7 | 11.7 | 10.4 | 12.2 | 11.4 | 10.4 |
| 1977 | 11.8 | 12.6 | 13.1 | 13.6 | 13.4 | 12.6 | 12.7 | 13.1 | 14.1 | 12.4 | 12.0 | 12.4 | 13.9 | 11.8 | 11.5 | 12.4 | 11.3 | 13.1 | 12.3 | 11.5 |
| 1978 | 12.1 | 13.0 | 13.4 | 13.9 | 13.7 | 12.9 | 13.1 | 13.5 | 14.4 | 12.8 | 12.5 | 12.9 | 14.4 | 12.3 | 12.1 | 13.0 | 12.0 | 13.7 | 13.1 | 12.3 |
| 1979 | 12.9 | 13.8 | 14.2 | 14.8 | 14.6 | 13.9 | 14.1 | 14.5 | 15.4 | 13.9 | 13.6 | 14.1 | 15.6 | 13.6 | 13.5 | 14.5 | 13.5 | 15.3 | 14.8 | 14.2 |
| 1980 | 13.6 | 14.5 | 14.9 | 15.5 | 15.4 | 14.6 | 14.9 | 15.3 | 16.2 | 14.8 | 14.6 | 15.0 | 16.5 | 14.7 | 14.6 | 15.6 | 14.8 | 16.5 | 16.1 | 15.6 |
| 1981 | 13.6 | 14.5 | 14.9 | 15.4 | 15.3 | 14.6 | 14.9 | 15.3 | 16.2 | 14.8 | 14.6 | 15.0 | 16.4 | 14.7 | 14.6 | 15.5 | 14.8 | 16.4 | 16.0 | 15.5 |
| 1982 | 14.0 | 14.8 | 15.2 | 15.8 | 15.7 | 15.0 | 15.3 | 15.7 | 16.5 | 15.2 | 15.0 | 15.5 | 16.9 | 15.2 | 15.1 | 16.1 | 15.4 | 16.9 | 16.6 | 16.2 |
| 1983 | 14.6 | 15.4 | 15.9 | 16.4 | 16.3 | 15.7 | 16.0 | 16.4 | 17.2 | 16.0 | 15.8 | 16.3 | 17.7 | 16.1 | 16.1 | 17.0 | 16.4 | 17.9 | 17.6 | 17.3 |
| 1984 | 14.0 | 14.8 | 15.2 | 15.7 | 15.6 | 15.0 | 15.2 | 15.6 | 16.4 | 15.1 | 15.0 | 15.4 | 16.7 | 15.1 | 15.1 | 15.9 | 15.2 | 16.7 | 16.3 | 16.0 |
| 1985 | 14.3 | 15.0 | 15.4 | 15.9 | 15.8 | 15.2 | 15.5 | 15.9 | 16.6 | 15.4 | 15.3 | 15.7 | 16.9 | 15.5 | 15.4 | 16.2 | 15.6 | 17.0 | 16.7 | 16.4 |
| 1986 | 14.1 | 14.8 | 15.2 | 15.7 | 15.6 | 15.0 | 15.2 | 15.6 | 16.3 | 15.2 | 15.0 | 15.4 | 16.6 | 15.1 | 15.1 | 15.9 | 15.3 | 16.6 | 16.3 | 15.9 |
| 1987 | 13.5 | 14.2 | 14.5 | 15.0 | 14.8 | 14.3 | 14.4 | 14.8 | 15.5 | 14.3 | 14.1 | 14.5 | 15.6 | 14.2 | 14.1 | 14.8 | 14.2 | 15.4 | 15.1 | 14.7 |
| 1988 | 13.7 | 14.4 | 14.7 | 15.2 | 15.0 | 14.5 | 14.7 | 15.0 | 15.7 | 14.6 | 14.4 | 14.7 | 15.8 | 14.5 | 14.4 | 15.1 | 14.5 | 15.7 | 15.4 | 15.0 |
| 1989 | 13.6 | 14.3 | 14.6 | 15.0 | 14.9 | 14.4 | 14.5 | 14.9 | 15.5 | 14.4 | 14.3 | 14.6 | 15.7 | 14.3 | 14.3 | 14.9 | 14.4 | 15.5 | 15.2 | 14.8 |
| 1990 | 12.7 | 13.3 | 13.6 | 14.0 | 13.9 | 13.3 | 13.4 | 13.7 | 14.3 | 13.3 | 13.1 | 13.3 | 14.3 | 13.0 | 12.9 | 13.5 | 12.9 | 13.9 | 13.5 | 13.2 |

## Table C-2 (Page 4 of 5)

### Small Company Stocks Total Returns
Rates of Return for all holding periods
Percent per annum compounded annually

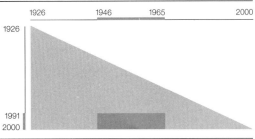

from 1926 to 2000

| To the end of | From the beginning of | | | | | | | | | | | | | | | | | | | |
|---|---|---|---|---|---|---|---|---|---|---|---|---|---|---|---|---|---|---|---|---|
| | 1946 | 1947 | 1948 | 1949 | 1950 | 1951 | 1952 | 1953 | 1954 | 1955 | 1956 | 1957 | 1958 | 1959 | 1960 | 1961 | 1962 | 1963 | 1964 | 1965 |
| 1991 | 13.3 | 13.9 | 14.2 | 14.6 | 14.5 | 14.0 | 14.1 | 14.4 | 15.0 | 14.0 | 13.8 | 14.1 | 15.1 | 13.8 | 13.8 | 14.4 | 13.8 | 14.8 | 14.5 | 14.2 |
| 1992 | 13.5 | 14.1 | 14.4 | 14.8 | 14.7 | 14.2 | 14.3 | 14.6 | 15.2 | 14.2 | 14.1 | 14.4 | 15.3 | 14.1 | 14.0 | 14.6 | 14.1 | 15.1 | 14.8 | 14.5 |
| 1993 | 13.6 | 14.2 | 14.5 | 14.9 | 14.8 | 14.3 | 14.5 | 14.8 | 15.4 | 14.4 | 14.3 | 14.5 | 15.5 | 14.3 | 14.2 | 14.8 | 14.3 | 15.3 | 15.0 | 14.7 |
| 1994 | 13.4 | 14.0 | 14.3 | 14.7 | 14.6 | 14.1 | 14.2 | 14.5 | 15.1 | 14.1 | 14.0 | 14.2 | 15.1 | 14.0 | 13.9 | 14.5 | 14.0 | 14.9 | 14.6 | 14.3 |
| 1995 | 13.8 | 14.4 | 14.7 | 15.1 | 15.0 | 14.5 | 14.6 | 14.9 | 15.5 | 14.6 | 14.4 | 14.7 | 15.6 | 14.5 | 14.4 | 15.0 | 14.5 | 15.4 | 15.2 | 14.9 |
| 1996 | 13.9 | 14.4 | 14.7 | 15.1 | 15.0 | 14.6 | 14.7 | 15.0 | 15.5 | 14.6 | 14.5 | 14.8 | 15.6 | 14.6 | 14.5 | 15.1 | 14.6 | 15.5 | 15.3 | 15.0 |
| 1997 | 14.0 | 14.6 | 14.9 | 15.3 | 15.2 | 14.7 | 14.9 | 15.2 | 15.7 | 14.8 | 14.7 | 15.0 | 15.8 | 14.8 | 14.7 | 15.3 | 14.8 | 15.7 | 15.5 | 15.2 |
| 1998 | 13.6 | 14.1 | 14.4 | 14.8 | 14.7 | 14.2 | 14.4 | 14.6 | 15.1 | 14.3 | 14.1 | 14.4 | 15.2 | 14.2 | 14.1 | 14.6 | 14.2 | 15.0 | 14.8 | 14.5 |
| 1999 | 13.9 | 14.4 | 14.7 | 15.0 | 15.0 | 14.5 | 14.7 | 14.9 | 15.4 | 14.6 | 14.5 | 14.7 | 15.5 | 14.5 | 14.5 | 15.0 | 14.5 | 15.4 | 15.1 | 14.9 |
| 2000 | 13.5 | 14.0 | 14.3 | 14.7 | 14.6 | 14.1 | 14.3 | 14.5 | 15.0 | 14.2 | 14.0 | 14.3 | 15.0 | 14.1 | 14.0 | 14.5 | 14.0 | 14.8 | 14.6 | 14.4 |

# Table C-2 (Page 5 of 5)

## Small Company Stocks Total Returns
Rates of Return for all holding periods
Percent per annum compounded annually

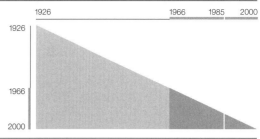

from 1926 to 2000

| To the end of | 1966 | 1967 | 1968 | 1969 | 1970 | 1971 | 1972 | 1973 | 1974 | 1975 | 1976 | 1977 | 1978 | 1979 | 1980 | 1981 | 1982 | 1983 | 1984 | 1985 |
|---|---|---|---|---|---|---|---|---|---|---|---|---|---|---|---|---|---|---|---|---|
| 1966 | -7.0 | | | | | | | | | | | | | | | | | | | |
| 1967 | 30.7 | 83.6 | | | | | | | | | | | | | | | | | | |
| 1968 | 32.4 | 58.0 | 36.0 | | | | | | | | | | | | | | | | | |
| 1969 | 14.8 | 23.2 | 0.9 | -25.1 | | | | | | | | | | | | | | | | |
| 1970 | 7.5 | 11.5 | -5.6 | -21.3 | -17.4 | | | | | | | | | | | | | | | |
| 1971 | 9.0 | 12.5 | -0.5 | -10.3 | -1.9 | 16.5 | | | | | | | | | | | | | | |
| 1972 | 8.3 | 11.1 | 0.5 | -6.9 | 0.2 | 10.3 | 4.4 | | | | | | | | | | | | | |
| 1973 | 2.4 | 3.8 | -5.6 | -12.3 | -8.7 | -5.6 | -15.1 | -30.9 | | | | | | | | | | | | |
| 1974 | -0.4 | 0.5 | -7.8 | -13.6 | -11.1 | -9.4 | -16.7 | -25.6 | -19.9 | | | | | | | | | | | |
| 1975 | 4.0 | 5.3 | -1.8 | -6.3 | -2.7 | 0.6 | -3.1 | -5.4 | 10.6 | 52.8 | | | | | | | | | | |
| 1976 | 8.0 | 9.6 | 3.5 | 0.0 | 4.2 | 8.4 | 6.8 | 7.4 | 24.4 | 55.1 | 57.4 | | | | | | | | | |
| 1977 | 9.3 | 10.9 | 5.5 | 2.6 | 6.7 | 10.6 | 9.7 | 10.8 | 24.6 | 44.5 | 40.5 | 25.4 | | | | | | | | |
| 1978 | 10.4 | 11.9 | 7.0 | 4.5 | 8.4 | 12.2 | 11.6 | 12.8 | 24.4 | 38.9 | 34.6 | 24.4 | 23.5 | | | | | | | |
| 1979 | 12.4 | 14.1 | 9.7 | 7.5 | 11.5 | 15.3 | 15.1 | 16.7 | 27.4 | 39.8 | 36.7 | 30.5 | 33.1 | 43.5 | | | | | | |
| 1980 | 14.1 | 15.8 | 11.7 | 9.9 | 13.8 | 17.5 | 17.6 | 19.4 | 29.1 | 39.8 | 37.4 | 32.8 | 35.3 | 41.7 | 39.9 | | | | | |
| 1981 | 14.1 | 15.6 | 11.9 | 10.2 | 13.8 | 17.2 | 17.3 | 18.8 | 27.1 | 35.8 | 33.1 | 28.7 | 29.6 | 31.7 | 26.2 | 13.9 | | | | |
| 1982 | 14.9 | 16.4 | 12.9 | 11.4 | 14.9 | 18.1 | 18.2 | 19.7 | 27.2 | 34.8 | 32.4 | 28.6 | 29.3 | 30.8 | 26.8 | 20.7 | 28.0 | | | |
| 1983 | 16.1 | 17.6 | 14.4 | 13.1 | 16.5 | 19.6 | 19.9 | 21.4 | 28.4 | 35.3 | 33.3 | 30.1 | 31.0 | 32.5 | 29.9 | 26.7 | 33.7 | 39.7 | | |
| 1984 | 14.8 | 16.1 | 13.0 | 11.7 | 14.8 | 17.5 | 17.6 | 18.7 | 24.7 | 30.4 | 28.1 | 24.8 | 24.8 | 25.0 | 21.6 | 17.4 | 18.6 | 14.2 | -6.7 | |
| 1985 | 15.3 | 16.6 | 13.7 | 12.5 | 15.4 | 18.0 | 18.1 | 19.2 | 24.7 | 29.9 | 27.8 | 24.8 | 24.8 | 24.9 | 22.1 | 18.8 | 20.1 | 17.6 | 7.9 | 24.7 |
| 1986 | 14.8 | 16.1 | 13.3 | 12.1 | 14.8 | 17.2 | 17.3 | 18.3 | 23.2 | 27.8 | 25.7 | 22.9 | 22.6 | 22.5 | 19.8 | 16.7 | 17.3 | 14.8 | 7.5 | 15.4 |
| 1987 | 13.6 | 14.7 | 12.0 | 10.9 | 13.3 | 15.5 | 15.4 | 16.2 | 20.6 | 24.4 | 22.3 | 19.6 | 19.0 | 18.5 | 15.7 | 12.6 | 12.4 | 9.5 | 3.0 | 6.5 |
| 1988 | 14.0 | 15.1 | 12.5 | 11.5 | 13.8 | 15.9 | 15.8 | 16.6 | 20.7 | 24.3 | 22.4 | 19.8 | 19.3 | 18.9 | 16.5 | 13.8 | 13.8 | 11.6 | 6.7 | 10.4 |
| 1989 | 13.8 | 14.8 | 12.4 | 11.4 | 13.6 | 15.6 | 15.5 | 16.2 | 20.0 | 23.3 | 21.5 | 19.1 | 18.5 | 18.1 | 15.8 | 13.4 | 13.4 | 11.4 | 7.3 | 10.3 |
| 1990 | 12.2 | 13.0 | 10.7 | 9.6 | 11.7 | 13.3 | 13.2 | 13.7 | 17.1 | 19.9 | 18.0 | 15.6 | 14.8 | 14.1 | 11.8 | 9.3 | 8.8 | 6.6 | 2.6 | 4.2 |
| 1991 | 13.3 | 14.2 | 11.9 | 11.0 | 13.0 | 14.7 | 14.6 | 15.1 | 18.5 | 21.2 | 19.5 | 17.3 | 16.7 | 16.2 | 14.2 | 12.1 | 12.0 | 10.3 | 7.1 | 9.2 |
| 1992 | 13.6 | 14.5 | 12.4 | 11.5 | 13.4 | 15.1 | 15.0 | 15.5 | 18.7 | 21.3 | 19.7 | 17.7 | 17.2 | 16.7 | 14.9 | 13.0 | 13.0 | 11.6 | 8.8 | 10.9 |
| 1993 | 13.9 | 14.7 | 12.7 | 11.8 | 13.7 | 15.3 | 15.3 | 15.8 | 18.8 | 21.3 | 19.8 | 17.9 | 17.4 | 17.0 | 15.3 | 13.6 | 13.6 | 12.4 | 10.0 | 12.0 |
| 1994 | 13.5 | 14.3 | 12.3 | 11.5 | 13.3 | 14.8 | 14.7 | 15.2 | 18.0 | 20.3 | 18.8 | 17.0 | 16.5 | 16.1 | 14.5 | 12.8 | 12.8 | 11.6 | 9.3 | 11.1 |
| 1995 | 14.1 | 14.9 | 13.0 | 12.3 | 14.0 | 15.5 | 15.5 | 16.0 | 18.7 | 21.0 | 19.6 | 17.8 | 17.4 | 17.1 | 15.6 | 14.2 | 14.2 | 13.2 | 11.2 | 13.0 |
| 1996 | 14.2 | 15.0 | 13.2 | 12.4 | 14.1 | 15.6 | 15.5 | 16.0 | 18.7 | 20.8 | 19.5 | 17.8 | 17.5 | 17.1 | 15.7 | 14.4 | 14.4 | 13.5 | 11.7 | 13.4 |
| 1997 | 14.5 | 15.3 | 13.5 | 12.8 | 14.4 | 15.8 | 15.8 | 16.3 | 18.8 | 20.9 | 19.6 | 18.1 | 17.7 | 17.4 | 16.1 | 14.9 | 14.9 | 14.1 | 12.5 | 14.1 |
| 1998 | 13.8 | 14.5 | 12.8 | 12.1 | 13.6 | 14.9 | 14.9 | 15.3 | 17.7 | 19.6 | 18.3 | 16.8 | 16.4 | 16.0 | 14.8 | 13.5 | 13.5 | 12.6 | 11.0 | 12.4 |
| 1999 | 14.2 | 14.9 | 13.3 | 12.6 | 14.1 | 15.4 | 15.4 | 15.8 | 18.1 | 20.0 | 18.8 | 17.3 | 17.0 | 16.7 | 15.5 | 14.3 | 14.3 | 13.6 | 12.1 | 13.5 |
| 2000 | 13.7 | 14.3 | 12.7 | 12.0 | 13.5 | 14.7 | 14.7 | 15.0 | 17.2 | 19.0 | 17.8 | 16.4 | 16.0 | 15.7 | 14.5 | 13.3 | 13.3 | 12.5 | 11.1 | 12.3 |

| To the end of | 1986 | 1987 | 1988 | 1989 | 1990 | 1991 | 1992 | 1993 | 1994 | 1995 | 1996 | 1997 | 1998 | 1999 | 2000 |
|---|---|---|---|---|---|---|---|---|---|---|---|---|---|---|---|
| 1986 | 6.9 | | | | | | | | | | | | | | |
| 1987 | -1.6 | -9.3 | | | | | | | | | | | | | |
| 1988 | 6.0 | 5.6 | 22.9 | | | | | | | | | | | | |
| 1989 | 7.0 | 7.1 | 16.4 | 10.2 | | | | | | | | | | | |
| 1990 | 0.6 | -0.9 | 2.0 | -7.0 | -21.6 | | | | | | | | | | |
| 1991 | 6.9 | 6.9 | 11.3 | 7.7 | 6.5 | 44.6 | | | | | | | | | |
| 1992 | 9.1 | 9.4 | 13.6 | 11.4 | 11.9 | 33.6 | 23.3 | | | | | | | | |
| 1993 | 10.5 | 11.0 | 14.8 | 13.3 | 14.1 | 29.2 | 22.2 | 21.0 | | | | | | | |
| 1994 | 9.6 | 10.0 | 13.1 | 11.5 | 11.8 | 22.1 | 15.4 | 11.7 | 3.1 | | | | | | |
| 1995 | 11.9 | 12.5 | 15.5 | 14.5 | 15.3 | 24.5 | 19.9 | 18.8 | 17.7 | 34.5 | | | | | |
| 1996 | 12.4 | 13.0 | 15.8 | 14.9 | 15.6 | 23.3 | 19.5 | 18.5 | 17.7 | 25.8 | 17.6 | | | | |
| 1997 | 13.2 | 13.8 | 16.5 | 15.8 | 16.5 | 23.3 | 20.0 | 19.4 | 19.0 | 24.8 | 20.2 | 22.8 | | | |
| 1998 | 11.5 | 11.9 | 14.1 | 13.2 | 13.6 | 18.9 | 15.7 | 14.4 | 13.2 | 15.8 | 10.2 | 6.7 | -7.3 | | |
| 1999 | 12.7 | 13.2 | 15.3 | 14.6 | 15.1 | 20.1 | 17.3 | 16.5 | 15.8 | 18.5 | 14.8 | 13.9 | 9.7 | 29.8 | |
| 2000 | 11.6 | 11.9 | 13.7 | 13.0 | 13.3 | 17.5 | 14.8 | 13.8 | 12.8 | 14.5 | 10.9 | 9.2 | 5.1 | 11.9 | -3.6 |

# Table C-3 (Page 1 of 5)

## Long-Term Corporate Bonds Total Returns
Rates of Return for all holding periods
Percent per annum compounded annually

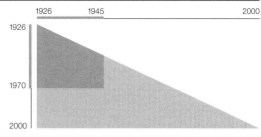

### from 1926 to 2000

| To the end of | 1926 | 1927 | 1928 | 1929 | 1930 | 1931 | 1932 | 1933 | 1934 | 1935 | 1936 | 1937 | 1938 | 1939 | 1940 | 1941 | 1942 | 1943 | 1944 | 1945 |
|---|---|---|---|---|---|---|---|---|---|---|---|---|---|---|---|---|---|---|---|---|
| 1926 | 7.4 | | | | | | | | | | | | | | | | | | | |
| 1927 | 7.4 | 7.4 | | | | | | | | | | | | | | | | | | |
| 1928 | 5.9 | 5.1 | 2.8 | | | | | | | | | | | | | | | | | |
| 1929 | 5.2 | 4.5 | 3.1 | 3.3 | | | | | | | | | | | | | | | | |
| 1930 | 5.8 | 5.4 | 4.7 | 5.6 | 8.0 | | | | | | | | | | | | | | | |
| 1931 | 4.4 | 3.9 | 3.0 | 3.1 | 2.9 | -1.9 | | | | | | | | | | | | | | |
| 1932 | 5.3 | 5.0 | 4.5 | 4.9 | 5.5 | 4.3 | 10.8 | | | | | | | | | | | | | |
| 1933 | 6.0 | 5.8 | 5.5 | 6.0 | 6.7 | 6.3 | 10.6 | 10.4 | | | | | | | | | | | | |
| 1934 | 6.8 | 6.7 | 6.6 | 7.3 | 8.1 | 8.1 | 11.7 | 12.1 | 13.8 | | | | | | | | | | | |
| 1935 | 7.1 | 7.0 | 7.0 | 7.6 | 8.3 | 8.4 | 11.2 | 11.3 | 11.7 | 9.6 | | | | | | | | | | |
| 1936 | 7.1 | 7.0 | 7.0 | 7.5 | 8.1 | 8.1 | 10.3 | 10.1 | 10.0 | 8.2 | 6.7 | | | | | | | | | |
| 1937 | 6.7 | 6.6 | 6.5 | 7.0 | 7.4 | 7.4 | 9.0 | 8.6 | 8.2 | 6.3 | 4.7 | 2.7 | | | | | | | | |
| 1938 | 6.6 | 6.6 | 6.5 | 6.9 | 7.3 | 7.2 | 8.6 | 8.2 | 7.8 | 6.3 | 5.2 | 4.4 | 6.1 | | | | | | | |
| 1939 | 6.4 | 6.4 | 6.3 | 6.6 | 6.9 | 6.8 | 8.0 | 7.6 | 7.1 | 5.8 | 4.9 | 4.3 | 5.0 | 4.0 | | | | | | |
| 1940 | 6.2 | 6.2 | 6.1 | 6.3 | 6.6 | 6.5 | 7.5 | 7.0 | 6.6 | 5.4 | 4.6 | 4.1 | 4.5 | 3.7 | 3.4 | | | | | |
| 1941 | 6.0 | 5.9 | 5.8 | 6.1 | 6.3 | 6.1 | 7.0 | 6.6 | 6.1 | 5.0 | 4.3 | 3.8 | 4.0 | 3.4 | 3.1 | 2.7 | | | | |
| 1942 | 5.8 | 5.7 | 5.6 | 5.8 | 6.0 | 5.8 | 6.6 | 6.2 | 5.7 | 4.7 | 4.0 | 3.6 | 3.8 | 3.2 | 2.9 | 2.7 | 2.6 | | | |
| 1943 | 5.6 | 5.5 | 5.4 | 5.6 | 5.8 | 5.6 | 6.3 | 5.8 | 5.4 | 4.5 | 3.9 | 3.5 | 3.6 | 3.1 | 2.9 | 2.7 | 2.7 | 2.8 | | |
| 1944 | 5.6 | 5.5 | 5.4 | 5.5 | 5.7 | 5.5 | 6.1 | 5.8 | 5.3 | 4.5 | 4.0 | 3.6 | 3.8 | 3.4 | 3.3 | 3.2 | 3.4 | 3.8 | 4.7 | |
| 1945 | 5.5 | 5.4 | 5.3 | 5.5 | 5.6 | 5.4 | 6.0 | 5.6 | 5.2 | 4.5 | 4.0 | 3.7 | 3.8 | 3.5 | 3.4 | 3.4 | 3.6 | 3.9 | 4.4 | 4.1 |
| 1946 | 5.3 | 5.2 | 5.1 | 5.3 | 5.4 | 5.2 | 5.7 | 5.3 | 5.0 | 4.3 | 3.8 | 3.5 | 3.6 | 3.3 | 3.2 | 3.1 | 3.2 | 3.3 | 3.5 | 2.9 |
| 1947 | 5.0 | 4.9 | 4.7 | 4.8 | 4.9 | 4.7 | 5.2 | 4.8 | 4.4 | 3.7 | 3.3 | 2.9 | 3.0 | 2.6 | 2.4 | 2.3 | 2.2 | 2.2 | 2.0 | 1.1 |
| 1948 | 4.9 | 4.8 | 4.7 | 4.8 | 4.9 | 4.7 | 5.1 | 4.8 | 4.4 | 3.8 | 3.3 | 3.0 | 3.1 | 2.8 | 2.6 | 2.5 | 2.5 | 2.5 | 2.4 | 1.9 |
| 1949 | 4.9 | 4.8 | 4.6 | 4.7 | 4.8 | 4.6 | 5.0 | 4.7 | 4.3 | 3.7 | 3.3 | 3.1 | 3.1 | 2.8 | 2.7 | 2.6 | 2.6 | 2.6 | 2.6 | 2.2 |
| 1950 | 4.8 | 4.7 | 4.5 | 4.6 | 4.7 | 4.5 | 4.9 | 4.5 | 4.2 | 3.6 | 3.2 | 3.0 | 3.0 | 2.8 | 2.6 | 2.6 | 2.6 | 2.6 | 2.5 | 2.1 |
| 1951 | 4.5 | 4.3 | 4.2 | 4.3 | 4.3 | 4.2 | 4.5 | 4.1 | 3.8 | 3.2 | 2.9 | 2.6 | 2.6 | 2.3 | 2.2 | 2.1 | 2.0 | 2.0 | 1.8 | 1.4 |
| 1952 | 4.4 | 4.3 | 4.2 | 4.2 | 4.3 | 4.1 | 4.4 | 4.1 | 3.8 | 3.3 | 2.9 | 2.7 | 2.7 | 2.4 | 2.3 | 2.2 | 2.2 | 2.1 | 2.0 | 1.7 |
| 1953 | 4.4 | 4.3 | 4.2 | 4.2 | 4.3 | 4.1 | 4.4 | 4.1 | 3.8 | 3.3 | 2.9 | 2.7 | 2.7 | 2.5 | 2.4 | 2.3 | 2.3 | 2.2 | 2.2 | 1.9 |
| 1954 | 4.4 | 4.3 | 4.2 | 4.3 | 4.3 | 4.2 | 4.4 | 4.1 | 3.8 | 3.4 | 3.1 | 2.9 | 2.9 | 2.7 | 2.6 | 2.5 | 2.5 | 2.5 | 2.5 | 2.2 |
| 1955 | 4.3 | 4.2 | 4.1 | 4.1 | 4.2 | 4.0 | 4.3 | 4.0 | 3.7 | 3.2 | 2.9 | 2.7 | 2.7 | 2.5 | 2.4 | 2.4 | 2.4 | 2.3 | 2.3 | 2.1 |
| 1956 | 3.9 | 3.8 | 3.7 | 3.7 | 3.7 | 3.6 | 3.8 | 3.5 | 3.2 | 2.8 | 2.4 | 2.2 | 2.2 | 2.0 | 1.9 | 1.8 | 1.7 | 1.6 | 1.6 | 1.3 |
| 1957 | 4.1 | 4.0 | 3.8 | 3.9 | 3.9 | 3.7 | 4.0 | 3.7 | 3.4 | 3.0 | 2.7 | 2.5 | 2.5 | 2.3 | 2.2 | 2.2 | 2.1 | 2.1 | 2.1 | 1.9 |
| 1958 | 3.9 | 3.8 | 3.6 | 3.7 | 3.7 | 3.5 | 3.7 | 3.5 | 3.2 | 2.8 | 2.5 | 2.3 | 2.3 | 2.1 | 2.0 | 1.9 | 1.9 | 1.8 | 1.8 | 1.6 |
| 1959 | 3.7 | 3.6 | 3.5 | 3.5 | 3.5 | 3.4 | 3.6 | 3.3 | 3.0 | 2.6 | 2.3 | 2.2 | 2.1 | 1.9 | 1.8 | 1.8 | 1.7 | 1.7 | 1.6 | 1.4 |
| 1960 | 3.9 | 3.8 | 3.7 | 3.7 | 3.7 | 3.6 | 3.7 | 3.5 | 3.3 | 2.9 | 2.6 | 2.4 | 2.4 | 2.3 | 2.2 | 2.1 | 2.1 | 2.1 | 2.0 | 1.8 |
| 1961 | 3.9 | 3.8 | 3.7 | 3.7 | 3.7 | 3.6 | 3.8 | 3.5 | 3.3 | 2.9 | 2.7 | 2.5 | 2.5 | 2.4 | 2.3 | 2.2 | 2.2 | 2.2 | 2.2 | 2.0 |
| 1962 | 4.0 | 3.9 | 3.8 | 3.8 | 3.9 | 3.7 | 3.9 | 3.7 | 3.5 | 3.1 | 2.9 | 2.7 | 2.7 | 2.6 | 2.5 | 2.5 | 2.5 | 2.5 | 2.5 | 2.3 |
| 1963 | 4.0 | 3.9 | 3.8 | 3.8 | 3.8 | 3.7 | 3.9 | 3.6 | 3.4 | 3.1 | 2.9 | 2.7 | 2.7 | 2.6 | 2.5 | 2.5 | 2.5 | 2.5 | 2.5 | 2.3 |
| 1964 | 4.0 | 3.9 | 3.8 | 3.8 | 3.8 | 3.7 | 3.9 | 3.7 | 3.5 | 3.1 | 2.9 | 2.8 | 2.8 | 2.7 | 2.6 | 2.6 | 2.6 | 2.6 | 2.6 | 2.5 |
| 1965 | 3.9 | 3.8 | 3.7 | 3.7 | 3.7 | 3.6 | 3.8 | 3.6 | 3.3 | 3.0 | 2.8 | 2.7 | 2.7 | 2.5 | 2.5 | 2.5 | 2.4 | 2.4 | 2.4 | 2.3 |
| 1966 | 3.8 | 3.7 | 3.6 | 3.6 | 3.6 | 3.5 | 3.7 | 3.5 | 3.2 | 2.9 | 2.7 | 2.6 | 2.6 | 2.5 | 2.4 | 2.4 | 2.4 | 2.3 | 2.3 | 2.2 |
| 1967 | 3.6 | 3.5 | 3.4 | 3.4 | 3.4 | 3.3 | 3.4 | 3.2 | 3.0 | 2.7 | 2.5 | 2.3 | 2.3 | 2.2 | 2.1 | 2.1 | 2.1 | 2.0 | 2.0 | 1.9 |
| 1968 | 3.5 | 3.4 | 3.3 | 3.4 | 3.4 | 3.2 | 3.4 | 3.2 | 3.0 | 2.7 | 2.5 | 2.3 | 2.3 | 2.2 | 2.2 | 2.1 | 2.1 | 2.1 | 2.0 | 1.9 |
| 1969 | 3.3 | 3.2 | 3.1 | 3.1 | 3.1 | 2.9 | 3.1 | 2.9 | 2.7 | 2.4 | 2.2 | 2.0 | 2.0 | 1.9 | 1.8 | 1.7 | 1.7 | 1.7 | 1.6 | 1.5 |
| 1970 | 3.6 | 3.5 | 3.4 | 3.4 | 3.4 | 3.3 | 3.4 | 3.2 | 3.1 | 2.8 | 2.6 | 2.5 | 2.5 | 2.3 | 2.3 | 2.3 | 2.2 | 2.2 | 2.2 | 2.1 |

# Table C-3 (Page 2 of 5)

## Long-Term Corporate Bonds Total Returns
Rates of Return for all holding periods
Percent per annum compounded annually

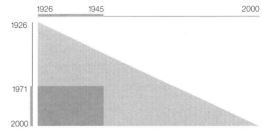

from 1926 to 2000

| To the end of | From the beginning of 1926 | 1927 | 1928 | 1929 | 1930 | 1931 | 1932 | 1933 | 1934 | 1935 | 1936 | 1937 | 1938 | 1939 | 1940 | 1941 | 1942 | 1943 | 1944 | 1945 |
|---|---|---|---|---|---|---|---|---|---|---|---|---|---|---|---|---|---|---|---|---|
| 1971 | 3.7 | 3.6 | 3.6 | 3.6 | 3.6 | 3.5 | 3.6 | 3.4 | 3.3 | 3.0 | 2.8 | 2.7 | 2.7 | 2.6 | 2.6 | 2.5 | 2.5 | 2.5 | 2.5 | 2.4 |
| 1972 | 3.8 | 3.7 | 3.6 | 3.7 | 3.7 | 3.6 | 3.7 | 3.5 | 3.4 | 3.1 | 2.9 | 2.8 | 2.8 | 2.7 | 2.7 | 2.7 | 2.7 | 2.7 | 2.7 | 2.6 |
| 1973 | 3.7 | 3.7 | 3.6 | 3.6 | 3.6 | 3.5 | 3.6 | 3.5 | 3.3 | 3.0 | 2.9 | 2.8 | 2.8 | 2.7 | 2.6 | 2.6 | 2.6 | 2.6 | 2.6 | 2.5 |
| 1974 | 3.6 | 3.5 | 3.4 | 3.4 | 3.5 | 3.4 | 3.5 | 3.3 | 3.1 | 2.9 | 2.7 | 2.6 | 2.6 | 2.5 | 2.5 | 2.4 | 2.4 | 2.4 | 2.4 | 2.3 |
| 1975 | 3.8 | 3.7 | 3.7 | 3.7 | 3.7 | 3.6 | 3.7 | 3.6 | 3.4 | 3.2 | 3.0 | 2.9 | 2.9 | 2.8 | 2.8 | 2.8 | 2.8 | 2.8 | 2.8 | 2.7 |
| 1976 | 4.1 | 4.0 | 3.9 | 4.0 | 4.0 | 3.9 | 4.0 | 3.9 | 3.7 | 3.5 | 3.4 | 3.3 | 3.3 | 3.2 | 3.2 | 3.2 | 3.2 | 3.2 | 3.2 | 3.2 |
| 1977 | 4.0 | 4.0 | 3.9 | 3.9 | 3.9 | 3.9 | 4.0 | 3.8 | 3.7 | 3.5 | 3.3 | 3.2 | 3.2 | 3.2 | 3.2 | 3.1 | 3.2 | 3.2 | 3.2 | 3.1 |
| 1978 | 4.0 | 3.9 | 3.8 | 3.8 | 3.9 | 3.8 | 3.9 | 3.7 | 3.6 | 3.4 | 3.2 | 3.2 | 3.2 | 3.1 | 3.1 | 3.1 | 3.1 | 3.1 | 3.1 | 3.0 |
| 1979 | 3.8 | 3.7 | 3.7 | 3.7 | 3.7 | 3.6 | 3.7 | 3.6 | 3.4 | 3.2 | 3.1 | 3.0 | 3.0 | 2.9 | 2.9 | 2.9 | 2.9 | 2.9 | 2.9 | 2.8 |
| 1980 | 3.7 | 3.6 | 3.5 | 3.5 | 3.6 | 3.5 | 3.6 | 3.4 | 3.3 | 3.1 | 2.9 | 2.8 | 2.8 | 2.8 | 2.7 | 2.7 | 2.7 | 2.7 | 2.7 | 2.7 |
| 1981 | 3.6 | 3.5 | 3.4 | 3.5 | 3.5 | 3.4 | 3.5 | 3.3 | 3.2 | 3.0 | 2.8 | 2.8 | 2.8 | 2.7 | 2.6 | 2.6 | 2.6 | 2.6 | 2.6 | 2.6 |
| 1982 | 4.2 | 4.1 | 4.1 | 4.1 | 4.1 | 4.0 | 4.1 | 4.0 | 3.9 | 3.7 | 3.6 | 3.5 | 3.5 | 3.4 | 3.4 | 3.4 | 3.5 | 3.5 | 3.5 | 3.5 |
| 1983 | 4.2 | 4.1 | 4.1 | 4.1 | 4.1 | 4.1 | 4.2 | 4.0 | 3.9 | 3.7 | 3.6 | 3.5 | 3.6 | 3.5 | 3.5 | 3.5 | 3.5 | 3.5 | 3.6 | 3.5 |
| 1984 | 4.4 | 4.4 | 4.3 | 4.3 | 4.3 | 4.3 | 4.4 | 4.3 | 4.2 | 4.0 | 3.9 | 3.8 | 3.8 | 3.8 | 3.8 | 3.8 | 3.8 | 3.8 | 3.9 | 3.8 |
| 1985 | 4.8 | 4.7 | 4.7 | 4.7 | 4.8 | 4.7 | 4.8 | 4.7 | 4.6 | 4.4 | 4.3 | 4.3 | 4.3 | 4.3 | 4.3 | 4.3 | 4.3 | 4.4 | 4.4 | 4.4 |
| 1986 | 5.0 | 5.0 | 4.9 | 5.0 | 5.0 | 5.0 | 5.1 | 5.0 | 4.9 | 4.7 | 4.6 | 4.6 | 4.6 | 4.6 | 4.6 | 4.6 | 4.7 | 4.7 | 4.8 | 4.8 |
| 1987 | 4.9 | 4.9 | 4.8 | 4.9 | 4.9 | 4.9 | 5.0 | 4.9 | 4.8 | 4.6 | 4.5 | 4.5 | 4.5 | 4.5 | 4.5 | 4.5 | 4.6 | 4.6 | 4.6 | 4.6 |
| 1988 | 5.0 | 5.0 | 4.9 | 5.0 | 5.0 | 5.0 | 5.1 | 5.0 | 4.9 | 4.7 | 4.6 | 4.6 | 4.6 | 4.6 | 4.6 | 4.6 | 4.7 | 4.7 | 4.8 | 4.8 |
| 1989 | 5.2 | 5.2 | 5.1 | 5.2 | 5.2 | 5.1 | 5.3 | 5.2 | 5.1 | 4.9 | 4.8 | 4.8 | 4.8 | 4.8 | 4.8 | 4.9 | 4.9 | 5.0 | 5.0 | 5.0 |
| 1990 | 5.2 | 5.2 | 5.1 | 5.2 | 5.2 | 5.2 | 5.3 | 5.2 | 5.1 | 5.0 | 4.9 | 4.8 | 4.9 | 4.9 | 4.9 | 4.9 | 4.9 | 5.0 | 5.0 | 5.1 |
| 1991 | 5.4 | 5.4 | 5.4 | 5.4 | 5.4 | 5.4 | 5.5 | 5.4 | 5.3 | 5.2 | 5.1 | 5.1 | 5.1 | 5.1 | 5.1 | 5.2 | 5.2 | 5.3 | 5.3 | 5.3 |
| 1992 | 5.5 | 5.4 | 5.4 | 5.5 | 5.5 | 5.5 | 5.6 | 5.5 | 5.4 | 5.3 | 5.2 | 5.2 | 5.2 | 5.2 | 5.2 | 5.3 | 5.3 | 5.4 | 5.4 | 5.4 |
| 1993 | 5.6 | 5.6 | 5.5 | 5.6 | 5.6 | 5.6 | 5.7 | 5.6 | 5.5 | 5.4 | 5.3 | 5.3 | 5.4 | 5.3 | 5.4 | 5.4 | 5.5 | 5.5 | 5.6 | 5.6 |
| 1994 | 5.4 | 5.4 | 5.4 | 5.4 | 5.4 | 5.4 | 5.5 | 5.4 | 5.3 | 5.2 | 5.1 | 5.1 | 5.1 | 5.1 | 5.2 | 5.2 | 5.2 | 5.3 | 5.3 | 5.3 |
| 1995 | 5.7 | 5.7 | 5.6 | 5.7 | 5.7 | 5.7 | 5.8 | 5.7 | 5.7 | 5.5 | 5.5 | 5.4 | 5.5 | 5.5 | 5.5 | 5.5 | 5.6 | 5.7 | 5.7 | 5.7 |
| 1996 | 5.6 | 5.6 | 5.6 | 5.6 | 5.7 | 5.6 | 5.7 | 5.7 | 5.6 | 5.5 | 5.4 | 5.4 | 5.4 | 5.4 | 5.4 | 5.5 | 5.5 | 5.6 | 5.6 | 5.6 |
| 1997 | 5.7 | 5.7 | 5.7 | 5.7 | 5.8 | 5.7 | 5.9 | 5.8 | 5.7 | 5.6 | 5.5 | 5.5 | 5.5 | 5.5 | 5.6 | 5.6 | 5.7 | 5.7 | 5.8 | 5.8 |
| 1998 | 5.8 | 5.8 | 5.8 | 5.8 | 5.8 | 5.8 | 5.9 | 5.9 | 5.8 | 5.7 | 5.6 | 5.6 | 5.6 | 5.6 | 5.6 | 5.7 | 5.7 | 5.8 | 5.9 | 5.9 |
| 1999 | 5.6 | 5.6 | 5.6 | 5.6 | 5.6 | 5.6 | 5.7 | 5.6 | 5.6 | 5.4 | 5.4 | 5.4 | 5.4 | 5.4 | 5.4 | 5.4 | 5.5 | 5.5 | 5.6 | 5.6 |
| 2000 | 5.7 | 5.7 | 5.7 | 5.7 | 5.7 | 5.7 | 5.8 | 5.7 | 5.7 | 5.6 | 5.5 | 5.5 | 5.5 | 5.5 | 5.5 | 5.6 | 5.6 | 5.7 | 5.7 | 5.7 |

# Table C-3 (Page 3 of 5)

## Long-Term Corporate Bonds Total Returns
Rates of Return for all holding periods
Percent per annum compounded annually

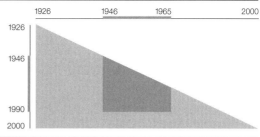

from 1926 to 2000

| To the end of | From the beginning of | | | | | | | | | | | | | | | | | | | |
|---|---|---|---|---|---|---|---|---|---|---|---|---|---|---|---|---|---|---|---|---|
| | 1946 | 1947 | 1948 | 1949 | 1950 | 1951 | 1952 | 1953 | 1954 | 1955 | 1956 | 1957 | 1958 | 1959 | 1960 | 1961 | 1962 | 1963 | 1964 | 1965 |
| 1946 | 1.7 | | | | | | | | | | | | | | | | | | | |
| 1947 | −0.3 | −2.3 | | | | | | | | | | | | | | | | | | |
| 1948 | 1.1 | 0.8 | 4.1 | | | | | | | | | | | | | | | | | |
| 1949 | 1.7 | 1.7 | 3.7 | 3.3 | | | | | | | | | | | | | | | | |
| 1950 | 1.8 | 1.8 | 3.2 | 2.7 | 2.1 | | | | | | | | | | | | | | | |
| 1951 | 1.0 | 0.9 | 1.7 | 0.9 | −0.3 | −2.7 | | | | | | | | | | | | | | |
| 1952 | 1.4 | 1.3 | 2.0 | 1.5 | 0.9 | 0.4 | 3.5 | | | | | | | | | | | | | |
| 1953 | 1.6 | 1.6 | 2.3 | 1.9 | 1.6 | 1.4 | 3.5 | 3.4 | | | | | | | | | | | | |
| 1954 | 2.0 | 2.1 | 2.7 | 2.5 | 2.3 | 2.4 | 4.1 | 4.4 | 5.4 | | | | | | | | | | | |
| 1955 | 1.9 | 1.9 | 2.4 | 2.2 | 2.0 | 2.0 | 3.2 | 3.1 | 2.9 | 0.5 | | | | | | | | | | |
| 1956 | 1.1 | 1.0 | 1.4 | 1.0 | 0.7 | 0.5 | 1.1 | 0.5 | −0.4 | −3.2 | −6.8 | | | | | | | | | |
| 1957 | 1.7 | 1.7 | 2.1 | 1.8 | 1.7 | 1.6 | 2.3 | 2.1 | 1.8 | 0.6 | 0.7 | 8.7 | | | | | | | | |
| 1958 | 1.4 | 1.3 | 1.7 | 1.4 | 1.2 | 1.1 | 1.7 | 1.4 | 1.0 | −0.1 | −0.3 | 3.1 | −2.2 | | | | | | | |
| 1959 | 1.2 | 1.2 | 1.5 | 1.2 | 1.0 | 0.9 | 1.3 | 1.0 | 0.6 | −0.3 | −0.5 | 1.7 | −1.6 | −1.0 | | | | | | |
| 1960 | 1.7 | 1.7 | 2.0 | 1.8 | 1.7 | 1.7 | 2.2 | 2.0 | 1.8 | 1.2 | 1.4 | 3.5 | 1.8 | 3.9 | 9.1 | | | | | |
| 1961 | 1.9 | 1.9 | 2.2 | 2.1 | 2.0 | 2.0 | 2.4 | 2.3 | 2.2 | 1.7 | 1.9 | 3.8 | 2.6 | 4.2 | 6.9 | 4.8 | | | | |
| 1962 | 2.2 | 2.3 | 2.6 | 2.5 | 2.4 | 2.4 | 2.9 | 2.9 | 2.8 | 2.5 | 2.8 | 4.5 | 3.6 | 5.1 | 7.3 | 6.4 | 7.9 | | | |
| 1963 | 2.2 | 2.3 | 2.6 | 2.5 | 2.4 | 2.4 | 2.9 | 2.8 | 2.7 | 2.4 | 2.7 | 4.1 | 3.4 | 4.5 | 6.0 | 5.0 | 5.0 | 2.2 | | |
| 1964 | 2.4 | 2.4 | 2.7 | 2.6 | 2.6 | 2.6 | 3.0 | 3.0 | 2.9 | 2.7 | 2.9 | 4.2 | 3.6 | 4.6 | 5.7 | 4.9 | 4.9 | 3.5 | 4.8 | |
| 1965 | 2.2 | 2.3 | 2.5 | 2.4 | 2.4 | 2.4 | 2.8 | 2.7 | 2.6 | 2.4 | 2.6 | 3.7 | 3.1 | 3.8 | 4.7 | 3.8 | 3.6 | 2.1 | 2.1 | −0.5 |
| 1966 | 2.1 | 2.1 | 2.4 | 2.3 | 2.2 | 2.2 | 2.6 | 2.5 | 2.4 | 2.2 | 2.4 | 3.3 | 2.7 | 3.4 | 4.0 | 3.2 | 2.9 | 1.7 | 1.5 | −0.1 |
| 1967 | 1.8 | 1.8 | 2.0 | 1.9 | 1.8 | 1.8 | 2.1 | 2.0 | 1.9 | 1.6 | 1.7 | 2.5 | 1.9 | 2.4 | 2.9 | 2.0 | 1.5 | 0.3 | −0.2 | −1.8 |
| 1968 | 1.8 | 1.8 | 2.0 | 1.9 | 1.9 | 1.8 | 2.1 | 2.0 | 1.9 | 1.7 | 1.8 | 2.5 | 2.0 | 2.4 | 2.8 | 2.1 | 1.7 | 0.7 | 0.4 | −0.7 |
| 1969 | 1.4 | 1.4 | 1.6 | 1.4 | 1.3 | 1.3 | 1.5 | 1.4 | 1.3 | 1.0 | 1.1 | 1.7 | 1.1 | 1.4 | 1.7 | 0.9 | 0.4 | −0.6 | −1.1 | −2.2 |
| 1970 | 2.0 | 2.0 | 2.2 | 2.1 | 2.1 | 2.1 | 2.3 | 2.3 | 2.2 | 2.0 | 2.1 | 2.8 | 2.4 | 2.7 | 3.1 | 2.5 | 2.3 | 1.6 | 1.5 | 0.9 |
| 1971 | 2.4 | 2.4 | 2.6 | 2.5 | 2.5 | 2.5 | 2.8 | 2.7 | 2.7 | 2.5 | 2.7 | 3.3 | 3.0 | 3.4 | 3.7 | 3.3 | 3.1 | 2.6 | 2.6 | 2.3 |
| 1972 | 2.5 | 2.6 | 2.8 | 2.7 | 2.7 | 2.7 | 3.0 | 2.9 | 2.9 | 2.8 | 2.9 | 3.6 | 3.2 | 3.6 | 4.0 | 3.6 | 3.5 | 3.0 | 3.1 | 2.9 |
| 1973 | 2.5 | 2.5 | 2.7 | 2.6 | 2.6 | 2.6 | 2.9 | 2.9 | 2.8 | 2.7 | 2.8 | 3.4 | 3.1 | 3.5 | 3.8 | 3.4 | 3.3 | 2.9 | 2.9 | 2.7 |
| 1974 | 2.3 | 2.3 | 2.5 | 2.4 | 2.4 | 2.4 | 2.6 | 2.6 | 2.5 | 2.4 | 2.5 | 3.1 | 2.7 | 3.0 | 3.3 | 2.9 | 2.8 | 2.4 | 2.4 | 2.1 |
| 1975 | 2.7 | 2.7 | 2.9 | 2.9 | 2.8 | 2.9 | 3.1 | 3.1 | 3.1 | 3.0 | 3.1 | 3.6 | 3.4 | 3.7 | 4.0 | 3.7 | 3.6 | 3.3 | 3.3 | 3.2 |
| 1976 | 3.2 | 3.2 | 3.4 | 3.4 | 3.4 | 3.4 | 3.7 | 3.7 | 3.7 | 3.6 | 3.8 | 4.3 | 4.1 | 4.5 | 4.8 | 4.5 | 4.5 | 4.3 | 4.4 | 4.4 |
| 1977 | 3.1 | 3.2 | 3.3 | 3.3 | 3.3 | 3.4 | 3.6 | 3.6 | 3.6 | 3.5 | 3.7 | 4.2 | 4.0 | 4.3 | 4.6 | 4.4 | 4.3 | 4.1 | 4.2 | 4.2 |
| 1978 | 3.0 | 3.1 | 3.2 | 3.2 | 3.2 | 3.2 | 3.5 | 3.5 | 3.5 | 3.4 | 3.5 | 4.0 | 3.8 | 4.1 | 4.4 | 4.1 | 4.1 | 3.8 | 4.0 | 3.9 |
| 1979 | 2.8 | 2.8 | 3.0 | 3.0 | 2.9 | 3.0 | 3.2 | 3.2 | 3.2 | 3.1 | 3.2 | 3.6 | 3.4 | 3.7 | 3.9 | 3.7 | 3.6 | 3.4 | 3.4 | 3.3 |
| 1980 | 2.6 | 2.7 | 2.8 | 2.8 | 2.8 | 2.8 | 3.0 | 3.0 | 2.9 | 2.8 | 2.9 | 3.4 | 3.1 | 3.4 | 3.6 | 3.3 | 3.3 | 3.0 | 3.1 | 2.9 |
| 1981 | 2.5 | 2.5 | 2.7 | 2.6 | 2.6 | 2.6 | 2.8 | 2.8 | 2.8 | 2.7 | 2.8 | 3.2 | 3.0 | 3.2 | 3.4 | 3.1 | 3.0 | 2.8 | 2.8 | 2.7 |
| 1982 | 3.4 | 3.5 | 3.7 | 3.6 | 3.7 | 3.7 | 3.9 | 3.9 | 3.9 | 3.9 | 4.0 | 4.5 | 4.3 | 4.6 | 4.8 | 4.6 | 4.6 | 4.5 | 4.6 | 4.6 |
| 1983 | 3.5 | 3.6 | 3.7 | 3.7 | 3.7 | 3.8 | 4.0 | 4.0 | 4.0 | 4.0 | 4.1 | 4.5 | 4.4 | 4.6 | 4.9 | 4.7 | 4.7 | 4.6 | 4.7 | 4.7 |
| 1984 | 3.8 | 3.9 | 4.1 | 4.1 | 4.1 | 4.1 | 4.4 | 4.4 | 4.4 | 4.4 | 4.5 | 5.0 | 4.8 | 5.1 | 5.3 | 5.2 | 5.2 | 5.1 | 5.2 | 5.2 |
| 1985 | 4.4 | 4.5 | 4.7 | 4.7 | 4.7 | 4.8 | 5.0 | 5.1 | 5.1 | 5.1 | 5.3 | 5.7 | 5.6 | 5.9 | 6.2 | 6.1 | 6.1 | 6.1 | 6.2 | 6.3 |
| 1986 | 4.8 | 4.9 | 5.0 | 5.1 | 5.1 | 5.2 | 5.4 | 5.5 | 5.6 | 5.6 | 5.7 | 6.2 | 6.1 | 6.4 | 6.7 | 6.6 | 6.7 | 6.6 | 6.8 | 6.9 |
| 1987 | 4.7 | 4.7 | 4.9 | 4.9 | 5.0 | 5.0 | 5.3 | 5.3 | 5.4 | 5.4 | 5.5 | 6.0 | 5.9 | 6.2 | 6.4 | 6.3 | 6.4 | 6.3 | 6.5 | 6.6 |
| 1988 | 4.8 | 4.9 | 5.0 | 5.1 | 5.1 | 5.2 | 5.4 | 5.5 | 5.5 | 5.5 | 5.7 | 6.1 | 6.0 | 6.3 | 6.6 | 6.5 | 6.5 | 6.5 | 6.7 | 6.7 |
| 1989 | 5.0 | 5.1 | 5.3 | 5.3 | 5.4 | 5.5 | 5.7 | 5.7 | 5.8 | 5.8 | 6.0 | 6.4 | 6.3 | 6.6 | 6.9 | 6.8 | 6.9 | 6.8 | 7.0 | 7.1 |
| 1990 | 5.1 | 5.2 | 5.3 | 5.4 | 5.4 | 5.5 | 5.7 | 5.8 | 5.8 | 5.8 | 6.0 | 6.4 | 6.3 | 6.6 | 6.9 | 6.8 | 6.9 | 6.8 | 7.0 | 7.1 |

## Table C-3 (Page 4 of 5)

### Long-Term Corporate Bonds Total Returns
Rates of Return for all holding periods
Percent per annum compounded annually

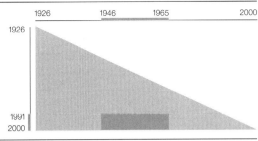

from 1926 to 2000

| To the end of | From the beginning of 1946 | 1947 | 1948 | 1949 | 1950 | 1951 | 1952 | 1953 | 1954 | 1955 | 1956 | 1957 | 1958 | 1959 | 1960 | 1961 | 1962 | 1963 | 1964 | 1965 |
|---|---|---|---|---|---|---|---|---|---|---|---|---|---|---|---|---|---|---|---|---|
| 1991 | 5.4 | 5.5 | 5.6 | 5.7 | 5.7 | 5.8 | 6.0 | 6.1 | 6.2 | 6.2 | 6.4 | 6.8 | 6.7 | 7.0 | 7.3 | 7.2 | 7.3 | 7.3 | 7.4 | 7.5 |
| 1992 | 5.5 | 5.5 | 5.7 | 5.8 | 5.8 | 5.9 | 6.1 | 6.2 | 6.3 | 6.3 | 6.5 | 6.8 | 6.8 | 7.1 | 7.3 | 7.3 | 7.3 | 7.3 | 7.5 | 7.6 |
| 1993 | 5.6 | 5.7 | 5.9 | 5.9 | 6.0 | 6.1 | 6.3 | 6.4 | 6.4 | 6.5 | 6.6 | 7.0 | 7.0 | 7.2 | 7.5 | 7.4 | 7.5 | 7.5 | 7.7 | 7.8 |
| 1994 | 5.4 | 5.4 | 5.6 | 5.7 | 5.7 | 5.8 | 6.0 | 6.1 | 6.1 | 6.1 | 6.3 | 6.7 | 6.6 | 6.9 | 7.1 | 7.0 | 7.1 | 7.1 | 7.2 | 7.3 |
| 1995 | 5.8 | 5.9 | 6.0 | 6.1 | 6.1 | 6.2 | 6.4 | 6.5 | 6.6 | 6.6 | 6.8 | 7.1 | 7.1 | 7.4 | 7.6 | 7.6 | 7.6 | 7.6 | 7.8 | 7.9 |
| 1996 | 5.7 | 5.8 | 5.9 | 6.0 | 6.0 | 6.1 | 6.3 | 6.4 | 6.5 | 6.5 | 6.6 | 7.0 | 6.9 | 7.2 | 7.4 | 7.4 | 7.5 | 7.4 | 7.6 | 7.7 |
| 1997 | 5.8 | 5.9 | 6.1 | 6.1 | 6.2 | 6.3 | 6.5 | 6.5 | 6.6 | 6.6 | 6.8 | 7.1 | 7.1 | 7.3 | 7.6 | 7.5 | 7.6 | 7.6 | 7.8 | 7.9 |
| 1998 | 5.9 | 6.0 | 6.2 | 6.2 | 6.3 | 6.3 | 6.5 | 6.6 | 6.7 | 6.7 | 6.9 | 7.2 | 7.2 | 7.4 | 7.7 | 7.6 | 7.7 | 7.7 | 7.8 | 7.9 |
| 1999 | 5.6 | 5.7 | 5.9 | 5.9 | 6.0 | 6.0 | 6.2 | 6.3 | 6.4 | 6.4 | 6.5 | 6.9 | 6.8 | 7.0 | 7.2 | 7.2 | 7.3 | 7.2 | 7.4 | 7.5 |
| 2000 | 5.8 | 5.8 | 6.0 | 6.0 | 6.1 | 6.2 | 6.4 | 6.4 | 6.5 | 6.5 | 6.7 | 7.0 | 6.9 | 7.2 | 7.4 | 7.3 | 7.4 | 7.4 | 7.5 | 7.6 |

# Table C-3 (Page 5 of 5)

## Long-Term Corporate Bonds Total Returns
Rates of Return for all holding periods
Percent per annum compounded annually

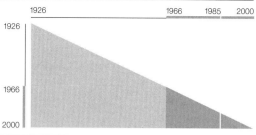

### from 1926 to 2000

| To the end of | From the beginning of 1966 | 1967 | 1968 | 1969 | 1970 | 1971 | 1972 | 1973 | 1974 | 1975 | 1976 | 1977 | 1978 | 1979 | 1980 | 1981 | 1982 | 1983 | 1984 | 1985 |
|---|---|---|---|---|---|---|---|---|---|---|---|---|---|---|---|---|---|---|---|---|
| 1966 | 0.2 | | | | | | | | | | | | | | | | | | | |
| 1967 | -2.4 | -5.0 | | | | | | | | | | | | | | | | | | |
| 1968 | -0.8 | -1.3 | 2.6 | | | | | | | | | | | | | | | | | |
| 1969 | -2.7 | -3.6 | -2.9 | -8.1 | | | | | | | | | | | | | | | | |
| 1970 | 1.2 | 1.5 | 3.7 | 4.3 | 18.4 | | | | | | | | | | | | | | | |
| 1971 | 2.8 | 3.3 | 5.5 | 6.5 | 14.6 | 11.0 | | | | | | | | | | | | | | |
| 1972 | 3.4 | 4.0 | 5.8 | 6.7 | 12.1 | 9.1 | 7.3 | | | | | | | | | | | | | |
| 1973 | 3.1 | 3.6 | 5.0 | 5.6 | 9.3 | 6.4 | 4.2 | 1.1 | | | | | | | | | | | | |
| 1974 | 2.4 | 2.7 | 3.9 | 4.1 | 6.7 | 3.9 | 1.7 | -1.0 | -3.1 | | | | | | | | | | | |
| 1975 | 3.6 | 4.0 | 5.1 | 5.5 | 8.0 | 6.0 | 4.8 | 4.0 | 5.4 | 14.6 | | | | | | | | | | |
| 1976 | 4.9 | 5.4 | 6.6 | 7.1 | 9.4 | 8.0 | 7.4 | 7.5 | 9.7 | 16.6 | 18.6 | | | | | | | | | |
| 1977 | 4.6 | 5.0 | 6.1 | 6.5 | 8.4 | 7.1 | 6.4 | 6.3 | 7.6 | 11.4 | 9.9 | 1.7 | | | | | | | | |
| 1978 | 4.2 | 4.6 | 5.5 | 5.8 | 7.5 | 6.2 | 5.5 | 5.2 | 6.0 | 8.4 | 6.4 | 0.8 | -0.1 | | | | | | | |
| 1979 | 3.6 | 3.9 | 4.7 | 4.8 | 6.2 | 5.0 | 4.2 | 3.8 | 4.3 | 5.8 | 3.7 | -0.9 | -2.1 | -4.2 | | | | | | |
| 1980 | 3.2 | 3.4 | 4.1 | 4.2 | 5.4 | 4.2 | 3.4 | 3.0 | 3.2 | 4.3 | 2.4 | -1.4 | -2.4 | -3.5 | -2.8 | | | | | |
| 1981 | 2.9 | 3.1 | 3.7 | 3.8 | 4.8 | 3.7 | 3.0 | 2.5 | 2.7 | 3.5 | 1.8 | -1.3 | -2.1 | -2.7 | -2.0 | -1.2 | | | | |
| 1982 | 4.9 | 5.2 | 5.9 | 6.1 | 7.3 | 6.5 | 6.0 | 5.9 | 6.5 | 7.7 | 6.8 | 4.9 | 5.6 | 7.0 | 11.0 | 18.7 | 42.6 | | | |
| 1983 | 5.0 | 5.2 | 5.9 | 6.1 | 7.2 | 6.4 | 6.1 | 6.0 | 6.4 | 7.6 | 6.7 | 5.1 | 5.7 | 6.9 | 9.8 | 14.4 | 23.1 | 6.3 | | |
| 1984 | 5.6 | 5.9 | 6.5 | 6.8 | 7.9 | 7.1 | 6.9 | 6.8 | 7.4 | 8.5 | 7.8 | 6.5 | 7.2 | 8.5 | 11.2 | 15.0 | 21.0 | 11.4 | 16.9 | |
| 1985 | 6.7 | 7.0 | 7.7 | 8.0 | 9.1 | 8.5 | 8.4 | 8.5 | 9.1 | 10.3 | 9.8 | 8.9 | 9.8 | 11.3 | 14.1 | 17.9 | 23.2 | 17.3 | 23.3 | 30.1 |
| 1986 | 7.3 | 7.6 | 8.3 | 8.7 | 9.7 | 9.2 | 9.1 | 9.2 | 9.9 | 11.0 | 10.7 | 9.9 | 10.9 | 12.4 | 14.9 | 18.2 | 22.5 | 18.0 | 22.1 | 24.9 |
| 1987 | 6.9 | 7.2 | 7.9 | 8.2 | 9.2 | 8.6 | 8.5 | 8.6 | 9.1 | 10.1 | 9.8 | 9.0 | 9.7 | 10.9 | 12.9 | 15.4 | 18.4 | 14.1 | 16.1 | 15.9 |
| 1988 | 7.1 | 7.4 | 8.0 | 8.3 | 9.2 | 8.7 | 8.6 | 8.7 | 9.2 | 10.2 | 9.8 | 9.1 | 9.8 | 10.9 | 12.7 | 14.8 | 17.3 | 13.5 | 15.0 | 14.5 |
| 1989 | 7.4 | 7.8 | 8.4 | 8.7 | 9.6 | 9.1 | 9.0 | 9.1 | 9.7 | 10.6 | 10.3 | 9.7 | 10.3 | 11.3 | 13.0 | 14.9 | 17.1 | 13.9 | 15.2 | 14.9 |
| 1990 | 7.4 | 7.7 | 8.3 | 8.6 | 9.4 | 9.0 | 8.9 | 9.0 | 9.5 | 10.3 | 10.0 | 9.4 | 10.1 | 11.0 | 12.4 | 14.1 | 15.9 | 13.0 | 14.0 | 13.5 |
| 1991 | 7.9 | 8.2 | 8.8 | 9.0 | 9.9 | 9.5 | 9.4 | 9.5 | 10.0 | 10.9 | 10.6 | 10.1 | 10.7 | 11.6 | 13.0 | 14.6 | 16.3 | 13.7 | 14.7 | 14.4 |
| 1992 | 7.9 | 8.2 | 8.8 | 9.1 | 9.9 | 9.5 | 9.4 | 9.5 | 10.0 | 10.8 | 10.6 | 10.1 | 10.6 | 11.5 | 12.8 | 14.2 | 15.7 | 13.3 | 14.1 | 13.7 |
| 1993 | 8.1 | 8.4 | 9.0 | 9.2 | 10.0 | 9.7 | 9.6 | 9.7 | 10.2 | 10.9 | 10.7 | 10.2 | 10.8 | 11.6 | 12.8 | 14.1 | 15.5 | 13.3 | 14.0 | 13.7 |
| 1994 | 7.6 | 7.9 | 8.4 | 8.6 | 9.3 | 9.0 | 8.9 | 9.0 | 9.3 | 10.0 | 9.8 | 9.3 | 9.8 | 10.4 | 11.4 | 12.5 | 13.7 | 11.5 | 12.0 | 11.6 |
| 1995 | 8.2 | 8.5 | 9.0 | 9.2 | 10.0 | 9.6 | 9.6 | 9.7 | 10.1 | 10.8 | 10.6 | 10.2 | 10.7 | 11.3 | 12.4 | 13.5 | 14.6 | 12.7 | 13.2 | 12.9 |
| 1996 | 8.0 | 8.2 | 8.7 | 9.0 | 9.6 | 9.3 | 9.2 | 9.3 | 9.7 | 10.3 | 10.1 | 9.7 | 10.1 | 10.7 | 11.7 | 12.7 | 13.7 | 11.8 | 12.3 | 11.9 |
| 1997 | 8.1 | 8.4 | 8.9 | 9.1 | 9.8 | 9.4 | 9.4 | 9.5 | 9.8 | 10.4 | 10.2 | 9.9 | 10.3 | 10.9 | 11.8 | 12.7 | 13.6 | 11.9 | 12.3 | 12.0 |
| 1998 | 8.2 | 8.5 | 8.9 | 9.1 | 9.8 | 9.5 | 9.4 | 9.5 | 9.9 | 10.4 | 10.3 | 9.9 | 10.3 | 10.9 | 11.7 | 12.6 | 13.4 | 11.8 | 12.2 | 11.9 |
| 1999 | 7.7 | 7.9 | 8.4 | 8.6 | 9.2 | 8.9 | 8.8 | 8.8 | 9.2 | 9.7 | 9.5 | 9.1 | 9.4 | 9.9 | 10.7 | 11.4 | 12.2 | 10.6 | 10.9 | 10.5 |
| 2000 | 7.8 | 8.1 | 8.5 | 8.7 | 9.3 | 9.0 | 8.9 | 9.0 | 9.3 | 9.8 | 9.6 | 9.2 | 9.6 | 10.0 | 10.8 | 11.5 | 12.2 | 10.7 | 11.0 | 10.6 |

| To the end of | From the beginning of 1986 | 1987 | 1988 | 1989 | 1990 | 1991 | 1992 | 1993 | 1994 | 1995 | 1996 | 1997 | 1998 | 1999 | 2000 |
|---|---|---|---|---|---|---|---|---|---|---|---|---|---|---|---|
| 1986 | 19.8 | | | | | | | | | | | | | | |
| 1987 | 9.3 | -0.3 | | | | | | | | | | | | | |
| 1988 | 9.8 | 5.1 | 10.7 | | | | | | | | | | | | |
| 1989 | 11.4 | 8.7 | 13.4 | 16.2 | | | | | | | | | | | |
| 1990 | 10.4 | 8.2 | 11.2 | 11.4 | 6.8 | | | | | | | | | | |
| 1991 | 12.0 | 10.4 | 13.3 | 14.2 | 13.1 | 19.9 | | | | | | | | | |
| 1992 | 11.6 | 10.3 | 12.5 | 13.0 | 11.9 | 14.5 | 9.4 | | | | | | | | |
| 1993 | 11.8 | 10.7 | 12.6 | 13.0 | 12.2 | 14.1 | 11.3 | 13.2 | | | | | | | |
| 1994 | 9.7 | 8.5 | 9.8 | 9.6 | 8.4 | 8.8 | 5.3 | 3.3 | -5.8 | | | | | | |
| 1995 | 11.3 | 10.4 | 11.8 | 12.0 | 11.3 | 12.2 | 10.4 | 10.7 | 9.5 | 27.2 | | | | | |
| 1996 | 10.4 | 9.5 | 10.6 | 10.6 | 9.8 | 10.3 | 8.5 | 8.3 | 6.7 | 13.6 | 1.4 | | | | |
| 1997 | 10.6 | 9.8 | 10.8 | 10.9 | 10.2 | 10.7 | 9.2 | 9.2 | 8.2 | 13.4 | 7.0 | 12.9 | | | |
| 1998 | 10.6 | 9.9 | 10.8 | 10.9 | 10.3 | 10.7 | 9.5 | 9.5 | 8.7 | 12.7 | 8.3 | 11.8 | 10.8 | | |
| 1999 | 9.2 | 8.4 | 9.2 | 9.0 | 8.4 | 8.5 | 7.2 | 6.9 | 5.9 | 8.4 | 4.1 | 5.0 | 1.2 | -7.4 | |
| 2000 | 9.4 | 8.7 | 9.5 | 9.4 | 8.8 | 9.0 | 7.8 | 7.6 | 6.8 | 9.1 | 5.8 | 6.9 | 5.0 | 2.2 | 12.9 |

## Table C-4 (Page 1 of 5)

### Long-Term Government Bonds Total Returns
Rates of Return for all holding periods
Percent per annum compounded annually

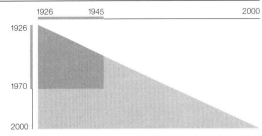

from 1926 to 2000

| To the end of | From the beginning of | | | | | | | | | | | | | | | | | | | |
|---|---|---|---|---|---|---|---|---|---|---|---|---|---|---|---|---|---|---|---|---|
| | 1926 | 1927 | 1928 | 1929 | 1930 | 1931 | 1932 | 1933 | 1934 | 1935 | 1936 | 1937 | 1938 | 1939 | 1940 | 1941 | 1942 | 1943 | 1944 | 1945 |
| 1926 | 7.8 | | | | | | | | | | | | | | | | | | | |
| 1927 | 8.3 | 8.9 | | | | | | | | | | | | | | | | | | |
| 1928 | 5.5 | 4.4 | 0.1 | | | | | | | | | | | | | | | | | |
| 1929 | 5.0 | 4.1 | 1.7 | 3.4 | | | | | | | | | | | | | | | | |
| 1930 | 4.9 | 4.2 | 2.7 | 4.0 | 4.7 | | | | | | | | | | | | | | | |
| 1931 | 3.1 | 2.2 | 0.6 | 0.8 | −0.5 | −5.3 | | | | | | | | | | | | | | |
| 1932 | 5.0 | 4.5 | 3.7 | 4.6 | 5.0 | 5.2 | 16.8 | | | | | | | | | | | | | |
| 1933 | 4.4 | 3.9 | 3.1 | 3.7 | 3.7 | 3.4 | 8.1 | −0.1 | | | | | | | | | | | | |
| 1934 | 5.0 | 4.6 | 4.0 | 4.7 | 4.9 | 5.0 | 8.7 | 4.9 | 10.0 | | | | | | | | | | | |
| 1935 | 5.0 | 4.7 | 4.1 | 4.7 | 5.0 | 5.0 | 7.8 | 4.9 | 7.5 | 5.0 | | | | | | | | | | |
| 1936 | 5.2 | 4.9 | 4.5 | 5.1 | 5.3 | 5.4 | 7.7 | 5.5 | 7.5 | 6.2 | 7.5 | | | | | | | | | |
| 1937 | 4.8 | 4.5 | 4.1 | 4.5 | 4.7 | 4.7 | 6.4 | 4.5 | 5.6 | 4.2 | 3.8 | 0.2 | | | | | | | | |
| 1938 | 4.8 | 4.6 | 4.2 | 4.6 | 4.8 | 4.8 | 6.3 | 4.6 | 5.6 | 4.5 | 4.4 | 2.8 | 5.5 | | | | | | | |
| 1939 | 4.9 | 4.7 | 4.4 | 4.7 | 4.9 | 4.9 | 6.3 | 4.8 | 5.7 | 4.8 | 4.8 | 3.9 | 5.7 | 5.9 | | | | | | |
| 1940 | 5.0 | 4.8 | 4.5 | 4.9 | 5.0 | 5.0 | 6.2 | 5.0 | 5.7 | 5.0 | 5.0 | 4.4 | 5.9 | 6.0 | 6.1 | | | | | |
| 1941 | 4.7 | 4.5 | 4.2 | 4.5 | 4.6 | 4.6 | 5.7 | 4.5 | 5.1 | 4.4 | 4.3 | 3.7 | 4.6 | 4.3 | 3.5 | 0.9 | | | | |
| 1942 | 4.6 | 4.5 | 4.2 | 4.5 | 4.5 | 4.5 | 5.5 | 4.4 | 4.9 | 4.3 | 4.2 | 3.6 | 4.3 | 4.0 | 3.4 | 2.1 | 3.2 | | | |
| 1943 | 4.5 | 4.3 | 4.0 | 4.3 | 4.4 | 4.3 | 5.2 | 4.2 | 4.6 | 4.0 | 3.9 | 3.4 | 3.9 | 3.6 | 3.1 | 2.1 | 2.6 | 2.1 | | |
| 1944 | 4.4 | 4.2 | 4.0 | 4.2 | 4.3 | 4.2 | 5.0 | 4.1 | 4.5 | 3.9 | 3.8 | 3.3 | 3.8 | 3.5 | 3.0 | 2.3 | 2.7 | 2.4 | 2.8 | |
| 1945 | 4.7 | 4.6 | 4.3 | 4.6 | 4.6 | 4.6 | 5.4 | 4.6 | 5.0 | 4.5 | 4.5 | 4.1 | 4.6 | 4.5 | 4.3 | 3.9 | 4.7 | 5.1 | 6.7 | 10.7 |
| 1946 | 4.5 | 4.3 | 4.1 | 4.3 | 4.4 | 4.3 | 5.0 | 4.2 | 4.6 | 4.1 | 4.0 | 3.7 | 4.1 | 3.9 | 3.6 | 3.2 | 3.7 | 3.8 | 4.4 | 5.2 |
| 1947 | 4.1 | 4.0 | 3.7 | 3.9 | 4.0 | 3.9 | 4.5 | 3.8 | 4.0 | 3.6 | 3.5 | 3.1 | 3.4 | 3.2 | 2.8 | 2.4 | 2.6 | 2.5 | 2.6 | 2.5 |
| 1948 | 4.1 | 4.0 | 3.7 | 3.9 | 3.9 | 3.9 | 4.5 | 3.7 | 4.0 | 3.6 | 3.5 | 3.1 | 3.4 | 3.2 | 2.9 | 2.5 | 2.7 | 2.6 | 2.7 | 2.7 |
| 1949 | 4.2 | 4.1 | 3.8 | 4.0 | 4.1 | 4.0 | 4.6 | 3.9 | 4.1 | 3.8 | 3.7 | 3.4 | 3.7 | 3.5 | 3.2 | 2.9 | 3.2 | 3.2 | 3.4 | 3.5 |
| 1950 | 4.0 | 3.9 | 3.7 | 3.8 | 3.9 | 3.8 | 4.3 | 3.7 | 3.9 | 3.5 | 3.4 | 3.1 | 3.4 | 3.2 | 2.9 | 2.6 | 2.8 | 2.8 | 2.9 | 2.9 |
| 1951 | 3.7 | 3.6 | 3.3 | 3.5 | 3.5 | 3.4 | 3.9 | 3.3 | 3.4 | 3.1 | 3.0 | 2.7 | 2.8 | 2.6 | 2.4 | 2.0 | 2.1 | 2.0 | 2.0 | 1.9 |
| 1952 | 3.6 | 3.5 | 3.3 | 3.4 | 3.4 | 3.3 | 3.8 | 3.2 | 3.3 | 3.0 | 2.8 | 2.6 | 2.7 | 2.5 | 2.3 | 1.9 | 2.0 | 1.9 | 1.9 | 1.8 |
| 1953 | 3.6 | 3.5 | 3.3 | 3.4 | 3.4 | 3.3 | 3.8 | 3.2 | 3.3 | 3.0 | 2.9 | 2.6 | 2.8 | 2.6 | 2.4 | 2.1 | 2.2 | 2.1 | 2.1 | 2.0 |
| 1954 | 3.7 | 3.6 | 3.4 | 3.5 | 3.6 | 3.5 | 3.9 | 3.4 | 3.5 | 3.2 | 3.1 | 2.9 | 3.0 | 2.9 | 2.7 | 2.4 | 2.6 | 2.5 | 2.5 | 2.5 |
| 1955 | 3.6 | 3.4 | 3.2 | 3.4 | 3.4 | 3.3 | 3.7 | 3.1 | 3.3 | 3.0 | 2.9 | 2.6 | 2.8 | 2.6 | 2.4 | 2.2 | 2.3 | 2.2 | 2.2 | 2.2 |
| 1956 | 3.3 | 3.1 | 2.9 | 3.0 | 3.0 | 3.0 | 3.3 | 2.8 | 2.9 | 2.6 | 2.5 | 2.2 | 2.3 | 2.2 | 1.9 | 1.7 | 1.7 | 1.6 | 1.6 | 1.5 |
| 1957 | 3.4 | 3.3 | 3.1 | 3.2 | 3.2 | 3.1 | 3.5 | 3.0 | 3.1 | 2.8 | 2.7 | 2.5 | 2.6 | 2.4 | 2.2 | 2.0 | 2.1 | 2.0 | 2.0 | 1.9 |
| 1958 | 3.1 | 3.0 | 2.8 | 2.9 | 2.8 | 2.8 | 3.1 | 2.6 | 2.7 | 2.4 | 2.3 | 2.1 | 2.1 | 2.0 | 1.8 | 1.5 | 1.6 | 1.5 | 1.4 | 1.3 |
| 1959 | 2.9 | 2.8 | 2.6 | 2.7 | 2.7 | 2.6 | 2.9 | 2.4 | 2.5 | 2.2 | 2.1 | 1.9 | 1.9 | 1.8 | 1.6 | 1.3 | 1.4 | 1.3 | 1.2 | 1.1 |
| 1960 | 3.2 | 3.1 | 2.9 | 3.0 | 3.0 | 2.9 | 3.2 | 2.8 | 2.9 | 2.6 | 2.5 | 2.3 | 2.4 | 2.3 | 2.1 | 1.9 | 2.0 | 1.9 | 1.9 | 1.8 |
| 1961 | 3.2 | 3.0 | 2.9 | 3.0 | 2.9 | 2.9 | 3.2 | 2.7 | 2.8 | 2.6 | 2.5 | 2.3 | 2.4 | 2.2 | 2.1 | 1.9 | 1.9 | 1.9 | 1.8 | 1.8 |
| 1962 | 3.3 | 3.1 | 3.0 | 3.1 | 3.1 | 3.0 | 3.3 | 2.9 | 3.0 | 2.7 | 2.6 | 2.5 | 2.5 | 2.4 | 2.3 | 2.1 | 2.2 | 2.1 | 2.1 | 2.1 |
| 1963 | 3.2 | 3.1 | 2.9 | 3.0 | 3.0 | 3.0 | 3.2 | 2.8 | 2.9 | 2.7 | 2.6 | 2.4 | 2.5 | 2.4 | 2.2 | 2.1 | 2.1 | 2.1 | 2.1 | 2.0 |
| 1964 | 3.2 | 3.1 | 2.9 | 3.0 | 3.0 | 3.0 | 3.2 | 2.8 | 2.9 | 2.7 | 2.6 | 2.4 | 2.5 | 2.4 | 2.3 | 2.1 | 2.2 | 2.1 | 2.1 | 2.1 |
| 1965 | 3.2 | 3.0 | 2.9 | 3.0 | 3.0 | 2.9 | 3.2 | 2.8 | 2.9 | 2.6 | 2.6 | 2.4 | 2.5 | 2.4 | 2.2 | 2.1 | 2.1 | 2.1 | 2.1 | 2.0 |
| 1966 | 3.2 | 3.1 | 2.9 | 3.0 | 3.0 | 2.9 | 3.2 | 2.8 | 2.9 | 2.7 | 2.6 | 2.4 | 2.5 | 2.4 | 2.3 | 2.1 | 2.2 | 2.1 | 2.1 | 2.1 |
| 1967 | 2.9 | 2.7 | 2.6 | 2.7 | 2.6 | 2.6 | 2.8 | 2.4 | 2.5 | 2.3 | 2.2 | 2.0 | 2.1 | 2.0 | 1.8 | 1.7 | 1.7 | 1.7 | 1.6 | 1.6 |
| 1968 | 2.8 | 2.7 | 2.5 | 2.6 | 2.6 | 2.5 | 2.7 | 2.4 | 2.4 | 2.2 | 2.1 | 2.0 | 2.0 | 1.9 | 1.8 | 1.6 | 1.6 | 1.6 | 1.6 | 1.5 |
| 1969 | 2.6 | 2.5 | 2.3 | 2.4 | 2.4 | 2.3 | 2.5 | 2.1 | 2.2 | 2.0 | 1.9 | 1.7 | 1.8 | 1.7 | 1.5 | 1.4 | 1.4 | 1.3 | 1.3 | 1.2 |
| 1970 | 2.8 | 2.7 | 2.5 | 2.6 | 2.6 | 2.5 | 2.7 | 2.4 | 2.5 | 2.3 | 2.2 | 2.0 | 2.1 | 2.0 | 1.9 | 1.7 | 1.7 | 1.7 | 1.7 | 1.6 |

# Table C-4 (Page 2 of 5)

## Long-Term Government Bonds Total Returns
Rates of Return for all holding periods
Percent per annum compounded annually

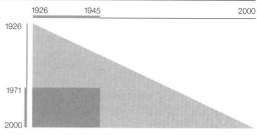

### from 1926 to 2000

| To the end of | From the beginning of 1926 | 1927 | 1928 | 1929 | 1930 | 1931 | 1932 | 1933 | 1934 | 1935 | 1936 | 1937 | 1938 | 1939 | 1940 | 1941 | 1942 | 1943 | 1944 | 1945 |
|---|---|---|---|---|---|---|---|---|---|---|---|---|---|---|---|---|---|---|---|---|
| 1971 | 3.0 | 2.9 | 2.8 | 2.8 | 2.8 | 2.8 | 3.0 | 2.7 | 2.7 | 2.5 | 2.5 | 2.3 | 2.4 | 2.3 | 2.2 | 2.1 | 2.1 | 2.1 | 2.1 | 2.0 |
| 1972 | 3.1 | 3.0 | 2.8 | 2.9 | 2.9 | 2.8 | 3.1 | 2.7 | 2.8 | 2.6 | 2.6 | 2.4 | 2.5 | 2.4 | 2.3 | 2.2 | 2.2 | 2.2 | 2.2 | 2.2 |
| 1973 | 3.0 | 2.9 | 2.8 | 2.8 | 2.8 | 2.8 | 3.0 | 2.6 | 2.7 | 2.5 | 2.5 | 2.3 | 2.4 | 2.3 | 2.2 | 2.1 | 2.1 | 2.1 | 2.1 | 2.1 |
| 1974 | 3.0 | 2.9 | 2.8 | 2.8 | 2.8 | 2.8 | 3.0 | 2.7 | 2.7 | 2.6 | 2.5 | 2.4 | 2.4 | 2.4 | 2.3 | 2.1 | 2.2 | 2.2 | 2.2 | 2.1 |
| 1975 | 3.1 | 3.0 | 2.9 | 3.0 | 3.0 | 2.9 | 3.1 | 2.8 | 2.9 | 2.7 | 2.7 | 2.6 | 2.6 | 2.5 | 2.4 | 2.3 | 2.4 | 2.4 | 2.4 | 2.4 |
| 1976 | 3.4 | 3.3 | 3.2 | 3.2 | 3.2 | 3.2 | 3.4 | 3.1 | 3.2 | 3.0 | 3.0 | 2.9 | 3.0 | 2.9 | 2.8 | 2.7 | 2.8 | 2.8 | 2.8 | 2.8 |
| 1977 | 3.3 | 3.2 | 3.1 | 3.2 | 3.2 | 3.1 | 3.3 | 3.0 | 3.1 | 3.0 | 2.9 | 2.8 | 2.9 | 2.8 | 2.7 | 2.6 | 2.7 | 2.7 | 2.7 | 2.7 |
| 1978 | 3.2 | 3.1 | 3.0 | 3.1 | 3.1 | 3.0 | 3.2 | 2.9 | 3.0 | 2.9 | 2.8 | 2.7 | 2.8 | 2.7 | 2.6 | 2.5 | 2.6 | 2.5 | 2.6 | 2.6 |
| 1979 | 3.1 | 3.0 | 2.9 | 3.0 | 3.0 | 2.9 | 3.1 | 2.9 | 2.9 | 2.8 | 2.7 | 2.6 | 2.7 | 2.6 | 2.5 | 2.4 | 2.5 | 2.4 | 2.5 | 2.4 |
| 1980 | 3.0 | 2.9 | 2.8 | 2.9 | 2.8 | 2.8 | 3.0 | 2.7 | 2.8 | 2.6 | 2.6 | 2.5 | 2.5 | 2.4 | 2.3 | 2.3 | 2.3 | 2.3 | 2.3 | 2.3 |
| 1981 | 3.0 | 2.9 | 2.8 | 2.8 | 2.8 | 2.8 | 3.0 | 2.7 | 2.7 | 2.6 | 2.5 | 2.4 | 2.5 | 2.4 | 2.3 | 2.2 | 2.3 | 2.3 | 2.3 | 2.2 |
| 1982 | 3.5 | 3.5 | 3.4 | 3.4 | 3.4 | 3.4 | 3.6 | 3.3 | 3.4 | 3.3 | 3.2 | 3.1 | 3.2 | 3.2 | 3.1 | 3.0 | 3.1 | 3.1 | 3.1 | 3.1 |
| 1983 | 3.5 | 3.4 | 3.3 | 3.4 | 3.4 | 3.4 | 3.5 | 3.3 | 3.3 | 3.2 | 3.2 | 3.1 | 3.2 | 3.1 | 3.0 | 3.0 | 3.0 | 3.0 | 3.0 | 3.0 |
| 1984 | 3.7 | 3.6 | 3.5 | 3.6 | 3.6 | 3.6 | 3.7 | 3.5 | 3.6 | 3.4 | 3.4 | 3.3 | 3.4 | 3.4 | 3.3 | 3.2 | 3.3 | 3.3 | 3.3 | 3.3 |
| 1985 | 4.1 | 4.0 | 3.9 | 4.0 | 4.0 | 4.0 | 4.2 | 4.0 | 4.0 | 3.9 | 3.9 | 3.8 | 3.9 | 3.9 | 3.8 | 3.8 | 3.8 | 3.9 | 3.9 | 3.9 |
| 1986 | 4.4 | 4.3 | 4.3 | 4.3 | 4.3 | 4.3 | 4.5 | 4.3 | 4.4 | 4.3 | 4.3 | 4.2 | 4.3 | 4.3 | 4.2 | 4.2 | 4.3 | 4.3 | 4.3 | 4.4 |
| 1987 | 4.3 | 4.2 | 4.1 | 4.2 | 4.2 | 4.2 | 4.4 | 4.2 | 4.3 | 4.2 | 4.1 | 4.1 | 4.2 | 4.1 | 4.1 | 4.0 | 4.1 | 4.1 | 4.2 | 4.2 |
| 1988 | 4.4 | 4.3 | 4.2 | 4.3 | 4.3 | 4.3 | 4.5 | 4.3 | 4.4 | 4.3 | 4.2 | 4.2 | 4.3 | 4.2 | 4.2 | 4.2 | 4.2 | 4.2 | 4.3 | 4.3 |
| 1989 | 4.6 | 4.5 | 4.4 | 4.5 | 4.5 | 4.5 | 4.7 | 4.5 | 4.6 | 4.5 | 4.5 | 4.4 | 4.5 | 4.5 | 4.5 | 4.4 | 4.5 | 4.5 | 4.6 | 4.6 |
| 1990 | 4.6 | 4.5 | 4.5 | 4.5 | 4.6 | 4.6 | 4.7 | 4.5 | 4.6 | 4.5 | 4.5 | 4.5 | 4.5 | 4.5 | 4.5 | 4.5 | 4.5 | 4.6 | 4.6 | 4.7 |
| 1991 | 4.8 | 4.7 | 4.7 | 4.8 | 4.8 | 4.8 | 5.0 | 4.8 | 4.9 | 4.8 | 4.8 | 4.7 | 4.8 | 4.8 | 4.8 | 4.7 | 4.8 | 4.8 | 4.9 | 4.9 |
| 1992 | 4.8 | 4.8 | 4.7 | 4.8 | 4.8 | 4.8 | 5.0 | 4.8 | 4.9 | 4.8 | 4.8 | 4.8 | 4.9 | 4.8 | 4.8 | 4.8 | 4.9 | 4.9 | 5.0 | 5.0 |
| 1993 | 5.0 | 5.0 | 4.9 | 5.0 | 5.0 | 5.0 | 5.2 | 5.0 | 5.1 | 5.0 | 5.0 | 5.0 | 5.1 | 5.1 | 5.1 | 5.0 | 5.1 | 5.2 | 5.2 | 5.3 |
| 1994 | 4.8 | 4.8 | 4.7 | 4.8 | 4.8 | 4.8 | 5.0 | 4.8 | 4.9 | 4.8 | 4.8 | 4.8 | 4.8 | 4.8 | 4.8 | 4.8 | 4.9 | 4.9 | 4.9 | 5.0 |
| 1995 | 5.2 | 5.1 | 5.1 | 5.2 | 5.2 | 5.2 | 5.4 | 5.2 | 5.3 | 5.2 | 5.2 | 5.2 | 5.3 | 5.2 | 5.2 | 5.2 | 5.3 | 5.3 | 5.4 | 5.5 |
| 1996 | 5.1 | 5.0 | 5.0 | 5.1 | 5.1 | 5.1 | 5.3 | 5.1 | 5.2 | 5.1 | 5.1 | 5.1 | 5.1 | 5.1 | 5.1 | 5.1 | 5.2 | 5.2 | 5.3 | 5.3 |
| 1997 | 5.2 | 5.2 | 5.1 | 5.2 | 5.2 | 5.2 | 5.4 | 5.2 | 5.3 | 5.3 | 5.3 | 5.2 | 5.3 | 5.3 | 5.3 | 5.3 | 5.4 | 5.4 | 5.5 | 5.5 |
| 1998 | 5.3 | 5.3 | 5.2 | 5.3 | 5.3 | 5.4 | 5.5 | 5.4 | 5.4 | 5.4 | 5.4 | 5.3 | 5.4 | 5.4 | 5.4 | 5.4 | 5.5 | 5.5 | 5.6 | 5.7 |
| 1999 | 5.1 | 5.1 | 5.0 | 5.1 | 5.1 | 5.1 | 5.3 | 5.1 | 5.2 | 5.1 | 5.1 | 5.1 | 5.2 | 5.2 | 5.2 | 5.2 | 5.2 | 5.3 | 5.3 | 5.4 |
| 2000 | 5.3 | 5.3 | 5.2 | 5.3 | 5.3 | 5.4 | 5.5 | 5.4 | 5.4 | 5.4 | 5.4 | 5.3 | 5.4 | 5.4 | 5.4 | 5.4 | 5.5 | 5.5 | 5.6 | 5.6 |

# Table C-4 (Page 3 of 5)

## Long-Term Government Bonds Total Returns
Rates of Return for all holding periods
Percent per annum compounded annually

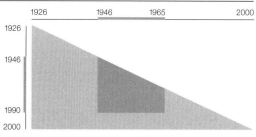

## from 1926 to 2000

| To the end of | From the beginning of 1946 | 1947 | 1948 | 1949 | 1950 | 1951 | 1952 | 1953 | 1954 | 1955 | 1956 | 1957 | 1958 | 1959 | 1960 | 1961 | 1962 | 1963 | 1964 | 1965 |
|---|---|---|---|---|---|---|---|---|---|---|---|---|---|---|---|---|---|---|---|---|
| 1946 | -0.1 | | | | | | | | | | | | | | | | | | | |
| 1947 | -1.4 | -2.6 | | | | | | | | | | | | | | | | | | |
| 1948 | 0.2 | 0.3 | 3.4 | | | | | | | | | | | | | | | | | |
| 1949 | 1.7 | 2.3 | 4.9 | 6.4 | | | | | | | | | | | | | | | | |
| 1950 | 1.4 | 1.8 | 3.3 | 3.2 | 0.1 | | | | | | | | | | | | | | | |
| 1951 | 0.5 | 0.6 | 1.4 | 0.8 | -2.0 | -3.9 | | | | | | | | | | | | | | |
| 1952 | 0.6 | 0.7 | 1.4 | 0.9 | -0.9 | -1.4 | 1.2 | | | | | | | | | | | | | |
| 1953 | 1.0 | 1.1 | 1.7 | 1.4 | 0.2 | 0.2 | 2.4 | 3.6 | | | | | | | | | | | | |
| 1954 | 1.6 | 1.8 | 2.5 | 2.4 | 1.6 | 1.9 | 4.0 | 5.4 | 7.2 | | | | | | | | | | | |
| 1955 | 1.3 | 1.5 | 2.0 | 1.8 | 1.1 | 1.3 | 2.6 | 3.1 | 2.9 | -1.3 | | | | | | | | | | |
| 1956 | 0.7 | 0.8 | 1.1 | 0.9 | 0.1 | 0.1 | 0.9 | 0.9 | 0.0 | -3.5 | -5.6 | | | | | | | | | |
| 1957 | 1.2 | 1.4 | 1.8 | 1.6 | 1.0 | 1.1 | 2.0 | 2.2 | 1.8 | 0.0 | 0.7 | 7.5 | | | | | | | | |
| 1958 | 0.6 | 0.7 | 1.0 | 0.8 | 0.2 | 0.2 | 0.8 | 0.7 | 0.2 | -1.5 | -1.6 | 0.5 | -6.1 | | | | | | | |
| 1959 | 0.4 | 0.5 | 0.7 | 0.5 | -0.1 | -0.1 | 0.4 | 0.3 | -0.2 | -1.7 | -1.8 | -0.5 | -4.2 | -2.3 | | | | | | |
| 1960 | 1.3 | 1.4 | 1.7 | 1.5 | 1.1 | 1.2 | 1.8 | 1.9 | 1.6 | 0.7 | 1.2 | 2.9 | 1.5 | 5.5 | 13.8 | | | | | |
| 1961 | 1.3 | 1.3 | 1.6 | 1.5 | 1.1 | 1.2 | 1.7 | 1.8 | 1.6 | 0.8 | 1.1 | 2.5 | 1.3 | 3.9 | 7.2 | 1.0 | | | | |
| 1962 | 1.6 | 1.7 | 2.0 | 1.9 | 1.5 | 1.7 | 2.2 | 2.3 | 2.1 | 1.5 | 1.9 | 3.2 | 2.4 | 4.7 | 7.1 | 3.9 | 6.9 | | | |
| 1963 | 1.6 | 1.7 | 1.9 | 1.8 | 1.5 | 1.6 | 2.1 | 2.2 | 2.0 | 1.5 | 1.8 | 3.0 | 2.2 | 4.0 | 5.6 | 3.0 | 4.0 | 1.2 | | |
| 1964 | 1.7 | 1.8 | 2.0 | 1.9 | 1.6 | 1.8 | 2.2 | 2.3 | 2.2 | 1.7 | 2.0 | 3.0 | 2.4 | 3.9 | 5.2 | 3.1 | 3.8 | 2.4 | 3.5 | |
| 1965 | 1.6 | 1.7 | 2.0 | 1.9 | 1.6 | 1.7 | 2.1 | 2.2 | 2.1 | 1.6 | 1.9 | 2.8 | 2.2 | 3.4 | 4.4 | 2.6 | 3.1 | 1.8 | 2.1 | 0.7 |
| 1966 | 1.7 | 1.8 | 2.0 | 2.0 | 1.7 | 1.8 | 2.2 | 2.3 | 2.2 | 1.8 | 2.1 | 2.9 | 2.4 | 3.5 | 4.3 | 2.8 | 3.2 | 2.3 | 2.6 | 2.2 |
| 1967 | 1.2 | 1.2 | 1.4 | 1.3 | 1.1 | 1.1 | 1.5 | 1.5 | 1.3 | 0.9 | 1.1 | 1.7 | 1.1 | 2.0 | 2.5 | 1.0 | 1.0 | -0.1 | -0.5 | -1.8 |
| 1968 | 1.1 | 1.2 | 1.4 | 1.3 | 1.0 | 1.1 | 1.4 | 1.4 | 1.2 | 0.8 | 1.0 | 1.5 | 1.0 | 1.7 | 2.2 | 0.8 | 0.8 | -0.2 | -0.4 | -1.4 |
| 1969 | 0.9 | 0.9 | 1.1 | 1.0 | 0.7 | 0.7 | 1.0 | 1.0 | 0.8 | 0.4 | 0.5 | 1.0 | 0.5 | 1.1 | 1.4 | 0.2 | 0.1 | -0.9 | -1.2 | -2.1 |
| 1970 | 1.3 | 1.3 | 1.5 | 1.4 | 1.2 | 1.3 | 1.5 | 1.6 | 1.4 | 1.1 | 1.3 | 1.8 | 1.3 | 2.0 | 2.4 | 1.3 | 1.3 | 0.7 | 0.6 | 0.1 |
| 1971 | 1.7 | 1.8 | 2.0 | 1.9 | 1.7 | 1.8 | 2.1 | 2.1 | 2.1 | 1.8 | 2.0 | 2.5 | 2.1 | 2.8 | 3.2 | 2.3 | 2.5 | 2.0 | 2.1 | 1.9 |
| 1972 | 1.9 | 1.9 | 2.1 | 2.1 | 1.9 | 2.0 | 2.3 | 2.3 | 2.3 | 2.0 | 2.2 | 2.7 | 2.4 | 3.0 | 3.4 | 2.6 | 2.8 | 2.4 | 2.5 | 2.3 |
| 1973 | 1.8 | 1.8 | 2.0 | 1.9 | 1.8 | 1.8 | 2.1 | 2.2 | 2.1 | 1.8 | 2.0 | 2.5 | 2.2 | 2.7 | 3.1 | 2.3 | 2.4 | 2.0 | 2.1 | 2.0 |
| 1974 | 1.8 | 1.9 | 2.1 | 2.0 | 1.9 | 1.9 | 2.2 | 2.3 | 2.2 | 1.9 | 2.1 | 2.6 | 2.3 | 2.8 | 3.2 | 2.5 | 2.6 | 2.2 | 2.3 | 2.2 |
| 1975 | 2.1 | 2.2 | 2.3 | 2.3 | 2.1 | 2.2 | 2.5 | 2.5 | 2.5 | 2.3 | 2.5 | 2.9 | 2.7 | 3.2 | 3.5 | 2.9 | 3.0 | 2.7 | 2.9 | 2.8 |
| 1976 | 2.5 | 2.6 | 2.8 | 2.8 | 2.6 | 2.7 | 3.0 | 3.1 | 3.1 | 2.9 | 3.1 | 3.6 | 3.4 | 3.9 | 4.3 | 3.7 | 3.9 | 3.7 | 3.9 | 3.9 |
| 1977 | 2.4 | 2.5 | 2.7 | 2.7 | 2.5 | 2.6 | 2.9 | 2.9 | 2.9 | 2.7 | 2.9 | 3.3 | 3.1 | 3.7 | 4.0 | 3.4 | 3.6 | 3.4 | 3.5 | 3.5 |
| 1978 | 2.3 | 2.4 | 2.6 | 2.5 | 2.4 | 2.5 | 2.7 | 2.8 | 2.8 | 2.6 | 2.7 | 3.1 | 2.9 | 3.4 | 3.7 | 3.2 | 3.3 | 3.1 | 3.2 | 3.2 |
| 1979 | 2.2 | 2.3 | 2.4 | 2.4 | 2.3 | 2.3 | 2.6 | 2.6 | 2.6 | 2.4 | 2.6 | 2.9 | 2.7 | 3.2 | 3.5 | 2.9 | 3.1 | 2.8 | 2.9 | 2.9 |
| 1980 | 2.0 | 2.1 | 2.2 | 2.2 | 2.1 | 2.1 | 2.3 | 2.4 | 2.3 | 2.2 | 2.3 | 2.6 | 2.4 | 2.8 | 3.1 | 2.6 | 2.7 | 2.4 | 2.5 | 2.5 |
| 1981 | 2.0 | 2.1 | 2.2 | 2.2 | 2.1 | 2.1 | 2.3 | 2.4 | 2.3 | 2.2 | 2.3 | 2.6 | 2.4 | 2.8 | 3.0 | 2.6 | 2.6 | 2.4 | 2.5 | 2.4 |
| 1982 | 2.9 | 3.0 | 3.2 | 3.1 | 3.0 | 3.1 | 3.4 | 3.5 | 3.4 | 3.3 | 3.5 | 3.9 | 3.7 | 4.1 | 4.4 | 4.0 | 4.2 | 4.0 | 4.2 | 4.2 |
| 1983 | 2.8 | 2.9 | 3.1 | 3.1 | 3.0 | 3.1 | 3.3 | 3.4 | 3.4 | 3.2 | 3.4 | 3.7 | 3.6 | 4.0 | 4.3 | 3.9 | 4.0 | 3.9 | 4.0 | 4.0 |
| 1984 | 3.2 | 3.2 | 3.4 | 3.4 | 3.3 | 3.4 | 3.6 | 3.7 | 3.7 | 3.6 | 3.8 | 4.1 | 4.0 | 4.4 | 4.7 | 4.3 | 4.5 | 4.4 | 4.5 | 4.6 |
| 1985 | 3.8 | 3.9 | 4.0 | 4.1 | 4.0 | 4.1 | 4.4 | 4.5 | 4.5 | 4.4 | 4.6 | 5.0 | 4.9 | 5.3 | 5.6 | 5.3 | 5.5 | 5.4 | 5.6 | 5.7 |
| 1986 | 4.2 | 4.3 | 4.5 | 4.6 | 4.5 | 4.6 | 4.9 | 5.0 | 5.0 | 5.0 | 5.2 | 5.6 | 5.5 | 5.9 | 6.3 | 6.0 | 6.2 | 6.1 | 6.4 | 6.5 |
| 1987 | 4.1 | 4.2 | 4.3 | 4.4 | 4.3 | 4.4 | 4.7 | 4.8 | 4.8 | 4.7 | 4.9 | 5.3 | 5.2 | 5.6 | 5.9 | 5.6 | 5.8 | 5.8 | 6.0 | 6.1 |
| 1988 | 4.2 | 4.3 | 4.5 | 4.5 | 4.4 | 4.6 | 4.8 | 4.9 | 4.9 | 4.9 | 5.1 | 5.4 | 5.4 | 5.8 | 6.0 | 5.8 | 6.0 | 5.9 | 6.1 | 6.2 |
| 1989 | 4.5 | 4.6 | 4.8 | 4.8 | 4.8 | 4.9 | 5.1 | 5.2 | 5.3 | 5.2 | 5.4 | 5.8 | 5.7 | 6.1 | 6.4 | 6.2 | 6.4 | 6.4 | 6.6 | 6.7 |
| 1990 | 4.5 | 4.6 | 4.8 | 4.8 | 4.8 | 4.9 | 5.2 | 5.3 | 5.3 | 5.3 | 5.5 | 5.8 | 5.7 | 6.1 | 6.4 | 6.2 | 6.4 | 6.3 | 6.5 | 6.7 |

## Table C-4 (Page 4 of 5)

### Long-Term Government Bonds Total Returns
Rates of Return for all holding periods
Percent per annum compounded annually

from 1926 to 2000

| To the end of | From the beginning of | | | | | | | | | | | | | | | | | | | |
|---|---|---|---|---|---|---|---|---|---|---|---|---|---|---|---|---|---|---|---|---|
| | 1946 | 1947 | 1948 | 1949 | 1950 | 1951 | 1952 | 1953 | 1954 | 1955 | 1956 | 1957 | 1958 | 1959 | 1960 | 1961 | 1962 | 1963 | 1964 | 1965 |
| 1991 | 4.8 | 4.9 | 5.1 | 5.2 | 5.1 | 5.2 | 5.5 | 5.6 | 5.7 | 5.6 | 5.8 | 6.2 | 6.1 | 6.5 | 6.8 | 6.6 | 6.8 | 6.8 | 7.0 | 7.1 |
| 1992 | 4.9 | 5.0 | 5.2 | 5.2 | 5.2 | 5.3 | 5.6 | 5.7 | 5.7 | 5.7 | 5.9 | 6.2 | 6.2 | 6.6 | 6.8 | 6.6 | 6.8 | 6.8 | 7.0 | 7.1 |
| 1993 | 5.2 | 5.3 | 5.4 | 5.5 | 5.5 | 5.6 | 5.8 | 6.0 | 6.0 | 6.0 | 6.2 | 6.5 | 6.5 | 6.9 | 7.2 | 7.0 | 7.2 | 7.2 | 7.4 | 7.5 |
| 1994 | 4.9 | 5.0 | 5.1 | 5.2 | 5.2 | 5.3 | 5.5 | 5.6 | 5.7 | 5.6 | 5.8 | 6.1 | 6.1 | 6.4 | 6.7 | 6.5 | 6.7 | 6.7 | 6.8 | 7.0 |
| 1995 | 5.3 | 5.5 | 5.6 | 5.7 | 5.7 | 5.8 | 6.0 | 6.1 | 6.2 | 6.2 | 6.4 | 6.7 | 6.7 | 7.1 | 7.3 | 7.1 | 7.3 | 7.3 | 7.5 | 7.7 |
| 1996 | 5.2 | 5.3 | 5.5 | 5.5 | 5.5 | 5.6 | 5.9 | 6.0 | 6.0 | 6.0 | 6.2 | 6.5 | 6.5 | 6.8 | 7.1 | 6.9 | 7.1 | 7.1 | 7.3 | 7.4 |
| 1997 | 5.4 | 5.5 | 5.7 | 5.7 | 5.7 | 5.9 | 6.1 | 6.2 | 6.3 | 6.2 | 6.4 | 6.7 | 6.7 | 7.1 | 7.3 | 7.1 | 7.3 | 7.3 | 7.5 | 7.6 |
| 1998 | 5.6 | 5.7 | 5.8 | 5.9 | 5.9 | 6.0 | 6.2 | 6.3 | 6.4 | 6.4 | 6.6 | 6.9 | 6.9 | 7.2 | 7.5 | 7.3 | 7.5 | 7.5 | 7.7 | 7.8 |
| 1999 | 5.3 | 5.4 | 5.5 | 5.6 | 5.6 | 5.7 | 5.9 | 6.0 | 6.0 | 6.0 | 6.2 | 6.5 | 6.5 | 6.8 | 7.0 | 6.8 | 7.0 | 7.0 | 7.2 | 7.3 |
| 2000 | 5.5 | 5.7 | 5.8 | 5.9 | 5.8 | 6.0 | 6.2 | 6.3 | 6.3 | 6.3 | 6.5 | 6.8 | 6.8 | 7.1 | 7.3 | 7.2 | 7.4 | 7.4 | 7.5 | 7.7 |

# Table C-4 (Page 5 of 5)

## Long-Term Government Bonds Total Returns
Rates of Return for all holding periods
Percent per annum compounded annually

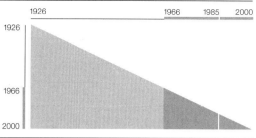

### from 1926 to 2000

| To the end of | From the beginning of 1966 | 1967 | 1968 | 1969 | 1970 | 1971 | 1972 | 1973 | 1974 | 1975 | 1976 | 1977 | 1978 | 1979 | 1980 | 1981 | 1982 | 1983 | 1984 | 1985 |
|---|---|---|---|---|---|---|---|---|---|---|---|---|---|---|---|---|---|---|---|---|
| 1966 | 3.7 | | | | | | | | | | | | | | | | | | | |
| 1967 | −3.0 | −9.2 | | | | | | | | | | | | | | | | | | |
| 1968 | −2.1 | −4.8 | −0.3 | | | | | | | | | | | | | | | | | |
| 1969 | −2.8 | −4.9 | −2.7 | −5.1 | | | | | | | | | | | | | | | | |
| 1970 | 0.0 | −0.9 | 2.0 | 3.2 | 12.1 | | | | | | | | | | | | | | | |
| 1971 | 2.1 | 1.8 | 4.7 | 6.4 | 12.7 | 13.2 | | | | | | | | | | | | | | |
| 1972 | 2.6 | 2.4 | 4.9 | 6.2 | 10.3 | 9.4 | 5.7 | | | | | | | | | | | | | |
| 1973 | 2.1 | 1.9 | 3.9 | 4.7 | 7.3 | 5.8 | 2.2 | −1.1 | | | | | | | | | | | | |
| 1974 | 2.4 | 2.2 | 3.9 | 4.7 | 6.7 | 5.4 | 2.9 | 1.6 | 4.4 | | | | | | | | | | | |
| 1975 | 3.0 | 3.0 | 4.6 | 5.3 | 7.1 | 6.2 | 4.5 | 4.1 | 6.7 | 9.2 | | | | | | | | | | |
| 1976 | 4.2 | 4.3 | 5.9 | 6.7 | 8.5 | 7.9 | 6.8 | 7.1 | 10.0 | 12.9 | 16.8 | | | | | | | | | |
| 1977 | 3.8 | 3.8 | 5.2 | 5.8 | 7.3 | 6.6 | 5.5 | 5.5 | 7.2 | 8.2 | 7.7 | −0.7 | | | | | | | | |
| 1978 | 3.4 | 3.4 | 4.6 | 5.1 | 6.3 | 5.6 | 4.5 | 4.4 | 5.5 | 5.8 | 4.6 | −0.9 | −1.2 | | | | | | | |
| 1979 | 3.1 | 3.0 | 4.1 | 4.5 | 5.5 | 4.8 | 3.8 | 3.5 | 4.3 | 4.3 | 3.1 | −1.0 | −1.2 | −1.2 | | | | | | |
| 1980 | 2.6 | 2.5 | 3.5 | 3.8 | 4.6 | 3.9 | 2.9 | 2.6 | 3.1 | 2.9 | 1.7 | −1.8 | −2.1 | −2.6 | −3.9 | | | | | |
| 1981 | 2.5 | 2.5 | 3.3 | 3.6 | 4.4 | 3.7 | 2.8 | 2.5 | 2.9 | 2.7 | 1.7 | −1.1 | −1.1 | −1.1 | −1.1 | 1.9 | | | | |
| 1982 | 4.4 | 4.5 | 5.5 | 5.9 | 6.8 | 6.4 | 5.8 | 5.8 | 6.6 | 6.8 | 6.5 | 4.9 | 6.0 | 7.9 | 11.2 | 19.6 | 40.4 | | | |
| 1983 | 4.2 | 4.3 | 5.2 | 5.5 | 6.3 | 5.9 | 5.3 | 5.3 | 6.0 | 6.1 | 5.8 | 4.3 | 5.1 | 6.4 | 8.4 | 12.9 | 18.9 | 0.7 | | |
| 1984 | 4.8 | 4.9 | 5.7 | 6.1 | 6.9 | 6.6 | 6.1 | 6.1 | 6.8 | 7.0 | 6.8 | 5.6 | 6.5 | 7.9 | 9.8 | 13.5 | 17.7 | 7.8 | 15.5 | |
| 1985 | 6.0 | 6.1 | 7.0 | 7.5 | 8.3 | 8.0 | 7.7 | 7.8 | 8.6 | 9.0 | 9.0 | 8.2 | 9.3 | 10.9 | 13.1 | 16.8 | 20.9 | 15.0 | 23.0 | 31.0 |
| 1986 | 6.8 | 6.9 | 7.9 | 8.3 | 9.2 | 9.0 | 8.7 | 8.9 | 9.8 | 10.2 | 10.3 | 9.7 | 10.9 | 12.5 | 14.6 | 18.1 | 21.6 | 17.3 | 23.5 | 27.7 |
| 1987 | 6.3 | 6.5 | 7.3 | 7.7 | 8.5 | 8.3 | 8.0 | 8.1 | 8.8 | 9.2 | 9.2 | 8.5 | 9.5 | 10.7 | 12.3 | 14.9 | 17.2 | 13.0 | 16.3 | 16.6 |
| 1988 | 6.5 | 6.6 | 7.4 | 7.8 | 8.5 | 8.4 | 8.1 | 8.2 | 8.9 | 9.2 | 9.2 | 8.6 | 9.5 | 10.6 | 12.0 | 14.2 | 16.1 | 12.5 | 15.0 | 14.9 |
| 1989 | 6.9 | 7.1 | 7.9 | 8.3 | 9.0 | 8.8 | 8.6 | 8.8 | 9.4 | 9.8 | 9.8 | 9.3 | 10.2 | 11.3 | 12.6 | 14.6 | 16.3 | 13.2 | 15.5 | 15.5 |
| 1990 | 6.9 | 7.0 | 7.8 | 8.2 | 8.9 | 8.7 | 8.5 | 8.6 | 9.2 | 9.6 | 9.6 | 9.1 | 9.9 | 10.8 | 12.0 | 13.7 | 15.2 | 12.3 | 14.1 | 13.9 |
| 1991 | 7.4 | 7.5 | 8.3 | 8.7 | 9.3 | 9.2 | 9.0 | 9.2 | 9.8 | 10.1 | 10.2 | 9.7 | 10.5 | 11.5 | 12.6 | 14.2 | 15.6 | 13.1 | 14.8 | 14.6 |
| 1992 | 7.4 | 7.5 | 8.3 | 8.6 | 9.3 | 9.1 | 9.0 | 9.1 | 9.7 | 10.0 | 10.0 | 9.6 | 10.4 | 11.2 | 12.2 | 13.7 | 14.9 | 12.6 | 14.0 | 13.8 |
| 1993 | 7.8 | 7.9 | 8.6 | 9.0 | 9.6 | 9.5 | 9.4 | 9.5 | 10.1 | 10.4 | 10.5 | 10.1 | 10.8 | 11.7 | 12.7 | 14.1 | 15.1 | 13.1 | 14.4 | 14.3 |
| 1994 | 7.2 | 7.3 | 8.0 | 8.3 | 8.9 | 8.7 | 8.6 | 8.7 | 9.2 | 9.4 | 9.4 | 9.0 | 9.6 | 10.4 | 11.2 | 12.3 | 13.2 | 11.2 | 12.2 | 11.9 |
| 1995 | 7.9 | 8.1 | 8.7 | 9.1 | 9.7 | 9.6 | 9.4 | 9.6 | 10.1 | 10.4 | 10.4 | 10.1 | 10.8 | 11.5 | 12.4 | 13.5 | 14.4 | 12.6 | 13.7 | 13.5 |
| 1996 | 7.6 | 7.8 | 8.4 | 8.7 | 9.3 | 9.2 | 9.0 | 9.1 | 9.6 | 9.8 | 9.9 | 9.5 | 10.1 | 10.8 | 11.5 | 12.6 | 13.3 | 11.6 | 12.5 | 12.3 |
| 1997 | 7.9 | 8.0 | 8.6 | 9.0 | 9.5 | 9.4 | 9.2 | 9.4 | 9.9 | 10.1 | 10.1 | 9.8 | 10.4 | 11.0 | 11.8 | 12.8 | 13.5 | 11.9 | 12.7 | 12.5 |
| 1998 | 8.0 | 8.2 | 8.8 | 9.1 | 9.6 | 9.5 | 9.4 | 9.5 | 10.0 | 10.2 | 10.3 | 10.0 | 10.5 | 11.1 | 11.8 | 12.8 | 13.5 | 12.0 | 12.8 | 12.6 |
| 1999 | 7.5 | 7.6 | 8.2 | 8.5 | 8.9 | 8.8 | 8.7 | 8.8 | 9.2 | 9.4 | 9.4 | 9.1 | 9.5 | 10.1 | 10.7 | 11.5 | 12.1 | 10.6 | 11.3 | 11.0 |
| 2000 | 7.9 | 8.0 | 8.5 | 8.8 | 9.3 | 9.2 | 9.1 | 9.2 | 9.6 | 9.8 | 9.9 | 9.6 | 10.0 | 10.6 | 11.2 | 12.0 | 12.6 | 11.2 | 11.8 | 11.6 |

| To the end of | From the beginning of 1986 | 1987 | 1988 | 1989 | 1990 | 1991 | 1992 | 1993 | 1994 | 1995 | 1996 | 1997 | 1998 | 1999 | 2000 |
|---|---|---|---|---|---|---|---|---|---|---|---|---|---|---|---|
| 1986 | 24.5 | | | | | | | | | | | | | | |
| 1987 | 10.1 | −2.7 | | | | | | | | | | | | | |
| 1988 | 9.9 | 3.3 | 9.7 | | | | | | | | | | | | |
| 1989 | 11.9 | 8.0 | 13.8 | 18.1 | | | | | | | | | | | |
| 1990 | 10.8 | 7.6 | 11.2 | 12.0 | 6.2 | | | | | | | | | | |
| 1991 | 12.1 | 9.8 | 13.2 | 14.4 | 12.6 | 19.3 | | | | | | | | | |
| 1992 | 11.5 | 9.5 | 12.1 | 12.8 | 11.0 | 13.5 | 8.1 | | | | | | | | |
| 1993 | 12.4 | 10.7 | 13.1 | 13.8 | 12.8 | 15.1 | 13.0 | 18.2 | | | | | | | |
| 1994 | 9.9 | 8.2 | 9.9 | 9.9 | 8.3 | 8.9 | 5.6 | 4.4 | −7.8 | | | | | | |
| 1995 | 11.9 | 10.6 | 12.4 | 12.8 | 11.9 | 13.1 | 11.6 | 12.8 | 10.2 | 31.7 | | | | | |
| 1996 | 10.7 | 9.4 | 10.8 | 11.0 | 10.0 | 10.6 | 9.0 | 9.2 | 6.4 | 14.2 | −0.9 | | | | |
| 1997 | 11.1 | 10.0 | 11.3 | 11.5 | 10.7 | 11.4 | 10.1 | 10.5 | 8.7 | 14.8 | 7.1 | 15.9 | | | |
| 1998 | 11.3 | 10.2 | 11.5 | 11.7 | 11.0 | 11.6 | 10.5 | 10.9 | 9.5 | 14.3 | 9.1 | 14.4 | 13.1 | | |
| 1999 | 9.7 | 8.6 | 9.6 | 9.6 | 8.8 | 9.1 | 7.9 | 7.8 | 6.2 | 9.2 | 4.3 | 6.0 | 1.5 | −9.0 | |
| 2000 | 10.4 | 9.5 | 10.5 | 10.5 | 9.9 | 10.3 | 9.3 | 9.5 | 8.3 | 11.2 | 7.5 | 9.7 | 7.7 | 5.2 | 21.5 |

## Table C-5 (Page 1 of 5)

### Intermediate-Term Government Bonds Total Returns
Rates of Return for all holding periods
Percent per annum compounded annually

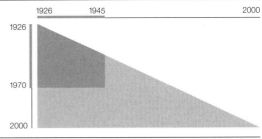

from 1926 to 2000

| To the end of | From the beginning of 1926 | 1927 | 1928 | 1929 | 1930 | 1931 | 1932 | 1933 | 1934 | 1935 | 1936 | 1937 | 1938 | 1939 | 1940 | 1941 | 1942 | 1943 | 1944 | 1945 |
|---|---|---|---|---|---|---|---|---|---|---|---|---|---|---|---|---|---|---|---|---|
| 1926 | 5.4 | | | | | | | | | | | | | | | | | | | |
| 1927 | 4.9 | 4.5 | | | | | | | | | | | | | | | | | | |
| 1928 | 3.6 | 2.7 | 0.9 | | | | | | | | | | | | | | | | | |
| 1929 | 4.2 | 3.8 | 3.4 | 6.0 | | | | | | | | | | | | | | | | |
| 1930 | 4.7 | 4.5 | 4.5 | 6.4 | 6.7 | | | | | | | | | | | | | | | |
| 1931 | 3.5 | 3.1 | 2.8 | 3.4 | 2.1 | -2.3 | | | | | | | | | | | | | | |
| 1932 | 4.2 | 4.0 | 3.9 | 4.7 | 4.3 | 3.1 | 8.8 | | | | | | | | | | | | | |
| 1933 | 3.9 | 3.7 | 3.6 | 4.1 | 3.7 | 2.7 | 5.3 | 1.8 | | | | | | | | | | | | |
| 1934 | 4.5 | 4.4 | 4.3 | 4.9 | 4.7 | 4.2 | 6.5 | 5.4 | 9.0 | | | | | | | | | | | |
| 1935 | 4.7 | 4.7 | 4.7 | 5.2 | 5.1 | 4.8 | 6.6 | 5.9 | 8.0 | 7.0 | | | | | | | | | | |
| 1936 | 4.6 | 4.5 | 4.5 | 4.9 | 4.8 | 4.5 | 5.9 | 5.2 | 6.3 | 5.0 | 3.1 | | | | | | | | | |
| 1937 | 4.3 | 4.2 | 4.2 | 4.6 | 4.4 | 4.1 | 5.2 | 4.4 | 5.1 | 3.8 | 2.3 | 1.6 | | | | | | | | |
| 1938 | 4.5 | 4.4 | 4.4 | 4.7 | 4.6 | 4.3 | 5.3 | 4.7 | 5.3 | 4.4 | 3.6 | 3.9 | 6.2 | | | | | | | |
| 1939 | 4.5 | 4.4 | 4.4 | 4.7 | 4.6 | 4.3 | 5.2 | 4.7 | 5.2 | 4.5 | 3.8 | 4.1 | 5.4 | 4.5 | | | | | | |
| 1940 | 4.4 | 4.3 | 4.3 | 4.6 | 4.4 | 4.2 | 5.0 | 4.5 | 4.9 | 4.2 | 3.7 | 3.8 | 4.6 | 3.7 | 3.0 | | | | | |
| 1941 | 4.1 | 4.0 | 4.0 | 4.2 | 4.1 | 3.9 | 4.5 | 4.0 | 4.3 | 3.7 | 3.1 | 3.1 | 3.5 | 2.6 | 1.7 | 0.5 | | | | |
| 1942 | 4.0 | 3.9 | 3.9 | 4.1 | 3.9 | 3.7 | 4.3 | 3.8 | 4.1 | 3.4 | 3.0 | 2.9 | 3.2 | 2.5 | 1.8 | 1.2 | 1.9 | | | |
| 1943 | 3.9 | 3.8 | 3.8 | 4.0 | 3.9 | 3.6 | 4.1 | 3.7 | 3.9 | 3.4 | 2.9 | 2.9 | 3.1 | 2.5 | 2.0 | 1.7 | 2.4 | 2.8 | | |
| 1944 | 3.8 | 3.7 | 3.7 | 3.9 | 3.7 | 3.5 | 4.0 | 3.6 | 3.7 | 3.2 | 2.8 | 2.8 | 2.9 | 2.4 | 2.0 | 1.8 | 2.2 | 2.3 | 1.8 | |
| 1945 | 3.7 | 3.6 | 3.6 | 3.8 | 3.6 | 3.4 | 3.8 | 3.5 | 3.6 | 3.1 | 2.7 | 2.7 | 2.9 | 2.4 | 2.0 | 1.8 | 2.2 | 2.3 | 2.0 | 2.2 |
| 1946 | 3.6 | 3.5 | 3.5 | 3.6 | 3.5 | 3.3 | 3.6 | 3.3 | 3.4 | 2.9 | 2.6 | 2.5 | 2.7 | 2.2 | 1.9 | 1.7 | 2.0 | 2.0 | 1.7 | 1.6 |
| 1947 | 3.5 | 3.4 | 3.3 | 3.5 | 3.3 | 3.1 | 3.5 | 3.1 | 3.2 | 2.8 | 2.4 | 2.4 | 2.5 | 2.1 | 1.8 | 1.6 | 1.8 | 1.7 | 1.5 | 1.4 |
| 1948 | 3.4 | 3.3 | 3.3 | 3.4 | 3.2 | 3.1 | 3.4 | 3.0 | 3.1 | 2.7 | 2.4 | 2.3 | 2.4 | 2.0 | 1.8 | 1.6 | 1.8 | 1.8 | 1.6 | 1.5 |
| 1949 | 3.4 | 3.3 | 3.2 | 3.3 | 3.2 | 3.0 | 3.3 | 3.0 | 3.1 | 2.7 | 2.4 | 2.3 | 2.4 | 2.1 | 1.8 | 1.7 | 1.9 | 1.8 | 1.7 | 1.7 |
| 1950 | 3.3 | 3.2 | 3.1 | 3.2 | 3.1 | 2.9 | 3.2 | 2.9 | 2.9 | 2.6 | 2.3 | 2.2 | 2.3 | 2.0 | 1.7 | 1.6 | 1.7 | 1.7 | 1.5 | 1.5 |
| 1951 | 3.1 | 3.1 | 3.0 | 3.1 | 3.0 | 2.8 | 3.0 | 2.7 | 2.8 | 2.4 | 2.2 | 2.1 | 2.1 | 1.8 | 1.6 | 1.5 | 1.6 | 1.5 | 1.4 | 1.3 |
| 1952 | 3.1 | 3.0 | 2.9 | 3.0 | 2.9 | 2.7 | 3.0 | 2.7 | 2.7 | 2.4 | 2.1 | 2.1 | 2.1 | 1.8 | 1.6 | 1.5 | 1.6 | 1.6 | 1.4 | 1.4 |
| 1953 | 3.1 | 3.0 | 2.9 | 3.0 | 2.9 | 2.7 | 3.0 | 2.7 | 2.8 | 2.4 | 2.2 | 2.1 | 2.2 | 1.9 | 1.7 | 1.6 | 1.7 | 1.7 | 1.6 | 1.6 |
| 1954 | 3.1 | 3.0 | 2.9 | 3.0 | 2.9 | 2.7 | 3.0 | 2.7 | 2.8 | 2.5 | 2.2 | 2.2 | 2.2 | 2.0 | 1.8 | 1.7 | 1.8 | 1.8 | 1.7 | 1.7 |
| 1955 | 2.9 | 2.9 | 2.8 | 2.9 | 2.8 | 2.6 | 2.8 | 2.6 | 2.6 | 2.3 | 2.1 | 2.0 | 2.0 | 1.8 | 1.6 | 1.5 | 1.6 | 1.6 | 1.5 | 1.5 |
| 1956 | 2.8 | 2.8 | 2.7 | 2.8 | 2.6 | 2.5 | 2.7 | 2.4 | 2.5 | 2.2 | 2.0 | 1.9 | 1.9 | 1.7 | 1.5 | 1.4 | 1.5 | 1.5 | 1.4 | 1.3 |
| 1957 | 3.0 | 2.9 | 2.9 | 2.9 | 2.8 | 2.7 | 2.9 | 2.6 | 2.7 | 2.4 | 2.2 | 2.2 | 2.2 | 2.0 | 1.9 | 1.8 | 1.9 | 1.9 | 1.8 | 1.8 |
| 1958 | 2.9 | 2.8 | 2.7 | 2.8 | 2.7 | 2.5 | 2.7 | 2.5 | 2.5 | 2.3 | 2.1 | 2.0 | 2.0 | 1.8 | 1.7 | 1.6 | 1.7 | 1.7 | 1.6 | 1.6 |
| 1959 | 2.8 | 2.7 | 2.6 | 2.7 | 2.6 | 2.4 | 2.6 | 2.4 | 2.4 | 2.2 | 2.0 | 1.9 | 1.9 | 1.7 | 1.6 | 1.5 | 1.6 | 1.5 | 1.5 | 1.4 |
| 1960 | 3.0 | 2.9 | 2.9 | 3.0 | 2.9 | 2.7 | 2.9 | 2.7 | 2.7 | 2.5 | 2.3 | 2.3 | 2.3 | 2.2 | 2.0 | 2.0 | 2.1 | 2.1 | 2.0 | 2.1 |
| 1961 | 3.0 | 2.9 | 2.9 | 2.9 | 2.8 | 2.7 | 2.9 | 2.7 | 2.7 | 2.5 | 2.3 | 2.3 | 2.3 | 2.1 | 2.0 | 2.0 | 2.1 | 2.1 | 2.0 | 2.0 |
| 1962 | 3.0 | 3.0 | 2.9 | 3.0 | 2.9 | 2.8 | 3.0 | 2.8 | 2.8 | 2.6 | 2.4 | 2.4 | 2.4 | 2.3 | 2.2 | 2.2 | 2.2 | 2.2 | 2.2 | 2.2 |
| 1963 | 3.0 | 2.9 | 2.9 | 3.0 | 2.9 | 2.8 | 2.9 | 2.7 | 2.8 | 2.6 | 2.4 | 2.4 | 2.4 | 2.3 | 2.2 | 2.1 | 2.2 | 2.2 | 2.2 | 2.2 |
| 1964 | 3.0 | 3.0 | 2.9 | 3.0 | 2.9 | 2.8 | 3.0 | 2.8 | 2.8 | 2.6 | 2.5 | 2.4 | 2.5 | 2.3 | 2.2 | 2.2 | 2.3 | 2.3 | 2.3 | 2.3 |
| 1965 | 3.0 | 2.9 | 2.9 | 2.9 | 2.9 | 2.7 | 2.9 | 2.7 | 2.7 | 2.6 | 2.4 | 2.4 | 2.4 | 2.3 | 2.2 | 2.2 | 2.2 | 2.2 | 2.2 | 2.2 |
| 1966 | 3.0 | 3.0 | 2.9 | 3.0 | 2.9 | 2.8 | 2.9 | 2.8 | 2.8 | 2.6 | 2.5 | 2.5 | 2.5 | 2.4 | 2.3 | 2.3 | 2.3 | 2.3 | 2.3 | 2.3 |
| 1967 | 3.0 | 2.9 | 2.9 | 2.9 | 2.8 | 2.7 | 2.9 | 2.7 | 2.8 | 2.6 | 2.4 | 2.4 | 2.4 | 2.3 | 2.2 | 2.2 | 2.3 | 2.3 | 2.3 | 2.3 |
| 1968 | 3.0 | 3.0 | 2.9 | 3.0 | 2.9 | 2.8 | 2.9 | 2.8 | 2.8 | 2.6 | 2.5 | 2.5 | 2.5 | 2.4 | 2.3 | 2.3 | 2.4 | 2.4 | 2.4 | 2.4 |
| 1969 | 2.9 | 2.9 | 2.8 | 2.9 | 2.8 | 2.7 | 2.8 | 2.7 | 2.7 | 2.5 | 2.4 | 2.4 | 2.4 | 2.3 | 2.2 | 2.2 | 2.2 | 2.3 | 2.2 | 2.3 |
| 1970 | 3.2 | 3.2 | 3.1 | 3.2 | 3.1 | 3.0 | 3.2 | 3.0 | 3.1 | 2.9 | 2.8 | 2.8 | 2.8 | 2.7 | 2.7 | 2.6 | 2.7 | 2.7 | 2.7 | 2.8 |

## Table C-5 (Page 2 of 5)

### Intermediate-Term Government Bonds Total Returns
Rates of Return for all holding periods
Percent per annum compounded annually

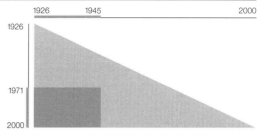

## from 1926 to 2000

| To the end of | From the beginning of 1926 | 1927 | 1928 | 1929 | 1930 | 1931 | 1932 | 1933 | 1934 | 1935 | 1936 | 1937 | 1938 | 1939 | 1940 | 1941 | 1942 | 1943 | 1944 | 1945 |
|---|---|---|---|---|---|---|---|---|---|---|---|---|---|---|---|---|---|---|---|---|
| 1971 | 3.3 | 3.3 | 3.3 | 3.3 | 3.3 | 3.2 | 3.3 | 3.2 | 3.2 | 3.1 | 2.9 | 2.9 | 3.0 | 2.9 | 2.8 | 2.8 | 2.9 | 2.9 | 3.0 | 3.0 |
| 1972 | 3.4 | 3.3 | 3.3 | 3.4 | 3.3 | 3.2 | 3.4 | 3.2 | 3.3 | 3.1 | 3.0 | 3.0 | 3.0 | 3.0 | 2.9 | 2.9 | 3.0 | 3.0 | 3.0 | 3.1 |
| 1973 | 3.4 | 3.4 | 3.3 | 3.4 | 3.3 | 3.2 | 3.4 | 3.3 | 3.3 | 3.1 | 3.0 | 3.0 | 3.1 | 3.0 | 3.0 | 3.0 | 3.0 | 3.1 | 3.1 | 3.1 |
| 1974 | 3.4 | 3.4 | 3.4 | 3.4 | 3.4 | 3.3 | 3.4 | 3.3 | 3.3 | 3.2 | 3.1 | 3.1 | 3.2 | 3.1 | 3.0 | 3.0 | 3.1 | 3.2 | 3.2 | 3.2 |
| 1975 | 3.5 | 3.5 | 3.5 | 3.5 | 3.5 | 3.4 | 3.5 | 3.4 | 3.5 | 3.3 | 3.2 | 3.2 | 3.3 | 3.2 | 3.2 | 3.2 | 3.3 | 3.3 | 3.3 | 3.4 |
| 1976 | 3.7 | 3.7 | 3.7 | 3.7 | 3.7 | 3.6 | 3.7 | 3.6 | 3.7 | 3.5 | 3.5 | 3.5 | 3.5 | 3.4 | 3.4 | 3.4 | 3.5 | 3.6 | 3.6 | 3.6 |
| 1977 | 3.7 | 3.6 | 3.6 | 3.7 | 3.6 | 3.6 | 3.7 | 3.6 | 3.6 | 3.5 | 3.4 | 3.4 | 3.5 | 3.4 | 3.4 | 3.4 | 3.5 | 3.5 | 3.5 | 3.6 |
| 1978 | 3.7 | 3.6 | 3.6 | 3.7 | 3.6 | 3.6 | 3.7 | 3.6 | 3.6 | 3.5 | 3.4 | 3.4 | 3.5 | 3.4 | 3.4 | 3.4 | 3.5 | 3.5 | 3.5 | 3.6 |
| 1979 | 3.7 | 3.6 | 3.6 | 3.7 | 3.6 | 3.6 | 3.7 | 3.6 | 3.6 | 3.5 | 3.4 | 3.4 | 3.5 | 3.4 | 3.4 | 3.4 | 3.5 | 3.5 | 3.5 | 3.6 |
| 1980 | 3.7 | 3.6 | 3.6 | 3.7 | 3.6 | 3.6 | 3.7 | 3.6 | 3.6 | 3.5 | 3.4 | 3.4 | 3.5 | 3.4 | 3.4 | 3.4 | 3.5 | 3.5 | 3.5 | 3.6 |
| 1981 | 3.8 | 3.7 | 3.7 | 3.8 | 3.7 | 3.7 | 3.8 | 3.7 | 3.7 | 3.6 | 3.6 | 3.6 | 3.6 | 3.6 | 3.5 | 3.6 | 3.6 | 3.7 | 3.7 | 3.7 |
| 1982 | 4.2 | 4.1 | 4.1 | 4.2 | 4.2 | 4.1 | 4.2 | 4.2 | 4.2 | 4.1 | 4.0 | 4.1 | 4.1 | 4.1 | 4.1 | 4.1 | 4.2 | 4.2 | 4.3 | 4.3 |
| 1983 | 4.2 | 4.2 | 4.2 | 4.3 | 4.2 | 4.2 | 4.3 | 4.2 | 4.3 | 4.2 | 4.1 | 4.1 | 4.2 | 4.2 | 4.1 | 4.2 | 4.3 | 4.3 | 4.4 | 4.4 |
| 1984 | 4.4 | 4.4 | 4.4 | 4.4 | 4.4 | 4.4 | 4.5 | 4.4 | 4.5 | 4.4 | 4.3 | 4.3 | 4.4 | 4.4 | 4.4 | 4.4 | 4.5 | 4.5 | 4.6 | 4.7 |
| 1985 | 4.6 | 4.6 | 4.6 | 4.7 | 4.7 | 4.6 | 4.8 | 4.7 | 4.7 | 4.7 | 4.6 | 4.6 | 4.7 | 4.7 | 4.7 | 4.7 | 4.8 | 4.9 | 4.9 | 5.0 |
| 1986 | 4.8 | 4.8 | 4.8 | 4.9 | 4.8 | 4.8 | 4.9 | 4.9 | 4.9 | 4.8 | 4.8 | 4.8 | 4.9 | 4.9 | 4.9 | 4.9 | 5.0 | 5.1 | 5.2 | 5.2 |
| 1987 | 4.8 | 4.8 | 4.8 | 4.8 | 4.8 | 4.8 | 4.9 | 4.8 | 4.9 | 4.8 | 4.8 | 4.8 | 4.9 | 4.8 | 4.8 | 4.9 | 5.0 | 5.1 | 5.1 | 5.2 |
| 1988 | 4.8 | 4.8 | 4.8 | 4.8 | 4.8 | 4.8 | 4.9 | 4.9 | 4.9 | 4.8 | 4.8 | 4.8 | 4.9 | 4.9 | 4.9 | 4.9 | 5.0 | 5.1 | 5.1 | 5.2 |
| 1989 | 4.9 | 4.9 | 4.9 | 5.0 | 5.0 | 4.9 | 5.1 | 5.0 | 5.1 | 5.0 | 4.9 | 5.0 | 5.0 | 5.0 | 5.0 | 5.1 | 5.2 | 5.2 | 5.3 | 5.4 |
| 1990 | 5.0 | 5.0 | 5.0 | 5.1 | 5.0 | 5.0 | 5.1 | 5.1 | 5.1 | 5.1 | 5.0 | 5.1 | 5.1 | 5.1 | 5.1 | 5.2 | 5.3 | 5.3 | 5.4 | 5.5 |
| 1991 | 5.1 | 5.1 | 5.1 | 5.2 | 5.2 | 5.2 | 5.3 | 5.2 | 5.3 | 5.2 | 5.2 | 5.2 | 5.3 | 5.3 | 5.3 | 5.4 | 5.5 | 5.5 | 5.6 | 5.7 |
| 1992 | 5.2 | 5.2 | 5.2 | 5.2 | 5.2 | 5.2 | 5.3 | 5.3 | 5.3 | 5.3 | 5.2 | 5.3 | 5.4 | 5.3 | 5.4 | 5.4 | 5.5 | 5.6 | 5.6 | 5.7 |
| 1993 | 5.3 | 5.3 | 5.3 | 5.3 | 5.3 | 5.3 | 5.4 | 5.4 | 5.4 | 5.4 | 5.3 | 5.4 | 5.5 | 5.4 | 5.5 | 5.5 | 5.6 | 5.7 | 5.7 | 5.8 |
| 1994 | 5.1 | 5.1 | 5.1 | 5.2 | 5.2 | 5.1 | 5.2 | 5.2 | 5.2 | 5.2 | 5.2 | 5.2 | 5.3 | 5.2 | 5.3 | 5.3 | 5.4 | 5.5 | 5.5 | 5.6 |
| 1995 | 5.3 | 5.3 | 5.3 | 5.3 | 5.3 | 5.3 | 5.4 | 5.4 | 5.4 | 5.4 | 5.3 | 5.4 | 5.4 | 5.4 | 5.5 | 5.5 | 5.6 | 5.7 | 5.7 | 5.8 |
| 1996 | 5.2 | 5.2 | 5.2 | 5.3 | 5.3 | 5.2 | 5.4 | 5.3 | 5.4 | 5.3 | 5.3 | 5.3 | 5.4 | 5.4 | 5.4 | 5.4 | 5.5 | 5.6 | 5.6 | 5.7 |
| 1997 | 5.3 | 5.3 | 5.3 | 5.3 | 5.3 | 5.3 | 5.4 | 5.4 | 5.4 | 5.4 | 5.3 | 5.4 | 5.4 | 5.4 | 5.4 | 5.5 | 5.6 | 5.6 | 5.7 | 5.8 |
| 1998 | 5.3 | 5.3 | 5.3 | 5.4 | 5.4 | 5.4 | 5.5 | 5.4 | 5.5 | 5.4 | 5.4 | 5.5 | 5.5 | 5.5 | 5.5 | 5.6 | 5.7 | 5.7 | 5.8 | 5.9 |
| 1999 | 5.2 | 5.2 | 5.2 | 5.3 | 5.3 | 5.3 | 5.4 | 5.3 | 5.4 | 5.3 | 5.3 | 5.3 | 5.4 | 5.4 | 5.4 | 5.4 | 5.5 | 5.6 | 5.6 | 5.7 |
| 2000 | 5.3 | 5.3 | 5.3 | 5.4 | 5.4 | 5.4 | 5.5 | 5.4 | 5.5 | 5.4 | 5.4 | 5.4 | 5.5 | 5.5 | 5.5 | 5.6 | 5.6 | 5.7 | 5.8 | 5.8 |

# Table C-5 (Page 3 of 5)

## Intermediate-Term Government Bonds Total Returns
Rates of Return for all holding periods
Percent per annum compounded annually

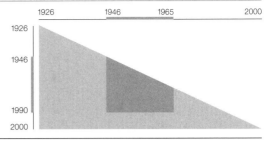

from 1926 to 2000

| To the end of | From the beginning of | | | | | | | | | | | | | | | | | | | |
|---|---|---|---|---|---|---|---|---|---|---|---|---|---|---|---|---|---|---|---|---|
| | 1946 | 1947 | 1948 | 1949 | 1950 | 1951 | 1952 | 1953 | 1954 | 1955 | 1956 | 1957 | 1958 | 1959 | 1960 | 1961 | 1962 | 1963 | 1964 | 1965 |
| 1946 | 1.0 | | | | | | | | | | | | | | | | | | | |
| 1947 | 1.0 | 0.9 | | | | | | | | | | | | | | | | | | |
| 1948 | 1.3 | 1.4 | 1.8 | | | | | | | | | | | | | | | | | |
| 1949 | 1.5 | 1.7 | 2.1 | 2.3 | | | | | | | | | | | | | | | | |
| 1950 | 1.4 | 1.4 | 1.6 | 1.5 | 0.7 | | | | | | | | | | | | | | | |
| 1951 | 1.2 | 1.2 | 1.3 | 1.1 | 0.5 | 0.4 | | | | | | | | | | | | | | |
| 1952 | 1.3 | 1.3 | 1.4 | 1.3 | 0.9 | 1.0 | 1.6 | | | | | | | | | | | | | |
| 1953 | 1.5 | 1.6 | 1.7 | 1.6 | 1.5 | 1.7 | 2.4 | 3.2 | | | | | | | | | | | | |
| 1954 | 1.6 | 1.7 | 1.8 | 1.8 | 1.7 | 2.0 | 2.5 | 3.0 | 2.7 | | | | | | | | | | | |
| 1955 | 1.4 | 1.4 | 1.5 | 1.5 | 1.3 | 1.4 | 1.7 | 1.7 | 1.0 | −0.7 | | | | | | | | | | |
| 1956 | 1.2 | 1.3 | 1.3 | 1.2 | 1.1 | 1.1 | 1.3 | 1.2 | 0.5 | −0.5 | −0.4 | | | | | | | | | |
| 1957 | 1.8 | 1.8 | 1.9 | 1.9 | 1.9 | 2.1 | 2.3 | 2.5 | 2.3 | 2.2 | 3.6 | 7.8 | | | | | | | | |
| 1958 | 1.5 | 1.6 | 1.6 | 1.6 | 1.5 | 1.6 | 1.8 | 1.9 | 1.6 | 1.3 | 2.0 | 3.2 | −1.3 | | | | | | | |
| 1959 | 1.4 | 1.4 | 1.5 | 1.4 | 1.3 | 1.4 | 1.5 | 1.5 | 1.2 | 1.0 | 1.4 | 2.0 | −0.8 | −0.4 | | | | | | |
| 1960 | 2.1 | 2.1 | 2.2 | 2.3 | 2.2 | 2.4 | 2.6 | 2.8 | 2.7 | 2.7 | 3.4 | 4.3 | 3.2 | 5.5 | 11.8 | | | | | |
| 1961 | 2.0 | 2.1 | 2.2 | 2.2 | 2.2 | 2.3 | 2.5 | 2.7 | 2.6 | 2.6 | 3.1 | 3.8 | 2.9 | 4.3 | 6.7 | 1.8 | | | | |
| 1962 | 2.2 | 2.3 | 2.4 | 2.5 | 2.5 | 2.6 | 2.8 | 2.9 | 2.9 | 2.9 | 3.5 | 4.1 | 3.4 | 4.6 | 6.3 | 3.7 | 5.6 | | | |
| 1963 | 2.2 | 2.3 | 2.4 | 2.4 | 2.4 | 2.5 | 2.7 | 2.8 | 2.8 | 2.8 | 3.2 | 3.8 | 3.1 | 4.0 | 5.1 | 3.0 | 3.6 | 1.6 | | |
| 1964 | 2.3 | 2.4 | 2.5 | 2.5 | 2.5 | 2.6 | 2.8 | 2.9 | 2.9 | 2.9 | 3.3 | 3.8 | 3.2 | 4.0 | 4.9 | 3.3 | 3.7 | 2.8 | 4.0 | |
| 1965 | 2.2 | 2.3 | 2.4 | 2.4 | 2.4 | 2.5 | 2.7 | 2.8 | 2.7 | 2.7 | 3.1 | 3.5 | 3.0 | 3.6 | 4.2 | 2.8 | 3.1 | 2.2 | 2.5 | 1.0 |
| 1966 | 2.4 | 2.4 | 2.5 | 2.5 | 2.6 | 2.7 | 2.8 | 2.9 | 2.9 | 2.9 | 3.2 | 3.6 | 3.1 | 3.7 | 4.3 | 3.1 | 3.4 | 2.8 | 3.2 | 2.8 |
| 1967 | 2.3 | 2.4 | 2.4 | 2.5 | 2.5 | 2.6 | 2.7 | 2.8 | 2.8 | 2.8 | 3.0 | 3.4 | 2.9 | 3.4 | 3.9 | 2.8 | 3.0 | 2.5 | 2.7 | 2.2 |
| 1968 | 2.4 | 2.5 | 2.5 | 2.6 | 2.6 | 2.7 | 2.8 | 2.9 | 2.9 | 2.9 | 3.2 | 3.5 | 3.1 | 3.5 | 4.0 | 3.0 | 3.2 | 2.8 | 3.0 | 2.8 |
| 1969 | 2.3 | 2.3 | 2.4 | 2.4 | 2.4 | 2.5 | 2.6 | 2.7 | 2.6 | 2.6 | 2.9 | 3.1 | 2.8 | 3.1 | 3.5 | 2.6 | 2.7 | 2.3 | 2.4 | 2.1 |
| 1970 | 2.8 | 2.9 | 3.0 | 3.0 | 3.1 | 3.2 | 3.3 | 3.4 | 3.4 | 3.5 | 3.8 | 4.1 | 3.8 | 4.2 | 4.6 | 3.9 | 4.2 | 4.0 | 4.4 | 4.4 |
| 1971 | 3.0 | 3.1 | 3.2 | 3.3 | 3.3 | 3.4 | 3.6 | 3.7 | 3.7 | 3.8 | 4.1 | 4.4 | 4.1 | 4.5 | 5.0 | 4.4 | 4.6 | 4.5 | 4.9 | 5.0 |
| 1972 | 3.1 | 3.2 | 3.3 | 3.3 | 3.4 | 3.5 | 3.7 | 3.8 | 3.8 | 3.9 | 4.1 | 4.4 | 4.2 | 4.6 | 5.0 | 4.4 | 4.7 | 4.6 | 4.9 | 5.0 |
| 1973 | 3.2 | 3.2 | 3.3 | 3.4 | 3.4 | 3.6 | 3.7 | 3.8 | 3.8 | 3.9 | 4.1 | 4.4 | 4.2 | 4.6 | 5.0 | 4.5 | 4.7 | 4.6 | 4.9 | 5.0 |
| 1974 | 3.2 | 3.3 | 3.4 | 3.5 | 3.5 | 3.6 | 3.8 | 3.9 | 3.9 | 4.0 | 4.2 | 4.5 | 4.3 | 4.7 | 5.0 | 4.5 | 4.7 | 4.7 | 5.0 | 5.1 |
| 1975 | 3.4 | 3.5 | 3.6 | 3.6 | 3.7 | 3.8 | 4.0 | 4.1 | 4.1 | 4.2 | 4.4 | 4.7 | 4.5 | 4.8 | 5.2 | 4.8 | 5.0 | 4.9 | 5.2 | 5.3 |
| 1976 | 3.7 | 3.8 | 3.9 | 4.0 | 4.0 | 4.1 | 4.3 | 4.4 | 4.5 | 4.5 | 4.8 | 5.1 | 4.9 | 5.3 | 5.6 | 5.2 | 5.5 | 5.5 | 5.8 | 5.9 |
| 1977 | 3.6 | 3.7 | 3.8 | 3.9 | 3.9 | 4.0 | 4.2 | 4.3 | 4.3 | 4.4 | 4.6 | 4.9 | 4.7 | 5.1 | 5.4 | 5.0 | 5.2 | 5.2 | 5.5 | 5.6 |
| 1978 | 3.6 | 3.7 | 3.8 | 3.8 | 3.9 | 4.0 | 4.2 | 4.3 | 4.3 | 4.4 | 4.6 | 4.8 | 4.7 | 5.0 | 5.3 | 4.9 | 5.1 | 5.1 | 5.3 | 5.4 |
| 1979 | 3.6 | 3.7 | 3.8 | 3.9 | 3.9 | 4.0 | 4.2 | 4.2 | 4.3 | 4.4 | 4.6 | 4.8 | 4.7 | 4.9 | 5.2 | 4.9 | 5.1 | 5.0 | 5.2 | 5.3 |
| 1980 | 3.6 | 3.7 | 3.8 | 3.9 | 3.9 | 4.0 | 4.1 | 4.2 | 4.3 | 4.3 | 4.5 | 4.8 | 4.6 | 4.9 | 5.2 | 4.8 | 5.0 | 5.0 | 5.2 | 5.2 |
| 1981 | 3.8 | 3.9 | 4.0 | 4.0 | 4.1 | 4.2 | 4.3 | 4.4 | 4.5 | 4.5 | 4.7 | 4.9 | 4.8 | 5.1 | 5.3 | 5.1 | 5.2 | 5.2 | 5.4 | 5.5 |
| 1982 | 4.4 | 4.5 | 4.6 | 4.7 | 4.8 | 4.9 | 5.0 | 5.2 | 5.2 | 5.3 | 5.5 | 5.8 | 5.7 | 6.0 | 6.3 | 6.0 | 6.2 | 6.3 | 6.5 | 6.7 |
| 1983 | 4.5 | 4.6 | 4.7 | 4.8 | 4.8 | 5.0 | 5.1 | 5.2 | 5.3 | 5.4 | 5.6 | 5.8 | 5.8 | 6.1 | 6.3 | 6.1 | 6.3 | 6.3 | 6.6 | 6.7 |
| 1984 | 4.7 | 4.8 | 4.9 | 5.0 | 5.1 | 5.2 | 5.4 | 5.5 | 5.6 | 5.7 | 5.9 | 6.1 | 6.1 | 6.3 | 6.6 | 6.4 | 6.6 | 6.7 | 6.9 | 7.1 |
| 1985 | 5.1 | 5.2 | 5.3 | 5.4 | 5.5 | 5.6 | 5.8 | 5.9 | 6.0 | 6.1 | 6.3 | 6.6 | 6.5 | 6.8 | 7.1 | 6.9 | 7.2 | 7.2 | 7.5 | 7.7 |
| 1986 | 5.3 | 5.4 | 5.5 | 5.6 | 5.7 | 5.9 | 6.0 | 6.2 | 6.3 | 6.4 | 6.6 | 6.9 | 6.8 | 7.1 | 7.4 | 7.2 | 7.5 | 7.5 | 7.8 | 8.0 |
| 1987 | 5.3 | 5.4 | 5.5 | 5.6 | 5.7 | 5.8 | 6.0 | 6.1 | 6.2 | 6.3 | 6.5 | 6.7 | 6.7 | 7.0 | 7.2 | 7.1 | 7.3 | 7.4 | 7.6 | 7.8 |
| 1988 | 5.3 | 5.4 | 5.5 | 5.6 | 5.7 | 5.8 | 6.0 | 6.1 | 6.2 | 6.3 | 6.5 | 6.7 | 6.7 | 6.9 | 7.2 | 7.0 | 7.2 | 7.3 | 7.5 | 7.7 |
| 1989 | 5.5 | 5.6 | 5.7 | 5.8 | 5.9 | 6.0 | 6.1 | 6.3 | 6.4 | 6.5 | 6.7 | 6.9 | 6.9 | 7.1 | 7.4 | 7.3 | 7.5 | 7.5 | 7.8 | 7.9 |
| 1990 | 5.5 | 5.7 | 5.8 | 5.9 | 5.9 | 6.1 | 6.2 | 6.4 | 6.4 | 6.5 | 6.8 | 7.0 | 7.0 | 7.2 | 7.5 | 7.3 | 7.5 | 7.6 | 7.8 | 8.0 |

## Table C-5 (Page 4 of 5)

### Intermediate-Term Government Bonds Total Returns
Rates of Return for all holding periods
Percent per annum compounded annually

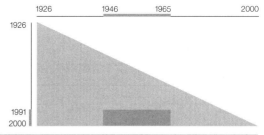

from 1926 to 2000

| To the end of | From the beginning of 1946 | 1947 | 1948 | 1949 | 1950 | 1951 | 1952 | 1953 | 1954 | 1955 | 1956 | 1957 | 1958 | 1959 | 1960 | 1961 | 1962 | 1963 | 1964 | 1965 |
|---|---|---|---|---|---|---|---|---|---|---|---|---|---|---|---|---|---|---|---|---|
| 1991 | 5.8 | 5.9 | 6.0 | 6.1 | 6.2 | 6.3 | 6.5 | 6.6 | 6.7 | 6.8 | 7.0 | 7.2 | 7.2 | 7.5 | 7.7 | 7.6 | 7.8 | 7.9 | 8.1 | 8.2 |
| 1992 | 5.8 | 5.9 | 6.0 | 6.1 | 6.2 | 6.3 | 6.5 | 6.6 | 6.7 | 6.8 | 7.0 | 7.2 | 7.2 | 7.5 | 7.7 | 7.6 | 7.8 | 7.8 | 8.1 | 8.2 |
| 1993 | 5.9 | 6.0 | 6.1 | 6.2 | 6.3 | 6.4 | 6.6 | 6.7 | 6.8 | 6.9 | 7.1 | 7.3 | 7.3 | 7.6 | 7.8 | 7.7 | 7.9 | 8.0 | 8.2 | 8.3 |
| 1994 | 5.7 | 5.8 | 5.9 | 5.9 | 6.0 | 6.2 | 6.3 | 6.4 | 6.5 | 6.6 | 6.8 | 7.0 | 6.9 | 7.2 | 7.4 | 7.3 | 7.5 | 7.5 | 7.7 | 7.8 |
| 1995 | 5.9 | 6.0 | 6.1 | 6.2 | 6.3 | 6.4 | 6.5 | 6.6 | 6.7 | 6.8 | 7.0 | 7.2 | 7.2 | 7.4 | 7.7 | 7.5 | 7.7 | 7.8 | 8.0 | 8.1 |
| 1996 | 5.8 | 5.9 | 6.0 | 6.1 | 6.2 | 6.3 | 6.4 | 6.5 | 6.6 | 6.7 | 6.9 | 7.1 | 7.1 | 7.3 | 7.5 | 7.4 | 7.6 | 7.6 | 7.8 | 7.9 |
| 1997 | 5.8 | 5.9 | 6.0 | 6.1 | 6.2 | 6.3 | 6.5 | 6.6 | 6.7 | 6.7 | 6.9 | 7.1 | 7.1 | 7.3 | 7.5 | 7.4 | 7.6 | 7.6 | 7.8 | 7.9 |
| 1998 | 5.9 | 6.0 | 6.1 | 6.2 | 6.3 | 6.4 | 6.5 | 6.7 | 6.7 | 6.8 | 7.0 | 7.2 | 7.2 | 7.4 | 7.6 | 7.5 | 7.6 | 7.7 | 7.9 | 8.0 |
| 1999 | 5.8 | 5.9 | 6.0 | 6.0 | 6.1 | 6.2 | 6.4 | 6.5 | 6.5 | 6.6 | 6.8 | 7.0 | 6.9 | 7.2 | 7.4 | 7.2 | 7.4 | 7.4 | 7.6 | 7.7 |
| 2000 | 5.9 | 6.0 | 6.1 | 6.2 | 6.2 | 6.4 | 6.5 | 6.6 | 6.7 | 6.8 | 6.9 | 7.1 | 7.1 | 7.3 | 7.5 | 7.4 | 7.5 | 7.6 | 7.7 | 7.8 |

## Table C-5 (Page 5 of 5)

### Intermediate-Term Government Bonds Total Returns
Rates of Return for all holding periods
Percent per annum compounded annually

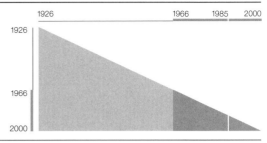

### from 1926 to 2000

| To the end of | From the beginning of | | | | | | | | | | | | | | | | | | | |
|---|---|---|---|---|---|---|---|---|---|---|---|---|---|---|---|---|---|---|---|---|
| | 1966 | 1967 | 1968 | 1969 | 1970 | 1971 | 1972 | 1973 | 1974 | 1975 | 1976 | 1977 | 1978 | 1979 | 1980 | 1981 | 1982 | 1983 | 1984 | 1985 |
| 1966 | 4.7 | | | | | | | | | | | | | | | | | | | |
| 1967 | 2.8 | 1.0 | | | | | | | | | | | | | | | | | | |
| 1968 | 3.4 | 2.8 | 4.5 | | | | | | | | | | | | | | | | | |
| 1969 | 2.3 | 1.6 | 1.9 | -0.7 | | | | | | | | | | | | | | | | |
| 1970 | 5.1 | 5.2 | 6.6 | 7.7 | 16.9 | | | | | | | | | | | | | | | |
| 1971 | 5.7 | 5.9 | 7.2 | 8.0 | 12.7 | 8.7 | | | | | | | | | | | | | | |
| 1972 | 5.6 | 5.8 | 6.8 | 7.3 | 10.1 | 6.9 | 5.2 | | | | | | | | | | | | | |
| 1973 | 5.5 | 5.6 | 6.4 | 6.8 | 8.7 | 6.1 | 4.9 | 4.6 | | | | | | | | | | | | |
| 1974 | 5.5 | 5.6 | 6.3 | 6.6 | 8.1 | 6.0 | 5.2 | 5.1 | 5.7 | | | | | | | | | | | |
| 1975 | 5.7 | 5.9 | 6.5 | 6.8 | 8.1 | 6.4 | 5.8 | 6.0 | 6.8 | 7.8 | | | | | | | | | | |
| 1976 | 6.4 | 6.5 | 7.2 | 7.5 | 8.7 | 7.4 | 7.2 | 7.7 | 8.8 | 10.3 | 12.9 | | | | | | | | | |
| 1977 | 5.9 | 6.1 | 6.6 | 6.8 | 7.8 | 6.6 | 6.2 | 6.4 | 6.9 | 7.3 | 7.0 | 1.4 | | | | | | | | |
| 1978 | 5.8 | 5.8 | 6.3 | 6.5 | 7.3 | 6.2 | 5.8 | 5.9 | 6.2 | 6.3 | 5.8 | 2.4 | 3.5 | | | | | | | |
| 1979 | 5.6 | 5.7 | 6.1 | 6.3 | 7.0 | 5.9 | 5.6 | 5.7 | 5.8 | 5.9 | 5.4 | 3.0 | 3.8 | 4.1 | | | | | | |
| 1980 | 5.5 | 5.6 | 5.9 | 6.1 | 6.7 | 5.7 | 5.4 | 5.4 | 5.6 | 5.5 | 5.1 | 3.2 | 3.8 | 4.0 | 3.9 | | | | | |
| 1981 | 5.8 | 5.8 | 6.2 | 6.3 | 6.9 | 6.1 | 5.8 | 5.9 | 6.0 | 6.1 | 5.8 | 4.4 | 5.2 | 5.8 | 6.6 | 9.5 | | | | |
| 1982 | 7.0 | 7.2 | 7.6 | 7.8 | 8.5 | 7.8 | 7.7 | 8.0 | 8.4 | 8.7 | 8.8 | 8.2 | 9.6 | 11.2 | 13.7 | 18.9 | 29.1 | | | |
| 1983 | 7.0 | 7.2 | 7.6 | 7.8 | 8.4 | 7.8 | 7.7 | 7.9 | 8.3 | 8.6 | 8.7 | 8.1 | 9.2 | 10.4 | 12.1 | 14.9 | 17.8 | 7.4 | | |
| 1984 | 7.4 | 7.5 | 7.9 | 8.2 | 8.8 | 8.2 | 8.2 | 8.4 | 8.8 | 9.1 | 9.2 | 8.8 | 9.9 | 11.0 | 12.5 | 14.7 | 16.5 | 10.7 | 14.0 | |
| 1985 | 8.0 | 8.2 | 8.6 | 8.8 | 9.5 | 9.0 | 9.0 | 9.3 | 9.7 | 10.1 | 10.3 | 10.0 | 11.2 | 12.3 | 13.7 | 15.8 | 17.4 | 13.8 | 17.1 | 20.3 |
| 1986 | 8.3 | 8.5 | 8.9 | 9.2 | 9.8 | 9.4 | 9.4 | 9.7 | 10.1 | 10.5 | 10.7 | 10.5 | 11.6 | 12.6 | 13.9 | 15.7 | 17.0 | 14.1 | 16.5 | 17.7 |
| 1987 | 8.1 | 8.2 | 8.6 | 8.8 | 9.4 | 9.0 | 9.0 | 9.2 | 9.6 | 9.9 | 10.1 | 9.8 | 10.7 | 11.5 | 12.5 | 13.8 | 14.5 | 11.8 | 12.9 | 12.5 |
| 1988 | 8.0 | 8.1 | 8.5 | 8.7 | 9.2 | 8.8 | 8.8 | 9.0 | 9.4 | 9.6 | 9.8 | 9.5 | 10.3 | 11.0 | 11.8 | 12.8 | 13.3 | 10.8 | 11.5 | 10.9 |
| 1989 | 8.2 | 8.4 | 8.7 | 8.9 | 9.4 | 9.0 | 9.1 | 9.3 | 9.6 | 9.9 | 10.0 | 9.8 | 10.5 | 11.2 | 11.9 | 12.8 | 13.3 | 11.2 | 11.8 | 11.4 |
| 1990 | 8.3 | 8.4 | 8.8 | 8.9 | 9.4 | 9.1 | 9.1 | 9.3 | 9.6 | 9.8 | 10.0 | 9.8 | 10.5 | 11.1 | 11.7 | 12.5 | 12.9 | 11.0 | 11.5 | 11.1 |
| 1991 | 8.5 | 8.7 | 9.0 | 9.2 | 9.7 | 9.4 | 9.4 | 9.6 | 9.9 | 10.2 | 10.3 | 10.2 | 10.8 | 11.4 | 12.0 | 12.8 | 13.1 | 11.5 | 12.0 | 11.7 |
| 1992 | 8.5 | 8.6 | 9.0 | 9.1 | 9.6 | 9.3 | 9.3 | 9.5 | 9.8 | 10.0 | 10.1 | 10.0 | 10.6 | 11.1 | 11.6 | 12.3 | 12.6 | 11.0 | 11.5 | 11.1 |
| 1993 | 8.6 | 8.7 | 9.0 | 9.2 | 9.7 | 9.4 | 9.4 | 9.6 | 9.8 | 10.1 | 10.2 | 10.0 | 10.6 | 11.1 | 11.6 | 12.2 | 12.5 | 11.1 | 11.4 | 11.1 |
| 1994 | 8.1 | 8.2 | 8.5 | 8.6 | 9.0 | 8.7 | 8.7 | 8.9 | 9.1 | 9.3 | 9.3 | 9.1 | 9.6 | 10.0 | 10.4 | 10.9 | 11.0 | 9.6 | 9.8 | 9.4 |
| 1995 | 8.4 | 8.5 | 8.8 | 8.9 | 9.3 | 9.0 | 9.0 | 9.2 | 9.4 | 9.6 | 9.7 | 9.5 | 10.0 | 10.4 | 10.8 | 11.3 | 11.4 | 10.1 | 10.4 | 10.1 |
| 1996 | 8.2 | 8.3 | 8.5 | 8.7 | 9.0 | 8.7 | 8.7 | 8.9 | 9.1 | 9.2 | 9.3 | 9.1 | 9.6 | 9.9 | 10.3 | 10.7 | 10.8 | 9.6 | 9.7 | 9.4 |
| 1997 | 8.2 | 8.3 | 8.5 | 8.7 | 9.0 | 8.7 | 8.7 | 8.9 | 9.1 | 9.2 | 9.3 | 9.1 | 9.5 | 9.8 | 10.2 | 10.5 | 10.6 | 9.5 | 9.6 | 9.3 |
| 1998 | 8.2 | 8.3 | 8.6 | 8.7 | 9.1 | 8.8 | 8.8 | 8.9 | 9.1 | 9.3 | 9.3 | 9.2 | 9.5 | 9.9 | 10.2 | 10.5 | 10.6 | 9.5 | 9.7 | 9.4 |
| 1999 | 7.9 | 8.0 | 8.2 | 8.4 | 8.7 | 8.4 | 8.4 | 8.5 | 8.7 | 8.8 | 8.8 | 8.7 | 9.0 | 9.3 | 9.5 | 9.8 | 9.9 | 8.8 | 8.9 | 8.6 |
| 2000 | 8.0 | 8.1 | 8.4 | 8.5 | 8.8 | 8.5 | 8.5 | 8.7 | 8.8 | 8.9 | 9.0 | 8.8 | 9.2 | 9.4 | 9.7 | 10.0 | 10.0 | 9.0 | 9.1 | 8.8 |

| To the end of | From the beginning of | | | | | | | | | | | | | | |
|---|---|---|---|---|---|---|---|---|---|---|---|---|---|---|---|
| | 1986 | 1987 | 1988 | 1989 | 1990 | 1991 | 1992 | 1993 | 1994 | 1995 | 1996 | 1997 | 1998 | 1999 | 2000 |
| 1986 | 15.1 | | | | | | | | | | | | | | |
| 1987 | 8.8 | 2.9 | | | | | | | | | | | | | |
| 1988 | 7.9 | 4.5 | 6.1 | | | | | | | | | | | | |
| 1989 | 9.2 | 7.3 | 9.6 | 13.3 | | | | | | | | | | | |
| 1990 | 9.3 | 7.9 | 9.7 | 11.5 | 9.7 | | | | | | | | | | |
| 1991 | 10.3 | 9.4 | 11.1 | 12.8 | 12.6 | 15.5 | | | | | | | | | |
| 1992 | 9.9 | 9.0 | 10.3 | 11.4 | 10.7 | 11.2 | 7.2 | | | | | | | | |
| 1993 | 10.1 | 9.3 | 10.5 | 11.3 | 10.9 | 11.2 | 9.2 | 11.2 | | | | | | | |
| 1994 | 8.2 | 7.4 | 8.1 | 8.4 | 7.5 | 6.9 | 4.2 | 2.7 | -5.1 | | | | | | |
| 1995 | 9.1 | 8.4 | 9.1 | 9.6 | 9.0 | 8.8 | 7.2 | 7.2 | 5.3 | 16.8 | | | | | |
| 1996 | 8.4 | 7.8 | 8.3 | 8.6 | 8.0 | 7.7 | 6.2 | 5.9 | 4.2 | 9.2 | 2.1 | | | | |
| 1997 | 8.4 | 7.8 | 8.3 | 8.6 | 8.0 | 7.8 | 6.5 | 6.4 | 5.2 | 8.9 | 5.2 | 8.4 | | | |
| 1998 | 8.6 | 8.0 | 8.5 | 8.7 | 8.3 | 8.1 | 7.1 | 7.0 | 6.2 | 9.2 | 6.8 | 9.3 | 10.2 | | |
| 1999 | 7.8 | 7.2 | 7.6 | 7.7 | 7.2 | 6.9 | 5.9 | 5.7 | 4.8 | 6.9 | 4.6 | 5.5 | 4.0 | -1.8 | |
| 2000 | 8.1 | 7.6 | 8.0 | 8.1 | 7.7 | 7.5 | 6.6 | 6.6 | 5.9 | 7.9 | 6.2 | 7.2 | 6.8 | 5.2 | 12.6 |

## Table C-6 (Page 1 of 5)

### U.S. Treasury Bills Total Returns
Rates of Return for all holding periods
Percent per annum compounded annually

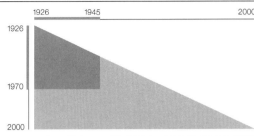

from 1926 to 2000

| To the end of | From the beginning of 1926 | 1927 | 1928 | 1929 | 1930 | 1931 | 1932 | 1933 | 1934 | 1935 | 1936 | 1937 | 1938 | 1939 | 1940 | 1941 | 1942 | 1943 | 1944 | 1945 |
|---|---|---|---|---|---|---|---|---|---|---|---|---|---|---|---|---|---|---|---|---|
| 1926 | 3.3 | | | | | | | | | | | | | | | | | | | |
| 1927 | 3.2 | 3.1 | | | | | | | | | | | | | | | | | | |
| 1928 | 3.3 | 3.3 | 3.6 | | | | | | | | | | | | | | | | | |
| 1929 | 3.7 | 3.8 | 4.2 | 4.7 | | | | | | | | | | | | | | | | |
| 1930 | 3.4 | 3.5 | 3.6 | 3.6 | 2.4 | | | | | | | | | | | | | | | |
| 1931 | 3.0 | 3.0 | 2.9 | 2.7 | 1.7 | 1.1 | | | | | | | | | | | | | | |
| 1932 | 2.7 | 2.6 | 2.5 | 2.3 | 1.5 | 1.0 | 1.0 | | | | | | | | | | | | | |
| 1933 | 2.4 | 2.3 | 2.2 | 1.9 | 1.2 | 0.8 | 0.6 | 0.3 | | | | | | | | | | | | |
| 1934 | 2.2 | 2.0 | 1.9 | 1.6 | 1.0 | 0.6 | 0.5 | 0.2 | 0.2 | | | | | | | | | | | |
| 1935 | 2.0 | 1.8 | 1.7 | 1.4 | 0.8 | 0.5 | 0.4 | 0.2 | 0.2 | 0.2 | | | | | | | | | | |
| 1936 | 1.8 | 1.7 | 1.5 | 1.2 | 0.7 | 0.5 | 0.4 | 0.2 | 0.2 | 0.2 | 0.2 | | | | | | | | | |
| 1937 | 1.7 | 1.5 | 1.4 | 1.1 | 0.7 | 0.4 | 0.3 | 0.2 | 0.2 | 0.2 | 0.2 | 0.3 | | | | | | | | |
| 1938 | 1.5 | 1.4 | 1.2 | 1.0 | 0.6 | 0.4 | 0.3 | 0.2 | 0.2 | 0.2 | 0.2 | 0.1 | 0.0 | | | | | | | |
| 1939 | 1.4 | 1.3 | 1.1 | 0.9 | 0.6 | 0.3 | 0.3 | 0.2 | 0.1 | 0.1 | 0.1 | 0.1 | 0.0 | 0.0 | | | | | | |
| 1940 | 1.3 | 1.2 | 1.1 | 0.9 | 0.5 | 0.3 | 0.2 | 0.1 | 0.1 | 0.1 | 0.1 | 0.1 | 0.0 | 0.0 | 0.0 | | | | | |
| 1941 | 1.3 | 1.1 | 1.0 | 0.8 | 0.5 | 0.3 | 0.2 | 0.1 | 0.1 | 0.1 | 0.1 | 0.1 | 0.0 | 0.0 | 0.0 | 0.1 | | | | |
| 1942 | 1.2 | 1.1 | 0.9 | 0.8 | 0.5 | 0.3 | 0.2 | 0.1 | 0.1 | 0.1 | 0.1 | 0.1 | 0.1 | 0.1 | 0.1 | 0.2 | 0.3 | | | |
| 1943 | 1.2 | 1.0 | 0.9 | 0.7 | 0.4 | 0.3 | 0.2 | 0.2 | 0.2 | 0.1 | 0.1 | 0.1 | 0.1 | 0.1 | 0.2 | 0.2 | 0.3 | 0.3 | | |
| 1944 | 1.1 | 1.0 | 0.9 | 0.7 | 0.4 | 0.3 | 0.2 | 0.2 | 0.2 | 0.2 | 0.2 | 0.2 | 0.1 | 0.2 | 0.2 | 0.3 | 0.3 | 0.3 | 0.3 | |
| 1945 | 1.1 | 1.0 | 0.8 | 0.7 | 0.4 | 0.3 | 0.2 | 0.2 | 0.2 | 0.2 | 0.2 | 0.2 | 0.2 | 0.2 | 0.2 | 0.3 | 0.3 | 0.3 | 0.3 | 0.3 |
| 1946 | 1.0 | 0.9 | 0.8 | 0.7 | 0.4 | 0.3 | 0.3 | 0.2 | 0.2 | 0.2 | 0.2 | 0.2 | 0.2 | 0.2 | 0.2 | 0.3 | 0.3 | 0.3 | 0.3 | 0.3 |
| 1947 | 1.0 | 0.9 | 0.8 | 0.7 | 0.4 | 0.3 | 0.3 | 0.2 | 0.2 | 0.2 | 0.2 | 0.2 | 0.2 | 0.2 | 0.3 | 0.3 | 0.4 | 0.4 | 0.4 | 0.4 |
| 1948 | 1.0 | 0.9 | 0.8 | 0.7 | 0.4 | 0.3 | 0.3 | 0.3 | 0.3 | 0.3 | 0.3 | 0.3 | 0.3 | 0.3 | 0.3 | 0.4 | 0.4 | 0.4 | 0.5 | 0.5 |
| 1949 | 1.0 | 0.9 | 0.8 | 0.7 | 0.5 | 0.4 | 0.3 | 0.3 | 0.3 | 0.3 | 0.3 | 0.3 | 0.3 | 0.4 | 0.4 | 0.5 | 0.5 | 0.5 | 0.6 | 0.6 |
| 1950 | 1.0 | 0.9 | 0.8 | 0.7 | 0.5 | 0.4 | 0.4 | 0.4 | 0.4 | 0.4 | 0.4 | 0.4 | 0.4 | 0.4 | 0.5 | 0.5 | 0.6 | 0.6 | 0.7 | 0.7 |
| 1951 | 1.0 | 0.9 | 0.9 | 0.7 | 0.6 | 0.5 | 0.4 | 0.4 | 0.4 | 0.4 | 0.5 | 0.5 | 0.5 | 0.5 | 0.6 | 0.6 | 0.7 | 0.7 | 0.8 | 0.8 |
| 1952 | 1.1 | 1.0 | 0.9 | 0.8 | 0.6 | 0.5 | 0.5 | 0.5 | 0.5 | 0.5 | 0.5 | 0.5 | 0.6 | 0.6 | 0.6 | 0.7 | 0.8 | 0.8 | 0.9 | 0.9 |
| 1953 | 1.1 | 1.0 | 0.9 | 0.8 | 0.7 | 0.6 | 0.6 | 0.5 | 0.6 | 0.6 | 0.6 | 0.6 | 0.6 | 0.7 | 0.7 | 0.8 | 0.8 | 0.9 | 1.0 | 1.0 |
| 1954 | 1.1 | 1.0 | 0.9 | 0.8 | 0.7 | 0.6 | 0.6 | 0.6 | 0.6 | 0.6 | 0.6 | 0.6 | 0.7 | 0.7 | 0.7 | 0.8 | 0.9 | 0.9 | 0.9 | 1.0 |
| 1955 | 1.1 | 1.0 | 0.9 | 0.8 | 0.7 | 0.6 | 0.6 | 0.6 | 0.6 | 0.6 | 0.7 | 0.7 | 0.7 | 0.7 | 0.8 | 0.8 | 0.9 | 1.0 | 1.0 | 1.1 |
| 1956 | 1.1 | 1.1 | 1.0 | 0.9 | 0.8 | 0.7 | 0.7 | 0.7 | 0.7 | 0.7 | 0.7 | 0.8 | 0.8 | 0.8 | 0.9 | 0.9 | 1.0 | 1.1 | 1.1 | 1.2 |
| 1957 | 1.2 | 1.1 | 1.1 | 1.0 | 0.8 | 0.8 | 0.8 | 0.8 | 0.8 | 0.8 | 0.9 | 0.9 | 0.9 | 1.0 | 1.0 | 1.1 | 1.1 | 1.2 | 1.3 | 1.3 |
| 1958 | 1.2 | 1.1 | 1.1 | 1.0 | 0.9 | 0.8 | 0.8 | 0.8 | 0.8 | 0.9 | 0.9 | 0.9 | 0.9 | 1.0 | 1.0 | 1.1 | 1.2 | 1.2 | 1.3 | 1.3 |
| 1959 | 1.3 | 1.2 | 1.1 | 1.1 | 0.9 | 0.9 | 0.9 | 0.9 | 0.9 | 0.9 | 1.0 | 1.0 | 1.0 | 1.1 | 1.1 | 1.2 | 1.3 | 1.3 | 1.4 | 1.4 |
| 1960 | 1.3 | 1.2 | 1.2 | 1.1 | 1.0 | 1.0 | 0.9 | 0.9 | 1.0 | 1.0 | 1.0 | 1.1 | 1.1 | 1.2 | 1.2 | 1.3 | 1.3 | 1.4 | 1.5 | 1.5 |
| 1961 | 1.3 | 1.3 | 1.2 | 1.1 | 1.0 | 1.0 | 1.0 | 1.0 | 1.0 | 1.0 | 1.1 | 1.1 | 1.1 | 1.2 | 1.3 | 1.3 | 1.4 | 1.4 | 1.5 | 1.6 |
| 1962 | 1.4 | 1.3 | 1.3 | 1.2 | 1.1 | 1.0 | 1.0 | 1.0 | 1.1 | 1.1 | 1.1 | 1.2 | 1.2 | 1.3 | 1.3 | 1.4 | 1.4 | 1.5 | 1.6 | 1.6 |
| 1963 | 1.4 | 1.4 | 1.3 | 1.2 | 1.1 | 1.1 | 1.1 | 1.1 | 1.1 | 1.2 | 1.2 | 1.2 | 1.3 | 1.3 | 1.4 | 1.4 | 1.5 | 1.6 | 1.6 | 1.7 |
| 1964 | 1.5 | 1.4 | 1.4 | 1.3 | 1.2 | 1.2 | 1.2 | 1.2 | 1.2 | 1.2 | 1.3 | 1.3 | 1.4 | 1.4 | 1.5 | 1.5 | 1.6 | 1.7 | 1.7 | 1.8 |
| 1965 | 1.5 | 1.5 | 1.4 | 1.4 | 1.3 | 1.3 | 1.3 | 1.3 | 1.3 | 1.3 | 1.4 | 1.4 | 1.5 | 1.5 | 1.6 | 1.6 | 1.7 | 1.8 | 1.8 | 1.9 |
| 1966 | 1.6 | 1.6 | 1.5 | 1.5 | 1.4 | 1.3 | 1.4 | 1.4 | 1.4 | 1.4 | 1.5 | 1.5 | 1.6 | 1.6 | 1.7 | 1.7 | 1.8 | 1.9 | 1.9 | 2.0 |
| 1967 | 1.7 | 1.6 | 1.6 | 1.5 | 1.5 | 1.4 | 1.4 | 1.4 | 1.5 | 1.5 | 1.6 | 1.6 | 1.7 | 1.7 | 1.8 | 1.8 | 1.9 | 2.0 | 2.0 | 2.1 |
| 1968 | 1.7 | 1.7 | 1.7 | 1.6 | 1.5 | 1.5 | 1.5 | 1.6 | 1.6 | 1.6 | 1.7 | 1.7 | 1.8 | 1.8 | 1.9 | 2.0 | 2.0 | 2.1 | 2.2 | 2.2 |
| 1969 | 1.8 | 1.8 | 1.8 | 1.7 | 1.7 | 1.6 | 1.7 | 1.7 | 1.7 | 1.8 | 1.8 | 1.9 | 1.9 | 2.0 | 2.0 | 2.1 | 2.2 | 2.3 | 2.3 | 2.4 |
| 1970 | 2.0 | 1.9 | 1.9 | 1.9 | 1.8 | 1.8 | 1.8 | 1.8 | 1.8 | 1.9 | 1.9 | 2.0 | 2.1 | 2.1 | 2.2 | 2.3 | 2.3 | 2.4 | 2.5 | 2.6 |

## Table C-6 (Page 2 of 5)

### U.S. Treasury Bills Total Returns
Rates of Return for all holding periods
Percent per annum compounded annually

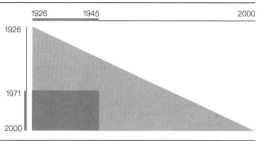

from 1926 to 2000

| To the end of | From the beginning of 1926 | 1927 | 1928 | 1929 | 1930 | 1931 | 1932 | 1933 | 1934 | 1935 | 1936 | 1937 | 1938 | 1939 | 1940 | 1941 | 1942 | 1943 | 1944 | 1945 |
|---|---|---|---|---|---|---|---|---|---|---|---|---|---|---|---|---|---|---|---|---|
| 1971 | 2.0 | 2.0 | 1.9 | 1.9 | 1.8 | 1.8 | 1.9 | 1.9 | 1.9 | 2.0 | 2.0 | 2.1 | 2.1 | 2.2 | 2.3 | 2.3 | 2.4 | 2.5 | 2.6 | 2.6 |
| 1972 | 2.0 | 2.0 | 2.0 | 2.0 | 1.9 | 1.9 | 1.9 | 1.9 | 2.0 | 2.0 | 2.1 | 2.1 | 2.2 | 2.2 | 2.3 | 2.4 | 2.4 | 2.5 | 2.6 | 2.7 |
| 1973 | 2.1 | 2.1 | 2.1 | 2.1 | 2.0 | 2.0 | 2.0 | 2.0 | 2.1 | 2.1 | 2.2 | 2.2 | 2.3 | 2.4 | 2.4 | 2.5 | 2.6 | 2.7 | 2.7 | 2.8 |
| 1974 | 2.3 | 2.2 | 2.2 | 2.2 | 2.1 | 2.1 | 2.2 | 2.2 | 2.2 | 2.3 | 2.3 | 2.4 | 2.4 | 2.5 | 2.6 | 2.7 | 2.7 | 2.8 | 2.9 | 3.0 |
| 1975 | 2.3 | 2.3 | 2.3 | 2.3 | 2.2 | 2.2 | 2.2 | 2.3 | 2.3 | 2.4 | 2.4 | 2.5 | 2.5 | 2.6 | 2.7 | 2.8 | 2.8 | 2.9 | 3.0 | 3.1 |
| 1976 | 2.4 | 2.4 | 2.3 | 2.3 | 2.3 | 2.3 | 2.3 | 2.3 | 2.4 | 2.4 | 2.5 | 2.5 | 2.6 | 2.7 | 2.7 | 2.8 | 2.9 | 3.0 | 3.1 | 3.1 |
| 1977 | 2.4 | 2.4 | 2.4 | 2.4 | 2.3 | 2.3 | 2.4 | 2.4 | 2.4 | 2.5 | 2.5 | 2.6 | 2.7 | 2.7 | 2.8 | 2.9 | 3.0 | 3.0 | 3.1 | 3.2 |
| 1978 | 2.5 | 2.5 | 2.5 | 2.5 | 2.4 | 2.4 | 2.5 | 2.5 | 2.5 | 2.6 | 2.6 | 2.7 | 2.8 | 2.8 | 2.9 | 3.0 | 3.1 | 3.1 | 3.2 | 3.3 |
| 1979 | 2.7 | 2.6 | 2.6 | 2.6 | 2.6 | 2.6 | 2.6 | 2.7 | 2.7 | 2.8 | 2.8 | 2.9 | 2.9 | 3.0 | 3.1 | 3.2 | 3.3 | 3.3 | 3.4 | 3.5 |
| 1980 | 2.8 | 2.8 | 2.8 | 2.8 | 2.7 | 2.7 | 2.8 | 2.8 | 2.9 | 2.9 | 3.0 | 3.1 | 3.1 | 3.2 | 3.3 | 3.4 | 3.5 | 3.5 | 3.6 | 3.7 |
| 1981 | 3.0 | 3.0 | 3.0 | 3.0 | 3.0 | 3.0 | 3.0 | 3.1 | 3.1 | 3.2 | 3.2 | 3.3 | 3.4 | 3.5 | 3.5 | 3.6 | 3.7 | 3.8 | 3.9 | 4.0 |
| 1982 | 3.1 | 3.1 | 3.1 | 3.1 | 3.1 | 3.1 | 3.2 | 3.2 | 3.3 | 3.3 | 3.4 | 3.5 | 3.5 | 3.6 | 3.7 | 3.8 | 3.9 | 4.0 | 4.1 | 4.2 |
| 1983 | 3.2 | 3.2 | 3.2 | 3.2 | 3.2 | 3.2 | 3.3 | 3.3 | 3.4 | 3.4 | 3.5 | 3.6 | 3.6 | 3.7 | 3.8 | 3.9 | 4.0 | 4.1 | 4.2 | 4.3 |
| 1984 | 3.3 | 3.3 | 3.3 | 3.3 | 3.3 | 3.3 | 3.4 | 3.4 | 3.5 | 3.6 | 3.6 | 3.7 | 3.8 | 3.9 | 3.9 | 4.0 | 4.1 | 4.2 | 4.3 | 4.4 |
| 1985 | 3.4 | 3.4 | 3.4 | 3.4 | 3.4 | 3.4 | 3.5 | 3.5 | 3.6 | 3.6 | 3.7 | 3.8 | 3.9 | 3.9 | 4.0 | 4.1 | 4.2 | 4.3 | 4.4 | 4.5 |
| 1986 | 3.5 | 3.5 | 3.5 | 3.5 | 3.4 | 3.5 | 3.5 | 3.6 | 3.6 | 3.7 | 3.8 | 3.8 | 3.9 | 4.0 | 4.1 | 4.2 | 4.3 | 4.3 | 4.4 | 4.5 |
| 1987 | 3.5 | 3.5 | 3.5 | 3.5 | 3.5 | 3.5 | 3.5 | 3.6 | 3.7 | 3.7 | 3.8 | 3.9 | 3.9 | 4.0 | 4.1 | 4.2 | 4.3 | 4.4 | 4.5 | 4.6 |
| 1988 | 3.5 | 3.5 | 3.5 | 3.5 | 3.5 | 3.5 | 3.6 | 3.6 | 3.7 | 3.8 | 3.8 | 3.9 | 4.0 | 4.1 | 4.1 | 4.2 | 4.3 | 4.4 | 4.5 | 4.6 |
| 1989 | 3.6 | 3.6 | 3.6 | 3.6 | 3.6 | 3.6 | 3.7 | 3.7 | 3.8 | 3.8 | 3.9 | 4.0 | 4.1 | 4.1 | 4.2 | 4.3 | 4.4 | 4.5 | 4.6 | 4.7 |
| 1990 | 3.7 | 3.7 | 3.7 | 3.7 | 3.7 | 3.7 | 3.7 | 3.8 | 3.8 | 3.9 | 4.0 | 4.1 | 4.1 | 4.2 | 4.3 | 4.4 | 4.5 | 4.6 | 4.7 | 4.8 |
| 1991 | 3.7 | 3.7 | 3.7 | 3.7 | 3.7 | 3.7 | 3.8 | 3.8 | 3.9 | 3.9 | 4.0 | 4.1 | 4.2 | 4.2 | 4.3 | 4.4 | 4.5 | 4.6 | 4.7 | 4.8 |
| 1992 | 3.7 | 3.7 | 3.7 | 3.7 | 3.7 | 3.7 | 3.8 | 3.8 | 3.9 | 3.9 | 4.0 | 4.1 | 4.1 | 4.2 | 4.3 | 4.4 | 4.5 | 4.6 | 4.7 | 4.7 |
| 1993 | 3.7 | 3.7 | 3.7 | 3.7 | 3.7 | 3.7 | 3.8 | 3.8 | 3.9 | 3.9 | 4.0 | 4.1 | 4.1 | 4.2 | 4.3 | 4.4 | 4.4 | 4.5 | 4.6 | 4.7 |
| 1994 | 3.7 | 3.7 | 3.7 | 3.7 | 3.7 | 3.7 | 3.8 | 3.8 | 3.9 | 3.9 | 4.0 | 4.1 | 4.1 | 4.2 | 4.3 | 4.4 | 4.4 | 4.5 | 4.6 | 4.7 |
| 1995 | 3.7 | 3.7 | 3.7 | 3.7 | 3.7 | 3.7 | 3.8 | 3.8 | 3.9 | 3.9 | 4.0 | 4.1 | 4.1 | 4.2 | 4.3 | 4.4 | 4.5 | 4.5 | 4.6 | 4.7 |
| 1996 | 3.7 | 3.7 | 3.8 | 3.8 | 3.7 | 3.8 | 3.8 | 3.8 | 3.9 | 4.0 | 4.0 | 4.1 | 4.2 | 4.2 | 4.3 | 4.4 | 4.5 | 4.5 | 4.6 | 4.7 |
| 1997 | 3.8 | 3.8 | 3.8 | 3.8 | 3.8 | 3.8 | 3.8 | 3.9 | 3.9 | 4.0 | 4.1 | 4.1 | 4.2 | 4.3 | 4.3 | 4.4 | 4.5 | 4.6 | 4.6 | 4.7 |
| 1998 | 3.8 | 3.8 | 3.8 | 3.8 | 3.8 | 3.8 | 3.8 | 3.9 | 3.9 | 4.0 | 4.1 | 4.1 | 4.2 | 4.3 | 4.3 | 4.4 | 4.5 | 4.6 | 4.6 | 4.7 |
| 1999 | 3.8 | 3.8 | 3.8 | 3.8 | 3.8 | 3.8 | 3.9 | 3.9 | 4.0 | 4.0 | 4.1 | 4.1 | 4.2 | 4.3 | 4.3 | 4.4 | 4.5 | 4.6 | 4.6 | 4.7 |
| 2000 | 3.8 | 3.8 | 3.8 | 3.8 | 3.8 | 3.8 | 3.9 | 3.9 | 4.0 | 4.0 | 4.1 | 4.2 | 4.2 | 4.3 | 4.4 | 4.4 | 4.5 | 4.6 | 4.7 | 4.7 |

# Table C-6 (Page 3 of 5)

## U.S. Treasury Bills Total Returns
Rates of Return for all holding periods
Percent per annum compounded annually

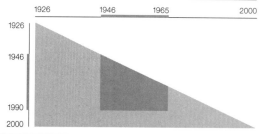

### from 1926 to 2000

| To the end of | From the beginning of | | | | | | | | | | | | | | | | | | | |
|---|---|---|---|---|---|---|---|---|---|---|---|---|---|---|---|---|---|---|---|---|
| | 1946 | 1947 | 1948 | 1949 | 1950 | 1951 | 1952 | 1953 | 1954 | 1955 | 1956 | 1957 | 1958 | 1959 | 1960 | 1961 | 1962 | 1963 | 1964 | 1965 |
| 1946 | 0.4 | | | | | | | | | | | | | | | | | | | |
| 1947 | 0.4 | 0.5 | | | | | | | | | | | | | | | | | | |
| 1948 | 0.6 | 0.7 | 0.8 | | | | | | | | | | | | | | | | | |
| 1949 | 0.7 | 0.8 | 1.0 | 1.1 | | | | | | | | | | | | | | | | |
| 1950 | 0.8 | 0.9 | 1.0 | 1.1 | 1.2 | | | | | | | | | | | | | | | |
| 1951 | 0.9 | 1.0 | 1.2 | 1.3 | 1.3 | 1.5 | | | | | | | | | | | | | | |
| 1952 | 1.0 | 1.1 | 1.3 | 1.4 | 1.4 | 1.6 | 1.7 | | | | | | | | | | | | | |
| 1953 | 1.1 | 1.2 | 1.3 | 1.5 | 1.5 | 1.7 | 1.7 | 1.8 | | | | | | | | | | | | |
| 1954 | 1.1 | 1.2 | 1.3 | 1.4 | 1.4 | 1.5 | 1.4 | 1.3 | 0.9 | | | | | | | | | | | |
| 1955 | 1.1 | 1.2 | 1.3 | 1.4 | 1.4 | 1.5 | 1.5 | 1.4 | 1.2 | 1.6 | | | | | | | | | | |
| 1956 | 1.3 | 1.3 | 1.4 | 1.5 | 1.6 | 1.6 | 1.7 | 1.7 | 1.6 | 2.0 | 2.5 | | | | | | | | | |
| 1957 | 1.4 | 1.5 | 1.6 | 1.7 | 1.8 | 1.9 | 1.9 | 2.0 | 2.0 | 2.4 | 2.8 | 3.1 | | | | | | | | |
| 1958 | 1.4 | 1.5 | 1.6 | 1.7 | 1.7 | 1.8 | 1.9 | 1.9 | 1.9 | 2.2 | 2.4 | 2.3 | 1.5 | | | | | | | |
| 1959 | 1.5 | 1.6 | 1.7 | 1.8 | 1.9 | 1.9 | 2.0 | 2.0 | 2.1 | 2.3 | 2.5 | 2.5 | 2.2 | 3.0 | | | | | | |
| 1960 | 1.6 | 1.7 | 1.8 | 1.9 | 1.9 | 2.0 | 2.1 | 2.1 | 2.2 | 2.4 | 2.5 | 2.6 | 2.4 | 2.8 | 2.7 | | | | | |
| 1961 | 1.6 | 1.7 | 1.8 | 1.9 | 2.0 | 2.0 | 2.1 | 2.1 | 2.2 | 2.3 | 2.5 | 2.5 | 2.3 | 2.6 | 2.4 | 2.1 | | | | |
| 1962 | 1.7 | 1.8 | 1.9 | 1.9 | 2.0 | 2.1 | 2.1 | 2.2 | 2.2 | 2.4 | 2.5 | 2.5 | 2.4 | 2.6 | 2.5 | 2.4 | 2.7 | | | |
| 1963 | 1.8 | 1.9 | 2.0 | 2.0 | 2.1 | 2.2 | 2.2 | 2.3 | 2.3 | 2.5 | 2.6 | 2.6 | 2.5 | 2.7 | 2.7 | 2.7 | 2.9 | 3.1 | | |
| 1964 | 1.9 | 2.0 | 2.0 | 2.1 | 2.2 | 2.3 | 2.3 | 2.4 | 2.4 | 2.6 | 2.7 | 2.7 | 2.7 | 2.9 | 2.8 | 2.9 | 3.1 | 3.3 | 3.5 | |
| 1965 | 2.0 | 2.1 | 2.1 | 2.2 | 2.3 | 2.4 | 2.4 | 2.5 | 2.5 | 2.7 | 2.8 | 2.9 | 2.8 | 3.0 | 3.0 | 3.1 | 3.3 | 3.5 | 3.7 | 3.9 |
| 1966 | 2.1 | 2.2 | 2.3 | 2.4 | 2.4 | 2.5 | 2.6 | 2.7 | 2.7 | 2.9 | 3.0 | 3.0 | 3.0 | 3.2 | 3.3 | 3.4 | 3.6 | 3.8 | 4.1 | 4.3 |
| 1967 | 2.2 | 2.3 | 2.4 | 2.5 | 2.5 | 2.6 | 2.7 | 2.8 | 2.8 | 3.0 | 3.1 | 3.2 | 3.2 | 3.3 | 3.4 | 3.5 | 3.7 | 3.9 | 4.1 | 4.3 |
| 1968 | 2.3 | 2.4 | 2.5 | 2.6 | 2.7 | 2.8 | 2.8 | 2.9 | 3.0 | 3.1 | 3.3 | 3.3 | 3.3 | 3.5 | 3.6 | 3.7 | 3.9 | 4.1 | 4.3 | 4.5 |
| 1969 | 2.5 | 2.6 | 2.7 | 2.8 | 2.9 | 3.0 | 3.0 | 3.1 | 3.2 | 3.4 | 3.5 | 3.6 | 3.6 | 3.8 | 3.9 | 4.0 | 4.3 | 4.5 | 4.7 | 4.9 |
| 1970 | 2.7 | 2.8 | 2.9 | 3.0 | 3.0 | 3.1 | 3.2 | 3.3 | 3.4 | 3.6 | 3.7 | 3.8 | 3.8 | 4.0 | 4.1 | 4.3 | 4.5 | 4.7 | 5.0 | 5.2 |
| 1971 | 2.7 | 2.8 | 2.9 | 3.0 | 3.1 | 3.2 | 3.3 | 3.4 | 3.4 | 3.6 | 3.7 | 3.8 | 3.9 | 4.0 | 4.1 | 4.3 | 4.5 | 4.7 | 4.9 | 5.1 |
| 1972 | 2.8 | 2.9 | 3.0 | 3.0 | 3.1 | 3.2 | 3.3 | 3.4 | 3.5 | 3.6 | 3.7 | 3.8 | 3.9 | 4.0 | 4.1 | 4.2 | 4.4 | 4.6 | 4.8 | 4.9 |
| 1973 | 2.9 | 3.0 | 3.1 | 3.2 | 3.3 | 3.4 | 3.5 | 3.6 | 3.6 | 3.8 | 3.9 | 4.0 | 4.1 | 4.2 | 4.3 | 4.4 | 4.6 | 4.8 | 5.0 | 5.1 |
| 1974 | 3.1 | 3.2 | 3.3 | 3.4 | 3.5 | 3.6 | 3.7 | 3.8 | 3.8 | 4.0 | 4.1 | 4.2 | 4.3 | 4.5 | 4.6 | 4.7 | 4.9 | 5.1 | 5.3 | 5.4 |
| 1975 | 3.2 | 3.3 | 3.4 | 3.5 | 3.6 | 3.7 | 3.7 | 3.8 | 3.9 | 4.1 | 4.2 | 4.3 | 4.4 | 4.5 | 4.6 | 4.8 | 5.0 | 5.1 | 5.3 | 5.5 |
| 1976 | 3.2 | 3.3 | 3.4 | 3.5 | 3.6 | 3.7 | 3.8 | 3.9 | 4.0 | 4.1 | 4.2 | 4.3 | 4.4 | 4.6 | 4.7 | 4.8 | 5.0 | 5.1 | 5.3 | 5.4 |
| 1977 | 3.3 | 3.4 | 3.5 | 3.6 | 3.7 | 3.8 | 3.9 | 3.9 | 4.0 | 4.2 | 4.3 | 4.4 | 4.4 | 4.6 | 4.7 | 4.8 | 5.0 | 5.1 | 5.3 | 5.4 |
| 1978 | 3.4 | 3.5 | 3.6 | 3.7 | 3.8 | 3.9 | 4.0 | 4.1 | 4.2 | 4.3 | 4.4 | 4.5 | 4.6 | 4.7 | 4.8 | 4.9 | 5.1 | 5.3 | 5.4 | 5.5 |
| 1979 | 3.6 | 3.7 | 3.8 | 3.9 | 4.0 | 4.1 | 4.2 | 4.3 | 4.4 | 4.5 | 4.7 | 4.8 | 4.8 | 5.0 | 5.1 | 5.2 | 5.4 | 5.5 | 5.7 | 5.8 |
| 1980 | 3.8 | 3.9 | 4.0 | 4.1 | 4.2 | 4.3 | 4.4 | 4.5 | 4.6 | 4.8 | 4.9 | 5.0 | 5.1 | 5.3 | 5.4 | 5.5 | 5.7 | 5.9 | 6.0 | 6.2 |
| 1981 | 4.1 | 4.2 | 4.3 | 4.4 | 4.5 | 4.7 | 4.8 | 4.9 | 5.0 | 5.1 | 5.3 | 5.4 | 5.5 | 5.7 | 5.8 | 5.9 | 6.1 | 6.3 | 6.5 | 6.7 |
| 1982 | 4.3 | 4.4 | 4.5 | 4.6 | 4.7 | 4.8 | 4.9 | 5.1 | 5.2 | 5.3 | 5.5 | 5.6 | 5.7 | 5.9 | 6.0 | 6.1 | 6.3 | 6.5 | 6.7 | 6.9 |
| 1983 | 4.4 | 4.5 | 4.6 | 4.7 | 4.8 | 4.9 | 5.1 | 5.2 | 5.3 | 5.4 | 5.6 | 5.7 | 5.8 | 6.0 | 6.1 | 6.2 | 6.4 | 6.6 | 6.8 | 7.0 |
| 1984 | 4.5 | 4.6 | 4.8 | 4.9 | 5.0 | 5.1 | 5.2 | 5.3 | 5.4 | 5.6 | 5.7 | 5.8 | 5.9 | 6.1 | 6.2 | 6.4 | 6.6 | 6.8 | 6.9 | 7.1 |
| 1985 | 4.6 | 4.7 | 4.8 | 4.9 | 5.1 | 5.2 | 5.3 | 5.4 | 5.5 | 5.7 | 5.8 | 5.9 | 6.0 | 6.2 | 6.3 | 6.4 | 6.6 | 6.8 | 7.0 | 7.1 |
| 1986 | 4.6 | 4.8 | 4.9 | 5.0 | 5.1 | 5.2 | 5.3 | 5.4 | 5.5 | 5.7 | 5.8 | 5.9 | 6.0 | 6.2 | 6.3 | 6.4 | 6.6 | 6.8 | 6.9 | 7.1 |
| 1987 | 4.7 | 4.8 | 4.9 | 5.0 | 5.1 | 5.2 | 5.3 | 5.4 | 5.5 | 5.7 | 5.8 | 5.9 | 6.0 | 6.2 | 6.3 | 6.4 | 6.6 | 6.7 | 6.9 | 7.0 |
| 1988 | 4.7 | 4.8 | 4.9 | 5.0 | 5.1 | 5.2 | 5.3 | 5.4 | 5.5 | 5.7 | 5.8 | 5.9 | 6.0 | 6.2 | 6.3 | 6.4 | 6.6 | 6.7 | 6.9 | 7.0 |
| 1989 | 4.8 | 4.9 | 5.0 | 5.1 | 5.2 | 5.3 | 5.4 | 5.5 | 5.6 | 5.8 | 5.9 | 6.0 | 6.1 | 6.2 | 6.3 | 6.5 | 6.6 | 6.8 | 6.9 | 7.1 |
| 1990 | 4.9 | 5.0 | 5.1 | 5.2 | 5.3 | 5.4 | 5.5 | 5.6 | 5.7 | 5.8 | 5.9 | 6.0 | 6.1 | 6.3 | 6.4 | 6.5 | 6.7 | 6.8 | 6.9 | 7.1 |

## Table C-6 (Page 4 of 5)

### U.S. Treasury Bills Total Returns
Rates of Return for all holding periods
Percent per annum compounded annually

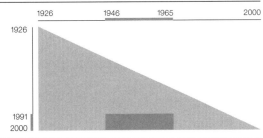

from 1926 to 2000

| To the end of | From the beginning of | | | | | | | | | | | | | | | | | | | |
| | 1946 | 1947 | 1948 | 1949 | 1950 | 1951 | 1952 | 1953 | 1954 | 1955 | 1956 | 1957 | 1958 | 1959 | 1960 | 1961 | 1962 | 1963 | 1964 | 1965 |
|---|---|---|---|---|---|---|---|---|---|---|---|---|---|---|---|---|---|---|---|---|
| 1991 | 4.9 | 5.0 | 5.1 | 5.2 | 5.3 | 5.4 | 5.5 | 5.6 | 5.7 | 5.8 | 5.9 | 6.0 | 6.1 | 6.3 | 6.4 | 6.5 | 6.6 | 6.8 | 6.9 | 7.0 |
| 1992 | 4.8 | 4.9 | 5.0 | 5.1 | 5.2 | 5.3 | 5.4 | 5.5 | 5.6 | 5.7 | 5.9 | 6.0 | 6.0 | 6.2 | 6.3 | 6.4 | 6.5 | 6.7 | 6.8 | 6.9 |
| 1993 | 4.8 | 4.9 | 5.0 | 5.1 | 5.2 | 5.3 | 5.4 | 5.5 | 5.5 | 5.7 | 5.8 | 5.9 | 6.0 | 6.1 | 6.2 | 6.3 | 6.4 | 6.5 | 6.7 | 6.8 |
| 1994 | 4.8 | 4.9 | 5.0 | 5.1 | 5.2 | 5.2 | 5.3 | 5.4 | 5.5 | 5.6 | 5.7 | 5.8 | 5.9 | 6.0 | 6.1 | 6.2 | 6.3 | 6.4 | 6.5 | 6.6 |
| 1995 | 4.8 | 4.9 | 5.0 | 5.1 | 5.2 | 5.2 | 5.3 | 5.4 | 5.5 | 5.6 | 5.7 | 5.8 | 5.9 | 6.0 | 6.1 | 6.2 | 6.3 | 6.4 | 6.5 | 6.6 |
| 1996 | 4.8 | 4.9 | 5.0 | 5.1 | 5.2 | 5.2 | 5.3 | 5.4 | 5.5 | 5.6 | 5.7 | 5.8 | 5.9 | 6.0 | 6.1 | 6.2 | 6.3 | 6.4 | 6.5 | 6.6 |
| 1997 | 4.8 | 4.9 | 5.0 | 5.1 | 5.2 | 5.2 | 5.3 | 5.4 | 5.5 | 5.6 | 5.7 | 5.8 | 5.9 | 6.0 | 6.0 | 6.1 | 6.3 | 6.4 | 6.5 | 6.5 |
| 1998 | 4.8 | 4.9 | 5.0 | 5.1 | 5.2 | 5.2 | 5.3 | 5.4 | 5.5 | 5.6 | 5.7 | 5.8 | 5.8 | 5.9 | 6.0 | 6.1 | 6.2 | 6.3 | 6.4 | 6.5 |
| 1999 | 4.8 | 4.9 | 5.0 | 5.1 | 5.1 | 5.2 | 5.3 | 5.4 | 5.5 | 5.6 | 5.7 | 5.7 | 5.8 | 5.9 | 6.0 | 6.1 | 6.2 | 6.3 | 6.4 | 6.4 |
| 2000 | 4.8 | 4.9 | 5.0 | 5.1 | 5.2 | 5.2 | 5.3 | 5.4 | 5.5 | 5.6 | 5.7 | 5.7 | 5.8 | 5.9 | 6.0 | 6.1 | 6.2 | 6.3 | 6.3 | 6.4 |

## Table C-6 (Page 5 of 5)

### U.S. Treasury Bills Total Returns
Rates of Return for all holding periods
Percent per annum compounded annually

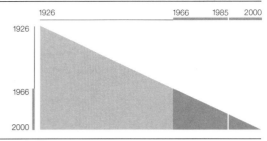

### from 1926 to 2000

| To the end of | From the beginning of | | | | | | | | | | | | | | | | | | | |
|---|---|---|---|---|---|---|---|---|---|---|---|---|---|---|---|---|---|---|---|---|
| | 1966 | 1967 | 1968 | 1969 | 1970 | 1971 | 1972 | 1973 | 1974 | 1975 | 1976 | 1977 | 1978 | 1979 | 1980 | 1981 | 1982 | 1983 | 1984 | 1985 |
| 1966 | 4.8 | | | | | | | | | | | | | | | | | | | |
| 1967 | 4.5 | 4.2 | | | | | | | | | | | | | | | | | | |
| 1968 | 4.7 | 4.7 | 5.2 | | | | | | | | | | | | | | | | | |
| 1969 | 5.2 | 5.3 | 5.9 | 6.6 | | | | | | | | | | | | | | | | |
| 1970 | 5.5 | 5.6 | 6.1 | 6.6 | 6.5 | | | | | | | | | | | | | | | |
| 1971 | 5.3 | 5.4 | 5.7 | 5.8 | 5.5 | 4.4 | | | | | | | | | | | | | | |
| 1972 | 5.1 | 5.1 | 5.3 | 5.3 | 4.9 | 4.1 | 3.8 | | | | | | | | | | | | | |
| 1973 | 5.3 | 5.4 | 5.6 | 5.6 | 5.4 | 5.0 | 5.4 | 6.9 | | | | | | | | | | | | |
| 1974 | 5.6 | 5.7 | 5.9 | 6.0 | 5.9 | 5.8 | 6.2 | 7.5 | 8.0 | | | | | | | | | | | |
| 1975 | 5.6 | 5.7 | 5.9 | 6.0 | 5.9 | 5.8 | 6.1 | 6.9 | 6.9 | 5.8 | | | | | | | | | | |
| 1976 | 5.6 | 5.6 | 5.8 | 5.9 | 5.8 | 5.7 | 5.9 | 6.4 | 6.3 | 5.4 | 5.1 | | | | | | | | | |
| 1977 | 5.5 | 5.6 | 5.7 | 5.8 | 5.7 | 5.6 | 5.8 | 6.2 | 6.0 | 5.3 | 5.1 | 5.1 | | | | | | | | |
| 1978 | 5.7 | 5.7 | 5.9 | 5.9 | 5.9 | 5.8 | 6.0 | 6.3 | 6.2 | 5.8 | 5.8 | 6.1 | 7.2 | | | | | | | |
| 1979 | 6.0 | 6.1 | 6.2 | 6.3 | 6.3 | 6.3 | 6.5 | 6.9 | 6.9 | 6.7 | 6.9 | 7.5 | 8.8 | 10.4 | | | | | | |
| 1980 | 6.3 | 6.4 | 6.6 | 6.7 | 6.7 | 6.8 | 7.0 | 7.4 | 7.5 | 7.4 | 7.8 | 8.5 | 9.6 | 10.8 | 11.2 | | | | | |
| 1981 | 6.8 | 7.0 | 7.2 | 7.3 | 7.4 | 7.5 | 7.8 | 8.2 | 8.4 | 8.4 | 8.9 | 9.7 | 10.8 | 12.1 | 13.0 | 14.7 | | | | |
| 1982 | 7.0 | 7.2 | 7.4 | 7.6 | 7.6 | 7.7 | 8.0 | 8.5 | 8.6 | 8.7 | 9.1 | 9.8 | 10.8 | 11.7 | 12.1 | 12.6 | 10.5 | | | |
| 1983 | 7.1 | 7.3 | 7.5 | 7.6 | 7.7 | 7.8 | 8.1 | 8.5 | 8.6 | 8.7 | 9.1 | 9.7 | 10.4 | 11.1 | 11.3 | 11.3 | 9.7 | 8.8 | | |
| 1984 | 7.3 | 7.4 | 7.6 | 7.8 | 7.9 | 7.9 | 8.2 | 8.6 | 8.8 | 8.8 | 9.2 | 9.7 | 10.4 | 10.9 | 11.0 | 11.0 | 9.7 | 9.3 | 9.8 | |
| 1985 | 7.3 | 7.4 | 7.6 | 7.8 | 7.8 | 7.9 | 8.2 | 8.5 | 8.7 | 8.7 | 9.0 | 9.5 | 10.0 | 10.4 | 10.5 | 10.3 | 9.2 | 8.8 | 8.8 | 7.7 |
| 1986 | 7.3 | 7.4 | 7.5 | 7.7 | 7.7 | 7.8 | 8.1 | 8.4 | 8.5 | 8.5 | 8.8 | 9.1 | 9.6 | 9.9 | 9.8 | 9.6 | 8.6 | 8.1 | 7.9 | 6.9 |
| 1987 | 7.2 | 7.3 | 7.4 | 7.6 | 7.6 | 7.7 | 7.9 | 8.2 | 8.3 | 8.3 | 8.5 | 8.8 | 9.2 | 9.4 | 9.3 | 9.0 | 8.1 | 7.6 | 7.3 | 6.4 |
| 1988 | 7.1 | 7.2 | 7.4 | 7.5 | 7.6 | 7.6 | 7.8 | 8.1 | 8.1 | 8.1 | 8.3 | 8.6 | 8.9 | 9.1 | 8.9 | 8.7 | 7.8 | 7.4 | 7.1 | 6.4 |
| 1989 | 7.2 | 7.3 | 7.4 | 7.5 | 7.6 | 7.6 | 7.8 | 8.1 | 8.1 | 8.2 | 8.3 | 8.6 | 8.9 | 9.0 | 8.9 | 8.6 | 7.9 | 7.5 | 7.3 | 6.8 |
| 1990 | 7.2 | 7.3 | 7.5 | 7.6 | 7.6 | 7.7 | 7.8 | 8.1 | 8.1 | 8.1 | 8.3 | 8.5 | 8.8 | 8.9 | 8.8 | 8.5 | 7.9 | 7.6 | 7.4 | 7.0 |
| 1991 | 7.1 | 7.2 | 7.4 | 7.5 | 7.5 | 7.6 | 7.7 | 7.9 | 8.0 | 8.0 | 8.1 | 8.3 | 8.6 | 8.7 | 8.5 | 8.3 | 7.7 | 7.3 | 7.2 | 6.8 |
| 1992 | 7.0 | 7.1 | 7.2 | 7.3 | 7.3 | 7.4 | 7.5 | 7.7 | 7.7 | 7.7 | 7.8 | 8.0 | 8.2 | 8.3 | 8.1 | 7.9 | 7.3 | 6.9 | 6.7 | 6.4 |
| 1993 | 6.9 | 6.9 | 7.0 | 7.1 | 7.1 | 7.2 | 7.3 | 7.5 | 7.5 | 7.5 | 7.6 | 7.7 | 7.9 | 7.9 | 7.7 | 7.5 | 6.9 | 6.6 | 6.4 | 6.0 |
| 1994 | 6.8 | 6.8 | 6.9 | 7.0 | 7.0 | 7.0 | 7.1 | 7.3 | 7.3 | 7.3 | 7.4 | 7.5 | 7.6 | 7.7 | 7.5 | 7.2 | 6.7 | 6.3 | 6.1 | 5.8 |
| 1995 | 6.7 | 6.8 | 6.9 | 6.9 | 7.0 | 7.0 | 7.1 | 7.2 | 7.2 | 7.2 | 7.3 | 7.4 | 7.5 | 7.5 | 7.4 | 7.1 | 6.6 | 6.3 | 6.1 | 5.7 |
| 1996 | 6.7 | 6.7 | 6.8 | 6.9 | 6.9 | 6.9 | 7.0 | 7.1 | 7.2 | 7.1 | 7.2 | 7.3 | 7.4 | 7.4 | 7.2 | 7.0 | 6.5 | 6.2 | 6.0 | 5.7 |
| 1997 | 6.6 | 6.7 | 6.8 | 6.8 | 6.8 | 6.8 | 6.9 | 7.1 | 7.1 | 7.0 | 7.1 | 7.2 | 7.3 | 7.3 | 7.1 | 6.9 | 6.4 | 6.1 | 6.0 | 5.7 |
| 1998 | 6.6 | 6.6 | 6.7 | 6.8 | 6.8 | 6.8 | 6.9 | 7.0 | 7.0 | 6.9 | 7.0 | 7.1 | 7.2 | 7.2 | 7.0 | 6.8 | 6.3 | 6.1 | 5.9 | 5.6 |
| 1999 | 6.5 | 6.6 | 6.6 | 6.7 | 6.7 | 6.7 | 6.8 | 6.9 | 6.9 | 6.8 | 6.9 | 7.0 | 7.1 | 7.1 | 6.9 | 6.7 | 6.2 | 6.0 | 5.8 | 5.5 |
| 2000 | 6.5 | 6.5 | 6.6 | 6.7 | 6.7 | 6.7 | 6.8 | 6.9 | 6.9 | 6.8 | 6.9 | 6.9 | 7.0 | 7.0 | 6.8 | 6.6 | 6.2 | 6.0 | 5.8 | 5.6 |

| To the end of | From the beginning of | | | | | | | | | | | | | | |
|---|---|---|---|---|---|---|---|---|---|---|---|---|---|---|---|
| | 1986 | 1987 | 1988 | 1989 | 1990 | 1991 | 1992 | 1993 | 1994 | 1995 | 1996 | 1997 | 1998 | 1999 | 2000 |
| 1986 | 6.2 | | | | | | | | | | | | | | |
| 1987 | 5.8 | 5.5 | | | | | | | | | | | | | |
| 1988 | 6.0 | 5.9 | 6.3 | | | | | | | | | | | | |
| 1989 | 6.6 | 6.7 | 7.4 | 8.4 | | | | | | | | | | | |
| 1990 | 6.8 | 7.0 | 7.5 | 8.1 | 7.8 | | | | | | | | | | |
| 1991 | 6.6 | 6.7 | 7.0 | 7.3 | 6.7 | 5.6 | | | | | | | | | |
| 1992 | 6.2 | 6.2 | 6.3 | 6.3 | 5.6 | 4.5 | 3.5 | | | | | | | | |
| 1993 | 5.8 | 5.7 | 5.7 | 5.6 | 4.9 | 4.0 | 3.2 | 2.9 | | | | | | | |
| 1994 | 5.5 | 5.5 | 5.5 | 5.3 | 4.7 | 4.0 | 3.4 | 3.4 | 3.9 | | | | | | |
| 1995 | 5.6 | 5.5 | 5.5 | 5.4 | 4.9 | 4.3 | 4.0 | 4.1 | 4.7 | 5.6 | | | | | |
| 1996 | 5.5 | 5.5 | 5.5 | 5.3 | 4.9 | 4.4 | 4.2 | 4.4 | 4.9 | 5.4 | 5.2 | | | | |
| 1997 | 5.5 | 5.4 | 5.4 | 5.3 | 5.0 | 4.6 | 4.4 | 4.6 | 5.0 | 5.4 | 5.2 | 5.3 | | | |
| 1998 | 5.4 | 5.4 | 5.4 | 5.3 | 5.0 | 4.6 | 4.5 | 4.6 | 5.0 | 5.2 | 5.1 | 5.1 | 4.9 | | |
| 1999 | 5.4 | 5.3 | 5.3 | 5.2 | 4.9 | 4.6 | 4.5 | 4.6 | 4.9 | 5.1 | 5.0 | 4.9 | 4.8 | 4.7 | |
| 2000 | 5.4 | 5.4 | 5.4 | 5.3 | 5.0 | 4.7 | 4.6 | 4.8 | 5.1 | 5.2 | 5.2 | 5.2 | 5.1 | 5.3 | 5.9 |

# Table C-7 (Page 1 of 5)

## Inflation
Rates of Return for all holding periods
Percent per annum compounded annually

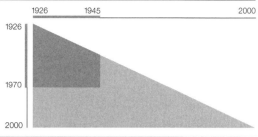

from 1926 to 2000

| To the end of | From the beginning of 1926 | 1927 | 1928 | 1929 | 1930 | 1931 | 1932 | 1933 | 1934 | 1935 | 1936 | 1937 | 1938 | 1939 | 1940 | 1941 | 1942 | 1943 | 1944 | 1945 |
|---|---|---|---|---|---|---|---|---|---|---|---|---|---|---|---|---|---|---|---|---|
| 1926 | -1.5 | | | | | | | | | | | | | | | | | | | |
| 1927 | -1.8 | -2.1 | | | | | | | | | | | | | | | | | | |
| 1928 | -1.5 | -1.5 | -1.0 | | | | | | | | | | | | | | | | | |
| 1929 | -1.1 | -1.0 | -0.4 | 0.2 | | | | | | | | | | | | | | | | |
| 1930 | -2.1 | -2.2 | -2.3 | -3.0 | -6.0 | | | | | | | | | | | | | | | |
| 1931 | -3.4 | -3.7 | -4.2 | -5.2 | -7.8 | -9.5 | | | | | | | | | | | | | | |
| 1932 | -4.4 | -4.9 | -5.4 | -6.5 | -8.6 | -9.9 | -10.3 | | | | | | | | | | | | | |
| 1933 | -3.8 | -4.1 | -4.5 | -5.1 | -6.4 | -6.6 | -5.0 | 0.5 | | | | | | | | | | | | |
| 1934 | -3.2 | -3.4 | -3.6 | -4.0 | -4.8 | -4.5 | -2.7 | 1.3 | 2.0 | | | | | | | | | | | |
| 1935 | -2.6 | -2.7 | -2.8 | -3.0 | -3.5 | -3.0 | -1.3 | 1.8 | 2.5 | 3.0 | | | | | | | | | | |
| 1936 | -2.2 | -2.3 | -2.3 | -2.5 | -2.9 | -2.3 | -0.8 | 1.7 | 2.1 | 2.1 | 1.2 | | | | | | | | | |
| 1937 | -1.8 | -1.8 | -1.8 | -1.9 | -2.1 | -1.6 | -0.2 | 2.0 | 2.3 | 2.4 | 2.2 | 3.1 | | | | | | | | |
| 1938 | -1.9 | -1.9 | -1.9 | -2.0 | -2.2 | -1.7 | -0.6 | 1.2 | 1.3 | 1.1 | 0.5 | 0.1 | -2.8 | | | | | | | |
| 1939 | -1.8 | -1.8 | -1.8 | -1.8 | -2.0 | -1.6 | -0.6 | 0.9 | 1.0 | 0.8 | 0.2 | -0.1 | -1.6 | -0.5 | | | | | | |
| 1940 | -1.6 | -1.6 | -1.6 | -1.6 | -1.8 | -1.3 | -0.4 | 0.9 | 1.0 | 0.8 | 0.4 | 0.2 | -0.8 | 0.2 | 1.0 | | | | | |
| 1941 | -0.9 | -0.9 | -0.8 | -0.8 | -0.9 | -0.4 | 0.6 | 1.9 | 2.0 | 2.0 | 1.9 | 2.0 | 1.7 | 3.3 | 5.2 | 9.7 | | | | |
| 1942 | -0.3 | -0.3 | -0.2 | -0.1 | -0.1 | 0.4 | 1.3 | 2.6 | 2.8 | 2.9 | 2.9 | 3.2 | 3.2 | 4.8 | 6.6 | 9.5 | 9.3 | | | |
| 1943 | -0.2 | -0.1 | 0.0 | 0.1 | 0.1 | 0.6 | 1.5 | 2.6 | 2.9 | 2.9 | 2.9 | 3.2 | 3.2 | 4.4 | 5.7 | 7.3 | 6.2 | 3.2 | | |
| 1944 | 0.0 | 0.0 | 0.2 | 0.2 | 0.2 | 0.7 | 1.5 | 2.6 | 2.8 | 2.9 | 2.8 | 3.1 | 3.0 | 4.1 | 5.0 | 6.0 | 4.8 | 2.6 | 2.1 | |
| 1945 | 0.1 | 0.2 | 0.3 | 0.4 | 0.4 | 0.8 | 1.6 | 2.6 | 2.7 | 2.8 | 2.8 | 3.0 | 2.9 | 3.8 | 4.5 | 5.2 | 4.2 | 2.5 | 2.2 | 2.3 |
| 1946 | 0.9 | 1.0 | 1.2 | 1.3 | 1.3 | 1.8 | 2.6 | 3.6 | 3.9 | 4.0 | 4.1 | 4.4 | 4.5 | 5.5 | 6.4 | 7.3 | 6.8 | 6.2 | 7.3 | 9.9 |
| 1947 | 1.2 | 1.4 | 1.5 | 1.7 | 1.7 | 2.2 | 3.0 | 4.0 | 4.2 | 4.4 | 4.5 | 4.8 | 5.0 | 5.9 | 6.7 | 7.5 | 7.2 | 6.8 | 7.7 | 9.6 |
| 1948 | 1.3 | 1.4 | 1.6 | 1.7 | 1.8 | 2.3 | 3.0 | 3.9 | 4.1 | 4.3 | 4.4 | 4.6 | 4.8 | 5.6 | 6.2 | 6.9 | 6.5 | 6.1 | 6.7 | 7.8 |
| 1949 | 1.2 | 1.3 | 1.4 | 1.5 | 1.6 | 2.0 | 2.7 | 3.5 | 3.7 | 3.8 | 3.9 | 4.1 | 4.2 | 4.9 | 5.4 | 5.9 | 5.5 | 4.9 | 5.2 | 5.8 |
| 1950 | 1.3 | 1.5 | 1.6 | 1.7 | 1.8 | 2.2 | 2.9 | 3.7 | 3.9 | 4.0 | 4.0 | 4.2 | 4.3 | 4.9 | 5.4 | 5.9 | 5.5 | 5.0 | 5.3 | 5.8 |
| 1951 | 1.5 | 1.6 | 1.8 | 1.9 | 2.0 | 2.4 | 3.0 | 3.8 | 4.0 | 4.1 | 4.1 | 4.3 | 4.4 | 5.0 | 5.5 | 5.9 | 5.5 | 5.1 | 5.4 | 5.8 |
| 1952 | 1.5 | 1.6 | 1.8 | 1.9 | 1.9 | 2.3 | 2.9 | 3.6 | 3.8 | 3.9 | 4.0 | 4.1 | 4.2 | 4.7 | 5.1 | 5.5 | 5.1 | 4.7 | 4.9 | 5.2 |
| 1953 | 1.5 | 1.6 | 1.7 | 1.8 | 1.9 | 2.2 | 2.8 | 3.5 | 3.6 | 3.7 | 3.8 | 3.9 | 4.0 | 4.4 | 4.8 | 5.1 | 4.7 | 4.3 | 4.4 | 4.7 |
| 1954 | 1.4 | 1.5 | 1.6 | 1.7 | 1.8 | 2.1 | 2.7 | 3.3 | 3.4 | 3.5 | 3.5 | 3.7 | 3.7 | 4.1 | 4.4 | 4.7 | 4.3 | 3.9 | 4.0 | 4.2 |
| 1955 | 1.4 | 1.5 | 1.6 | 1.7 | 1.7 | 2.1 | 2.6 | 3.2 | 3.3 | 3.4 | 3.4 | 3.5 | 3.5 | 3.9 | 4.2 | 4.4 | 4.0 | 3.6 | 3.7 | 3.8 |
| 1956 | 1.4 | 1.5 | 1.6 | 1.7 | 1.8 | 2.1 | 2.6 | 3.2 | 3.3 | 3.3 | 3.3 | 3.5 | 3.5 | 3.8 | 4.1 | 4.3 | 3.9 | 3.6 | 3.6 | 3.7 |
| 1957 | 1.5 | 1.5 | 1.7 | 1.8 | 1.8 | 2.1 | 2.6 | 3.2 | 3.3 | 3.3 | 3.3 | 3.4 | 3.5 | 3.8 | 4.0 | 4.2 | 3.9 | 3.5 | 3.6 | 3.7 |
| 1958 | 1.5 | 1.6 | 1.7 | 1.8 | 1.8 | 2.1 | 2.6 | 3.1 | 3.2 | 3.3 | 3.3 | 3.4 | 3.4 | 3.7 | 3.9 | 4.1 | 3.8 | 3.4 | 3.4 | 3.5 |
| 1959 | 1.5 | 1.6 | 1.7 | 1.8 | 1.8 | 2.1 | 2.5 | 3.0 | 3.1 | 3.2 | 3.2 | 3.3 | 3.3 | 3.6 | 3.8 | 3.9 | 3.6 | 3.3 | 3.3 | 3.4 |
| 1960 | 1.5 | 1.6 | 1.7 | 1.7 | 1.8 | 2.1 | 2.5 | 3.0 | 3.1 | 3.1 | 3.1 | 3.2 | 3.2 | 3.5 | 3.7 | 3.8 | 3.5 | 3.2 | 3.2 | 3.3 |
| 1961 | 1.4 | 1.5 | 1.6 | 1.7 | 1.8 | 2.0 | 2.4 | 2.9 | 3.0 | 3.0 | 3.0 | 3.1 | 3.1 | 3.4 | 3.5 | 3.7 | 3.4 | 3.1 | 3.1 | 3.1 |
| 1962 | 1.4 | 1.5 | 1.6 | 1.7 | 1.7 | 2.0 | 2.4 | 2.8 | 2.9 | 3.0 | 3.0 | 3.0 | 3.0 | 3.3 | 3.4 | 3.6 | 3.3 | 3.0 | 3.0 | 3.0 |
| 1963 | 1.4 | 1.5 | 1.6 | 1.7 | 1.7 | 2.0 | 2.4 | 2.8 | 2.9 | 2.9 | 2.9 | 3.0 | 3.0 | 3.2 | 3.4 | 3.5 | 3.2 | 2.9 | 2.9 | 2.9 |
| 1964 | 1.4 | 1.5 | 1.6 | 1.7 | 1.7 | 2.0 | 2.3 | 2.8 | 2.8 | 2.9 | 2.9 | 2.9 | 2.9 | 3.1 | 3.3 | 3.4 | 3.1 | 2.8 | 2.8 | 2.9 |
| 1965 | 1.4 | 1.5 | 1.6 | 1.7 | 1.7 | 2.0 | 2.3 | 2.7 | 2.8 | 2.8 | 2.8 | 2.9 | 2.9 | 3.1 | 3.2 | 3.3 | 3.1 | 2.8 | 2.8 | 2.8 |
| 1966 | 1.5 | 1.6 | 1.7 | 1.7 | 1.8 | 2.0 | 2.4 | 2.8 | 2.8 | 2.8 | 2.8 | 2.9 | 2.9 | 3.1 | 3.2 | 3.3 | 3.1 | 2.8 | 2.8 | 2.8 |
| 1967 | 1.5 | 1.6 | 1.7 | 1.8 | 1.8 | 2.0 | 2.4 | 2.8 | 2.8 | 2.8 | 2.8 | 2.9 | 2.9 | 3.1 | 3.2 | 3.3 | 3.1 | 2.8 | 2.8 | 2.8 |
| 1968 | 1.6 | 1.7 | 1.8 | 1.8 | 1.9 | 2.1 | 2.4 | 2.8 | 2.9 | 2.9 | 2.9 | 3.0 | 3.0 | 3.1 | 3.3 | 3.4 | 3.1 | 2.9 | 2.9 | 2.9 |
| 1969 | 1.7 | 1.8 | 1.9 | 1.9 | 2.0 | 2.2 | 2.5 | 2.9 | 3.0 | 3.0 | 3.0 | 3.0 | 3.0 | 3.2 | 3.4 | 3.5 | 3.2 | 3.0 | 3.0 | 3.0 |
| 1970 | 1.8 | 1.9 | 2.0 | 2.0 | 2.1 | 2.3 | 2.6 | 3.0 | 3.0 | 3.1 | 3.1 | 3.1 | 3.1 | 3.3 | 3.4 | 3.5 | 3.3 | 3.1 | 3.1 | 3.1 |

# Table C-7 (Page 2 of 5)

## Inflation
Rates of Return for all holding periods
Percent per annum compounded annually

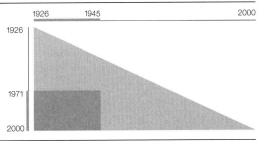

from 1926 to 2000

| To the end of | From the beginning of 1926 | 1927 | 1928 | 1929 | 1930 | 1931 | 1932 | 1933 | 1934 | 1935 | 1936 | 1937 | 1938 | 1939 | 1940 | 1941 | 1942 | 1943 | 1944 | 1945 |
|---|---|---|---|---|---|---|---|---|---|---|---|---|---|---|---|---|---|---|---|---|
| 1971 | 1.8 | 1.9 | 2.0 | 2.1 | 2.1 | 2.3 | 2.6 | 3.0 | 3.0 | 3.1 | 3.1 | 3.1 | 3.1 | 3.3 | 3.4 | 3.5 | 3.3 | 3.1 | 3.1 | 3.1 |
| 1972 | 1.9 | 1.9 | 2.0 | 2.1 | 2.1 | 2.3 | 2.6 | 3.0 | 3.1 | 3.1 | 3.1 | 3.1 | 3.1 | 3.3 | 3.4 | 3.5 | 3.3 | 3.1 | 3.1 | 3.2 |
| 1973 | 2.0 | 2.1 | 2.2 | 2.2 | 2.3 | 2.5 | 2.8 | 3.1 | 3.2 | 3.2 | 3.2 | 3.3 | 3.3 | 3.5 | 3.6 | 3.7 | 3.5 | 3.3 | 3.3 | 3.3 |
| 1974 | 2.2 | 2.3 | 2.4 | 2.4 | 2.5 | 2.7 | 3.0 | 3.3 | 3.4 | 3.4 | 3.4 | 3.5 | 3.5 | 3.7 | 3.8 | 3.9 | 3.7 | 3.6 | 3.6 | 3.6 |
| 1975 | 2.3 | 2.4 | 2.5 | 2.5 | 2.6 | 2.8 | 3.1 | 3.4 | 3.5 | 3.5 | 3.5 | 3.6 | 3.6 | 3.8 | 3.9 | 4.0 | 3.8 | 3.7 | 3.7 | 3.7 |
| 1976 | 2.3 | 2.4 | 2.5 | 2.6 | 2.6 | 2.8 | 3.1 | 3.4 | 3.5 | 3.6 | 3.6 | 3.6 | 3.6 | 3.8 | 3.9 | 4.0 | 3.9 | 3.7 | 3.7 | 3.8 |
| 1977 | 2.4 | 2.5 | 2.6 | 2.7 | 2.7 | 2.9 | 3.2 | 3.5 | 3.6 | 3.6 | 3.6 | 3.7 | 3.7 | 3.9 | 4.0 | 4.1 | 3.9 | 3.8 | 3.8 | 3.9 |
| 1978 | 2.5 | 2.6 | 2.7 | 2.8 | 2.8 | 3.0 | 3.3 | 3.6 | 3.7 | 3.7 | 3.8 | 3.8 | 3.8 | 4.0 | 4.1 | 4.2 | 4.1 | 3.9 | 4.0 | 4.0 |
| 1979 | 2.7 | 2.8 | 2.9 | 3.0 | 3.0 | 3.2 | 3.5 | 3.8 | 3.9 | 4.0 | 4.0 | 4.0 | 4.1 | 4.2 | 4.4 | 4.4 | 4.3 | 4.2 | 4.2 | 4.3 |
| 1980 | 2.9 | 3.0 | 3.1 | 3.2 | 3.2 | 3.4 | 3.7 | 4.0 | 4.1 | 4.1 | 4.2 | 4.2 | 4.2 | 4.4 | 4.5 | 4.6 | 4.5 | 4.4 | 4.4 | 4.5 |
| 1981 | 3.0 | 3.1 | 3.2 | 3.3 | 3.3 | 3.5 | 3.8 | 4.1 | 4.2 | 4.2 | 4.3 | 4.3 | 4.4 | 4.5 | 4.6 | 4.7 | 4.6 | 4.5 | 4.5 | 4.6 |
| 1982 | 3.0 | 3.1 | 3.2 | 3.3 | 3.3 | 3.5 | 3.8 | 4.1 | 4.2 | 4.2 | 4.2 | 4.3 | 4.3 | 4.5 | 4.6 | 4.7 | 4.6 | 4.5 | 4.5 | 4.6 |
| 1983 | 3.0 | 3.1 | 3.2 | 3.3 | 3.3 | 3.5 | 3.8 | 4.1 | 4.2 | 4.2 | 4.2 | 4.3 | 4.3 | 4.5 | 4.6 | 4.7 | 4.6 | 4.5 | 4.5 | 4.6 |
| 1984 | 3.0 | 3.1 | 3.2 | 3.3 | 3.4 | 3.5 | 3.8 | 4.1 | 4.2 | 4.2 | 4.2 | 4.3 | 4.3 | 4.5 | 4.6 | 4.7 | 4.6 | 4.5 | 4.5 | 4.5 |
| 1985 | 3.1 | 3.1 | 3.2 | 3.3 | 3.4 | 3.5 | 3.8 | 4.1 | 4.2 | 4.2 | 4.2 | 4.3 | 4.3 | 4.5 | 4.6 | 4.7 | 4.5 | 4.4 | 4.5 | 4.5 |
| 1986 | 3.0 | 3.1 | 3.2 | 3.3 | 3.3 | 3.5 | 3.8 | 4.0 | 4.1 | 4.1 | 4.2 | 4.2 | 4.2 | 4.4 | 4.5 | 4.6 | 4.5 | 4.4 | 4.4 | 4.4 |
| 1987 | 3.0 | 3.1 | 3.2 | 3.3 | 3.3 | 3.5 | 3.8 | 4.0 | 4.1 | 4.1 | 4.2 | 4.2 | 4.2 | 4.4 | 4.5 | 4.6 | 4.5 | 4.4 | 4.4 | 4.4 |
| 1988 | 3.1 | 3.1 | 3.2 | 3.3 | 3.4 | 3.5 | 3.8 | 4.0 | 4.1 | 4.1 | 4.2 | 4.2 | 4.3 | 4.4 | 4.5 | 4.6 | 4.5 | 4.4 | 4.4 | 4.4 |
| 1989 | 3.1 | 3.2 | 3.3 | 3.3 | 3.4 | 3.5 | 3.8 | 4.1 | 4.1 | 4.2 | 4.2 | 4.2 | 4.3 | 4.4 | 4.5 | 4.6 | 4.5 | 4.4 | 4.4 | 4.4 |
| 1990 | 3.1 | 3.2 | 3.3 | 3.4 | 3.4 | 3.6 | 3.8 | 4.1 | 4.2 | 4.2 | 4.2 | 4.3 | 4.3 | 4.4 | 4.5 | 4.6 | 4.5 | 4.4 | 4.4 | 4.5 |
| 1991 | 3.1 | 3.2 | 3.3 | 3.4 | 3.4 | 3.6 | 3.8 | 4.1 | 4.1 | 4.2 | 4.2 | 4.2 | 4.3 | 4.4 | 4.5 | 4.6 | 4.5 | 4.4 | 4.4 | 4.5 |
| 1992 | 3.1 | 3.2 | 3.3 | 3.4 | 3.4 | 3.6 | 3.8 | 4.1 | 4.1 | 4.2 | 4.2 | 4.2 | 4.2 | 4.4 | 4.5 | 4.5 | 4.4 | 4.3 | 4.4 | 4.4 |
| 1993 | 3.1 | 3.2 | 3.3 | 3.3 | 3.4 | 3.6 | 3.8 | 4.0 | 4.1 | 4.1 | 4.1 | 4.2 | 4.2 | 4.3 | 4.4 | 4.5 | 4.4 | 4.3 | 4.3 | 4.4 |
| 1994 | 3.1 | 3.2 | 3.3 | 3.3 | 3.4 | 3.5 | 3.8 | 4.0 | 4.1 | 4.1 | 4.1 | 4.2 | 4.2 | 4.3 | 4.4 | 4.5 | 4.4 | 4.3 | 4.3 | 4.4 |
| 1995 | 3.1 | 3.2 | 3.3 | 3.3 | 3.4 | 3.5 | 3.7 | 4.0 | 4.0 | 4.1 | 4.1 | 4.1 | 4.2 | 4.3 | 4.4 | 4.4 | 4.3 | 4.3 | 4.3 | 4.3 |
| 1996 | 3.1 | 3.2 | 3.3 | 3.3 | 3.4 | 3.5 | 3.7 | 4.0 | 4.0 | 4.1 | 4.1 | 4.1 | 4.1 | 4.3 | 4.4 | 4.4 | 4.2 | 4.2 | 4.3 | 4.3 |
| 1997 | 3.1 | 3.2 | 3.2 | 3.3 | 3.4 | 3.5 | 3.7 | 3.9 | 4.0 | 4.0 | 4.0 | 4.1 | 4.1 | 4.2 | 4.3 | 4.4 | 4.3 | 4.2 | 4.2 | 4.2 |
| 1998 | 3.1 | 3.1 | 3.2 | 3.3 | 3.3 | 3.5 | 3.7 | 3.9 | 4.0 | 4.0 | 4.0 | 4.0 | 4.1 | 4.2 | 4.3 | 4.3 | 4.2 | 4.1 | 4.2 | 4.2 |
| 1999 | 3.1 | 3.1 | 3.2 | 3.3 | 3.3 | 3.5 | 3.7 | 3.9 | 3.9 | 4.0 | 4.0 | 4.0 | 4.0 | 4.2 | 4.2 | 4.3 | 4.2 | 4.1 | 4.1 | 4.2 |
| 2000 | 3.1 | 3.1 | 3.2 | 3.3 | 3.3 | 3.5 | 3.7 | 3.9 | 3.9 | 4.0 | 4.0 | 4.0 | 4.0 | 4.1 | 4.2 | 4.3 | 4.2 | 4.1 | 4.1 | 4.2 |

## Table C-7 (Page 3 of 5)

### Inflation
Rates of Return for all holding periods
Percent per annum compounded annually

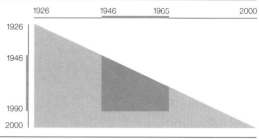

from 1926 to 2000

| To the end of | From the beginning of 1946 | 1947 | 1948 | 1949 | 1950 | 1951 | 1952 | 1953 | 1954 | 1955 | 1956 | 1957 | 1958 | 1959 | 1960 | 1961 | 1962 | 1963 | 1964 | 1965 |
|---|---|---|---|---|---|---|---|---|---|---|---|---|---|---|---|---|---|---|---|---|
| 1946 | 18.2 | | | | | | | | | | | | | | | | | | | |
| 1947 | 13.5 | 9.0 | | | | | | | | | | | | | | | | | | |
| 1948 | 9.8 | 5.8 | 2.7 | | | | | | | | | | | | | | | | | |
| 1949 | 6.8 | 3.2 | 0.4 | -1.8 | | | | | | | | | | | | | | | | |
| 1950 | 6.6 | 3.8 | 2.2 | 1.9 | 5.8 | | | | | | | | | | | | | | | |
| 1951 | 6.5 | 4.3 | 3.1 | 3.2 | 5.8 | 5.9 | | | | | | | | | | | | | | |
| 1952 | 5.6 | 3.7 | 2.6 | 2.6 | 4.2 | 3.3 | 0.9 | | | | | | | | | | | | | |
| 1953 | 5.0 | 3.2 | 2.3 | 2.2 | 3.3 | 2.4 | 0.8 | 0.6 | | | | | | | | | | | | |
| 1954 | 4.4 | 2.8 | 1.9 | 1.8 | 2.5 | 1.7 | 0.3 | 0.1 | -0.5 | | | | | | | | | | | |
| 1955 | 4.0 | 2.5 | 1.7 | 1.6 | 2.1 | 1.4 | 0.3 | 0.2 | -0.1 | 0.4 | | | | | | | | | | |
| 1956 | 3.9 | 2.5 | 1.8 | 1.7 | 2.2 | 1.7 | 0.8 | 0.8 | 0.9 | 1.6 | 2.9 | | | | | | | | | |
| 1957 | 3.8 | 2.6 | 2.0 | 1.9 | 2.3 | 1.9 | 1.2 | 1.3 | 1.4 | 2.1 | 2.9 | 3.0 | | | | | | | | |
| 1958 | 3.6 | 2.5 | 1.9 | 1.9 | 2.3 | 1.8 | 1.3 | 1.3 | 1.5 | 2.0 | 2.5 | 2.4 | 1.8 | | | | | | | |
| 1959 | 3.5 | 2.4 | 1.9 | 1.8 | 2.2 | 1.8 | 1.3 | 1.4 | 1.5 | 1.9 | 2.3 | 2.1 | 1.6 | 1.5 | | | | | | |
| 1960 | 3.3 | 2.4 | 1.9 | 1.8 | 2.1 | 1.8 | 1.3 | 1.4 | 1.5 | 1.8 | 2.1 | 1.9 | 1.6 | 1.5 | 1.5 | | | | | |
| 1961 | 3.2 | 2.2 | 1.8 | 1.7 | 2.0 | 1.7 | 1.3 | 1.3 | 1.4 | 1.7 | 1.9 | 1.7 | 1.4 | 1.2 | 1.1 | 0.7 | | | | |
| 1962 | 3.1 | 2.2 | 1.7 | 1.7 | 1.9 | 1.6 | 1.3 | 1.3 | 1.4 | 1.6 | 1.8 | 1.6 | 1.3 | 1.2 | 1.1 | 0.9 | 1.2 | | | |
| 1963 | 3.0 | 2.2 | 1.7 | 1.7 | 1.9 | 1.6 | 1.3 | 1.3 | 1.4 | 1.6 | 1.8 | 1.6 | 1.4 | 1.3 | 1.3 | 1.2 | 1.4 | 1.6 | | |
| 1964 | 2.9 | 2.1 | 1.7 | 1.6 | 1.9 | 1.6 | 1.3 | 1.3 | 1.4 | 1.6 | 1.7 | 1.6 | 1.4 | 1.3 | 1.2 | 1.2 | 1.4 | 1.4 | 1.2 | |
| 1965 | 2.8 | 2.1 | 1.7 | 1.7 | 1.9 | 1.6 | 1.3 | 1.4 | 1.4 | 1.6 | 1.7 | 1.6 | 1.4 | 1.4 | 1.4 | 1.3 | 1.5 | 1.6 | 1.6 | 1.9 |
| 1966 | 2.9 | 2.2 | 1.8 | 1.8 | 2.0 | 1.7 | 1.5 | 1.5 | 1.6 | 1.7 | 1.9 | 1.8 | 1.6 | 1.6 | 1.6 | 1.7 | 1.9 | 2.0 | 2.2 | 2.6 |
| 1967 | 2.9 | 2.2 | 1.9 | 1.8 | 2.0 | 1.8 | 1.6 | 1.6 | 1.7 | 1.8 | 2.0 | 1.9 | 1.8 | 1.8 | 1.8 | 1.9 | 2.1 | 2.2 | 2.4 | 2.8 |
| 1968 | 3.0 | 2.3 | 2.0 | 2.0 | 2.2 | 2.0 | 1.7 | 1.8 | 1.9 | 2.0 | 2.2 | 2.1 | 2.0 | 2.1 | 2.1 | 2.2 | 2.4 | 2.6 | 2.8 | 3.3 |
| 1969 | 3.1 | 2.5 | 2.2 | 2.2 | 2.4 | 2.2 | 2.0 | 2.0 | 2.1 | 2.3 | 2.5 | 2.4 | 2.4 | 2.4 | 2.5 | 2.6 | 2.9 | 3.1 | 3.4 | 3.8 |
| 1970 | 3.2 | 2.6 | 2.3 | 2.3 | 2.5 | 2.3 | 2.2 | 2.2 | 2.3 | 2.5 | 2.7 | 2.6 | 2.6 | 2.7 | 2.8 | 2.9 | 3.2 | 3.4 | 3.7 | 4.1 |
| 1971 | 3.2 | 2.6 | 2.4 | 2.4 | 2.5 | 2.4 | 2.2 | 2.3 | 2.4 | 2.6 | 2.7 | 2.7 | 2.7 | 2.7 | 2.8 | 3.0 | 3.2 | 3.4 | 3.6 | 4.0 |
| 1972 | 3.2 | 2.7 | 2.4 | 2.4 | 2.6 | 2.4 | 2.3 | 2.3 | 2.4 | 2.6 | 2.7 | 2.7 | 2.7 | 2.8 | 2.9 | 3.0 | 3.2 | 3.4 | 3.6 | 3.9 |
| 1973 | 3.4 | 2.9 | 2.6 | 2.6 | 2.8 | 2.7 | 2.6 | 2.6 | 2.8 | 2.9 | 3.1 | 3.1 | 3.1 | 3.2 | 3.3 | 3.4 | 3.7 | 3.9 | 4.1 | 4.4 |
| 1974 | 3.7 | 3.2 | 3.0 | 3.0 | 3.2 | 3.1 | 3.0 | 3.1 | 3.2 | 3.4 | 3.5 | 3.6 | 3.6 | 3.7 | 3.9 | 4.0 | 4.3 | 4.6 | 4.8 | 5.2 |
| 1975 | 3.8 | 3.3 | 3.1 | 3.1 | 3.3 | 3.2 | 3.1 | 3.2 | 3.4 | 3.5 | 3.7 | 3.7 | 3.8 | 3.9 | 4.1 | 4.2 | 4.5 | 4.7 | 5.0 | 5.4 |
| 1976 | 3.8 | 3.4 | 3.2 | 3.2 | 3.4 | 3.3 | 3.2 | 3.3 | 3.4 | 3.6 | 3.8 | 3.8 | 3.8 | 4.0 | 4.1 | 4.3 | 4.5 | 4.8 | 5.0 | 5.3 |
| 1977 | 3.9 | 3.5 | 3.3 | 3.3 | 3.5 | 3.4 | 3.3 | 3.4 | 3.6 | 3.7 | 3.9 | 3.9 | 4.0 | 4.1 | 4.2 | 4.4 | 4.7 | 4.9 | 5.1 | 5.4 |
| 1978 | 4.1 | 3.7 | 3.5 | 3.5 | 3.7 | 3.6 | 3.5 | 3.6 | 3.8 | 3.9 | 4.1 | 4.2 | 4.2 | 4.3 | 4.5 | 4.7 | 4.9 | 5.1 | 5.4 | 5.7 |
| 1979 | 4.3 | 3.9 | 3.8 | 3.8 | 4.0 | 3.9 | 3.9 | 4.0 | 4.1 | 4.3 | 4.5 | 4.5 | 4.6 | 4.8 | 4.9 | 5.1 | 5.4 | 5.6 | 5.9 | 6.2 |
| 1980 | 4.5 | 4.2 | 4.0 | 4.1 | 4.3 | 4.2 | 4.2 | 4.3 | 4.4 | 4.6 | 4.8 | 4.9 | 4.9 | 5.1 | 5.3 | 5.5 | 5.7 | 6.0 | 6.2 | 6.6 |
| 1981 | 4.7 | 4.3 | 4.2 | 4.2 | 4.4 | 4.4 | 4.3 | 4.4 | 4.6 | 4.8 | 4.9 | 5.0 | 5.1 | 5.3 | 5.4 | 5.6 | 5.9 | 6.1 | 6.4 | 6.7 |
| 1982 | 4.6 | 4.3 | 4.2 | 4.2 | 4.4 | 4.3 | 4.3 | 4.4 | 4.5 | 4.7 | 4.9 | 5.0 | 5.1 | 5.2 | 5.4 | 5.5 | 5.8 | 6.0 | 6.2 | 6.5 |
| 1983 | 4.6 | 4.3 | 4.2 | 4.2 | 4.4 | 4.3 | 4.3 | 4.4 | 4.5 | 4.7 | 4.9 | 4.9 | 5.0 | 5.1 | 5.3 | 5.5 | 5.7 | 5.9 | 6.1 | 6.4 |
| 1984 | 4.6 | 4.3 | 4.1 | 4.2 | 4.4 | 4.3 | 4.3 | 4.4 | 4.5 | 4.7 | 4.8 | 4.9 | 5.0 | 5.1 | 5.2 | 5.4 | 5.6 | 5.8 | 6.0 | 6.3 |
| 1985 | 4.6 | 4.3 | 4.1 | 4.2 | 4.3 | 4.3 | 4.3 | 4.4 | 4.5 | 4.6 | 4.8 | 4.9 | 4.9 | 5.0 | 5.2 | 5.3 | 5.5 | 5.7 | 5.9 | 6.1 |
| 1986 | 4.5 | 4.2 | 4.1 | 4.1 | 4.3 | 4.2 | 4.2 | 4.3 | 4.4 | 4.5 | 4.7 | 4.7 | 4.8 | 4.9 | 5.0 | 5.2 | 5.4 | 5.5 | 5.7 | 5.9 |
| 1987 | 4.5 | 4.2 | 4.1 | 4.1 | 4.3 | 4.2 | 4.2 | 4.3 | 4.4 | 4.5 | 4.7 | 4.7 | 4.8 | 4.9 | 5.0 | 5.1 | 5.3 | 5.5 | 5.6 | 5.8 |
| 1988 | 4.5 | 4.2 | 4.1 | 4.1 | 4.3 | 4.2 | 4.2 | 4.3 | 4.4 | 4.5 | 4.7 | 4.7 | 4.8 | 4.9 | 5.0 | 5.1 | 5.3 | 5.4 | 5.6 | 5.8 |
| 1989 | 4.5 | 4.2 | 4.1 | 4.1 | 4.3 | 4.2 | 4.2 | 4.3 | 4.4 | 4.5 | 4.7 | 4.7 | 4.8 | 4.9 | 5.0 | 5.1 | 5.3 | 5.4 | 5.6 | 5.7 |
| 1990 | 4.5 | 4.2 | 4.1 | 4.2 | 4.3 | 4.3 | 4.2 | 4.3 | 4.4 | 4.6 | 4.7 | 4.8 | 4.8 | 4.9 | 5.0 | 5.1 | 5.3 | 5.4 | 5.6 | 5.8 |

## Table C-7 (Page 4 of 5)

**Inflation**
Rates of Return for all holding periods
Percent per annum compounded annually

from 1926 to 2000

| To the end of | From the beginning of 1946 | 1947 | 1948 | 1949 | 1950 | 1951 | 1952 | 1953 | 1954 | 1955 | 1956 | 1957 | 1958 | 1959 | 1960 | 1961 | 1962 | 1963 | 1964 | 1965 |
|---|---|---|---|---|---|---|---|---|---|---|---|---|---|---|---|---|---|---|---|---|
| 1991 | 4.5 | 4.2 | 4.1 | 4.1 | 4.3 | 4.3 | 4.2 | 4.3 | 4.4 | 4.5 | 4.7 | 4.7 | 4.8 | 4.8 | 5.0 | 5.1 | 5.2 | 5.4 | 5.5 | 5.7 |
| 1992 | 4.5 | 4.2 | 4.1 | 4.1 | 4.3 | 4.2 | 4.2 | 4.3 | 4.4 | 4.5 | 4.6 | 4.7 | 4.7 | 4.8 | 4.9 | 5.0 | 5.1 | 5.3 | 5.4 | 5.6 |
| 1993 | 4.4 | 4.2 | 4.1 | 4.1 | 4.2 | 4.2 | 4.1 | 4.2 | 4.3 | 4.4 | 4.6 | 4.6 | 4.6 | 4.7 | 4.8 | 4.9 | 5.1 | 5.2 | 5.3 | 5.5 |
| 1994 | 4.4 | 4.1 | 4.0 | 4.1 | 4.2 | 4.2 | 4.1 | 4.2 | 4.3 | 4.4 | 4.5 | 4.5 | 4.6 | 4.7 | 4.8 | 4.9 | 5.0 | 5.1 | 5.2 | 5.4 |
| 1995 | 4.4 | 4.1 | 4.0 | 4.0 | 4.2 | 4.1 | 4.1 | 4.2 | 4.2 | 4.4 | 4.5 | 4.5 | 4.5 | 4.6 | 4.7 | 4.8 | 4.9 | 5.0 | 5.1 | 5.3 |
| 1996 | 4.3 | 4.1 | 4.0 | 4.0 | 4.1 | 4.1 | 4.1 | 4.1 | 4.2 | 4.3 | 4.4 | 4.5 | 4.5 | 4.6 | 4.7 | 4.8 | 4.9 | 5.0 | 5.1 | 5.2 |
| 1997 | 4.3 | 4.0 | 3.9 | 4.0 | 4.1 | 4.0 | 4.0 | 4.1 | 4.2 | 4.3 | 4.4 | 4.4 | 4.4 | 4.5 | 4.6 | 4.7 | 4.8 | 4.9 | 5.0 | 5.1 |
| 1998 | 4.2 | 4.0 | 3.9 | 3.9 | 4.0 | 4.0 | 4.0 | 4.0 | 4.1 | 4.2 | 4.3 | 4.3 | 4.4 | 4.4 | 4.5 | 4.6 | 4.7 | 4.8 | 4.9 | 5.0 |
| 1999 | 4.2 | 4.0 | 3.9 | 3.9 | 4.0 | 4.0 | 3.9 | 4.0 | 4.1 | 4.2 | 4.3 | 4.3 | 4.3 | 4.4 | 4.5 | 4.5 | 4.6 | 4.7 | 4.8 | 4.9 |
| 2000 | 4.2 | 3.9 | 3.9 | 3.9 | 4.0 | 4.0 | 3.9 | 4.0 | 4.1 | 4.2 | 4.2 | 4.3 | 4.3 | 4.4 | 4.4 | 4.5 | 4.6 | 4.7 | 4.8 | 4.9 |

# Table C-7 (Page 5 of 5)

## Inflation
Rates of Return for all holding periods
Percent per annum compounded annually

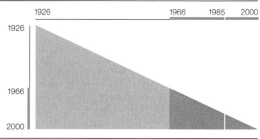

from 1926 to 2000

| To the end of | From the beginning of 1966 | 1967 | 1968 | 1969 | 1970 | 1971 | 1972 | 1973 | 1974 | 1975 | 1976 | 1977 | 1978 | 1979 | 1980 | 1981 | 1982 | 1983 | 1984 | 1985 |
|---|---|---|---|---|---|---|---|---|---|---|---|---|---|---|---|---|---|---|---|---|
| 1966 | 3.4 | | | | | | | | | | | | | | | | | | | |
| 1967 | 3.2 | 3.0 | | | | | | | | | | | | | | | | | | |
| 1968 | 3.7 | 3.9 | 4.7 | | | | | | | | | | | | | | | | | |
| 1969 | 4.3 | 4.6 | 5.4 | 6.1 | | | | | | | | | | | | | | | | |
| 1970 | 4.5 | 4.8 | 5.4 | 5.8 | 5.5 | | | | | | | | | | | | | | | |
| 1971 | 4.3 | 4.5 | 4.9 | 5.0 | 4.4 | 3.4 | | | | | | | | | | | | | | |
| 1972 | 4.2 | 4.3 | 4.6 | 4.6 | 4.1 | 3.4 | 3.4 | | | | | | | | | | | | | |
| 1973 | 4.8 | 5.0 | 5.3 | 5.4 | 5.2 | 5.2 | 6.1 | 8.8 | | | | | | | | | | | | |
| 1974 | 5.6 | 5.9 | 6.3 | 6.5 | 6.6 | 6.9 | 8.1 | 10.5 | 12.2 | | | | | | | | | | | |
| 1975 | 5.7 | 6.0 | 6.4 | 6.6 | 6.7 | 6.9 | 7.8 | 9.3 | 9.6 | 7.0 | | | | | | | | | | |
| 1976 | 5.6 | 5.9 | 6.2 | 6.4 | 6.4 | 6.6 | 7.2 | 8.2 | 8.0 | 5.9 | 4.8 | | | | | | | | | |
| 1977 | 5.7 | 5.9 | 6.2 | 6.4 | 6.4 | 6.6 | 7.1 | 7.9 | 7.7 | 6.2 | 5.8 | 6.8 | | | | | | | | |
| 1978 | 6.0 | 6.2 | 6.5 | 6.7 | 6.7 | 6.9 | 7.4 | 8.1 | 7.9 | 6.9 | 6.9 | 7.9 | 9.0 | | | | | | | |
| 1979 | 6.5 | 6.7 | 7.0 | 7.3 | 7.4 | 7.6 | 8.1 | 8.8 | 8.8 | 8.1 | 8.4 | 9.7 | 11.1 | 13.3 | | | | | | |
| 1980 | 6.9 | 7.1 | 7.4 | 7.7 | 7.8 | 8.1 | 8.6 | 9.3 | 9.3 | 8.8 | 9.2 | 10.3 | 11.6 | 12.9 | 12.4 | | | | | |
| 1981 | 7.0 | 7.2 | 7.6 | 7.8 | 7.9 | 8.1 | 8.6 | 9.2 | 9.3 | 8.9 | 9.2 | 10.1 | 10.9 | 11.5 | 10.7 | 8.9 | | | | |
| 1982 | 6.8 | 7.0 | 7.3 | 7.5 | 7.6 | 7.8 | 8.2 | 8.7 | 8.7 | 8.2 | 8.4 | 9.0 | 9.5 | 9.6 | 8.3 | 6.4 | 3.9 | | | |
| 1983 | 6.6 | 6.8 | 7.1 | 7.2 | 7.3 | 7.5 | 7.8 | 8.2 | 8.2 | 7.7 | 7.8 | 8.2 | 8.5 | 8.4 | 7.2 | 5.5 | 3.8 | 3.8 | | |
| 1984 | 6.5 | 6.7 | 6.9 | 7.0 | 7.1 | 7.2 | 7.5 | 7.9 | 7.8 | 7.3 | 7.4 | 7.7 | 7.8 | 7.6 | 6.5 | 5.1 | 3.9 | 3.9 | 4.0 | |
| 1985 | 6.4 | 6.5 | 6.7 | 6.8 | 6.9 | 7.0 | 7.2 | 7.5 | 7.4 | 7.0 | 7.0 | 7.3 | 7.3 | 7.1 | 6.1 | 4.8 | 3.8 | 3.8 | 3.9 | 3.8 |
| 1986 | 6.1 | 6.2 | 6.4 | 6.5 | 6.5 | 6.6 | 6.8 | 7.1 | 6.9 | 6.5 | 6.5 | 6.6 | 6.6 | 6.3 | 5.3 | 4.2 | 3.3 | 3.2 | 2.9 | 2.4 |
| 1987 | 6.0 | 6.2 | 6.3 | 6.4 | 6.4 | 6.5 | 6.7 | 6.9 | 6.8 | 6.3 | 6.3 | 6.4 | 6.4 | 6.1 | 5.2 | 4.2 | 3.5 | 3.4 | 3.3 | 3.1 |
| 1988 | 6.0 | 6.1 | 6.2 | 6.3 | 6.3 | 6.4 | 6.5 | 6.7 | 6.6 | 6.2 | 6.1 | 6.3 | 6.2 | 5.9 | 5.1 | 4.3 | 3.6 | 3.6 | 3.5 | 3.4 |
| 1989 | 5.9 | 6.0 | 6.2 | 6.2 | 6.2 | 6.3 | 6.4 | 6.6 | 6.5 | 6.1 | 6.0 | 6.1 | 6.1 | 5.8 | 5.1 | 4.3 | 3.7 | 3.7 | 3.7 | 3.7 |
| 1990 | 5.9 | 6.0 | 6.1 | 6.2 | 6.2 | 6.3 | 6.4 | 6.6 | 6.5 | 6.1 | 6.0 | 6.1 | 6.1 | 5.8 | 5.2 | 4.5 | 4.0 | 4.0 | 4.1 | 4.1 |
| 1991 | 5.8 | 5.9 | 6.0 | 6.1 | 6.1 | 6.1 | 6.2 | 6.4 | 6.3 | 5.9 | 5.9 | 5.9 | 5.9 | 5.6 | 5.0 | 4.4 | 3.9 | 3.9 | 3.9 | 3.9 |
| 1992 | 5.7 | 5.8 | 5.9 | 5.9 | 5.9 | 6.0 | 6.1 | 6.2 | 6.1 | 5.7 | 5.7 | 5.7 | 5.7 | 5.4 | 4.8 | 4.2 | 3.8 | 3.8 | 3.8 | 3.8 |
| 1993 | 5.6 | 5.7 | 5.8 | 5.8 | 5.8 | 5.8 | 5.9 | 6.0 | 5.9 | 5.6 | 5.5 | 5.6 | 5.5 | 5.2 | 4.7 | 4.1 | 3.7 | 3.7 | 3.7 | 3.7 |
| 1994 | 5.5 | 5.6 | 5.7 | 5.7 | 5.7 | 5.7 | 5.8 | 5.9 | 5.8 | 5.4 | 5.4 | 5.4 | 5.3 | 5.1 | 4.6 | 4.0 | 3.6 | 3.6 | 3.6 | 3.6 |
| 1995 | 5.4 | 5.5 | 5.5 | 5.6 | 5.5 | 5.6 | 5.6 | 5.7 | 5.6 | 5.3 | 5.2 | 5.2 | 5.2 | 4.9 | 4.4 | 3.9 | 3.6 | 3.5 | 3.5 | 3.5 |
| 1996 | 5.3 | 5.4 | 5.5 | 5.5 | 5.5 | 5.5 | 5.6 | 5.6 | 5.5 | 5.2 | 5.1 | 5.1 | 5.1 | 4.8 | 4.4 | 3.9 | 3.6 | 3.5 | 3.5 | 3.5 |
| 1997 | 5.2 | 5.3 | 5.3 | 5.4 | 5.3 | 5.3 | 5.4 | 5.5 | 5.3 | 5.1 | 5.0 | 5.0 | 4.9 | 4.7 | 4.2 | 3.8 | 3.4 | 3.4 | 3.4 | 3.3 |
| 1998 | 5.1 | 5.1 | 5.2 | 5.2 | 5.2 | 5.2 | 5.3 | 5.3 | 5.2 | 4.9 | 4.8 | 4.8 | 4.7 | 4.5 | 4.1 | 3.6 | 3.3 | 3.3 | 3.3 | 3.2 |
| 1999 | 5.0 | 5.1 | 5.1 | 5.1 | 5.1 | 5.1 | 5.2 | 5.2 | 5.1 | 4.8 | 4.7 | 4.7 | 4.6 | 4.4 | 4.0 | 3.6 | 3.3 | 3.3 | 3.2 | 3.2 |
| 2000 | 5.0 | 5.0 | 5.1 | 5.1 | 5.1 | 5.0 | 5.1 | 5.2 | 5.0 | 4.8 | 4.7 | 4.7 | 4.6 | 4.4 | 4.0 | 3.6 | 3.3 | 3.3 | 3.2 | 3.2 |

| To the end of | From the beginning of 1986 | 1987 | 1988 | 1989 | 1990 | 1991 | 1992 | 1993 | 1994 | 1995 | 1996 | 1997 | 1998 | 1999 | 2000 |
|---|---|---|---|---|---|---|---|---|---|---|---|---|---|---|---|
| 1986 | 1.1 | | | | | | | | | | | | | | |
| 1987 | 2.8 | 4.4 | | | | | | | | | | | | | |
| 1988 | 3.3 | 4.4 | 4.4 | | | | | | | | | | | | |
| 1989 | 3.6 | 4.5 | 4.5 | 4.6 | | | | | | | | | | | |
| 1990 | 4.1 | 4.9 | 5.1 | 5.4 | 6.1 | | | | | | | | | | |
| 1991 | 4.0 | 4.5 | 4.6 | 4.6 | 4.6 | 3.1 | | | | | | | | | |
| 1992 | 3.8 | 4.3 | 4.2 | 4.2 | 4.0 | 3.0 | 2.9 | | | | | | | | |
| 1993 | 3.7 | 4.0 | 4.0 | 3.9 | 3.7 | 2.9 | 2.8 | 2.7 | | | | | | | |
| 1994 | 3.6 | 3.9 | 3.8 | 3.7 | 3.5 | 2.8 | 2.8 | 2.7 | 2.7 | | | | | | |
| 1995 | 3.5 | 3.7 | 3.6 | 3.5 | 3.3 | 2.8 | 2.7 | 2.7 | 2.6 | 2.5 | | | | | |
| 1996 | 3.4 | 3.7 | 3.6 | 3.5 | 3.3 | 2.9 | 2.8 | 2.8 | 2.8 | 2.9 | 3.3 | | | | |
| 1997 | 3.3 | 3.5 | 3.4 | 3.3 | 3.1 | 2.7 | 2.6 | 2.6 | 2.6 | 2.5 | 2.5 | 1.7 | | | |
| 1998 | 3.2 | 3.3 | 3.2 | 3.1 | 3.0 | 2.6 | 2.5 | 2.4 | 2.4 | 2.3 | 2.2 | 1.7 | 1.6 | | |
| 1999 | 3.1 | 3.3 | 3.2 | 3.1 | 2.9 | 2.6 | 2.5 | 2.5 | 2.4 | 2.4 | 2.3 | 2.0 | 2.1 | 2.7 | |
| 2000 | 3.1 | 3.3 | 3.2 | 3.1 | 3.0 | 2.7 | 2.6 | 2.6 | 2.6 | 2.5 | 2.5 | 2.3 | 2.6 | 3.0 | 3.4 |

Stocks, Bonds, Bills, and Inflation

Volatility\ˌvä-lə-'ti-lə-tēl
1: The extent to which an asse
returns fluctuate from period
period.

# Glossary

**Ibbotson**Associates

# Glossary

## All Growth Stocks

A portfolio of stocks constructed by setting a book-to-market ratio cutoff at the bottom 30 percent of NYSE stocks and selecting all NYSE, AMEX, and NASDAQ stocks with a book-to-market ratio lower than the cutoff.

## All Value Stocks

A portfolio of stocks constructed by setting a book-to-market ratio cutoff at the top 30 percent of NYSE stocks and selecting all NYSE, AMEX, and NASDAQ stocks with a book-to-market ratio higher than the cutoff.

## American Stock Exchange (AMEX)

One of the largest stock exchanges in the U.S. Securities traded on this exchange are generally of small to medium-size companies.

## Arbitrage Pricing Theory (APT)

A model in which multiple betas and multiple risk premia are used to generate the expected return of a security.

## Arithmetic Mean Return

A simple average of a series of returns.

## Asset Class

A grouping of securities with similar characteristics and properties. As a group, these securities will tend to react in a specific way to economic factors (e.g., stocks, bonds, and real estate are all asset classes).

## Balanced Mutual Fund

Fund that seeks both income and capital appreciation by investing in a generally fixed combination of stocks and bonds.

## Basic Series

The seven primary time series representing Stocks, Bonds, Bills and Inflation: large company stocks, small company stocks, long-term corporate bonds, long-term government bonds, intermediate-term government bonds, U.S. Treasury bills, and inflation.

## Beta

The systematic risk of a security as estimated by regressing the security's returns against the market portfolio's returns. The slope of the regression is beta.

## Book-to-Market Ratio

The ratio of total book value to total market capitalization. Value companies have a high book-to-market ratio, while growth companies have a low book-to-market ratio.

## Callable Bonds

Bonds that the issuer has the right to redeem (or call) prior to maturity at a specified price.

## Capital Appreciation Return

The component of total return which results from the price change of an asset class over a given period.

## Capital Asset Pricing Model (CAPM)

A model in which the cost of capital for any security or portfolio of securities equals the riskless rate plus a risk premium that is proportionate to the amount of systematic risk of the security or portfolio.

## Convexity

The property of a bond that its price does not change in proportion to changes in its yield. A bond with positive convexity will rise in price faster than the rate at which yields decline, and will fall in price slower than the rate at which yields rise.

## Correlation Coefficient

The degree of association or strength between two variables. A value of +1 indicates a perfectly positive relationship, −1 indicates a perfectly inverse relationship, and 0 indicates no relationship between the variables.

## Cost of Capital

The discount rate which should be used to derive the present value of an asset's future cash flows.

## Coupon

The periodic interest payment on a bond.

## Decile

One of 10 portfolios formed by ranking a set of securities by some criteria and dividing them into 10 equally populated subsets. The New York Stock Exchange market capitalization deciles are formed by ranking the stocks traded on the Exchange by their market capitalization.

## Derived Series

The components or elemental parts of the returns of the seven primary Stocks, Bonds, Bills, and Inflation asset classes. The two categories of derived series are: risk premia, or payoffs for taking various types of risk, and inflation-adjusted asset returns.

## Discount Rate

The rate used to convert a series of future cash flows to a single present value.

## Dow Jones Industrial Average

The oldest stock price index beginning in 1884 with 11 stocks currently consisting of 30 representative large stocks.

## Duration (Macauley Duration)

The weighted average term-to-maturity of a security's cash flows. The weights are the present values of each cash flow as a percentage of the present value of all cash flows.

## Efficient Frontier

The set of portfolios that provides the highest expected returns for their respective risk levels. The efficient frontier is calculated for a given set of assets with estimates of expected return and standard deviation for each asset, and a correlation coefficient for each pair of asset returns.

## Geometric Mean Return

The compound rate of return. The geometric mean of a return series is a measure of the actual average performance of a portfolio over a given time period.

## Histogram

A bar graph in which the frequency of occurrence for each class of data is represented by the relative height of the bars.

## Income Return

The component of total return which results from a periodic cash flow, such as dividends.

## Index Value

The cumulative value of returns on a dollar amount invested. It is used when measuring investment performance and computing returns over non-calendar periods.

## Inflation

The rate of change in consumer prices. The Consumer Price Index for All Urban Consumers (CPI-U), not seasonally adjusted, is used to measure inflation. Prior to January 1978, the CPI (as compared with CPI-U) was used. Both inflation measures are constructed by the U.S. Department of Labor, Bureau of Labor Statistics, Washington.

## Inflation-Adjusted Returns

Asset class returns in real terms. The inflation-adjusted return of an asset is calculated by geometrically subtracting inflation from the asset's nominal return.

## Intermediate-Term Government Bonds

A one-bond portfolio with a maturity near 5 years.

## Large Company Stocks

The Standard and Poor's 500 Stock Composite Index® (S&P 500).

## Large Growth Stocks

A portfolio of stocks constructed by setting a book-to-market ratio cutoff at the bottom 30 percent of NYSE stocks and a market capitalization cutoff at the median of NYSE stocks and selecting all NYSE, AMEX, and NASDAQ stocks with a book-to-market ratio lower than the book-to-market cutoff and a market capitalization greater than the market capitalization cutoff.

## Large Value Stocks

A portfolio of stocks constructed by setting a book-to-market ratio cutoff at the top 30 percent of NYSE stocks and a market capitalization cutoff at the median of NYSE stocks and selecting all NYSE, AMEX, and NASDAQ stocks with a book-to-market ratio higher than the book-to-market cutoff and a market capitalization greater than the market capitalization cutoff.

## Logarithmic Scale

A scale in which equal percentage changes are represented by equal distances.

## Lognormal Distribution

The distribution of a random variable whose natural logarithm is normally distributed. A lognormal distribution is skewed so that a higher proportion of possible returns exceed the expected value versus falling short of the expected value. In the lognormal forecasting model, one plus the total return has a lognormal distribution.

## Long-Term Corporate Bonds

Salomon Brothers long-term, high-grade corporate bond total return index.

## Long-Term Government Bonds

A one-bond portfolio with a maturity near 20 years.

## Low-cap Stocks

The portfolio of stocks comprised of the 6-8th deciles of the New York Stock Exchange.

## Market Capitalization

The current market price of a security determined by the most recently recorded trade multiplied by the number of issues outstanding of that security. For equities, market capitalization is computed by taking the share price of a stock times the number of shares outstanding.

## Mean-Variance Optimization (MVO)

The process of identifying portfolios that have the highest possible return for a given level of risk or the lowest possible risk for a given return. The inputs for MVO are return, standard deviation, and the correlation coefficients of returns for each pair of asset classes.

## Micro-cap Stocks

The portfolio of stocks comprised of the 9-10th deciles of the New York Stock Exchange.

## Mid-cap Stocks

The portfolio of stocks comprised of the 3-5th deciles of the New York Stock Exchange.

## National Association of Securities Dealers Automated Quotation System (NASDAQ)

A computerized system showing current bid and asked prices for stocks traded on the Over-the-Counter market, as well as some New York Stock Exchange listed stocks.

## New York Stock Exchange (NYSE)

The largest and oldest stock exchange in the United States, founded in 1792.

## Over-the-Counter Market (OTC)

A market in which assets are not traded on an organized exchange like the New York Stock Exchange, but rather through various dealers or market makers who are linked electronically.

## Price-Weighted Index

An index in which component stocks are weighted by their price. Thus, higher-priced stocks have a greater percentage impact on the index than lower-priced stocks.

## Quintile

One of 5 portfolios formed by ranking a set of securities by some criteria and dividing them into 5 equally populated subsets. The micro-cap stocks are a market capitalization quintile.

## R-squared

Measures the "goodness of fit" of the regression line and describes the percentage of variation in the dependent variable that is explained by the independent variable. The R-squared measure may vary from zero to one.

## Return

see Total Return

## Risk

The extent to which an investment is subject to uncertainty. Risk may be measured by standard deviation.

## Riskless Rate of Return

The return on a riskless investment; it is the rate of return an investor can obtain without taking market risk.

## Risk Premium

The reward which investors require to accept the uncertain outcomes associated with securities. The size of the risk premium will depend upon the type and extent of the risk.

## Rolling Period Returns

A series of overlapping contiguous periods of returns defined by the frequency of the data under examination. In examining 5-year rolling periods of returns for annual data that starts in 1970, the first rolling period would be 1970–1974, the second rolling period would be 1971–1975, the third rolling period would be 1972–1976, etc.

## Rolling Period Standard Deviation

A series of overlapping contiguous periods of standard deviations defined by the frequency of the data under examination. In examining 5-year rolling periods of standard deviation for annual data that starts in 1970, the first rolling period would be 1970-1974, the second rolling period would be 1971-1975, the third rolling period would be 1972-1976, etc.

## Serial Correlation (Autocorrelation)

The degree to which the return of a given series is related from period to period. A serial correlation near +1 or -1 indicates that returns are predictable from one period to the next; a serial correlation near zero indicates returns are random or unpredictable.

## Small Company Stocks

A portfolio of stocks represented by the fifth capitalization quintile of stocks on the NYSE for 1926–1981 and the performance of the Dimensional Fund Advisors (DFA) Small Company Fund thereafter.

## Small Growth Stocks

A portfolio of stocks constructed by setting a book-to-market ratio cutoff at the bottom 30 percent of NYSE stocks and a market capitalization cutoff at the median of NYSE stocks and selecting all NYSE, AMEX, and NASDAQ stocks with a book-to-market ratio lower than the book-to-market cutoff and a market capitalization smaller than the market capitalization cutoff.

## Small Value Stocks

A portfolio of stocks constructed by setting a book-to-market ratio cutoff at the top 30 percent of NYSE stocks and a market capitalization cutoff at the median of NYSE stocks and selecting all NYSE, AMEX, and NASDAQ stocks with a book-to-market ratio higher than the book-to-market cutoff and a market capitalization smaller than the market capitalization cutoff.

## S&P 500®

Stock index including 500 of the largest stocks (in terms of stock market value) in the United States representing 88 separate industries. Prior to 1957, it consisted of 90 of the largest stocks.

## Standard Deviation

A measure of the dispersion of returns of an asset, or the extent to which returns vary from the arithmetic mean. It represents the volatility or risk of an asset. The greater the degree of dispersion, the greater the risk associated with the asset.

## Systematic Risk

The risk that is unavoidable according to CAPM. It is the risk that is common to all risky securities and cannot be eliminated through diversification. The amount of an asset's systematic risk is measured by its beta.

## Total Return

A measure of performance of an asset class over a designated time period. It is comprised of income return, reinvestment of income return and capital appreciation return components.

## Treasury Bills

A one-bill portfolio containing, at the beginning of each month, the bill having the shortest maturity not less than one month.

## Unsystematic Risk

The portion of total risk specific to an individual security that can be avoided through diversification.

## Volatility

The extent to which an asset's returns fluctuate from period to period.

## Yield

The yield to maturity is the internal rate of return that equates the bond's price with the stream of cash flows promised to the bondholder. The yield on a stock is the percentage rate of return paid in dividends.

Stocks, Bonds, Bills,
and Inflation

G
A
L
C
M
D
R

# Index

**Ibbotson**Associates

# Index

# M

# IBBOTSON INVESTMENT TOOLS + RESOURCES

## SBBI Report Subscriptions

Receive the most up-to-date data available when you subscribe to our SBBI reports on a monthly, quarterly or semi-annual basis. The SBBI reports contain year-to-date data on a calendar year basis. These reports feature:

- Updated returns and index values available on a monthly basis for six U.S. asset classes plus inflation.
- Inflation-adjusted returns and index values plus other derived series.
- Quarterly updates to the Stocks, Bonds, Bills, and Inflation index graph.
- Market commentary on a semi-annual basis.
- Prompt delivery of time-sensitive market data via fax.
- All report subscriptions include a 2001 Classic Edition Yearbook and can begin at any time throughout the year.

**SBBI Classic Edition Yearbook with Monthly Reports\* $695**
**SBBI Classic Edition Yearbook with Quarterly Reports\*\* $280**
**SBBI Classic Edition Yearbook with Semi-Annual Report\*\*\* $160**

## The Cost of Capital Center Web Site

Visit Ibbotson's enhanced valuation web site, The Cost of Capital Center, where you can conveniently purchase cost of capital information online. Located at **http://valuation.ibbotson.com**, the site enables you to purchase Cost of Capital Quarterly analysis on over 300 industries, purchase individual company betas from the Beta Book database of 5,000 companies, and purchase risk premia and company tax rate reports.

## 2001 Cost of Capital Yearbook

Providing data on over 300 industries, the Cost of Capital Yearbook is an invaluable reference for anyone performing discounted cash flow analysis. The yearbook contains critical statistics you need to analyze corporations and industries and includes:

- Five separate measures of cost of equity.
- Weighted average cost of capital.
- Detailed statistics for sales, profitability, capitalization, beta, multiples, ratios, equity returns and capital structure.

Published annually, the Cost of Capital Yearbook is updated with data through March 2001. For the most frequent data available, subscribe to the Cost of Capital Yearbook with Cost of Capital Quarterly™ updates.

**Cost of Capital Yearbook with 3 Quarterly Updates $995**
**Cost of Capital Yearbook $395** *(Shipped in June)*

*\* Last report ships in December with data through November.*
*\*\* Last report ships in October with data through September.*
*\*\*\* Report ships in July with data through June.*

## Ibbotson SalesBuilder™ Presentation System

The SalesBuilder Presentation System features Ibbotson charts and presentations packaged three ways–in Microsoft PowerPoint as a complete Asset Allocation Library or 11 different SalesBuilder Presentation Modules, or individually as 8$\frac{1}{2}$" x 11" laminated prints of our 13 most popular graphs.

**SalesBuilder Asset Allocation Library $800**
**SalesBuilder Presentation Module $100 each**
**SalesBuilder Individual Laminated Prints $25 each**

## 2001 Stocks, Bonds, Bills, and Inflation® Valuation Edition Yearbook

Since its introduction in 1999, the SBBI® Valuation Edition has earned a reputation as the industry standard in valuation reference materials. Filled with real world examples and useful graphs to illustrate the analyses, the SBBI Valuation Edition will help you make the most informed decisions in your cost of capital estimation.

The Valuation Edition covers the topics that come up most often when performing valuation analysis, including:

- Tables that enable you to calculate equity risk premia and size premia for any time period.
- Evidence of size premia by industry.
- Alternative methods of calculating equity risk premia, size premia and beta.
- New developments in the field of cost of capital estimation.
- Problems and possible solutions in estimating the cost of capital for international markets.

The Valuation Edition also contains an easy-to-understand overview and comparison of the build-up method, CAPM (Capital Asset Pricing Model), Fama-French 3-factor model, and the DCF (discounted cash flow) approach.

**2001 SBBI Valuation Edition Yearbook $110**

## Ibbotson Beta Book

The Beta Book is an invaluable resource for modeling stock performance and accurately pricing securities. With data on over 5,000 companies, the book provides statistics critical for calculating cost of equity with the CAPM and the Fama-French 3-factor model. Employing the most current methods, the Beta Book contains traditional 60-month levered beta calculations, unlevered betas, betas adjusted for thinly traded securities and betas adjusted toward peer group averages. Published semi-annually, the First Edition provides data through December 2000 and the Second Edition provides data through June 2001.

**2001 First Edition $625** *(Shipped in February)*
**2001 Second Edition $625** *(Shipped in August)*
**Both Editions $1,000**

## Ibbotson Software + Data

We have developed a line of software that allows you to discover, understand and present the tradeoffs that must be considered when working toward the right balance between risk and reward for your clients.

## Ibbotson Analyst™

Ibbotson Analyst is designed to help you look at the historical behavior of a variety of asset classes. Create graphs, charts and tables of statistical data from as early as 1926 to explore fundamental investment concepts and alternatives, communicate these concepts to clients and present diversified investment choices to clients. Choose from a wide selection of Ibbotson data or import your own. Series are updated monthly via our web site, **www.ibbotson.com.**

**First year subscription $1,500**

## Ibbotson Portfolio Strategist™

Changing client needs and objectives, unique constraints, and a variety of risk tolerances—all these factors must be considered when you are designing, implementing and monitoring asset allocation strategies for your clients. Portfolio Strategist can help you build better portfolios for your clients and help determine the asset mix that offers the best chance of achieving the highest return for a given level of risk.

Portfolio Strategist also integrates seamlessly with Ibbotson Fund Strategist to move from classifying security holdings to recommending an asset allocation to implementing the plan with mutual funds, using the exclusive Ibbotson Security Classifier and Ibbotson Fund Optimizer applications.

**First year subscription $1,100**

## Ibbotson Fund Strategist®

Selecting funds to implement an asset allocation policy can be difficult, especially when you encounter outdated or abbreviated holdings, changing managers and objectives, and most importantly, drifting, shifting or mislabeled styles. Fund Strategist simplifies the process and helps you strengthen your approach to mutual fund selection with the returns-based style analysis in this easy-to-use software tool.

Fund Strategist analysis results are presented in a concise, fact sheet-style format. The full color, one-page fund profiles include descriptive tables and graphs highlighting the fund's style and performance over time. Financial advisors can use the sheets with clients, while mutual fund companies can use them as fund fact sheets with distributors.

Fund Strategist also integrates seamlessly with Ibbotson Portfolio Strategist to move from classifying security holdings to recommending an asset allocation to implementing the plan with mutual funds, using the exclusive Ibbotson Security Classifier and Ibbotson Fund Optimizer.

**First year subscription $600**

## Ibbotson EnCorr™

Designed for money managers, plan sponsors and consultants, the EnCorr software system embodies sophisticated investment concepts within an easy-to-use framework. EnCorr is a modular system that integrates historical data analysis, strategic asset allocation, forecasting, style analysis, performance measurement, portfolio attribution and a wide array of statistical and graphical analyses into one family.

**Prices begin at $2,000**

For more information or to request a product catalog, call 800 758 3557 or visit our web site at **www.ibbotson.com.**